Public Budgeting

and

Financial Management

(Indian Experience)

(For the Students of MBA and Postgraduate Diploma Courses in Public Policy and Management)

Prof. Nand Dhameja

Management Development Institute, Gurgaon

Formerly, Professor and Senior Consultant

Indian Institute of Public Administration, New Delhi

S. CHAND & COMPANY PVT. LTD.

(AN ISO 9001 : 2008 COMPANY)

RAM NAGAR, NEW DELHI - 110 055

S. CHAND & COMPANY PVT. LTD.

(An ISO 9001 : 2008 Company)

Head Office: 7361, RAM NAGAR, NEW DELHI - 110 055
Phone: 23672080-81-82, 9899107446, 9911310888
Fax: 91-11-23677446
Shop at: **schandgroup.com;** e-mail: **info@schandgroup.com**

Branches:

AHMEDABAD	:	1st Floor, Heritage, Near Gujarat Vidhyapeeth, Ashram Road, **Ahmedabad** - 380 014, Ph: 27541965, 27542369, ahmedabad@schandgroup.com
BENGALURU	:	No. 6, Ahuja Chambers, 1st Cross, Kumara Krupa Road, **Bengaluru** - 560 001, Ph: 22268048, 22354008, bangalore@schandgroup.com
BHOPAL	:	Bajaj Tower, Plot No. 2&3, Lala Lajpat Rai Colony, Raisen Road, **Bhopal** - 462 011, Ph: 4274723, 4209587. bhopal@schandgroup.com
CHANDIGARH	:	S.C.O. 2419-20, First Floor, Sector - 22-C (Near Aroma Hotel), **Chandigarh** -160 022, Ph: 2725443, 2725446, chandigarh@schandgroup.com
CHENNAI	:	No.1, Whites Road, Opposite Express Avenue, Royapettah, **Chennai** - 600014 Ph. 28410027, 28410058, chennai@schandgroup.com
COIMBATORE	:	1790, Trichy Road, LGB Colony, Ramanathapuram, **Coimbatore** - 6410045, Ph: 2323620, 4217136 coimbatore@schandgroup.com **(Marketing Office)**
CUTTACK	:	1st Floor, Bhartia Tower, Badambadi, **Cuttack** - 753 009, Ph: 2332580; 2332581, cuttack@schandgroup.com
DEHRADUN	:	1st Floor, 20, New Road, Near Dwarka Store, **Dehradun** - 248 001, Ph: 2711101, 2710861, dehradun@schandgroup.com
GUWAHATI	:	Dilip Commercial (Ist floor), M.N. Road, Pan Bazar, **Guwahati** - 781 001, Ph: 2738811, 2735640 guwahati@schandgroup.com
HYDERABAD	:	Padma Plaza, H.No. 3-4-630, Opp. Ratna College, Narayanaguda, **Hyderabad** - 500 029, Ph: 27550194, 27550195, hyderabad@schandgroup.com
HALDWANI	:	Bhatt Colony, Talli Bamori, Mukhani, **Haldwani** -263139 (Marketing Office) Mob. 09452294584
JAIPUR	:	1st Floor, Nand Plaza, Hawa Sadak, Ajmer Road, **Jaipur** - 302 006, Ph: 2219175, 2219176, jaipur@schandgroup.com
JALANDHAR	:	Mai Hiran Gate, **Jalandhar** - 144 008, Ph: 2401630, 5000630, jalandhar@schandgroup.com
KOCHI	:	Kachapilly Square, Mullassery Canal Road, Ernakulam, **Kochi** - 682 011, Ph: 2378740, 2378207-08, cochin@schandgroup.com
KOLKATA	:	285/J, Bipin Bihari Ganguli Street, **Kolkata** - 700 012, Ph: 22367459, 22373914, kolkata@schandgroup.com
LUCKNOW	:	Mahabeer Market, 25 Gwynne Road, Aminabad, **Lucknow** - 226 018, Ph: 4076971, 4026791, 4065646, 4027188, lucknow@schandgroup.com
MUMBAI	:	Blackie House, IInd Floor, 103/5, Walchand Hirachand Marg, Opp. G.P.O., **Mumbai** - 400 001, Ph: 22690881, 22610885, mumbai@schandgroup.com
NAGPUR	:	Karnal Bagh, Near Model Mill Chowk, **Nagpur** - 440 032, Ph: 2720523, 2777666 nagpur@schandgroup.com
PATNA	:	104, Citicentre Ashok, Mahima Palace , Govind Mitra Road, **Patna** - 800 004, Ph: 2300489, 2302100, patna@schandgroup.com
PUNE	:	Sadguru Enclave, Ground floor, Survey No. 114/3, Plot no. 8 Alandi Road , Vishrantwadi **Pune** – 411015 Ph: 64017298 pune@schandgroup.com
RAIPUR	:	Kailash Residency, Plot No. 4B, Bottle House Road, Shankar Nagar, **Raipur** - 492 007, Ph: 2443142,Mb. : 09981200834, raipur@schandgroup.com (Marketing Office)
RANCHI	:	Shanti Deep Tower, Opp. Hotel Maharaja, Radium Road, **Ranchi** - 834001 Mob. 09430246440 ranchi@schandgroup.com
SILIGURI	:	122, Raja Ram Mohan Roy Road, East Vivekanandapally, P.O., Siliguri, **Siliguri** -734001, Dist., Jalpaiguri, (W.B.) Ph. 0353-2520750 **(Marketing Office)** siliguri@schandgroup.com
VISAKHAPATNAM	:	No. 49-54-15/53/8, Plot No. 7, 1st Floor, Opp. Radhakrishna Towers, Seethammadhara North Extn., **Visakhapatnam** - 530 013, Ph-2782609 (M) 09440100555, visakhapatnam@schandgroup.com **(Marketing Office)**

First Edition 2014

ISBN : 978-81-928300-9-4 **Code :** 07 574

PRINTED IN INDIA

By Rajendra Ravindra Printers Pvt. Ltd., 7361, Ram Nagar, New Delhi -110 055 and published by S. Chand & Company Pvt. Ltd., 7361, Ram Nagar, New Delhi -110 055.

T.N. CHATURVEDI
Former Governor of Karnataka & Kerala
Former Member of Parliament (R.S.)
Former Comptroller & Auditor General of India

सत्यमेव जयते

PRAKASHALAYA
A-4, Sector-17, Noida-201301, U.P.
Tel.: 0120-4214025
E-mail : tnchaturvedi@gmail.com

FOREWORD

Public finance is one of the more important and difficult areas of governance. It has been so all along but with increasing complexities of countries in the global world and internal economic relations, it assumes a more pronounced plank in governance. Budgeting, sound and progressive, and as may facilitate development, is the key to good governance. How and from whom the resources are raised become crucial questions, particularly in a democratic government which is parliamentary in character. Apart from equity, justice and fairness, the issues of accountability and transparency have great social significance. From another angle, the problems of budgeting even a presidential system are no less acute. The need for maximisation and optimal utilisation of limited resources in the context of enhanced political consciousness of citizens in India and their rising expectations and aspirations poses a big , challenge to good budgeting. Budgeting as a concept, and as an operational exercise, is not some fixed or static model, suitable for all times and climes. The changing economic perspectives and political compulsions do condition the overall character of budgeting from time to time so as to validate its relevance.

In India, since the commencement of budgeting process in the modern form more than a century ago, there have been a number of experiments and a good deal of experience has been garnered. As was naturally expected after the attainment of independence, the introduction of the Constitution! and adoption of the democratic system of planned economy, budgetary experiments and innovations gathered a new momentum. The policy of liberalisation, privatisation and globalisation as was initiated by the Indian Government in 1991 was bound to have a profound impact requiring rethinking on the subject, as has been evident in recent years. Thus, we have at our disposal a very wide gamut of experience, experiments and innovations.

It is time that we took stock of the situation, and have a relook at various developments in the field of public budgeting and financial management consciously initiated from time to time keeping in view in an objective manner. This is what Prof Nand Dhameja, presently Professor of Management Development, has comprehensively done in his present book. Professor Dhameja is an academic with extensive experience in this area in different situations, institutions and organisations. He is well-versed in the processes of budgeting and financial management, both in the private and public sectors in our country. As an academic he has not only of the intellectual grasp of issues but also intricacies of application. He has all along been an effective and successful teacher. His forte has been the area of public budgeting and financial management. In his book he discusses and expounds on the subject both in a historical framework as well as in an analytical manner. In his Preface, while introducing the book, Prof. Dhameja outlines succinctly as to how he has dealt with this complex area. It is not necessary therefore for me to go into any details of his exposition, which I do find both informative and interesting. His approach shows his intensive and wide familiarity with the subject. He always takes great pains to keep himself in touch with the latest developments. This is what lends great value to his books.

I have known Prof Nand Dhameja for fairly long. I have had opportunity to see his earlier works. As his biographical data will indicate he continues to build on his varied experience with considerable intellectual vigour and expertise. This is amply reflected in his present contribution which will be welcomed not only by students, scholars, management trainees and researchers in universities, but also by policymakers who want to comprehend and appreciate the so-called mysteries of budgetary and financial management in a holistic manner, as integral to good governance. I thank Prof Dhameja for inviting me to pen these few observations. I wish him all the best in his future endeavours and contributions to this highly significant area.

T. N. Chaturvedi

(T.N. CHATURVEDI)

November 17, 2013

PREFACE

There have been various developments in the area of public budgeting and financial management. Budgeting in governments has moved from Appropriation Budgeting, to Performance Budgeting, to Zero-Base-Budgeting, to Outcome Budgeting and to Gender budgeting over the years. The present book discusses these budgeting approaches, outlines the process of each approach, its format and guidelines for its development. These approaches are described as a marketing strategy to popularize budget principles and to reinforce the need and significance of budgeting in the minds of government employees. Budgeting is similar to construction plan of a building, the 'Construction Plan' and the 'Working Plans' are two different approaches to a construction activity, the former is mandatory, is required by the authorities, while the latter ones are not mandatory and are for planning, and monitoring of construction activity by the builder and owner. Similarly, budgeting has various approaches, one, 'Annual Financial Statement Receipts and Payments', which is required to be placed before the Parliament for approval under Article 112 of the Constitution. The other budgets drawn from the former are for managerial decision making. The other budget statements include performance budget, Zero-base-budget, Outcome budget, etc. are not mandatory and are for managerial decision making.

The book emphasizes that these different approaches be not taken as separate budgeting systems, rather there is a need to integrate all these approaches into one, to use budget as a tool for planning and control.

The book is divided into three parts. The first part gives a detailed account of budget developments in India and raises various policy issues like, budgeting and planning process, budgetary approaches and budget format and documents, grants and loan to states, classification of plan and non-plan expenditure, practice of bunching of end-of year-spending and need of biennial budgeting, budgeting as an economic and political exercise and future of budget reforms. This is the subject matter first chapter.

The second part spread over chapters two to seven presents in detail, planning and budgeting process and mechanics of various approaches of budgeting as evolved over the years. Planning and budgeting process, and budget meaning, its principles, classifications, mechanism and budgeting in a commercial organization are discussed in chapter two.

Budget approaches discussed in the following six chapters namely, three to eight include, appropriation budgeting, performance budgeting, Zero-base-budgeting, outcome budgeting and outcome gender budgeting. Chapter four and its sub chapters present in detail, the meaning, significance, classification structure, performance evaluation and financial management system relating to performance budgeting. Mechanics and process and also implementation issues concerning Zero-base budgeting are detailed in chapter five and its sub-chapters. Chapter six presents a case study to illustrate the adoption of zero-base-budgeting in a research & development organization, its focuses on the commitment of top management and involvement of concerned officials for the success of ZBB. It also raises certain policy issues for the success of ZBB. The chapter seven discusses the outcome budgeting approach introduced during 2005-06, and raises various policy issues like, need for the definition and concept clarity of the term outcome, or how does it differ from performance budgeting, or role of outcome budgeting system in the country, or how outcome budgeting is going to be integrated with other budget approaches? Chapter eight gives an overview of gender budgeting in India, points to an issue: is it a budgetary approach, a process os authorization of executive s to execute plans?

Part three relates to financial management practice of a government. It is spread over two chapters –nine and ten and covers Fiscal Responsibility and Budget Management (FTBM) as a step to control fiscal deficit and a road map towards adoption of accrual accounting. Chapter nine discusses fiscal responsibility requirements as detailed in the FRBM Act and FRBM Rules in India and various other countries and raises the issue of effectiveness of fiscal responsibility legislation. Chapter ten discusses the mechanics of accrual accounting, or how does it differ from cash basis of accounting and lays down the road map for the adoption of accrual accounting.

The book has been developed out of the consultancy work and teaching of financial management and budgeting in MBA and Public Policy courses and various Management Development Programmes (MDPs).

The book provides an in-depth description and analysis of major areas of budgeting and financial management of public sector and will be useful to senior executives involved in policy formulation and implementation. Public administration practioners and academicians will also find the book useful.

The book will also be useful in

- MBA and Post-Graduate Courses in Public Policy
- Mid-career training programmes for managers, consultants and civil servants organised by various Central and State-Level Training Institutes

The author welcomes comments and suggestions from readers so that any future work will benefit their responses.

Prof. Nand Dhameja

ACKNOWLEDGEMENT

I would like to express my gratitude to Shri T. N. Chaturvedi, former Governor Karnataka and Kerala, and former Comptroller and Auditor General of India. He is currently Chairman of the Indian Institute of Public Administration, New Delhi and is guiding various academic and professional institutions. He has agreed to write a Foreword to the book and has always been a source of inspiration and expert guide on various topics which figure in the book.

I am indebted to Dr. G. R. Dalvi, the then Executive Director National Productivity Council, New Delhi for enticing me with the performance budgeting assignment of a state government. My thanks are also due to Ms. Praveen Tripathi, Financial Adviser, Council for Scientific and Industrial Research, India, for associating me on implementation of Zero-Base Budgeting in its various laboratories and divisions. I am grateful to Mr. M. C. Gupta, the then Director, Indian Institute of Public Administration, New Delhi, for his encouragement and also facilitating the work on ZBB.

My special thanks are due to Dr. Mukul P. Gupta, Director Management Development Institute, Gurgaon for his encouragement, valuable advise and suggestions that shaped the presentation of the book. Mr. Anthony Jose, librarian MDI, Gurgaon provided all help in locating material and references and I am thankful to him.

I would like to convey my heartfelt thanks to participants of various training programmes for their queries and comments which sharpened my thoughts on public budgeting and as such this book is the outcome.

I profusely thank my publishers for timely presenting the book.

Comments and suggestions from readers are welcome.

Prof. Nand Dhameja

CONTENTS

CHAPTER 1

Budgeting in India : Developments and Perspectives

Budgeting for a government is a constitutional requirement; it is an economic event and outlines economic planning for the Government for the next year. Similarly, budget is prepared by every enterprise; even a family also prepares a budget, though it may not be in writing. Under Article 112 of the Constitution, the Union Government submits before the Parliament every year a statement of estimated receipts and expenditure of the Government for approval, referred to as the "Annual Financial Statement"; the financial statement is a budget in the common parlance. Similarly, each State Government maintains its own budget which is to be approved by the State Legislature.

History of budgeting in India goes back to 1860 when the first budget was presented by James Wilson who was pioneer in the development of budget system and was the first member of the finance department. He developed the budget system in India on the lines of the British budgetary system whereby the financial estimates of each year were arrayed, considered and approved by the Legislative Council and he is regarded as the father of the budgetary system in India [i]. Since till 1857, the country was in the possession of the East India Company, and the Finance Department for administration of finances of the country, though created during 1843-44, suited to the commercial practices of the East India Company. However, the public finances as evidenced by Chanakya's (also known as Kautilya) Arthashastra were system of orderly administration during 2000 BC; and Mauryan, Gupta and *Mughal* emperors had rudimentary budgetary system suiting their whims and fancies. Since then there have been various developments in the budgeting approaches in India, though principles of budgeting have been the same throughout. The word 'budget' is derived from the French word '*bougette*' which means a small leather bag or pouch. It contains all incoming cash; or cash drawn as per the laid down procedure for financing of proposals carried to the Parliament for approval. Presentation of estimates of cash inflows or cash outflows for various items is referred to as, '*appropriation budget*' or a line item budget. Developments in this regards over the years include adoption of various approaches of budgeting like, Performance budgeting, Zero-base budgeting, Outcome budgeting, Gender budgeting, though they lack cohesiveness and integration, these budget approaches as followed in India are discussed in this chapter. Mechanics and process of each approach are detailed in the following chapters.

Railway finances in India were separated from the general finances as per the Legislative Assembly decision in 1924. This was with the objective 'to secure stability for civil estimates by providing for an assured contribution from Railway revenues and to introduce flexibility in the administration of the Railway finance'. As such, the first Railway Budget was presented in 1925-26 and under the terms of Convention of 1924, the Central Exchequer was entitled to receive from the

---

i. [Sudarsanan C N Government Budgeting : Principles and Practices (Sree Sudarsan Publications, Chennai 2001)]

Railways a sum equal to one percent of the loan capital invested in the Railway; though this has increased over the year. Since then the railway budget is presented separately that from the main budget.

The first budget for Independent India was presented by the India's first Finance Minister Sir R. K. Shanmugham Chetty on November 26, 1947 and since then budget is presented every year normally on the last day of February. Until the year 2000, the budget was announced at 5.00 pm on the last working day of February. This practice was inherited from the Colonial Era, when the British Parliament would pass the budget in the noon followed by India in the evening of the day. This practice was changed to presentation of the budget at 11.00 am in the year 2001.

The annual budget has to be passed by the House of the Parliament before it comes into effect on April 1, the start of the India's financial year. The Indian Parliament has approximately one month to review and modify the government's budget proposal and during this period various Standing Committees of the Parliament review the budget proposal and then finally it is discussed and approved by the Parliament.

Further, as per Article 112 of the Constitution, budget shall show expenditure as

(*a*) '*Charged*' or **(*b*)** '*Voted*':

(*a*) Expenditure '*charged*' upon the Consolidated Fund of India is to meet expenditure as laid down in the Constitution; these include expenses of the Constitutional bodies like, Comptroller & Auditor General, Election Commission, Supreme Court Judges, President and Vice-President. These charged expenses though can be discussed in the Parliament, are not subject to vote by the Parliament.

(*b*) Other expenditure estimates submitted in the form of Demands for Grants which are drawn from the 'Annual Financial Statements' are submitted to the Parliament for approval. Each Demand or combination of demands relate to a single Ministry. The "Annual Financial Statement" together with the 'Demands for Grants' constitute the Budget for the year. Once the Parliament approves the 'Voted' portion of proposed expenditure, the funds required to meet the voted grants together with the expenditure 'Charged' on the Consolidated Fund are allowed to be withdrawn from the Consolidated Fund under the authority of an Appropriation Act passed by the Parliament. The fiscal measures for raising of resources required for meeting the expenditure budgeted for, are embodied in a Finance Act passed by the Parliament. Thus budget submitted to the Parliament is subject to four stages of review:

- General discussion;
- Discussion and Voting on Demands for Grants;
- Passing of the Appropriation Bill; and
- Passing of the Finance Bill

Budgeting Procedure, in brief, is presented in Box 1 below

APPROPRIATION BUDGET

The budget for a department/organization, in general, is presented in terms of objects of expenditure like, salaries, wages, travel, materials, utilities and office expenses without highlighting the purpose or the end result expected. The budget is to ensure accountability, to facilitate itemized financial control and to show sources of funds and objects of expenditures. For illustration of appropriation budget see Exhibit 3.1 and Exhibit 3.2 in chapter three. The appropriation budget indicates items of expenses but does not reflect activities or purposes for which money is spent or the end result of the expenditure. This highlights the need for adoption of performance budgeting.

BOX 1

Starting with October- November, the Finance Ministry officials begin consultations with various stakeholders-Industry associations, chambers of commerce, consumer lobby groups, farmers' associations, economists and employees' unions- in the North Block on Raisina Hill, the seat of power. Each group comes armed with demands for tax breaks and fiscal sops.

In January, with barely two months to go, meetings are held with the stakeholders, chaired by the Finance Minister. Finally, plans and programmes are carefully dovetailed to mirror the political leanings of the ruling party or coalition, marrying ideology with economics.

Every year, seven days before the Budget is presented, top officials of the Finance Ministry, experts, printing press technicians and stenographers are led into the North Block for a period of quarantine. For a week, they are totally cut off from the outside world, including their families. Only the finance minister can enter or exit the quarantined basement area where these officials will work and live.

A team of intelligence Bureau officials maintain round the-clock vigilance. Cell phones are banned. The stenos' computers are delinked from the server to rule out the possibility of cyber-theft. In case of a family emergency, relatives may leave a message on a landline number given to them, but at no point can they directly speak to the official inside.

The finance minister's speech is the most closely guarded document. It is usually handed over to the printers at midnight, about two days before the Budget is to be announced.

Initially, Budget papers were printed at Rashtrapati Bhavan. But in 1950, the Budget was leaked and the printing venue shifted to a press at Minto Road. Since 1980, the Budget has been printed in the basement of the North Block.

Source; Hindustan Times, New Delhi, July 5, 2009

PERFORMANCE BUDGETING

In India, plea for the introduction of Performance Budgeting was made in 1954 in the Lok Sabha debates on the Finance Ministry's control over expenditure. The Estimates Committee of the Lok Sabha in its 20th Report (1958) suggested that performance budget should be the goal and that a beginning might be made in a few selected Ministries and projects. The Administrative Reforms Commission 1968 (ARC) in its report titled "Finance Accounts and Audit" recommended that performance budgeting be introduced at the Centre as well as States.

Performance budgeting is similar to Planning Programming Budgeting System (PPBS) which was first introduced in the United States of America (USA) on the recommendation of the First Hoover Commission's Report (1949). The Second Hoover Commission's Report (1956) further stressed the concept. Since then substantial progress has been made and the concept has been applied with various modifications in the US. Many developing countries also adopted the technique of performance budgeting with certain modifications.

To quote from the Administrative Reforms Commission Report (1968) [ii] :-

"The present budgetary system serves well the twin purposes of Parliamentary accountability and control of expenditure but it is deficient as an instrument of management and evaluation of

ii. [Administrative Reform Commission Report, 'Finance Accounts and Audit (1968), GOI] performance. A system of budgeting which would inter-relate financial outlays with physical targets and achievements has become absolutely necessary. We have accordingly recommended the introduction of performance budgeting. Performance budgeting is, in essence, a technique for presenting estimates and expenditure in terms of functions, programmes, activities and projects. It would help create a built-in-mechanism for watching the progress in attaining programme targets and taking timely corrective action when things go away. It will also help reinforce the principle of accountability to Parliament."

Referring to the estimates for 'Demands for Grants', the Administrative Reform Commission in its Report (Jan. 1968, p 6) observed that the "Budget no doubt contains notes on important schemes as a supplement to Demands for Grants. But such a narrative description given separately cannot be a substitute for the inclusion of fuller data, relating to estimated inputs and expected outputs, as an integral part of the budget". As stated by the Working Group[iii] of the Administrative Reform Commission on Performance Budgeting, "from the point of view of Plan implementation, our budget have failed to provide an adequate link between the financial outlays and physical targets, notwithstanding the growing amount of data now being supplied in the budget documents". There is, therefore, an urgent need to introduce a system which will provide such a link and that link must take the form of a "Performance Budget". The Commission further recommended that "We feel, however, that the scheme, instead of being introduced in stages over a period of years as suggested by the Working Group, should be introduced as soon as possible in all the departments the activities of which are developmental in character".

As a consequence, performance budget was prepared by all the Union Government Ministries and by most of the State Governments for major projects/programmes each costing ₹ 100 crore or more. Performance budgeting system was also introduced in nationalised banks in India around 1972, though the manner and pace of performance budgeting system had not been the same in various banks. In general, the performance budgets were prepared by each branch of a bank on the basis of its past performance, environmental data and the policy guidelines issued by the head office. Regional budgets were developed on the basis of the branch budgets. Similarly, the bank budget was formulated after meetings and discussions of regional managers and managers from the central office and was a consolidation of regional budgets. As such, performance budget system in banks was an integral part of the budgeting system.

Similarly, budgets for the Railway Ministry in India are presented before the Parliament every year. The Budget Statement shows the total revenue receipts of Railways; revenue expenditure and Works Expenditure; distribution of the Railways' surplus; position of the various funds that the Railways are keeping with the Central Government like, Depreciation Reserve Fund, Development Fund, Pension Fund, etc.

In short, performance budget entails:

Laying down physical targets and finances involved;

What the government is doing and at what cost?

What are we accomplishing from the money spent?

(For illustration of performance budget see Exhibit 4.1 and Exhibit 4.2 in chapter four)

We discuss certain aspects relating to performance budgeting in the following pages:

- Format of performance budget
- Classification structure for performance budget and accounts
- Structure of accounts in Government in India

FORMAT OF PERFORMANCE BUDGET: In general, performance budget was presented under following broad heads:

---

iii. [Working Group of the Administrative Reform Commission on Performance Budgeting, Administrative Reform Commission Report, 'Finance Accounts and Audit (1968), GOI]

1. **Introduction :** gives a brief overview of the organization and department
2. **Review of the overall performance and Programmes ahead :** gives targets and achievements for the year in terms of broad physical dimensions and financial outlays; outlook for the next year is also presented
3. **Appraisal of performance** of major projects, programmes of the Ministry/department indicating growth of the programmes along with achievements and necessary remedial steps
4. **Financial requirements :** budgetary requirements in financial terms for major projects/ programmes each costing ₹ 100 crore or more are presented
5. **Explanation of financial requirement :** presents the narrative explanations justifying the financial requirements for each programme indicating physical data, targets, achievements, relevant workload factors and performance ratios

The format of a performance budget is illustrated by presenting performance budget of a department in Annexure A at the end of the Chapter. Details of the performance budgeting approach, its meaning, significance, classification structure, performance evaluation and financial management system are presented in chapter four and its sub-chapters four A and four B.

BUDGET AND ACCOUNTS : CLASSIFICATION STRUCTURE

A five-tier classification is followed for the presentation of budget and accounts in India. This is shown below in Exhibit 1.1

Exhibit – 1.1

Sectors of the Economy

⇓

Major Head (or Function or Major Programme)

⇓

Minor Head (or Programme)

⇓

Sub-head (or Activities or Schemes)

⇓

Detailed Head (or Object-wise Classification)

SECTORAL CLASSIFICATION :

The sectoral classification is the aggregation of the operations of the Government or is the grouping of the functions of the Government with reference to the characteristics of services provided by a function.

For this purpose, the economy is classified into four sectors:

(*a*) General Services

(*b*) Social & Community Services

(*c*) Economic Services

(*d*) Grant-in-Aid and Contributions

(a) General Services : General services include services indispensable to the existence of an organised State, such as, Police, Defence, District Administration, Fire Protection, etc. This sector is sub-divided into six sub-sectors namely,

- Organs of State (Parliament, Head of State, Judiciary, Audit, Council of Ministers and Elections),
- Fiscal Services (Agencies for collection of taxes),
- Interest payments and debt services,
- Administrative Services, such a Public Service Commission, District Administration, Police, Jails, etc.,

- Pensions and Miscellaneous General Services and
- Defence Services.

(*b*) **Social and Community Services :** Social and Community Services deal with programmes connected with the provision of basic social services to consumers such as, education, medical relief, housing, social security and welfare and services needed for community living such as, public health, urban development, broadcasting, information and publicity.

(*c*) **Economic Services :** Economic services deal with programmes and activities in the fields of production and trade towards economic growth of the nation. It is divided into seven sub-sectors, namely,

(1) General Economic Services (Foreign Trade and Export Promotion)
(2) Agriculture and Allied Services (Agriculture Cooperation, Planning Statistics, etc.)
(3) Industry and Minerals (Large and Medium Industries – Village and Small Industries, Mines and Minerals)
(4) Water and Power Development
(5) Transport and Communication (Port, Light-houses and Shipping Civil)
(6) Railways, and
(7) Posts and Telegraphs.

(*d*) **Grant-in-aid and Contributions :** Grant-in-aid and contribution record the transfer of resources in the form of grant-in-aid from the Centre to the States and to the Union Territories and from the State Government to the local bodies and Panchayati Raj Institutions.

Major Head, Minor Head, Sub-head and Detailed Head :

Each sector is further sub-divided into Major head → called Functions
Major head is further divided into 'Minor head' → called Programmes.
Minor Head is further divided as Sub-head → called Activities
Sub-head is divided as detailed head → object-wise classification of expenses

Thus Sectors, Major head, Minor head, Sub-head and Detailed head together constitute a five-tier arrangement of classification structure of Government Accounts.

Major head of accounts generally corresponds to 'Functions' such as Defence, Public Works, Agriculture; while Minor head, sub-ordinate to major head identifies the 'Programme' undertaken to achieve the objectives of the function. A programme may consist of a number of schemes or activities and these generally correspond to 'sub-heads' below the minor head represented by the programme. In certain cases, especially in regard to non-developmental expenditure, or expenditure of an administrative nature, the sub-heads denote the components of a programme, such as 'Organisation' or the different 'Wings of Administration'

A 'detailed head' also termed as an object-wise classification is primarily meant for itemized control over expenditure and indicates the object or nature of expenditure on a scheme or activity in terms of inputs such as 'salaries', 'office expenses', 'Grant-in-aid', 'Loans', 'Investments'.

Structure of Government Accounts in India:

The accounts of expenditure and revenues of India or State governments, and Union territories are recorded in the following three parts:

Part I	Consolidated Fund
Part II	Contingency Fund
Part III	Public Account

I. Consolidated Fund : It contains all revenues received, loans raised or the recoveries of the loan granted form the consolidated fund. Similarly, Government expenses are incurred from this fund with the authorization from the Parliament. There is a separate consolidated fund for the Union Government and for each state or for each Union Territory.

The Consolidated fund, where in all revenues and expenses are recorded after due process of law, is relevant for management purposes, has three main divisions, namely:-

Revenue,
Capital, and
Debt

The first division, **'Revenue'**, comprises of 'revenue receipt' and 'revenue expenditure' which arise from the operations of the enterprise. Revenue receipts include proceeds of taxation, and other receipts classed as revenue; and the net result after deduction of the revenue expenditure from the revenue receipts is shown as revenue surplus or deficit for the year.

The second division, **'Capital'** comprises of 'Capital Receipts' and 'Capital expenditure'*. The Capital expenditure is incurred either to increase or create assets of a material character, or to reduce recurring liabilities like, payment of capitalized value of the future pensions; these are normally not related to the operations of the enterprise. Such expenditure usually are met from borrowed funds.

The third division **'Debt'** comprises of public debt, loans and advances and inter-state settlements. Debt may be for the Union and State Governments and includes loan raised. Loans of a purely temporary nature are classed as 'Floating Debt' (Treasury Bills and Ways and Means Advances are the examples of Floating Debt), or loans are also 'Permanent Debt'. Loan also includes the repayment of the temporary loan and the recoveries of the 'Permanent Debt'; or 'Loans from the Union Government' and 'Loans and Advances by the Union Territories'.

II. **Contingency Fund :** The contingency fund is an imprest placed at the disposal of the President to meet urgent unforeseen expenditure pending authorization from the Parliament. Parliament approval for such expenditure and for withdrawal of an equivalent amount from the Consolidated fund is subsequently obtained and the amount spent from the contingency fund is recouped to the fund. Each state and union territory has its own contingency fund. At present the Contingency Fund has a corpus of ₹ 500 crore.

III. **Public Account :** The transactions like, provident fund, small savings and other deposits etc. for which the Government acts as a banker are kept in the public account. Such funds do not belong to the Government and have to be repaid back to the owners and the Parliamentary authorization is not required for such payments.

The above three divisions namely, revenue, capital and debt, are clubbed with the five-tier classification discussed above.

Code numbers: Scheme of Codification:

(1) **'Revenue'** transactions are denoted by a **Single** letter as 'A'
Capital transactions are denoted by double letter as 'AA'

(2) **Major Heads** in the Revenues and capital divisions are numbered serially:
- **Receipt Side** – is denoted by Roman **numerals**
- **Disbursement** – is denoted by Arabic **numerals** side

Principles and purposes of Account classifications:

The structural classification of accounts of Government in India, as discussed above, is based on the principle that a receipt or payment should be entered into the head of account which has a close reference to the department in which it is occurred, rather than to its objects. Since April 1st, 1976, the Departmentalized accounting system introduced in all the Ministries/Departments of Central Government are compiled by all Principal Accounts Office in the Ministry/ Department Concerned and are submitted to the Director of Audit Central Revenues (or any other final compiling authority

* ***In one view, the distinction between revenue and capital expenditure disguises useless expenditure and has lost all utility, so distinction instead be made between 'static expenditure' such as salaries and pensions which change nothing, and 'dynamic expenditure' which increases capacity of the economy to grow and cope with the future. (Ashok V. Desai, Business World March 19, 2012).***

as may be prescribed for the purpose of the accounts of the Union Government as a whole).

The decentralized accounting system with elaborate classification has been adopted to ensure uniformity of accounting in India, to have reliable comparison between the accounts of different Governments and periods, to assist in the realistic budget estimates or forecasts of receipts and payments, and to have meaningful comparison of actual with budgets.

ZERO-BASE BUDGETING

With the objective to control growth in public expenditure, the Seventh Five Year Plan document suggested various steps including modification of planning and budgetary procedures so as to take integrated view of developmental outlays regardless of whether they are new schemes of the current Plan or on-going schemes started in earlier plans. One of the steps suggested was to introduce Zero Base Budgeting approach both for the non-developmental and developmental expenditure; and the Government decided to adopt ZBB approach in the Central Government departments with effect from the budget for the year 1987-88. In this regard, the Finance Ministry sent on July 10, 1986 a ZBB manual under the title, 'Introduction of ZBB in the Government of India', to all ministries, departments, public sector undertakings and state governments. The manual presents guidelines for implementing ZBB. (The Manual is reproduced in Annexure B at the end of the chapter)

As a result, a number of Ministries at the Centre adopted ZBB approach. In addition, many State governments also adopted the ZBB approach.

Maharashtra Government was one of the States which initiated steps for the implementation in all the 40 departments including health, agriculture, and urban development and issued instructions dated October 27, 1986 and also issued a circular dated December 16, 1986 for the introduction of ZBB[iv]. These are presented in Appendix I and Appendix II respectively at the end.

Objective and approach of ZBB in India as laid down in the guidelines issued by the Finance Ministry in 1986 referred to above are summarized as under:

- ZBB was intended to help both in the judicious allocation of scarce resources at the national level and in deriving the optimum benefits out of the resources allocated. The objective was not to just cut expenditure, but to make public expenditure programmes more effective by a more purposive allocation of resources to various programmes.
- Under the ZBB approach, the existing programmes would not be treated as immutable but would be examined afresh as to their continued utility and effectiveness, thereby freeing resources for new programmes. Accordingly, new proposals and the funds required therefore and also on-going activities and the funds for them were required to be justified. In other words, both plan as well as non-plan schemes (latter are normally on going schemes) would be subject to review and justification under ZBB.
- Preparation and presentation of Performance Budget to the Parliament along with Demand for Grants of respective Departments would continue as before and with the adoption of ZBB, no separate set of documents would be presented to the Parliament, but the Performance Budget document would be further refined so as to increase its usefulness.
- Central Monitoring Group, as an analytical and advisory group had been constituted for introduction of ZBB and for dissemination of knowledge and expertise on the subject. The Group would, whenever required, analyse the data received from various Ministries for putting up to higher authorities for taking a final view on allocation of resources. The Group comprised Financial Advisor and officers of Ministry of Finance and Joint Secretary (Budget) as the Convener. Proforma seeking information on schemes/programmes of various Ministries so as to review, their usefulness, their continuance, and their ranking in order of their priority had been sent to various Ministries/Departments.
- Public Sector Undertakings, Departmental undertakings and autonomous bodies under the administrative control of various Ministries had been impressed upon to adopt ZBB approach in the sphere of their Revenue Budgets with the objective to cut down costs.

iv. ***[Joshi P L, ZBB Technology in Government (Dhruv & Deep Books, 1987)]***

As against the above detailed approach of ZBB, there was a simplified approach called, '*target-based-budget*', wherein a certain percentage of existing funds were made available for reallocation towards new Industrial Research activities. This approach was adopted in research and development organizations like, Council for Scientific and Industrial Research (see Chapter VI). Zero-base budgeting approach, its meaning, characteristics, mechanics, process and implementation issues are detailed in chapter five and its sub-chapters five A and five B.

■ OUTCOME BUDGET

Governments spend hundreds of crore of rupees on various projects or programmes and in order to know, 'how effectively each rupee is spent', or 'what is the benefit or outcome of the money spent', outcome budget was adopted.

Outcome budget is an exercise to convert 'outlays' into 'outcome', or to find out how effectively each rupee of government expenditure is spent. The outcome budget measures the development outcomes of government programmes; or develops linkage between the money spent and the results which follow; or converts financial outlays into physical outcomes, measurable and monitorable targets. This is to ensure that budget is an exercise to be cost-effective, to focus not on money spent but on the result of the money spent or on 'achievement' or 'accomplishment' and to account for 'value for money'. Thus outcome budget is used as an important tool for effective management of programmes and towards accountability; it is to inform the public about the money spent by various ministries.

To start, outcome budget was adopted during 2005-06 for plan schemes where it was easier to link expenditure with results for such investment programmes. To quote, Forward to Outcome Budget 2005-06[v], "This exercise has been taken up only for Plan expenditure at this stage. From the next year the outcome budget will be prepared for the Non-Plan expenditure too. Over a period of time, the outcome budget is expected to reflect the 'annual budget' in terms of intended outcome". Non-plan expenditure includes salary and pension for government employees, defence expenditure, interest payments on government debt and subsidies; and the non-plan expenditure of the Central Government accounts for approximately 70% of the total.

From the fiscal year 2006-07, the outcome budget was planned to become a part of the regular budgetary process and every ministry would present its preliminary outcome budget, while proposing its demand for grants to the Ministry of Finance. Thus, outcome budget becomes a sort of examination of expenditure before they are made, instead of a post-expenditure scrutiny; so at every stage of planning a programme, there would be mechanism of checks and balances, and this would result in reducing of unnecessary expenses. To quote from the Finance Minister Speech for the year 2006-07, "Government has shifted the emphasis from sheer 'quantity to the quality' of the outcome of the various social sector programmes. To ensure value for public expenditure, an outcome budget was presented on August 25, 2005. Government intends to present a Performance Budget on the first outcome budget before the end of the budget session. The outcome budget for 2006-07 was placed before the Parliament in 2007. This new approach underscores our resolve to ensure that the intended services in the right quantity and quality are delivered to the "aam admi". Accordingly, the Expenditure Finance Committee, which sanctions plans up to ₹ 100 crores would ask for clear definition of outcomes at the stage of planning a programme itself. Programme and Response Monitoring Division of the Planning Commission will co-ordinate the initiative towards outcome budget, and will try to bring a fair degree of uniformity of approach across the ministries, and develop yardsticks of reflecting outcomes with due regard to the special nature of their collective responsibilities, programmes and projects.

Developmental programmes, in general, have quantifiable outcomes and pace of expenditure has to be closely monitored so as to translate the outlays into outcomes. Outcome budget focuses not on how much has been spent but rather on what has been achieved by that expenditure. Converting

v. ***[Forward to Outcome Budget by P. Chidambaram, Union Finance Minister, GOI dated August 25, 2005***

outlays into outcomes, entails identification of result expected, and quantification of the result, which is a complex process and differs from ministry to ministry. It is more complex and complicated for administrative ministries involved in maintenance of law and order or for policy making relating to socio-economic matters. Thus making outcome budgeting a success becomes a challenging exercise; in particular, as the non-plan expenditure is a sizeable share of the total. For example, it is relatively easy to check if defence ministry has spent the funds allocated to buy new weapons but it is much harder to figure out how the sum spent on a village would help to lift the rural community above the poverty line.

As per the Revised Guidelines[vi] for the preparation of Outcome Budget 2009-10, "Outcome budgets have become an integral part of the budgeting process since 2005-06. For the regular budget of 2009-10, there will be one single document titled OUTCOME BUDGET 2009-10. This will broadly indicate the physical dimensions of the financial budgets as also the actual physical performance in 2007-08, performance for the full preceding year (2008-09) and targeted performance during 2009-10". As such performance budget and the outcome budget hitherto presented separately by Ministries/Departments, were merged with effect from the financial year 2007-08 and are presented as a single document titled, "Outcome Budget". It was with a view that the performance budget document lacked clear one-to-one relationship between the financial budget and the performance budget and inadequate target-setting in physical terms for the ensuing year. Further, there had also been a growing concern about the need to track not just the intermediate physical "outputs" that were more readily measurable but also the "outcomes", which were the end objectives of State intervention.

In other words, the Outcome Budget documents is prepared separately by each Ministry/ Department in respect of all Demands/Appropriations controlled by them except those exempted. (A List of exempted Demands/Appropriations is enclosed at Annexure C). However, even the Ministries/Departments and other authorities 'exempted' were requested to carry out this exercise for internal use and voluntarily decide to place it in public domain fully or partially.

As per the the Guidelines, the Outcome Budget 2009-10 will be prepared on the basis of Budget 2009-10 in the form of a document, separate for each Ministry/Department; the document is spread over six chapters which are summarized below:(For details of the outcome budgeting approach, various issues relating to outcome budget and its integration with other budget approaches see chapter seven)

Executive summary : Apart from summarizing relevant Chapters, this portion prominently highlight the details of the monitoring mechanism to regularly monitor physical and financial progress during the course of the year and to inform the general public about it.

Chapter I : It contains a brief introductory note on the functions of the Ministry/Department, organizational set up, list of major programmes/schemes implemented by the Ministry/department, its mandate, goals and policy framework. It also highlights goals, or major programmes or schemes in respect of women/gender equality, if any.

Chapter II : It contains a tabular format, which may be visualized as "vertical compression and horizontal expansion" of the Statement of Budget Estimate (SBE) included in the Expenditure Budget Vol. II (With suitably adapted format for Railways).

The main objective is to establish a one-to-one correspondence between the (finance) Budget and Outcome Budget for the year. The details comprise of the financial outlays, projected physical outputs and projected/budgeted outcomes (intermediate/partial and final, as the case may be), projected physical output are disaggregated by sex, wherever possible and appropriate i.e. where delivery is to individuals.

Chapter III : Presents reform measures and policy initiative, if any, taken by the Ministry/ department and how they relate to the intermediate outputs and final outcomes in areas such as public- private partnerships, alternate delivery mechanisms, social and women's empowerment processes, greater decentralization, transparency, etc.

---

vi ***Revised Guidelines for Preparation of Outcome Budget 2009-10, Office Memorandum dated May 6, 2009 No. 2(1(Pers/E.Cord/OB/2005 Ministry of Finance GOI***

Chapter IV : Review of past performance: It indicates the performance during the previous two years namely, 2007-08 and 2008-09 in terms of targets already set. The analysis of physical performance Scheme-wise with the reasons for variations; explaining the scope and objectives of individual programs/schemes, giving their physical targets and achievements, indicators of performance relating to individuals are disaggregated.

Chapter V : It contains financial review covering overall trends in expenditure vis-à-vis budget estimates/revised estimates in recent years, including the current year. Data is segregated scheme-wise, object head-wise, and institution wise in the case of autonomous Institutions. Position of outstanding utilization certificates and unspent balances with States and implementation agencies should is be brought out.

Chapter VI : It gives review of performance of Statutory and Autonomous Bodies under the administrative control of the Ministry/department.

To sum up, though outcome budget emphasises on results, or achievements, or accomplishments, it is similar to performance budget, it (the former) should be a welcome exercise as it is expected to change the mind set of officials to focus on results or outcome of the project and to ensure value for money rather than simply outlay of the project. In other words, outcome budget is just like putting of old wine in new bottles; in a way it could be a marketing strategy to re-label the performance budget to make it acceptable, operational and successful. However, since budgeting involves more of behavioural issues arising from laying down realistic targets, responsibility fixing and making executives accountable, performance budgeting, in that respect has not been effective, or is a non-starter despite its existence for over the decades, will outcome budget not have the similar fate?

GENDER BUDGET

Gender budgeting is one tool to promote women's equality and empowerment by allocating funds to implement policies for the development and empowerment of women. It is also called 'women's budget', or 'gender sensitive budget', or 'applied gender budget analysis'. "Gender budget is based on the modern idea that budget is not simply an accounting or book -keeping exercise. Instead, budgeting is key part of planning and implementation process. Thus budgets should follow policies rather than policies being determined by budgets. And among the policies that budgets should follow, is Government of India's commitment to promoting gender equality".

Gender budgeting is not to have a separate budget to address women's or gender concerns. Rather it has the objective to ensure that every part of the government budget takes gender differences into account, and special allocations for women and gender are helpful in addressing to their special needs.

Gender Budget Statement in India was first introduced in Budget 2005-06 considering the request of women's groups and on the recommendation of the Expert Group on "Classification System of Government Transactions". This statement has received an impetus over the last eight budgets with growing awareness of gender sensitivities. Gender Budgeting is an evolving area where, with better understanding and appreciation of the subject, more and more Ministries/Departments are reviewing programmes and schemes to address the quantum of resources that have the budgetary potential to impact and address the development needs of women. This Statement indicates, in two parts, the budget provisions for schemes that are substantially meant for the benefit of women. Part A details schemes in which 100% provision is for women, Part B reflects schemes where the allocations for women constitute at least 30% of the provision. Though gender budgeting is in the gestation stage, it raises a question, is it a budgetary approach, a process of authorisation of executives to execute plans; or a fund allocated for women and gender to address to their special needs? For details of gender budgeting and various issues relating to this budgeting see chapter eight.

BUDGETARY SYSTEM : ISSUES

Having discussed developments in budgeting and various budget approaches, namely, appropriation budgeting, performance budget, Zero-base budgeting, outcome budgeting and gender budgeting followed in India, certain issues concerning the budgeting approaches are discussed in the following pages. However, before that we present a list of the main documents submitted to the Parliament in connection with the Central Budgeting in Annexure D at the end of the chapter.

Budgetary approach, Planning Process and Budget documents

A question is raised about linkage of budgeting process and the planning process. For example, the performance budgeting as a technique for planning, implementation and reporting both in financial and physical terms was viewed as a duplication of the process of planning since our planning process also covered these aspects. The above contention that performance budgeting had also the virtues of the planning process was an over simplification of the concept of performance budgeting. According to the Report of the Working Group on Performance Budgeting of the Administrative Reform Commission, experience had shown that in our planning process, there was an absence of rapport between the financial and physical aspects of a programme; budgetary estimates were either under pitched or over pitched affecting allocation of resources. As such, "the technique of performance budgeting is something more than a mere bridge between financial and physical aspects of a programme". No doubt planning process covered programmes, targets outlays etc, there was a lacuna in the existing system in that there was no well organised framework. The performance budget tended to supply such framework to strengthen the planning process.

A number of documents presented before the Parliament contain information regarding physical and financial aspects for various programmes/projects. Was there a need for performance budgeting in that context?

It is true that the various documents (Explanatory Memorandum, Demand for Grants, Economic Survey etc.) presented to the Parliament provided a great deal of information and there had been various development towards giving more information. But in the absence of a comprehensive scheme for budgetary reform and also that these documents were often the results of attempts at meeting the requirements from different quarters, the information tended to be diffused, inadequate, disjointed. The performance budget provided co-ordinated and well knit, purposeful and cohesive, whole information at one place for formulation of programmes, or in the evaluation for performance; in that context the Administrative Reform Commission, 1968, reported the nature and extent of changes in the budget documents under the performance budgeting as compared to the then existing ones.

Budget approaches: Need for Integration

Various developments in budget approaches in India over the years, in a way, have been adopted that from the western countries, though after in-depth analysis and deliberations. For example, performance budget was similar to that of Planning, Programming and Budgeting System (PPBS) or Programme Budget in the US and was on the recommendations of the Administrative Reform Commission 1968 to link-up physical targets with financial involvement and to focus on 'achievements' and end results of the money spent. Similarly, ZBB was adopted in India in 1986, as it had been followed in the US (as discussed in chapter five) in Texas Instrumentation and Georgia State; its focus was to do away with the principle of incrementalism and to review both – ongoing programmes as well as new programmes so as to priortise activities, to weed out non-significant ones and to have better allocation of resources. Further, outcome budget was adopted in India in 2005–06 to emphasise on the outcome of the money spent, though both the performance budget and outcome budget are similar. Need for the adoption of outcome budget, rather than strengthening of the performance budgeting, and further defining of the term 'outcome', its conceptual aspects require detailed deliberations.

The above budgetary approaches were confined mainly to plan expenditure, without much review of the non-plan expenditure, the latter one accounts for about two-third of the total government expenditure. As such, these budget approaches have the same objective i.e. to have optimal allocation of funds, or to have value for money, or to weed out unproductive low priority activities. It is contended that the developments in budget approaches were with the intention to reinforce the need and significance of budgeting in the minds of government employees. In fact, budgeting is the same and different approaches are a marketing strategy to popularize the budgeting principles. As such, it is like putting of the same wine in bottles with different attractive labels.

Further, a question is raised: what should be the format of budgeting, should not budgeting system integrate all these approaches to avoid duplication and excess paper work? For example, ZBB was integrated with the budgeting system in vogue at that time, as no separate set of documents was reported to be presented to the Parliament, and performance budget was so refined so as to increase its usefulness. However, performance budget earlier or outcome budget now are separate documents presented to the Parliament; these are not contained in the Key Budget Documents presented to the Parliament (list is given in Annexure D at the end of this chapter) and also are not mandatory. In the context of performance budgeting, the Working Group on Performance Budgeting of the Administrative Reform Commission[vii] reported that it would not be sufficient to have the performance budget document as a supplementary one to the existing set of documents, as in that case, it would not have any impact whatsoever on the existing system and would be some what of fifth wheel to the coach. In that context, it may be mentioned that the private business houses or commercial enterprises integrate the principles of performance budgeting and Zero-base budgeting in their budgetary system and they usually don't use the jargons, performance budget or zero base budget, or outcome budget.

Similarly, the outcome budget introduced in 2005-06 was a separate document for various demands exceeding ₹ 100 crore and above, though the Revised Guidelines for the outcome budgeting 2009-10 laid down that for the regular budget of 2009-10, there will be 'one single document titled outcome budgeting 2009-10'. Further, the revised guidelines also read (para 4), "The outcome budget 2009–10 will be "prepared on the basis of Budget 2009-10 in the form of a document, separate for each Ministry/Department." In other words, the financial budget is drawn first and outcome budget is developed there from; it indicates that financial budget and outcome budget are two separate documents, the former one in the form of Annual Financial Statement is submitted to the Parliament for approval. As such, budgeting is similar to construction plan of a building, the 'Construction Plan' and the 'Working Plans' are two different approaches to a construction activity, the former is mandatory, is required by the authorities, while the latter ones are not mandatory and are for planning, and monitoring of construction activity by the builder and owner. Similarly, budgeting has various approaches, one, 'Annual Financial Statement of Receipts and Payments', which is required to be placed before the Parliament for approval under Article 112 of the Constitution. The other budgets drawn from the former are for managerial decision making. The other budget statements include performance budget, Zero-base-budget, Outcome budget, etc, these are not mandatory and are for managerial decision making.

Grants and loans to States and Budgeting

A bulk of the expenditure incurred by the Ministries of Industry, Agriculture, and Education, etc. is in the form of grants and loans to the states, or loans and investment in the share capital of State Public Enterprises. It was contended that it would be difficult to evaluate the results of such loans and grants through the Central Budget. In the opinion of the Study Team of the Administrative Reform Commission[viii], "if a suitable note is added in the budget explaining the purposes for which the grants are given and if this is supplemented by other administrative devices for obtaining regular periodical reports about performance from the receiving and spending agencies, the need and

---

vii [ibid]

viii [The Study Team on Financial Administration of the Administrative Reform Commission on Performance Budgeting, Administrative Reform Commission Report, 'Finance Accounts and Audit (1968), GOI (p 181)]

requirements of the situation would be met. Moreover, their actual utilization for the purposes for which money was given is also ensured in the audit". The Study Team also stated that, "the grants and loans may conveniently be shown as such and that no performance measurement or evaluation need be attempted in the budgets at the giving end. This is the case in the federal budget of the U. S. A also"

Plan and Non-plan classification

Government expenditure is normally classified as plan and non-plan; plan expenditure, in general, signify development expenditure while non-plan expenditure deals with essential outlays pertaining to debt repayment, salary and other administrative expenditure. Government budgets also follow the same classifications. Such classification is in addition to revenue and capital. Planning Commission prepares and monitors Five Year Plans and the budget contains every year expenses for plan as well as non-plan items. Such classification is unique in India so as to give greater emphasis to planning.

It may be mentioned that the Planning Commission is a non statutory as well extra constitutional body. It was set up by Jawaharlal Nehru on 15 March 1950, by an executive order to formulate India's Five-Year Plans, It makes periodic assessment of all resources in the country, boosts up insufficient resources and formulates plans for the most efficient and judicious utilization of resources. As a result, expenditure provisions in budget as well as accounts are made under the heads; 'plan' and 'non-plan'.

A Committee under the Chairmanship of Dr. C. Rangarajan was set up in April 2010 to suggest steps to improve management of the public expenditure. The Committee Report[ix] recommended that Plan and Non-Plan distinction in the budget is neither able to provide a satisfactory classification of developmental and non-developmental dimensions of government expenditure nor an appropriate budgetary framework and such Plan and Non-Plan distinction in the budget should be removed. The Committee also recommended that all public expenditure should be split into 'capital' and 'revenue' expenditure. The Committee noted that compartmentalisation of plan and non-plan expenditure has resulted in a situation in which the country has schools without teachers and hospitals without doctors because doctors and teachers are part of non-plan expenditure while schools and hospitals are part of plan expenditure. While the Planning Commission should be responsible for formulation of the Five-Year Plan, the task of firming up annual budgets should be entrusted to the Finance Ministry based on inputs from the Plan panel.

The Committee further reported that:

- While the finance ministry will become the primary agency deciding and disbursing resources for government sectors and programmes after the declassification, the planning commission will function as an advisory body that will seek to ensure that the spending is in accordance with the developmental priorities of the government.
- Ministry of Finance may be responsible for guiding the fiscal policy, preparation of budget and financial decisions. The planning commission may be responsible, for sake of convenience and domain knowledge, to guide the overall development priorities of the Government.
- The finance ministry will be the primary agency deciding the sectoral outlays for the five-year period for state and central plans, erasing the need for any other plan-budget link document
- States will not have to come to the Planning Commission for approval of state plans but directly implement programmes according to available resources. However, to check misuse of funds and increase accountability, all spending at the state level should come

ix *[Report of the High Level Expert Committee on Efficient Management of Public Expenditure, Planning Commission, Government of India, New Delhi (July, 2011) Website : www.planningcommission.gov.in]*

under the purview of Comptroller Auditor General of India (CAG) instead of local audits for directly transferred funds.

- There should be modification in the accounting classification with a view to strengthen the framework for transfer of funds from centre to the states.
- The proposed classification should provide uniform codes for central programmes, sub-programmes and schemes being implemented in the states.
- The Central Plan Monitoring System (CPMS) should be strengthened and citizens should be empowered to seek information on flow of resources and utilisation with a view to promote transparency and accountability.
- There should a basic shift in budgeting approach from "one-year horizon to a multi-year horizon and from input based budget to outputs and outcomes".

As a step to cut total expenditure, in the words of Ashok V. Desai, 'abolish the distinction between Plan and non-Plan expenditure, that will save expenditure on the Planning Commission, a parking place for economists and sleepwalkers' (see Business World March 19, 2012).

The recommendations of the C. Rangarajan Committee to abolish the distinction between Plan and non-Plan expenditure have far reaching policy implications in terms of role of the Planning Commission and Finance Ministry and implementation of the recommendations will require acceptance by the Planning Commission and majority of the states. Notwithstanding the above, till the plan and non-plan expenditure distinction continues, why not the budgetary exercise and the budgetary approach– whether performance budget, or ZBB or outcome budgeting– should cover both plan and non-plan expenditure?

As emphasised by the Finance Minister in the budget speech for the year 2000-01, the composition of Central Government expenditure had become rigid and prone to large, precommitted increases; and the on-going schemes mostly in the nature of non-plan expenditure, which account in about two-third of the total expenditure, should be subjected to rigor of ZBB, or outcome budget scrutiny.

Budgeting : An Economic and Political Exercise

As stated earlier, budget is an exercise for allocation of resources for various projects or programmes, it is a policy document indicating the context and direction for future. A question is raised, is budget an economic exercise or a political document? Budgetary exercise though should be based on principle of optimal allocation of resources, many a time economic reality is set aside, and budget is to serve more of political agenda. For example, in the US, as a process of budgetary reforms, legislation was enacted with an objective of reducing the annual deficit to zero by 1991, (which later was extended to 1993), it quickly became 'an excuse for accounting gimmickry and economic sophistry' witnessing the book-keeping gymnastic and political brinkmanship.[x] The same has been the approach of over-estimation of revenues and under-estimation of expenses for the coming year. For example, in India, for the budgetary exercise for the 2011-12, there was optimism in estimation of receipts which were expected to increase by 17.4 percentages over the previous year, while growth in expenses only by 3.3 percentage.

Budgeting : Practice of Funding of end-of-year spending and budgeting as a Biennial Exercise

Budget at present is an annual exercise and as mentioned earlier, is a constitutional requirement and all funds voted by the Legislature lapse when the financial year end, known as the 'rule of lapse'[xi]. At times, appropriations and release of funds made at fag end of the year lead to the practice

x *[Joseph C. Pilegge, Budget Reforms in Handbook of Public Budgeting (E) Jack Rabin (marcle dekker inc, New York 1992)]*

of end-of-year spending rush so as to exhaust the funds allocated. Thus the executives avoid refund of unutilized funds and to have lower allocation the next year. This is in a way against the principle of 'value for money' or importance of 'output and results'. The Administrative Reform Commission (1968) considered the following three suggestions to overcome the deleterious effects of rule of lapse and the practice of end-of-year spending rush so as to exhaust the funds allocated:

- Abrogation of the rule of lapse
- An eighteen months' or 24 months' budget instead of a 12 months' one
- The funds may be sanctioned annually with the provision that funds may not lapse at the end of the year but may be available for utilization by the executive for a limited period of say, three to four months in the succeeding year on the principle of spill-over[xii].

The ARC did not find favour any of the above and recommended that "in order to overcome the reluctance of the Ministries/Departments to surrender funds in time the Finance Ministry should give an assurance through a circular that under spending in one year would not prejudice the budget estimates for the next year."

However, it may be mentioned that some of the local governments in the US adopt a "budget system with fewer line items, more authority for managers to move among line items, and freedom for agencies to keep some or all of what they save – thus minimizing the incentive for year-end spending sphere". Further, a practice to carry forward a portion of unutilized funds to the next year is followed in Canada. In this regard, the National Performance Review Report[xiii] (1993) recommends, "allow agencies to roll over 50 percent of unobligated year-end balances in all appropriations for operations" and also allow agencies to use up to two percentage of rolled over funds to finance bonus for employees involved.

As regards the suggestion to have longer period budget of eighteen months' or twenty four months', the ARC (1968) was of the view that the year would then cease to be the unit of Government account and there would be one budget, one Finance Act, one Appropriation Act every eighteen months or two years and no longer one of each in every year. Neither in expenditure, nor in revenue it is possible to estimate with accuracy for a two year period. However, the National Performance Review Report (1993) recommended biennial budgets and multi-year authorization. Further, some states in the US have biennial budgets and Sweden has three year budget frame. In this regard, as mentioned earlier, the C. Rangarajan Committee recommended that there should be a basic shift in budgeting approach from "one-year horizon to a multi-year horizon and from input based budget to outputs and outcomes". Similarly, Ashok V. Desai is of the view that instead of the budget estimates for the coming one year, it should give projections for the next five years so as to spread out expensive investments and to have detailed planning for the coming years. (Business World March 19, 2012).

Future of Budget Reform

"The budget is a mythical beanbag. Congress votes mythical beans into it, and then tries to reach in and pull real beans out"— ***Will Rogers***

Gleckman has described the budgetary exercise "as an excuse for accounting gimmickry and economic sophistry" [xiv] As against this, according to Richard Rose, "like PPBS, and Management by Objectives, Zero-Base-Budgeting has "evaporated". Gone but not forgotten, it survives in pockets of

---

xi ***[Administrative Reform Commission Report, 'Finance Accounts and Audit (1968), GOI (p. 17)]***

xii ***[Ibid (p 18)]***

xiii ***[National Performance Review Report, (September 1993), Creating a Government That Works Better & Costs Less (AL Gore, USA)]***

xiv ***[Gleckman H, The bottom line: Graman-Rudman isn't working (Business Week , 3099- 36, 1989) in Joseph C. Pilegge, Budget Reforms in Handbook of Public Budgeting (E) Jack Rabin (marcle dekker inc, New York 1992)]***

the federal bureaucracy and in altered form, in some 20 states. What these all three executive branch budgetary reforms had in common was emphasis on analysis. But analysis was either unwelcome or unnecessary"[xv]

There have been continued and renewal efforts at budgetary innovations. Most of the efforts have been aimed at finding technical and procedural – not policy- solutions. Caiden suggested that "the search for new approaches to budgeting is a task for each generation as it confronts changing economic and fiscal conditions". The budgetary approaches or budgetary innovations should not remain as distinct and disjoint rather should be integrated into one. As such, performance budget, or ZBB or outcome budget, or gender budget are distinct budgetary approaches each focusing on a certain aspect and naming them as a budget would be an oversimplification. Budget as a policy document operationalises the plan, is an instrument of planning, control and decision making, and authorizes the executives; as such only one budget integrated with various approaches can be a policy document. Budgeting is similar to a construction plan of a building; 'Building Construction Plan' is a policy document, the 'Working Plans' are distinct approaches, each focusing on a certain aspect for the guidance of the builder. To conclude, we quote Joseph C. Pilegge[xvi], " All of these (approaches) – along with such concepts as envelop budgeting, target-based budgeting, revenue budgeting, and others still in the gestation stage, can be expected to occupy the debate over managing the nation's finances into the twenty-first century.

---

xv ***[Rose R Implementation and evaporation. The recod of MBO. Public Administration Review 37: 64 0 77 (1977) in Joseph C. Pilegge, Budget Reforms in Handbook of Public Budgeting (E) Jack Rabin (marcle dekker inc, New York 1992)]***

xvi ***[Joseph C. Pilegge, Budget Reforms in Handbook of Public Budgeting (E) Jack Rabin (marcle dekker inc, New York 1992)]***

Annexure A

Performance Budget - Format

A performance budget is a comprehensive document with an object to provide cohesive information both in physical and financial terms at one place for formulation of programmes and for evaluation for performance of each programme. The contents and the presentation of performance budget are thus extremely important and are as under:

1. **Introduction:** This part gives a brief overview of the organisation/department. It starts with the origin, set-up and scope of work of the organisation/department to give an idea of its functioning. The objectives, range of work in terms of broad programme classifications and broad organisation structure of the departments/agencies involved with the implementation of the programmes are also enunciated in this part.
2. **Review of the overall Performance and Programmes Ahead :** This part gives a review of the performance dealing with the targets and achievements for the year in terms of broad physical dimensions and financial outlays. The outlook for the next year in terms of physical dimension and financial outlays are also presented.
3. The next part gives appraisal of performance of major projects, programmes of the Ministry/department indicating growth of the programmes along with achievements and necessary remedial steps taken so far during the course of the programme.
4. **Financial requirements :** The budgetary requirements in financial terms for major projects/programmes each costing ₹ 100 crore or more are presented in this part. The information normally included in this part are :-
   (*a*) Programmes and activities budgeted for the organisation/department and the physical targets for each programme.
   (*b*) Financial needs for each programme.
   (*c*) Funds required for various inputs or objects of expenses, like salaries, establishment, etc.
   (*d*) Sources of funds indicating the Demand Numbers and Major Heads under which the funds are provided for the various programmes.

   The total of funds required under the functional classification (presented in 'b' above) and under object wise classification (presented in 'c' above) are same.

   The above information, in addition to that of the budgeted year, also includes revised estimates for the current year, and actual for the immediate past year.
5. **Explanation of financial requirement:** This part presents the narrative explanations justifying the financial requirements for each programme. The narrative explanations are in terms of physical data, targets, achievements, relevant workload factors and performance ratios.

   This part is essential for the necessary development of performance budget, since it provides necessary data in physical and financial terms for purposes of performance evaluation.

Annexure B

Introduction of Zero - Base Budgeting in the Government of India

Circular on Zero Base Budgeting Dated July 10, 1986

Copy of D.O. Letter No. F2(90)~B(PB)/86 dated 10th July 1986 of Shri R. Ganapati, Secretary to the Government of India, Ministry of Finance, Department of Expenditure, New Delhi, Addressed to the Secretaries to the other Ministries/Departments of the Government of India.

1. As you are no doubt aware, the Seventh Five Year Plan has been drawn up in the context of severe resource constraints being faced by the Central and State Governments. The Plan document has, therefore, delineated a framework of fiscal management to underpin the efforts to successfully implement the Plan. The document has suggested several steps to control public expenditure, including;

(*a*) strengthening the procedures for the scrutiny of expenditure proposals and subjecting them to the discipline of cost effectiveness analysis;

(*b*) administrative reforms to eliminate unnecessary work, reduce overlap and simplify procedures;

(*c*) fuller utilisation of the facilities already created through better maintenance adopting a cost effective approach in public services;

(*d*) modification of the planning and the budgetary procedures so as to take an integrated view of developmental outlays regardless of whether they are on new schemes of the current Plan or on the maintenance of schemes started in earlier Plans;

(*e*) re-examination of the rationale for various subsidies taking into account the possibility of leakages, the economic status of beneficiary groups and cost-benefit analysis of the subsidies;

(*f*) elimination of all Non-Plan support, including subsidies and Non-Plan loans to cover cash losses, to public sector enterprises; and

(*g*) introduction of Zero Base Budgeting which requires the expenditure on even the on-going activities to be justified; it is to be applied to both non-development and development expenditure.

It has accordingly been decided to adopt Zero Base Budgeting (ZBB) approach in the Central Government Departments with effect from the Budget for 1987 - 88.

2. ZBB requires identification and sharpening of objectives; those objectives; selecting the best alternative through cost-benefit and cost effectiveness analysis; prioritisation of objectives and programmes; switching of resources from programmes with lower priority to those with higher priority; and identification and elimination of programmes which have out lived their utility.

3. In ZBB, a Ministry / Department or an organisation is required to justify not only the new proposals and the funds therefore but also the on-going activities and the funds for them. In other words, provisions for existing programmes are also required to be justified in the budget rather than adding them in the budget as a matter of routine. As such, under the ZBB approach, the existing programmes will not be treated as immutable but will be examined afresh as to their continued utility and effectiveness thereby freeing resources for new programmes.

4. ZBB is intended to help both in the judicious allocation of scarce resources at the national level, and in deriving the optimum benefits out of the resources thus allocated. The objective is not to just cut expenditure, but to make public expenditure programmes more effective by a more purposive allocation of resources to various programmes. If budgetary cuts become inevitable, ZBB will provide a more logical basis for effecting them as compared to *ad hoc* and across the board cuts. An explanatory note on the concepts and procedures of

ZBB is given in academic literature. We would, however, prefer to adopt the ZBB approach without placing undue emphasis on the jargon and without creating a mass of paper work.

5. It is not intended that as a result of this exercise a separate set of documents will be presented to Parliament. The preparation and presentation of Performance Budgets to the Parliament along with Demands for Grants of the respective Departments will continue as heretofore. As you will readily agree, with the adoption of ZBB approach, Performance Budget document can be further refined so as to increase its usefulness.
6. We are fully conscious of the fact that each Department will have to develop its own methodology for achieving the objectives of the ZBB. The Finance Ministry will only act as a catalyst. I have separately constituted a Group of Financial Advisers and officers of the Ministry of Finance, with Joint Secretary (Budget) as the Convener, which will function as the Central Monitoring Group for introduction of ZBB. The Central Monitoring Group will only be an analytical and advisory group which, whenever required, will analyse the data received from various Ministries for putting up to higher authorities for taking a final view on allocation of resources. It will also act as the core centre for dissemination of knowledge and expertise on the subject. You may now constitute a Group of senior officers with the Financial Advisor, (FA) as the Convener to interact with the Central Monitoring Group and at the same time ensure that the ZBB exercise undertaken is specifically tailored to suit the culture and requirements of your Ministry/Department. This Group will review the existing programmes, both Plan and Non-Plan, with reference to the basic objectives of the Seventh Plan including the development perspective towards the year 2000 outlined in the Plan document.
7. One of the advantages sought in ZBB approach is the involvement of top level officers in the budgetary process. Conversely, it is also true that without their participation and support, the ZBB exercise would not produce the desired results. I would, therefore, request you to impress upon all your officers to actively participate in the ZBB exercise. While your FA. may act as the nodal point for this purpose, you will agree with me that the introduction of ZBB cannot be left to the FA. alone, it needs your personal involvement and that of your senior colleagues.
8. Looking at the various steps involved in ZBB, we are of the view that it may be implemented in the best possible manner only by the people who are actually administering/executing the various schemes/programmes/activities of your department. Hence, we recommend that no outside consultants need be appointed for this purpose at this stage. We are, however, planning to hold some workshops, seminars, etc. for training the key officials of the Ministries on ZBB process. We shall let you know about this in due course.
9. The Central Monitoring Group has prepared a model Questionnaire **(Form A, Appendix I)** for seeking information on the schemes/programmes/activities of the various Ministries so that a meaningful review about their usefulness and further continuance could be undertaken. The various aspects covered in the questionnaire may kindly be answered in their proper perspective. The proforma of another form **(Form B, Appendix II)** for preparing a ranking of the various programmes in order of their priority is also enclosed. Programmes with smaller outlays of, say, less than a crore of rupees per year, may be grouped together. It may kindly be ensured that the total number of programmes/groups of programmes for which the information is furnished does not become unwieldy. The questionnaire may kindly be completed in respect of each scheme / programme / activity, other than those relating to investments in and loans to Public Sector Enterprises, and returned along with Form B to Shri K.S. Sastry, Joint Secretary (Budget), Department of Economic Affairs, Ministry of Finance by 31st August, 1986.

10. In so far as the Public Sector Enterprises are concerned, it may be impressed upon them that they apply ZBB concept in preparation of their Budgets. While their Capital Budgets involving investment decisions are normally appraised by a number of agencies in the Government before a final decision is taken, it is in the sphere of their Revenue Budgets that there appears to be considerable application of this technique to cut down the costs. The Revenue Budgets should be prepared, say, by the end of December and got approved by the Board of Directors well in advance of the commencement of the new financial year. Apart from financial outlays, the Revenue Budget should clearly indicate the physical targets for the various goods and services proposed to be produced by the undertakings during the next years. The estimates of expenditure going into the Revenue Budget should be fully supported by the relevant cost data. The target for overall capacity utilisation and efficiency as well as consumption norms for all the key factors of production should be fixed and put up to the Board of Directors along with the Revenue Budget. At the time of approving the Revenue Budget, the Board of Directors may also like to prioritise the various activities of the undertakings so that, if necessary, the activities with lower priority may be dispensed with and more funds may be made available for financing the activities with higher priority. The introduction of ZBB approach in finalisation of the Revenue Budgets of Public Sector Enterprises may be monitored through the Government Directors and the Financial Advisor working in your Department.

11. As regards Departmental undertakings and autonomous bodies under your administrative control the above procedure may be adopted mutatis -' mutandis keeping in view the nature of their function and the extent of autonomy granted to them by the Government.

12. I also look forward to your suggestions, if any, for successful implementation of ZBB in the Government of India and Central Public Enterprises.

APPENDIX -I

FORM 'A'

ZERO BASE BUDGETING QUESTIONNAIRE

(To be filled separately for each programme/group of programmes)

1. Name of the programme/group of programmes
2. What are the objectives of the Programmes? (to be specified in short, pithy phrases)
3. How are the objectives related to the goals and objectives specified in the Seventh Plan document for the Seventh Plan period as well as for the year 2000?
4. Why should the stated objectives be achieved only through the instrument of public expenditure programmes? (The idea is to see whether the same cannot be achieved through other instruments of public policy e.g. legal and administrative controls, tax/subsidy mechanism, credit policy, promotion of voluntary effort, etc)
5. What are the other departments/agencies funded by the Central Government working to achieve the same objectives? Please specify their budget allotments for the year 1986-87. What mechanisms exist to coordinate with them?
6. What are the programmes of other departments/agencies (whether funded by the Central Government or not) on whose successful implementation depends the success of this programme? What mechanisms exist to ensure their successful implementation?
7. Would you like some changes in the existing organisational structure for effective implementation of this programme? If so, please give your suggestions.
8. Would you like some changes in the existing systems and procedures within the Government for taking decisions relating to implementation of this programme? If so, please give your suggestions.

9. Would you like some changes in the existing personnel management systems and practices (including recruitment, training and career development) in relation to implementation of this programme? If so, please give your suggestions for improvements.

10. Since inception (please specify the year) how many times has the implementation of this programme been evaluated? With what result? (note to be taken of the observations made by the Parliamentary Committee as well as the Comptroller and Auditor-General of India)

11. Whether the programme is funded from external assistance; if so, to what extent?

12. Whether the programme is the result of a statutory requirement; if so, spell out the requirement?

13. Are there any factors (like natural increase in the number of beneficiaries) which make it imperative to increase the allotment of funds to the programme in coming years?

14. Whether any norms have been fixed for regulating the expenditure on the programme or specific components thereof?

15. If additional allotment of funds, say, 25 percent is made for this programme, how would you expand the programme? How soon can you expand? What will be the benefits flowing from such expansion?

16. If allotment of funds for this programme is cut, say by 25 percent, how would you contract the programme? How soon can you contract? what will be the adverse consequences of such contraction?

17. Any other information that you consider relevant for taking a decision on the Budget allotments to the programme in the four years ending 1989-90.

18. Budget allotment for 198X- 199X

	Plan	Non – Plan	Total
Revenue Gross			
Receipts & Recoveries* Net			
Capital (including Loans) Gross			
Receipts & Recoveries* Net			
Total (to be carried over to Form B)			

19. What is the break-up of the Budget allotment under the following heads:

(*a*) Staff salaries, etc. (please specify the number of staff)

(*b*) Travel expenses (only tour/transfer T A expenses to be given here. LTC expenses to be given under (*a*) above)

(*c*) Office expenses

N.B. In respect of (*a*), (*b*) and (*c*) please include information on autonomous agencies for which maintenance grants are given by the Department.

(*d*) Equipment

(*e*) Materials and supplies

(*f*) Maintenance expenses

(*g*) Transfers to State and Union Territory Governments (Please indicate the pattern of financing)

(*h*) Transfers to Public Enterprises

(*i*) Transfer to autonomous bodies (excluding maintenance grants included under (*a*), (*b*) and (*c*) above)

(*j*) Works expenditure (Please specify separately the allotment for work expenditure include in the Budget of the executing agency e.g. Central Public Works department)

(*k*) Others.

---

* ***Whether they appear in the accounts as reduction of expenditure or on the receipt side.***

APPENDIX - II

FORM 'B'

ZERO BASE BUDGETING

Ranking of Programme I Group of Programmes Budget
Allotment for 198X - 199X

1.

2.

3.

N.B.

1. A programme with a budget allotment of less than ₹ One crore may not be listed separately; analogous programmes to be grouped; list not to exceed 30.
2. Programmes to be arranged in descending order of priority.

Annexure C

List of exempted Demands/Appropriations in respect of which Outcome Budget is not mandatory

The outcome budget 2009-10 is intended to cover the entire Central Plan Outlay (Gross Budget support and Internal and Extra Budgetary Resources) and connected non-Plan provisions that are amenable to Outcome Budgeting. In general, a Ministry/Department may exclude the "*Assistance to State Plan*" component of its Plan Budget from the scope of Outcome Budget. The following demand/appropriations are specifically exempted from the purview of outcome budgeting:

Ministry of Defence
Defence Pensions
Defence Services - Army
Defence Services - Navy
Defence Services - Air Force
Defence Ordnance Factories
Defence Services - Research and Development
Capital Outlay on Defence Services
Interest Payments
Transfer to State and Union Territory Governments
Loan to Government Servants, etc.
Repayment of Debt
Pensions
Indian Audit and Accounts Department
Cabinet
Transfer to Union Territory Governments
Election Commission
Supreme Court
Ministry of Parliamentary Affairs
Ministry of Personnel, Public Grievance sand Pensions
Staff, Household and Allowances of the President
Lok Sabha
Rajya Sabha
Union Public Service Commission
Secretariat of the Vice-President
Andaman & Nicobar Islands
Chandigarh
Dadra & Nagar Haveli
Daman & Diu
Lakshadweep

Annexure D

KEY TO BUDGET DOCUMENTS: BUDGET 2013 - 2014

1. The Budget documents presented to Parliament comprise, besides the Finance Minister's Budget Speech, the following:
   A. Annual Financial Statement (AFS)
   B. Demands for Grants (DG)
   C. Appropriation Bill
   D. Finance Bill
   E. Memorandum Explaining the Provisions in the Finance Bill, 2013
   F. Macro-economic framework for the relevant financial year
   G. Fiscal Policy Strategy Statement for the financial year
   H. Medium Term Fiscal Policy Statement
   I. Medium Term Expenditure Framework Statement
   J. Expenditure Budget Volume-1
   K. Expenditure Budget Volume-2
   L. Receipts Budget
   M. Budget at a glance
   N. Highlights of Budget
   O. Status of Implementation of Announcements made in Finance Minister's Budget Speech of the previous financial year.

The documents shown at Serial A, B, C and D are mandated by Art. 112,113, 114(3) and 110(a) of the Constitution of India respectively, while the documents at Serial F, G, H and I are presented as per the provisions of the Fiscal Responsibility and Budget Management Act, 2003. Other documents are in the nature of explanatory statements supporting the mandated documents with narrative or other content in a user friendly format suited for quick or contextual references.

(i) In addition to the above, individual Departments/Ministries also prepare and present to Parliament their Detailed Demands for Grants, Outcome Budget, and their Annual Reports. The Economic Survey which highlights the economic trends in the country and facilitates a better appreciation of the mobilization of resources and their allocation in the Budget is brought out by the Economic Division of Department of Economic Affairs, Ministry of Finance. The Economic Survey is presented to Parliament in advance of the Union Budget. *As such, Performance Budget, Zero-base Budget and Outcome Budget are not mandatory under the provisions of the Constitution.*

(ii) To monitor the performance management of various Ministries/Departments, Result Framework Document (RFD) system has been adopted by the Government. The RFD system is being implemented in the various Ministries/Departments in phased manner. In Phase I of the implementation, RFD was implemented to 59 Ministries/Departments for the year 2009-10. In Phase II, 62 Ministries/Departments prepared RFD for the year 2010-11. Performance Management in the Government is a new concept which determines the performance index based upon the agreed objectives, policies, programs and projects/ schemes. To ensure the success in achieving the agreed objectives and implementing agreed policies, programs and projects, the RFD also includes a commitment for required resources and necessary operational autonomy.

CHAPTER 2

Planning and Budgetary Process

"Planning is a continuous movement towards desired goals"

Pt. Jawaharlal Nehru

"Five year plans are formulated in the perspective of long term development. This enables us to raise the national efforts to match specific goals and meet critical challenges, annual plans give us operational meaning to the exercise. Monitoring, review and evaluation procedures help to keep the vessel in the course. The voyage has been longer and rougher than we have imagined but there is little doubt about the rightness of the courses we have charted".

Smt. Indira Gandhi

PLANNING

Planning is the designing of future course of action. During the period of technological and scientific advancements, when every organization and economy wants to accelerate its rate of development, planning assumes significant role. In a developing economy, planning is essential for the optimum development and equitable distribution of resources. It is to ensure best use of scarce resources to avoid wastages, to reduce economic inequalities and to quicken the pace of national development.

Thus planning, bridges the gap from where we are to, where we want to go and is concerned with taking action in the immediate present to prevent becoming obsolete in the future. External factors like, technological and social change, inter-dependence and complexity has impact on organization's functioning and planning is concerned with adaptability to variations in the external factors.

John Kenneth Galbraith has emphasized the significance of planning in the New Industrial State employing modern technology. It requires a massive and inflexible commitment of resources to the introduction of innovation in the process of production of goods and services and such commitment is not possible without a meticulous and detailed research and planning[i]. To quote Dr. Dubashi, "Planning has become a passport to success of an enterprise. It has become the first and most important technique of modern management. Absence of planning is absence of preparation and therefore, the path of failure".[ii] As the saying goes, if you fail to plan, you are planning to fail'

Planning is considered essential in every economic system. In a western capitalist economic system, planning is used as an instrument of correcting or countervailing the aberrations, imbalances and malfunctioning of the marketing economy, like unemployment, monopoly, inequality or social costs of private enterprises. In a socialist economy, planning is used as a means for management of socially owned means of production; and in a developing country, planning is an instrument of accelerating the pace of economic development.

The need for planning in India, a developing country, becomes clear when we look ahead at the potentials and the utilization of its resources;

i [John Kenneth Galbraith, The New Industrial State]

ii [Dubashi, P.R., Grammar of Planning]

- with a population of 121 crore; over 2 crore of unemployed and above 26 percent being below poverty line;
- of the land under cultivation, less than 20 percent is irrigated;
- with 9 crore cubic meter per annum of utilizable water resources, only 40 percent are put to use;
- hydro electric power generation accounts for only 15 percent of the potential of 216 million kilowatt hours per annum.

Thus planning is essential to tap the potentials, and to put them to optimal use for economic development (*).

Planning, thus, provides benefits like —

- identification of problems or opportunities;
- improvement in the decision making process;
- focus specially on future directions, values and objectives of the economy or organization; and
- helping the executives in assuring the growth, survival of enterprises.

BUDGETS AND PLANNING PROCESS

A budget is an instrument which operationalises the plan and lays down the path to be followed for achievement of the planed objectives. A budget, thus, is a pre-determined plan expressed in financial terms. Concepts involved in a budget are: looking ahead with a purpose, numerical estimation of inflows and out flows, and balancing of inflows and outflows. The word 'budget' is derived from the French word '*bougette*', which means "small leather bag"[iii] or pouch, referring to proposals for financing of government expenditure carried to the Parliament for approval. In other words, it implies planning for the sources and spending of money from the bag with the Parliament approval for achieving the objectives.

Planning, as discussed above, attempts to translate long-term objectives into medium term, operational sub-objectives and to have an optimal allocation of human, physical and financial resources for attainment of objectives. It is a dynamic process, needs constant review and redefinition of objectives and plans. The budgeting system, on the other hand, provides mechanism for laying down standards, achieving and implementing plans and provides feed back information on the attainment or otherwise of planned targets and standards; it is a process of authorization of executives to execute plans, it is a process of authorization of executives to execute plans. In short, the budgetary system provides dynamism to planning.

For example, a manager's job comprises of following four tasks:

Accept Task
⇓
Decide How To Do It
⇓
Delegation
⇓
Check Result

iii ***[Sudarshan C.N., Government Budgeting: Principles and Practices, Sree Sudarshan Publication, Chennai,2001*]**

* **Note:** *It is appropriate to distinguish between growth and development. While growth is merely a quantitative concept and implies simply an increase in the gross national product, development is a qualitative as well as the quantitative concept, considers increase in the standard of living, and involves changes in attitudes, institutions, organizations, manpower and other resources required for mobilization of the potential of the economy.*

These tasks are true of managers at all level, across all departments and functions, whether senior most level or at lower level (see Box-1).

Box: 1

Manager's Job: Four Phases

Accept Task
↓
Decide How to Do it ⇒ Planning
↓
Delegate
↓
Check Results ⇒ Control

Box: 2

Management

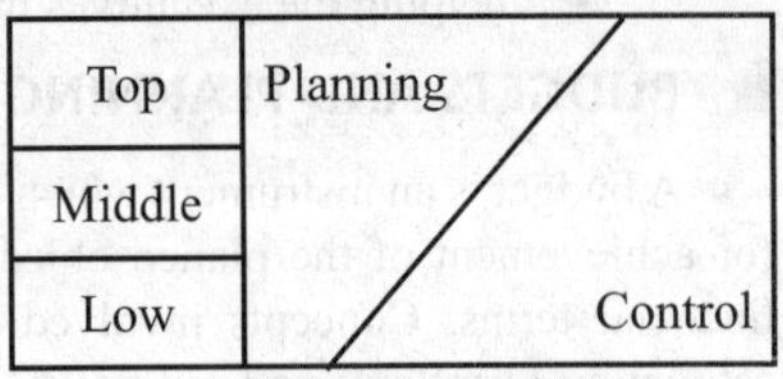

Involvement of Time

Task two above, '*Decide How to Do it*' and task four '*Check Results*' are planning and control, respectively. In other words, 'planning' and 'control' are inbuilt at all levels of management. At senior level, a manager devotes relatively a greater percentage of his time for planning, while control involves lesser of his time (see box-2).

■ BUDGET: MEANING AND PROCESS

Budgeting process, as discussed latter, requires approval of the competent authority, namely Board of Directors in case of a company, or Parliament in case of the Central Government. As per Article 112 of the Constitution of India, the executives have to place before the Parliament, estimates of expected receipts and expected payments. Once these are approved by the Parliament, it becomes a budget passed by the Parliament. Thus budget authorizes the executives to take up activities and spend money while a plan does not give any such authority.

Oxford English Dictionary defines budget as: a statement of probable revenue and expenditure for the ensuing year with financial proposals founded thereon annually submitted by the Exchequer for the approval of the House of Commons.

Other definitions of budget and budgeting are: Budget is a "document that spells out annual business plans in financial terms, serves as a co-coordinating centre for the actions of the different sections of the business, and assists managers in controlling the activities for which they are responsible".

Budgeting is defined as a process of preparation and administration of budgets, encompasses planning and control. It has following three broad stages:

(*i*) Budget Formulation
(*ii*) Budget Finalisation and Settlement;
(*iii*) Performance Monitoring and Review

As such budget is prepared in all enterprises, whether individual, commercial or a government department. Further budgeting process entails:

I. **Formulation** of budget proposals for various projects/ programmes/ activities for the coming year. This is normally coordinated by a Budget Committee or Finance Director.

II. **Finalisation of Budget:** Budget proposals, as formulated above, are discussed, approved and finalised. As such, budget involves allocation of resources to various activities or projects approved.

III. **Review:** budget is reviewed periodically, may be monthly, quarterly or half yearly. As such budget for the period is compared with the actuals to analyse the variances and to initiate control action. This enables the enterprise to monitor the progress of the work and to see linkages with the organizational objectives.

In other words, budgeting is a continuous process, a process which goes on throughout the year.

As discussed above, a budget thus operationalises the plan, is essentially a blueprint for action. It lays down in quantitative terms, financial as well as non financial, results to be expected in future. It is different from 'forecast' or a 'projection' or a 'guess' as it is an 'active estimate' which emphasizes on the "target" to be achieved while forecast or projection is a passive estimate without any specific 'target' in view. Budgeting thus is a process of allocation of funds to various programmes or activities, and is a means of priortisation of various programmes and activities.

Budgeting, a planning and a control mechanism, is required in every organization. Discussion of budgeting in every situation can be under two broad heads:

I. **Principles of budgeting** – these are true in all cases. These focus on 'what is' budgeting and 'why' budgeting.

II. **Budgeting Mechanism or Design** – This deals with budget format or budget presentation. This focuses on 'how' aspect of budgeting which encompasses different formats of budget presentation. These include appropriation budget, programme budget, performance budget, outcome budget, zero-base budget,gender budget or integration of these approaches. The budget presentation varies in different organizations, depending upon size and nature of business, needs and attitude of management. Management may adopt 'top down' or 'bottom up' approach towards planning. Accordingly, presentation of budget varies from that of private enterprise to public enterprise.

BUDGETING PRINCIPLES

Budgeting as a planning and control technique has certain principles, and these are true in all cases. These principles relate to:

- Organization Objectives and organization structure. Every organization is divided into responsibility centres and divisions.
- Management Commitment towards budgeting, whatever approaches whether 'top down' or 'bottom up' is followed.
- Budget as a process of authorization of executive to take up activities
- Budgeting as a process of prioritization of activities and programmes, and allocating fund so as to have optimal utilization of funds or to have value for the money.
- Budget Classifications: Capital and Revenue budgets.
- Budget Estimates be realistic. Alternatively, the estimates can be conservative or optimistic.
- Budgeting approach may be: Flexible budget approach or fixed budget approach.
- System of Record keeping and accounting.
- Developing of norms, yardsticks or standards for inputs or outputs for various programmes/ jobs.
- Ascertaining Variances and initiating control action
- Effective communication, timely feedback and corrective action

BUDGET CLASSIFICATIONS

Capital and Revenue budgets: Budgets are normally classified as capital budget and revenue budget. Capital budgets relate to planning for the acquisition or construction of infrastructure like, building, machines or projects, while revenue budgets cover planning for activities of recurring nature or activities relating to operation of the enterprise. Operating budgets also called functional budgets, *i.e.* Sales budgets, Production budgets, Material budgets, Marketing budgets are examples of Revenue budget. The operating budgets and capital budgets are summerised into a Master budget. In other words, Master budget is a consolidated summery of all functional budgets and capital budgets, *i.e.* a blueprint showing the proposed activities and anticipated financial results of the activities. These are projected Balance Sheet, and projected Income Statement for a commercial enterprise.

Fixed budget Vs Flexible budget: Fixed budget relates to a given capacity or level of activity while flexible budget considers changed scenario and is tailored to any different levels of activities. It is based on the principle that it is a bad plan that admits no modification. Fixed and variable classification is a dynamic approach to budgeting and cost control.

BUDGET MECHANISM OR BUDGET PRESENTATION

There have been variations in the presentation of budget over the years. This is particularly so in government budgeting, as governments have followed over the years different formats or approaches for budget presentation to focus on principles of budgeting. These formats can be broadly discussed under following heads:

- Conventional budgeting or appropriation budgeting
- Performance budgeting
- Zero Base Budgeting (ZBB)
- Outcome budgeting
- Gender budgeting

These formats have been evolved over the years, focusing on budget principles. All these formats can be integrated to have value of money.

It would be appropriate to state that these different formats are emphasized mainly in the government and these labels are normally unheard of in the private sector enterprises though the latter prepare budget with the principle to have 'value from money'.

Before we discuss the format, significance and process of different budget approaches, we discuss below budgeting process in commercial organizations and in governments.

BUDGET IN A COMMERCIAL ORGANISATION

In commercial organisations, budget is used as technique of planning and control, to fix production and sales targets in relation to the objectives of the organization. Budgets are drawn for the organization as a whole covering all functions and services. In other words, budgets are drawn for sales, production, purchase, personnel and other functions fixing the targets for each. These budgets are also classified in broad terms as revenue and capital. All the functional and services budgets are consolidated into master budget in the form of budgeted Profit & Loss Statement, and budgeted Balance Sheet. The functional budgets laying down the targets to be achieved by the functional heads provide a mechanism for evaluating the performance of the respective functional head or divisional head. Each functional budget, in turn is the result of the detailed budget, laying down the targets for the lower level executives in that function. In short, there is a hierarchy of budgets, lower level budgets are aggregated into higher level budget and all functional budgets are consolidated into master budget. The hierarchy of the budgets is used as a planning and control techniques at various levels in the organization.

BUDGETARY PROCESS IN A COMMERCIAL ORGANIZATION

For budgeting as a process to operationalise the plan, starting point is to have an understanding of long range plan and the organization structure. This should be followed by scanning of current business environment, *i.e.* trends in socio, political, cultural spheres and their effects on the organization. Since budget is normally prepared for one year, goal/objective for the budget period should be defined. Following additional steps for budget preparation are:

Determine limiting factor or key factor, *i.e.* a variable which is a constraint for the implementation of the budget. This factor affects the overall objective of the organization, *i.e.* profit maximization.

For example, for a commercial enterprise, sales is a limiting factor, as it affects production and operations of the enterprise.

- Establish budget centres, responsibility centres also called divisions or departments that are involved in the exercise of budget preparation. Introduce responsibility accounting system.
- Constitute a budget committee
- Develop budget manual and guidelines for the preparation of budgets
- Formulate budget for various responsibility centres
- Approval of the Board of Directors (BOD)-policy making body
- Review periodically
  - Recording of actuals
  - Ascertain variances-compare actual with the budgets
- Initiate control action

BUDGET PREPARATION

As stated above, for operating budgets preparation, sales may be a limiting factor. In that case, budget preparation will start with the sales budget. However, in many cases availability of raw material, or production capacity may be a limiting factor, budget preparation in that case should start with that limiting factor. Let us discuss, various operating budgets, given sales as a limiting factor.

Sales Budget: Sales budget is more than a sales forecast for the coming period. A forecast is merely a 'passive estimate' while budget reflects the 'positive actions', influences further events and indicates: units to be sold, selling price, sales volume, selling expenses- fixed and variable.

Production Budget: Production budget is the next in sequence of budget preparation. Sales plan of individual products are the basis of production budget. It results in production plan for individual products, that is planning for

(*a*) Number of units to be produced
(*b*) Number of units to be sold plus/minus
(*c*) Change in inventory levels
(*d*) Direct material cost
(*e*) Direct labour cost
(*f*) Manufacturing overheads- fixed and variable

Various other operating budgets are;

Direct Material Cost Budget: Indicates various materials – in quantity and cost required.

Materials Purchase Budget: Direct and indirect material consumption plan, and inventory level desired are the bases of material purchase budget. It indicates foreign exchange requirements in case of imports, or units to be bought, prices and cost of purchase.

Direct Labour Budget:

- Plan for the number and expenses on direct labour personnel
- Plan for overtime and incentive expenses on the basis of production budget and manpower budget.

Production budget is the basis of direct labour budget.

Manpower Budget: It indicates number of personnel under various categories and the expenses to be incurred on salaries and wages on the basis of production and sales plans for the period. Based on manpower budgets and policies, the training expenses budget and the recruitment expense, etc. are formulated.

Administrative Expenses Budget: This covers expenses of corporate office, finance, personnel marketing and sales expenses.

Cash Budget: It is a plan for expected cash receipts and cash payments derived from the above operation budgets and also the capital budgets. The cash flows are from cash sales, collection from receivables and other incomes; and payments for purchases, manpower and other expenses; cash flows from capital receipts and capital payments. Cash budget is important for planning purposes.

Master Budget: It is the consolation of all budgets, and it is budgeted Profits and Loss account and budgeted Balance Sheet.

Budget process is illustrated below under (*a*) Fixed budget process and (*b*) Flexible budget process.

ILLUSTRATIONS: FIXED AND FLEXIBLE BUDGET APPROACHES

Budget Preparation Process

M/S SHONE EXPRESS Co.		Budget for the year X001
Budgeted Sale: Units		10,000
@ ₹. 20	₹.	2, 00,000
Budgeting Cost: Total Cost	₹.	1,80,000
(Of which Fixed Cost is ₹. 60,000)		
Budget Profit	₹.	20,000

Prepare budget under a) Fixed budget approach or b) Flexible budget approach

(*a*) Budget under Fixed Budgeting Approach:

	Budget	Actuals	Variance
Budget Sale-Unit	10,000	11,500	1,500 (F)
		@ ₹ 19.50	
-₹.	2, 00,000	2, 24,250	24,250 (F)
Cost (fixed)	60,000	67,000	7,000 (U)
(Variable)	1, 20,000	1, 31,100	11,100 (U)
		@ ₹. 11.40	
Budget Total Cost	₹ 1, 80,000	1, 98,100	18,100 (U)
Budgeted Profit	₹. 20,000	26,150	6,150 (F)

* (U) refers to unfavourable; (F) refresh Favourable

(*b*) Budget under Flexible Budget Approach: – X001

Level of Operations

Budgeted Sales Units (No)	8,000	9,000	10,000	11,000	12,000
Sales ₹.@ ₹.20 (in ₹.)	1,60,000	1,80,000	2,00,000	2,20,000	2,40,000
Variable cost (in ₹)	12	12	12	11.5	11.3
Variable cost / unit(₹)	96,000	1,08,000	1,20,000	1,26,500	1,35,600
Contribution/ unit ₹	8	8	8	8.5	8.7
Contribution ₹	64,000	72,000	80,000	93,000	1,04,400
Fixed Cost ₹.	48,000	60,000	60,000	60,000	70,000
Budgeted Profit ₹.	16,000	12,000	20,000	33,500	34,400

M/S SHONE EXPRESS Co.

		Flexible Budget	Actuals	Varience
Sale-Unit		11,500	11,500	
	₹.	2, 30,000	2, 24,250	5,750(U)
Cost				
Variable Cost	₹.	1, 32,250	1, 31,100	1,150 (F)
Contribution		97,750	93,150	4,600 (F)
Fixed cost	₹.	70,000*	67,000	3,000(F)
Profit		27,750	26,150	1,600(U)

Note: Variable cost is worked in proportion to total

* Fixed cost for an activity level beyond 11,000 units is ₹. 70,000

BUDGET PROCESS: ILLUSTRATED

I. Fixed budget for M/S Shone Express has been drawn for the year X001 with target sale of 10,000 units. In value terms, sales targets are ₹. 2,00,000.

II. Budgeted costs have been worked out taking various types of materials and other inputs. Cost has been distinguished as fixed costs and variable costs.

III. Under Fixed budget approach, budgeted profit thus is ₹. 20,000

IV. Under Fixed budget approach, variances are worked out with favorable profit variance of ₹. 6,150. On the other hand, flexible budget gives an unfavorable profit variance of ₹. 1,600.

V. Under fixed budget approach, favourable budget variance of ₹. 6,150 is analysed as under:

Sales unit variance	=		1,150 (F)
Sales price unit variance	=		₹. 0.50 (U) per unit
Sales variance	=		₹. 24,250 (F)
Sales Quantity Variance	=	(1500 @ ₹ 20)	₹. 30,000 (F)
Sales Rate Variance	=	(11,500 @ ₹. 0.50)	₹. 5,750 (U)
Total Cost Variance	=		₹. 18,100 (U)
Fixed Cost variance	=		₹. 7,000 (U)
Variable Cost variance	=		₹. 11,100
Variable Cost Rate variance	=	(11,500 @ ₹. 0.60)	₹. 6,900 (F)
Variable Cost Quantity Variance	=	(1,500 @ ₹. 12)	₹ 18,000 (U)

VI. With the approach of flexible budget, the budgets have been drawn at different levels of activity, *i.e.* from 8,000 units to 12,000 units. Accordingly, profits and variances have been worked out at these levels of activities. At 11,500 units level of actual sales, unfavourable profit variance of ₹ 1600 is analysed as under:

Sales price unit variance:	₹. 0.50 (U) per unit
Sales variance	₹. 5,750 (U)
Fixed Cost variance:	₹. 3000 (F)
Variable Cost Rate variance:	₹. 0.10 per unit
Variable Cost variance:	₹. 1150 (F)

VII. Variances are analysed in terms of responsibility accounting system, executive responsible for variances are identified distinguishing controllable and non-controllable expenses. Control action is initiated, having performance oriented control system.

VIII. In short, flexible budgeting approach identifies variances in the changed scenario and is appropriate for planning and control.

Hence, a budget, as a technique of planning and control, has various benefits which can be summarized as follows. A budget:

- Defines the objectives of the organizations and translates those objectives into plans and programmes for various levels of the organization,
- Is a means to facilitate communication and coordination of plans among various executives,
- Provides yardsticks to measure efficiency for various functions, divisions, sections,
- Shows the extent to which actual results have deviated form the defined objectives,
- Provides a guide for corrective action, and
- Facilitates control and delegation of responsibilities.

In short, budgets facilitate, planning, coordination, communication and control of the various activities at various levels in the organization.

CHAPTER 3

Budgeting in Government: Conventional Budget and other Formats of Budget

Every government has to obtain the authority of the Parliament to raise revenue and to take up activities and incur expenditure. This is done through budgeting by estimating expenditure and revenues for the coming year and getting these approved by the legislature, *i.e.* Parliament. Budget is described as a "financial blueprint for a specified period, normally twelve months. It is one of the chief instruments of financial control as well as the authorization whereby the administration is enabled to carry out its policies and programmes".[i]

Thus budget authorizes the executives to take up activities. To quote Bridges Lord, " Whatever else a government may or may not do, one thing it cannot avoid doing each year if it is to continue to exist, and that is to obtain the authority of the Parliament to raise revenue, to meet expenditure, which is done by the Budget and the accompanying Finance Bill".[ii]

In India as mentioned earlier, the first budget was presented in 1860 by James Wilson, and since then the form and the contents of budget have undergone substantial changes. Article 112 of the Constitution requires the Union Government to place before the Parliament, every year the 'Annual Financial Statement' covering estimates of receipts and payments of the Government for the coming year. In simple form, budget is a financial blue print for a specified period, normally, one year, it contains proposals of expenditure and revenues; it is one of the chief instruments of financial control and authorization whereby executive is enabled to carry out its programmes and policies. This financial instrument is called 'appropriation budget'.

As stated earlier, the formats of budget in government can be discussed under following heads:

- Conventional budgeting or appropriation budgeting
- Performance budgeting
- Zero Base Budgeting (ZBB)
- Outcome budgeting
- Gender budgeting

These formats have been evolved over the years, focusing on budget principles. All these formats can be integrated to have value of money. To iterate, these different formats are emphasized mainly in the government and are normally unheard of in the private sector enterprises which prepare budget with the principle to have 'value from money'.

■ CONVENTIONAL BUDGET

The budgets are mainly designed to ensure 'legislature control and accounting scrutiny' with the objectives to ensure that funds are raised and money spent by specific authorities according to legislative sanctions. These conventional budgets are framed in terms of various Ministries/ Departments with expenditures broken down into the broad objects constituting the primary units

i. [Report of the Study Team on Financial Administration, Administrative Reforms Commission (GOI May 1967 p.7)]

ii. [Bridges Lord, "The Treasury" (Allen & Unwin, 1964, p 188)]

of appropriation such as pay of officers, payments for establishment, allowances and honoraria. The budgets are conceived largely in financial terms and emphasise the financial outlays and not much on the results of the proposed outlays. In other words, the conventional budget is accountability oriented and is intended to facilitate itemized financial control; it shows various sources from where the money is to be raised and objects where money is to be spent.

The budget serves following three functions in administration,

(*a*) A **Financial Plan** for realizing the objectives of the department. The budget lays down the expected expenditure in the coming year on various items.

(*b*) A means of **Approval** of the Legislature: A budget giving plans of expenditure and revenue is submitted for approval of the Parliament or Legislative Assembly.

(*c*) A main instrument to ensure **Financial Accountability and Control:** The budget is a principal mechanism to provide accountability of the executives to the legislature to ensure that the amount spent for various purposes has been within the limits laid down, and it is a principal device for implementation of the programme and objectives laid out in the plan. It also provides a chief source of data that will facilitate the decisions on fiscal and economical matters.

(*d*) To illustrate, we present below budget estimates for various items of expenses for the Delhi Milk Scheme in Exhibit 3.1. Similarly, Exhibit 3.2 presents the estimates of various items of expenses for the Ministry of Food Processing Industries for the year 1998—99.

Exhibit : 3.1 Delhi Milk Scheme

Appropriation Budget Illustration

	Years		**(₹ Crore)**
Item of Expenses :	X_0	X_1	
Materials		1770	
Salaries/Wages		215	
Stores		220	
Travel		5	
Publicity		2	
Machines		100	
Land and Equipment		20	
Total		**2332**	
Inflows :			

Exhibit : 3.2 Ministry of Food processing Industries

Budget Estimates 1998—99

Objectwise Classification

(₹ Crore)

	Plan	**Non- Plan**	**Total**
Salaries	0.40	2.55	2.95
Wages	--	0.01	0.01
Overtime allowance (OT)	--	0.03	0.03
Domestic Travel Expenses	0.05	0.23	0.28
Foreign Travel Expenses	0.05	0.16	0.21
Office expenses	0.10	0.96	1.06

Publications	--	0.04	0.04
Other Admin. Expenses	--	0.03	0.03
Advertising & Publicity	1.50	0.03	1.53
Professional Services	--	0.01	0.01
Grant-in-aid	32.20	0.01	32.21
Subsidies	--	0.60	0.60
Lump sum Provision	--	0.06	0.06
Investments	1.00	--	1.00
Loans & Advances	8.80	--	8.80
TOTAL	**44.10**	**4.72**	**48.82**

The budgets illustrated above reveal what the organizations purchase? Or What are their items of expenses but the budgets do not bring out, why do they buy? Or what business they are in? Or what are their activities? Or what is the cost of each activity?

In fact, if the organizations names are not disclosed, it can not be known, what these organizations do? What business they are involved in? These budgets can better be described as, Appropriation budget or Financial Budget, or line-item budget and have the following main characteristics as:

- Oriented towards financial or money aspects.
- Emphasis is mainly on inputs like, salaries, rent, stationary and not on purpose of the expenses. The over-riding consideration of this type of budget is that financial accountability per- meates the entire budgetary process.
- Focus is on the exhaustion of funds provided in the budget rather than on performance or on result of the money spent as related with the objective, and
- Realise heavily on cash basis of payment rather than utilization of the inputs and results of those inputs.

In short, budget is the most important annual item on the agenda of the Parliament. It serves purposes namely, fiscal, financial, and economic, administrative, and developmental. It is a document for parliamentary action and instrument of Parliamentary control. In fact, "line item or object classification was a product of an era in which legislators and the general public distrust administrators"[iii] , and detailed listing of objects of expenditure, greatly reduced the discretionary power of administrators[iv]

A significant characteristic of planning, particularly in developing countries has been the increase in the functions of the State. Earlier, State was entrusted mainly with the function of maintenance of law and order and protection of individual right to property. Now with the heavy emphasis on economic development and increase in developmental activities, the State is performing the function of 'protector' of the rights of weaker sections, a stabilizer, a pioneer, an innovator, and an entrepreneur. In order to provide economic services to weaker sections and to reduce inequality of income, the state is entering into the function of entrepreneurship and has started a number of commercial enterprises for the betterment of the society. This has resulted in significant importance accorded to public sector whose growth has become a dominant factor in the development process. The importance of the State is reflected by the significant increase in the public outlays in the developing countries. For India, total government outlay as a percent of GDP has increased over

---

iii ***[Burkehead, J Government Budgeting John Wiley & Sons, New York 1956), in Joseph C. Pilegge. Budget Reforms, in Jack Rabin (ed) Handbook of Public Budgeting (Marcel dekker inc. New York, 1992)]***

iv ***[Schick A, Control patterns in state budget execution Public Administration Review 26, 1964) in Jack Rabin, ibid]***

the years from approximately 30 percent of GDP in early years of twenty first century to 51 percent during 2011-12. (Exhibit 3.3) The share of development outlay to total outlay has also increased from 50 percent to approximately 60 percent over the years.

With the increase in the function of the State and heavy outlay on development activity, it becomes necessary that the budget should show the purposes for which the money is being spent, show what the government is doing; how much and at what cost. In other words, the budget should not only show financial outlays, but should also show the physical results expected of the financial outlays and this emphasises the need for, or requires a budget, known as Performance Budgeting which is discussed in the next chapter.

Exhibit : 3.3 The Share of Development Outlay of Total Outlay

(₹ Crore)

Year	Total Outlay of Government*	GDP**	Outlay % of GDP
1990-91	176,548	1347,889	13
2003-04	803,274	2777,813	29
2004-05	896,096	2971,464	30
2005-06	1044,509	3253,073	32
2006-07	1225,149	3564,364	34
2007-08	1431,960	3896,636	37
2008-09	1721,651	4158,676	41
2009-10	2070,959	4516,071	45
2010-11RE	2458,842	4937,006	50
2011-12 BE	2694,145	5243,582	51

* *Total outlay of Government reflects budgetary transactions of the Central Government, State Governments, Union Territories including internal and extra-budgetary resources of public sector undertakings for their plans*

** *GDP at factor cost*

Source: Economic Surveys, GOI

Exhibit : 3.4 Growth Oriented Young Executive Enterprise

Considering growth opportunities arising from the liberalization measures introduced by the government, Manisha Singh who recently graduated from a leading business school in North formed a business enterprise to deal in computer parts, accessories and other related items. Manisha discussed her business plans with her friends and relatives who agreed to loan to the business ₹ 100 lakh at the rate of 12%. Manisha along with her family contributed another ₹ 300 lakh as owner's equity.

She opened a bank account with State Bank of India in the name of the firm and deposited the amount of the loan and her equity contribution.

For its administrative arrangements, the firm acquired a building (measuring 1000 sqft) for ₹ 100 lakh and furniture and equipment costing another ₹ 50 lakh, the payment was made by cheque. Stock of inventory meant for sale was procured in bulk to have benefits of quantity discount, the goods costed ₹ 200 lakh. However, the supplier allowed six months credit of ₹ 40 lakh. A team of five members was entrusted with the task of managing the affairs of the enterprise.

Before launching business operations to public, Manisha reviewed the position of bank balance which is summarized as under:

Bank Account

Receipts		Payments	
Equity Contribution	300	Building	100
12% Loan	100	Furniture and Equipment	50
		Goods Inventory	160
		Bank Balance	90

The management launched its business operations and details for the six month ending March 31, 2012 are as under:

- Sold half of its stock of goods for ₹ 350 lakh, (of this ₹ 280 lakh was received and ₹ 70 lakh remained outstanding)
- The firm suffered due to strike by employees which lasted for one month.
- Payment for Purchase of computer ₹ 40 lakh
- Employees remuneration paid 40 lakh
- Repairs and other expenses 10 lakh
- Payment of Warehouse rent 20 lakh
- Interest and bank charges 6 lakh

Further, it was ascertained that:

- Building and furniture are depreciated @ 10 % pa.
- Salary for one of the employee ₹ 6 lakh remained unpaid
- Warehouse rent already paid includes ₹ 4 lakh which pertains to the next year
- There was an offer for the sale of the building for ₹ 180 lakh, as such the value of building is increased to ₹ 180 lakh
- Remaining inventory stock of ₹ 100 has a market value of ₹ 156 lakh.

There was good news of Manisha wedding which she celebrated by inviting her colleagues and friends and spent ₹ 20 lakh from her own personal account.

Issues for discussion :

- What issues interest you from the above case ?
- What name would you suggest for the firm ?
- Identify inflows and outflows of cash.
- What are the assets of the firm ?
- What are its sources of funds ?
- What is the bank balance as on March 31, 2012 ?
- What accounting principles have we followed ?
- Indicate two aspects of various transactions in the case.
- What books of accounts do you think could be prepared ?
- What Financial Statement emerge from the above ?
- How would you report on the operations of the enterprise for the year ?
- How would you report on the financial condition of the enterprise ?
- Would you describe say business venture of Manisha as a success ?

CHAPTER 4

Performance Budgeting : Meaning, Need and Mechanism

Appropriation budget, as discussed in the previous chapter, focuses on financial outlays, presents expenses in terms of inputs or items of expenditures like salaries, rent, establishment, etc. It shows various sources from where the funds are to be raised, and objects where money is to be spent; and reveals *what* the organization purchases. It does not indicate the purpose of the expense or, *why* does it buy; or what business is it in?

As an illustration, under appropriation budget, funds are allocated to various departments like, education, or to public works, or power; and the funds are drawn from the treasury for the purposes assigned for items of expenditures like, salaries, rent, establishment, etc., so long as the actual withdrawals do not exceed the budgeted amount sanctioned. Later, what happens to this money is nobody's concern. This is the reason that the amounts have been budgeted and spent on projects, but there is no trace of the project or 'accomplishment'. This is because the budgetary control process only looks at the financial aspects, *i.e.* that the money has been spent, and there is no emphasis on physical achievement. Similarly, no question is raised regarding the result or outcome of the money spent on higher education, or on roads; or how many engineers have been trained, or how much roads have been constructed?

This highlights the need for performance budget which basically presents purposes and objectives for which funds are required, the costs of various programmes and activities proposed for achieving the objectives. To quote the Study Team on Financial Administration of the Administration Reform Commission,[i] "Performance budgeting is essentially a technique of presenting Government operations in terms of functions, programmes, activities and projects". By means of the function-programme-activity classification, the individual items which make up the budget are sought to be shown not only in financial terms but as far as possible, in physical terms as well. Federal Government in the US adopted performance budgeting on the recommendation of the first Hoover Commission[ii], the recommendation was that the "whole budgetary concept of the Federal Government should be refashioned by the adoption of a budget based on functions, activities and projects". The Commission observed that "such an approach would focus attention upon the general character and relative importance of the work to be done or upon the service to be rendered, rather than upon the things to be acquired, such as personal services, supplies, equipment, and so on. These latter objects are, after all, only the means to an end. The all important thing in budgeting is the work or the service to be accomplished, and what that work or service will cost". To put it in other words, performance budget links physical targets with financial outlays and presents the programmes and activities giving physical targets and financial outlays required. In the words of Prof. Jesse Burkehead[iii]. "A Performance Budget is one which presents the purposes and objectives

i ***[Report of the Study Team on Financial Administration, Administrative Reforms Commission (GOI May 1967)]***

ii ***[Hoover Commission on the Organisation of the Executive Branch of the Government, Federal Government (1949)]***

iii ***[Jess Burkehead, Government Budgeting, (John Wiley, New York 1956)]***

for which funds are requested, the costs of programmes proposed for achieving these objectives, and quantitative data measuring the accomplishments and work performed under each programme"*

The above definition shows that a performance budget presents:

(*i*) *Purposes or objectives* for which funds are requested.

(*ii*) *Programmes or activities* with their costs, for achieving these objectives.

(*iii*) *Quantitative data measuring the work performed* or services rendered or result accomplished under each programme or activity.

Thus, performance budget is a comprehensive operational document and it presents for the next year, a work plan containing programmes, projects and activities specifying the targets in physical terms and the finance required therefore, by the agency concerned. Its focus is on the work and the result expected of the money to be spent in the next year rather than on the nature of *expenses or on the agency who is incurring* those expenses. In other words, the performance budgeting is a budgeting approach which lays emphasis on '*accomplishment*' rather than '*means of accomplishment*'. It is primarily concerned with the ends to be served by the Government or the organization rather than with the money to be spent on several objects or items of expenses. The important thing under this technique is the precise definition of the work to be done or service to be rendered and a correct estimate of what that work or service will cost. This technique would make executives accountable to the legislature or subordinate accountable to his superior in physical as well as financial terms. In short, performance budget has three important functions in administration;

(*a*) It is a financial plan for realizing the objectives of the department:

(*b*) It is a means by which that approval of the legislature for incurring of the expenditure is obtained; and

(*c*) It is an instrument for ensuring financial accountability and control.

Purposes of Performance budgeting :

- Co-relates the physical and financial aspects of programmes and activities,
- Brings closely together annual objectives and developmental plans through common language,
- Measures progress towards long term objectives as envisaged in the plans,
- Facilitates better appreciation and review by the legislature,
- Improves budget formulation, review and decision-making at all levels of management in the organization, and thus serves as an effective instrument of planning and control for managers,
- Makes possible more effective performance audit.

To illustrate, we present below in Exhibits 4.1 and 4.2 performance budgets for Delhi Milk Scheme and the Ministry of Food Processing Industries. The conventional budgets for these organizations were presented in the previous chapter in Exhibits 3.1 and 3.2. The Exhibit 4.1 indicates the tasks performed by the Delhi Milk Scheme in terms of its functions as:

- Procurement of Milk or milk powder
- Processing of Milk
- Distribution of Milk
- Administrative aspects

Similarly, for the Ministry of Food Industries, various programmes are presented in Exhibit 4.2.

* **Note.** *Performance budgeting with different manifestations with titles as project budgeting, Planning Programming and Budgeting system (PPBS) were adopted in the US (for details see pp 73-78, Joseph C. Pilegge . Budget Reforms, in Jack Rabin (ed.) Handbook of Public Budgeting (Marcel dekker inc. New York, 1992)*

Exhibit : 4.1 Delhi Milk Scheme

Performance Budgeting : Illustration

Programmes : Activities		**Years**
Procurement	Qty.	₹ 1801
• Milk Powder		
• Milk		
• Butter oil		
Processing		155
Distribution		170
Administration		186
Machines		100
Land and Building		20
Total		**2332**
Inflows		

Exhibit : 4.2 Ministry of Food Processing Industries

Budget Estimates 1998—99

Programmes (₹ Crore)

		Plan	**Non-Plan**	**Total**
1	Policy Formation & Administration	2.50	3.07	5.57
2	Fisheries	12.00	--	12.00
3	Food Storage and warehousing	28.10	1.05	29.15
4	Consumer Industries	1.50	0.60	2.10
	Total	44.10	4.72	48.82

Sub-programmes and activities and their budget estimates for each of the above four Programmes for the Ministry of Food Processing Industries, are annexed at the end of the chapter as Annexure A.

NEED FOR PERFORMANCE BUDGETING

Governments were originally involved with the task of maintenance of law and order and protection of individual's rights and property. With the increasing emphasis on balanced economic development, the State is vested with greater economic activities for the benefit of weaker sections of the society. As a result, the State acts as a stabilizer, a pioneer, an entrepreneur and total outlays by the State has increased over the year. It becomes essential to ascertain the purposes of the money spent by the government, what is '*accomplishment*' or the '*impact*' of such expenditure. As mentioned in the previous chapter, the share of Government expenditure to total GDP has increased from about 30% in early years of 2000 to about 51% during 2011-12. In such a situation, a budget simply in financial terms without any relationship with physical work will not indicate the effectiveness of the money spent or the extent of development attained due to heavy outlay. Thus, in situations where the outlays by the State have significantly increased over the years, budget must show what Government is *doing, how much* and at *what cost it is doing*. Performance budget reflects these and shows the physical targets and financial outlay for the year.

PERFORMANCE BUDGETING INSTALLATION: SYSTEMS APPROACH

Performance budget is not one shot activity, it is a continuous process to translate organization's objectives into operational terms. It translates the objectives in terms of programmes and activities, lays down targets both in financial and physical terms of programmes and activities, and evaluates the actual working in terms of these targets. The systematic approach for developing Performance Budget as illustrated in the Exhibit 4.3 involves the following:

Exhibit : 4.3 Systematic Approach to Performance Budgeting

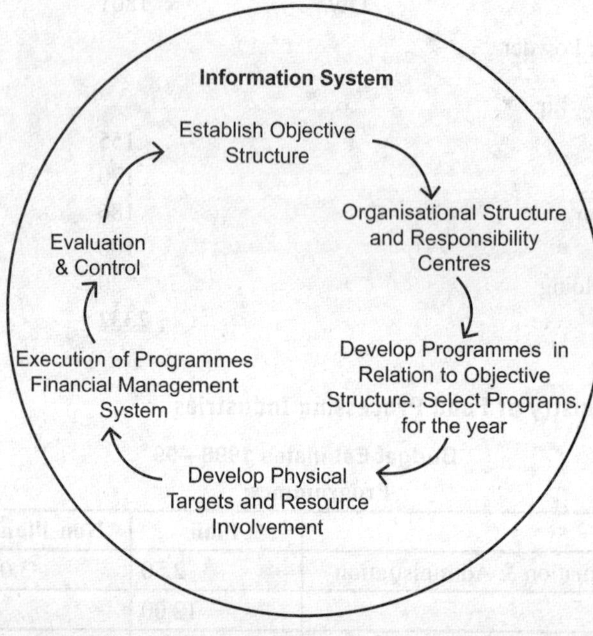

I. **Define objectives and goals** of the organization in quantitative and precise terms, as far as possible. The objective structure should be developed to identify the corporate objective and the objectives subordinate to it.

II. **Organization structure** should be linked up with the objective structure to identify responsibility and authority at various levels. Decide a level in the organization structure for which the performance budgeting exercise will start.

III. **Develop a meaningful Function- Programme-Activity** classification for the department with reference to its goals and objectives. Determine sequence of these activities and allocation of resources by means of network analysis.

IV. **Identify various alternative** programmes for the achievement of objectives and select programmes for the period under consideration in relation to the structure. This requires application of the Cost-Benefit Analysis technique for appraisal of various alternative programmes and selection of a few programmes for the coming year.

V. **Develop financial management system** in relation to the above classification to ensure use of funds for the purpose intended.

VI. **Develop norms, indices,** yardsticks, input-output ratios, work measurement as performance indicators for evaluation and control.

VII. **Develop information system** for purposes of budget formulation, review and decision making for the above aspects.

Understanding and developing of the aforesaid aspects are must for every progressive organization, and are pre-requisite for the performance budgeting system to be successful and effective. The aspects relating to organization structure, classification structure, performance evaluation norms and accounting and financial system are discussed in the following two chapters, namely, chapter IV A and chapter IV B.

Conditions Necessary for the Success of Performance Budgeting

I. Budgeting should be a continuous process and be linked to be the objectives of the organization. In other words, it should not be in isolation to the objectives of the organization.

II. Budgeting should not be considered as an activity to be done outside the organization or an activity which is done only at corporate office as a ritual to comply with the legislature requirements. In fact, it should be considered as an operational tool to be used by management.

III. Budgeting should percolate downward to various levels of management in the organization. Budgets drawn at lower level should be aggregated at the middle level and the budgets at middle level should be consolidated at the top level.

IV. Following from the preceding point III above, there is a need to identify various management levels in the organizational structure and to decide a level from that upward, the performance budget should be drawn either following bottom up or top down approach.

V. Evolve necessary financial data through the accounting system in terms of programmes and activities. The existing accounting system should be modified so as to meet the requisite characteristics of performance budgeting.

VI. There should be a systematic effort to evolve work performance units, or norms, or performance indicators in order to measure the physical progress or accomplishment.

VII. There should be a systematic planning for the government operations for long period. No doubt, the development expenditure on various projects is formulated for five years, having annual break-down indicating operations, tasks, time schedules, targets and other aspects, the non-development expenditure should also be a subject to such planning.

VIII. Budgeting and administrative authority of a programme must be one and the same. The concerned administrative machinery should be able to formulate budgets without the interference of an outside agency.

IX. There should a system of performance reporting at regular intervals. The physical and financial aspects must be inter-woven into a single report giving projections of costs in future. Such reporting system enables the formulation of policy and programmes and facilitates appraisal thereof.

All the above conditions may not hold true at a given time, but a start must be made to introduce performance budgeting, with an attempt to refine and improve on the given situations, till we reap the full benefits of performance budgeting. To quote from the UN Manual[iv]

"It's (performance budgeting) total application assumes an existence of a number of factors or facilities. In its ultimate application, this approach involves sound budgetary operations, financial discipline, skilled and responsible manpower both for budget formulation and execution, a frequent and efficient system of recording and reporting financial and physical data. Some or all of these conditions may not exist in a given country. Their development must be given a continuing attention in considering and introducing the performance techniques".

LIMITATIONS OF PERFORMANCE BUDGET

Like any other management techniques, performance budget has following limitations:

(*a*) Performance budgeting enables only a quantitative and financial evaluation of programmes and activities. It does not provide qualitative evaluation.

(*b*) Its usefulness is limited in respect of programmes that are not measureable, even in such non-measurable areas, suitable bases can be developed to explain performance and to ascertain the effectiveness of the money spent.

(*c*) For an effective use of performance budgeting, a well-defined functions-programmes-

iv ***United Nations, A Manual for Programme and Performance Budgeting (United Nations, Dept. Of Economic and Social Affairs, 1965,)***

activity need to be developed for a concerned organization, which may not be easier, however, it can be refined over the years as we experience with the use of performance budgeting.

Annexure A

Ministry of Food processing Industries : Sub-programmes and Activities for Various Programmes as per Exhibit 4.2

1. Programme : Policy Formation & Administration —Activities are as under

1.1	Establishment of Monitoring Cell	0.60	--	0.60
1.2	Promotion of Food processing Industries	1.60	--	1.60
1.3	Strengthening of Nodal Agencies	0.30		0.30
1.4	Establishment Expenditure of Secretariat		3.07	3.07
	TOTAL	2.50	3.07	5.57

2. Programme: Fisheries- Activities are as under

2.1	Strengthening of Traditional Fish processing technologies/marketing	0.50		0.50
2.2	Infrastructutral facilities for food processing Industries	11.20		11.20
2.3	Utilisation of low value fish	0.30	--	0.30
	TOTAL	12.00	--	12.00

3. Programme : Food Storage and warehousing – Sub- Programmes and Activities are as under

3.1	**Research & Evaluation**		**0.70**	**0.21**	**0.91**
	3.1.1 Modernisation of Rice Milling Industry---				
	Activities as:				
	i.	Post Harvest Technology Centre IIT Khargpur			
	ii.	Regional Extension Service Centre			
	iii.	Paddy Processing Research Centre, Thanjavur			
	iv.	Rice Mill Machinery Testing Centres			
	v.	Extension Service Centre at CFTRI, Mysore			
3.2	**Food processing-Activities as:**		**15.75**	**0.84**	**16.59**
	i.	Assistance for Setting-up/expansion/up gradation of Food Processing Inds.	10.00		
	ii.	Assistance for manpower development in Food Processing Industries	2.50		
	iii.	Generic Advertising on processed foods and for providing marketing assistance	0.90		
	iv.	Assistance for setting up of Demonstration Unit/Pilot projects	0.30		
	v.	Assistance for strengthening of backward linkages	0.95		

	vi.	Continuous Inspection of Fruit products		0.51	
	vii.	Establishment Fruit Products Control Order		0.27	
	vii.	Consultancy Service Cell		0.06	
3.3	**Meat & Poultry processing- Activities:**		**6.25**		**6.25**
	i.	Development of Meat processing (Pork, sheep, Goat, Rabbit, & buffalo Meat)	3.50		
	ii.	Development of Poultry & Egg processing	2.00		
	iii.	Development of marketing facilities infrastructure and transport	0.75		
	iv.	Assistance for Live Stock Development Council	--		
3.4	**Milk Based Industries–Activities as;**		**5.40**		
	Activities as ;		5.00		
	i.	Assistance for Research and Development in Food processing Industries			
	ii.	Assistance for Setting up Innovative Dairy products	0.40		

4. Programme : Consumer Industries- Sub- Programmes and Activities are as under

4.1	**Investment in Public Enterprises**		**2.10**		**2.10**
	i.	Equity Investment in Modern Food Industries (India) ltd.	0.50		
	ii.	Equity Investment in NERAMAC	0.50		
	Loan to Public Enterprises				
	i.	Loans to Modern Food Industries (India) ltd.	1.50		
	ii.	Loan to NERMAC	0.60		
	Other Programmes				
	i.	Subsidy to NERAMAC for working Capital			

CHAPTER 4A

Performance Budgeting : Organisation & Classification Structure; Performance Evaluation & Physical Measurement

As discussed in the previous chapter, the broad purposes of performance budgets are:-

I. To highlight the accountability of the executives to the legislatures and to reflect what the Government is doing, how much is it doing and at what cost? and

II. To use the budget as an operational document by the management for planning, control and decision making.

For the purpose, there is a need to understand the organization structure and to develop classification structure under which the budget is to be presented and also to develop performance evaluation system laying down the physical measurements linking with the organization and classification structures. The present chapter discusses the above aspects of organization and functional structures and performance evaluation system.

ORGANISATION STRUCTURE

In every organisation, there is a hierarchy of management; at the apex, the top management is the overall in charge; next is the middle management, the divisional or functional managers who are responsible for their respective divisions or functions; and they supervise the managers reporting to them. A simplified hierarchical organization management structure is illustrated in Exhibit 4 A. I.

For purposes of performance budget, the organisation structure is linked up with the objective structure to identify aims and means for managers at different levels and also to develop physical targets and financial involvements at various levels.

Understanding of the organisation structure is useful to identify the level of managers that will interact in the budgeting process. For the purpose, the top level management must decide a level in the organisation, the managers from that level upwards will interact in the budgeting process. This would depend upon the role of the managers and their involvement with the organizational objectives. The selection of the manager's level from where upward the performance budgeting exercise will start, depends upon the following two factors:

- the level should not be too low and nor too high in the organisation hierarchy to prevent meaningful review or analysis;
- the managers who interact in performance budgeting make significant decisions on the amount of spending and the scope of direction or quality of work to be performed.

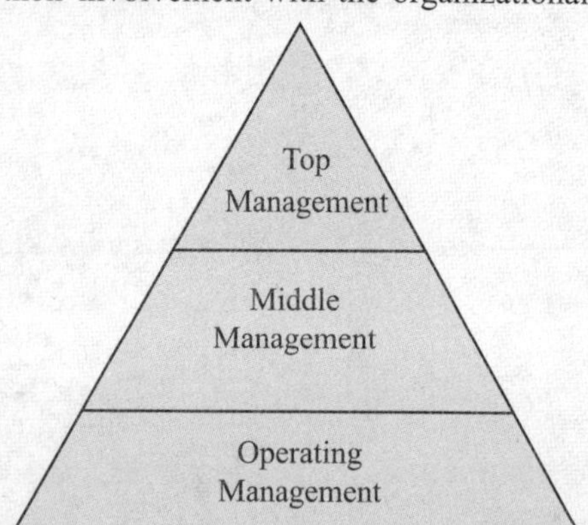

Exhibit : 4A. 1

Hierarchical Management Structure

The managers involved in the exercise of preparation of performance budget on the basis of above two factors will have authorities and responsibilities for discharge of their duties. The performance budget dovetailing physical targets and financial expenditure for various organisation units or centres must identify objectives for each unit (or centre). The objectives of the organisational unit (or centre) must correspond with the mission, corporate objectives and sub-objectives. In other words, the organisation structure must be linked with the objective structure by identifying the objective(s) to be achieved by managers at the various levels.

For example, from the organisation structure of a State Public Works Department (PWD) given in Exhibits 4A.2, the top management has to decide from which level onwards the performance budgeting exercise should start.

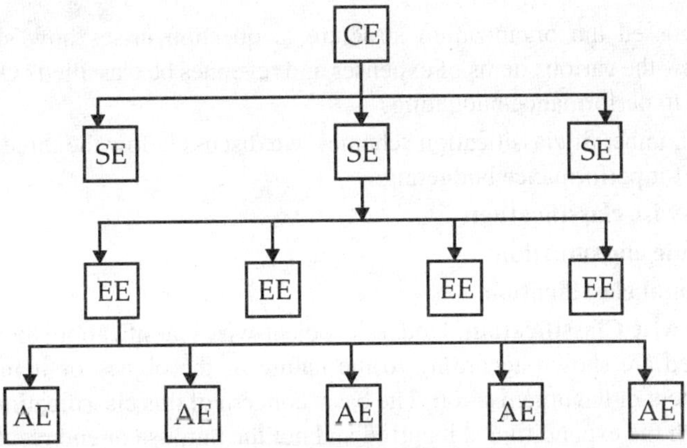

Exhibit : 4A. 2

Organisation Structure of State PWD

CE stands for Chief Engineer SE stands for Superintendent Engineer

EE stands for Executive Engineer AE stands for Assistant Engineer

In PWD, the performance budgeting exercise can start from the Junior Engineer level, or Assistant Engineer or Executive Engineer level or at a level higher to that. The guiding factor in such matter is that the level from which performance budget exercise starts, must have significance role in the decision making process of the organisation in the spending and the quantity of work of the organisation.

The level of executive engineer may be good enough to start performance budget as he makes significant decisions, has financial power to sanction say ₹ 5,00,000 while the lower level of assistant engineer has a very small financial power of say ₹ 50,000 and contributes little in the decision making process.

Once the level of executive engineer for purposes of stating performance budgeting exercise is decided, it is necessary to identify, the objectives, authorisation and responsibilities for the various levels in the organisation. It will facilitate timing of physical targets and financial requirements.

Thus, in the above example of PWD, the performance budget may be prepared for the level of executive engineer and above. The budgets at the executive engineer level will be consolidated which will be a budget for the higher level i.e. superintendent engineer. Similarly, consolidation of the budgets of the superintendent engineers will give the master performance budget for the whole organisation to be used by the chief engineer. Thus the budgets at the level of executive engineers are more detailed and give physical targets, financial requirements and can be used for planning and control by the executive engineers. The higher level budgets at the superintendent engineers level are in less details and are useful for planning and control by superintendent engineers.

In other words, there is one master budget for the organisation to be used by the chief of the organisation. This budget is the consolidation of the budgets at the various lower levels. The lower level budgets are more detailed and give physical targets and financial involvements at the corresponding levels for purposes of planning and control.

In short, a performance budgeting for the organisation is a comprehensive operational document useful for managerial planning and control.

CLASSIFICATION STRUCTURE

Having discussed the organization structure, a question arises how should the budget be presented? Or how the various items of expenses and revenues be classified? Or which classification scheme is suited to performance budgeting?

There are a number of classification schemes, we discuss below the three schemes to highlight the one required for performance budgeting:-

(*a*) Object-wise classification

(*b*) Economic classification

(*c*) Functional classification

(*a*) Object-wise Classification: Under the object-wise classification, the data relating to funds requested are shown according to the nature or the object, or items of expenses in the department or the organisation. The basic concern of this classification is to show the items on which the expenditure is incurred and not the purpose or end results served by it.

This classification enables to identify the inputs required for the work involved and furnishes a uniform basis for review of funds required for a programme or output at various levels of management. It serves the purpose of financial accountability of the executive to the legislature and also ensures observance of accountability on the part of each sub-ordinate authority within the executives. Object-wise classification of expenses for a department is illustrated below:

- Salaries of officers
- Wages of workers
- Travel Expenses
- Office Expenses
- Professional and Specialised Services
- Rent, Rate & Taxes
- Publication
- Machinery & Equipment
- Motor Vehicle
- Write off of losses
- Other Charges

Total:

Appropriation budget of Delhi Milk Scheme as presented in Exhibit 3.1 or of Ministry of Food Processing Industries as presented in Exhibit 3.2 in chapter III are examples of object wise classification.

The above classification of expenses does not reflect the purposes of the expenses, or of the organization, and it fails to help the management in the implementation of their developmental task. Further, it does not assist the management in decision making process of planning and control, particularly when huge amounts are being spent on developmental tasks.

(*b*) **Economic Classification:** The economic classification is used to provide data required for examining the economic effects of the expenditure proposed on the economy. For example, it is important to know how much of the expenditure on a particular service is of a current nature or of short term nature and how much will be of lasting benefit and will create new facilities. The expenditure of latter category leads to capital formation, has lasting or long term effects, and is called '*Capital expenditure*' while the former type is of significance for the current year and is termed as '*Revenue expenditure*'. To illustrate, a budget has two parts: Capital Budget proposes expenditures and revenues of lasting effects, while current budget proposes expenditures and revenues of short term effects. The current budget concerns normal operations and maintenance expenses in relation to broad economic objectives of the Government; operating expenses of various government institutions are the examples. On the other hand, the capital budget includes expenses and revenues on various projects or infrastructure, which create assets having long term effects on the economy. (For details of revenue and capital classification see chapter 1, p7)

For example, Indian Railways, present their budget separately for 'Revenue Account' and for 'Works Account'. Revenue Account Budget gives ordinary working expenses which include: General superintendence and services, repairs and maintenance, operating expenses for traffic and fuel, etc. Works Account Budget includes items like: New Lines, Gauge conversion, Rolling stock, Electrification projects, staff quarters, setting-up workshops, etc.

In short, Economic classification focuses on the economic effects – short term or long term – of various proposals but this classification is devoid of the purposes of performance budgeting of accountability and managerial tool of planning and control.

(*c*) **Functional Classification:** The functional classification is defined to include all expenditures which are related in a meaningful way to specific purposes. The purpose of this classification is to show that the expenditure is according to objectives, or purposes served—immediate or short run.

Under functional classification, the expenditure is linked up with objectives and functions of the organisation rather with the agency incurring the expenditure. The budget under this classification shows various functions or services rendered by the Government, such as education, agriculture, health, defence, justice and law, public works. All expenses incurred on education are presented under the function education irrespective of the agency incurring it. Similarly, all expenses entrusted with the construction of buildings, road and bridges are presented under the head '*Public Works*'.

Thus the functional classification enables to have information regarding aggregate expenditure on particular function or service irrespective of the agency incurring that expenditure; wherein a function is an aggregation of the programmes related to the function; while a programme is aggregation of various related activities. The terms functions, programme and activity are defined as under:

A '*function*' is major division of the total organised effort of the Government, the purpose of which is to provide a distinct and separate service. It relates to the objective of the government and thus, education, agriculture, national defence, public healths are examples of various functions serving different government purposes.

A '*programme*' represents an identifiable segment of the function and produces products or services. It produces end results, the purposes for which the organisation was set up and is the highest level of classification of work performed by an organisation or agency. To illustrate, for education as a function, the various programmes are: elementary education, secondary education, higher education, technical education and vocational education.

An '*activity*' represents the division of the programme into homogenous types of work. So for various programmes in education function, number of classes, number of students, training of teachers are examples of activities.

Illustration

The function, programme activity classification is illustrated as follows:

Function	Programmes	Activities
Education	• Primary Education	-Training of Teachers
		- Number of Classes
		-Number of students taught
	• Secondary Education	
	• Technical Education	
	• Vocational Education	
Agriculture	• High Yielding Variety	-Development of Rice
	• Warehousing or Storage	
Public Health	• Control of Communicable Diseases,	- DDT Spraying
	• Eradication of Malaria	
Public Works	• Construction of Building	
	• Construction of Bridges	
	• Construction of Roads	-Land Acquisition
	- National Highways	- Earth Work
	- State Highways	- Bridges & Culverts
	- Lateral Roads	- Sole Coat
	Missing Links of Roads	- Inner Coat
	Improvement to Roads	- Top Coat
	Widening of Roads	
	- Strategic Roads	
	- By-passes	
	- Major District Roads	
	- Construction of New Roads:	
	- Village Road	

The terms functions, programmes and activities, defined and illustrated above, can be used inter-changeable, however, there must be consistency in the use of such terms in the budgets.

Classification based on functions, programmes, activities in relation to the organisation structure defines the job structure at various levels of management and thus enables the management to plan and control work at different levels.

Using the above classification scheme, the top management of the organisation is concerned with the function of construction and development of roads while the second level management may be responsible for one or more of the programmes related to the function. So the top management may hold the immediate next level managers responsible for the programme(s) entrusted, say, National Highways. Similarly, the next lower level managers may be entrusted with some activity/activities of the programmes. Thus, this process of classification makes it possible to link programme or activities with the level of management and establishes relationship between inputs and output at corresponding level of the management and classification structure.

The aforesaid function classification, no doubt, relates to the purpose of the organisation and is useful for managerial planning and control, it fails to serve the purpose of financial accountability. In short, every classification scheme has certain advantages.

For accountability purposes, expenditure is usually charged according to the immediate subject of expenditure at the time the money is spent, like wages and salaries, materials, travel expenses, grants to another body, loans and so forth, whereas the economic classification groups these primary items of expenditure as per their economic character, the functional classification groups them according to the particular purpose they serve[i].

PERFORMANCE EVALUATION AND PHYSICAL MEASUREMENT

Having discussed the organization and classification structure, let us develop performance evaluation system laying down the physical measurement for each programme and activity for an effective performance budgeting. For that purpose, the performance evaluation system should be linked with the classification structure. In other words, physical as well as financial units of measure are determined and meaningful indicators of performance for each function, programme as well as various activities are developed so as to be used as a tool of internal management.

Physical measurement would include:

(*a*) Measurement of accomplishment showing the effect of the work and the achievement of objectives and programme, e.g. reduction of poverty level, or increase in literacy on account of expense on education;

(*b*) In some cases, the measurement may relate to output or end result of programme or activity, e.g. number of houses constructed or meter of roads constructed, or number of classes held;

(*c*) Measure of workload bringing out the volume of work and time. Such measurements would relate to inputs or work involved. For the purpose, work studies are carried out by the concerned departments, or other agencies. Measure of staffing pattern or workload under each programme and activity is an example.
Work study may indicate that a financial analyst for a bank involved in granting loans, would analyse 15 loan applications a day.

(*d*) Develop unit cost data and productivity ratios relating to programme /activity classification. For example:
- Cost per meter of road,
- Cost per day per patient
- Doctor: staff ratio
- Number of bus breakdown per 10000 km.
- Employees per bus
- Waiting time for patients in OPD

(*e*) Establish norms and standards on the basis of (c) above for purposes of comparison.

The work measurement unit and indicators of performance may be of two types : -

1. Unit cost or unit cost ratio

2. Work measurement ratios. These, in turn, can of three types:-

(*a*) **Measurement of workload:** It identifies volume of work and relates to internal action of the agency to secure desired results. For example, number of classes held in a school. It is adequate for agency having operation of a routine and administrative type.
These are to be supplemented by time and costs involved.

(*b*) **Measurement of end product:** It reflects results of work performed and relates to completed actions of the agency and constitutes direct service to the clients.

(*c*) **Measurement of Accomplishment:** It shows effect of the work performed and relates to the goal or objective of public policy. For example, raising of literacy level among the pupils.

---

i ***United Nations, A Manual for Programme and Performance Budgeting (United Nations, Dept. Of Economic and Social Affairs, 1965, Chapter IV).***

An illustrative list of performance indicators for a large hospital having in patient and OPD facilities is given in Box 4.A.

BOX 4. A

- **Capacity utility of the hospital and its department :** Average number of patients per day in the hospital divided by the total bed strength of the hospital. Similarly, for a hospital department, average number of patients per day in that particular department divided by the bed strength of that department.
- Length of stay for in-patients
- Waiting time of patients
- Number of operations performed or patients treated
- Ratio of doctor : nurses

To quote from the UN Manual, "In its ultimate application, performance budgeting employs physical measures and ratios reflecting resources utilisation in all operating organisations in which the approach is feasible and the cost of obtaining the desired data does not exceed the benefits to management. At the beginning of such an application, however, minimum measures of work in significant programmes areas maybe sufficient to meet immediate needs. Action later can be taken on the basis of experience to develop additional measures and ratios and to refine existing measurement practices so as to better serve budget requirements and performance analysis needs. In any event, the possible adoption of programme and performance budgeting in individual countries should not be abandoned because of the lack of existing data on physical measures. Such measures can be developed and refined after steps have been taken towards the establishment of suitable programme classification for the government budget, and the related adjustment of financial management system to provide appropriate financial data and techniques for budget formulation, presentation and execution"[ii]. (UN MANUAL)

ii ibid

CHAPTER 4B

Performance Budgeting : Financial Management System

Having discussed organisation and classification structures, the next step in the installation of performance budgeting is the financial management system. The financial management system for performance budgeting is like a mirror that reflects the stage of completion of the project, and thus the success of performance budgeting depends upon the financial management system in use. Further, accounting being a significant part of information and reporting system, a well developed accounting system signifies the good information system which is essential for the success of performance budgeting and for achievement of its objectives, namely:

- effective legislative control over financial aspects;
- correlation of long term and annual plans;
- implementation and evaluation of programmes and activities at various levels; and
- decision making process in the organization.

Thus performance budgeting system to be effective would require:

- an integrated accounting and budgeting structure,
- accounting classification similar to the budget classification structure

Further, with the increase in developmental expenditure of the government, accounting and costing information at various stages of programmes and activities is required by the management for purposes of accountability and managerial decision making. Within these broad purposes, the accounting system should;

I. facilitate accountability, financial as well as legal, both from the executive to the legislature and within the executive from lower to higher levels,

II. provide information which could be related to broad functional areas served by the government for rational determination of the allocation resources among the several functions,

III. serve as a tool for the executives to ensure financial control,

IV. facilitate an independent audit,

V. provide timely information for planning, programming and directing several programmes and activities to management at all levels, and

VI. facilitate economic analysis of governmental operations and their impact on the national economy.

Basis of Accounting: accounting is generally concerned with recording and classifying data pertaining to transactions in the form of stocks, machinery and equipment, funds flow. As such, accounting can be based on any one of the following four phases of a transaction:-

(*i*) Order or commitment

(*ii*) Receipt of goods or services

(*iii*) Disbursement or payment of cash

(*iv*) Consumption of goods or services

The above four phases may take place simultaneously or at different intervals in any possible order. Which one of these phases is most suited for purposes of performance budgeting?

Order or obligation: Ordering of goods or services as a basis of accounting takes into consideration the obligations or commitments in connection with that order but it ignores delivery, payment and consumption of goods. This basis is vital for control of funds

Receipt of goods and accrued expenditure: Procurement of goods or services and the liability accrued for payment is the basis of accounting. This basis ignores the time of the order, consumption or payment.

Disbursement or cash payment: Represents the payment of cash without regard to the receipt or consumption of services or goods. This phase considers the payment requirements in relation to cash available. Cash being an asset of first performance, it is the simplest and common basis of accounting in government.

Accrual or consumption: Represents accounting at the point of use of goods or services irrespective of order, receipt or disbursement.

To illustrate the four phases at different time intervals, these four phases may take place at different timings as under:-

Order	-	March, 2012
Receive	-	June, 2012
Payment	-	August, 2012
Accrual	-	April, 2013

For an organization having April- march as financial year, the expenses in the above illustration will be booked in different years depending upon the phase as a basis of accounting. This can be shown as under: -

Phase	Month	Financial year
Order	March, 2012	2011 -12
Receive	June, 2012	2012 -13
Payment	August, 2012	2012 -13
Accrual	April, 2013	2013 - 14

Thus, with the different bases of accounting, the expenses are booked for different years and it affects performance for various years, particularly, when the transaction under consideration is quite voluminous relating to a purchase of costly asset or property.

In other words, a transaction for purchase of costly equipment, or a transaction relating to development expenditure involving heavy outlay, will be booked in accounts and budget depending upon the basis of accounting adopted. This raises an important question: will such booking of expenses be in conformity with the targets and progress of programmes and activities in physical terms?

When a government is involved in administrative and routine type of functions, following of cash basis of accounting serves the purposes of financial accountability and control of legislative over executives. However, in case the Government is engaged in numerous developmental tasks involving expenditure on projects yielding social and economic benefits for a long period, the accrual basis of accounting is suitable to ascertain cost, performance and progress at various stages of the project. Accrual or commercial accounting is based on double entry system where both the aspects of a transaction are recorded; expenses are matched with the revenues generated and thus the expenses are considered at the time of consumption of goods or services.(see chapter X for details)

For example, for a transaction relating to purchase of equipment for cash, the two aspects recorded are:

- Equipment Purchase:- Addition of equipment asset
- Cash payment;- Reduction of Cash Balance

Similarly, for the payment of salaries for the year, the two aspects are:-

- Salary...................... as an expense
- Cash Payment ....reduction of cash balance

The accrual basis of accounting reflects:

- **Assets:** Inventories, equipment, cash & Bank and other resources available
- **Use of available resources** represented by salaries to employees, rent, electricity and utility charges, including use of resources in relation to works performed in a given period;
- **Liabilities** – borrowings, owners' funds, and amount dues

To sum up, as regards the basis of accounting for performance budgeting, the Working Group on Performance Budgeting constituted by the Study Team on Budgetary Reforms of the Administrative Reforms Commission[i], recommended that, "in the initial stages, accounts should not be unduly disturbed. Refinements such as accrual accounting, allocation of overheads like, general administration and common services, etc., may also be deferred to later stage. The introduction of performance budgeting elsewhere not be made contingent on shift from cash to accrual basis. The advantage to be gained by having total or full or accrued cost may not be commensurate with the cost and labour involved in a radical departure immediately from the long established accounting systems and practices. In fact, for a major part of governmental expenditure, cash basis of accounting may meet the requirement."

SYSTEM OF ACCOUNTING

Accounting as a means of information reporting and control should be designed in a manner which is flexible, is not primarily geared to the issue of legality and is an effective tool of management. For this purpose, the accounting has to be goal oriented, should be developed in relation to function, programme and activity classification, and should give preference to substance over form.

There are mainly two systems of accountings: product accounting and responsibility accounting. Under product accounting, the costs related to a product are accumulated irrespective of an individual or a departmental head responsible for those costs. Under responsibility accounting, on the other hand, costs are accumulated for a centre or unit and each centre or a unit is headed by a responsible official. Thus, responsibility accounting intends to tag officials in the organization as a centre of authority, responsibility and accountability.

The accounting system suited to performance budgeting is the responsibility accounting and various steps in installation of responsibility accounting are:

I. **Identify Responsibility centers:** Divide the organization into various departments or centres in line with functions, programme, activity, classification. Each centre is to be headed by a responsible official who is responsible for its functioning. The responsibility centre can be of following four types:

   (i) Cost centres or expense centre or input centre
   (ii) Revenue centre
   (iii) Financial performance or profit centre
   (iv) Investment centre.

i. Report of the Study Team of Administrative Reform Commission (May 1, 1977) GOI (p177)

II. Accumulate costs for each centre

III. Distinguish between controllable and non-controllable costs: While accumulating costs for each centre or sub-centre, distinction should be drawn between controllable and non-controllable costs.

IV. Build hierarchy of responsibility centers

The responsibility accounting system based on accrual basis would provide cost information at various stages of programmes and activities.

In short, a good financial management system for purposes of performance budgeting must ensure the following: -

I. Correlation between the developmental heads in the national plan and the budget,
II. Integration of accounting and budget structure,
III. Switch over to accrual basis of accounting, particularly, for developmental works,
IV. Adopting responsibility accounting system.

CHAPTER 5

Zero–Base Budgeting: Meaning & Characteristics

As discussed in earlier chapters, budget is a predetermined plan expressed in financial terms and is essentially a blue print for action. It lays down in quantitative terms, financial as well as non-financial results to be expected in future.

Handbook of Public Administration by UN (1961) describes national budget as "both the compass indicating the course a Government should take in its financial administration and the wheel with which it can steer that course. It has many aspects. It is an instrument for scheduling and evaluating government activities. The document in which it is summarized is of unusual public interest and importance. Through that document, the manner in which the country's financial resources are to be utilized, obtains approval and consent at the highest executive and legislative level"[i]

Budget is a device for allocation of scarce resources to various activities envisaged and is an instrument of authourisation and planning and control. There has been an increase in government expenditure over the years. For example, Central Government annual expenditure has increased from ₹ 24,170 crore in 1980-81 to ₹ 3.62 lakh crore in 2001-02 to ₹ 8.6 lakh crore in 2008-09 to ₹ 12.58 lakh crore (BE) in 2011-12 i.e. 52 time over 31 years (from 1981-82 to 2011-2012) or 3.5 times over ten years (from 2001-02 to 2011-12). This increase is particularly so in the non-plan expenditure. Budget has been used as an instrument to control growth of public expenditure in the country.

The Seventh Five Year Plan document, in order to control public expenditure, suggested various steps including modification of planning and budgetary procedures so as to take an integrated view of developmental outlays regardless of whether they are on new schemes of the current Plan or on the maintenance of schemes started in earlier plans.

Adoption of Zero Base Budgeting (ZBB) was one of the steps for allocation of resources so as to control both non development and development expenditure[ii] . We discuss in the present chapter the concept, and process of ZBB. Aspects relating to ranking and evaluation of decision packages and implementation of ZBB are discussed in the next two chapters. ZBB implementation in India is illustrated by discussing a case study of a research and development organizations in the subsequent chapter (VI).

■ ZERO BASE BUDGET : CONCEPT

ZBB is an approach to budgeting with an objective to have an optimal allocation of given resources or to have 'value for money'. It is a management concept linking planning, budgeting,

i. United Nations, (1961) A Handbook of Public Administration, New York pp.78-79
ii. Dhameja Nand, Zero Base Budgeting in India – Some Issues, The Chartered Accountant, April 1987

review and operational decision making into a single process. It attempts to shift the traditional approach of fund allocation towards a new mode of thinking and operations. Traditionally, budgets are developed by taking the current level of funding for the existing programmes and increasing the expenditures to fund new programmes which are generally scrutinized closely. However, under ZBB, existing programmes and activities are subjected to the same kind of analysis and justification usually reserved for new programmes.

In other words, the traditional budget subjects the new schemes or programmes a close scrutiny and funds the on-going schemes at the current level with some increments. The ZBB, on the other hand, does away with the principle of incrementalism and subjects all programmes both, new and on-going with close review and justification. It may be mentioned that the term 'programme' is also referred to as a 'decision package'.

This is made clear by following Exhibit-5.1

Exhibit : 5.1

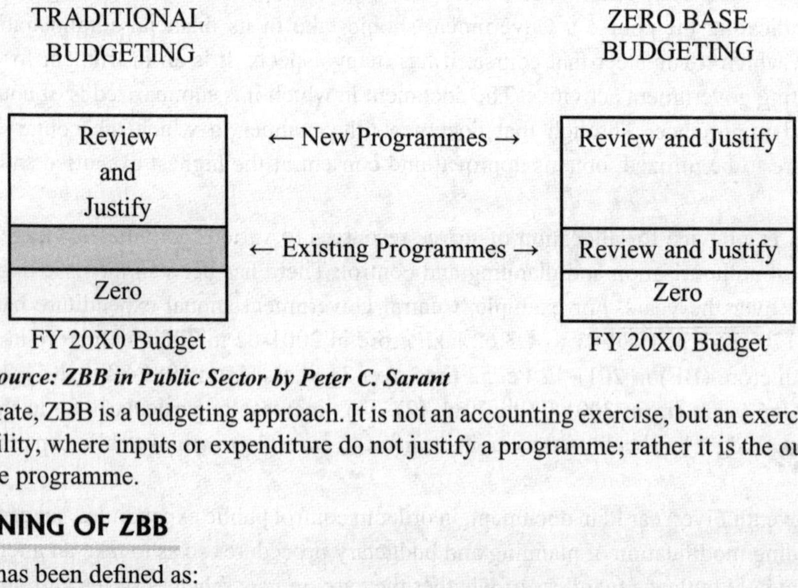

Source: ZBB in Public Sector by Peter C. Sarant

To iterate, ZBB is a budgeting approach. It is not an accounting exercise, but an exercise towards accountability, where inputs or expenditure do not justify a programme; rather it is the output which justifies the programme.

■ MEANING OF ZBB

ZBB has been defined as:

"Zero-base budgeting is a management process that provides for systematic consideration of all programmes and activities in conjunction with the formulation of budget requests and programme planning"[iii].

"ZBB is a system whereby each governmental programme, regardless of whether it is new or existing programme, must be justified in its entirety each time a new budget is formulated"[iv].

"Zero-base budgeting is a management tool ......a method of more efficient use of limited resources in the pursuit of specified goals. The goal, as with any planning-budgeting process, is to identify the output desired, and the input resources required to obtain it. This need not involve a reduction of expenditures. An increase, if it efficiently contributed to the attainment of the desired goal, might be an alternative"[v].

---

iii. ***Executive Office of the President, Office of Management and Budgeting, Zero-Base Budgeting Bulletin 77-9, April 19, 1977.***

iv. ***Pyhrr, Peter A., Zero-Base Budgeting, A Practical Management Tool for Evaluation Expenses, 1973. (John Wiley and sons, Inc.)***

v. ***Wilson, Charls H., "Zero-Base Budgeting, Will it Work or is it Another Buzzword?" Congressnal Record – House, January 31, 1977***

"In the most literal sense, zero-base budgeting implies constructing a budget without any reference to what has gone before, based on a fundamental reappraisal of purposes, methods, and resources"[vi].

"ZBB is a technique which complements and links the existing planning, budgeting, and review process. It identifies alternative and efficient methods of utilizing limited resources in the effective attainment of selected benefits. It is a flexible management approach which provides a credible rationale for allocating resources by focusing on the systematic review and justification of the funding and performance levels of current programmes or activities"[vii].

ZBB is a flexible approach to budget formulation by which budget analysis and justification shifts away from 'increments' for the existing programmes to detailed justification for the existing as well as new programmes. Thus thrust of ZBB is:

- That budget is not based on the last year
- That it examines ongoing activities just as closely as proposed activities
- That the principle of increment is not followed in fund allocations.
- That it deals with all elements of budget requests, not just increments or changes or the previous year

Therefore, ZBB is a management tool which provides a systematic method for evaluating all operations and programmes current or new; it allows for budget reductions and expansions in a rational manner and it allows the reallocation of resources from low to high priority programmes.

Under ZBB approach, questions are raised as:

- Are the current activities efficient and effective?
- Should current activities be eliminated or reduced to fund higher priorities new programmes or to reduce the current budget?
- Thus ZBB involves:
  - Evaluation of all programmes
  - Evaluation may occasionally lead to completely rethinking or redirect a programme, in which we do throw everything out and start over again.

Characteristics of Zero-Base Budgeting

Zero-base budgeting has characteristics as:

- Justify the resources requirements for various levels of existing activities as well as for new activities;
- Focus the justification on the evaluation of discrete programmes, activities, or other functions of each decision unit;
- Establish for all managerial levels in an agency, objectives against which accomplishments can be identified and measured;
- Assess alternative methods of accomplishing objectives;
- "Decision packages" are the major tool for budgetary review, analysis, and decision making; and
- Decision packages are ranked to allocate resources available[viii].

---

vi. *Taylor, Graeme M., "Introduction to Zero Base Budgeting," The Bureaucrat, Spring 1977*

vii. *Sarant, Peter; 'Zero Base Budgeting in the Public Sector: A Pragmatic Approach' Addison-Wesley Publishing Company, Inc. Philippine, 1978*

viii. *Executive Office of the President, Office of Management and Budgeting, Zero-Base Budgeting Bulletin 77-9, April 19, 1977.*

Benefits of Zero-Base Budgeting

ZBB, a mammoth approach to budgeting, provides benefits as:[ix]

- The budget process focuses on a comprehensive analysis of objectives and development of plans to accomplish the desired activities;
- Combines planning, evaluation, and budgeting into a single process;
- Encourages lower level management participation in planning, evaluation, and budgeting;
- Managers at all levels are required to evaluate in detail the cost effectiveness of their operations and specific activities – both new and old – all of which are clearly identified;
- Alternative ways to meet objectives are identified;
- Provides managers at all levels with better information on the relative priority associated with budget requests and decisions"

A survey of department heads and their budget analysts of the State of Georgia in the United States, which was one of the first users of ZBB, indicated three primary advantages and three disadvantages associated with the ZBB as under.[x]

Three primary advantages associated with ZBB were described as:

I. Focus on financial planning phase prior to budget preparation;

II. Improvement in the quality of management information; and

III. Involvement of managers at all levels in the budgeting exercise.

Disadvantages of ZBB were described as under:

I. Increase in time and effort required for budget preparation. This was reported to be a very serious problem in budget preparation.

II. ZBB did not significantly affect the allocation of funds. Eleven of the thirteen department heads indicated that there had been no apparent reallocation of financial resources as a result of ZBB.

III. Ineffectiveness of the decision package ranking to meet the changes in the level of funding.

ZBB is a more detailed budgeting exercise wherein a manager is required to justify requirement of funds for every activity, whether existing or new. Accordingly, less priority activities are weeded out and activities having relatively high benefit cost ratio are included for allocation of funds in the budget.

ZBB: Historical Perspective

Origin of the ZBB concept is traced to Bastable,[xi] who in his book, *Public Finance*, emphasised that past figures should not be used as the basis for estimates and there was a need to look afresh at causative factors. To quote:

"One very natural course in the infancy of Finance was to take the figures of the preceding or some other year, generally the last for which the accounts are made up, as the basis. Another method nearly as mechanical is to take the increases during preceding years and count on a like result in the future. In reality, these facts should only be regarded as elements in the calculation. The revenue and expenditure of a State do not move in a definite course: they are acted on by many distinct causes, and it is on these that the financier should frame his estimates".

---

ix. ***Ibid***

x. ***Minmer George, S. and Hermanson, R.H., 'A Look at Zero-Base Budgeting- The Georgia Experience' Atlanta Economic Review, July –August-1976***

xi. ***Bastable, C.F., 'Public Finance' Macmillan Press, London, 1892 (As referred to by Geoff Burrows and Barbara Syme, ZBB: Origin and Pioneers, Department of Accounting and Finance, Australia University Press, Melboune)***

Further, there was a proliferation of ZBB thought and practice during the 1911-17 periods from the activities of the British Treasury. In this regard observations by Hillary Higgs,[xii] and Hilton Young' are worth mentioning. Hillary Higgs opened his Financial System of the United Kingdom with a discussion on the preparation of estimates and the role of Treasury. The circular in this regard (dated October 2, 1911, for the year 1912- 13) contained a section which reads as follows:

"*My [Treasury] Lords desire to impress upon Departments the fact that a sufficient explanation is necessary for a duly authorised service even when it does not exceed the estimate of the preceding year. The habit of regarding each year's estimate as the starting-point for the next is one against which special vigilance is needed in the case of services upon which the expenditure is in some degree discretionary, and My Lord think it necessary to warn Departments, especially those whose expenditure is of this charter, that they must be prepared to subordinate such expenditure to the financial exigencies of each year*".

Similarly, Hilton Young[xiii] in the first edition of his *System of National Finance* described the preparation of the estimates and referred to a circular letter from the Treasury emphasising that the state of public revenue demands utmost economy and warned against assuming last year's estimates as the starting point for those of the next.

As against the genesis of ZBB during the early years of 20th Century in British Treasury programme, the concept of ZBB was popularised by the President Jimmy Carter, President of USA during the early stages of his Presidency, it had widespread use in cities and states and no contemporary budget reform has received more widespread media coverage than ZBB. The purpose in instituting ZBB was to show governmental decision-makers where money would do the most good and to determine the value of existing programmes. Duplicate programmes hopefully would be weeded out. In principle, "ZBB provides budgeting from the ground up". Every proposed expenditure comes under review as though the budget were prepared for the first time.[xiv] The National Performance Report[xv] in the US emphasised that budgeting should be a managerial process that sets direction for management improvement and efficiency. It should be a financial process that assimilates and ties together a wealth of financial data. It should be a marketing process, by which the government sells its programmes and services. And finally, it should be an accountability process, through which government communicates its decisions about priorities and expected performance. ZBB is reported to be the most current of the budget reforms; the method has direct relevance to the subject of budgeting as an expression of power because it theoretically allows for examination and re-justification of the whole programme each year.

ZBB was first introduced in US in a number of government departments and commercial enterprises in the early sixties. Since then, it was adopted in a number of countries. Texas Instruments was one of the first enterprises to adopt ZBB in its Research and Development department in 1968 and in the subsequent years it was adopted in the whole organization. Peter A. Phyrr was instrumental in the adoption of ZBB in the Texas Instruments. Georgia State which was experiencing huge budgetary deficit at that time, adopted ZBB for its all 65 agencies. Jimmy Carter, the then Governor, Georgia State, was impressed with the successful use of ZBB, included it in his election manifesto for the President ship of the US, that if elected, he will introduce ZBB in the US. On his election

xii. Higgs, Hillary, 'The Financial System of United Kingdom' Macmillan Press, London, 1914 (As referred to by Geoff Burrows and Barbara Syme, opcit)

xiii. Young, Hilton, 'The System of National Finance' (London Smith Elder, 1915) As referred to by Geoff Burrows and Barbara Syme, op cit

xiv. Horgren, C.T, Fosler Datar G., Blackt, S.M. and Gray, P., 'Cost Accounting in Australia: A Management Emphasis, Prientece-Hall, Sydney, 1966

xv. National Performance Review Report: Creating A Government That Works Better and Costs Less, Al Gore Committee Report, 1983.

of US President, President Carter brought the ZBB to the White House with him and on Valentines Day, February 14, 1977, issued an order establishing ZBB through the Federal Government and requested that each agency develop a zero base budgeting system (see Annexure A at the end of the chapter for the Order).

Once the ZBB was adopted in the US, it travelled in other countries. As a result it was introduced in many countries like the UK, France and many developing countries.

SUMMING UP

ZBB is a more detailed budgeting exercise wherein fund allocation is not done on the basis of past years and executive is required to justify requirements of funds for every activity, whether on-going or new, without reference to the last year appropriations; such evaluation may occasionally lead to complete rethinking in which we throw everything out and start over again. Accordingly, the lesser priority activities are weeded out and activities having a relatively high benefit cost ratio are included for funds appropriations.

In short, the top management sets broad goals and general guidelines on available resources and decentralises the responsibility for preparation of "decision packages" down to middle managers, who are actually responsible for putting together their own pictures of what parts of their programmes they want to keep and those which they see as relatively less desirable in order to accomplish the goals which they are charged to accomplish.

Theoretically, ZBB is similar to the approach that decision-makers should consider more than a single recommended level of spending for various programmes.[xvi] In this sense, ZBB is a form of *alternative* budgeting. It requires executives to consider not only alternative levels of funding and service output, but alternative means for achieving the objectives.

According to Richard Rose, "like PPBS and Management by Objectives, Zero-base budgeting has 'evaporated', gone but not forgotten, it survives in pockets of the federal bureaucracy and, in altered form, in some 20 states. What all three of these executive branch budgetary reforms had in common was an emphasis on analysis. But analysis was either unwelcome or unnecessary.[xvii]

ZBB of the form described above is relatively rare, in part because executives assume a knowledge of programme costs that may not be present, and in part because they open the whole budget, much of which is not really likely to change owing to such prioritisation. As a result, simplified ZBB, called *target-based budgets*, has been used. Such budgets create a pool of money for reallocation by taking new money and a percentage of existing funds. Agencies cut themselves by a given percentage and propose what they would do with new money and why. These proposals are rank-ordered and funded as far down the list as the money available allows. This procedure forces a clear statement of priorities and links the goals of the governmental unit with the budget presented. It allows for some reallocation without creating unnecessary chaos or insecurity.[xviii]

Another simplified version of ZBB could be to adopt it selectively and occasionally to particular activities considering: status quo should not be the starting point for the following year budget; and review the existing level of expenditure, not necessarily a total.

Another version of ZBB emerged from what the Core Group appointed to review ZBB exercise in science and technology departments had recommended. The Core Group recommended that budgeting (see details in chapter-VI) exercise by a department should bring its current level

---

xvi. Joseph C. Pilegge, "Budget Reforms" (p 79). in Jack Rabin (edited), A Handbook of Public Budgeting, Marcel Decker, New York, 1992.

xvii. Richard, Rose., "Implementation and Evaporation: The Record of MBO" Public Administration Review, July – August, 1977 in . Jack Rabin (edited), A Handbook of Public Budgeting, Marcel Decker, New York, 1992.

xviii. Ruben S. Iren, "Budgeting: Theory, Concepts Methods and Issues", in Jack Rabin(edited), A Handbook of Public Budgeting, Marcel Decker, New York, 1992.

expenditure down by 30 per cent by removing programmes/projects/tasks which have either not fructified or which could be accorded lower priority. Of this 30 percent savings, half could be deployed for strengthening the programmes identified to be retained; the strengthening may be either to accelerate some priority programmes or to raise them from sub-critical funding. The other half could be utilized for initiating new programmes or taking new initiative which have been considered as priority, especially in view of the changing situations including the WTO regime coming into effect.

In short, ZBB is a comprehensive approach to redesign the work structure and costs associated thereto. For example, it is argued that healthcare industry which has been passing through turbulence state, can be transformed through adoption of the ZBB approach. It would entail re-envisioning the business and asking what activities and resources are needed, as opposed to what needs to be trimmed or removed. ZBB examines every area of spending with a more complete set of tools than targeted cost cutting. The approach analyses which activities should be performed at what levels and frequency, as well as how they could be better performed – potentially moved offshore, outsourced, streamlined, standardized or automated with refined organizational structure and responsibilities.[xix]

ZBB PROCESS

Exhibit : 5.2

Zero Base Budgeting: A participative Approach

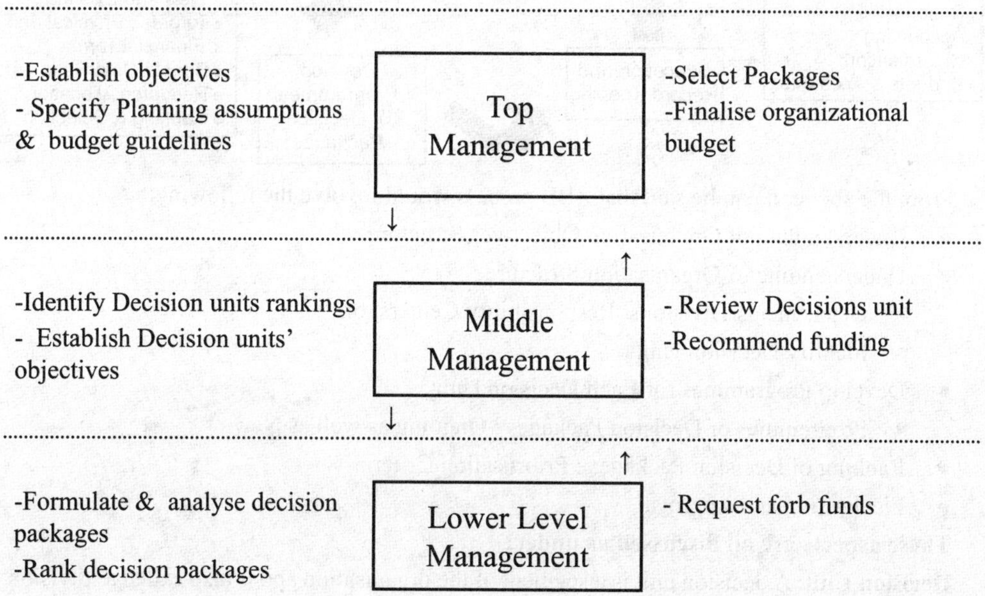

ZBB is a top-to-bottom-to-top approach to budgeting. As illustrated in Exhibit 5.2, it requires participation of managers at all levels in the organisation. The top management establishes goals and objectives, and issues guidelines to the middle level/lower level managers for formulation of budget. Budget programmes are formulated, ranked and evaluated by the middle level/lower level managers and these are submitted to the top management which finalises the budget for the organisation. Under ZBB approach, every scheme, whether new or on-going, is subject to review before committing funds to it for the ensuing year and thus it bids goodbye to the system of 'incrementalism' whereby

---

*xix. **Karan Singh, Paul Cichocki and Molly Kerr, Turbulence in Healthcare: Has the Time come for radical redesign through Zero-based budgeting? Business India (December 9, 2-12)***

funds are allocated to on-going schemes on the basis of their performance during the previous year by adding (or deducting) a certain percent thereon. Thus, ZBB system allocates funds to various schemes-both new as well as existing, on the basis of their utility or desirability in future. In the words of Merewitz and Sosnick[xx] "perhaps the essence of zero base budgeting is simply that an agency provides a defence for its budget request that makes no reference to the level of previous appropriations".

Systematic approach for developing ZBB can be presented as under in Exhibit 5.3

Exhibit : 5.3

Zero-Base Budgeting Process

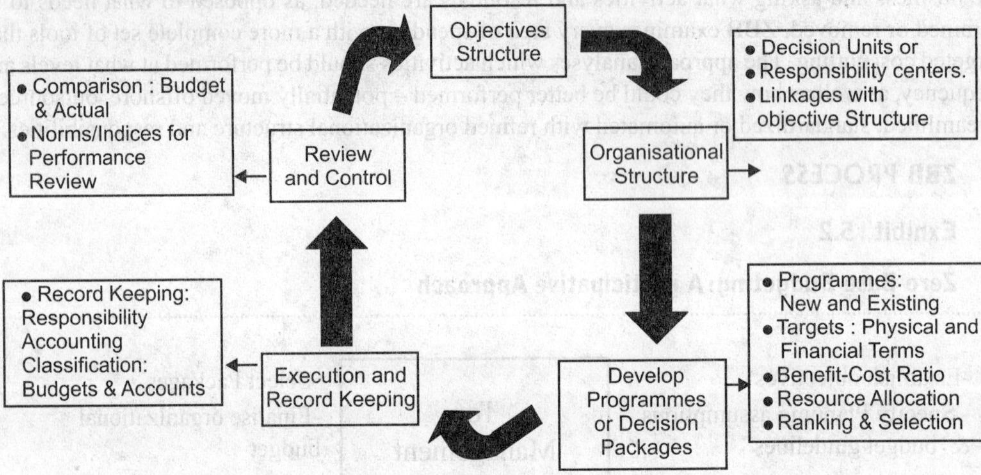

From the above, it can be said that ZBB process would involve the following:

- Understanding of Organisation Objectives Structure
- Understanding of Organisation Structure :
  - Departments/Divisions/ Responsibility Centers; or
  - Identify Decision Units
- Develop Programmes for Each Decision Unit :
  - Programmes or Decision Packages : Ongoing as well as New
- Ranking of Decision Packages : Priortisation Criteria
- Finalisation and Approval

These aspects are all discussed as under:

Decision Unit: A decision unit is a segment of the organisation and is also called a 'division' or a 'department' or a 'responsibility centre' for which the budget is prepared and which is headed by an executive. For purpose of ZBB, management of an organisation has to decide of decision units, *i.e.* level in the organisation structure from which budgeting exercise is to start. As such, a decision unit should neither be at such a low level in the organisation structure as to have enormous paper work, nor be at such a high level as not to have meaningful involvement of managers in formulation and review of budgets. The level in the organisation so decided from which the budgetary exercise would start, should have authority commensurate with responsibilities.

Decision Packages: Every decision unit manager prepares packages which represent budget

xx. ***Merewitz, Leonard and Sosnick Stephen H. 'The Budget's New Clothiers: A Critic of Planning, Programming, Budgeting and Benefit Cost Analysis' (Chicago, Markham, 1971)***

request for the unit. A decision package (DP) refers to a 'programme' and it contains a description of the programme, its objectives, benefits, relevance to organisation objectives, estimated costs, phased outlays and consequences of its not being funded. Anderson[xxi] defines a decision package as: 'a summary (operational plan) which usually includes a statement of the expected business results or purpose of the activity, its costs, personnel required, measures of performance, alternative course of action and an evaluation from a corporate or organisational perspective of the benefits of performance and consequence of non-performance.'

Design of a decision package and its description enables management to evaluate it against other similar packages. To quote Phyrr[xxii], 'the decision packages is a document that identifies and describes a specific activity in such a manner that management can (*a*) evaluate it and rank it against other activities competing for the same or similar limited resources, and (*b*) decide whether to approve it or disapprove it"

Decision packages can be categorised as:

- Business- as-usual packages or ongoing packages
- New packages
- Research and Development Packages
- Service and Support Facilities Packages
- Capital Expenditure Packages
- Overhead and Infrastructure Packages
- Obligatory or Statutorily Required Packages
- Business Related Packages

The decision packages may be 'mutually exclusive' or 'incremental'. Of the mutually exclusive packages, a package with maximum benefits is selected and then decision is made among various incremental packages reflecting different levels of efforts depending upon the return expected and the funds involved. The incremental packages may be 'base package' or 'higher level package'. A 'base package' represents the minimum level of effort below which the budget unit is not 'viable' or 'effective'. Normally, the 'base package' includes functions and costs that are required by law and represents unavoidable obligation. On the other hand, higher level packages reflect higher levels of efforts expanded on a specific function. A decision unit manager uses decision package to define his objectives and responsibilities and how these can be performed at various levels of effectiveness.

Ranking and Evaluation of Decision Packages: The decision packages for every decision unit are reviewed and ranked in the order of priority or in terms of their cost–benefit analysis. These then are consolidated with those of other decision units through the management hierarchy and thus budget for the organisation is finalised. Various approaches of ranking are discussed in the next chapter.

Review and Revision of Budget during the Year

The budget once formulated, should in order to be a complete mechanism of planning and control, be revised and used during the year by the management at various levels to assess performance, to ascertain deviations and to check how far these deviations are controllable and who is responsible for them.

---

xxi. Anderson Donald N., 'Zero-Base Budgeting: How it Get Rid of Corporate Crabgrass, Management Review, October 1976

xxii. Phyrr Peter, op. cit

The above ZBB framework presumes that the hierarchy of organisation's objectives is clearly defined and is also matched with various levels of organisation structure. In other words, it requires that every decision unit manager is clear about his objectives, responsibilities and authorities.

Annexure A

THE WHITE HOUSE

WASHINGTON

February 14, 1977

MEMORANDUM FOR THE HEADS OF EXECUTIVE DEPARTMENTS AND AGENCIES

During the campaign, I pledged that immediately after the inauguration I would issue an order establishing zero-base budgeting throughout the Federal Government. This pledge was made because of the success of the zero-base budget system adopted by the State of Georgia under my direction as Governor.

A zero-base budgeting system permits a detailed analysis and justification of budget requests by an evaluation of the importance of each operation performed.

An effective zero-base budget system will benefit the Federal Government in several ways. It will:

-Focus the budget process on a comprehensive analysis of objectives and needs.

-Combine planning and budgeting into a single process.

-Cause managers to evaluate in detail the cost-effectiveness of their operation.

-Expand management participation in planning and budgeting at all levels of the Federal Government.

The Director of the Office of Management and Budget will review the Federal budget process for the preparation, analysis, and justification of budget estimates and will revise those procedures to incorporate the appropriate techniques of the zero-base budgeting system. He will develop a plan for applying the zero-base budgeting concept to preparation, analysis, and justifications of the budget estimates of each department and agency of the executive branch.

I ask each of you to develop a zero-base system within your agency in accordance with the instructions to be issued by the Office of Management and Budget. The fiscal year 1979 budget will be prepared using this system.

By working together under zero-base budgeting system, we can reduce costs and make the Federal Government more efficient and effective.

Jimmy Carter

Source. *Zero-Base Budgeting in the Public Sector by Peter C. Sarant (Addission-Wesley Publishing Company, 1978 p.10)*

CHAPTER 5A

Z B B : Decision Packages – Ranking and Evaluation Approaches

As a process of ZBB, decision packages formulated for various decision units, as described in the previous chapter, are to be ranked in order of priority, keeping in view the objectives of the organization. Ranking determines allocation of resources and the decision packages of higher priority are given preference.

For the purpose, ranking is defined as a process by which managers arrange programmes, or also termed as decision packages, in decreasing order of priority and the ranking process identifies the relative priority assigned to each package based on benefits expected or costs involved.

Ranking of the decision packages is normally done at various levels in the organization. Initially ranking is done by the decision unit manager who has developed decision packages, these are subsequently reviewed through the management hierarchy along with the other decision packages of other decision units. All the decision packages are finally consolidated at the top management level.

Such ranking at different management levels may be done by one manager or a group of managers; this may be done on a single parameter or a number of parameters. To be effective and to introduce objectivity, the ranking should be done by a group on the bases of number of parameters, each parameter having a pre-determined weight.

There could be various approaches of prioritisation. An approach of prioritisation followed in ranking of decision packages and finalisation of budget formulation should minimise subjectivity and personal bias. In other words, the ranking approach adopted should be objective one to reflect the laid down goals and objectives. As a principle, the approach of prioritisation should be finalized by the management before the budget formulation process begins.

We discuss below four approaches of prioritisation:

1. Cut off Points approach
2. Paired-Comparison approach
3. Degree of Urgency approach
4. Two-Dimensional Priority Rating Matrix approach

The last three approaches have been illustrated for functions and schemes of a local government. The functions of a local government are broadly categorised as:

I. Obligatory functions

II. Desirable functions

Various schemes formulated both under obligatory functions and desirable functions are prioritised to finalise the schemes and budget for the coming year.

Functions of a local government are laid by an Act passed by the legislature, *e.g.* The Delhi Municipal Corporation Act 1957, lays down functions of the Corporation in Sections 41 to 43 of Chapter III. Some of the functions are 'obligatory' and it is incumbent on the Corporation to make a provision for each of these functions. Other functions, called 'discretionary' ones are to be provided for either wholly or in part.

An illustrative list of obligatory and discretionary functions of a Municipal Corporation is given in Exhibit 5A.1. These functions are drawn from the Delhi Municipal Corporation Act, 1957, and the Budget documents for the year 1988-89.[i]

PRIORITISATION APPROACHES

1. Cut off Points approach

Under this approach, a cut off point of expenditure is set for each level of management, starting from higher level to lower levels before the budgeting exercise commences. The cut off points of expenditure for various levels of management are laid down on the basis of last year budget or on the basis of budgeted expenses for the last six month of the current year and actual expenditure of six months of the current year. The choice of cut off points is based on levels of organizational hierarchy and the desired degree of budget authority at different levels. As a matter of principle, the cut off points are more stringent at the higher levels of management and the cut off points of expenditure are laid out before the budgeting exercise starts.

As an illustration, the cut off points for various levels could be as under :

Levels of Management		Cut off Point as % of Total
Level A	Top Management	100 %
Level B	Middle Management	80% cut off
Level C	Lower Level	50 % cut off
Level D	Lowest Level	Nil

As per the above, the procedure for ranking for various management levels would be as:

- **Lowest Level D :** Rank all Decision Packages and hand over the same to the next higher level C
- **Lower Level C :** Take packages as ranked by the manager at level D above.
  - Skim the top ones up to a Total value of 50 % of the last year expenditure
  - Evaluate and consolidate the rest. Handover the packages with new ranking to the next level B.
- **Middle Level B :** Glance over the packages received from Level C
  - Skim the top ones up to 80 % of the expenditure of the last year
  - Evaluate and consolidate the rest.
  - Hand over the packages with new ranking to the higher level manager at level A.
- **Top Level A :** Glance over the packages received from Level B
  - Skim over the ranking and finalise the same.

The cut off point of expenditure is illustrated in Exhibit 5A.2

2. Paired-Comparison Approach

Compare programmes in a pair of two programmes at a time to determine their priorities and to produce a numerical expression of relative importance. A forced Choice-matrix is used to make a series of comparisons in which a pair of two programmes are considered at a time, to determine which one of the two programmes being compared is "better" or "more deserving" to be given higher priority.

---

i. The Delhi Municipal Corporation Act. 1957 and Budget Document for the year 1988-89.

Steps for the Paired-Comparison approach[ii] towards prioritisation are discussed below with the help of a forced-choice-matrix worksheet given in Exhibit 5A.3.

I. On the vertical axis, various programmes to be prioritised are listed in the column heading '*Schemes*'. On the horizontal axis, various programmes to be compared are listed under the head '*compared to*'. Twelve programmes (1 to 12) on the vertical axis and eleven programmes (2 to 12) on the X-axis are listed.

II. The first programme in the list is compared with the second programme, and the assessment is entered in the appropriate cell in the "*Compared To*" column;

- If first programme is more important than second programme, number '1' is posted in row 1, column 2; or
- If programme one is less important than the second programme, a zero is posted in row 1, column 2.
- Thereafter, the first programme is compared with the third programme, if the first one is more important than the third one, a number 1 is posted in row 1, column 3: otherwise a zero (0) is posted. Similarly, the first programme is compared with the fourth, the first with the fifth and so on.

III. The same procedure is continued, the second programme is compared with each of the programme following it and '1' or '0' is posted as required. All such comparisons are completed.

IV. In the vertical columns '*compared to*', we have either '1' or '0'. Number of zeros in each column is counted and their number is posted in each column's total box, indicated by an asterisk. This comparison is done for the entire column. For example '4' is posted in column eight; and '9'is posted in column twelve in Exhibit 5A. 3

V. For *each* horizontal row, add all the numbers including the number in the asterisked total box (arrived at by point IV above). Row total is entered in the total column. For example, '11'is entered in row 1; '8'in row 7; and '1' in row eleven in Exhibit 5A.3

A programme with highest total is given top most priority (rank number 1: the programme with the second highest total is prioritised number 2, and so on. This determines priorities for various programmes.

Under paired-comparison approach, illustrated in Exhibit 5A.3, twelve programmes of a municipality are prioritised by comparing programmes in a pair of two at a time. For example, Programme 1 (Public health & Medical relief) is compared with programme 2 (Water supply) and 1 is 'Considered better than 2, and number (1) is posted in row 1, column 2. Similarly, programme 1 is compared with other programme turn by turn and number '1' '0' is pasted in the corresponding column.

This way, every programme in the first column is compared in a pair of two with the successive programmes (which has not been previously compared) on the horizontal axis. For example, programme 10, when compared to programme 11, the former, is considered to be better than 11, and number '1' is casted in 10 row 11 th column. Further, on comparison of programme 10, with programme 12, programme 10 is found to be less important than programme 12, number '0' is posted in row 10 column 12.

Now number of zeros (0's) appearing in each vertical column are entered in the respective

---

ii. ***Austin Allan L. and Cheek Logan ·M.: Zero Base Budgeting -A Decision Package Manual (AMA, 1979).***

column's total box marked asterisk (*).

All numbers appearing in each of the horizontal rows, including the number in the asterisk total box, (as arrived at point IV above) are added and entered in the 'total' column.

Thus the programme 1 (Public Health, Medical Relief) having highest total has highest priority; programmes 2 and 12 (Water supply, and Scavenging, Drains & Sewers respectively) having next highest totals are given 2nd and 3rd priority, respectively. Programme 3 (Supply of Unfiltered water) having lowest total is given the lowest priority.

The Paired-comparison approach though adopts logical sequencing for prioritisation, relies heavily on the judgment of executives or a committee enterested with the task of prioritisation and thus does not have the advantage of being an objective one.

Further, paired comparison approach being one-dimensional, a programme having low priority gets dropped. Though it may be of importance from social welfare viewpoint.

Lastly, this approach is easily applicable, where the number of programmes to be prioritised is smaller. In situation where the number becomes large, (more than fifty) the whole exercise becomes unwieldy.

3. Degree of Urgency Approach

Programmes differ in terms of their urgency which can be measured in terms of various factors like, legal requirements, public health, economic reasons, etc. and these can be the bases of prioritisation. Some of the factors which indicate degree of urgency are as under:

Statutory Obligation : required by legislation or government instructrions

Safety Requirements : required to eliminate hazards to public health and safety

Inter-developmental Requirements : required for purposes of coordination with other departments as a part of operations

Economic Grounds : provides economic benefits in terms of increasing benefits: or reducing costs improvement in efficiency or standard of service

Welfare or Social Benefits : required for the welfare of public or for some social benefits

Replacement or Addition of Assets : brings in additional assets or replaces existing ones to add to available capacity and its utilization:

Convenience : brings in extra convenience, comfort or other facilities.

In a number of local governments in U.S.A, priority rating system is used for ranking of proposals[iii], Exhibit 5A.4 gives a familiar form of rating system. It ranks proposals into groups according to their degree of urgency, giving first priority to proposals that are obligatory by statute or directive of governments, followed by removal of hazards to health and safety, down through proposals that merely increase comfort or convenience.

---

iii. Simpson C.R. 'Municipal Budgeting- A Case for priorities Governmental Finance 5, No.3 (1976) (Reprinted in Readings in Government and Non-Profit Accounting, Richard J. Vargo (Wadsworth Publishing Co. California, 1977)

Degree of urgency as indicated by various factors can be quantified by assigning some weights and various schemes or programmes in the budget are prioritised on the basis of their total weights.

To illustrate, weights for each factor of urgency are assigned as under : (Factors of urgency and weights for each are suggestive one):

Factors	**Weights Points**
- Statutorily Required	25
- Safety	25
- Economic Grounds	15
- Inter-developmental Requirements	13
- Welfare & Social benefits	12
- Replacement or Expansion	10

For every proposal or scheme, degree of urgency is estimated in terms of various factors and their weight points, and that is the basis of its prioritisation.

Prioritisation on the basis of scale of weight points could be categorized as under:

Category	**Weight Points**	**Range**
Essential	I	61 – 100
Highly desirable	II	31 - 60
Desirable	III	10 – 30

This approach of prioritisation on the basis of degree of urgency was common among a number of organizations, like petroleum companies, research and development organisations.

To illustrate, we assign weights for two programmes namely Water Supply and Libraries. These are as under:

Factors of urgency	**Weight points**	
	Water Supply	**Libraries**
-Statutorily Required	20	2
-Safety	20	2
-Economic Grounds	10	10
-Inter-departmental Requirements	13	4
-Welfare & Social Benefits	10	8
- Replacement or Expansion	2	2
Total Weights	75	28

On the basis of total weight points, both the schemes would be prioritised as under:

	Weight Points	**Category**	**Priority**
Water Supply	75	Essential	Top-I
Libraries	21	Desirable	Desirable-III

Under this approach, weight points for a programme are estimated on the basis of urgency measured in terms of various factors. To iterate, weight points are decided well before the budget formation exercise starts and these are uniformly followed for all programmes by various divisions. Determining of various factors, and their weight points by department heads or a committee, should be approved by the Civic body. These should be reviewed and updated periodically. This approach would minimize subjectivity in prioritisation of various programmes. As illustrated in chapter VI, the Council for Scientific and Industrial Research follows the Degree of Urgency Approach and ranks various programmes on the basis of weights assigned.

4 .Two-Dimensional Priority Rating Matrix Approach

In the previous two approaches, ranking is based either on priority of functions, or on degree of urgency and these two approaches are single dimensional, where only one factor is the basis of prioritisation. There are situations where a programme having a low ranking under one approach, may be of higher importance when reviewed by another approach. For example, the programme on Fair & Exhibitions has, as discussed above, low ranking under the Paired-Comparison approach, and may get excluded due to fund constraints. However, the same programme has high priority due to the urgency factor say, Safety requirements or Government circulars. This leads us to a method, where two factors are the bases of prioritisation.

Priority Rating Matrix Systems[iv] considers two factors simultaneously for purposes of prioritisation and is thus two dimensional. It is illustrated in Exhibit 5A.5. Two factors (a) priority of functions, and (b) degree of urgency are ranked independently and their, multiple rating is the basis of ranking.

Priority of Functions: First factor of ranking is the priority of functions. As discussed earlier, a municipality is required to perform certain services which can be ranked in order of their importance as "basic needs", followed by "essential wants" and "essential amenity". The ranking of services or programmes would resemble that under the Paired-Comparison approach.

Ranking of Programmes should be done by a Committee or departmental heads, and be approved by the Council of legislatures. The ranking should be reviewed periodically by the Council to reflect changing times and circumstances.

Degree of Urgency: Urgency is the second factor to determine prioritisation : and degree of urgency is estimated in terms of various factors like, statutory requirements, economic grounds, public health, etc. These factors are assigned weights to indicate their importance, and this would resemble with that of second approach discussed earlier.

In Exhibit 5A.5 one factor is measured on x-axis and the second factor on y-axis. These factors are assigned weights; for simplicity, weights are assigned by simple sequence of consecutive numbering, successive number indicating lower weights.

Since programmes falling within the first degree of urgency, i.e. statutorily required or required by Government Circulars-shall not be excluded, this clause is given distinct number to ensure that it always gets preference over others. Below this clause, the priority rating of any given programme is the product of the numerical rating assigned to the two appropriate factors, the highest priority for the lowest possible number. Priority Rating Matrix (Exhibit 5A.5) is a matrix of two factors- priority of functions and degree of urgency-and the priority number is a multiple of priorities of both the numbers. This way it is an improvement over both the previous approaches, which are simply one-dimensional rating systems. Exhibit 5.A.6 indicates priority of functions on x-axis which resembles the Paired-Comparison approach discussed above. Similarly, degree of urgency is reflected on the y-axis.

iv. 3 Simpson C.R. 'Municipal Budgeting- A Case for priorities Governmental Finance 5, No.3 (1976) (Reprinted in Readings in Government and Non-Profit Accounting, Richard J. Vargo (Wadsworth Publishing Co. California, 1977) 4. Simpson C.R. Ibid, Priority Rating Matrix System is being followed by a number of Municipalities

On comparing, the Two-Dimensional Priority Rating approach with the Paired-Comparison approach, one finds that programme of Unfiltered water supply (programme No 3) has the least priority, *i.e.* 12th rank under the latter approach and may get excluded in times of funds conservancy. On the other hand, under the Two-Dimensional Rating system, the programme 'Unfiltered Water Supply' has weights ranging from 12 to 135 depending upon the degree of urgency.

Funds available will be allocated for various programmes depending upon their weights. In Exhibit 5A.6 schemes of lowest weight will be given highest priority. If for example, fund available allows inclusion of schemes having weights up to "75", all schemes with weights less than "75" would get included. This way "scheme of Unfiltered Water Supply" would get included in the budget as it is a scheme with a degree of urgency required.

The system of Priority Rating Matrix discussed above is a simple one, as it introduces weights to both functions and urgency in a simple consecutive numerical values. It can be modified by varying the relative numerical weights of various categories of functions or urgency to reflect changes in the relative importance of functions or urgency.

SUMMING UP

Local Governments allocate their limited resources to various programmes or proposals. Since their working is subjected to political pressures, a well defined framework and system of allocation of resource would provide a more objective approach to the decision making process. The present chapter has discussed four possible approaches towards such a framework. The fourth approach of two dimensional Priority Rating System in its simple form is useful in fixing Priorities or resource allocation. The approach can be modified by altering the relative importance of various factors and by revising the relative weights for them. To quote Simpson[v] on prioritisation,

"The priority rating system, even in its present primitive state has proven to be a useful accessory to the budget formulation process, and the principles embodied in the system, appear to have the potential for wider application to problems or resources allocation generally. It will never be a total substitute for the free interplay of the many forces and pressures that are brought to bear in the resolution of these problems. The workings of the political process are probably far too complex ever to be captured in a mathematical formula. Such a system can, however, provide a framework for a more rational definition and discussion of the issues and thereby bring about a more objective approach to the decision making process."

Exhibit : 5A.1

FUNCTIONS OF A MUNICIPAL CORPORATION
AN ILLUSTRATIVE L1ST*

Obligatory Functions

Water supply : Supply of pure & wholesome water

Education : Establishment, maintenance & aid to, schools for primary education

Public health : Preventing & checking the spread of dangerous diseases

Medical Relief : Public Vaccination and inoculation

Conservancy, Street cleansing & Road watering,

Scavenging, Drains and Sewers,

---

v. ibid

Roads and public lighting

Buildings, Land acquisition & management

Fire brigade-maintenance brigade & protection of life, & property in case of fire

Licensing, removal of encroachment on public streets, places & bridges

Garden & open spaces - layout & maintenance

Municipal Markets & slaughter houses

Discretionary Functions

Education-physical & cultural education, other than primary education

Libraries: Establishment & Maintenance

Museums, Art galleries, botanical or zoological collections Stadia, gymnasia's, akhras & places of sports & games Census of population-registration of marriages, Providing of music or other entertainment in public places

Organising and managing fair & exhibition

Construction & maintenance of rest houses, poorhouses, children's home, shelters for destitute & disabled persons

Construction & maintenance of dwelling houses for officer's corp. Destitute & Disable persons-relief & construction of shelters Construction & maintenance & management of swimming pools, public wash houses, bathing places

Veterinary hospitals

Organising and managing of cottage industries, handicraft centers, and sales 'emporia',

Construction of warehouses and godowns of garages sheds & stands of vehicles and cattle biers.

* ***Source: The Municipal Corporation Act, 1957 & Budget Document. 1,988-89***

Exhibit : 5A. 2

Cut off Points : Ranking approach

Lowest Management Level D	**Lower Management Level C**	**Middle Management Level B**	**Top Management Level A**
Rank all packages & handover to Level C	Glance over all packages received from D	Glance over all packages received from C	Glance over all packages received from level B
	Skim top ones up to 50 % of previous year expense.	Skim top ones up to 80 % of previous year expense.	Skim over the ranking & finalise the same
	Evaluate the rest	Evaluate the rest	
	Consolidate the new ranking & handover to Level B	Consolidate the new ranking & handover to Level A	

Exhibit : 5A.3

Forced-Choice-Matrix-Showing Paired Comparison for Municipality's Functions and Priorities

S. No.	SCHEMES	COMPARED TO												
		2	3	4	5	6	7	8	9	10	11	12	TOTAL	RANK
1	Public Health and Medical Relief	1	1	1	1	1	1	1	1	1	1	1	11	1
2	Water Supply	0*	1	1	1	1	1	1	1	1	1	1	10	2
3	Unfiltered water		0*	0	0	0	0	0	0	0	0	0	0	12
4	Roads & Public Lighting			1*	1	1	0	0	1	1	1	0	6	6
5	Encroachment Public Places				1*	1	0	0	1	1	1	0	5	7
6	Municipal Markets Slaughter House					1*	0	0	1	1	1	0	4	8
7	Conservancy Street Cleaning						4*	1	1	1	1	0	8	4
8	Education							4*	1	1	1	0	7	5
9	Libraries								1*	1	1	0	3	9
10	Swimming Pools									1*	1	0	2	10
11	Fair & Exhibition										1*	0	1	11
12	Scavenging Drains & Sewerage											9*	9	3

Exhibit : 5A.4

Priority Groupings According to Degree of Urgency

Priority Group 1

(*a*) Required by legislation or action of other governmental jurisdiction

(*b*) On instruction from or arising out of instruction from Local Governments

Priority Group 2

(*a*) Eliminates a provision or obvious hazard to public health or safety

(*b*) Replaces a clearly obsolete facility or maintains and better utilizes an existing facility

(*c*) Directly benefits the City's economic base by increasing property values

(*d*) Results in reduced operating costs and/or potentially better service

Priority Group 3

(*a*) Prevents a substantial reduction in an existing standard of service due to population growth

(*b*) Eliminates a potential hazard to health or safety, or eliminates nuisance conditions

Priority Group 4

(*a*) Provides a new facility or asset, or improves an existing standard of service

(*b*) Provides programms or projects having primary social, cultural, historic or aesthetic value

(*c*) Provides programms or projects designed primary to increase public convenience or comfort

Exhibit : 5A.5

Two Dimensional Priority Rating Matrix

PRIORITY OF FUNCTIONS													
Priority Rating System													
MATRIX	Numerical Value	Public Health & Medical Relief	Water Supply	Scavenging Drains & Sewers	Conservancy Street Cleaning	Education	Roads & Public Lighting	Encroachment Public Places	Municipal Markets & Slaughter Houses	Libraries	Swimming Pools	Fair & Exhibition	Unfiltered Water Supply
Degree of Urgency : Statutory Obligation		1	2	3	4	5	6	7	8	9	10	11	12
Numerical Value		4	5	6	7	8	9	10	11	12	13	14	15
Safety requirements	4	16	20	24	28	32	36	40	44	48	52	56	60
Inter-departmental Requirements	5	20	25	30	35	40	45	50	55	60	65	70	75
Economic Grounds	6	24	30	36	42	48	54	60	66	72	78	84	90
Welfare or Social Benefits	7	28	35	42	49	56	60	70	77	84	91	98	105
Replacement or Addition of Assets	8	32	40	48	56	64	72	80	88	96	104	112	120
Convenience	9	36	45	54	63	72	81	90	99	108	117	126	135

Exhibit : 5A.6

Two Dimensional Priority Rating Matrix

PRIORITY OF FUNCTIONS													
Priority Rating System													
MATRIX	Numerical Value	Public Health & Medical Relief	Water Supply	Scavenging Drains & Sewers	Conservancy Street Cleaning	Education	Roads & Public Lighting	Encroachment Public Places	Municipal Markets & Slaughter Houses	Libraries	Swimming Pools	Fair & Exhibition	Unfiltered Water Supply
Degree of Urgency													
Statutory Obligation		1	2	3	4	5	6	7	8	9	10	11	12
Numerical Value		4	5	6	7	8	9	10	11	12	13	14	15
Safety requirements	4	16	20	24	28	32	36	40	44	48	52	56	60
Inter-departmental Requirements	5	20	25	30	35	40	45	50	55	60	65	70	75
Economic Grounds	6	24	30	36	42	48	54	60	66	72	78	84	90
Welfare or Social Benefits	7	28	35	42	49	56	60	70	77	84	91	98	105
Replacement or Addition of Assets	8	32	40	48	56	64	72	80	88	96	104	112	120
Convenience	9	36	45	54	63	72	81	90	99	108	117	126	135

CHAPTER 5B

Z B B : Implementation Issues and Problem Areas

ZBB is a mammoth exercise for better allocation of resources to improve decision making process and to facilitate planning and reduction of costs. It can be adopted for all activities involving allocation of resources. However, it is more suited for activities or departments involving costs for which there is no rational way of estimating the 'right amount' of costs, or for which there is not any engineering standard, and the amount spent is a matter of judgment. Such costs are termed '*discretionary costs*' or '*managerial costs*'. These activities normally are service or supportive activities like, finance, marketing, research & development, quality control, production planning, etc. for which there is absence of a definite relationship between level of expenses and the expected benefits; or where the manager has discretion to choose between different levels of activities and can influence benefits by changing such levels of activities. ZBB is recommended for such activities. On the other hand, in other activities like, manufacturing, where there exists inputs-output relationship, or there is an engineering standard of expenses and expected benefits and the manager's judgment cannot influence benefits by changing the level of expenditure, this gigantic exercise of budgeting is not worth the cost involved in its application.

In short, ZBB is more suited for activities having 'discretionary' or 'managerial' expenses; and is not warranted for engineering expenses

In not-for-profit organisations, particularly those which do not produce goods but provide services to public and where discretionary expenses account for a larger proportion of total expenses, ZBB is more suited to their activities.

We discuss below various problems and issues relating to successful implementation of ZBB, a means of planning and control.

Foremost, the effective implementation of ZBB would require that the following be ensured;

1. Support of top management in the budgetary process: the top management must believe in the ZBB approach, must be committed to it, and should involve lower level people.
2. Effective design of budgetary system suited to the needs of the enterprise: constitute a Task Force or a Committee for implementation of ZBB, manuals, procedures and formats for budgeting, and arrange training of the people.
3. Effective management of the system including MIS.

This would entail issue of planning assumptions and guidelines; determining of workloads and work indices; comparison of actuals with budgets and initiating necessary corrective actions for variances.

PROBLEMS AND ISSUES

ZBB has been adopted in a number of organizations and there are situations where it has not been a success because of certain problems in its implementation. Problems and issues relating to ZBB implementation are discussed under the following four heads.

1. **Structural Issues**
2. **Accounting Issues**
3. **Administrative and Behavioural Issues**
4. **Policy Issues**

1. Structural Issues

Introduction of ZBB involves a detailed exercise in the formulation of budgets which in turn requires decisions regarding various aspects of ZBB. Various issues relating to ZBB formulations can be grouped as,

I. Determining of Decision Units
II. Decision Packages Formulation Problems
III. Ranking Process Problems

Various problem areas relating to each are discussed as under:

I. Determining of Decision Units: One of the first step in ZBB is the identification of entities or divisions in the organisation who will prepare initial decision packages. Such decision units are determined on the basis of information needs of higher level management. As a principle, the decision units should not be so low as to involve excessive paperwork nor should it be so high as to mar important consideration and prevent meaningful review of work performed. Further, there should be linkages of objectives of each decision unit with the overall corporate objectives and the manager of a decision unit should have authority commensurate with his responsibilities.

II. Decision Packages Formulation Problems: A decision package contains details of the proposed programme, its objectives, costs, benefits and relevance to objectives and is designed as to enable management to evaluate it against other similar packages. Various problems relating to decision package formulation are:

(*a*) Identification of activities, functions or operations for which decision packages are to be developed. For example, for a police department, a decision unit having 45 patrol posts and 600 people on roll, is involved in patrolling the roads and highways with the objective to detect, investigate and apprehend those committing crimes and to safeguard life and property of the public. Functions performed by the decision unit comprise of;

- Operating stations- attending calls, or other administrative works;
- Obligatory Services- like taking inmates to the courts;
- Preventive patrol; and
- Other services.

Three possible alternative decision packages for the decision unit to perform the above functions are:

1. Decision Packages for the Highway Patrol as a whole;
2. Decision Packages for each Patrol Post with all functions in each decision package;
3. Decision Packages for each function

The issue to be decided is: Which of the above three alternatives should be adopted for developing decision packages?

(*b*) For each Decision Package, various levels of packages, *i.e.* minimum level, current level and higher levels are to be developed.

This requires that the manager developing the decision packages should have fuller view of the packages. However, various problems confronted by managers include, they normally, find it difficult to think of a minimum level package, a package below the current level package. Further, while estimating costs for resources at minimum level packages, manpower is normally taken at current level.

(*c*) Identifying work measurement and evaluating data for a service activity where benefits are difficult to quantify, makes the task of evaluating decision packages difficult. There is a normal tendency to add fat in the budget so as to provide safety cushion at the times of control, which results in over estimation of costs in the budget.

(*d*) How many packages should be formulated in each decision unit? As a principle, a larger number of packages makes the ranking process difficult.

III. Ranking Process Problems: Problems relating to ranking process are include :

(***a***) To determine who will do the ranking? Ranking by top management is true theoretically. There may be multi-tier ranking process depending upon the levels of decision units in the organisation. In that case, what will be the ranking process at various levels? In order to introduce an element of objectivity, ranking should be done by a committee on the basis of weights assigned to various attributes. Forming of a committee and determining of voting process are the issues to be decided in advance.

(***b***) Ranking becomes difficult when decision packages of dissimilar functions like, research projects and administrative projects, are to be ranked, particularly when ranking is to be done for projects having higher priorities.

2. Accounting Issues

ZBB requires quantification to the extent possible, of various inputs and expected benefits and converting the same in financial terms in decision packages. For this purposes, the following problems need to be sorted out:

(***a***) **Basis of Accounting:** What should be the basis of accounting? Cash payment, receipt of goods, order of goods, and consumption are the four alternative bases for accounting. 'Consumption' or 'accrual' basis is recommended for accounting and for budgeting. This requires recording of assets, provision of depreciation on fixed assets, matching of expenses with revenues, and treatment for outstandings or prepaid. However, at present, in many organisations, particularly not-for-profit organisations-cash basis is adopted for accounting purposes and there is a need to convert the same to accrual accounting to portray financial information in relation to each quantity of work, *i.e.* linkages of physical work and the finances involved therein. However, as mentioned earlier, the Administrative Reform Commission mentioned that cash basis of accounting may meet the requirement for purposes of performance budgeting and adoption of accrual accounting may be deferred to a later stage[i]. Since about five decades have passed, and we are on a path towards development, the need for accrual accounting, in particular for developmental projects, is of utmost importance.

(***b***) **Responsibility Accounting and Accounting Classification:** Having identified various decision units for purposes of ZBB, accounts should be maintained in relation to the decision units so as to facilitate comparison of budget and accounts. Accounting classification and account codes followed should be same in the plan, budget and account books.

i. Report of the Study Team of Administrative Reform Commission (May 1, 1977) GOI, p 177

(*c*) Estimates of expenses or receipts for the coming year for purposes of budgeting can be made as per the following alternatives:
- actuals for the last three years; or
- actuals for the current year period plus budget for the remaining months of the current year; or
- actuals for the previous year.

The alternative selected for the estimates of expenses or receipts should be representative one and should be followed consistently.

3. Administrative and Behavioural Issues

ZBB has not been found acceptable or has been dropped in number of organisations mainly because of various administrative and behavioural problems. There is a need to look into these problems and to take steps to overcome the same. Some of these problems are:

(*a*) Many managers develop apathy towards ZBB. They feel threatened by the new system and do not cooperate. In fact, there is a need to involve managers in the budgeting exercise, as it is a tool for the managers' use. Since large number of managers, both technical as well financial, are involved in the ZBB exercise, communication becomes a difficult problem and needs to be looked into.

(*b*) The problem gets accentuated where there is absence of formalised policy and planning assumptions by the top management for the guidance of middle or lower level managers who are involved in the preparation of decision packages.

(*c*) ZBB requires more time and effort in budget formulation particularly in the first year of its application. It is reported that ZBB generates too much of paper work, it requires inordinate numbers of personnel, and is said to be very serious problem in ZBB[ii]. "ZBB persists in perpetuating the mindless '*mountain of paperwork*', not to mention the massive methodological problems that are implicit in the procedure". As regards time, formulation of ZBB in Taxes Instruments and in Georgia State took about three months longer than that of under the other budget system. Further, the experience of ZBB in Georgia State shows that there were 11,000 decision packages accompanied by 33 pages of instructions and 24 different forms. It was estimated that if the governor allotted four hours every day for two months, he could spend about one minute on each decision package, not enough time to read it, let alone analyse it[iii] . However, as per another estimate, ZBB requires approximately 20 to 30 per cent more paper work and budget personnel than traditional budgeting; this does not seem inordinate considering that ZBB is intended to produce more analysis and better information. Such things are not free. The question is whether additional benefits are worth the additional costs[iv],[v] . In India, no separate set of documents on account of ZBB[vi] was required to be presented to the Parliament, as the performance budget, as discussed in chapter 1, was required to be refined so as to take care of the issue of increased paperwork in various decision units. Similarly, the question how many copies to make of a decision package, has to be looked into; since, decision packages are to be evaluated and ranked by a number

ii. J. Havemann, 'The tale of how one agency used ZBB and lived to tell about it' (National Journal, February 18, 1978)

iii. R. Anthony, 'Zero Base Budgeting is a Fraud' (The Wall Street Journal, April 27, 1977)

iv. Carl Grafton and Anne Permal Off, 'Budgeting Reforms in Perspective' in Jack Robin and D. Lynch Thomas (eds) Handbook on Public Budgeting and Financial Management, New York Marcel Dekker, 1983)

v. George S. Minmier and R. H. Hermansion, A Look at Zero Bas Budgeting – The Georgia Experience, (Atlanta Economic Review, July – August 1976)

vi. GOI Ministry of Finance, D.O Letter No. 2. F. 2 (90) B(PB)/86 dated July 10, 1986

of persons. Number of copies of the decision packages, though facilitates early evaluation, it results in enormous paper work and creates an administrative problem.

(*d*) Information flows are necessary for the success of a business. It has been said that the recipe for a good decision is "90 per cent information and 10 per cent inspiration". Information is the ingredient that coalesce ZBB, correct and timely information is necessary for formulation of decision packages and their ranking. Lack of cost and other information has been reported to be a problem in implementation of ZBB. This focuses on the need to develop budget manuals and forms and communicate the same to the managers involved in ZBB; to develop systems to assist managers in determining cost of each function; to workout financial outlays for various levels of decision packages and formulate reports for top management.

4. Policy Issues

(*a*) Should the ZBB be implemented in the entire organisation or in a certain selected departments?

This policy issue has to be decided by the management considering various factors like size, location, commitment of managers, etc. To mention some applications: ZBB in Taxes Instruments was adopted in the Staff and Research Division in 1969 and in the subsequent year it was adopted by all the divisions; the State of Georgia adopted ZBB in all its 65 executive agencies in the first year despite their size and location. Further, a survey has indicated that approximately one third of the organisations using ZBB used it to supplement the existing budget system; another one-third of the user firms adopted ZBB throughout the orgnisation as a replacement for the previous budget system, and the remaining firms used ZBB in certain specific departments[vii].

(*b*) Should this gigantic exercise of budgeting be done every year? Various alternatives to be considered in this regard are:

- every year or
- after a gap of two or three years or
- select some activities in one year and other activities in subsequent years. Thus every activity would get covered by this system once in 2 to 3 years.

Every alternative has its advantage. To economise on cost and time, this detailed budgeting exercise need not be repeated every year, if following two conditions are fulfilled:

(*i*) management is satisfied that operations are efficient and effective,

(*ii*) work environment is reasonably stable, without major changes in work load problems.

Surplus Manpower: The main objective of ZBB is to allocate funds over projects of higher importance and weed out projects of lower importance. ZBB as a management tool, indicates projects of lower importance, and the decision to weed out the same or to close down the same, rests upon the management.· Similarly, the issue of surplus or redundant manpower would be a managerial decision, whether to transfer, or terminate or to wait for normal turnover of manpower.

(c) **Participation:** ZBB requires participation by managers at all levels in the organisation. A successful participative budget induces proper motivation and acceptance of specific goals, and provides for linkage of reward or punishment with performance. For participation to be effective, it should not merely be restricted to the act of participation enabling

vii. Suver D. James and Brown L. Ray, ' Where does Zero Base Budgeting Work' (Harvard Business Review, Nov. –Dec. 1977)

the participants to know one another and leading to increased cohesiveness, but should also involve discussions among participants towards gaining acceptance of the new set objectives.

(*d*) **Role of ZBB:** No doubt, the Government of India adopted ZBB in its 1987-88 budget, but what was its role in the budgeting system in the country? It was stated to be integrated with the performance budgets presented to the legislation, as no separate set of documents would be presented to the Parliament on account of ZBB, and performance budget documents would be further refined so as to increase its usefulness. Since the performance budget prepared by the departments were included in the existing budget documents, the issue to be considered is that ZBB to be useful in the decision making process, should it not be integrated with the existing budgetary process?

CHAPTER 6

ZBB : Implementation in India - A Case Study of Research and Development Organisation

In the budget speech for the year 2000-01, the Finance Minister emphasized that over the years, the composition of Central Government expenditure had become rigid and prone to large, pre-committed increases. More than half of the annual budget outlays are transfer payments. Interest payments, defence, internal security, major subsidies, salaries, allowances and pensions and non plan grants to states accounted for about 95 per cent of non-plan expenditure and about 70 per cent of total expenditure. To curb built-in expenditure growth and bring about structural changes in the composition of expenditure, it was proposed that "all ongoing schemes will be subjected to rigorous Zero Base Budgeting (ZBB) scrutiny". Starting from the year 1999-2000, the exercise towards ZBB was completed in eight departments and 69 schemes were to be discontinued or merged.

Pursuant to the emphasis on ZBB implementation by the government, a number of departments including those involved in agricultural, scientific, technology, industrial and medical research, namely ICAR, ICMR, CSIR, initiated steps towards ZBB implementation exercise. We present below, in brief, a case exercise towards ZBB adoption in research and development agencies namely Council for Scientific & Industrial Research (CSIR) and Indian Council for Medical Research (ICMR); steps involved in ZBB implementation, various problem areas and the issues concerning such exercise. It may be mentioned here that the ZBB implementation exercise in CSIR started during 2000-01 and budgets at its laboratories and its headquarter level had been formulated by following the ZBB principles.

It may also be mentioned that a Core Group was set up in early 2001 by the Principal Scientific Advisor to the Government to review the ZBB exercise in the science and technology departments and to provide guidelines for the ZBB exercise in future. The Core Group comprised of members from Scientific Advisory Committee to the Cabinet (SAC-C), Consultative Group of Eminent Senior Scientists (CGESS), Planning Commission Ministry of Finance and Scientific and Technology departments. The Core Group observed that the CSIR had done a detailed exercise for its labs and divisions and had generated documents relating thereto. The Group laid down general guidelines for the preparation of ZBB by the science and technology departments. The extracts from the Guidelines are reproduced in **Exhibit 6.1.** The salient features of the Guidelines are as under:

- For ZBB exercise to be meaningful, plan and non-plan budgets be taken together and ZBB exercise should encompass all activities covered by them.

Adopted from the author's paper "Zero Base Budgeting : Re-emphasised in India - A Case study of Research and Development Organisation published in IJPA Jan-March 2002. The paper was based on ZBB implementation in various laboratories and its divisions of the CSIR. The author acknowledges the CSIR for his involvement in the implementation process. The author is grateful to the CSIR for allowing to use its data/details to illustrate the adoption of ZBB in its various laboratories and the organisation as a whole. The author expresses his thanks to Ms. Praveen Tripathi, Financial Advisor, and Shri A.K. Verma, Senior Deputy Advisor, CSIR for their comments on the earlier drafts and also for their suggestions on various stages of the project study.

- Budgeting exercise by a department should bring its current level expenditure down by 30 per cent by removing programmes/ projects/tasks which have either not fructified or which could be accorded lower priority. Of this 30 per cent savings, half could be deployed for strengthening the programmes identified to be retained; the strengthening may be either to accelerate some priority programmes or to raise them from sub-critical funding. The other half could be utilised for initiating new programmes or taking new initiative which have been considered as priority especially in view of the changing situations including the WTO regime coming into effect.
- The current level say, 2000-01, may be kept as baseline for evolving budget proposals for the next year and the same procedure be followed for the succeeding year.
- Departments should show ratio of salary expense to total expense and should evolve a healthy ratio so as to induct new personnel.
- The Departments should be encouraged to use the savings available through the ZBB exercise to create new R&D centres operated jointly with private sector or by foreign MNCs.

The CSIR and ICMR are autonomous research organizations registered under the Registration of Societies Act XXI of 1860 and are funded by government. The CSIR was headed by the Director General who was also Secretary to the Government of India, Department of Scientific and Industrial Research. It was among the world's largest publicly funded R&D organisations having a chain of 40 world class R&D laboratories with 80 field stations spread across India, with the total staff strength of 21,000 including 8,500 highly qualified scientists, technical officers and engineers. Its range of activities covered practically the entire spectrum of industrial R&D ranging from aerospace to mining to micro-electronics to metallurgy. As such, the organisation was described as a global R&D resource as its patrons and partners hailed from over 50 countries. It had total budget of around ₹ 1000 crore during 2001-02, of which 40 per cent was the plan budget. Each laboratory was headed by a Director who was responsible for its management and control. Each laboratory got budget allocations from the headquarters; however, the Director was in charge of the budgetary exercise for the laboratory.

CSIR had a detailed review mechanism for the activities/ programmes undertaken in different laboratories and its divisions. There were Research Council (RC) and Management Council (MC) for each Lab: these comprised of scientists and specialists, external as well as internal, from different fields and industries and they approved the new research activities.

ICMR was the apex body in the country for formulation, coordination and promotion of biomedical research in India. The council achieved this through *intramural* research (*i.e.*, it constitutes totally funded and owned by the ICMR) and *extramural* research (*i.e.*, through grants-in-aid given to projects largely outside the ICMR). The ICMR had a network of 21 permanent national-level research centres which were generally disease specific and conducted mission- oriented research, six Regional Medical Research Centers, which addressed to regional health problems and were located in different geographical areas and a large number of field stations spread across all the states in India. A major endeavour of the Council was to strengthen indigenous capabilities and develop a broad based and balanced cadre of able research personnel and facilities to cope with the present and ongoing health problems of India. The Council budget for the year 2001-02 amounted to ₹ 200 crore. Intramural Projects of the ICMR were reviewed by a Scientific Advisory Committee comprising of eminent biomedical research scientists as its members, while extramural projects, were reviewed by appropriately constituted Expert Committees and Project Review Committees. The Scientific Advisory Board, the top most advisory body of the ICMR, provided guidelines in the scientific and technical matters. The Board met every year to review the on-going activities and to approve of the programmes and budget for the coming year. The Board also critically examined the continuation or otherwise of projects on the basis of and recommendations of various committees. In addition, each technical division of the Headquarters had a Scientific Advisory Group, which met annually to review the intra and extramural research done during the course of the year and examined the plan of action and budget requirements for the next year.

Zero-Base Budgeting Initiation

ZBB was initiated in ICMR during the year 2000-01, by a letter to the Directors of the Regional Centres and the Divisional Chiefs to prepare their budgets for the year 2001-02 according to the principles of ZBB. Similarly, CSIR initiated steps to implement ZBB at its Headquarter and also at its 40 labs. We present below the procedure followed for the implementation of ZBB at CSIR.

ZBB AT CSIR

Communication from the Chief Executive

ZBB implementation exercise at the CSIR started during 2000-01, with a communication from the Chief Executive (CEO) to the Directors of Laboratories and Divisions emphasising the need, benefits and urgency of ZBB for purposes of finalisation of the revised estimates for the current year and proposal for budget estimates for the next year. He familiarised about its prevalence earlier in the organisation and in its laboratories in some form and constituted a Task Force. The Task Force was to hold consultations, externally and internally, to finalise the ZBB at Headquarter after having received various programmes/proposals from individual laboratories and its Divisions- the programmes/proposals which had been prepared in the light of the guidelines issued in this regard. He also constituted an Implementation Group for implementation of ZBB in CSIR laboratories/ institutions. The group comprised of senior scientists, financial advisor, executives in the area of finance and an outside expert. The group was entrusted with the responsibility to:

- provide guidelines and procedure on ZBB,
- organise familiarisation/interaction programmes on regional basis facilitating the implementation of ZBB in the laboratories, and
- consolidate information/inputs received for consideration of the Task Force constituted for the purpose.

The chief executive also mentioned about the detailed guidelines, instructions and proforma being circulated by the Financial Adviser for understanding and implementation of ZBB. A copy of the letter dated July 20, 2000 addressed to directors of various laboratories is annexed as Exhibit 6.2

Communication from Financial Adviser and Director Planning

Communication from the CEO was followed up by a communication by the next higher level management, namely, Financial Advisor, Director Planning in the form of detailed guidelines, manuals and formats for the preparation of ZBB. The communication from the Financial Advisor is given in Exhibit 6.3; the detailed guidelines, manuals and formats annexed to the Financial Advisor's letter are reproduced as Annexures 6.1 to 6.4.

The Financial Advisor suggested that

- Each Lab should constitute a High Level Committee (HLC), with the Director as the Chairman, four senior scientists as members and senior F & AO as the Member Convenor. The Committee would have the overall responsibility to review the entire activities/ programmes of the laboratory based on the duly 'ranked' Decision Packages submitted by each of the Decision Units/Divisions at the Lab.
- All Decision Units/Divisions in the laboratory would examine individually all the new as well as on-going programmes in the division and would accord a rank/priority to them in the prescribed format.

HLC would then rank/priorities all the programmes in the Laboratory. The Task Force at headquarter would pursue all the programmes and their priorities as received from all the laboratories and would accord a headquarter level ranking.

Allocation of budgetary support to various laboratories would then be made, depending upon the funds in the organisation, on the basis of their priorities.

Familiarization/Interaction Workshops and Programmes

Next details of the ZBB implementation exercise comprised of familiarization/interaction workshops and programmes on zonal basis for various laboratories and establishments in the zone. The workshops were to be attended by heads of respective laboratories and establishments, their scientists, technologists and planning and finance executives. The Implementation Group from the headquarters facilitated by their attendance, the workshop to share its experiences and to clarify various points for completion of the formats towards finalisation of Decision Units, Decision Packages and steps towards their ranking.

These workshops/programmes were followed by Second Level Workshops within the labs/ establishments for other scientists, technologists and planning and finance executives. This was to familiarise executives at the grassroots level with the intricacies of ZBB.

Decision Package

Every lab/division was advised to prepare Decision Packages for each Decision Unit, and a format prescribed for the purpose was to be filled for each package. A decision package as a budget request, contained information namely, dates of start and completion, cost, expected benefits, manpower requirements and desired envisaged results/output in terms of:

- Advancement of knowledge
- Number of scientific papers expected,
- Application of knowledge
- Number of patents, development of technology, knowledge societal welfare
- Quality of life improvement, and
- Facilitation of Policy Decision making.

The other information related to sources of alternate funding; consequences of no-funding; or in case of additional allotment of funds, (or cut in allotment of funds), say 25 per cent, how and how soon would the programme expand, (or contract), and what would be the benefits (or demerit) of such expansion (or contraction).

Ranking/ Prioritisation Procedure

Ranking in case of CSIR was done firstly at each laboratory on the basis of laid out criteria and final ranking could be accorded by the Task Force at headquarter.

At each laboratory, ranking was done at two levels as: amongst the decisions packages at the decision unit level; and amongst the decision units at the laboratory level by the high level committee.

The logic of the above multi-tier ranking system was that a decision package before its being funded, had to compete both at the decision unit levels as well as at the organisational level.

Programme ranking/prioritisation was normally based on certain parameters depending upon the nature of activities in each laboratory, with due consideration of local/regional relevance and that too conforming to the overall organisation working. Further efforts were made to make the ranking criteria and the various parameters therein transparent to minimise subjectivity. As an illustration, performance criteria developed for a laboratory is given below. (The criteria for ranking and budget allocation was developed before the commencement of the budgeting and ranking exercise and thus the decision unit heads were having the knowledge of the criteria)

Ranking and Performance Criteria:

Parameters		Weight
External Cash Flow	Maximum	30
> = 100 per cent Target		30
91 per cent -- 100 per cent		20
71 per cent-- 90 per cent		15
Technologies	Maximum	25
Lab		10
Consultancy		15
Synthesis/Reports		8
Publications	Maximum	25
Indian> 3 Per paper		15
Foreign>4 Per Paper		15
Patents	Maximum	10
Indian per Patent		5
Foreign per Patent		10
Productivity Factors		10
(Based on the above factors in relation to Lab Average)		

CONCLUSIONS AND ISSUES FOR CONSIDERATION

ZBB exercise in research and development agencies, multi-division and multi location giant scientific and technical organizations, illustrates the emphasis attached to planning of ongoing as well as new activities and prioritisation of the same. However, the following issues need consideration:

- Scientist/technocrat as the head of the centre or the lab has a dual role of specialist-cum-administrator, he should accept ZBB, be committed to ZBB and its process involving evaluating and prioritising the ongoing and new activities. Communication from CEO CSIR and FA CSIR are illustrative of the commitment towards ZBB. This is particularly so, as scientists and technocrats are normally committed to their area of research; and the salary and other committed expenses which account for a significant part of the total budget, make it difficult to bring in modifications in the existing rigid budgetary expenditure.
- Ranking of research programmes and administration/service programmes would warrant determination of *inter-se* priority between the two categories. Should there be separate ranking for the two category programmes? or Should these be ranked together? and How should ranking be finalized? Such questions would require policy decisions and involvement of specialists and others.
- Research and development agencies normally have an elaborate review and monitoring mechanism and this would be required to be dovetailed with that necessitated under the ZBB process. For example, at CSIR Research Committee (RC) and Management Committee (MC), the reviewing committees already existed in each lab; whereas the Task Force, and the High Level Committee were newly constituted for purposes of prioritization and finalisation of ZBB; it necessitated coordination between the existing and the newly constituted committees. Similarly, the existing appraisal and review mechanism would require integration with the ZBB mechanism.
- Information system to ascertain cost for different programmes, and that too at different levels of their funding was required for purposes of ZBB.
- The amount of time and effort spent in the initial years of installation of ZBB and the documents developed in the process should be made useful in the coming years. In other words, ZBB process should not merely confine to planning and preparation of budget

document but also should be a step towards control and be useful for the successive years for allocation and control of expenses, whether by following a comprehensive system or a simpler version of the ZBB process.

- Budgetary exercise to encompass review of all activities should cover both plan and non-plan expenditure.
- Issue of surplus manpower and to bring in mobility in the existing personnel between the Labs/Divisions would require a policy decision.
- What would be the role of ZBB vis-a-vis performance budgeting or other budgetary formats? How ZBB would be integrated with the other monitoring and control techniques used? As a tool of planning, control and fund allocation, ZBB process should not merely result in a separate budget document but be integrated with the prevailing budgeting system.

Exhibit : 6.1

Core group setup by Principal Scientific Advisor to the Government
Guidelines by the Core Group on ZBB on Research & Scientific Organisations : Extracts

Office of the Principal Scientific Adviser to the Government of India

Vigyan Bhavan Annexe,

Maulana Azad Road, New Delhi-110 001

Guidelines resulting from the meeting of the Core Group on Zero–Based Budgeting of Scientific Departmentalist Agencies held on February 1, 2001

At the request of the Finance Minister, the Principal Scientific Adviser to the Government of India set up a Core Group to review the Zero–Base Budgeting exercise of the following department/ agencies:

Department of Science and Technology (DST), Department of Biotechnology (DBT), Department of Scientific and Industrial Research (DSIR)/Council of Scientific and Industrial Research (CSIR), Department of Ocean Development (DOD), Indian Council of Agricultural Research (ICAR), Department of Atomic Energy (DAB), Department of Space (DOS) and Defence Research Development Organisation (DRDO). A Core Group was formed from select members of Scientific Advisory Committee to the Cabinet (SAC-C), Consultative Group of Eminent Senior Scientists (CGESS), representative of Planning Commission and ministry of Finance and also the focal persons from the Department/ Agencies concerned along with their Financial Adviser.

Guidelines for preparation of ZBB are given in Part-l and Part-II. Part-I pertains to General Guidelines applicable to all S&T departments/agencies and Part-II is specific to Departments.

General Guidelines Part I are reproduced below:

GENERAL GUIDELINES : PART I

(*i*) "Zero base budgeting exercise will be meaningful only if the Plan and non-Plan Budget are taken together and the exercise encompasses all activities covered by them. Correspondingly, the agencies would need flexibility in operating non-Plan and Plan as a full entity without any special financial procedure for Plan and non-Plan separately.

(*ii*) "If the budget of the department (non-Plan plus Plan) is equal to 100 units for the year BE 2000-2001, the exercise should be done by the department/agency to bring it down by 30% by removing programmes / certain S&T tasks and projects which have either not fructified or or which can be accorded lower priority in view of other competing programmes or technologies. This 30% should be considered as savings: Of this about half may be deployed for strengthening the programmes identified to be retained; the strengthening may be either to accelerate some priority programmes or to raise them from sub-critical funding. The other half may be utilized for initiating new programmes or taking new initiative which have been considered as priority specially in view of the changing situations including the WTO regime coming into effect". (It may be mentioned that this approach of ZBB called target-base-budgets has been discussed in the earlier chapter V)".

"Such an exercise done for BE 2000-01 should be kept as the baseline for evolving the budget proposals for BE 2001-02, with only certain increase over BE 2001-02 for the priority programmes and the new initiatives. Again before formulating BE 2002- 03 zero base budget such an approach can be used somewhere around August- September, 2002 and detailed exercises can begin".

(*iii*) "All departments have to indicate in their budget papers the achievements in research fructified for application or production during the last two years i.e. 1999 - 2000 and 2000-2001. It may also be done through a flow chart as to how their research activities/ technologies have flown into actual market place through productionisation. Such a flow chart may be limited to a few select examples while they can give overall approximate figures for the department/agencies in terms of research investments fructifying into commercial products".

(*iv*) "In order to evolve a healthy ratio for salary to budgets, it was decided that all departments/ agencies will show the total money for salary and the total amount of scientific programmes. Again the approach will be to show both non-Plan and Plan together. It was also noted that a single uniform ratio cannot be prescribed because various agencies do different types of work: some mainly concentrate on extramural funding, some agencies do all their work in-house, some agencies have a mix of R&D, scientific services, education, etc. However, this ratio is vital to study in detail. It was also noted that over a period we should evolve a policy looking beyond the ratios because induction of new personnel is important as otherwise most departments/agencies may have an average age of 50-55 soon".

(*v*) "It was considered essential that if one has to implement zero base budgeting effectively then there will be a need of mobility of scientific personnel and in fact some of the facilities as well. It will be better that scientific departments/agencies give some thought to this aspect and enunciate their approach towards this".

While using the above five as general guidelines, the departments may also use the specific guidelines which are given at Part-II.

One recommendation that emerged which can be applicable to all departments is that the departments may be encouraged to use the savings available through the zero base budgeting exercise on the lines given in Part-I, to create new R&D centers operated jointly with private sector which will have the standard of the R&D centers being opened by foreign MNCs in the country. Such centers could have private sector investment more than 51 %. The management of the R&D centers may be such as to create new structures/labs or use some of the existing institutions with totally modified methods of working mandated through amendment of existing rules. Such initiatives by departments or by multiple departments together as consortia would be very essential because of the opening up of the economy and the WTO regime coming into force. For the financial year BE 2001-02, a creation of a few entities like, these from the money saved specially from the zero base budgeting would be of immense value and shall go a long way to make Indian R&D globally competitive and also to attract S&T talents in the' country and to increase private sector investments for S &T. Such joint R&D centers may be given special tax benefits for ten years.

Exhibit : 6.2

COUNCIL OF SCIENTIFIC & INDUSTRIAL RESEARCH
Anusandhan Bhawan, 2, Rafi Marg, New Delhi

R.A. MASHELKAR, F.R.S.
DIRECTOR GENERAL, CSIR
& Secretary, Government of India
Department of Scientific & Industrial Research

DO No
Date: 20th July, 2000.

Dear Dr.

You will recall that the Hon'ble Finance Minister, in his budget speech 1999, had indicated that in preparation for the next year's budget, he would initiate the system of Zero Base Budgeting (ZBB) in all Government Departments. Soon thereafter, Ministry of Finance issued detailed guidelines for adopting and implementing ZBB in the Government. Pursuant to this, I constituted a Task Force under the Chairmanship of Dr. .... to help implement the Government guidelines. The Task Force has had wide ranging consultations externally and internally and has now worked out a suitable mechanism and guidelines for adopting this system in CSIR.

Let me hasten to add that Zero Base Budgeting is essentially a tool which links planning, budgeting, review and operational decision making into a single integrated process. It is primarily based on a fundamental appraisal of purpose, methods and resources. We are fortunate that in CSIR we already have a system of review and appraisal of R&D Projects and activities. Thus, the implementation of ZBB will not at all be difficult. Rather I believe the effort will be beneficial to us.

The Finance Ministry is insisting that it will not accept consider our Revised Estimates for the current year and Budget Estimates for the next Financial Year unless we implement the ZBB. Indeed, in the meeting of the FAs taken by the Finance Minister on 4th July, he even said that budget allocations for 2000-01 will not be made unless this exercise of ZBB had been gone through. Hence my request to you to kindly accord priority to adopting the system in your Laboratory at the earliest.

Financial Adviser, CSIR is writing and sending you separately the detailed guidelines, instructions and proformae for ZBB. I am sure her colleagues and she will be available to you for any assistance you may need in understanding and implementing ZBB.

With warm regards,

Yours sincerely
(R.A. MASHELKAR)

Dr.
Director
Lab CSIR,

Exhibit : 6.3

Council of Scientific & Industrial Research
Anusandhan Bhavan, Rafi Ahmed Kidwai Marg,
New Delhi - 110 001

PRAVIN TRIPATHI **DO No.**
FINANCIAL ADVISOR **Date: 24th July, 2000**

Dear Dr.

1. The Director General, CSIR vide his D.O. letter of even number dated 20th]uly, 2000 has already written to you explaining and emphasising the need to initiate Zero Base Budgeting (ZBB) System in your Laboratory for all the projects partially or wholly funded by CSIR itself. You would appreciate that this will help in judicious allocation of scarce resources so as to derive the optimum benefits/ returns. I may emphasise that ZBB approach does not prohibit taking up new projects rather it provides ample opportunities for initiating more important new programmes by deferring or dropping those programmes which are of low priority/ranking and outlived their utility.
2. I would suggest that to help you to undertake the exercise you may like to constitute a High Level Committee (HLC) under your Chairmanship of around four Senior Scientists, Head, PME /RBPD as members and Sr. F&AO /F&AO as the Member Convenor. This Committee could be entrusted the overall responsibility to review the entire activities / programmes of the Laboratory based on the duly 'ranked' Decision Packages submitted by each of the Decision Units/ Divisions (see Annexure).
3. The overall system would then be as follows:-
   - **I.** All Decision Units/ Divisions in the Laboratory will examine individually all the new/ ongoing programmes in the Division and accord a rank/priority to them in the Form 'B'.
   - **II.** The HLC will then rank /prioritise all the programmes in the Laboratory in Form 'A' duly backed up/ supported with the required information as provided in Form "B".
   - **III.** Forms 'A' and 'B' from all the Labs. would be perused by the Task Force at CSIR level and all programmes accorded a CSIR level ranking.
   - **IV.** The allocation of budgetary support would then be made depending upon the availability of funds to CSIR on the basis of priority.
4. We have devised four background notes to facilities the undertaking of the exercise in your Lab namely:-

(*i*) Zero-Base Budgeting- An Outline	Annexure- 6.1
(*ii*) Detailed concept of ZBB alongwith necessary guidelines to review projects and accord ranking	Annexure- 6.2
(*iii*) Format of Decision Packages for scrutiny and ranking	Annexure- 6.3
(*iv*) Proforma for sending input to CSIR	Annexure- 6.4 Form A & Form B

The success of this exercise centers on you. With your support your colleagues too will be able to objectively rank all the ongoing/ new programmes/ activities. My colleagues at CSIR Headquarters Shri ……………………………….. and I are at your service anytime for any assistance that you may need. I now look forward to receive the Forms 'A' & 'B' completed by 20th August, 2000. Do not hesitate to contact us.

Wishing you personal regards,

Yours sincerely,

(PRAVIN TRIPATHI)

Dr.
Director
Lab, CSIR.

Annexure 6.1
Zero Base Budget (ZBB) - An Outline

- Essentially a Management concept which links planning, budgeting, review and operation decision making into a single integrated process and is an integral part of the budgetary process.
- ZBB implies constructing a budget without any reference to what has gone before based on a fundamental reappraisal of purposes, methods and resources.
- Every programme or task should be subjected to ZBB scrutiny to see if it could be done more cost effectively or if it could be eliminated altogether because of introduction of other schemes or it has out lived its utility.
- Under ZBB the existing programmes are not treated as immutable but are examined afresh as to their continued utility and effectiveness thereby freeing resources for new programmes.
- The objective is not to just cut expenditure but make public expenditure programmes more effective by a more purposive allocation of resources of various programmes.
- If the budgetary cuts become inevitable, ZBB will provide a logical basis for effecting them as compared to ad-hoc & across the board cuts.
- ZBB is intended to help both in the judicious allocation of scarce resources and deriving the optimum benefits out of resources allocate.

Annexure 6.2

Detailed Concept on ZBB Along with Necessary Guidlines to Review Projects and Accord Ranking

Conventional Budgeting

The nature, philosophy and practice, of conventional budgeting system as it is practiced now is as follows:

- It is accounting oriented without any specific output -input linkages, presented in the form of a departmental budget - the funds being allocated to certain aggregated budget heads rather than to certain specific activities / programmes;
- It is an 'aggregated expenditure budget'; it does not provide to the top management any basis for restricting expenditure, in case affordability prevents its total funding. Hence the arbitrary across the board cuts affecting high and low priority tasks equally.

It is an extrapolation of the last year's budget by:

- Incrementing it for an assumed rate of inflation.
- Providing for wages and salaries increases.
- Adding new projects/ programmes or activities.
- Realistic submissions - imprudent if not foolish - also get the inevitable cuts, and get less than necessary.
- Across-the-board cuts are made again clever got what they wanted.
- Cleverer learn their lesson and deliberately inflate their budget submission in future.

- It accepts status quo as the fate-accompli, all the activities- old and new - that have been included in the next year's budget:
  - Are equally essential in achieving the objectives; and
  - Are currently being performed in the most cost-effective manner.

Zero–Base Budgeting

The economics of ZBB is implicit in its concept and philosophy itself, which requires every organisation and its activities to justify their very existence and effectiveness. Being, in essence, an ex-ante rather than post-facto cost-benefit analysis of all decision making in an organisation/unit, ZBB seeks to reverse the whole process of conventional budgeting by its unequivocal assertion that *it is not the expenditure that should justify the output. Instead, it should be the output that must justify the expenditure; its implementation requirements and implications*.

At the government level, the objective of ZBB exercise is to optimise the cost of governance by making the public expenditure more effective and need-based. Thus the Government of India has reiterated its intention of implementing ZBB while presenting the budget for the year 1999-2000.

It is necessary for top management to examine and endorse foundational assumptions of ZBB. The basic tenets of ZBB are:

- Notwith standing the prosperity of an organisation, there will always be a gap between desirability and affordability. In other words, all what is desirable may not be affordable.
- As a corollary to the above, the greatest challenge to the decision makers, therefore, lies in identifying the 'Desirable' within the limits of 'affordability'.
- "There is no room for improvements" is an operating philosophy of "Doom-Sayers". In reality "even best can be improved" provided there is a WILL to do so.
- Uncritical acceptance of past priorities, strategies, precedents, policies, procedures, etc. is inimical to growth as its sets inertia, and prevents organisational renewal.
- Past activities do not exist simply because they have acquired a history. They shall exist,

only if, there is a need for their existence and at the same time someone can take the responsibility of justifying the need for their existence.

- Future activities must fit into the organisational objectives and strategy and must pass the test of 'necessity' and cost-benefit analysis.
- It is not the expenditure that should justify the output; it should be the output that must justify the expenditure.
- Budgeting is not accounting, It is accountability. As such it is not the exclusive responsibility of Finance Manager or the top executive. Instead it commits everyone who has to or wishes to take a decision.
- It is not for certain budget heads that funds are required. Instead, it is for implementing certain decisions (programmes) that funds are needed.

In essence, ZBB is an integration of Planning and Budgeting into a single process with sole objective of development and redeployment of scarce resources through a rigorous and rational scrutiny. Thus, it is a management tool which provides a systematic method for evaluating all operations and programmes, old or new, allows for budget reductions and expansions within the limits of affordability in a rational manner and permits the re-allocation of resources from low to high priority programmes. Finally, ZBB is the ex-ante cost-benefit analysis of all decision-making in an organistion.

ZBB requires each manager to:

- Establish objectives of his or her functions consistent with organizational objectives and gain agreement on them;
- Define and devise alternative ways of achieving the objectives;
- Select the most practical and effective alternative from the above;
- Break the chosen alternatives into incremental levels of efforts;
- Assess the cost and benefits of each incremental level:
- Describe the consequences of disapproval of the activity
- Rank all the activities of his function according to the importance of each one of them in achievement of functional objectives.

In Zero–Base Budgeting approach one reconstructs the operation from zero or scratch. Each activity competes for funds on equal footing and the funding decisions are, as per the relative importance.

Zero–Base Budgeting (ZBB) can be used in any area on which cost benefit analysis can be carried out and for which standard costs and norms are not available.

The process of formulation of zero-base budget consists of the following steps:

- Identification of 'Decision Units'.
- Preparation of 'Decision Packages'.
- Ranking/prioritisation - of decision packages within a decision unit.
- Ranking /prioritisation of decision packages of various decision units.
- Allocation of resources for the chosen decision packages under each decision Unit.
- Monitoring and Evaluation.

Decision Unit: Each distinct cost centre can be a decision unit. Decision unit should be such where a particular activity or a group-of activities can be independent and meaningfully identified and evaluated. Further there is no overlapping between the activities of one decision unit and the other. The decision unit should be managerially viable.

Decision Packages: A decision package is a document, which identifies a discrete activity, function or operation in a definitive manner for management evaluation and comparison with other activities. In other words each decision package should be 'stand alone'. Essentially, a decision package is a budget request ideally containing the following information for thc higher management.

- Identification data: Decision Unit, programme activity for which the package is made, accountability, etc.
- Objective of the decision unit
- Objective of the decision package
- Feasibility Assessment

Is the programme legally required?
Is the programme technically feasible?
Is the programme operationally viable?
The benefit-cost analysis:

- Benefit / output (tangible) at existing / threshold/optimum level.
- Tangible costs at the existing/ threshold and optimum level.
    - Yearly phasing of the proposed expenditure
    - Consequence of its non-funding.
    - Alternatives considered before choosing the recommended mode of achieving the stated objective
    - In case of additional allotment of funds, (or cut in allotment of funds), say 25 per cent, how and how soon would the programme expand, (or contract), and what would be the benefits (or demerit) of such expansion (or contraction).

Ranking/Prioritisation

Ranking or prioritisation of each decision package is done at two levels:

- Amongst the decision packages at the decision unit level.
- Among the decision units at the higher management level.

The logic of the two tier ranking system is simple. Implicit in it is the intention that a decision package before being funded has to compete both at the decision unit levels as well as at the organizational level.

The criteria or basis for ranking a decision package is implicit in the objectives of decision unit, on the one hand, and that of the organisation, on tile other. In an R&D organisation enterprise the simple most criteria for prioritisation could be on the basis of:

- Statutory / legally /internationally / national committed activities/programmes.
- Emergent activities /programmes arising from national events.
- Advancement of knowledge and/or
- Application of knowledge and /or
- Development of Technology/Know how and /or
- Societal Welfare/quality of life improvement and/ or
- Facilitation of policy/decision making

Funding Decision

Once all the decision packages have been ranked on the basis of pre-determined criteria, the stage is set for the funding decisions by the top management. If the cost of total decision packages is higher than the affordable level, the low priority activities/programmes are cut retaining the high prioritised activities / programmes. While funding a decision package, it is necessary for the management to indicate also the level at which the activity/programme should be carried out, *i.e.* existing /threshold optimum level.

Monitoring & Evaluation

Needless to say that the whole process of ZBB affords the top management and cost centres manager's two opportunities for evaluating the programmes and activities of their organisation and departments/divisions. In the first place, an ex-ante, *i.e.* before committing the funds-exercise is done requiring the cost centre managers to evaluate their total activities - both old and new - together with justification for their continuance. In fact it is this scrutiny which makes ZBB a distinct management technique of effectively utilising the resources by their redeployment from low to high priority areas.

Since all the decision packages have to compete amongst themselves for funding only those, which are most relevant to the organisation are funded. The post facto monitoring and evaluation is done on the basis of the contents and particularly the outputs envisaged in the decision packages with fixed accountability.

Annexure- 6.3

Decision Package Form for use at Lab. Level

(One for each Project/Activity funded wholly/partially In-house)

1. Name of Decision Unit/ Division
2. Name of Project/Activity
3. IMPACT Project No.
   (If given indicate full Project No.)
4. Description of Project/Activity
   (in not more than 10 lines)
5. (*a*) Date of Start (Month & Year)
   (*b*) Date of Completion (Month & Year)
6. Manpower Resource Deployment

Category & Designation	Existing Nos.	% of time deployed	Nos.Required 2001-02	% of time deployed	Change sought in 2001-02: Justification
Scientific Sci. B/C Sci. EI/EII Sci. F Sci. G/H					
Technical Group III Group II Group I					
Administrative Group A Group B Group C Group D Others					
Total					

7. Desired Envisaged Results/Outputs

□ ADVANCEMENT OF KNOWLEDGE NO. OF SCIENTIFIC PAPERS EXPECTED

□ APPLICATION OF KNOWLEDGE IPR/ PATENT FILING IN NOS.

□ DEVELOPMENT OF TECHNOLOGY/ KNOW HOW DETAILS:

□ SOCIETAL WELFARE /QUALITY OF LIFE IMPROVEMENT DETAILS:

□ FACILITATION OF POLICY/DECISION MAKING DETAILS:

□ OTHER (SPECIFY):

8. Benefits accruing by retaining the Project/Activity (Give Quantitative details under appropriate diverse heading :,)

□ SCINTIFIC □ TECHNOLOGICAL
□ SOCIETAL □ FINANCIAL
□ ECONOMIC □ STRATEGIC
□ OTHERS

9. (*a*) Alternatives to In-house (Government) Funding:
WHETHER EXPLORED? IF SO DETAILS THEREOF AND OUTCOMES.

(*b*) Consequences of Non Funding of Project/Activity (Give details under appropriate diverse heading :,)

□ SCINTIFIC □ TECHNOLOGICAL
□ SOCIETAL □ FINANCIAL
□ ECONOMIC □ STRATEGIC
□ OTHERS

10. Financial requirements if funding for Project/Activity is to be continued.

Items	Actual Expenditure 1999-2000	Envisaged Expenditure 2000-2001	% change over 1999-2000	Envisaged Expenditure 2001-2002	% change over 2000-2001
A. REVENUE (Recurring)					
Salaries					
Chemicals & Consumables					
TA					
Contingency					
Maintenance					
Human Resource Development					
Other Expenses					
TOTAL REVENUE					
B. CAPITAL					
Works & Services					
Equipment					
Computer/Software Library books					
Other Capital items					
TOTAL CAPITAL					
TOTAL (A+B)					

11. Prepared by

(Name) (Signature)

12. (*a*) Ranking by Head Decision Unit: □ □ □

(Indicate Non repetitive Number within the Division/Unit)

______________ ______________

(Name) (Signature)

Date:

(*b*) Ranking by HLC: □ □ □

(Indicate overall non repetitive Number within the Laboratory)

______________ ______________

(Name) (Signature)

Date:

Annexure 6.4

FORM 'A

Laboratory Name

INVENTORY OF PROGRAMMES AND THEIR RANKIN*

(₹ Crore)

Name of the Programmes/ Activity/ Task	Year of commencement	Date of Approval and Approving Activity RCM/ MC/Director/ CSIR	Expenditure (1999-2000)	Projected 2000-01	Projected 2001-02
(i)					
(ii)					
(iii)					
(iv)					
(v)					
(vi)					
(vii)					

Please provide information for continuing programme as well as proposed new programmes

FORM 'B'

Laboratory Name

ZERO–BASE BUDGETING QUESTIONNAIRE

(To be filled separately for each programme/group of programmes)

1. Name of the programme/group of programmes
2. What are the objectives of the Programme?
   (*to be specified in short pithy phrases*)
3. How are the objectives related to the goals and objectives specified in the Ninth Plan document for the Ninth Plan period as well as for the years to come?
4. Why should the stated objectives be achieved only through the instrument of public expenditure programme?
   (*The idea-is to be whether the same cannot be achieved through other instruments of public policy, i.e. Legal and administrative controls, tax/subsidy mechanism, credit policy, promotion of voluntary efforts*)
5. What are the other programmes, if any funded by the Central Government to achieve the same objectives? Please specify their budget allotments for the year 2000-2001. What mechanism exists to ensure their successful implementation?
6. What are the programmes of other Departments/agencies (whether funded by the Central Government or not) on whose success depends the success of this programme? What mechanism exists to ensure their successful implementation?
7. Would you like some changes in the existing organisational structure for effective implementation of this programme? If so, please give your suggestions.
8. Would you like some changes in the existing system and procedures within the Government for taking decisions relating to implementation of this programme? If so, please give your suggestions.

9. Would you like some changes in the existing personnel management systems and practices (including requirement, training and career development) in relation to implementation of this programme? If so, please give your suggestions for improvement.
10. Since inception (please specify the year) how many times has the implementation of this programme been evaluated? With what results?

    (*note to be taken of the observations made by Parliamentary Committee as well as the Comptroller and Auditor General of India*)
11. Whether the programme is funded from external assistance; if so to what extent?
12. Whether the programme is the result of statutory requirement; it so, spell out the requirement?
13. Are there any factors (like natural increase in the number of beneficiaries) which make it imperative to increase the allotment of funds to the programme in the coming years?
14. Whether any norms have been fixed for regulating the expenditure on the programme or specific component thereof?
15. If additional allotment of funds, say 25%, is made for this programmne, how would you expand the programme? How soon can you expand? What w1l1 be the benefits flowing from such expansion?
16. If additional allotment of funds for this programme is cut, say by 25%, how would you like to contract the programme? How soon can you contract? What will be the adverse consequences of such contraction?
17. Any other information that you consider relevant for taking a decision on the Budget allotments to the programme in the 2000-2001 (RE) and 2001-2002.
18. Budget allotment for 2000-2001 & 2001-2002

REVENUE	2000-2001	2001-2002
CAPITAL		
TOTAL		

Whether they appear in the accounts as reduction of expenditure or on the receipt side.

19. What is the breakup of the Budget allotment under the following heads?

(*a*)	Staff Salaries			
	(Please specify the number of staff)			
(*b*)	Travel Expenses			
(Only tour /transfer TA Expenses to be given here LTC expenses to be given under (*a*) above).				
(*c*)	Office expenses (Contingency)			
N.B: In respect of (*a*), (*b*) and (*c*), please include information on autonomous agencies under which maintenance grants are given by the department.				
(*d*)	Equipment			
(*e*)	Material and Supply			
(*f*)	Maintenance expenses			
(*g*)	Land & Works expenditure			
(*h*)	Others HRD and R & D Support			
(*i*)	Other capital- Like Buses/Vehicle etc			

20. If the Scheme envisages provision of services. or any user charges levied. If so give annual realisations and the date when the user charges were last revised.

CHAPTER 7

Outcome Budgeting

Having discussed performance budgeting and zero base budgeting in earlier chapters, we discuss and illustrate the outcome budgeting approach. Governments spend hundreds of crores of rupees on various projects, programmes or activities; for example, as mentioned earlier, total budgetary outlay of Central, State Governments and Union Territories is approximately 50 percent of GDP. One would like to know: how effectively each rupee was spent; or what is the benefit or outcome of the money spent? Projects are normally monitored by the outlays, or by the exhaustion of funds budgeted; and there is not much emphasis on the 'outcome' or the 'benefits' expected from the expenditure; or to ascertain whether money is being spent for larger good. Outcome, if ascertained, is evaluated post-expenditure and is communicated to the Parliamentary Committees.

Under the outcome budgeting approach, allocation of funds is based on outcomes instead of inputs; this approach is addressed to the statement, 'Government must be responsible for its actions and accountable for results'. Outcome budgeting has been characterized as a potential major budgetary reform of the 21st Century.[i] . The outcome budgeting was originally adopted sometimes in mid 20th Century as an alternative to inputs-oriented budgeting. It was called by different names with varying goals and objectives like, entrepreneurial budgeting, mission-driven budgeting.[ii]

Various issues relating to outcome budget vis-à-vis performance budgeting, Zero-Based-Budgeting is presented to highlight that outcome budget is similar to performance budgeting and is an exercise to change the mindset of officials to focus on results and to ensure value for money; however, its success depends upon behavioural, technical and policy issues.

The Finance Minister, Government of India in his budget speech for the year 2005-06 said, "I must caution that outlays do not necessarily mean outcomes, the people of the country are concerned with the outcomes" and there is a need to improve the quality of implementation and enhance the need to improve the efficiency and accountability of the delivery mechanism. The Finance Minister also said that programmes and schemes are not allowed to be continued indefinitely from one plan period to the next without an independent and in-depth evaluation. The mechanism to measure the development outcomes of all major programmes would be set-up together with the Planning Commission.[iii]

Accordingly, outcome budget for the year 2005-06 was presented to the Parliament in August 2005; the 725 page document spelt out desired outcomes of projects under 44 ministries and 61 departments. It was a comprehensive document that presented what each department hoped to

i. Miller G .J and Willoughby K. "Introduction" in Miller G .J & others (eds.)"Performance-Based Budgeting" (Boulder Co.: West view Press 2001) in Mwabilu L. Ngoyo; Gerald J. Miller and Marc Holzer, 'Outcome Budgeting : Conceptual Definition' ngoyil3@aol.com; geraldmiller@comeast.net; mholzer@pipeline.com

ii. For details see Mwabilu L. Ngoyo; Gerald J. Miller and Marc Holzer, 'Outcome Budgeting : Conceptual Definition' ngoyil3@aol.com; geraldmiller@comeast.net; mholzer@pipeline.com

iii. Outcome Budget 2005 – 06, GOI Foreword by the Finance Minister, Circular dated August 25, 2005

accomplish with the funds provided; or what would be delivered by the government to the public and by what time. To be more specific, outcome budget for every Ministry or Department presented details for programmes/schemes. The details related to:

- Objective/outcome
- Quantifiable
- Financial outlay
- Processes/timeliness
- Remarks/risk factor

Details of some of the programmes are illustrated in Exhibit 7.I

As an example, outcome budget for the National Programme for Control of Blindness, Ministry of Health & Family Welfare are summarized as under:

- Objective/Outcome:
  (*a*) Reduction in the prevalence of blindness to 0.8% by the end of 10th Plan
- Plan Outlay 2005-06:
  (*a*) GOI Share - ₹ 89.00 cr
  (*b*) State Share - Nil
- Quantifiable Deliverables:
  (*a*) Cataract Surgery 41 lakhs
- Schools Eye Screening Programme Targets:
  (*a*) Children to be screened- 350 lakhs
  (*b*) Free spectacles-7.35 Iakhs
  (*c*) Eye Banking Targets:
  Eyes to be collected- 30,000
- Infrastructure Strengthening:
  (*a*) RIO-4
  (*b*) Medical Colleges- 10
  (*c*) District Hospital-20
  (*d*) Sub- District Hospital-25
  (*e*) PHC & Vision Centres- 1000
- Training of Eye Surgeons/ Nurses- 950
- To release assistance to about 25 State Government. Hospitals located on National Highways- maximum limit- ₹ 5 crores
- Processes
- Timelessness
  (*a*) Strengthen services of other causes of blindness like corneal blindness
  (*b*) Shift from eye camp to fixed facility surgical approach
  (*c*) Strengthen capacities of eye care infrastructure
  (*d*) Strengthen participation of Voluntary organisations.
  (*e*) Proposals received through State Governments considered for release of funds
- Remarks
  (*a*) Risk Factors
  Release of funds depends on receipts of compete proposals from State Governments

Outcome budget is an exercise to convert 'outlays' into 'outcomes', or to find out how effectively each rupee of government expenditure is spent. The outcomes identified and targets set by the Ministries/Departments are compiled by the Planning Commission and the Ministry of Finance, Department of Expenditure. The outcome budget measures the development outcomes of government programmes; develops linkage between the money spent and the results which follow; or it converts financial outlays into physical outcomes measurable and monitorable targets. This is to ensure that budget is an exercise to be cost-effective, to focus not on money spent but on the result of the money spent or on 'achievement' or 'accomplishment' and to account for 'value for money'. Thus outcome budget is used as an important tool for effective management of programmes and towards accountability; it is to inform the public about the money spent by various ministries.

To start, outcome budget was adopted in India, as mentioned earlier, during 2005-06 for plan schemes where it was easier to link expenditure with results for such investment programmes; and "from the next year the outcome budget will be prepared for the Non-Plan expenditure too. Over a period of time, the outcome budget is expected to reflect the 'annual budget' in terms of intended outcome"[iv].

Outcome budget is a sort of examination of expenditure before they are made, instead of a post-expenditure scrutiny; so at every stage of planning a programme, there would be mechanism of checks and balances, and this would result in reducing of unnecessary expenses. Thus the emphasis has shifted from sheer 'quantity to the quality' of the outcome of the various social sector programmes. Accordingly, the Expenditure Finance Committee, which sanctions plans up to ₹ 100 crores would ask for clear definition of outcomes at the stage of planning a programme itself. Programme and Response Monitoring Division of the Planning Commission co-ordinates the initiative towards outcome budget, and tries to bring a fair degree of uniformity of approach across the ministries, and develop yardsticks of reflecting outcomes.

Developmental programmes, in general, have quantifiable outcomes and pace of expenditure has to be closely monitored so as to translate the outlays into outcomes. Outcome budget focuses not on how much has been spent but rather on what has been achieved by that expenditure. Converting outlays into outcomes, entails identification of result expected, quantification of the result, and it is a complex process which differs from ministry to ministry. It is more complex and complicated for administrative ministries involved in maintenance of law and order or policy making relating to socio-economic matters. As these are not easily and objectively identifiable or are not subject to measurement and thus making the outcome budgeting a success becomes a challenging exercise, in particular, as stated earlier, non-plan expenditure is a sizeable share of the total. For example, it is relatively easy to check if defence ministry has spent the funds allocated to buy new weapons and it is much harder to figure out how a particular sum spent on a village helped to lift the rural community above the poverty line.

Further, for the government to meet 21st century challenges and to regain the confidence of tax payers and to see that every rupee spent has output, the budget focuses on 'results and output' rather than on inputs. As mentioned earlier, the outcome budget was introduced in 2005-06; and with effect from the Financial year 2007 -08, the Performance Budget and the Outcome Budget hitherto presented to the Parliament separately by Ministries/Departments, are merged and presented as a single document titled, 'Outcome Budget' by each Ministry/Department in respect of all Demands/ Appropriations controlled by them except those exempted from this requirement.[v] The Outcome Budget will cover non-plan expenditure so far as possible[vi]. The outcome budget is laid before the Parliament after final approval of the Minister-in-charge to ensure that the process is complete during the Session when the Regular Budget is presented.

---

iv. ibid

v. Outcome Budget: Revised Guidelines 2009-10. Office Memorandum No. 2(1)Pers/E.Cord/OB/2005, dated May 6, 2009 Monostry of Finance, GOI.

vi. Central Government Budget 2009

Outcome Budget – Steps Involved

In continuation of the budgeting process discussed in the earlier chapters, preparation of outcome budget would require:

- Outcomes should be specifically defined in measurable and monitorable terms;
- Intermediate outputs should also be defined wherever required;
- Benchmark the standards/quality of outcome and services;
- Capacity-building for requisite efficiency at all levels in terms of equipment, technology, knowledge and skills;
- Ensure flow of right amount of money at right time to the right level with neither delay nor "parking" of funds;
- Involvement of the community/target-groups/recipients of the service, with easy access and feedback systems.

Outcome Budget - Expectations

Adoption of outcome budget is expected to change the mindset of government officials and make them become more result oriented instead of merely being outlay - centric. With the outcome budget, the ministry officials would look for results expected or performance; or focus on planning for projects; or on benefits expected from the money to be spent and this would enforce an element of accountability.

In short, benefits expected from outcome budget include:

- Change government officials' mindset, to be more result oriented instead of being outlay centric.
- Making administrative ministries to be committed to outlays and lay down yardsticks or benchmarks at different levels of capacities or efficiencies.
- Ensure optimal fund allocation and to have value for money.
- Have effective monitoring and evaluation system so as to indicate the areas requiring further calibration and honing of processes to deliver the intended outcomes.
- Involvement of the community or target groups for whom the schemes are meant.

Outcome Budget- Academic Debate

A research study, "Outcome Budgeting : Conceptual Definition" by Mwabilu L. Ngoyi; Gerald J. Miller and Marc Holzer[vii] presents findings of a survey administered to budget and finance officers, analysts, and auditors to assess their perspective about the conceptual definition of outcome budgeting. Findings of the study are summed as under:

- The survey was carried out to assess response by asking questions which included-
  - Whether an outcome budgeting system requires a strategic plan?
  - Whether an outcome budgeting system requires an annual performance plan?
  - Whether outcome budgeting audit is listed in a Stock Exchange?
- Result of the survey suggested lack of an agreement about the conceptual definition of outcome budgeting across government levels.
- Implementation of outcome budget has been impeded by the confusion about the basic definition of outcome budgeting.
- Researchers refuse to view it little more than performance budgeting or Programme,

---

vii. Mwabilu L. Ngoyo; Gerald J. Miller and Marc Holzer, 'Outcome Budgeting : Conceptual Definition' ngoyil3@aol.com; geraldmiller@comeast.net; mholzer@pipeline.com

Planning and Budgeting System (PPBS)[viii] (Forrester, 2001).

- "Outcome budgeting is similar in many aspects to earlier fiscal practices, such as, Planning-Programming- Budgeting System, Management by Objectives, and Zero Base Budgeting System. However, unlike these past reforms, which aimed to optimise programmes, outcome budgeting seeks to improve organization."
- Outcome based budgeting aims to stimulate motivation and seeks to achieve organisational goals through decentralised incentives that allow programme managers greater authority and exercise of their creativity in the detailed use of resources, while holding them accountable for the results.
- "In contrast to performance budgeting, which places an emphasis on outputs, economy and efficiency, outcome budgeting is concerned with outcomes and effectiveness". 'While other budget systems targeted internal stakeholders, outcome budgeting attempts to communicate' with and educate stakeholders about government accomplishments and the costs of achievements and the costs of achieving these results.
- "An outcome-based budgeting system places more emphasis on strategic and performance plans with measurable results, performance budgets, on accountability process, a performance evaluation that de-emphasises micro-managing of line-item spending, and annual reports communicating to stakeholders".
- Overall, the findings from the research can be a matter of concern. The results suggesting the lack of agreement in perception across level of government about the conceptual definition are not consistent with the characteristics of the amalgam of proposals which emerge in the current budgetary reform. Thus outcome budgeting would not gain widespread acceptance if the concept were not well defined and agreed upon by many government stakeholders.
- To quote Ngoyi; Miller and Holzer[ix], " Unfortunately, the implementation efforts have been impeded by the confusion about its definition. Furthermore, the research on outcome budgeting is still very weak, particularly in public administration and generally in the management literature, because researchers refuse to view it as more than performance budgeting of old or Programme, Planning and Budgeting System (PPBS). This fact might partly explain the difficulties in defining outcome budgeting. On the other hand, while the theory is clear, it is important to point out that there is no standard definition of this system in public administration literature"….. " Outcome budgeting would not gain widespread acceptance if the concept were not well defined and agreed upon by many government stakeholders.".

OUTCOME BUDGET – ISSUES

In short, budgeting in government as a constitutional requirement under Article 112 is the 'Annual Financial Statement' containing estimated receipts and expenditure for the coming year for the Central Government, it has to be laid before both the Houses of Parliament. Further, estimates in the form of demands for grants are also submitted to the Parliament. Over the years, the budgeting exercise, with the objective of optimal allocation and better use of resources, has been subjected to certain different approaches. Performance budget contained physical targets and financial requirements in terms of functions, programmes and activities. The performance budget

viii. Forrester J " Current State of Research on Outcome Budgeting" (personal Communication, August 13, 2001, in Mwabilu L. Ngoyo; Gerald J. Miller and Marc Holzer, 'Outcome Budgeting : Conceptual Definition' ngoyil3@aol.com; geraldmiller@comeast.net; mholzer@pipeline.com

ix. ibid

laid emphasis on performance, on achievements rather than on exhaustion of funds or on outlays, it developed linkages between physical targets and financial requirements. Further, in order to review the on-going schemes and to have judicious allocation of funds, Zero-Base Budgeting approach had been emphasized from time to time.

ZBB, as mentioned in earlier chapters, is an approach towards accountability, output rather than inputs is the justification of budget proposal. In this regard, the outcome budget adopted emphasising on results, or achievements, or accomplishments, was similar to that of performance budget. To that extent, outcome budget should be a welcome exercise as it is expected to change the mindset of officials to focus on results or outcome of the project and to ensure value for money rather than on spending of money.

Thus outcome budget is just like putting of old wines in new bottles; in a way, it could be a marketing strategy to re - label the performance budget to make it acceptable, operational and successful. However, since budgeting involves more of behavioural issues arising from laying down realistic targets, responsibility fixing and making executives accountable; for the outcome budgeting to be effective, there is a need to define the concept and to have conceptual clarity of the definition of outcome, in particular for administrative ministries/departments involved in providing of services or maintenance of law and order or policy making which involve about 70 percent of total government expenditure.

To sum up, there is a need to look into policy issues like,

- What would be the role of outcome budgeting in the budgeting system of the country?
- How outcome budget is going to be integrated with the existing budgeting practices?
- Need for research on the definition and conceptual clarity of the meaning of the term outcome among various stakeholders of the government

Exhibit : 7.I

Outcome Budget for Programmes for certain Departments- (Illustrative List)

Statement of Outlays and outcomes/Targets: Annual Plan 2005-06 (₹ Crore)

1. Programme: Development of Marine Fisheries- Department of Husbandry and Dairying

Objective/ Outcome	Plan Outlay 2005-06	Quantifiable Deliverables	Processes/ Timeliness	Remarks/ Risk Factors
Development of traditional mechanised and deep sea fishing to Small Sectors including safety of fishermen	₹ 32.5 crore	I. Traditional craft motorised = 4000 II. Intermediate craft of improved design introduced = 200 III. Resources specific Deep Sea = 5 IV. No. of boats for which subsidised HSD provided = 1800	April 2005 to March 2006	i. Readiness of State Government to provide matching share. ii. Timely completion of formalities by State agencies.

II. Department of Elementary Education & Literacy Sarva Shiksha Abhiyan (SSA)

Objective/ Outcome	Plan Outlay 2005-06	Quantifiable Deliverables	Processes/ Timeliness	Remarks/ Risk Factors
Enrolling all Children of 6-14 years in	₹ 780.00 crore (Include	I. Enrolling all the 8.13m out of school children in regular	To be reported by 31/12/2005	Proper updating of
Elementary Schools/EGS/ AlE Centre	amount allocable for NE)	2. Reducing drop out rate Primary level (class I-V) by 5% points	Annual Reporting	Village education
Improving access, enrolment, retention and quality of elementary education		3. School infrastructure- *a)* Sanction of new schools *b)* Construction of school buildings,	Annual Reporting	Registers by State Govts.
		c) Construction of ACR	Teachers	
		d) Drinking water facilities		Vacancies/ absenteeism
		e) Construction of toilets		
		f) Quality education		Inadequate
		- Supply of books Teachers appointments Training of Teachers	ECCE, Child Labour Time Overruns State Releasing its Share	Logistec Court Cases

III. Department of Secondary and Higher Education National Institutes of Technology (NITS)

Objective/ Outcome	Plan Outlay 2005-06	Quantifiable Deliverables	Processes/ Timeliness	Remarks/ Risk Factors
To provide institutions & research of high quality in different branches of engineering & technology	₹ 90.00 crore	• 18 NITs are being run to impart quality technical education for 33,000 students which is likely to increase by 15-20% p.a. • With the conversion of RECs into NITs, infrastructure facilities will be strengthened & faculty positions to be filled up • A NIT will be on the pattern of IIT Act 1961- bill to be introduced in Parliament	• MHRD provides 100% assistance. • For proper fund utilisation, budget meetings are held periodically • Funds released after ensuring proper utilisation of funds already with the institutions	• Facilities were pathetic at the time of conversion. • Ministry provides funds for upgradation of infrastructure facilities & monitoring the position

IV. AICTE & Its Schemes

Objective/ Outcome	Plan Outlay 2005-06	Quantifiable Deliverables	Processes/ Timeliness	Remarks/ Risk Factors
Planned & coordinated development of technical education system. Overall quality improvement, regulation & maintenance of forms & students	₹ 100.00 crore	AICTE continues to regulate functioning of around 5,000 Institutions imparting technical education in different disciplines with an intake capacity of about 6.23 lakh students	Time taken in accreditation varies from Institute to Institute	Accreditation programmes are based on the initiatives of the Institutions, though AICTE provided incentives to institutes for seeking accreditation

V. National Programme for Control of Blindness-Ministry of Health & Family Welfare

Objective/ Outcome	Plan 2005-06 Outlay		Quantifiable Deliverables	Processes/ Timeliness	Remarks/ Risk Factors
	GOI Share	State Share			
Reduction in the prevalence of blindness to 0.8% by the end of 10th Plan	₹ 89.00 crore	Nil	Cataract Surgery- 44 lakh Schools Eye Screening Programme Targets: Children to be screened- 350 lakh Free spectacles- 7.35 lakh Eye Banking Targets: Eyes to be collected- 30.000 Infrastructure Strengthening: RIO- 4 Medical Colleges- 10 District Hospital-20 Sub- District Hospital-25 PHC & Vision Centers- 1000 Training Of Eye Surgeons/ Nurses- 950 To release assistance to about 25 State Govt. Hospitals located on National Highways- maximum limit- ₹ 1.5 crore	Strengthen services of other causes of blindness like corneal blindness Shift from eye camp to fixed facility surgical approach Strengthen capacities of eye care infrastructure Strengthen participation of Voluntary organisation Proposals received through State Governments Considered for release of funds	Release of funds depends on receipts of compete proposals from State Governments

CHAPTER

8 Gender Budgeting

Budgeting, to iterate, is a policy document, it operationalises the plans and allocates resources for various schemes/projects/programmes for human development and development of the economy. Since women and girls comprise a large part of valuable human resources of the country (roughly account for half of the population), and their socio-economic development steps the foundation for sustained growth of the economy and society as a whole. Women in general face disparity as reflected by indicators like, health, nutrition, literacy, education, skill level, occupational status. Further, there are gender specific barriers which prevent them from gaining access to their rightful share of public goods and services and there is an imperative need to address to these barriers in the planning and development process for the growth of the economy.

Gender budgeting is one tool to promote women's equality and empowerment by allocating funds to implement policies for the development and empowerment of women. It is also called 'women's budget', or 'gender sensitive budget', or 'applied gender budget analysis'. "Gender budget is based on the modern idea that budget is not simply an accounting or book-keeping exercise. Instead, budgeting is key part of planning and implementation process. Thus budgets should follow policies rather than policies being determined by budgets. And among the policies that budgets should follow, is Government of India's commitment to promoting gender equality".[i]

To quote, the Handbook[ii], the gender budgeting serves varied purposes which include:

- Indentifying the felt needs of women and reprioritizing and/or increasing expenditure to meet these needs;
- Supporting gender mainstreaming in macroeconomics;
- Strengthening civil society participation in economic policy making;
- Enhancing the linkages between economic and social policy outcomes;
- Tracking public expenditure against gender and development policy commitments; and
- Contributing to the attainment of the Millennium Development Goals (MDGs).

A budget focuses on policies and programmes planned for the next year for the people in general; gender budget, on the other hand focuses on the needs of women and girls as they are usually at disadvantage as compared to men and boys. However, gender budget is not about allocating government money 50 – 50 between men and boys on one hand, and women and girls on the other. Rather, it looks at every part of the government budget to assess how it will address to the different needs of women and girls.

Put it in other words, gender budgeting is not simply to have a separate budget to address women's or gender concerns. Rather it has the objective to ensure that every part of the government budget takes gender differences into account, and special allocations for women and gender would be helpful in addressing to their special needs

i. ***[Gender Budgeting Handbook for Government of India Ministries & Department]***
ii. ***[ibid]***

The Handbook addresses to the question, why does gender budgeting focuses on women as[iii]: around the world, gender budgeting tends to focus on women because:

- Women are a greater proportion of the illiterate people in the world,
- Maternal mortality continues to be a leading cause of death for women of reproductive age in developing countries ;
- Women are under-represented in decision-making especially at senior levels in both government and business sectors;
- Women's 'economic' work continues to be very different in nature from men's; they are engaged in less formal, lower status types of work and receive less pay than men for the same work;
- Women also continue to be involved most of the unpaid work of bearing, rearing and caring for children and other citizens.

Gender Budget Statement in India was first introduced in Budget 2005-06 on considering the request of women's groups and on the recommendation of the Expert Group on "Classification System of Government Transactions"[iv]. In order to make further refinement to the Statement, every year the Ministries/Departments are requested through the Annual Budget Circular to highlight the quantum of public expenditure earmarked in budget for women. On the basis of the information thus furnished by the Ministries/Departments, the Gender Budget Statement is prepared. This Statement indicates, in two parts, the budget provisions for schemes that are substantially meant for the benefit of women. Part A details schemes in which 100% provision is for women, Part B reflects schemes where the allocations for women constitute at least 30% of the provision.

The rationale of Gender Budgeting arises from the recognition of the fact that the national budget impacts various sections of the society differently, through the pattern of resource allocation and priority accorded to competing sectors. Gender Budgeting in its simplest connotation is 'Gender Analysis' of the budget aimed at examining the budgetary allocation through a gender lens. The purpose of gender budgeting is to monitor expenditure and public service delivery from a gender perspective, as a means of mainstreaming women's concerns in all activities and improving their access to public resources. The gender budget statement has received an impetus over the last eight budgets with growing awareness of gender sensitivities. Gender Budgeting is an evolving area where with better understanding and appreciation of the subject, more and more Ministries/Departments are reviewing programmes and schemes to address the quantum of resources that have the budgetary potential to impact and address the development needs of women.

Gender Budget for the year 2013-14 is presented under Statement 20 in the Expenditure Budget Vol. I, 2013-2014. This Statement is reproduced in at the end of the chapter as Exhibit 8.1. This Statement has two parts as:

- Part A: contains schemes in which 100% provision is for women;
- Part B reflects schemes where the allocations for women constitute at least 30% of the provision.

Ananlysis of the Statement indicates that for the year 2013-14:

- 30 Ministries/Departments and 5 Union territories Governments have made allocations for gender budget statement;
- there is18.6% increase for 100% women specific programmes which have gone up from ₹ 22,969 crore in BE 2012-13 to ₹ 27,248 crore in BE 2013-14;
- taking parts A and B together, there is an increase of 10.2% from ₹ 88,143 crore in BE 2012-13 to ₹ 97,134 crore in BE 2013-14.

---

iii. [ibid]

iv. [Finance Minister Budget Speech for the year 2004-05 para 76]

In short gender budget is beneficiary-oriented budget – women and girls beneficiaries, being a larger and important segment of population, It highlights the programmes and allocations of funds thereof for the development of this segment of the population. Similar can be approach for other segments of the society, or for certain specific regions, like north-east region, or functions like, railways. Though gender budgeting exercise is in the gestation stage, a issue is raised, is it a budgetary approach, a process of authorization of executives to execute plans ; a fund allocated for women and gender to address to their special needs?

Exhibit : 8.1

PART A - 100% Women specific programmes

(*In crores of Rupees*)

Ministry/Department	2012-2013 *Budget* Plan	*Non-Plan*	*Total*	2012-2013 *Revised* Plan	*Non-Plan*	*Total*	2013-2014 *Budget* Plan	*Non-Plan*	*Total*
Demand No. 2									
Department of Agriculture Research & Education									
1 Directorate of Women in Agriculture	1.50	3.67	5.17	1.50	3.50	5.00	4.90	3.78	8.68
2 All India Co-ordinated Research Project on Home Science	11.50	....	11.50	11.50	....	11.50	15.61	....	15.61
Total	**13.00**	**3.67**	**16.67**	**13.00**	**3.50**	**16.50**	**20.51**	**3.78**	**24.29**
Demand No. 14									
Department of Telecommunications									
1 Amenities to staff	....	0.10	0.10	....	0.15	0.15	....	0.25	0.25
2 Universal Service Obligation Scheme	2.20	....	2.20	....	....	....	1 50	....	1.50
Total	**2.20**	**0.10**	**2.30**	....	**0.15**	**0.15**	**1.50**	**0.25**	**1.75**
Demand No. 32									
Ministry of External Affairs									
1 Establishing five Vocational Training Centres in Africa for Women Solar Engineers in collaboration with Barefoot College, Tilonia, Ajmer	....	....	....	....	0.15	0.15	....	12.27	12.27
2 Strengthening African civil society & NGOs through microfinance, micro-enterprise & livelihood promotion in collaboration with Self Employed Women's Association (SEWA)	....	....	....	....	0.90	0.90	....	2.05	2.05
3 Construction of Girls' hostel building for Pokhara University, Lekhnath, Kaski, Nepal	....	....	....	....	0.88	0.88	....	088	0.88
4 Construction of Maternity Centre for Tribhuvan University Teaching Hospital, Kathmandu, Nepal	....	....	....	....	....	....	....	028	028
5 Girls Hostel building for Nepal APF School, Kathmandu, Nepal	....	....	....	....	....	....	....	243	243
6 Construction of Anim Shedra (Nunnery) in Bhutan	....	....	....	....	1.93	1.93	....	....	....
7 Construction of Labour Room and									

* *Source: Statement 20- Expenditure Budget Vol I, 2013-14 (GOI)*

traditional medicine unit at Chumey BHU-II, Bhutan	....	....	....	....	....		....	0.03	0.03
Total		....			**3.86**	**3.86**	....	**17.94**	**17.94**
Demand No. 47									
Department of Health & Family Welfare									
1 Reproductive & Child Health (RCH) Flexible Pool	4938.51	....	4938.51	3857.00	....	3857.00	5347.01	....	.5347.01
2 Infrastructure Maintenance									
(a) Rural Family Welfare Services	4031.00	....	4031.00	4295.46	....	4295.46	4146.00	....	4146.00
(b) Training Institutions under States/ Basic Training for ANM/LHV	115.00	....	115.00	10852	....	108.52	....	....	....
Total	**9084.51**	....	**9084.51**	**8260.98**	....	**8260.98**	**9493.01**	....	**9493.01**
Demand NO.53									
Ministry of Home Affairs									
Engaging women employees on contract basis	....	0.10	0.10	....	0.10	0.10	....	010	0.10
Demand No. 55- Police									
(i) ITBP									
Opening of Creche, Day Care Centre. Gender Sensitization, Health Care Centre, Nutritional Care Centre, Women's Rest rooms (furniture and fixtures) /Washing Drying/ women's Laundry	....	0.21	0.21	....	0.12	012	....	004	004
(ii) CRPF									
1 Women's hostel	....	40.00	40.00	....	40.00	40.00	....	100.00	100.00
2 Other schemes like Day care centre, Gender Sensitization, Health nutritional Care Centre etc	....	37.00	37.00	....	37.00	37.00	....	41.50	41.50
Total	....	**77.00**	**77.00**	....	**77.00**	**77.00**	....	**141.50**	**141.50**
(iii) Sashastra Seema Bal									
Scheme like Day care centre, Gender Sensitization, Health and Nutritional Care	....	1.00	1.00	....	0.15	0.15	....	0.42	0.42
(iv) CISF									
Construction of Family Welfare Centres at RTC Ananthpur and Arakkonam exclusively for the benefit of women	1.30	....	1.30	0,48	....	0,48	0.45	....	0.45
(v) Bureau of Police Research & Development (BPR&D)									
5th Women National Conference for Women in Police	....	0.10	0.10	....	0.10	0.10	....	0.10	0.10
2 Research study proposed by Crime and Criminology Division	0.25	0.10	0.35	0.09	0.10	0.19	....	0.28	0.28
3 Women Training Programmes viz course on Self Development and Conflict Management for women police officers of the rank of Dy. SP to ASI	....	0.09	0.09	....	0.08	0.08	0.01	0.26	0.27

4 Organising courses on crime against women vis a vis Human Rights, Juvenile Justice & Investigation of female foeticide cases	....	0.10	0.10	0.02	0.07	0.09	0.06	0.14	0.20
5 Organising the Workshop/Seminar on Trafficking in the States to sensitise Police Officers on these issues	....	0.20	0.20	0.06	0.62	0.68	0.12	0.44	0.56
6 Organising the Virtual Interactive Courses for IPS & other senior police officers to sensitise them on issues relating to Gender Categories	....	0.20	0.20	....	0.13	0.13	....	0.15	0.15
7 Research projects on women related issues by the women professionals proposed by the Correctional Administration Division	....	0.01	0.01	....	0.01	0.01	....	0.01	0.01
8 Provision for the infrastructure in Women's Rest Room and creche and for women health care centres.	....	0.05	0.05	0.04	0.09	0.13	0.03	0.06	0.09
9 Schemes like creation of Rest room for women trainee, creation of creche for women employees, hostel room, etc.	....	0.60	0.60	016	0.47	0.63	0.32	0.65	0.97
Total	**0.25**	**1.45**	**1.70**	**0.37**	**1.67**	**2.04**	**0.54**	**2.09**	**2.63**
(vi) BSF									
Schemes like Women accommodation with toilets, cook house cum dining hall	0.40	....	0.40	....	....	....	....	....	....
(vii) Intelligence Bureau									
Creche Facilities, Yoga Centre & Health Mela	....	....	....	....	0.05	0.05	....	0.05	0.05
Total Police	**1.95**	**79.66**	**81.61**	**0.85**	**78.99**	**79.84**	**0.99**	**144.10**	**145.09**
Demand No. 59									
Department of School Education and Literacy									
1 Mahila Samakhya for women	60.00	....	60.00	60.00	....	60.00	60.00	....	60.00
2 National Scheme for Incentive to the Girl Child for Secondary Education	100.00	....	100.00	100.00	....	100.00	100.00	....	100.00
3 Scheme for construction and running of Girls Hostels for students of Secondary and Higher Secondary schools	450.00	....	450.00	327.00	....	327.00	450.00	....	450.00
Total	**610.00**	....	**610.00**	**487.00**	....	**487.00**	**610.00**	....	**610.00**
Demand No. 60									
Department of Higher Education									
1 Women's Hostel in Polytechnic	100.00	....	100.00	70.00	....	70.00	....	....	....
Demand No. 66									
Ministry of Micro, Small & Medium Enterprises									
1 Trade Related Entrepreneurship Assistance Programme	....	....	....	2.30	....	2.30	253	....	2.53

2 Mahila Coir Yojna	3.00	....	3.00	2.91	....	2.91	3.45	....	3.45
Total	**3.00**	....	**3.00**	**5.21**	....	**5.21**	**5.98**	....	**5.98**
Demand No. 68									
Ministry of Minority Affairs									
1 Scheme for Leadership Development of Minority Women	15.00	....	15.00	12.80	....	12.80	15.00	....	15.00
2 Free Cycles for Girl Students of Class IX	5.00	....	5.00	0.04	....	0.04	....	....	....
3 Scheme for containing population decline of small minorities	....	....	....	0.01	....	0.01	2.00	....	2.00
Total	**20.00**	....	**20.00**	**12.85**	....	**12.85**	**17.00**	....	**17.00**
Demand No. 70									
Ministry of Overseas Indian Affairs									
1 Legal assistance to Indian Women facing problems in NRI marriages	....	0.75	0.75	....	0.65	0.65	....	0.75	0.75
Demand No. 83									
Department of Rural Development									
Rural Housing - Indira Awas Yojana	11075.00	....	11075.00	9024.00	....	9024.00	15184.00	....	15184.00
Demand No. 85									
Department of Science & Technology									
1 Women Component Plan	40.00	....	40.00	....	....	....	....	....	....
2 Disha Programme for Women in Science	49.00	....	49.00	47.24	....	47.24	53.00	....	53.00
Total	**89.00**	....	**89.00**	**47.24**	....	**47.24**	**53.00**	....	**53.00**
Demand No.87									
Department of Biotechnology									
Biotechnology Programmes for Women	3.50	....	3.50	2.80	....	2.80	3.50	....	3.50
Demand No. 89									
Ministry of Social Justice & Empowerment									
1. Girls Hostel for SCs	95.00	....	95.00	14.00	....	14.00	50.00	....	50.00
Demand No. 95									
Ministry of Tribal Affairs									
Strengthening of Education among ST girls in low literacy Districts	40.00	....	40.00	40.00	....	40.00	40.00	....	40.00
Demand No. 96									
Andaman and Nicobar Islands	7.75	3.20	10.95	7.31	3.20	10.51	13.81	2.77	16.58
Demand No. 97									
Chandigarh	21.84	34.20	56.04	14.37	4.94	19.31	18.90	5.06	23.96
Demand No. 98									
Dadra and Nagar Haveli	3.00	0.05	3.05	3.00	0.05	3.05	3.25	0.05	3.30
Demand No. 99									
Daman and Diu	0.38	....	0.38	0.38	....	0.38	0.31	....	0.31
Demand No. 100									
Lakshadweep	3.09	....	3.09	3.09	....	3.09	3.65		3.65
Demand No. 105									
Ministry of Women & Child Development									
1 Hostels for Working Women	10.00	....	10.00	8.30	....	8.30	20.00	....	20.00

2 Support to Training & Employment Programme (STEP)	20.00	....	20.00	7.50	....	7.50	20.00	....	20.00
3 Central Social Welfare Board	60.00	20.85	80.85	45.30	19.18	64.48	50.00	20.85	70.85
4 Rashtriya Mahila Kosh	100.0	....	100.00	....	....	....	20.00	....	20.00
5 Swadhar	100.0	....	100.00	55.00	....	55.00	75.00	....	75.00
6 Relief to and Rehabilitation of Rape Victims	20.00	....	20.00	....	....	....	85.00	....	85.00
7 National Commission for Women	11.00	4.13	15.13	12.27	3.30	15.57	15.00	4.13	19.13
8 Gender Budgeting	1.00	....	1.00	0.71	....	0.71	1.00	....	1.00
9 Conditional Cash Transfer for girl child with Insurance cover (Dhanlakshmi)	5.00	....	5.00	5.00	....	5.00	10.00	....	10.00
10 Comprehensive scheme for combating trafficking (Ujjawala)	12.00	....	12.00	7.40	....	7.40	13.00	....	13.00
11 Priyadarshini Scheme	15.00	....	15.00	14.00	....	14.00	15.00	....	15.00
12 Rajiv Gandhi Scheme for Empowerment of Adolescent Girls (SABLA)	750.00	....	750.00	504.00	....	504.00	650.00	....	650.00
13 Indira Gandhi Matritva Sahyog Yojna (IGMSY)	520.00	....	520.00	84.00	....	84.00	500.00	....	500.00
14 National Mission for Empowerment of Women	25.00	....	25.00	11.00	....	11.00	55.00	....	55.00
Total	**1649.00**	**24.98**	**1673.98**	**754.48**	**22.48**	**776.96**	**1529.00**	**24.94**	**1553.98**
Total (PART A-100% women specific programmes)	**22822.22**	**146.71**	**22968.93**	**18760.56**	**117.92**	**18878.48**	**27048.41**	**199.78**	**27248.19**

PART B-30% Women specific programmes

Demand No. 1									
Department of Agriculture & Cooperation									
1 Technology Mission on Cotton	4.50	....	4.50	3.78	....	3.78	4.50	....	4.50
2 Jute Technology Mission	3.00	....	3.00	1.70	....	1.70	2.10	....	2.10
3 Integrated Oilseeds Oilpalm /Pulses and Maize Development	120.00	....	120.00				90.00	....	90.00
4 Support to State Extension Services	180.00	....	180.00	75.00	....	75.00	83.00	....	83.00
5 National Food Security Mission	555.00	...	555.00	529.00	....	529.00	675.00	....	675.00
6 Extension Support to Central Institutions	5.40	....	5.40	0.70	....	0.70	1.00	....	1.00
7 Mass Media Support to Agricultural Extension	57.00	....	57.00	50.00	....	50.00	60.00	....	60.00
8 Establishment of Agri-Clinic and Agri-business Centres	6.00	....	6.00	1.70	....	1.70	2.00	....	2.00
Total	**930.90**	....	**930.90**	**661.88**	....	**661.88**	**917.60**	....	**917.60**
Demand No. 15									
Department of Electronics and Information Technology									
Department of Electronics-Accredited Computer Courses	0.60	....	0.60	0.60	....	0.60	0.70	....	070
2 National Institute of Electronics arid Information lechnology	2.50	....	2.50	2.50	....	2.50	....	....	....
3 C-DAC						0.10	....	0.10	
4 Manpower Development (including Skill Development and IT for Masses						2.00	....	200	
Total	**3.10**		**3.10**	**3.10**		**3.10**	**2.80**	....	**2.80**
Demand No. 17									
Department of Food & Public Distribution									
Village Grain Bank Scheme	2.40		2.40	0.30		0.30	0.60		0.60
Demand No. 19									
Ministry of Culture									
1 Zonal Culture Centres	9.30		9.30	9.30		9.30	11.85		11 85
2 Financial Assistance for Professionals & Individual for Specified Performing Art Projects	11.29	0.47	11.76	11.29	0.42	11.71	12.80	0.47	13.27
Total	**20.59**	**0.47**	**21.06**	**20.59**	**0.42**	**21.01**	**24.65**	**0.47**	**25.12**
Demand No. 30									
Ministry of Earth Sciences									
Atmospheric Processes and modeling and services	79.00		79.00	1000		10.00	25.00		25.00
2 Ocean Science & Services	91.00		91.00	24.00		24.00	30.00		30.00
3 Ocean Technology	89.00		89.00	22.00		22.00	30.00		30.00
Total	**259.00**		**259.00**	**56.00**		**56.00**	**85.00**		**85.00**
Demand No. 32									
Ministry of External Affairs									
Training of foreign nationals under Indian Technical and Economic Cooperation (ITEC) programme					120.00	120.00		140.00	140.00
2 Training of foreign nationals under Special Commonwealth									

	Assistance for Africa Programme (SCAAP)	....	....	....	....	20.00	20.00	....	25.00	2500
3	Training of foreign nationals under TCS Colombo Plan	....	....	....	....	4.60	4.60	....	4.60	4.60
	Total	....	....	....	....	**144.60**	**144.60**	....	**169.60**	**169.60**
Demand No. 47										
	Department of Health & Family Welfare									
1	Safdarjunq Hospital, New Delhi	146.19	117.60	263.79	135.38	117.60	252.98	190.12	131.96	322.08
2	Dr. RML Hospital, New Deihl	77.98	5106	129.04	71.49	5254	124.03	100.10	60.13	160.23
3	All India Institute of Medical Sciences, New Delhi	241.74	331.50	573.24	252.96	402.24	655.20	280.50	402.90	683.40
4	Lady Hardinge Medical College & S. K. Hospital	69.00	98.25	167.25	47.36	96.24	143.60	146.25	100.88	247.13
5	Post Graduate Institute of Medical Education & Research, Chandigarh	61.18	146.30	207.48	57.00	148.20	205.20	76.00	165.30	241.30
6	Jawaharlal Institute of Post Graduate Medical Education & Research, Puducherry	65.21	83.70	148.91	67.37	90.72	158.09	86.40	99.90	186.30
7	National Cancer Control Programme	178.56	7.20	185.76	108.00	7.06	115.06	175.20	8.16	183.36
8	Grants to Kasturba Health Society, Wardha	25.50	....	25.50	25.50	....	25.50	25.50	....	25.50
9	National Vector Borne Disease Control Programme (including Filaria & Kala Azar)	234.52	3.14	237.66	186.55	3.30	189.85	234.52	3.45	237.97
10	National TB Control Programme	255.65	0.83	256.48	200.57	....	200.57	255.65	....	255.65
11	National Leprosy Eradication Programme	16.83	....	16.83	12.98	....	12.98	16.83	....	16.83
12	National Blindness Control Programme	159.50	....	159.50	132.00	....	132.00	159.50	....	159.50
13	Development of Nursing Services	23.75	....	23.75	10.45	....	10.45	19.00	....	19.00
14	National Institute of Mental Health & Neuro-Sciences, Bengaluru	38.15	28.00	66.15	38.15	30.24	68.39	46.48	35.00	81.48
15	All India Institute of Speech & Hearing, Mysore	13.80	4.80	18.60	12.49	4.72	17.21	32.46	5.32	37.78
16	Infrastructure Maintenance									
	(a) Direction and Administration	415.44	10.07	425.51	454.52	16.93	471.45	708.98	17.34	726.32
	(b) Urban Family Welfare Services	....	....	....	221.03	....	221.03	....	....	....
17	Discretionary Grant	....	7.35	7.35	....	0.53	0;53	....	0.53	0.53
18	National Medical Library	8.06	1.24	9.30	8.06	1.24	8.30	8.60	1.32	9.92
19	Central Government Health Scheme	44.16	288.00	332.16	45.34	330.24	375.58	48.58	330.72	379.30
20	Contraception	119.33	....	119.33	113.83	....	113.83	119.33	....	119.33
21	Urban Family Welfare Services	197.80	....	197.80	....	....	....	....	....	....

22	Mission Flexible Pool	2896.99	....	2866.99	2067.80	....	2067.80	2824.36	282436
	Total	**5259.34**	**1179.04**	**6438.38**	**4268.83**	**1301.80**	**5570.63**	**5554.36**	**1362.91**	**6917.27**
Demand No.48										
	Department of A YUSH									
	Central Council for Research in Ayurvedic Sciences	16.00	....	16.00	1.50	....	1.50	6.00	....	6.00
2	Rashtriya Ayurveda Vidyapeeth, New Delhi	1.42	0.13	1.55	1.67	0.13	1.80	1.25	0.15	1.40
3	Central Council for Research in Homoeopathy	20.48	9.97	30.45	27.62	11.02	38.64	44.27	9.80	54.07
4	Central Counol for Research in Unani Medicine	13.12	8.50	21.62	12.66	8.69	21 35	15.60	8.76	24.36
5	Central Council for Research in Yoga & Naturopathy	3.30	....	3.30	....	....	....	....	....	....
6	National Institute of Naturopathy, Pune	1.31	....	1.31	....	....	....	....	....	....
	Total	**55.63**	**18.60**	**74.23**	**43.45**	**19.84**	**63.29**	**67.12**	**18.71**	**85.83**
Demand No.50										
	Department of AIDS Control									
	National AIDS Control Programme	510.00	....	510.00	527.87	....	527.87	535.50	....	535.50
Demand No. 55- Police										
	(i) ITBP									
	Opening of Creche, Day Care Centre, Gender Sensitization, Health Care Centre, Nutritional Care Centre, Women's Rest rooms (furniture and fixtures)/Washing Drying/women's Laundry	....	0.06	0.06	....	0.12	0.12	....	0.04	0.04
2	Construction of Barracks, toilets, bathrooms							0.17	....	0.17
	Total	....	**0.06**	**0.06**	....	**0.12**	**0.12**	**0.17**	**0.04**	**0.21**
	(ii) CISF									
	Construction of Familly Welfare Centres at RTC Ananthpur exclusively for the benefit of women	0.39	....	0.39	....	....	....			....
2	Construction of Family Welfare Centres at RTC Deoli and Creche facilities	....	....	....	0.48	....	0.48	0.45		0.45
	Total	**0.39**	....	**0.39**	**0.48**	....	**0.48**	**0.45**	....	**0.45**
	(iii) Bureau of Police Research & Development (BPR&D)									
	Fellowship scheme for doctoral work in Criminology and Police Science for women, award etc.	....	....	....	....	10.44	10.44	....	8.51	851
2	Pandit Gobind Ballabh Pant Award Scheme for books in Hindi	....	....	....	....	0.84	0.84	....	0.84	0.84
	Total	....	....	....	....	**11.28**	**11.28**	....	**9.35**	**9.35**
	Total Police	**0.39**	**0.06**	**0.45**	**0.48**	**11.40**	**11.88**	**0.62**	**9.39**	**10.01**

Demand No.58										
	Ministry of Housing & Urban Poverty Alleviation									
1	Swarnajayanl Shahari Rozgar Yojana	251.40	....	251.40	211.33	....	211.33	285.00	....	285.00
Demand No. 59										
	Department of School Education and Literacy									
1	Strengthening of Teachers Training Institution	160.00	....	160.00	93.44	....	93.44	160.00	....	160.00
2	Support to NGOs/Institutes /SRCs for Adult Education and Skill Development	65.10	0.02	65.12	49.87	....	49.87	62.00	....	62.00
3	Adult Education and Skill Development Scheme	505.69	....	505.69	360.74	....	360.74	490.26	....	490.26
4	Kendriya Vidyalayas Sangathan	105.00	625.87	730.87	105.00	631.30	736.30	105.00	674.77	779.77
5	Navodaya Vidyalayas Samiti	437.50	162.38	599.88	437.50	141.42	578.92	437.50	149.49	586.99
6	Vocationalization of Education	30.00	....	30.00	24.00	....	24.00	24.03	....	2403
7	Information & Communication Technology In Schools	105.00	....	105.00	105.00	....	105.00	105.00	....	105.00
8	Access & Equity	0.03	....	0.03	0.01	....	0.01			
9	Sarva Shiksha Abhiyan (SSA)	12368.62	....	12368.62	11444.18	....	11441.18	13192.87	....	13192.87
10	National Programme of Nutritional Support to Primary Education (Mid-Day Meal Scheme)	5013.54	....	5013.54	4830.00	....	4830.00	5550.30	....	5550.30
11	National Council of Educational Research & Training (NCERT)	4.50	63.81	68.31	3.51	52.96	56.47	4.50	68.49	72.99
12	National Institute of Open Schooling	0.03	....	0.03	0.01	....	0.01	0.03	....	0.03
13	Central Tibetian School Society Administration	1.80	12.04	13.84	1.49	12.79	1428	1.80	13.84	1564
14	Joint Indo Mongolian School (Mongolia)	0.30	....	0.30	0.25	....	0.25	....	....	....
15	Rashtriya Madhyamik Shiksha Abhiyan (RMSA)	1374.56	....	1374.56	1395.96	....	1395.96	1477.52	....	1477.52
16	National Means cum Merit Scholarship Scheme	21.00	....	21.00	21.00	....	21.00	21.00	....	21.00
17	Centrally Sponsored Scheme of appointment of Language Teachers	1.74	....	1.74	0.57	....	0.57	1.74	....	1.74
18	Scheme for Providing Quality Education in Madrass	52.50	....	52.50	58.50	....	58.50	52.50	....	52.50
19	Scheme for Infrastructure Development in Minority Institutions	15.00	....	15.00	8.52	....	8.52	15.00	....	15.00
20	National Bal Bhawan	4.20	2.14	6.34	1.64	2.05	3.69	2.40	2.30	4.70
21	Scheme for setting up of 6000 Model Schools at Block level as Bench Mark of Excellence	486.00	....	486.00	337.50	....	337.50	450.00	....	450.00

22	Inclusive Education for the Disabled at Secondary School	21.00	....	21.00	8.42	....	8.42	15.00	....	15.00
23	Directorate of Adult Education	2.70	0.85	3.55	1.19	0.84	203	2.70	0.91	3.61
24	National Literacy Mission Authority	0.60	0.02	0.62	0.21	0.01	0.22	0.60	0.01	0.61
	Total	**20776.41**	**867.13**	**21643.54**	**19288.51**	**841.37**	**20129.88**	**22171.75**	**909.81**	**23081.56**
Demand No.60										
	Department of Higher Education									
1	University Grants Commission	1911.50	1408.25	3319.75	1694.21	1419.89	3114.10	1715.20	1520.02	3235.22
2	Indira Gandhi National Open University	31.50	0.30	31.80	31.50	0.27	31.77	37.50	0.30	37.80
3	Community Polytechnics	45.00	....	45.00	18.00	....	18.00	....	....	....
4	National Institute of Technical Teacher's Training & Research	10.50	18.24	28.74	9.60	16.44	26.04	10.50		10.50
5	Sant Longowal Institute of Engineering & Technology	4.80	8.36	13.16	3.15	7.37	10.52	....	....	....
6	Upgradation of Existing/ Setting up of new Polytechnic	252.00	....	252.00	126.00	....	126.00	....	....	....
7	National Council for Promotion of Urdu Langauge	8.40	....	8.40	12.00	....	12.00	....	....	....
8	Rashtnya Sanskrit Sansthan	18.00		18.00	26.84	16.84	43.68			
9	Central Institute of Indian Language	15.42	3.56	18.98	15.42	3.41	18.83	....	....	....
10	Kendriya Hindi Sansthan	3.00	4.62	7.62	3.00	6.12	9.12	....	....	....
11	Central Hindi Directorate	4.50	0.93	5.43	4.50	344	7.94	....	....	....
12	North Eastern Regional Institute of Science and Technology, Itanagar	3.00	10.92	13.92	1.34	1128	12.62	....	....	....
13	Central Institute of Technology, Kokrajhar	6.60	....	6.60	15.00	....	15.0	....		
14	Scholarship for College & University Students	125.00	....	125.00	79.06	....	79.06	175.00		175.00
15	Education Loan Interest Subsidy	240.00	....	240.00	300.00	....	300.00			
16	National Mission in Education through Information and Communication Technology	255.00	....	255.00	66.60	....	66.60	120.00	....	120.00
17	Indian Institutes of Technology	523.64	359.40	883.04	581.24	394.68	975.92	1047.27	435.03	1482.30
18	Indian Institutes of Management	75.60	11.56	87.16	47.80	9.80	57.60	147.00	12.23	159.23
19	Indian Institute of Science, Bengaluru	45.00	65.56	110.56	54.00	65.56	119.56	....	69.88	69.88
20	Indian Institute of Information Technology (Design & Manufacturing), Kanchipuram	24.00	.....	24.00	24.00	....	24.00	....	....	....
21	National Institute for Industrial Engineering, Mumbai	11.10	9.20	20.30	1.80	7.65	9.45	1.80	8.18	9.98
22	National Institute for Forge and Foundary Technology, Ranchi	3.43	4.23	7.66	5.14	6.28	11.42	....	6.88	6.88
23	Indian School of Mines, Dhanbad	33.00	13.98	46.98	40.50	16.17	56.67	33.00	17.42	50.42

24	Indian Institutes of Information Technology	7.50	....	7.50	2.40	....	2.40	....	....	....
25	Indian Institutes of Science for Education and Research	195.00	....	195.00	204.00	....	204.00	....	....	....
26	National Institutes of Technology	326.37	209.77	536.14	281.62	224.74	506.36	424.29	242.72	667.01
27	Schools of Planning and Architecture	8.70	5.83	14.53	1.89	5.83	7.72	....	772	772
28	Grants for promotion of Indian languages	....	....	....	....	....	....	69.00	24.97	93.97
29	Support for the Polytechnics in the States	....	....	....	....	....	....	280.00	....	280.00
30	Support to Indian Institute of Science (IISC) and Indian Institute (s) of Science Education & Research (IISER)	....	....	....	....	....	....	257.85	69.88	327.73
31	Interest Subsidy and contribution for guarantee fund	....	....	....	....	....	....	330.00	....	330.00
32	Assistance to other institutes including SLIET, NERIST Ranchi, CIT Kokrajhar	....	....	....	....	....	....	20.40	26.98	47.38
33	New SPA							25.50	6.29	3179
	Total	**4187.56**	**2134.71**	**6322.27**	**3650.61**	**2215.77**	**5866.38**	**4694.31**	**2448.50**	**7142.81**
Demand No. 62										
	Ministry of Labour									
	Improvement in working conditions of child women labour	150.00	....	150.00	132.00	....	132.00	200.00	....	200.00
Demand No. 66										
	Ministry of Micro, Small & Medium Enterprises									
	Prime Minister's Employment Generation Programme	382.88	....	382.88	382.88	....	382.88	425.48	....	425.48
2	Workshed Scheme for Khadi Artisans (Now merged into SFURTI)	30.00	....	30.00	4.96	....	4.96	6.00	....	6.00
3	Scheme for enhancing Productivity and Competitiveness for Khadi Industries Artisans (Now merged into SFURTI)	....	....	....	....	....	....	4.50	....	4.50
4	Rejuvenation, Modernisation and Technology Upgradation of Coir Industries	4.80	....	4.80	1.50	....	1.50	4.80		480
5	Scheme of fund for Regeneration of Traditional Industries	....	....	....	1.50	....	1.50	16.64	....	16.64
6	Strengthening of Infrastructure of existing									

	weak Khadi Institutions and Assistance for marketing Infrastructure (Now merged into SFURTI)	....	....	....	1.80	....	1.80	2.25	....	2.25
7	Khadi Reform Development Package (ADS Assistance)	15.00	....	15.00	....	....	....	15.00		15.00
8	Interest Subsidy Eligibility Certificate for Khadi and Polyvastra	7.80	....	7.80	....	....	....	....	....	....
9	SFURTI (Corr)	0.60	....	0.60	....	....	....	....	....	....
10	Market Promotion (including Export Promotion) & Publicity (inclusive of new component of marketing/plazas and Modified MDA	36.00	....	36.00	....	....	....	....	....	....
11	Khadi Grant	....	....	....	50.49	....	50.49	35.49		35.49
	Total	**477.08**	....	**477.08**	**443.13**	....	**443.13**	**510.16**	....	**510.16**
Demand No. 68										
	Ministry of Minority Affairs									
	Merit -curn-Means scholarships for professional & technical courses of undergraduate & post-graduate level	220.00	....	220.00	184.07	....	184.07	270.00	....	270.00
2	Pre-Matric Scholarship for Minorities	900.00	....	900.00	795.78	....	795.78	950.00	....	950.00
3	Post-Matric Scholarship for Minorities	500.00	....	500.00	340.75	....	340.75	548.50	....	548.50
4	Maulana Azad National fellowship for minority students	7000	....	70.00	66.00	....	66.00	90.00	....	90.00
5	Interest subsidy on educational loans for overseas studies	....	....	....	0.02	....	0.02	2.00	....	2.00
6	Free Coaching and Allied Scheme	20.00	....	20.00	14.42	....	14.42	25.00	....	25.00
7	Support of students clearing Preliminary conducted by UPSC, SSC, State Public Services Commissions etc.	4.00	....	4.00	0.02		0.02	3.00	....	300
	Total	**1714.00**	....	**1714.00**	**1401.06**		**1401.06**	**1888.50**	....	**1888.50**
Demand No. 69										
	Ministry of New & Renewable Energy									
1	Biogas Programme	154.00	....	154.00	118.00	....	118.00	123.00	....	123.00
2	Cook Stove	14.00	....	14.00	3.50	....	3.50	5.00	....	500
3	Solar Cooker	5.00	....	5.00	0.50	....	0.50	300	....	300
	Total	**173.00**	....	**173.00**	**122.00**	....	**122.00**	**131.00**	....	**131.00**
Demand No.71										
	Ministry of Panchayati Raj									
	Panchayat Mahila Evam Yuva Shakti Abhiyan (now subsumed in RGPSA)	....	....	....	1.75	....	1.75	....	....	....
2	Rashtriya Gram Swaraj Yojna (now subsumed in RGPSA)				90.00		90.00			

3	Rajiv Gandhi Panchayat Sashaktikaran Abhryan (RGPSA)	106.00	....	106.00	50.00	....	50.00	455.00	....	455.00
	Total	**106.00**	....	**106.00**	**141.75**	....	**141.75**	**455.00**	....	**455.00**
Demand No.83										
	Department of Rural Development									
	Mahatma Gandhi National Rural Employment Guarantee Scheme	10989.00	....	10989.00	9794.68	....	9794.68	11000.00	....	11000.00
2	Aajeevika	1757.50	....	1757.50	1300.00	....	1300.00	2000.00	....	2000.00
	Total	12746.50	....	12746.50	11094.68	....	11094.68	13000.00	....	13000.00
Demand No. 89										
	Ministry of Social Justice & Empowerment									
	Special Central Assistance for Scheduled Castes Sub Plan	352.80	....	352.80	308.40	....	308.40	309.00	....	309.00
2	Post Matric Scholarship for SCs	441.00	....	441.00	438.60	....	438.60	441.00	....	441.00
3	Machinery for Implementation of PCR Act 1955 & Prevention of Atrocities Act 1989	29.40		29.40	24.60	....	24.60	26.40	....	26.40
4	Assistance to Voluntary Organisations for SCs	14.70	....	14.70	4.35	....	4.35	8.25	....	8.25
5	Grants to Non- Government institutions for running pre-examination Training Centre for SCs renamed as Free Coaching of SCs and OBCs	3.30	....	3.30	1.60	....	1.60	3.45	....	3.45
6	Nalional Commission for SCs	....	3.83	3.83	....	3.49	3.49	....	3.77	3.77
7	Rajv Gandhi National Fellowship for SCs	36.90	....	36.90	720	....	7.20	29.40	....	29.40
8	Share Capital to SCs Development Corporation	6.00	....	6.00	1.50	....	1.50	6.00	....	6.00
9	Self Employment Scheme -Liberation and Rehabilitation of Scavengers	29.40	....	29.40	6.00	....	6.00	167.10	....	167.10
10	Top Class Education for SCs	7.20	....	7.20	4.35	....	4.35	6.00	....	6.00
11	Boys and Girls Hostels for BCs	12.00	....	12.00	6.00	....	6.00	12.00	....	12.00
12	Post Matric Scholarship for BCs	195.30	....	195.30	194.21	....	194.21	243.00	....	243.00
13	Assistance to voluntary organisations for BCs	1.35	....	1.35	0.40	....	0.40	1.35	....	1.35
14	Deendayal Disabled Rehabilitation Scheme	30.90	....	30.90	19.80	....	19.80	32.06	....	32.06
15	National Institute of Social Defence	2.70	0.38	3.08	1.35	0.33	1.68	270	040	3.10

16	National Institute for Disabled/handicapped	18.90	13.01	31.91	16.10	13.08	29.18	20.10	13.95	34.05
17	Aids and appliances for the Handicapped	26.40	....	26.40	19.90	....	19.90	28.80	....	28.80
18	Spinal Injury Centre	0.60	....	0.60	0.60	....	0.60	0.60	....	0.60
19	Implementation of the Persons with Disability Act	28.50	....	28.50	5.40	....	5.40	29.70	....	29.70
20	Distribution Expenses of Commodity Assistance under bilateral agreement	....	0.30	0.30	....	0.27	0.27	....	0.27	0.27
21	Assistance to Voluntary Organisation for Old Age home	10.80	....	10.80	4.80	....	4.80	12.00	....	12.00
22	Scheme of Assistance for Establishment of Old Age Home for Indigent Senior Citizens	21.60	....	21.60	....	....	....	....	....	....
23	Scheme for Monitoring of the schemes through States and District level VMCs	2.10	....	2.10	....	....	....	....	....	....
24	Assistance to Voluntary Organisation for providing Social Defence services	1.50	....	1.50	0.90	....	0.90	0.90	....	0.90
25	Information and Mass Education Cell	8.10	....	8.10	0.90	....	0.90	12.00	....	12.00
26	National Handicapped Finance & Development Corporation	8.10	....	8.10	6.00	....	6.00	9.30	....	9.30
27	Employment of Physically Challenged	1.20	....	1.20	0.15	....	0.15	1.20	....	1.20
28	National Finance & Development Corporation for weaker section	65.70	....	65.70	54.00	....	54.00	71.10	....	71.10
29	Lump sum allocation for NE & Sikkim	73.80	....	73.80	56.75	....	56.75	85.32	....	85.32
30	Other Scheme under Ministry of Social Justice and Empowerment benefiting Women	50.55	10.50	61.05	6.24	3.12	9.36	53.00	3.57	56.57
31	Pradhan Mantri Adarsh Gram Yojana	0.30	....	0.30	....	....	....	30.00	....	30.00
	Total	**1481.10**	**28.02**	**1509.12**	**1190.10**	**20.29**	**1210.39**	**1641.73**	**21.96**	**1663.69**
Demand No.93										
	Ministry of Textiles									
1	Integrated Handloom Development Scheme	52.43	....	52.43	....	....	....	....	....	....
2	Marketing and Export Promotion Scheme	15.84	....	15.84	....	....	....	....	....	....
3	Handloom Weavers Comprehensive Welfare Scheme	42.00	....	42.00	42.00	....	42.00	28.50	....	28.50
4	Mill Gate Price Scheme	94.42	....	94.42	40.00	....	40.00	30.00	....	30.00
5	Diversified Handloom Development Scheme	4.56	....	4.56	....	....	....	....	....	....
6	Ambedkar Hastshilp Vikas Yojana	15.00	....	15.00	15.00	....	15.00	1.20	....	1.20

7	Design & Technology Upgradation	4.20	....	4.20	6.00	....	6.00	8.40	....	8.40
8	Marketing Support, Services & Export Promotion	16.50	....	16.50	16.50	....	16.50	13.50	....	13.50
9	Research & Development	3.85	....	3.85	3.85	....	3.85	3.00	....	3.00
10	Handicraft Artisans Comprehensive Welfare Scheme	7.80	....	7.80	7.80	....	7.80	11.70	....	11.70
11	Human Resource Development Scheme	6.54	....	6.54	6.54	....	6.54	7.80	....	7.80
12	R&D, Training & IT Initiatives	11.70	....	11.70	11.70	....	11.70	10.20	....	10.20
13	Seed Organisation and HRD	10.80	....	10.80	10.80	....	10.80	12.80	....	12.80
14	Catalytic Development Programme	65.76	....	65.76	65.76	....	65.76	70.00	....	70.00
15	Quality Certificate Systems	1.70	....	1.70	1.70	....	170	2.00	....	2.00
16	CFC for Integrated Wool Processing	1.20	....	1.20	1.70	....	1.70	2.00	....	2.00
17	Other Schemes of the Ministry	3.30	....	3.30	3.30	....	3.30	4.00	....	4.00
18	Comprehensive Handloom Weavers' Scheme				67.80	....	67.80	35.10	....	35.10
	Total	**357.60**	....	**357.60**	**300.45**		**300.45**	**240.20**	....	**240.20**
Demand No. 95										
	Ministry of Tribal Affairs									
1	SCA to Tribal Sub-Plan	360.00	....	360.00	304.50	....	304.50	360.00	....	360.00
2	Grants under Artide 275(1) of the Constitution	395.10		395.10	333.38		333.38	395.10	....	395.10
3	Post Matric Scholarship	374.25		374.25	410.84		410.84	374.25	....	374.25
4	Upgradation of Merit	0.75		0.75	1.05		1.05	0.75	....	0.75
5	Pre-Matric Scholarship	40.50		40.50	25.00		25.00	40.50	....	40.50
6	Establishment of Ashram School	37.50		37.50	37.50		37.50	3750	....	37.50
7	Boys and Girls Hostel	39.00		39.00	39.00		39.00	39.00	....	39.00
8	Vocational Training Centres in Tribal Areas	3.00	....	3.00	3.00	....	3.00	3.00	....	3.00
9	Rajiv Gandhi National Fellowship	45.00	....	45.00	42.47	....	42.47	45.00	....	45.00
10	Top Class Education	6.50	....	6.50	3.50	....	3.50	6.50	....	6.50
11	National Overseas Scholarship	0.50	....	0.50	0.50	....	0.50	0.50	....	0.50
12	Research Education & Mass Education Tribal Festivals and others (Component: Exchange of visits)	0.13	....	0.13	0.11	....	0.11	0.13	....	0.13
13	Grants-in-Aid to NGOs for STs including Coaching and Allied Scheme and Award for Exemplary Service	18.00	....	18.00	18.00	....	18.00	18.00	....	18.00
	Total	**1320.23**	....	**1320.23**	**1218.85**	....	**1218.85**	**1320.23**	....	**1320.23**
Demand No. 96										
	Andaman and Nicobar Islands	3.00	....	3.00	3.00	....	3.00	7.00	....	7.00

Demand No. 97									
Chandigarh	83.80	143.36	227.16	69.72	96.68	166.40	8706	105.44	192.50
Demand No. 98....									
Dadra and Nagar Haveli	8.53	....	8.53	8.53	....	8.53	0.02		0.02
Demand No. 99									
Daman and Diu	0.43	....	0.43	0.43	....	0.43	0.50	....	0.50
Demand No. 100									
Lakshadweep	0.48	....	0.48	0.48	....	0.48	0.63	....	0.63
Demand No. 105									
Ministry of Women & Child Development									
1 Rajiv Gandhi National Creche Scheme	55.00	....	55.00	53.75	....	53.75	55.00	....	55.00
2 Scheme for the Welfare of Working Children in need of care & Protection	5.00	....	5.00	4.25	....	4.25	5.00	....	5.00
3 Integrated Child Development Scheme (ICDS)	9351.50	....	9351.50	9351.50	....	9351.50	10443.00	....	10443.00
4 Integrated Child Protection Scheme (ICPS)	200.00	....	200.00	136.60	....	136.60	150.00	....	150.00
5 National Nutrition Mission	125.00	....	125.00	41.50	....	41.50	150.00	....	150.00
6 National Institute of Public Cooperation & Child Development	6.00	8.25	14.25	5.50	8.12	13.62	6.50	8.87	15.37
7 National Commission for the Protection of Child Rights	6.00	....	6.00	5.25	....	5.25	6.50	....	6.50
8 Central Adoption Resource Agency	4.50	1.05	5.55	3.75	0.95	4.70	4.50	0.95	5.45
9 Innovative Work on Women & Children	1.50	....	1.50	0.55	....	0.55	1.50	....	1.50
10 Nutrition Education Scheme (Food & Nutrition Board)	5.00	6.17	11.17	5.00	6.11	11.11	6.50	6.50	13.00
11 World Bank ICDS-IV Project	51.40	....	51.40	4.00	....	4.00	73.00	....	73.00
Total	**9810.90**	**15.47**	**9826.37**	**9611.65**	**15.18**	**9626.83**	**10901.50**	**16.32**	**10917.82**
Demand No.106									
Ministry of Youth Affairs and Sports									
1 Nehru Yuva Kendra Sangathan	31.50	8.85	40.35	31.91	8.54	40.45	31.91	9.63	41.54
2 National Service Scheme	21.78	2.07	23.85	21.78	2.36	24.14	22.65	2.50	25.15
3 Youth Hostels	0.60	....	0.60	0.60	....	0.60	0.45	....	0.45
4 Scouting & Guiding	0.49	....	0.49	0.49	....	0.49	0.30	....	0.30
5 Rajiv Gandhi National Institute of Youth Development	6.00	0.27	6.27	6.00	0.51	6.51	6.00	0.51	6.51
6 Scheme relating to Talent Search and Training	0.19	....	0.19	....	....	....	3.00	....	3.00
7 National Programme for Youth and Adolescent Development	6.83	....	6.83	6.83	....	6.83	6.83	....	6.83
8 National Youth Corps	19.06	....	19.06	15.81	....	15.81	15.78	....	15.78
Total	**86.45**	**11.19**	**97.64**	**83.42**	**11.41**	**94.83**	**86.92**	**12.64**	**99.56**

CHAPTER

9

Fiscal Responsibility and Budget Management: A Step towards Financial Discipline

"Physicians say of cancer, that in the early stages of this disease it is easy to cure but difficult to diagnose; whereas later on, if it has not been recognized and treated at the beginning, it becomes easy to diagnose and difficult to cure. The same thing happens in affairs of State." Machiavelli

The Central Government had been borrowing endlessly from the Reserve Bank of India; internal debt for India was among the highest in the world, while the external debt was low than most others. "Weak revenue performance and lack of expenditure control at both the Central and state government levels caused the consolidated deficit of the public sector to rise sharply to around 11 per cent of GDP in FY 1999/00, with public sector debt exceeding 80 per cent of GDP."[i]

Fiscal problem in India had arisen early 1980s onwards, as in the early 1980s there were revenue surplus for the states and also for the consolidated accounts of the Centre and the states. The deficit started mounting up in late 1980s. "Worsening of deficit came about through a combination of weak tax revenue, a sharp increase in the wage bill, rising interest payment and rising subsidies"[ii]. The combined total expenditure exceeded the combined total current receipts, resulting in a gap known as gross fiscal deficit. This gap has been financed largely through capital receipts namely,

(*a*) internal receipts: borrowings from the market, mobilization of small savings, provident fund collections, etc. and

(*b*) external loans and grants from governments, international institutions and commercial borrowings

The total outstanding liabilities of the Central government comprising internal and external liabilities as a percentage of GDP are estimated at 50.1 percent for the year 2012-13, though the corresponding percentage was 56.9 percent in the year 2007-08. As against this, the short term debt as a percent of GDP increased over the year from 3.67 percent in 2000-01 to 24.6 percent in 2012-13. Deficit indicators in the Central Government in India, as summarized in Exhibit 9.1 below has the following features:

(*a*) Despite attempts to contain revenue deficit, it has been rising over the years and is above three percent of GDP for the last five years.

(*b*) Fiscal deficit has been high and still is around 5.0 percent during the last three years and there have been pressure from the multi-national funding agencies to control it.

i. Shruti Rajagopalan, Fiscal Responsibility and Budget Management Bill 2000, Working Paper no. 0074 The Indian Economy (centre for Civil Society)

ii. Government of India, Ministry of Finance, (July 2004), Report of the ask Force on Implementation of the Fiscal Responsibility and Budget Management Act, 2003 (Also known as Kelkar Committee Report)

Exhibit : 9.1

Deficit Indicators

(₹ in crores)

Year	Revenue deficit	Fiscal deficit	Primary deficit
1990-91	18,560 (3.2)	44,630 (7.7)	23,130 (4.0)
1994-95	31,030 (3.0)	57,700 (5.6)	13,640 (1.3)
1995-96	29,730 (2.4)	60,240 (4.9)	10,200 (0.8)
1997-98	46,450 (3.3)	88,940 (6.3)	23,300 (1.6)
2007-08	52,569 (4.1)	126,912 (2.5)	(–0.9)
2008-09	253,539 (4.5)	336,992 (6.0)	NA (2.6)
2009-10	338,988 (5.2)	418,482 (6.5)	NA (3.2)
2010-11	252,252 (3.2)	373,592 (4.8)	NA (1.8)
2011-12	394,951 (4.3)	521,980 (5.7)	NA (2.6)
2012-13	350,424 (3.5)	513,590 (5.1)	NA (1.9)

Note: Figures in brackets are percentages of GDP.

Sources: Economic Survey, Government of India, Budget at a Glance, GOI.

Deficit financing is helpful and a valuable instrument in promoting economic development in the initial sages, but extreme caution is necessary in using deficit financing as it is intrinsically inflationary in character. As the saying goes, 'deficit financing, like fire, is a good servant but a bad master'. [iii]

As such, deficit and debt had attracted focused attention because of the following deficit problems:

- deficit had been a large proportion of GDP;
- deficit comprised of revenue deficit arising due to higher current consumption expenditure of the government, and the primary deficit, which was the fiscal deficit less interest payments;
- growing debt, which was the accumulated deficit from the past;
- growing interest burden on public debt, an obligatory expenditure that constrained the flexibility available with the government for resource allocation; and
- financing a part of the high deficit through borrowings from the Reserve Bank of India.

For example, interest expenditure of the Central Government increased 51 times over the two decades from 1979-80 as a result of mounting debt and accumulated deficit over the years. Interest payments of ₹ 902 billion by the Central Government preempted 40 per cent of gross tax and non-tax revenues in 1999-2000. Taking together the defence revenue expenditure, major subsidies and transfer to the States, the Center had to borrow to meet interest burden and other items of revenue expenditure. This emphasized the desperate need for legislation on the ceiling of the expenditure of the Central Government and to put a cap on Government borrowings.

The persistent fiscal deficit and the steadily high Debt/GDP ratio constituted the most important challenges affecting India's growth prospects. In response to this challenge, the Government constituted on 17th January, 2000, a Committee on Fiscal Responsibility Legislation to go into various aspects of the fiscal system. The Committee recommended draft legislation on fiscal responsibility. This was followed by an announcement in the Budget 2000-2001 for a strong institutional mechanism embodied in a "Fiscal Responsibility Act" and to bring the necessary legislative proposals to the House during the course of the year. Accordingly, the Fiscal Responsibility and Budget Management Bill, 2000 was introduced in Lok Sabha in December 2000.

iii. International Monetary Fund: India' Experience with Fiscal Rules- Working Paper August 2009 (WP/09/1750 prepared by Alejandro Sergio Simone and Petia Topalova)

The proposed law casted an obligation on the Government itself to strengthen the institutional framework for conduct of prudent and accountable fiscal policy and paved the way for promoting greater macro-economic stability. The proposed Fiscal Responsibility and Budget Management legislation was to provide a legal and institutional framework to bring down the fiscal deficit, contain the growth of public debt and stabilise debt as a proportion of GDP over the medium term. It would bind future governments to a pre-specified path of fiscal consolidation. This covered only the finances of the Central Government. The matter regarding similar legislation at State level would be for State Governments to pursue.

The Fiscal Responsibility and Budget Management (FRBM) Act was enacted by the Parliament in 2003 to bring in fiscal discipline. The Act came into effect on July 5, following the issue by the Finance Ministry of the notification and the FRBM Rules 2004 made under the Act. A central requirement of the FRBM Act concerned the revenue deficit in 2007 -8: it required that government undertake[iv]:

> "*appropriate measures to reduce the fiscal deficit and revenue deficit so as to eliminate revenue deficit by 31st March 2008 and thereafter build up adequate revenue surplus*"

This date was extended to March 31, 2009 by an amendment to the FRBM Act.

The FRBM Rules imposed limits on fiscal and revenue deficit and also on borrowings by the Government.

Exhibit 9.2 below summarises the main requirements under the FRBM Act 2003 and under the FRBM Rules.

Exhibit : 9.2

Requirements of the FRBM

Requirement	FRBM Act	FRBM Rules
• *Revenue deficit*		
Date for elimination	31 March, 2008	
Minimum annual gain		0.5% of GDP
• *Fiscal deficit to GDP*		
Ceiling		3% by 31 March, 2008
Minimum annual gain		0.3% of GDP
• *Guarantees*		
Maximum annual issuance		0.5% of GDP
Total liabilities		incremental flow capped at 9 percent of GDP in 2004- 05; this ceiling to be reduced by 1 percentage point of GDP every year.
• *RBI primary market purchases of GOI bonds*	Cease on 1/4/2006	

Source: Dr. Vijay Kelkar Report (2004)

The FRBM Act has four main requirements.

First, it required the Government to place before the Parliament every year three statements along, with the Budget, covering

iv. ***Kannan, R., and Lahiri, Ashok. 2002. India's fiscal deficits and their Sustainability in perspective. New Delhi: National Institute of Public Finance and Policy.***

(*a*) Medium Term Fiscal Policy Statement,
(*b*) Fiscal Policy Strategy Statement
(*c*) Macroeconomic Framework Statement

These were intended to bring in improvements in the area of transparency and medium-term fiscal planning.

(*a*) **The Medium-term Fiscal Policy Statement** covered a three-year rolling target for four specific fiscal indictors in relation to GDP at market prices namely,
   (*i*) Revenue Deficit
   (*ii*) Fiscal Deficit
   (*iii*) Tax to GDP ratio and
   (*iv*) Total outstanding debt at the end of the year.

   The statement included the underlying assumptions, an assessment of sustainability relating to balance between revenue receipts and revenue expenditure and use of capital receipts including market borrowings for generation of productive assets.

(*b*) **Fiscal Policy Strategy Statement :** This statement specifies the policy measures pertaining to taxation, expenditure, subsidies, administered prices borrowing and guarantees. This statement also explains how current policies are in conformity with sound fiscal management principles and gives the rationale for any major deviation in key fiscal measures.

(*c*) **Macroeconomic Framework Statement** This report shows the underlying assessment of growth prospects of the economy and the underlying assumptions. It contains assessment regarding the GDP growth rate, the fiscal balance of the Central Government and the external sector balance of the economy.

Second, the Act laid down fiscal management principles, making it incumbent on the Centre to "reduce the fiscal deficit" (no target is mentioned in the Act, but the Rules prescribe three percent of GDP) and, more categorically, to "eliminate revenue deficit" by March 31, 2008, (later by an amendment of the FRBM Act, the date was extended to March 31, 2009). It required the Government to set a ceiling on guarantees (the rules prescribe 0.5 percent of GDP). The Act provided that the ceilings might be exceeded on grounds of "national security or national calamity or such other exceptional grounds as the Central Government may specify"

Third, the Act prohibited the Centre from borrowing from the Reserve Bank of India, *i.e.* it banned deficit financing through money creation. The RBI was also barred from subscribing to primary issues of Central Government securities though temporary Ways and Means advances to tide over cash flow problems are permitted. This provision would not apply till April 2006. Exceptions were also allowed whenever the Government declares an exceptional situation.

Fourth, the Finance Minister was required to keep Parliament informed through quarterly reviews of receipts and expenditure, and place the outcome of these reviews before Parliament. He was also required to make a statement in Parliament explaining the reasons for deviations from the FRBM Act obligations, and remedial measures that were proposed to be taken in order to overcome these.

FRBM ACT AND TASK FORCE

The Government set up a Task Force under the chairmanship of Dr. Vijay Kelkar on the implementation of the Fiscal Responsibility and Budget Management. The Task Force was primarily required to 'fix annual targets, indicating the path of adjustment and required measures'. But it appears that the Task Force has assumed wider role and has made recommendations to bring about a radical transformation of the Indian Tax System.

The Task Force favoured a 'Revenue-led' approach to raise resources rather than the existing approach to reduce government expenditure to achieve fiscal consolidation. To justify, the Task Force stated that reducing government spending "would be contractionary for the macro economy", whereas "raising revenues is likely to be less contractionary." Further, the government should enhance capital expenditure "in order to counter-balance the contractionary effects of fiscal consolidation". The Task Force favoured revenue mobilization through low and few tax rates, alongside widening of the tax base and shifting the incidence of taxation on consumption. For the purpose, the Task Force proposed radical changes both in direct taxes and indirect taxes.

FISCAL RESPONSIBILITY: INTERNATIONAL EXPERIENCE

Fiscal responsibility, world wide has been accorded a greater focus over the years. Approaches followed towards fiscal responsibility could be put under two broad categories.

1. Fiscal Responsibility: by Pursuing Fiscal Reforms

First approach, a more generic one comprised of pursuing fiscal reforms and having some specific objective(s) in terms of deficit target (followed by Canada, Austria, Denmark, France,) and/ or limit on government borrowings (followed by Greece, Italy, UK); and/or target for expenditure growth (followed by Finland, Canada, Greece, Italy, Germany, Netherlands,) over the years. This approach had been followed widely by a large number of countries. The European Union and the Growth and Stability Pact of 1999, which bound members to bring down and then keep their deficits below three per cent of GDP was another example involving fiscal reforms. Strictly, this was a 'fiscal responsibility treaty' rather than an Act, but nevertheless legally binding. In the Years before the introduction of the euro, the Treaty appeared to have succeeded in achieving deficit reductions. Since then, however, its record had been awful, the Treaty had almost totally unravelled during this period, with the two biggest Euro countries *i.e.* France and Germany being in breach of the ceiling.

The Treaty even had provisions for a penalty in the form of a no interest bearing deposit of 0.2 per cent of GDP to be paid by defaulting countries, to be later treated as a fine if the problem remained unremedied in two years. However, the European Council of Ministers chose not to enforce the provisions, by disagreeing with the recommendation of the European Commission (the executive wing). This decision was taken with full transparency (as required by the Pact) and detailed written reasons, even disclosing who voted for and against.

On July 12, 2004 the European Court of Justice held that countries could not simply waive the provisions, but the Council nevertheless does have the right to desist from collecting the penalty. Infact, the Treaty has become more of a statement of good intentions than a binding legal obligation. This raises questions:

Whether a government not politically committed to a particular level of fiscal prudence can be restrained by the passing of fiscal responsibility legislation? The answer is clearly, 'no'. Does the Act serve any purpose at all? Perhaps it does.

In other words, it has the barking dog effect on outsiders, as house owners know, barking dogs do have value even if they do not bite. Part of the value of the Act lies in its apparent strictness. The barking dog could perhaps impress Moody's and Standard & Poor's and international onlookers as a credible commitment to fiscal responsibility, with consequent benefits for borrowing costs.

2. Fiscal Responsible Legislation

Second approach involved fiscal responsibility legislation to impose fiscal discipline. This approach was intended to have transparency of fiscal policy process and had taken two routes as:

(a) Fiscal Responsible Legislation: *Generic objectives* – New Zealand Fiscal Responsibility Act 1994[v] was the most notable and the first example of legislation designed to impose

v. ***OECD: Budgeting for Results: Perspectives on Public Expenditure Management, OECD Governance (vol. 1995, No.2, August 2009),***

fiscal discipline largely through legislated fiscal reporting requirements that increased the transparency of fiscal policy process. It set a general range of objectives based on the principle of prudence and stability. The New Zealand Act had been hailed by many experts as a model, and from an economist's point of view, it was conceptually and theoretically elegant. However, enactment was passed by a government that gave up control over its Central bank, and was already strongly committed to a tight fiscal policy and indeed to all the elements of conservative economic orthodoxy. Further, the New Zealand Act provided a generic range of objectives and also a very large degree of flexibility, this perhaps is more than the Indian FRBM Act.

The New Zealand Act did not set specific targets, rather it required governments to set targets and follow broad principles of economic management. The New Zealand Government's long-term objectives included:

- reducing net public debt to below 20 per cent of GDP; achieving at least fiscal balance over the economic cycle once net public debt was below 20 per cent of GDP;
- maintaining a broad-base and low-rate tax environment;
- reducing current outlays to below 30 per cent of GDP;
- restoring net worth to significantly positive levels and reducing risks to the fiscal position.
- benefits from the New Zealand Act reported included :
  - enhanced credibility of the fiscal policy process
  - improved focus on decision-making
  - a focus on balance sheet concepts and a related attention to the efficiency of asset use
  - identification of formerly hidden contingent liabilities
  - an acceptance of the principles of risk management in government
  - increased pressure on the New Zealand Treasury to improve its forecasting performance arising from the Act's transparency and accountability requirements

(*b*) **Fiscal Responsible Legislation:** *Specific and Measurable Fiscal Objectives-* France and the United States and later India had been exponents of the other approach of legislation which laid down more specific and measurable fiscal objectives and also put a ceiling on the deficit. In keeping with the trade-off between flexibility and the binding nature of constraints, the New Zealand approach would enable a more flexible fiscal policy response to changes in economic conditions while the approach of laying specific and measurable fiscal objectives in theory, may provide more certainty that fiscal policy would follow a particular course. The US followed another route of Fiscal Responsibility Legislation which though put a ceiling on the deficit and forced the US Government to reduce it (the so-called Gramm-Rudman-Hollings Act of the Reagan era), was an abject failure. This was largely because the cuts required to enforce the Act became impractical in the face of unavoidable increases in expenditure on mandatory items like, social security. The Act was simply violated and the deficit continued to rise. This gave rise to the Budget Enforcement Act which was enacted in 1990 in an effort to control future budgetary actions, having the limits to laydown on discretionary spending, and the pay-as-you-go process to require that any legislative action on direct spending or revenues, which would increase the deficit, be offset.

Fiscal responsibility laws in Latin America [vi], with special attention to their provisions for

vi. ***Webb, Steven B., Fiscal responsibility laws for subnational Discipline : The Latin American experience World Bank Policy Research Paper 3309, May 2004 (World Bank Washington DC)***

fiscal discipline by sub national governments is useful-to help resolve the coordination problem in getting diverse governments to avoid overusing the common national credit market and to help individual governments make a time-consistent commitment for fiscal prudence. The same was true of the cases of Brazil, Colombia, Peru, and Argentina, as well as the case of Mexico where other types of laws and regulations aim to achieve the same objectives of solidifying incentives for fiscal discipline at all levels of government.

FRBM AND AUTONOMY OF CENTRAL BANK

One of the important aspects of Fiscal Responsibility legislation was to give more autonomy to the Central Bank of the country. The Central Bank autonomy generally related to three areas, *i.e.* (*a*) personnel matters referring to autonomy of management officials, their appointment, or the governing board; (*b*) financial aspects, which referred to access of the Government to Central bank credit; and (*c*) conduct of policy related to flexibility to the Central bank in the formulation and execution of monetary policy.

Reserve Bank in India was divested of ownership functions in commercial banking, development finance and securities trading entities. It was recommended to divestiture RBI of the supervisory functions about co-operative banks, non-banking financial companies and also of commercial banks. Lastly, to separate the Government Debt management functions from the monetary policy, the Government had decided to create an independent debt management office (DMO) to consolidate all debt management functions of the government. The DMO was planned to be operational by 2012. This would enable the RBI to primarily focus on its role as monetary authority and enhance the possibility of a move towards greater autonomy. In order to make the FRBM Act effective, following are the recommendations:

- Central Government should not borrow from the RBI
- To have Expenditure Reduction Act along with the FRBM Act
- Follow the recommendations of the Expenditure Reform Commission to cut non-productive expenditure on government departments
- To stop State Government guarantees
- RBI to make prescriptions on each state on its finances
- To stop monetizing budget deficits
- To adopt accrual basis of accounting for all the government departments
- To rely on other indicators such as, interest rates, saving rates, currency rates, etc.
- To give the RBI more autonomy in personnel matters, financial matters and conduct of policy

FRBM ACT AND RULES IN INDIA

The FRBM Act in India was unusual. Act of Parliament is usually directed at prescribing the law to be followed by the public or a class of persons or by the government in its dealings with others, either the public at large or a section of it.

The FRBM Act, on the other hand, was aimed at fettering the Centre itself from doing things that Parliament did not want it to do. No party other than the government itself was legally bound by the Act. The Rules were even more unusual; the Centre was to issue them in order to constrain itself.

As regards the issue of effectiveness of the legislative, one view was that Rules were 'largely cosmetic'; the Government could itself amend them. If the three per cent fiscal deficit target was found unrealistic, a notification from the Finance Ministry could change it to any other figure say, four percent; if more guarantees were to be issued, the target could be raised to any desired level. Requirement of placing of three statements before the Parliament was not much of a difficulty as the Economic Survey and the Budget Speech would suffice to prepare all three of the new statements.

However, a firm target of eliminating the revenue deficit by 2008 (later on extended to 2009 by an amendment) in the Act was welcome and uncontroversial objective; and the target could be relaxed, by the Government. For examples, a bad monsoon or an international recession or an oil crisis might well qualify as a "national calamity" or at least as an "other exceptional circumstance". In such a situation, the other hard provision *i.e.* prohibition on deficit financing was also lifted. All these did not require an amendment of the Act. In other words, the FRBM Act could be amended routinely by simply adding a clause to the annual Finance Act, the way the Income Tax Act or Sales Tax Act is amended. Further, psychologically, any amendment in the Act, as a routine clause would not result in fall of the Government. The fact is that, the first amendment was introduced by the Finance Minister within three days of the Act coming into force, to postpone the date for elimination of revenue deficit from March 2008 to March 2009. Overall effect of the Act had been likened as a :

"pact between a heavy smoker and his wife, in which the Wife (concerned for his health) prescribes the maximum number of cigarettes per day with a gradual reduction to nil; after giving him the agreed number, she would lock away the cigarette box, but leave the key with him in case of 'emergency' smoking needs, the only condition being that he should tell her after each emergency. Also, if he really felt bad, she would even amend the ceiling for a while, till he felt better".

Further, concerns had been expressed at the rising fiscal deficit, to reduce the scope for window dressing in government finances; to reduce opportunities for creative accounting and biased forecasts. For example, the fiscal deficit of the Central government, in the budget documents for the year 2008-09 was 6.2 percent of gross domestic product (GDP) for 2008-09, in practical terms it worked out to eight percent after taking into account the off-budget expenses, especially the oil bonds. Lastly, the IMF had said that the FRBM framework should "define precisely the accounting framework and definitions for target fiscal indicators".

CHAPTER 10

Accrual Accounting in Government : Concept and Roadmap

Importance of accounting method can be emphasized by the statement, 'there cannot be adequate accounting without adequate record keeping, and there cannot be adequate management without adequate accounting'.

CASH BASIS

Accounting system in government is normally cash based wherein economic events are recorded according to movement of cash. Under this system, revenues are recorded and accounted for when cash is received, expenses when cash is paid irrespective of the accounting period in which the service is rendered or the benefits are received. It does not record accounts for assets, or their usage; or does not record accruals or outstanding. Cash basis of accounting is consistent with the budget approval by the legislature; it puts limit on expenditure and is a means of control over government expenditure. The financial year for a government in India commences on April 1, and ends on March 31 of the next year; the budgetary outlay not spent by the end of the year is not carried forward to the next financial year and the amount lapses. In other words, any cash transaction that takes place after 31 March is not included in accounts of the previous year.

To illustrate, for every transaction, there are four phases;

(*a*) Issue of order or contract for the supply of goods/services;

(*b*) Receipts of goods/services and commencement of liability;

(*c*) Settlement of the liability by payments of the amount due;

(*d*) Usage or consumption of goods/service

In addition, there is a management decision to spend money arising from the budget approval which precedes the above four phases. These four phases may occur at the same time or at different times; under cash basis, accounting records when cash is paid. In other words, accounting system does not take cognition of any phase other than cash; *i.e.* when order is placed, or when assets are received, or assets are put to use. To put it in other words, every transaction has two aspects and only cash received or paid is recorded under cash basis of accounting, and the other aspect is not considered in accounting. For examples,

Transaction		Cash Basis Aspect Recorded
i). Purchase of machinery for cash ₹ 5 lakh: two aspects are:		
a). cash paid ₹ 5 lakh	*b*) machinery acquired ₹ 5 lakh	*a*). cash paid ₹ 5 lakh
ii). Purchase of machinery on credit: the two aspects are:		
a). outstanding liability;	*b*) machinery acquired	None

iii). Salary @ ₹ 60,000 pm, payment made to a manager for his services during the year ₹ 7,20,000: two aspects are : *a*). cash paid ₹ 7,20,000 *b*). salary expense ₹ 7,20,000	*a*). cash paid ₹ 7,20,000
iv). Salary @ ₹ 60,000 pm, payment made to a manager for his services during the year ₹ 6,00,000 & ₹ 1,20,000 remains as an outstanding liability: two aspects are : *a*). cash paid ₹ 6,00,000 *b*). salary expense ₹ 7,20,000 and (Outstanding liability ₹1,20,000)	*a*). cash paid ₹ 6,00,000

In the above four examples, the only cash received or paid aspects are recorded in accounts while the other aspects are not recorded in the account records.

In other words, for transactions (*i*), (*iii*) and (*iv*) above, accounts under cash basis will record, only (*one*) aspect as

(*i*) ₹ 5 lakh cash paid
(*iii*) cash paid ₹ 7,20,000
(*iv*) cash paid ₹ 6,00,000

Thus there is no accounting record for the machinery acquired, or outstanding liability, or salary expense, or salary outstanding liability. This system is also known as single entry system as it records only one aspect of the transaction; or is also termed as 'incomplete system' of accounting as it does not record both the aspects of a transaction. In other words, cash basis has the primary shortcoming that it fails to capture, aspects other than the cash receipt or cash payment.

Cash basis is simple, economical to administer and provides information to assess compliance with the legislative requirements and to control expenditure. In addition, it provides following advantages[i]:

- it promotes accountability and control as it facilitates comparison between budgeted and actual cash expenditure;
- it facilitates legislative control of expenditure;
- it is unambiguous and presents factual financial information;
- it concentrates on disbursement of money and is consistent with the cash; cash movement in and out of government.

However, cash basis of accounts lacks in respects of the following:

- does not generate information about asset management, as a result we don't know, what is the total value of assets owned by the government or its department;
- does not generate information to assess the long-term economic impact of the current policies;
- makes no allowance for usage of asset;
- does not generate information regarding cost of a service provided, like, cost per unit of electricity generated, or cost per unit of drinking water supplied, or cost per bed per day of a hospital;
- produces a very imperfect measure of economic cost and is inadequate for certain types of decision making concerning costs, efficiency and resource usage;
- doesn't provide information regarding the performance of a programme or a government department;

i. ***United Nations (1988), Government Accounting and Financial Reporting in Developing Countries, (New York)***

- makes no allowance for stocks held at period-end;
- distorts currents year's cost because of consumption, paid for in previous or subsequent years
- does not provide information of the amount recoverable, or amount payables.

In other words, to quote the United Nations, "At the operational level, the cash basis of accounting has been identified as the major cause for unnecessary operational rush at the year end to carry out procurement transactions, and to process payments. Such avoidable rush and associated side-tracking of normal administrative procedure are aimed at exhausting budgetary allocations or reducing the level of unspent balances which would otherwise lapse at the period end"[ii]

ACCRUAL BASIS

Under accrual approach, accounting recognizes transactions and events as they occur rather than when cash is received or paid. For example, in the above four transactions i), ii), iii), & iv), both the aspects are recorded in accounts and so it is also known as 'double entry system' or commercial accounting and is mandatory for commercial enterprises. In other words, for the above four transactions, both the aspects recorded will be as:

Transaction	Accrual Basis: Aspects Recorded
(*i*) Purchase of machinery for cash ₹ 5 lakh: two aspects are: (*a*) cash paid ₹ 5 lakh (*b*) machinery acquired ₹ 5 lakh	(*a*) cash paid ₹ 5 lakh (*b*) machinery acquired ₹ 5 lakh
(*ii*) Purchase of machinery on credit: the two aspects are: (*a*) outstanding liability; (*b*) machinery acquired	(*a*) outstanding liability; (*b*) machinery acquired
(*iii*) Salary @ ₹ 60,000 pm paid to a manager for his services during the year ₹ 7,20,000: two aspects are : (*a*) cash paid ₹ 7,20,000 (*b*) salary expense ₹ 7,20,000	(*a*) cash paid ₹ 7,20,000 (*b*) salary expense ₹ 7,20,000
(*iv*) Salary @ ₹ 60,000 pm, payment made to a manager for his services during the year ₹ 6,00,000 & ₹ 1, 20,000 remains as an outstanding liability: two aspects are : (*a*) cash paid ₹ 6,00,000 (*b*) salary expense ₹ 7,20,000 (Outstanding liability ₹1,20,000)	(*a*) cash paid ₹ 6,00,000 Salary Outstanding liability ₹ 1,20,000) (*b*) salary expense ₹ 7,20,000

The accrual basis of accounting would result in accounting for cash receipts and paid, receivables, payables or outstanding liabilities, and assets like, machinery, building, furniture and also a charge for the usage of fixed assets, known as depreciation. In other words, accrual accounting reflects income earned, expenses incurred during the period, or cost of service rendered and revenue earned from that service. Thus it shows surplus or deficit for the period; assets owned, or net worth as on a date. These are reflected in the two financial statements namely, balance sheet and Income & Expenditure Statement (or also called profit and loss account). For example, for a department, say, Delhi Jal Board, accrual account will provide information relating to expenses incurred for providing water, revenue earned on account of water supply, funds deployed in various assets of the Jal Board, amount due to and due by the Jal Board, its liabilities, its net worth and also changes in its net worth over the period.

The information generated would be useful to assess the financial performance and long-term sustainability of the policies of the Jal Board. In other words, the accrual basis captures all the four phases of transactions and thus is called 'complete system of accounting'.

ii. ibid

Accrual basis of accounting has following advantages:

- It measures inputs in terms of resources consumed;
- It makes possible the identification of economic cost i.e, the consumption of resources either paid for in prior years or to be paid for in the future, both are considered in the annual result of operations to the relevant year;
- It provides an accurate and comprehensive picture of financial position at the end of the period than that given by the cash basis.

To quote Das[iii], "Accrual accounting has highlighted issues about financial policy and performance, for the government as a whole, including assessment of the government's net worth and changes in it over time. It has also provided information on the long-term sustainability of policies, taking into account the future expenditure implications of the decisions. By recording unfunded pension liabilities and taking them into account while presenting the financial position of the government, accrual accounting has made transparent the transfer of costs to future generations. By providing such information, accrual accounting has been able to underpin intergenerational equity issues"

To compare cash basis and the accrual basis, we present below the financial information captured at each phase for both the bases, and also present the relevant need which this type of information satisfies. To iterate the accrual basis accounts for information for all phases of a transaction and is also known as a complete system of accounting

	Cash Basis	Accrual Basis
Type of Information captured: (*a*) Issue of order or contract for the supply of a good/ services;	No	Yes
(*b*) Receipts of good/service and commencement of liability;	No	Yes
(*c*) Settlement of the liability by payments of the amount due;	Yes	Yes
(*d*) Usage or consumption of goods/service	No	Yes
	• cash basis is needed to Manage Cash and Debt	• Accural basis is needed to plan programmes effectively and manage them efficiently • Control and manage Inventory • Manage Cash and Debt

New Zealand has accounting and accounting reports based on accrual system and many other countries like United States, UK, Australia, Sweden are moving towards accrual accounting. In India a number of municipalities like, Bengaluru, Ahmedabad, Delhi, Tamil Nadu, Hyderabad

iii. Das S K, Rethinking Public Accounting: Policy and Practice of Accrual Accounting in Government, (Oxford University Press, 2006)

have introduced accrual accounting. All these and many other organizations have adopted accrual accounting at the behest of the World Bank or other multi-national funding agencies which provided finances for various projects. All these examples of adoption of accrual accounting have been stand-alone exercises as there was no uniform accounting system that these municipal bodies could follow and these exercises have involved time-over-run.

Considering the imperative need to adopt accrual accounting, the Government in India has set up Government Accounting Standards Advisory Board (GASAB) in the office of the Comptroller and Auditor General of India (C&AG) to recommend an operational framework and a detailed road map for adoption of accrual accounting.

The Twelfth Finance Commission (TFC), recognizing the need for improvements in accounting and financial reporting, recommended a gradual shift to accrual accounting by the Union Government. The Central Government has accepted the recommendation in principle. In addition, eighteen State Governments have also accepted the idea of accrual accounting. Pursuant to Government's directions the GASAB has laid out a framework for transition from existing cash based accounting to accrual based accounting by the government. The framework provides a phased approach to the transition, as recommended by the TFC and broad guidance on the issues peculiar to government accounting.

The Roadmap prepared by GASAB for transition to accrual accounting envisages a period of 10-12 years for completing the transition. It prescribes setting up of a Task Force or Cell or a designating a nodal agency for coordination and overseeing the implementation. The broad framework for transition to accrual accounting as presented in Exhibit 10.1 is spread over five stages as under.[iv]:

Stage I – *Introduce Accrual based recognition Principle for current expenses*:

- Differentiate between revenue and capital transactions; which is being followed at present.
- Recognise revenue expenses on accrual basis and as a result recognize outstanding expenses as liabilities and expenses prepaid as assets;
- Recognise revenue receipts, like tax revenues, and non-tax revenue to be recognized on cash basis; and
- Capital transactions- both receipts and payments should be continued to be accounted for on cash basis as at present.

Stage II – *Non-tax revenues to be recognized on accrual basis:*

- Tax revenue to be recognized on cash basis, while non-tax revenue are to recognized on accrual basis
- Military assets are to be recognized on accrual basis, while remaining capital expenditure continue to be recognized on cash basis

Stage III – *Recognise all expenses on accrual basis including recognition of depreciation but not of provisions:*

- Recognise all revenue expenses on accrual basis, including depreciation
- Don't recognise provisions
- Tax revenue to be recognized on cash basis
- Recognise all physical and financial assets (including inventories) on accrual basis with the exception of infrastructure like, land, heritage, intangibles
- Disclose all explicit contingent liabilities

Stage IV – *Recognise all expenses on accrual basis (as Stage III above) & also recognize provisions and infrastructure*

iv. ***Government Accounting Standards Advisory Board (GASAB), C&AG (GOI), Operational Framework of Accrual Basis of Accounting in Governments in India (February 2007)***

Stage V – *Introduce full accrual accounting for all the four elements namely, expense, revenues, assets, and liabilities*

Exhibit : 10.1

Roadmap for transition to Accrual accounting

	Revenue Expenses (Current)	**Revenue Income (Current)**	**Capital: Assets**	**Capital: Liabilities**	**Contingent Liabilities**
Stage I	Distinction: (*a*) Revenue Expenses & (*b*)Capital Expense (a) Accrual basis; (b) Cash basis	(*a*) Tax Revenue & (*b*) Non-tax Revenue (*a*) & (*b*) on Cash basis	Cash Basis– Assets acquired or disposed of.	Public debt & Borrowings on public a/c- Cash basis	Guarantees– Cash basis
Stage II	As in Stage I above	(*a*) On cash basis (*b*) On accrual basis	Cash basis– Assets Acquired and Disposed off. Accrual basis– Military assets	Public debt & Borrowings on public a/c- Payables + All other Liabilities: on cash basis	Same as above
Stage III	Accrual Basis - All revenue expenses (a) & (b) including depreciation	(*a*) On cash basis (*b*) On accrual basis	Accrual basis All physical and financial assets (excluding infrastructure, land, heritage, intangible assets)	Accrual Basis : All liabilities (except provisions & superannuation benefits)	Disclose all explicit contingent liabilities
Stage IV	Accrual Basis - All revenue expenses (a) & (b) including depreciation	(*a*) On cash basis (*b*) On accrual basis	Accrual Basis - All physical and financial assets, and infrastructure excluding heritage and intangibles	Accrual Basis : All liabilities including provisions	Same as above
Stage V	All Revenue expenses on Accrual Basis	All revenues on Accrual basis	All Assets : On Accrual Basis	All Liabilities on Accrual Basis	Same as above

As regards presentation of accounts, the Parliamentary Committee on Papers in its Sixtieth Report (March 1998) observed that there has not been any set standards of presentation of accounts of the institutions/organizations receiving grants-in-aid from the Government. The method of presentation of accounts of statutory boards/corporations/organizations is totally dismal and is not in keeping with the requirement of transparency and exposure of professional skill of these organizations. They do not give a lucid presentation of their accounts and large number of items of accounts of all such organizations generally remain incomplete, unscrutinised and in arrears for several years. (Committee of Experts on Uniform Format of Accounts, 2000)[v].

Recommendations of the Committee are as:[vi]

- All the autonomous organizations should follow one common format for its accounting and presentation of accounting information.
- Within the common format of accounts, further additional information might be given/ prescribed for the Central Universities & other Educational Institutions and for the District Rural Development Agencies.
- The Financial Statements and its Schedules would provide full disclosure of the organization and all the accounting information.
- Provision for depreciation on fixed assets was to be made applicable in respect of all autonomous organizations.
- The accounting would be based on the principles of accrual system of accounting and the concept of 'going concern' would have to be maintained.
- Financial Statements of the Central Autonomous organizations as recommended, would contain balance sheet, income & expenditure account, statement of receipts and payments. The formats prescribed should be made applicable for all accounting years commencing on or after 1.4.2001. Earlier application was encouraged.

Similarly, the Supreme Court, in response to a writ petition before it, ordered[vii] in 2001 that the Municipal Corporation of Delhi (MCD) and the New Delhi Municipal Corporation. "will be required to maintain accounts as per the mercantile system (accrual system) of accounting and stated that the necessary amendments to the regulations be carried out by the Government of India for the same". Further, the Government of India through the budgetary provisions for fiscal 2002, recommended that the Development Authorities and Housing Boards be brought under the tax net and therefore amended Section 10 (20A) of the Income Tax Act 1961. So in order to determine income tax liability of the Development Authorities and Housing Boards, accounting on accrual system became a pre-requisite. As such accrual system of accounting has been implemented in a number of organizations namely, Delhi Municipal Corporation, Kolkata Municipal Corporation, Bengaluru Municipal Corporation, Hyderabad Municipal Corporation Ahmedabad Municipal Corporation, Controller General of Accounts, Department of Post, Municipal Bodies in Tamil Nadu (*i.e*, five Municipal Corporations, and 102 municipalities)

ACCRUAL ACCOUNTING IMPLEMENTATION

For adoption of accrual accounting, a certain number of conditions are pre-requisite, these include[viii]:

- participation of the accountancy profession and joint development of accounting standards,

---

v. Committee of Experts on Uniform Format of Accounts for Central Autonomous Bodies, Report of, A Committee Constituted by the Government on the recommendations of the Parliamentary Committee on Papers (Nov.2000)

vi. ibid

vii. Implementing Accrual Based Accounting System, The Chartered Accountant, (July 2010).

viii. Hepworth Noel (2000), Changing to accrual accounting in Central Government, (with particular regards to the experiences of the United Kingdom), Norway: Institute of Public Finance Limited (IPF), FEE

- an appropriate cultural approach and commitment of top management to accrual accounting,
- a robust audit process,
- an IT capacity

Given the above conditions, steps for introduction of accrual accounting are as under:

- Prepare Accounting Manual and Guidelines
- Develop Chart of Accounts in which account heads are grouped logically under a functional hierarchy of main heads, sub heads and sub-sub-heads
- Distinguish between capital and revenue accounts
- Identify and locate assets,
  - Defining methods of valuation of the assets
  - Ascertain the original cost of the assets, or define the method of their valuation, or useful life, and so ascertain their opening balances
  - Similarly, identify, locate and value various liabilities
  - Arrange training of employees.

From above, prepare opening balance sheet indicating assets, liabilities, prepaid expenses or outstanding liabilities.

- Prepare balance sheet and profit & Loss accounts for the period:
- Carry revenue items (revenue expenses and revenue receipts) pertaining to the period to the income & expenditure statement
- There may be items of revenue expenses which do not pertain to a particular year rather these relate to a number of years and are known as deferred revenue expenses and are spread over in the income & expenditure statement for the years.
- Provide depreciation on fixed assets at the rates prescribed.
- Carry the assets and liabilities in the balance sheet.

ACCOUNTING AND FINANCIAL REPORTING FORMAT RECOMMENDED MODIFIED CASH BASIS[ix]

With the objective to bring in transparency and uniformity in financial reporting by NPOs, mainly of smaller size and of having associational structure, accrual accounting may not be agreeable as it would involve time and efforts, modified cash basis of financial reporting system could be recommended with the following main features. This is a stop-gap arrangement, till the time NPOs are equipped to switch over to accrual accounting and such switch over should be cost-effective to their requirements. Necessary training and development of manuals towards accrual accounting should be the responsibility of professional bodies.

- Distinction should be made between revenue and capital transactions. Revenue incomes and expenses for the period should be recorded in the income and expenditure statement on receipt basis. Incomes or revenue contributions are shown on receipts rather than on accrual, without any adjustment for outstanding or for receipts in advance. However, adjustments be made for bills received for goods or services procured, by showing such items as expenses in income statement and also as a liability in the balance sheet.
- Fixed asset created on incurring an expenditure exceeding certain amount, say ₹ 1,000, and that asset having an estimated economic life of more than one year be shown at 'cost'. These should not be adjusted for depreciation and depreciation be not reflected as an

ix. ***Dhameja Nand NPOs- Accounting & Financial Reporting Framework (Indian Journal of Public Administration December. 2005)***

expense in the income & expenditure statement. It is on the ground that, depreciation being a non-cash item, does not involve out flow of cash, its estimation is influenced more by judgment, is open to diverse estimation and has been a source of creative accounting.

- Materials should be shown as consumed as and when purchased, as such there is no inventory stock in the balance sheet
- Thus NPOs should prepare following three financial statements:
  - Income and Expenditure Statement
  - Balance Sheet
  - Receipt and Payment Account

There should be a prescribed format for balance sheet and details of all assets and liabilities, incomes and expenses be given in separate schedules which should be integral part of balance sheet and income and expenditure account.

Statement of Accounting Policies should contain all significant policies followed.

In short, modified cash basis is a simpler accounting and financial reporting system, primarily following cash basis having the distinction of revenue and capital items; adjusting for prepaid or outstanding expenses for which bills have been received; recording materials purchased as consumed, and recording fixed assets on cost, without any provision for depreciation.

Lastly, referring to web-sites of various municipal corporations, one finds details about their management, organization structure, functions and activities, but there is little information about their finances, *i.e.* assets, liabilities, expenses and incomes; may be accrual accounting system, as discussed above, is only on paper and the accounting reports are meant for internal use.

APPENDIX - I

Introduction of Zero Base Budgeting

Government of Maharashtra

Finance Department

Instructions dated

27th October, 1986

Preamble

The Seventh Five-year Plan has to be implemented in the context of severe resource constrains being faced by the State Government. It is, therefore necessary that strenuous efforts are made for pruning of wasteful expenditures. Existing procedures for the scrutiny of expenditure proposals will have to be strengthened and subjected to the discipline of cost-effectiveness. Administrative reforms to eliminate unnecessary work, reduce overlap and simplify procedures will have to be hastened. There is a need to re-examine planning and budgetary procedures, so that an integrated view is taken of developmental outlays, regardless of whether they are on new schemes of the current plan or on the maintenance of schemes started in the earlier plans. It is further necessary that the rationale for each subsidy proposal is examined thoroughly taking into account the possibility of leakages, the economic status of beneficiary groups and the cost-benefit of the subsidy. All existing staff norms will have to be carefully reviewed. Additional resources for investments will have to be found largely by close scrutiny of schemes and programmes sanctioned in the past, their costs and benefits and their relevance for continuance in the future. Past committed levels of expenditure need not be considered as sacrosanct any longer.

As one of the means of achieving the objectives mentioned in the preamble above, Government is pleased to issue to following directions.

Resolution

1. The Zero Base Budgeting (ZBB) approach should be adopted by all departments of Government while formulating budget proposals with effect from the Budget for 1987-88.
2. Zero Base Budgeting (ZBB) requires identification and sharpening of objectives; examination of various alternative ways of achieving those objectives; selecting the best alternative through cost-benefit and cost-effectiveness analysis; prioritisation of objectives and programmes; switching of resources from programmes with lower priority to those of higher priority; and identification and elimination of programmes which have outlived their utility. It is proposed to carry out a continuous review of all on -going activities of the Government on this basis.
3. Each of the Administrative Departments should, to begin with, assume their total 1987-88 "Non-Plan Funding" to be only 80 per cent of the level of funding they have received in 1986-87. Police, Law and Judiciary and Jails Department, may assume their "Non-Plan Funding" for 1987-88 to be at the same level as the current year's level of funding. However, Zero Base Review will have to be conducted in respect of each scheme/activity by these departments also. Assuming a 20 per cent budget reduction, each of the Administrative Departments must identify lowest priority activities and functions, which might be considered for merging, reduction or elimination. Funds for any new items of expenditure which departments would like to propose will have to be largely found by pruning activities of lower priority in their own departments. All Administrative Department should prepare

their "Minimum Level Non-Plan Budget Package" as indicated above immediately for adoption while framing non-plan budget for 1987-88.

4. The Zero-Base budgeting technique should be applied not only to items of non-development expenditure but also to those of development expenditure. As far as the 1987-88 budget is concerned, the exercise may, if necessary and if absolutely unavoidable, be restricted to the "Non-Plan" part of the budget. While formulating budgets for subsequent years (i,e., 1988-99 onwards). plan schemes and programmes should also be brought within the purview of Zero-Base Review.
5. Staff rendered surplus as a result of Zero-Base Review will be pooled in the "Surplus Cell" in the General Administration Department for redeployment elsewhere.
6. Saving effected by the Administrative Departments due to Zero-Base Budgetary reviews will, to the maximum extent feasible, be given to the respective Departments as additional outlays for duly approved plan schemes.
7. Zero-Base Budgeting will succeed only if it is used as a management tool and does not deteriorate into a mindless form-filling exercise. Towards this end, it has been decided that Secretaries of all Administrative Departments should be made personally responsible for its implementation and success. With continued determination and perseverance, the Zero-Base Budgeting approach will be an excellent method to prune fat and allocate resources more scientifically. To ensure continued commitment to Zero-Base Budgeting approach, the annual performance of all officers on this item should be monitored periodically. The annual performance appraisal of all Senior Officers would be based, among other criteria, on the achievement of the officers in this important area of Government's new initiative.
8. As regards Department Undertakings and Autonomous Bodies under each Administrative Department, the above procedure may be adopted *mutatis mutandis* keeping in view the nature of their functions and the extent of autonomy granted to them by the Government.

By order and in the name of the
Government of Maharashtra.

MADHAV GODBOLE
Secretary to Government,
Finance Department.

APPENDIX - II

Introduction of Zero Base Budgeting

Government of Maharashtra
Finance Department
Circular
16th December, 1986

The State is going through a severe resource constraint in spite of a substantial resource mobilisation effort undertaken during the current year, we would still have serious difficulty in having an annual plan of reasonable size for 1987-88. With a view to getting more out of every rupee of Government expenditure, Government has introduced Zero Base Budgeting in all its departments with effect from the Budget for 1987-88.

In traditional budgeting, we accept last year's expenditure figures as the base. We then increment them to account for inflation, increase in salary, etc. We assume a further reasonable increase while admitting new items of expenditure for a particular department. Every year the budgeting exercise starts with the previous year's expenditure figures as the base. Such traditional budgeting system makes two assumption :-

(*a*) Schemes and programmes sanctioned in the past need to be continued without any further examination when the budget is prepared.

(*b*) The methods used for achieving a particular task are perhaps the best methods and there is no scope for alternative cost-effective methods.

These two assumptions behind traditional budgeting are not always the valid assumptions. There must obviously be a great deal which we should be able to give up from the schemes started long time ago.

Instructions regarding introduction of Zero-Base Budgeting have already been issued on 27th October 1986. Broadly speaking, Zero Base Budgeting is a continuous search for alternatives. It should be viewed as an approach to resource allocation rather than a uniform set of procedures. Note A to this circular gives the broad methodology of Zero Base Budgeting and lists out the steps involved in a Zero Base Budgeting exercise.

Due to anticipated shortfall for financing the Annual Plan for 1987-88, a certain percentage of plan outlays of various plan sectors is proposed to be kept unbudgeted. The provisions against these unbudgeted outlays could be made by way of supplementary demands **only after and to the extent** the saving in non-plan provisions agreed to be affected are identified and decisions thereon are taken by the Government. It will, therefore, be in the interest of the departments concerned that they complete the exercise as expeditiously as possible and intimate reductions in non-plan provisions of 1987-88 to the Planning Department and the Finance Department.

Due to certain commitments of Government, there will be a shortfall in the resources available for the Annual Plan for 1986-87. It has therefore, become necessary to effect cuts to the plan outlays of the current year under various sectors. The Planning Department will intimate the cuts applied to the various provisions to the departments concerned separately. However, as a result of the Zero Base Budgeting exercise, if the departments are in a position to indicate positive savings in the remaining period of the current year, the cuts applied to the plan provision for the current year could be restored to that extent.

Zero Base Budgeting will be a continuous process. This process will act as a prelude to the actual framing of the budget every year. Zero Base Budgeting will succeed only if it is ensured that it received support at the top level. Secretaries of Administrative Departments are, therefore, requested to motivate all the officers of their Departments to adopt Zero Base Budgeting and identify the possible savings on priority basis.

By order and in the name of the
Governor of Maharashtra

MADHAV GODBOLE
Secretary to Government,
Finance Department

Note A

Methodology be adopted for Zero Base Budgeting and the broad steps in Zero Base Budgeting exercise.

1. Methodology for Zero Base Budgeting

(*a*) The top management in each department must identify the "Decision Units" in the organisation i.e., levels of management where decision involving expenditure are made. It should also specify and communicate to all decision units, the overall objectives and missions of the department.

(*b*) Each "Decision Unit" should explore the various alternative ways of achieving its own objectives and do a cost-benefit analysis of these alternatives, wherever possible.

(*c*) Each "Decision Unit" should then proceed to do the ranking of the above alternatives or "Decision Packages".

(*d*) The next higher level of management should then scrutinise the "Decision Packages" and do its own ranking in respect of all Decision Units under its control and so no, at the various higher level of decision making in the hierarchy.

(*e*) A large number of Government schemes/ programmes/activities are socio-economic and welfare programmes and hence need to be viewed differently as compared with private companies which are generally purely profit-oriented. Hence, it will not be practicable to subject all the schemes/ programmes/activities to rigid scrutiny based on quantifiable cost to be incurred on and benefit to be derived from them.

II. Broad Steps in a Zero Base Budgeting exercise

Step 1. Define the objectives, mission and key result areas of your department. Communicate these to all implementing officers and other "Decision Units" (A "decision unit" is a programme or organisational entity for which budgets are prepared and for which an officer/manager makes significant decisions on the amount of spending and the scope or quality of work to be performed).

Step 2. Let each "decision unit" list out all their activities. Activities will include programmes, schemes as well as support activities (e.g., Legal Cell, Statistical Unit, Audit Wing, Inspection Unit, Typing Pool, etc.)

Step 3. Prima facie identify those activities which have outlived their utility and so can be eliminated, straight away.

Step 4. Identify activities that can be conveniently merged with other activities.

Step 5. With reference to the objectives to be achieved, prioritize and rank the activities in decreasing order of priority (This should be done by using the approach of cost benefit analysis wherever feasible).

Step 6. For each Activity, ask the further question, as to whether these are alternative methods of achieving the intention/or object of that activity, assuming that the current method is but one amongst various possible alternative methods. For each alternative method, one can prepare a "Decision Package" and choose the best "Decision Package" i.e., the one which is most cost-effective.

"Decision Package" may be formulated in either of two ways, as:-

- **Mutually Exclusive Packages -** Which identify alternative means of performing the same function. The alternative are ranked and the best one chosen. The other packages are discarded.
- **Incremental Packages -** Which identify sequential levels of effort and funding that may be expended on a specific function.

Although a function may be described in terms of mutually exclusive packages, once the best alternative is chosen, the task remains of identifying incremental activities which would meet and exceed the minimum basic requirements of the function. For each function there generally will exist several approaches to accomplish it, these are mutually exclusive. But within each of the several choices, incremental level of activities in achieving the ultimate objective of the function can be identified.

Step 7. For each activity after choosing most cost-effective amongst a set of mutually exclusive "Decision Packages", develop a few "Incremental Decision Package" starting with a "Minimum level funding package" for that activity.

Step 8. Once again rank all "Decision Packages" finally selected in order of decreasing priority.

Step 9. Steps 2 to 8 should be done by each "Decision Unit". The steps should then be repeated at the next higher level in the hierarchy and so on.

Step 10. The final ranking of schemes/activities should be done at the level of the Secretary to each department. Depending on the reasource constraint, there will be a cut-off line. Schemes/ activities (i.e., "Decision Packages") falling below the cut off line will not be funded.

APPENDIX - III

Glossary of Budget Terms

Accrual Basis of Accounting: wherein accounting recognizes transactions and events as they occur rather than when cash is received or paid. it is also known as 'double entry system' or commercial accounting and is mandatory for commercial enterprises.

Annual Financial Statement : A statement of estimated receipts and expenditure of the Government for a financial year from April 1 to March 31 next. The Financial statement is required under Article 112 of the Constitution to be laid before the Parliament for approval. The Financial Statement is the budget for the Government

Appropriation Budget: The budget presented in terms of objects of expenditure like, salaries, wages, travel, materials, utilities and office expenses without highlighting the purpose or the end result expected. The appropriation budget is to ensure accountability, to facilitate itemized financial control and to show sources of funds and objects of expenditures. The budget indicates items of expenses but does not reflect activities or purposes for which money is spent or the end result of the expenditure. It is also termed as conventional budgeting or line item budgeting.

Basis of Accounting: Four alternative bases for accounting include, cash payment, receipt of goods, order of goods, and consumption or accrual. Cash basis is commonly followed in government departments, while accrual basis is mandatory for commercial enterprises.

Budget: Quantitative expression of proposed plan of action by the government for the next year. The word 'budget' is derived from the French word 'bougette' which means a small leather bag or pouch. It contains all incoming cash; or cash drawn as per the laid down procedure for financing of proposals carried to the Parliament for approval. The budgeting system provides mechanism for laying down standards, achieving and implementing plans and provides feed back information on the attainment or otherwise of planned targets and standards; it is a process of authorization of executives to execute plans, As such, the budgetary system provides dynamism to planning.

Capital Receipts & Payments: These comprise of 'Capital Receipts' and 'Capital expenditure'. The Capital expenditure is incurred either to increase or create assets of a material character, or to reduce recurring liabilities like, payment of capitalized value of the future pensions; these are normally not related to the operations of the enterprise. On the other hand, such expenditure usually are met from borrowed funds. Capital receipts comprise of borrowings or proceeds from issue of bonds or receipts of grant for creation of assets of material character.

Capital and Revenue Budgets: Capital budget relates to planning for the acquisition or construction of infrastructure like, building, machines or projects, while revenue budget covers planning for activities of recurring nature or activities relating to operation of the enterprise. Operating budgets also called functional budgets i.e. sales budgets, production budgets, material budgets, marketing budgets are examples of revenue budget

Charged Expenditure : Expenses proposed in the budget are presented as 'Charged expenses' and 'Voted expenses'. Expenses 'charged' upon the Consolidated Fund of India as laid down in the Constitution include expenses of the constitutional bodies like, Comptroller & Auditor General of India, Election Commission, Supreme Court Judges, President and Vice-President. These charged expenses though can be discussed in the Parliament, are not subject to vote by the Parliament.

Cash Basis of Accounting: Under cash basis, economic events are recorded according to movement of cash, wherein revenues are recorded and accounted for when cash is received, expenses when cash is paid irrespective of the accounting period in which the service is rendered or the benefits are received. It does not record accounts for assets, or their usage; or does not record accruals or outstanding. Cash basis is simple, easy to administer and provides information to assess compliance with the legislative requirements and to control expenditure. It is commonly followed in government accounts.

Consolidated Fund: All revenues received, loans raised or the recoveries of the loan granted by the government form the consolidated fund. Similarly, Government expenses are incurred from this fund with the authorization from the Parliament. There is a separate Consolidated fund for the Union Government and for each state or for each Union Territory. It records all revenues and expenses after the due process of law and has three main divisions, namely, Revenue, Capital, and Debt

Contingency Fund: The contingency fund is an imprest placed at the disposal of the President to meet urgent unforeseen expenditure pending authorization from the Parliament. Parliament's approval for such expenditure and for withdrawal of an equivalent amount from the Consolidated fund is subsequently obtained and the amount spent from the contingency fund is recouped to the fund. Each state and union territory has its own contingency fund. At present the Contingency Fund has a corpus of Rs. 50 crore.

Cut off Points Approach of Prioritisation: It is one approach followed in ranking of decision packages or programmes under ZBB. Under this approach, a cut off point of expenditure is set for each level of management, starting from higher level to lower levels before the budgeting exercise commences. As a matter of principle, the cut off points are more stringent at the higher levels of management.

Decision Packages: Every decision unit manager prepares packages or programmes. which represent budget request for the unit. A decision package (DP) contains a description of the programme, its objectives, benefits, relevance to organisation objectives, estimated costs, phased outlays and consequences of its not being funded. It is defined as, 'a summary (operational plan) which usually includes a statement of the expected business results or purpose of the activity, its costs, personnel required, measures of performance, alternative course of action and an evaluation from a corporate or organisational perspective of the benefits of performance and consequence of non-performance'.

Design of a decision package and its description enables management to evaluate it against other similar packages. As such, 'the decision package is a document that identifies and describes a specific activity in such a manner that management can (a) evaluate it and rank it against other activities competing for the same or similar limited resources, and (b) decide whether to approve it or disapprove it'.

Decision Unit: A decision unit is a segment of the organisation and is also called a 'division' or a 'department' or a 'responsibility centre' for which the budget is prepared and which is headed by an executive. For purpose of ZBB, management of an organisation has to decide of decision unit, i.e. level in the organisation structure from which budgeting exercise is to start. As such, a decision unit should neither be at such a low level in the organisation structure as to have enormous paper work, nor be at such a high level as not to have meaningful involvement of managers in formulation and review of budgets. The level in the organisation so decided from which the budgetary exercise would start, should have authority commensurate with responsibilities.

Degree of Urgency Approach of Prioritisation: It is one approach followed in ranking of decision packages or programmes under ZBB. Programmes differ in terms of their urgency which is measured in terms of various factors like, legal requirements, public health, economic reasons etc. and these are the bases of prioritisation. Factors indicating degree of urgency normally include, Statutory Obligation, Safety Requirements; Inter-developmental Requirements; Econômic Grounds; Welfare of Social Benefits, replacement or Addition of Assets; Convenience.

Engineering Costs: These are the costs for which there exist inputs-output relationship, or there is an engineering standard of expenses and expected benefits and the manager's judgment cannot influence benefits by changing the level of expenditure.

Finance Bill: Proposal of Government for levy of new taxes, modification of the existing tax structure are submitted to the Parliament for approval. Financial year for a government in India commences on April 1, and ends on March 31 of the next year.

Five-tier Presentation of Budget : A five-tier classification followed for the presentation of budgets and accounts in India include: Sectors of the Economy; Major Head (or Function or Major Programme); Minor Head (or Programme); Sub-head (or Activities or Schemes); Detailed Head (or Object-wise Classification).

Flexible Budget : Budget developed using budgeted revenue and cost based on the level of output achieved or likely to be achieved in the budget period.

Fiscal Deficit : Excess of all payments (both revenue and capital payment) of the government for the year, over receipts other than the borrowings

Gender Budgeting: a tool to promote women's equality and empowerment by allocating funds to implement policies for the development and empowerment of women. It is also called 'women's budget', or 'gender sensitive budget', or 'applied gender budget analysis'. It focuses on the needs of women and girls as they are usually at disadvantage as compared to men and boys; and it looks at every part of the government to assess how it will address to the different needs of women and girls.

Managerial Costs or Discretionary Costs: These are the costs for which there is no rational way of estimating the 'right amount' of costs, or for which there is not any any engineering standard, and the amount spent is a matter of manager's judgment. Such costs relate to activities or supportive activities like, finance, marketing, research & development, quality control, production planning etc. for which there is absence of a definite relationship between level of expenses and the expected benefits.

Outcome Budgeting: Under the outcome budgeting approach, allocation of funds is based on outcomes instead of inputs, the focus is on output rather than on outlay. Outcome budgeting is similar to performance budgeting and is an exercise to change the mindset of officials to focus on results and to ensure value for money. It measures the development outcomes of government programmes; or develops linkage between the money spent and the results which follow; or converts financial outlays into physical outcomes, measurable and monitorable targets. Outcome budget was introduced in India in 2005-06; and with effect from the Financial year 2007 -08, the Performance Budget and the Outcome Budget hitherto presented to the Parliament separately by Ministries/ Departments, are merged and presented as a single document titled oucome budget,

Paired-Comparison Approach of Prioitisation: It is one approach followed in ranking of decision packages or programmes under ZBB. Pair of two programmes are compared at a time to determine their priorities and to produce a numerical expression of relative importance.

Performance Budgeting: A system of budgeting which inter-relates financial outlays with physical targets and achievements and presents estimates and expenditure in terms of functions, programmes, activities and projects. It helps create a built-in-mechanism for watching the progress in attaining programme targets and taking timely corrective action when things go away and also reinforces the principle of accountability to Parliament.

Plan and Non-plan Classification: Government expenditure is normally classified as plan and non-plan; plan expenditure, in general, signifies development expenditure while non-plan expenditure deals with essential outlays pertaining to debt repayment, salary and other administrative expenditure. Government budgets also follow the same classifications. Such classification is in addition to revenue and capital. Planning Commission prepares and monitors Five Year Plans and the budget contains every year expenses for plan as well as non-plan items. Such classification is unique in India so as to give greater emphasis to planning. A Committee under the Chairmanship of Dr. C. Rangarajan recommended that Plan and Non-Plan distinction in the budget is neither able to provide a satisfactory classification of developmental and non-developmental dimensions of government expenditure nor an appropriate budgetary framework and such plan and non-plan distinction in the budget should be removed.

Planning: Planning is the designing of future course of action. It bridges the gap from where we are to, where we want to go and is concerned with taking action in the immediate present to prevent becoming obsolete in the future. External factors like, technological and social change, inter-dependence and complexity has impact on organization's functioning and planning is concerned with adaptability to variations in the external factors

Product Accounting: Costs related to a product are accumulated irrespective of an individual or a departmental head responsible for those costs.

Public Account: The transactions like, provident fund, small savings and other deposits etc. for which the Government acts a banker are kept in the public account. Such funds do not belong to the Government and have to be repaid back to the owners and the Parliamentary authorization is not required for such payments.

Ranking of Decision Packages: Ranking is a process by which managers arrange programmes or decision packages in decreasing order of their priority. As such, the ranking process identifies the relative priority assigned to each package based on benefits expected or costs involved. Ranking or prioritization approach adopted should be objective one to reflect the laid down goals and objectives. As a principle, the approach of prioritisation should be finalized by the management before the budget formulation process begins. Ranking approaches include cut-off point approach, paired comparison approach, degree of urgency approach and two dimensional priority rating matrix approach.

Responsibility Accounting : Costs are accumulated for a centre or unit and each centre or a unit is headed by a responsible official. The responsibility accounting intends to tag officials in the organization as a centre of authority, responsibility and accountability. The accounting system suited to performance budgeting is the responsibility accounting

Revenue Deficit: It is excess of revenue payments of the government for the year over its revenue receipts

Revenue Receipts & Payments: All receipts and payments are categorized as 'revenue' and 'capital'. Revenue comprises of 'revenue receipt' and 'revenue expenditure' which arise from the operations of the enterprise. Revenue receipts for a government include proceeds of taxation, and other receipts classed as revenue; and after deduction of the revenue expenditure from the revenue receipts, the net result is shown as revenue surplus or revenue deficit for the year.

Sectoral Classification: Sectoral classification is the aggregation of operations of the Government or is grouping of the functions of Government with reference to the characteristics of services provided by a function. For budget purposes, the economy is classified into four sectors namely,: General Services; Social & Community Services; Economic Services, and Grant-in-Aid and Contributions.

Target-base Budgeting: An approach which simplifies the zero-base budgeting approach wherein a certain percentage of existing funds are made available for reallocation towards new activities. This approach was adopted in India in research and development organizations like, Council for Scientific and Industrial Research

Two Dimensional Priority Rating Matrix Approach: It is one approach followed in ranking of decision packages or programmes under ZBB. Under this approach two factors are considered simultaneously for purposes of prioritisation and is thus two dimensional. Two factors considered include (a) priority of function, and (b) degree of urgency; decision packages are ranked independently on the basis of these two factors and their multiple rating is the basis of ranking.

Voted Expenses : Expenses proposed in the budget are presented as 'Charged expenses' and 'Voted expenses'. Expenses other than 'charged' are submitted in the form of Demands to the Parliament for approval. Each Demand or combination of demands relate normally to a single Ministry. Once the Parliament approves the 'Voted' portion of proposed expenditure, the funds required to meet the voted grants together with the expenditure 'Charged' on the Consolidated Fund constitute budget for the year and are allowed to be withdrawn from the Consolidated Fund under the authority of an Appropriation Act passed by the Parliament.

ZBB : ZBB is a budgeting approach whereby each governmental programme, regardless of whether it is new or existing programme, must be justified in its entirety each time a budget is formulated. ZBB is a flexible approach to budget formulation by which budget analysis and justification shifts away from 'increments' for the existing programmes to detailed justification for the existing as well as new programmes.

INDEX

3e

Ancient and Medieval India

For UPSC and State Civil Services Examinations

Now with **Enriched Digital Resources**

Poonam Dalal Dahiya

McGraw Hill Education (India) Private Limited

Published by McGraw Hill Education (India) Private Limited
Registered Office: Anjana Complex No: 5/90 A, Butt Road, St. Thomas Mount, Chennai – 600016

Ancient and Medieval India, 3e

Third reprint 2026

Print Edition
ISBN-(13 digits): 978-93-6444-710-2
ISBN-(10 digits): 93-6444-710-7

Print Edition
ISBN-(13 digits): 978-93-6444-790-4
ISBN-(10 digits): 93-6444-790-5

04 05 06 07 08 RAJ 30 29 28 27 26

Typeset at APS Compugraphics, 4G, PKT 2, Mayur Vihar, Phase-III, Delhi - 96 and printed and bound in India at Rajkamal Electric Press, Kundli, Haryana.

Cover Image Source: Shutterstock

Visit us at: www.mheducation.co.in

Write to us at: support.india@mheducation.com

CIN: U80302TN2010PTC111532
Toll free Number: 1800 103 5875

Dedicated to my late father
Sh. Randhawa Singh Dalal
who taught me to dream big

Preface

The syllabus of the General Studies for the UPSC and State Service examinations is pretty exhaustive in nature and Ancient and Medieval History has emerged as one of the important component of this syllabus. Many aspirants find history a boring factual subject that has to be crammed and is not a fun to learn. It is indeed difficult for any new aspirant to cover it comprehensively in a short span of time. The very purpose of writing this book is to break this myth and to make learning of history a joyful process.

This book has a completely new approach towards study of Ancient and Medieval History. It attempts **to make the learning of history simple and interesting** and provides a one-stop solution to all your history needs. The book is structured in a way that it is in sync with **each and every topic in the syllabus**. The information is given in an interesting format to make one comfortable with history.

Special Features of this Book

1. Comprehensive coverage of entire syllabus pertaining to Ancient and Medieval History demanded for UPSC, State Services and other competitive examinations.
2. Inclusion of two comprehensive detachable quick revision charts each pertaining to Ancient and Medieval history to simplify the learning process.
3. In every chapter, the keywords have been highlighted so that it becomes easy for the reader to make a quick reference to important points.
4. Ample diagrams, maps and tabular information is included in the chapters to provide conceptual clarity about historic events.
5. Along with the repository of last year's questions (both Prelims and Mains), practice questions are provided for each chapter to make students practice, assess and master the particular topic.
6. Use of simple and lucid language to cater to the needs of students of different backgrounds.
7. Trend Analysis of UPSC CSE Prelims Questions.

I sincerely hope that all the readers of the book will appreciate and benefit from its contents and find it useful for their preparation.

Any remarks/recommendations towards improving the content and its richness will be most welcome and eagerly awaited. Your valuable suggestions will go far in enhancing this book in the future. You may reach me at poonamrandhawasingh@gmail.com.

All the very Best!

Poonam Dalal Dahiya

Acknowledgements

I wish to thank a multitude of people whose lives have intersected with mine in one way or the other and inspired me to write this book. To begin with, I would like to express my heartfelt gratitude for my dear husband Mr. Aseem Dahiya, who has been a source of constant inspiration and encouragement ever since I have known him and who has seen from close quarters the crests and troughs of my struggle, all the while prodding me to never give up. Without his unflinching support, I would not have been able to complete this challenging task or anything else in life. He, along with my son Vikramaditya, has given a new meaning and purpose to my life, wherein I find myself obligated to return to the society in no small measure, what I have gained from it.

My gratitude is also due to my mother Smt. Sudesh and my brothers Amit and Ajay who have always believed in me and motivated me to develop my notes written over the years during preparation of various examinations into this work. I would also like to thank my whole family, especially my in-laws, teachers, colleagues and friends who in their own unique ways have helped me to form my views on various issues as delineated in this book and without their support it would not have been possible for me to research and write this book.

I am also indebted to every teacher of mine who has not only relentlessly mentored me in this endeavour but also helped me during the course of my own UPSC preparation, specially Pavan Sir (of Pavan Kumar IAS Academy), Ravindran Sir (of Vajiram and Ravi), Praveen Bansal Sir (of Abhimanu IAS Study Group) and Anil Narula Sir (of Anil Narula's IAS Study Center). I am also sincerely thankful to Shri D.S. Mishra, IAS, Dr. Dinesh Arora, IAS, Shri Maheswar Dayal, IPS, and Dr. Ajay Chikkara, IRS who have always supported me through this journey of mine, and have encouraged and helped me in their own ways in completing this work on time.

I would also like to express my true appreciation to McGraw Hill Education, India, and their entire team who gave consistent support and helped me in the creation and development of the book. My special thanks to Mr. Tanmoy Roy Chowdhury, Mr. Tanweer Ahmad, Mr. Nikhil Wadhera, Ms. Aparna Kumar, Ms. Aarooshi Garg, Mr. Atul Gupta and Mr. Suhaib Ali for their continued support all through this venture.

I finally hope that this book will help the readers in a better conceptual understanding of the Ancient and Medieval History of India and help all those civil service aspirants who have fire in their eyes and who dare to dream.

Poonam Dalal Dahiya

Trend Analysis of UPSC CSE Prelims Questions from Ancient and Medieval India (2009–2023)

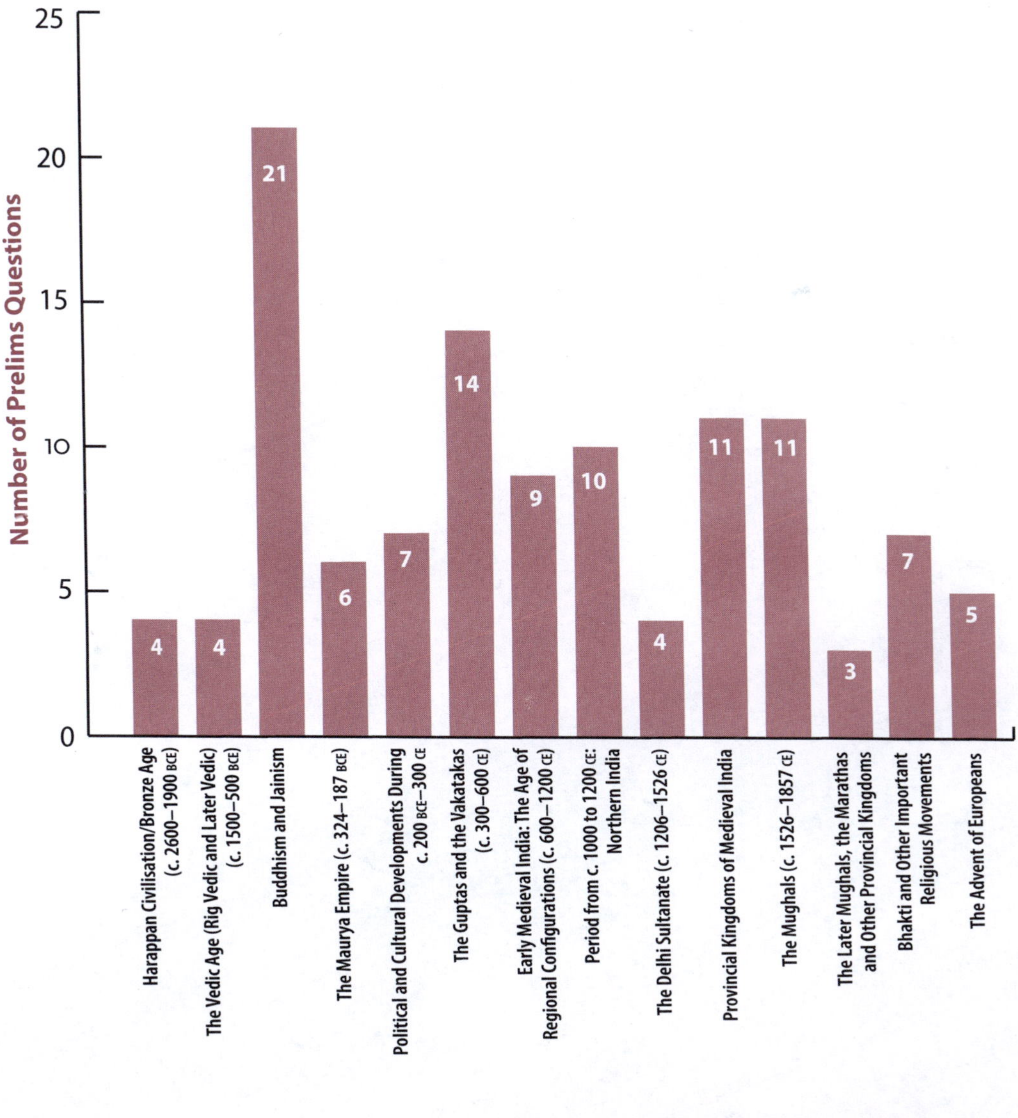

Contents

CHAPTER

1

Pre-Historic India

History

The English word '**history**' comes from the Greek word *historia,* meaning 'inquiry, knowledge acquired by investigation'. History corresponds to the study of the past and throws light on various past events of significance which shaped and evolved human experiences. It is further divided into *pre-history, proto-history,* and *history*.

Pre-history	Proto-history	History
Events that occurred before the invention of writing are considered the domain of **pre-history**, which is generally represented by the three stone ages.	Defining proto-history is rather difficult as it has different connotations. Generally, it refers to a period between pre-history and history, during which a culture or civilisation had not yet developed writing but were mentioned in the written records of a contemporary literate civilisation. For example, the script of the Harappan civilisation remains undeciphered; however, since its existence is noted in Mesopotamian writings, it is considered a part of proto-history. Similarly, the Vedic civilisation from c. 1500–600 BCE had an oral literary tradition, though they did not take to literary writing – they can thus be considered a part of proto-history as well. Archaeologists consider Neolithic and Chalcolithic cultures to be a part of proto-history	The study of the past after the invention of writing and the study of literate societies based on the written and archaeological sources constitutes **history**.

Sources of Reconstructing History

Literary Sources		Non-Literary Sources
(i) **Religious Literature** throwing invaluable light on the social and economic conditions of the ancient Indian period such as (a) The four **Vedas**, mostly assigned to c.1500–500 BCE, namely The Rig Veda (mainly consisting of prayers) and The Sama, Yajur and Atharva – containing prayers, rituals, magic and mythological stories.	(ii) **Secular Literature** such as (a) ***Dharmashastras*/ Law books** which prescribe the duties for different social groups such as *Manu Smriti*. (b) **Kautilya's** '*Arthashastra*' which provides great information about the Mauryan period polity and economy. (c) '*Ashtadhyayi*', an important work on grammar written by **Panini**.	(i) **Inscriptions/*Prashastis***: Writings engraved on hard surface such as stone and metal like copper which usually record some achievements or ideas help us in understanding different religious and administrative policies of ancient times. For instance, inscriptions detailing state policy issued by **Ashoka** and inscriptions recording the land grants by the **Satavahans,** kings of the Deccan. (ii) **Coins**: Coins provide useful information not only on the economic history of different dynasties but also provide input on different parameters involved such as the script, art and religion of the time, as well as the progress made in terms of metallurgy and science and technology. For instance, the earliest coins found in India were **punch-marked coins** and contained only certain symbols and were made of silver and copper, whereas later on the Indo-Greeks introduced **gold coins** and issued the coins which bore the names and images of rulers.

Literary Sources		Non-Literary Sources
(b) **Upanishads** also referred to as Vedanta and containing philosophical discussions on '*Atma*' and '*Pramatma*'. (c) **Sutras** such as *Shrautasutras* and *Grihyasutras* containing ritual literature on moral values. (d) **Epics** of *Ramayana* and *Mahabharata*. (e) **Buddhist religious texts** written in Pali and commonly known as *Tripitakas* (three baskets), i.e. *Suttapittaka*, *Vinayapitaka* and *Abhidhammapitaka*. (f) **Jaina's religious texts** written in Prakrit commonly called *Angas* containing philosophical concepts of the Jainas.	(d) Compositions of **Kalidasa** such as '*Abhijananashakuntalam*', '*Ritusamhara*' and '*Meghadutam*' which provide us valuable information about the social and cultural life of the Guptas. (e) '*Rajataranagini*' written by **Kalhana** tells about the social life of 12th CE Kashmir. (f) ***Charita's* or biographies** written by court poets in praise of their patron rulers such as '*Harshacharita*', written by Banabhatta in praise of King Harshavardhana. (g) **Sangam literature**, the earliest south Indian literature produced by poets who joined together in assemblies (Sangam), provides valuable insight about the period from 300 BCE till 300 CE. This Tamil literature contains literary gems of '*Silappadikaram*' and '*Manimekali*', both shedding light on south Indian society, economy and polity of those times.	(iii) **Archaeology**: On the basis of the excavated remains, Archaeology enables us to form an idea of the material life of the ancient people. For example, excavated sites belonging to the **Harappan period** let us know about the life of people living in that era. Similarly, in south India the graves known as **Megaliths** throw light on the life of the people living in the Deccan and south India before 300 BCE. (iv) **Geological and Biological Studies**: The faunal (animal) and floral (plant) sources too complement the archaeological studies in understanding the ancient way of life. For instance, through an examination of plant residues, and especially through **pollen analysis**, inference can be drawn about the farming practiced by Stone Age people. Similarly, **mitochondrial DNA** provides information on pre-historic migrations. (v) **Account of Foreign Travellers**: India was visited by many travellers since times immemorial and among them the notable ones, i.e. Greek, Roman and Chinese visitors, have left behind a rich account of our historical past. Some of the notables among them were: (a) Greek Ambassador **Megasthenes** wrote '*Indica*' and provided valuable information about the Mauryan society and administration. (b) Similarly, '*The Periplus of the Erythrean Sea*' and Ptolemy's '*Geography*' both written in Greek provide valuable data regarding Indian ports and commodities of trade between India and the Roman Empire. (c) Buddhist traveller **Fa-hien** who came to India in the 500 CE have left a vivid account of the age of Guptas. (d) Another noted Buddhist pilgrim **Hsuan Tsang** visited India in the 700 CE and gave details of India under the reign of king Harshvardhana and glory of Nalanda University.

Pre-Historic India

The history and identity of human settlements in India go back to the pre-historic times. As discussed above that pre-historic period is the period before the development of script, therefore our knowledge of this period is based only on the materials found in the archaeological excavations. The credit for doing an early extensive study of Indian pre-history goes to Robert Bruce Foote, who discovered what was probably the first palaeolithic tool discovered in India – the Pallavaram handaxe. Later, he discovered a large number of pre-historic sites in south India. The contribution of Sir Mortimer Wheeler is equally significant, as his efforts greatly contributed towards our knowledge of the pre-historical cultures of India and their sequence.

This phase of human development is also referred to as the Stone Age[1]. On the basis of geological age, the type and technology of stone tools, and subsistence base, the Indian Stone Age* is classified primarily into three types:

- Old Stone Age, Palaeolithic Age (5,00,000–10,000 BCE)
- Late Stone Age, Mesolithic Age (10,000–6,000 BCE)
- New Stone Age, Neolithic Age (6,000–1,000 BCE)

**A general time range is specified as there is a great deal of variation in the dates for different sites.*

Palaeolithic Age[2] (Hunters and Food Gatherers)

The Palaeolithic Age is the earliest period of the Stone Age, which developed in the Pleistocene period or the Ice Age[3]. It was spread in practically all parts of India **except** the alluvial plains of the Indus and Ganga, southern Tamil Nadu and the hilly areas of the Western Ghats. The pre-historic man who belonged to the species of *Homo erectus*[4] did not have a complex language culture and might have expressed a few sounds or words and used a sign language.

Way of Life and Main Characteristics

(a) The Palaeolithic men of India are said to have belonged to the Negrito race and lived in open air, river valleys, caves and rock shelters.

---

[1] It is called so, as the earliest man living during this period made tools and implements of stone found in his surroundings and these tools helped him to hunt and gather food in order to satisfy his hunger.

[2] The term *'Palaeolithic'* is derived from the Greek word *'palaeo'*, which means old and *'lithic'*, which means stone. Therefore, the term Palaeolithic Age refers to the Old Stone Age.

[3] The Pleistocene period is the geological period of the age when the earth's surface was covered with ice, and weather was so cold that human or plant life could not survive. But in the tropical region, where ice melted, the earliest species of men could exist.

[4] Stages of human evolution: *Australopitheuss atarensis* < *Homo habilis* < *Homo erectus* < *Homo neanderthalensis* < *Homo sapiens*.

(b) They were food gathering people who lived on hunting and gathered wild fruits and vegetables.

(c) They had no knowledge of agriculture, house building, pottery, or any metal. It was only in later stages that they attained the knowledge of fire.

(d) In the Upper Palaeolithic period, evidence of art appears in the form of paintings.

(e) Man, during this period, used tools of unpolished, undressed rough stones – mainly hand axes, cleavers, choppers, blades, burins, and scrapers. Since the stone tools were made of a hard rock called 'quartzite', Palaeolithic men are therefore also called 'Quartzite men' in India.

Palaeolithic Tools

FIGURE 1.1 Palaeolithic Tools

The Palaeolithic Age is divided into three phases according to the nature of stone tools used (Fig. 1.1). They are:

Early or Lower Palaeolithic	Middle Palaeolithic	Late or Upper Palaeolithic
Use of hand axes, choppers, and cleavers, mainly for chopping, digging, and skinning. These stone tools were rough and heavy.	Use of stone tools made of **flakes,** mainly scrapers, borers, points, and blade-like tools. These tools became smaller and there was a decrease in the use of hand axes in relation to other tools.	This period is marked by innovation in tools and technology. Parallel-sided blades, burins, and some instances of bone tools.
Found in Soan and Sohan river valley (now in Pakistan), Kashmir, Thar Desert (Didwana, Rajasthan), Hiran Valley (Gujarat), rockshelters of Bhimbetka (M.P.), and Belan Valley Mirzapur (U.P.). See Fig. 1.2.	Found in Soan, Narmada and Tungabhadra river valleys, Potwar plateau (between Indus and Jhelum), Sanghao Cave (near Peshawar, Pakistan).	Found in Andhra Pradesh, Karnataka, Maharashtra, Central MP, Southern UP and Chhotanagpur Plateau. Bone tools found only at cave sites of Kurnool and Muchchatla Chintamani Gavi in Andhra Pradesh whereas Incised ostrich eggshell. Shell and stone beads have been found in Andhra Pradesh and Patna in Maharashtra.

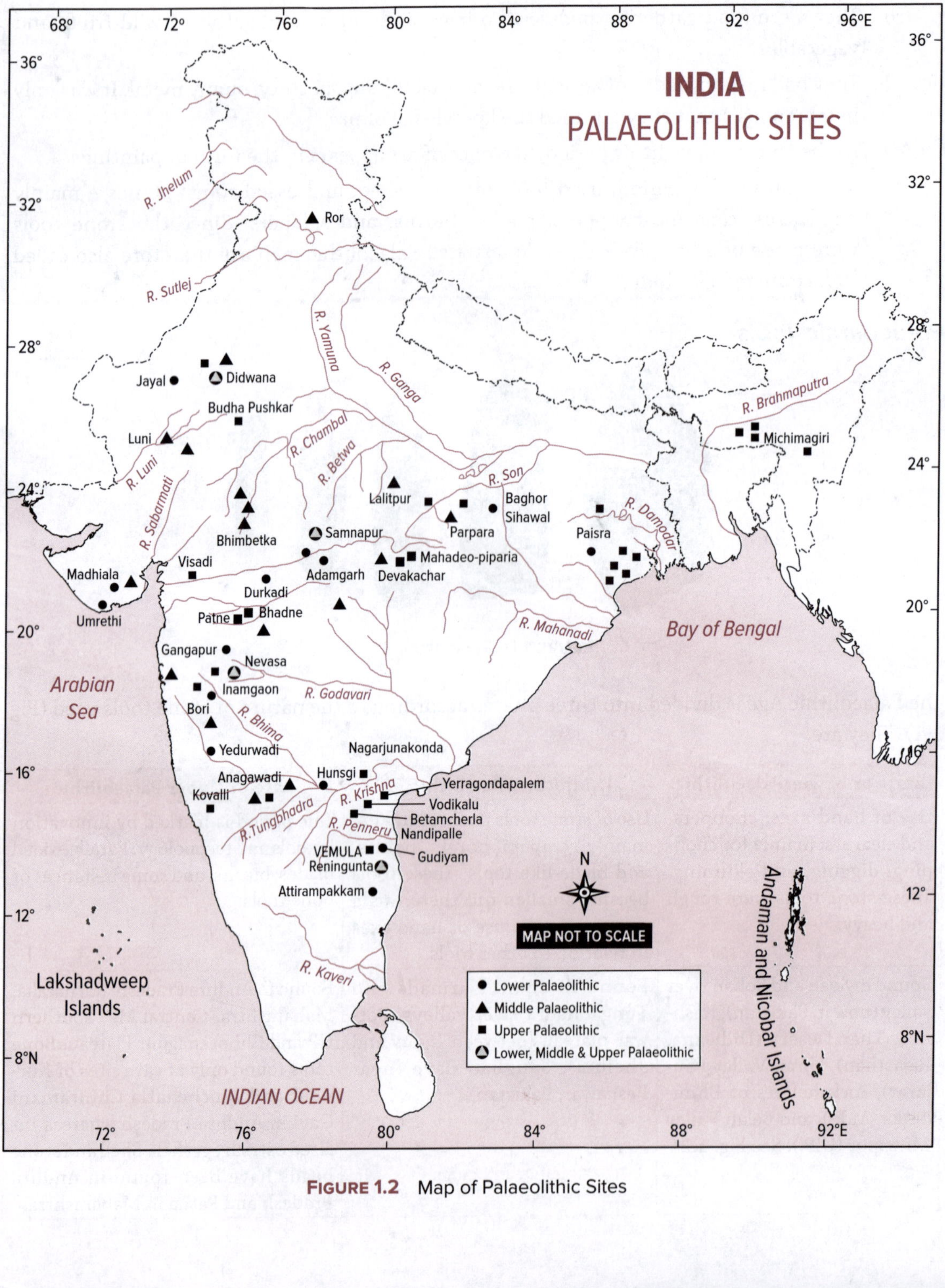

FIGURE 1.2 Map of Palaeolithic Sites

Early or Lower Palaeolithic	Middle Palaeolithic	Late or Upper Palaeolithic
5,00,000 BCE–50,000 BCE	3,85,000 BCE–40,000 BCE	40,000 BCE–10,000 BCE
Covers the greater part of the Ice Age.	Established only in 1960 by H.D. Sankalia and was named Nevasan industry after the site of Nevasa, Maharashtra.	*Homo sapiens* first appeared at the end of this phase thereby marking increase in cognitive capability of humans. This phase also coincided with the last phase of the Ice Age, when the climate became comparatively warmer and less humid.

Mesolithic Age[5] (Hunters and Herders)

The Mesolithic Age represents the intermediate stage in Stone Age culture. Both Mesolithic and Neolithic cultures belong to the Holocene era[6] (which succeeded the Pleistocene era around 10,000 years ago). One of the key aspects of the Mesolithic Age was the reduction in size of well-established tool types. The characteristic tools of this age were **microliths** (miniature stone tools usually made of crypto-crystalline silica, chalcedony, or chert, both of geometrical and non-geometrical shapes) (Fig. 1.3). They were not only used as tools in themselves but were also used to make composite tools, spearheads, arrowheads, and sickles after hafting them on wooden or bone handles. The microliths enabled the Mesolithic man to hunt smaller animals and birds.

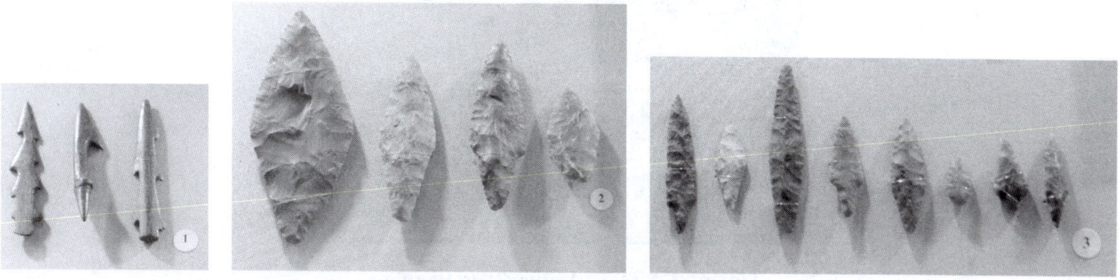

FIGURE 1.3 Tools of the Mesolithic Age

Way of Life and Main Characteristics

(a) The Mesolithic people lived in semi-permanent and temporary settlements along with occupying caves and open grounds.

[5] The term '*Mesolithic*' is a combination of two words, '*meso*' and '*lithic*'. In Greek, '*meso*' means middle and '*lithic*' means stone. Hence, the Mesolithic stage of pre-history is also known as the Middle Stone Age.

[6] During this era, there was a rise in temperature, as a result of which the climate became warm which further resulted in melting of ice and brought certain changes in flora and fauna. With the advent of global warming, human groups became highly mobile and began to occupy various eco zones.

(b) They survived on hunting, fishing, food gathering, and in later stages, also domesticated animals along with cultivation of plants thus paving the way for Neolithic way of life. This culture is thus assigned to pre-agricultural times in most areas. These people used fire and perhaps roasted food too.

(c) They buried the dead and sometimes with grave goods which suggests their beliefs in life after death.

(d) They had artistic skill and the Mesolithic era initiated rock art in pre-history. In 1867, the first rock paintings in India were discovered at Sohagighat (Kaimur Hills, UP). Now, over 150 Mesolithic rock art sites have been discovered across India, with rich concentration in Central India such as the Bhimbetka caves (Fig. 1.4), Kharwar, Jaora, and Kathotia (M.P.), Sundargarh and Sambalpur (Orissa), Ezhuthu Guha (Kerala). Animals dominate the scenes at most Mesolithic rock art sites. However, no snakes are depicted in Mesolithic paintings. Also, certain rock paintings give ideas about the development of religious practice along with reflecting the division of labour on the basis of gender.

FIGURE 1.4 Bhimbetka Cave Painting[7]

IMPORTANT MESOLITHIC SITES

S. No.	Site	Importance
1.	Bagor (Rajasthan) on River Kothari	One of the largest and best documented Mesolithic sites in India.
2.	Adamgarh in Madhya Pradesh	Provides the earliest evidence for the domestication of animals.

[7] The various themes of paintings of Bhimbetka include hunting, fishing, dancing, family and burial scenes, honey and plant food collection. However, the most prominent are the hunting scenes in which both men and women are depicted participating and different animals like bison, buffalo, tiger, elephant, rhinoceros, deer and Nilgai can be seen. Birds are also painted, but perching birds which generally feed on grains in the field are not seen in earlier times but in later times. The weapons used are bows and arrows, pointed stick and a barbed sphere. The paintings are made in a stick line fashion and most commonly red and white colours are used which were either mineral in nature or were extracted from plants.

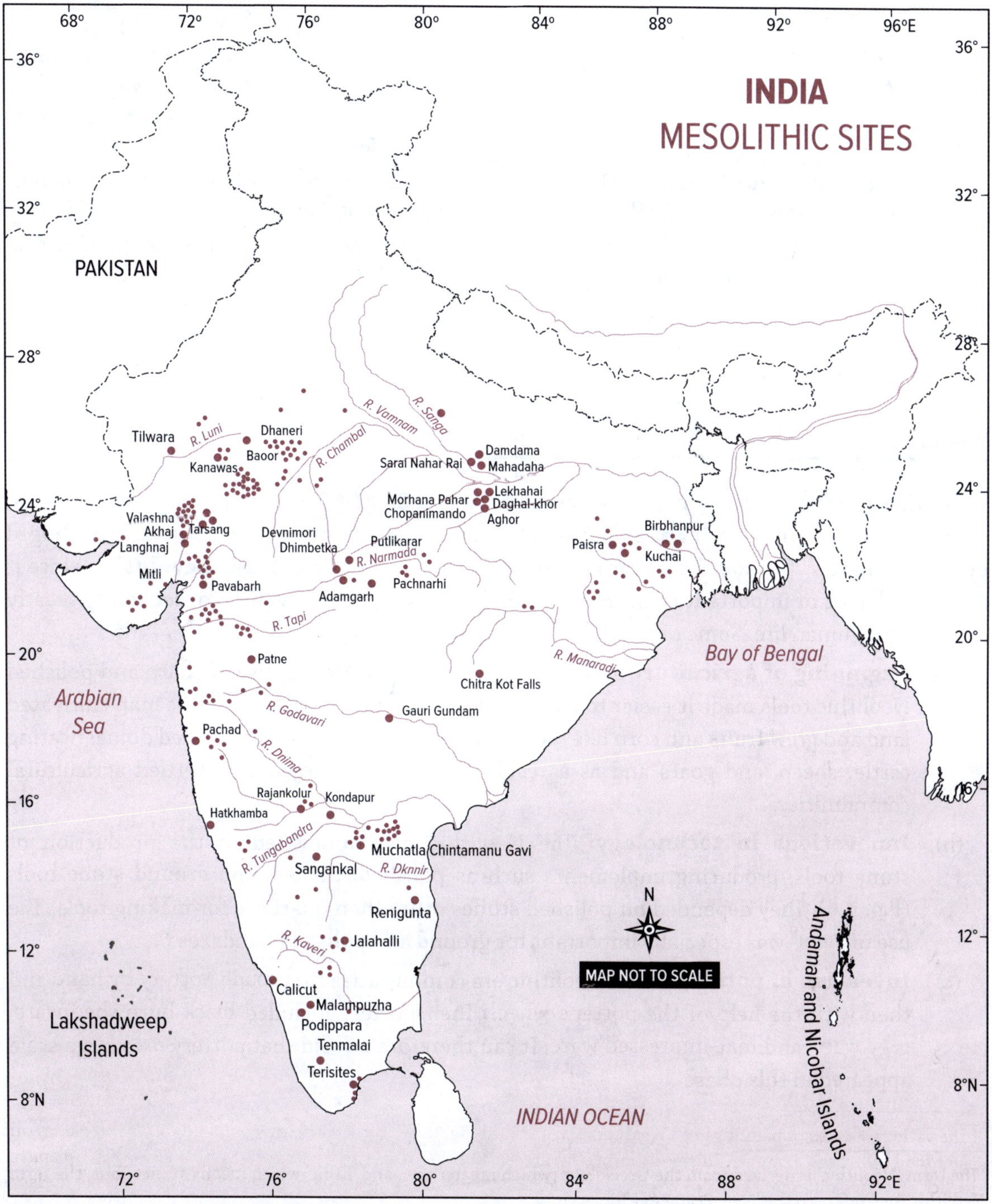

FIGURE 1.5 Mesolithic Sites in India

S. No.	Site	Importance
3.	Mahadaha (U.P.)	Bone artefacts are found, including arrowheads and bone ornaments. Finding of a burial having a man and woman buried together.
4.	Langhnaj, district Mehsana in Gujarat and in the Kaimur region of Mirzapur (U.P.)	Though pottery is absent at most Mesolithic sites, it is present at both these sites.
5.	Chotanagpur Region, Central India South of River Krishna (Tinnevelly in Tamil Nadu) Birbhanpur (in West Bengal) Langhnaj (near Gujarat) Sarai Nahar Rai (near Allahabad Pratapgarh area)	Prominent sites in these concerned states.

Neolithic Age[8] (Food-Producing Stage)

In northern India, the Neolithic age emerged around c.8000–6000 BCE. But at some places in southern and eastern India, it was as late as 1000 BCE. Its significance in pre-history can be gauged by the fact that V. Gordon Childe termed the Neolithic phase as **Neolithic Revolution** since it introduced a lot of important changes in man's socio-economic life which consequently greatly affected the human life. Some of the innovations were:

(a) **Beginning of agriculture** and **animal domestication:** The use of sharp and polished Neolithic tools made it easier to cultivate the soil and thus, the Neolithic man cultivated land and grew fruits and corn like *ragi* and horse gram (*kulathi*). He started domesticating cattle, sheep, and goats and as a result, there was emergence of settled agricultural communities.

(b) **Innovations in technology:** The Neolithic man innovated in the production of stone tools, producing implements such as polished, pecked, and ground stone tools (Fig. 1.6). They depended on polished stones other than quartzite for making tools. The use of celts[9] was especially important for ground and polished handaxes.

(c) **Invention of pottery[10]:** The Neolithic era communities first made pottery by hand and then with the help of the potter's wheel. Their pottery included black burnished ware, grey ware, and mat-impressed ware. It can therefore be said that pottery on a large-scale appeared in this phase.

[8] The term 'Neolithic' is derived from the Greek 'neo' which means new, and 'lithic' which means stone. Thus, the term 'Neolithic Age' refers to the 'New Stone Age'.

[9] Celts were tools with handles which made the tools much more effective and efficient.

[10] The need to store food grains compelled man to make pottery.

FIGURE 1.6 Relics of Late Neolithic Period, Authur M. Sackler Museum of Art and Archaeology, Peking University, Beijing, China

(d) **Emergence of self-sufficient village communities:** In the later phases of the Neolithic era, people led a more settled life. They lived in circular and rectangular houses made of mud and reed. They also knew how to make boats and could spin cotton, wool and weave cloth.

(e) **Division of labour based on sex and age:** As society was progressing, the need for additional labour was recognised and thus labour was procured from other non kin groups too.

Neolithic Regional Cultures	
(i) Neolithic Culture of North-Western India	In the north-western part of India, the Neolithic culture began at a very early date. For instance, the site of Mehrgarh has produced evidence of early Neolithic times dating to c. 7000 BCE and this culture preceded Indus Valley civilisation.
(ii) Neolithic Culture of Kashmir	The Neolithic culture in Kashmir was contemporary to the Harappan civilisation. The people lived in pit houses (about 4 m in depth) in order to escape the cold weather.
(iii) Neolithic Culture of Ganges Valley and Central India	These Neolithic sites were characterised by cord marked pottery. Important sites are Koldiwa, Chirand, Senuwar and Mahagara.
(iv) Neolithic Culture of Eastern India	These Neolithic sites are found in Bihar and West Bengal and show similarities with the Neolithic complexes of east and south-east Asia.
(v) Neolithic Culture of Southern India	These sites have been found mainly in Andhra Pradesh and Karnataka and in the north-western Tamil Nadu. These sites have ash mounds in the centre with settlements around them.
(vi) Neolithic Culture of North Eastern India	The Neolithic culture in north-eastern India appears at a very late period and generally dates from 2500–1500 BCE or even later.

It is also pertinent to note that the Neolithic cultures of India are divided into various regional cultures and they flourished in different time periods.

Important Neolithic Sites

S. No.	Site	Importance
1.	Burzahom (Jammu and Kashmir)	Unique rectangular chopper. Domestic dogs buried with their masters in graves.
2.	Gufkraal (Jammu and Kashmir)	Famous for pit dwelling, stone tools and graveyard in house.
3.	Maski, Brahmagiri, Piklihal and Takkalakota (Karnataka)	Proof of cattle herding.
4.	Budihal (Karnataka)	Proof of community food preparation and feasting.
5.	Chirand (Bihar)	Considerable bone implements specially made of antlers, i.e. horns of deer.
6.	Belan Valley which is located on the northern spurs of the Vindhyas and middle part of Narmada valley	All the three phases of Palaeolithic age followed by Mesolithic and Neolithic in sequence.
7.	Koldihwa (in Belan valley)	Reveals a three-fold cultured sequence of Neolithic, Chalcolithic and Iron Age.
8.	Chopani – Mando (Belan valley)	Provides earliest evidence of use of pottery.
9.	Mehrgarh (Breadbasket of Baluchistan, a province of Pakistan)	Earliest Neolithic site. Evidence of houses built of sun-dried bricks by Neolithic people. Evidence of cultivation of crops like wheat, barley and cotton. Earliest example of dentistry, i.e. drilling of human tooth.
10.	Koldihwa and Mahagara (lying south of Allahabad)	Have many strata of circular huts along with crude hand-made pottery. Also, evidence of rice (this is the oldest evidence of rice cultivation, not only in India but anywhere in the world).
11.	Paiyampalli in Tamil Nadu Utnur, Nagarjunakonda, Budihal in Andhra Pradesh Amri, Kotdiji in Sindh, Punjab Garo Hills in Meghalaya Saraikhola (near Taxila on Potwar plateau)	Prominent sites in these concerned states.

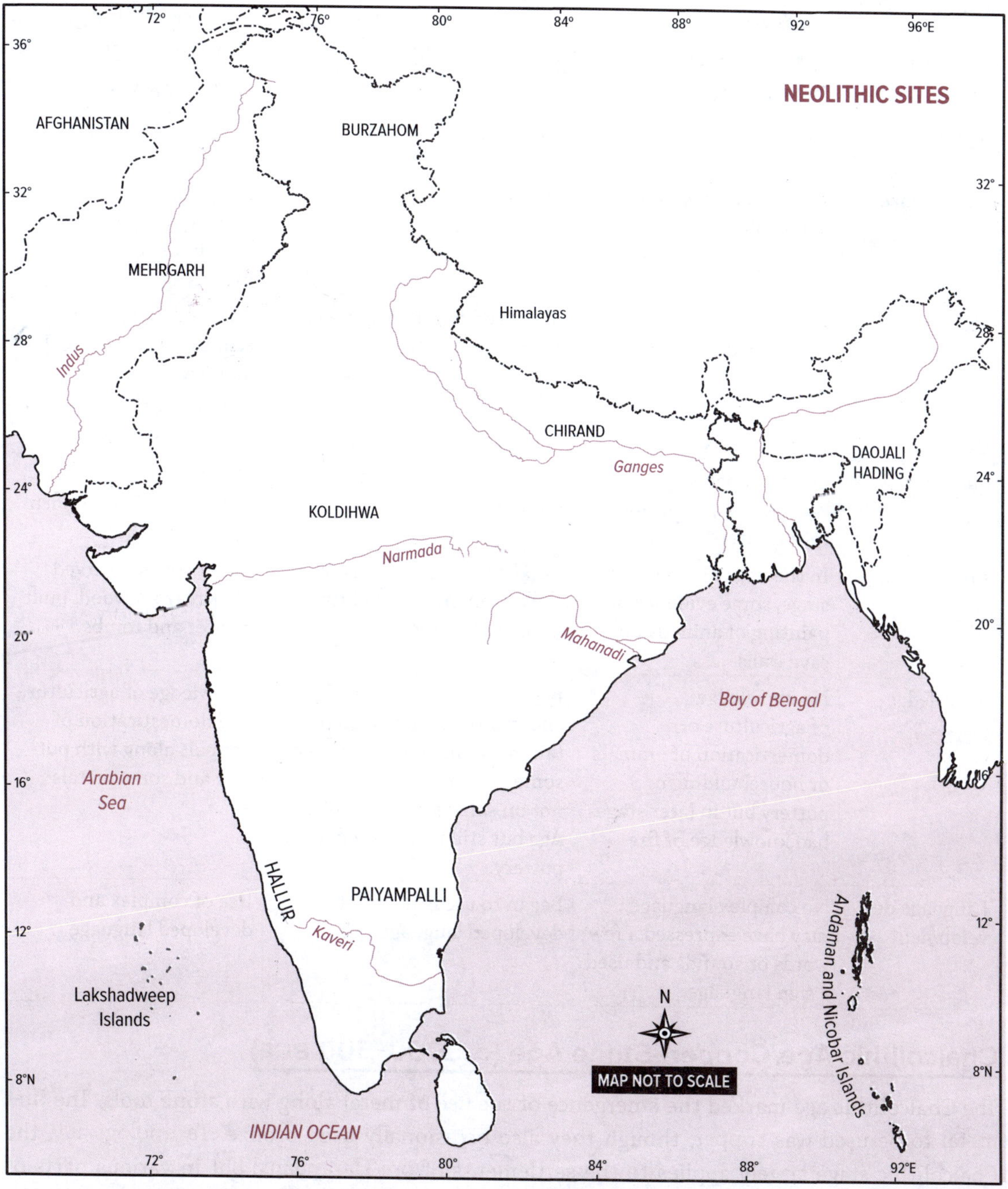

FIGURE 1.7 Map of Neolithic Sites

	Palaeolithic Age	Mesolithic Age	Neolithic Age
Time period	5,00,000–10,000 BCE	10,000–6000 BCE	6000–1000 BCE
Also known as	Old Stone Age	Late/Middle Stone Age	New Stone Age
Age of	Hunters and food gatherers	Hunters and herders	Food producers
Subsistence	Food gathering, hunting and fishing	Pre-agricultural times	Agriculture, livestock rearing complemented with hunting and gathering
Stone tools	Rough, crude, big and unpolished stone tools	Improved polished stone tools such as microliths	Polished and pecked stone tools such as celts along with needles, scrappers, etc.
Existence	Nomadic existence	Transition stage	Settled existence
Shelter	Lived in open spaces, river valleys, caves and rock shelters	Lived in semi-permanent and temporary settlements	People started living in permanent houses such as thatched huts
Art and craft	In the upper Palaeolithic stage, some evidence of painting of animals on cave walls	Good evidences of artistic skills as many cave paintings have been found belonging to this era	Made pottery, carved objects from wood, built shelter and tombs
Knowledge	No knowledge of agriculture or domestication of animals or housebuilding or pottery but in later stages had knowledge of fire	Began to use controlled fire, and in later stages started taming animals and initiated some plant cultivation though not on same scale as Neolithic Age but still no knowledge of pottery.	Knowledge of agriculture and domestication of animals along with pottery and some metals
Language development	No complex language, may have expressed a few words or sounds and used a sign language	Began to use little bit of developed language	Use of complex and developed language

Chalcolithic Age/Copper–Stone Age (c. 3000–500 BCE)

The Chalcolithic age marked the emergence of the use of metal along with stone tools. The first metal to be used was copper, though they also occasionally used bronze. Technologically, the Chalcolithic stage largely applies to the settlements of pre-Harappans, but in various parts of country, it appears after the end of the bronze Harappan culture. Some Chalcolithic cultures are contemporary of Harappan culture and some of pre-Harappan cultures, though it is possible to say that most Chalcolithic cultures are post-Harappan. It was mostly concentrated in western

India; covering parts of Gujarat, Rajasthan, MP and Maharashtra, because copper was mostly found there.

Chalcolithic	Harappan
Primarily rural	Primarily urban
Used mostly copper	Used bronze
Lived near hilly land or rivers	Attained urbanisation on the basis of produce from flood plains in Indus valley

Way of Life and Main Characteristics

(a) Chalcolithic people subsisted on agriculture and cattle rearing, besides practising hunting and fishing. The people of the Chalcolithic phase produced wheat and rice as their staple, barley, *bajra*, several pulses such as lentil, black gram, green gram, and grass pea, while those living in eastern regions lived on fish and rice. They practiced more slash-burn or *jhum* cultivation. However, neither the plough nor the hoe has been found at any site of this period. It is pertinent to note that major parts of this culture flourished in the zone of black soil, useful mainly for growing cotton.

(b) They domesticated cows, sheep, goats, pigs and buffaloes and hunted deer but were not acquainted with horses. They cooked their food and ate beef too. However, quite interestingly, the domesticated animals were slaughtered for food and not milked for dairy products (this practice still continues among the *Gond people of Bastar)*.

(c) Pottery was well advanced during chalcolithic period and the potteries are the most valuable source of information of chalcolithic culture as no written records of this phase has been found. They used different types of pottery, of which black and red pottery and ochre coloured pottery (OCP) were the most popular. This was made using the potter's wheel and was painted with white line design. Equally interesting is the fact that female potters did not use the potter's wheel, only men did.

(d) They were characterised by rural settlements and were not acquainted with burnt brick, and generally lived in thatched houses made of mud bricks. Their economy was a village-based economy. Also, one can note the beginnings of social inequalities in Chalcolithic societies, as chiefs who lived in rectangular houses dominated others who lived in round huts. Along with the difference in the size of houses, the difference in the types of items found in graves indicate towards the social stratification as some graves have yielded gold, silver ornaments and semi-precious stones while in some graves cheap pottery and earthen beads have been found.

(e) Their villages were small, with huts close to each other. People lived in rectangular and circular houses with mud walls and thatched roofs. Most of the houses were single roomed but some had two or three rooms. Existence of public buildings like fort and dam in chalcolithic settlements indicates towards some type of public authority but nothing definite is known about the nature and character of public authority.

(f) Small clay images of earth goddesses have been found from Chalcolithic sites. It is thus possible to say that they venerated the Mother Goddess. The bull was probably the symbol of their religious cult (based on stylised bull terracottas of Malwa and Rajasthan). However, male figurines were rare in the discoveries of chalcolithic culture thus indicating towards the inferior status of male deities as compared to female deities. Also, with the discovery of items of common use from graves indicate that chalcolithic people believed in the idea of life after death.

(g) Chalcolithic people were fond of ornaments and decoration. The women wore ornaments of shell and bone and carried finely worked combs in their hair. They manufactured beads of semi-precious stones such as carnelian, steatite and quartz crystal. They practised trade and commerce through barter system.

(h) The Chalcolithic-era people were expert coppersmiths. They knew the art of copper-smelting and were good stone workers as well. They knew spinning and weaving too. However, they did not know the use of writing.

(i) Infant mortality was very high among Chalcolithic people, as evident from the burial of a large number of children in western Maharashtra.

FIGURE 1.8 Chalcolithic Sites in India

Chalcolithic settlements have been found in south-eastern Rajasthan, western M.P., western Maharashtra, as well as other parts of southern and eastern India. There are definite regional differences in terms of cereals produced and consumed, pottery made, and so on. For instance, eastern India produced rice, whereas western India cultivated barley and wheat. In Maharashtra, the dead were buried in the north–south direction, whereas in southern India they were buried in the east–west direction. In eastern India, fractional burial was practiced.

Major Chalcolithic Cultures	Associated Key Sites
(a) Banas culture (2600 BCE–1900 BCE) in south–east Rajasthan	Flourished in valley of River Banas (Rajasthan). Most prominent sites are Ahar near Udaipur and Gilund.
(b) Kayatha culture (2100 BCE–2000 BCE)	Flourished in valley of River Kalisind (Madhya Pradesh). Most prominent site is Kayatha in Chambal.
(c) Malwa culture (1700 BCE–1400 BCE)	Most prominent site is Navdatoli on the banks of River Narmada in Western Madhya Pradesh. Was also present in parts of Gujarat and Rajasthan.
(d) Jorwe culture (1400 BCE–700 BCE)	Flourished in valley of River Parvara (tributary of River Godavari, Maharashtra). Most prominent site are Inamgaon, Jorwe, Daimabad and Chandoli near Pune in Maharashtra
(e) Prabhas culture (1800 BCE–1400 BCE)	Flourished around Prabhas Patan (modern Somnath, Gujarat).

Important Chalcolithic Sites

S. No.	Site	Importance
1.	Ahar (Banas Valley, Rajasthan)	People practised smelting and metallurgy. Lived in stone-built houses.
2.	Gilund (Banas Valley, Rajasthan)	Seldom use of burnt bricks
3.	Nevasa (Jorwe, Maharashtra) and Eran (M.P.)	Non-Harappan culture.
4.	Navdatoli	Cultivated almost all food grains.
5.	Daimabad	Largest Jorwe culture site in Godavari valley. Famous for recovery of bronze goods such as bronze. Rhinoceros, elephant, two-wheeled chariot with a rider and a buffalo.
6.	Songaon, Inamgaon and Nasik (Maharashtra)	Large mud houses with ovens and circular pit houses.
7.	Kayatha (M.P.)	Mud-plastered floors. Pre-Harappan elements in pottery along with copper objects with sharp cutting edges.
8.	Malwa (M.P.)	Richest Chalcolithic ceramics. Spindle whorls. Non-Harappan culture.
9.	Chirand, Senuar, Sonpur (Bihar) Mahishdal (West Bengal)	Prominent sites in these concerned states.

QUESTIONS FROM LAST YEAR'S MAINS

1. Mesolithic rock cut architecture of India not only reflects the cultural life of the times but also a fine aesthetic sense comparable to modern painting. Critically evaluate this comment. **(2015)**

PRACTICE QUESTIONS – PRELIMS

1. Match the following:

Column A	Column B
i. Palaeolithic Age	A. Copper
ii. Neolithic Age	B. Discovery of fire
iii. Chalcolithic Age	C. Microliths
iv. Mesolithic Age	D. Tools for harvesting crops

(a) i. A ii. C iii. D iv. B
(b) i. C ii. A iii. D iv. B
(c) i. B ii. D iii. A iv. C
(d) i. D ii. C iii. A iv. B

2. Consider the following statements and identify which are specific to the Neolithic period.

i. Domestication of animals and growing of wild varieties of crops.
ii. People used copper and bronze to make a lot of tools.
iii. Making of specialised tools by flaking stones, which were pointed in one end.

(a) 1 only (b) 1, 2, 3
(c) 1, 3 only (d) 1, 2 only

3. Match the historical period and archaeological sites.

Period	Site
i. Palaeolithic	A. Bhimbetka
ii. Mesolithic	B. Belan
iii. Neolithic	C. Navada Toli
iv. Chalcolithic	D. Mehrgarh

(a) i. A ii. C iii. D iv. B
(b) i. C ii. A iii. D iv. B
(c) i. B ii. A iii. D iv. C
(d) i. D ii. C iii. A iv. B

4. Which of the following are characteristic of the Neolithic age?

i. Use of very finely flaked small stone stools, blades, and burins.
ii. Domestication of cattle, horses, and other farm animals.
iii. Painting and decorating pottery.

(a) i, ii, iii, only (b) i, ii only
(c) ii, iii, only (d) None of the above

5. Consider the following statements and choose the appropriate one.

i. Technologically, the Chalcolithic stage refers to pre-Harappans but in various parts of the country it appears after the end of the bronze Harappan culture.
ii. All Chalcolithic cultures are not necessarily pre-Harappan cultures, but all pre-Harappan cultures are necessarily Chalcolithic cultures.
iii. All Chalcolithic cultures are necessarily pre-Harappan cultures, but pre-Harappan cultures are not necessarily Chalcolithic cultures.

(a) i only (b) i, iii only
(c) i, ii, iii (d) i, ii only

6. Which of the following statements is correct regarding pre-historic art?
(a) Palaeolithic and Mesolithic people practised painting.
(b) Pre-historic art does not appear at the Bhimbetka caves.
(c) Many figures regarding the solar system were painted.
(d) The paintings depict the religious beliefs of the people.

7. Which was the first metal used by man?
(a) Copper (b) Silver
(c) Bronze (d) Iron

8. With which of the following periods do we associate the 'microlith' implements?
(a) Palaeolithic (b) Chalcolithic
(c) Neolithic (d) Mesolithic

9. With which period do we associate the 'megaliths'?
(a) Pleistocene
(b) Neolithic-Chalcolithic
(c) Mesolithic
(d) None of the above

10. What was the earliest metal tool used for?
(a) Pot-making
(b) House-building
(c) Clearing jungles
(d) Making wheels

11. The first animals to be domesticated during Stone Age were:
(a) Dogs, goat, sheep
(b) Dogs, horses, goat
(c) Horses, sheep, goat
(d) Sheep, elephant, dog

12. Nomadic man started settling in:
(a) Palaeolithic Age
(b) Mesolithic Age
(c) Neolithic Age
(d) Chalcolithic Age

13. Man moved from food-gathering to food-producing in the:
(a) Palaeolithic Age
(b) Mesolithic Age
(c) Chalcolithic Age
(d) Neolithic Age

14. The greatest innovation of man in the Palaeolithic age was
(a) Metal implements
(b) Potter's wheel
(c) Discovery of fire
(d) Spinning and weaving

15. During the Chalcolithic age, the only metal known to man was:
(a) Iron (b) Gold
(c) Copper (d) Silver

16. Which one of the following statements is not correct?
(a) The Chalcolithic men in India were acquainted with burnt bricks.
(b) Palaeolithic man in the later stages knew about fire.
(c) Bhimbetka Caves are a treasure house of pre-historic paintings.
(d) Man came to practice agriculture in Neolithic era.

17.

Sites		Age	
i.	Ahar and Gilund	A.	Chalcolithic
ii.	Mohenjodaro	B.	Harappa
iii.	Burzahom	C.	Neolithic
iv.	Bagor	D.	Mesolithic

(a) i. A ii. C iii. B iv. D
(b) i. C ii. A iii. D iv. B
(c) i. A ii. B iii. C iv. D
(d) i. D ii. C iii. A iv. B

18. Consider the following statements regarding the economy of the Neolithic period:

i. The economy of the early Neolithic cultures was based on agriculture and animal domestication
ii. The Neolithic man knew about iron

Which of the following statement(s) is/are correct?

(a) Only i (b) Both i and ii
(c) Only ii (d) None of the above

19. Consider the following statements regarding Chalcolithic people:

i. Chalcolithic communities traded and exchanged materials with other contemporary communities
ii. Large settlements like Ahar, Gilund, Navdatoli, Eran, Rangpur, Daimabad, and Inamgaon served as major centres of trade and exchange
iii. Ahar people, settled close to the copper source, supplied copper tools and objects to other contemporary communities in Malwa and Gujarat

Which of the following statement(s) is/are correct?

(a) Only i (b) i and ii
(c) ii and iii (d) All of the above

20. Consider the following statements regarding the status of technology during the Chalcolithic period:

i. The Chalcolithic people were expert coppersmiths and had made considerable progress in metal technology.
ii. The painted pottery was well made.

Which of the following statement(s) is/are correct?

(a) Only i (b) i and ii
(c) Only ii (d) None of the above

21. Consider the following statements regarding the Chalcolithic cultures in India:

i. Some of the Chalcolithic cultures were contemporary with the Harappan culture and others were post-Harappan.
ii. The Chalcolithic culture is characterised by painted pottery, usually red and black.
iii. It was urban as compared to rural Harappan.

Which of the following statement(s) is/are correct?

(a) Only i (b) i and ii
(c) i and iii (d) All of the above

22. Which of the following pairs is incorrectly matched?

i. Lower Palaeolithic – Handaxe and cleaver industries
ii. Middle Palaeolithic – Tools made on flakes
iii. Upper Palaeolithic – Tools made on blades and burins.

(a) Only i
(b) Only i and ii
(c) All of the above
(d) None of the above

23. Consider the following statements regarding tools and technology of the middle Palaeolithic culture:

i. The middle Palaeolithic period is characterised basically by the flakes obtained by striking them out from pebbles or cobbles.
ii. The tools included various kinds of scrapers, borers, and knives.

Which of the above statement(s) is/are correct?

(a) Only i (b) i and ii
(c) Only ii (d) None

24. Which of the following archaeological sites have Palaeolithic, Mesolithic and Neolithic remains?

(a) Belan valley (b) Bhimbetka
(c) Nevasa (d) Pushkar

ANSWERS

1. (c)	2. (a)	3. (c)	4. (a)	5. (a)	6. (a)	7. (a)	8. (d)
9. (b)	10. (c)	11. (a)	12. (c)	13. (d)	14. (c)	15. (c)	16. (a)
17. (c)	18. (a)	19. (d)	20. (b)	21. (b)	22. (d)	23. (b)	24. (a)

PRACTICE QUESTIONS – MAINS

1. Explain the different phases of the Stone Age, specifying their characteristic features and prominent sites related to each.

2. Why does the Neolithic Age hold a unique place in the evolution of mankind? Elaborate with five examples.

3. 'Technologically, the Chalcolithic phase refers to pre-Harappan cultures, but in various parts of the country, the Chalcolithic phase appears after the end of bronze Harappa culture'. Does this statement hold any authenticity? Specify with reasons.

4. In the absence of a written script, Chalcolithic pottery provides us fascinating information about the culture and lifestyle of people of those times. Comment critically.

CHAPTER

2

Harappan Civilisation/Bronze Age (c. 2600–1900 BCE)

The Harappan civilisation was the first urban civilisation in South Asia, contemporaneous with the civilisations of Mesopotamia and Egypt. Of the three aforementioned civilisations, the Harappan civilisation occupied most area (about 37 acres). Earlier historians had called this civilisation the Indus Valley Civilisation, but since then, major settlements have been excavated in the Ghaggar-Hakra belt that spread far beyond the Indus region. Harappa, as the first archaeological site to be discovered, therefore gives its name to the entire civilisation. It forms a part of the proto-history of India and belongs to the Bronze Age. While it is classified as a civilisation that is older than Chalcolithic civilisations, in many ways it was far more developed than settlements in the Chalcolithic Age. The Harappan civilisation can be classified in three phases*:

(i) Early/Pre-Harappan phase (c. 3200–2600 BCE)
(ii) Mature Harappan phase (c. 2600–1900 BCE)
(iii) Late Harappan phase (c. 1900–1300 BCE)

A general time range is specified as there is a great deal of variation in the dates for different phases.

There exists an undeniable cultural continuity among all the phases of the Harappan civilisation, yet they differ slightly from each other.

Early Harappan Phase	Mature Harappan Phase	Late Harappan Phase
Also known as the Regionalisation Era. It was the formative, proto-urban phase of the Harappan civilisation. In this phase, the people lived in large villages and there was a gradual growth of towns. It was thus a transitional phase from rural to urban life.	Also known as the Integration Era. It was **the urban phase of the Harappan civilisation,** which shows the characteristics of a full-fledged civilisation. During this phase, great cities emerged. It is pertinent to note that the unqualified term, 'Harappan Culture' or 'Harappan Civilisation', primarily refers to this mature urban phase.	The last phase of the Harappan civilisation, which is also known as the Localisation Era, was the post-urban phase defined by a decline in the cities. This is the final period in the Harappan civilisation and refers to the fragmentation of the culture of the Integration Era.
It is related to the Hakra phase of settlements, and the settlements in this period are marked by their: (a) Fortifications, (b) Fairly high level of expertise in specialised crafts such as stone-working, bead-making, and metal-crafting, (c) The use of wheeled transport, and the existence of trade networks. However, it is pertinent to note that this phase did not have the large cities that defined the mature Harappan phase, neither did it have as much expertise in craft specialisation. However, most raw materials except jade, which has not been found in the early Harappan settlements, are similar to the ones used in the mature Harappan phase.	It is equally important to understand the fact that the use of term 'Harappan Culture' or 'Harappan Civilisation' for all the excavated sites does not mean that all the other sites are identical to Harappa. It only pertains to the fact that the other sites have the same basic set of Harappan material traits, such as the typical red and black pottery, terracotta figurines, standardised brick size in 1:2:4 ratio, and so on.	Late Harappan settlements were smaller compared to mature Harappan ones. The transition from the mature phase does not show any sudden discontinuity as such, but there is a gradual change in seals, pottery confined writing, in the frequency of cubical weights, and so on.

Early Harappan Phase	Mature Harappan Phase	Late Harappan Phase
Some of the early Harappan archaeological sites are Padri in Gujarat, Kalibangan in Rajasthan, Dholavira in Kutch, Harappa in West Punjab, Balakot, Amri, and Bhirrana in Haryana, Kot Diji and Gumla in Pakistan. It is **noteworthy** to add that there are no early Harappan sites in the active Indus plain.	Some of the important sites belonging to this phase are Harappa in West Punjab, Mohenjo-Daro, Chanhudaro and Suktagendor in Pakistan, Lothal in Gujarat, Kalibangan in Rajasthan, Dholavira in Kutch, Banawali and Rakhigarhi in Haryana.	The Late Harappan phase comprises five geographical zones each having distinct phases: (a) The West Punjab Phase (Cemetery-Harappan Culture), (b) The East Punjab Phase, (c) The Jhukar Phase: Important Jhukar sites are Jhukar, Chanhudaro and Amri. (d) The Rangpur Phase: Prominent Rangpur phase sites are in Kutch, Saurashtra and mainland Gujarat. (e) The Ganga–Yamuna Doab Phase: It should be noted that even though the Late Harappan settlements were more in number, yet they were smaller and more rural, though marked by a diverse agricultural base.

General Features of the Mature Harappan Phase

Archaeological evidence reveals a great deal about the Harappan civilisation, which is marked by both cultural homogeneity as well as diversity. There is still no totally accepted theory on the origin of Harappan culture but generally it is believed to have either emerged from pre-Harappan/indigenous village culture (which may be the more reasonable view), or, as argued by diffusionist theorists, it owes its origin to the Mesopotamian Civilisation. The area occupied by the Harappan civilisation was triangular in shape and was the largest among the three ancient urban civilisations, the other two being ancient Egypt and Mesopotamaia (present day Iraq). It roughly covers modern day Rajasthan, Punjab, Haryana, Gujarat and Pakistan.

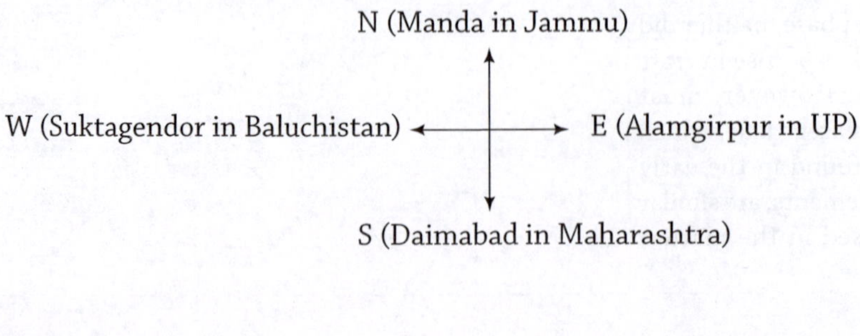

Town Planning

Harappan civilisation is known for its urban outlook and sophisticated sense of civic planning and organisation. In most cases the Harappan city was divided into two parts:

- Citadel/Raised Part – This part occupied a smaller area, and was mostly situated to the west of the city. Rulers of the city lived here. It also contained public buildings, granaries, and important workshops.
- Lower Part – The common citizenry lived and carried on their professional lives in this part of the city.

Distinguishing aspects of Harappan town planning are as follows:

(a) The streets were wide, the main street being ten metres wide which divided the town into rectangular and square blocks. There were lamp-posts at intervals.

(b) Burnt bricks of good quality were used and the unique feature of this brick was its identical ratio of 1:2:4 in terms of thickness:width:length across all Harappan structures. Equally striking was the uniformity in the average size of bricks – 7 × 14 × 28 cm for houses and 10 × 20 × 40 cm for city walls.

(c) They had an excellent underground drainage system – drains were made of mortar, lime and gypsum and covered with large brick or stone slabs for easy cleaning. All the houses were connected to the street drains which were built on either side of the roads. The street drains were made of baked brick with special shaped bricks to form corners. They were well aware of the principles of waterproofing as the bricks were closely fitted and sealed with mud mortar to prevent the leakage of dirty water. Alongwith it, small settling pools and traps were also built at regular intervals to allow only water to flow away, thereby maintaining a check on the solid wastes and other sediments from being washed away with the water.

(d) Houses were often of two or more storeys, though varied in size but quite monotonous. The houses had tiled bathrooms and some houses had their own wells but no window faced the streets.

The town planning roughly followed a grid pattern and streets ran from north and cut at right angles. The Harappans collected rain water in water reservoirs as evident at Dholavira.

Society and Polity

(a) The Harappan society was an urban society, comprising mostly of the middle class. The houses excavated suggest at least three distinct social groups: **ruled**, **rich merchants** and **poor labourers** who lived in the lower part of the city.

(b) The Harappan people followed diverse professions such as priests, warriors, peasants, traders and artisans, etc. The structural remains at sites such as Harappa[1] and Lothal[2] indicate that different types of buildings were used as residence by different classes. Social differentiation is also attested by different residential structures, with the number of rooms varying from one to twelve.

(c) Nothing is known definitely about the nature of polity. But, based on the predominance of mercantile class in Harappan cities, it is presumed that the Harappa was possibly ruled by a class of merchants who were probably more concerned with commerce than with conquest. However, fortification is evident in several cities. For instance, Dholavira, in particular, had forts within forts.

(d) It seems that the Harappan civilisation had urban administrative bodies similar to modern *Municipal Committees* since the planned layout of cities, construction and maintenance of public buildings would have been virtually impossible in the absence of such bodies.

(e) The Harappan society appears to be **matriarchal** in nature as indicated by the finding of a large number of terracotta female figurines and also based on the popularity of the mother goddess in Harappan culture but still not much is known about the nature of inheritance in Harappan society.

(f) Harappan people generally wore garments of cotton, silk and wool. A piece of woven cloth has been found at Mohenjo-Daro while the discovery of spindles and needles at many sites attest to the practice of spinning and weaving among the Harappan people. Their dress styles can be inferred from the terracotta figurines and stone sculptures belonging to that period, wherein men are mostly shown wearing a dress wrapped round the lower half of the body with one end worn over the left shoulder and under the right arm.

Agriculture and Animal Domestication

Agriculture was the important source of subsistence for the Harappans. The Harappans[3] grew wheat (especially in Mehrgarh), barley, horse gram, peas, melon, watermelon, sesame, dates, millets, grapes, henna (*mehndi*), garlic, mustard, rice (Lothal). They produced sufficient food grains to feed themselves and the surplus food grains[4] were stored in granaries as evident from the discovery of granaries at sites of Harappa, Mohenjo-Daro and Lothal.

---

[1] The presence of a class of workmen is proved by the workmen quarters near the granary at Harappa.

[2] Similarly, the workshops and houses meant for coppersmiths and beadmakers have been discovered at Lothal.

[3] The Harappan societies of Sindh and Punjab largely consumed wheat and barley while those of Rangpur and Surkotda consumed rice and millets.

[4] In all probability, the food grains were received as taxes from peasants and stored in granaries for the payment of wages as well as for use during emergencies.

The characteristic features pertaining to the agricultural practices of the Harappans were:

(a) The Harapppan people ploughed fields, possibly with the help of wooden ploughs; the same have been discovered at Kalibangan. Terracotta models of plough have been found at Banawali and Bahawalpur.

(b) Harappans, in general, did not use canals and rather practised flood irrigation. In Indus plain, people sowed seeds in the flood plains in November, when the flood water receded they reaped their harvests of wheat and barley in April, before the advent of the next flood.

(c) The Harappan civilisation was the earliest known civilisation to produce cotton. This cotton was known as '*Sindon*' by the Greeks as it was from Sindh.

(d) The Harappans relished non-vegetarian food and thus exploited riverine and marine resources wherever possible. For example, fish-eating was common and molluscs were an important protein-rich food element of the people in the coastal sites of Gujarat. Apart from non-vegetarian food, the Harappan people also consumed milk and curd.

(e) The Harappans domesticated animals on a large scale. Besides cattle (oxen, buffaloes, goats, humped bulls, sheep, pigs, asses, camels) cats and dogs were also domesticated. It is pertinent to note here that Harappan culture was not horse-centred. They were well acquainted with the elephant and the rhinoceros but horse was not used regularly.

Industries and Crafts

The Harappans showed good masterly skills in a variety of arts and crafts. Their major crafts included bead and ornament making, shell bangle making, ivory carving and metal working. The Harappans also practised boat making and seal making. Terracotta[5] manufacturing and bricklaying were also other important crafts. They were well aware of civil engineering as evident by the various structures like dams and forts. Their medical knowledge was also advanced as revealed by the evidence of skull surgery found at Kalibangan and Lothal. They also refined the art of bead making and made beads and ornaments out of shell, carnelian, jasper, crystal, steatite and metals like copper, bronze, gold and terracotta in innumerable designs and decorations. Bead makers' shops have been excavated at Chanhudaro and Lothal.

The characteristic features associated with industries and craft production were:

(a) The jewellery excavated includes gold and silver jewellery, which includes ornaments of all sorts such as necklaces, bracelets, pendants, earrings and brooches. For instance, at Allahdino (near Karachi), a lot of necklaces made of gold, silver, carnelian and semi-precious stones have been found. Harappans were the first to use silver in the world.

[5] The terracotta pieces (fire baked earthen clay) represent unsophisticated artistic works while the seals and images were manufactured with great skill.

(b) Harappan people loved to decorate themselves and hair dressing by both men and women is evident from figurines found at different sites.

(c) A lot of terracotta items have been found at many sites, including terracotta figurines of males and females, figurines of animals such as bulls, buffaloes, dogs, monkeys and various models of terracotta toy carts. It is important to note that more female figurines have been uncovered in comparison to male figurines.

(d) The Harappan people knew and used almost all the metals such as copper, bronze, silver and gold but it seems that they did not have any knowledge of iron.

(e) They were also good at metallurgy and producing alloys. The craftsmen used to make artifacts out of both pure copper and bronze such as spears, knives, short swords, mirrors, axes, needles, rings and bangles. The Harappan artisans also made beautiful images of metal, as exhibited in the famous 'dancing girl' bronze idol found at Mohenjo-Daro. It is rather interesting that the number of pure copper artifacts was far greater than alloyed bronze ones, but it does not mean technological backwardness rather points towards cultural preference in all likelihood. It is also important to note that the weapons produced by the Harappans were mostly defensive in nature as there is no evidence of weapons like swords, etc.

(f) Another well-known piece of art of the Harappan period is the stone sculpture of a bearded man, probably the bust of a priest discovered at Mohenjo-Daro, which is having an embroidered cloak across his left shoulder and his eyes are half closed indicating a posture of meditation (Fig. 2.1).

FIGURE 2.1 Stone Sculpture of Bearded Man

Pottery

The Harappans were experts in the use of the potter's wheel and used diverse varieties of pottery for daily use which were well baked and fine in decorations. Primarily red black pottery, the red ware pottery painted with black designs were popular. The painted motifs generally noticed on the pottery are horizontal lines of varied thickness, leaf patterns, palm and *pipal* trees, intersecting circles, geometrical motifs with both floral and faunal patterns such as figurines of birds, fishes and animals like rabbits, peacocks, ducks, pigeons, wild fowl and monkeys. The pottery is shaped like dish-on-stands, S-shaped jars, plates, dishes, bowls and pots. Some of these pots were used for storing grain or water, while some perforated pots were probably used for brewing fermented alcoholic beverages (Fig. 2.2).

FIGURE 2.2 **Harappan pottery (3300–1300 BCE) showcases sophisticated artistry, diverse designs, and trade insights.**

Script

The Harappan script was pictographic and logosyllabic (each symbol stood for a word/syllable). It is believed that they used ideograms, i.e. a graphic symbol or a character to convey the idea directly. Harappan writing was boustrophedon, that is to say, right to left and left to right in alternate lines. The number of signs is between 400 and 600, of which 40 or 60 are basic and the rest are their variants. Although the earliest specimen of the Harappan script was discovered in 1853 and the complete script by 1923, yet it has not been deciphered so far. The evidence of a common script however points to great cultural integration, and its virtual disappearance by c.1700 BCE hints at the lack of sufficient downward percolation of writing.

Economy

The inferences about the Harappan economy have been derived from its flourishing trade relations with its contemporary Mesopotamian and Persian civilisations. The Mesopotamians called the Indus Region '*Meluhha*'. The Mesopotamian texts speak of three intermediate trading stations called *Dilmun* (probably Bahrain on Persian Gulf), Makan (probably the Makran coast, Oman) and *Meluhha*. They also indicate that Mesopotamia imported copper, carnelian, ivory, shell, lapis-lazuli, pearls and ebony from 'Meluhha'. The export from Mesopotamia to Harappans included items[6] such as garments, wool, perfumes, leather products and silver. The trading network was not limited to external (foreign) network but included internal network (within the country) also.

There was no metallic money in circulation and trade was conducted by means of barter. Inland transport primarily employed bullock carts (Fig. 2.3) while they navigated the regions located on Arabian Sea by boat.

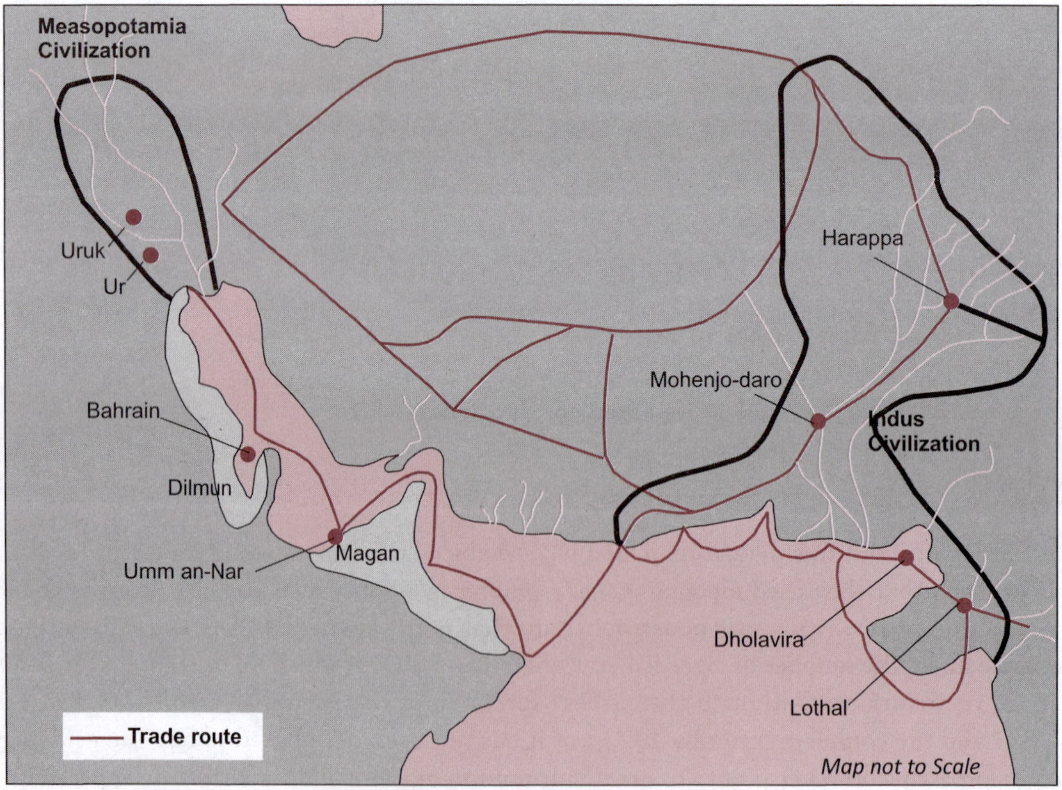

FIGURE 2.3 Trade Routes of Indus Valley

[6] The probable reason behind the lack of remains of these goods at Harappan sites is that except silver, all these products are perishable.

The key aspects of Harappan trade networks and economy are as follows:

(a) Seals hold a special significance in the Harappan context (Fig. 2.4). Every merchant probably had a seal bearing an emblem, often of a religions character and a name/brief description on one side. The standard Harappa seal was a square/oblong plaque made of steatite stone. It is noteworthy that while the seals depict a number of animals there is no representation of horse on these while Bull and Fish are the most commonly depicted animals. Though its primary purpose is inferred to mark the ownership of property, they may also have served as amulets.

(b) Harappan seals have been found in Mesopotamian cities like Susa and Ur. In Nippur, a seal has been found bearing Harappan script and a unicorn. Recently, some ancient sites in the Persian Gulf like Failaka and Bahrain have also yielded Harappan seals. In Mohenjo-Daro, three cylindrical seals of the Mesopotamian type have been found, which underline their trading relations.

(c) In Lothal, a button seal has been found. There were bead-making factories at Chanhudaro and Lothal. The products of these factories were items of export. A dockyard has been excavated in Lothal and sea ports have been found at Rangpur, Somnath and Balakot.

(d) A remarkable aspect of the Harappan culture was its standardisation and accuracy in the context of weights and measures. Weights followed a binary system in the lower denominations – 1, 2, 8, 16, 32 to 64, and then in decimal multiples of 160 like 160, 320, 640, 1600, 3200, and so on. Weights were made of chert, limestone and steatite and were generally cubical in shape.

(e) Measures of length were based on the foot (37.6 cm) and the cubit (51.8 to 53.3 cm). A shell scale has been found at Mohenjo-Daro, a shell object probably used to measure angles has been found at Saurashtra, and an ivory scale has been discovered at Lothal.

FIGURE 2.4 Stamp of Mohenjo-Daro

Harappan Imports

Metals	Source Region
Gold	Afghanistan, Iran, Kolar (South India)
Copper	Khetri (Rajasthan), Baluchistan, Oman
Tin	Afghanistan, Iran
Lapis lazuli	Shortughai (Afghanistan)
Jade	Pamir (Central Asia)
Turquoise	Khorasan (Central Asia)
Steatite	Tapi Chahya (Iran), South Rajasthan
Bitumin	Baluchistan, Mesopotamia
Lead	South India
Silver	Zawar Mines of Rajasthan, Mesopotamia

Religion

Harappan civilisation is considered a secular society because not a single structure qualifying as temple has been found. Sacred ritual spots included the Great Bath at Mohenjo-Daro[7], where the elite in all likelihood undertook ritual activity that included ceremonial bathing (Fig. 2.5). The Harappan religion is normally termed as animism, i.e. worship of trees, stones, etc. Considering the extensive discovery of amulets, the Harappans probably believed in the existence of ghosts and evil forces and therefore used amulets against them.

FIGURE 2.5 The Great Bath at Mohenjo-Daro

[7] The Great Bath measures 11.88*7.01 m and is 2.43 m deep. Flights of steps at either end lead to the surface and there were side rooms for changing clothes. The floor of the bath was made of burnt bricks and water was probably drawn from a large well in an adjacent room while an outlet from the corner of the bath led to a drain.

Other key inferences about the Harappan religious practices are as follows:

(a) Idolatry was practiced. The Harappan people generally worshipped:

- Mother goddess (Fig. 2.6)
- Pashupati Mahadeva or proto-Shiva (mostly an upper-class preference, seals depict him in a yogic posture)
- Lingam (phallus) and yoni worship (cult of fertility)
- Pipal tree
- Humped bull
- Birds (dove and pigeon)
- One-horned unicorn (may in fact be the rhinoceros)

(b) Fire altars have been found in Kalibangan and Lothal.

(c) The seal of Pashupati Mahadeva is surrounded by an elephant, a tiger, a rhino, a buffalo and a deer and it is likely that these animals were also worshipped (Fig. 2.7).

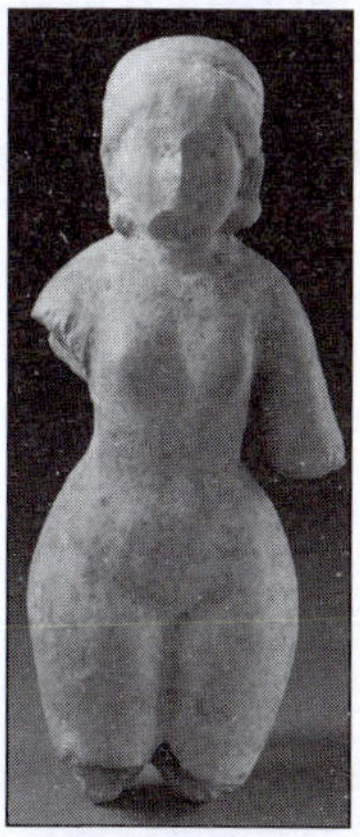

FIGURE 2.6 Fertility Goddess

Figure 2.7 Pashupati Shiva

(d) Dead bodies were placed in a north–south direction and were generally accompanied by objects including food, pottery, ornaments and tools. These items were not as expensive in comparison to those in contemporary Mesopotamian or Egyptian cultures. However, there is still no clear idea among historians about the nature of inheritance in Harappan society.

(e) Three methods of burial were used:

- Complete burial
- Fractional burials (where the bones were gathered and buried after exposure of the body to birds and beasts)

- Cremation followed by burial of the ashes

(f) In Harappa, coffins containing bodies have been found. In Kalibangan, small circular pits containing large urns and pottery have been found. Furthermore, a triangular terracotta cake has been discovered, which has a horned deity on one side and an animal being dragged by a human on the end of a rope on the other, pointing towards animal sacrifice in all likelihood.

(g) Remains of horses at Surkotda and dogs with men in graves at Ropar have been discovered. At Lothal, a pair of male and female skeletons have been discovered together.

Decline

The Harappan decline is roughly dated around 1900 BCE, but no archaeological evidence accurately provides an explanation for the de-urbanisation. The Mature phase was followed by the late Harappan phase. There is, however, no unanimous view pertaining to the cause for the decline of the Harappan Culture. Possible theories for decline of the Harappan civilisation are as follows:

Possible Causes for Decline of Harappan Civilisation

(a) Aryan invasion
(b) Ecological disturbance
(c) Change in river course
(d) Low rainfall
(e) Flood
(f) Drying of Ghaghar and increasing aridity
(g) Earthquake
(h) Natural calamities

Famous Harappan Sites

Site	State	River	Excavator	Specialities
Harappa	Pakistan (Punjab)	Ravi	Dayaram Sahini (1921), Vats (1940)	- Two rows of six granariets - Evidence of coffin burial and cemetery 'H' culture - Single-room barracks - Two red stone idols of a dancing girl and naked bust of male, female genitalia

Site	State	River	Excavator	Specialities
				- Evidence of direct trade interaction with Mesopotamia - Post-cremation burials more numerous
Mohenjo-Daro 'Mound of the dead'	Pakistan (Sindh)	Indus	R. D. Banerji (1922) Marshall (1931), Kashinath Dixit, Sir John, E. Makay (1938)	- Multi-pillared assembly hall - Great Bath (a public venue) - College of priests - Large granary - Piece of woven cotton cloth - Superficial evidence of horse - Bronze dancing girl - Violent death of some inhabitants (discovery of human skeletons together) - Seal representing Mother Goddess, Pashupati, bearded man and a woman to be sacrificed - Evidence of ship/big boat - Bangles of clay
Lothal	Gujarat (Ahmedabad District, at the head of the Gulf of Cambay)	Bhogava and Sabarmati river confluence	S.R. Rao (1957)	- Dockyard - Important sea trade centre and bead-making factory - Town not divided into two sectors - City divided into six sectors and each section was built on a wide platform of unique brick - Remains of rice husks - Houses with entrances on the main street (houses of all other sites had side entries) - Painting on a jar resembling the story of the cunning fox in *Panchatantra* - Evidence of double burial (male and female together). - Brick-built tank-like structure - Seal from Mesopotamia found here - Ivory scale found here - Terracotta model of ship found here - The lower part of the city is walled - Fire altars

Site	State	River	Excavator	Specialities
Kaliban-gan 'Black Bangles'	Rajasthan (Hanuman-garh Distt.)	Ghaggar	Amlanand Ghosh (1953) Dr. B. B. Lal and B. K. Thapar (1961)	- Ploughed field - Fire altars showing practice of cult of sacrifice - Remains of massive brick wall around both citadel and lower town - Bones of camel - Not as well-planned and organised as Mohenjo-Daro; did not even have a drainage system - Burials in circular and rectangular graves - Provides evidence of pre-Harappan civilisation at lower layer of excavation and mature Harappan at upper layer of excavation - Decorative bricks used in flooring only at this site
Chanhu-Daro	Pakistan (Sindh), near Mohenjo-Daro	Indus	N.G. Mazumdar (1931) and E. Makay	- Remains of both pre-Harappan and Mature Harappan culture. - Bead factory site as lots of beads, seals, ornaments unearthed - Residents were good craftsmen - No fortified structure - Only Harappan city without a citadel - Evidence of human sacrifice - Clay model of four-wheeler - Bronze model of roofed chariot
Rangpur (near Lo-thal)	Gujarat	Bhadar	M.S. Vatsa (1931) S.R. Rao (1953–1954)	- Remains of both pre-Harappan and Mature Harappan culture - Flakes - Yellow and grey color pots of pre Harappan people.
Banawali (Hisar)	Haryana	Rangoi	R.S. Bist (1973–1974)	- Centre of pre-Harappan, Mature Harap-pan as well as Late Harappan civilisation - High quality barley - Ceramics, steatite seal - Fire altars - Clay model of plough - Seals found only in lower town and not in citadel

Site	State	River	Excavator	Specialities
Alamgir-pur	Meerut (U. P.)	Hindon	Y.D. Sharma (1958)	- Late-Harappan culture - Impression of cloth on a trough - Pottery and beads
Kot-Diji	Sindh (Pakistan)	Sindh	Ghurey (1935) Fazal Ahmed Khan (1955)	- Pre-Harappan site - House made of stone - City destroyed by force
Amri	Sindh (Pakistan)	Indus	N.G. Majumdar (1929)	- Pre-Harappan settlement - Transitional culture between pre- and post-Harappan culture - Actual remains of rhinoceros, trace of Jhangar culture in Late Harappan civilisation and fire altars
Ropar	Punjab (India)	Sutlej	Y.D. Sharma (1955–1956)	- Cemetery, seal, earthen pot Buildings mainly of stone and soil - Evidence of burying dog below human
Surkotada	Gujarat (Kutch)	Sabar-mati	J.P. Joshi (1964)	- Bones of horse and graveyard
Suktagen-dor	Sindh (Pakistan) Baluchistan	Dasht/ Dashak river	A Stein, George Dales (1929)	- Ash filled pot, copper axe, earthen bangles and pottery - Originally a port but later cut off from sea due to coastal uplift - Had trade links with Babylon.
Dholavira	Gujarat (Kutch)	Luni River	J.P. Joshi (1968) Excavation between 1990–2005 was carried out by R.S. Bisht	- Giant water reservoir - Unique water harvesting system – An inscription comprising ten large sized signs of the Harappan script similar to a signboard - Shows all three phases of Harappan culture - Large-scale use of sandstone along with mud brick - Megalith burial has been found. - Evidences of Irrigation, dams and Embankments.

Site	State	River	Excavator	Specialities
Rakhigarhi (near Hisar), Bhirrana (Fate-hgarh)	Haryana	Ghaggar River Plain	Amarendra Nath	- Over 350 hectares with new finds of two additional mounds, making it the largest Indus Valley civilisation site and town in the world - Shows all three phases of Harappan Culture - At Bhirrana a fragmented artefact of a thick, sturdy red ware with an incised female figure has been found, with a pose similar to the bronze Mohenjo-Daro 'dancing girl'

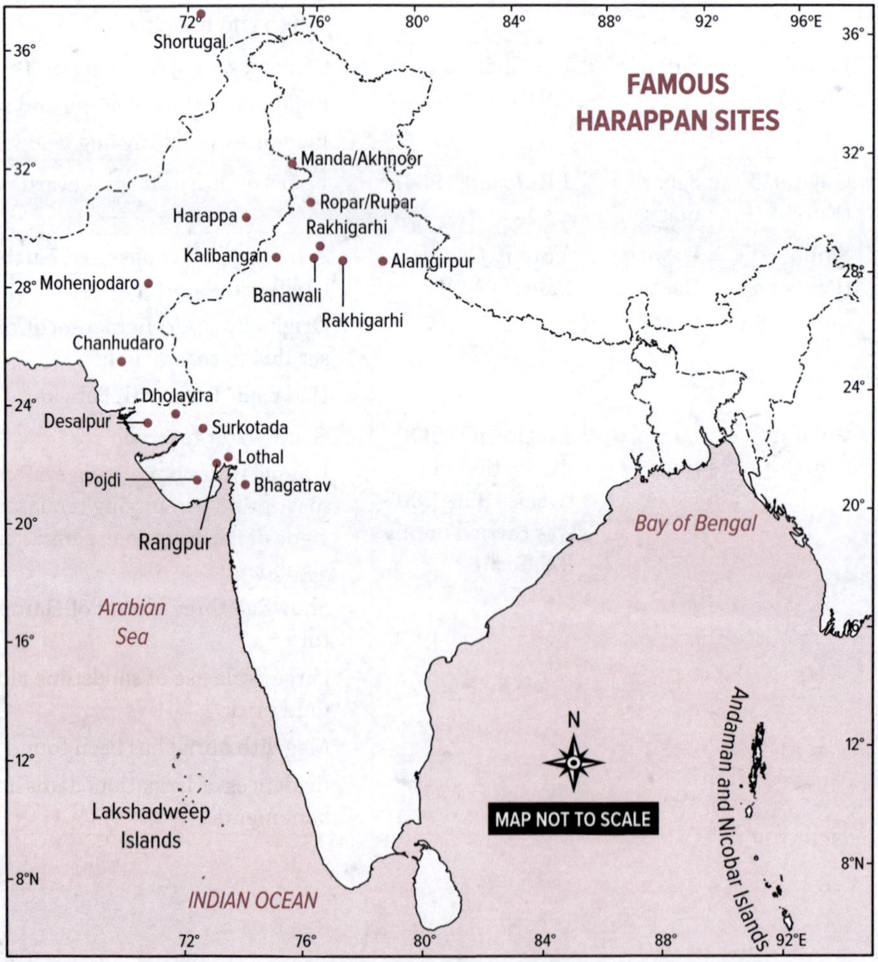

FIGURE 2.8 Famous Harappan Sites

DISTINGUISHING FEATURES OF HARAPPAN AND MESOPOTAMIAN CIVILSATIONS

Harappan	Egyptian/Mesopotamian
1. Planned towns with chess board system, excellent drainage system	1. Towns show a haphazard growth
2. Rectangular houses with brick-lined bathrooms and wells together with their stairways are found in all Harappan cities	2. Such town planning absent
3. Produced their own characteristic pottery and seals	3. No such unique aspect
4. Invented their own typical script, which bears no resemblance to the Egyptian and Mesopotamian scripts	4. Mesopotamia has cuneiform script and the Egyptian script is known as hieroglyphics. Both scripts have been deciphered, which tell a lot about the civilisations
5. Script mostly on seals	5. Mesopotamians pressed letters onto moist clay tablets while Egyptians wrote on papyrus sheets made of reeds
6. No signs of existence after 1900 BCE	6. Continued to exist even after 1900 BCE
7. Spread over a wider area	7. Less area as compared to Harappa
8. Produced rice and domesticated elephants	8. Not the case with the Mesopotamians

Post-Urban Phase of Harappan Culture/Late Harappan Phase (c. 1900 BCE–1300 BCE)

The Mature Harappan phase was followed by the Late Harappan phase, which was marked by the decline of urban life and the diversification of agriculture. The stylistic homogeneity of Harappan civilisation disappeared and the post-Harappan stage was marked by sharp stylistic diversity. There was a complex interplay of change and continuity. Elements of urbanism like seals, specialised crafts, cities, long distance trade, and so on, declined but did not completely disappear. Some of the few urban centres surviving in the Late Harappan were Kudwala in Cholistan, Bet Dwarka in Gujarat and Daimabad. A key development in this phase was the beginning of double cropping – wheat and barley were grown as winter crops and rice, millets and sorghum were grown as summer crops. Other key features of this period were:

- The declining culture in this phase is also referred to as sub-Indus culture.
- The rural settlements of this phase are primarily Chalcolithic in nature.
- The post-urban Harappans lived in villages, subsisting on agriculture, stock-raising, hunting and fishing.

- In this period, painted Harappan pottery is replaced with less intricate designs and painted grey ware (PGW). All Late Harappan sites lack human figurines. In comparison with Mature Harappan pottery, the pottery in this phase was less bright. The pots were thicker and sturdier and many peculiar Harappan shapes like perforated jars, s-shaped jars disappeared.
- No object for measuring length is noticed.
- This period marks the end of the Harappan trade with West Asian centres, as lapis lazuli, chert, carnelian beads, copper and bronze vessels are either absent or scarce as trade items.
- Important places pertaining to this phase are Prabhas Patan (Somnath), Rangpur (Gujarat), Swat Valley, Manda in Jammu, Sanghol in Punjab, Daulatpur in Haryana, Alamgirpur, Hulas in Uttar Pradesh.

LATEST DEVELOPMENTS

a. In 2021, UNESCO included Dholavira in Gujarat as India's 40th world heritage site. It is the first site of Harappan civilisation in India to be included in the coveted list. Dholavira in Gujarat and Rakhigarhi in Haryana are also among the five[8] archaeological sites to be developed as 'iconic' Destinations in 2020 (Fig. 2.9).

FIGURE 2.9 Dholavira in Gujarat

[8] The other sites are Adhichanallur in Tamil Nadu, Hastinapur in Uttar Pradesh, and Sivasagar in Assam.

b. Two ancient mounds at Rakhigarhi[9] in Haryana are identified as sites of national importance. Rakhigarhi Museum and Interpretation Centre, showcasing largest collection of Harappan artefacts, is also being built at Rakhigarhi.

c. Scientists from IIT-Kharagpur and the Archaeological Survey of India (ASI) have uncovered evidence that the Indus Valley Civilisation is at least 8,000 years old, and not 5,500 years old, taking root well before the Egyptian (7000 BC–3000 BC) and Mesopotamian (6500 BC–3100 BC) civilisations. What's more, the researchers have found evidence of a pre-Harappan civilisation that existed for at least 1,000 years before this.

d. The civilisation proliferated to other Indian sites like Bhirrana and Rakhigarhi in Haryana, apart from the known locations of Harappa and Mohenjo-Daro in Pakistan and Lothal, Dholavira and Kalibangan in India.

e. The scientists believe they also know why the civilisation ended about 3,000 years ago – climate change. The Indus Valley people were very resolute and flexible and continued to evolve even in the face of declining monsoon. The people shifted their crop patterns from large-grained cereals like wheat and barley during the early part of intensified monsoon to drought-resistant species like rice in the latter part. As the yield diminished, the organised large storage system of the Mature Harappan period gave way to more individual household-based crop processing and storage systems that acted as a catalyst for the de-urbanisation of the civilisation rather than an abrupt collapse, they say.

DO YOU KNOW?

a. Burnt Bricks: Harappa Dried Bricks: Egypt Baked Bricks: Mesopotamia/Sumeria

b. At the time of the Harappan civilisation, Sindh and Rajasthan were not desert areas as they are today.

c. The Great Bath at Mohenjo-Daro served ritual bathing.

d. Contemporary Sumerian cities also produced the same food grains and domesticated the same animals as Harappans, but the Harappan people in Gujarat produced rice and domesticated elephants, which was not the case with the people of Mesopotamian cities.

e. The Harappans knew the use of wheel but not that of the spoked wheel.

f. No temples or religious structures (except the Great Bath) have been found at Harappa. It is very likely that no priests ruled in Harappa, as they did in Mesopotamia.

[9] Rakhigarhi is now considered to be the largest Harappan site in the Indian subcontinent overtaking Mohenjo-Daro. Recently, DNA was isolated from the skeleton of a Harappan lady at Rakhigarhi and from its results, it was established that the dominant gene in most south Asians is 25–30% Harappan. By craniofacial reconstruction, it was found that Harappans resembled contemporary Haryanvis.

g. The Harappans did not have in weapons.

h. The Inhabitants of the Indus region worshipped gods in the form of trees, animals, and human beings, but the gods were not placed in temples as was done in ancient Egypt and Mesopotamia.

i. Although Harappan culture was a Bronze Age Culture, yet they used bronze on a limited scale, and largely continued to use stone implements.

j. Ragi or Finger Millets have not been found in any Harappan site in North India.

k. Shortughai is a Harappan trading post in Afghanistan.

l. Pre-Harappan Phase – Kot Digi, Amri, Harappan, Kalibangan, Banwali; Mature Phase – Harappa, Mohanjo-Daro, Chanhudaro, Kalibangan.

m. A. Cunningham, a British engineer, who later became a great excavator and explorer, noticed a Harappan seal for the first time in 1853 but he did not realise its significance then. It was only in 1921 that the potentiality of the Harappan site was appreciated when an Indian archeologist Daya Ram Sahni started excavating it.

QUESTIONS FROM LAST YEAR'S PRELIMS

1. Which one of the following ancient towns is well known for its elaborate system of water harvesting and management by building a series of dams and channelising water into connected reservoirs? **(2021)**

(a) Dholavira (b) Kalibangan
(c) Rakhigarhi (d) Ropar

2. Which one of the following is not a Harappa site? **(2019)**

(a) Chanhudaro (b) Kot Diji
(c) Sohagaura (d) Desalpur

3. Which of the following characterises/characterise the people of the Indus Valley Civilisation? **(2013)**

i. They possessed great palaces and temples.
ii. They worshipped both male and female deities.
iii. They employed horse-drawn chariots in warfare.

Select the correct statement/statements using the codes given below.

(a) i and ii only
(b) ii only
(c) i, ii and iii
(d) None of the statements given above is correct.

4. Regarding the Indus Valley Civilisation, consider the following statements: **(2011)**

i. It was predominantly a secular civilisation and the religious element, though present, did not dominate the scene.
ii. During this period, cotton was used for manufacturing textiles in India.

Which of the statements given above is/are correct?

(a) i only
(b) ii only
(c) Both i and ii
(d) Neither i nor ii

5. Match List I with List II and select the correct answer using the codes given below: **(2002)**

	Ancient Site		Finding
(A)	Lothal	i.	Ploughed Field
(B)	Kalibangan	ii.	Dockyard
(C)	Dholavira	iii.	Terracota replica of a plough
(D)	Banawali	iv.	An Inscription comprising ten large sized signs of the Harappan Script.

Codes

(a) A–i; B–ii; C–iii; D–iv
(b) A–ii; B–i; C–iv; D–iii
(c) A–i; B–ii; C–iv; D–iii
(d) A–ii; B–i; C–iii; D–iv

6. Which of the following animals was not represented in seals and terracotta art of Harappan Sculpture? **(2002)**

(a) Cow (b) Elephant
(c) Rhinoceros (d) Tiger

ANSWERS

1. (a) 2. (c) 3. (b) 4. (c) 5. (b) 6. (a)

QUESTIONS FROM LAST YEAR'S MAINS

1. The ancient civilisation in the Indian subcontinent differed from those of Egypt, Mesopotamia, and Greece in that its culture and traditions have been preserved without a breakdown to the present day. Comment. **(2015 GS1)**

2. To what extent has the urban planning and culture of the Indus Valley Civilisation provided inputs to present day urbanisation? Discuss. **(2014**

3. Write about the chief feature planning in Indus Valley

PRACTICE QUESTIONS – PRELIMS

1. Terracotta model of ship is found at

(a) Lothal (b) Harappa
(c) Mohenjo-Daro (d) Alamgirp

2. A stone-cut reservoir has been at:

(a) Surkotada (b) Kalibar
(c) Dholavira (d) Harap

(b) A–i, B–ii, C–iii, D–iv
(c) A–iv, B–iii, C–ii, D–i
(d) A–iii, B–i, C–ii, D–iv

4. Consider the following statements and mark the option which is correct.
i. The first man-made port was found in Harappa.
ii. The main crops of the Indus Valley Civilisation were wheat and barley.
iii. The largest Harappan settlement in India is Rakhigarhi in Haryana.
iv. The largest number of settlements are in the Ghaggar-Hakar valley.
(a) i and ii (b) all of the above
(c) ii, iii and iv (d) none of the above

5. Match the following:

A.	Mohenjo-Daro	i.	Daya Ram Sahni
B.	Chanhu-Daro	ii.	S.R. Rao
C.	Harappa	iii.	R.D. Banerjee
D.	Lothal	iv.	N.G. Majumdar

(a) A–iii, B–iv, C–i, D–ii
(b) A–iii, B–i, C–iv, D–ii
(c) A–i, B–ii, C–iii, D–iv
(d) A–i, B–ii, C–iv, D–iii

6. Match the following:

i.	Ghaggar	A.	Mohenjo-Daro
ii.	Ravi	B.	Kalibangan
iii.	Indus	C.	Lothal
iv.	Bhogava	D.	Harappa

A–i, B–ii, C–iii, D–iv
...i, B–iv, C–i, D–ii
...i, C–iv, D–ii
...–iv, D–i

7. Co... ...ing statements and mar... ...correct.
i ... an...
ii. Evid... in fl... Kaliban... ...d from Lothal
... used
... at

iii. A clay model of plough has been discovered from Banawali.
iv. The steatite figure of a bearded man has been recovered from Mohenjo-Daro.
(a) All of the above
(b) ii and iii
(c) None of the above
(d) i, ii and iii

8. Match the following:

i.	Mohenjo-Daro	A.	Great Bath
ii.	Chanhu-Daro	B.	Without citadel
iii.	Lothal	C.	Dockyard
iv.	Harappa	D.	Sandstone-make dancer

(a) A–i, B–ii, C–iii, D–iv
(b) A–iii, B–i, C–ii, D–iv
(c) A–ii, B–iii, C–iv, D–i
(d) A–i, B–iii, C–ii, D–iv

9. Consider the following statements and mark the option which is correct.
i. Broken ivory was used as a scale in Chanhu-Daro.
ii. During burial, bodies were laid down in north-south direction.
iii. The Great Bath of Mohenjo-Daro.
(a) i, ii and iii (b) ii and iii
(c) i and ii (d) All of the above

10. Consider the following statements and mark the option which is correct.
i. The fertility goddess denotes people's faith in fertility cult.
ii. The area occupied by the Harappan civilisation was triangular in shape.
iii. Remains of the horse have been discovered from Surkotada.
iv. Painting on a jar resembling the story of the cunning fox from the *Panchtantra* has been found in Lothal.
(a) i and iv
(b) All of the above

(c) None of the above
(d) iii only

11. Consider the following statements and choose the appropriate options from the answers.

i. Harappan script is regarded as pictographic.
ii. The script was boustrophedon, written from left to right and right to left in alternate lines.
iii. The script of the Harappans is not deciphered till now.

(a) i, ii, iii (b) ii, iii only
(c) i, iii only (d) None of the above

12. Consider the following statements about Harappan sites and choose the appropriate one.

i. Harappans knew about horses but it was not horse-centred.
ii. A series of circular platforms has been found between granary and the citadel, which was used for the pounding of grain.
iii. The citadel and the platform were crowded one-room dwellings which suggest slave habitats.
iv. The floor is made of bricks along with gypsum and mortar.

(a) i, ii, iii only (b) ii, iii, iv only
(c) i, ii, iv only (d) i, ii, iii, iv only

13. Match the following sites and their founders:

i.	Chanhundro	A.	S.R. Rao
ii.	Kalibangan	B.	N.G. Majumdar
iii.	Lothal	C.	A. Gosh
iv.	Banwali	D.	R. S. Visht

(a) i – C ii – A iii – D iv – B
(b) i – A ii – B iii – C
(c) i – B ii – C iii –
(d) i – B ii – A

14. Consider the following statements and choose appropriate answer about Harappan pottery.

i. Harappan pottery is dark red or bright red and is well-baked and uniformly sturdy.
ii. Harappan pottery is chiefly wheel-made, consists of both painted and plain ware, the plain variety being more common.
iii. Harappan pottery was less utilitarian in character.

(a) i, ii, iii only (b) ii, iii, only
(c) i, ii, only (d) None of these

15. Consider the following statements about the religious practices of Indus Valley Civilisation.

i. Indus people worshipped gods in the forms of trees and animals.
ii. People believed in evil forces and used amulets as protection against them.
iii. Pashupati was represented in seals as sitting in a yogic posture.
iv. There is sufficient evidence for the prevalence of phallic worship.

(a) i, ii, iv only (b) ii, iii, iv only
(c) i, iii only (d) i, ii, iii, iv only

16. Consider the following statements ... the Indus Valley Civilisation. ... of the ... tes.

i. Barley has been fou... y Civilisation Indus Valley C...
ii. People ... Valley Civilisation ... with other countries.

... statement is/are true about ... Valley Civilisation?

... only
... i, ii and iii (b) ii only
(d) iii only

17. Which of following statements is incorrect about the Indus Valley Civilisation?
(a) People of Indus Valley Civilisation used to practice metallurgy.
(b) No site of this civilisation has been found in Haryana region.
(c) Animals known to people of Indus Valley Civilisation include humped bull, rhinoceros, elephant, horse.
(d) All of the above.

18. Which one is the biggest site of the Harappan Civilisation?
(a) Rakhigarhi (b) Harappa
(c) Lothal (d) Dholavira

19. Which of the following statements regarding the Indus valley Civilisation is not true?
(a) The excavations at Harappa are attributed to R.B. Daya Ram Sahani.
(b) The Indus Valley people were not acquainted with the art of spinning and weaving.
(c) Generally, houses had an open courtyard and well.
(d) The Bronze Dancing Girl was discovered at Mohenjo-Daro.

20. The main characteristic of the Indus Valley Civilisation was
Town planning
iii. inage system
(a) i
(b) i on out roads
(c) i, ii, iii
(d) None of

21. Rice cultivation a
with the Harappan s
ociated

(a) Kalibangan (b) Harappa
(c) Ropar (d) Lothal

22. The Indus Valley people knew the use of
(a) Gold, copper, bronze but not iron
(b) Silver, iron, gold but not bronze
(c) Silver, lead, iron but not copper
(d) Gold, tin, bronze but not silver

23.

	Site	Meaning
i.	Mohenjo-Daro	Mound of the Dead
ii.	Kalibangan	Bangles of Clay

(a) Both are correctly matched
(b) Only i is correct
(c) Only ii is correct
(d) None of them is correctly matched

24.

Metal	Source
(A) Lapis lazuli	(i) Khetri
(B) Jade	(ii) Afghanistan
(C) Copper	(iii) Kolar
(D) Gold	(iv) Pamir

(a) A–i, B–ii, C–iii, D–iv
(b) A–iii, B–i, C–ii, D–iv
(c) A–ii, B–iv, C–i, D–iii
(d) A–i, B–iv, C –iii, D–iii

25. Of the following Harappan sites those in India are
(a) Mohenjo-Daro and Harappa
(b) Banwali and Chanhu-Daro
(c) Lothal and Kalibangan
(d) Lothal and Kot Diji

26. During the Indus valley Civilisation period, the dominant number used for weights and measures was
(a) 2 (b) 4
(c) 8 (d) 16

CHAPTER

3

The Vedic Age (Rig Vedic and Later Vedic) (c. 1500–500 BCE)

Harappan culture was followed by another great civilisation and culture known as Vedic culture. It is called the Vedic Age as its reconstruction is primarily based on using Vedic texts as sources. However, archaeological sources have also supplemented the texts, though not comprehensively. Indo-Aryans are believed to be the composers of Vedic texts. The term 'Indo-Aryans' is basically a linguistic term and refers to speakers of a sub group of the Indo-Iranian branch of the Indo-European family of languages. *Rig Veda* composers describe themselves as *Arya*, a cultural/ethnic term etymologically derived from '*ar*' meaning to cultivate, literally meaning kinsmen or companion, in Sanskrit it means favourably disposed newcomers and later it implied men of good family 'noble'. There is still no consensus on the original home of Aryans and different theories are postulated which further continue the debate. The different theories are as follows:

ANSWERS

1. (a)	2. (c)	3. (d)	4. (c)	5. (a)	6. (c)	7. (a)	8. (a)
9. (d)	10. (b)	11. (a)	12. (c)	13. (c)	14. (a)	15. (d)	16. (c)
17. (b)	18. (a)	19. (b)	20. (c)	21. (d)	22. (a)	23. (a)	24. (c)
25. (c)	26. (d)						

PRACTICE QUESTIONS – MAINS

1. The lifestyle of the Harappan people in all aspects – social, economic (agriculture, trade and commerce), religious – was marked by an aura of advancement not only over past Stone Age cultures, but it also overshadowed its contemporary civilisations. Elaborate with suitable examples.

2. Identify various important Harappan sites and the significance they hold.

3. Trade was as relevant in Harappan era as it is today. Elucidate specifying about different aspects related to Harappan economy such as seals, weights, different Harappan imports.

4. What were the possible reasons behind the Harappan civilisation's decline? Also, mention the key features of the post-Harappan phase.

Theory	Postulates	Supported by
European theory	Continent of Europe is the home land of Aryans. The Indo-Aryans came to India from Eurasia. They were semi-nomadic people and came from the plains of Eastern Europe, especially the area north of Black Sea. On the basis of comparative linguistics of Greek, Latin, German, Gothic, Celtic and Sanskrit (Indo-European family of languages), we find certain structural similarities and cognates (similar related words). For example, the Sanskrit words *matri* and *pitri* are similar to the Latin *mater* and *pater*. Similarly, *Inar* of the Hittite (Turkey) language is similar to *Indra* of the Vedas. *Suryyas* and *Maruttash* of the Kassite (Mesopotamia) inscriptions are equivalent of the Vedic *Surya* and *Marut*.	Sir William Jones (1786) Giles – Hungary Shroeder – France P. Nehring – Steppes (S. Russia) Morgan – Western Siberia
Central Asian theory	Central Asia is the homeland of the Aryans. With the comparative study of the '*Avesta*' (Iranian text) and the '*Vedas*', one finds striking linguistic relationship between them of not just words but of concepts too. The interchangeability between 'h' and 's' and incredible consistency in this change as *hepta hindu* (*sapta sindhu*), *Ahura* (*asura*), *haoma* (*soma*), *daha* (*dasa*) further substantiate the claim.	Max Muller – Central Asia E-Meyer Herzfeld
Arctic Region theory	Northern Arctic region is the homeland of Aryans, as the Vedas speak about 6 months each of long days and long nights, which happens only in the Arctic region.	Bal Gangadhar Tilak
Tibet theory	Tibet is the original home of Aryans with reference to the Vedas and other Aryan texts.	Swami Dayanand Saraswati
Indian theory	Indigenous to the subcontinent. There are definite literary evidences in the Vedas that the Aryans regarded the Sapta Sindhu as their original home. Sanskrit, more than any other European language, contains the largest number of original Indo-European vocables. It had greater contact with the parent language of the Aryans than any other European languages. The sacrificial rituals of the Vedic Aryans point to their Indian origin. The geographical data found in the Rig Veda fit in with the geography of Punjab and the neighbouring regions. The river hymns in the Rig Veda mention the names of the rivers of the region. The flora and fauna mentioned is mostly similar to the Himalayan region.	Sampurnanand and A.C. Das – Sapta Sindhu Region Ganganath Jha – Brahmarishi Desa (situated in the confluence of the Ganges and the Yamuna) L.D. Kala – Kashmir R.B. Pandey – Madhya Pradesh

The dominant and mostly accepted view is that instead of an Aryan invasion, there was a series of Indo-Aryan immigrations[1] and they came to the sub-continent as immigrants. It is also inferred that the earliest Aryans lived in the land of the **Sapta Sindhu** (Sindhu is the river par excellence of the Aryans) and probably because of their use of horse chariots and superior military technology, they could establish their political dominance in the region. The region was drained by the seven rivers, *viz*., the Indus (*Sindhu*), and its five tributaries, namely, the **Jhelum** (***Vatista***), **Beas** (***Vipasa***), **Chenab** (***Askini***), **Ravi** (***Purushni***), **Sutlej** (***Sutudri***); and the **Saraswati** (**modern Ghaggar Hakra**), which covered mostly the areas of eastern Afghanistan, Punjab and fringes of western UP (Fig. 3.1). The rare mention of the river Yamuna (twice) and Ganga (only once) is pointer to the fact that Rig Vedic Aryans had not inhabited that region as yet.

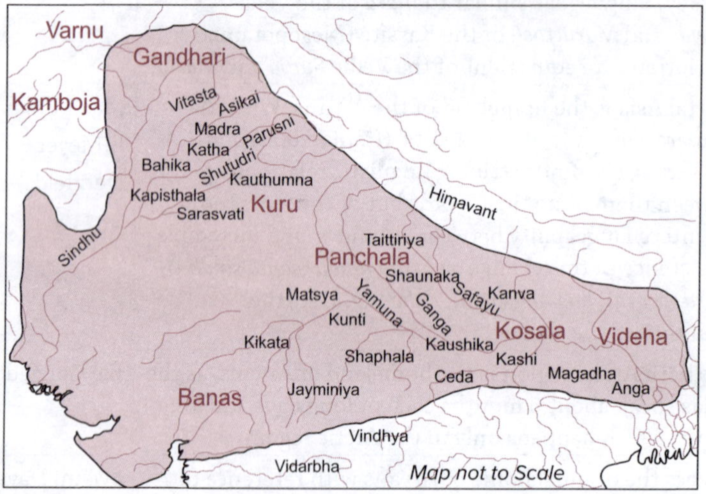

FIGURE 3.1 Vedic Age Map

Rig Vedic Culture (c. 1500–1000 BCE)/Early Vedic Civilisation

The Vedic corpus is generally divided into Early Vedic and Later Vedic texts. However, recently, on the basis of internal chronology, more complex classification has been adopted, which divides the Vedic literature as:

[1] The archaeological evidence of the migrations comes from what is known as Andronovo culture situated in Southern Siberia. This culture flourished in the second millennium BCE. From here, people moved to the north of Hindukush (the area known as Bactria–Margiana Archaeological Complex) and from here they entered India. Evidences of horses, spoked wheels, fire cults, and cremation (which formed important parts of Aryan life in India) during the period between 1900 BCE and 1500 BCE, were found in these regions. Apart from these, the artifacts and ceramics also suggest movement of people from Central Asian region to South Asian region.

a. Early Vedic Literature/Rig Vedic Culture (c. 1500–1000 BCE): Includes the Rig Veda Samhita and other texts of the family. They are called 'family books' as their composition is attributed to the families of certain seer poets, such as Vishvamitra, Atri, Gritsamada, Vasishtha and Bharadvaja.

b. Later Vedic Literature/Later Vedic Culture (c. 1000–500 BCE): Includes Books 1, 8, 9, and 10 of the *Rig Veda Samhita*, the Samhitas of the *Sama Veda*, the *Yajur* and the *Atharva Vedas* and the *Brahmanas*, *Aranyakas* and *Upanishads* attached to all the four Vedas.

Vedic Literature

The word *Veda* has been derived from the root *'vid'*, which means to know/knowledge. They hold the status of *Shruti* (which has been heard) and have been transmitted orally for many centuries. Later, they were written down, and the earliest surviving manuscript belongs to the 11th century. There are four Vedas and every Veda generally has four parts: *Samhita*, *Brahmana*, *Aranyaka* and *Upanishad*.

The four Vedas are:

- Rig Veda
- Sama Veda
- Yajur Veda
- Atharva Veda

Veda	Remarks
Rig Veda	The Rig Veda is a collection of 1,028 hymns, divided into 10 *Mandals* (books). They are the earliest compositions and hence, they depict the life of the early Vedic people in India. Recently, the Rig Veda has been included by the UNESCO in the list of literature signifying World Human Heritage. • Earliest Mandals, i.e., II to VII are called family books as they are ascribed to particular families of seers/*rishis*. • Mandal VIII – Mostly relate to Kanva's family. • Mandal IX – Compilation of Soma hymns. • Mandal I and X – Are later additions and contain the *Purusashukta* which explains the four *varnas*. • The priests related to the Rig Veda are *Kotri* or *Motri*, and the *Upveda* of the Rig Veda is the Ayurveda. • Only surviving recension of the Rig Veda is the *Shakala shakha*.
Sama Veda	The *Sama Veda* is the collection of verses mostly taken from the *Rig Veda*, but arranged in a poetic form to facilitate singing. It is a collection of 1,810 melodies, and also contains the famous Dhrupada raga, later sung by Tansen. The *Upveda* of the *Sama Veda* is the Gandharva Veda. Recensions (*Shakhas*) of the Sama Veda are *Kauthuma*, *Jaiminiya* (*Talavakara*) and *Ranayaniya*.

Veda	Remarks
Yajur Veda	The Yajur Veda deals with the procedure for the performance of sacrifices. The texts are further divided into: a. *Shukla* Yajur Veda/White Yajur Veda/*Vajasaneya* (contains only the *mantras*). It contains the *Madhyandina* and *Kanva* recensions. b. *Krishna* Yajur Veda/Black Yajur Veda (contains both *mantras* and prose explanations/commentary) It contains the *Kathaka, Maitrayani, Taittiriya* and *Kapishthala* recensions. The *Upveda* of the Yajur Veda is the Dhanur Veda.
Atharva Veda	The Atharva Veda is a collection of magic spells and charms to ward off the evil spirits and diseases. It is the last Veda and is considered a non-Aryan work divided into 20 *kandas* (books), with 731 hymns. It contains the Gopatha Brahmana. The *Shaunaka* and *Paippalada* are the recensions of the Atharva Veda. The *Upveda* of the Atharva Veda is the Shilpa Veda.

Brahmanas

The Brahmanas describe the rules for the performance of sacrificial ceremonies. They, however, explain the hymns of the Vedas in an orthodox manner. Each Veda has several Brahmanas attached to it. The most important Brahmana is the *Satpatha Brahmana*, which is attached to the Yajur Veda and is the most exhaustive. It recommends 'one hundred sacred paths'.

Aranyakas

Aranyakas are called the 'forest books' as they were written mainly by hermits living in the jungles for their pupils. They deal with mysticism and philosophy and oppose sacrifice. They emphasise meditation and are considered to be the concluding portion of the Brahmanas, and interpret rituals in a philosophical way.

Upanishads

The literal meaning of 'Upanishad' is 'to sit near someone'. There are 108 Upanishads, of which 13 are the most prominent. The Upanishads dwell on the '***Atman***' and '***Brahman***', and focus a lot on the philosophy about life, universe, self, body, sacrifice, etc. They emphasise that the knowledge of the self or *atman* should be acquired and that the relation of the *atman* with the *Brahman* should be properly understood.

- The Mandukyopanishad '*Satyamev jayate*' is the largest of all Upanishads.
- The Chhandogya Upanishad – clearly refers to the first three *ashrams* and discusses the types of marriage (mainly two).

- *Anuloma* marriage – The marriage of a man in his own *varna* or below his *varna*. It is the most accepted and common form of marriage in the society.
- *Pratiloma* marriage – The marriage of a girl/woman in a *varna* lower than her own, deemed rare and not sanctioned by the Vedas.

Vedanta

Vedanta literally signifies the 'end of the Vedas', as they reveal the final aim of the Vedas. They condemn sacrifices and ceremonies and denote the last phase of the Vedic period.

Vedanga

The word '*Vedanga*' means the 'limbs of the Vedas'. They are the supplementary texts that aid in the proper recitation and understanding of the Vedas. However, these do not qualify as *Shruti* as they are considered of human origin (not revealed by the gods) and are written in the form of *Sutras*. *Sutras* are very short condensed statements that are used to express varied ideas. There are six *Sutras* which are:

1. *Shiksha* (Phonetics)
2. *Kalpa* (Ritualistic science)
3. *Jyotisha* (Astronomy)
4. *Vyakaran* (Grammar)
5. *Nirukta* (Etymology)
6. *Chhanda* (Metrics)

The *Kalpasutra* is further divided into:

a. *Shrautasutra*: concerned with Vedic sacrifices that require three or more fires.
b. *Grihyasutra*: concerned with comparatively simpler domestic sacrifices, which require only one fire. It includes rituals pertaining to crucial life stages (*Samskaras*) such as *Upanayana* (initiation), *Vivaha* (marriage) and *Antyeshti* (funerary practices).
c. *Dharmasutra*: concerned with the rituals' *Dharma*.

Puranas

The word 'puranas' literally means 'old'. They were the religious sectarian literature of later times (around 4th–6th centuries) which had a well-defined perception of the past traditions. They reflect the Brahmanical social and religious values and also shed light on the emergence and development of Hindu religious practices. The Puranas generally discuss five topics in the time span of four ages/*yugas (Satya, Treta, Dvapara and Kali)*:

1. *Sarga* (Deals with the creation of the world)

2. *Pratisarga* (Recreation)
3. *Manvantaras* (Periods of the various Manus)
4. *Vamsha* (Genealogies of the gods and *rishis*)
5. *Vamshanucharita* (Texts relating to royal dynasties, both the Suryavanshis – who claimed their descent from the Sun – and Chandravanshis – who claimed their descent from the Moon).

- Traditionally, the Puranas are considered to be composed by Vyasa and it is commonly accepted that the four *yugas* make up a *mahayuga*, that 1000 *mahayugas* make a *kalpa*, that and every *kalpa* is further divided into 14 *manvantaras* which are presided over by a specific Manu. Each *Yuga* is periodically destroyed and again, the recreation of world occurs with the cyclical decline and revival of Dharma.
- The Puranas are further divided into 18 *Mahapuranas* (great *Puranas* such as *Brahma, Vishnu, Narada, Bhagavata, Padma, Garuda, Varaha, Matsya, Kurma, Linga, Shiva, Skanda, Agni, Vamana*, etc.) and numerous *Upapuranas* (secondary Puranas).
- Some *Puranas* such as the *Brahma, Matsya, Harivamsha, Vishnu, Brahmanda* and *Vayu* provide useful information on historical dynasties (of Haryankas, Shishunagas, Nandas, Mauryas, Shungas – till the Guptas). They also contain detailed accounts of historical geography such as mountains, rivers, etc.

Dharamshastra

Dharmashastra are the Sanskrit texts dealing specifically with Dharma (code of conduct that conceptually signifies 'a righteous moral law' which is in consonance with the universal natural law). Dharma also refers to the fulfillment of *Purusharthas* (life goals) such as Dharma (righteous conduct), Artha (material well-being), Kama (sensual pleasure) and Moksha (liberation from the cycle of life and death). The *Dharmashastras* are further subdivided into *Dharmasutras* (composed during c.600–300 BCE) and *Smritis* (composed during c.200 BCE–900 CE). They recognise three sources of Dharma, namely, the Vedas (*Shruti*), *Smriti* (that which is remembered) texts and *Shistachara* (good mannerisms and practices of decent cultured people). A person's Dharma was dependent on many factors such as gender, marital status, *varna* and *ashram*. Out of the four *varnas*, three *varnas*, i.e. *Brahmanas, Kshatriyas* and *Vaishyas* were considered *Dvija* (twice born, as they had the right to the sacred thread ceremony considered akin to second birth), while the *Shudras* were burdened with many civil disabilities.

The four ashrams dividing the life of a *dvija* male were:

a. *Brahmacharya* (Celibate studenthood)
b. *Grihastha* (Household caretaker)
c. *Vanaprastha* (Partial renunciation)

d. *Sanyasa* (Complete renunciation)

It should be noted that the different *ashram* stages were not followed rhetorically by all and it was not even applicable to women or *shudras*.

Epics

The two Sanskrit epics, the Mahabharata and the Ramayana, are part of both oral and written traditional history. The link between the *Puranas* and the epics is that the heroes and clans who are the actors in the epics are the descendants of Manu's progeny. The two epics were clearly aware of each other as the Mahabharata has a section called *Ramopakhyana*, detailing the story of Rama, and the Ramayana mentions the *Kurus and* Hastinapur but does not mention the Mahabharata war.

Mahabharata War and Ramayana

Mahabharata	Ramayana
(a) Roughly composed between c. 400 BCE–400 CE.	(a) Roughly composed between c. 400 BCE–300 CE.
(b) The Mahabharata is said to be composed by Ved Vyasa and consists of 18 *Parvas* (books) and has around 1 lakh verses. It is considerably longer than Ramayana.	(b) Ramayana is considered as the *Adi-Kavya* (first conscious poetry) composed by Valmiki and it consists of seven *Kandas* (books) having around 24,000 verses. It is much shorter than the Mahabharata, despite later additions.
(c) Traditionally, the war is believed to have happened in the *Dvapara yuga*. But, historians consider the events and social character of the Mahabharata corresponding to an earlier stage of development than the Ramayana, as the Mahabharata setting pertains to the Indo-Gangetic divide and upper Ganga valley.	(c) Traditionally, it is considered that Rama lived in the *Treta yuga*, i.e. earlier than the Mahabharata. Since the setting of Ramayana shifted eastwards to the middle Ganga valley, and the language of the Ramayana is more polished and its concepts are more closely related to later societies, historians consider it of a later stage than the Mahabharata.

Varied Aspects of Rig Vedic Culture

Based on the inferences drawn from different Rig Vedic hymns, the political, social and economic aspects of Rig Vedic life are as discussed further.

Political Life of Rig Vedic Aryans

Rig Vedic society was a tribal society and its people lived a semi-nomadic life. Since the concept of state was absent, a definite territorial identity was absent. Aryan tribes were called *Janas*. Their chief (*rajan*) was known as the *Gopati* or *Gopa* (protector of cows), and the chief queen was called the *Mahisi*. The *Janas* often had conflicts with the Panis, who used to hide the cattle of Aryans in the forest and were thus deemed the enemies of Aryans. In order to get their cattle back, the Vedic God 'Indra' was invoked and many battles known as *Gavisthi*, *Gaveshana*, *Goshu* or *Gavyat* (to search for cows) were fought between the Aryans and the *Panis*. The main function of the *rajan* was thus to protect the *jana* and cattle from the enemies along with offering prayers to gods on behalf of the *jana*.

Certain aspects related to polity and administration

(a) The society's political structure was somewhat similar to the monarchial form, but the *Gopati*'s office was not hereditary and he was selected from among the clan's men and was perhaps elected by the assembly called *samiti*. Thus, democratic elements and republican polity were present in the political life of the Rig Vedic times.

(b) Some important tribal assemblies of this period were:

a. *Sabha* Smaller body meant for elites (exclusive body)

b. *Samiti* Broad-based folk assembly, presided over by the *Rajan*

c. *Vidatha* Tribal assembly with diverse functions such as distributing war booty among the members of the tribe

d. *Gana* Highest advisory body

c. *Parishad* Legislative body where common issues were discussed

(c) The polity was liberal, progressive and egalitarian in character as there was hardly any difference in political status of common people and political functionaries. In fact, the power and prestige of the crown was not so high and his main role was to lead the tribe during the offensive and defensive battles. Other functions of the state were yet to emerge.

(d) Some of the important functionaries of Rig Vedic societies were:

- *Purohit* (priest): *The purohita* assisted and advised the chief on various matters. In exchange for their ritualistic services, the priests received *dana* (gifts) and *dakshina* (sacrificial offering).
- *Senani* (Chief of army)
- *Gramini* (Leader of the village and fighting unit)
- *Vrajapati* (Officer who controlled the territory)

It is pertinent to note that there is no mention of any officer for administering justice though Rig Vedic society was not an ideal society as there were cases of theft and burglary. Similarly, there is no evidence of tax collecting officers and it perhaps seems that the people offered to the chief a voluntary contribution called '*bali*'.

(d) Vedic society was militaristic and military technique was much advanced as they possessed chariots driven by horses. The Rig Vedic charioteers used varma (coats of mail) and sipra/sironastra (helmets) and went to combat equipped with asi (swords), hanas (arrows) and ilhianus (bows). The *sena* was not a permanent fighting group and consisted of able-bodied tribesmen who were mobilised at the time of the wars and later, the king redistributed the tributes and booty collected from war among them. Cattle lifting was the most common type of conflict.

(e) The Aryans were engaged in two types of battles:

1. With pre-Aryans (probably referred to them as *Dasas/Dasyus*)
2. Amongst themselves: There have been mentions of two such battles:
   a. A battle occurred between a Bharata King Divodasa (winner) and *Dasa* ruler Shambara.
   b. The 'battle of ten kings'(*dasharajna*): This was fought between the Bharata chief Sudas, grandson of Divodasa (winner) on one side, and ten other tribes including the famous five tribes (*Punch-jana*), namely, the Yadu, Turvasha, Puru, Anu and Druhyu on the banks of the river Paurushni (Ravi). Later, the Bharatas joined hands with the Purus to form the Kuru tribe who further allied with Panchalas and established their control over the Upper Ganga valley.

Social Life of Rig Vedic Aryans

All the social units were based on brotherhood. *Kula* (Family) was the basic social unit and *Kulapa* was the head of the family who also represented the members of the family in political activities. Largely, there were joint families in the Rig Vedic age, which followed the patrilineal system. A number of families together constituted *Grama* and *Gramini* was its head who were part of a larger grouping called *vis* or clan headed by *Vishpati*. One or more than one clans made *jana* or tribe. The *jana* was the largest social unit and the highest political unit was headed by *Janeshya/Gopati*, who was equivalent to a King.

Certain aspects related to Rig Vedic society

(a) The society was patriarchal in nature, though the women had important positions in the society since they were educated and had access to the assembly. Women like *Apala, Ghosa, Lopamudra* and *Vishwavara* composed hymns and received *Upanayana*. Women attended the meetings of the *Vidatha*. Girls were free to choose their life partners and there were no instances of child marriage, *sati* or *purdah* in the Rig Veda. There were though few instances of levirate (marrying the husband's younger brother on the death of husband) and widow remarriage. Marriage was usually monogamous, though some references to polygyny and polyandry are also found in the Rig Veda. However, interestingly in the Rig Veda, no desire is expressed for daughters, though the desire for children and cattle is a recurrent theme in the hymns. One of the probable reason behind preference for the birth of a son was because of the martial nature of the society, which required male members for their clashes to establish dominance over the territories.

(b) The society was not divided on caste lines and occupation was not based on birth. Everyone, be it the *Rajans*, the *Purohits or* the artisans, etc., was part of the clan networks and the members of a family could adopt different occupations. This is indicated by the following verse in the Rigveda: *'I am a poet, my father is a physician, and my mother grinds grain upon the stone. Striving for wealth, with varied plans, we follow our desires like cattle'*. Thus, social mobility was of very high order as a person could change their Varna status by changing the profession.

(c) However, certain differences did exist during the period. *Varna* or colour was the basis of initial differentiation between the Vedic and non-Vedic people. The Vedic people were fair whereas the non-Vedic indigenous people were dark in complexion and spoke a different language. Authors of Rig Veda distinguished themselves from other groups whom they called *'dasyus'* or *'dasas'*. The *dasas* were also referred as *a-vrata* (who do not obey the ordinances of the gods) and *a-kratu* (those who do not perform sacrifices). The Aryans were more hostile towards *Dasyus* than the *Dasas*, probably due to the fact that *Dasyus* were non-Aryan indigenous people while the *Dasas* were the early Aryan groups who had lost their skin colour to some extent due to intermarriages with indigenous people.

(d) Thus, even though a socially organised *'varna* system' was not prevalent and tribal elements were stronger in the society, yet Rig Vedic society can still not be considered a totally egalitarian society as social stratification was based on the division of labour and gender. The only mention of the four *varnas* was found in the *Purusashukta* of the tenth *mandal* of the Rig Veda, which makes one conclude that the *varna* system was probably introduced at the end of the Rig Vedic age and that there was social mobility and the absence of strict social hierarchy. However, the Rig Vedic people were familiar with slavery.

Rig Vedic Economy

Since the Rig Vedic society was a pastoral society, cattle rearing was their dominant activity. The chief measure of wealth was cattle and a wealthy man was known as *Gomat*, that is to say, one who owned many cattle. A large number of words are derived from the word *'gau'*, meaning cow. It is pertinent to note that even the donations to the priests were mainly cows and women slaves but not land, which reveals the importance of pastoralism. Evidence of trade and commerce[2]

[2] Trade and commerce were practised but monetisation of economy was absent. Barter system was followed.

is meagre and there was no concept of private property based on land ownership. The clan as a whole enjoyed right over the resources.

Certain aspects related to Rig Vedic economy

(a) The unit of currency was *niskha*, which was made of gold. Barter was the model of exchange and the cow was an important unit of value. There was no regular revenue system and the kingdom was maintained by the voluntary tribute (*bali*) of subjects and bounty won in a battle.

(b) Gift exchange and redistribution had an important economic role in the Rig Vedic society. Such exchanges, known as 'prestations', were done not on an individual level but at the group level. Apart from economic goods, this also included the exchange of other things such as women, courtesies, hospitality and military assistance.

(c) Shifting agriculture was practiced and fire was used to burn down forest cover and the patch of land thus cleared was then sown. Apart from *yava* or barley, no other grain is mentioned. The field was known as *kshetra* and the term *krishi* referred to ploughing. The Rig Vedic people used wooden plough (*phala*, *langala* and '*sira*'). Vedic god Indra is also described as Urvarajit (winner of fertile fields), and there are also references to Kshetrapati (guardian deity of agricultural fields).

(d) The term *ayas* in the Rig Veda refers to copper and bronze and not iron. Thus, they did not use iron technology, but were familiar with copper. Also, there have been very less references to metallurgical activities.

(e) A lot of other crafts such as cart-making, carpentry, tanning, sewing and weaving find mention, though the chariot-maker enjoyed a special status in Rig Vedic society. Chariot-racing and dice gambling were popular pastimes.

(f) For transport, bullock carts, horses and horse-drawn chariots were used. There are also references to the sea (*samudra*) and boats (*nau*).

Rig Vedic Religion

There was neither temple nor idol worship in the Early Vedic age. The Rig Veda reflects naturalistic polytheism (similar to primitive animism) as they venerated natural forces like the wind, rain, water, thunder, etc. Very few temple divinities were venerated. They generally worshipped in the open air through *yajnas*. Vedic texts refer to meat eating and also the sacrificial killing of animals except the cow, which was considered *aghnya* (not to be killed). A peculiar case of Henotheism[3]

[3] In Henotheism, one particular god is held supreme on a particular occasion and the same status is accorded to another deity on some other occasion.

or Kathenotheism is found in Rig Vedic religion, wherein the deity being invoked in a particular hymn is considered the supreme god.

Other peculiar features of Rig Vedic Religion were as follows:

(a) Rituals and ceremonies though formed the crux of the Vedic religion, they were simple in nature, devoid of any rigidities or complexities. Also, they were performed mainly for attainment of materialistic goals like for attaining victory in a battlefield, for cattle wealth and for more sons.

(b) There was no exclusive monopoly of Brahmans in the priestly class. Rather, there were 16 other categories of priestly class other than Brahmans. Also, the role of priestly class was not too important in religious life and even the householder was considered priest of 17th category who could perform all rituals and sacrifices.

(c) The philosophical elements were in nascent stage of development during Rig Vedic Age. In fact, the concepts of soul and salvation emerged much later.

(d) Male deities enjoyed higher status than female deities.

Some of the deities worshipped by the Rig Vedic people were as follows:

Rig Vedic God	Remarks
Indra	• Greatest god of the Aryans • 250 hymns are attributed to him • Called Purandhar (Breaker of forts), Maghavan (bounteous) and Vritrahan (Slayer of Vritra, chaos)
Agni	• Second most important god; the god of fire • 200 hymns are attributed to him • The son of earth and heaven • Intermediary between gods and men
Varuna	• Third most important god; the god of personified water • Looked after *rita* or the cosmic order • Ethically, the highest of all Rig Vedic gods
Soma	• *God of plants*/king of gods/special god of the Brahmanas • All hymns of the 9th *mandal* assigned to him • Aryans knew Himalaya (*Munjavat*) as the source of the *soma* plant • Considered the wise god who inspires the poets to compose hymns
Yama	• Lord of death
Rudra	• Amoral archer god whose arrows brought diseases • Lived in the mountains and the guardian of healing herbs • Resembled Greek god Apollo and identified as Protosiva

Rig Vedic God	Remarks
Pushan	• The god of jungle paths, herdsmen and cattle • Aided the transformation of day to night and vice versa
Surya	• Son of Dyaus, who drives away darkness and spreads light.
Savitri	Solar deity to whom the famous *Gayatri Mantra* is attributed to in the third *mandal* of the Rig Veda
Aditi	Goddess of eternity and the mother of the gods, invoked to bestow freedom from evil, harm and sickness
Prithvi	Earth goddess
Vishnu	Benevolent god, but mentioned very infrequently in the Rig Veda
Marutas	The sons of Rudra who personified storms
Vayu	God of wind
Ashvins	The twin gods of war and fertility
Usha	Goddess of dawn and is mentioned around 300 times in the Rig Veda hymns
Sinivali	Bestows children

Apart from the above mentioned gods, there is mention of some ***Demi-gods*** such as:

1. Gandharvas (Divine musicians)
2. Apsaras (Mistress of gods)
3. Vishwadevas (Intermediate deities)
4. Aryaman (Guardian of compacts and marriages)

Terms used in Rig Vedic Age	Meaning
(a) Godhuli Samgava	Measure of time (Dusk) Morning
(b) Gavyuti	Measure of distance
(c) Duhitri	Daughter who milks cows
(d) Gotra	Kinship units
(e) Vish	Clan/people in general
(f) Gana	Lineage
(g) Grama	Village
(h) Gauri/gavala	Buffalo
(i) Gojit	Winner of cows/Hero
(j) Vap	To sow
(k) Srini	Sickle
(l) Ksehtra	Cultivated field

Terms used in Rig Vedic Age	Meaning
(m) Urvara	Fertile fields
(n) Dhanya	Cereals
(o) Ghrita	Butter
(p) Soma/Sura	Intoxicating drink
(q) Goghna	Guest; one who is fed on cattle
(r) Sita	Furrow created by ploughing
(s) Siri	Yarn
(t) Takshan	Carpenter

Later Vedic Culture and Civilisation (c. 1000–500 BCE)

The Later Vedic Age is characterised by more complexities in social, political and economic life. There was gradual eastward expansion of the Aryans, as they expanded[4] from the north-west Punjab to the south-east Uttar Pradesh in the Ganga-Yamuna doab including both eastern Uttar Pradesh (Kosala) and north Bihar (Videha)[5] during the Later Vedic period. The later Vedic texts speak about the region of *Kuru Panchala* which falls in the Indo-Gangetic divide and the Upper Ganga valley along with mention of Saraswati and Dhristavati rivers and tribes of Kurus, Panchalas, Vashas and Ushinaras.

Political Life of Later Vedic Aryans

In terms of the political context, the tiny tribal settlements of the Vedic period were replaced by comparatively stronger kingdoms while royal power increased. The territorial formations and the development of lineages became stronger during the Later Vedic period. The concept of state emerged during the Later Vedic Age and thus, the definite territorial identity developed. The term '*Rashtra*' first appeared in this period. The wars were no longer fought for cows, but for territories. It was slowly turning in its later stages to an *age of the 'janapadas'* instead of *'janas'*. Chiefs grew at the expense of the tribal peasantry and handsomely rewarded the *purohits*[6] who helped them in maintaining their authority. For instance, *Aitreya Brahamana* points out that the king has to provide 1000 pieces of gold and cattle to the Brahmana who anoints him. The king was addressed

[4] Perhaps this expansion was induced by the need for water and land resources, fresh, less occupied territories and population pressures.

[5] Around 1000 BCE, the Vedic Aryans moved towards Kosala region in eastern Uttar Pradesh and Videha in North Bihar, where the Vedic people encountered the local people following Chalcolithic material culture, however by the end of the Vedic period, both the regions were Aryanised.

[6] Attained the meaning of 'one who places the king in the forefront' and became very important in the establishment of polity and kingship.

by different names across different regions. For instance, in northern regions, he was known as Virat, in eastern regions he was called Samrat while in western and southern regions, he was addressed as Svarat and Bhoja, respectively.

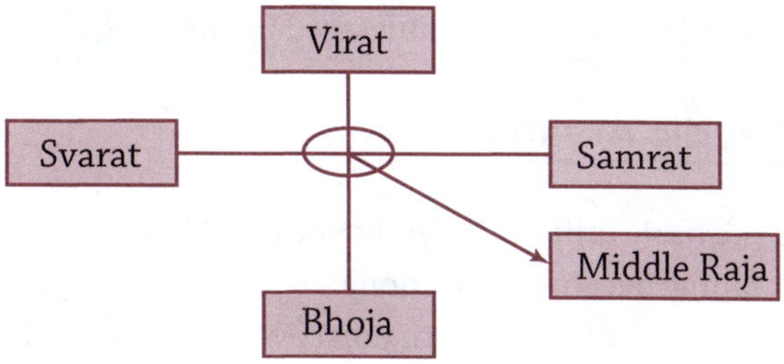

Certain aspects related to polity and administration

(a) The king was usually a *kshatriya* and the office of the monarch was made almost hereditary. Traces of election of the chief or king appear in late Vedic texts, but hereditary kingship was emerging. The king gradually emerged as the controller of the social order too.

(b) The king's influence was further strengthened by ritual enactments such as the *Rajasuya* (which was royal consecration and conferred supreme power on the king), *Vajapeya* (literally meaning drink of strength; it had a chariot race in which royal chariot was made to win against all kinsmen) and *Aswamedha* (unquestioned control over an area in which the royal horse ran uninterrupted). Due to the dominance of the rituals, the power and influence of the *Rajanyas,* the warrior nobles and the *Brahmanas* increased, while the king was distanced from the *vis*. The concept of divine monarchy had also developed among the people of Later Vedic Age as evident by mention of King Parikshit as *Aradhadeva* (half god) in Atharva Veda.

(c) As the chiefs became more powerful, the authority of the popular assemblies started waning. *Sabha* and *Samities* continued to hold ground, though not like the Rig Vedic Age, but the *Vidatha* completely disappeared. The functions of the popular assemblies were gradually replaced now by the officers who served as advisors to the chief and were appointed by him to help him in administration. Thus, the bureaucracy evolved significantly and as many as 16 officials are mentioned in the later Vedic texts. Some of the prominent among them were :

- *Senani*
- *Purohita*
- *Yuvaraja*
- *Akshawapa* (King's companion in game of dice)

- *Rakshin* (Police chief)
- *Palaghar* (Ambassador)

(d) It should be however noted that even in Later Vedic times, the king did not possess a standing army and tribal units were mustered in times of war.

Social Life of Later Vedic Aryans

The family still remained the basic unit of the Vedic society. However, its composition underwent a change. The Later Vedic family became large enough to be called a joint family, with three or four generations living together. The rows of hearths discovered at Atranjikhera and at Ahichchhtra (both in western Uttar Pradesh) show that these were meant for communal feeding or for cooking the food of large families.

Certain aspects related to Later Vedic society

(a) In the family, a patrimonial (authority of father) system developed and women were generally confined to household chores and subordinate positions. As compared to the Rig Vedic age, women lost importance in the society and there have been references to rare instances of *sati* and child marriage. In one text, women have been counted as a vice along with dice and wine. In another text, a daughter has been said to be the source of all sorrows. Assemblies were then dominated by nobles and affluent men and women were no longer permitted to attend assemblies.

(b) One of the most important changes from the Rig Vedic society was the rise and growth of social differentiation in the form of the *varna* system. The Later Vedic society was clearly divided into four *varnas*: Brahmanas, Rajanyas or Kshatriyas, Vaishyas and Shudras (Fig. 3.3). The increasing cult of sacrifices added enormously to the power of the Brahmanas while the position of Shudras deteriorated as they were ordained to be in the service of the three upper varnas and were thus denied almost all the privileges. Even they could not recite the Gayatri mantra.

(c) Another important institution that began to take shape was *ashrama* or the different stages of life, *Brahmacharya* (student life), *grihastha* (householder), *vanaprastha* (hermitage) and the fourth stage *sanyasa*. Together with *varna*, Later Vedic society came to be known as *Varna-ashrama-dharma* society. Though *Ashrama* or the four stages of life were prescribed, but were not religiously followed. It is pertinent to note here that the first reference of Ashrama System is found in Chandogaya Upanishad but reference is limited to just first 3 ashrams. However, the first reference to all the four ashramas is found in Jabala Upanishad.

(d) The upper three classes known as *Dvija* (twice born) discriminated against both *Shudras* and *Chandalas*. Education was largely confined to *dvija* castes and began with the investiture ceremony (i.e. the wearing of sacred thread) (*Upanayana*), although women were also initiated at times. This can be construed as the beginning of the imposition of disabilities on the shudras as well as the beginning of the concept of ritual pollution.

(e) The institution of *gotra* appeared in the Later Vedic culture. Literally it means 'cow pen' or the place where cattle belonging to whole clan are kept, but in course of time it meant descent from a common ancestor. Marriage between persons of the same *gotra* was forbidden. There were legendary seers, such as, Kashyapa, Vashista, Bhrigu, Gautama, Bhardwaj, Attri, Vishwamitra and Agastya, after whom the *gotras* were named. Kshatriyas and Vaishyas took the same *gotra* names of the families of Brahmans who traditionally performed their domestic rituals. There is mention of the *Chandrayana* penance for men marrying women of the same *gotra*.

(f) Caste exogamy was extensively practiced and a rigid social hierarchy developed, which restricted the social mobility of the earlier period.

(g) Interestingly, certain craft groups managed to attain higher status. For example, the *Rathakaras*, the chariot makers had the right to wear the sacred thread.

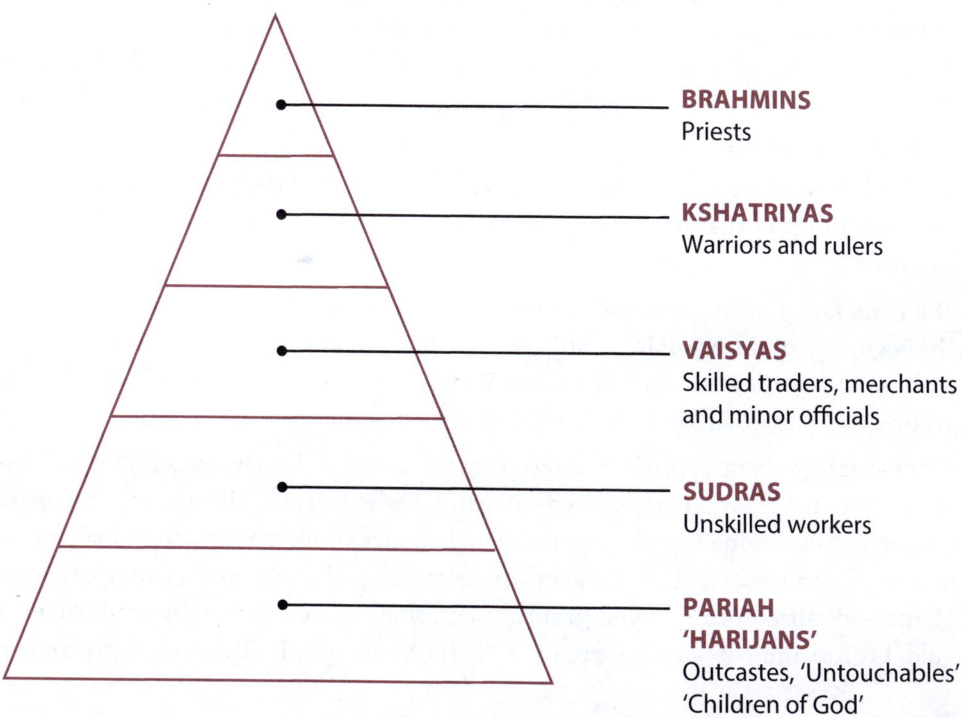

FIGURE 3.2 Later Vedic Castes

Later Vedic Age Economy

The economic activities of Later Vedic period were quite diversified. Agriculture, pastoralism, craft production and trade contributed to the economic development. The predominantly pastoral society of Early Vedic times had become agricultural and agriculture emerged as the chief means of livelihood of the Later Vedic people. The *Satapatha Brahmana* mentions rituals related to ploughing undertaken by the kings and this suggests the importance given to cultivation by the rulers, and the shift to agriculture to support the increasing population. The forests were cleared by burning the trees, which is also mentioned in the *Satapatha Brahamana* (ruler Videha Madhava burnt the forests between river Saraswati and river Sedanira or Gandak). Cultivation was done by the plough and mixed farming (cultivation along with herding) was one of the prime occupations of the Later Vedic people.

Certain aspects related to Later Vedic economy

(a) The land was still communally owned over which the '*vish*' (clan) had many participatory rights, but it was recognised as property and the head of the household who owned the land was termed as '*Grahpati*'.

(b) Rice *(Vrihi)* and wheat *(Godhuma)* became the staple diet of the people and apart from barley, the Later Vedic people now started growing wheat, rice, pulses, lentils, millet, sugarcane and lentils. Also, with the beginning of food production, agricultural produce began to be offered in the rituals. The items of *dana* and *dakshina* included cooked rice. *Tila*, from which the first widely used vegetable food-oil was derived increasingly, came to be used in rituals.

(c) The society was largely rural. However, towards the end of the period, there are traces of the beginning of urbanism (as *nagar* in the sense of a town is mentioned in the *Taittiriya Aranyaka*).

(d) The main factor in the expansion of the Aryan culture during the Later Vedic period was the beginning of the use of iron, which was introduced around 1000 BCE and is mentioned as *Krishna Ayas/Shyama Ayas*. The Later Vedic culture is also called as PGW– Iron Phase culture, as a particular kind of pottery (painted grey ware) was used during that phase.

(e) Diverse arts and crafts proliferated during the Later Vedic age and craft specialization took deep roots, when compared to early Vedic period, since more occupational groups are mentioned in this period. For instance, bow makers, rope makers, arrow makers, hide dressers, stone breakers, physicians, goldsmiths and astrologers are some of the specialised professional groups mentioned in the texts. Tin, lead, silver, iron, gold, bronze and copper were known to Later Vedic people. There were probably good smiths and smelters as a lot of copper objects have been found at PGW sites. People had obtained knowledge of glass manufacturing too. *Shresthins* indicate the guilds or organisation of merchants.

(f) Exchange was still via barter, but *niskha* was used as a convenient unit of value although not as a typical currency. Wagons drawn by oxen were probably the most used mode of transport.

(g) Unlike the Rig Vedic age where only voluntary offerings were taken and per se no revenue collection was done, in the Later Vedic age, collection of taxes and tributes was made mandatory and Bali thus became a regular tax and was collected by *Balisadhaks* while the treasurer was known as *Sangrihitri*. *Bhaga* signified King's share in agricultural produce which was collected by *Bhagadughas* while *Bhoga* signified ceremonial gifts. It is equally interesting to note that the Vaishyas appear to be the only tribute payers in Later Vedic times.

(h) The Later Vedic people were acquainted with four types of pottery:

 (i) Painted Grey Ware

 (ii) Black and Red Ware

 (iii) Black-slipped Ware

 (iv) Red Ware

Later Vedic Age Religion

Changes in the material life naturally resulted in a change in their attitude towards gods and goddesses as well. The two most important Rig Vedic gods, Indra and Agni, lost their importance and instead of them, **Prajapati** (the creator) became supreme. Some of the other minor gods became prominent, such as **Vishnu** (conceived as the preserver and protector of people) and **Rudra** (the god of animals). Idolatry appears in Late Vedic phase and just as the society was divided in the Later Vedic phase in terms of social classes, similarly some of the social orders too adopted their own deities. For example, **Pushan** (who was supposed to look after cattle) came to be regarded as the god of the Shudras. The Later Vedic culture was focused on the centrality of the cult of sacrifice. Rituals and sacrifices became more important and elaborate, and assumed both public and domestic character. There was an increase in the frequency and number of the *yajnas*, which generally involved the killing of animals on a large scale and the destruction of cattle wealth. This was probably the result of the growing importance of a class of Brahmanas and their efforts to maintain their supremacy in the changing society. These *yajnas* brought to them a large amount of wealth in the form of *dana* and *dakshina*. Some of the important *yajnas* were – *Ashvamedha*, *Vajapeya*, *Rajasuya*, etc. The purpose of these *yajnas* was two-fold:

(a) Firstly, it established the authority of the chiefs over the people, and

(b) Secondly, it reinforced the territorial aspect of the polity since people from all over the kingdom were invited to these sacrifices.

Philosophical dimensions of religion emerged during Later Vedic Age and concepts like heaven, hell, rebirth, soul, transmigration and salvation attained popularity. However, towards the end of Later Vedic age, a strong reaction began to emerge against priestly domination, against cults and sacrifices, especially in the land of Panchala and Videha where, around 600 BCE, the Upanishads were compiled and later also led to the development of heterodox faiths such as Buddhism and Jainism which emphasised correct human behaviour and discipline.

Comparative Analysis of Rig Vedic Age and Later Vedic Age

	Rig Vedic Age	Later Vedic Age
Time Period	c.1500–1000 BCE	c.1000–500 BCE
Area	The core geographical area of the Rig Vedic texts corresponds to Eastern Afghanistan, Punjab and western Uttar Pradesh.	The core geographical area of Later Vedic texts corresponds to the Kuru–Panchala region, which comprised the Indo-Gangetic divide and the upper Ganga valley.
Political Sphere	(a) The chief was known as *Rajan/Gopati* and was selected among the clan's men. His office was thus not hereditary. (b) The wars were primarily fought for the protection of cattle, i.e. cows. (c) It was the age of '*janas*'. (d) The Rajan was helped in his administrative task by the tribal assemblies known as *Sabha*, *Samiti* or the *Vidatha* and thus, these assemblies in a way limited the powers of the chiefs.	(a) Hereditary kingship emerged and the chiefs grew at the expense of the tribal peasantry. There was also emergence of idea of the divine nature of kingship. (b) The wars were no longer fought for cows but for territories. The term *'Rashtra'* first appeared in this period. (c) In the later stages, it was slowly turning into the age of the '*janapads*'. (d) The tribal assemblies lost their privileged status and gradually became subordinated to king. Instead of them, now emerged an elaborate administrative machinery headed by key officials who assisted the king in administrative work.

Rig Vedic Age	Later Vedic Age	
	(e) There was no taxation system as only voluntary offerings were taken and per se no revenue collection was done.	(e) In the Later Vedic age, taxation system developed and collection of taxes and tributes was made mandatory and were done by *Sangrihitri*.
Social Sphere	(a) Society was simple and largely egalitarian wherein there was social mobility and absence of strict social hierarchy. The society was not divided on caste lines and occupation was not based on birth. (b) Women enjoyed equal rights and had access to tribal assemblies, i.e. *Sabha* and *Samiti*. (c) Women received education. (d) Child marriage, Sati system did not exist. (e) Prevalence of widow remarriage.	(a) Emergence of rigid class distinctions and rise and growth of social differentiation in the form of *Varna* system. The Later Vedic Society was divided into 4 Varnas: *Brahmans, Kshatriyas, Vaishyas and Shudras* and there was absence of social mobility. The caste system now became hereditary and thus the occupation was based on birth. (b) There was significant decline in the status of women as they assumed subordinate position to men and lost access to both *Sabha* and *Samiti*. (c) Education was restricted to women and only few women received education. (d) There were rare instances of Sati and Child marriage. (e) Widows were not allowed to remarry.
Economic Sphere	(a) Mainly Pastoral economy supplemented by agriculture. Barley (yava) was the only grain grown. (b) Cattle was chief measure of wealth and there was no concept of private property based on land ownership. (c) The Rig Vedic people knew of a metal called *ayas*, which was either copper or bronze but they had no knowledge of iron.	(a) Agriculture became chief occupation supplemented by Pastoralism along with other different occupations. Other grains like rice, wheat, millets, sugarcane etc. were grown along with barley. (b) Cattle lost its importance and land emerged as important measure of wealth. (c) The Later Vedic period was the beginning of use of iron called *Krishna Ayas* which helped a lot in the expansion of the Aryan culture. The Later Vedic period is also known as Iron Phase Culture.

Rig Vedic Age	Later Vedic Age	
Religious Sphere	(a) There was neither temple nor idol worship during Rig Vedic period. (b) The Rig Vedic people venerated natural forces and worshipped primarilsy deities of Indra, Agni, Varuna, Soma etc. (c) Rituals and sacrifices were not of much significance to their religious practices.	(a) Idolatry and temple worship appears in the later stages of Later Vedic period. (b) The two important Rig Vedic gods, '*Indra*' and '*Agni*' lost their importance and instead some minor gods such as *Rudra* and some new gods such as *Prajapati* and *Vishnu* became supreme during the Later Vedic period. (c) The Later Vedic Culture was focused on the centrality of the cult of sacrifice and was immensely based on both priestly domination and ritual dogmas.

Key Concepts	Source
(a) *Gotra*	Atharva Veda
(b) *Purusashukta* hymn (Four-fold division of society)	Rig Veda (Tenth *Mandala*)
(c) First three *ashramas* (*Brahmacharya, Garhasthya, Vanaprastha*)	*Chhandogya Upanishad*
(d) Four *ashrams* (*Brahmacharya, Garhasthya, Vanaprastha, Sannyas*)	*Jabala Upanishad*
(e) *Samsara* (Transmigration of soul)	*Brahadarankya Upanishad*
(f) Sabha and Samiti as the twin daughters of Prajapati	Atharva Veda
(g) '*Satyamev Jayate*'	*Mundak Upanishad*
(h) Doctrine of 'Trimurti'	*Maitrayani Upanishad*
(i) Mention of the 'Great Flood'	*Satpatha Brahamana*
(j) Kshatriyas' precedence over Brahmanas	*Atreya Brahamana*
(k) Mention of the eastern and western seas	*Satpatha Brahmana*
(l) Origin of the Universe	Rig Veda (Tenth *Mandala*)

DO YOU KNOW?

(a) Unlike *Shruti* texts (Vedas), *Smriti* (Remembered) texts includes the Puranas, epics such as the Ramayana, the Mahabharata, *Vedanga, Nitishastra*, and *Dharamashastra*.

(b) The *Kali* age is believed to start from the day Lord Krishna died, about 20 years after the Mahabharata war.

(c) The Ramayana has many versions. Different versions have different beginnings and endings, such as:

(i) The Paumachariu of Vimalasuri in Prakrit is a Jaina version, in which Ravana is killed by Lakshmana, and not by Rama, as Rama, being a true Jaina, embodies non-violence.

(ii) The *Dasharatha Jataka* in Pali (a Buddhist version)

(iii) The *Iramavataram* in Tamil (by Kamban)

(iv) The *Ramcharitmanas* in Hindi (by Tulsidas).

(d) There are primarily four families of languages spoken in India:

(i) Indo-European (spoken by around 75%): It includes Hindi, Bengali, Marathi, Urdu, Gujarati, Oriya, Punjabi, Assamese, Sindhi, Nepali, Kashmiri, etc.

(ii) Dravidian (spoken by around 22%): It includes Telugu, Tamil, Kannada, Malayalam, and Tulu. Largely spoken in South India, except Gondi (Central India), Brahui (Baluchistan, Pakistan), and Malto (Rajmahal Hills, Eastern India).

(iii) Austro-Asiatic (spoken by around 1%): It includes Khasi, Santhali, Mundari, Ho, Savara, Kharia, etc.

(iv) Tibeto-Burmese (spoken by around 1%): It includes Manipuri, Bodo, Tripuri, Garo, Lushai, Sema, Karbi, Ao, Adi, Nissi, etc.

(e) Classical Sanskrit refers to the language whose rules were codified by Grammarian *Panini* in his famous volume *Ashtadhyayi*.

(f) *Patanjali's Mahabhasya* is another important text of Sanskrit grammar.

(g) *Tolkappiyam* is the oldest surviving Tamil grammar.

(h) Among the Dravidian languages, Tamil has the oldest literature followed by Kannada.

(i) Pali and Prakrit both, like Sanskrit, belong to the Indo-Iranian branch of the Indo-European family.

(j) Oldest surviving Prakrit grammar is *Prakritaprakasha* of Vararuchi.

(k) Magathi and Shauraseni are the dialects of Prakrit.

QUESTIONS FROM LAST YEAR'S PRELIMS

1. With reference to the difference between the culture of Rigvedic Aryans and Indus Valley people, which of the following statements is/are correct? **(2017)**

(1) Rigvedic Aryans used the coat of mail and helmet in warfare whereas the people of Indus Valley Civilization did not leave any evidence of using them.

(2) Rigvedic Aryans knew gold, silver and copper whereas Indus Valley people knew only copper and iron.

(3) Rigvedic Aryans had domesticated the horse whereas there is no evidence of Indus Valley people having been aware of this animal.

Select the correct answer using the code given below:

(a) 1 only
(b) 2 and 3 only
(c) 1 and 3 only
(d) 1, 2 and 3

2. The religion of Early Vedic Aryans was primarily of: **(2012)**

(a) *Bhakti*
(b) Image worship and *Yajnas*
(c) Worship of nature and *Yajnas*
(d) Worship of nature and *Bhakti*

3. The national motto of India, '*Satyameva Jayate*', inscribed below the Emblem of India is taken from **(2012)**

(a) *Katha Upanishad*
(b) *Chhandogya Upanishad*
(c) *Aitareya Upanishad*
(d) *Mandukya Upanishad*

4. With reference to the '*dharma*' and '*rita*' depict a central idea of the ancient Vedic civilisation of India; in this context, consider the following statements: **(2011)**

I. *Dharma* was a conception of obligations and of the discharge of one's duties to oneself and to others.

II. *Rita* was the fundamental moral law governing the functioning of the universe and all it contained.

Which of the statements given above is/are correct?

(a) I only (b) II only
(c) Both I and II (d) Neither I nor II

ANSWERS

1. (a) 2. (c) 3. (d) 4. (c)

QUESTIONS FROM LAST YEAR'S MAINS

1. What are the main features of Vedic society and religion? Do you think some of the features are still prevailing in Indian society? **(2023 GS1)**

PRACTICE QUESTIONS – PRELIMS

1. Consider the following statements regarding the source of Vedic civilisation:

I. The most important source of Vedic civilisation is the Vedas.

II. The Vedas are neither any individual religious work nor a collection of definite number of books compiled at a particular time.

III. The Mahabharata and the Ramayana are great epics.

Which of the following statement(s) is/are correct?

(a) Only I (b) I and II
(c) II and III (d) All of these

2. What was the main difference between the Indus Valley civilisation and Vedic civilisation?

(a) Indus Valley civilisation was urban whereas the Vedic civilisation was rural.
(b) Indus Valley civilisation believed in non-violence whereas Vedic civilisation in sacrifices.
(c) The main emphasis in the Indus Valley civilisation was on trade, whereas in the Vedic age, it was on religion.
(d) None of the above

3. *'The world is God and God is my soul'* is the philosophy contained in the:

(a) Upa Vedas (b) Puranas
(c) Brahmanas (d) Upanishads

4. The Gayatri Mantra contained in the Rig Veda is dedicated to which deity?

(a) Agni (b) Savitri
(c) Surya (d) Varuna

5. Rig Veda is divided into ten books/ *Mandalas*. Which among the following book(s) is/are the oldest?

(a) I (b) VIII
(c) II–VII (d) III–IX

6. Which of the following statement(s) is/are not correct?

(a) The Rig Vedic people believed in primitive animism.
(b) The Rig Vedic women were highly respected and that most of the religious ceremonies were considered incomplete unless wives joined their husbands.
(c) The Later Vedic people used painted grey ware pottery.
(d) The Rig Vedic Aryans were by and large urban people.

7. Match the following:

A.	Rig Veda	i.	Melodic Verses
B.	Sama Veda	ii.	Spells and Charms
C.	Atharva Veda	iii.	Oldest Veda
D.	Yajur Veda	iv.	*Shakala* and *Krishna*

(a) A–ii, B–i, C–iii, D–iv
(b) A–i, B–ii, C–iii, D–iv
(c) A–iv, B–iii, C–ii, D–i
(d) A–iii, B–i, C–ii, D–iv

8. Consider the following statements and mark the option which is correct.

I. The Indra deity signified *rita*/cosmic order.

II. Agni, the fire god, was the god of the home and was considered as an intermediary between gods and men.

III. Soma was associated with plants and herbs.

IV. Pushan was the god of the roads, herdsmen, and cattle.

(a) I and II
(b) All of these

(c) II, III and IV
(d) None of these

9. Consider the following statements and choose the appropriate option from the answers for the correct statement(s).

I. Colour (*varna*) was the basis of class differentiation among Aryans.
II. Boustrophedon script was written from right to left in one line and then from left to right in the next line.
III. The family of the Rig Vedic Aryans was matrilineal.

(a) All of these (b) II and III
(c) I and III (d) I only

10. Consider the following statements about the religious practices of Later Vedic culture.

I. Vishnu and Rudra which were smaller deities in the Rig Veda became extremely important.
II. People did not believe in idolatry.
III. People worshipped Gods in the forms of trees and animals.
IV. Some of the important *yajnas* were ashvamedha, vajapeya, rajasuya, etc.

Which of the above statements are true?

(a) I, II, and IV (b) II, III and IV
(c) I and IV (d) All of these

11. Consider the following statements and mark the option which is correct.

I. The Puranas contain thoughts on the mystery of life and universe mythology.
II. The main crop of Rig Vedic civilisation was Barley.
III. Rig Veda does not throw light on the beliefs and practices of the non-Aryans.

(a) I and II (b) III only
(c) All of these (d) None of these

12. Consider the following statements regarding the Vedic states and their territory:

I. The term *Rashtra* came to be important during Later Vedic phase.
II. The battle of the ten kings gives us the names of ten kings who participated in a war against the Sudas, and involved the states of the Purus, Yadus, Turvasas, Anus, and Druhyus.

Which of the following statement(s) is/are correct?

(a) Only I
(b) Only II
(c) Both the statements
(d) Neither of the statements

13. Which of the correct ascending order of Political structure of Rig Vedic India?

(a) *Grama* > *Kula* > *Vis* > *Rashtra* > *Jana*
(b) *Kula* > *Grama* > *Vis* > *Jana* > *Rashtra*
(c) *Rashtra* > *Jana* > *Grama* > *Kula* > *Vis*
(d) *Jana* > *Grama* > *Kula* > *Vis* > *Rashtra*

14. The chief impact of Vedic culture on Indian history was the

(a) Progress of philosophy
(b) Rise of other-worldly outlook
(c) Consolidation of caste system
(d) Growth of Sanskrit

15. Which subject is not dealt with in the Puranas?

(a) Arithmetic
(b) Genealogies of the gods
(c) Primary creation
(d) Secondary creation

16. Match the following:

A.	*Gavyuti*	(i)	Chief
B.	*Gopati*	(ii)	Guest
C.	*Godhuli*	(iii)	Measure of Distance
D.	*Goghna*	(iv)	Measure of Time

(a) A–i, B–ii, C–iii, D–iv
(b) A–iii, B–iv, C–i, D–ii
(c) A–iii, B–i, C–iv, D–ii
(d) A–ii, B–iii, C–iv, D–i

17. Consider the following statements about the Later Vedic civilisation?

I. Sacrifices became more important.
II. People of the Later Vedic civilisation used to have painted grey ware pottery.
III. There was no standing army with the king though revenue collection was done.

Which of the above statement(s) is/are true?

(a) I only (b) II only
(c) All of these (d) III only

18. The main characteristics of the Later Vedic people were:

I. Town planning and excellent drainage system.
II. Worshipped Prajapati and believed in idolatry.
III. Strongly believed in *Varna* System.

(a) I and II (b) I only
(c) II and III (d) All of these

19. Consider the following statements about Rig Veda period:

I. There was widespread use of horses.
II. Agriculture was the predominant economic activity.

Which of the above statement(s) is/are correct?

(a) I only (b) II only
(c) Both I and II (d) Neither I nor II

20. The ninth *mandala* of the Rig Veda Samhita is devoted wholly to

(a) Varuna and cosmic order
(b) Soma and the God who is named after the drink
(c) Urvashi and the Heaven
(d) Indra and his elephant

ANSWERS

1. (d)	2. (a)	3. (d)	4. (b)	5. (c)	6. (d)	7. (d)	8. (c)
9. (d)	10. (c)	11. (a)	12. (c)	13. (b)	14. (c)	15. (a)	16. (c)
17. (c)	18. (c)	19. (a)	20. (b)				

PRACTICE QUESTIONS – MAINS

1. Give a comparative analysis of the different aspects of Rig Vedic and Later Vedic Ages, emphasising on social, political, economic, and religious aspects.

2. To what extent did the word '*gau*' hold significance in the lives of Rig Vedic people. Explain, giving suitable examples.

3. Discuss certain aspects of Vedic Age (both Rig Vedic and Later Vedic) *vis-a-vis* the Indus Valley civilisation. Are they similar or dissimilar? Conduct suitable analysis.

CHAPTER

4

The Mahajanapadas of the Indo-Gangetic Plain (c. 600–300 BCE)

The sixth century BCE is known as an era of 'Second Urbanisation'[1] in the Indian Subcontinent. After the decline of the Harappan towns and nearly after a gap of more than a thousand years, urban centres emerged again but not in the Indus plain. The centre of economic and political activity shifted from the North-West Punjab, Haryana and Western U.P. to Eastern U.P. and Bihar (Ganga Basin). This region was not only fertile on account of better rainfall and river

[1] The first phase of urbanisation was witnessed under Harappan Civilisation. The second phase of urbanisation was the outcome of all-round development made in the material, socio-cultural and political sphere.

(a) The agricultural expansion created huge amount of surplus which prepared a solid material base for the emergence of urban centres.

(b) Due to increasing use of iron in Arts and Crafts, a number of new crafts emerged which further resulted in the emergence of urban craft centres.

systems, but was also closer to the iron production centres. As has been detailed in the earlier chapters, in the Later Vedic period, people had started agriculture, which made them settle down at a particular place. The new iron agricultural tools and implements (such as the ploughshare) enabled the people to clear thick forest cover and cultivate the hard soil of this area. Also, iron weapons made the warrior class more important, and slowly, people gained a strong allegiance to the territory they belonged to rather than the *Jana* or tribe. These permanent settlements led to the foundation of the Janapadas or territorial states, under the control of the king. The use of better iron tools and weapons enabled some territorial states to become very large, and they came to be called **Mahajanapadas** (large territorial states) in North India (cities and states became visible in South India a few centuries later). Most of the Mahajanapadas were situated in the north of Vindhyas, between Bihar in the east to the north-west frontier of the subcontinent. From c. 600 BCE, the political history of India is the history of struggles between these states for supremacy. According to Buddhist texts, *Anguttara Nikaya* (the land between Himalayas and Narmada) was divided into **16 independent states (Mahajanapadas)** as shown below:

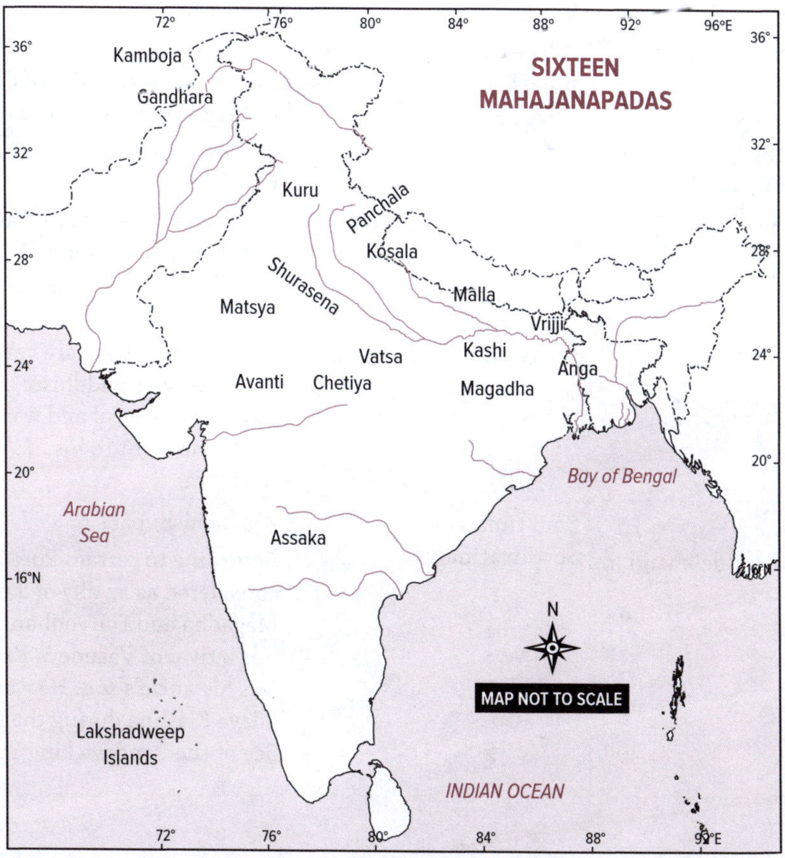

FIGURE 4.1 Mahajanapadas

State	Capital	King/Other Related Unique Aspect(s)
Anga (Modern districts of Monghyr and Bhagalpur, Bihar)	Champa (located at the confluence of Ganga and Champa rivers)	Champa was an important commercial centre on the trade routes and merchants sailed from here to Suvarnabhumi (South-East Asia).
Kashi	Varanasi (Modern Banaras)	Kashi was eventually captured by Kosala.
Kosala (Eastern U.P., included Ayodhya and the tribal republican territory of Shakyas of Kapilavastu)	Sarayu river divided the state into two parts: Northern part's capital: Shravasti and Southern part's capital: Kushavati	King: Prasenjit (Buddha's contemporary) The tribal republic of the Shakyas of Kapilavastu included Lumbini, which is the birthplace of Gautama Buddha.
Vajji* (North of Ganga in the division of Tirhut) *Confederacy of eight or nine clans of which the Lichchhavis (capital: Vaishali), Videhans (capital: Mithila), Jnatrikas (based in Kundapura), and Vajjis (capital: Vaishali) were important.	Vaishali (Modern Basarh in North Bihar)	King: Chetaka [Brother of Trishala (mother of Mahavira) and father of Chellana (wife of Magadha King Bimbisara)]. Mahavira belonged to the Jnatrikas Clan. The Vajjis were defeated and assimilated in the Magadha empire by Ajatshatru.
Mallas	Kushinara and Pava	Kusinara and Pava are very important in the history of Buddhism, since Buddha took his last meal and was taken ill at Pava, and went to his *Mahaparinirvana* at Kusinara.
Cheti or Chedi (Eastern part of Bundelkhand in Central India)	Shuktimati or Sotthivatinagara	King: Shishupala According to certain Puranas, he is considered as an ally of Jarasandha of Magadha and Duryodhana of Kuru. He was a rival of Vasudeva Krishna, who was his uncle's son. He was killed by Vasudeva Krishna during the *Rajasuya* sacrifice of the Pandava king Yudhishthira.

State	Capital	King/Other Related Unique Aspect(s)
Vatsa* (on the banks of river Yamuna) *Vatsa was known for its fine cotton textiles.	Kaushambi (at the confluence of the Ganga and Yamuna, near Allahabad)	King: Udayana Udayana was the hero of three Sanskrit dramas, *viz.*, *Svapnavasavadatta* of Bhasa, *Priyadarshika* and *Ratnavali* of Harsha. Legends recount a rivalry between Udayana and Pradyota of Avanti, and refer to a love affair between Udayana and Vasavadatta (Pradyota's daughter).
Kuru (Western U.P.)	Indraprastha	The epic poem, the Mahabharata, tells of a conflict between two branches of the reigning Kuru clan.
Panchala (Western U.P.)	Ganga river divided the state into two parts: Northern part's capital: Ahichchhatra (modern Bareilly, U.P.) and Southern part's capital: Kampilya (modern Farukkhabad, U.P.)	The famous city of Kannauj was situated in the kingdom of Panchala.
Matsya (Jaipur, Alwar and Bharatpur area of Rajasthan)	Viratanagara (Modern Bairat)	Founder: Virata
Shurarena	Mathura (on banks of Yamuna)	King: Avantipura Disciple of Buddha.
Avanti (Central Malwa)	Divided by the Vindhyas North Avanti Ujjain and South Avanti Mahishmati	King: Pradyota Father-in-law of Udayana.
Gandhara (Modern Peshawar and Rawalpindi, Pakistan, and the Kashmir Valley)	Takshashila/Taxila (Major centre for trade and learning)	King: Pushkarasarin Had cordial relation with Magadha and waged a successful war against Avanti. The Behistun Inscription of the Achaemenid Emperor Darius mentions that Gandhara was conquered by the Persians in the later part of 6th century BCE.

State	Capital	King/Other Related Unique Aspect(s)
Kamboja [Rajori and Hajra (Kashmir) and North-West Frontier Province of Pakistan]	Pooncha	The Kambojas were famous in ancient times for their excellent breed of horses and as remarkable horsemen located in the Uttarapatha or North-West.
Ashavaka/Assaka (Located on the banks of the Godavari river, between the rivers Godavari and Manjira)	Potali (Modern Bodhan, district Nizamabad, and parts of Adilabad in Telangana)	It was the only Mahajanapada situated to the south of the Vindhya Range, and was in Dakshinapatha.
Magadha (Modern Patna and Gaya)	Rajagriha or Girivraja	Haryanka dynasty

It should be noted that the most powerful states in the 6th century were Magadha, Kosala, Vatsa, and Avanti and two of the Mahajanapads, the Vajji and Malla were *Gana-Sanghas*. The *Gana-Sanghas* (literally meaning an assembly of Gana, those who claim to be of equal status) were an alternative polity to the kingdoms. Unlike kingdoms where they had a single hereditary monarch, the *Gana-Sanghas* had a government by assembly and within this assembly too, they had an oligarchy. Some of the *Ganas* were of one clan, e.g. the Shakyas and the Mallas; while the others were confederation of several clans, e.g. Vajjis.

Gana-Sanghas (Chiefdoms and Oligarchies)	Kingdoms
(a) The chief office was not hereditary and was known as *Ganapati or Ganaraja. The* power was vested in an aristocratic council comprising heads of leading Kshatriya families and the authority structure of *ganas* had greater elements of tribal organisation.	(a) Kingdoms registered a centralised government with king as sovereign and all the power was vested in him and ruling family. The ruling family became a dynasty with hereditary succession and mostly following primogeniture.
(b) Most of the *ganas* were located in or near the Himalayan foothills in eastern India, which also suggests that probably their establishment predated the transition to kingdoms as clearing wooded low-lying hills was comparatively easier than the marshy jungles of the plain.	(b) Major kingdoms generally occupied the fertile alluvial tracts of the Ganga valley.

Gana-Sanghas (Chiefdoms and Oligarchies)	Kingdoms
(c) The corporate aspect of government was a major attribute of *Gana-Sanghas*. They were based in smaller geographical areas and had more representative government. The discussion matters were placed before the assembly who met in a hall, called *Santhagara*. ***Gana-Puraka*** was responsible for ensuring quorum required for major deliberations. The council discussed and debated the issues and they were put to vote, if a unanimous decision could not be reached. Voting was done with the pieces of wood known as *salakas* and *salaka-gahapaka* (the collector of votes) ensured honesty and impartiality.	(c) Political power was concentrated in the king who was advised and assisted by ministers, advisory councils such as *Parishad* and *Sabha*. However, with the emergence of the concept of 'divinity of king' and more emphasis on priestly rituals, the centrality of the popular assemblies was reduced.
(d) The Gana-Sanghas had only two strata – the *kshatriya rajakula* (ruling families) and the *dasa-karmakara* (slaves and labourers).	(d) Clan loyalty weakened in the kingdoms and more focus was on caste loyalties and loyalty towards the king.
(e) *Gana-Sanghas* were more ready to tolerate unorthodox views and more open to individualistic or independent opinion than the kingdoms. This tolerance was the major reason that two of the most venerated gurus of the heterodox sects, i.e. Mahavira (Jainism, belonged to Vajji confederacy) and Buddha (Buddhism, belonged to Shakya clan) were able to propagate their philosophy in a more unrestricted way in *Gana-Sanghas* as compared to kingdoms.	(e) The Brahmanical political, social and religious theory was more deeply entrenched in kingdoms.

Political Conflicts and the Pre-Eminence of Magadha

The political conflict among the Mahajanapadas ultimately led to the emergence of Magadha as the most powerful state and the centre of a vast empire. Magadha's rise to political supremacy began with **Bimbisara,** who belonged to the Haryanka dynasty, and ruled for 52 years, from 544 to 492 BCE. In the *Mahavamsa,* it is stated that he was anointed as the king by his father at the age of 15, which suggests that he was not the founder of his dynasty. He was a contemporary of both Buddha and Mahavira, and paid equal respect to them. Through his conquests and diplomacy, Bimbisara made Magadha the paramount power. He pursued a three-pronged policy, namely, matrimonial alliances, friendship with strong rulers and conquest of weak neighbours to expand the empire.

Haryanka Dynasty (Magadha)

Founder: Probably the grandfather of Bimbisara (566 BCE)

Actual foundation by Bimbisara (544–492 BCE)

- Contemporary of Buddha and Mahavira.
- Capital at Rajgriha (Girivraja), which was an impressive city and almost impregnable as surrounded by five hills, the openings in which were closed by stone walls on all sides.
- Also known as Seniya, Sreniya was the first king to have a standing army.
- Earlier, had rivalry with Avanti's king Pradyota, but later became friends and Bimbisara even sent his royal physician Jivaka to Ujjain (along *Dakshinapatha to Avanti*) when Pradyota had Jaundice.
- Conquered Anga (East Bihar) by defeating its ruler Brahmadatta. Anga, and especially its capital, Champa, were important for inland and maritime trade.
- Strengthened his position by three matrimonial alliances. Marriage relations with the different princely families gave enormous diplomatic prestige and paved the way for expansion of Magadha westward and northward. He took three wives:
    - His first wife was from Kosala named Mahakoshala (sister of Prasenjit), who brought in dowry the territory of Kashi, which yielded a revenue of 1,00,000 coins.
    - His second wife was the Lichchhavi Princess Chellana from Vaishali, who gave birth to Ajatashatru.
    - His third wife was the daughter of the chief of the Madra clan (Punjab).
- It is believed that Gandhara ruler of Taxila, Pukkusati (Pushkarasarin) sent an embassy to Bimbisara.

Ajatashatru (492–460 BCE)

- Son of Bimbisara, being impatient to rule Magadha, is believed to have killed his father and seized the throne.
- Most powerful and aggressive ruler of Haryanka dynasty and followed his father's expansionist policy through military conquest.
- Annexed Kosala[2] (ruled by Prasenjit).

---

[2] Ajatashatru first came into conflict with his maternal uncle Prasenjit, who was aggrieved by the treatment meted out to Bimbisara. He asked Ajatashatru to return the territory of Kashi, which was given to his mother in dowry. Ajatashatru refused, and it was only after a fierce battle that Prasenjit agreed to leave Kashi with Magadha. Similarly, he fought with his maternal grandfather, Chetak, the chief of Vaishali and after 16 long years of war Ajatashatru succeeded in breaking the might of Vaishali. Therefore, he not only retained Kashi, but also added Vaishali to Magadha.

- Used two innovative military weapons:
    - War engine, which was used to throw stones like catapults (*Mahashilakantaka*).
    - Chariot with mace for mass-killing (*Rathamusala*).
- Began the fortification of Rajgriha to meet the danger of invasion posed by the ruler of Avanti (who had earlier defeated the Vatsas of Kaushambi).
- The Buddha died during his reign.
- Arranged the first Buddhist council.

Udayabhadra (Udayin) (460–444 BCE)

- Founded the new capital at Pataliputra (modern Patna), situated at the confluence of Ganga and Son rivers. Pataliputra had a very strategic location as it lay at the centre of the Magadhan kingdom, which then extended from the Himalayas in the north to the Chhotanagpur Hills in the south.
- Probably was murdered at the instigation of Palaka, the king of Avanti.

Shishunaga Dynasty (around 412–345 BCE)

Shishunaga

- Shishunaga was earlier a Viceroy/*Amatya* (high ranking official) at Varanasi (Banaras), and it is believed that the people of Magadha, outraged by the successive parricides of the successors of Udayin, appointed Shishunaga as king.
- Temporarily shifted capital to Vaishali.
- The most important achievement of Shishunaga was to defeat Avanti (Pradyota Dynasty) and make it a part of Magadha. This brought an end to 100-year-old rivalry between Magadha and Avanti.

Kalasoka

- Son and successor of Shishunaga.
- Also known as Kakarvarna (according to the Puranas).
- Second Buddhist Council held at Vaishali.
- Shifted capital back to Pataliputra from Vaishali.

Nanda Dynasty (First non-Kshatriya dynasty) (345–321 BCE)

Mahapadma Nanda

- Also called Ugrasena in Pali texts, because of his large army.
- According to the Brahmanical texts, he belonged to a low caste or at least a non-Kshatriya caste, while according to the Puranas, he was the son of a king of the Shishunaga dynasty by a Shudra woman, and thus the Nandas were considered *adharmika* (those who do

not follow the norms of Dharma). Buddhist texts describe the Nandas as belonging to *annatakula* (of unknown lineage).

- The first empire builder of India, and claimed to be the *ekarat*, the sole sovereign who destroyed all other ruling princes, and *sarva-kshatrantaka,* uprooter of the Kshatriyas.
- Added Kalinga to Magadha and brought an image of *Jina* as a victory trophy.
- Also acquired Kosala, which had, in all likelihood, rebelled against him.
- Made methodical collection of taxes by regularly appointing officials. He also built canals and did a lot of irrigation work.

Dhanananda

- Last important king of the Nanda dynasty.
- Identified with the Agrammes or Xandrames of Greek classical writers.
- Credited with a huge army; it is believed that Alexander attacked Punjab during his reign but his huge army checked them from advancing towards Magadha.
- Credited with the invention of *Nandopakramani* (a particular measure).
- He is believed to be an arrogant and oppressive ruler who imposed heavy taxes on the common man. His greed and exploitation made him quite unpopular among the masses, and ultimately Chandragupta Maurya under the able guidance of Kautilya, took the advantage of this public resentment and uprooted the Nanda rule and set up the Maurya empire.

Maurya Dynasty (321 BCE)

Causes of Magadha's Success

Magadha could gradually establish its dominance over all other Mahajanapads on account of several factors:

(a) **Firstly,** Magadha enjoyed an advantageous geographical position. Due to its proximity and control over richest iron deposits (found around south Bihar), Magadhan weapons were far superior and effective. Also, both of its capitals, Rajgriha and Patliputra, were situated at very strategic points. Girivraja or Rajagriha was surrounded by five hills, which helped it to provide natural fortification and was almost impregnable. Similarly, Pataliputra was more like a water fort, since it was situated at the confluence of the rivers Son and Ganga.

(b) **Secondly,** Magadha lay at the centre of the middle Gangetic plain, which had fertile alluvium and received heavy rainfall. Thus, this area could be made more productive even without much irrigation. These fertile river plains provided a vast amount of agricultural surplus, which was essential for raising a vast standing army. Further, forests in southern areas provided timber and elephants, which gave a special military advantage to Magadha as all the other Mahajanapads effectively used horses and chariots in warfare. Magadha was the first state to use elephants on a large scale against its neighbours. Elephants could be used in storming fortresses and in marching over areas lacking roads or other means of communication.

(c) **Thirdly,** Magadha certainly benefited from numerous able and ambitious rulers such as Bimbisara, Ajatashatru and Mahapadma Nanda. They employed all fair and foul means at their disposal to enlarge their kingdoms.

(d) **Fourthly,** because of the rise of trade, towns, and metal money, the tolls levied too added to the treasury of Magadhan kings, which again helped them to maintain the huge army.

(e) **Finally,** the unorthodox character of Magadhan society infused in it more enthusiasm for expansion than any other kingdoms.

North-West India: Persian and Macedonian Invasions

In north-east India, Magadha emerged as a formidable power and gradually smaller principalities and republics merged within it. The situation in north-western India did not allow for such consolidation. The Mahajanapads of Kamboja, Madra and Gandhara were continuously fighting with each other. Thus, a powerful kingdom like Magadha could not emerge in the north-west frontier. Taking advantage of this political disunity, the Persian (Iranian) empire in the 6th century BCE penetrated into north-western India. The Achaemenid king Cyrus (558–529 BCE) was the first ruler to invade the sub-continent. He led a military expedition that destroyed the city of Kapisha (lying south east of the Hindu Kush mountains) and received tribute from the people of Kamboja and Gandhara. Later, Persian king Darius, in 518 BCE, annexed Punjab, the west of Indus, and Sindh. The Greek historian Herodotus (considered as the father of Western history-writing) mentions about Gandhara that '*this area was the twentieth and the most prosperous satrapy (province) of the Persian empire, and paid a tribute of 360 talents of gold, which was not only more than that from all other 20 provinces put together, but was also about one-third of the total revenue of Iran from its Asian provinces. Indian provinces provided mercenaries for the Persian armies fighting against the Greeks in the 5th century BCE. In fact, the army of Xerxes (the successor of Darius) included soldiers from Gandhara*'. It appears that till Alexander's invasion of India (around c. 330 BCE), the north-western part of the subcontinent was under Persian rule.

Persian Impact on India

(a) The introduction of the Kharoshthi script, which was derived from Aramaic (the official script of the Persian empire, written right to left like Arabic) in north-western India is a fine example highlighting the Persian impact. Some of the Ashokan inscriptions in north-western India are written in this script.

(b) Persian *sigloi*-type coins were copied in India.

(c) It is possible that the rock inscriptions used by Ashoka in the 3rd century BCE were inspired by the Persian King Darius. The monuments of Ashoka's time, especially the bell-shaped capitals and the preamble of Ashoka's edicts, have a lot of Iranian influence.

The 200 years of Indo-Persian contact resulted in not only political influence, but also socio-economic acculturation. Along with providing impetus to Indo-Persian trade and commerce, it resulted in forging cultural ties.

Alexander's Invasion (327–326 BCE)

Alexander (356–326 BCE) was the son of Philip of Macedonia (Greece), who invaded India in 326 BCE. It is considered that in the 4th century, the Greeks and the Persians fought for the supremacy of the world. After decisively defeating the Persian army led by Darius, the Macedonian conqueror marching across the Persian empire, entered the Indian provinces. Alexander was attracted towards India not only because of its fabulous wealth, but being a passionate student of geographical inquiry and natural history, he also wanted to solve the problem of the ocean, the limits of which were a puzzle to Greek geographers. The political situation of north-western India suited his plans, as at that time, the region was split up into a number of small independent states like Taxila, Punjab (Kingdom of Porus), Gandhara, etc., and no major united and strong resistance was put across to Alexander. Alexander entered India through the Khyber Pass in 326 BCE. Except Porus[3], who fought the famous battle of Hydaspas (on Jhelum), all other kings submitted meekly. King Ambhi of Taxila was the first to surrender. When Alexander reached Beas, his soldiers, being war-weary, homesick and diseased, refused to go further. Therefore, he was forced to retreat. To mark the farthest point of his advance, he erected 12 huge stone altars on northern bank of Beas. He remained in India for 19 months and on his way back home, had military encounters with *Gana-Sanghas* such as the Malloi (Malavas). He died at Babylon (in 323 BCE). Since he barely had time to organise his conquests in India, most of the conquered states were restored to their rulers who submitted to his authority, and his territorial possessions were divided into three parts, each placed under a Greek governor. North-western India was placed under Seleucus Nikator.

[3] Although Alexander defeated Porus, impressed by his courage and bravery, he restored his kingdom.

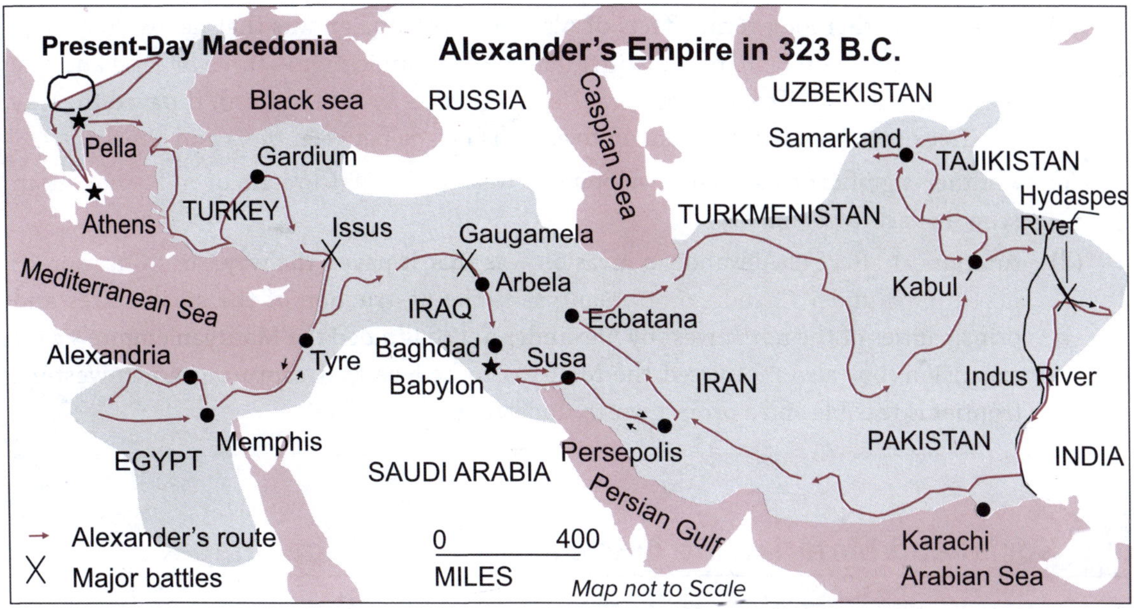

FIGURE 4.2 Alexander's Invasion of India

Effect of Alexander's Invasion

Alexander's invasion was the first occasion when ancient Europe came into close contact with ancient India and it produced significant outcomes.

Effect of Alexander's Invasion

(a) One of the most important outcomes of the invasion was the establishment of direct contact between India and Greece in different fields. Alexander's historians have left valuable geographical and historical/chronological accounts of ancient Indian history. The clearly dated accounts of Alexander's campaign enabled us to build the Indian chronology for subsequent events on a definite basis. The crucial socio-economic information provided in these travelogues help us know and understand diverse ancient societal practices such as 'autonomous cities' (probably referring to the *Gana-Sanghas*), *sati* system, the sale of girls in market places by poor parents, the fine breed of oxen in north-western India (in fact, it is said that Alexander ordered 2 lakh oxen to be sent to Macedonia), and so on.

(b) One of the other long-term effects of Alexander's campaign was that he exposed India to Europe by opening up four distinct lines of communication – three by land and one by sea (as Alexander sent his admiral Nearchus via sea route to Iran). It paved the way for Greek merchants and craftsmen to establish trade between India and Greeks.

(c) Another significant cultural development was the establishment of a cosmopolitan school of arts at Gandhara.

(d) An indirect effect of Alexander's invasion was that it paved the way for unification of north India under Chandragupta Maurya, as the destruction of the small states and principalities of the north-west by Alexander not only aided the Mauryan empire's easy expansion, but also motivated the Mauryas to believe that capturing north-western frontier is feasible and a project worth undertaking.

Social and Material Life in the Age of the Mahajanapadas

Archaeologically, 6th century BCE is marked by the beginning of NBPW phase and the second urbanisation in India (after the Harappan Civilisation). This is derived on the basis of literary testimony of the early Buddhist Pali texts, Sanskrit Sutra literature, and archaeological evidence from early NBPW sites. NBPW refers to Northern Black Polished Ware, which was a glossy, shining type of pottery made from very fine fabric and probably used as tableware by the wealthy. It is rather interesting to note that NBPW is not always black (as it is found in other shades and colours too), also found in Southern India (identified at Amravati in Andhra Pradesh, though there is a concentration of sites in northern India), and not necessarily always polished (although it is well-fired, wheel-made, deluxe pottery, having a glossy surface). The NBPW is usually unpainted, but there are some instances of designs like wavy lines, concentric and intersecting circles, bands, dots, etc., painted on in yellow and light vermillion.

Social and Material Life in the Age of Mahajanapads

(a) The NBPW phase also marks the beginning of the use of money in the sub-continent, as early series of punch-marked coins have been excavated from NBPW sites. Along with metal money, burnt bricks and ring wells too appeared in the middle of the NBPW phase.

(b) During c. 600–300 BCE, there was significant expansion in the number and size of village settlements, towns, and corresponding population growth in the Ganga Valley. Numerous villages and towns are mentioned in the Pali and Sanskrit texts. There was a great degree of differentiation in case of towns:

(i) *pura* or *nagaṛa* meant a fortified town or city;

(ii) *nigama* referred to a market town which was at an intermediate level between *grama* and *nagara*;

(iii) *rajdhani* referred to capital city;

(iv) *nagarka* was a small town and

(v) *mahanagara* was a big city.

Some of the prominent towns (*mahanagaras*) were Kashi, Kaushambi, Rajgriha, Pataliputra, Shravasti, Ayodhya, Vaishali, Champa and Kapilavastu.

(c) Not only were these towns seats of government, but they also served as major hubs of trade and commerce and were inhabited by many artisans and merchants who were organised into their respective guilds. The guilds not only managed markets, checked the quality of manufactured goods, fixsed the price of goods, looked after the welfare of its members, facilitated the transfer of vocational knowledge from generation to generation but also maintained troops for safety of its members and enjoyed judicial powers over its members. The *setthi* was a high level businessman, associated with trade and money lending. Both artisans and merchants lived in fixed localities in towns known as *vessas* (merchant streets). Generally, crafts were hereditary and the son used to learn his family trade from his father.

(d) Craft products like textile goods, ivory products, pots, etc., were exported over long distances by merchants. All the major cities were situated on river banks and trade routes, and were connected with each other. The two major trans-regional routes of the time were known as *Uttarapatha* (of northern India, stretching from the north-west across the Indo-Gangetic plains to the port city of Tamralipti on the Bay of Bengal) and *Dakshinapatha* (of southern India, stretching from Pataliputra in Magadha to Pratishthana on the Godavari, and connected to ports on the western coast). The internal trade routes joined the external trade routes, and there are evidences of flourishing trade of the subcontinent along both eastern (Bengal with Myanmar) and western (Taxila with Afghanistan, Iran and Mesopotamia) regions.

(e) The major items of import included precious stones such as gold, lapis lazuli, jade, silver, etc., while finished crafts, textile goods, sandalwood and pearls were major items of export.

(f) Pali texts also mention sea travel and trade. Custom officials (*Kammikas*) and Toll officials (*Shaulkika/Shulkadhyaksha*) levied taxes on merchandise, and special royal officials called *Rajabhatas* were deputed to safeguard the lives and property of travellers.

(g) Trade was facilitated by use of money termed *Nishka* and *Satamana.* The earliest coins are punch-marked (called so as pieces of metals were punched with certain marks such as hill, tree, bull, fish, crecent, elephant, etc.) and made of silver, though a few copper coins are also found. The Pali texts further refer to the plentiful use of money and its use to pay wages and prices. Panini's *Ashtadhyayi* also mentions wage (*vetan*) and wage-earners (*vaitanika*). The knowledge of script further facilitated the growth of trade and commerce as now the accounts of the transactions could be maintained.

(h) Both towns and villages mutually supported each other as the non-agriculturists living in towns were fed by the agriculturists living in villages, and in return, artisans and traders living in towns made tools, cloth, etc., available to rural folk. The Pali texts (especially the *Vinay Pitaka*) suggests three types of villages (*grama*):

  (i) Typical villages, inhabited by various castes, communities and headed by a headman called *gramabhojaka, gramini or gramakas.* The majority of the villages belonged to this category. The village headman enjoyed considerable importance and had direct links with the kings. They not only collected taxes from the villagers, but also maintained law and order in their locality.

  (ii) Suburban villages, which were in the nature of craft villages. For example, carpenters' village (*vaddhaki-grama*), reedmakers' village (*nalakara-grama*), saltmakers' village (*lonakara-grama*) and chariotmakers' villages are mentioned in the texts of the period. These villages served as markets for other villages and linked the towns with the countryside.

  (iii) Border villages *(aramika-grama),* which were situated on the periphery of the countryside and merged into forests. People living in these villages were mainly hunters and fowlers, who mostly lived on primitive subsistence methods like food gathering.

(i) The village lands were divided into cultivable plots and were allotted family-wise, though the size of land holdings varied. The plots were cultivated by the family on its own as well as with hired agricultural labourers (*dasa-kammakara*). Rich peasants were known as *'Gahapati'*. Irrigation channels were dug collectively under the supervision of village headman.

(j) One-sixth (1/6) of the produce was paid by peasants as tax, which was collected by royal agents. There were generally no intermediaries between peasants and the state, though some villages were granted to Brahmanas (*brahmadeyas*) and big merchants for their own use. It should be noted that the beneficiaries were granted only the revenue of these lands and not administrative authority.

(k) There was an emergence of the notion of private property, as there are references to the gift and sale of land.

It is equally noteworthy that during this period, because of the use of the iron ploughshare and good fertility of alluvial soil, agriculture made great advances. Perhaps for the first time, there was land and agrarian expansion, which aided in the emergence of an advanced food-producing economy. Rice was the staple cereal and paddy transplantation was widely practiced. Along with rice, barley, pulses, millets, cotton and sugarcane were also produced. The excavated site of Atranjikhera (Etah, U.P.) provides valuable information about the transition from rural to urban life.

Administrative System

The king enjoyed the highest official status and ruled with the help of officials. Higher officials were called *Mahamatras/Amatyas,* who probably had executive, judicial and military functions such as those of judge, chief accountant, head of the royal household, minister (*Mantrin*) and commander (*Senanayaka*), and were assisted by *Ayuktas.* It appears that high officers and ministers were largely recruited from the priestly class of Brahmanas, and yielded considerable authority. The Buddhist text *Mahaparinibbana Sutta* mentions an influential minister named Vassakara of Magadha, who enabled Ajatashatru to conquer the *Gana-Sangha* of Vajjis by effectively creating dissension in the ranks of the Lichchhavis of Vaishali. The real increase in state power is indicated by the formation of a large professional army. In order to sustain such a huge army, a robust fiscal system was required. *Bali,* a voluntary payment made by the tribesmen to their chiefs in the Vedic times, became a compulsory payment, and special officers called *balisadhakas* were appointed to collect it. As mentioned earlier, it was 1/6th of the produce. The advent of writing may have helped in the assessment and collection of taxes. In addition to taxes, peasants, artisans and traders were subjected to forced labour for royal purposes. Popular assemblies like the *sabha* and the *samiti* almost disappeared, and instead, a small body called the *parishad,* consisting exclusively of the Brahmanas, served as an advisory council to the king.

Legal and Social System

This period marks the origin of the Indian legal and judiciary systems. Earlier, people were governed by tribal law, which did not recognise any class distinction, but now since the caste groups and the *varna* system were strongly entrenched in social life, the legal system was also partially disposed towards the higher *varnas*. The civil and criminal law was based on the *varna* division. The higher *varnas* were considered purer, and a higher order of moral conduct was expected from the higher *varnas*. All disabilities were imposed on Shudras. They were not only relegated to lower positions of the society but also deprived of religious and legal rights. Crimes committed by Shudras against Brahmanas and others were punished severely, while crimes committed against Shudras were punished lightly. Civil and criminal law was administered by royal agents, who followed retributive law (criminal offences were governed by the idea of revenge, i.e. 'a tooth for a tooth' and 'an eye for an eye').

Despite the emergence of socio-economic disparities, kinship ties continued to be extremely important, and were eventually incorporated in the caste hierarchy. Extended kin groups were referred as *Nati* and *Nati-kulani*. *Kula* denoted extended patrilineal family, while *Natakas* included relatives on both mother's and father's side. The importance of kinship ties can be gauged by the fact that although Buddhist monks were supposed to have renounced family ties, monastic rules were bent to make allowances for them. The strengthening of patriarchal control within the household led to the increased subordination of women. Strict control over women's sexuality was considered essential for not only the patrilineal transmission of property, but also for maintaining and perpetuating endogamous caste system. Different Brahmanical, Buddhist and Jain texts point towards the low status of women. They prescribe an ideal code of conduct for women and define their expected roles. Given the increasingly patriarchal nature of the household, it is not surprising that the preference for sons over daughters continued. The son was considered necessary for the continuation of lineage, and the performance of the father's and ancestors' funerary rites. In the *Samyutta Nikaya,* the Buddha is presented as consoling Prasenjit (king of Kosala), who was upset at the birth of a daughter. Buddha tells him, '*Don't worry, she may prove better than a male offspring. She will grow up wise and virtuous. She will honour her mother-in-law and will be faithful to her husband. The boy she may bear may do great deeds.*' These words sum up the expected roles associated with womanhood.

The society was clearly divided into four *varnas* – Brahmans, Kshatriyas, Vaishyas and Shudras. The functions of each *varna* were clearly laid down. According to this system, rulers and warriors were called Kshatriyas, priests and teachers formed the Brahmanical order, peasants and taxpayers were called Vaishyas, and those who served all classes were called Shudras. Members of higher *varnas* not only avoided the company of the Shudras, but also refused to enter into marital relations with them. A Shudra was not allowed to be appointed to any higher post, and was meant to only serve the *dvijas* (Brahmins, Kshatriyas and Vaishyas) as a slave, artisan and agricultural labourer.

QUESTIONS FROM LAST YEAR'S MAINS

1. Explain the role of geographical factors towards the development of Ancient India. **(2023 GS1)**

PRACTICE QUESTIONS – PRELIMS

1. Match the following:

A. *Mahamatras*	i. Tax collector	C. *Gahapati*	iii. High-ranking official
B. *Balisadhaka*	ii. Wealthy landlord	D. *Setthi*	iv. Rich merchant

(a) A–ii, B–i, C–iii, D–iv
(b) A–i, B–ii, C–iii, D–iv
(c) A–iv, B–iii, C–ii, D–i
(d) A–iii, B–i, C–ii, D–iv

2. Consider the following statements and mark the option which is correct.

(i) The first coins were punch-marked silver and copper coins.
(ii) The main crops of the Age of the Mahajanapads were wheat and barley.
(iii) The PGW phase was followed by NBPW phase.
(iv) The tax was collected by the ***Senanayaka***.

(a) i and iii (b) All of these
(c) ii, iii and iv (d) None of these

3. Match the following:

A.	Magadha	i.	Champa
B.	Anga	ii.	Varanasi
C.	Kosala	iii.	Rajgriha
D.	Kashi	iv.	Shravasti

(a) A–i, B–ii, C–iii, D–iv
(b) A–iii, B–iv, C–i, D–ii
(c) A–iii, B–i, C–iv, D–ii
(d) A–ii, B–iii, C–iv, D–i

4. Consider the following statements about the NBPW phase, and mark the option which is correct.

(i) Rice was the staple diet of the NBPW phase.
(ii) Peasants knew about paddy transplantation.
(iii) The NBPW phase marked the beginning of the second urbanisation.
(iv) Burnt bricks and ring wells were used in the NBPW phase.

(a) All of these (b) ii and iii
(c) None of these (d) i, ii and iii

5. Match the following:

A.	Bimbisara	i.	Matrimonial alliances
B.	Ajatashatru	ii.	Aggressive policy
C.	Udayin	iii.	Built Fort at Pataliputra
D.	Shishunaga	iv.	Shifted Capital to Vaishali

(a) A–i, B–ii, C–iii, D–iv
(b) A–iii, B–i, C–ii, D–iv
(c) A–ii, B–iii, C–iv, D–i
(d) A–i, B–iv, C–iii, D–iii

6. Consider the following statements and choose whether it was a result of Persian influence:

(i) Bell-shaped capital of Ashoka's rock edits.
(ii) The Kharosthi script written from right to left in one line and then from left to right in the next line.
(iii) The Influence on Mauryan Sculpture.

(a) All of these (b) ii and iii
(c) i and iii (d) None of these

7. Consider the following statements about the religious practices of the people of the Mahajanapadas.

(i) The people worshipped gods in the forms of trees and animals.
(ii) Generally, people believed in the Brahmanical order and Shudras were exploited by all.
(iii) The Society was clearly divided into four varnas.
(iv) There is sufficient evidence of the prevalence of the *sati* system and the sale of girls by poor parents.

(a) i, ii and iv (b) ii, iii and iv
(c) i and iii (d) All of these

8. Consider the following statements about the Alexander's Invasion and state which is correct.

(i) Through the Persians, the Greeks came to know about the great wealth of India.

(ii) Alexander invaded India around 326 BCE.
(iii) The ruler of Taxila, Porus, fought gallantly with Alexander, while King Ambhi submitted meekly before Alexander.
(iv) Alexander conquered Magadha.
(a) i, ii and iv (b) ii, iii and iv
(c) i and ii (d) All of these

9. Consider the following statements about the Persian invasion and state which is correct.
(i) Indo-Persian contact lasted almost for 200 years before the Greeks invaded India.
(ii) Cyrus was the first ruler to invade India.
(iii) The north-western province of Gandhara was the 20th *satrapy* of Persian empire.
(iv) Indian subjects were also enrolled in the Persian Army.
(a) i, ii and iv (b) ii, iii and iv
(c) i and iii (d) All of these

10. Match the following:

A.	Bimbisara	i.	Haryanka Dynasty
B.	Ajatashatru	ii.	Shifted capital to Vaishali
C.	Ashoka	iii.	Maurya Dynasty
D.	Shishunaga	iv.	Probably killed his father

(a) A–i, B–ii, C–iii, D–iv
(b) A–iii, B–i, C–ii, D–iv
(c) A–ii, B–iii, C–iv, D–i
(d) A–i, B–iv, C–iii, D–ii

11. Match the following:

A.	Kosala	i.	Birth place of Buddha, Lumbini, is situated.
B.	Mallas	ii.	Buddha passed away at Kusinara, which is a part of this kingdom.
C.	Vajjis	iii.	Mahavira belonged to this confederacy of clans.
D.	Vatsa	iv.	King Udayin is from this place, who the hero of three major dramas.

(a) A–i, B–ii, C–iii, D–iv
(b) A–iii, B–i, C–ii, D–iv
(c) A–ii, B–iii, C–iv, D–i
(d) A–i, B–iv, C–iii, D–ii

12. Match the following:

A.	Pataliputra	i.	Capital of Kosala
B.	Rajgriha	ii.	Water fort
C.	Ujjain	iii.	Impregnable, as surrounded by five hills
D.	Shravasti	iv.	Capital of Avanti

(a) A–i, B–ii, C–iii, D–iv
(b) A–iii, B–i, C–ii, D–iv
(c) A–ii, B–iii, C–iv, D–i
(d) A–i, B–iv, C–iii, D–ii

13. Consider the following statements and mark the option which is incorrect.
(i) Iron implements and technology aided in the development of large kingdoms.
(ii) The four most powerful Mahajanapads were that of Magadha, Kosala, Vatsa and Avanti.
(iii) The Mahajanapads were mostly situated in the north of the Vindhyas.
(iv) The people now had allegiance to ***Janapada*** rather than the ***Jana***.
(a) i and iii
(b) All of these
(c) ii, iii and iv
(d) None of these

14. Consider the following statements and mark the option which is correct.

(i) The founder king of the Haryanka dynasty was Bindusara (or Bimbisara).

(ii) Ajatashatru added Vaishali to his kingdom.

(iii) Shishunaga's greatest achievement was the destruction of the power of Avanti.

(iv) Mahapadma Nanda took the title of ***Ekarat***.

(a) i and iii (b) All of these

(c) ii, iii and iv (d) None of these

15. Consider the following statements and mark the option which justifies the reason behind Magadha's success:

(i) Magadha had a high income on account of the fertile plains of Ganga basin.

(ii) The first capital of Magadha, Rajgriha, was a water fort.

(iii) The second capital, Pataliputra, was located in a strategic position on the confluence of Ganga and Son.

(iv) The unorthodox character of Magadhan people too aided in the state's rise to glory.

(a) i, iii and iv (b) All of these

(c) ii, iii and iv (d) None of these

16. Match the following:

A.	***Nishka***	i.	Coin
B.	***Vessas***	ii.	State official
C.	***Gramini***	iii.	Village Head
D.	*Ayuktas*	iv.	Merchant streets

(a) A–i, B–ii, C–iii, D–iv

(b) A–iii, B–i, C–ii, D–iv

(c) A–ii, B–iii, C–iv, D–i

(d) A–i, B–iv, C–iii, D–ii

17. Match the following:

A.	Cheti	i.	Shishupala
B.	Magadha	ii.	Bindusara
C.	Taxila	iii.	Ambhi
D.	Avanti	iv.	Pradyota

(a) A–i, B–ii, C–iii, D–iv

(b) A–iii, B–i, C–ii, D–iv

(c) A–ii, B–iii, C–iv, D–i

(d) A–i, B–iv, C–iii, D–ii

18. Consider the following statements and mark the option which is incorrect.

(i) The Shishunagas were succeeded by the Haryankas.

(ii) Ajatashatru fought with Alexander.

(iii) Shishunaga's greatest achievement was the destruction of the power of Avanti.

(iv) Mahapadma Nanda acquired Kalinga.

(a) i and ii (b) All of these

(c) ii, iii and iv (d) None of these

19. Consider the following statements and mark the option which is correct.

(i) Bimbisara sent his royal physician, Jivaka, to Ujjain for helping the king of Avanti, who was suffering from jaundice.

(ii) Ajatashatru introduced two new military weapons in his fight against Vaishali.

(iii) Magadhans were the first to use elephants on big scale.

(iv) Mahapadma Nanda defeated Udayin.

(a) i, ii and iii (b) All of these

(c) ii, iii and iv (d) None of these

20. Consider the following statements about the social life of pre-Mauryan times and mark the option which is correct.

(i) The legal and social system was partially biased against the Shudras.

(ii) Women were highly respected and enjoyed considerable freedom.

(iii) The popular assemblies of *Sabha* and *Samiti* lost their importance.

(iv) The polity and social life of the *Gana-Sanghas* was not as rigid as that of the kingdoms.

(a) i and iii (b) i, iii and iv

(c) ii, iii and iv (d) None of these

ANSWERS

1. (a)	1.	(d)	2. (a)	3. (c)	4. (a)	5. (a)	6. (c)
7. (b)	8. (c)	9. (d)	10. (d)	11. (a)	12. (c)	13. (d)	14. (c)
15. (a)	16. (d)	17. (a)	18. (a)	19. (a)	20. (b)		

PRACTICE QUESTIONS – MAINS

1. The 6th Century BCE saw the rise of big territorial states called the Mahajanapads. What were the reasons facilitating the rise of such big states? Which were the major Mahajanpadas and which emerged the most powerful amongst them? Explain giving suitable examples.

2. Describe the effects of Persian and Macedonian invasion on India.

3. Discuss the reasons behind Magadha's success, specially outlining the role of its major rulers.

4. Describe the social, political, and administrative life of pre-Mauryan times. Was trade a major factor in the second urbanisation? If yes, then what were the major routes followed by traders and what were the general trading goods? Address all these issues in your answer.

5. How did the *Gana-Sanghas* differ from the kingdoms? Elucidate.

CHAPTER

5

Buddhism and Jainism

Sixth century BCE was a period of great religious upheaval. Great teachers like Confucius in China, Zoroaster in Iran, and Parmenides in Greece questioned the established socio-religious norms and focused more on ethical and moral values. In India, the scenario was no different. India witnessed the growth of two great alternative religions: Buddhism and Jainism. These religions emphasised that true happiness does not lie in material prosperity or performance of rituals, but in non-violence, charity, frugality and good social conduct. Various reasons are attributed to the origin and popularity of these two important and potent religious reform movements.

Causes of Origin

Some of the significant causes of origin of these alternative religions are listed below.

a. The Kshatriyas' reaction against domination of the Brahmanas: The post Vedic society was clearly divided into four *varnas*: Brahmanas, Kshatriyas, Vaishyas and Shudras. Kshatriyas (who functioned as rulers and warriors) were ranked second in the *varna* hierarchy. They reacted strongly against the ritualistic domination of the Brahmanas and the various privileges enjoyed by the priestly class (such as receiving gifts and exemption from taxation and punishment). It is rather unsurprising that both Buddha and Mahavira (key leaders of Buddhism and Jainism), who strongly disputed the authority of the Brahmanas, belonged to the Kshatriya *varna*. Equally interesting is the fact that Buddhist Pali texts frequently reject the Brahmanical claim to innate superiority and reverses the Brahmanical order of rank, thus placing Kshatriyas higher than the Brahmanas.

b. Rise of new agricultural economy which demanded animal husbandry: In the sixth century BCE, as noted earlier, the centre of economic and political activity shifted from Haryana and Western UP to Eastern UP and Bihar, which had more rainfall and more fertile land. Since it was now easier to exploit the iron ore resources of Bihar and adjoining regions, people started using more and more iron tools and ploughshare to clear the thick forest cover and cultivate the hitherto unexplored areas. The agricultural economy based on iron ploughshare required the use of bullocks, and thus could only flourish with animal husbandry. But the Vedic practice of animal sacrifice resulted in killing of cattle indiscriminately and stood in the way of the progress of the new agricultural economy. Thus, for the stability and prosperity of the new agrarian economy, this slaughtering of animals had to be stopped. Since both Buddhism and Jainism advocated non-violence and were strongly against any form of sacrifices, they were found promising to the peasant masses.

c. Patronising of Buddhism and Jainism by Vaishyas and other mercantile groups who wanted better social status and a reign of peace: As we are well aware, the sixth century BCE is known as the era of second urbanisation in the Indian sub-continent. Expansion of agriculture resulted in improved food supply and helped in the development of craft production, trade and urban centres. The development of trade is reflected in discovery of thousands of silver and copper **Punch-Marked Coins** (**PMC**) by the numismatists. More than sixty towns and cities such as Patliputra, Rajagriha, Shravasti, Varanasi, Vaishali, Champa, Kaushambi and Ujjaini developed between 600 and 300 BCE. These cities became centres of craft production and trade, and were inhabited by a large number of artisans and merchants. This general economic progress had led to the rise of the Vaishyas and other mercantile groups, who wanted better social position than what the Brahmanas gave them. Since Buddhism and Jainism did not attach any importance to the existing *varna* system, it was preferred to patronise non-Vedic religions like Buddhism and Jainism through substantial donations. Also, both Buddhism and Jainism preached the gospel of non-violence, which could put an end to wars between different kingdoms, and consequently promote further trade and commerce, which was beneficial for this economic class.

d. Ready acceptance of simple, ascetic, peace-centred principles of Buddhism and Jainism by general folk (laity): The improvement in agriculture and development of trade, money and urbanisation had an impact on the society as well. Due to these changes, traditional equality and brotherhood gave way to inequality and social conflict. People wanted some kind of reprieve from the increasing social problems like violence, cruelty, theft, hatred and falsehood. Common people yearned to return to simple, primitive and uncorrupt life. Therefore, when new religions such as Buddhism and Jainism preached the concept of peace and social equality, simple and puritan ascetic living, people welcomed it.

Gautama Buddha and Buddhism

Early Buddhist Literature

Our understanding of Gautama Buddha and various other facets of Buddhism is derived mostly from early Buddhist literature. Early Buddhist literature is generally divided into canonical and non-canonical texts:

a. Canonical texts are those texts that are directly linked to Gautama Buddha in one way or another. However, differences exist among various Buddhist schools as to which texts are canonical. They can simply be understood as books which lay down the basic tenets and principles of Buddhism, such as, the *Tipitakas* (three *Pitakas*, also known as the Pali canon).

b. Non-canonical texts or semi canonical texts are texts that are not the sayings of the Buddha, but commentaries and observations on canonical texts, treatise on the Dharma/ *Dhammapada*, historical information, quotes, definitions, grammars and other writings in Pali, Tibetan, Chinese and other East Asian languages. Some important non-canonical texts are:

- *Milindapanho* (written in Pali, it consists of a dialogue on various philosophical issues between the Indo-Greek king Milinda/Menander and the monk Nagasena),
- *Nettipakarana* (The Book of Guidance, which gives a connected account of the Buddha's teachings),
- *Visuddhimagga* (The Path to Purity, written by Buddhaghosa, deals with development from purity of discipline to *nibanna*/enlightenment),
- *Nidanakatha* (first connected life story of Buddha),

- the *Dipavamsa* and the *Mahavamsa* (written in Pali, both contain historical cum mythical account of the Buddha's life, Buddhist councils, Ashoka and arrival of Buddhism to Sri Lanka), and
- *Mahavastu* (written in mixed Sanskrit–Prakrit, it lays down the sacred biography, i.e. hagiography of the Buddha).

The Tipitakas

The *Tipitaka* (in Pali) and *Tripitaka* (in Sanskrit) meaning 'The Three Baskets/Collections' is one of the earliest compilations of Buddhist teachings written (originally) on long, narrow leaves. The Buddhist monks transcribed and categorised the Buddha's teachings in three baskets, which is how the name 'Three Baskets' originated. All branches of Buddhism have the *Tripitaka* as part of their core scriptures, which comprises three books – the *Sutta* (conventional teaching), the *Vinaya* (disciplinary code) and the *Abhidhamma* (moral psychology).

a. The *Sutta Pitaka* (*Sutra*/Basket of Discourses): This contains the Buddha's discourses on various doctrinal issues in dialogue form. These texts are also known as '*Buddha Vacana*' or 'the word of the Buddha', as it refers to texts that are supposed to contain *what the Buddha himself said*. With the exception of few *sutras*, the authority of this text is accepted by all Buddhist schools. These discourses were arranged on the basis of the manner in which they were delivered.

b. The *Vinaya Pitaka* (Discipline Basket): This contains rules for monks and nuns of the monastic order (*Sangha*). It includes the *Patimokka* – a list of transgressions against monastic discipline and atonements for these. Apart from monastic rules, the *Vinaya* texts also include doctrinal expositions, ritual texts, biographical stories and some elements of the '*Jatakas*' or 'birth stories'.

c. The *Abhidhamma Pitaka* (Basket of Higher Teachings): This contains a thorough study and systemisation of the teachings of the *Sutta Pitaka* through summaries, questions and answers, lists, etc.

The three *Pitakas* are divided into *Nikayas* (books). For instance, the *Sutta Pitaka* consists of five *Nikayas*: *Digha Nikaya* (collection of long discourses), *Majjhima Nikaya* (collection of medium-length discourses), *Samyutta Nikaya* (collection of kindred sayings), *Anguttara Nikaya* (collection of discourses arranged in accordance with number) and *Khuddaka Nikaya* (smaller collection). The *Khuddaka Nikaya* is further subdivided into fifteen books, the prominent among them being the *Jatakas* (stories of the previous births of the Buddha), *Dhammapada* (verses dealing with ethical sayings), *Niddesa* (expositions), *Buddhavamsa* (the history of Buddha), *Patisambhida* (analytical knowledge), the *Theragatha* and *Therigatha* (songs of Buddhist monks and nuns).

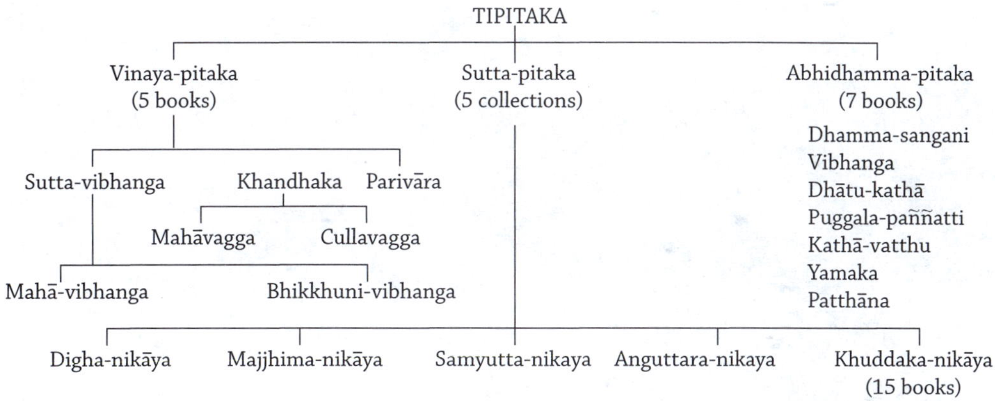

Life of the Buddha

The *hagiography* (sacred biography) of Buddha is briefed in the *Sutta* and *Vinaya Pitakas*, which is further explained in a more detailed and connected way in later texts of *Buddhacharita, Mahavastu* and *Nidanakatha*. According to tradition, Gautama Buddha (also known as Sakyamuni/Tathagata) was born as Siddhartha in 563 BCE on Vaishakha Poornima day at Lumbini (near Kapilavastu, Nepal) to Suddhodana (chief of republican Sakya clan, who ruled from Kapilavastu in the Kosala Kingdom). His mother Mahamaya (princess of the Kosala dynasty), gave birth and died seven days after his birth. Siddhartha was thus raised by his step-mother Gautami. It is believed that soon after he was born, certain Brahmanas saw the 32 marks of a *Mahapurusha* (great man) on his body and predicted that either he would be a world conqueror or a world renouncer. His father wanted to keep him away from the path of renunciation, hence he shielded him from all sorrows, and brought him up in luxury and comfort.

At the early age of 16 years, he was married to Yashodhara and had a son named Rahula. However, at the age of 29, after seeing an old man, a sick man, a corpse and an ascetic, he decided to become a wanderer and left his palace with Channa, the charioteer, and his favourite horse, Kanthaka, in search of truth (*Mahabhinishkramana*/Great Renunciation) and wandered for six years. He meditated with established teachers of that era – firstly with Alara Kalama and then with Uddaka Ramaputta – but was not convinced with their instructions that man could obtain liberation from sorrow by mental discipline and knowledge only. Later on, accompanied by five wandering ascetics – Kondanna, Bhaddiya, Vappa, Mahanama and Assaji – he practiced severe austerities until his body was almost emsaciated. Realising that austerities could not lead to realisation, he abandoned them. His five ascetic companions, disgusted at his seeming failure, deserted him and left for Sarnath. He then moved towards the village of Senani, where he was offered a bowl of milk-rice by a low-caste village girl, Sujata. Accepting from a grass-cutter a gift of *kusa* grass for a mat, he took a seat under a *Peepal* tree facing east. Here he resolved not to rise again until enlightenment was attained.

FIGURE 5.1 The Buddha

'Here on this seat my body may shrivel up,
my skin, my bones, my flesh may dissolve,
but my body will not move from this seat
until I have attained Enlightenment,
so difficult to obtain in the course of many kalpas'.

As Gautama sat in deep meditation, Mara, the Lord of Illusions, perceiving that his power was about to be broken, rushed to distract him from his purpose. Gautama touched the earth, calling it to bear witness the countless lifetimes of virtue that had led him to this place of enlightenment. When the earth shook, confirming the truth of Gautama's words, Mara unleashed his army of demons. In the epic battle that ensued, Gautama's wisdom broke through the illusions and the power of his compassion transformed the demons' weapons into flowers. Mara and all his forces fled in disarray. Thus, at the age of 35, he ultimately attained Nirvana/Enlightenment at Gaya, Magadha (Bihar) under a Peepal tree at Uruvela, on the banks of river Niranjana, and came to be known as the Buddha, the Enlightened One. The Peepal tree was known as the famous Bodhi tree. It is believed that Asoka's queen Tissarakkha was jealous of the tree, and three years after she became queen (i.e. in the nineteenth year of Ashoka's reign) she caused the tree to be killed by means of *mandu* thorns. The tree, however, grew again. The tree was again cut down by King Pushyamitra Shunga in the second century BCE, and by King Shashanka in 600 CE. Every time the tree was destroyed, a new tree was planted at the same place; and this tree at Bodh Gaya is still revered by Buddhists.

The Buddha delivered his first sermon on deliverance from suffering to his five former companions in a deer park at Sarnath. This event is known as *'DhammaChakka-Pavattana'* meaning *'turning the wheel of dharma'*. His five disciples soon realised the truth themselves and became *Arhats*. The Buddha wandered about, teaching his doctrine for over four decades, and established an order of monks and nuns known as the *Sangha*. He finally attained *Parinibbana* at the age of 80 at Kusinara (lying in Mallas). It is believed that his last words were, 'All composite things decay, strive diligently'.

Buddha is represented in five forms:

- Lotus and Bull – Birth
- Horse – Renunciation
- Bodhi Tree – Mahabodhi
- *Dhammachakra Pravartana* – First sermon
- Footprints – Nirvana

Doctrines of Buddhism

The core of Buddha's doctrine is expressed in the *Ariya-Sachchani* (Four Noble Truths), *Ashtangika-Marga* (Eight-Fold Path), Middle Path, Social Code of Conduct and Attainment of *Nibbana*/ *Nirvana*. Buddha explains that his teachings are just like a raft, which helps one to cross over the turbulent river of life and suffering. Once across, we do not need to cart the raft around with us. In other words, Buddha urges that one should not cling to anything, including his teachings. The teachings are only *Upaya* (skillful means or expedient tools) and are thus not dogma: '*It is fingers pointing at the moon and one should not confuse the finger for the moon*'.

His teachings contain three important pillars:

- Buddha – Founder/Teacher
- *Dhamma* – Teachings
- *Sangha* – Order of Buddhist monks/nuns (who act as torch bearers of *Dhamma* worshippers or *Upasakas* and are a major factor in the dissemination of the Buddha's doctrine)

While struggling for Enlightenment, Buddha had discovered Dhamma/Four Noble Truths which form the central teachings of Buddhism. The Four Noble Truths are given in the following picture:

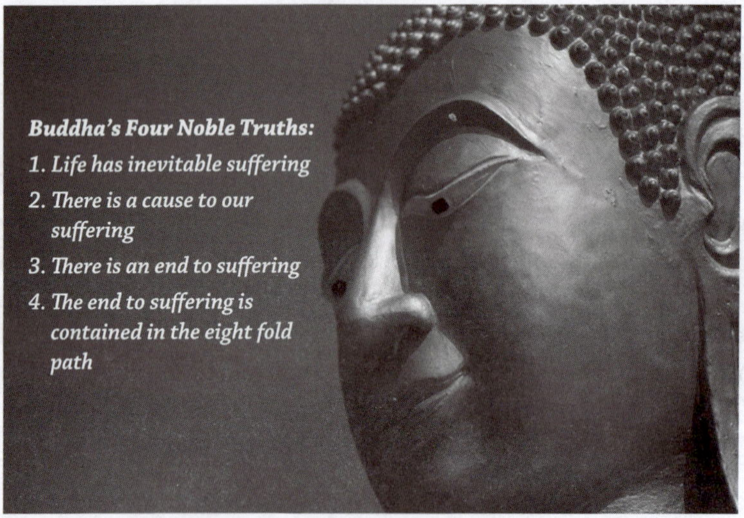

FIGURE 5.2 Buddha's Four Noble Truths

a. *The Truth of Suffering (Dukkha)*: Buddha taught that everything is suffering (*sabbam dukkham*). It refers not only to the actual pain and sorrow experienced by an individual, but also to the potential to experience these things.

b. *The Truth of the Cause of Suffering (Samudaya):* Suffering is part of living and there is a reason behind it. Desire (*Trishna*) is main cause of suffering.

c. *The Truth of the End of Suffering (Nirodha):* This suffering can be ended by attaining Nirvana/*Nibbana*.

d. *The Truth of the Path Leading to the End of Suffering (Astangika-Marga)*: There is a path that leads to the end of suffering.

Buddha urged people to study, meditate, think and act in ways that can help them come to a full understanding of each of these Four Noble Truths and to stay on the path that will lead them to peace and happiness. Paradoxically, the Eight-Fold Path is more about unlearning rather than learning, i.e. to learn in order to unlearn and uncover. This path consists of eight interconnected activities and is a process that helps one to move beyond the conditioned responses that obscure his/her true nature. The *Astangika-Marga (Fig. 5.3) comprises the following:*

1. Right Vision (*Samma-Ditthi*): It signifies perfect view or understanding of the nature of reality and the path of transformation.
2. Right Thought or Attitude (*Samma-Sankappa*): It signifies having an emotional intelligence and acting from love and compassion.
3. Right or Whole Speech (*Samma-Vaca*): It signifies clear, truthful, uplifting and non-harmful communication.

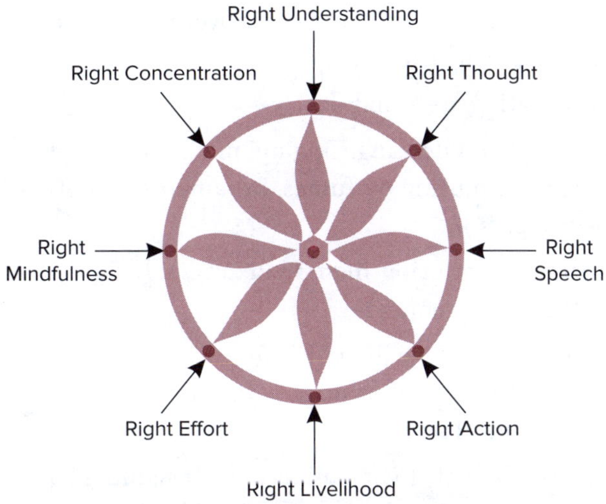

FIGURE 5.3 Astangika-Marga

4. Right or Integral Action (*Samma-Kammanta*): It signifies an ethical foundation of life, based on the principle of non-exploitation of oneself and others. It includes The Five Precepts (training rules), which are like an ethical code of conduct governing the behaviour of members of the monastic order and the laity. Following are the Five Precepts:
   a. Do not commit violence (to undertake the training to avoid taking the life of beings): This precept applies to all living beings and not just humans, as all beings have a right to their lives and that right should be respected.
   b. Do not covet the property of others (to undertake the training to avoid taking things not given): This precept goes further than mere stealing, as it preaches that one should avoid taking anything unless one is totally sure that it is intended for him only.
   c. Do not indulge in corrupt practices or sensual behaviour (to undertake the training to avoid sensual misconduct): This precept covers overindulgence in any sensual pleasure, such as gluttony or misconduct of a sexual nature. For laity, celibacy was replaced by chastity.
   d. Do not speak a lie (to undertake the training to refrain from false speech): This precept covers slander, lying, deceiving and speech that is not beneficial to the welfare of others.
   e. Do not use intoxicants (to undertake the training to abstain from substances which cause intoxication and heedlessness): This precept is in a special category as it does not infer any intrinsic evil in, say, alcohol itself, but believes that indulgence in such a substance could be the cause of breaking the other four precepts.

In addition to these, monks and nuns were supposed to strictly observe three additional precepts, which are:

i. To avoid eating after mid-day
ii. To abstain from dancing, singing, music and other entertainment, as well as to refrain from using perfumes, ornaments and other items used to adorn or beautify a person
iii. To abstain from using high or luxurious beds, and from handling gold and silver (including money)

5. Right Livelihood or Proper Livelihood (*Samma-Ajiva*): It signifies a livelihood based on correct action and on the ethical principal of non-exploitation. According to Buddha, it formed the basis of an ideal society.
6. Right Effort or Energy/Vitality (*Samma-Vayama*): It signifies consciously directing our life energy to the transformative path of creative and healing action that fosters wholeness, thus moving towards conscious evolution.
7. Right Mindfulness or Complete/Thorough Awareness (*Samma-Sati*): It signifies developing awareness about oneself and keenly watching self behaviour. Buddha says that 'if you hold yourself dear, watch yourself well'.
8. Right Concentration or Meditation (*Samma-Samadhi*): It signifies '*Samadhi*' in the sense of enlightenment or Buddhahood. *Samadhi* literally means to be fixed, absorbed in or established at one point, thus the first level of meaning is concentration, when the mind is fixed on a single object. The second level of meaning goes further and represents the establishment, not just of the mind, but also of the whole being in various levels or modes of consciousness and awareness.

The path taught by the Buddha is often referred to as the Middle Path (the one between extreme indulgence and extreme asceticism.) It should be noted that 'Right' here signifies 'proper', 'whole', 'thorough', 'integral', 'complete' and 'perfect'. It does not necessarily mean 'right', as opposed to 'wrong'. For instance, the opposite of 'Right Awareness' is not necessarily 'Wrong Awareness'. It may simply be 'incomplete'. Buddha had emphasised that if a person follows this Eight-Fold Path, then he will reach his destination of attaining *Nibbana*/Nirvana without the machinations of the priests. *Nibbana*/Nirvana is the ultimate goal of Buddha's teachings. The Pali word *Nibbana* is formed of '*Ni*' and '*Vana*'. '*Ni*' is a negative particle and '*Vana*' means lusting or craving. It is called *Nibbana*, as it is a departure from the craving or lusting. Literally, *Nibbana* means non-attachment. It does not mean physical death; rather, it signifies dying out or extinction of desire, attachment, greed, ignorance, hatred and even the sense of ego.

It should be noted that Buddhism accepts the transmigration and impermanence, but rejects the idea of God and soul (*atman*). According to Buddha, the soul is a myth. In the Buddhist universe, there are many realms (worlds) and many different kinds of beings; one can be born as any one of them. Traditionally, Buddhism teaches the existence of the ten realms of being. At the top is Buddha and the scale descends as follows: *Bodhisattva*[1] (an enlightened being destined to be a Buddha, but purposely remaining on earth to teach others), *Pratyeka Buddha* (a Buddha on their own), *Sravaka* (direct disciple of Buddha), heavenly beings (superhuman angels), human beings, *Asura* (fighting spirits), beasts, *Preta* (hungry ghosts) and depraved men (hellish beings). These ten realms are 'mutually immanent and mutually inclusive, each one having in it the remaining nine realms'. For example, the realm of human beings has all the other nine states (from hell to Buddhahood). Man is at the same time capable of real selfishness, creating his own hell, or is truly compassionate, reflecting the compassion of Buddha. Buddhism states that man is characteristically placed at the midpoint of the ten stages; he can either lower himself abruptly or gradually into hell, or rise to the enlightened state of the Buddha through discipline, cultivation and the awakening of faith. The connection between different lives is established by *Karma*. As opposed to ritual action of Brahmanical tradition, *Karma* in Buddhist tradition is result of an action depending on the intention more than the action itself. Buddhism entails less feelings of guilt and puts great emphasis on 'mind'. Buddha stresses that it is mental anguish, such as remorse, anxiety, guilt, etc., which is to be avoided in order to cultivate a calm and peaceful mind. Rebirth is governed by the cumulative results of the *Karma* of a particular life. It is rather interesting to note that even though Buddhism emphasises on non-violence (*ahimsa*), yet it does not necessarily entail vegetarianism; and monks were not forbidden from eating meat.

Buddhism and Women

It is equally interesting to note that women did not participate in the early beginnings of Sangha as it is believed that initially Buddha was reluctant to have females in Sangha and thought that they would corrupt the monks and would destroy it. The same aspect is very clearly visible in his debates[2] with his disciple Ananda over the admission of women. It was Ananda who finally persuaded Buddha to at least allow[3] his own mother Maha Prajapati Gautami to the Sangha.

[1] The several stages along the Bodhisattva path involved the attainment of a number of perfections known as 'Paramitas'. Originally listed as six and later expanded to ten; they consisted of generosity, good conduct, patient forbearance, mental strength, meditation, wisdom, skilfulness in means, determination, power and knowledge.

[2] Buddha once told Ananda, *"If women were not admitted into the monasteries, Buddhism would have continued for one thousand years, but because this admission has been granted, it will last only five hundred years."*

[3] Buddha agreed on the condition that she should accept the eight rules. He made these eight rigid rules hoping that Maha Prajapati would refuse to accept these conditions. On the contrary, Maha Prajapati accepted them at once and thus became the first woman to be initiated into the Sangha.
They were:
(a) A Bhikkhuni, however senior she may be by age and experience, should always salute a Bhikkhu;
(b) A Bhikkhuni should not spend the rainy season in a district in which there is no Bhikkhu;
(c) Every half month, the Bhikkhunis should take a lesson from a male Bhikkhu;
(d) After the rainy season is over, every Bhikkhuni has to confess to a joint meeting of Bhikkhunis and Bhikkhus what has been seen, what has been heard, and what has been suspected;

Gradually, recognising the abilities and talents of the women in the Sangha, Buddha gave them responsible positions in the Bhikkhuni Sangha. Over time, the *Bhikkhunis* like Dhammadinna, Sumangala, Mathika, Vasanti, Sumedha, Khema and Utpalavarna started preaching *Dhamma*. Later, several sex workers who were looked down upon by society also joined the Sangha and acquired a respectable place. For instance, Padmavati of Ujjain, Arthakasi of Kasi and Ambapali (Amrapali) of Vaishali came from this background and enjoyed a high reputation. In fact, Buddha eventually insisted that there should be Buddhist nuns as well as monks. In his words, "*I will not take final Nirvana until I have nuns and female disciples who are accomplished...until I have lay women followers...who will....teach the Dhamma.*"

Thus, in spite of all the limitations and conditions the Sangha imposed on women, their admission, nevertheless, liberated them as individuals having equal spiritual worth, equally capable of realising the Truth.

Buddhism and Brahmanism

The Buddhist monks considered *varna* based on action, unlike the Brahmanas, who conferred on it a divine sanction, dividing people based on birth. In *Anguttara Nikaya*, it is mentioned that when a person joins the *Sangha*, he becomes *vevanniyanti* (without *varna*). The *Sangha* had members from all castes, such as Mahakassapa, Sariputta, Mahamoggallana (prominent Brahmana monks), the Buddha, Ananda, Aniruddha (prominent Kshatriya monks), Upali (a barber), Chunda (blacksmith who fed the Buddha his last meal). The Pali canon also reverses the order of rank and places the Kshatriya *varna* higher than the Brahmana.

Even though Buddhism was certainly more inclusive than the Brahmanical tradition, yet it supported social order based on classes and did not aim at abolishing social differences. Certain Buddhist tradition rules tried to maintain the status quo. For instance, there were a number of conditions for entry, such as the ban on the entry of debtors, slaves and soldiers without permission from their respective masters. This was naturally biased against these social dropouts. Similarly, both Brahmanism and Buddhism emphasised on the virtues of carrying out familial obligations, protecting private property and respecting political authority. Both also did not participate directly in production and lived on alms given by society.

Buddhism and Upanishads

Both Upanishads and Buddhism emerged as a reaction against Brahmanical dominance. They both condemn priestly dominance as well as rituals and ceremonies. They both emphasise on

(e) A Bhikkhuni who is guilty of a severe offence shall be punished in a joint meeting;
(f) A Bhikkhuni has to go through two years probation and will get full membership only when a joint meeting approves it;
(g) Under no circumstances should a Bhikkhuni revile or abuse a Bhikkhu;
(h) Officially, no Bhikkhuni shall be granted the right to admonish a Bhikkhu, but a Bhikkhu can admonish a Bhikkhuni.

non-violence and efficacy of path of knowledge for the attainment of salvation. However, both differ also in certain respects:

Buddhism	Upanishads
(a) Buddhism does not believe in existence of soul.	(a) Upanishads believe in idea of soul and transmigration of soul.
(b) Buddhism rejected the idea of God.	(b) Upanishadic philosophy revolves around the idea of one supreme deity known as 'Brahma' and every individual is considered an expression of Brahma.
(c) In Buddhist philosophy, salvation is known as 'Nirvana' which is extinction of desire. A person can attain Nirvana within lifetime itself. On death, a person attains 'Mahaparinirvana'.	(c) In Upanishadic philosophy, salvation is 'Moksha' which signifies merging of individual soul with supreme soul, i.e., Brahma.
(d) There is no concept of 'heaven' or 'hell' in Buddhism and it says nothing about the creation of Universe or its sustenance.	(d) Upanishadic philosophy does contain ideas of heaven and hell and it believes that Brahma is the creator and ssustainer of Universe.

Reasons for Spread and Popularity of Buddhism

Buddhism left an abiding mark[4] on the history of India and it gradually became popular in Magadha and other parts of the country. With the support of Emperor Ashoka[5], it further spread its wings to Central Asia, West Asia and Sri Lanka, gradually transforming into a world religion. Various reasons are attributed to its spread:

a. Buddhism appealed to the common man as, unlike Brahmanism, it was far more liberal and democratic. Since it attacked the *varna* system and did not deprecate manual labour, it particularly won the support of the lower classes. It was open to people of all castes, and even women were admitted to the Sangha. This section of the society was neither given sacred threads nor was allowed to read Vedas, so conversion to Buddhism freed them from marks of inferiority. Buddhism also found a virgin soil for conversion in terms of the non-Vedic people. The people of Magadha readily accepted Buddhism as they were earlier looked down upon by the orthodox Brahmanas, who considered Magadha to be out of the holy *Aryavarta*.

---

[4] UNESCO World Heritage sites in India related to Buddhism:
(a) Mahabodhi Temple Complex, Bodhgaya
(b) Sanchi Stupa
(c) Ajanta Caves
(d) Nalanda

[5] Ashoka sent his son Mahendra and daughter Sangmitra to Sri Lanka, Buddha's missionaries Sona and Uttara went to Suvaranabhumi (South east Asian peninsula comprising Myanmar and Thailand), Mahadev went to Mysore, Dharamarakshit went to Himalayan region and Maharakshit went to the land of Greeks.

b. The Buddha's personality and his rationale doctrine helped immensely in the popularity of Buddhism. He tried to win over opponents by his wit and presence of mind, and by maintaining poise and calm under difficult situations[6]. Buddhism taught the people to judge and reason based on the merits and logic.

c. Unlike Brahmanism, whose texts were in Sanskrit and hence accessible only to a few Brahmanas, the Buddha's teachings were in Pali (the language of the common man), which further aided in the spread of Buddhism.

d. The patronisation by monarchies of Magadha, Kosala, Kaushambi, and several other *Gana-Sanghas* and their people contributed to its further popularity. Many Buddhist monks[7] were invited by the rulers of neighbouring countries which further helped in the spread of Buddhism.

e. Buddhism tried to mitigate the evils resulting from the new material life of the sixth century BCE. Since the Buddhists had a keen awareness of the problems (social and economic disparities), they presented innovative solutions to these concerns. Buddhism asked people not to accumulate wealth, indulge in cruelty or violence – ideas that were welcomed by the people.

Reasons for the Decline of Buddhism

It is rather ironical that from early 12th century, Buddhism began to disappear from the land of its birth. Various reasons are responsible for this:

a. Buddhism succumbed to the same rituals and dogmas which it had originally denounced. In the beginning, it was inspired by the spirit of reform. But gradually it became victim to the same evils of Brahmanism which it had earlier fought. It changed for worse over period of time. The Buddhist monks gave up Pali, the language of the people, and took to Sanskrit, the language of a few intellectuals.

b. Later, from first century CE, they also practised large scale idol worship[8] and received numerous offerings from the devotees. This resulted in corruption of the ascetic life of

---

[6] It is said that on one occasion,an ignorant person abused him. Buddha listened on silently, and when the person had ended his abuse, Budhha asked: "My friend, if a person does not accept a present, what will happen to it? The person replied: "It remains with the person who has offered it." Budhha, then said, "My friend, I do not accept your abuse."

[7] For instance:

(a) In the Ist century, Chinese rulers sent his ambassadors to India to invite Buddhist monks. These ambassadors carried Dharamrakshit and Kashyap Matanga to China who later translated Buddhist literature to Chinese.

(b) Kumarajiva was a prominent Buddhist scholar who went to China in 401 CE and became the president of Buddhist scholars there.

(c) Dharamdeva was another prominent Buddhist scholar who went to China in 1001 CE.

(d) Later,Chinese travellers like Fa-Hien and Huen Tsang visited India and took back Buddhist literature.

[8] Mahayana Buddhism transformed Buddha into God.

Buddhist monks. The principles prescribed by Buddha were conveniently forgotten, and thus started the degradation of the Buddhist monks and their preaching.

c. Some Brahmana rulers, such as Pushyamitra Shunga, the Huna King Mihirakula (worshipper of Shiva) and Shaivite Shashank of Gauda persecuted the Buddhists on a large scale. The liberal donations to the monasteries gradually declined. Also, some rich monasteries were specially targeted by the Turkish and other invaders. The loss of royal patronage[9] also contributed to the decline of Buddhism.

d. Revival of Brahmanical religion in a new form, known as Vaishvanism, attracted common masses towards it as it was free from rituals, sacrifices, and priestly domination and emphasised a direct relationship between God and devotees through Bhakti.

Key Term/Concept	Meaning/Purpose
(a) Chaityas	Prayer halls of monks
(b) Viharas	Monasteries
(c) Pravrajya	Ceremony to mark a person's going forth from home into homelessness and his/her becoming a novice under a preceptor. Involved shaving the head and donning ochre robes.
(d) Upasampada	Ordination ceremony when the novice becomes a full-fledged member of the monastic community.
(e) Uposatha	Ceremony held on full moon and new moon.
(f) Parajika	Literally meaning defeat, it included four most serious offences involving expulsion from the *Sangha* (sexual intercourse, taking what is not given, killing someone and making false claim of spiritual attainment).
(g) Pavarana	*Pavarana* is a Buddhist holy day celebrated on *Aashvin* full moon of the lunar month. It marks the end of the rainy season, sometimes called 'Buddhist Lent'. On this day, each monk must come before the community of monks (*Sangha*) and atone for an offense he may have committed during the *Vassa* (rainy season).
(h) Upasakas	Male followers who have taken refuge in the Buddha, *Dhamma* and *Sangha, but who have not taken monastic vows.*
(i) Upasikas	Female followers who have taken refuge in the Buddha, *Dhamma* and *Sangha*, but who have not taken monastic vows.
(j) Boddhisattva	Enlightened beings who have renounced their own salvation and put off entering paradise in order to help others attain enlightenment. They devote all their power and energy to save suffering beings in this world. As deities of compassion, Bodhisattvas are typically represented with precious jewellery, elegant garments, and graceful postures.
(k) Bhikkhu Sangha	*Sangha* of monks

[9] Gupta rulers patronised Vaishnavism.

Key Term/Concept	Meaning/Purpose
(l) Bhikkhuni Sangha	*Sangha* of nuns
(m) Theragatha	Verses of elder monks
(n) Therigatha	Verses of elder nuns
(o) Shramana/Samana	One who strives to realise the truth.
(p) Paribbajaka/Pari-vrajaka	Wanderer
(q) Shakra	God Indra
(r) Sarvastivadin	One of the popular schools of Theravada, which basically relies on the dictum that '*everything whether internal as well as external exist continuously in all the three phases of time*'.
(s) Sautrantika	Those who consider only the Sutras as valid (teachings of the Buddha) and not the commercial literature. So, among the texts of the *Tripitaka*, the Sautrantikas hold only the *Suttapitaka* and *Vinaypitaka* to be valid teachings of Lord Buddha.
(t) Sammitiya	One of the early Buddhist schools.
(u) Pradakhshina	An important ritual and devotional practice in Buddhism involving walking around the Stupa.
(v) Torana	The entrance gate of a Stupa

Stupas

Stupas can be understood as the burial mounds hemispheric structure where the dead's relics and ashes were kept. They were also significant as pilgrimage sites and as objects of reverence and meditation. Since Vedic times, the stupas were common throughout India, but they attained the status of cult worship during King Ashoka's reign who broke up the Buddha's existing body relics and created monuments to enshrine them. According to Buddhist tradition, nine stupas[10] were originally built following Buddha's death, eight over the relics and one over the vessel in which the relics were first put. The stupas are generally made up of a **cylindrical drum** and a circular **Anda**[11] with a **Harmika**[12] and a **Chhatra**[13] on top. The core of the stupa was made of unburnt brick while the outer surface was made by using **burnt bricks**, which were then covered with a thick layer of plaster and medhi and the torana (gateway) usually decorated with wooden sculptures.

[10] At Rajagriha, Vaishali, Kapilvastu, Allakapa, Ramagrama, Vethadipa, Pava, Kushinagar, and Pippalvina.

[11] **Anda:** Hemispherical mound symbolic of the mound of dirt used to cover Buddha's remains (in many stupas actual relics were used).

[12] **Harmika:** Square railing on top of the mound.

[13] **Chhatra:** Central pillar supporting a triple umbrella form.

Types of Stupas

Type of Stupa	Utility
(a) Relic Stupa	• In which the relics or remains of the Buddha, his disciples are kept.
(b) Object Stupa	• In which the items or objects belonging to the Buddha or his disciples, such as a begging bowl or robe, or important Buddhist scriptures are kept.
(c) Commemorative Stupa	• Built to commemorate events in the lives of Buddha or his disciples.
(d) Symbolic Stupa	• Built to symbolise aspects of Buddhist theology; for instance, Borobudur is considered to be the symbol of 'the Three Worlds (dhatu) and the spiritual stages (bhumi) in a Mahayana bodhisattva's character.'
(e) Votive Stupa	• Beginning in the 7th century CE in India, small miniature terracotta stupas became popular as votive offerings. • They are often carved from stone or cast in bronze.

Some Important Stupas

Stupa Name	Significance
(a) Sanchi Stupa (Madhya Pradesh)	• It was constructed in the 3rd century BCE by Ashoka. • The stupa has four entrances, with the southern one being the first to be completed. Others were added subsequently. The gateways are ornately carved and ornamented with statues. • Since 1989, Sanchi Stupa has been a UNESCO World Heritage Site.
(b) Dhamek Stupa, Sarnath (Uttar Pradesh)	• Dhamek Stupa was commissioned by Ashoka in 249 BCE at the site of Rishipattana, where after obtaining enlightenment, Buddha gave his first sermon to his first five students revealing his Eightfold Path leading to Nirvana. • It was rebuilt again in 500 CE.
(c) The Great Stupa of Amravati (Dhanyakataka, Andhra Pradesh)	• The Amravati Stupa is a damaged Buddhist monument, which was probably built in phases between the third century BCE and about 250 CE.
(d) Barhut Stupa (Madhya Pradesh)	• The Bharhut stupa was originally erected by Ashoka and it is believed that Sungas later adopted the Stupa. • According to inscriptions on the railings, the reliefs and figures in Bharhut stupa were provided by lay people, monks, and nuns unlike the Mauryas imperial art.
(e) Piprahwa (Uttar Pradesh)	• Piprahwa contains a massive stupa, as well as the ruins of many monasteries. • It is considered to be the site of the Buddha's ashes being handed to his own Sakya clan.

Stupa Name	Significance
(f) Nagarjunakonda (Andhra Pradesh)	• Nagarjunakonda is an important Buddhist site situated west of the Amaravati Stupa and has been home to the remnants of various Mahayana Buddhist and Hindu sanctuaries.
(g) Sonari (Madhya Pradesh)	• Sonari like Sanchi Stupa is a Buddhist stupa complex with two major and five minor stupas.

Buddhist Councils

Buddhist Council	Time	Place	Ruler	President	Specificity
First	483 BCE	Rajgriha	Ajatashatru	Mahakassappa	Held soon after the death of the Buddha, it was at this council that the Buddha's teachings were divided into three categories or 'baskets' (*pitaka*): discourses, discipline and higher knowledge. **Vinay Pitaka*, rules of the order, recited by Upali. **Sutta Pitaka*, great collection of Buddha's sermons, by Ananda.
Second	383 BCE	Vaishali	Kalasoka	Sabbakami	The objective was to settle a debate on certain practices of Buddhist monks, especially in western India Division: *Sthaviravadins* and Mahasanghikas. The group who stayed called themselves the Elders (*Thera* in Pali). They felt they were in keeping with the original spirit of the Buddha's teachings. The other group, the Great Community (*Mahasanghika* in Sanskrit), interpreted Buddha's teachings more liberally, but in a way that they felt was truer to his intentions. These two groups would eventually evolve into *Theravada* and *Mahayana* Buddhism.

Buddhist Council	Time	Place	Ruler	President	Specificity
Third	250 BCE	Patliputra	Ashoka	Mogaliputta Tissa	The objective of the council was to purify the Buddhist movement from opportunistic factions. Origin of *Theravada* school. *Tripatika* coded in Pali language. Sent Buddhist missionaries to other countries.
Fourth	1st Century CE	Kashmir	Kanishka	Vasumitra	Buddhism divided into the Mahayana sect and the Hinayana sect. Some believe that the Fourth Buddhist Council is the name of two separate Buddhist council meetings. The *Theravada* had a Fourth Buddhist Council in the first century BCE in Tambapanni, i.e. Sri Lanka, at Aloka Lena (now Alu Vihara) during the time of King Vattagamani-Abaya. The second one was held by the Sarvastivadin school, in Kashmir around the 1st century CE.

Important Buddhist Writers

Important Buddhist Writers

(a) Asvaghosha: Author of the '*Buddhacharita*' in Sanskrit. Contemporary of Kanishka. He was a poet, dramatist, musician, scholar, and debater.

(b) Nagarjuna: He is considered to be the founder of the *Madhyamaka* school of Mahayana Buddhism. He was a friend and contemporary of Satvahana King Gautamiputra of Andhra.

(c) Asanga and Vasubandhu: Two brothers who flourished in the Punjab region in the fourth century CE. Asanga was the most important teacher of *Yogachara* or *Vijnanavada* school founded by his guru, Maitreyanatha. Vasubandhu's greatest work, *Abhidharmakosa*, is still considered an important encyclopaedia of Buddhism.

(d) Buddhaghosa: He lived in the fifth century and was a great Pali scholar. His best-known work is the *Visuddhimagga* 'Path of Purification', a comprehensive summary and analysis of the *Theravada* understanding of the Buddha's path to liberation.

(e) Dinnaga: The last mighty intellectual of the fifth century, also well known as the founder of the Buddhist logic.

(f) Dharmakirti: He lived in the seventh century CE; and was another great Buddhist logician, a subtle philosophical thinker and dialectician.

Different Schools of Buddhism

Hinayana (Theravada)	Mahayana	Vajrayana
(a) Literally means '*the Lesser Path*' and *Theravada* signifies 'Doctrine of the Elders'.	Literally means '*the Greater Path*'. The terms 'Mahayana' and 'Hinayana' were given by the Mahayana school.	Literally means '*Vehicle of Thunderbolt*'. The Vajrayana or 'Diamond Vehicle' is also referred to as *Mantrayana, Tantrayana, Tantric* or *esoteric* Buddhism. The period of Indian Vajrayana Buddhism has been classified as the final period of Buddhism in India. It marks the transition from Mahayana speculative thought to the enactment of Buddhist ideas in individual life. The term '*vajra*' is used to signify the absolutely real and indestructible in a human being, as opposed to the fictions an individual entertains about himself and his nature; '*Yana*' is the spiritual pursuit of the ultimately valuable and indestructible.
(b) It is considered the orthodox school and to be truer to Gautama Buddha's teachings than Mahayana. *Theravada* was the original school of Buddhist philosophy.	It is the heterodox school of Buddhist philosophy. It originated later than Hinayana. It has two chief philosophical schools: the *Madhyamika* and *Yogachara*.	It was a form of Buddhism, which appeared in eastern India in the eighth century and was finally established in Tibet in the 11th century, as a result of a mission sent from the great Vajrayana monastery of Vikramshila. The 'Two Truths Doctrine' is the central concept of the Vajrayana practice path and lays down the philosophical basis for its methods. The 'Two Truths' identifies 'conventional' and 'ultimate' truths. Conventional truth is the truth of consensus reality, and common sense notions of what does and does not exist. Ultimate truth is reality as viewed by an awakened, or enlightened mind.
(c) Its scriptures are in Pali, the language that Buddha taught in.	Its scriptures are in Sanskrit, the language of Indian scholasticism.	Most of the terms originated in the Sanskrit language of tantric Indian Buddhism, but since it deals with inner experiences, the Vajrayana texts use a highly symbolic language '*samdhya-bhasa*' or 'Twilight Language', that aims at helping the followers of its disciplines to evoke within themselves experiences considered to be the most valuable available to human beings. Thus, Vajrayana attempts to recapture the enlightenment experience of the historical Buddha.

Hinayana (Theravada)	Mahayana	Vajrayana
(d) A School of Buddhism which treats Buddha as nothing more than a human being. Does not believe in idol worship and tries to attain individual salvation through self-discipline and meditation. Ultimate aim of Hinayana is thus nirvana.	A school of Buddhism which treats Buddha as god and worships idols of Buddhas and Bodhisattvas embodying Buddha nature. Mahayana believes in universal liberation from suffering for all beings (hence the '*Great Vehicle*'). Ultimate aim of Mahayana is 'spiritual upliftment'. It allows salvation to be alternatively obtained through the grace of the Amitabh Buddha by means of faith and devotion to mindfulness of the Buddha. It believes in *mantras*.	It is an esoteric extension of Buddhist thought and practice which sees itself as a quicker, more effective path to enlightenment. Its followers believed that salvation can be best attained by acquiring the magical power, which they called *Vajra*. As with Mahayana Buddhism, the Vajrayana emphasises the role of the Bodhisattva, but the tradition tends to favour fierce deities known as the *Taras*. Vajrayana ritual and devotion employs *mantras* (esoteric verbal formulas), *mandalas* (diagrams and paintings used in visualisation practices) and a complex array of other rituals. Great emphasis is placed on the role of the *guru* in the Vajrayana; these are religious teachers who have mastered the philosophical and ritual tradition. The Tibetan translation of guru is '*lama*', and the various Tibetan schools of the Vajrayana trace long lineages of *gurus* who serve both as religious and political leaders (the Dalai Lama is the most well-known of Tibet's lamas).
(e) At present, *Theravada* Buddhism is to be found in Sri Lanka, its main bastion, and also in Myanmar, Thailand, and other parts of South East Asia. Ashoka patronised Hinayana.	At present, Mahayana Buddhism is to be found in Japan, China, and other Asian countries. Kanishka patronised Mahayana and later, Harsha Vardhana supported it as well.	It became popular in eastern India, particularly Bengal and Bihar and is predominant in the Himalayan nations of Tibet, Nepal, Bhutan, and also Mongolia.

Eight Great Bodhisattvas

Bodhisattva	Role	Appearance and Depiction
Manjushri	The Bodhisattva of wisdom and insight.	Usually depicted with a sword in his right and a text in his left hand. In his right hand, Manjushri holds a flaming sword that symbolises the wisdom that cuts through ignorance. In his left hand, he holds the *Prajnaparamita sutra,* a scripture that signifies his mastery of *prajna*. Often, he appears sitting on a lion or lion skin. The lion symbolises the wild mind, which Manjushri shows can be tamed through wisdom.

Bodhisattva	Role	Appearance and Depiction
Avalokiteshvara/ Padmapani/ Lokesvara	The Bodhisattva of infinite compassion. He is also considered as the manifestation of *Amitabha*, the Buddha of Infinite Light.	Usually depicted as white in colour and holding a lotus.
Vajrapani	The Bodhisattva that represents power and forceful energy.	Usually depicted as blue in colour and holding a Vajra (a lightning bolt) in his right hand. Among all the serene, meditative bodhisattvas, Vajrapani is wreathed in flame with a fierce pose and fiercer face. He is usually depicted standing in a warrior pose and surrounded by fire, which represents the power of transformation.
Maitreya	The Bodhisattva who has not lived yet, but who is predicted to arrive in the future as a saviour figure expected to bring true Buddhist teachings back into the world after their decline. Also known as the Future Buddha.	Since Maitreya is currently waiting to enter the world, he is usually depicted sitting and waiting and is often painted orange or light yellow wearing a *khata* (a traditional scarf made of silk) and holding an orange bush, symbolising his ability to clear away distracting and destructive emotions.
Kshitigarbha	The Bodhisattva is famous for bowing to save the souls of all beings between Buddha's death and the age of Maitreya, including the souls of children who died young and those in hell.	As opposed to most bodhisattvas who appear wearing the luxurious robes of royalty, the bodhisattva of Kshitigarbha wears simple monk's robes and carries a staff which he uses to open up the gates of hell in one hand, and in another he holds a jewel called a *cintamani* that has the power to light up darkness and grant wishes.
Akashagarbha	The Bodhisattva has the ability to purify transgressions and is known as the twin brother of Kshitgarbha.	Usually depicted with either blue or green skin wearing ornate robes and with a halo around his head. He generally appears in a peaceful meditation pose sitting cross-legged on a lotus flower or standing calmly on a fish in the middle of the ocean and carries a sword to cut through negative emotions.

Bodhisattva	Role	Appearance and Depiction
Samantabhadra	Meaning '*Universal Worthy*,' the Bodhisattva refers to fundamental and unchanging goodness. Alongside Shakyamuni Buddha (also known as Gautama Buddha) and the bodhisattva Manjusri, he forms part of the Shakyamuni Trinity. and is famous for his ten great vows.	He is almost always riding an elephant with six tusks, or three elephants at once. Symbolically, these six texts represent the *Paramitas* (Six Perfections): charity, morality, patience, diligence, contemplation and wisdom.
Sarvanivarana-Vishkambhin	The Bodhisattva purifies wrong-doing and obstructions, both internal and external, that people face on the path to enlightenment.	Usually depicted with the deep blue skin (associated with royalty) and is seated on a lotus and holding a wheel of jewels. In addition to blue, the Bodhisattva may also appear white, when his role is to relieve calamities, or yellow, when his role is to provide sufficient provisions.

It is pertinent to note that out of these eight, Manjusri, Avalokitesvara and Vajrapani are part of the 'Three Family Protectors', i.e. the three bodhisattvas who makes of the trinity that protects the Buddha and represents his key virtues as Manjusri represents the Buddha's wisdom, Avalokitesvara represents his compassion and Vajrapani his power.

Vardhaman Mahavira and Jainism

Early Jain Literature

Jaina teachings were first preserved as an oral tradition, but later they were collated and recorded. In olden times, monks strictly followed the five great vows of Jainism. Even religious scriptures were considered possessions and therefore knowledge of the religion was never documented. Later Jaina teachers realised that it was extremely difficult to keep memorising the entire Jain literature compiled by the many scholars of the past and present. In fact, significant knowledge was already lost and the rest was polluted with modifications and errors. Hence, they decided to document the Jaina literature as known to them. The word 'canon' for the Jaina holy writings is increasingly felt to be inadequate, for it implies an unchanging body of texts sanctioned by a central authority. The sacred books of the Jainas are known as *Siddhanta or Agama* ('what has come down to us' or tradition) and these earliest texts are in an eastern dialect of Prakrit known as *Ardh-Magadhi*. To a large extent, the concepts of *Siddhanta* and *Agama* denote fluid groupings that are open to change. The complication of the entire canon is traditionally believed to have taken place in the fifth or sixth century CE at a council presided over by Devarddhi Kshamashramana held in Vallabhi in Gujarat. Compilations such as *Acharanga Sutra*, *Sutrakritanga and the Kalpasutra* are regarded as the early texts. Jainism around third century CE split into two major sects, the *Digambara*/Sky-clad or naked and the *Shvetambara*/Clad in white.

Lord Mahavira's immediate disciples were known as *Ganadharas* (these disciples were mendicants, as the Jina is, and have followed him since before his enlightenment). All *Ganadharas* possessed perfect knowledge (*keval-gyan*). They orally compiled the direct preaching of Lord Mahavira into 12 main texts (*sutras*). These texts are known as *Angas* (limbs or main texts) and are the oldest religious scriptures and the backbone of Jaina literature. Monks who had knowledge of a minimum of ten *Purvas* (means 'early' or 'previous texts' which are considered original teachings of the *Jinas*) were known as *Srut-kevlis*. The *Srut-kevlis* wrote many texts (*sutras*) expanding the subject matter defined in the *Angas*. Collectively, these texts are called *Angbahyas* (meaning outside of *Angas*). The *Shvetambara* canon includes the 12 *Angas*; 12 *Upangas* (scriptures which provide further explanation of *Angas*); 10 *Prakirnas* (scriptures which describe independent or miscellaneous subjects of the Jaina religion); six *Cheda Sutras* (subject matter described in these is only for monks and nuns and not for lay people; it relates to the conduct and behaviour of monks and nuns and also explains how they can repent for their sins and mistakes); four *Mula Sutras* (scriptures which are essential for monks and nuns to study in the earlier stages of their monkhood); and a number of individual texts such as the *Nandi Sutra* and *Anuyogadvara*. Believing that all the original *Angas* have been lost for centuries, the *Digambaras* have a different canon (known as *Siddhanta*). It should be noted that *the Tattvartha Sutra* contains the main doctrines of Jaina faith, though the two main sects have slightly different versions and composition dates.

Jainas believe that each *Jina* reveals the same essential truths, according to the needs of the society and in the era in which he is born. When he reaches omniscience, he can make the *divya-dhvani* (divine sound), through which he transmits his teachings to all sentient beings (*samavasarana*). The *Digamabara* and *Shvetambara* sects interpret the notion of the divine sound differently. *Digamabaras* consider it to be an unarticulated sound, which is monotone and can be compared to the sound of 'OM'. Whereas, *Shvetambaras* call it 'divine' because all beings can hear it, including five-sensed animals with understanding and spiritual abilities. It is considered to be a human language that takes the form of Ardha-Magadhi Prakrit.

The non-canonical (commentaries on the canonical) Jaina works are partly in Prakrit dialects (such as Maharashtri) and partly in Sanskrit. Jaina texts include vast collection of lyrical poetry, hymns and *katha* (didactic story) in different languages like Prakrit, Sanskrit, Apabhramsha and Kannada. These texts not only offer glimpses of cultural history of that era, but also tell us a great deal about the history and doctrines of Jainism, its rival schools, the *Sangha*'s life, etc. It is rather unfortunate that Jaina texts have not been studied as extensively as Buddhist texts. Some important non canonical works are:

a. The Jaina *Puranas* (called *Charitas* by *Shvetambaras*) are the hagiographies of the Jaina saints/*Tirthankaras* (literally meaning 'ford makers', who build fords that help people across the ocean of suffering).
   - The *Adi Purana* compiled in 9th century is the hagiography of Jaina founder Rishabha (Adinatha).
   - The 8th century *Harivamsha Purana* gives a Jaina version of the stories of Krishna, Balarama, Pandavas, and Kauravas, among others.
   - The 9th century Jinasena and Gunabhadra authored *Trishashtilakshana Mahapurana* contains not only life stories of various Jaina saints, kings and heroes, but also contains discussions on topics like interpretation of dreams, life-cycle rituals, duties of a king and warrior, etc.

b. The 12th century *Parishishtaparvan* by Hemachandra gives details about political history and provides the earliest account of Jaina teachers.

Life of Vardhamana Mahavira

Vardhamana is considered the 24th and last *Tirthankara or Jina* (meaning victor, one who has attained infinite knowledge and now can help others to attain liberation from the cycle of rebirth, i.e. '*Moksha*'). He came to be known as *Mahavira* (great hero; Fig. 5.4). He was also known by the names of Jitendriya (one who has conquered his inner desires) and Arihant (worthy). He possessed *avadhijnana* (superhuman insight and cognition).

FIGURE 5.4 Mahavira

According to tradition, he was a contemporary of the Buddha and was born in c. 599 BCE at a village named Kundagrama near Vaishali (capital of Videha). Like the Buddha, he was born in a Kshatriya clan. His father Siddhartha was the chief of the Jnatjriya clan and his mother Trishala was Lichchavi's King Chetaka's sister. His family was connected with the royal family of Magadha, as Chetaka's daughter was married to Bimbisara (Haryanka Dynasty of Magadha). Initially, he led a householder's life, married Yashoda, and had a daughter named Priyadarshana. But he renounced the world in search of truth at the age of 30 and became an ascetic. He wandered for 12 years, practising severe austerities, fasting and meditation. At the age of 42, it is believed that on the banks of Rijupalika river, outside the town of Jrimbhikagrama, and in the fields of a householder named Samaga, he attained *kevalajnana* (omniscience or infinite knowledge). He passed away and became a *siddha* (fully liberated) at the age of 72 years in c. 527 BCE at Pavapuri near Patna.

Doctrines of Jainism

The Jaina doctrine is much older than Buddhism and it is accepted that in each half cycle of time there are total 24 Tirthankaras. It is rather interesting to note that the Jaina conception of time is divided into endless sequence of progressive (*utsarpinis*) and regressive half cycles (*avasarpinis*) in terms of degree of happiness. These vast spans of time are further divided into 6 kalas (stages). The first founder Tirthankara Rishabhadeva (symbol – bull), whose reference is also found in Rig Veda and Vayu Purana, belongs to our current half cycle of *avasarpini* (i.e. a period of regressive happiness). The historicity of all the Tirthankaras is not easy to establish. Neminatha belonging to Saurashtra (Gujarat) is believed to be the 22nd Tirthankara, and the 23rd Tirthankara is believed to be Parshvanatha (of Benaras) having the emblem of the snake. The 24th Tirthankara was Mahavira, who had the emblem of the lion.

The core of Jaina doctrine is expressed in the principle of

a. *Anekantavada* (doctrine of manifold nature of reality),
b. *Syadavada* (the theory of conditioned predication),
c. *Nayavada* (theory of partial standpoints),
d. *Triratna* (three gems),
e. *Pancha Mahavrata* (five great vows), and
f. *Ahimsa* (doctrine of non-violence).

Opposed to the philosophy of *ekanta* (one-sidedness or solitary attribute), Jaina doctrine of *Anekantavada* is literally the doctrine of 'non-one-sidedness' or 'manifoldness' or 'non-absolutism'. It is one of the basic principles of Jainism that encourages acceptance of relativism and pluralism. According to this doctrine, *truth and reality are perceived differently from different points of view, and no single point of view is the complete truth*. Jainas compare all attempts to proclaim absolute truth with *adhgajanyayah* (the '*maxim of the blind men and elephant*'). In this story, one man felt the trunk, another felt the ears, while the third felt the tail. All the blind men claimed to explain the true appearance of the elephant, but could only partly succeed, due to their narrow perspectives. Jaina doctrine states that objects have infinite modes of existence and qualities, so they cannot be completely grasped in all aspects and manifestations by finite human perception. Only the *Kevalins* – the omniscient beings – can comprehend objects in all aspects and manifestations, while all others are capable of only partial knowledge.

The doctrine of *Syadavada* (doctrine of 'may be') emphasises on the relativity of all knowledge. According to this doctrine, all judgments are conditional, holding good only in certain conditions, circumstances, or senses. All that is possible is a number of partially true statements about any reality but the whole reality cannot be determined for certain. Every statement about reality should be prefixed with *syat* (meaning 'may be'). The doctrine of *Nayavada* signifies the system of describing reality from different points of view. '*Naya*' can be understood as partially true statements but they cannot lay claim to absolute validity. '*Naya*' can also be defined as a particular opinion framed with a viewpoint, a viewpoint which does not rule out other different viewpoints, and is, therefore, expressive of a partial truth about an object, as entertained by a knowing agent.

Jainism believes in the concept of Karma and Salvation. According to Jain philosophy, the bad deeds of a person get attached to the soul. The bondage of these deeds (Karma) is responsible for the cycle of life and death. In order to attain salvation (Nirvana), the inflow of Karma towards soul has to be stopped and the already accumulated Karmas have to destroyed to liberate the soul. To achieve liberation of the soul, a Jaina must follow the three jewels of Jaina ethics, popularly called *Triratna*. They are:

a. Right faith (*Samyag darshana*): This does not mean believing what you are told, but means seeing (hearing, feeling, etc.) things properly, and avoiding preconceptions and superstitions that get in the way of seeing clearly.

b. Right knowledge (*Samyag jnana*): This means having an accurate and sufficient knowledge of the real universe – this requires a true knowledge of the five (or six) substances and nine truths of the universe – and having that knowledge with the right mental attitude.

c. Right conduct (*Samyag charitra*): This means living one's life according to Jaina ethical rules; to avoid doing harm to living things; and freeing oneself from attachment and other impure attitudes and thoughts.

In order to help attain *Triratna* one must observe *Pancha Mahavrata* (five great vows):

i. Non-violence (*Ahimsa*): Among these five vows, non-violence (*ahimsa*) is the cardinal principle of Jainism, and hence it is known as the cornerstone of Jainism. Non-violence is the supreme religion (*Ahimsa parmo dharma*). According to Jainism, all living beings, irrespective of their size, shape, or different spiritual developments, are equal and have souls[14]. No living being has the right to harm, injure, or kill any other living being, including animals, insects and plants. Jainism recognises four forms of existence – that of gods (*deva*), humans (*manushya*), hell beings (*naraki*) and animals and plants (*tiryancha* who are further divided on the basis of the faculty of sense into smaller sub-categories: *ekendriyas* (single-sense bodies); and *nigodas* (lowest of *ekendriya* having sense of only touch, who are born in clusters and whose lives last only a fraction of a second). The general laity following Jainism is supposed to avoid harming beings with two or more senses, but the

[14] Interestingly, Jains believe that even some non-living things like air and water have souls.

monks/renunciants are supposed to refrain from harming even *ekendriyas* and element bodies (*sthavara* – which are slightly higher than *nigodas*). It is more painful if a life of the higher forms (with more than one sense) is killed. Since all non-vegetarian food is made by killing a living being with two or more senses, Jainism preaches strict vegetarianism, and prohibits non-vegetarian foods. In Jainism, it is the intention to harm, the absence of compassion, unawareness and ignorance that makes an action violent. Violence is not defined by actual harm, for this may be unintentional. Without violent thought there can be no violent action. Non-violence is to be observed in action, speech and thought. One should not be violent, ask others to do so, or approve of such an activity. Jainism prohibited the practice of war, and even agriculture for its followers. Eventually Jainas, confined themselves to trade and mercantile activities.

ii. Truth (*Satya*): Jainism insists that one should not only refrain from falsehood, but should always speak the truth, which should be wholesome and pleasant. One should remain silent if the truth causes pain, hurt, anger, or death of any living being. Anger, greed, fear and jokes are the breeding grounds of untruth. To speak the truth requires moral courage. Only those who have conquered greed, fear, anger, jealousy, ego and frivolity can speak the truth. Truth is to be observed in speech, mind and deed.

iii. Non-stealing (*Achaurya or Asteya*): Stealing consists of taking another's property without his consent, or by unjust or immoral methods. It does not entitle one to take away a thing, which may be lying unattended or unclaimed. One should observe this vow very strictly, and should not touch even a worthless thing, which does not belong to him. When accepting alms, help, or aid, one should not take more than what is the minimum requirement. To take more than one's need is also considered theft in Jainism.

iv. Celibacy/Chastity (*Brahmacharya*, added by Mahavira): Total abstinence from sensual pleasure and the pleasure of all five senses is called celibacy. Sensual pleasure is an infatuating force, which sets aside all virtues and reason at the time of indulgence. This vow of controlling sensuality is very difficult to observe in its subtle form. One may refrain from physical indulgence, but may still think of sensual pleasures, which is prohibited in Jainism. Monks are required to observe this vow strictly and completely. They should not enjoy sensual pleasures and pleasure of all five senses. There are several rules laid down for observing this vow for householders. They should not indulge in any physical relationship other than with one's own spouse, and that too of limited nature.

v. Non-attachment/Non-possession (*Aparigraha*): An attachment to worldly objects results in the bondage to the cycle of birth and death. Therefore, one who desires spiritual liberation should withdraw from all attachments to objects that please any of the five senses. Jainism believes that the more worldly wealth a person possesses, the more he is likely to commit sin to acquire and maintain the possession, and in the long run he may be unhappy. Worldly wealth creates attachment, which will continuously result in greed, jealousy, selfishness, ego, hatred, violence, etc. Mahavira has said that 'wants and desires have no end, and only the sky is the limit for them'.

It should be noted that if these *vratas* or vows are very strictly observed, they are known as '*Mahavratas*', i.e. great or full vows; and normally these are meant for the ascetics. Laymen, however, cannot observe the vows so strictly and therefore they are allowed to practice them as far as their conditions permit. The same *vratas* or vows – when partially observed – are termed as '*Anuvratas*', i.e. small or partial vows. The highest form of death[15] achieved by a person, whether a monk or a layman, involved death by meditating and fasting.

Buddhism and Jainism

Both Buddhism and Jainism had some similarities in their teachings. For instance, both rejected the authority of Vedas, emphasised on renunciation and human effort as the means of obtaining salvation, and established a monastic order for both men and women. Like Buddhism, Jainism is fundamentally atheistic; though it recognises the existence of gods, yet it refuses to give them importance in the universal scheme of themes and places the Gods lower than Jina (the conqueror). Like Buddhist texts, Jaina texts criticise the Brahmanas, their practice of animal sacrifices and ritual authority giving preference to Brahmanas. Both Jainism and Buddhism focus on the superiority of the Kshatriya *varna* over all other *varnas* including Brahmanas. They both attempted to give a new connotation to the meaning of Brahmana, shifting the emphasis from an ascribed status to one achieved by good deeds. They use the word '*Brahmana*' in the sense of acknowledging a wise person who possesses true knowledge and lives an exemplary life. Like Buddhism monastic order, people of all castes and social backgrounds were welcomed in Jainism. There are frequent mentions of a learned Jaina monk named Harikeshiya who belonged to a *Chandala* family. Brahmana *varna* was represented by Bhadrabahu, Divakara, Jinasena and Haribhadra. Similarly, Jainism opened its doors to women mendicants who were addressed as *aryika* or *sadhvi*.

Spread and Influence of Jainism

Jainism gradually spread to western India where the Brahmanical religion was weak. The early Jainas adopted Prakrit language of the common people to preach their doctrines and discarded Sanskrit language (which was mainly patronised by the Brahmanas). This greatly helped in widening the follower base of Jainism. And, with the support of kings who greatly patronised Jainism, like Chandragupta Maurya (he himself became a Jaina ascetic and spent his last years in Karnataka), it became popular in southern India too. The great famine that occurred in Magadha after 200 years of the death of Mahavira also contributed to its spread in southern India. According to tradition, the famine lasted for about 12 years; and in order to protect themselves, many Jaina

---

[15] Attainment of death through fasting is known as '*Salekhana*' in Jainism.

followers under the leadership of Bhadrabahu (who later came to be known as *Digambaras*) went South and spread Jainism there. Around 4th century BCE, it also spread to Kalinga and was greatly popularised by its king Kharavela. In about 2nd and 1st centuries BCE, it reached as far as the southern districts of Tamil Nadu. Later, it penetrated Malwa, Gujarat, and Rajasthan. It is rather interesting to note that even though Jainism did not win as much state patronage as Buddhism, and was not as fast to spread as Buddhism in early times, it still retains its hold in many areas of the Indian sub-continent, whereas Buddhism has practically disappeared from the land of its birth.

Different Schools of Jainism

Digambara	Shvetambara
(a) Literally means 'sky clad'. *Digambaras* stress the practice of nudity as an absolute pre-requisite to the mendicant's path and to the attainment of salvation.	Literally means 'white clad'. *Shvetambaras* assert that the practice of complete nudity is not essential to attain liberation.
(b) According to tradition, during the famous Magadha famine (200 years after the death of Mahavira), they are the ones who under the leadership of Bhadrabahu migrated south and lived in the old traditional way.	According to tradition, during the famous Magadha famine, they are the ones who under the leadership of Sthalabahu had stayed back at Magadha. When the Jainas who had migrated south returned, they accused this group of violating rules of Jainism on account of wearing white clothing.
(c) On the point of liberation of women, *Digambara* tradition holds that a woman lacks the body and rigid will necessary to attain *moksha*, i.e. liberation, hence she has to be reborn as a man before such an attainment is possible. For instance, the 19th Tirthankara of the *Shvetambara* tradition is not accepted as female by them, rather as a male named Mallinatha, born into a royal family as a prince, who after taking vows of *Digambara* monk, eventually became a Tirthankara.	Whereas, *Shvetambaras* acknowledge the possibility of women attaining Jina-hood and maintain that women are capable in the present lifetime of the same spiritual accomplishments as men. For instance, in the *Shvetambara* tradition, the 19th Tirthankara is a female named Malli, who is the only female Tirthankara.
(d) According to *Digambara* tradition, on attaining enlightenment, an omniscient is freed from the needs of ordinary existence such as, hunger, thirst, sleep, disease, or fear.	Whereas, *Shvetamabara* tradition holds that even the omniscient requires food.

Digambara	Shvetambara
(e) Regarding hagiography of Mahavira, both differ to a great extent. For example, regarding the embryo of Mahavira, *Digambara* tradition rubbishes the claim of *Shvetamabaras* and dismiss the whole episode as unreliable and absurd.	The *Shvetambaras* believe that Mahavira was born of a Kshatriya lady, Trishala, though conception took place in the womb of a Brahman lady, Devananda. The change of embryo is believed to have been affected by God Indra on the eighty-third day after conception.
(f) Regarding marriage of Mahavira, *Digambara* tradition holds that Mahavira never married and renounced the world while his parents were alive.	The *Shvetambaras* believe that Mahavira married Princess Yashoda at a fairly young age and had a daughter from her named Priyadarshana, and that Mahavira led a full-fledged householder's life till he was thirty. It was only after his parents' death that he became an ascetic.
(g) Regarding idols of Tirthankaras, *Digambara* tradition represents the idols of Tirthankaras as nude, unadorned and with downcast eyes in the contemplative mood.	Whereas, the *Shvetambara* tradition depicts the idols of Tirthankaras as wearing a loin-cloth, bedecked with jewels and with glass eyes inserted in the marble.
(h) Regarding canonical literature, *Digambaras* hold that the original and genuine texts were lost long ago. The *Digambaras* also refuse to accept the achievements of the first council which met under the leadership of Acharya Sthulabhadra and consequently the recasting of the *angas*.	Whereas, the *Shvetambaras* believe in the validity and sacredness of canonical literature, that is, the 12 *angas* and *sutras*, as they exist now.
(i) The *Digambaras* make use of the term '*Purana*' for the hagiographies.	Whereas, the *Shvetambaras* use the term '*Charita*'.
(j) Regarding food of ascetics, the *Digambara* monks take food standing and with the help of knotted upturned palms and in one house only where their *sankalpa* (preconceived idea) is fulfilled.	Whereas, the *Shvetambara* monks collect their food from different houses.
(k) Regarding possessions of ascetics, the *Digambara* ascetic must renounce all possessions, including clothes and is allowed only two possessions: *Rajoharana* (a small peacock-feather broom for brushing insects away) and a *Kamandalu* (a wooden water-pot for toilet hygiene).	Whereas, the *Shvetambara* ascetic is allowed to have fourteen possessions including loin-cloth, shoulder-cloth, etc.

THE DIGAMBARA SUB-SECTS

	Major Sub-Sects			Minor Sub-Sects	
	Bisapantha	**Terapantha**	**Taranapantha or Samaiyapantha**	**Gumanapantha**	**Totapantha**
(a)	The followers of *Bisapantha* support the Dharma-gurus, i.e. religious authorities known as *Bhattarakas*, the heads of *Jaina Mathas*	In North India, since it arose as a revolt against the domination and conduct of the *Bhattarakas*, i.e. so consequently, the institution of *Bhattarakas* lost its importance in North India, however in South India the *Bhattarakas* continue to play an important role.	The sub-sect is also called *Samaiyapantha as* its followers worship *Sarnaya*, i.e. sacred books and not the idols. Their three main traits are: (i) the aversion to idol worship, (ii) the absence of outward religious practices, and (iii) the ban on caste distinctions.	The sub-sect stresses on the purity of conduct and self-discipline and strict adherence to the precepts.	The Totapanthis (i.e. sixteen and a half) came into existence as a result of differences between the Bisa (i.e. twenty) Pantha and Tera (i.e. thirteen) pantha sub-sects and thus the followers believe to some extent in the doctrines of Bisapantha and to some extent in those of Terapantha.
(b)	They worship the idols of *Tirthankaras* and also the idols of *Ksetrapala*, *Padmavati* and other deities in their temples.	They worship the idols of *Tirthankaras* and **not** of *Ksetrapala*, *Padmavati* and other deities in their temples.	They thus, strongly refute idolatry but have their own temples in which they keep their sacred books for worship.	They strictly prohibit the lighting of candles or lamps in the Jaina temples as they regard this as a violation of the fundamental doctrine of Jaina religion, viz. non-violence.	

	Major Sub-Sects			Minor Sub-Sects	
	Bisapantha	Terapantha	Taranapantha or Samaiyapantha	Gumanapantha	Totapantha
(c)	They worship these idols with saffron, flowers, fruits, sweets, scented incense sticks, etc. While performing these worships, they sit on the ground and do not stand. They perform Arati, i.e. waving of lights over the idol, in the temple even at night and distribute *prasada*.	They worship the idols not with flowers, fruits and other green vegetables (known as sachitta things), but with sacred rice called '*Aksata*', cloves, sandal, almonds, dry coconuts, dates, etc. While worshipping they stand and do not sit. They do not perform Arati or distribute prasada in their temples.	They do not offer articles like fruits and flowers at the time of worship. They give more importance to spiritual values and the study of sacred literature.	They only visit and view the image in the temples and do not make any offerings to them.	
(d)	Followers include all Digambara Jainas from Maharashtra, Karnataka and South India and also a large number of Digambara Jainas from Rajasthan and Gujarat.	Followers of *Terapanthis* are more numerous in Uttar Pradesh, Rajasthan and Madhya Pradesh.	The *Taranapanthis* are few in number and are mostly confined to Bundelkhand, Malwa area of Madhya Pradesh and Khandesh area of Maharashtra.	The followers are mostly concentrated in Rajasthan, specifically Jaipur.	The followers are extremely few in number and are now found in some pockets in Madhya Pradesh.

THE SVETAMBARA SUB-SECTS

	Murtipujaka	Sthanakvasi	Terapanthi
(a)	The followers are the thorough worshipers of idols and offer flowers, fruits, saffron, etc. to their idols and invariably adorn them with rich clothes and jeweled ornaments. They stay in temples or in the specially reserved buildings known as *upasrayas*.	The *Sthanakvasis* do not believe in idol-worship at temples and thus do not have temples at all instead they have 'sthanakas', that is, prayer halls, where they carry on their religious fasts, festivals, practices, prayers, discourses, etc. They also do not have faith in the places of pilgrimage and do not participate in the religious festivals of Murtipujaka Svetambaras.	They are non-idolatrous and are very finely organised under the complete direction of one *Acharya*, that is, religious head, one code of conduct and one line of thought. All the monks and nuns of the *Terapantha* scrupulously follow the orders of their Acharya, preach under his guidance and carry out all religious activities in accordance with his instructions. They also attach importance to the practice of meditation.
(b)	Four main attributes: (i) Pujera (worshipers) (ii) Deravasi (temple residents) (iii) Chaityavasi (temple residents) (iv) Mandira-margi (temple goers)	Two main attributes: (i) Dhundhiya (searchers) (ii) Sadhumargi (followers of Sadhus, i.e. ascetics)	The *Terapanthis* are considered reformists as they emphasise simplicity in religion. For instance, the Terapanthis do not even construct monasteries for their monks, who inhabit a part of the house which the householders build for themselves.
(c)	Largely concentrated in Gujarat.	They are found mainly in Gujarat, Punjab, Haryana and Rajasthan.	They are concentrated mainly in Bikaner, Jodhpur and Mewar areas of Rajasthan.

* *It is pertinent to note that even though the name* ***Terapantha*** *sub-sect appears both among the Digambara and the Svetambara sects, still the two Terapanthis are entirely different from each other as while the Digambara Terapanthis believe in nudity and idol-worship, the Svetambara Terapanthis are quite opposed to both.*

Jaina Councils

Council	Year	Place	Achievement	President
1	310 BCE	Patliputra	Compilation of 12 *angas* to replace *Purvas* (Rejection by Digambaras)	Sthulabhadra
2	512 CE	Vallabhi (Gujarat)	Final compilation of 12 *angas* and 12 *Upangas*	Derridhiganj

Key Term/Concept	Meaning/Purpose
(a) *Basadis*	Jaina monastic establishment
(b) *Avadhijnana*	Super human cognition
(c) *Ganadharas*	Chief disciplines of Mahavira
(d) *Siddha*	Fully liberated
(e) *Dravya*	Substance
(f) *Guna*	Quality
(g) *Paryaya*	Mode
(h) *Jiva*	Soul
(i) *Eva*	In fact
(j) *Pudgala*	Aggregates of atoms which have form, colour, taste and smell, and can be touched and felt
(k) *Chaitanya*	Consciousness
(l) *Virya*	Energy
(m) *Mohaniya*	Delusion causing karmas
(n) *Asarva*	Flow
(o) *Nirjara*	Wearing out
(p) *Gunasthanas*	Stages of purification
(q) *Arhat*	Who has entered the stage of *kevalajnana*
(r) *Tirthankara*	*Arhat* who has already acquired the capability of teaching the doctrine

Ajivikas

Buddhism and Jainism were not the only religions, which challenged Brahmanical dominance. According to the Buddhist sources, more than 62 sects and philosophies flourished in this period. One of these sects, known as the Ajivikas or 'Followers of the way of life,' were an ascetic order that started at the time of Buddha and Mahavira, and lasted until the 14th century.

Ajivika was founded by Makkhali Gosala. Ajivikas were very popular in Magadha in the third century BCE and Mauryan kings donated several caves in the honour of Ajivika monks. According to tradition, it is believed that for some six years, Mahavira's hardship was shared by Gosala, but ultimately the two quarreled and Gosala left Mahavira to found the sect of the *Ajivikas* (pre-determinism or '*niyati*'). His doctrines and those of his followers are known only from Buddhist and Jaina sources, which state that he was lowborn and died after a quarrel with Mahavira shortly before the Buddha died.

The Ajivikas, who were rigid fatalists and determinists, supposedly held that the affairs of the entire universe were ordered by a cosmic force called *niyati* (meaning 'rule' or 'destiny' in Sanskrit) that determined all events, including an individual's fate, to the last detail and that barred personal efforts to change or accelerate improvement toward one's spiritual destiny. No human effort could have any effect against *niyati*, and therefore *karma* is a fallacy. Nirvana was only reached after living through an immense number of lives, which proceeded automatically like the unwinding of a ball of thread, the last life being as an Ajivika monk. As a result of this static and melancholy view of the human condition, the Ajivikas practiced austerities rather than pursue any purposeful goal. Some later Ajivikas worshipped Gosala as a divinity, and the tenet of *niyati* developed into the doctrine that all change was illusory and that everything was eternally immobile.

QUESTIONS FROM LAST YEAR'S PRELIMS

1. In which one of the following regions was Dhanyakataka, which flourished as a prominent Buddhist centre under the Mahasanghikas, located? **(2023)**

(a) Andhra (b) Gandhara
(c) Kalinga (d) Magadha

2. 'Souls are not only the property of animal and plant life, but also of rocks, running water and many other natural objects not looked on as living by other religious sects.' The above statement reflects one of the core beliefs of which one of the following religious sects of ancient India? **(2023)**

(a) Buddhism (b) Jainism
(c) Shaivism (d) Vaishnavism

3. With reference to the ancient India, consider the following statements: **(2023)**

1. The concept of stupa is Buddhist in origin.
2. Stupa was generally a repository of relics.
3. Stupa was a votive commemorative structure in Buddhist tradition.

How many of the statement(s) given above is/are correct?

(a) 1 only (b) 2 only
(c) All three (d) None

4. With reference to Indian history, consider the following texts: **(2022)**

1. Nettipakarana
2. Parishishtaparvan
3. Avadanashataka
4. Trishashtilakshana Mahapurana

Which of the above are Jaina texts?

(a) 1, 2 and 3 (b) 2 and 4 only
(c) 1, 3 and 4 (d) 2, 3 and 4

5. With reference to Indian history, consider the following pairs: **(2022)**

Historical person	known as
1. Aryadeva	Jaina scholar
2. Dignaga	Buddhist scholar
3. Nathmuni	Vaishnava scholar

How many pairs given above are correctly matched?

(a) None of the pairs
(b) Only one pair

(c) Only two pairs
(d) All three pairs

6. With reference to the cultural history of India, which one of the following is the correct description of the term 'paramitas'? **(2020)**
(a) The earliest Dharmashastra texts written in aphoristic (sutra) style
(b) Philosophical schools that did not accept the authority of Vedas
(c) Perfections whose attainment led to the Bodhisattva path
(d) Powerful merchant guilds of early medieval South India

7. With reference to the religious history of India, consider the following statements: **(2020)**
1. Sthaviravadins belong to Mahayana Buddhism.
2. Lokottaravadin sect was an offshoot of Mahasanghika sect of Buddhism.
3. The deification of Buddha by Mahasanghikas fostered Mahayana Buddhism.

Which of the statements given above is/are correct?
(a) 1 and 2 only (b) 2 and 3 only
(c) 3 only (d) 1, 2 and 3

8. Consider the following statements: **(2019)**
i. Deification of the Buddha.
ii. Trading the path of Bodhisattvas.
iii. Image worship and rituals.

Which of the statements given above are the features of Mahayana Buddhism
(a) i only (b) i and ii only
(c) ii and iii only (d) i, ii and iii

9. With reference to the religious practices in India, the 'Sthanakvasi' sect belongs to: **(2018)**
(a) Buddhism (b) Jainism
(c) Vaishnavism (d) Shaivism

10. With reference to India history, who among the following is future Buddha, yet to come to save the world? **(2018)**
(a) Avalokiteshvara
(b) Lokesvara
(c) Maitreya
(d) Padmapani

11. With reference to the religious history of India, consider the following statements: **(2017)**
1. Sautrantika and Sammitiya were the sects of Jainism.
2. Sarvastivadin held that the constituents of phenomena were not wholly momentary, but existed forever in a latent form.

Which of the statement(s) given above is/are correct?
(a) 1 only (b) 2 only
(c) Both 1 and 2 (d) Neither 1 nor 2

12. The painting of Bodhisattva Padmapani is one of the most famous and of illustrated paintings at **(2017)**
(a) Ajanta (b) Badami
(c) Bagh (d) Ellora

13. With reference to the religious history of India, consider the following statements: **(2016)**
i. The concepts of Bodhisattva is central to Hinayana sect of Buddhism.
ii. The Bodhisattva is the compassionate one on his way to enlightenment.
iii. The Bodhisattva delays achieving his own salvation to help all sentient beings on their path to it.

Which of the statement(s) given above is/are correct?
(a) i only (b) ii and iii only

(c) ii only (d) i, ii and iii

14. With reference to the cultural history of India, the memorising of chronicles, dynastic histories and epic tales was whose profession among the following?

(a) *Shramana* (b) *Parivraajaka*
(c) *Agrahaarika* (d) *Maagadha*

15. Which of the following kingdoms were associated with the life of the Buddha? **(2015 and 2014)**

i. Avanti ii. Gandhara
iii. Kosala iv. Magadha

Select the correct answer using the code given below.

(a) i, ii and iii (b) ii and iv
(c) iii and iv only (d) i, iii and iv

16. Which of the following statement(s) is/are applicable to Jaina doctrine? **(2013)**

i. The surest way of annihilating *Karma* is to practice penance.
ii. Every object, even the smallest particle has a soul.
iii. *Karma* is the bane of the soul and must be ended.

Select the correct answer using the codes given below.

(a) i only (b) ii and iii only
(c) i and iii only (d) i, ii and iii

17. Some Buddhist rock-cut caves are called Chaityas, while the others are called Viharas. What is the difference between the two? **(2013)**

(a) Vihara is a place of worship, while Chaitya is the dwelling place of the monks.
(b) Chaitya is a place of worship, while Vihara is the dwelling place of the monks.
(c) Chaitya is the *stupa* at the far end of the cave, while Vihara is the hall axial to it.
(d) There is no material difference between the two.

18. Which one of the following describes best the concept of Nirvana in Buddhism? **(2013)**

(a) The extinction of the flame of desire.
(b) The complete annihilation of self.
(c) A state of bliss and rest.
(d) A mental stage beyond all comprehension.

19. With reference to the history of ancient India, which of the following was/were common to both Buddhism and Jainism? **(2012)**

i. Avoidance of extremities of penance and enjoyment.
ii. Indifference to the authority of the Vedas.
iii. Denial of efficacy of rituals.

Select the correct answer using the codes given below:

(a) i only (b) ii and iii only
(c) i and iii only (d) i, ii and iii

20. Lord Buddha's image is sometimes shown with the hand gesture called '*Bhumisparsha Mudra*'. It symbolises **(2012)**

(a) Buddha's calling of the Earth to watch over Mara and to prevent Mara from disturbing his meditation.
(b) Buddha's calling of the Earth to witness his purity and chastity despite the temptations of Mara.
(c) Buddha's reminder to his followers that they all arise from the Earth and finally dissolve into the Earth, and thus this life is transitory.
(d) Both the statements (a) and (b) are correct in this context.

21. The Jaina philosophy holds that the world is created and maintained by **(2011)**

(a) Universal law
(b) Universal truth
(c) Universal faith
(d) Universal soul

22. Which among the following was not a contemporary of the other three? **(2005)**
(a) Bimbisara (b) Gautam Buddha
(c) Milinda (d) Prasenjit

23. With reference to ancient Jainism, which one of the following statements is correct? **(2004)**
(a) Jainism was spread in south India under the leadership of Sthalabahu.
(b) The Jainas who remained under the leadership of Bhadrabahu were called *Shvetamabaras* after the council held at Patliputra.
(c) Jainism enjoyed the patronage of the Kalinga king Kharvela in the first century bc.
(d) In the initial stages of Jainism, the Jainas worshipped images unlike Buddhists.

24. Consider the following statements: **(2003)**
i. Vardhamana Mahavira's mother was the daughter of Lichchavi chief Chetaka.
ii. Gautama Buddha's mother was a princess from the Kosalan Dynasty.
iii. Parshavanatha, the 23rd Tirthankara, belonged to Benaras.

Which of the following statement(s) is/are correct?
(a) Only i (b) Only ii
(c) ii and iii (d) i, ii and iii

25. In ancient Indian Buddhist monasteries, a ceremony called *Pavarala* used to be held. It was the: **(2002)**
(a) Occasion to elect the *Sanghaparinayaka* and two speakers – one on *Dhamma* and the other on *Vinaya*.
(b) Confession by the monks of their offences committed during their stay in the monasteries during the rainy season.
(c) Ceremony of initiation of new person into the Buddhist *Sangha* in which the head is shaved and yellow robes are offered.
(d) Gathering of Buddhist monks on the next day to the full moon day of Ashadha when they take up a fixed abode for the next four months of rainy season.

26. Which of the following presided over the Buddhist council held during the reign of Kanishka at Kashmir? **(2001)**
(a) Parsva (b) Nagarjuna
(c) Sudarka (d) Vasumitra

27. Assertion (A): The emphasis of Jainism on non-violence prevented agriculturists from embracing Jainism.

Reason (R): Cultivation involved killing of insects and pests. **(2000)**
(a) If both Assertion and Reason are true and reason explains Assertion.
(b) If both Assertion and Reason are true but reason cannot explain Assertion.
(c) If Assertion is true and Reason is not true
(d) If Assertion is not true and reason is true.

28. The concept of Eight-fold path forms the theme of: **(1998)**
(a) *Dipavamsa*
(b) *Divyavadana*
(c) *Mahaparinibbana Sutta*
(d) *Dharma-Chakra Pravartna Sutta*

29. *Milindapanho* is in the form of a dialogue between the king Menander and the Buddhist monk **(1997)**

(a) Nagasena (b) Nagarjuna
(c) Nagabhatta (d) Kumaribhatta

30. Which of the following were common to both Buddhism and Jainism? **(1996)**

i. Avoidance of extremities of penance and enjoyment.
ii. Indifference to the authority of the Vedas.
iii. Denial of efficacy of rituals.
iv. Non-injury to animal life.

Select the correct answer using the codes given below:

(a) i, ii, iii and iv (b) ii, iii and iv
(c) i, iii and iv (d) i and ii

31. Which one of the following is not a part of early Jaina literature? **(1996)**

(a) *Therigatha* (b) *Acarangasutra*
(c) *Sutrakritanga* (d) *Brihatkalpasutra*

32. The concept of *Anuvrata* was advocated by **(1995)**

(a) Mahayana Buddhism
(b) Hinayana Buddhism
(c) Jainism
(d) The Lokayukta school

ANSWERS

1. (a)	2. (b)	3. (b)	4. (b)	5. (c)	6. (c)	7. (b)	8. (d)
9. (b)	10. (c)	11. (b)	12. (a)	13. (b)	14. (d)	15. (d)	16. (d)
17. (b)	18. (a)	19. (b)	20. (b)	21. (a)	22. (c)	23. (c)	24. (c)
25. (b)	26. (d)	27. (a)	28. (d)	29. (a)	30. (b)	31. (a)	32. (c)

QUESTIONS FROM LAST YEAR'S MAINS

1. Early Buddhist Stupa art, while depicting folk motifs and narratives, successfully expounds Buddhist ideals. Elucidate. **(2016 GS1)**

2. How far is it correct to say that changes in the post-Vedic economy gave birth to new religious movements in India? **(2015, History optional)**

3. The Buddha's teachings to a large extent could be helpful in understanding and resolving the problems of today's society. Analyse critically. **(2014, History optional)**

4. Taxila university was one of the oldest universities of the world with which were associated a number of renowned learned personalities of different disciplines. Its strategic location caused its fame to flourish, but unlike Nalanda, it is not considered as a university in the modern sense. Discuss. **(2014 GS1)**

5. Assess the importance of Jaina tenets and their relevance to humanity. **(2011, History optional)**

PRACTICE QUESTIONS – PRELIMS

1. Match the following:

(A)	Eight fold path	i. Tantras
(B)	Vajrayana	ii. Jainism
(C)	Digambara	iii. Buddhism
(D)	Buddha's first sermon	iv. Sarnath

(a) (A)–ii, (B)–i, (C)–iii, (D)–iv
(b) (A)–i, (B)–ii, (C)–iii, (D)–iv
(c) (A)–iv, (B)–iii, (C)–ii, (D)–i
(d) (A)–iii, (B)–i, (C)–ii, (D)–iv

2. Consider the following statements and mark the option which is correct.

i. The women were not admitted in the Buddhist *Sanghas*.
ii. The Middle Path was laid down by the Buddha.
iii. The Buddha was born at Lumbini.
iv. According to the Buddha, desire is the root cause of all evils.

(a) i and ii (b) All of the above
(c) ii, iii and iv (d) None of the above

3. Consider the following statements and mark the option which is correct.

i. Mahavira was a contemporary of Buddha.
ii. The first Buddhist council was held during the reign of king Ashoka.
iii. Buddhism accepted the superiority of Brahmanas.

(a) i and ii (b) ii only
(c) ii and iii (d) i only

4. Consider the following statements and mark the option which is correct.

(i) Jainas believed in the existence of god but placed it below their Jina.
(ii) Buddhists believe in the concept of god but do not believe in *atman* (soul).

(a) Both are true (b) Only i is true
(c) Only ii is true (d) None of the above

5. Consider the following statements and mark the option which is correct.

i. Both Buddhism and Jainism were formed by Kshatriyas.
ii. Mahayana Buddhism believes in idol worship while Hinayana does not.
iii. The *Shvetambaras* are naked while *Digambaras* are white clad.

(a) i and ii (b) ii only
(c) ii and iii (d) i and iii

ANSWERS

1. (d) 2. (c) 3. (d) 4. (b) 5. (a)

PRACTICE QUESTIONS – MAINS

1. Identify the points of both similarity and dissimilarity between Buddhism and Brahmanism.

2. Discuss the causes for the emergence of new religions in the sixth century BCE?

3. Why did Buddhism decline, whereas Jainism spread to other parts? What are the basic similar principles in both Jainism and Buddhism? Elucidate.

CHAPTER

6

The Maurya Empire (c. 324–187 BCE)

The Maurya period is a remarkable period in the early history of Indian subcontinent. It not only marks the establishment of the first sub-continental empire, but also the development of innovative and comparatively stable governance strategies. **Leaving** Kerala, Tamil Nadu and some parts of north-eastern India, the Mauryas ruled over the whole of the sub-continent. The sources of the Maurya period are more varied and considered more authentic than the earlier periods. For the first time now, we have at our disposal a number of sources (literary sources like *Arthashastra* of Kautilya, *Indica* of Megasthenes and the Junagarh Inscription of Rudradaman I, which attributes to the beginning of construction of a Sudarshana lake during Chandragupta's reign), and edicts issued by Ashoka that throw a clearer light on the history of this period.

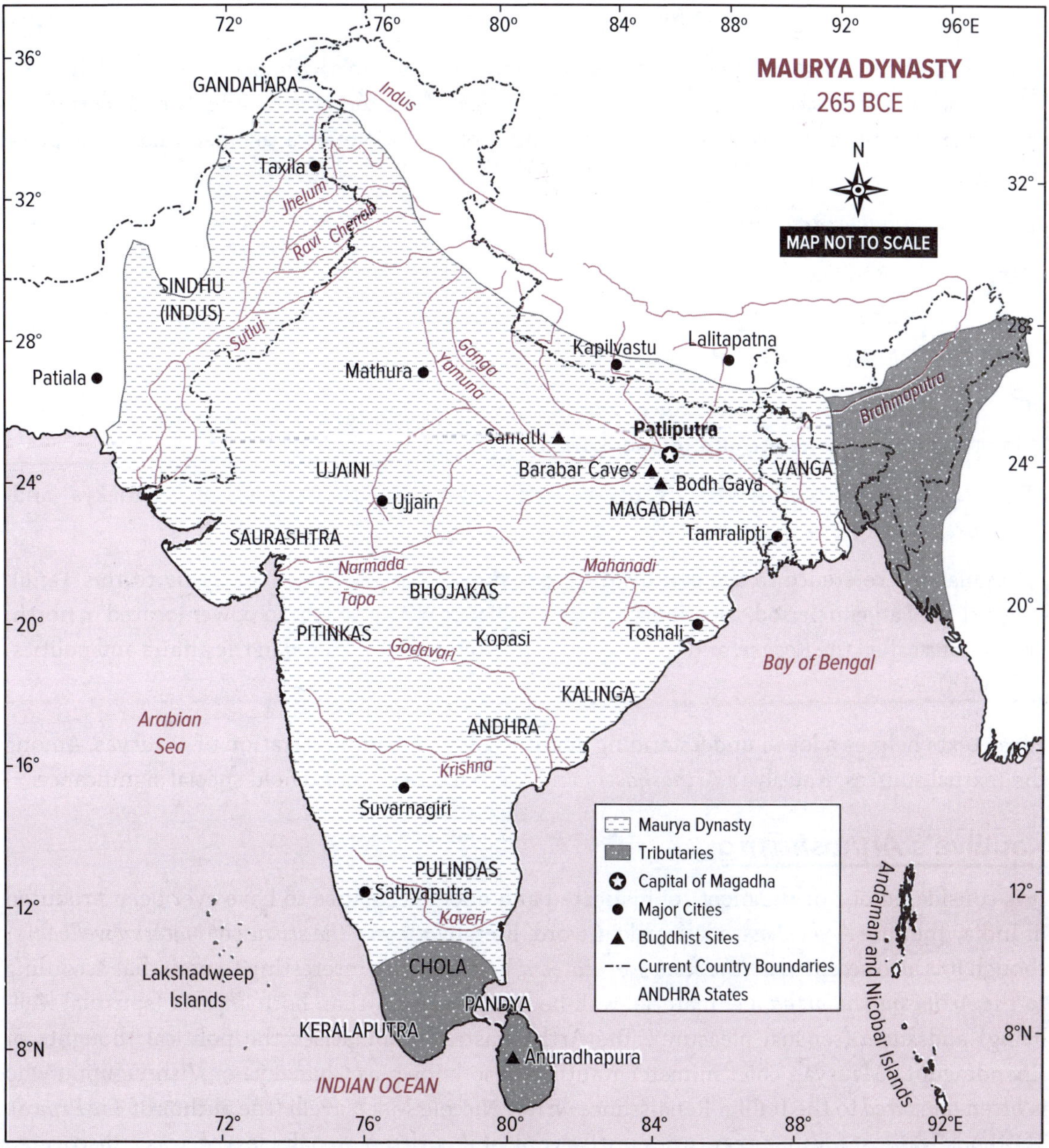

FIGURE 6.1 Map of Maurya Dynasty

The other major literary sources for the period include:

Hemachandra's *Parishishtaparvan* (establishing Chandragupta's connections with Jainism). Vishakhadatta's *Mudrarakshasa* from the 5th century written during the Gupta period (a historical drama describing the clever machinations of Chanakya against Chandragupta's enemies).

Dandin's *Dashakumaracharita.*

Banabhatta's *Kadambari.*

The trinity of Buddhist texts that give us an account of Chandragupta's life, namely, the *Mahavamsa*, *Milindapanho* and *Mahabhashya.*

The Buddhist *Dipavamsa*, *Ashokavadana*, *Divyavadana* (these three texts, as well as the Mahavamsa, give us an account of Ashoka).

The *Vamsatthapakasini* (a 10th century commentary on the legend of Chanakya and Chandragupta).

Mamulanar's reference to the southward expansion of the Mauryas (according to this Tamil poet of the Sangam period, the Mauryas had an alliance with a southern power located in north Karnataka called the *Koshar*, and the Mauryas continuously interfered in the affairs and politics of south).

These texts help us a lot in understanding about the life and administration of Mauryas. Among the textual sources, Kautilya's *Arthashastra* and Megasthenes's *Indica* hold special significance.

Kautilya's *Arthashastra*

It is considered one of the most sophisticated and detailed treatise to have ever been produced in India. The title *Arthashastra*, a Sanskrit word, literally means '*the science of material wellbeing*', though it is also accepted as '*the science of statecraft*'. It is rather interesting to note that according to the *Arthashastra*, *artha*, i.e. material well-being, is superior than both *dharma* (spiritual well-being) and *kama* (sensual pleasure). The Arthashastra[1] summarises the political thoughts of Chandragupta Maurya's chief minister Kautilya, also known as Chanakya or Vishnugupta, who is often *compared* to the Italian Renaissance writer Niccolo Machiavelli (the author of *The Prince*). This book was lost for many centuries until a copy of it, written on palm leaves, was rediscovered in India in c. 1905 CE by R. Shamashastry. This edition is dated to approximately c. 250 CE, many centuries after the time of Kautilya, but it is generally accepted that the main ideas in this book are largely of Kautilya himself. The book contains detailed information about specific

[1] It consists of 15 books (*Adhikaranas*), out of which the first five deal with *tantra* (internal administration), and next eight with *avapa* (interstate relations). The final two books deal with other miscellaneous topics.

topics that are relevant for rulers who wish to run an effective government. Diplomacy and war (including military tactics) are the two points treated in most detail but the work also includes recommendations on law, prisons, taxation, irrigation, agriculture, mining, fortifications, coinage, manufacturing, trade, administration and spies.

The ideas expressed by Kautilya in the *Arthashastra* are completely practical and unsentimental. Kautilya openly writes about controversial topics such as assassinations, when to kill family members, how to manage secret agents, when it is useful to violate treaties, and when to spy on ministers. However, he also writes about the moral duty of the king and stresses on paternal despotism as he summarises the duty of a ruler, saying, *'The happiness of the subjects is the happiness of the king; their welfare is his. His own pleasure is not his good but the pleasure of his subjects is his good'.*

FIGURE 6.2 Chanakya

Megasthenes' Indica

Indica is an account left by a Greek ambassador, Megasthenes, sent by Seleucus Nikator to the court of Chandragupta Maurya who lived in the Mauryan capital of Pataliputra. This book has not survived, but its fragments are preserved in later Greek and Latin works of Diodorus (historian who describes Alexander's Indian campaign and provides a general description of India), Strabo (geographer whose books deal with geography of India and Persia), Pliny (Roman scholar who cites Megasthenes' observations) and Arrian (statesman and soldier who provides us with an account of Alexander's campaign and also of Admiral Nearchus's voyage back to Babylon). *Indica* describes the sub-continent in terms of its size and shape (India is a *quadrilateral-shaped country*, bound by the ocean on the southern and the eastern side), soil, climate, rivers, plants, animals (contains lengthy descriptions of elephants, horses and monkeys as it appears that Greeks were specially captivated by Indian animals), produce, administration, society, legends and folklore. The Greeks referred to the Indians' worship of Lord Krishna and addressed him as Dionysus and Herakles/Hercules. They portrayed Indians as honest (since theft was rare) and having great character and moral values. Megasthenes was also greatly impressed by the contentment and prosperity of the Indian people.

'Famine has never visited India and that there has never been a general scarcity in the supply of nourishing food and even in times of war the Indians would never ravage the cultivated soil as was done by other nations but would fight their battles, away from agricultural fields allowing the tillers of the soil to carry on cultivation even when battles were raging.'

The major faults of Megasthenes' work were mistakes in details, the uncritical acceptance of Indian folklore and a tendency to idealise Indian culture by the standards of Greek philosophy. For instance, Megasthenes, influenced by Herodotus' classification of the Egyptian society into seven classes based on the professional criterion, mentioned existence of seven castes in India too (viz., philosophers, held in high esteem and consisting of *Brahmanas* and *Shramanas*; farmers, herdsmen and hunters; artisans and traders; soldiers; overseers; and the king's counsellors), which obviously was a division with reference to the professional pursuits of different sections of the society, and was rather contrary to the traditional fourfold division of the caste system then prevalent. However, Megasthenes did identify two of the most important aspects of the Indian caste system: endogamy and hereditary occupation. Strabo also wrongly states that Indians were ignorant of writing and smelting, and never drank wine except at sacrifices. Even with these faults, Megasthenes' *Indica* along with Kautilya's *Arthashastra* provides valuable insight on one of the most powerful and prominent dynasties of that time: the Mauryan dynasty.

The Mauryan Dynasty

The founder of the Mauryan dynasty, Chandragupta Maurya (324/321–297 BCE) inherited a large army of the Nandas, which he used to conquer almost whole of north, the north-west and a large part of the peninsular India. There is a lot of ambiguity about the origins and caste of Maurya family, and they vary from text to text. The Buddhist texts such as the *Digha Nikaya*, *Mahavamsa* and *Divyavadana*, speak of the Mauryas as belonging to a branch of the Kshatriya Moriya clan associated with the Shakyas, probably to give the family a higher status; but *Brahmanical sources* consider them Shudras and heretics, presumably because each king was strong patron to a heterodox sect. The family has also been believed to be associated with the Nandas, as according to the *Vishnu Purana*, Chandragupta was the eldest son of Maurya, son of the Nanda king Sarvarthasiddhi, by Mura, daughter of a hunter (*vrishala*).

Chandragupta Maurya (324/321–297 BCE)

- Mauryan dynasty founded by Chandragupta Maurya with the help of his mentor Chanakya/Kautilya.
- Chandragupta in all likelihood first established himself in Punjab and then moved eastwards until he gained control over the Magadha region. According to traditional belief, Chandragupta adopted this strategy on the basis of a moral drawn from an instance *where he witnessed a woman scolding her child for eating from the centre of a dish, because it is bound to be hotter than the sides*.
- Called *Sandrocottus* by the Greek scholars (identified by William Jones). Greek sources even suggest a meeting between Chandragupta and Alexander (who invaded north-west India during 327–326 BCE). They also account for the conflict between Chandragupta Maurya and Seleucus Nikator (who was one of the generals of Alexander, and after his death had succeeded in gaining control over most of the eastern Asiatic provinces). Chandragupta defeated him around 301 BCE and Seleucus was compelled to yield *Arachosia* (Qandahar area of south-east Afghanistan), *Gedrosia* (south Baluchistan) and *Parapomisadai* (area between Afghanistan and the Indian sub-continent, such as Kabul, Herat, Gandhara) to him in return for 500 elephants.
- Seleucus sent an ambassador to the Mauryan court, Megasthenes (who wrote the *Indica*).
- He was the chief architect of the Mauryan empire and built a vast empire, which included Bihar, Nepal, western and north-western India and the Deccan.
- According to Jain texts and tradition, Chandragupta adopted Jainism and went to the hills of Shravana Belagola (near Mysore) with Bhadrabahu and committed *Sallekhana* (death by slow starvation).

Bindusara (297–273 BCE)

- Greek writers address him as *Amitrochates* (destroyer of foes), while the *Mahabhasya* refers to him as *Amitraghat* (killer of enemies). It is rather strange that Buddhist sources are silent on Bindusara. However, stories from the Ajivika sect do mention of a fortuneteller who prophesied to Bindusara about his son Ashoka's future greatness.
- Conquered 'the land between the two seas', i.e. the Arabian sea and the Bay of Bengal. The Tibetan monk Taranatha (who wrote a 17th century history of Indian Buddhism) states that one of Bindusara's great lords, Chanakya, destroyed the nobles and kings of 16 towns and made him master of all the territory between the eastern and western seas.

- Greek sources also mention of his diplomatic relations with western kings. According to Strabo, Antiochus (Syrian king) sent Deimachus as an ambassador to Bindusara's court. Similarly, Pliny mentions that King Ptolemy II Philadelphus of Egypt sent Dionysius as an ambassador to India.
- In *Divyavadana*, probably during his reign, there is a mention of his son Ashoka, who quelled a rebellion against wicked ministers at Taxila.
- Believed to have joined the Ajivika sect.
- Under his rule, almost the entire sub-continent (as far south as Karnataka) was under Mauryan suzerainty.

Ashoka (268–232 BCE)

- After Bindusara's death in 273 BCE, there was a four-year succession conflict. According to *Divyavadana*, Bindusara wanted his son Susima to succeed him, and Ashoka was the choice of Bindusara's ministers. Later, with the help of a minister named Radhagupta, and after killing 99 brothers, Ashoka finally acquired the Magadha throne and thus, after four years, came his formal consecration.
- He was appointed the Viceroy of Taxila and Ujjain (both cities handled commercial activities) during the reign of Bindusara.
- Regarded as one of the greatest kings of all times, and probably was the first ruler to maintain direct contact with his people through his inscriptions. The various names of the emperor include *Buddhashakya* and *Ashoka* (in the Maski edict), *Dharmasoka* (Sarnath inscription), *Devanampiya* (meaning beloved of the gods) and *Piyadassi* (meaning of pleasing appearance) given in the Sri Lankan Buddhist chronicles *Dipavamsa* and *Mahavamsa*).
- According to the Buddhist text *Ashokavadana*, Ashoka's mother was daughter of a Brahmana of Champa named Subhadrangi. According to belief, Ashoka got his name (literally meaning '*without sorrow*') from the fact that his birth resulted in the reunion of his mother and father, who were otherwise separated due to a palace intrigue. It is from her exclamation, '*I am now without sorrow*', that the child Ashoka got his name.
- Buddhist texts such as the *Dipavamsa* and *Mahavamsa* provide a detailed account of his queens. According to legend, Ashoka had a love marriage with his wife Mahadevi (daughter of a merchant of Vidisha, who later became the mother of Mahendra/Mahinda and Sanghamitra/Sanghamitta, the celebrated children of Ashoka who helped in the propagation of the Buddhist religion). These two texts also mention the queens Asandhimitta, Padmavati, Tissarakhita (who tried to get the Bodhi tree cut) and Karuvaki (only queen to be mentioned in the Queen's edict/Allahabad-Kosam pillar edict, where she is described as *the mother of prince Tivara*, the only son of Ashoka to be mentioned by name in inscriptions).

- His empire covered the whole territory from Hindukush to Bengal, and extended over Afghanistan, Baluchistan, and the whole of India including Kashmir and the valleys of Nepal (the first empire to do so), with the exception of a small area in the far south (which, according to rock edict 13, were inhabited by the Cholas and Pandyas, and according to rock edict 2, by the *Keralaputras* and *Satiyaputras*).
- His Hellenistic contemporaries were Antiochius II of Syria, Ptolemy II of Egypt, Antigonus of Macedonia, Magas of Cyrenaica (Libya) and Alexander of Epirus, as all of them are mentioned in the edicts of Ashoka. Ashoka exchanged missions, both diplomatic and other, with them. '*The conquest by Dharma has been won here, on the borders, and even six hundred yojanas* (5,400–9,600 km) *away, where the Greek king Antiochius rules, beyond there where the four kings named Ptolemy, Antigonus, Magas and Alexander rule, likewise in the south among the Cholas, the Pandyas, and as far as Tamraparni* (*Sri Lanka*),' says the 13th Rock Edict).
- Was a great proponent of Buddhism. According to tradition, and as mentioned in the *Mahavamsa* and *Dipavamsa*, he was converted to Buddhism by his nephew *Nigrodha* (who had become a monk at the tender age of 7). According to the *Divyavadana*, Samudra (a merchant-turned monk) converted him. Buddhism for the first time went outside India during his reign. He sent his son Mahendra and daughter Sanghamitra to Ceylon (Sri Lanka).
- Appointed *Dharma Mahamattas* to propagate dharma among various social groups including women (in the 14th year of his reign).
- Organised the third Buddhist council at Pataliputra (in the 18th year of his reign), after which he sent Buddhist missionaries to Ceylon and Suvarnabhumi.
- In the course of his second Dharmayatra tour (in the 21st year of his reign), he visited Lumbini (the birth place of Buddha).
- Banned animal sacrifice, regulated the slaughter of animals for food, and established *dharmashalas*, hospitals and *sarais* throughout his kingdom.

Brihadratha

The Maurya empire declined rapidly after Ashoka and the later kings had very short reigns. The empire became weak and fragmented, and the Mauryan dynasty came to an end when the last king, Brihadratha, was killed by his military commander, Pushyamitra Sunga, in 187 BCE.

Sunga Dynasty (187 BCE)

Ashokan Inscriptions and Ashoka's Dhamma

The history of Ashoka is reconstructed on the basis of his inscriptions. These inscriptions throw light not only on the reign of Ashoka, but also reveal his external and domestic policies, his views

about *dhamma*, and the extent of his empire. As statements of his personal concerns, they are remarkable documents vividly describing the ambience of his time. There are total 33 inscriptions and are primarily classified into:

- Major Rock Edicts,
- Minor Rock Edicts,
- Separate Rock Edicts,
- Major Pillar Edicts and
- Minor Pillar Edicts.

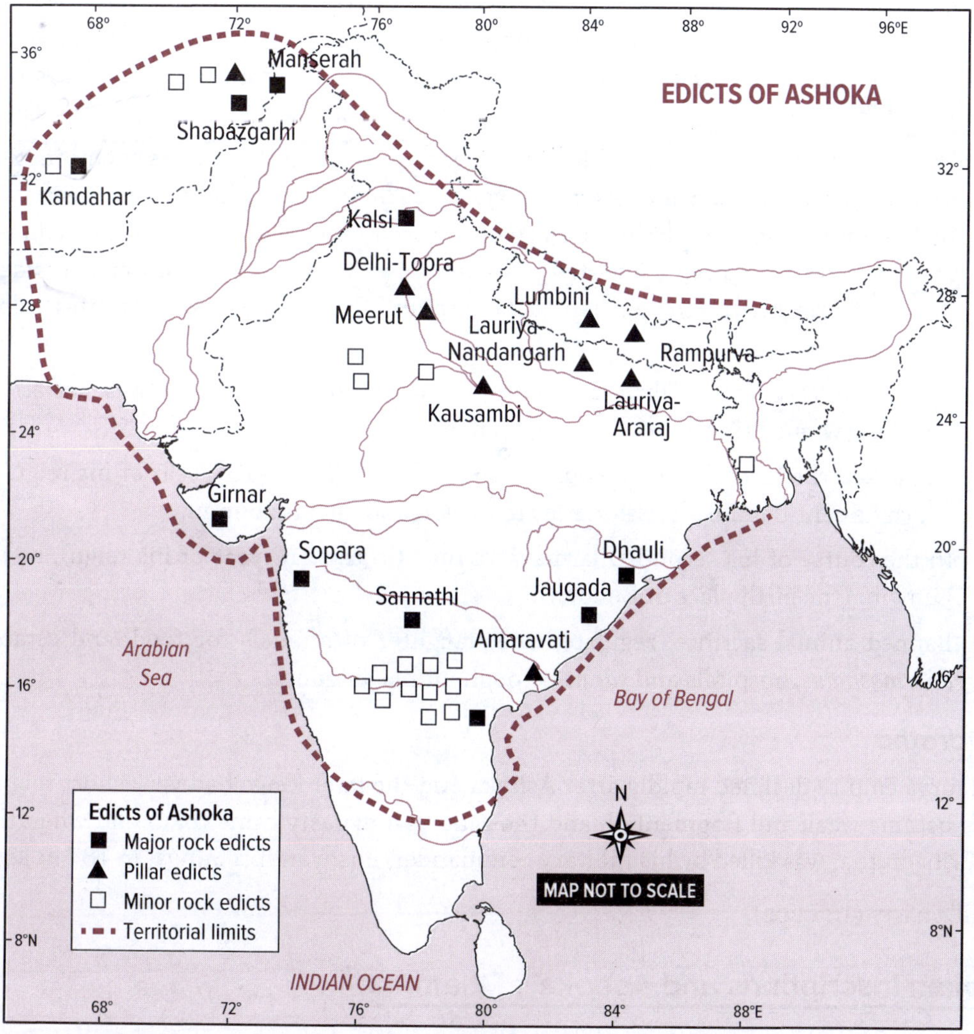

FIGURE 6.3 Map showing Edicts of Ashoka's Empire

The edicts of the earlier half of his reign were inscribed on conveniently located rock surfaces and were widely distributed throughout the empire, especially in the areas of public settlements where people can easily read these edicts, and are thus referred to as the minor and major rock edicts. On the other hand, pillar edicts were mostly inscribed in the latter parts of his reign and instead of rocks were on well-polished sandstone monolithic pillars (quarried from the sites of Chunar, near Varanasi), each surmounted with a finely sculpted animal capital involving great technological expertise in cutting and engraving, and were largely confined to the Ganges plain (since they were transported by river).

In his inscriptions, Brahmi, Kharosthi, Prakrit, Aramaic and Greek languages (deciphered by James Prinsep in c. 1837 CE) have been used. There is interestingly no reference to the teachings of the Buddha in the Greek and Aramaic versions (mostly found around the north-western borders such as the Shar-i-Kuna Greek-Aramaic inscription). Equally fascinating is the fact that some concepts in these edicts are drawn from the philosophical discourses of that language. For instance, *the edicts in Aramaic are better understood if read in the context of some Zoroastrian concepts*. Also, it is true that Ashoka's inscriptions do not contain certain key ideas associated with the Buddha's teaching, such as the Eight-Fold Path, the Four Noble Truths and the goal of *Nibbana*. Nevertheless, there is definite Buddhist core ideology in his dhamma-focused inscriptions.

Most of the Ashoka's inscriptions are about *dhamma* (Prakrit form of dharma, literally meaning the universal law or righteousness or social and religious order), and it was clearly inspired by the Buddhist *upasaka dhamma* (i.e. the Buddha's teaching for the laity), but it was not a mirror image of it. Ashoka's *dhamma* was a set of teachings that could not be identified with just narrow sectarian belief, rather it encompassed a social and intellectual code of ethics influencing many aspects of social life, and even a lot more than that. It emphasised on non-violence, mutual respect and understanding between people of different sects and beliefs. Ashoka did not see *dhamma* as piety, resulting from good deeds that were inspired by formal religious beliefs, but as conformity to a social ethic. His *dhamma* was aimed at creating an attitude of mind having primacy of ethical behaviour and the recognition of the dignity of human life. He repeatedly asked *the people to extend respect, consideration, compassion and tolerance towards slaves and servants, respect for teachers, obedience to parents, generosity towards friends and relatives, regard and donations to Brahmanas and Shramanas, a concern for all living beings and an abstention from destroying life*. His policy of *dhamma* included the state's concern for the welfare of its people. It was a code of conduct or ideal social behaviour common to all religions of the world, which he appealed to his subjects to follow. A closer look at Ashokan edicts illustrates that basic attributes of *dhamma* included compassion *(daya)*, *charity* (dana), *truthfulness*, *purity* and *gentleness*.

Fourteen Major Rock Edicts and Their Corresponding Messages

Rock Edict	Corresponding Message
First Edict	Declared prohibition of animal sacrifice.
Second Edict	Medical treatment of human and animals, planting beneficial medicinal herbs and roots, fruits and the digging of wells.
Third Edict	Mentions *Pradeshikas*, *Rajukas* and *Yuktas* and their need for going on tours of inspection every five years as part of their other duties, preaching *dhamma*, and also adopting liberal attitude towards *Brahmanas* and *Shramanas*.
Four Edict	*Bheri Ghosha* (war drum) replaced by *Dhamma Ghosha* and King Ashoka attached greatest value to this duty.
Fifth Edict	Appointment of *Dhamma Mahamattas*, a special cadre of officials entrusted to spread dhamma within the kingdom.
Sixth Edict	Mantri parishad and officers like *Pulisani* and *Pativedakas* (reporters).
Seventh Edict	Religious tolerance amongst all sects and welfare measures for public not only in his own kingdom but also in the neighbouring kingdoms of Cholas, Pandyas and that of Antiochus in the north-west.
Eighth Edict	Royal pleasure tours (*Vihara-yatras*) replaced by *dhamma* tours (*dhamma-yatras*). Ashoka himself went to Sambodhi at Bodhgaya.
Ninth Edict	Criticism of the uselessness of various ceremonies, instead lays stress on dhamma and moral conduct.
Tenth Edict	King desires no more fame or glory.
Eleventh Edict	Announces that the gift of dhamma being the best of all gifts and the policy of *Dhamma* is the best policy to follow. *Dhamma* included giving respect to elders, and good behaviour towards slaves.
Twelfth Edict	Mention of *Ithijika Mahamatta* (*mahamattas* in charge of women's welfare) and appeals for not only tolerance amongst sects, but also for people to honour and understand the dhamma of others.
Thirteenth Edict	• The Kalinga war (261 BCE, occurred in the ninth year after Ashoka's consecration) changed his attitude and Ashoka, who was the worshipper of Shiva, turned towards Buddhism. *Digvijay* was replaced by *Dhamma Vijay*, the sword was replaced by *dhamma*, the war drum (*Bheri Ghosha*) became law (*Dhamma Ghosha*). His *dhamma* contained the essence (good qualities) of all the religions of the world. The king considered victory by *dhamma* to be the foremost victory; mention of victory by *dhamma* on his Hellenistic neighbours like Antiochus, and others like the Cholas and Pandyas. But, in this rock edict itself, he sternly warns the forest tribes against any intransigence. • The information provided by 13th Edict also helped in understanding the territorial extent of the Mauryan Empire and also contains references to its neighbours Cholas (Northern Tamil Nadu), Cheras (Kerala) and Pandayas (Southern Tamil Nadu).
Fourteenth Edict	Purpose of rock edicts.

Pillar Edicts and their Corresponding Messages

The majestic free-standing Ashokan pillars probably signify the axis of the world (*axis mundi*) that separated heaven and earth. Pillar edicts have been found at Lauriya-Araraj, Lauriya Nandangarh, Rampurva, Nigali Sagar, Sarnath, Topra and Meerut. It is rather interesting to note that two pillars, one from Topra and the other from Meerut, were shifted to Delhi by Feroz Shah Tughlaq. There are pillars without inscriptions such as the bull capital pillar at Rampurva, the pillar with the lion capital at Vaishali and the Kolam pillar, which is also without a capital. The Ashokan pillars have the following features:

FIGURE 6.4 Ashokan Pillar at Vaishali

a. Mostly, the pillars are similar in form and dimensions, and are made of sandstone quarried from Chunar.

b. Mostly monoliths (i.e. carved out of a single piece of stone) and have a lustrous, polished surface.

c. Do not have a base, and the plain, smooth cylindrical shaft tapers slightly upwards to a height of 12–14 m. A cylindrical bolt joins the top of the shaft to the capital, and have a bell capital (a stone carved in the shape of an inverted lotus).

d. On top of bell capital is a platform (abacus) which is intended to support the crowned animal. The abacus is square and plain in earlier pillars, and circular and curved in later ones. All the parts of the pillars are carved on all sides, i.e. in the round, probably meant to be viewed from all around.

The motifs associated with the Ashokan pillars have a rich and varied symbolism in resonance with many prevailing Indian religious traditions. For instance, the most found motifs were of lotus (symbolised purity and fecundity in Indian tradition), lion (is a solar symbol and represents the Buddha too, as he is referred to as *Sakya-simha*, i.e. lion among the Sakyas), bull (symbol of fertility), elephant (relevant in Buddhism as according to Buddhist tradition, Buddha entered his mother's womb in the form of a white elephant), spoked wheel (represents *dharmachakra*, i.e. the wheel of dharma and also associated with sovereignty) and horse (symbolises departure of Siddhartha from his home). Some of the important pillar edicts feature the following:

Pillar Edict	Corresponding Message
First Pillar Edict	Social code
Second Pillar Edict	Describes *dhamma* as consisting of least amount of sin, performing virtuous deeds, having compassion, purity and truthfulness
Third Pillar Edict	Soul and sin
Fourth Pillar Edict	*Rajukas*
Fifth Pillar Edict	Popularly known as the Delhi-Topra pillar edict, it features prohibitions regarding animal killing
Sixth Pillar Edict	Welfare of people
Seventh Pillar Edict	*Dhamma Mahamattas*

FIGURE 6.5 Delhi Topra Pillar

Other Relevant Inscriptions and Important Edicts

Edict/Inscription	Remarks
Allahabad – Kosam/Queen's Edict/ Kausambi or Schism Edict	Ashoka warns members of the *Sangha* against causing division in the ranks. Samudragupta's inscription is on this edict itself. Jahangir was probably responsible for its removal to the fort at Allahabad.
Girnar Rock Inscription of Rudradaman (Kathiawar)	Mentions the Sudarshan Lake constructed by Pushyagupta, a *rashtriya* (means provincial governor) of Saurashtra during Chandragupta Maurya's reign.
Kandahar Inscription	Bilingual Greek, Aramaic inscription
Nigali Sagar Inscription (Nepal)	To record the first enlargement of stupa (14 years after his consecration) and later Ashoka's visit to the site (20 years after his consecration).
Rummindei Inscription (Nepal)	To commemorate the birthplace of the Buddha, Ashoka visited Lumbini, worshipped here and gave tax concessions to the villagers. It records that *the village of Lumbini was exempted from bali and was to pay only one-eighth of bhaga.*
Sannati Inscription (Karnataka)	Site of all 14 major rock edicts as well as two separate Kalinga edicts.
Kalinga Edict (Bhauli and Jaugada)	Mentions '*All men are my children*'.
Saugaura Copper Plate Inscription and Mahasthan Inscription of Chandragupta Maurya	Mentions relief measures adopted during famine in Magadha.
Minor Rock Edict 1	Indicates that Ashoka turned towards Buddhism gradually (nearly after 2.5 years in power), and not suddenly.
Minor Rock Edict 3	Ashoka greets the *Sangha*, professes his deep faith in the Buddha, *dhamma*, and *Sangha* and recommends six Buddhist texts for monks, nuns and the general laity.
Inscriptions at Shahbazgarhi and Mansehra	Written in Kharosthi script.
Brahmagiri Minor Rock Edicts I and II	Talks about local administration.

FIGURE 6.6 Rummindei Pillar

Ashoka's Legacy

Ashoka was not only a great missionary ruler in the history of ancient India, but of the world too. He has great and path-breaking innovative achievements to his credit, such as:

a. Political unification of the country: He not only added Kalinga to Mauryan dynasty but also bound the whole country together by one *dhamma*, one language, and practically one script of Brahmi (which is used in most of his inscriptions).

FIGURE 6.7 Kanaganahalli Stone Portrait of Ashoka which Mentions Ashoka as 'Ranyo Ashoka'

b. Spread of tolerance and respect: He adopted and preached tolerance in not only the religious sphere (did not try to force his Buddhist faith on his subjects and made gifts to non-Buddhist sects as well, such as, donating Barbara caves to Ajivika ascetics), but in the case of scripts (other than Brahmi, he respected other scripts like Kharosthi, Aramaic and Greek), and languages (Greek, Prakrit and Sanskrit) too.

c. Promotion of cultural contacts: He not only brought innovative administrative changes, but also promoted cultural contacts between Indian states, and between India and the outer world too. It would not be an exaggeration if Ashoka is considered the first global cultural ambassador of India.

d. Policy of peace and non-aggression: Ashoka is famous in history for his policy of peace, non-conquest and non-aggression. In this sense, he was much ahead of his time and generation.

Mauryan Administration

The Maurya period was marked by innovative administrative changes and an elaborate administration. It is generally believed that the Mauryas had a vast and highly centralised bureaucratic rule with king as the fountainhead of all powers; though it is claimed that Mauryan kings (especially Ashoka) claimed paternal despotism rather than divine rule. Ashoka's empire was probably divided into provinces with a viceroy in each province. In the *Arthashastra*, Kaulitya notes down the concept of *saptanga rajya* according to which, a state comprises seven inter-related and interlocked *angas* or *prakritis* (elements):

1. Svamin (king)

Soul of all the seven elements. According to Kautilya, the king was the *Dharmapravakta* (promulgator of social orders as he issued *Rajasasana*, i.e. royal rescripts and maintained *porana pakiti*, i.e. ancient rules and customs). Even though in his daily affairs he was assisted by a council of ministers, yet the king himself took all final decisions regarding revenue, law and order, war, or any other matter related to administration. He was expected to be agile and accessible to his officials at all times. In one of his rock edicts, Ashoka had declared that even common people could meet him any time. He also declared that *all his subjects were like his children and he desired their happiness in this and the other world*. The *Arthashastra* also asserts that the king should maintain helpless children, old people, childless women, and other destitute and vulnerable people. The king also tried to ensure people's welfare by planting trees along roads, digging wells, and providing medical care for both men and animals.

> *'Chandragupta was a very hard-working official. He remained in court whole day, did not sleep at day time and even when he would have his body massaged or his hair combed and dressed, he would attend to public business and gave audience to his ambassadors.'*
>
> **Megasthenes**

In Mauryan times, the king also had to exercise great vigilance to safeguard his life and position. *Arthashastra* contains a great detail about the multiple secret emergency exits and about different examination techniques employed to check all the things going in and out of the palace complex. Interestingly, there is also mention of female personal bodyguards of the king, who were skilled in archery. Kautilya also mentions the dangers of assassination and thus suggests ways to guard the king against poison, fire and snakes; and to muster an effective ring of spies who can sniff out even the slightest whiff of sedition (such as *sanstha* or stationary spies who were posted permanently at a particular region and *sanchara* or wandering spies who wandered from place to place for collecting secret information). Chandragupta maintained a body of spies called *Overseers* (the *Episcopoi* of the Diodorus or *Ephori* of Strabo and Arrian) who kept watch on events going on throughout the country and regularly reported to the King. Strabo says that the *Ephori* were appointed from the most faithful persons. There is also mention of *Pativedakas* and *Pulisani* who functioned as special reporters of the king and kept him informed of public opinion.

2. Amatya (all high officials, counsellors and executive heads of departments/ ministers)

The king appointed a council of ministers to assist him in day-to-day administration called *Mantriparishad* (a larger body as compared to the *Mantra-parishad*, which was a small consultative body of mantris). According to *Megasthenes* and later Greek writers like Diodorus, Starbo, Arrian, etc., the *Mantriparishad* was very influential. Besides advising the king in matters of administration, it exercised great influence in the appointment of governors, viceroys, deputy governors, treasurers, generals, admirals, judges, chief magistrates and other high officials. The meeting of the *Mantriparishad* was also attended by the *Maha-Mantrins* or the high ministers, who were handsomely paid. This is borne out by the fact that while the *Mantrins* received 48,000 panas as salary per annum, the members of the Mantriparishad received only 12,000 panas per annum.

There were also bodies of *Nikayas* (trained officials) who looked after the ordinary affairs of the realm. The Arthashastra refers to the highest functionaries at the centre as the eighteen *Tirthas*, the chief among them were the *Mantrin* (chief minister), *Purohita* (high priest), *Yuvaraja* (heirapparent) and *Senapati* (commander-in-chief). There were various other officials who were in charge of important portfolios. These officials were known as *Amatyas* (who filled the highest administrative and judicial appointments), *Mahamattas* and *Adhyakshas*. The *Adhyakshas* (or superintendents, whom Megasthenes called the *Astynomoi*, the *magistrates* of Strabo) were high-ranking officials next to the Tirthas, concerned mostly with economic functions and some military duties. The *Arthashastra* provides a list of 27 *Adhyakshas* who were responsible for running various economic departments like agriculture, mining, weaving, trade, etc. For instance, the magistrates who looked after towns and cities were called *Nagaradhyaksha*, and those looking after the military were called *Baladhyakshas*. Quite strikingly, there were enormous gaps in terms of salary between the highest and lowest category of government officers. For instance, the ratio of the clerk's/soldier's salary to that of the chief minister/commander of the army works out at 1:96.

Among all the executive officials, *Samahartri* (chief collector of revenue) was the most important and his responsibility involved maintaining accounts and collection of taxes from all types of sources. Most of the superintendents mentioned above functioned on his orders. There was also the office of *Samnidhatri* (treasurer) who was also in charge of the royal stores, *akshapatala* (records-cum-audit office) and *dauvarika* (chief of the palace attendants). It is rather interesting to note that Kautilya laid down certain specific tests to determine the suitability of appointment of persons as different *Amatyas*, and only those whose character had been tested under all kinds of allurements and not just one kind, were to be promoted to still higher position of advisers to the king. For instance, in case that the *Amatyas* in charge of civil and criminal justice might be sufficiently religious-minded to adjudicate cases impartially, they had to be purified by religious tests (*Dharmopadhasuddha*). Likewise, those to be appointed as chancellor of the exchequer (Samaharta) had to be purified by a money test (*Arthopadhasuddha*); those appointed to the pleasure gardens, had to be purified by a love test (*Kamopadhasuddha*); and those who had to be employed in work which needed bold and immediate steps had to be purified by a fear test (*Bhayopadhasuddha*).

3. *Janapada* (territory and population)

Apart from Magadha with its capital at Pataliputra, the Mauryan Empire was divided into four other provinces, with capitals at Taxila (north-western India), Suvarnagiri (southern India), Tosali (eastern India) and Ujjain (western India). During Ashoka's reign, a fifth province of Kalinga was added. The head of the provincial administration was viceroy, who was in charge of law and order and collection of taxes for the centre. He was generally a prince from the royal family (*kumara or aryaputra*) and was assisted by *Mahamattas* and a council of ministers. Besides imperial provinces, there were a number of territories that enjoyed some measure of autonomy.

State	Capital
Uttarapatha	Taxila
Dakshinapatha	Suvarnagiri
Eastern India	Tosali
Avantiratha	Ujjain
Kalinga	Tasali/Dhauli

The provinces were further divided into divisions headed by *Pradeshikas*, who had no advisory council. Divisions were divided into districts under officials called *Rajukas* (derived from *rajju*, meaning rope, and probably referring to the measurement of land using ropes). He was assisted by *Yuktas* (clerks) in accounting, secretarial and other miscellaneous works. Districts were in turn divided into groups of 5 or 10 villages headed by *Sthanikas* (who collected taxes), and were assisted by *Gopas* (who maintained proper records and accounts). *Nagrika* was the city administrative chief while *Pradeshtha* was the city judge and *Rakshin* was the police chief in the city. The lowest administrative unit was the village, headed by *Gramini*/*Gramika* on the consultation of *Grama-vriddhas* (village elders). The Maurya administration was thus structurally in the nature of a pyramid with the Gramini at the bottom and the king at the top. However, it is not sure whether the entire Indian sub-continent had similar type of administration. It seems that while the central province of Magadha was under strict supervision of the king, other far-flung areas might have witnessed varied degree of administrative control.

Sthaniya ⟶ *Drona* ⟶ *Mukha* ⟶ *Kharvatika* ⟶ *Samgrahana*

Administrative unit of 800 villages ⟶ 400 villages ⟶ 200 villages ⟶ 10 villages

The municipal administration of Pataliputra, the capital city of Mauryas, was of a unique character. The city administration of Pataliputra, according to Megasthenes and corroborated by *Arthashastra*, was conducted by six committees of five members each. Each committee was assigned different subjects such as industry, foreigners, birth and death registration, trade and market regulations and tax collection to look after.

Committee/Board	Function
1. Industry	This committee had to look after production of commodities, keep watch on the quality of raw materials used, decide the fair value of the articles produced and stamp the finished articles as evidence of their suitability to be marketed.
2. Foreigners	Both Strabo and Diodorus state that the Mauryan Government took special care of the foreigners. The duty of this board was to see that no foreigner was wronged. The board used to send physicians to attend and take care of any foreigner who was not keeping well, and if he died, they buried him and delivered the property he had left behind to his family.

Committee/Board	Function
3. Vital statistics (birth and death registration)	This board would enquire when and how deaths occurred and register every birth and death with a view of not only levying a tax, but also in order that birth and deaths among both high and low may not escape the cognizance of the government.
4. Trade, commerce and market regulations	It kept watch over the weights and measures and made sure that commodities were sold out before their quality deteriorated. It also ensured that seasonal products were sold by public notice and no one was allowed to deal in more than one commodity (however, one could do so by paying double or three times the tax according to the number of commodities dealt with). Kautilya even suggested that the dues realised in the form of grain should be kept as buffer stock to be used in time of food shortage.
5. Manufactured articles	The fifth board supervised that public notice was given for the sale of manufactured articles. This board kept strict watch so that newly manufactured articles were not mixed or piled with the old stock.
6. Tax collection	The sixth board was in charge of collecting one-tenth of the prices of the articles or produce sold as tax. Any fraud in payment of this tax was punishable with death penalty.

4. Durga (Fortified capital)

The Mauryans maintained a huge army. According to Greek writer Justin, *Chandragupta had 6,00,000 infantry, 30,000 cavalry, 9,000 elephants and 8,000 chariots*. Although, it seems to be an exaggerated figure, but the possession of a large army by the Mauryas cannot be doubted. Higher officers called *Anta-Mahamattas* were responsible for the security of frontier forts. Kautilya gave detailed directions for the construction of the main fort in the capital city. He recommends that troops should be stationed along the approaches to the fort and the fort walls should be surrounded by not one but three moats filled with lotuses and crocodiles. He also suggests that the fort should be provided with plenty of supplies to tide over sieges and should have numerous secret escape routes. Kautilya strongly approves of a standing army, which was supposed to be recruited from all four *varnas*, adequately trained and maintained by the state. *Senapati* and *Nayaks* were important military officers under whom there were several *Adhyakshas*/superintendents of different wings and units of the army. Megasthenes reports that the administration of different branches of the army was carried through a War Office comprising 30 members, obviously experts in different branches of military art and science. It was divided into six boards of five members each:

(i) The Board of Admiralty: In charge of the navy, though interestingly Kautilya does not mention the navy.

(ii) The Board of Infantry: Headed by *Padadhyaksha*

(iii) The Board of Cavalry: Headed by *Asvadhyaksha*

(iv) The Board of War Chariots: Headed by *Rathadhyaksha*

(v) The Board of War Elephants: Headed by *Hastyadhyaksha*

(vi) The Board of Transport and Supervision of Equipment

In addition to these, there is also mention of periodic levies of troops such as *Maula* (hereditary warriors), *Bhartiakas* (mercenaries), and forest tribe soldiers, and allies (furnished by friends).

5. Kosha (Treasury)

As discussed above, the Mauryas maintained a huge standing army and employed a large number of state officials. Since these soldiers and officials were paid in cash, the state taxes were not considered sufficient to meet all the needs of the state. Hence it had to undertake and regulate numerous economic activities to generate more and more resources. Taxes were levied in both cash and kind. The mainstay of economy in this period was agriculture (animal husbandry and trade were other main occupations), and the land revenue was the main source of income. Principal crops were various varieties of rice, barley, millet, wheat, sugarcane, and most of the pulses, peas, and oilseeds. The notion of private property of *Kshetra* (land which could be sold under certain regulations) had emerged and got established during this time. The *kshetrika* (land-owner) was distinguished from the *upasava* (tenant). In case of land disputes where neither side could prove its claim, the property went to the king. Peasants paid one-sixth of produce as *bhaga* and extra tax *bali* as tribute. The *bali* (land tax or tax on the area of land) was the main item of revenue and was levied at the rate of one-sixth of the produce. Peasants had to pay many other taxes like *Pindakara* (assessed on groups of villages), *Hiranya* (paid only in cash), *Kara* (levied on fruits and flower gardens), etc., but the exact nature of all of them is still not very clear. Land tax was collected by a class of officials called *Agranomoi* (by Megasthenes).

The importance of irrigation was fully realised and peasants had to pay *more tax on irrigated land* known as *udaka-bhaga* (water rate, and generally levied at one-fifth to one-third of the produce). State assistance was provided to the peasants to dig wells for irrigation.

Megasthenes refers to various other classes of officials who superintended the rivers, measured the land, and inspected the sluices by which water is let out from the main canals into their branches so that everyone may have an equal supply of it. In order to augment the resource base, the Mauryan state founded new agricultural settlements to bring virgin land under cultivation (*Shunyanivesha*). People from overpopulated areas, slaves and prisoners of war were brought to these new settlements to work on the fields. These villages belonged to the king and were looked after by government officials called *Sitadhyaksha* (Superintendent of agriculture). Share-cropping existed on both state-owned and privately-owned land. Kautilya refers to different kinds of share-croppers working on the state-owned land such as the *Ardhasitikas* (kept half of the produce) and the *Svaviryopajivins* (kept one-fourth or one-fifth of the produce). It should be noted that there is no reference in any text of taking away the land of the farmers in case of non-payment of taxes. Kautilya also mentions certain emergency taxes (*Pranaya*) or additional levies that the state could impose if the treasury got depleted. These included a tax on farmers (ranging from one-fourth to one-third of the produce depending on the quality of their land), an additional levy on the traders, and taxes on the income of actors, singers and prostitutes. State also paid attention to the development of animal wealth. Pastures were maintained by state. *Vivita Adyaksha* was in-charge of pasture land while Sun Adyaksha was in-charge of slaughter houses[2].

Trade and urban economy received great impetus under the Mauryas and influenced almost all parts of the empire. The main centres of textile manufacturing were *Varanasi*, *Mathura*, *Bengal*, *Gandhara* and *Ujjain*. The state also functioned as entrepreneur and state-run textile workshops were placed under *Sutradhyaksha*, and chariot workshops under a *Rathadhyaksha*. Mining and metallurgy were another important economic activities and the mine officer was called *Akaradhyaksha*. Kautilya describes forests, pastures and mines as state property. Trade was conducted through land and river routes. Pataliputra was also connected through various trade routes with all parts of the subcontinent. The main centre of trade in the northwest was Taxila, which was further connected with central Asian markets. Tamralipti (Tamluk in West Bengal) in the east and Broach in the west were important seaports. Craft activities were also a major source of revenue to the state. Artisans living in towns had to pay taxes either in cash or kind or work free for the king (*visthi*, i.e. forced labour). Arthashastra mentions wage labour (*karamakara*), bonded labour and slave labour (*dasas* and *ahitakas*, i.e. those pledged to creditors when contracting a debt). Traders and artisans were organised in corporate associations called *shrenis* or guilds or *puga* to protect their rights. The guilds were headed by *Jesthaka*. The Mauryas were responsible for introduction of iron on a large scale in different parts of the sub-continent. They maintained a monopoly over the production of iron, which was in great demand by the army, industry and agriculture. It was done through the official called *Loha-adyaksha*. Urban taxes included *Shulka* (duties on imported and exported goods) and excise duties on local manufactures. Certain important officials were:

a. *Panyadhyaksha* (Officer in charge of trade, price fixation and sale of goods produced by state-run manufacturing units)
b. *Sansthadhyaksha* (Superintendent of markets)
c. *Rupadarshaka* (Inspector of coins)
d. *Pautavadhyaksha* (In charge of standardised weights and measures)

A considerable part of the revenue was spent for the maintenance of the army, war horses, war elephants and war chariots. The artisans also received maintenance from the royal exchequer. Herdsmen were paid grains from the royal granary for their labour for clearing the land of wild beasts and fowls. The philosophers, i.e. the *Brahmanas* and the *Shramanas*, received unused land as royal gifts but such land could not be sold or mortgaged by the beneficiaries. For instance, Pillar

[2] According to Arthashastra, milch cattle was not allowed to be slaughtered.

Edict 3 refers to the gifts of mango groves, gardens and alms houses by queen Karuvaki, while inscriptions in the Barabar and Nagarjuni hills account for the gift of caves to Ajivika ascetics by king Ashoka and his successor Dasaratha. The children of *Brahmanas* and handicapped people were exempted from paying taxes. Construction of roads, buildings, forts, repairs of the existing constructions, etc. claimed a good part of the expenditure during the rule of Chandragupta. There has been no evidence of any banking system but *usury* (lending of money at high interest rate) is often mentioned, though ironically, Megasthenes claimed that Mauryans did not know about money lending. Punch-marked silver coins which carried the symbol of peacock, hill and regent formed the imperial currency of the Mauryans. Thus, there was not only extensive state participation in the economy, but the state also exercised great regulation and control over the economy.

6. *Danda/Bala* (Justice or force)

As far as judicial administration is concerned, the king was the supreme authority. He personally adjudicated the cases that came before him. Judging of cases consumed a great part of his time in the court. He would never keep his petitioners waiting. He obviously followed the exhortations of Kautilya, his minister, who observed in his Arthashastra that '*when in the court, he (the king) shall never cause his petitioners to wait at the door, for when a king makes himself inaccessible to the people and entrusts his work to his immediate officers, he may be sure to engender confusion in business, and to cause thereby public disaffection, and himself a prey to his enemies*'.

Judges were called *Dharmasthas* (though Ashokan inscriptions mention city *Mahamattas* who were also given judicial functions), and *Pradeshtris* were the officers responsible for the suppression of criminals. Various civil as well as criminal courts functioned at the local level right from village to province. It seems most of the cases were disposed off at the village level by village elders. Police headquarters were present in all principal centres and *Bandhanagara* meant proper jail while *Charka* refers to police lock up. From the classical sources, we can establish that the judges also decided with utmost care the cases in which foreigners were concerned, and would come down sharply on those who took unfair advantage of them. Punishments to persons held guilty by the court were very severe. Decapitation, amputation of limbs, fines and forfeitures were the different types of punishment prevalent at that time. The nature of the punishment depended on the nature, gravity, circumstances and also on the *varna* of the offender and the plaintiff. Generally, the *dvija*/higher varnas were given lighter punishment than the lower ones, though in Pillar Edict 4 Ashoka claims that he had introduced *samata* (fairness) in judicial procedures. The same edict refers to a three-day respite for those who were condemned to death to appeal the decision, which indicates that death penalty was present even during Ashoka's time.

Four sources of law are mentioned by Kautilya:

- *Dharma* (sacred law) (royal proclamations)
- *Vyavahara* (usage)
- *Charitam* (custom and precedents)
- *Rajasasana* (royal edicts or orders)

7. Mitra (ally)

From the point of the *Vijigishu* (the would-be-conqueror) Kautilya discusses the inter-state policy and takes into account all possible circumstances. He lists *Shad-gunya* (six policies) that the king should follow in these circumstances:

a. Policy of *Sandhi* (peace treaty): If one is weaker than the enemy
b. Policy of *Vigraha* (hostility): If one is stronger than the enemy
c. Policy of *Asana* (keeping quiet): If one's power is equal to that of the enemy
d. Policy of *Yana* (marching on a military expedition): If one is much stronger than the enemy
e. Policy of *Samshraya* (seeking shelter with another king or in a fort): If one is very weak
f. Double policy of *Dvaidhibhava* (sandhi with one king and vigraha with another): If one can fight the enemy with the help of an ally

The Mauryas had great diplomatic relations with various Hellenistic kingdoms and even South Asian countries. Probably they had a full-fledged department of foreign affairs for the same. In Arthashastra, there is mention of certain diplomatic posts of:

a. *Nisriharthaduta* → Full-fledged ambassador
↓
b. *Parimitarthaduta* → Could not go beyond his instruction in negotiation
↓
c. *Sasanharaduta* → Special messenger

The Mauryan Society

As far as the society is concerned, despite the challenge posed by Buddhism and Jainism, the *varna* system continued to exist and *Brahmanas* and *Kshatriyas* dominated the social hierarchy. However, as a result of greater trade and commerce, there was improvement in the social status of Vaishyas or trading communities and Shudras. Now Shudras could be involved in the agricultural and artisanal activities. This period also saw increase in the number of untouchables, i.e. *Chandalas* and *Shvapakas* (dog breeders), also called *Antavasayin* (literally meaning living at the end). Surprisingly, there is no mention of either *Varna* or *Sati* in the Ashokan edicts.

Even though Megasthenes lauds the Indian society for not having any slaves, yet ironically, the fact is that slavery existed in India at that time. This is borne out by the *Arthashastra* which says that '*no Arya or freeman could be reduced to slavery*'. Reference to *dasas* (the slaves) in Ashokan inscriptions also bear testimony to the existence of the institution of slavery in Mauryan India. Ashokan edicts, while discussing *dhamma*, demands courteous behaviour towards dasas and *bhatakas/bhritakas* (servants). Kautilya lists various rules and penalties (if rules are broken) for the treatment of male and female slaves. For example, a man could not be a slave either by birth, by voluntarily selling himself, by being captured in war, or as a result of judicial punishment. Certain punishments were prescribed for selling or mortgaging a pregnant woman slave without arranging for her maternity. There is also reference of manumission[3] of slaves on payment of money. There were also instances of release from enslavement when a dasi bore her master a son, and the child was also considered the father's legitimate child.

Mauryan Art and Sculpture

The magnanimous Mauryan power was also visible in monumental stone sculptures and structures. Important beginnings were made in rock-cut and *stupa* architecture. In the Mauryan period, stone culture dramatically emerged as the principal medium of Indian arts. The Mauryan art was strongly linked with political and religious ideology of that time. The Maurya kings, especially Ashoka, highly patronised different art forms such as stone sculptures, ring stones, disc stones, terracotta figurines and *stupa* architecture. Ashoka played a major role in popularising the *stupa* cult. He not only redistributed the Buddha's relics to every important town, but also ordered construction of stupas over them. It is roughly estimated that he got built approximately 84,000 stupas. Ashoka's greatest innovation was the substitution of stone for wood and brick. Ashokan pillars at Rampurva, Lauriya Nandangarh and Sarnath present excellent examples of stone sculptures that developed in this period. All these pillars are circular and monolithic, and are made of sandstone found at *Chunar*, near Mirzapur in U.P. The Maurya period also saw the beginning of rock-cut architecture. The rock-cut architecture of Lomasha Risi cave in the Barabara hills near Gaya, and the majestic Dhauli caves (near Bhubaneswar, Odisha which contains the rock sculpture of the front part of an elephant) is magnificent. The famous *Vajrasana* (throne of meditation) at the Mahabodhi temple at Bodh Gaya probably belonged to this period. Among several stone and terracotta sculptures of this period, the polished stone sculpture of a female known as the Didarganj *Yakshini* (demi-gods and spirits; *Yakshinis* are generally regarded as fertility deities, and the female counterpart of Yakshas, who were the deities connected with water, trees, forest, wilderness and fertility) is the most famous one. Another important polished Chunar sandstone sculpture is of the torso of a nude male figure found at Lohanipur in Patna. The

[3] Act of freeing slaves by their owners.

stone portrait of Ashoka found at Kanaganahalli (near Sannati, Karnataka) is also spectacular. Universities of Taxila, Ujjain and Varanasi were the famous centres of learning. In the field of literature, Bhadrabahu's *Kalpasutra* is attributed to the Mauryan period. Lomasha Risi and Sudama caves of Gaya are other great examples of wooden architectural heritage. A large number of carved ring stones and disc stones which probably had religious and ritualistic significance have been found at various sites in northern India, such as Delhi, Patna, Taxila, Mathura, Vaishali and Kaushambi. They have different carvings arranged in two or more concentric circles and have different designs and geometric patterns.

FIGURE 6.8 Sanchi Stupa

FIGURE 6.9 Commemorative postal stamp of India depicting Didarganj Yakshi

The Maurya period also witnessed rapid development of material culture in the Gangetic plains. The new material culture of Gangetic basin was based on the intensive use of iron and iron implements (such as socketed axes, sickles, ploughshare and spoked wheel), prevalence of writing, use of punch-marked coins, NBPW pottery artifacts, introduction of burnt bricks and timber in construction (as reported by Megasthenes in his writings about the wooden structure at the Mauryan capital of Pataliputra) and ring wells (which supplied water to people for domestic use and also served as soak pits in congested settlements). The existence of inscriptions, occasional NBPW potsherds and punch-marked coins in parts of Bangladesh (Bogra district), Odisha (Sisupalgarh), Andhra (Amravati) and Karnataka points towards the spread of material culture to these peripheral areas too. Our national emblem is adopted from the four-lion capital (Fig. 6.10) of Ashokan pillar at Sarnath near Benaras. Megasthenes has described the grandeur of the Mauryan palace at Pataliputra.

FIGURE 6.10 Lion emblem on Ashoka Pillar, Hanging Garden, Maharashtra

Some remains of this palace, including the 80-pillared hall have been found at Kumrahar near Patna. The high technical skill attained by the Mauryan artisans is evident in the stone pillars' polish, which is as shining as the Northern Black Polished Ware (NBPW).

Mauryan art is also believed to have Achaemenid/Persian influence since the pillar inscriptions of Ashoka are very similar in form and style to the Persian king Darius' inscriptions. In fact, even the words *lipi* and *dipi* occur in the inscriptions of both Ashoka and Darius, and the inscriptions of both kings begin in the third person and then move to the first person. The polished surface and animal capitals of Ashokan pillars present another similarity. However, there are also differences between the Mauryan and Persian pillars as the Persian pillars stand on bases, either shaped like a bell (i.e. inverted lotus) or a plain rectangular or circular block while in case of Mauryan pillars the base is absent and the inverted lotus appears at the top of the shaft. The shape and ornamentation of the Mauryan lotus (typical bulge) is also different from the Persian ones (bulge is absent). Most of the Persian pillars have a fluted surface while Mauryan pillars are smooth. The Mauryan type abacus and independent animals carved in the round crowning are absent in the Persian context. The Mauryans thus made a remarkable contribution to art and architecture.

Decline of the Mauryas

The Mauryan empire began to disintegrate soon after the death of Ashoka around 232 BCE. Ashoka was succeeded by a chain of weak rulers since, surprisingly, after Ashoka, only one of the later Mauryas, i.e. king Dasaratha is known to have issued inscriptions. Several factors can be delineated which brought about the decline and fall of the Mauryan empire, such as:

a. Brahmanical reaction: The anti-sacrifice attitude of Buddhism and deriding of the superfluous rituals performed by them by Ashoka must have brought loss to the income and livelihood options of Brahmanas who used to live on the varied gifts made to them. Also, the appointment of *Dhamma Mahamattas* would have come in conflict with the *Brahmanas'* prestige as custodians of social morality and order. This naturally must have made Brahmanas hostile towards the Mauryas. They wanted a ruler who would uphold their existing interests and privileges. It is rather interesting to note that some of the new kingdoms that arose on the ruins of the Maurya empire were ruled by Brahmanas such as the Shungas and the Kanvas in Central India and the Satavahanas in the Deccan. Ashoka's pacifist policy also resulted in lack of preparedness of the army, and may have been a factor responsible for the success of Greek invasion. Harprasad Shastri too corroborates this view and holds Ashoka's pro-Buddhist and pacifist (peace) policy responsible for annoying the Brahmanas and resulting in the fall of Mauryan empire.

b. Oppressive rule in provinces: There have been instances of complaints by citizens of certain provinces regarding misrule by corrupt officials. The appointment of Ashoka as the viceroy of Taxila during Bindusara's reign to redress the grievances of citizens against *dushtamatyas* (wicked bureaucrats) is a good example. Similarly, the Kalinga edicts also point towards the fact that Ashoka was very concerned about oppression in the provinces and therefore advises his *Mahamattas* not to torture townsmen without due cause. The disturbing and outrageous fact that the last Maurya king Brihadratha was assassinated by his commander of army during an inspection of the troops, and there was probably not much hue and cry on the murder, further substantiates the claim that the later Mauryas were not very popular with the public.

c. Financial crisis: The enormous expenditure on maintaining such a large army and bureaucracy must have created a financial crisis for the Mauryan empire. The cost of establishing settlements on the newly cleared lands also must have strained the treasury (as the people settling on these lands initially were exempted from tax). D.D. Koshambi supports this view and feels that heavy economic pressure due to a vast army and bureaucracy may have resulted in a crisis.

d. Spread of material culture and new knowledge in the outlying areas: Once the new knowledge of iron tools and weapons spread in the peripheral areas, Magadha lost its special advantage. On the basis of material culture acquired from Magadha, new kingdoms such as the Shungas and Kanvas in Central India, the Chetis in Kalinga and the Satavahanas in the Deccan were founded and developed.

e. Neglect of the north-west frontier and absence of a boundary structure such as the Great Wall of China: The neglect of safeguarding of the passage on the north-west frontier cost the Mauryans dearly. In the third century BCE, a number of Central Asian nomadic tribes such as the Scythians were in a state of flux, and moved towards the settled empires of China and India in search of new terrains. The Chinese ruler Shih Huang Ti (247–210 BCE) in about 220 BCE constructed the Great Wall of China to protect his empire against the Scythian attack. Since such measures were not taken by Ashoka on the north-western frontier of India, in order to escape the Scythians, the Parthians, the Shakas and the Greeks were forced to move towards India. The Greeks were first to invade India in 206 BCE and they set up their kingdom in north Afghanistan called *Bactria*.

QUESTIONS FROM LAST YEAR'S PRELIMS

1. According to Kautilya's Arthashastra, which of the following are correct? **(2022)**

1. A person could be a slave as a result of a judicial punishment.
2. If a female slave bore her master a son, she was legally free.
3. If a son born to a female slave was fathered by her master, the son was entitled to the legal status of the master's son.

Which of the statements given above are correct?

(a) 1 and 2 only (b) 2 and 3 only
(c) 1 and 3 only (d) 1, 2 and 3

2. Consider the following pairs: **(2022)**

Site of Ashoka's major rock edicts		*Location in the State of*
1 Dhauli	–	Odisha
2 Erragudi	–	Andhra Pradesh
3 Jaugada	–	Madhya Pradesh
4 Kalsi	–	Karnataka

How many pairs given above are correctly matched?

(a) Only one pair
(b) Only two pairs
(c) Only three pairs
(d) All four pairs

3. Who among the following rulers advised his subjects through this inscription? **(2020)**

"Whosoever praises his religious sect or blames other sects out of excessive devotion to his own sect, with the view of glorifying his own sect, he rather injures his own sect very severely."

(a) Ashoka
(b) Samudragupta
(c) Harshavardhana
(d) Krishnadeva Raya

4. In which of the following relief sculpture inscriptions 'Ranyo Ashoka' (King Ashoka) mentioned along with the stone portrait of Ashoka? **(2019)**

(a) Kanganahalli (b) Sanchi
(c) Shahbazgarhi (d) Sohgaura

5. Who of the following had first deciphered the edicts of Emperor Ashoka? **(2016)**

(a) Georg Buhler (b) James Prinsep
(c) Max Muller (d) William Jones

6. With reference to the art and archaeological history of India, which one among the following was made earliest? **(2015)**

(a) Lingaraja Temple at Bhubaneswar
(b) Rock-cut elephant at Dhauli
(c) Rock-cut monuments at Mahabalipuram
(d) Varaha image at Udaygiri

7. The ancient Indian play Mudrarakshasa of Visakhadutta has its subject as **(2002)**

(a) a conflict between Gods and demons of ancient Hindu lore
(b) a romantic story of an Aryan prince and a tribal woman
(c) the story of the power struggle between two Aryan tribes
(d) the court intrigues at the time of Chandragupta Maurya

8. The Ashokan major edicts which tell us about the Sangam kingdom include rock edicts **(1998)**

(a) I and X (b) I and XI
(c) II and XIII (d) II and XIV

9. Which one of the following ancient Indian records is the earliest royal order to preserve food grains to be utilised during the crises in the country? **(1998)**

(a) Saugaura Copper Plate
(b) Rummindei Pillar edict of Ashoka
(c) Prayaga Prashati
(d) Mehrauli Pillar inscription of Chandra

10. Which one of the following edicts mentions the personal name of Ashoka? **(1998)**

(a) Kalsi
(b) Rummindei
(c) Special Kalinga edict
(d) Maski

11. Which one of the following scripts of ancient India was written from right to left? **(1997)**

(a) Brahmi (b) Nandnagiri
(c) Sharada (d) Kharosthi

12. Which one of the following statements regarding Ashokan stone pillars is incorrect? **(1997)**
(a) These are highly polished.
(b) These are monolithic.
(c) The shaft of pillars is tapering in shape.
(d) These are parts of architectural structures.

13. The name by which Ashoka is generally referred to in his inscriptions is **(1995)**
(a) Chakravarti (b) Dharmadeva
(c) Dharmakirti (d) Piyadassi

ANSWERS

1. (b)	2. (b)	3. (a)	4. (a)	5. (b)	6. (b)	7. (d)	8 (c)
9. (a)	10. (d)	11. (d)	12. (d)	13. (d)			

QUESTIONS FROM LAST YEAR'S MAINS

1. Discuss the significance of the lion and bull figures in Indian mythology, art and architecture. **(2022 GS1)**

2. Delineate the nature and impact of India's contact with western Asia and the Mediterranean world during the Mauryan period. **(History optional, 2015)**

3. Discuss different interpretations of historians about the nature of Ashoka's 'dhamma'. Did his principle of dhamma-vijaya render the Mauryan empire militaristically weak?
(History optional, 2014)

4. Examine the role of adhyaksha in the Mauryan administration.
(History optional, 2012)

5. Assess the role of guilds and trade organisations in the development of early Indian economy.
(History optional, 2010)

PRACTICE QUESTIONS – PRELIMS

1. In which one among the following Ashokan edicts is the Kalinga war mentioned?
(a) Pillar edict 6 (b) Rock edict 13
(c) Rock edict 11 (d) Pillar edict 1

2. Which of the following statements are true about Ashoka?
(i) He was viceroy of Taxila before he became king.
(ii) Kalinga war fought in 261 BCE changed his outlook towards violence.
(iii) In his inscriptions, he is mostly referred to as Ashoka and not Piyadassi.
(iv) He sent his son Mahinda to China for propagating Buddhism.
(a) i and ii (b) All of the above
(c) ii, iii and iv (d) None of the above

3. Consider the following statements and mark the option which is correct.
(i) Slavery did not exist during Mauryan times.
(ii) The Mauryas had an elaborate administrative structure.
(iii) Generally royal princes were appointed as viceroys.
(iv) Certain tests were conducted to test the suitability of the officers for different jobs.
(a) All of the above
(b) ii, iii and iv
(c) None of the above
(d) i, ii and iii

4. Match the following:

(i)	Mahamattas	(A)	Village headmen
(ii)	Adhyaksha	(B)	Ministers/high officials
(iii)	Anta-mahamattas	(C)	Superintendent
(iv)	Gramika	(D)	Frontier areas in-charge

(a) (A)–i, (B)–ii, (C)–iii, (D)–iv
(b) (A)–iii, (B)–i, (C)–ii, (D)–iv
(c) (A)–iv, (B)–i, (C)–ii, (D)–iii
(d) (A)–i, (B)–iv, (C)–iii, (D)–iii

5. Match the following:

(i)	Dhamma Mahamatta	(A)	District level officers
(ii)	Akshapatala	(B)	Special cadre of dhamma-preaching officers
(iii)	Rajukas	(C)	Audit and records office
(iv)	Yuktas	(D)	Clerks

(a) (A)–i, (B)–ii, (C)–iii, (D)–iv
(b) (A)–iii, (B)–i, (C)–ii, (D)–iv
(c) (A)–ii, (B)–iii, (C)–iv, (D)–i
(d) (A)–i, (B)–iv, (C)–iii, (D)–iii

6. Consider the following statements and mark the option which is incorrect.
(i) Chanakya wrote Indica and Arthashastra.
(ii) The Mauryas had a great standing army and people from all varnas were recruited in the army.
(iii) Taxes were paid in cash only.
(iv) Salaries were paid in kind.
(a) All of the above
(b) ii and iii
(c) None of the above
(d) i, iii and iv

7. Consider the following statements and mark the option which is correct.
(i) Kautilya laid down a Saptanga theory of administration.
(ii) Ashoka believed in autocratic rule and not paternal despotism.
(iii) Bindusara is also known as the conqueror of the land between two seas.
(iv) Indica is survived in fragments and tells us about the Mauryan ways and life.
(a) All of the above
(b) i, iii and iv
(c) None of the above
(d) i, ii and iii

8. Match the following:

(i)	Bindusara	(A)	Amitraghat
(ii)	Ashoka	(B)	Devanam Piyadassi
(iii)	Chandragupta Maurya	(C)	Sandrocuttus
(iv)	Chanakya	(D)	Vishnugupta

(a) (A)–i, (B)–ii, (C)–iii, (D)–iv
(b) (A)–iii, (B)–i, (C)–ii, (D)–iv

(c) (A)–ii, (B)–iii, (C)–iv, (D)–i
(d) (A)–i, (B)–iv, (C)–iii, (D)–iii

9. Match the following:

(i)	Bindusara	(A)	Propagated Buddhism to Ceylon
(ii)	Ashoka	(B)	Converted to Jainism
(iii)	Chandragupta Maurya	(C)	Great statesman
(iv)	Chanakya	(D)	Joined Ajivika Sect

(a) (A)–i, (B)–ii, (C)–iii, (D)–iv
(b) (A)–iii, (B)–i, (C)–ii, (D)–iv
(c) (A)–ii, (B)–iii, (C)–iv, (D)–i
(d) (A)–i, (B)–iv, (C)–iii, (D)–iii

10. Consider the following statements and mark the option which is correct.
(i) Inscriptions of Ashoka were written in Pali and Prakrit only.
(ii) Girnar inscription relates to a provincial governor, Pushyamitra Sunga, of Chandragupta's reign.
(iii) Rummindei inscription mentions of Ashoka's visit to Lumbini.
(iv) Nigali Sagar Inscription mentions of enlargement of Stupa.
(a) All of the above
(b) i, iii and iv
(c) iii and iv
(d) i, ii and iii

11. Consider the following statements and mark the option which is incorrect.
(i) Dashratha was the last Maurya king who was killed by Pushyamitra Sunga.
(ii) Girnar inscription of Saurashtra relates to a provincial governor, Pushyagupta, of Chandragupta's reign.
(iii) Chandragupta had defeated Seleucus Nikator.
(iv) Ashoka preached about non-violence and disbanded his army.
(a) All of the above
(b) ii and iii
(c) iii and iv
(d) i, ii and iii

ANSWERS

1. (b) 2. (a) 3. (a) 4. (c) 5. (b) 6. (d) 7. (b) 8. (a)
9. (c) 10. (c) 11. (b)

PRACTICE QUESTIONS – MAINS

1. What were the probable reasons of decline of the Mauryan empire? Elucidate.

2. Describe the contribution of the Mauryas to the field of art and architecture, and the significance of Mauryan empire in the history of India.

3. Ashoka's dhamma was different than the Brahmanical dharma or Buddhist dhamma. Do you agree with this statement? Give reasons for your answers.

4. Explain the administrative structure of the Mauryan empire giving references from Kautilya's saptanga theory.

CHAPTER

7

Political and Cultural Developments During c. 200 BCE–300 CE

The period between c. 200 BCE–300 CE did not witness the emergence of a large empire like that of the Mauryas, but it is notable for many other historical, political and cultural achievements. This period is marked by a shift in political focus from Magadha to north-western India. It saw a series of invasions and the rise of many regional kingdoms, as well as the emergence of new traditions of governance such as joint rule and subordinate rule. This is also a period when cities expanded and urban culture gained a certain predominance. There was an increase in specialised crafts and a marked expansion of trade networks. The economy saw an increasing use of currency. This was, furthermore, a period defined by the intermingling and influence of new cultures, vibrant doctrinal debates, the rise in devotional worship of images and the institutionalisation of religious activity. The period also saw the emergence of sophisticated sculptural and architectural styles. The period, in short, contributed much to the rich and versatile heritage of the sub-continent as we know it today.

Political History of North India

As we have discussed earlier, the last Maurya king Brihadartha was murdered in 187 BCE by his own commander-in-chief, Pushyamitra Sunga while he was inspecting his troops. The Maurya rule thus came to an end and the Sunga Dynasty was established as the rulers of Magadha. It is pertinent to note that Pushyamitra's empire extended over only part of the erstwhile Maurya empire, including Pataliputra, Ayodhya, Vidisha and some parts of modern day Punjab (like Jalandhar and *Sakala*, or Sialkot as it is known now). The Sungas are considered *Brahmanas* in their caste origins, and they are referred to in both Buddhist and Brahminical texts such as the *Harshacharita*, the *Brihadaranyaka Upanishad*, Panini's *Ashtadhyayi*, Kalidasa's *Malavikaagnimitram*, *Divyavadana* and Tarantha's (a Buddhist scholar) account. The ten Sunga kings ruled, in all likelihood, for a total of 112 years.

Sunga Dynasty (185 BCE–148 BCE)

Brihadratha (last Mauryan ruler)

Pushyamitra Sunga (killed Brihadratha, founder of the Sunga Dynasty)

- Formerly the commander-in-chief of the Mauryan Army.
- He performed two Ashvamedha sacrifices, as mentioned in the Ayodhya stone inscription of King Dhana.
- His dominions extended as far as the Narmada river to the south, and included cities such as Pataliputra, Ayodhya and Vidisha. The drama *Malavikaagnimitram* mentions the conflict between Pushyamitra and Yajnasena, the king of Vidarbha (eastern Maharashtra) and the victory of the Sungas over them.
- He defeated the Bactrian Greek king, Demetrius. This encounter is mentioned in Patanjali's works (who refers to the *yavanas*, that is, foreigners from west coming up to Ayodhya and Chittor) as well as in Kaildasa's *Malavikaagnimitram* (which narrates the incident of the challenging of Pushyamitra's Ashvamedha horse by the *yavanas*, which led to a military encounter between prince Vasumitra, the son of Agnimitra, and the *yavana* army).
- Patanjali, the notable grammarian who wrote the *Mahabhasya* was a contemporary of Pushyamitra Sunga.
- The Divyavadana gives an account of Pushyamitra's cruelty towards Buddhists and his hatred towards Buddhism.

Agnimitra

- The hero of Kalidasa's *Malavikagnimitram*, described in this drama as the viceroy of Vidisha.

Bhagabhadra/Bhagavata

- Probably the fifth king Kasiputa Bhagabhadra, or the ninth king Bhagavata, as indicated by the notable Besnagar Pillar inscription[1] of Heliodorus. Heliodorus was the Greek Ambassdor of the Indo-Greek ruler Amtalakita/Antialkidas of Taxila, who probably stayed at Sunga's court. In this inscription *he describes himself as a Bhagavata, that is, a worshipper of Lord Krishna and Garuda (Vishnu's vehicle), and declares that he had set up this pillar in honour of this god.*

FIGURE 7.1 Heliodorus Pillar at Vidisha

Devabhuti

- Also known as Devabhumi and was the last ruler of the Sunga Dynasty.
- According to the *Harschcharita*, he was killed by his *Brahmana* minister Vasudeva Kanva, who founded the Kanva dynasty. In parts of the central India, remnants of the Sunga empire were replaced by the Satavahanas.

[1] Also known as *Garudadhawaja* Inscription.

Kanva Dynasty

Vasudeva

- Supposed to be a descendent of Rishi Kanva and ruled from Pataliputra.
- We know virtually nothing about the Kanvas except for the rather cursory references to them in later texts.
- Also described as the *Sungabhrityas* (literally meaning 'servants of the Sungas').
- They made way for the Mitras in c. 30 BCE, who were eventually dislodged by the Shakas in Magadha.

According to some scholars, the last Kanva ruler Susharman was overthrown by a successor of Simuka of the Satavahana dynasty. Around the same time, that is, 200 BCE, there were invasions by various groups of people based in Central Asia and western China. These were *Indo-Greeks*, the *Scythians* or the *Shakas*, the *Parthians* or the *Pahlavas* and the *Kushanas*. These invasions not only changed the political structure of north-west India, but also aided in the transmission and transformation of cultural elements of both India and the central Asian region.

Indo–Greeks/Bactrian Greeks

After the death of Alexander in 323 BCE, many Greeks came to settle on the north-western borders of India with Bactria (presently northern part of Afghanistan, the area lying to the south of the Oxus river and to the north-west of the Hindu Kush mountains). The rulers of Bactria came to be called the Bactrian Greeks, because of their Hellenistic (Greek) ancestry as they were originally *satraps* (subordinate rulers) of the Seleucid Empire of West Asia. Around the 3rd century BCE, Diodotus I (the governor of Bactria) revolted against the Antiochus, the Seleucid king, and established an independent Bactrian Greek kingdom. Later, around c.145 BCE, on account of growing pressure from the Scythian tribes, the Bactrian Greeks lost their hold over Bactria, but continued to rule for few decades over the north-western part of the sub-continent. These Bactrian Greeks who ruled over parts of north-west India between the 2nd century BCE and the early 1st century BCE are known as the Indo-Greeks.

As we have discussed in the earlier chapter, with the construction of Chinese Wall, the Scythians were pushed back from the China and they turned their attention towards the neighbouring Greeks and Parthians. Thus, in order to escape the wrath of the nomadic Scythian tribes, the Bactrian Greeks were forced to invade India. Since the successors of Ashoka were too weak to hold ground, a series of invasions on the north-western border of India started. In the beginning of the 2nd century BCE, the Indo-Greeks were the first to invade India. They occupied a large part of north-western India, much larger than that conquered by Alexander, and it is believed that they pushed forward to as far as Ayodhya and Pataliputra. They were the first to issue gold coins and much of their lineage is determined on the basis of excavated coins which include coins of silver, copper and nickel as well. It is rather interesting to note that out of the 42 Indo-Greek kings, as many as 34 are known only through their coins. The large number of kings within a short span of time suggests that some of them ruled concurrently, and thus it is probable that two Greek dynasties ruled the north-western India on parallel lines simultaneously.

Demetrius (King of Bactria)

- Invaded India around 190 BCE and probably also came into conflict with Pushyamitra Shunga.
- Conquered a considerable part of the Mauryan empire in north-western India and extended Bactrian rule to the south of the Hindu Kush.

Menander/Milinda/Minedra (165 BCE–145 BCE)

- The most celebrated Indo-Greek ruler who not only stabilised Indo-Greek power, but also extended his empire's frontiers in India.
- His empire extended over parts of both Bactria and north-western India and appears to have included southern Afghanisthan and Gandhara, the region west of the River Indus.
- Had his capital at *Sakala* (modern Sialkot, Punjab), and it is believed that he also invaded and conquered the Ganga-Yamuna doab but failed to retain it for long. Another important city under his domain was Mathura.
- He was converted to Buddhism by Nagasena who has been identified with the King Milinda mentioned in the famous Buddhist text *Milindapanho* (*Question of Milinda*), which contains philosophical questions that Milinda asked Nagasena (the Buddhist author of the text). The text claims that impressed by the answers, the king accepted Buddhism[2] as his religion.
- He is also identified with King Minedra mentioned in a fragmented Kharosthi inscription found on a casket at Bajaur (presently in the North-West Frontier Province of Pakistan), which refers to the enshrining of relics of the Buddha, probably in a *stupa*, during his reign.

Hermaius (Last ruler of this dynasty)

- He was defeated by the Parthians around the last quarter of the 2nd century BCE, which led to the end of Greek rule in Bactria and the area to the south of the Hindu Kush.

However, it should be noted that Indo-Greek rule continued in north-western India for some more time. There is mention of Queen Agathokleia (probably one of the queens of Menander I) and her son Strato, whose joint coins have been found. This north-west Gandhara region was also lost to Parthians and Shakas in due course of time. Later, in the late 1st century BCE or the early 1st century CE, the remaining part of their territory, that is, the area to the east of the Jhelum was also ceded to the Kshatrapa ruler Rajuvula.

[2] Became follower of Mahayana Buddhism.

Impact of Indo-Greek Rule

a. The Indo-Greeks were the first rulers in India to issue coins (gold, silver, copper and nickel) which can be definitely attributed to any dynasty and were also the first to issue gold coins in India (which increased in number under the Kushanas). Interestingly, the coins of the Shakas, Parthians and the Kshatrapas followed the basic features of Indo-Greek coinage, including the bilingual and bi-script legends. Indo-Greek coins were miniatures of aesthetic excellence, of precise economic value and also providing useful information on emerging religious sects and cults (specially *Shaiva* and *Bhagvata* sects) that were prominent in that area. Coinage was also adjusted to region and requirement. For instance:

The Indo-Greek coins which were circulated to the north of the Hindu Kush	The Indo-Greek coins which were circulated to the south of the Hindu Kush
(a) Were made of gold, silver, copper and nickel	Were made of silver and copper, and were often square in shape
(b) Followed the Attic weight standard and had Greek legends.	Had bilingual inscriptions in Greek and Kharoshthi (rarely in Brahmi) and followed an Indian weight standard.
(c) Had royal portraits on the obverse and images of Greek deities (such as Zeus, Apollo and Athena) on the reverse along with the name and title of the king.	Royal portrait occurs on the obverse side, but the motifs on the reverse include religious symbols that were Indian rather than Greek in inspiration.

b. They introduced new features of Hellenistic art and literature such as Gandhara art in the north-west frontier of India, which was not purely Greek, but rather it was the outcome of the intermingling and influence of both Indian and central Asian contacts. A striking instance of this mingling is the Besnagar Pillar inscription of Heliodorus. New terms which had the influence of Greek terminology began to be used in the sub-continent. For instance, the term '*horshastra*' used for astrology in Sanskrit is derived from Greek word 'horoscope'.

c. The Hellenistic Greeks are also known for their monumental buildings and their small, finely-crafted objects. Excavation of the cities of Ai-Khanoum (located on the confluence of the Oxus and the Kokcha of modern Balkh), Antioch, and Sirkap at Taxila, reveal a great talent of urban planning.

FIGURE 7.2 Gandhara Image of Buddha

d. The Indo-Greeks also introduced practice of military governorship (the governors were called strategos/*satraps*).

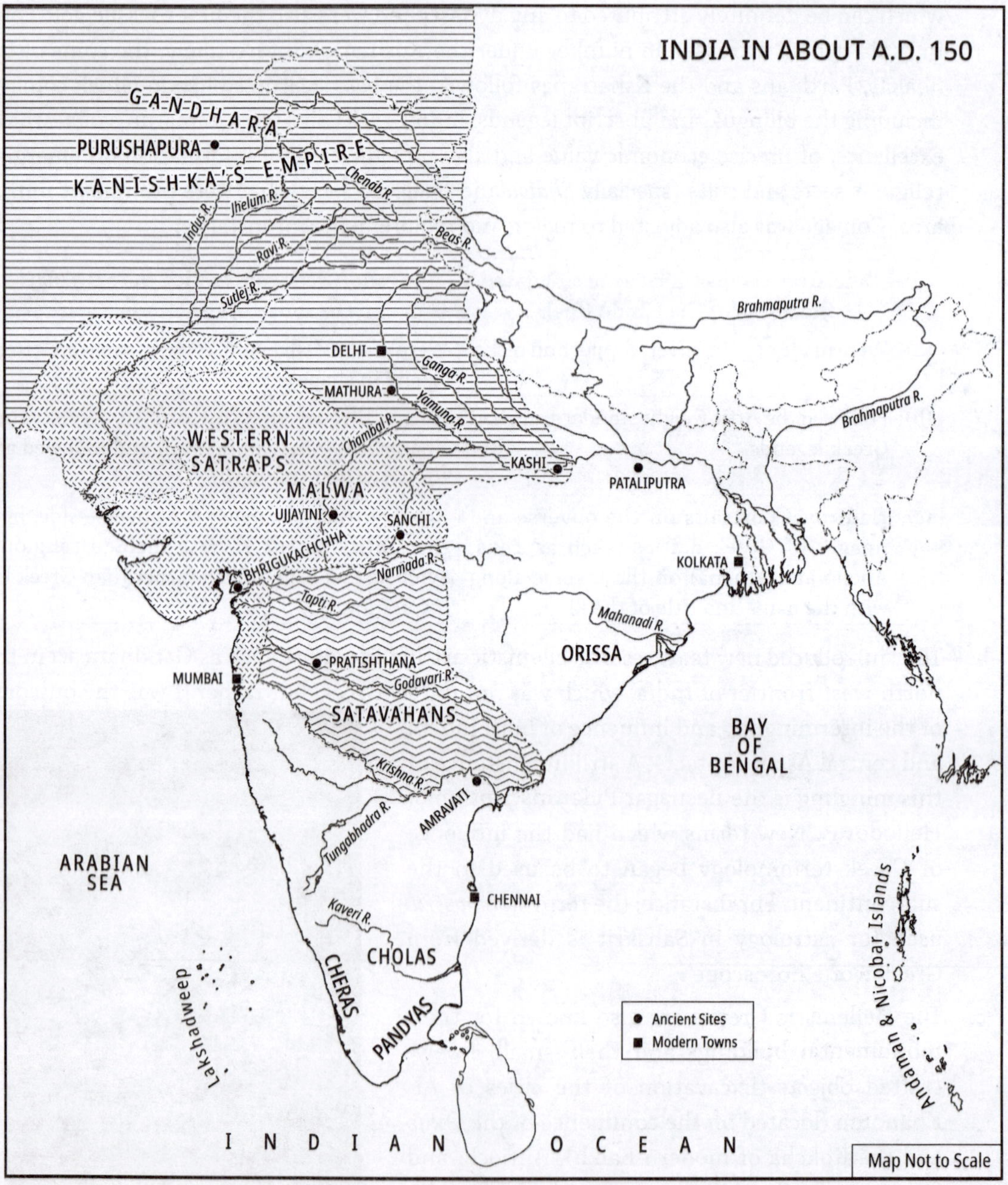

FIGURE 7.3 Indo Scythian Kingdom

The Shakas/Scythians

'Shaka' is the Indian term used for the people called the Scythians, who originally belonged to Central Asia. Interestingly, Patanjali in his Mahabhasya refers to the Shakas as 'Anirvasita (pure) Shudras'. The Greeks were followed by the Shakas to India, and they controlled a much larger area as compared to the Greeks. In the late 2nd century BCE, as we have discussed earlier, the decline of the Greek kingdoms (Seleucid empire) in the north-west coincided with the attack on Bactria by nomadic tribal people from central Asia, that is, the Hsiung-nu/Xiongnu, Wu-sun and Yueh-chis (the tribal stock to which the Kushanas too belonged). It is believed that in the first century BCE, on account of excessive snow and continuous raids by their neighbours, the Hsiang-nu suffered famine. This led to their migration and the displacement of the Yueh-Chis, who were driven from their best lands and had to migrate to distant places. The Yueh-Chis were further split into two branches, the Little Yueh-chis (who settled in northern Tibet) and the Great Yueh-chis who went further west, to the shores of the Aral Sea and the plains of the Syr Darya (Jaxartes), displacing the original inhabitants of that area, that is, the Scythians/the Shakas. The Shakas advanced into Bactria, Parthia and the Indus plains. There were five branches of the Shakas who finally settled with their seats of power in different parts of India and Afghanistan:

a. One branch of the Shakas settled in Afghanistan. Prominent rulers of this branch were Vonones and Spalirises.

b. The second branch settled in Punjab with Taxila as their capital. Maues was a prominent ruler.

c. The third branch settled in Mathura, where it ruled for about two centuries. Azilises was a prominent ruler.

d. The fourth branch established its hold over western India where they ruled until 4 century CE. They ruled for the maximum period on account of a flourishing economy based on the sea-borne trade in Gujarat and thus issued a large number of silver coins. One of the prominent rulers was Rudradaman I, belonging to the Shaka Kshatrapas of western Indian lineage.

e. The fifth branch of the Shakas established its power in the upper Deccan.

These complicated migrations and movements of people from central Asia had a ripple effect in the polity of the Indian sub-continent.

Hsiung-nu ⟶ Yueh-Chis ⟶ The Great Yueh-chis ⟶ The Shakas ⟶ The Parthians

The history of Shaka rule is known largely through inscriptions and coins. On the basis of coins, certain kings who can be identified are Vonones (the earliest independent Parthian ruler of eastern Iran), Spalirises, Azes I, Azilises and Azes II. Some coins even suggest the practice of conjoined rule as well. For instance, Spalirises and Azes I were probably co-rulers, as were Azes I and Azilises. Some prominent Shaka kings are:

Maues/Moga/Moa (c. 80 BCE)

- Probably the first Shaka king in India who established power in Gandhara.
- Inscription found at Taxila mentions a Shaka king, Moga, and his *kshatrapa/satrap* (governor), Patika. His name also appeared on several copper and silver coins. His coins carried figures of typically Indian deities like *Abhisheka Laxmi*.

Azes

- Successfully annexed the territory in northern India of the last of the Indo-Greek king Hippostratos.
- He is also believed to be associated with the Vikram Samvat era of 58 BCE, which is used to mark Azes' accession. This era was earlier reckoned with the victory of an Ujjain king named Vikramaditya over the Shakas. It is believed that Vikramaditya effectively fought against the Shakas when all other Indian rulers surrendered in front of them and from that time onwards, '*Vikramaditya*[3]' became a coveted title just like '*Caesar*' for Romans.

The Shakas and Scytho-Parthians ruled through *kshatrapas* (governors) or *mahakshatrapas* (subordinate rulers), who aided a lot in the expansion of the empire. For instance, during the reign of the Scytho-Parthian ruler Azilises, a *kshatrapa* Rajuvula aided a lot in the eastward expansion of his empire. Later, he took title of *mahakshatrapa* and functioned as an independent ruler of the Mathura region and was succeeded by his son Sodasha to the throne of Mathura. It is pertinent to note that these *kshatrapas* had a more independent status than was normal for an administrative governor, since they not only issued their own inscriptions in whatever era they wished to observe, but were also permitted to mint their own coins. Another official title, *meridarch*, was used for an officer in charge of a designated area.

The Scytho-Parthians/*Shaka-Pahlavas*

In mid-1st century CE, the Shakas' domination in north-west India was followed by that of the Parthians, though in comparison with the Greeks and the Shakas they occupied a very small portion of north-western India. In many ancient Sanskrit texts, they are mentioned together as the *Shaka-Pahlavas*. Interestingly, for some time, both ruled concurrently. Generally, the term *Shaka-Pahlava*/Scytho-Parthians is used for different groups of invaders who came from Parthia into north-west India in the 1st century CE. Originally, the Parthians lived in Iran and invaded India at the beginning of the Christian era. Gondophernes/Guduvhara (mentioned in an inscription dated 45 CE found at Takht-i-Bahi, recovered from Mardan near Peshawar) was the most famous and important Parthian king and it was during his reign that St. Thomas came to

[3] Whoever achieved anything great adopted this title just as the Roman emperors adopted the title Caesar to demonstrate their great power. As a result of this practice, we have as many as 14 Vikramaditya in Indian history, with Chandrgupta II of the Gupta dynasty being the most famous of them.

India to propagate Christianity. On his coins, there is also mention of his nephew Abdagases, his governors Sapadana and Satavastra, his military governors Aspavarman and Sasa. In due course of time, the Parthians, like the Shakas, became assimilated into the Indian society and became an integral part of it. The Kushanas ultimately ousted the successors of Gondophernes from north-western India.

The Kushanas

The Kushanas were also referred as *Yueh–Chis* (Moon tribe) or *Tocharians*, who were one of the five clans (Kuei-shang) into which the *Yue-chi* tribe was divided. They were nomadic tribal people who were originally from the steppes of north Central Asia. The Kushanas first occupied Bactria (or north Afghanistan), where they displaced the Shakas, and gradually seized Gandhara, replacing the rule of the Greeks and the Parthians in these areas. Ultimately, they set up their authority over the lower Indus basin and the greater part of the Gangetic basin. Their empire extended from the river Oxus to the river Ganga, from Khorasan in Central Asia to Varanasi in Uttar Pradesh (almost the area of nine modern countries).

Kujula Kadphises/Kadphises I (15 CE–64 CE)

- He amalgamated the five clans of *Yue-chi* tribe and laid the foundations of a unified Kushana empire.
- He minted coins in copper and believed to have imitated the Roman '*aurei*' type coins to facilitate trade.
- His coins have been found south of the Hindu Kush, which suggest that during his reign the Kushanas probably started their movement towards Indian sub-continent.
- His coins also suggest an association with Buddhism.
- He adopted the epithet '*dharmathida*' and '*sachadharmathida*'.

Vima Kadphises/Wema Kadphises II (64 CE–78 CE)

- He was the son of Kadphises I and started as a co-ruler with his father for some time but later also ruled independently. He conquered Gandhara from the Parthians and further spread the kingdom to the east of the Indus till Mathura region. The political significance of Kanishka's rule lies in the fact that he integrated central Asia with north India as a part of a single empire. It resulted in the intermingling of different cultures and increase in inter-regional trading activities.
- He issued a large number of gold coins.
- He was a firm devotee of Shiva and proclaimed himself as 'Mahishvara' on his coins.
- All his coins (both gold and copper) have unmistakable sign of Shiva with his trident bull.

Kanishka (78 CE–101 CE)

- He was the son of Kadphises II and is perhaps the most famous Kushana king, under whose reign the Kushana empire reached its zenith. It expanded from Central Asia to Afghanistan and north-western India to further east into the Ganga valley and southwards into the Malwa region, and included Varanasi, Kaushambi and Shravasti in Uttar Pradesh and Sanchi in Madhya Pradesh. The centre of this huge empire was Bactria, as evident in the use of the Bactrian language in Kanishka's coins and inscriptions.

FIGURE 7.4 Kanishka Coin

- The famous Rabatak inscription (in modern Baghran province, Afghanistan) presents valuable information on Kanishka.
- Adopted the title of 'Devputra', and has been shown wearing a 'peaked helmet' on some coins.
- Kanishka had two capitals:
    - Purushapura (present day Peshawar): He built a giant *stupa* to house the Buddha's relics in the city of Purushpura. The building was still intact with all its magnificence when the Chinese pilgrim Fa-Hien visited the area later in the early fifth century CE.
    - Mathura
- He is remembered for two major reasons:
    - Started the Shaka era (78 CE), which is accepted as the beginning of his reign, and which is now used by the Government of India for its calendar. The probable explanation as to why the name Shaka era and not Kushana era probably lies in the belief that either Kanishka was mistakenly considered a Shaka, or that the era was in continuous use throughout the reigns of the Shakas *kshatrapas* of Western India, who acknowledged the overlordship of the Kushanas.
    - Held the fourth Buddhist council at Kundalavana (near Srinagar in Jammu and Kashmir) under the presidency of Vasumitra. Kanishka was a great patron of Buddhism[4]. It was in this council that Buddhism was split into two schools – the Hinayana and the Mahayana. According to legends, it was Passa, a Buddhist monk who advised Kanishka to commence the fourth Buddhist Council.

[4] Kanishka was a great patron of Mahayana Buddhism.

- He patronised great scholars and eminent personalities of that era such as:
  a. Ashvagosha: A Buddhist scholar who wrote the hagiographic *Buddhacharita* (the sacred biography of the Buddha) and composed the *Saundarananda* (a Sanskrit *kavya*).
  b. Charaka: He is known as the father of Ayurveda who wrote a book on medicine called *Charaksamhita* and also wrote the *Sasruta*.
  c. Vasumitra: An eminent philosopher who authored the encyclopaedia of Buddhist philosophy called *Mahavibhasa*.
  d. Nagarjuna: He is often termed an Indian Einstein who proposed the Theory of Relativity in his time in the form of a *Sutra*, the *Prajna Parimata Sutra*. He was also a great exponent of the Mahayana doctrine and propounded the *Madhyamaka* (also known as *Sunyavada* school) which focuses on *sunyata* or *emptiness*
  e. Mathara: He was a minister who was noted for his unusual intelligence.
  f. Ageoilaus: A Greek engineer under whose guidance, it is believed, the great *stupa* of Purushapura was built.
- Kanishka also patronised the Gandhara and Mathura schools of sculpture. At Mathura, a headless statue of Kanishka depicting him as a warrior been found.
- He controlled the famous Silk Route in Central Asia.

China → Central Asia → Afghanistan → Iran → Western Asia (part of the Roman Empire)

- Another striking aspect of Kanishka's personality was his attitude of religious tolerance as the king's coinage depicts motifs drawn from a great variety of religious traditions: Indian (the motifs of the *Shiva* and the *Buddha*), Greek (motifs of Greek deities such as *Helios*, a sun god and *Selene*, moon goddess), and West Asian (such as motifs of Persian gods *Atash*, fire god, and *Mithra*, sun god).
- Towards the end of his long reign, it appears that he led an unsuccessful military expedition into Central Asia against the Chinese and was defeated by General Pan-chao and was forced to pay tribute to Chinese emperor Ho-ti.

Vasudeva II (last Kushana emperor)

- The immediate successors of Kanishka were Vasishka, Huvishka, Kanishka II (who adopted the title of 'Kaiser') and Vasudeva I, who during his reign, around the mid-2nd century CE took the title *Shaono Shao Vasudevo Koshano*, which indicates that by this time the Kushanas were totally Indianised. Also, it was during his reign that the empire started declining. The names of these rulers and those of various *kshtatrapas* and *mahakshtrapas* are found on a number of Kharoshthi inscriptions on a massive rock at Hunza (located between the Karakoram highway and the Hunza river).

Kushana power gradually declined from the early third century CE. The Kushana empire in Afghanistan and in the area west of the Indus was supplanted by the Sassanian power[5] (of Iran) in the mid-3rd century CE. However, some remnants of the Kushanas lingered on in the Kabul valley, Kapisa and Bactria till as late as the 4th century. The decline of the Kushanas led to the resurfacing of several polities of both monarchies and Ganas in different parts of north India (as evident from the coins, seals and inscriptions) which had been temporarily subdued by them such as:

a. The Shaka Kshatrapas in western and central India.
b. The Arjunayanas in Bharatpur and Alwar area.
c. The Malavas in Punjab and some portions of adjacent Rajasthan.
d. The Yaudheya *Gana* in Eastern Punjab and the adjoining areas of Uttar Pradesh and Rajasthan.
e. The Naga Kings in and around Padmavati region (identified with Pawaya in modern Gwalior district, Madhya Pradesh).

The Shaka Kshatrapas of Western India

As discussed earlier, the Syctho-Parthians ruled through their *kshatrapas* (viceroys) and *mahakshatrapas* (subordinate rulers). In the early centuries CE, there were two important lines of *kshatrapa* rulers - *the* Kshaharatas and *the* Kardamakas who continued to have a hold over parts of western India during and after the Kushana period.

The Kshaharatas

The prominent rulers belonging to this dynasty included:

Bhumaka (around c.78 CE)

- Originally owed allegiance to Kanishka.
- His coins, with legends in Brahmi and Kharoshthi, have been found at Malwa, Ajmer area and coastal Gujarat.

Nahapana (c.119–25 CE)

- Progressed in his career from *kshatrapa* to *mahakshatrapa* and ultimately to *rajan* (king).
- His kingdom probably had its capital at Minnagara (modern Doha located between Ujjain and Broach) and included Malwa, Gujarat, Saurashtra, northern Maharashtra, parts of Rajasthan and lower Indus valley. An inscription of one of his *amatyas* named Aryaman has been found at Pune district.

[5] A Sassanian Inscription of 262 CE uses the term Hindustan for this region. Thus, the term Hindustan used for India in Mughal and modern times was first used in the 3rd century CE.

- His coins have been found at Ajmer, Rajasthan and Nashik, Maharashtra. Some of his donative inscriptions have been found in Nashik and the Karle caves of Maharashtra.
- It is believed that the Shaka Kshatrapas were involved in continuous conflict with the Satavahanas over the suzerainty over the Deccan and control over the western seaport areas frequently changed hands. For instance, the Nashik and Pune areas seem to have been conquered by either Nahapana or his predecessors from the Satavahanas. Later, around 125 CE, Nahapana is believed to have been killed by the Satavahana ruler, Gautamiputra Satkarni, who not only restruck Nahapana's coins but also *mentioned his victory over Nahapana in his inscriptions in the Nashik and Pune districts*. This victory is also mentioned in his mother, Gautami Balashri's, inscription.
- One inscription mentions that *a field for providing food was granted to Buddhist monks by Ushavadata (Nahapana's son-in-law)*.

The Kardamakas

The Kardamakas are another line of the Shaka *kshatrapas* who ruled western India after the Kshaharatas dynasty came to an end. The prominent rulers belonging to this dynasty included:

Chashtana (around c.120 CE)

- Founder of the *Kardamaka* dynasty. Originally ruled in the Sind area as a subordinate of the Kushanas and was probably the *kshatrapa* of the South-western provinces of the Kushana empire at the time of Nahapana.
- The Kardamakas had the practice of senior (*mahakshatrapa*) and junior (*kshatrapas*) rulers. For instance, during the lifetime of Chashtana (the *mahakshatrapa*), his son Jayadaman and later his grandson Rudradaman I were *kshatrapas*.
- He was succeeded by the most famous ruler of his dynasty and his grandson Rudradaman I.

Rudradaman I (c.130 CE–152 CE)

- The most famous of all the Shaka *kshtarapa* rulers, who ruled in the middle of second century CE.
- His empire was spread over almost whole of western India which included Sindh, Gujarat, Konkan, Narmada Valley, Malwa and Kathiawar except the Nashik and Pune areas.
- He is famous in history because of the repairs he undertook to improve the Sudarshan Lake from Chandragupta Maurya's reign, located in the semi-arid zone of Kathiawar, and this task is described in the famous Junagarh or Girnar inscription (dated in the Shaka year 72, i.e. 150–151 CE). This inscription happens to be the first chaste Sanskrit royal inscription of early India, when all others were generally composed in Prakrit.

- His other achievements are also described through this inscription. The inscription mentions that he defeated Gautamiputra Satkarni, the lord of the *Dakshinapatha*, twice, but did not destroy him as he was a close relative. Rudradaman's daughter was married to Gautamiputra Satakarni's son Vasishthiptra Pulumavi.
- Vishvasena (Last Kshatrapa ruler who ruled at the end of 3rd century BCE and belonged to the Chashtana lineage).

The Impact and Contribution of Contacts with Central Asia

The *Shaka-Kushana* phase introduced various new elements to trade and agriculture, to administrative organisation, to art and literature, sculpture and pottery, science and technology, and to the Indian society at large. In fact, Central Asian influence was felt in almost all spheres and aspects of social life. For instance:

a. Pottery and Architecture: They introduced the use of burnt bricks for flooring and tiles for both flooring and roofing. The period is marked by the construction of brick walls. Red pottery techniques, which were widely used in Central Asia, were replicated in the Indian subcontinent too. The typical pottery of this period was red ware, both plain and polished with medium to fine fabric. The distinctive pots of this period are sprinklers and spouted channels.

b. Trade and Agriculture: Due to the establishment of intimate contacts between Central Asia and India, trade between the two regions also flourished. India imported a good deal of gold from the Altai mountains of Central Asia. Due to the extensive control of the Kushanas on the Silk Route, the economy of the Kushanas was replenished with the tolls levied from the traders and this income helped in building a large prosperous empire. Embassies were sent from India to the court of the Roman emperor Augustus in 27–28 CE and also to the Roman Emperor Trajan in 110–20 CE. It is rather pertinent to note that even though it was the Indo-Greeks who introduced gold coins in India, it was the Kushanas who were the first rulers in India to issue the gold coins[6] on such a wide scale. The Kushanas also promoted agriculture. It is believed that the Kushanas were the pioneers in introducing and extending the areas under the large-scale irrigation[7].

c. Military Knowledge and Equipments: Being excellent horsemen[8] themselves, the Shakas and the Kushanas introduced better cavalry and popularised the use of riding horses on a large scale. They made common the use of reins, saddles and *toe-stirrups* made of rope,

[6] In fact, the metallic purity of the gold coins issued by the early Kushan Kings was much better than the Gupta gold coins.

[7] The earliest archaeological traces of large scale irrigation in Pakistan, Afghanistan, and western Central Asia date to the Kushan period.

[8] Their passion for horsemanship is shown by numerous equestrian terracotta figures of Kushan times discovered from Begram in Afghanistan.

which facilitated the movement of the rider. They also brought in caps, helmets and boots used by warriors. The Shakas and Kushanas introduced new dressing styles such as the turban, the tunic, trousers, heavy long coats and long boots, which were adopted not only by warrior classes but also by certain other sections of the society. The practice of making leather shoes began in India during this period in all likelihood.

d. Administrative Organisation: The Central Asian conquerors introduced new styles in administration. For instance, the Indo-Greeks introduced the practice of military governorship wherein they appointed military governors called *strategos* while the Kushanas introduced the '*Satrap*' system of government, under which the empire was divided into numerous *satrapis* and each *satrapi* was placed under the rule of a *satrap*. These systems led to the development of a feudatory[9] organisation wherein these Central Asian conquerors established their supremacy over numerous small princes who regularly paid tributes to them. The Shakas and the Kushanas strengthened the idea of the divine origin of kingship. They took the title of 'Deviputra', that is, the sons of god.

e. Indian Society. One of the striking aspects about the Central Asian conquerors was that not only did they assimilate with the India society, but they also added new ingredients to Indian culture and enriched it immensely. They completely identified themselves with Indian culture. Since they did not have their own script, written language or any organised religion, they adopted these components of culture from India. It would be not wrong to state that in no other period of ancient history were foreigners assimilated in Indian society on such a large scale as they were in the post-Maurya period. Since most of them came as conquerors they were absorbed as *kshatriyas*. Even in the *Manusmriti*, the Shakas and Parthians are described by Manu as the *vratya-kshatriyas* (second class kshatriyas) who had deviated from their duties of sacrificial rituals and thus fallen in status.

The rulers not only adopted the Indian societal norms but also adopted the popular religions of that time. For instance, some of them converted to Vaishnavism (the worship of Vishnu), as in the case of Greek ambassador Heliodorus who set up a pillar in honour of Vasudeva. A few others adopted Buddhism, as in the case of the Greek ruler Menander who became a Buddhist. Similarly, the Kushana rulers worshipped both Shiva and the Buddha and the images of these two gods appeared on the Kushana coins.

The origin of Mahayana Buddhism owes a lot to the Central Asian influence. The monks and nuns could not afford to lose the cash donations from the growing body of traders and artisans and thus now started accepting gold and silver, took to non-vegetarian food and wore elaborate robes (as substantiated by the discovery of large number of coins in the monastic areas of Nagarjunakonda in Andhra Pradesh). The disciplined life of the *sangha* was also deserted by a few to resume their householder's life and earlier the things

[9] Kushans adopted the pompous title of 'king of kings', which indicates they collected tributes from numerous small princes.

associated with the Buddha which were worshipped as his symbols were replaced with his images. This new form of Buddhism which venerated and worshipped images of the Bodhisattvas came to be called Mahayana Buddhism and Kanishka was a great patron of this form of Buddhism who not only organised the fourth Buddhist Council but also set up many other *stupas* to perpetuate the memory of the Buddha. The fundamental difference between Mahayana and Hinayana school can be seen in the following box.

Hinayana	Mahayana
It considers the highest goal of human life should be to achieve *nibbana*/ Nirvana and become an *arhat*.	It considers the attainment of *nibbana* to be a lesser goal, rather according to it the higher goal is to follow the path of Bodhisattva and attain Buddhahood.
According to them, an *arhat* is one who after attaining *nibbana* disappears from the cycle of *samsara*.	According to them, the *Bodhisattva* is the one who has attained great wisdom but decides to postpone his *nibbana* and help others to become the Buddha. The Bodhisattva should have the ten virtues of *dana* (generosity), *shila* (good conduct), *kshanti* (patient forbearance), *virya* (mental strength), *dhyana* (meditation), *prajna* (wisdom), *upayakaushalya* (skillfulness in means), *pranidhana* (determination), *bala* (power) and *jnana* (knowledge).
In Hinayana, the Buddha is considered a *mahapurusha* (superior man), the unequalled teacher par excellence who had become enlightened and became an *arhat*.	Mahayana increased the gulf between the becoming of an *arhat* and a Buddha. It introduced the idea of transcendent Buddhas and Bodhisattvas who stood in between *nibbana* and *samsara*. It conceived of many Buddhas and Bodhisattvas such as *Maitreya*, *Avalokiteshvara* and *Manjushri*, all of whom helped others in deliverance in their respective Buddha-*kshetras*.

f. Art and Literature: Art in the post-Mauryan period was predominantly religious. Two most important features concerning art and architecture of this period are the construction of stupas and development of regional schools of sculpture.

   i. *Stupas*: A *stupa* is a large *hemispherical dome* with a central chamber in which relics of the Buddha or some Buddhist monk is kept in a small casket. The base was surrounded by a path for *pradakshina* (clockwise circumambulation), enclosed by wooden railings which were later made in stone. Three prominent *stupas* of this period are at Bharhut (which dates to the middle of the second century BCE and is significant for its sculptures; its railings are made of red stone), Sanchi (three big *stupas* were constructed at Sanchi in this period; the biggest of the three, which was built originally by emperor Ashoka, was enlarged to twice its size sometime in the second century BCE), and Amravati and Nagarjunkonda (both in Andhra Pradesh). A number of *stupas* were also constructed in south India during this period but none has survived in its entirety.

ii. Schools of Sculptural Art: Idols of the Buddha were carved out for the first time in this period. The Central Asian rulers became enthusiastic patrons of Indian art and literature and showcased great zeal in establishing new schools of art. There was a synthesis of both local (Indian) and Central Asian elements in the new images of Buddha. The Kushana empire brought together masons and artisans trained in different art forms and belonging to different nationalities, which further enriched the diverse cultures. There were three major schools of sculptural art which developed in this period. These were: Gandhara[10] School of Art, Mathura school of Art and Amravati school of Art.

Gandhara School of Art	Mathura School of Art	Amravati School of Art
Gandhara school had foreign influence as it was based on Graeco-Roman norms wherein the theme of sculptures is predominantly Buddhist but their style is Greek. It is therefore also known as Graeco- Buddhist School of art. This school assimilated various traits of Acamenian, Parthian and Bactrian traditions into the local traditions.	The Mathura school of art was primarily a centre of an indigenous school of art having no foreign influence. It is believed to have evolved from representation of *yakshas* (indigenous male deities). Also, presentation of female beauty as a vehicle of art was a novel experiment of Mathura school.	The Amravati school of art was also indigenous in nature.
It is said to have flourished between 100 CE and 700 CE.	It is said to have flourished between 100 BCE and 600 CE.	It is said to have flourished between 150 BCE and 350 CE.
Found primarily in North-west India.	Found primarily in Mathura, Sonkh and Kanaklitila (part of North India).	It flourished in Andhra Pradesh between the lower valleys of the rivers Krishna and Godavari.
The main patrons of this art form were the Kushanas.	The main patrons of this art form were the Kushanas.	The main patrons of this art form were the Satavahanas, but it carried on even later, patronised by their successor Ikshavaku rulers.

[10] Indian craftsmen came into contact with the central Asians, Greeks and Romans, especially in the north-western frontier of India in Gandhara. This gave rise to a new kind of art form known as Gandhara school of art.

Gandhara School of Art	Mathura School of Art	Amravati School of Art
Influence of Buddhism and Hellenistic realism. So, in Gandhara school mainly Buddhist images are found. The famous *Bamyan Buddha* of Afghanistan belong to this school of Art.	Influence of all three religions. (Buddhism, Jainism and Brahmanism). Mathura not only produced beautiful stone images of Buddha and Mahavira but also of Brahmanical deities too. For instance, during the Kushana period, a number of sculptures of Brahmanical deities were carved, which included *Kartikeya*, *Vishnu*, *Kubera* alongwith the headless erect statue of Kanishka. Mathura has also yielded large numbers of sculptures of Jaina deities besides the *ayagapatas* or stone slabs to place objects of worship and *Sarvatobhadrika* image of four Jain *Jinas*. Other striking examples of Mathura school include figures of *yakshas* and *yakshis*, *nagas* and *naganis* and sensual females.	Mainly Buddhist images are found. The thematic representations include the stories from the life of the Buddha, mostly from *jatakas*.
Chief characteristics of the Gandhara school of Art: (a) Sculpture in spiritual state. (b) Fewer ornaments. (c) Great detailing and rich carving. (d) Realistic images. (e) Expressive images. (f) Lean body.	Chief characteristics of the Mathura school of Art: (a) Sculpture in delighted mood. (b) Lacking spiritual look. (c) Energetic. (d) Having strong muscular structure. (e) Not much attention to detailed sculpting. (f) Images are less expressive.	An important characteristic of the Amravati school is the 'narrative art'. The medallions were carved in such a manner that they depict an incident in a natural way. For example, one medallion depicts a whole story of 'taming of an elephant by the Buddha'. There is a prominence of human figures in comparison to figures drawn from nature.
Features of Buddha sculpture: (a) Spiritual Buddha. (b) Sad Buddha. (c) Bearded Buddha. (d) Buddha in yogi postures. (e) Buddha is depicted with a garment draped in Graeco-Roman fashion, with wavy hairs, large forehead and long ears.	Features of Buddha sculpture: (a) Delighted Buddha. (b) Lacking spiritual look. (c) With no beard or moustache. (d) Shaven head and face. (e) Graceful posture of Buddha. (f) Seated in Padmasana. (g) The *halo* around the Buddha was profusely decorated with geometrical motifs.	Sculptures of this school are mainly found on the railings, plinths and other parts of *stupas*.

Gandhara School of Art	Mathura School of Art	Amravati School of Art
(f) Halo not decorated. Different *Mudras* portrayed: (a) Abhaya *mudra* (Don't fear) (g) Bhumisparsha *mudra* (Touching the earth) (h) Dhayan *mudra* (Meditation) (i) Dharmachakra *mudra* (Preaching pose)	(h) Buddha surrounded by two monks: Padmapani (holding lotus) and Vajrapani (holding Vajra). (i) The Standing Buddha of the Sravasti and Kausambhi.	
The stone used for making idols of Buddha and Bodhisattava was predominantly blue-grey schist.	The Mathura artists used local red stone with black spots to make the images.	Another important feature of Amravati art is the use of white marble-like stone to carve out the figures.

FIGURE 7.5 Gandhara School of Art

FIGURE 7.6 Mathura School of Art

FIGURE 7.7 Amravati School of Art

A lot of stone sculpture belonging to both the Gandhara and Mathura schools of art were produced in the Kushana period and formed a part of the great cultural heritage of India. Along with the stone sculptures, beautiful Buddhist caves were also constructed out of rocks in Maharashtra and Andhra Pradesh. Numerous rock panels depicting different stories connected with Buddha are found at Nagarjunakonda, Gaya, Sanchi, Bharhut and Amravati.

The Central Asian rulers also patronised and helped in the growth of Sanskrit literature. The earliest specimen of *kavya* style and that too in chaste Sanskrit is found in the Junagadh Inscription of Rudradaman I. Some of the great creative authors such as Ashvaghosha enjoyed the patronage of the Kushanas. Some of the important Buddhist texts such as *Mahavastu* and *Divyavadana* belonged to this period. The progress of Mahayana Buddhism led to the composition of numerous *avadanas*[11] which were aimed to popularise the Mahayana sect and were composed in Buddhist hybrid Sanskrit. The Greeks contributed to the development of the Indian theatre[12] by introducing the use of the curtain, which was called *yavanika*. One of the most classic works on the rhetoric and dramaturgy, Bharata's *Natyashastra*, probably belonged to the same period. One of the earliest erotic works on sex and love making, the *Kamasutra*[13], was composed during this time by Vatsyayana, which is also one of the best examples of secular literature of this period.

g. Science and Technology: Post-Mauryan Indian astronomy and astrology has a huge Greek influence. The term '*horashastra*' used for astrology in Sanskrit was derived from the Greek term 'horoscope'. The Greek coins, which were properly shaped and stamped, were a great improvement on punch marked coins. The largest number of copper coins were issued by the Kushanas. Working in glass-making during this period was especially influenced by foreign practices and in no other period in ancient India did glass-making make such progress as it did during this period.

The Satavahanas

As we have discussed earlier, that the Maurya rule was succeeded by the Sungas and the Kanvas in the north. However, in Deccan and in central India, the Satavahanas succeeded the Mauryas though after a gap of almost 100 years. On the basis of unearthing of many local rulers' coins (such as coins of the Kura rulers found at Brahmapuri, other local rulers such as Gobhadra, Samigopa, Chimuka, Kamvaya and Narana coins found at different locations), it is generally accepted that after the decline of the Mauryas and before the advent of the Satavahanas, there must have been

[11] Life history and history.

[12] Both outdoor and indoor theatres appear in the caves of Ramgarh hill, 160 miles south of Banaras, and there is also a rest house for an actress.

[13] It is based on the life of a city-bred person or Nagaraja who lived in the period of thriving urbanism.

numerous small political principalities that were ruling in different parts of the Deccan. Probably, the *Rathikas* and *Bhojikas* mentioned in the Ashokan inscriptions gradually progressed into the *maharathis* and *mahabhojas* of pre-Satavahana times.

The Satavahanas are considered identical with the 'Andhras' of the *Puranas*. However, interestingly, neither the name *Andhra* appears in Satavahana inscriptions, nor do the *Puranas* speak of the Satavahanas (only refer to *Andhras*). According to some *Puranas*, the *Andhras* ruled for 300 years with their capital at Pratishthana (modern Paithan) on the Godavari in Aurangabad district. This is also the period designated to the Satavahana Dynasty. The earliest Satavahana inscriptions belong to the 1st century BCE, when they defeated the Kanvas and established their rule over parts of central India. It is also pertinent to note that the early Satavahana kings appeared not in Andhra but in north Maharashtra (the fertile basin of the upper Godavari valley), where their earliest coins and inscriptions have been found. Gradually, they extended their power over Karnataka and Andhra. Their greatest competitors were the Shaka Kshatrapas of Western India, who had established themselves in the upper Deccan and western India. Control of the prominent seaports such as *Bhrigukachcha* (Broach), Kalyan and *Suparaka* (Sopara) must have been a bone of contention between the two.

The Satavahanas claimed *Brahmana* descent and performed Vedic rituals and worshipped gods like Krishna, Vasudeva, as evident in the Naneghat cave inscription of Naganika (1st century BCE), which mentions the great sacrifices performed by Satkarni I. Another striking feature of the kings pertaining to this dynasty was that they used matronyms such as Gautamiputra and Vashishthiputra, although they were not matrilineal or matriarchal in any sense. The Satavahanas assumed the title of *Dakshinapathapati* (*Lord of the Dakshinapatha*). The Satavahanas are also known in history for starting the practice of giving royal grants of land to Brahmanas and Buddhist monks, including those associated with tax exemptions. It is mentioned in one of the inscriptions of Gautamiputra Satkarni that *the land gifted to the Brahmanas was not to be entered or disturbed by the royal troops, was not to be dug for salt, was free from the control of state officials, and was to enjoy all sorts of pariharas (immunities)*. They also promoted Buddhism by granting land to the monks.

Simuka

- Founder of the Satavahana Dynasty and was immediately active after Ashoka's death.
- Built Jain and Buddhist temples.

Gautamiputra Satkarni (c.106–130 CE)

- It appears initially the Shaka Kshatrapas of Western India succeeded in dislodging the Satavahanas from the western and central region, but later the fortunes of the Satavahanas were revived by its most famous ruler, Gautamiputra Satkarni. He not only defeated the Shakas but also raised the power and prestige of the Satvahanas to greater heights. It was under his reign that the empire was at its peak.

- He claimed to have destroyed the Kshaharta lineage, to which his adversary Nahapana belonged, and restruck under his name more than 8000 silver coins of Nahapana. He also wrested Malwa and Kathiawar from the Shakas. His empire extended from Malwa in the north to Karnataka in the south, having general authority over the present day Andhra region.
- His achievements are described and eulogised after his death, during his son Pulumayi II's reign, in a Nashik inscription of his mother Gautami Balashri (written in Prakrit). In this inscription, *he is described as the destroyer of the Shakas, Pahlavas, and the Yavanas, as the uprooter of the Kshaharatas and as the restorer of the glory of the Satvahanas.*
- In the Nashik inscription, he is also described as *ekabamhana* (a peerless Brahmana) and *khatiya-dapa-manamada* (one who destroyed the high handedness and pride of the Kshatriyas).
- He donated land to the Buddhist monks, the *Mahasamghikas*, at Karle (the Karle inscription mentions the grant of 'Karajika' village near modern Pune, Maharashtra) and at Nashik (as evident in the Nashik inscription, dated in the 18th year of Gautamiputra's reign which mentions that this piece of land was earlier in the possession of Nahapana's son-in-law Ushavadata).
- He assumed titles of *Rajaraja* and *Maharaja*.
- In the later period of his reign, he probably lost some of the conquered Kshaharata territories to the Kardamaka line of the Shaka Kshatrapas of Western India, as evident in the Junagadh inscription of the Rudradaman I.

Vashishthiputra Pulumayi (c. 130–154 CE)

- His coins are found in the various parts of Andhra.
- The Shakas Kshatrapas of Western India probably recovered some of their territories due to his engagements in the east.
- According to the Junagadh inscription, he married the daughter of Rudradaman I.

Yajna Sri Satakarni (c. 165–194 CE)

- One of the later kings who recovered north Konkan and Malwa from the Shaka rulers.
- Lover of trade and navigation, as evident from the motif of ship on his coins.

The successors of Yajnashri Satakarni included Gautamiputra Vijaya Satakarni, Chanda Satakarni, Vasisthiputra Vijaya Satkarni, Pulumavi and Hala (probably the 17th king in the line, also a great poet who authored the *Gatha Sattasai*, which is a collection of 700 erotic poems in the Maharashtri Prakrit dialect). In the mid-3rd century CE, the Satavahana dynasty came to an end and various forces came into power in their stead: the Vakatakas in the Deccan, the Kadambas in Mysore, the Abhiras in Maharashtra and the Ikshvakus in Andhra emerged as the main rulers.

Important Aspects of the Satavahanas

Polity and Administration

The Satavahana king was represented as the upholder of *dharma* and he generally strove for the royal and divine ideal set forth in the *dharmashastras*. In order to attribute divinity to kingship, most kings were represented as possessors of supernatural powers and of qualities of mythical heroes such as Rama, Arjuna, Bhima, and so on. The Satavahanas retained some of the administrative units of Ashokan times. The kingdom was divided into subdivisions called *aharas* or *rashtras*, meaning districts. There were also officers called *amatyas/mahamatras* who were perhaps ministers or advisors of the king. But, unlike Mauryan times, certain military and feudal traits are found in the administration of the Satavahanas. For instance, the *senapati* was appointed provincial governor. It was probably done to keep the tribal people who were not thoroughly Brahmanised under strong military control. The lowest level of administration was a *grama (village)*, which was under the charge of a *gaulmiku (village headman)*, who was also the head of a military regiment consisting of nine chariots, nine elephants, 25 horses and 45 foot soldiers. The military character of the Satavahanas is also evident with the use of terms like *kataka* and *skandhavaras* in their inscriptions, which denote military camps and settlements attached to a particular king and also served as administrative centres. The Satavahana kingdom had three grades of feudatories:

a. *Raja* (who had right to strike coins)

b. *Mahabhoja*

c. *Senapati*

According to Pliny, they maintained an army of 100,000 infantry, 2000 cavalry and 1000 elephants. This presupposes a large rural population, and it appears that the peasants produced enough to support this military strength. Revenue was collected both in cash and kind. The Satavahana kings were the first in Indian history to make tax-free land grants to Buddhists and Brahmanas to gain religious merit. This practice became more prominent in succeeding periods.

Material Culture

As the Satavahanas acted as a bridge between North and South India, similarly their material culture was a fusion of both local Deccan elements as well as northern ingredients. Through contacts with the north, the people of Deccan learnt the use of coins, burnt bricks, ring-wells, the art of writing, and so on. There was regular use of fire-baked bricks and the use of flat, perforated roof tiles which must have aided in the longevity of the construction. For instance, in Karimnagar, as many 22 brick walls have been discovered. The drains were covered and were also underground to lead waste water into soakage pits. They were also fairly acquainted with the use of iron and agriculture. They probably exploited the rich mineral resources of Deccan such as iron ores from

Karimnagar and Warangal and gold from Kolar fields. Unlike the gold coins of the Kushanas, they mostly issued lead coins[14] (which they probably imported from the Romans) apart from copper and bronze coins. The Deccan developed a very advanced rural economy. The people knew about the art of paddy transplantation and especially the area on the confluence of the rivers Krishna and Godavari formed a great rice bowl. The Satavahanas also produced cotton and in different foreign accounts, Andhra was famous for its cotton products.

Social Organisation

Since the Andhras are identified with the early Satavahanas, they were probably a local Deccan tribe who were gradually Brahamnised. The Satavahana kings (such as Gautamiputra Satkarni) claimed to be Brahmans and considered it their primary duty to uphold the *varna* system, that is, the four-fold division of social structure determined by caste. Kings and queens performed Vedic sacrifices and worshipped Vaishnava gods such as Krishna and Vasudeva. Though they made liberal sacrificial fees to the Brahmanas, they also promoted Buddhism by granting land to Buddhist monks, especially to Mahayana Buddhists. Nagarjunakonda and Amravati in Andhra Pradesh and Nashik and Junar areas of Maharashtra became important Buddhist sites under the Satavahanas and their successors, the Ikshvakus. Due to flourishing trade and commerce, merchants and artisans formed an important, social strata. Merchants generally named themselves after the towns to which they belonged. Both artisans[15] and merchants made generous donations to the Buddhist cause.

FIGURE 7.8 Nagarjunakonda Buddha

[14] It seems that the Satavahanas probably used gold as bullion.

[15] Among the artisans, the *gandhikas* or perfumers are repeatedly mentioned as donors. At a later stage, the term *gandhika* became so general as to connote all kinds of shopkeepers. The modern title Gandhi is derived from this ancient term.

Architecture

During the Satavahana phase, many *chaityas* (sacred shrines) and *viharas* (monasteries) were cut out of the solid rock in the north-western Deccan or Maharashtra with great precision and skill. The Karle Chaitya in the western Deccan belongs to this era. The Nashik inscriptions of Nahapana and Gautamiputra Satakarni, which are on the walls of the three *viharas*, is another important architectural site belonging to this period. Two famous stupas of this period are Amravati[16] and Nagarjunakonda[17]. The official language of the Satavahanas was Prakrit, though the script was Brahmi. One famous Prakrit text, *Gathasattasai*, is attributed to a Satavahana king called Hala, which consisted of 700 verses all written in Prakrit.

FIGURE 7.9 Chaitya at Karle

Early State of Kalinga

It is well-known that the Deccan as well as eastern India were parts of Ashoka's empire. He had conquered Kalinga through a violent battle in which the loss of men and property was enormous. After Ashoka, Kalinga became prominent under the kings of Chedi dynasty. Unfortunately, not much information about the kings of the dynasty is available except Kharavela, who probably lived in the first century BCE. His achievements are recorded in an inscription, known as the Hathigumpha inscription, situated in the Udaigiri hills near Bhubaneswar in Odisha.

[16] The construction of Amravati Stupa started around 200 BCE but it was completely reconstructed in the second half of the 200 CE. It is full of sculptures that depict various scenes from the life of the Buddha.

[17] Nagarjunakonda prospered most in the second and third centuries under the patronage of the Ikshvakus, the successors of the Satavahanas. It possesses both Buddhist monuments and the earliest brahmanical brick temples.

King Kharavela (c. 1st century BCE)

- Probably belonged to *The Mahameghavahanas* of Kalinga.
- Seems to have wrested Kalinga from Mauryans and founded an independent line of kings, the Chedis /Chetis of Kalinga.
- He is also known as Bhikshu-Raja, and he constructed a great palace known as the 'Palace of Victor'.
- Famous for the Hathigumpha inscription, which is engraved on the Udaigiri hills near Bhubaneswar. It is the second inscription by Naganika after his Nanaghat inscription.
- Follower of Jainism and provided cave shelters for Jaina monks in Udaigiri hills. The Hathigumpha inscription proves that Jainism entered Orissa and probably became the state religion within 100 years of death of Mahavira. The inscription is so named because the image of an elephant is carved out of stone next to the boulder carrying the inscription. The inscription tells us that *he was a follower of Jainism and had fought many successful battles against his neighbours*.

Early Historical Period of South India: From Megalithic to the State Polities of Chera, Cholas and Pandyas

The Megalithic background of South India

As we know, the prehistoric age (the pre-writing phase) is generally followed by the historical period which is normally marked by the beginning of writing and written literature, more settled and stable community life, agriculture by means of iron ploughshare, the gradual rise of state system, the use of metal money and a flourishing economy, and so on. However, interestingly, all these phenomena do not emerge in a linear fashion in southern India, especially at the tip of the peninsula with the Kaveri delta as the nucleus zone, until about the 2nd century BCE. The Neolithic phase of south India, which was highlighted by the use of polished stone axe and blade tools, was succeeded by the Megalithic phase (around 1200 BCE–300 BCE). The upper portions of the peninsula were inhabited by people who were called the Megalith builders. Quite strangely, these people are identified not from their actual settlements, which are rare, but from their graves. These graves are called Megaliths, as they were encircled with mega/big pieces of stones and were, in most cases, located outside the settlement area. These Megalith burial sites have yielded the first iron objects from south India (which include arrowheads, daggers, swords, spearheads, tridents, battle axe, hoes, ploughshares, sickles, etc.). Besides these, lot of black and red ware pottery has been found buried in these Megaliths. These artifacts, along with food grains such as wheat and rice found at various Megalithic sites, indicate that the Megalithic people followed agro-pastoral and hunting activities for their livelihood. They did not, in all likelihood, practice an advanced type of agriculture, since the number of agricultural tools found in the grave sites are lesser in number in comparison to tools meant for fighting and hunting. These Megaliths have been found in all upland areas of the peninsula, but their concentration is more in eastern Andhra and in Tamil Nadu. Prominent sites that have yielded Megalithic burials include Brahmagiri, Maski (Karnataka), Adichallanur (Tamilnadu) and Junapani near Nagpur (Maharashtra). It is highly likely that the Cholas, the Pandyas and the Keralaputras (Cheras) mentioned in the Ashokan inscriptions probably belonged to the last phase of Megalithic culture. The Megalithic period in south India was followed by the Sangam age.

FIGURE 7.10 Megalithic Burial

The Sangam Age and Literature (3rd century BCE–3rd century CE)

By the 3rd century BCE, the Megalithic people moved from the uplands into the fertile river basins and reclaimed the marshy deltaic areas. On account of the influence of both material (iron technology, which promoted forest clearing and plough cultivation, distribution of punch-marked coins of the *janapadas* due to a flourishing north-south trade) and cultural contacts from north (as result of the interactions of traders, conquerors, Jaina, Buddhist, Ajivikas and Brahmana missionaries), these Megalithic communities came to practice wet paddy cultivation, founded numerous villages and towns and came to have social classes. In due time, the state system also developed in the southern India. Three early kingdoms, that of the Cholas, the Pandyas and the Cheras, emerged in the rice-growing areas of *Tamilakam* (the land between the Tirupati hills and the southernmost tip of peninsula). It is for this reason that the advent of the historical period in south India is generally dated to the 3rd century BCE, though with recent archaeological excavations at Kodumanal, the dates can be pushed backwards to at least the 4th century BCE.

The major sources of information on the political history of this time are the laudatory poems of the Sangam age literature, which is also referred to as early Classical Tamil literature. The

Sangam age refers to that period in the early history of south India, when large number of poems in Tamil were composed by a number of authors. The term 'Sangam' refers to an assembly or 'meeting together' of Tamil poets. Traditionally, three Sangams or assemblies are believed to have been convened one after the other at different places under the patronage of the Pandya kings of Madurai. The poems were modeled on the bardic songs of older times, and were orally transmitted for an indefinite period before they were finally written down by poets who came from both cities and villages, had varied social and professional backgrounds which included both dignitaries of that time such as kings, ministers, merchants, astrologers as well as common folk such as teachers, soldiers, goldsmiths, blacksmiths and carpenters. Sangam literature is primarily secular, and due to their varied themes and authorship, Sangam poems offer rich, diverse vantage points of looking at everyday themes in a *Tamilakam* context.

Sangam Literature (Corresponds to the Post-Maurya and Pre-Gupta Period)

Sangam	Place of Organisation		Outcome/Relevant fact
First	Thenmadurai	Agastya	Its works did not survive.
Second	Kapatapuram	Agastya Tolkappiyar (a disciple of Agastaya)	Only the *Tolkappiyam* (a Tamil grammar) by Tolkappiyar survives
Third	Madurai	Nakkirar	Forms the entire corpus of existing Sangam Literature

The Sangam corpus includes six of the eight anthologies of poems included in the *Ettutokai* (The Eight Collections), and nine of the ten *pattus* (songs) of the *Pattuppattu* (The Ten Songs). The style and certain historical references in the poems suggest that this literature is most likely composed between 3rd century BCE and 3rd century CE. Around mid-8th century, they were compiled into anthologies, which were further collected into the super-anthologies (the anthologies of anthologies) called the *Ettutokai* and the *Pattuppattu*. It is rather interesting to note that the anthologies include a total of 2381 poems ascribed to 473 poets, out of whom 30 poets were women. Apart from these poems, the first two books of the *Tolkappiyam* (a book on Tamil grammar and poetics written by Tolkappiyar) are also a part of the corpus of Sangam Literature. There is also mention of the *Agattiyam*, which was the first known book on Tamil grammar. It was supposedly written by the sage Agathiyar, and is believed to be lost beyond redemption. The sage Agathiyar, according to Hindu legends, brought the Tamil language and its syntax to the Tamil people from god Shiva. It is believed that Tolkappiyar, the author of *Tolkappiyam*, was the disciple of Agathiyar. Poems within Sangam literature were composed on two broader themes of *akam* (love) and *puram* (mostly based on war but also included public poetry such as poems on good and evil, community and kingdom). A remarkable feature of Sangam literature is its vivid portrayal of the contemporary society and culture of *Tamilakam* and its peaceful and harmonious interactions with the northern (Aryan) culture.

Sangam literature can be divided into two groups: narrative and didactic. The narrative texts are called Melkannakku (18 Major Works consisting of eight anthologies and ten idylls), and are considered works of heroic poetry in which heroes are glorified and perpetual wars and cattle raids are frequently mentioned. The didactic works are called Kilkanakku (18 Minor Works). A large number of Tamil didactic works such as Tiruvalluvar's *Tirukkural* (famous work on ethics, philosophy, polity and love, and considered the fifth Veda of Tamil Nadu), Tamil epics such as *Silappadikaram* (considered the brightest gem of early Tamil literature which deals with love story of Kovalan, who prefers a courtesan Madhavi of Kaveripattnam to his noble wedded wife Kannagi) and *Manimekalai* (a sequel to *Silappaddikaram* and is considered the 'Odyssey of Tamil poetry', which deals with the adventures of the daughter born of the union of Kovalan and Madhavi and her subsequent conversion to Buddhism) were written in the period between the 5th and 6th centuries.

The Three Early Kingdoms: The Pandyas, the Cholas and the Cheras

The southern end of the Indian peninsula situated south of the Krishna river was divided amongst three early kingdoms and a large number of chieftains wherein the chieftainship was hereditary. The important *vendar* (crowned kings) who dominated the Tamilakam region during the Sangam Age were the Pandyas in the valleys of the Tamrapani (Sri Lanka) and Vaigai, the Cholas in the lower Krishna valley and the Cheras on the Kerala coast. These kings had their own particular insignia of royalty such as the special umbrella, the drum and the staff. The Cholas, Pandyas and Cheras had several subordinate chiefs known as *velir* (chieftains), who used to pay a regular tribute to the king. The kings and chieftains often formed alliances with one another and fought each other. Internecine conflict was the norm of the day and this probably also gave large scope to the Sangam poets to compose poems on war.

Kingdom	Capital	Emblem	Premium Port
The Pandyas (covers modern Tirunelveli, Madurai, Ramnad districts and south Travancore)	Madurai	Fish	Korkai
The Cholas (covers modern Tanjore and Trichinopoly district of Tamil Nadu)	Uraiyur	Tiger	Puhar (modern Kaveripattanam)
The Cheras (covers mostly Kerala coast)	Vanji/Karuvur	Bow	Tondi and Muchiri

The Pandyas

The Pandya territory occupied the southern-most and the south-eastern portion of the Indian peninsula. The Pandyas are first mentioned by Megasthenes in his *Indica*, wherein he refers to a Pandya kingdom famous for pearls and ruled by a woman (which may suggest some matriarchal influence in the Pandya society). Even Sangam Literature mentions Pandya rulers and describes the Pandya kingdom as wealthy and prosperous. The Pandya kings profited from trade with Roman Empire and even sent embassies to the Roman emperor Augustus. They performed Vedic sacrifices and the Brahmanas in their territory enjoyed considerable influence. The early Pandya kings were Nediyon, Palshalai Mudukudumi, and other prominent Pandya kings were:

Nedunjeliyan I

- It is believed that he died of remorse due to his tragic role (as he ordered the execution) in the death of Kovalan, the hero and the husband of Kannagi of the *Silappadikaram*.

Nedunjeliyan II

- He is one of the most important Pandya kings and is credited with many major military victories and acquiring territories from other chieftains.
- It is believed that at a very young age, he defeated a confederacy of Cheras, Cholas and five other chieftains in the battle of *Talaiyalanganam*. In this battle, the Chera king was taken prisoner.
- Two Tamil Brahmi inscriptions from Mangulam pertaining to early 2nd century BCE mentions that a subordinate and relative of Nedunjeliyan presented gifts to Jaina monks.

A 1st century BCE inscription from Alagarmalai mentions about a person called Katumara Natan, who appears to be either a Pandyan prince or subordinate.

The Cholas

The Chola kingdom (which in early medieval times was also known as Cholamandalam/ Coromandel) was situated to the north-east of the territory of the Pandyas and between the Penner and the Velar rivers. Their chief centre of political power and capital Uraiyur was famous for cotton trade. They also maintained an efficient navy. It also appears that in the middle of 2nd century BCE, a Chola king named Elara conquered Sri Lanka and ruled it over for nearly 50 years. The Cholas were also rich and prosperous and the main source of their wealth was their trade in cotton cloth.

Karikala

- One of the greatest of all Chola kings, who founded its port city Puhar (modern Kaveripattanam which was a great centre of trade and commerce and had a large dock) and constructed 160 km of embankment along Kaveri river. It is mentioned that this was built with the labour of 12,000 slaves brought as captives from Sri Lanka.
- Credited with having defeated a confederacy of Pandyas, Cheras and their allies at the battle of Venni. It is mentioned in Sangam texts that *11 rulers lost their drums in the field* (which is significant as the royal drum was an important insignia of royal power) *and the Chera king who suffered a wound in the back died of vattakirutal (ritual starvation).*
- He is also credited with another major victory at Vahaipparandalai in which, according to Sangam texts, several chieftains lost their umbrellas.

Tondaiman Ilandiraiyan

- Another important Chola ruler who ruled from Kanchi either as an independent ruler or as a subordinate ruler of Karikala.
- He was a gifted poet, and in one of his poems he has emphasised on the personal character of the king. He says that *in order to rule well a king should possess a strong personal character*.
- Under Karikala's successors (especially Nalangilli and Nedungilli who fought bitterly among themselves for the throne), the Chola power rapidly declined and it is believed that their neighbouring powers expanded their empire at their cost. Later, the Pallavas from north wrested a lot of their territories. From the 4th to 9th century CE, the Cholas played a marginal role in south Indian history.

The Cheras

The Cheras were situated to the west and north of the Pandyas. It was an important and prosperous kingdom owing to its trade with the Romans. It appears that the Romans had in fact set up two regiments at Muziris/Muchiri (near modern Kochi) to protect their interests and also built a temple of Augustus. The history of the Cheras was marked with continuous battles with the Cholas and the Pandyas.

Udiyanjeral

- Earliest known Chera king.

Nedunjeral Adan

- One of the prominent kings of Chera dynasty, who probably defeated seven crowned kings and won the coveted title of *adhiraja*.
- It is also claimed that he not only defeated an enemy on the Malabar coast but also captured several *yavana* traders and later released them after taking ransom.
- He is also believed to have fought a war against a Chola king. However, in this war unfortunately both the principal adversaries (that is to say the Chola king and Nedunjeral) lost their lives.
- Kuttuvan, the younger brother of Nedunjeral Adan, conquered Kongu and extended the power of the Cheras up to the eastern and western oceans.
- One of Adan's sons is also described as an *adhiraja* who claimed to wore a garland of seven crowns and was victorious against Anji (a chieftain of Tagadur).

Senguttuvan

- Was Nedunjeral Adan's son and according to Chera poets was their greatest king who is also known as the Red or Good Chera. He led many successful military expeditions. He won a battle against the Mokur chieftain.

- He has been mentioned in the post-Sangam text, *Silappadikaram*, which describes his military conquest against Viyalur in the land of Nannan and capture of the Kodukur fortress in Kongu country.
- He also successfully backed one of the claimants in a Chola succession conflict, killing the nine others.
- He also claimed to have invaded the north, and fought against an Aryan chieftain in order to obtain stone for an image of Kannagi (the heroine of the *Silappadikaram* and considered the goddess of chastity), and crossed the Ganga and had a bath in the Ganga before bringing the stone back to his country.

Kudakko Ilanjeral Irumporai

- One of the last Chera kings mentioned in the Sangam texts, who is also believed to have won wars against the Cholas and Pandyas.

After the 2nd century CE, the Chera power declined and not much is known of their history till 8th century CE.

The Sangam poets also eulogise various chieftains such as Ay, Andiran and Pari for their heroism and generosity.

The Administration and Social Life in the Three Early Kingdoms

The Economy in Sangam Age

The whole *Tamilakam* in this period was divided into five *tinais*, or eco-zones based on their economic resources. These were: *kurinji* (hilly region); *palai* (arid zone); *mullai* (pastoral tracts); *marudam* (wet lands); and *neital* (seacoast). These zones were not clearly demarcated, and were scattered all around the region. Because of their different geographical contexts and ecological specialties, people in different *tinais* had their own modes of subsistence. For example, in *kurinji*, it was hunting and gathering; in *palai*, where people could not produce anything, they took to raiding and plundering; in *mullai* people practiced animal husbandry; in *marudam* it was plough agriculture; and in *neital* people took to fishing and salt making.

The people were engaged in various economic activities such as agriculture, crafts and trade. Rice was the most important crop. It formed the main part of peoples' diet and also served as a medium of barter exchange for inland trade. The top of the peninsula and the adjacent regions were extremely fertile and produced paddy, ragi, sugarcane, fruit, pepper and turmeric. Since the Tamil region does not have perennial rivers, the chiefs, wherever possible, encouraged agricultural activities by making tanks and dams. The Chola king Karikala of the Sangam age is credited with constructing a dam on the river Kaveri. It is considered to be the earliest dam in the country.

Among the crafts, the most important one was spinning and weaving of textiles, cotton as well as silk. Salt manufacture was another important activity.

The most important feature of the Sangam economy was flourishing trade with the Roman[18] world. The best account of Indo-Roman trade is given in the book called the *Periplus of the Erythrean Sea*, which was written in the first century CE by an anonymous author. Another Roman writer, Pliny, complains in his account '*Natural History*' that Rome was drained of gold on account of her trade with India. Major items of export to the Romans were the Indian products such as spices (included *yavanapriya* or pepper), perfumes, jewels, ivory and fine textiles (muslin especially), several precious and semi-precious stones like diamond, carnelian, turquoise, agate, sapphire, and so on, besides pearls, indigo, sandalwood, iron and steel cutlery. Against this import, Romans exported gold and silver to India. It is confirmed by the recovery of a large number of Roman gold coins in south India. Other important items of export from the Roman empire included wine, which is indicated by wine amphorae and shards of Roman wares found in significant numbers at Arikamedu in south India. Besides these, the western traders also brought tin, lead, coral and slave girls to the subcontinent.

After the discovery of the monsoons by Hippatus, a Greek navigator, in 45 CE, more and more sea voyages were used for trading purposes. The discovery of the monsoons and the use of a direct sea route between Indian coasts and the western world as well as south-east Asia was the main reason for the growth of trade. Important ports of India on the western coast were Bharukachchha (Broach), Sopara, Kalyana and Muziris. Ships from these ports sailed to the Roman Empire through the Red Sea. Trade with south-east Asia was conducted through the sea. Prominent ports on the eastern coast of India were Tamralipti (West Bengal), Arikamedu (Tamil Nadu Coast), and so on. Sea trade was also conducted between Bharukachchha and the ports of south-east Asia.

The economy of all the three kingdoms flourished due to large-scale local and long distance trade. It led to rise of important towns and craft centres in the Tamil region. Vanji, the capital of the Cheras, was an important centre of trade and craft. Muziris/Muchiri on the south-west coast was the foremost port of the Cheras. It is believed that the Roman ships laden with gold used to land here and took back large amounts of pepper. An interesting 2nd century document, the *Vienna Papyrus*, records *an agreement regarding transportation of goods between two merchants based in Alexandria and Muchiri*. Madurai, the capital of the Pandyas, was an important centre of fine textile and ivory working. Korkai, in the Tirunnelveli district of Tamil Nadu, was an important Pandya port which was famous for its pearls. Uraiyur (Tiruchirapalli in Tamil Nadu), the capital of the Cholas, was a grand city with magnificent buildings. Kaveripattinam or Puhar was the main Chola port. The Sangam poems refer to the busy markets guarded by soldiers who in order to ensure the safety of merchants and prevent smuggling, used to maintain constant vigil on the

[18] It is believed that the Romans first started trade with the southernmost part of India, as their earliest coins are found in the Tamil kingdoms which lay outside the Satvahana dominions.

trade routes. Transit duties were collected from merchants who moved their goods from place to place. Tribute from subordinate chiefs along with plunder and spoils of the war were the main sources of revenue.

Social Structure and Organisation

In the Tamil Brahmi inscriptions found at several places, kings are addressed as *ko* and chieftains as *ko* or *kon*. The *Brahmanas* first appeared in the Tamil land in the Sangam age. Many *Brahmanas* functioned as poets and were generously rewarded by the king. Though the concept of *varna* was known, social classes in the early Sangam period were not marked by acute caste distinctions (this phenomenon appeared in later stages). For instance, *Brahmanas* were present in the society and they performed Vedic ceremonies and sacrifices and also acted as advisers to the chief, but they enjoyed no special privileges and also took meat and wine. The *Kshatriyas* and *Vaishyas* appear as regular *varna* in the Sangam texts. The more relevant basis of stratification was *kuti* (clan-based descent groups) where there was no real restriction on inter-dining and social interaction among the *kuti* groups. The ruling class was called *arasar*, and its members had marriage relation with the *vellalas* (rich peasants), which formed the fourth caste of peasants. The *vellalas* held the bulk of land, and employed *kadaisiyan* (agricultural labour) to do the manual farm work. Some agricultural labourers known as *pariyars* also worked in animal skins and used them as mats. People were known on the basis of their occupation they followed, such as artisans, salt merchants, textile merchants, etc. There were sharp social inequalities in the age of the Sangam. The rich lived in well-decorated brick houses and wore costly clothes whereas the poor lived in mud huts and had scanty clothes to wear.

The class of warriors was an important element in polity and society. Commanders of the army were credited with the title of *enadi* at a formal ceremony. The state maintained a rudimentary army which consisted of chariots drawn by oxen, elephants, cavalry and infantry. Elephants played an important role in war while horses were imported by sea. War heroes occupied a special position in society, and memorial stones called *nadukal or virukkal* were raised in honour of those who died in fighting, and they were worshipped as god.

In the domain of religion, the Sangam period witnessed a close and peaceful interaction between north Indian and south Indian traditions. The *Brahmanas* who performed religious ceremonies popularised the worship of Indra, Vishnu and Shiva in south India. The Sangam poems reflect the emergence of new bases of royal prestige and legitimacy by performing Brahmanical sacrifices. For instance, a Pandya ruler, Mudukudumi, took the title *Palshalai* (one who has many sacrificial halls). There are also references to the presence of Buddhists and Jainas in Tamil region. The local people, particularly those of the hills, worshipped a deity called *Murugan*, which was identified with Kartikeya, a war god in northern India and was later called Subramaniya in Medieval times.

The Megalithic practice of providing for the dead continued in the Sangam Age too, as people offered rice to the dead. Cremation was also introduced. Sangam texts also reflect a belief in sacred or magical forces called *ananku*, that were supposed to inhabit different objects. The job of carrying out rites and rituals to correct the *ananku* was entrusted to lower castes of *pariyans, pananas* and *velans* who were generally associated with ritualistic dancing, singing, with lighting the cremation fire and worshipping *natukal* (memorial stones). *Ananku* was also believed to cling to women and it was generally believed that if a woman was chaste, her *ananku* would be under control and had auspicious potential.

Women in the Sangam period appear to have been educated. This is testified by many poems contributed by women poets to the corpus of Sangam Literature. Women are also described as engaged in various economic activities such as paddy plantation, cattle rearing, basket-making, spinning, etc. However, the cruel practice of Sati was also prevalent in Tamil society, and it was known as *tippayadal*. But it was not obligatory as there are references to widows present in society. However, the position of widows was miserable as they were prohibited to decorate themselves or participate in any form of amusement. Sangam poems also mention of *chevilittai*, who were like foster mothers and seem to be closely associated with family members.

Key Terms	Meaning
Kalatika	Superintendent of pearl fisheries
Kanatikan	Chief of scribes
Nalakars	Reed workers
Lonakaras	Salt makers
Koluvanikan	Trader in ploughshares
Kolu	Hard iron tip fixed to a wooden ploughshare
Ur	Assembly of village elders
Emporium (a Greco-Roman term).	Coastal town associated with foreign trade
Pattinam	Port
Satthavahakula	Family of caravan traders
Kumbhakarakula	Family of potters
Setthikula	Family of merchants cum bankers
Kammarakula	Family of metalsmiths
Atavirakkhikakula	Family of forest guards
Dhannavanijakula	Family of grain merchants
Pannikakula	Family of greengrocers
Pasanakottakakula	Family of stone grinders
Satthavahaputta	Son of caravan trader
Nisadaputta	Son of hunter
Vaddhakiputta	Son of carpenter

Key Terms	Meaning
Shailalakas/Selavadhaki	Stone masons
Kamara	Blacksmith
Gadhika	Perfumer
Karshapana	Copper coin
Niyamakjettha	Head of the sailor's guild
Katikai	Assembly of learned persons

Crafts, Trade and Towns in the Post Mauryan Age

The period pertaining to the Shakas, the Kushanas, the Satavahanas and the three early kingdoms (that is, the period from 3rd century BCE to 2nd century CE) was the most flourishing period in the history of crafts and commerce in ancient India. Production of crafts started growing in this period with tremendous impetus, as trade and commerce, both internal and foreign, was dependent to a great extent on the craft activities. The *Digha Nikaya*, which belongs to pre-Maurya times, mentions nearly two dozen occupations but the *Mahavastu*, which belongs to this period catalogues 36 kinds of workers. Similarly, the *Milindapanho* mentions 75 occupations, of which 60 were associated with crafts. A Tamil text known in English as *The Garland of Madurai* supplements the information provided in the two Buddhist texts. The level of specialisation was very high and as many as eight crafts were associated with the working of gold, silver, lead, tin, copper, brass, iron and precious stones or jewels, which employed separate artisans working in each craft. The technological advancement in iron is evident by the excavation of sophisticated iron artifacts, specially from the Karimnagar and Nalgonda districts of Telangana region. Indian iron and steel, including cutlery, were exported to as far as Abyssinian ports and were in high demand in western Asian countries.

The manufacturing in textiles, silk-weaving, arms, luxury articles, handicrafts and terracotta figurines, made rapid progress during this period. The textile industry was a prominent industry. Mathura (famous for a special type of cloth called *shataka*) and Vanga (eastern Bengal) were famous for variety of cotton and silk textiles. The discovery of some dyeing vats at some sites in south India such as Uraiyur and Arikamendu indicates that dyeing was a thriving craft in the area during this period. Ujjain was a prominent bead-making centre. The shell industry was in a thriving state, and many shell products belonging to the Kushana period have been excavated. Coin-minting[19] was an important craft, and this period is noted for numerous types of coins made of gold, silver, copper, bronze, potin and lead. Interestingly, the craftsmen even made fake

[19] The period between 200 BCE and 300 CE evidences the largest number of coins as supported by the discovery of highest number of dies and coin moulds in both north and in the Deccan. In fact, a coin mould from a Satvahana level shows that it could turn out half a dozen coins at a time. Thus, in no other period had the money economy penetrated the lives of common people so deeply.

Roman coins. The beautiful pieces of terracotta found in profuse quantities in almost all Kushana and Satavahana sites, especially Yelleshwaram in Nalgonda district, are truly masterpieces. It is generally believed that terracotta was meant mostly for the use of upper classes in towns. The artisans in this period touched new heights of prosperity, and there are numerous inscriptions which refer to the donations made by artisans to monasteries.

The communities of merchants were organised in groups known as *shreni* or guilds under the head called *sreshthi*. Another type of mercantile group was called *sartha*, which signified mobile or caravan trading corporation of interregional traders. The leader of such a guild was called *sarthavaha*. Like merchants, almost all craft vocations were also organised into guilds, each under a headman called *jetthaka/pamukkha*. These included weavers, corn dealers, bamboo workers, oil manufacturers, potters, etc. The guilds were associations of merchants and craftsmen following the same profession or dealing in the same commodity. They elected their head and framed their own rules regarding prices and quality to regulate their business on the basis of mutual goodwill. They also served as banks and received deposits from the public on a fixed rate of interest. It is interesting to note that around the 2nd century CE, in Maharashtra, lay devotees of Buddhism deposited money with the guilds of potters, oil millers and weavers for providing robes and other necessities to the monks. Similarly, at Mathura at the same time, there is mention of deposit of money with a chief of flour guild for serving daily to the Brahmanas. The *Yajnavalkya Smriti* refers to the qualifications and powers of guild officers and also hints towards judicial role of guilds. The guilds heads used to have a good rapport with the king, and according to some Buddhist texts, they used to accompany the king as a part of the official entourage. Sometimes, they were also appointed as *mahamatta*. Certain officials known as the *bhandagarika* were appointed to keep a record of the transactions and conventions of guilds, as mentioned in the *Nigrodha Jataka*. These royal officers had some authority over the guilds. Some guilds also had a *shrenibala*, which was some sort of a corporate organisation of warriors maintained by these guilds. The importance of the guilds can be gauged by the fact that some guilds also issued coins and seals. Some coins found at Taxila have the legend *negama*, while two copper coins found at Kaushambi bear the legend *gadhikanam*. Some seals with the captions *nigama, nigamasya* have been found at the sites of Rajghat (seals with the legend of *gavayaka*, signifying guild of milkmen), Bhita (seals with the legend of *shulaphalayikanam*, signifying guild of makers of arrowheads), and Ahichchhatra (seals with the legend of *kumhakara*, signifying guild of potters).

One of the most important features of the post-Mauryan period was the growth of trade and commerce, both internally as well as externally. As we have discussed earlier, there were two major internal land routes in ancient India – Uttarapatha, which connected northern and eastern parts of India with the northwestern fringes, and Dakshinapatha, which connected peninsular India with the western and northern parts of India. The Dakshinapatha started from Kaushambi near Allahabad, ran through Ujjaiyini (modern Ujjain) extended further up to Bhrigukaccha or Broach, an important port on western coast. The Dakshinapatha was further connected with

Pratishthana (modern Paithan), the capital of the Satavahanas. We have already discussed about the flourishing trade and the different items of import and export of the three early southern kingdoms with Rome and south-east Asia. Interestingly, in addition to the articles directly supplied by India, certain articles were brought to India from China and Central Asia and then sent to the eastern part of the Roman empire. For instance, earlier silk was directly sent from China to the Roman empire through the famous Silk Route, but after the annexation of Iran by Parthians, silk was diverted to the western Indian ports through the north-western part of the subcontinent and sometimes it was also transported via the east coast to west coast of the subcontinent. Thus, the period c. 200 BCE–300 CE was marked by urban prosperity all over India. More is known about the urban centres than the villages of this period.

QUESTIONS FROM LAST YEAR'S PRELIMS

1. With reference to ancient South India, Korkai, Poompuhar and Muchiri were well known as **(2023)**

(a) capital cities
(b) ports
(c) centres of iron-and-steel making
(d) shrines of Jain Tirthankaras

2. Which one of the following explains the practice of Vattakirutal' as mentioned in Sangam poems? **(2023)**

(a) Kings employing women bodyguards
(b) Learned persons assembling in royal courts to discuss religious and philosophical matters
(c) Young girls keeping watch over agricultural fields and driving away birds and animals
(d) A king defeated in a battle committing ritual suicide by starving himself to death

3. With one of the following statements about Sangam literature in ancient South India **(2022)**

(a) Sangam poems are devoid of any reference to material culture.
(b) The social classification of Varna was known to Sangam poets.
(c) Sangam poets have no reference to warrior ethic.
(d) Sangam literature refers to magical forces as irrational.

4. Which one of the following books of ancient India has the love story of the son of the founder of Sunga dynasty? **(2016)**

(a) Swapnavasavadatta
(b) Malavikaagnimitra
(c) Meghdoota
(d) Ratnavali

5. With reference to the religious history of India, consider the following statements:

i. The concept of Bodhisattva is central to Hinayana sect of Buddhism.
ii. Bodhisattva is a compassionate one on his way to enlightenment.
iii. Bodhisattva delays achieving his own salvation to help all sentient beings on their path to it.

Which of the statements given above is/are correct? **(2016)**

(a) i only (b) ii and iii only
(c) ii only (d) i, ii and iii

6. Some Buddhist rock-cut caves are called Chaityas, while the others are called Viharas. What is the difference between the two? **(2013)**

(a) Vihara is a place of worship, while Chaitya is the dwelling place of the monks.

(b) Chaitya is a place of worship, while Vihara is the dwelling place of the monks.

(c) Chaitya is the stupa at the far end of the cave, while Vihara is the hall axial to it.

(d) There is no material difference between the two.

7. With reference to the guilds (*shreni*) of ancient India that played a very important role in the country's economy, which of the following statements is/are correct? **(2012)**

i. Every guild was registered with the central authority of the state and the king was the chief administrative authority on them.

ii. The wages, rules of work, standards and prices were fixed by the guild.

iii. The guild had judicial powers over its own members.

Select the correct answer using the codes given below:

(a) i and ii only (b) iii only

(c) ii and iii only (d) i, ii and iii

8. With reference to the invaders in ancient India, which one of the following is the correct chronological order? **(2006)**

(a) Greeks-Shakas-Kushanas

(b) Greeks-Kushanas-Shakas

(c) Shakas-Greeks-Kushanas

(d) Shakas-Kushanas-Greeks

9. Consider the following statements:

i. The last Mauryan ruler Brihadratha was assassinated by his commander-in-chief Pushyamitra Sunga.

ii. The last Sunga king Devabhuti was assassinated by his Brahmana minister Vasudeva Kanva who usurped the throne.

iii. The last ruler of the Kanva dynasty was deposed by the Andhras.

Which of these statements is/are correct? **(2003)**

(a) i and ii (b) Only ii

(c) Only iii (d) i, ii and iii

10. Who among the following presided over the Buddhist Council held during the reign of Kanishka at Kashmir? **(2001)**

(a) Parsva (b) Nagarjuna

(c) Sudarka (d) Vasumitra

11. The practice of military governorship was first introduced in India by the **(2000)**

(a) Greeks (b) Shakas

(c) Parthians (d) Mughals

12. The Indo-Greek kingdom set up in north Afghanistan in the beginning of the second century BC was **(1999)**

(a) Bactria (b) Scythia

(c) Zedrasia (d) Aria

13. What is the correct chronological order in which the following appeared in India? **(1998)**

i. Gold Coins

ii. Punch marked silver coins

iii. Iron plough

iv. Urban culture

Select the correct answer using the codes given:

(a) iii, iv, i, ii (b) iii, iv, ii, i

(c) iv, iii, i, ii (d) iv, iii, ii, i

14. Many of the Greeks, Kushanas and Shakas embraced Buddhism rather than Hinduism because **(1998)**
(a) Buddhism was in the ascendant at that time
(b) They had renounced the policy of war and violence
(c) Caste-ridden Hinduism did not attract them
(d) Buddhism provided easier access to Indian Society

15. Which one of the following was a corporation of merchants in ancient India? **(1997)**
(a) Chaturvedimangalam
(b) Parishad
(c) Ashtadikgaja
(d) Manigrama

16. The term 'Yavanapriya' mentioned in ancient Sanskrit texts denoted **(1995)**
(a) A fine variety of Indian muslin
(b) Ivory
(c) Damsels sent to Greek courts for dance performance
(d) Pepper

ANSWERS

1. (b)	2. (d)	3. (b)	4. (b)	5. (b)	6. (b)	7. (d)	8. (a)
9. (d)	10. (d)	11. (a)	12. (a)	13. (b)	14. (d)	15. (d)	16. (d)

QUESTIONS FROM LAST YEAR'S MAINS

1. Highlight the Central Asian and Greco-Bactrian elements in Gandhara art. **(2019 GS1)**

2. Delineate the nature and impact of India's contact with Western Asia and the Mediterranean world during the Mauryan period. **(History Optional 2015)**

3. 'Not only does ancient Tamil literature furnish an accurate picture of widely disparate classes; it also describes the social condition of Tamil country as it was.' Discuss. **(History Optional 2015)**

4. Trace the role of guilds and trade organisations in the development of early Indian economy. **(History Optional 2015)**

5. The ancient civilization in Indian sub-continent differed from those of Egypt, Mesopotamia and Greece in that its culture and traditions have been preserved without a breakdown to the present day. Comment. **(2015 GS1)**

6. Gandhara sculpture owed as much to the Romans as to the Greeks. Explain. **(2014 GS1)**

7. In what ways can the Megalithic culture be considered foundational phase of the history of peninsular India? **(History Optional 2014)**

8. Though not very useful from the point of view of a connected political history of South India, the Sangam literature portrays the social and economic conditions of its time with remarkable vividness. Comment. (2013 GS1)

8. Justify Pliny's statement that the Rome was being drained out of its gold by India during the first century of the Christian era.

(History Optional 2012)

PRACTICE QUESTIONS – PRELIMS

1. Match the following:

Column I	Column II
i. Vatsayana	A. Engineer
ii. Agesilaus	B. Medical Science
iii. Vasumitra	C. Kamasutra
iv. Charaka	D. Philosopher

(a) i–A ii–C iii–D iv–B
(b) i–C ii–A iii–D iv–B
(c) i–B ii–D iii–A iv–C
(d) i–D ii–C iii–A iv–B

2. Consider the following statements:

i. The last Mauryan ruler Brihadratha was assassinated by his commander-in-chief Pushyamitra Sunga.
ii. Pushyamitra Sunga was succeeded by King Devabhuti.
iii. The most famous ruler of the Satavahana dynasty was Gautamiputra Satkarni.

Which of these statements is/are correct?

(a) i and iii (b) Only ii
(c) Only iii (d) i, ii and iii

3. Consider the following statements:

(i) Kalinga rose under King Kharvela of the Chedi dynasty.
(ii) The Sunga dynasty was followed by the Kanva dynasty
(iii) The Junagadh inscription pertains to Pushyamitra Sunga.

Which of these statements is/are correct?

(a) i and ii (b) Only ii
(c) Only iii (d) i, ii and iii

4. Match the following:

Column I	Column II
i. Chola	A. Nedunjeliyan
ii. Chera	B. Karikala
iii. Pandya	C. Kharvela
iv. Chedi	D. Senguttuvan

(a) i–A ii–C iii–D iv–B
(b) i–C ii–A iii–D iv–B
(c) i–B ii–D iii–A iv–C
(d) i–D ii–C iii–A iv–B

5. Match the following:

Column I	Column II
i. Chola	A. Uraiyur
ii. Chera	B. Kalinga
iii. Pandya	C. Muziris
iv. Chedi	D. Madurai

(a) i–A ii–C iii–D iv–B
(b) i–C ii -A iii–D iv–B
(c) i–B ii–D iii–A iv–C
(d) i–D ii–C iii–A iv–B

6. Consider the following statements:

i. Official language of the Satvahanas was Prakrit written in Brahmi script.
ii. The Satavahanas mostly used lead coins.
iii. The Satvahanas were the first to grant tax free land to Brahmanas and Buddhists.

Which of these statements is/are correct?

(a) i and ii (b) Only ii
(c) Only iii (d) i, ii and iii

7. Consider the following statements:

i. The Gandhara School of art is an indigenous school as compared to the Mathura school, which had Greek influences.

ii. Mahayana Buddhism developed due to Central Asian influence.

iii. The Bodhisattvas are important component of Mahayana philosophy.

Which of these statements is/are incorrect?

(a) i and ii (b) Only i

(c) Only iii (d) i, ii and iii

ANSWERS

1. (b) 2. (a) 3. (a) 4. (c) 5. (a) 6. (d) 7. (b)

PRACTICE QUESTIONS – MAINS

1. What was the overall impact of Central Asian influence on different aspects of Indian sub-continent? Elucidate giving adequate examples.

2. The period from 2nd Century BCE to 3rd Century BCE was the most flourishing period for trade and commerce in ancient India. Do you agree? What were the reasons behind this growth?

3. Describe the system of administration and social organisation of the Satvahanas.

4. Describe the key differences between the basic philosophy of Mahayana and Hinayana branches of Buddhism.

5. What were the reasons for the invasion of Central Asian people on Indian sub-continent? Elucidate giving their chronological arrival in the sub-continent.

CHAPTER

8

The Guptas and the Vakatakas (c. 300–600 CE)

As we have discussed earlier, after the fall of the Maurya empire, the Kushans in the North and the Satavahanas in the Deccan emerged as the two major political powers. They not only brought political unity and economic prosperity to these regions, but were also great stabilising forces in their respective areas. Around c. 230 CE, the Kushans' reign ultimately came to an end in northern India, and a considerable part of its empire came under the suzerainty of the Murundas (possibly kinsmen of the Kushans). The Murundas ruled for a short time span of about 25–30 years. Around the last decades of the 3rd century CE (around 275 CE), a new empire arose on the ruins of the Kushan empire and established its sway over a good part of the former dominions of both the Kushans and the Satavahanas. This was the Gupta empire, which kept northern India politically united for more than a century.

The Guptas are believed to be feudatories of the Kushans[1]. They are most likely Vaishyas[2] in origin, and they ruled over fertile parts of the *madhyadesha*, that is, *anuganga* (the middle Gangetic basin), *saketa* (modern Ayodhya, Uttar Pradesh) and *magadha* (mostly Bihar). Prayag (modern Allahabad, Uttar Pradesh) was probably their important centre of power, which, due to its strategic location, further aided in the expansion of the empire. The Guptas could easily exploit the iron ore deposits of central India and southern Bihar, and also took advantage of their proximity to the areas of north India which carried on silk trade with the Byzantine empire (Eastern Roman empire). 'Garuda' was probably their state seal. Historians often consider the Gupta period as the 'golden age' of India's past as it is often remembered for certain key classical features, such as the political unification of a large part of the subcontinent under a mostly centralised government, the production of exceptional Sanskrit literary works, sophisticated stone sculpture and architecture, and innovative developments in the field of science and technology. The political history of the Guptas is largely reconstructed on the basis of certain excavated inscriptions and coins.

Gupta Dynasty

Maharaja Gupta/Sri Gupta (Founder of Gupta Dynasty)

- Founder of Gupta dynasty.

Maharaja Ghatotkacha

- Like his father, he was not documented by his own inscriptions. The earliest description of him is found in his grandson's Samudragupta's Allahabad pillar inscription.

Chandragupta – I (c. 319–335/336 CE)

- First important king of the Gupta Dynasty; laid the foundations of the Gupta empire and claimed the title of *maharajadhiraja* (king of kings).
- Started Gupta era in 319–320 CE, which presumably marks his accession date.
- His empire included parts of modern Bihar, Uttar Pradesh and Bengal, with its capital which was at Pataliputra.
- Enhanced his power and prestige by marrying Kumaradevi, princess of Lichchhavi clan of Nepal (since the Guptas were probably Vaishyas by caste, marriage into a Kshatriya clan granted legitimacy, prestige and strength to the Guptas). Coins were struck in the joint names of the Emperor, his queen, and the Lichchhavi nation, thereby acknowledging this marital alliance. In fact, Samudragupta was referred to as *Lichchhavi-dauhitra* (grandson of the Lichchhavis) in the famous *Allahabad prashasti*.

[1] It is highly likely that the Guptas learnt the use of saddles, reins, buttoned coats, trousers, and boots from the Kushans and became excellent horsemen themselves.

[2] Different titles are recommended for the different varnas by the Dharmashastras. The title '*Sharman*' or auspicious is recommended for the *Brahmana*, '*Varman*' or armour for the *Kshatriya*, '*Gupta*' or hidden for the *Vaishya*, and *Dasa* or servile for the '*Shudra*'.

Samudragupta (c. 335/336–375 CE)

- Son of Chandragupta I, who followed a policy of war and conquest and enormously enlarged his kingdom. His rule was one of expansion marked first by the conquest of his immediate neighbours and then by campaigns to the east and the south, where chiefdoms and kingdoms were subdued and forced to pay tribute to him. Due to this policy of his, the historian V. A. Smith has called him the 'Napoleon' of India.
- Had a disputed accession to the throne. It is generally believed that his father had chosen him successor even though he had several elder brothers, which led to a struggle for succession after his father's death. It is presumed that Samudragupta prevailed after subduing his rival, Kachagupta, an obscure prince of the dynasty who was also his brother.
- His achievements are recorded in a long inscription (a eulogy) engraved on the Allahabad pillar (Prayaga-prashasti), whose surface also contains inscriptions of Ashoka and later, the Mughal emperor Jahangir. Unlike the Ashokan inscription which stresses on peace and non-violence, Samudragupta's inscription extolling his deeds and virtues stresses on violence and military conquest, and gives us information about his different conquests.

  It was composed in pure Sanskrit by Harisena, who was not only his court poet but was also a *kumaramatya*, that is, a high-ranking official who described himself by different titles such as *sandhivigrahika* (minister for peace and war) and *mahadandanayaka* (judicial/military officer).
- According to the inscription, *Samudragupta exerted direct or indirect control over much of the Indian subcontinent, stretching from kingdoms in Nepal and Punjab in the north to the Pallava kingdom at Kanchipuram in the south-east*. The last vestiges of Kushan rule, like the Shakas, the Murundas, and even the faraway independent territory of *Simhala* (present day Sri Lanka), accepted his suzerainty as well.
- The *prashasti* divides Samudragupta's opponents into four categories: rulers slain, whose dominions Samudragupta annexed outright; 'frontier' kings, who were forced to pay homage; rulers defeated, but reinstated as tributaries; and 'distant' kings, who acknowledged Samudragupta as an emperor by sending him embassies. He adopted a different policy for each category. In the first category, located in the Ganga-Yamuna doab, he followed a policy of annexation. He defeated nine Naga rulers and incorporated their kingdoms in the Gupta empire. In the second category, consisting of neighbouring frontier kingdoms and nine republican states of Punjab and western India, Samudragupta's conquests awed the frontier kings into submission and they agreed to pay tribute and taxes to him and obey his orders without any fight. He conquered the *atavika rajyas*, that is, forest kingdoms of central India and forced their rulers into servitude.
- The Vindhyan forest kingdoms had a strategic value as they held the key of the route to south India. This enabled him to proceed to the south along the eastern coast, conquering

twelve kings on the way and reached as far as Kanchi near present day Chennai. The Prayag *prashasti* mentions the defeat of the twelve south Indian rulers (together) by Samudragupta (including Vishnugopa of Kanchi). It is pertinent to note that Virasena was the commander of Samudragupta during his southern campaign. However, instead of annexing the southern kingdoms, he adopted the policy of political conciliation and reinstated the defeated kings on their thrones. It is generally presumed that this policy was adopted since he knew the limitation of not being able to keep them under control and subservience after returning to his capital in the north. Therefore, it was enough for him that these states recognised his suzerainty and paid him tributes and presents. Lastly, the Shaka satraps of western India and Kushan rulers of northwest India and Afghanistan seem to have paid him homage. The ruler of Ceylon sent an embassy to secure privileges for Sinhalese monks at Bodh Gaya. The inscription adds that *Samudragupta also received tributes from many kings of south-east Asia*. It is generally believed that though he had spread his influence over a vast area, Samudragupta exercised direct administrative control mainly over Indo-Gangetic basin.

- He celebrated his conquests by performing an *ashvamedha* (horse sacrifice) and by issuing *ashvamedha* coins (portraying the scene of the sacrifice) marking the occasion.
- He was called *Anukampavan* (full of compassion) as he granted permission to the Buddhist king of Ceylon, Meghavarman, to build a monastery and rest house for pilgrims from Ceylon at Bodh Gaya. The magnificence of this monastery was described in the 7th-century works of Hieun Tsang/Xuanzang.
- He is depicted on his coins both as a muscular warrior (flaunting his victories on hundreds of battlefields) as well as a poet, a musician and a patron of learning. He was a great patron of art and adopted the title of Kaviraja (king among poets).
- His love for music is attested by his coins that represent him playing on the veena (lyre) on occasion.
- Legends on his coins include epithets such as *parakramah* (brave), *apratirathah* (invincible), *vyaghra-parakramah* (brave as a tiger) and *ashvamedha-parakramah* (powerful enough to perform the *ashvamedha*).
- Though Hindu by practice, he extended his patronage to other religions, and one of his ministers was the great Buddhist philosopher Vasubandhu. Samudragupta is remembered for his patronage of art and literature.

Chandragupta II (c. 376–413/15 CE)

- According to some legends, Samudragupta was succeeded by his elder son Ramagupta, but Chandragupta II killed him. It is also believed that during Ramagupta's tenure, the Gupta empire was invaded by a powerful Shaka king. Ramagupta lost the battle and signed a humiliating treaty that allowed his wife to be sent to the enemy camp. It is said that Chandragupta II had to kill his brother and marry his wife, Dhruvadevi, to safeguard the honour of the Gupta dynasty.

- The peak of the territorial expansion of the Gupta empire was reached during Chandragupta II's reign (also known as Chandragupta Vikramaditya), who extended the limits of his empire by conquests and marital alliances with other royal dynasties of the period. He married Kuberanaga, the Naga princess, and had a daughter, Prabhavati, with her. Prabhavati was married to Rudrasena II of the ruling Vakataka dynasty in Deccan. After the death of her husband, Prabhavati ruled the territory as regent to her minor sons with the help of her father. During this twenty year period, the Vakataka realm was practically a part of the Gupta empire.
- Chandragupta thus exercised indirect control over the Vakataka kingdom, which proved very beneficial to him. With his great influence in this central Indian region, he was able to target his other enemies better. Thus, he conquered western Malwa and Gujarat from the Shaka satraps (one of them was Rudrasimha III) who had been in command in western India for about the past four centuries. This conquest took the expanse of the Gupta empire to the western sea coast, which was an important region for trade and commerce. This contributed to the prosperity of Malwa and its chief city Ujjain, which was also Chandragupta II's second capital.
- An iron pillar inscription[3] at Mehrauli in Delhi indicates that his empire included even north-western India and Bengal. He took the title of *Vikramaditya*, that is, the one who is as powerful as the sun, and *Simhavikrama*.
- He was the first ruler to issue silver coins. He also issued copper coins and is referred to as *Chandra* on his coins. He also issued gold coins called *dinara*.

FIGURE 8.1 Queen Kumaradevi and King Chandragupta I on a coin of their son Samudragupta

[3] On the iron pillar, the exploits of a king called Chandra are glorified who had established Gupta authority in north western India and in a substantial part of Bengal.

- The Udaigiri cave inscriptions refer to his *digvijaya*, that is, his conquest of the whole world.
- Fa Hien/Faxian, the famous Chinese traveler, visited India during his reign.
- His court at Ujjain was adorned by nine famous scholars known as the *Navaratnas* ('nine gems')

Navaratnas	
Kalidasa	Renowned classical Sanskrit poet and playwright of India and a peerless genius whose works such as *Abhijananashakuntalam*, *Malavikagnimitram*, *Vikramorvasiyam* became famous worldwide.
Amarasimha	Sanskrit lexicographer and poet, and his 'Amarakosha' is a vocabulary of Sanskrit roots, homonyms and synonyms. It is also called *Trikanda*, as it has three parts containing around ten thousand words.
Varahamihira	Renowned mathematician and astrologer who wrote three important books: (a) *Panchasiddhantika* (a treatise on mathematical astronomy which is a compendium of *Vedanga Jyotisha* as well as Hellenistic astronomy and summarises five earlier astronomical treatises, namely the (i) *Surya Siddhanta,* (ii) *Romaka Siddhanta,* (iii) *Paulisa Siddhanta,* (iv) *Vasishtha Siddhanta, and* (v) *Paitamaha Siddhanta*) (b) *Brihat Samhita* (compilation of wide-ranging topics such as astrology, planetary movements, eclipses, rainfall, clouds, architecture, growth of crops, manufacture of perfume, matrimony, domestic relations, gems, pearls and rituals, which also provides interesting details of the beliefs of those times), and (c) *Brihat Jataka* (considered the standard textbook on Vedic astrology).
Dhanvantri	Physician who is considered the father of Ayurveda (literally meaning 'knowledge for longevity').
Ghatakarapara	An expert in sculpture and architecture.
Shanku	An architect who wrote the *Shilpashastra*.
Kahapanaka	An astrologer who wrote the *Jyothisyashastra.*
Vararuchi	Grammarian and Sanskrit scholar and the author of the *Prakrit Prakasha*, which is first grammar of the Prakrit language.
Vetala Bhatta	A magician who wrote the *Mantrashastra*

Kumaragupta I (c. 415–455 CE)

- Adopted the title of *Shakraditya* and *Mahendraditya* and performed ashavmedha sacrifice.
- Founded the Nalanda University (near present day Patna).
- Worshipper of lord *Karttikeya* (son of Lord Shiva).
- During the last years of his reign, peace was disturbed on the north-west frontier due to the invasion of the Huns of Central Asia. In the mid-5th century, the *ye-tha*, known as White Huns (Hepthalites), became powerful in the Oxus valley. After occupying Bactria, the Huns crossed the Hindukush mountains and entered India by occupying Gandhara. Their first attack during his reign was repulsed by prince Skandagupta. The Guptas however could not protect their empire for long and the successive waves of Hun invasion made the Guptas very weak. This was one of the main factors which accelerated the disintegration of the Gupta empire.
- The Bilsad inscription is the oldest record of his reign and dates to Gupta year 96, which corresponds to 415 CE. Other inscriptions of Kumaragupta's reign are the Karandanda, Mandsor and Damodar Copper plate inscriptions (the latter mentions that *trade guilds served as banks for advancing loans and receiving deposits in Kumaragupta's reign*).

Skandagupta (c. 455–467 CE)

- Faced and repulsed the Huns successfully.
- Junagarh/Girnar inscription of his reign tells that *his governor* Parnadatta *got the* Sudarshan lake *repaired.*
- Adopted the title *Vikramaditya*.
- The Gupta empire continued to exist but central control weakened and local governors became feudatory kings with hereditary rights.
- Later Gupta kings included Purugupta, Kumaragupta II, Budhagupta, Narasimhagupta, Kumaragupta III and Vishnugupta. The Gupta empire declined due to a variety of factors.

Decline of the Guptas

Reasons for the decline of the Guptas	
Hun Invasions	As we have discussed earlier in this chapter, the Huns' further movement into the Indian territories was successfully repulsed by Skandagupta in the early 5th century. In the later half of the 5th century, weak successors of Skandagupta could not check growing Hun power and the Hun chief Toramana was able to conquer large parts of western India, stretching up to Eran near Bhopal in central India. Banabhatta in his *Harshcharitra* refers to the Huns invasion. The inscriptions issued by the Huns and

	numismatic evidence shows that by 485 CE, they had occupied what is present day Punjab, Rajasthan, Kashmir, eastern Malwa and a large part of central India. In 515 CE, Toramana was succeeded by his son Mihirkula, who was a tyrant and an iconoclast (Kalhana's *Rajataringini* mentions his cruelty; even Hieun Tsang mentions him as a fierce persecutor of Buddhists) who finally suffered defeat at the hands of Yashodharman of Malwa, Narasimhagupta Baladitya of the Gupta dynasty, and the Maukharis. However, this victory over the Huns could not revive the Gupta Empire.
Rise of Feudatories	The Guptas' power was severely curbed by the rise of feudatories. Yashodharman of Malwa, who belonged to Aulikara feudatory family, successfully challenged the authority of the Guptas after defeating Mihirkula, and set up 532 pillars of victory commemorating his conquest of almost the whole of northern India. Even though Yashodharman's rule was short-lived, it did cause a severe damage to the Gupta empire's reputation and image. Motivated and encouraged by these scheme of events, other feudatories too rose in rebellion against the Guptas and gradually declared themselves independent in Bihar, Bengal, Madhya Pradesh, Vallabhi, Gujarat, western Malwa, and so on. It is noteworthy that after the reign of Skandagupta, hardly any Gupta coin or inscription is found in western Malwa and Saurashtra.
Gradual Decline in Economic Prosperity	The gradual economic decline of the Gupta empire is indicated by the gold coins of later Gupta rulers, which have less of gold content and more of alloy. We also notice a gradual disappearance of coins in the post-Gupta period. It led the kings to make payments in form of land rather than cash. It is evident by the discovery of large scale land grant charters donating land to *brahmanas* and officers. This further aggravated the feudal tendencies of the empire and indicated lesser control on the part of the central government. Also, due to the loss of western India, the rich revenues from foreign trade and commerce also dropped and this further crippled the Guptas.

'*The migration of a guild of silk weavers from Gujarat to Malwa in 473 CE and their adoption of non-productive professions show that there was probably not much demand of cloth produced by them*' (as stated in Mandasor inscription).

The decline of the Gupta empire resulted in the emergence of numerous ruling dynasties in different parts of northern India. Prominent among them were the Pushyabhutis of Thanesar, Maukharies of Kannauj and the Maitrakas of Valabhi. The political scene in the Peninsular India was no different. The Chalukyas and the Pallavas emerged as strong regional powers in Deccan and northern Tamil Nadu, respectively.

The Vakatakas of the Deccan

In peninsular India, especially in northern Maharashtra and Vidarbha, the Satavahanas were succeeded by a local power known as the Vakatakas, who played an effective role in the political game of the Deccan for more than two and a half centuries. The Vakatakas were contemporaneous of the Guptas in northern India. The *Puranas* refer to the dynasty as the *Vindhyakas*. The Vakatakas, who were Brahmin themselves (belonging to the Vishnuvriddha gotra) were great champions of the Brahmanical religion and performed numerous Vedic sacrifices. Their history can be reconstructed on the basis of a large number of copper-plate land grant charters issued to the *brahmanas*. Even though they promoted Brahminism, they were liberal in outlook and patronised Buddhism as well.

The Vakatakas had matrimonial ties with the imperial Guptas (Rudrasena II of the royal Vakataka family was married to Prabhavatigupta, the daughter of Chandragupta II of the imperial Gupta family), the Nagas of Padmavati, the Kadambas of Karnataka and the Vishnukundins of Andhra. Culturally, the Vakataka kingdom is important because it became a channel to spread Brahminical culture to southern India. The Vakatakas are noted for having been patrons of the arts, architecture and literature. Their legacy in terms of public works and monuments has made significant contributions to Indian culture. The rock-cut Buddhist *viharas* and *chaityas* of the Ajanta Caves (a UNESCO World Heritage Site) were built under the patronage of the Vakataka king, Harisena. They are also credited with having built a few temples in Tigwa and Nachanakuthara. They made a remarkable contribution in the field of painting. Ajanta cave numbers XVI, XVII and XIX are the best examples of Vakataka excellence in the field of painting, in particular the painting titled *Mahabhinishkramana*. Not only the Vakataka rulers, but their ministers or governors like Hastibhoja and Varahadeva also extended their benevolent patronage to the Ajanta cave painters. Kings like Pravarasena II (celebrated author of the *Setubandhakavya*) and Sarvasena (author of the *Harivijaya*) were themselves poets of great repute in Prakrit. A style by name *Vaidharbhariti* was developed in Sanskrit during their rule, which was praised by the poets of the likes of Kalidasa, Banabhatta and Dandin. The Vakatakas had a stamp of their own in their rulership, which is truly unmatched.

Vakataka Dynasty

Vindhyashakti I (last quarter of the 3rd century, around c. 250–270 CE)

- Founder of the Vakataka dynasty, who probably ruled from Purika.
- He is credited to have performed a number of Vedic sacrifices and thus revived Brahminical rituals, which were in abeyance during the rule of the later Satavahanas.
- The Ajanta inscriptions of the time of Harisena describe him as a *dvija* and praise him for his military achievements. It is claimed that *the sun was obscured by the masses of dust raised by his horses' hooves, and he is compared with the gods Puramdara (Indra) and Upendra (Vishnu).*

Pravarasena (c. 270–330 CE)

- Vindhayasakti's son and successor, who is considered the founder of the real power and greatness of the Vakatakas. He extended the empire southwards into Vidarbha and adjoining areas of the Deccan, with his capital at Kanchanaka (modern Nachna).
- His son Gautamiputra married the daughter of the Naga king Bhavanaga, which cemented an important political alliance.
- By military exploits and matrimonial alliances, he extended his kingdom from Bundelkhand in the north to Hyderabad in the south, and to commemorate his victories, he performed an *asvamedha* sacrifice and a *vajapeya* sacrifice. He was the only Vakataka king who took the title of *samrat*, while all other kings took the modest title of maharaja.
- After the death of Pravarasena, his four sons divided the empire and ruled independently in separate provinces. Gautamiputra in all likelihood died during the lifetime of his father and hence, his son Rudrasena I succeeded his grandfather Pravarsena to the throne and ruled from Nandivardhana, near modern Nagpur. Sarvasena, another son of Pravarasena, started ruling independently from Vastugulma as his capital, which is identified as modern Bassien in Vidarbha. We do not have adequate knowledge of the two other sons of Pravarasena. By 340 CE, the Vakatakas were divided into two lines, one ruling from Nandivardhana and the other ruling from Vatsagulma.

  It is rather interesting to note that in spite of these divisions in the Vakataka kingdom, the contemporary Gupta rulers never attacked the Vakatakas. This may be due to the Guptas' belief that the Vakatakas could be useful to them in defeating the Western Kashtrapas.

NANDIVARDHANA BRANCH/LINE

Rudrasena I (c. 340–365 CE)

- Founder of the Vakataka Nandivardhana branch, which ruled from Nandivardhana (near Nagpur).
- Since no inscription belonging to his reign is available, not much is known about the events that took place during his reign. He is known to have been a worshipper of Lord *Mahabhairava*, the fierce form of Shiva.

Prithvisena I (c. 365–390 CE)

- Described in later Vakataka inscriptions as a righteous conqueror, he was compared to the epic hero Yudhishthira due to his comparable qualities of truthfulness, transparency, compassion and humility.
- Padmapura seems to have been an important administrative centre during his time.

- Spent most his time in consolidating his kingdom. The chief feature of his reign is a political alliance between Chandragupta II and himself, and together they defeated the Shaka *satraps* of Malwa and Kathiawar.
- During the later parts of his reign, the Guptas and the Vakatakas entered into a matrimonial alliance since Prithvisena's son Rudrasena II, the crown prince, was married to Prabhavatigupta, the daughter of Chandragupta II.
- Prithivisena also was a Shaiva like his father.

Rudrasena II (c. 390–395 CE)

- Ruled only for a period of five years as he died prematurely, leaving behind three minor sons Divakarasena, Damodarasena and Pravarasena. His wife Prabhavatigupta ruled as the regent until 410 CE. *Unfortunately*, Divakarasena also died prematurely and did not live long enough to ascend the throne but his younger brothers Damodarasena and Pravavarasena II did. In fact, the seal of Prabhavatigupta's Maregaon plates describes her as the '*mother of two kings*'.

Pravarasena II (c. 395–440 CE)

- Largest number of Vakataka inscriptions belong to his reign. A dozen copper-plate grants of his were discovered in different parts of Vidarbha, though Prabhavatigupta continued to issue inscriptions in her own right and died during the later part of her son's reign.
- He is credited with the founding of a new capital at Pravarapura, which is identified as Paunar in the present-day Wardha district.
- Even though he was a devotee of Shiva, he composed a Prakrit *kavya* glorifying Rama, the *Setubandha*/*Ravanavaha*, which is about Rama's journey to Lanka and his victory over Ravana.
- He entered into a matrimonial alliance with the contemporary Kadambas (near Mysore). His son Narendrasena was married to a princess of Kuntala, Ajihata Bhattarika, the daughter of Kakutsavarman of the Kadamba dynasty.

Narendrasena (c. 440–460 CE)

- It is believed that after the death of Pravarsena II, a struggle for succession happened in which Narendrasena emerged successful.
- He had to face the invasion of the Nala king, Bhavadottavarman, both in the beginning and at the end of his reign. In between, he made some conquests, and had to face the stiff opposition of the Nalas all along.

Prithivisena II (c. 460–480 CE)

- Last known ruler of Nandivardhana branch of the Vakataka dynasty, who is credited with the revival of the fallen fortunes of the Vakatakas. His inscriptions refer to his *having twice rescued the sunken fortunes of Vakatakas*.
- He had to face the invasion of Harisena of Vatsagulma line thrice, and the invasion of Bhavadottavarman of the Nala dynasty. He also appears to have fought with the Traikutaka king, Dahrasena of southern Gujarat.
- After Prithivisena II's death, it is presumed that Harisena of the Vatsagulma line of the Vakatakas conquered his successors and united the Nandivardhana line with his own.

VATSAGULMA BRANCH/LINE

- The second major Vakataka line was the Vatsagulma branch, which had its capital at Vatsagulma (modern Washim in Akola district, Maharashtra). The founder *of the* Vatsagulma line *of the* Vakatakas was Sarvasena, the son of Pravarasena I.

Sarvasena (c. 330–355 CE)

- Adopted the title *dharma-maharaja*.
- Was believed to be a renowned Prakrit poet, and his lost work, the *Harivijaya*, was lauded by later writers. Some of his verses were incorporated into the *Gathasattasai*.

Vindhyashakti II/Vindhyasena (c. 355–400 CE)

- He ruled for almost four decades and his kingdom seems to have included the Marathwada region comprising of the southern part of Vidarbha, the northern part of Hyderabad state, and some other adjoining territories.
- He is believed to have defeated the Kadambas of Banavasi, who ruled over Kuntala (north Karnataka).
- His son and successor Pravarasena II appear to have ruled for a period of fifteen years. Pravarasena II was followed by Devasena, who was a pleasure-seeking ruler, but luckily had the services of a very capable minister, Hasthibhoja. His successor Harisena was the ablest and the greatest ruler of this line.

Harisena (c. 475–500 CE)

- Last known king of the Vatsagulma line, who not only united the two Vakataka branches but also extended his territories by conquering Kuntala, Avanti, Kalinga, Kosala, Konkan and Andhra. His kingdom extended from Malwa in the north to southern Maharashtra in the south, and from the Bay of Bengal in the east to the Arabian Sea in the west.
- Dandin, a poet of the 6th century CE, described Harisena as *'powerful, truthful and bountiful, glorious, lofty, and a penetrating critic of ethical and economic compendia'*.

- The Thalner copper plates (which record the gifts of villages of bronze workers and goldsmiths) belong to his rein and many of the Ajanta caves were executed during his reign. In one of the inscriptions at cave XVI and the Ghatotkacha cave, there is mention of his minister Varahadeva.

With the death of Harisena II, the glory of the Vakatakas ended and the Nalas, the Kadambas, the Kalachuris and Yasodharman of Malwa occupied their territory.

Various Facets of Life under the Guptas and the Vakatakas

a. Administrative Organisation

The king was the focus of administration and Gupta kings adopted pompous titles[4] like *parameshwara*, *maharajadhiraja*, *parama-bhattaraka*, *parama-daivata* (the foremost worshipper of gods) and *paramabhagavata* (foremost worshipper of Vasudeva Krishna). The Gupta kings also tried to exalt their status by comparing them with gods. The *Allahabad prashasti* thus which describes Samudragupta as a god dwelling on earth, equal to the gods *Dhanada* (Kuber), *Varuna* (god of the waters), *Indra* and *Antaka* (Yama), who had no antagonist of equal power in the world. Unlike the Mauryan period, where the political authority was concentrated in the hands of the king, the Gupta administration was decentralised in nature and contained many feudatories[5] like local kings and smaller chiefs, who ruled over large parts of their empire. These lesser rulers adorned their names with titles like *raja* and *maharaja*. The kingship was normally hereditary but there was an absence of the practice of primogeniture (that is, throne always going to the eldest son).

The Gupta bureaucracy was less elaborate[6] as compared to that of the Mauryas. The most important officers under the Guptas were called the *kumaramatyas*, with an office of their own called the *adhikarana*. They were appointed by the king and were possibly paid in cash. All the important functionaries like the *mantri* and the *senapati* were recruited from this cadre. Administrative posts were not only hereditary, but often several offices were combined in the hands of the same person. For instance, Harisena, the composer of the *Allahabad pillar inscription* of Samudragupta, was a *mahadandanayaka* (chief judicial officer) as well as a *mahasandhivigrahika* (minister for war and peace), and also the son of *mahadandanayaka* Dhruvabhuti. Similarly, in the Vakataka

---

[4] These titles also signified that the Guptas ruled over many lesser kings in their empire.

[5] The feudatory chiefs had primarily three obligations to fulfil:

(a) They offered homage to the sovereign by personal attendance at his court;

(b) Paid regular tribute to him; and

(c) Presented the sovereign daughters in marriage.

[6] As their political system was more feudal since much of the imperial administration was managed by feudatories and beneficiaries, the rural and urban administration were supervised by elders while the leading artisans and merchants regulated most economic activities.

empire, both father Hasthibhoja and his son Varahadeva served as ministers under Devasena and Harisena, respectively. The hereditary nature of the post naturally weakened the royal control over the administration.

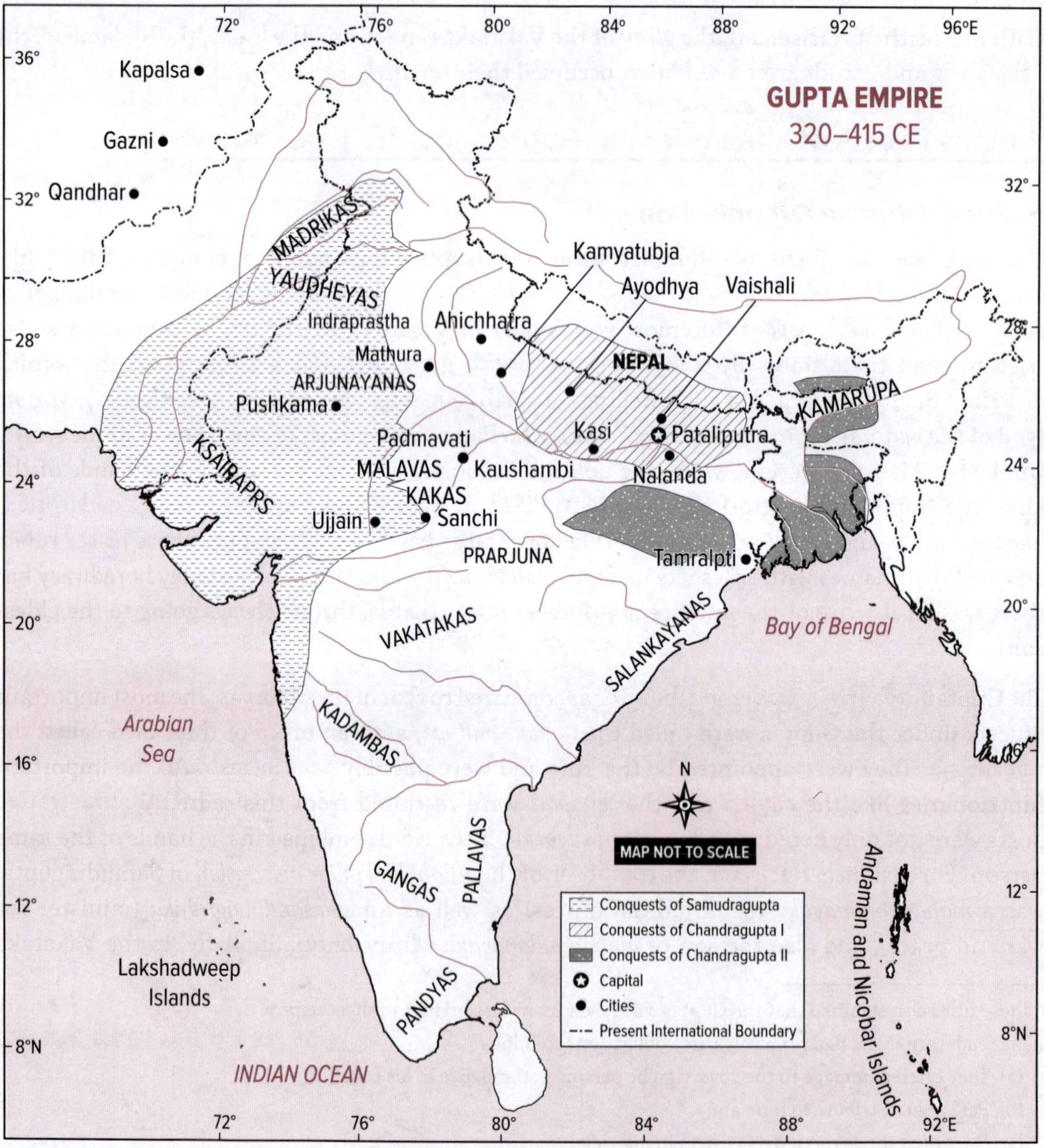

FIGURE 8.2 Gupta Empire

The Gupta empire was divided into provinces known as *deshas*, *rashtra* or *bhuktis* and their head was called *uparika*. Sometimes, crown princes were also made the viceroys of the provinces. The uparika was appointed directly by the king and he had the authority to appoint the head of the district administration and district town board. The provinces were further divided into a number of districts called *pradeshas* or *vishayas*, which were placed under the charge of *vishayapati*. In eastern India, the vishayas were divided into *vithis*, which were further divided into villages. The village headman called *gramadhyaksha/gramika* looked after the affairs of the village with the help of village elders. The position of village headman strengthened during Gupta times as no land transactions could be affected without his consent. In the case of the Vakatakas, less information is available about their administrative structure. However, it was very similar to the Guptas. Their empire was also divided into provinces called *rashtras* or *rajyas*, which were administered by governors known as *rajyadhikritas*. The provinces were further divided into *vishayas*, which were again divided into *aharas* and *bhogas/bhuktis*. An officer called *sarvadhyaksha* presumably appointed and directed subordinate officers known as *kulaputras*.

Empire Division Structure:

- *Bhukti* (province) → *Uparika* (viceroy)

  ↓

- *Vishayas* (district) → *Vishayapati*

  ↓

- *Vithis* (sub-districts)

  ↓

Gram (village) → *Gramika*

The urban administration included the additional feature of organised professional bodies. For instance, the Damodarpur copper-plates of the reign of Kumaragupta indicate that in the district of Kotivarsha (north Bengal), the *uparika* was assisted in his administrative duties by a corporate council including prominent members of the town – an *adhishthana adhikarana* (a board of five members). These members were: the *uparika*, the *nagara-sreshthin* (chief merchant), *sarthavaha* (chief caravan trader), *prathama-kulika* (chief artisan or merchant) and *prathama-kayastha* (chief in-charge of revenue collection).

The judicial system was far more developed under the Gupta rulers than in earlier times. For the first time, civil and criminal laws were clearly demarcated. Theft and adultery were subjects treated under criminal law. Disputes regarding various types of property formed the body of civil law. Elaborate laws were laid down about inheritance. However, like earlier periods, laws were based on the *varna* hierarchy. The supreme judicial power rested with king and he tried cases with the help of the *brahmana* priests. There was the office of *mahanadanyaka*, who probably functioned as chief justice. *Uparikas* and *Vishyapatis* in their respective territorial jurisdiction dispensed the judicial function. Interestingly, the guilds of merchants and artisans were governed by their own laws and enjoyed certain immunities. They could punish their members who violated the laws and customs of the guild, however capital punishment was not at all given (as reported by Fa-Hien).

Judicial Structure:

- *Mahanadanyaka* (chief justice)

↓

- *Uparikas* ⟶ provinces

↓

- *Vishyapatis* ⟶ at district level

The numerical strength of the Gupta army is not known, but it is accepted that the emperor had a standing army which must have been supplemented by the feudatories' forces in times of need. Thus, military organisation was feudal in character. Suprisingly, the standard term of *senapati* is not found in the Gupta inscriptions though it is mentioned in some Vakataka epigraphs. The commander-in-chief of the army was known as *mahabaladhikrita*. Horse chariots receded into the background and cavalry came to the forefront in this period. There is mention of the *bhatashvapati* (commander of infantry and cavalry). In case of the Vakatakas, *chhatras* denoted irregular troops while *batas* referred to regular troops who were not only responsible for maintaining law and order but also extracted revenue due to the state.

Key terms / Positions	Meaning
(a) *Mahapratihara*	Chief of the palace guards
(b) *Pratihara*	One who regulated ceremonies and granted the necessary permits for admission to the royal presence
(c) *Khadyatapakita*	Superintendent of the royal kitchen
(d) *Dutakas*	Spies
(e) *Dandapashika*	District level police officer
(f) *Vinayashitisthapaka*	One who maintains moral and social discipline
(g) *Akshapataladhikrita*	Keeper of royal records
(h) *Pustapalas*	Record keepers of land transfers
(i) *Shaulkika*	Collector of *shulka*
(j) *Khila*	Untilled land
(k) *Aprahata*	Cultivable wasteland

(l) *Aprada*	Unsettled land
(m) *Vastu*	Habitat land
(n) *Pataka*	Land measure equivalent to 60–80 acres
(o) *Modakas*	Modern *laddus*, which were a prized sweet of the Guptas
(p) *Panchayatan*	A style of temple construction

b. The Economy

The Gupta period was characterised by elements of continuity and change[7] in economic life. It witnessed an increase in land taxes but a decrease in trade and commerce taxes (such as *shulka* or tolls). The period from c. 4th century to 8th century was a period of agricultural expansion[8]. Due to the practice of granting lands to brahmanas[9] (*brahmadeyas*, *agraharas* or *shasanas*) and to some other officers, vast areas of virgin land were brought under cultivation and major improvements were made in the existing methods of production (such as use of iron ploughshare, irrigation and preservation of cattle wealth) to attain higher yield. The inscriptions refer to a variety of land types, including cultivable land (*Kshetra*), uncultivable land (*Khila*), forest land or jungle (*Aprahata*), Grazing land (Gopata Sarah) and habitable land (Vasti) while terms like *Kulyavapa (12–16 acres)*, *Dronavapa (1½–2 acres)*, and *Adhavapa (3/8–1/2 acre)* were related to land measurements. The king collected taxes varying from one-fourth to one-sixth of the produce. Two new agricultural taxes that appear in Gupta inscriptions are *uparikara* (probably a tax imposed on temporary tenants) and *udranga* (its exact nature is not clear, but might be water tax or a sort of police tax). There is also mention of *vata-bhuta* tax, which probably refers to cesses for the maintenance of rites performed for the winds and spirits, and *halirakara*, probably plough tax. In addition to these taxes, peasants were also subjected to *vishti* (forced labour) for serving the royal army and officials. Villagers were obliged to provide the royal officials on tour with food grains, items of daily maintenance such as grass for animals, hide for seats, charcoal for cooking, etc. Since most of the administration was managed by the feudatories and beneficiaries, so unlike the Mauryas, the Guptas did not regulate economic activities on a big scale. Vakataka inscriptions mention of *klipta* (purchase tax or sales tax) and *upaklipta* (additional minor tax).

The Gupta and post-Gupta period witnessed a comparative decline in the country's trade and commerce. Till 550 CE, India continued to have some trade with the Eastern Roman empire, to

---

[7] For instance, during the 1st half of the Gupta period (from around 300 CE till 450 CE), the process of economic growth continued but around the middle of the 5th century, the economy entered the phase of reversal.

[8] The decline of economic activities, specially towards the end of the 5th century, increased the economic significance of agriculture and due to the decline of secondary and tertiary activities, ruralisation of the Indian economy took place.

[9] Started in the Deccan by the Satvahanas, the practice of grating land free of tax to religious functionaries became a regular affair in Gupta times. The villages granted to the beneficiaries could not be entered by royal agents, retainers, and others and they were also empowered to punish criminals. The grant of fiscal and administrative concessions to priests and administrators further added to the feudal character of Guptas.

which it exported silk and spices. Around the sixth century, the Romans learnt the art of rearing silk worms, which adversely affected India's export foreign trade. The Mandasor inscription is testimony to the fact that a guild of silk weavers left their original home at Lata in western Gujarat and migrated to Mandasor, where they gave up their original occupation and took to other professions. The disruption of the north-western trade route by the Huns was another factor for this decline. India tried to make up for the loss by carrying on trade with South-East Asian countries, but it did not help revive the economy substantially. During the Gupta period, the north-Indian trade with south-east Asia was handled by the ports of the east coast i.e. Tamralipti, Ghantashala, and Kadura while those of the west coast, Broach, Chaul, Kalyan and Cambay, traded with the Mediterranean and west Asia but the more southerly of these ports were outside Gupta control. The loss in trade lessened the inflow of gold and silver into the country. It is confirmed by a general scarcity of gold coins after the Guptas. In ancient India, the Guptas issued a large number of gold coins[10] called *dinaras* though the gold content is not as pure as Kushan ones. However, the gold coins of each successive Gupta ruler, after Chandragupta II, contained less gold and more alloy. After the conquest of the western *satraps* of Gujarat, they issued a large number of silver coins (*rupyakas*) mainly for local exchange and very few copper coins.

There is frequent mention of artisans, merchants and guilds in different inscriptions and seals of both Guptas and Vakatakas, which point towards thriving urban crafts and trade. There is also mention of the flourishing conditions and philanthropic activities of guilds. For instance, the Indore plates of the Vakataka king Pravarasena mention of a *vanijaka* (merchant) named *Chandra who bought half of the village that was gifted by the king to the brahmanas*. Other inscriptions mention the construction of temples, shelter homes, assembly houses and gardens by merchants. In fact, they also took an active part in the town administration during the Gupta period. The same is affirmed even by Chinese traveller Fa-Hien who informs us that Magadha was full of cities and its rich people believed in benevolence and righteousness and supported charitable offerings.

c. Society

The structure of the society underwent change in the Gupta period. The *brahmana* supremacy not only continued but rather increased in Gupta times, as evident from the large number of land grants to the *brahmanas* not only from the rulers (*brahmadeya*) but from certain categories of other people too. In return of this favour and support, *brahmanas* presented the Gupta kings as possessing attributes of gods and tried to legitimise the position of the Guptas. The Guptas, who were originally *vaishyas*, came to be looked upon as *kshatriyas* by the *brahmanas*. Since the *brahmadeya* land was given along with administrative rights and tax exemptions, it resulted in creation of a new class of *brahmana* landlords. The castes proliferated into numerous sub-castes in this period due to primarily two reasons:

---

[10] The level of monetisation was highest during this Age because the largest numbers of gold coins were issued by Guptas in the entire Indian history.

i. Assimilation of large number of foreigners: A large number of foreigners had been assimilated into the Indian society and each foreigner was assigned a sub-caste. For instance, the various foreign ruling families of pre-Gupta period (of Greek/Scythian origins) were given semi-kshatriya status. Similarly, the Huns who invaded India during the early 5th century were also assimilated in Indian society as one of the 36 Rajput clans.

ii. Absorption of tribal communities into Brahminical society: With the extension of Brahminical culture in distant and different areas, a large number of tribal communities were assimilated in the Brahminical social structure of the *varna* system. It is rather interesting to note that *while the foreigners and tribal heads were included as kshatriyas, the ordinary tribals were given the status of shudras*.

The social and economic status of *shudras* improved during this period. They were now allowed to listen to the *Ramayana*, the *Mahabharata* and the *Puranas*. They could also perform some domestic rituals that were earlier prohibited for them and could now even worship a new god called Krishna. From the 7th century onwards they were generally represented as agriculturists. Now a distinction was made between shudras and untouchables, the latter being treated lower in status than the *shudras*. The practice of untouchability intensified (especially hatred for *chandalas*). The Chinese traveler Fa-Hien mentions in his memoirs that *the chandalas lived outside the village and had to maintain distance from the upper castes. The chandalas suffered such glaring lack of privilege that whenever they entered towns or market places they would strike a piece of wood to announce their arrival, so that the others might not touch them and get polluted*. In south India, the notion of untouchability seems to have arrived in the late Sangam age. For instance, in a famous text *Acharakkovai*, water touched by a *pulaiya* (untouchable) is seen as unfit for consumption by higher caste people, and even glancing at a *pulaiya* pollutes the upper caste people.

The status of women deteriorated further in the Gupta period. The main reason for the subordination of women was their complete dependence on men for their livelihood. It is rather ironical that the women from two lower *varnas* were free to earn their livelihood, which probably gave them some freedom, but the women from the two upper varnas were even denied[11] this liberty too. Similarly, widow remarriage was not allowed for the members of the higher orders, but the Shudras could practise both levirate[12] or *nagoya* and widow remarriage. However, they had full right on their *stridhana* (the presents received by the bride at the time of her marriage, both from her parents' side and also from her parents-in-law). A lawyer of the sixth century, *Katyayana*, held that a woman could sell and mortgage her immovable property along with her *stridhana,* which clearly implies that women received shares in landed property but in a patriarchal set-up, they were not allowed to inherit landed property. Women, thus, effectively lacked property rights

---

[11] As the members of the higher orders came to acquire more and more land, they became more polygamous and more property minded, to the extent that they started considering even women as items of property.

[12] The younger brother could marry the wife of the elder brother after the latter's death.

and the lack of property rights further resulted in their subordination and complete dependence on men for their livelihood.

The free representation of females in art suggest that there was no *purdah* system in the society. However, the first evidence of *sati* (immolation of a widow) around c. 510 CE is found in an inscription at Eran in Madhya Pradesh. In the *Harshacharita* of Banabhata, the queen performs *sati* on the death of her husband, king Prabhakaravardhana. *Dharamshastra* (law books) texts belonging to the period reflect a tendency towards lowering the age of marriage for girls and advocating a celibate and austere life for widows. The Sanskrit *kavya* literature refers to the courtesans as *ganikas*, who were admired for their beauty but could never attain social respectability.

References to slaves are found in the *dharamashastra* texts as well as the *Narada* Smriti[13], which mentions fifteen types of slaves. These include mainly the prisoners of war reduced to slavery, debt bondsmen and voluntary enslavement. Slaves are generally referred to as domestic servants or personal attendants.

d. Religion

The period c. 300–600 CE is often considered as the phase of consolidation of Brahmanical ideology as temple-based sectarian cults became popular and Sanskrit was firmly established as the language of royal inscriptions. In the Gupta period, *smarta* religious practices (practice based on the Smritis) became popular. Sectarian symbols such as the *linga*, *trishula*, *bull*, *Gaja-lakshmi*, *chakra* and *shankha* (conch shell) appeared on the royal *prashastis*, coins and seals. Hinduism acquired its present shape during Gupta age only.

The Gupta rulers gave patronage to Bhagvatism, which was centred around the worship of Bhagvat or Vishnu[14] and his incarnations. Later, Vishnu came to be identified with Krishna Vasudeva, a legendary hero of the Vrishni tribe who gave the historic sermon of *Bhagvat Gita* in the epic of *Mahabharata*. So Bhagvatism was also identified with Vaishnavism. It put emphasis on *bhakti* (loving devotion) and *ahimsa* (non-killing of animals, which is why it stresses more on vegetarianism) rather than Vedic rituals and sacrifices. The new religion was quite liberal, and assimilated the lower classes in its fold. According to the *Bhagvat Gita*, the chief text of Bhagvatism, whenever there was a social crisis, Vishnu would appear in a human form and save the people. Thus, ten incarnations of Vishnu were envisioned. The *Puranas* were written to popularise the virtues of each one of these incarnations. Thus, by the end of the Gupta period,

[13] A law book of *Narada*, a work of 5th century.

[14] Vishnu was a minor god in Vedic times who represented the sun and the fertility cult while Narayana originally was a non-Vedic tribal god called *bhagavata* who was conceived as a divine counterpart to the tribal chief, and his worshippers were called *bhagavatas*. Just as a tribal chief received presents from his kinsmen and distributed shares among them, Narayana was also supposed to bestow shares or good fortune (*bhaga*) on his *bhakta* or worshippers. In return, the *bhaktas* offered their *bhakti* or loving devotion to him. However, by the second century BCE, Vishnu and Narayana were merged and came to be known as Narayana-Vishnu.

Mahayana Buddhism was overshadowed by Bhagavatism and Vishnu became a member of the trinity of gods along with Shiva and Brahma. Idol worship became a common feature and the idols of different incarnations of Vishnu were housed in the temples constructed in the Gupta period. Many festivals also came to be celebrated. Interestingly, some of the Gupta kings proclaimed themselves as *Bhagavatas* (worshippers of Lord Krishna) and Garuda was their emblem, while most of the Vakatakas claimed to be devotees of Shiva and adopted the boar as their emblem. However, both Guptas and Vakatakas claimed to be devotees of Vishnu. There was also an emergence of worship of composite deities such as *Hari-hara*, who is a part Vishnu and part Shiva, and religious syncretism (for instance, the *incorporation of the Buddha as one of the ten Vishnu avatars*). This phase also saw the competitive relationship between various cults, as expressed graphically in the representations of the Devi trampling on the other Hindu gods, or Buddhist deities trampling Hindu ones, mostly Shiva.

This period also saw a myriad of local cults, beliefs and practices. The popular devotional worship included worship of stone and terracotta images of various demi-gods and demi-goddesses such as *yakshas*, *yakshini*, *nagas*, *gandharvas* and *apsaras*, but with one major difference. Even though the independent worship of *yakshas* and *nagas* continued (as evident by a *yaksha* temple at Padmavati, Madhya Pradesh, and a *naga* shrine at Cave XVI, Ajanta), the colossal sculptures of these *yakshas* and *nagas* as found in earlier times disappeared and they now appeared more often as subsidiary figures and more as *dvarapalas* (gate keepers of the great gods). This phenomenon clearly establishes the attempts of the dominant religious traditions to not only establish links with the popular cults but also points towards their efforts to subordinate them.

The Gupta kings were devout Hindus, but they followed a policy of tolerance towards other religious sects. The Chinese pilgrims Fa-Hien and Hiuen Tsang, who came to India during the reign of Chandragupta II and Harsha respectively, clearly give the impression that Buddhism was also flourishing. Though it is also true that Buddhism no longer received royal patronage, and its glory as in the days of Ashoka and Kanishka was nowhere to be found. However, some *stupas* and *viharas* were constructed and Nalanda developed as a great centre of education for Mahayana Buddhism during his time. Students from other countries also came to study in this university. According to Hiuen Tsang, *the revenues of one hundred villages supported it*.

There was also spread of Tantrism in India in this period. As we have discussed earlier, from the 5th century, the *brahmanas* had started receiving land in the tribal areas of Nepal, Assam, Bengal, Orissa, central India and Deccan. As a consequence, both tribal and Brahminical culture influenced each other. The tribals were assimilated in the Brahminical fold as *shudras*, and simultaneously, the tribal elements came to be assimilated in the *Brahminical* society. The *brahmanas* also adopted their rituals, gods and goddesses. It is this assimilation of Brahminical religion and tribal practices which resulted in the development of Tantrism. Some general features of Tantrism include the *importance attached to* rituals, yogic practices, terrifying deities, sexual rites and an emphasis on '*shakti*' (energy), which was conceived to be feminine. The Tantric path was supposed to be a secret one, which was divulged by preceptors to select initiates only, and involved the attainment of supernatural powers and a state of liberation. Certain diagrams known as *yantras*, *mandalas* or *chakras* and *mudras* (symbolic gestures) play an important role in Tantric rituals. It did not believe in any caste or gender bias and admitted both women and *shudras* in its ranks. The Tantric concepts affected Shaivism and Vaishnavism as well as Buddhism and Jainism. It resulted in the introduction of the worship of female deities in these religions.

e. Literature

The Gupta period is considered as the Golden Age of art and literature in ancient India. The literature in this period was written in Sanskrit. A huge body of religious and secular literature was compiled in this period. The two great epics, the *Ramayana* and the *Mahabharata*, were finally compiled in the 4th century CE. The stories of both the epics symbolise the victory of good over evil. Both Rama and Krishna came to be considered incarnations of Vishnu. It also marks the beginning of the writing of the *Puranas*. The major Puranas written in this period are the *Vishnu Purana*, *Vayu Purana* and the *Matsya Purana*. For the worship of Shiva, Shiv Purana was composed, whereas the various incarnations of Vishnu are glorified in the *Varaha Purana*, *Vamana Purana* and the *Narasimha Purana*. Some Smritis or law books were also compiled in the Gupta period. One of these, the *Narada Smriti* throws light on the general social and economic rules and regulations of the period. Several *dharamashastras* such as *Yajnavalkya*, *Narada*, *Katyayana* and *Brihaspati Smritis* were composed in this period. Kamandaka's *Nitisara*, which is a book on statecraft and Vatsayayana's *Kamasutra*, which is a treatise on sensual pleasure, belong to this period.

The secular literature gems of this period have greater emphasis on verse as opposed to prose, and they include classic works of the following:

i. Kalidasa: Kalidasa was one of the *navratnas* of Chandragupta II. His works are very famous and have been translated in many European languages. The notable features of his works include the display of an element of humour, with the characters of higher caste speaking in Sanskrit while those of lower caste and women speaking in Prakrit. Kalidasa invokes Shiva in the beginning of his works and names him Triloknath. Some of his works are listed in the table.

Important Works of Kalidasa	
Meghadutam	It is a classic poem by Kalidasa which details story about the *yaksha*, who has been exiled by King Kubera for not performing his duties, and who then requests a passing cloud to convey a message to his dear wife who lives on Mount Kailash.
Abhijyanashakuntalam	Considered a classic and one of the best hundred literary works in the world. It was first translated in English by Sir William Jones and is one of the most widely translated works.

Kumarasambhavam	Story about the birth of Shiva and Parvati's son and also contains references of Sati system.
Raghuvamsha	Depicts Vishnu as the origin and the end of the universe.
Ritusamhara	Poem describing the cycle of seasons.
Malvikagnimitram	First dramatic work of Kalidasa, for the celebration of Vasantutsava (spring festival).

ii. Shudraka: Writer of the play *Mrichchhkatikam* (Little Clay Cart), which deals with the love affair of a poor brahmana with the beautiful daughter of a courtesan.

iii. Vishakhadatta: Author of *Mudrarakshasa* and *Devichandraguptam*.

iv. Bharavi: Writer of a Sanskrit kavya in the 6th century, *Kiratarjuniya*, which describes the combat between Arjuna and Lord Shiva in the guise of a kirata or a mountain-dwelling hunter.

v. Dandin: Writer of *Kavyadarshana* and *Dasakumaracharita*.

vi. Amarshima: Author of the Sanskrit lexicon *Amarakosha*.

vii. Bhasa: Celebrated writer of 13 plays, including *Madhyamavyayoga*, *Duta-Ghatotkacha*, *Dutavakya*, *Balacharita* and *Charudatta*.

viii. Bhatti: Author of *Ravanavadha*, which illustrates the rules of grammar while telling the story of Rama's life.

ix. Vishnusharman: Author of the *Panchatantra*, which is a fine illustration of *nidarshana* (which tells what should and should not be done). It has an elegant prose style and is interspersed with witty verses. It was possibly composed in the Vakataka empire and contains satirical tales in which animals play an important role.

x. Mentha: Author of the *Hayagrivavadha*.

It is rather interesting to note that Sanskrit literature has produced five mahakavyas, all of which belong to Gupta Empire:

- *Raghuvamsham*
- *Kumarasambhavam* by Kalidasa
- *Kiratarjuniyam* by Bharavi
- *Shishupal-vadha* by Magha: Describes the slaying of Shishupala by Krishna.
- *Naisadhiyacharitam* by Sri Harsa: On the life of King Nala and Queen Damayanti.

f. Art and Architecture

Ancient Indian art was mainly inspired by religion. As in earlier times, Buddhism gave a great impetus to art in Gupta period as well. A life-sized bronze image of the Buddha (around 2 metres in height) belonging to the Mathura school has been found from Sultanganj in Bihar. Beautiful images of the Buddha were also created at Mathura and Sarnath. The finest examples of Buddhist art during Gupta period are the paintings of Ajanta caves[15], which are now included in the list of the World Heritage Sites by the UNESCO. Apart from narrative scenes connected with the Buddha, the *bodhisattvas* and the *Jatakas*, the Ajanta frescos depict religious scenes of *yakshas*, *gandharvas*, *apasaras*, and include scenes from everyday life as well. Surprisingly, these paintings with lustrous colors have not faded even after fourteen centuries. The Bagh cave paintings near Gwalior can be termed Buddhist art as well, and as compared with Ajanta, are simpler and plain.

FIGURE 8.3 Ajanta Caves

The Gupta period marks beginning of Indian temple architecture, as temples in the form of concrete structures were constructed in northern India for the first time. These temples were made in the architectural style known as *Nagara*, in which generally flat-roofed square temples were built. Two of these temples, in which the images of Vishnu are placed in the centre as a chief deity, are found at Bhitargaon in Kanpur (made of bricks), and the stone sculpture of *Nara Narayana* from the Dashavatara temple at Deogarh in Jhansi. Most of the other surviving stone temples belonging to this era are in a ruined state and are located in the hilly areas of Madhya Pradesh, such as the Vishnu temple of Tigawa and the Parvati temple of Nachna-Kuthara.

FIGURE 8.4 Dashavatara Temple, Deogarh

[15] Ajanta caves are a series of rock-cut caves on Waghora river near Aurangabad, Maharashtra. Although these paintings covered the period from the 1st century BCE to the seventh century CE, some of them relate to the Gupta period.

The sculptures pertaining to period of c. 300–600 CE not only show a continuation of earlier styles and trends derived from Mathura and Gandhara schools, but also show introduction of new styles. The inspiration of the themes for sculpture was drawn from Hindu, Buddhist and Jaina traditions. Many Vaishnava sculptures, which include images of the avatars such as boar, man-lion, dwarf and Vasudeva-Krishna, have been found at Mathura. One of the largest known free standing stone images belonging to this period is a colossal figure of Krishna effortlessly lifting up Govardhana mountain, found at Varanasi. A stone sculpture of a larger than life figure of a horse (probably representing an *ashavmedha* horse) carved out of beige sandstone found at Khairigarh in Uttar Pradesh too belongs to this period. The cave architecture of this period is almost entirely Buddhist, but there are a few exceptions such as the caves at Udaigiri, near Vidisha, which has the famous relief scene of Vishnu rescuing the earth from the waters in the form of *Nri-Varaha* (body of a man and head of a boar), and Elephanta caves, the largest one of which is dedicated to Shiva. The Buddha images of this period displayed a greater variety of *mudras* than before. For instance, the Buddha images from Sarnath differed in several ways (as robes have no folds) from those of Mathura. The spectacular Bamiyan Buddha sculptures which were tragically destroyed by the Taliban too belonged to this period. A dated stone image of a seated *tirthankara* belonging to 432 CE was excavated at Mathura, which was different from the seated figurines of preceding centuries.

FIGURE 8.5 Krishna Govardhana

FIGURE 8.6 Mahadeva of Elephanta Caves

FIGURE 8.7 Buddha-Head Stone

The Gupta coins are also pieces of art. They are well designed and meticulously crafted. They carry aesthetically impressive depictions of the activities of the rulers. At many places such as Kaushambi, Rajghat, Bhita and Mathura, terracotta figurines and plaques have been found.

g. Science and Technology

The Gupta period is unparalleled for its achievements in mathematics and astronomy. The roots of Indian mathematics can be traced to the *Shulvasutras*, which were the appendices to the *Shrautasutras*. The *Shulvasutras* were the manuals for the preparation of the site where Vedic sacrificial rituals were to be performed and they laid the foundations of geometry. The four major *Shulvasutras*, which are mathematically the most significant, are those composed by Baudhayana, Manava, Apastamba and Katyayana. The Pythagoras theorem and Pythagorean triples' earliest expression can be found in Baudhayana, which was composed around 600 BCE. The *ganita shastra* (mathematics) was far more advanced as the oldest datable evidence of the decimal place value system can be found in a 3rd century work on astrology called the *Yavanajataka* by Sphujidhvaja (which however, does not mention zero). But an even earlier work, the *Chhandasutra* of *Pingala*, mentions the zero symbol as a dot used in metrics. Varahamihira's *Panchsiddhanta*, which belonged to the Gupta period, is the earliest dateable text to use zero both as a symbol and a number. Some of the notable and eminent personalities belonging to this era are:

Notable and Eminent Personalities	
(a) Aryabhatta I	Father of Algebra and the earliest known astronomer of India, who probably resided at Pataliputra and wrote two astronomical texts: (a) *Aryabhatiya* (a text which deals with astronomy and mathematics) and (b) *Aryabhata-siddhanta* (which has not survived and is known only through references in later works). For instance, the 7th century commentator, Bhaskara I, who wrote a commentary on Aryabhatiya, calls the Aryabhatiya the *Ashmakatantra* and *Ashmakiya*, and the followers of Aryabhatta as *Ashmakiyas*.

Notable and Eminent Personalities	
	Aryabhatta has also written the *Suryasiddhanta*, which contains sine tables. His method of extracting the square root and cube root presupposes the decimal place value of numbers, which certainly shows that Indian mathematicians (started using the decimal system in the 5th century CE) were much ahead of Arabs and Europeans who started using the same in the 12th century after learning from Arabs. Even Arab writers like Ibn Washiya, Al-Masudi and Al-Biruni give credit for the discovery of the system to the Hindus. Aryabhatta I is noted for: i. He was first to discover that the earth rotates on its axis and also worked out the correct equation for calculating the orbit of a planet and gave extremely accurate estimate of the length of a year to 365.2586805 days. ii. First astronomer to give a scientific explanation of eclipses as he established that they are not caused by some demons but by the moon coming between the earth and the sun. He also worked out how to ascertain which part of moon would be obscured during an eclipse. iii. He found out the sine functions and used them in astronomy and laid foundations of trigonometry. He also made tables for the trigonometric ratio sine, for angles from 0 to 90 degrees. iv. He was the first to invent zero and to recommend the use of the decimal system. v. He described the various properties of a circle and gave a very accurate value of pi (p), correct to 4 decimal places at 3.1416. vi. He also perfected the methods of solving indeterminate equations in integers problems.
(b) Varahamihira	A 6th century astronomer, astrologer, mathematician and scholar, who was one of the *navratnas* of Chandragupta II and belonged to Avanti. As we have already discussed, his famous work *Panchasiddhantika* summarised five astronomical schools. *Brihatsamhita* is an encyclopaedic work dealing with diverse topics such as how to ascertain the value of precious metals and stones, how to sharpen swords, how to make trees bear fruit out of season, how to distinguish the good breeds of animals, how to foresee the location of water, explanation of seasons, and meteorological issues such as the correlation between the clouds, winds and amount of rainfall.
(c) Brahmagupta	Late 6th/7th century astronomer and well-known mathematician who made important contributions to geometry. He was the first mathematician to discuss the method of obtaining a cyclic quadrilateral having rational sides and determined the formulae to find the area of a cyclic quadrilateral, the circum diameter of a triangle, and the diagonals of a cyclic quadrilateral in terms of its sides. He also wrote the *Brahmasputasiddhanta* (628 CE), in which he hinted at the Law of Gravitation, and *Khandakhadyaka* (665 CE), covering such topics as the longitudes of the planets, diurnal rotation, lunar and solar eclipses, rising and setting of the sun, the moon's crescent and conjunctions of the planets. He also referred to *svayamvaha yantras* signifying complex automatic devices, which reflects an awareness of the idea of perpetual motion too.

Notable and Eminent Personalities	
(d) Mahavira	A famous 9th century mathematician of Karnataka who lived in the court of the Rashtrakuta king Amoghvarsha, and wrote a book called the *Ganitasarasangraha*, which deals with various mathematical problems. He produced formulae for the area and circumference of an eclipse, though these formulae were later discarded as incorrect.
(e) Bhaskara II	Author of the *Lilavati* written in the 12th century, which contains important ideas of calculus.
(f) Vagbhata	A disciple of Charaka and distinguished physician of Ayurvedic system of medicine from c. 600 CE. He wrote the *Ashtangahridaya* (meaning 'Heart of Medicine') and the *Ashtangasamgraha* (meaning 'Tome on Medicine').
(g) Maharishi Palakapya	He wrote the *Hastyayurveda*, a treatise dealing with the diagnosis and treatment of the major diseases of elephants through medication and surgery.
(h) Dhanvantri	He was famous for his knowledge of Ayurveda.
(i) Kashyapa	A 7th century physician who compiled his Ayurvedic knowledge in a compendium which dealt with the diseases of women and children.
(j) Sushruta	The famous author of the *Sushruta Samhita*, which deals with surgery. It contains six sections, mainly focusing on the treatment of wounds, extraction of splinters and arrows, suturing, embryology, anatomy, poisons, removal of cataracts, removal of stones in the bladder, etc. The text also refers to plastic surgery, with detailed references to rhinoplasty wherein a flap of skin is grafted to repair a severed nose and the repair of torn ear lobes. It also mentions of study of human anatomy by dissecting corpses.

Metallurgy also saw technological advancement in Gupta times. The bronze images of Buddha produced on a considerable scale during this period are an example of advanced technology. The iron pillar at Mehrauli, Delhi, standing in the open, which has surprisingly not gathered rust even after fifteen centuries, speaks volumes of the iron technology prevailing in the Gupta period. The wonderful paintings of Ajanta, still intact, indicate that the art of making colours was unmatched in this period.

QUESTIONS FROM LAST YEAR'S PRELIMS

1. Which one of the following statements is correct? **(2021)**

(a) Ajanta Caves lie in the gorge of Waghora river.

(b) Sanchi Stupa lies in the gorge of Chambal river.

(c) Pandu-lena Cave Shrines lie in the gorge of Narmada river.

(d) Amaravati Stupa lies in the gorge of Godavari river.

2. With reference to the history of India, the terms "kulyavapa" and "dronavapa" denote **(2020)**

(a) measurement of land

(b) coins of different monetary value

(c) classification of urban land
(d) religious rituals

3. With reference to the Scholars/literatures of ancient India, consider the following statements: **(2020)**

1. Panini is associated with Pushyamitra.
2. Amarsimha is associated with Harshavardhana.
3. Kalidasa is associated with Chandragupta-II.

Which of the above given statements is/are correct?

(a) 1 and 2 only (b) 2 and 3 only
(c) 3 only (d) 1, 2 and 3

4. With reference to the period of Gupta dynasty in ancient India, the towns Ghantasala, Kadura and Chaul were well known as

(a) Ports handling foreign trade
(b) Capitals of powerful kingdoms
(c) Places of exquisite stone art and architecture
(d) Important Buddhist pilgrimage centres

5. With reference to forced labour (Vishti) in India during the Gupta period, which one of the following statements is correct? **(2019)**

(a) It was considered as source of income for the State, a sort of tax paid by the people.
(b) It was totally absent in Madhya Pradesh and Kathiawar region of the Gupta Empire.
(c) The forced labourer was enticed to weekly wages.
(d) The eldest son of the labourers was sent as the forced labourer.

6. With reference to the art and archaeological history of India, which one among the following was made the earliest? **(2015)**

(a) Lingaraja Temple at Bhubaneswar
(b) Rock-cut Elephant at Dhauli
(c) Rock-cut Monuments at Mahabalipuram
(d) Varaha Image at Udayagiri

7. With reference to Indian history, which of the following(s) is/are the essential element/elements of the feudal system? **(2015)**

i. A very strong centralised political authority and a very weak provincial or local political authority.
ii. Emergence of administrative structure based on control and possession of land.
iii. Creation of lord-vassal relationship between the feudal lord and his overlord.

Which of the statement(s) given above is/are correct?

(a) i and ii only (b) ii and iii only
(c) iii only (d) i, ii and iii

8. With reference to the cultural history of India, the term 'Panchayatan refers to: **(2014)**

(a) An assembly of village elders
(b) A religious sect
(c) A style of temple construction
(d) An administrative functionary

9. With reference to the Indian history of art and culture, consider the following pairs: **(2014)**

Famous work of sculpture: Site

i. A grand image of Buddha's Mahaparinirvana with numerous celestial musicians above and the sorrowful figures of his followers below: Ajanta
ii. A huge image of Varaha Avatar (boar incarnation) of Vishnu, as he rescues

Goddess Earth from the deep and chaotic waters, sculpted on rock: Mount Abu

iii. 'Arjuna's Penance' 'Descent of Ganga' sculpted on the surface of huge boulders: Mamallapuram

Which of the pair(s) given above is/are correctly matched?

(a) 1 and 2 only (b) 3 only
(c) 1 and 3 only (d) 1, 2 and 3

10. With reference to the guilds (*shreni*) of ancient India that played a very important role in the country's economy, which of the following statement(s) is/are correct? **(2012)**

i. Every guild was registered with the central authority of the state and the king was the chief admin authority on them

ii. The wages, rules of work, standards and prices were fixed by the guild

iii. The guild had judicial powers over its own members.

Select the correct answer using the codes given below:

(a) 1 and 2 only (b) 3 only
(c) 2 and 3 only (d) 1, 2 and 3

11. With reference to the scientific progress of ancient India, which of the statements given below are correct? **(2012)**

i. Different kinds of specialised surgical instruments were in common use by 1st century AD.

ii. Transplant of internal organs in the human body had begun by the beginning of 3rd century AD.

iii. The concept of sine of an angle was known in 5th century AD.

iv. The concept of cyclic quadrilateral was known in 7th century AD.

Select the correct answer using the codes given below:

(a) 1 and 2 only
(b) 3 and 4 only
(c) 1, 3 and 4 only
(d) 1, 2, 3 and 4

12. The Nagara, the Dravida and the Vesara are the **(2012)**

(a) three main racial groups of the Indian subcontinent.
(b) three main linguistic divisions in to which the languages of India can be classified.
(c) three main styles of Indian temple architecture.
(d) three main musical *gharanas* prevalent in India.

13. There are only two known examples of cave paintings of the Gupta period in ancient India. One of these is the paintings of the Ajanta caves. Where is the other surviving example of Gupta paintings? **(2010)**

(a) Bagh Caves
(b) Ellora Caves
(c) Lomas Rishi Cave
(d) Nashik Caves

14. Why did Buddhism start declining in India in the early medieval times? **(2010)**

i. Buddha was by that time considered as one of the incarnations of Vishnu and thus became a part of Vaishnavism.

ii. The invading tribes from Central Asia till the time of last Gupta king adopted Hinduism and persecuted Buddhists.

iii. The kings of Gupta dynasty were strongly opposed to Buddhism.

Which of the statement(s) given above is/are correct?

(a) 1 only (b) 1 and 3 only
(c) 2 and 3 only (d) 1, 2, and 3

15. What does Baudhayan theorem (Baudhayan Sulva Sutra) relate to? **(2007)**
(a) Lengths of sides of a right-angled triangle.
(b) Calculation of the value of pi.
(c) Logarithmic calculations.
(d) Normal distribution curve.

16. Match List-I with List-II and select the correct answer using the code given below the lists: **(2006)**

List-I (Finding/Invention/ Calculation)	List-II (Ancient Indian Scholar)
(A) Time taken by the earth to orbit the Sun	i. Aryabhatta
(B) Calculation of the value of ('pi')	ii. Bhaskaracharya
(C) Invention of the digit zero	iii. Budhayana
(D) The game of snakes and ladders	iv. Gyandev

(a) A – ii, B – iv, C – i, D – iii
(b) A – ii, B – iii, C – i, D – iv
(c) A – i, B – iii, C – ii, D – iv
(d) A – i, B – iv, C – ii, D – iii

17. The Allahabad Pillar inscription is associated with which one of the following? **(2006)**
(a) Mahapadma Nanda
(b) Chandragupta Maurya
(c) Ashoka
(d) Samudragupta

18. Consider the following statements: **(2004)**
I. The Chinese pilgrim Fa-Hien attended the fourth Great Buddhist Council held by Kanishka.
II. The Chinese pilgrim Hiuen-Tsang met Harsha and found him to be antagonistic to Buddhism.

Which of these statement(s) given above is/are correct?
(a) 1 only (b) 2 only
(c) Both 1 and 2 (d) Neither 1 nor 2

19. 'Mrichchhakatika', an ancient Indian book written by Shudraka, deals with: **(2003)**
(a) The love affair of a rich merchant with the daughter of a courtesan.
(b) The victory of Chandragupta II over the Saka satraps of Western India.
(c) The military expeditions and exploits of Samudragupta.
(d) The love affair between a Gupta King and a Princess of Kamarupa.

20. From the third century AD, when the Hun invasion ended the Roman empire, the Indian merchants relied more and more on the: **(1999)**
(a) African trade
(b) West European trade
(c) South-east Asian trade
(d) Middle eastern trade

21. Which one of the following ports handled the north Indian trade during the Gupta period? (1999)
(a) Tamralipti (b) Broach
(c) Kalyan (d) Cambay

22. The silver coins issued by the Guptas were called: **(1997)**
(a) Rupaka (b) Karshapana
(c) Dinara (d) Pana

23. Who among the following is known for his work on medicine during the Gupta period? **(1996)**
(a) Saumilla (b) Sudraka
(c) Shaunaka (d) Susruta

24. Match the following: **(1996)**

(A)	Vishakhadatta	(i)	Medicine
(B)	Varahmihira	(ii)	Drama
(C)	Charaka	(iii)	Astronomy
(D)	Brahmagupta	(iv)	Mathematics

(a) A – i, B – iii, C – iv, D – ii
(b) A – ii, B – i, C – iii, D – iv
(c) A – ii, B – iii, C – i, D – iv
(d) A – iii, B – iv, C – i, D – ii

25. Zero was invented by **(1995)**
(a) Aryabhatta
(b) Varahamihira
(c) Bhaskara I
(d) an unknown Indian

ANSWERS

1. (a)	2. (a)	3. (c)	4. (a)	5. (a)	6. (b)	7. (b)	8. (c)
9. (c)	10. (d)	11. (c)	12. (c)	13. (a)	14. (a)	15. (a)	16. (c)
17. (d)	18. (d)	19. (a)	20. (c)	21. (a)	22. (a)	23. (d)	24. (c)
25. (a)							

QUESTIONS FROM LAST YEAR'S MAINS

1. Discuss the main contributions of Gupta period and Chola period to Indian heritage and culture. **(2022 GS1)**
2. Assess the importance of the accounts of the Chinese and Arab travellers in the reconstruction of the history of India. **(2018 GS1)**
3. How do you justify the view that the level of excellence of the Gupta numismatic art is not at all noticeable in later times? **(2017 GS1)**
3. Trace the role of guilds and trade organisations in the development of early Indian economy. **(History Optional 2015, 2010)**
4. Discuss the provincial and district administrative units of the Gupta Empire with the designation and functions of the officers. **(History Optional 2014)**

PRACTICE QUESTIONS – MAINS

1. Describe the religious conditions of India during the 3rd–6th century CE with special reference to new trends.
2. How was the social life during Guptas? Explain, focusing on condition of women and lower castes.
3. The Gupta period is rightly the golden period for science and technology. Do you agree? Explain with suitable examples.
4. What is meant by secular literature? Mention some prominent secular writers of Gupta Age.

CHAPTER

9

Early Medieval India: The Age of Regional Configurations (c. 600–1200 CE)

The term 'early medieval' denotes the intermediate transition period between the 'ancient' and the 'medieval'. The early medieval period in India is marked by feudalism, political fragmentation and the formation and proliferation of various states at regional level. This period in south India especially, is viewed more as a period of segmentary statehood, wherein the role of king was diminished and he acted more as a ritual head, neither having any firm revenue infrastructure or a standing army. For simpler understanding, the period from c. 600–1200 CE can be roughly classified into primarily two phases, different for north and south India*, respectively:

[*Kindly note that in order to ensure simplicity, the period of classification does not adhere to a specific time span but just presents a rough idea for conceptual clarity. For instance, in order to ensure continuity among the various kingdoms, the period from c. 600–750 CE may include kingdoms after c. 750 CE too.]*

a. The period from c. 600–750 CE in north India was dominated by the Pushyabhutis of Thaneswar and the Maukharis of Kannauj, whereas correspondingly, the period from c. 600–750 CE in south India included three major states, that of the Pallavas of Kanchi, the Chalukyas of Badami and the Pandyas of Madurai.

b. The period from c. 750–1200 CE in north India can be further divided into two phases:

    i. Phase I (c. 750–1000 CE): In north India, this phase was marked by the age of three important empires; the Gurjara Pratiharas in northern India, the Palas in eastern India and the Rashtrakutas in Deccan.

    ii. Phase II (c. 1000–1200 CE): This phase is primarily known as the age of conflict. All over the country, there was breakdown of the tripartite powers into many smaller kingdoms. For instance, in northern India, the Pratihara empire's disintegration brought to the forefront various Rajput states under the control of different Rajput dynasties such as the Chahamanas (Chauhans), Chandellas, Paramaras of Malwa, and so on. These states eventually fought and resisted the Turkish attacks from northwest India led by Mahmud Ghazni and Mohammad Ghori in the 11th and 12th centuries, but had to yield ultimately as they failed to stand united against the invaders. This section will be dealt with in the next chapter.

The period from c. 850–1200 CE in south India saw the supremacy of the Cholas.

Even though India was politically divided during these years, this era added new and rich cultural elements in the fields of art, literature and language. In fact, some of the best specimens of temple architecture and Indian literature belong to this period.

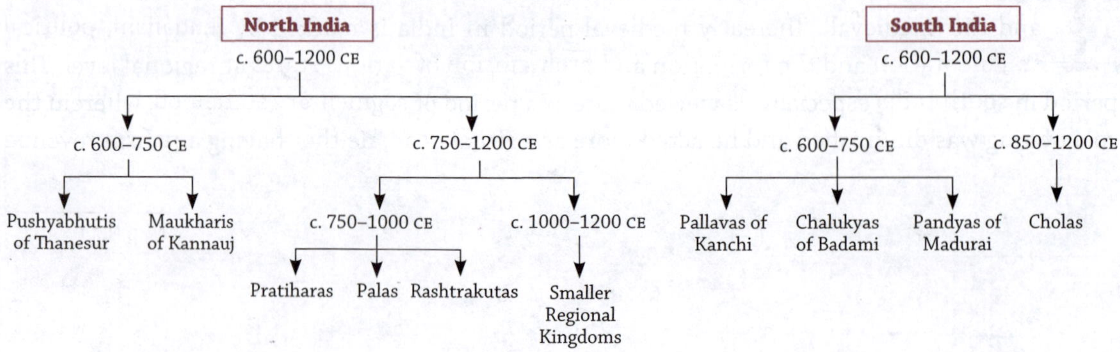

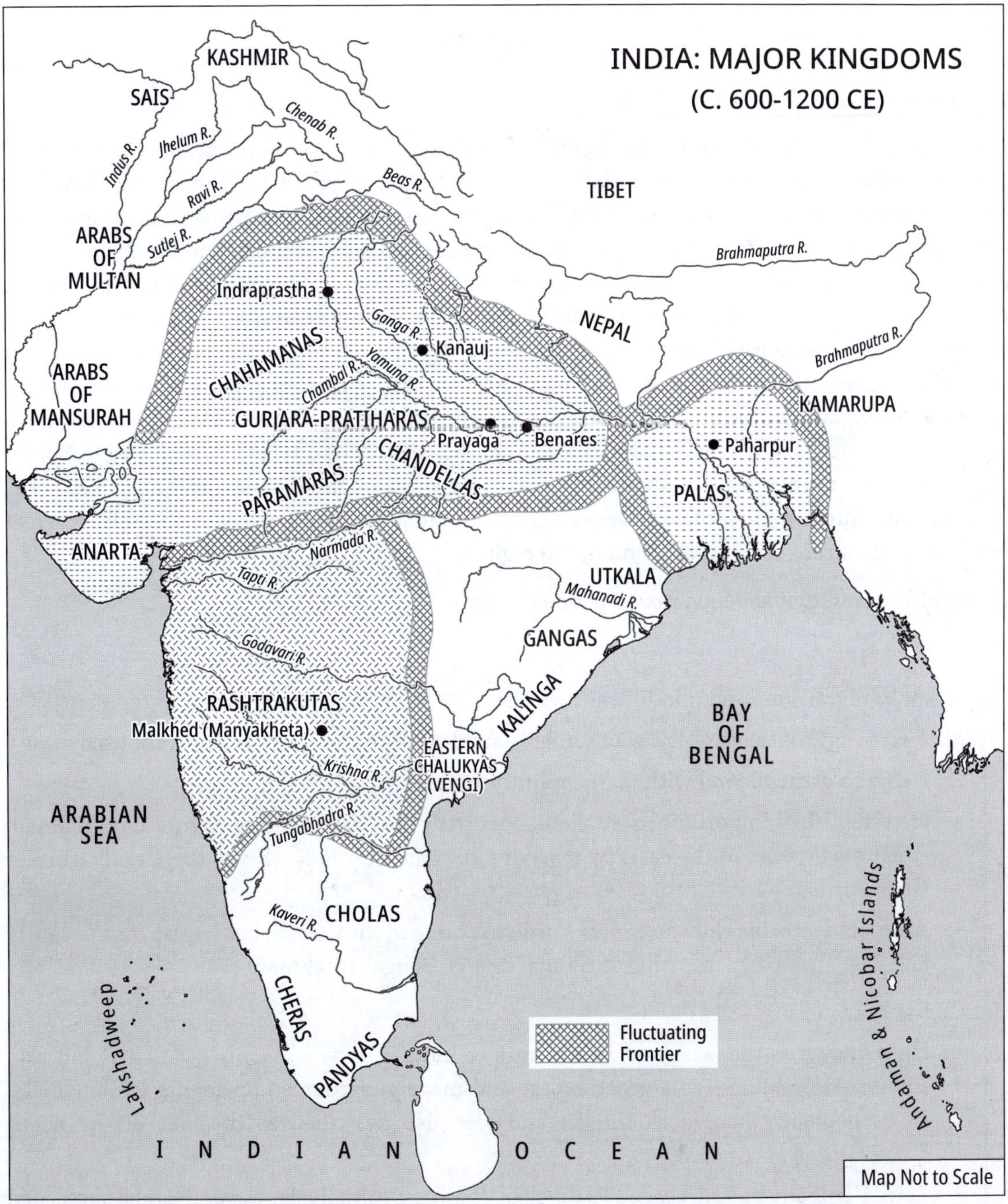

FIGURE 9.1 Major Kingdoms (c. 600–1200 CE)

Period from c. 600–750 CE: Northern India

Pushyabhutis of Thanesar

As we have discussed earlier, until the middle of the 6th century CE, the Gupta Empire had provided stability to the northern India – especially modern day Uttar Pradesh and Bihar – for about 160 years. The decline of the Gupta Empire had, however, resulted in the splitting of northern India into several kingdoms. Since the 5th century CE onwards Kashmir, Punjab and north west India had come under the sovereignty of the white Hunas, whereas from the middle of the 6th century CE, north and western India was ruled by different feudatories of the Guptas. An important ruling family to gain prominence after the fall of the Gupta was that of the Pushyabhutis, who had their capital at Thanesar (near Kurukshetra, Haryana). Two major historical sources which provide information regarding the Pushyabhuti dynasty are the *Harshacharita*, a biography of Harsha written by Harsha's court poet Banabhatta, and travelogues of the Chinese pilgrim Hsuan Tsang/ Xuanzang. Not much is known about the first three kings of the dynasty and most likely the dynasty came into prominence with the accession of Prabhakar Vardhana, who was able to defeat the Hunas and strengthen his position in the regions of Punjab and Haryana.

Pushyabhutis (Originally feudatories of the Guptas)

↓

Prabhakar Vardhana (around mid-6th century CE)

- Fourth king of the dynasty, who actually laid the foundations of the Pushyabhuti dynasty.
- He was a great general with many military victories.
- He established important marital alliances with the Maukharis of Kanyakubja/Kannauj (their neighbours to the east) by marrying his daughter Rajyashri to the Maukhari ruler Grahavarman.
- After his death, his elder son Rajya Vardhana came to the throne, but he was treacherously killed by Shashanka, the king of Gauda, that is, Bengal and Bihar.

Harsha Vardhana (c. 606–647 CE)

- He is known as the last great Hindu king of India, who was originally a Shaiva but also supported Buddhism to a great extent and made generous endowments to Buddhists. He is popularly known as Harsha and was also described as the lord of the north (*sakalauttarapathanatha*).
- Rajya Vardhana had succeeded Prabhakar Vardhana initially. However, Harsha succeeded his brother, when Rajya Vardhana left the reigns of governance in the hands of Harsha Vardhana as he had to undertake a campaign against the ruler of Malwa, Devagupta and Shashanka, the ruler of Gauda, who had imprisoned their sister Rajyashri and killed

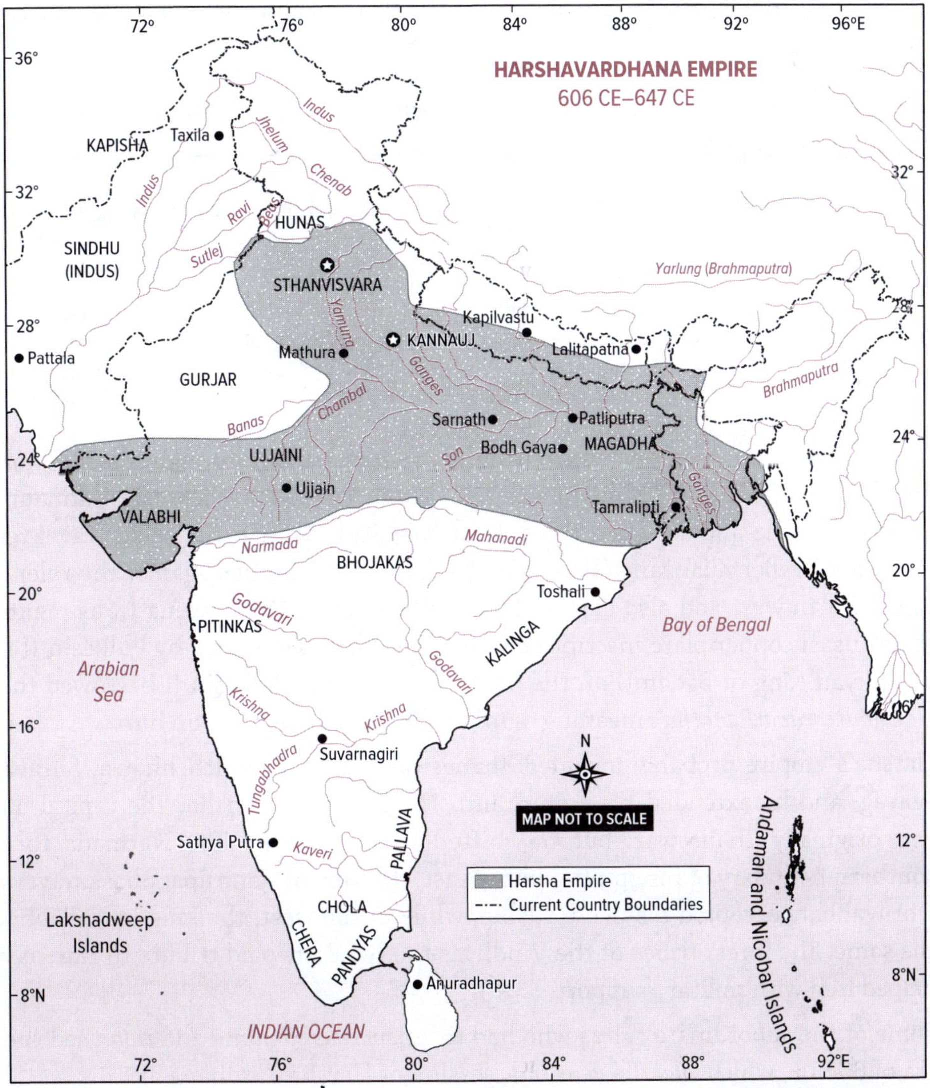

FIGURE 9.2 Harshvardhana Empire

her husband Grahavarman. He defeated the Malwa army and killed Devagupta, but was unfortunately killed by Shashanka, who also cut the Bodhi tree and occupied Kannauj. It was under these circumstances that Harsha then ascended the throne. He was only sixteen years of age at that time, but he still proved himself to be a great warrior and an able administrator. He immediately marched towards Kannauj and rescued his sister Rajyashri, who was believed to be on the verge of committing Sati. Kannauj subsequently came under the sovereignty of Pushyabhutis.

- Later, he also defeated Shashanka and extended his control over parts of Kongoda in Odisha.

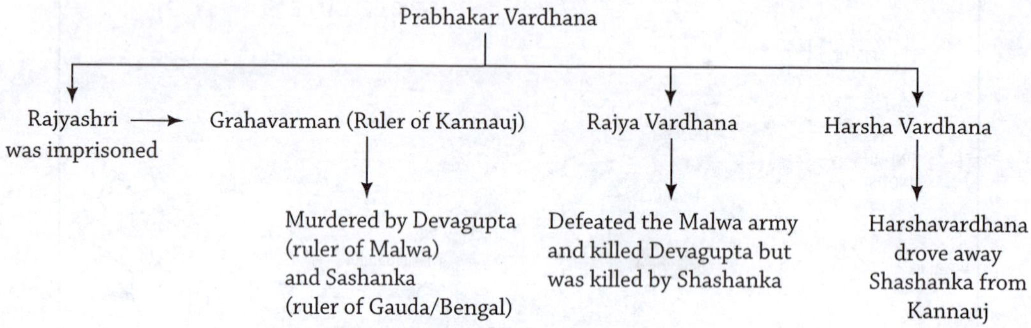

- Harsha's reign was marked by many military victories and he brought most of north India under his control as he brought the five 'Indies (regions)' – Punjab, Kannauj, Bengal, Odisha, Mithila and assumed the title of 'Siladitya' (as mentioned in travel records of Chinese traveller Xuanzang (Hsuan Tsang). He was victorious against the ruler of Sindh in the north west and also defeated the Vallabhi king, Dhruvasena II, as mentioned in the Nausasi copper plate inscription. However, he was defeated by Pulkesin II (western Chalukyan King of Badami) on the banks of Narmada. Pulkesin II bestowed the title of '*Sakalauttarapathanatha*', meaning 'Lord of the entire north', upon him.
- Harsha's empire probably included Thaneswar, Kannauj, Ahichchhatra, Shravasti, and Prayag, and he extended his empire into Magadha and Odisha. The capital of Harsha was originally Thaneswar, but he shifted it to Kannauj. The Narmada formed the southern boundary of his empire. In the east, the king of Kamrupa, Bhaskaravarman and Dhruvabhata accepted his overlordship, while in the west, the king of Vallabhi also did the same. The forest tribes of the Vindhyas too regularly paid tribute to Harsha and also helped him with military support.
- Some of the subordinate rulers who had titles such as *samanta* and *raja* used the Harsha era of 606 CE, which was the year of accession of Harsha Vardhana.
- The Chinese pilgrim Hsuan Tsang, who is also known as the Prince of Travellers and author of *Si-Yu-Ki,* visited India during 629–644 CE. He earned Harsha's friendship and left a vivid account of the beauty, grandeur and prosperity of Kannauj. He gives a detailed account of a grand assembly held at Kannauj in 643 CE, which was attended by the representatives of Hinduism, Jainism and Buddhism, in which Xuanzang along with others gave discourses on Mahayana doctrines. This grand conclave was also attended by various subordinate kings including those of Vallabhi and Assam. A huge tower with a golden statue of the Buddha was constructed for the occasion, which was later worshipped by Harsha himself.

- He also used to celebrate a solemn festival at Prayag (Allahabad) at the end of every five years and also held the *Mahamoksha Parishad* at Allahabad. The images of the Buddha, the Sun and Shiva were worshipped and gifts of valuable articles and clothing were distributed in charity.
- Harsha was a great patron of the arts and learning. He was very talented himself as it is believed that he wrote three dramas *Priyadarshika, Ratnavali* (both romantic comedies) and *Nagananda* (based on *Bodhisattva Jimutavahana*). He also has to his credit a work on grammar and two Sutra works. It is presumed that he himself composed the text of the two inscriptions Madhuban and Banskhera (they contain his signature and exhibit his calligraphic skills). According to Banabhatta, he was also an accomplished flute player.
- He established a large monastery at Nalanda. Banabhatta (author of *Harshacharita* and *Parvatiparinay*), Mayura (author of *Mayurashataka*), renowned grammarian Bhartrihari (author of *Vakapudiyu*) and Matanga Divakara were the accomplished writers at his court.
- He had diplomatic relations with the Chinese as his contemporary T'ang Emperor sent three embassies to his court. The last of these, under Wang-Hiuen-Tse, came to India in 647 CE when Harsha was no longer alive.

The death of Harsha was followed by a period of political confusion that continued up to the 8th century, when the Gurjara-Pratiharas and the Rajput rulers emerged as a big force in northern India.

Administration and Social Life under Harsha

Harsha governed his empire on almost the same lines as the Guptas, except that his administration was more feudal and decentralised. The leading feudatories of Harsha were Bhaskaravarmana of Kamarupa, Dhruvabhatta of Vallabhi, Purnavarman of Magadha and Udita of Jalandhara. He had the support of a large army, which was also supplemented by contributory forces from feudatories in the times of need. The army consisted of infantry, cavalry, chariots and elephants. The power shifted to military camps known as *skandhavaras*. Land grants to priests in lieu of their special services continued and it is generally presumed that land grants to officers by charters in lieu of their salary probably began with Harsha (as evident in the lesser number of coins issued by Harsha). These grants contained the same privileges as enjoyed by Brahmadeya lands. The maintenance of public records was another salient feature of Harsha' administration. '*Nilopitu*' referred to the archive of the Harsha period and was under the control of special officers who maintained the records of both good and bad events in it.

There was a sharp economic decline as compared to the Gupta period, as evident from the decreasing number of coins, decline of trade centres and fewer activities of merchant guilds. Due to the decline of trade and commerce, handicrafts and agriculture were also adversely affected. Hsuan Tsang states that people were taxed lightly and the revenues were divided into four parts:

- One part earmarked for the king
- Second part reserved for scholars
- Third part for the endowments of officials and public servants
- Fourth part for religious purposes

Harsha personally supervised the administration and according to the records of Hsuan Tsang, he divided his day into *three parts: attending to administrative duties during the first and devoting himself to religious work during the other two*. He used to have frequent tours of inspection around his kingdom. However, law and order suffered from some lacunae as inferred from the travel statements of Hsuan Tsang, wherein he states that *he was robbed as well*. The laws of the land were severe and generally robbery was considered as second only to treason, for which the right hand of robber was amputated. Hsuan Tsang condemned the trials as barbarous and superstitious. But later, it appears under the influence of Buddhism, the severity of punishment was mitigated and criminals were punished for life.

The Brahmanas and Kshatriyas were reported to lead a simple life, but the nobles and priests led a luxurious life. The Shudras were generally agriculturists and their status improved as compared to past. Earlier, they were meant to serve the other three varnas only, but they could now pursue agriculture independently. However, the state of untouchables such as the *Chandalas* continued to be pathetic and they suffered from all forms of disabilities. The position of women was not good due to the prevalence of Sati and dowry system. Remarriage of widows was not permitted, particularly among the higher castes. Hsuan Tsang mentions three ways of disposal of the dead—cremation, water burial and exposure in the woods. The forest guards were known as the Vanapalas and the chief of all the villages was an officer called *sarva-palli-patti.*

Hsuan Tsang pointed to the disintegration of the Buddhist sect into eighteen sects. However, Nalanda[1] emerged as a great centre of Buddhist studies and had a huge monastic establishment. Another Chinese traveller Yijing/I-Tsing also visited India in 670 CE and lived for ten years at the Nalanda monastery. He describes that Nalanda was supported by the revenues of 200 villages and there were around 3000 students on its rolls. It had an observatory and a great library and attracted scholars from various parts of the world. The brick temple of Lakshmana at Sirpur with its rich architecture is another legacy of the Harsha period. In terms of literary heritage, besides Harsha himself and his biographer Banabhatta, other literary figures who adorned his court were Matanga Divakara and the famous Barthrihari, who was a poet, philosopher and grammarian.

[1] The term 'Nalanda' means giver of knowledge and was founded by Kumaragupta I during the Gupta period, and was patronised by his successors and later by Harsha. It was a residential university and education was free, including boarding and lodging. Admission was by a competitive examination and it was so tough that only 30% of the aspirants could qualify. The medium of instruction was Sanskrit and though it was a Mahayana University, different religious subjects like Hinayana doctrine, Vedas, Sandhya and Yoga philosophies were also taught. The professors of the University were called pandits and some of the renowned professors were Dingnaga, Dharampala, Sthiramati and Silabadhra. Dharamapala later became the head of the Nalanda University.

The Maitrakas

The Maitrakas were tributary chiefs of the Guptas, who established an independent kingdom in western India ruling over Saurashtra in Gujarat. Dhruvasena II was the most important ruler of the Maitrakas, who was a contemporary of Harsha Vardhana and was married to his daughter. Hsuan Tsang tells us that Dhruvasena II attended Harsha's assembly at Prayaga (Allahabad). The Maitrakas developed Vallabhi as their capital, which was also an important centre of learning. Being on the Arabian Sea, it was also a port town having flourishing trade and commerce. The Maitrakas continued to rule until the middle of the 8th century when Arab attacks weakened their power.

The Maukharies

The Maukharies were also subordinate rulers of the Guptas and used the title of *samanta*[2]. They ruled over Kannauj, a city in western Uttar Pradesh, which gradually replaced Pataliputra as the political centre of northern India. Harsha Vardhana's sister Rajyashri was married to Grahavarmana. As we have discussed earlier, Shashanka, the ruler of Bengal (Gauda), and Devagupta, the ruler of Malwa jointly attacked Grahavarmana and killed him. After the successful expedition of Harsha Vardhana, the kingdom of Kannauj was then merged with that of the Pushyabhutis and Harsha shifted his capital from Thanesar (Kurukshetra) to Kannauj. The Maukharis are also mentioned in Patanjali's work.

Hari Varhmana Maukhari (mid-6th century CE)

- Had assumed the title 'Maharaja'; however, the extent of his kingdom is unknown.

Advaita Varmana

- He had succeeded his father, and is said to have assumed the title of Maharaja.

Ishanavarmana (c. 554 CE)

- The real founder of Maukhari supremacy and assumed the title '*Maharajadhiraja*' according to Asirgarh copper plate inscription.
- The Maukhari kingdom had stretched to Andhra Pradesh, Odisha and Gauda, under his reign. The Andhra king defeated by Ishanavarman may have been a member of the Visnukundin family. Ishanavarman had to face opposition from the later Guptas and there started a prolonged struggle with the later Guptas. He had to suffer crushing defeat at the hands of Kumaragupta.

---

[2] Samantas or subordinates were expected to be present at the kings' courts, to bring gifts for them and provide them with military support. As Samanta gained power and wealth, they would gradually declare them as maha-samanta or maha-mandaleshwara (the great lord of a circle or region).

- He is remembered in history for the resistance offered to the Hunas, resulting in the defeat of the Hunas. The Maukharis possibly fought with the Hunas as feudatories of Baladitya of the Imperial Gupta family. The Harsha inscription claims that Ishanavarmana had also defeated the Sulikas.
- The seals and coins of this ruler indicate that he was a learned person, a just ruler, a brave warrior and a patron of education.

Sarvavarmana (c. 560–585 CE)

- Probably the son of Ishanavarmana, who succeeded the throne after his father's death. Sarvavarmana did maintain his hold on Magadha and kept the later Guptas under subordination. The Asirgadh inscription in Nimar district of Madhya Pradesh narrates his victory over Damodargupta, and describes Nimar as a 'Maukhari outpost in the Deccan.'
- In the time of Sarvavarmana, the later Guptas created no trouble.

Avanti Varmana (c. 585–600 CE)

- The Nalanda seal shows that Sarvavarmana was succeeded by his son Avantivarmana who also took the title of *Maharajadhiraja* and extended the boundary of the kingdom by transferring the capital to the historical city of Kannauj.
- It was under him that the Maukhari empire reached at its peak.

Grahavarmana (around c. 600 CE)

- He succeeded Avantivarmana and was married to Rajyashri, the daughter of Prabhakar Vardhana of the Pushyabhuti family of Thanesara.
- Grahavarmana was killed by Deva Gupta of the later Gupta lineage.

Gradually the Maukhari family disappeared into obscurity.

Period from c. 600–750 CE: Southern India

As we have seen earlier, the period from c. 300–750 CE marks the second historical phase in the region south of the Vindhyas. It continued some processes from the first historical phase but it also differed from the first historical phase (c. 200 BCE–300 CE) in many respects such as:

First Historical Phase (c. 200 BCE–300 CE)	Second Historical Phase (c. 300–750 CE)
The major kingdoms were of the Satavahanas, the Cholas, the Cheras and the Pandyas.	The three major kingdoms of this era were of the Pallavas of Kanchi, the Chalukyas of Badami, the Pandyas of Madurai.
This period was marked by the appearance of numerous crafts, internal and external trade, widespread use of coins and a good number of towns.	Trade, towns and coinage declined in this phase, however, there was more expansion of agrarian economy.

First Historical Phase (c. 200 BCE–300 CE)	Second Historical Phase (c. 300–750 CE)
This period offered patronage to Buddhism as is evident in extensive Buddhist monuments in both Andhra and Maharashtra. Cave inscriptions also point to the existence of Jainism and Buddhism in the southern districts of Tamil Nadu.	There was more emphasis on Brahmanism and more instances of Vedic sacrifices by kings. Jainism was restricted to Karnataka. The culture of Megaliths paved way for temple construction.
The epigraphs were mostly written in Prakrit.	Sanskrit became the official language of the peninsula and most charters were prepared in it.

Deccan

The Western Chalukyas of Badami

As we have discussed earlier, in northern Maharashtra and Vidarbha (Berar), the Satavahanas were succeeded by the Vakatakas. The Vakaṭakas were followed by the Chalukyas of Badami, who played a prominent role in the history of Deccan and south India for about two hundred years from the beginning of the 6th century CE. The Chalukyas were a maritime power and they set up their kingdom in western Deccan with capital at Vatapi (modern Badami in Karnataka). Along with the Chalukyas of Badami (who are primarily called the Western Chalukyas), there were two other branches of the lineage who ruled independently – the Eastern Chalukyas of Vengi and the Chalukyas of Lata.

The Western Chalukyas, in order to acquire legitimacy and respectability, claimed Brahmanical origin as *Haritiputras* of the *Manavya gotra*. The founder king of this dynasty was Pulakeshin I, who established the independent power of this dynasty.

Pulkeshin I (c. 535–566 CE)

- Founded the kingdom with capital at Vatapi (Badami, Karnataka).
- Performed a number of *shrauta* sacrifices such as *ashavmedha*.

Kirtivarman I (c. 566–598 CE)

- Pulkeshin I's son, who further enlarged the kingdom and defeated the Kadambas of Banavasi (near Mysore), the Mauryas of the Konkan and the Nalas of the Bastar area.

Mangalesha (c. 598–609 CE)

- After Kirtivarman I's death, a war of succession broke out between his brother Mangalesha and nephew Pulakeshin II, in which Pulkeshin II emerged triumphant.

Pulkeshin II (c. 610–642 CE)

- The most powerful and famous king of this dynasty, who achieved many military successes. His eulogy was written by his court poet Ravikirti in the Aihole inscription, which describes his victories against the Kadambas of Banavasi, Alupas and Gangas of Mysore. He also led expeditions against eastern Deccan kingdoms, south Kosala and Kalinga.

- Contemporary of Harsha Vardhana and defeated him on the banks of river Narmada. He thus acquired the title of *dakshinapatheshvara* (lord of the south) and *Paramesvara*.
- Sent an embassy to Persian king Khusro II (the reception of this embassy is depicted in the Ajanta Caves).
- Hsuan Tsang visited his kingdom and he *described that even though Pulkeshin II was Hindu, he was tolerant towards Buddhism and Jainism.*
- He had conflicts with the Pallavas of Kanchi and annexed the region between Krishna and Godavari (popularly known as Vengi) from the Pallavas and placed it under his brother Vishnuvardhana (Chalukyas of Vengi/Eastern Chalukyas). Thus, the first expedition against the Pallavas, who were at the time ruled by Mahendravarman I, was a complete success. However, the second expedition against the Pallavas proved to be a complete failure as King Narsimhavarman of the Pallava dynasty killed Pulkeshin II and adopted the epithet of *Vatapikonda*.
- The Badami Chalukya dynasty went into a brief decline following the death of Pulakeshin II due to internal feuds. Badami was occupied by the Pallavas for a period of 13 years. It marked the beginning of a long-drawn political struggle between the Pallavas and Chalukyas, that continued with ups and down for more than a hundred years.

Vikramaditya I (c. 655–680 CE)

- Succeeded in pushing the Pallavas out of Badami and re-established authority over the whole kingdom. He not only defeated successive Pallava rulers but also captured their capital Kanchi.
- Vikramaditya I took the title '*Rajamalla*' (meaning 'the Sovereign of the Mallas' or Pallavas).
- Also defeated the Cheras, Cholas and Pandyas.

Vinayaditya I (c. 680–696 CE)

Vijayaditya (c. 696–733 CE)

- His 37-year rule was a prosperous one and is widely known for his prolific temple building activity.

Vikramaditya II (c. 733–743 CE)

- The Vatapi dynasty was at its peak again during the rule of the illustrious king Vikramaditya II, who is best known for his repeated invasions of the territory of *Tondaimandalam* and his subsequent victories over Pallava King Nandivarman II. He thus avenged the earlier humiliation of the Chalukyas by the Pallavas and in order to commensurate his victory got engraved a Kannada inscription on the victory pillar of the Kailasanath Temple.

- He is also known for benevolence towards the people and the monuments of Kanchipuram, the Pallava capital.
- During his reign, Arab intruders of the Umayyad Caliphate invaded southern Gujarat, which was under Chalukya rule, but the Arabs were defeated and driven out by Pulakesi, a Chalukya governor of Navsari.
- He later also overran the other traditional kingdoms of Tamil country, the Pandyas, the Cholas and the Cheras, in addition to subduing a Kalabhra ruler.

Kirtivarman II (c. 743–757 CE)

- Last ruler of this dynasty who was defeated by the Rashtrakuta king Dantidurga. Thus, Chalukyan rule came to an end in about 757 CE and one of the feudatories, the Rashtrakutas came into prominence.

Administration and Social Life under Chalukyas

Unlike the Pallavas and the Cholas, the Chalukyan administration was highly centralised and the village autonomy was completely absent. They had a small standing army but were a great maritime power. In fact, Pulkeshin II had 100 ships in his navy. The Badami Chalukyas were Brahmanical Hindus and accorded importance to Vedic rites and rituals, but they showed equal tolerance and respect to other religions. A number of temples in the honour of Vishnu, Shiva and other gods were also built during this period. Though Buddhism was on decline in western Deccan, Jainism was progressing steadily under the Chalukyas. In fact, Ravikirti, the court poet of Pulkeshin II, was a Jain scholar.

Culturally, Chalukyan period is noted for the growth of art and architecture in Deccan. Much of the paintings and sculpture of the Ajanta and Ellora caves were completed during the Chalukyan reign. Their style of architecture is called 'Chalukyan architecture'. They developed Deccan or Vesara style of temple-building, which reached its culmination under the Rashtrakutas and the Hoyasalas (13th century). Nearly a hundred monuments built by them, rock-cut (cave) and structural, are found in the Malaprabha river basin in modern Bagalkot district of northern Karnataka. They mostly used locally found reddish-golden sandstone in their monuments. Most of the Chalukyan temple-building activities were concentrated in a relatively small area of Aihole, Badami, Pattadakal and Mahakuta in modern Karnataka state. Their temple building activity can be categorised primarily into three phases:

Phases of Chalukyan temple building activity	
(a) The early phase (which began in the last quarter of the 6th century)	• In this phase, prominently cave temples were built, such as the three elementary cave temples at Aihole (one Vedic, one Jaina and one Buddhist which is incomplete), followed by four developed cave temples at Badami out of which three caves temples are Vedic and one belongs to Jaina tradition. • The noteworthy feature of these cave temples at Badami is that each has a plain exterior but an exceptionally well-finished interior, consisting of a pillared verandah, a columned hall (mandapa) and a *cella* (shrine, cut deep into rock) which contains the deity of worship. • The Vedic temples contain large well-sculpted images of *Harihara, Mahishasuramardhini, Varaha, Narasimha, Trivikrama, Vishnu seated on Anantha* (the snake) and *Nataraja* (dancing Shiva).
(b) The second phase	• This phase of temple building was at Aihole, where some 70 structures exist and has been called '*one of the cradles of Indian temple architecture*', and Badami. These are the Lad Khan Temple with its interesting perforated stone windows and sculptures of river goddesses, the Meguti Jain Temple which shows progress in structural design, and the Durga Temple with its northern Indian style tower. • Other Dravida style temples from this period are the Naganatha Temple at Nagaral, the Banantigudi Temple and the Mahakutesvara Temple.
(c) The mature phase	• The mature phase of Badami Chalukyan architecture includes the structural temples at Pattadakal, which were built in the 8th century and are now a UNESCO World Heritage Site. There are ten temples at Pattadakal, six in southern Dravida style and four in the northern Nagara style. Well known among these are the Sangamesvara Temple, the famous Virupaksha Temple of Karnataka which contains a lot of representations from the Mahabharata, and the Mallikarjuna Temple built in the southern style. • Inscriptional evidence suggests that *the Virupaksha and the Mallikarjuna Temples were commissioned by the two queens of King Vikramaditya II after his military success over the Pallavas of Kanchipuram*. The Bhutanatha group of temples at Badami are also from this period.

The Eastern Chalukyas of Vengi

In the second half of the 8th century, the Eastern Chalukyas established themselves in Vengi in Andhra Pradesh. As we have discussed earlier, Pulakesin II (c. 610–642 CE) conquered the Vengi region in eastern Deccan and in 624 CE appointed his brother Vishnuvardhana as the governor of this newly acquired territory. Probably after the death of Pulkeshin II, Vishnuvardhana declared independence and thus the Eastern Chalukyas of Vengi came into prominence. Initially, the capital of the Eastern Chalukyas was Vengi (near modern Eluru) but later it was moved to Rajamahendravaram (modern Rajamundry). Throughout their history, the Eastern Chalukyas were the cause of many wars between the more powerful Cholas and Western Chalukyas since they controlled the strategic Vengi country. The five centuries of the Eastern Chalukya rule of Vengi saw not only the consolidation of this region into a unified whole, but also saw the efflorescence of Telugu culture, literature, poetry and art during the latter half of their rule. They continued ruling the region as feudatories of the Cholas until 1189 CE. Their kingdom ultimately succumbed to the Hoysalas and the Yadavas.

Vishnuvardhana (around c. 624 CE)

↓

Vijayaditya II (c. 808–847 CE)

- One of the most important rulers of this dynasty, who led successful military expeditions against the Rashtrakutas, the Gangas, and also led campaigns into Gujarat. Even the Rashtrakuta inscriptions acknowledge their defeat at the hands of Vijayaditya and they admit *that the glory of their kingdom was 'drowned in the ocean of the Chalukyas'*.

Vijayaditya III (c. 848–892 CE)

- Another important ruler of this dynasty, who claimed to have won over not only the Pallavas, the Pandyas, the Gangas, the Rashtrakutas, the Kalachuris and South Kosala, but also gave shelter to a Chola king.

Bhima I (c. 892–922 CE)

- He was captured by the Rashtrakuta king but was later released.

Vijayaditya IV (around c. 922 CE, for a period of six months)

- From his reign, many succession disputes erupted in which the Rashtrakutas openly interfered and backed one or the other contenders. The later rulers thus had very short reigns, from six months to a mere fortnight too.
- Some political stability was restored during the reigns of Bhima II and Amma II, but it did not last for a long time and subsequently in 999 CE, the Eastern Chalukyas of Vengi were conquered by the Chola king Rajaraja.

The Chalukyas of Lata

Initially in their early years, they started as feudatories of the Western Chalukyas but gradually during the 10th and 11th centuries, with the diminishing power of the Western Chalukyas, they declared themselves independent and started ruling in the Lata region of present day Gujarat and were ultimately defeated by the Chalukyas of Gujarat (Solankis).

Nimbarka (Not much is known about him)

↓

Barappa (c. 970–990 CE)

- The dynasty's first prominent ruler, who earlier worked as a general of the Western Chalukya king Tailapa II and was subsequently made the governor of the Lata region by Tailapa.
- It is believed that a joint army of Barappa and the Shakambhari king defeated the Solanki ruler Mularaja.
- According to Hemachandra's Devyashraya Kavya, Mularaja's son Chamunda-raja invaded Lata and killed Barappa.

Gogi-raja (c. 990–1010 CE)

- Barappa's son Gogi-raja probably revived the family's fortune in the Lata region.

Kirti-raja (c. 1010–1030 CE)

- A 940 Shaka (1018 CE) copper plate inscription of Kirti-raja was discovered in Surat, which lists the names of his ancestors as Gogi, Barappa and Nimbarka.

Vatsa-raja (c. 1030–1050 CE)

- Vatsa is believed to have built a golden umbrella for the god Somanatha, and also established a free food canteen (*sattra*).

Trilochana-pala (c. 1050–1070 CE)

- Two copper plate inscriptions dated 972 Shaka (1050 CE Ekallahara and 1051 CE Surat) related to Trilochana-pala have been discovered. He is titled *Maha-Mandaleshvara* in these inscriptions.
- These inscriptions given an account of the mythical origin of the Chalukyas. According to these inscriptions, *the family's progenitor originated from the chuluka (a vessel or a folded palm to hold water) of the creator deity Virinchi. On the deity's advice, he married the Rashtrakuta princess of Kanyakubja.*
- The 1050 CE inscription records his donation of the Ekallahara village to a Brahmin named Taraditya.

However, by 1074 CE, the dynasty appears to have been vanquished by the Solankis.

Far South

The political history of the far south during this period was dominated by two prominent kingdoms, the Pallavas of Kanchi and the Pandyas of Madurai.

The Pallavas of Kanchi

On the ruins of the Satavahanas, in the eastern part of the peninsula (especially in the Krishna-Guntur region), arose the Ikshvakus. They were probably a local tribe who adopted the exalted name of the Ikshavakus to demonstrate the antiquity of their lineage. Many monuments and copper plate inscriptions at Nagarjunakonda and Dharanikota belonged to them. The Ikshvakus were supplanted by the Pallavas. The term Pallava means '*creeper*', which is a Sanskrit version of the word *tondi* and in Tamil they are synonymous to robber. So, the Pallavas[3] were probably a pastoral local tribe who established their authority in the land of creepers called *Tondaimandalam* (the land between the north Penner and north Vellar rivers), mostly comprising of southern Andhra Pradesh and northern Tamil Nadu with their capital at Kanchi. Kanchi (modern Kanchipuram) under them became an important temple town and a centre of trade and commerce.

Some inscriptions refer to early kings of this dynasty[4] such as Shivaskandavarman, who probably ruled in the early 4th century CE. But in the last quarter of the 6th century, the ruler who played a crucial role in the Pallavas' rise to power was Simhavishnu.

Simhavishnu

- He supposedly defeated the Ikshvakus and laid a firm foundation for the Pallava empire.
- Putting an end to the political disturbances caused by the Kalabhras, he conquered the land up to the Kaveri and set up capital at Kanchi (south of Chennai).
- Bore the title of '*Avanisimha*' (Lion of the Earth).
- The great Sanskrit scholar Bharavi lived during his reign.

Mahendravarman I (c. 590–630 CE)

- During his reign, conflict between the Chalukyas of Badami and the Pallavas heightened and he was defeated by Pulekshin II at Pullalur (near Kanchi) who annexed the northern part of the Pallava kingdom.
- Was a great patron of arts, was himself a poet and musician. He wrote the famous Sanskrit work *Mattavilasa Prahasanna* and adopted the title of Chitrakarapuli revealing his talents in painting. During his reign, a commentary called Dakshinchitra was also compiled. The music inscription at Kudumiyanmalai is ascribed to him and is testimony to his music talent.
- He was also a great builder of cave temples, as evident from the Mandagappattu inscription which hails him as Vichitrachitta who constructed a temple for Brahma, Vishnu and Shiva without the use of bricks, timber, metal and mortar. He initiated the construction

[3] They are believed to be identical with the Pulindas mentioned in the inscriptions of Ashoka.

[4] It is believed that there were probably three lines of Pallava rulers:

(a) First line of Pallava Rulers (250–350 CE): The early Pallava rulers who issued their charters in Prakrit and important rulers among them were Shivaskandavarman and Vijayaskandavarman.

(b) Second line of Pallava Rulers (350–550 CE): Issued their charges in Sanskrit and one of the most important ruler was Vishnugopa who was defeated by Samudragupta during his south Indian expedition.

(c) Third Line of Pallava Rulers (575 CE till 9th century): Issued their charters in both Sanskrit and Tamil, and Simhavishnu was the first ruler of this line.

of the famous cave temple at Mahabalipuram and his rock cut temples are found in a number of places like Vallam, Mahendravadi, Dalavanur, Pallavaram, Mandagappattu and Tiruchirappalli.

- Was earlier a Jaina but later took up Shaivism under the influence of Appar. He built a Shiva temple at Tiruvadi.

FIGURE 9.3 Mamallapuram Rock Carvings

Narasimhavarman I/Mahamalla[5] (c. 630–668 CE)

- Avenged his father's defeat and not only defeated Pulkeshin II[6] but also invaded the Western Chalukyan kingdom and captured Badami with the help of the Sri Lankan prince, Manavarma.
- Claimed to have won over not only the Chalukyas but also the Cholas, Cheras and the Kalabhras.
- Dispatched two naval expeditions to help his friend Manavarma, but subsequently Manavarma was defeated and he had to seek political refuge at his court.
- Enthusiastic patron of architecture and along with constructing the port of Mamallapuram, he also ordered the construction of the *rathas* at Mahabalipuram. It is in honour of Narasimhavarman I that Mahabalipuram is also known as Mamallapuram. It is during his reign that Hsuan Tsang visited the Pallava capital Kanchipuram, and later described Kanchi as '*a big and beautiful city, six miles in circumference. It had 100 Buddhist monasteries in which about 10,000 Buddhist monks lived. The people of Kanchi were great learners.*'

[5] Which means great wrestler.

[6] His victory over Pulakeshin II in the battle of Manimangalam near Kanchi is mentioned in Kuram copper plates. The Pallava army under General Paranjothi pursued the retreating Chalukyan army, entered Chalukyan territory, captured and destroyed the capital city of Vatapi and thus Narasimhavarman I assumed the title of 'Vatapikonda'.

FIGURE 9.4 Ratha Temple at Mahabalipuram

Mahendravarman II (c. 668–670 CE)

- The Pallava-Chalukya conflict continued for subsequent decades and Mahendravarman II died fighting the Chalukyas.

Parameshvaraman I (c. 670–695 CE)

- Defeated the Chalukya king Vikramaditya and also the Gangas.
- Built temple at Kanchi.

Narsimhavarman II/ Rajasimha (c. 700–728 CE)

- Constructed Rajasimheshvara/Kailashnatha Temple at Kanchipuram.
- Shore temple at Mahabalipuram.
- Famous Sanskrit scholar Dandin was at his court.
- Sent an ambassador to China.

Paramesdhvaraman II (c. 728–731 CE)

- During his reign, the Pallava capital Kanchi was attacked by the Chalukyas and he suffered a humilitating defeat.

Nandivarman II (c. 731–795 CE)

- Patronised Perundevanar who translated the Mahabharata as *Bharatavenba* in Tamil.

Dantivarman (c. 795–846 CE)

- During his reign, Rashtrakuta king Govind III invaded Kanchi.

Nandivarman III (c. 846–869 CE)

- Managed to defeat the Pandyas.

Aparajita (c. 880–893 CE)

- Last known Pallava king who, with the help of Western Gangas and Cholas, defeated the Pandyas in a battle at Shripurambiyam.

In c. 893 CE, the Pallavas were ultimately overthrown by the Chola king Aditya I and the area of *Tondaimandalam* passed under the suzerainty of the Cholas. Culturally, the reign of Pallavas is important for the growth of Tamil bhakti literature and the Dravidian style of art and architecture in south India. It was under them that Mahabalipuram emerged as an important centre of temple architecture.

Administration and Social Life under Pallavas

The Pallavas had a well-organised administrative system headed by a King who was assisted by able ministers. The state was divided into Kottams and each Kottam was administered by officers appointed by the King. A well-trained army was maintained by the King. The land grants provided to the temples by the King were known as *Devadhana* and to the Brahmanas were known as *Brahmadeya*, which were exempted from tax. Land tax was the primary source of the government revenue, though tax was also collected from carpenters, goldsmiths, oil pressers and weavers. The government had the primary responsibility of providing irrigation facilities and a number of irrigation tanks were dug by the Pallava kings. For instance, the irrigation tanks at Mahendravadi and Mamandoor were dug during the reign of Mahendravarman I. The village assemblies were called *Sabhas*, which looked after local affairs, maintained records of all village land and managed temples.

During the reign of Pallavas, however, the caste system became rigid in the Tamil society. The position of the Brahmans was further consolidated through the land grants by the kings and the nobles and they were also given the responsibility of looking after temples. During the Pallavas, Buddhism and Jainism suffered from a decline whereas Shaivism and Vaishnavism witnessed a rise. Much of the rise is attributed to the Bhakti movement, which we are going to study in detail in a later chapter. The *Devaram* composed by Nayannars and the *Nalayradivyaprabandam* composed by Alvars represent the rich religious literature of the Pallava period. Another important literary work belonging to Pallavas is *Nandikkalambagam*, but the name of the author of this work is unknown.

The Pallavas were also great patrons of learning and their capital Kanchi emerged as an ancient centre of learning. The *Ghatika* at Kanchi attracted students from both India and abroad. In fact, Diganaga, the famous Buddhist writer, came to study at Kanchi and Dharamapala belonged to Kanchi who later became the head of the Nalanda University. Under the patronage of the Pallavas, music, dance and painting, too, reached great heights. The Mamandur inscription contains a note on the notation of the vocal music whereas the Kudumianmalai inscription referred to musical notes and instruments. The famous Sittannavasal paintings belonged to Pallavas.

It was also a great age of temple building as the Dravidian style of temple architecture actually began under the Pallavas. The gradual evolution starting from the cave temples to monolithic rathas culminated in structural temples. In fact, the development of temple architecture can be traced primarily to four stages:

(a) **Rock Cut Temples:** The Pallavas under Mahendravarman I introduced the art of excavating temples from rocks. This style is visible at places like Mahendravadi, Mamandur, Mandagappattu, Dalavanur, Vallam, Tiruchirappalli, Tirukalukkunram and Siyamangalam.

(b) **Monolithic *Rathas* and *Mandapas*:** The second stage of Pallava architecture mostly pertains to the reign of Narasimhavarman I and is concentrated at Mamallapuram. The five *rathas*, popularly called the Panchapanadava rathas, signify five different styles of temple architecture.

(c) **Structural Temples:** The next stage belongs to the reign of Rajasimha who introduced structural temples built by using the soft sand rocks. The famous Kailashnatha Temple at Kanchi and the shore temple of Mamallapuram are the finest examples of this stage.

(d) **Structural temples built by later Pallavas:** The Vaikundaperumal temple, the Matagenswara temple and the Muktheeswara temple at Kanchipuram belong to this stage of architecture.

The Pallavas also contributed to the development of sculpture. The sculptural beauty of this period is witnessed in both the sculptures found in the temples and the 'Open Art Gallery' found at Mamallapuram. 'The Descent of the Ganges' and 'the Penance of Arjuna' are more like fresco paintings in stone owing to the minute details and to the theme of these sculptures.

Ellora Group of Caves	Ajanta Group of Caves	Mamallapuram
(a) The Ellora group of caves which were designated as a **UNESCO World Heritage Site** are famous for **sculptures**. (b) The **patrons** of these caves range from the dynasties of Chalukyas to Rashtrakutas. (c) These set of caves were developed during the period between the **5th** and **11th** centuries and are thus **newer** as compared to Ajanta Caves.	(a) The Ajanta group of caves were also designated as a **UNESCO World Heritage Site** and are famous for **paintings.** (b) They were inscribed by the Buddhist monks, under the patronage of the Vakataka kings – **Harisena** being a prominent one and certain inscriptions speak of the patrons who range from kings to merchants.	(a) Mamallapuram, also called Mahabalipuram or *Seven Pagodas*, was founded by a 7th-century **Pallava** King **Narasimhavarman,** also known as Mamalla – for whom the town was named. (b) The town's **Five Rathas**, or monolithic temples, are the remnants of seven temples, for which the

Ellora Group of Caves	Ajanta Group of Caves	Mamallapuram
(d) Each cave is having exquisite edifices which could have been created only with the knowledge of trigonometry, structural engineering, and metallurgy. Also, not only the animals, birds, trees, flowers are pictured elegantly, but even human emotions and character – greed, love, compassion are depicted with professional skill.	(c) These set of caves developed in two phases: (i) First phase (c. 200 BCE to 200 CE). (ii) The second phase (c. 200 CE to 400 CE). (d) Reference of the Ajanta caves is found in the travel accounts of Chinese Buddhist travellers **Fa Hien** (during the reign of Chandragupta II; 376–415 CE) and **Hsuan Tsang** (during the reign of emperor Harshavardhana; c. 606–647 CE).	town was known as Seven Pagodas. The entire assemblage collectively was designated as **UNESCO World Heritage Site**
The rock-cut cave temples in Ellora are in **34** caves and are related to *Ajivikas, Jainism, Buddhism* and *Brahmanism*: **17** caves: are dedicated to **Brahmanism**, **12** caves: are dedicated to **Buddhism** and **5** caves: are dedicated to **Jainism**. It is also pertinent to note that first the heterodox sects set the trend of creating this model of temples and later, the orthodox sects adopted it as a medium of disseminating religious ideologies.	There is a total of **29** caves and all are related to Buddhism: (i) **25** were used as *Viharas* or residential caves (ii) **4** were used as *Chaitya* or prayer halls.	The monolithic rathas are known as the *Panchapandava Rathas:* (a) *The Arjuna Ratha*: contains artistically carved sculptures of Siva, Vishnu, *mithuna* and *dwarapala*. (b) *The Dharmaraja Ratha*: One of the most exquisite of the five rathas, has a three-storied *vimana* and a square base. (c) *The Bhima Ratha:* is rectangular in plan and has beautiful sculptures of Harihara, Brahma, Vishnu, Skanda, Ardhanarisvara and Shiva as Gangadhara.

Ellora Group of Caves	Ajanta Group of Caves	Mamallapuram
Prominent features about caves of Vedic religions: (a) The earliest caves in these groups are mostly simple and square-shaped except Kailashnatha cave **(cave-16)**, which is a massive monolithic structure, carved out of a single solid rock. This temple which is said to represent **Kailash**, the abode of Lord Shiva, stands out remarkably and is two storeyed having the Kailasa temple on the first floor. The lower storey has carved life-size **elephants**, which give impression as if they are holding up the temple on their backs. The temple exterior has richly carved windows, images of deities from the Hindu scriptures and *Mithunas* (amorous male and female figures). Interestingly, most of the deities to the left of the temple entrance are *Shaivite* and the deities to the right of the entrance are *Vaishnavite*. (b) Some other beautiful specimens include: (i) The wedding ceremony of Siva-Parvati, (ii) The attempted lifting of the Kailasa mountain by *Ravana*, and (iii) The destruction of *Mahisasura* by the goddess *Durga*. (iv) The river goddess *Ganga* mounted on a crocodile and the river goddess *Yamuna* mounted on a tortoise.	Some peculiar features of mural paintings were: (a) The colours were extracted out of natural objects and minerals. The prominent colours used are black, red, white, yellow, blue and green. (b) Though a variety of human moods are presented, the dominant ones are of compassion and peace. (c) Light and shadow are intelligently used. (d) The story panels are attractive and informative and the central theme of the paintings involve scenes from the *Jataka* stories and select episodes from the life history of Buddha. (e) The celestial figures of *Kinnaras*, *Vidyadharas* and *Gandharvas* are depicted in paintings and sculptures. (f) Some beautiful specimens include: (i) The sculpture of Buddha in the *garba-griha* having image of the embodiment of benevolence. (ii) Sculptures of *Yakshis* and *Hariti* with children are significant. (iii) The popular Bodhisattva Avalokitesvara carved out independently is another beautiful feature.	Some of the prominent pieces of carving in Mamallapuram are: (a) The Descent of the Ganga (variously described as '*Bhagirata's Penance*' or '*Arjuna's Penance*'). (b) The sculptural panel in the Krishna *mandapa*, where village life with cows and cowherds is depicted with beauty and skill, is yet another artistic wonder to behold.

Ellora Group of Caves	Ajanta Group of Caves	Mamallapuram
Prominent features about Buddhist caves: (a) Every Buddhist cave temple is unique in terms of architecture and the panels in these caves portray scenes from the life of the Buddha. They were designed as monasteries for teaching and training the monks in religious treatises and scriptures. For instance, in cave no. 6, a man is reading a manuscript on a folding table. (b) Some famous sculptures include Buddha in three sagacious postures: (i) meditating (*dhyana mudra*), (ii) preaching (*vyakhyana mudra*) (iii) touching the earth by index finger of right hand (*bhumi-sparsha mudra*). (c) Another important aspect was that in Buddhist caves, the goddesses were represented by way of the carved images of *Tara, Khadiravani-tara, Chunda, Vajradhat-vishvari, Maha-mayuri, Sujata, Pandara and Bhrikuti*. For instance, in cave no. 12, a stout female figure is depicted wearing a waistband and headgear of a cobra. *Khadrivani-tara* also holds a cobra in one of her hands in the same cave. (d) A few Jain caves are also seen in Ellora group in which the figures of *Yaksha-matanga, Mahavira, Parsvanatha* and *Gomatesvara* are surrounded by attendants.	The methodology and technique employed was: (a) First, they plastered the ridged surface of the volcanic rock with the plaster which was made of vegetable fibres, paddy husk, rock-grit and sand. (b) Then the surface was overlaid with a thin layer of lime, ready to receive the pigment. (c) They also used a stretch of cloth to reinforce the application of pigment on the surface.	The iconic Shore Temple were constructed during the reign of Rajasimha (c. 700–728 CE) and comprises of three shrines dedicated to Shiva and Vishnu. It is pertinent to note that unlike other structures of the region, the Shore Temple is a five-storeyed rock-cut monolith. In fact, the monolithic *vimanas* are peculiar to Mamallapuram.

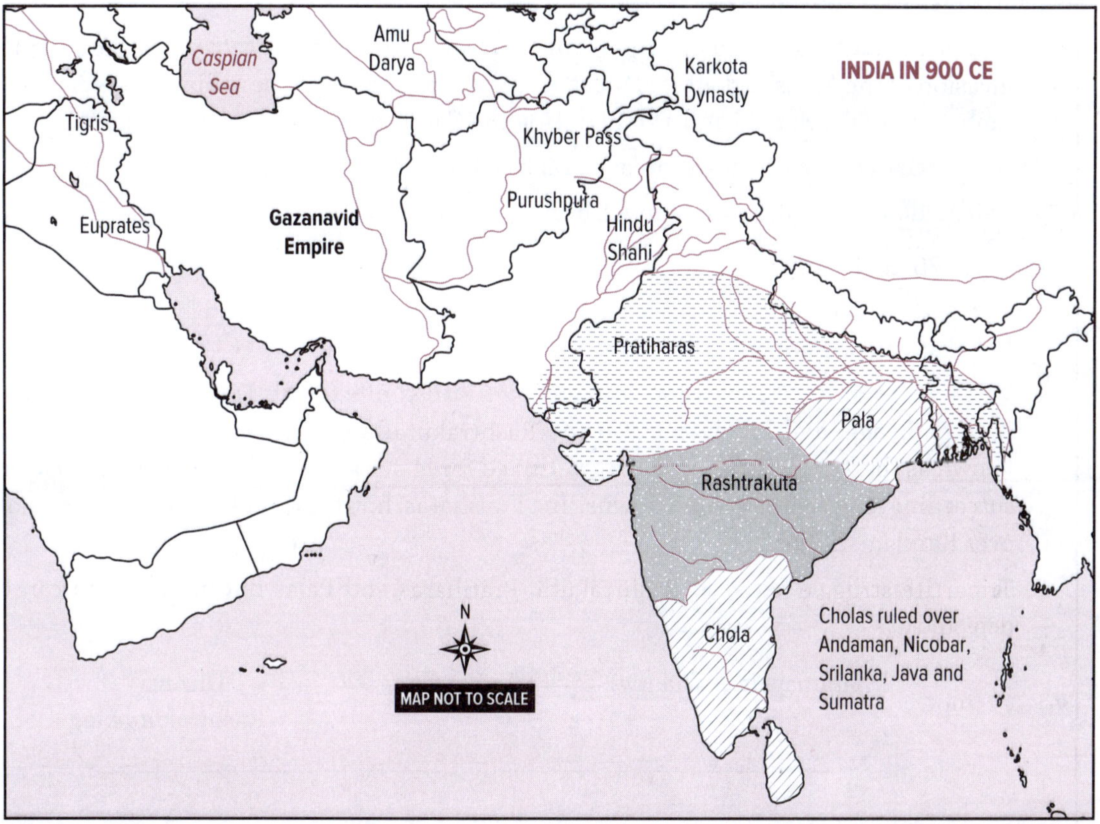

FIGURE 9.6 India in 900 CE

The Pratihara Dynasty

The Pratiharas were also known as the Gurjara–Pratiharas, as they originated from the Gurjaras who were primarily pastoralists and fighters. Since the early kings of this dynasty considered the epic hero Lakshmana as their hero, who had served as the door-keeper to his brother Rama, the Pratiharas took on their title which literally means '*door-keeper*'. The Gurjara–Pratiharas are known for their sculpture, their carved panels and the open pavilion style temples. The greatest development of the Gurjara–Pratihara style of temple building took place at Khajuraho (a UNESCO World Heritage Site). The dynasty was founded by a Brahmana named Harichandra in and around Jodhpur, south western Rajasthan. The Gurjara–Pratiharas were instrumental in containing Arab armies moving east of the Indus. They came to prominence in the second quarter of the 8th century, during the reign of Nagabhatta I.

Nagabhatta I (c. 730–760 CE)

- One of the most famous and prominent Pratihara kings, who is known for checking the invasion of the Arabs and offered most successful resistance to the Arabs. He defeated the Arab army under Junaid and Tamin during the Caliphate campaigns in India.
- He exercised control over the areas of Malwa, Rajputana and Gujarat.
- Defeated by the Rashtrakuta king, Dhruva.

Vatsaraja (c. 780–800 CE)

- One of the successors of Nagabhatta I, who extended his rule over to a large part of north India and made Kannauj in western U.P. his capital.
- Vatsaraja's policy of expansion brought him into conflict with Dharamapala, the Pala King of Bengal and Bihar and also the Rashtrakuta king Dhruva, thus began what is known as the 'tripartite struggle'. It continued for about another 350 years under various succeeding kings with ups and downs. The Pratiharas, however, could maintain their hold over Kannauj till the last.
- Tripartite struggle between Rashtrakuta, Pratiharas and Palas during his reign can be depicted as:

  Dharamapala (Pala king) —defeated by→ Vatsaraja —defeated by→ Dhruva Rashtrakuta king

  Both eyed Kannauj

Nagabhatta II (c. 800–833 CE)

- The tripartite struggle continued as:

  Dharamapala (Palas) —again defeated by→ Nagabhatta II —defeated by→ Govind III (Rashtrakuta).
- Nagabhatta II was succeeded by his son Ramabhadra, who ruled briefly, and was succeeded by his son Mihira Bhoja.

Bhoja I / Mihir Bhoja (c. 836–885 CE)

- Grandson of Nagabhatta II, who had a long reign of over 46 years and proved to be the most successful and popular ruler of Pratiharas.
- In the early years of his reign he was defeated by the Palas, Rashtrakutas and the Kalachuris, but he subsequently made a comeback. With the aid of feudatories such as the Chedis and the Guhilas, he won victories over the Palas and the Rashtrakutas.
- He had his capital at Kannauj, which was also called Mahodaya. In one of his earliest inscriptions, the Barah copper plate inscription, *there is mention of a military camp i.e., skandhavara at Mahodaya.*

- He is also identified with the king Juzr of the travel accounts of the 9th century Arab merchant, Sulaiman, who describes his great military power and riches. He was appreciated by the Arab writer for keeping his empire safe from robbers. He was called King Baura by another Arab traveller, Al-Masudi. According to Arab travellers, the Pratihara rulers had the best cavalry in India.
- Expansion checked by Sankarvarmen of Kashmir and Rashtrakuta Krishna II and Devapala
- Devotee of Vishnu and adopted the title of 'Adivaraha'.
- The Kalachuris, the Chandalas and the Arabs of Sindh acknowledged his supremacy.

Mahendrapala (c. 885–910 CE)

- Under Bhoja and his successor Mahendrapala I, the Pratihara empire reached its peak of prosperity and power. The extent of its territory was almost similar to that of the Guptas and by the time of Mahendrapala, the empire reached west to the border of Sindh, east to Bengal, north to the Himalayas and south past the Narmada.
- Fought a battle with the king of Kashmir but had to yield to him some of the territories in the Punjab won by Bhoja.
- Took the title *Maharajadhiraja* of *Aryavarta* (Great King of Kings of Northern India). His court was adorned by Rajashekhar, who was an eminent Sanskrit poet, dramatist and critic who wrote:
    - *Karpuramanjari:* A famous play written in Sauraseni Prakrit to please his wife, Avantisundari, a woman of taste and accomplishment. He is perhaps the only ancient Indian poet to acknowledge a woman for her contributions to his literary career.
    - *Kavya Mimansa* (around c. 880–920 CE): A practical guide for poets that explains the elements and composition of a good poem.
    - *Vidhasalabhanjika*
    - *Bhrinjika*
    - *Balaramayana*
    - *Prapanch Pandav*
    - *Balabharata*
    - Bhusan Kosh

Mahipala I (c. 913–944 CE)

- Defeated by the Rashtrakuta King Indra III, who completely devastated the city of Kannauj.
- Gujarat passed into the hands of the Rashtrakutas in this period, in all likelihood, as Al Masudi in his accounts mentions that *the Pratihara empire had no access to the sea.*

Rajyapala (c. 960–1018 CE)

- The Rashtrakuta king Krishna III invaded north India in about 963 CE and defeated the Pratihara ruler.
- Raid of Mahmud Ghazni on Kannauj; Rajyapala fled from battlefield.
- Murdered by Vindhyadhar Chandella.

Yashpala (c. 1024–1036 CE)

- Last ruler of this dynasty.
- By 1090 CE, the Gadhavalas conquered Kannauj.

Under a succession of rather obscure rulers, the Pratiharas never regained their former influence and gradually, their feudatories started asserting their independence and the empire disintegrated and was reduced to the area around Kannauj. Finally, in 11th century CE, they were wiped off from the political map by the Ghaznavids and their rule was succeeded by Chahamanas or Chauhans in Rajputana, Chalukyas or Solankis in Gujarat and the Paramaras or Pawars in Malwa.

The Palas of Bengal

In eastern India, after the death of king Shashanka[7] in c. 637 CE, a situation of political confusion prevailed in Bengal and adjoining areas. The region witnessed invasions by Yashovarmana of Kannauj, Lalitaditya of Kashmir, and even of a Chinese army. Bhaskaravarman, the ruler of Assam, conquered most of Bengal and the western territories of Bihar and Odisha came under the influence of Harsha. Subsequently, around 8th century CE, Gopala laid the foundation of Pala dynasty. As the names of all the succeeding kings ended with 'Pala' which meant 'protector' in the ancient language of Prakrit, this dynasty came to be known as the 'Pala' dynasty. The Pala kingdom included Bengal and Bihar, which included the major cities of Pataliputra, Vikrampura, Ramvati (Varendra), Monghyr (Munger), Tamralipti and Jaggadala. The tripartite struggle continued between the Palas, Rashtrakutas and Pratiharas and the area of Bihar and modern east U.P. remained a bone of contention between them, though Bihar, in addition to Bengal, remained mostly under the control of the Palas for most of the time.

The Pala kings were the followers of Buddhism, especially Mahayana and Tantric schools of Buddhism. They greatly promoted this religion by making monasteries (viharas) and temples in eastern India. The Pala legacy is still reflected in Tibetan Buddhism.

---

[7] Shasanka was the first significant ruler of Bengal who ruled between 606–637 CE and who could extend his political sovereignty over areas that lay far beyond the geographical boundary of Bengal, probably as far as Odisha. He established his capital at Karnasuvarna (near Murshidabad).

Gopala (around c. 750 CE)

- According to the Khalimpur copper plate inscription of Dharmapala, *Gopala, in order to rescue the people from matsya-nyaya (a period of anarchy), founded the Pala dynasty when he was elected the king by notable men of the realm*. He displaced the later Guptas of Magadha and Khadga dynasty of eastern Bengal.
- Gopala was an ardent Buddhist and according to Buddhist scholar Taranatha, Gopala built the famous monastery at Odantapuri.

Dharmapala (c. 770–810 CE)

- Though he initially suffered defeats at the hands of the Pratiharas and the Rashtrakutas (he was defeated by the Rashtrakuta king, Dhruva, who had earlier defeated the Pratihara ruler too), but later he conquered large parts of northern India and raised the Pala empire to great heights.
- Believed to have held a durbar at Kannauj, which was attended by many vassal chiefs, wherein he showcased his own power by installing his puppet ruler, Chakrayudha, on the throne. Thus, Kannauj functioned as a dependency and Dhramapala had Bengal and Bihar under his direct rule. His sovereignty was also accepted by the rulers of both west and south India such as those of Punjab, western hill states, Rajputana, Malwa and Berar.
- Dharmapala was again defeated by the Pratihara king, Nagabhatta II, near Monghyr.
- Founded the Vikramshila monastery near Bhagalpur in Bihar, and like Nalanda university, it also attracted students from all parts of India and from Tibet. Many Sanskrit texts were translated into tibetan language at this monastery. The most celebrated name associated with the Vikramshila University was that of the Buddhist scholar Dipankara (called Atisa), who was greatly respected in Tibet.
- He also founded the Somapuri monastery (near Paharpur, Bihar) and is also credited with the grant of 200 villages to Nalanda University.
- The renowned 8th century Buddhist scholar, Santarakshita, who is also considered as an abbot of Nalanda, belonged to his reign. Santarakshita founded the philosophical school known as *Yogacara-Svatantrika-Madhyamika,* which united the Madhyamaka tradition of Nagarjuna, the Yogacara tradition of Asanga and the logical and epistemological thought of Dharmakirti. He was also instrumental in the introduction of Buddhism and the Sarvastivadin monastic ordination lineage to Tibet.

Devapala (c. 810–850 CE)

- Extended the empire to include *Pragyoytishpur*/*Kamarupa* (Assam), parts of Odisha (*Utkala*) and modern Nepal. He claimed to have extracted tribute from the whole of northern India, from the Himalayas to the Vindhyas, and from the eastern to the western oceans.

- His inscriptions proclaim his victory over the Hunas, the lords of Gurjaras (probably Mihir Bhoja) and the Dravidas.
- Preferred Monghyr to Pataliputra.
- Was also a great patron of Buddhism. According to Buddhist tradition, the Sailendra dynasty king, Balaputradeva (ruler of Suvarnadvipa which corresponds to the Indonesian archipelago, including Malaya, Java, Sumatra and other neighbouring islands), requested him to grant five villages to the monastery at Nalanda. He granted the request and appointed Viradeva as the head of Nalanda Monastery.
- His court poet was a Buddhist scholar, Vajradatta, who is the author of the *Lokesvarasataka*.
- The Pala empire was called '*Ruhimi* or *Ruhma Dharma*' by the Arab merchant Sulaiman, who visited India in the middle of the 9th century. He claims that the Pala emperor was at war with the Pratiharas and Rashtrakutas and had more troops than his adversaries.
- The power of the Palas declined in the late 9th century and Pala control of North India was too ephemeral, as they struggled with the Gurjara-Pratiharas and the Rashtrakutas for the control of Kannauj and were defeated. The subordinate rulers of Assam and Odisha assumed independence.

Mahipala I (c. 977–1027 CE)

- After a short lived decline, the fortunes of the Palas were restored under Mahipala I in the late 10th century.
- He defended Pala bastions in Bengal and Bihar against Chola invasions, but was defeated by Rajendra Chola.

Ramapala (c. 1072–1126 CE)

- The last strong Pala ruler, who gained control of Kamarupa and Kalinga and again revived Pala fortunes in the 11th century.
- He was mentioned in Sandhyakar Nandi's *Ramcharita*, which describes *Kaivarta* peasant rebellion[8].

The empire was considerably weakened by the 11th century, with many areas engulfed in rebellion. The Palas power was destroyed by the resurgent Hindu Sena dynasty. The Sena dynasty, under

[8] Kaivarta Rebellion occupies an important place in the history of Bengal as it overthrew the Palas, ousting them from their ancestral territory of Varendra. Some historical studies considered it to be a revolt of Samantas, which occurred due to the weakening of the Palas while some historians like R.S. Sharma consider it as an instance of peasant revolt which emerged due to feudal suppression and excessive taxation imposed by the Palas rulers. The Kaivarta chief Divya rose in revolt against the reigning Pala king Mahipal. The Palas were ousted from Varendra and the King was killed. His younger brother Ramapala tried to get the support of the Samantas to recapture Varendra. Thereafter, Sivaraja, a subordinate of the King, raided Varendra and captured and devastated parts of it. Later, Rampal invaded Varendra and confronted Bhima, the nephew of Divya, and succeeded in recapturing Varendra. The rebellion eventually forced the Palas to follow a policy of appeasement towards the cultivators.

Vijaysena, dethroned the Pala Empire in the 12th century, thereby ending the reign of the last major Buddhist power in the subcontinent.

The Pala period is considered one of the golden eras in the history of Bengal. The Palas not only brought stability and prosperity to Bengal which was suffering due to centuries of civil war between warring divisions but they also advanced the achievements of previous Bengali civilisations and created outstanding works of art and architecture. They built great temples and monasteries, such as the famous Somapura Mahavihara. They also patronised the great universities of Nalanda and Vikramashila. In fact, the proto-Bengali language was developed under Pala rule as they laid the basis for the Bengali language, including its first literary work, the *Charyapada*, which is a collection of mystic Buddhist poems from the tantric tradition. The writers of Charyapada are called Mahasiddhas and they were from Bengal, Bihar, Odisha and Assam.

The Palas were also astute diplomats and great military conquerors. The Palas' army was noted for its vast war elephant cavalry while their navy performed both mercantile and defensive roles in the Bay of Bengal. The empire enjoyed relations with the Srivijaya Empire, the Tibetan Empire and the Arab Abbasid Caliphate. Their flourishing mercantile and intellectual contacts could be established by the Abbasid coinage found in Pala archaeological sites, as well as the records of Arab historians. In fact, as a result of increased trade between Bengal and the Middle East, Islam first appeared in Bengal during Pala rule.

The Rashtrakutas

The political history of the Deccan between c. 753 and 975 CE was marked by the rise of the Rashtrakutas, who for a long time provided stability to the region. 'Rashtrakuta' means the chief of a *rashtra* (a division or kingdom, depending on the context). Around c. 625 CE, they appeared to have migrated from the Latur area to Ellichpur (near the source of the Tapi, in modern M.P.) since one of the title used by kings of the main and subordinate lines was *lattalura-puraveshvara* (lord of the great city of Lattalura/Latur on the Maharashtra–Karnataka border). They are presumed to be a feudatory of the Chalukyas and their capital was Manyakheta or Malkhed near Sholapur. Despite the extensive use of Sanskrit in their inscriptions, Kannada was their mother tongue and they are believed to be of Kannada origin.

They achieved spectacular military successes in the north and south and in the tripartite struggle they mostly defeated the Palas and the Pratiharas. It is significant to note that although their raids did not result in the extension of the Rashtrakuta empire to the Gangetic valley, they brought rich plunder, and added to the fame of the Rashtrakutas. They also constantly fought against the eastern Chalukyas of Vengi (Andhra Pradesh), the Pallavas of Kanchi and the Pandyas of Madurai. The Arab accounts testify the liberal attitude of the Rashtrakuta kings as the Arab traders were allowed to build mosques and follow their religion without any hindrance.

Dantidurga (c. 733–756 CE)

- Feudatory of the Chalukya king, Kirtivarman II, who later founded the Rashtrakuta kingdom by taking control of the northern regions of the Chalukya empire and thus ascended[9] to the throne in c. 733 CE. However, the Rashtrakutas as a kingdom rose in power from c. 753 CE.
- His name 'Dantidurga' (meaning *he whose elephant is his fortress*) also signifies his military feats and accomplishments. In the earliest record of his reign, i.e., the Ellora inscription of 742 CE, he is mentioned as '*Prithivivallabha*' and '*Khagavaloka*' (he whose glances are as keen as the edge of a sword). Taking advantage of the disturbed condition of Lata and Malwa after the Arab invasions, he took control of these territories. He also attacked Kanchi, the capital of the Pallavas, and struck up an alliance with Nandivarmana who gave his daughter Reva in marriage to him.
- He later also helped his father-in-law, the Pallava King Nandivarmana, to regain Kanchi from the Chalukyas and also defeated the Gurjaras of Malwa, and the rulers of Kalinga, Kosala and Srisailam.

Krishnaraja I (c. 756–774 CE)

- Dantidurga's Uncle, who ascended the throne after a succession battle among different family members as Dantidurga, died childless. Mentioned as '*Shubhatunga*' (high in prosperity) and '*Akalavarsha*' (constant rainer) in Bhandak Inscription of 772 CE. Extended the Rashtrakuta empire and brought major portions of present day Karnataka and Konkan under his control. Also gave a final blow to Pallavas.
- The magnificent rock-cut Kailashnatha Temple at Ellora (near Aurangabad, Maharastra) was built during his reign. The temple is dedicated to Lord Shiva and is monolithic[10] i.e., made of one single piece of rock.
- After his death around 775 CE, a succession battle ensued between his two sons Govind II and Dhruva in which eventually Dhruva emerged victorious.

---

[9] According to Samangadh inscription of 754 CE, Dantidurga overthrew the last Chalukyan ruler of Badami Kirtivarman II and assumed full imperial rank. It is believed that he performed a ritual called *hiranya-garbha* (literally meaning the golden womb), which was thought to be a ritual which would lead to the rebirth of the sacrificer as a Kshatriya, even if he was not one by birth.

[10] Carved out of a massive block of rock having length of 200 feet and 100 feet in breadth and height. The temple consists of four parts – the main shrine, the entrance gateway, an intermediate shrine for Nandi and Mandala surrounding the courtyard. The temple stands on a lofty plinth 25 feet high and the central face of the plinth has imposing figures of elephants and lions, giving the impression that the entire structure rests on their back. It has a 3-tiered *Sikhara* or tower resembling the *Sikhara* of the Mamallapuram rathas. It is indeed an architectural marvel with its beautiful sculptures. For instance, the sculpture of Goddess Durga is shown as slaying Buffalo demon. In another sculpture, Ravana is making attempts to lift Mount Kailasha, the abode of Shiva. The scenes of *Ramayana* are also depicted on the walls.

Dhruva (c. 780–793 CE)

- During his reign, the kingdom expanded into an empire that encompassed all of the territory between the Kaveri river and central India. He led successful expeditions to Kannauj, the seat of northern Indian power where he defeated the Gurjara-Pratiharas (Nagabhatta II) and the Palas of Bengal (Dharmapala).
- He also brought the Eastern Chalukyas and Gangas of Talakad under his control. The Rashtrakutas became a pan-Indian power during his rule.

Govind III (c. 793–814 CE)

- Son of Dhruva, who took the Rashtrakutas to greater heights. He emerged victorious at the tripartite struggle. He made incursions to north India and defeated Pala king Dharmapala and also wrestled Malwa from Pratihara king Nagabhatta II. As mentioned in the Sanjan inscription of his reign, '*the horses of Govinda III drank from the icy waters of the Himalayan streams and his war elephants tasted the sacred waters of the Ganges.*'
- It is believed that the Rashtrakuta empire under his reign gradually spread over the areas from Cape Comorin to Kannauj and from Banaras to Bharuch. His military exploits have been compared to those of Alexander the Great and Arjuna of Mahabharata. Having conquered Kannauj, Gujarat and Kosala, he travelled south and not only humbled the Pallavas of Kanchi but also installed a ruler of his choice in Vengi and received two statues as an act of submission from the king of Ceylon (one statue of the king and another of his minister). The Cholas, the Pandyas and the Cheras all paid him tribute.

Amoghavarsha I (c. 814–878 CE)

- One of the most famous of the Rashtrakutas, who built a new capital city, that of Manyakheta (modern Malkhed).
- He defeated the invading Eastern Chalukyas at Vingavalli and assumed the title *Viranarayana*. Also made peace with the Western Gangas by giving them two of his daughters in marriage. It is interesting to note that unlike his father, he preferred to maintain friendly relations with his neighbours, the Gangas, the Eastern Chalukyas and the Pallavas with whom he also cultivated marital ties.
- He was a patron of literature and was an accomplished scholar in Kannada and Sanskrit himself. He wrote the *Kavirajamarga* – the earliest Kannada work on poetics and the *Prashnottara Ratnamalika* in Sanskrit, which is considered as a writing of high merit and was later translated into the Tibetan language.
- Because of his religious temperament, his interest in the arts and literature and his peace-loving nature, he is often compared to emperor Ashoka and called 'Ashoka of the South', and is also compared to Gupta king Vikramaditya in giving patronage to men of letters.

He was a follower of Jainism and Jinasena, the author of *Adipurana*,[11] and *Parsvabhudaya*[12] was his chief preceptor. He also patronised many Jain scholars.

Krishna II (c. 879–914 CE)

- Was not wholly successful in curbing rebellions and the only success of his reign was the termination of Lata viceroyalty. His expeditions against Vengi and Chills resulted in only disgrace and disaster and even exile for some time.

Indra III (c. 914–929 CE)

- Grandson of Amoghavarsha who crushed the different rebellions and reestablished the empire.
- He defeated Pratihara Mahipala I and sacked Kannauj in 915 CE, and emerged as the most powerful ruler of his times.

Krishna III (c. 939–967 CE)

- The last great Rashtrakuta ruler, who consolidated the empire so that it stretched from the Narmada river to Kaveri river and included the northern Tamil country (*Tondaimandalam*) while levying tribute on the king of Ceylon.
- He was engaged in a struggle against the Paramaras of Malwa and the Eastern Chalukyas of Vengi. In about 949 CE, he also defeated the Chola king Parantaka I and annexed the northern part of the Chola empire. He then marched towards Rameshwaram and set up a pillar of victory there and also built a temple.
- During his reign, Trivikrama composed '*Nalachampu*' and Halayudha wrote '*Kavirahasya*'.

After his death, all his opponents united against his successor and in 972 CE sacked the Rashtrakuta capital Malkhed and burnt it to ashes. This marks the end of the Rashtrakutas.

Rashtrakuta rule lasted in the Deccan for almost 200 years till the end of the 10th century. They were tolerant in their religious views and patronised not only Shaiviam and Vaishnavism but Jainism as well. The Rashtrakutas not only allowed Muslim traders to settle but also permitted Islam to be preached in their dominions. They are credited with the construction of the famous rock cut temple of Shiva at Ellora. The sculptural art of Rashtrakutas reached its zenith at Elephanta Caves[13]. They were also great patrons of art and letters. Their courts were

---

[11] Life stories of various Jaina Saints.

[12] Biography of Parsva in verses.

[13] Elephanta is an island near Bombay which was originally called Sripuri but the Portuguese, after seeing the large figure of an elephant, named it Elephanta. They showcase a close similarity with the sculptures at Ellora and were probably carved by the same craftsmen. At the entrance to the sanctum, there are huge figures of *Dwara-palakas*. In the walls of the *prakara* around the sanctum, there are niches containing the images of Shiva in various forms – *Nataraja*, *Gangadhara*, *Ardhanareesvara* and *Somasknada*. One of the most imposing figures of this temple is *Trimurti*, a sculpture about 6-metre high and said to represent the three aspects of Shiva – the Creator, the Preserver and the Destroyer.

adorned by not only Sanskrit scholars but also poets and authors who wrote in Prakrit and in the apabhramsha language. The great *apabhramsha* poet Swayambhu and his son probably lived at the Rashtrakuta court. Along with them, Saktayana, who wrote the grammar work called *Amogavritti*, and the great mathematician Viracharya, author of *Ganitasaram*, too, flourished under the patronage of the Rashtrakutas. The Kannada literature saw its beginning during the period of the Rashtrakutas. Pampa, the greatest of the Kannada poet, wrote '*Vikramasenavijaya*' while Ponna was another famous Kannada poet who wrote '*Santipurana*'.

General Overview of Life during These Three Kingdoms

The administration was run on similar pattern as that of the Guptas, the Pushyabhutis and the Chalukyas in the Deccan. The king was the epitome of all affairs and was not only the head of administration but also commander-in-chief of the armed forces. The court was not only a centre of cultural affairs and of justice, but of cultural life as well. The ladies of the king's durbar also attended the durbar on festive occasions and according to Arab writers, they did not veil their faces. The king's position was hereditary, and normally, the eldest son succeeded the father, but the succession rules were not so rigid. The princes were mostly appointed as provincial governors and in some rare cases, princesses were also appointed to government posts. For instance, *a Rashtrakuta princess, Chandrobalabbe, daughter of Amoghavarsha I, administered the Raichur doab for some time*. The kings were generally advised by ministers, who were chosen from the leading families and their position was more or less hereditary. *As in the case of the Pala kings, a Brahmana family supplied four successive chief ministers to Dharmapala and his successors*. From epigraphic and literary records, it appears that almost every kingdom had a minister of foreign affairs, revenue, treasurer, senapati, chief justice and purohita. All the ministers except the purohita were expected to lead military campaigns when called upon to do so.

All the three kingdoms had large and well-organised infantry and cavalry and large number of war elephants. The Palas had the largest number of elephants, the Pratiharas had the finest cavalry while the Rashtrakutas had a large number of forts, which were garrisoned by special troops and had their own independent commanders. The infantry consisted of both regular and irregular troops and of levies supplied by the vassal chiefs. The wars were frequent between kings and their vassals also known as *samantas*. For instance, the *Rashtrakutas had to constantly fight against the vassal chiefs of Vengi and Karnataka. Similarly, the Pratiharas had to constantly fight against the Paramaras of Malwa and the Chandellas of Bundelkhand*. The vassals ruled autonomously over the areas and were bound by the general obligation of loyalty, paying a fixed tribute, supplying a quota of troops and were required to fight along with the king in times of need or foreign attack. Sometime, a son of the vassal chief was required to stay in the attendance of the overlord to guard against any rebellion or at times they had to marry one of their daughters to the overlord or to one of his sons. The Palas and the Rashtrakutas had their own navies but more details are not known.

The directly administered territories were divided into:

a. *Rashtra* under the supervision of Rashtrapati or governor.

↓

b. *Bhukti* (provinces) under the supervision of *Uparika* who was expected to collect land revenue and maintain law and order

↓

c. *Mandalas or Visaya* (districts) whose head was called *Visyapati* and was expected to perform the functions of collection of revenue and maintaining law and order at district level.

↓

d. *Pattala* (much smaller unit of cluster of villages) which were headed by *Bhojapati.*

↓

e. Village headed by the village headman and village accountant whose posts were generally hereditary. He was often assisted by village elder called *grama-mahajana* or *grama-mahattara.* In certain villages there were village committees for managing local schools, tanks, temples, roads and also settling simple disputes. These sub-committees worked in close cooperation with the village headman and received a percentage of the revenue collection. Similar committees were also present in towns which had the participation of the heads of trade guilds too. The law and order in towns was the responsibility of the *kosha-pala* or *kotwal.*

It is noteworthy to add that, almost all the officials were paid by giving them grants of rentfree land and it also led to the rise of hereditary revenue officers called *nad-gavundas* or *desagramakutas.* Later, they were addressed as *deshmukhas* and *deshpandes* in Maharashtra. The revenue assignments called *bhoga* or *fief* granted by the rules to his officers were temporary in theory and were liable to be resumed whenever the ruler wanted but this was rarely practised except in case of outright rebellion or disloyalty. Subsequently, with the rise of power of these hereditary officials, the village communities became weaker and subsequently the control and authority of the kings over these officials also diminished. Thus, the government became feudalised.

The growth of feudal society had far-reaching effects as it not only weakened the position of the ruler making him more dependent on the feudal chiefs but also resulted in decline of trade and encouraged an economy in which small principalities emerged having largely self-sufficient villages. However, in the age of disorder and violence, these feudal states could also provide safety of life and property to the common folk.

In terms of religion, most of the kings were tolerant in their views and behaviour and generously patronised the Hinduism (some were devout followers of Shiva or Vishnu), Buddhism or Jainism.

Muslims were welcomed and allowed to propagate their faith by the Rashtrakuta kings. The kings like those of the earlier times were considered upholders of social hierarchy and generally the *Chaturvarna* system continued. However, the state was essentially secular as the politics and religion were in essence kept apart and kings were not dominated by the religious discourses.

Trade and Commerce

In northern India, the period from c. 750–1000 CE was considered to be period of stagnation and even of decline in terms of trade and commerce. This was primarily due to the collapse of the Roman Empire with which earlier India had flourishing trade relations. Also, the decline of the Sassanid Empire (Iranian) due to the rise of Islam, affected India's overland foreign trade. Since the wealth in gold and silver of India was more due to India's favourable foreign trade, hence, with decline in foreign trade there arose the paucity of gold coins in northern India between the 8th and 10th centuries. Interestingly, the trade between the south India and the countries of South-east Asia increased during this period.

Interestingly, the decline in trade and commerce was also reflected in some of the Dharmashastras written during this period wherein a ban was imposed on travel beyond the areas *where the munja grass does not grow or where the black gazelle does not roam* (*outside India*). *Travel across the salt seas was also considered polluting*. Presumly, the ban was meant to discourage Indians from going to areas dominated by the Islam in the west and Buddhism in the east so that the Brahmanas' stronghold was maintained. However, this ban was not taken that seriously by Indians as there are a lot of accounts of Indian merchants, philosophers, medical men and craftsmen visiting Baghdad and other Muslim towns in west Asia during this period. Gradually, from 10th century onwards, foreign trade and commerce was revived with the emergence of the extensive Arab empire in West Asia and North Africa. The demand for Indian fabrics, incenses and spices among the wealthy Arab rulers rejuvenated the trade again and Malwa and Gujarat emerged as major trade centres.

The Salama Dynasty of Assam (c. 800–1000 CE)

Assam, also known as Kamrupa or Pragjyotisha, remained under the authority of the Palas especially Devapala. However, in 800 CE, a local ruler of Kamarupa named Harjaravarman declared independence from the Palas and established the Salamba dynasty having capital at Haruppeshvara on the banks of river Brahmaputra (*Lauhitya*).

The Eastern Gangas of the Odisha

In late 6th century CE, the Shailodbhavas, who were earlier subordinates of Shashanka gradually asserted their authority over Kongoda (which covers modern Puri and Ganjam districts). However, in the 8th century the Shailodbhavas were replaced by the Gangas of Shvetaka who were originally migrants from Karnataka and established themselves in the north Ganjam area. Similarly, the Gangas of the Kalinganagara were also migrants from Karnataka who moved into Odisha towards the end of 5th century and established themselves in south Odisha specially the Vamsadhara and Nagavali valleys.

From the 10th century onwards, the Ganga kingdom rapidly expanded and the north and south Odisha were also unified. Probably their alliance with the Cholas also aided in their military expansion and in the early 12th century, the Ganga king Anantavarman Chodaganga displaced the Somavamshi ruler from lower Odisha. Interestingly, the mother and one of queens of Anantavarman were Chola princesses. However, military conflict also used to happen between the Gangas and the Cholas as evident from the fact that Chola king Kulothunga I twice sent military expedition against Kalinga.

Period from c. 850–1200 CE: Southern India

The Cholas

During c. 850–1200 CE, the Cholas[14] who were famous in Indian history for their local self-government, founded a mighty empire in southern India which brought under its control a large part of the peninsula. The Cholas also possessed a strong navy, which further aided them to develop sea trade in the Indian Ocean and to conquer Sri Lanka and the Maldives islands. They not only defeated Indian kings but also defeated the kings of Malaya, Java and Sumatra. It is believed that the Cholas came to power after over throwing the authority of the Pallavas in south India. The founder of the Chola dynasty was Vijayalaya (9th century CE).

Vijayalaya (around c. 850 CE)

- Founder of the Chola empire, earlier a feudatory of the Pallavas.
- He established his power in the area around Uraiyur, captured Tanjore and extended his kingdom along the lower Kaveri.

Aditya I (c. 871–907 CE)

- Successor of Vijayalaya who achieved significant military successes and expanded the Chola kingdom.
- At the battle of Shripurambiyam, he allied with the Pallavas and defeated Pandyas and as a recompense received some territories in the Tanjore area. Later in c. 893 CE, he defeated and killed his Pallava overlord Aparajita thus bringing *Tondaimandalam* (southern Tamil country) under his control.

[14] Interestingly, the relationship between these Cholas, called the 'Imperial Cholas of Tanjore', with the earlier Cholas mentioned in Sangam literature is not very clear.

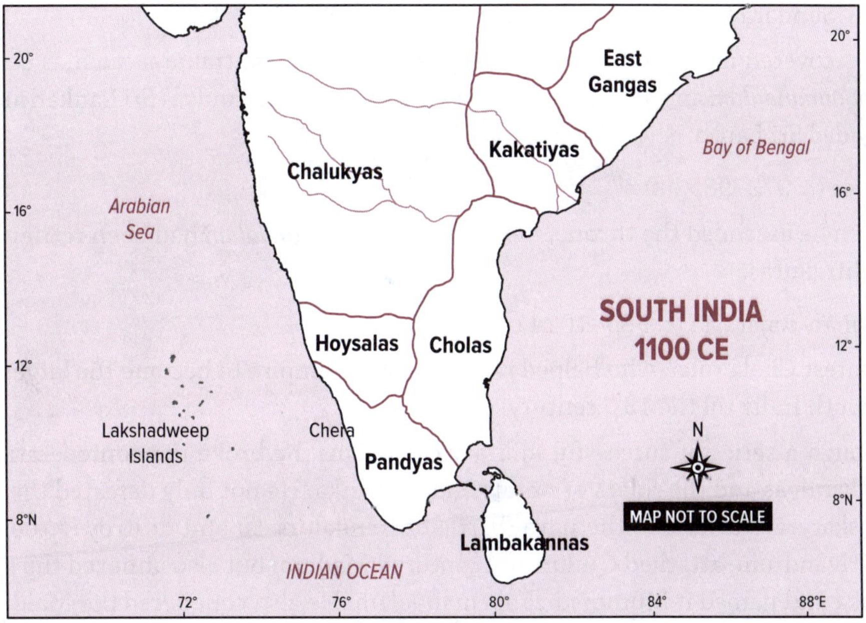

FIGURE 9.7 South India Map 1100 CE

- He also allied with the Cheras and conquered Kongudesha (probably Coimbatore and Salem districts) from Pandyas.
- He presumably also conquered Talked, which was the capital of the Western Gangas.
- He entered into a matrimonial alliance with the Pallavas by marrying a Pallava princess.

Parantaka I (c. 907–953 CE)

- Won several victories with the help of his allies such as the Western Gangas, the Kodumbalur chiefs and the ruler of Kerala.
- He captured Madurai and took the title of *Madurantaka* (destroyer of Madurai) and *Maduraikonda* (capturer of Madurai).
- At the famous battle of Vellur, he defeated the combined armies of the Pandyas and the king of Sri Lanka and thus Pandya territories became a part of the Chola empire.
- However, in c. 949 CE, he was defeated by the Rashtrakuta ruler Krishna III at the battle of Takkolam. Krishna III assumed the title of '*Conqueror of Kanchi and Tanjai*' and the Rashtrakuta army overran the Tondaimandalam.
- He was a great builder of temples and provided the vimhans of the famous Nataraja temple at Chidambaram with a golden roof. The two famous Uttiramerur inscriptions provide a detailed account of the village administration under his reign.

Parantaka II/Sundara Chola (c. 957–973 CE)

- He recovered most of the lost territories from the Rashtrakutas such as some parts of *Tondaimandalam* and also not only defeated a combined Pandya–Sri Lankan army but also invaded Sri Lanka.

Uttama Chola (c. 973–985 CE)

- When he ascended the throne, most of the *Tondaimandalam* had been retrieved from the Rashtrakutas.

Arumolivarman/Rajaraja I (c. 985–1014 CE)

- Greatest Chola ruler, who helped raise the Chola Empire to become the largest dominion in south India till the 13th century.
- Through a series of successful military campaigns, he broke the confederation between the Pandyas and the rulers of Kerala and Sri Lanka. He not only defeated the Chera ruler Bhaskararavivarman in the naval battle of Kandalursalai and destroyed the Chera navy at Trivandrum, attacked Quilon and captured Madurai but also annexed the northern Sri Lanka and named it Mummadichola mandalam. He also conquered the Maldives islands.
- He led a naval expedition against the Sailendra Empire (Malaya peninsula) and expanded Chola trade with China.
- He also achieved victories against the Western Chalukyas, the Rashtrakutas, later Chalukyas who had their capital at Kalyani and annexed the north-western parts of the Ganga region in north west Karnataka and also overran Vengi. However, he restored Vengi to its rulers after marrying the daughter of the king of the Vengi. It is pertinent to note that the Cholas and the later Chalukyas clashed for the overlordship of Vengi, the Tungabhadra doab and the Ganga country in the north-west Karnataka. Neither side was able to gain a decisive victory in this contest and ultimately it exhausted both the empires.
- In c. 1010 CE he constructed the Rajarajeshwara or Brihadishvara temple, dedicated to Shiva at Thanjavur (Tanjore). This temple is also called the Rajaraja temple as the Cholas were in the habit of installing the images of kings and queens in the temples in addition to the deity. He also helped in the construction of a Buddhist monastery at Nagapattinam.
- During his reign he developed and re-organised an excellent revenue system wherein land was surveyed and then revenue was assessed. Interestingly, he was referred to as *Ulakalanada Perumal* i.e., the great one who measured the earth, which, apart from being compared to God Vishnu can also point to his efforts of ordering a land survey.

FIGURE 9.8 Brihadishvara Temple

Rajendra I (c. 1014–1044 CE)

- Son of Rajaraja I, who carried forward his father's expansionist policy and continued the Chola territorial expansion.
- He completed the victory over Ceylon[15] by defeating the Sri Lanka king Mahinda V. The royal insignia of the king and the queen of Sri Lanka were captured and Sri Lanka was not able to free herself from the Chola control for another 50 years.
- He completely overran the Pandyas and Cheras and included them in his empire.
- In 1022 CE, he led an expedition to the north, crossed the Ganga following the same route which was taken by the great conqueror Samudragupta and defeated the Pala ruler, Mahipal I and the Western Chalukyas. To commemorate this occasion, he assumed the title of *Gangaikondachola* (meaning '*the Chola conqueror of Ganga*') and established a new capital named *Gangaikondacholapuram* (meaning '*the city of the Chola conqueror of the Ganga*') near the mouth of the river Kaveri. He built a Shiva temple here known as the famous Rajesvaram temple and excavated a large irrigation tank called Cholagangam. The river Tungabhadra was the northern boundary.
- In 1025 CE, a successful naval expedition was dispatched against the revived Sri Vijaya empire (which extended over the Malay peninsula, Sumatra, Java and the neighbouring islands and controlled the overseas trade route to China). The expedition led to the conquest of the *kadaram* or *kedah* and a number of other places in the Malay peninsula and Sumatra.

[15] The art of stone carving went to Sri Lanka and the paintings of Sigiriya were modelled on the Ajanta paintings.

- The rulers of the Sailendra dynasty were Buddhists and earlier had cordial relations with the Cholas. Infact, the Sailendra ruler had built a Buddhist monastery at Nagapattinam and at his instance, Rajendra I had endowed a village for its upkeep. The cause of breach between the two now was the Chola eagerness to remove obstacles to Indian traders and to expand Chola trade with China. It is noteworthy to add that the Chola navy was the strongest in the area for some time and the Bay of Bengal was converted into a 'Chola lake'.
- He was a great patron of learning and was known as *Pandita-chola*.

Rajadhiraja (c. 1044–1052 CE)

- He was a great warrior who always led from the front standing shoulder to shoulder with his men on front lines and earned the title of *Jayamkonda Chola* (the victorious Chola King). He ably defeated the Pandyas, Cheras and the ruler of Sri Lanka.
- He also sacked and plundered Chalukyan cities such as Kalyani and planted a Jaystambha at Yadgir. It is noteworthy to add that the Cholas had a blot on their history as they adopted a very harsh attitude towards both the king and general population of the places they sacked, since they mostly plundered and massacred the people including Brahmanas and children. For instance, the Cholas destroyed Anuradhapura, the ancient capital of Sri Lanka, and treated their king and queen very harshly; they did the same in Pandya country where they settled a military colony to overawe the population. However, once they had conquered the country, they tried to set up a sound system of administration in it.
- Was also known as *Vijaya Rajendra Chola* (i.e., 'the victorious Rajendra Chola king').
- He died in the battlefield while fighting in the battle of Koppam against Someshwar, a western Chalukyan king and from the manner of his death, Rajadhiraja came to be known as *Yanai-mel-thunjina Devar* (the *king who died on the back of an elephant*).

Rajendra II (c. 1054–1063 CE)

- Crowned in the battlefield.
- Defeated Someshwar, planted a Jaystambha at Kolhapur.

Virarajendra (c. 1063–1067 CE)

- Defeated Someshwar II and established a Vedic college of learning.

Athirajendra (c. 1067–1070 CE)

- Had to face many rebellions and died while suppressing one of them.

Kollutung I (c. 1070–1122 CE)

- The last important Chola king who adopted the title of *Shungam-tavirtta* (abolisher of tolls). Under him the Chola empire started disintegrating and shrunk to a much smaller area. During his reign, Sri Lanka became independent.

- In c. 1077 CE, a Chola embassy of 70 merchants were dispatched to China and they took tribute (articles taken for trade) such as glassware, camphor, brocades, rhinoceros horns and ivory. The kingdom also had flourishing trade with the kingdom of Shri Vijaya.
- He is credited with uniting the eastern Chalukyas of Vengi with the Cholas. It is presumed that he discarded wars and worked for peace as his reign was comparatively peaceful and it was only during the second half of his reign the kingdom faced hostility from the Chalukyas and Hoysalas.
- He was titled *Sungam Tavirtta Cholan* on account of abolition of taxes and remission of tolls during his reign.
- The classic writer Kamban (who wrote Ramayana in Tamil) was at his court.

The later rulers such as Kulottunga II, Rajaraja II and Kulottunga III tried to maintain the Chola empire but the Chola power gradually declined and the dynasty came to an end in the 13th century. The place of the Cholas was taken by the Pandyas and the Hoysalas in the south, and of the later Chalukyas by the Yadavas and the Kakatiyas. These states too extended patronage to arts and architecture. But unfortunately, they weakened themselves by continually fighting against each other, sacking towns and not even sparing the temples. Finally, in the beginning of 14th century, they were destroyed by the Sultans of Delhi.

Administration of the Cholas

The Chola inscriptions generally refer to the king as *ko*, *perumal*, *perumal adigal* (the great one), *raja-rajadhiraja* and *ko-konmai kondan* (king of kings). The king had all the authority rested in him and had a council of ministers to advise him. The different Chola inscriptions describe *the king as endowed with an attractive physical appearance, a great warrior and conqueror, a great patron of the arts and a generous giver of gifts (specially to Brahmanas), a protector of varnasharma dharma, a destroyer of the evils of the Kali age*. The kings were often compared with the gods either directly or with the use of double entendre. For instance, the Chola king Rajaraja was referred to as *Ulakalanada Perumal*, that is, *the great one who measured the earth like the God Vishnu who according to a famous myth encompassed the universe with his three strides*. The kings often undertook tours in order to keep in better touch with the administration. They were protected by bodyguards called *Velaikkarar* who were sworn to defend the kings even at the cost of their own lives. There was a hereditary element in their selection and they were given assignments of land revenue. The Venetian traveller Marco Polo, who visited Kerala in the 13th century writes that on the death of the monarch, all his body guards burnt themselves in the funeral pyre. The kings maintained large households and large palaces with banquet halls, spacious gardens and terraces.

The large number of terms for offices and officials in the Chola inscriptions as compared to those of the Pallavas, Pandyas and Cheras suggest an expansion of the administrative structure especially from the reign of Rajaraja I (early 11th century) and a decline after the reign of Kulothunga I, at which point the centralised bureaucracy declined and there was a gradual increase in the power of local chieftains. The various officials were called *perundanam* and *sirudanam*. The Cholas maintained a large army consisting of three limbs of elephants, cavalry and infantry (which was armed with spears). The royal troops were called *Kaikkolaperumpadai* and military cantonments were called *kadagams*. Special attention was given to the training of the army.

The empire known as *Rajyam* or *Rastrayam* was divided into eight *mandalams* (*provinces*) each governed by a governor/Viceroys, who were generally princes of the royal blood or of noble families. Officials were generally paid by giving them assignments of revenue-bearing lands. Some of the provinces were formed of principalities which had been annexed by the Cholas and some were the territories of the vassal princes, who paid tribute and rendered service to the king in emergent situations. The provinces were further divided into *Kottams* or *Valanadus* which were again divided into *Nadus* (*districts*), each of which again consisted of a number of autonomous villages that played a key role in the Chola administration system. The administration was also greatly facilitated by the *shrenis* or *pugas* (guilds), which were like some autonomous corporate organisations having persons belonging to the same craft.

- Mandalam/Province: Headed by Viceroy/Governor.
- Kottam/Valandu
- Nadus (district): Also known as agricultural land.
- Nattar: Assembly of the leading men of a Nadu or district.
- Nagarattar/Nagaram: Assembly of the Mercantile groups/Merchants.

The *nagaram* was specific to different trades and specialised groups. For instance, the *Saliya nagaram* and *Satsuma parishatta nagaram* was associated with the textile trade, the *Shankarappadi nagaram* represented oil and ghee suppliers, the *Paraga nagaram* was the corporate organisation of seafaring merchants and the *Vaniya nagaram* catered to the oil merchants. These corporate organisations were also referred to as *samaya,* that is, created through an agreement or contract and interestingly the members of *samaya* were governed by a code of conduct called *bananju-dharma*. One of the powerful guilds which was also among the largest supra-regional merchants association was the *Ayyavole* (The Five Hundred) which was established in the Aihole, Karnataka. Similarly, *Manigramam* was another prominent guild of the 13th century located in the Tamil country and was subordinated to the Ayyavole. Trading caravans used to move with armed protection and these guilds jointly fixed cesses and tolls. In due course of time, the merchant guilds became more and more powerful and independent. As the Cholas declined, the guilds too subsequently became less dependent on royal support.

Chola Village Administration

The Cholas were famous for their local self-government model, which can be considered as one of the earliest examples of the Panchayati Raj System. The village administration was very systematic and well developed. Regarding the assemblies of the villages, the Chola inscriptions mention:

a. Ur: The general assembly of the local residents of non-*brahmadeya* villages (or *vellanvagai* villages) to discuss matters without any formal rule or procedure. Nothing much is known about the composition of the Ur but, generally the members were less than ten. It dealt with various matters related to land maintenance such as land sale, gift and tax exemptions.

b. Sabha or Mahasabha: Exclusive assembly of *Brahmans*/gatherings of the adult male members in the *agraharas*, that is, rent free *brahmadeya* villages which enjoyed a large measure of autonomy. The membership was governed by different criteria such as property ownership, family antecedents, learning and good conduct. The Mahasabha possessed the propriety rights over communal lands and controlled the private lands within its jurisdiction. It could raise loans for the village and levy taxes with the right to realise the revenue in cases of default by selling the lands in question by public auction.

There were close links between some of the *Brahmana* Sabhas and the Chola court. Two inscriptions from Uttaramerur testify this fact and specify that *the resolution of the Sabha was made in the presence of an official specially deputed by the king*. In another inscription from Tanjavur, it appears that *Rajaraja I issued orders to the Sabhas of the Cholamandalam to perform various types of services in the Brihadeshvara temple*. The affairs of the village were managed by an executive committee to which educated persons owning property were elected either by drawing lots or by rotation. These members had to retire every three years. There were different committees which looked after different activities like law and order, justice, tank committee known as *erivariya* (which looked after the distribution of water to the fields).

Inscriptions and Texts

Who could be a member of a sabha? The Uttaramerur inscription lays down:

All those who wish to become members of the sabha should be owners of land from which land revenue is collected.

They should have their own homes.

They should be between 35 and 70 years of age.

They should have knowledge of the Vedas.

They should be well-versed in administrative matters and honest.

If anyone has been a member of any committee in the last three years, he cannot become a member of another committee. Anyone who has not submitted his accounts, and those of his relatives, cannot contest the elections.

While inscriptions tell us about kings and powerful men, here is an excerpt from the Periyapuranam, a twelfth century Tamil work, which informs us about the lives of ordinary men and women:

On the outskirts of Adanur was a small hamlet of Pulaiyas (a name used for a social group considered "outcastes" by Brahmanas and Vellalas), studded with small huts under old thatches and inhabited by agrarian labourers engaged in menial occupations. In the thresholds of the huts covered with strips of leather, little chickens moved about in groups; dark children who wore bracelets of black iron were prancing about, carrying little puppies ... In the shade of the marudu (arjuna) trees, a female labourer put her baby to sleep on a sheet of leather; there were mango trees from whose branches drums were hanging; and under the coconut palms, in little hollows on the ground, tiny-headed bitches lay after whelping. The red-crested cocks crowed before dawn calling the brawny Pulaiyar (plural) to their day's work; and by day, under the shade of the kanji tree spread the voice of the wavy-haired Pulaiya women singing as they were husking paddy ...

The Chola village assembly was the absolute proprietor of the village lands and also of the newly acquired lands. The main source of income of Chola Empire was the land revenue, which was normally $1/6^{th}$ of the produce. The royal dues were collected by the village assemblies and were paid either in cash or the kind or in both. The land revenue department was well organised and was called *puravuvarithinaikkalam*. The Chola government carried out land surveys (which were generally very accurate) periodically and record of holdings was maintained. Chola inscriptions mention different categories of land:

Type of Land	Utility
Vellanvagai	Land of non-Brahmana peasant proprietors
Brahmadeya	Land gifted to Brahmanas
Shalabhoga	Land for the maintenance of a school
Devadana or Tirunamattukkani	Land gifted to temples
Pallichchhandam	Land donated to Jaina Institutions

The different Chola inscriptions point out to several instances of land transfers via sale or gift, involving the transfer of *kani* rights, that is, the right of possession over land associated with certain other rights and obligations. These rights were further sub divided into:

a. *Karanmai* (right to cultivate): Further divided into two types–

   i. *Kudi Nikki*: Situation in which people previously settled in the village were either removed or deprived of their rights.

   ii. *Kudi Ninga*: Situation in which such people were not to be disturbed.

b. *Mitachi* (superior possessive right).

In certain inscriptions of Karnataka, there are interesting references to villages headed by women. For instance, in a 902 CE inscription, we learn that *the village Bharangiyur was headed by the wife of a man named Bittayya*, in another inscription of 1055 CE, *there is a reference to a woman named Chandiyabbe as agavundi*, that is, *village chieftain* and *another woman named Jakkiyabbe as her mantraki* (counsellor).

Chola Society and Economy

The society was divided on caste lines and the status of the *Paraiyar* (untouchables) continued to be pathetic. The *Vellallas* (farming groups) were identified with the Shudra varna but since they were land holders and were an economically powerful group they did not suffered from much discrimination or lower social status.

A crucial and unique development was the emergence of a supra caste dichotomy known as

a. *Idangai* (left hand caste groupings): Consisted mainly artisanal and trading groups.

b. *Valangai* (right hand caste groupings): Consisted mainly of agricultural groups.

Initially, these were not antagonistic to each other but gradually an element of conflict emerged between the two caste groupings. The position of women did not improve and the practice of Sati was prevalent among the royal families. The system of devadasi or dancing girls attached to temples emerged during this period.

An interesting aspect related to the religious sphere was a significant shift of royal patronage from *gifts to Brahmanas* to *gifts to temples*. Apart from the king, members of the royal family, rich merchants too contributed generously to the temples. Revenue from many surrounding and far-flung villages was assigned for the temples maintenance and in order to ensure transparency, the management of the financial resources was in the hands of Brahmana Sabhas of several villages. Both Shaivism and Vaishnavism continued to flourish during the Chola period.

There was an expansion in the agrarian economy and various factors attributed to it such as extension of the margin of agriculture through land reclamation, the spread of irrigation techniques and an expansion in the range of crops. The use of *agrahatta* (Persian wheel) also facilitated the already established smooth irrigation networks of tanks, canals, wells and sluices.

FIGURE 9.9 Agrahatta (Persian Wheel for Irrigation)

The early medieval period also marked a significant improvement in the craft techniques and various centres of craft production emerged. For instance, Kanchipuram emerged as important weaving industry centre. Kudamukku was a prominent centre of betel nut and areca nut cultivation as well as an important centre of crafts such as metal works, coin minting and textiles. Palaiyarai was another important administrative centre and residential capital of the Cholas. Another noteworthy aspect of the Chola period was the emergence of trading castes known as the *Garvares* who were the northern merchants who had migrated southwards in the 10th–11th centuries, *Gaudas*/*Gavundas* who were originally cultivators, *Heggades* who were initially revenue officials, *Kayasthas* (scribes, they specialised in drafting and writing land grant documents) and *Karanas* who also represented the occupational group of professional scribes.

The Chola kings maintained close commercial contact with south-east Asia and China.

Key Term/Concept	Meaning
Puravu-vari-tinaikkalam/ Shri-karanam	Revenue department.
Eccoru	Obligation of villagers to provide food for state officials.
Muttaiyal/Vetti/Kudimai	Obligation of villagers to provide labour services to state officials.
Kadamai	Land revenue collected in kind.
Antarayam	Rural tax realised in cash.
Dharmasana	Royal court of justice.
Ur-nattam or ur-irukkai	Residential quarter of the land owning farmers.
Kammanacheri	Residential quarter of the artisans.
Paraicheri	Residential quarter of the agricultural labourers.

Key Term/Concept	Meaning
Paraiyar	Socially and spatially segregated group of people who were considered ritually impure.
Vellalar	Cultivating groups.
Kaniyudaiyar	Land owning farmers.
Ulukudi	Tenant farmers.
Perudan	Highest officials.
Sirutaram	Lower officials.
Kasu	Gold coins.
Gaudas	Cultivators.
Nettal	Compulsory labour.
Nagarams	Market and commercial centres.
Erivirappattanas	Protected mercantile towns.
Samanta	Refers to a king who has been defeated but his kingdom has been restored to him, with the condition that he will continue to accept the over lordship of the conquering king and also pay regular tribute to him in cash or kind. He may also be asked to help with military assistance in times of need.
Eripatti	Land, revenue from which was set apart for the maintenance of the village tank.
Ghatikas	In the 7th and 8th centuries, 'ghatikas', or colleges attached to the temples emerged as new centres of learning which provided Brahmanical education in Sanskrit medium.
Taniyurs	Distinct revenue units under Cholas.
Peruvazhis	Trunk Roads

Chola Art and Literature

The temple architecture in the south reached its climax under the Cholas. The Dravida style of temple architecture came into vogue which laid emphasis on the building of storey upon storey above the chief deity room (*garbhagriha*). The temple had a pillared hall called *mandapa* with elaborately carved pillars and flat roof which was mostly used as an audience hall and a place for other activities such as ceremonial dances by devadasis. The temple, apart from serving as place of worship, also functioned as the hub of social and cultural life. The temple had lofty and elaborate gates called *gopurams*. A fine example of Dravida style architecture is the 8th century temple of Kailashnatha at Kanchipuram. Similarly, the Brihadeswara temple at Tanjore and the Shiva temple at Gangaikondacholapuram are another fine specimen of Dravida style. The *Airavathesvara* temple at Tanjore and *Kamphaharesvara* temple at Tribhuvanam are examples of later Chola temples. It is pertinent to note that after the fall of Cholas, temple building activity continued under the Chalukyas of Kalyani and the Hoysalas. The district of Dharwar and the Hoysala capital had large number of temples such as the magnificent temple of Hoysalesvara which is a fine example of Chalukyan style

In case of the Chalukyan style, that is, the Vesara style (which represents a mixed style of Nagara and Dravida), apart from the images of Gods and their attendants *Yaksh* and *Yaskhini*, the temples contained finely sculptured panels depicting panorama of life such as scenes of dance, music, love and war. These were mostly built under the patronage of the Chalukyas and are found at Pattadakal near Badami (Karnataka). The art of sculpture attained high standard during this period as evident in the giant statue of Gomateswar at Sravan Belgola. The Chola period is noted for the aesthetic and technical finesse of its metal sculpture. The dancing figure of Shiva called the Nataraja belongs to this period and is considered to be a bronze masterpiece.

FIGURE 9.10 Shravanabelagola Gommateshvara

There was also growth in literature of general parlance languages along with Sanskrit during this period. A number of *Alvars* (devotees of Vishnu) and *Nayannars* (devotees of Shiva) flourished in the *Tamilakham* between the 6th and 9th centuries who composed a lot in Tamil and other regional languages. The writings of these saints have been collected into 11 volumes under the name *Tirumurais* in the early 12th century and were considered to be so sacred that they were deemed the Fifth Veda. Kamban's *Ramayana* and *Periyapuranam* or *Tiruttondarpuranam* by Sekkilar are two classic gems of this period. The development of Tamil literature reached its peak during the Chola period. *Sivakasintamani*, written by Thiruthakkadevar and Kundalakesi, belonged to

10th century. Jayankondar's *Kalingattapparani* describes the Kalinga war foght by Kolutunga I. The Ottakuthar's *Moovarula* depicts the life of three Chola kings. Another notable products of Chola Age are the *Nalavenba* written by Pugalendi, *Kalladam* by Kalladanar, *Yapperungalam* by Jain scholar Amirthasagar, *Nannul* by Pavanandhi and *Virasoliyam* by Buddhamitra. Along with Tamil, a vast body of literature was also composed in Kannada with the aid of the patronage of the Rashtrakutas, Chalukyas and the Hoysalas. The famous Rashtrakuta king Amoghavarsha wrote a book on poetics in Kannada. The famous trinity of Pampa (who composed *Vikramarjunavijaya's* popularly known as *Pampa Bharat*), Ponna and Ranna were the three most priced jewels of Kannada poetry. Nanniah, who lived at the court of a Chalukyan king, started the Telugu version of the Mahabharata, which was completed in the 13th century by Tikkanna.

FIGURE 9.11 Chola Bronze Nataraja Idol

However, among the elites as a language of learning Sanskrit still retained a position of importance. The important works composed in Sanskrit around this period were:

(a) the *Kathasaritasagara*, which was a collection of stories,

(b) the *Rajtarangini*, a vivid account of the kings of Kashmir composed by Kalhana, and

(c) the *Gita Govinda*, a piece of devotional literature composed on the theme of love between Radha and Krishna, by Jayadeva in Bengal under the Pala kings.

Contact with South-East Asia and China

Indian contact with south-east Asia has been dated from the 5th century BCE, as there are references to Indians visiting *Suvarnadvipa* (Island of Gold, identified with Java) in the *Jatakas* (Buddhist fables). The early contacts with south-east Asia are also confirmed by recent archeological finds, that of pearls and ornaments of agate and carnelian, semi-precious stones of Indian origin, from coastal sites in Thailand, Vietnam, Indonesia, which have now further pushed the contact back to the 1st century BCE. Interestingly, according to Chinese traditions, the first kingdom in south-east Asia was founded at *Funan* (Cambodia) in the fourth century CE by a Brahmana known as Kaundinya, who had come from India and had married the local princess. However, Indian contact with south-east Asia increased from the 5th century CE onwards, when inscriptions in the Sanskrit language start appearing in many areas. It reached its peak during c. 800–1300 CE, when many kings and dynasties with Indian names emerge over all south-east Asia.

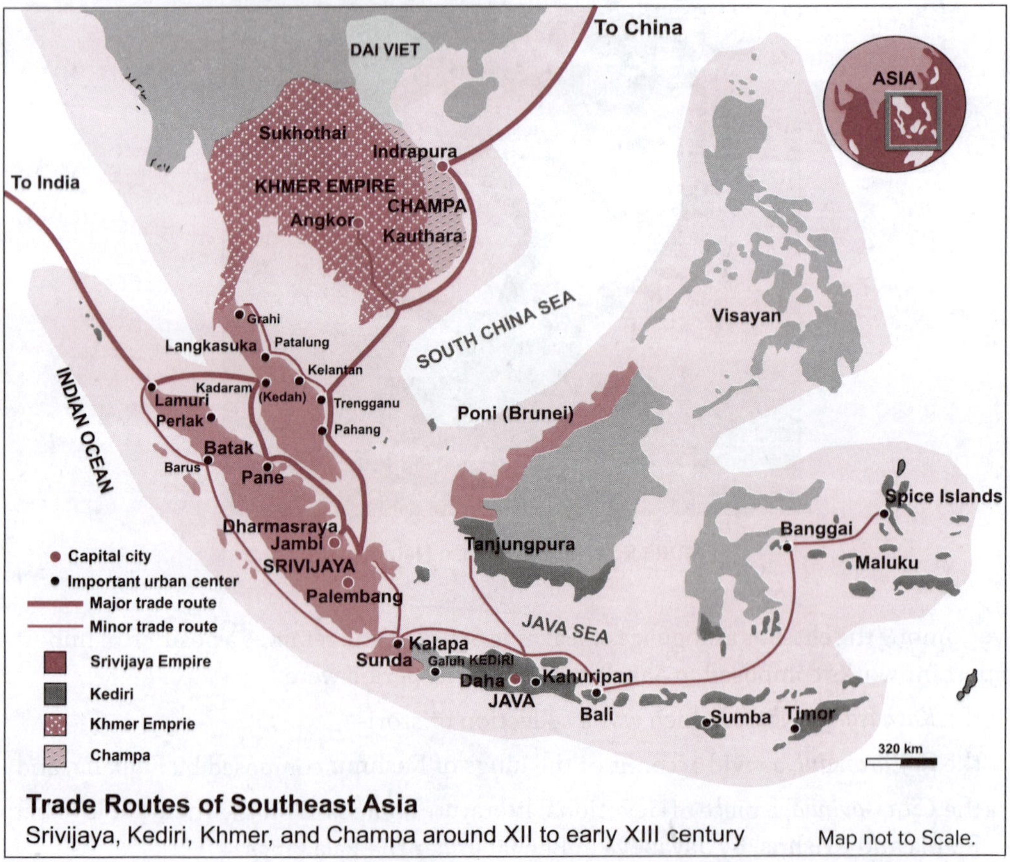

FIGURE 9.12 Trade Routes of Southeast Asia

We have discussed this earlier too, that while India's trade with the western areas declined, the trade with south-east Asia and China grew steadily till the 12th century. India's contact with south-east Asia was largely on account of trade and commerce and the leadership in this trade was taken by the kingdoms in south India and Bengal (the chief port being Tamralipti). The growth of India's foreign trade in the area was based on a strong naval tradition, including ship-building, and a strong navy and the skill and enterprise of its traders. South-east Asia was rich in cardamom, sandal-wood, camphor, cloves, and so on, which formed important items of trade between India and the West. With the decline of the Roman empire, China had become a main focus of trade in the Indian Ocean. The main seaport for foreign trade in China during this period was Canton or Kanfu as the Arab travellers called it. The Chinese accounts mention that *Canton river was full of ships from India, Persia and Arabia*. In Canton itself there were three Brahmana temples in which Indian Brahmanas resided. The presence of Indians in the Chinese sea is testified by the Japanese records which give the credit of introducing cotton into Japan to two Indians, who were carried over to the country by the black currents. Many Indian rulers, particularly the Palas and the Sena rulers of Bengal, and the Pallava and the Chola rulers of the south India, encouraged the trade relations by sending a series of embassies to the Chinese emperors. The Chola king Rajendra I even sent a naval expedition against Malaya and neighbouring countries to overcome their interference in the trade with China. Buddhist scholars like Gunabhadra, Dharmadeva, Vajrabothi and Dharmagupta also went from India to China and translated many Sanskrit works at the request of Chinese emperors.

Initially, Indian traders settled along the coast, but gradually they shifted their network to the interior parts of the countryside too. In order to meet the ritual requirements of the Indian settlers, the priests followed the traders and, in this way, both Buddhist and Hindu religions were introduced in the region. It also resulted in the interaction of Indian social and cultural elements with that of south-east Asia. It is however, noteworthy to understand that the uniqueness about this interaction was the fact that the local cultures of these countries was equally respected and maintained and there emerged a fine intermingling of both local and Indian cultural aspects, each learning from one another. For instance, while Sanskrit was accepted as a language of court and religion in South-east Asia, the regional languages continued to be used alongside, and many inscriptions in mixed Sanskrit and local language are found. The material prosperity of the south-east Asian countries was also based on the introduction of the Indian technique of irrigated rice cultivation.

Sailendra Empire and India Connection

The most important empire which came to be founded in south-east Asia in the 8th century CE was the Sailendra empire which comprised of Java, Sumatra, Malay Peninsula and other parts of the south-east Asian region. They were a leading naval power and on account of their geographical position controlled the trade between China and India as well as other countries in the west. The Sailendra kings were followers of Buddhism and had close contact with the Indian rulers.

(a) One of the kings of this empire built a monastery at Nalanda in the ninth century, and at his request, the Pala king, Devapala of Bengal, granted five villages for its upkeep.

(b) Similarly, in the eleventh century, another king was permitted by the Chola king Rajaraja I to build a Buddhist monastery at Nagapattam on the Tamil coast.

(c) The Sailendras also built a beautiful temple dedicated to Buddha at Barabodur in Java. It is situated on the top of a hillock and consists of nine gradually receding terraces.

FIGURE 9.13 Stupa Borobudur, Java

FIGURE 9.14 Angkor Vat, Cambodia

FIGURE 9.15 Rock Wall Carving, Mahabharata Battle Scene, Angkor Vat Temple

Besides Buddhism, the worship of Hindu gods such as Vishnu and Shiva was also quite popular in south-east Asia. The temples dedicated to them have been found at various places. They show distinct traces of Indian influence and inspiration. One of the most famous temples dedicated to Vishnu is the Angkorvat temple built in the 12th century by Surya Varman II, the king of Kambuja (Cambodia). It is surrounded by a moat, filled with water. It has a huge gopuram (gateway) and number of galleries, the walls of which are decorated with sculptures based on themes drawn from the Mahabharat and the Ramayana. Even in Siam or Thailand, the temples at Bangkok contain many sculptures depicting the Ramayana and even the traditional laws of that country were composed on the model of Dharmashastras. Similarly, Bali came under the rule of Hindu dynasties from 6th century. Even to this day, there is prevalence of the caste system.

QUESTIONS FROM LAST YEAR'S PRELIMS

1. Consider the following events in the history of India: **(2020)**

1. Rise of Pratiharas under King Bhoja.
2. Establishment of Pallava power under Mahendravarman-I.
3. Establishment of Chola power by Parantaka-I.
4. Pala dynasty founded by Gopala.

What is the correct chronological order of the above events, starting from the earliest time?

(a) 2 – 1 – 4 – 3 (b) 3 – 1 – 4 – 2
(c) 2 – 4 – 1 – 3 (d) 3 – 4 – 1 – 2

2. In the context of the history of India, consider the following pairs: **(2016)**

Term	Description
(1) Eripatti:	Land, revenue from which was set apart for the maintenance of the village tank
(2) Taniyurs:	Villages donated to a single Brahmin or a group of Brahmins
(3) Ghatikas:	Colleges generally attached to the temples

Which of the pairs given above is/are correctly matched?

(a) 1 and 2 (b) 3 only
(c) 2 and 3 (d) 1 and 3

3. What is/are common to the two historical places known as Ajanta and Mahabalipuram? **(2016)**

(1) Both were built in the same period.
(2) Both belong to the same religious denomination.
(3) Both have rock-cut monuments.

Select the correct answer using the code given below.

(a) 1 and 2 only
(b) 3 only
(c) 1 and 3 only
(d) None of the statements given above is correct.

4. With reference to the economic history of India, the term 'Araghatta' refers to: **(2016)**

(a) Bonded labour
(b) Land grants made to military officers
(c) Waterwheel used in the irrigation of land
(d) Wasteland converted to cultivated land

5. With reference to Indian history, which of the following is/are the essential elementary elements of the feudal system? **(2015)**

i. A very strong centralised political authority and a very weak provincial or local political authority.
ii. Emergence of administrative structure based on control and possession of land.
iii. Creation of lord-vassal relationship between the feudal lord and his overlord.

Select the correct answer using the code given below.

(a) i and ii only (b) ii and iii only
(c) iii only (d) i, ii and iii

6. The Chinese traveller Yuan Chwang (Hiuen Tsang) who visited India recorded the general conditions and culture of India at that time. In this context, which of the following statements is/are correct? **(2013)**

i. The roads and river-routes were completely immune from robbery.
ii. As regards punishment for offences, ordeals by fire, water and poison were the instruments for determining the innocence or guilt of a person.
iii. The tradesmen had to pay duties at ferries and barrier stations.

Select the correct answer using the codes given below.

(a) i only (b) ii and iii only
(c) i and iii only (d) i, ii and iii

7. With reference to the guilds (shreni) of ancient India that played a very important role in the country's economy, which of the following statements is/are correct? **(2012)**

i. Every guild was registered with the central authority of the state and the king was the chief admin authority on them.
ii. The wages, rules of work, standards and prices were fixed by the guild.
iii. The guild had judicial powers over its own members.

Select the correct answer using the codes given below:

(a) i and ii only (b) iii only
(c) ii and iii only (d) i, ii and iii

8. The Nagara, the Dravida and the Vesara are the **(2012)**

(a) Three main racial groups of the Indian subcontinent.
(b) Three main linguistic divisions in to which the languages of India can be classified.
(c) Three main styles of Indian temple architecture.
(d) Three main musical gharanas prevalent in India.

9. Where is the famous Virupaksha temple located? **(2009)**

(a) Bhadrachalam
(b) Chidambaram
(c) Hampi
(d) Srikalahasti

10. Consider the following statements: **(2006)**

(i) The Ikshvaku rulers of Southern India were antagonistic towards Buddhism.
(ii) The Pala rulers of Eastern India were patrons of Buddhism.

Which of the following statement(s) given above is/are correct?

(a) i only (b) ii only
(c) Both i and ii (d) Neither i nor ii

11. Who among the following laid the foundations of the Rashtrakuta Empire? **(2006)**
(a) Amoghvarsha I
(b) Dantidurga
(c) Dhruva
(d) Krishna I

12. The initial design and construction of which massive temple took place during the reign of Suryavarman II? **(2006)**
(a) Sri Mariammam Temple
(b) Angkor Vat
(c) Batu Caves Temple
(d) Kamakhya Temple

13. Consider the following statements: **(2003)**
(i) The Cholas defeated the Pandya and Chera rulers and established their domination over peninsular India in the early medieval times.
(ii) The Cholas sent an expedition against Sailendra empire of South-East Asia and conquered some of the areas.

Which of these statement(s) is/are correct?
(a) Only i (b) Only ii
(c) Both i and ii (d) Neither i nor ii

14. Emperor Harsha's southward march was stopped on the Narmada river by **(2003)**
(a) Pulkeshin I
(b) Pulkeshin II
(c) Vikramaditya I
(d) Vikramaditya II

15. Match the following: **(1997)**

(A)	Gupta	(i)	Badami
(B)	Chandella	(ii)	Panamalai
(C)	Chalukya	(iii)	Khajuraho
(D)	Pallava	(iv)	Deogarh

(a) A–iv, B–iii, C–i, D–ii
(b) A–iv, B–ii, C–iii, D–i
(c) A–ii, B–iii, C–iv, D–i
(d) A–iii, B–iv, C–i, D–ii

ANSWERS

1. (c)	2. (d)	3. (b)	4. (c)	5. (b)	6. (b)	7. (d)	8. (c)
9. (c)	10. (b)	11. (b)	12. (b)	13. (c)	14. (b)	15. (a)	

QUESTIONS FROM LAST YEAR'S MAINS

1. How will you explain the medieval Indian temple sculptures represent the social life of those days? **(2022 GS1)**

2. The rock-cut architecture represents one of the most important sources of our knowledge of early Indian art and history. Discuss. **(2020 GS1)**

3. Pala period is the most significant phase in the history of Buddhism in India. Enumerate. **(2020 GS1)**

4. Indian philosophy and tradition played a significant role in conceiving and shaping the monuments and their art in India. Discuss. **(2020 GS1)**

5. Assess the importance of the accounts of the Chinese and Arab travellers in the reconstruction of the history of India. **(2018 GS1)**

6. The Kailasha temple built at Ellora marks the culmination of rock-cut architecture in India. Elucidate. **(2015, History optional)**

7. How could the local self-government under the Cholas adjust with their centralised administrative structure? **(2015, History optional)**

8. Critically analyse the agricultural economy from 750–1200 CE. **(2014, History optional)**

9. Analyse the vibrant cultural activities in peninsular India during 550–750 CE. Compare and contrast it with the situation in contemporary North India. **(2013, History optional)**

10. Chola architecture represents a high watermark in the evolution of temple architecture. Discuss. **(2013 GS1)**

PRACTICE QUESTIONS – PRELIMS

1. What is the correct chronological order of the coming of following Chinese pilgrims?
   (i) Hsuan Tsang
   (ii) I-Tsing
   (iii) Fa-Hien

   Code:
   (a) i, ii, iii
   (b) ii, i, iii
   (c) iii, i, ii
   (d) iii, ii, i

2. Consider the following statements:
   (i) Mihir Bhoja was the greatest ruler of the Pratihara dynasty.
   (ii) The Rashtrakuta king Amoghvarsha wrote Kavirajamarga, the earliest Kannada work on poetics.
   (a) Only i (b) Only ii
   (c) i and ii (d) None

3. Consider the following statements:
   (i) Devapala founded Buddhist monastery at Vikramashila.
   (ii) The university which became famous in the post Gupta era was Nalanda.
   (a) Only i (b) Only ii
   (c) i and ii (d) None

4. Consider the following statements:
   (i) Banabhatta was the court poet of Harshavardhana.
   (ii) The Rathas of Mahabalipuram were built by Palas.
   (a) Only i (b) Only ii
   (c) i and ii (d) None

5. Consider the following statements:
   (i) Harshavardhana organised religious assembly at Prayag.
   (ii) The famous Brihadeshwara Temple was built by Cholas.
   (iii) The Pattakadal temples were mainly built by Chalukyas.
   (a) Only i and ii (b) Only ii and iii
   (c) All (d) i and iii

6. Match the following:
   (A) Rajaraja (i) Pushyabhuti
   (B) Dantidurga (ii) Rashtrakuta
   (C) Nagabhatta (iii) Pratiharas
   (D) Harshavardhana (iv) Chola
   (a) A–iv, B–iii, C–i, D–ii
   (b) A–iv, B–ii, C–iii, D–i

(c) A–ii, B–iii, C–iv, D–i
(d) A–iii, B–iv, C–i, D–ii

7. Match the following:

(A)	Kudimai	(i)	Brahmadeya village exclusive assembly
(B)	Ur	(ii)	Tank committee
(C)	Mahasabha	(iii)	Labour services
(D)	Erivariya	(iv)	Non-brahmadeya village assembly

(a) A–iv, B–iii, C–i, D–ii
(b) A–iv, B–ii, C–iii, D–i
(c) A–ii, B–iii, C–iv, D–i
(d) A–iii, B–iv, C–i, D–ii

8. Consider the following statements:
(i) The famous Aihole Inscription belongs to Pulkeshin.
(ii) The tripartite struggle was between the Palas, Rashrakutas and the Cholas.
(iii) Mihir Bhoja adopted the title of Adivaraha.
(a) Only i and ii
(b) Only ii and iii
(c) All
(d) i and iii

9. What is the correct chronological order in case of
(i) Simhavishnu
(ii) Mahendravarman I
(iii) Narsimhavarman I
(iv) Parameshvaraman I
(a) i, ii, iii, iv (b) ii, i, iv, iii
(c) ii, i, iii, iv (d) i, ii, iv, iii

ANSWERS

1. (c) 2. (c) 3. (b) 4. (a) 5. (c) 6. (b) 7. (d) 8. (d)
9. (a)

PRACTICE QUESTIONS – MAINS

1. Describe the highlights of the tripartite struggle, giving references to the major powers involved and important battles.

2. Describe the temple architecture of Pallavas and the Cholas.

3. The administration under Harshavardhana was more or less similar to that of Guptas. Elucidate.

4. Shed some light on the cultural contact of India with south-east Asia. Did trade and commerce have something to do with it? Explain, citing examples.

CHAPTER

10

Period from c. 1000 to 1200 CE: Northern India

As we have discussed in the last chapter, the period from c. 1000 to 1200 CE in northern India is primarily known as the age of conflict. It resulted in the breakdown of the tripartite powers (the Rashtrakutas, the Palas and the Pratiharas) into many smaller kingdoms all over the country. For instance, in northern India, the disintegration of the Pratihara empire resulted in the emergence of various Rajput states under the control of different Rajput dynasties, such as the Chahamanas (Chauhans), Chandellas, the Paramaras of Malwa, and so on. We will see later that these states fought and resisted the Turkish attacks from northwest India led by Mahmud of Ghazni and Mohammad Ghori in the 11th and 12th centuries, but their failure to stand united against the invaders eventually led to their defeat.

The Rajput Clans

In the early 12th century, the term *Rajaputa* came into prominence, which referred to certain specific lineage-based clans. The basis of Rajput society was the clan, and every clan traced its descent from a common ancestor (real or imaginary). Some historians believe that they were the descendants of various groups of foreign invaders such as the Shakas, the Kushanas, the Hunas, and so on, who had gradually settled down in the region of Rajasthan and, after intermingling with Indian society, emerged as a warrior class. Other historians consider them as a part of the Kshatriya *varna* of the Brahmanical system. Scholars like B. D. Chattopadhyaya consider that the Rajput clans emerged due to multiple factors like the expansion of the agrarian economy. The distribution of land among royal kinsmen allowed many local chiefs to acquire enough financial and political power to set up an independent authority. Meanwhile, inter-clan collaboration in the form of political and matrimonial alliances as well as the construction of fortresses on an unprecedented scale led to a consolidation of the clan structure. These clans dominated a compact territory. Attachment to land, family and 'honour' were the characteristic features considered important by the Rajput clans.

In order to acquire legitimacy and authenticity for their newly acquired position in the eyes of their subjects, the Rajput clans invited *Brahmanas* from the Gangetic delta and other regions to perform royal rituals and ceremonies. In return, they were given land and other things as *dakshina* (fee). The *Brahmanas* were also asked to write about the Rajput's illustrious ancestry, linking them with Lord Rama (of the *Suryavansha*) and Lord Krishna (of the *Chandravansha*) in order to claim a dignified position among the warrior classes. Certain clans also claimed *agnikula* origins for themselves, referring to a myth wherein these clans emerged out of the sacrificial fire of sage Vashishta on Mount Abu. The four *Agnikula* Rajput clans were:

a. The Pratiharas (who we have discussed in the last chapter).

b. The Chahamanas/Chauhans of Ajmer.

c. The Chandellas of Bundelkhand.

d. The Paramaras of Malwa.

Apart from them, according to medieval bardic traditions, there were about 36 Rajput clans which included Gahadavalas of Kannauj, the Tomaras of Delhi, the Solankis, the Chalukyas of Gujarat, and so on.

Rajput social organisation had its advantages as well as disadvantages. The sense of brotherhood and egalitarianism which prevailed among the Rajputs was both an advantage and a disadvantage as it also made it difficult to maintain discipline among the different clans. They treated war as a sport, which led to continuous warfare among themselves over struggle for land and cattle. Most of the Rajput rulers were staunch Hindus, though some of them patronised Jainism too.

The Chahamanas/Chauhans

The Chahamanas of Shakambhari, colloquially known as the Chauhans of Sambhar, ruled in parts of the present-day Rajasthan and its neighbouring areas between 7th and 11th centuries CE. They were the most prominent ruling family of the Chahamana clan. The Chahamanas originally had their capital at Shakambhari, which is identical to modern Sambhar near Jaipur in the Sapadalaksa country (part of present-day Rajasthan). However, the later rulers moved the capital to Ajmer, and for this reason, they are also known as the Chahamanas (Chauhans) of Ajmer. They were originally feudatories of the Pratiharas and assumed independence during the reign of King Simharaja.

Simharaja (c. 944–971 CE)

- Founded the Chahamana/Chauhan dynasty around 10th century CE and adopted the title of *Maharajadhiraja*.

Vigraharaja II (c. 971–998 CE)

- Defeated Mulraja I and overran Gujarat.
- Captured Chittor.

Ajayaraja II (c. 1110–1135 CE)

- Next important ruler who carried on the aggressive policy, defeated the Paramaras and captured their capital Ujjaini.
- Founded the city of *Ajayameru* (Ajmer).

Vigraharaja IV (c. 1150–1164 CE)

- Also known as Visaldev, who captured Delhi from the Tomaras in c. 1151 CE but allowed them to rule as feudatories. He also took possession of Eastern Punjab, sacked and plundered Gujarat. The records of his reign states that his kingdom extended in the north up to the Siwalik Hills and in the south up to Udaipur.
- Moved the capital from Shakambhari (Sambhar) to Ajmer.
- Also came in conflict with the Paramars of Malwa, which was probably ruled by their famous ruler Bhoja.
- Patronised literature and authored a famous play, *Harikeli Nataka*.
- The structure that was later converted into the Adhai Din Ka Jhopra mosque was constructed during his reign.

Prithviraj III (c. 1177–1192 CE)

- The most famous of all Chauhans, is popularly known as Prithviraj Chauhan or Rai Pithora in the folk legends. He scored victories over all his neighbours, including the Chandella king Paramardi, Chalukya Bhima II and Gahadvala Jayachandra.

FIGURE 10.1 Prithvi Raj Chauhan

- Ascended the throne at the young age of 11, after death of his father Someshvara, but took the reins of administration in his hands when he was 16.
- Led an expedition in Bundelkhand against the Chandella ruler and its capital Mahoba and it was in this struggle the famous Chandella warriors Alha and Udal lost their lives.
- Defeated Muhammad Ghori in the First Battle of Tarain in c. 1191 CE.
- In 1192 CE, Muhammad Ghori defeated Prithviraj Chauhan in the Second Battle of Tarain, and subsequently executed him. His defeat at Tarain is seen as a landmark event in the Islamic conquest of India, and has been described in several semi-legendary accounts, most notably the *Prithviraj Raso*.
- Two great poems, *Prithviraj Raso* and *Prithviraj Vijaya*, were written by his court poets Chandbardai and Jayanaka, respectively.

Hari-raja (c. 1193–1194 CE)

- Muhammad Ghori followed up his victory by the conquest of Ajmer and Delhi and placed the young son of Prithviraj, *Govinda*, as his vassal in Ajmer. Govinda was de-throned and banished by Prithviraja's brother Hari-raja for accepting Muslim suzerainty. Govinda then established the Chahamana branch of *Ranastambhapura* (Ranthambore). Hari-raja regained Ajmer and followed a policy of hostility against the conquerors of Delhi.
- Qutabuddin Aibak invaded Ajmer, overthrew Hari-raja and took the principality.

The Chauhan dynasty then retired to Ranthambhor and ruled there in diminishing glory. But in c. 1301 CE, Ala-ud-din Khilji captured Ranthambhor and uprooted the last stronghold of Chauhan power.

The Chandellas of Bundelkhand

The Chandellas of Bundelkhand trace their descent to a mythical ancestor named Chandratreya, born of the moon. The Chandellas initially ruled as feudatories of the Gurjara–Pratiharas of Kannauj, and were involved in conflicts with the Pratiharas, the Palas and the Kalachuris of Chedi (who bordered the Chandellas on the south). The Chandellas are well-known for their art and architecture, most notably for the fully developed Nagara-style temples at their original capital Khajuraho. During the reigns of Chandella rulers Yashovarman, Dhanga and Vidyadhara; the Lakshmana Temple (c. 930–950 CE), the Vishvanatha Temple (c. 999–1002 CE) and the Kandariya Mahadeva Temple (c. 1030 CE) were constructed respectively. They also commissioned a number of water bodies, palaces and forts at other places, including their strongholds of Jayapura-Durga (modern Ajaigarh), Kalanjara (modern Kalinjar) and their later capital Mahotsava-Nagara (modern Mahoba). In the first quarter of the 9th century CE, the dynasty was founded by Nannuka, who was the ruler of a small kingdom and established his capital at Kharjjuravahaka (Khajuraho).

Nannuka (c. 831–845 CE)

- Was the founder king of Chandellas.

Vakpati (c. 845–865 CE)

- According to the Chandella inscriptions, Nannuka's successor Vakpati defeated several enemies.

Jayashakti and Vijayashakti (c. 865–885 CE)

- Vakpati's sons Jayashakti (*Jeja*) and Vijayashakti (*Vija*) consolidated the Chandella power.
- According to a Mahoba inscription, the Chandella territory was named 'Jejakabhukti' after Jayashakti.

Rahila (c. 885–905 CE)

- In many eulogistic inscriptions, Vijayashakti's successor Rahila is credited with several military victories.

Shri Harsha (c. 905–925 CE)

- Around 914 CE, Rahila's son Harsha played an important role in restoring the rule of the Pratihara King Mahipala, possibly after a Rashtrakuta invasion by king Indra III.

Yashovarman (c. 925–950 CE)

- Around 10th century, Yashovarman became practically independent, although he continued to acknowledge Pratihara suzerainty.
- He conquered the important fortress of Kalanjara, and had several other military successes.

According to Khajuraho inscription dated c. 954 CE:

'He had several other military successes, including against the Gaudas (identified with the Palas), the Khasas, the Chedis (the Kalachuris of Tripuri), the Kosalas (possibly the Somavamshis), the Mithila (possibly a small tributary ruler), the Malavas (identified with the Paramaras), the Kurus, the Kashmiris and the Gurjaras'.

- His reign marked the beginning of the famous Chandella style art and architecture. He commissioned the famous Lakshmana Temple at Khajuraho.

Dhanga-Deva (c. 950–999 CE)

- The first independent Chandella king who took the title of *Maharajadhiraja* and under whose reign the Chandellas had become a sovereign power as unlike the earlier Chandella inscriptions, the records of Dhanga do not mention any Pratihara overlord.
- A Khajuraho inscription claims that *'the rulers of Kosala, Kratha (part of Vidarbha region), Kuntala and Simhala listened humbly to the commands of Dhanga's officers. It also claims that the wives of the kings of Andhra, Anga, Kanchi and Radha resided in his prisons as a result of his success in wars.'* These may be eulogistic exaggerations but they certainly suggest that Dhanga did undertake extensive military campaigns.
- Like his predecessor, Dhanga also commissioned a magnificent Vishvanatha Temple at Khajuraho.

FIGURE 10.2 Vishvanatha Temple at Khajuraho

Ganda-Deva (c. 999–1002 CE)

- Dhanga's successor Ganda appears to have retained the territory he inherited.

Vidyadhara (c. 1003–1035 CE)

- According to some legends, Vidyadhara killed the Pratihara king of Kannauj (possibly Rajyapala) who had fled his capital instead of fighting the invading Ghaznavid ruler, Mahmud of Ghazni.
- It is believed that Mahmud later invaded Vidyadhara's kingdom and the conflict between the two ended with Vidyadhara paying tribute to Mahmud.
- By the end of Vidyadhara's reign, the Ghaznavid invasions had weakened the Chandella kingdom and thus taking advantage of this, the Kalachuri king Gangeya-deva conquered eastern parts of the kingdom.
- Vidyadhara is noted for having commissioned the Kandariya Mahadeva Temple.

FIGURE 10.3 Kandariya Mahadeva Temple

Vijayapala (c. 1035–1050 CE)

- Vijayapala defeated Gangeya-deva in a battle. However, during his reign, the Chandella power started declining as evident by the giving up of allegiance by the Kachchhapaghatas of Gwalior during this period.
- One of the probable reasons behind decline in the power of Chandellas was the factor of constant struggle between them and their neighbours. For instance, they had to fight many battles with the neighbouring dynasties, especially the Paramaras of Malwa and the Kalachuris of Tripuri. Later, 11th century onwards, the Chandellas had to face raids by the northern Muslim dynasties, such as the Ghaznavids and the Ghurids. Eventually, around the beginning of the 13th century, following *Chahamanas* and *Ghurid* invasions the Chandella power effectively ended.

Paramardi-deva (c. 1165–1203 CE)

- Was the last powerful Chandella king.
- Around 1183 CE, the Chahamana ruler Prithviraj Chauhan invaded the Chandella kingdom and sacked Mahoba (as per the Madanpur stone inscriptions). It is believed that Paramardi, being scared and coward took shelter in the Kalanjara fort and consequently the Chandella force led by Alha, Udal and other generals was defeated in this battle.
- There are different versions of Paramardi's fate, as according to some legends Paramardi either committed suicide out of shame or retired to Gaya, while others account that Paramardi restored the Chandella power and ruled as a sovereign until around 1203 CE, when the Delhi Sultanate invaded the Chandella kingdom. Some other historians such as the 16th century historian Ferishta believe that disagreeing with the king's decision to surrender to the Delhi forces, Paramardi was assassinated by his own minister.

The Chandella power did not fully recover from their defeat against the Delhi Sultanate. The Chandella power thus continued to decline due to both rising Islamic influence, as well as the rise of other local dynasties, such as the Bundelas, the Baghelas and the Khangars. It is believed that one minor branch of the family continued ruling Kalanjara, whose ruler was eventually killed by Sher Shah Suri's army in 1545 CE, while another minor branch ruled at Mahoba, and according to certain texts, one of its princesses married into the Gond royal family of Mandla.

The Paramaras of Malwa

The Paramaras of Malwa were originally based in the Mount Abu area of Rajasthan. According to tradition, *the sage Vishwamitra stole Vashishtha's kama dhenu* (*wish-granting* cow). *In order to retrieve his cow, Vashishtha performed a sacrifice on Mount Abu and out of this sacrificial fire emerged a hero who seized his cow and was named* Paramara (*slayer of enemies*). He was thereafter crowned the king. The earliest known Paramara king, Upendra, was believed to be of the lineage of this hero. There are several branches of this dynasty, though the main branch ruled at Malwa, with its capital at Dhara (modern Dhar, M.P.).

According to the Harsola copper-plates issued by the Paramara king, Siyaka II in c. 949 CE, the early Paramara rulers were probably established in the 10th century CE and were the feudatories of the Rashtrakutas of Manyakheta. Interestingly, the Paramara power rose and declined several times owing to their struggles with the Chalukyas of Kalyani, Chalukyas of Gujarat, the Kalachuris of Tripuri and other neighbouring kingdoms. It is also believed that due to multiple times of the sacking of capital city 'Dhara' by their enemies, the later Paramaras had to move their capital to Mandapa-Durga (now Mandu). Under the Paramaras, Malwa enjoyed a great level of political and cultural prestige. The Paramaras were well-known for their patronage to poets and scholars and as in fact Bhoja was himself a renowned scholar. Most of the Paramara kings were Shaivites and built several Shiva temples, although they also patronised Jain scholars.

Upendra (around first quarter of the 9th century CE)

- It is believed that he was made ruler of Deccan by the Rashtrakuta king Govinda III, after the latter's successful military expedition in Malwa. He is considered to be the founder of Malwa's Parmara dynasty.
- The Paramaras were temporarily eclipsed when they lost Malwa to the Pratiharas and their power was revived in the mid-10th century by Vairasimha II and Siyaka II.

Siyaka II (c. 948–972 CE)

- Around 972 CE, Siyaka (also known as Harsha) threw off his allegiance to the Rashtrakutas. He not only defeated the Rashtrakuta king, Khottiga, at Kalighatta on the banks of the Narmada, but also sacked the Rashtrakuta capital Manyakheta and established the Paramaras as a sovereign power.

Munja (c. 972–990 CE)

- Also known as Utpala or Vakpatiraja II, who extended the empire and achieved many military successes such as that against the Kalachuris where he sacked their capital Tripuri. He led many expeditions into Rajputana and defeated the Hunas, sacked the capital of the Guhilas of Medapati Aghata, captured territories of the Chahamanas of Naddula, annexed Mount Abu and southern parts of Jodhpur from the other branch of Chahamanas and placed his sons and nephew in charge of the conquered territories. He also invaded the Chalukyan kingdom of Anahilapataka and Lata.
- He was finally defeated by the Western Chalukyan ruler, Tailapa II. As a result of this defeat, the Paramaras lost their southern territories (possibly the ones beyond the Narmada river) to the Chalukyas.
- Adopted the titles of Amoghavarsha/Prithvivallabha/Sri-vallabha. Apart from being an accomplished military leader, he was a poet and patron of the arts and literature. He constructed many tanks and temples during his reign.

Sindhuraja (c. 990–1010 CE)

- Munja's brother, who defeated the Western Chalukya king Satyashraya, and recovered the territories lost to Tailapa II. He also achieved military successes against a Huna chief, the Somavanshis of south Kosala, the Shilaharas of Konkana and the ruler of Lata (southern Gujarat).
- His court poet Padmagupta wrote his biography, *Nava-Sahasanka-Charita*.

Bhoja (c. 1010–1055 CE)

- Sindhuraja's son and Munja's nephew Bhoja, who is the most celebrated ruler of the Paramara dynasty, and under whom the dynasty reached its zenith. Under his reign, the Paramaras extended their kingdom from Chittor in the north to upper Konkan in the south, and from the Sabarmati river in the west to Vidisha in the east.
- Around 1018 CE, he defeated the Chalukyas of Lata in present-day Gujarat. Between 1018 CE and 1020 CE, he gained control of the northern Konkan, whose Shilahara rulers probably served as his feudatories for a brief period.
- Formed an alliance against the Kalyani Chalukya King Jayasimha II, with Rajendra Chola and Gangeya-deva Kalachuri.
- During the last years of Bhoja's reign, around 1042 CE, Jayasimha's son and successor, Someshvara I, invaded Malwa and sacked its capital Dhara. Though Bhoja re-established his control over Malwa soon after the departure of the Chalukya army, the defeat pushed back the southern boundary of his kingdom from Godavari to Narmada.
- His attempts to expand his kingdom eastwards was foiled by the Chandella king Vidyadhara. However, Bhoja was able to extend his influence among the Chandella feudatories, the Kachchhapaghatas of Dubkund. He also launched a campaign against the Kachchhapaghatas of Gwalior, possibly with the ultimate goal of capturing Kannauj, but his attacks were repulsed by their ruler Kirtiraja.
- Bhoja also defeated the Chahamanas of Shakambhari, killing their ruler Viryarama. However, he was forced to retreat by the Chahamanas of Naddula.
- Adopted the title of *Parameshvara-Paramabhattaraka*, which is considered to be identical to the title of Paramara-Deva. According to some medieval Muslim historians, after sacking Somnath, Mahmud of Ghazni changed his route to avoid confrontation with a Hindu king named Param Dev, who has been identified as Bhoja.
- It is also believed that Bhoja may have also contributed troops to support the Hindu Shahi ruler Anandapala's fight against the Ghaznavids. Around 1043 CE, he may have also been a part of the Hindu alliance that expelled Mahmud's governors from Hansi, Thanesar and other areas around.

- During the last year of Bhoja's reign, or shortly after his death, the Solanki king Bhimadeva and the Kalachuri king Karna attacked his kingdom. According to some historians, Bhoja died of a disease at the same time the allied army attacked his kingdom.
- He is considered a righteous scholar king who himself was a polymath. His writings cover a wide variety of topics such as grammar, poetry, architecture, yoga and chemistry. He patronised the arts, literature and the sciences. He established the *Bhoj Shala*, which was a centre for Sanskrit studies, and a temple of Sarasvati in present day Dhar.
- He is said to have founded the city of Bhojpur, credited with building of not only Bhojeshwar temple but also three dams in that area. He is often compared to the fabled Vikramaditya.

Jayasimha I (c. 1055–1070 CE)

- Bhoja's son and successor who faced the joint Kalachuri–Solanki invasion immediately after Bhoja's death. Bilhana's writings suggest that *he sought help from the Chalukyas of Kalyani*.

Lakshmadeva (c. 1086–1094 CE)

- Nagpur Prashasti inscription of c. 1105 CE credits him with extensive military conquests.

Mahalakadeva, the last known Paramara king, was defeated and killed by the forces of Ala-ud-din Khilji of Delhi in c. 1305 CE, although epigraphic evidence (an inscription from Udaipur) suggests that the Paramara rule continued for a few years after his death, until c. 1310 CE, at least in the north-eastern part of Malwa. A later inscription shows that the area had been captured by the Delhi Sultanate by c. 1338 CE.

The Chalukyas of Gujarat/The Solanki Rajputs

The Solanki Rajputs are also known as the Chalukya family of Gujarat, which was different from the earlier Chalukyan dynasty of Badami. They ruled parts of Gujarat and Kathiawar between c. 950 and 1300 CE. Unlike the Chalukyas of Kalyani and Vengi, the Solankis never claimed a shared descent or any other association with the original Chalukya dynasty. Interestingly, they never used the term 'Chalukya' to describe themselves, but chose to use its variant, '*Chaulukya*'. They had many branches, though three branches were the most prominent. The oldest branch ruled from Central India's Mattamayura and its earliest rulers were Simhavarman, Sadhanva and Avanivarman. The other branch was founded by Barappa in Lata (South Gujarat); the most prominent city of their kingdom was Bhrigukachchha (Broach). Another branch was founded by Mularaja I, whose capital was at *Anahilapataka* (or *Anahilavada*, which is identical to modern Patan, Gujarat).

Mulraja I (c. 940–995 CE)

- Mulraja I led many military expeditions against Saurashtra, Kutch, Abhiras, and so on. His power suffered a setback with the invasions of the Chahamanas and the Chalukyas of Lata.
- After being defeated by the Paramaras of Malwa, he took refuge with the Rashtrakuta king, Dhavala. Later, he recovered his kingdom, but his successors remained embroiled in conflicts with the Kalachuris and Paramaras.
- He was a Shaiva devotee, but also patronised Jainism as he built the *Mulavasatika* (Mula's residence) temple for the Digambaras and the *Mulanatha-jinadeva* (the Jina who is Mula's lord) temple for the *Shvetambaras*.

Bhima I (c. 1022–1064 CE)

- Grandson of Mulraja, and the next important ruler after Mularaja.
- During his reign, Mahmud of Ghazni overran Gujarat and plundered Somnath in 1025 CE.
- He built the Sun temple of Modhera. His wife Udaymati built the Rani-ki vav (Queen's step well) in his memory, which is on the list of UNESCO's World Heritage Sites.

It is pertinent to note that out of the five famous Dilwara temples, one Vimal Vasahi temple dedicated to Jain lord *Rishabha* was built in c. 1031 CE by Vimalsha, a minister of Bhima I.

Karan (c. 1065–1091 CE)

- He defeated a Bhil chieftain and founded Karnavati, which is now known as Ahmedabad.

Jayasimha Siddharaja (c. 1092–1142 CE)

- He ruled for about half a century, and enlarged the kingdom by conquering states like Saurashtra and Kutch.
- Jayasimha also conquered Malwa and its siege is premise of many Gujarat bards. One of the favourite is woven around the siege of Junagadh by Jayasimha. According to legends, the fort was ultimately captured by him along with Ranakdevi, wife of the Raja Rakhengar, the ruler of Junagadh. However, Ranakdevi preferred to commit sati on a pyre at Wadhwan rather than remarry Jayasimha. Ranakdevi temple still stands in Wadhwan at the site of her death.
- Hemachandra, a Jain monk, rose to prominence and had good relationship with the king. The Rudra Mahakala temple at Siddhapur was built during his reign.

Kumarapala (c. 1142–1171 CE)

- During Kumarapala's reign, Gujarat's prosperity was at its peak.
- He too shared good relationship with Hemachandra and graciously patronised Jainism during his rule in Gujarat.
- He rebuilt the Somnath temple.

Bhima II (c. 1177–1240 CE)

- He successfully repelled the incursions of Muhammad Ghori (at the battle of Kayadara), who had the ambition of repeating the act performed by Mahmud of Ghazni.
- In c. 1195–1197 CE, an army led by Aibak, Ghori's *deputy*, invaded again, but Bhima II defeated Aibak again and adorned himself as *Abhinav Siddharaj*.

After c. 1243 CE, the Solankis lost control of Gujarat to their feudatories, the Hindu Vaghela dynasty of Dholka, who established a short-lived (76 years) but powerful principality. After c. 1292 CE, the Vaghelas became tributaries of the Seuna (Yadava) dynasty of Devagiri in the Deccan Plateau. The dynasty ended when Khilji conquered Gujarat in c. 1297 CE. Another Dilwara temple, the Luna Vashi temple dedicated to Lord Neminath, was built in c. 1230 CE by two Porwad brothers – Vastupal and Tejpal, who were both ministers of Virdhaval, the Vaghela ruler of Gujarat.

The Tomaras

The Tomaras ruled the Hariyana (Haryana) country with their capital at Dhillika (Delhi) and they are believed to be a feudatory of the Pratiharas. Medieval bardic literature names the dynasty as 'Tuar', and classifies them as one of the 36 Rajput clans. They often had conflicts with the Chahamanas of Shakambhari, and later, their rule was followed by that of the Chahamanas. A 13th century Palam Baoli (step well) inscription records that *the land of Hariyanaka was first enjoyed by the Tomaras, then by the Chauhans, and thereafter by the Shakas (that is, the Delhi Sultans)*.

The iron pillar at Mehrauli carries an 11th century inscription which refers to one of the most famous kings of the Tomara dynasty, Anangapala Tomara who is widely believed as the ruler who established Delhi. The coins issued under his reign feature the horseman-and-bull figure, and also bear the title *'Shri Samanta-deva'*. It is pertinent to note that these coins are very similar to those of the Shakambhari Chahamana kings Someshvara and Prithviraja III, indicating that Anangapala was a contemporary of these 12th century kings. The Tomara Rajputs have a special connection with Delhi, and it is reflected in medieval legends too. According to a legend mentioned in the *Prithviraja Raso*, '*a Brahmana told the Rajput king Anangapala Tomar that the base of the iron pillar rested on the hood of the Vasuki, the king of serpents, and that his rule would last as long as the pillar stood upright. Out of curiosity, Anangapala dug out the pillar, only to find it smeared with the blood of Vasuki. Realising his mistake, the king ordered it to be re-instated, but it remained loose (dhili). Because of this, the area came to be known as 'Dhilli' (modern Delhi)*'.

The Tomaras were associated with the construction of the earliest surviving waterworks in the Delhi area. Anangapala II was the founder of the citadel of Lal Kot in the Mehrauli area and also built a tank known as the Anang Tal. Similarly, the famous Suraj Kund reservoir (near Faridabad, Haryana) is said to have been commissioned by a Tomara king named Surajpala.

The Gahadavalas of Kannauj

Beginning in the late 11th century, for approximately a hundred years, the kingdom of Kannauj was ruled by the Gahadvalas or Gaharwars, who claimed to be Suryavanshi kshatriyas. Interestingly, the Rathore clan of the Rajputs claimed descent from the Gahadvala dynasty. Chandradeva founded the Gahadavala dynasty of Kannauj around c. 1090 CE. They gradually squeezed the Palas out of Bihar and made Banaras a second capital.

Chandradeva (around c. 1090 CE)

- Founding ruler of this dynasty who successfully wrested Delhi from both the Pratiharas and the Rashtrakutas and annexed it to his state of Kannauj.

Govindchandra (c. 1114–1154 CE)

- Grandson of Chandradeva, who not only defeated the Ghaznavids and secured the release of his father Madan Chandra, but he also raised Kannauj to unprecedented glory as under his reign the state of Gaharwar reached the pinnacle of its power.
- His kingdom comprised much of the present day Uttar Pradesh and Bihar.
- Govindachandra was a patron of both Hindu temples and Buddhist monasteries and his wife Kumaradevi was a devout Buddhist.

Vijayachandra (c. 1154–1170 CE)

- Son of Govindachandra, who is identified with the names of Vijayapala/Malladeva and he successfully faced aggressions of the Ghaznavids.
- However, during his reign, Delhi was lost and the Tomara rulers stopped recognising Vijayachandra as their sovereign and probably aligned with the Chauhans of Ajmer.

Jaichandra (c. 1170–1194 CE)

- Son of Vijayachandra, who was the last great king of the Gahadavala dynasty. His power and extensive jurisdiction was noticed by even Muslim historians. During his reign, the Chauhans from Ajmer under Prathviraj Chauhan annexed Delhi. According to some legends, *Prithviraja loved Samyukta, daughter of Jaichandra. After opposition from her father, as Prithviraj was heir to the rival Chauhan Rajput kingdom to the west, Samyukta eloped with Prithviraj*. This further aggravated the dissension between the kingdoms, and Jaichandra then sought help from Muslims of the north to invade the Chauhans of Ajmer–Delhi. This romantic tale is the subject of a lot of folklore.
- Suffered a defeat at the hands of the king Lakshmansena of Bengal. After the fall of Delhi, around c. 1194 CE, the city of Kannauj was attacked by Muhammad of Ghori. It is believed that Jaichandra was defeated in the Battle of Chanawar and subsequently drowned in the Ganga. His kingdom was conquered and was sacked by Ghori's armies.

Some survivors, led by Jaichandra's son and grandson Siyaji (Shiv ji), fled west to the Marwar desert region of Rajasthan, where they established themselves as rulers in the early 13th century. They founded the Rathore clan, which ruled the princely state of Marwar or Jodhpur. The glory of Kannauj ended with the conquest of Iltutmish.

Kingdom of Kashmir and North-West

Much of the history of Kashmir and North-west India is deduced from the legendary and historical chronicle *Rajatarangini* (which means 'the river of kings'). It was probably written in 12th century CE in Sanskrit by a Kashmiri *Brahmana* called Kalhana, though not much is known about him apart from what is written in the book. It is possible that his father, Champaka, was the minister in the court of Harsha of Kashmir. This earliest historical source consists of 7826 verses, which are divided into eight books called *Tarangas* (waves).

In early 7th century, the Karkota dynasty rulers established their rule in Kashmir. The dynasty marked the rise of Kashmir as a power in Central Asia and Northern India. The Karkota dynasty (c. 625–855 CE) was founded by Durlabhvardhana during the lifetime of the Pushyabhuti king, Harshavardhana. The Karkota emperors were primarily Hindu, who have been known for building spectacular Hindu temples in their capital, Parihaspur. They, however, also patronised Buddhism, and some stupas, chaityas and viharas can be found in the ruins of their capital.

Karkota Dynasty

Durlabh Vardhana (c. 598–634 CE)

- Also known as Prajnaditya and during his rule, Hsuan Tsang visited Kashmir.

Lalitaditya/Muktapida (c. 697–733 CE)

- Most illustrious king of the Karkota dynasty. He was able to extend the power of Kashmir beyond the normal mountain limits. Lalitaditya was able to vanquish the Turks, Tibetans, Bhutias, Kambojas, and others. However, some historians believe that Kalhana highly exaggerated the conquests of Lalitaditya.
- His main success was against king Yasovarman of Kannauj.
- Built the famous Martand (Sun) temple in Anantnag district, Kashmir which is the oldest known Sun temple in India (Fig. 10.4) and was also one of the biggest temple complexes of that time.

Vajraditya (c.734–741 CE)

- During his reign, Arabs made frequent raids upon Kashmir.

FIGURE 10.4 Martand Sun Temple

Jayapida (c. 745–776 CE)

- One of the more powerful Karkota kings, who led many military expeditions. For instance, he led a three-year-long expedition against the eastern countries and claimed victory over the five chieftains of Gauda and ruler of Kannauj.
- It is believed that during the last years of his reign, he imposed excessive taxes on the advice of *Kayasthas*, and treated his subjects cruelly. It is said that he died because of a curse by a *Brahmana*.

The Karkota dynasty was followed by the Utpala dynasty. Avanti Varman ascended the throne of Kashmir on c. 855 CE, establishing the Utpala dynasty and ending the rule of the Karkota dynasty.

Utpala Dynasty

From the 8th to 10th century CE, the Kashmir region was ruled over by the Hindu Utpala dynasty. The kingdom was established by Avanti Varman, ending the rule of the Karkota dynasty in 855 CE. The political history of early medieval Kashmir is incomplete without special mention of the *tantrins* (a body of foot soldiers), *ekangas* (a body of royal body guards) and the *damaras* (landed chiefs), who played a crucial role in the politics of that time and at times acted as king-makers. The history of this region is also unique in one aspect of its tradition, namely, the legacy of powerful queens. The Rajatarangini mentions three women rulers, namely Yashovati of the

Gonanda dynasty, Sugandha of the Utpala dynasty and Didda of the Yashaskara dynasty (who had the longest and most eventful stint; she is discussed below).

Avanti Varman (c. 855–883 CE)

- He was the founder of the Utpala dynasty and was known as a great administrator. He took actions to stabilise the state and to regain the power. He controlled the powers of the *damaras*, rural aristocrats causing internal problems.
- Was a benevolent and beloved king, as he ensured the prosperity of the entire region. He was credited with taking major innovative works in the field of irrigation. For instance, he took steps to prevent the flood waters of the Mahapadma (Wular) lake from damaging crops.
- During his reign, the cities of Avantipur and Suyapur were founded, and many Hindu temples dedicated to both Vishnu and Shiva and Buddhist monasteries were built, notable of which is the Avantiswara and Avantiswami temples.

Sankara Varman (c. 883–902 CE)

- Son of Avanti Varman, who led military campaigns into the Punjab and Gujarat.
- His military operations led to the drain of wealth from the treasury, and as a result, heavy taxes were imposed on the people. Although he tried to regain some of the treasury's wealth by fiscal extortion, in acts such as plundering temples, the losses could not be recovered.

Yashaskara Dynasty

Queen Didda (c. 958–1003 CE)

- Her career is described in the sixth *taranga* of the *Rajatarangini*. She was the wife of king Kshemagupta and the daughter of Simharaja of Lohara (*which lay around the Pir Panjal range, on a trade route between western Punjab and Kashmir*), granddaughter of Bhima Shahi, one of the Hindu Shahis of Kabul.
- Didda ruled first as a regent for her son and various grandsons, and thereafter as the sole ruler in her own right. In fact, Kalhana disapproved of her; according to him, *her personality reflected the defects of womankind*. He has described her *as deficient in moral character, merciless by nature, and has further explained in detail how she ruthlessly killed her son and three grandsons before ascending the throne*. According to Kalhana, *she also had an affair with a courier and herdsmen named Tuna, who became her trusted confidante*. Even prior to becoming regent, Didda had considerable influence in state affairs, and coins have been found which appear to show both her name and that of Kshemagupta.
- She founded towns of Diddapura and Kankanapura and a temple called the Diddasvamin temple.

After ruling indirectly and directly, Didda placed Sangramaraja, the son of her brother on the throne, diverting the royal succession from the Yashaskaras to her natal family, and thus started the Lohara dynasty in Kashmir.

Hindu Shahi Dynasty

After the decline of the Kushana Empire in the 3rd century to the early 9th century CE, the Turkish Shahiya dynasty ruled over the Kabul valley (in eastern Afghanistan) and Gandhara (northern Pakistan and Kashmir). They were split into two eras: the Buddhist Shahis and the later Hindu Shahis, with the transition into Hinduism occurring around 870 CE. In the second half of the 9th century CE, Kallar, a *Brahmana* minister of King Lagaturman, overthrew the Shahiya king and laid the foundation of Hindu Shahi dynasty. The Shahis were rulers of predominantly Buddhist and Hindu populations and were thus patrons of numerous faiths, and various artifacts and coins from their rule have been found that display their multicultural domain.

Kallar (c. 890–895 CE)

- In the Rajatarangini, Kallar is referred to as *Lalliyashahi*, and was the Brahmana minister of the Shahi dynasty.
- He was not able to maintain control over the Kabul valley for long, and around c. 870 CE, he was forced to move his capital from Kabul to Udabhanda (modern day Und village in Rawalpindi district, Pakistan) after being defeated by the Arab, Sarrarid Yaqui ibn.

Jayapala (c. 964–1001 CE)

- He is celebrated as a hero for his struggles in defending his kingdom from the Turkish rulers of Ghazni. According to legends, King Jayapala was challenged by the armies of Sultan Sabuktigin in the Battle of Peshawar (c. 1000 CE), and later by his son, Sultan Mahmud of Ghazni.

Anandapala (c. 1001–1010 CE)

- The son of Jayapala, who was an able warrior and general. He led many battles prior to his ascension.
- However, during his reign as emperor, many losses were inflicted on his kingdom by the Ghaznavids. For instance, during the battle of Chach between Mahmud and Anandapala, some 30,000 *Gakhars* fought alongside as soldiers for the Shahi Emperor and incurred huge losses for the Ghaznavids. They still lost the battle and suffered much financial and territorial loss.
- He eventually signed a treaty with the Ghaznavid Empire in c. 1010 CE, and shortly a year later died a peaceful death.
- Out of respect for his resistance against Mahmud of Ghazni, some historians often compare him with King Porus, who bravely opposed Alexander.

Trilochanpala (c. 1010–1022 CE)

- He tried to expand his kingdom by conquering the Shivalik Hills, which was earlier the domain of the Rai of Sharwa. Thus, his kingdom extended from the River Indus to the upper Ganges valley.
- According to Al-Biruni, '*Initially Trilochanpala was honourable in his loyalty to his father's peace treaty to the Ghaznavids*'. However, eventually he rebelled against Sultan Mahmud but was later assassinated by some of his own mutinous troops in 1022 CE in an assassination which was believed to have been instigated by the Rai of Sharwa, who became his arch enemy due to his kingdom's expansion into the Shivalik ranges.
- In Punjabi folklore, he was romanticised as the last Punjabi ruler of Punjab.

Bheempala (c. 1022–1026 CE)

- He is referred by famous historian Utbi as the '*fearless*' due to his courage and valour. He is known to have personally commanded the Battle of Nandana, where he is said to have seriously wounded the commander of the Ghaznavid army, Muhammad bin Ibrahim.
- He was final Shahi Emperor of the famed dynasty.
- The kingdom was destroyed by Mahmud of Ghazni in the beginning of the 12th century CE. Their remaining army was eventually exiled into northern India.

The Chedis of Tripuri

The state of Chedi was situated between the Narmada and Godavari rivers, and was ruled by the Kalachuri dynasty. Like the Chandellas, the Kalachuris of Chedi (also known as the Kalachuris of Tripuri) were formerly subordinate to the Pratiharas, but around the middle of the 10th century CE, they asserted their independence. They ruled the historical Chedi region (also known as *Dahala-mandala*) with their capital at Tripuri, near modern Jabalpur, M.P. The Kalachuris of Tripuri fought several battles against the Chandellas of Jejakabhukti, and later had matrimonial alliances with them. They also had to defend their territory against the Palas, and a confederacy of the Cholas, Pallavas and the Pandyas.

Kokkala I (c. 845–885 CE)

- He was the founder of the dynasty and undertook many military campaigns. He invaded Northern Konkan and helped the Rashtrakuta king, Krishna II, against the Eastern Chalukyas and the Pratiharas.
- He married a Chandella princess and it is believed that after his death, his eldest son succeeded him on the throne while the others were appointed rulers of different mandalas/provinces. This led to the disintegration of the kingdom, as descendants of one of these founded a separate kingdom in South Kosala with its capital at Tummana.

Yuvaraja (c. 915–945 CE)

- Another important ruler who defeated and drove out the Rashtrakuta forces. In order to celebrate this great victory, the famous poet Rajasekara staged his drama *Viddhasalabhanjika*.
- The Kalachuri inscription credits *Yuvaraja with successful raids against Kashmir and the Himalayan region*.

Lakshmanaraja (around the third quarter of the 10th century CE)

- He was also a great conqueror as he not only invaded and defeated Vangala (south Bengal), and the Somavamsi king of South Kosala, but he also invaded Lata in the west, then ruled over by a feudatory of the Rashtrakutas, and defeated the king of Gurjara, probably Mularaja I, the founder of the Chalukya dynasty.

Gangeya-deva (c. 1019–1040 CE)

- One of the most important rulers of the Kalachuri dynasty, who, due to his military genius, made the Chedis one of the greatest political powers in India at the time. Owing to his great victories, he assumed the proud title of *Trikalingadhipati* (the Lord of *Trikalinga*) and also assumed the title of *Vikramaditya*.
- Some historians believe that an important factor in Gangeya deva's success was the fact that when most of the other great powers to its north and north-west were affected by the devastating raids of Sultan *Mahmud,* his kingdom never faced any such raid.
- He issued coins of different sizes, weights and metals such as in gold, silver gold, silver, silvery copper (billon) and copper. During his reign, the four-armed Lakshmi, seated cross-legged on the lotus, holding a lotus in the upper two hands, with inscriptions in Nagari script *'Shrimad-Ga/ngeyade/va'* on the reverse side was introduced.

Lakshmi-Karna (c. 1041–1073 CE)

- Also known as the Karna, and like his father was one of the greatest generals of his time. He was more successful than his father not only in the south but also in the north-west and carried his victorious arms along the eastern coast to as far as Kanchi.
- He is said to have defeated many dynasties in the south such as the Pallavas, Kungas, Muralas, Pandyas (South) and Someshvara I.

Yashkarna (c. 1073–1125 CE)

- His reign was marked by a series of invasions as the Chalukyas of Deccan raided his kingdom, and the Paramaras plundered his capital and encamped for some time on the Narmada. He was also defeated by the Chandellas. All these defeats gradually weakened the Kalachuris.

Vijayasimha (c. 1177–1211 CE)

- The last king of the dynasty when Chandella ruler Trailokyavarman conquered nearly the whole of the Kalachuri kingdom, included Baghelkhand and Dahala Mandala.

Towards the beginning of the 12th century CE, the Chedi possessions were also lost to rising dynasties such as the Ganpatis of Warangal, the Yadavas of Devagiri and the Vaghela Rajputs.

The Senas of Bengal

The Sena dynasty was a Hindu dynasty that ruled Bengal for little over a century (c. 1097–1225 CE). The empire at its peak covered much of the north-eastern region of the Indian subcontinent. Earlier, both Bihar and Bengal were under the domination of the Pala dynasty. They called themselves *Brahma Kshatriya*, and unlike the Palas who were Buddhist, the Sena rulers were staunch Hindus. The rulers of the Sena dynasty traced their origin to the south Indian region of Karnataka, as indicated by the Deopara inscription. The Deopara inscription speaks of one of the founders in the South, Samanta Sen, whose successor was Hemanta Sen, the first *of the family to whom royal epithets are given in the family records and who usurped power from the Palas and styled himself king in c. 1095 CE*. His successor, Vijay Sena, helped lay the foundations of the dynasty.

Vijaya Sena (c. 1095–1158 CE)

- Founder of the dynasty who had an unusually long reign of over 60 years, which restored peace and prosperity to Bengal and made a deep impression among its people. He is believed to have taken advantage of the revolt of Samantachakra in the Varendra region during the reign of Mahipala II, and gradually consolidated his position in western Bengal. He ultimately assumed an independent position during the reign of Madanapala.
- He conquered Vanga, defeating Bhojavarman.
- Vijaya Sena had two capitals:
  - Vikrampura
  - Vijaypura
- The famous poet, Sriharsha, composed the *Vijay Prasasti* (Eulogy of Vijay) in memory of Vijay Sena. The Deopara Prashasti is a stone inscription eulogising the Sena kings, particularly Vijaya Sena, composed by the court poet Umapati Dhara. Another inscription, the Barrackpore copper-plate, describes him as *Maharajadhiraja*.

Ballal Sena (c. 1158–1179 CE)

- The best-known Sena ruler who consolidated the kingdom. He conquered Mithila/portions of eastern Bihar. According to a tradition in Bengal, *Ballal Sena's kingdom consisted of the five provinces of Banga, Barendra, Rar, Bagri (possibly a portion of lower Bengal) and Mithila*. He made Nabadwip the capital as well.

- Ballal Sena is associated with the revival of orthodox Hindu practices in Bengal, in particular with the establishment of the reactionary tradition of Kulinism, although there is no historical authenticity to these accounts.
- He married Ramadevi, the princess of the Western Chalukya Empire, which indicates that the Sena rulers maintained close social contact with south India.
- Wrote the *Danasagara* and *Adbhutsagara*.

Lakshamana Sena (c. 1178–1207 CE)

- The military glory of the Sena dynasty reached its climax under Lakshmana Sena, who expanded the Sena Empire to Assam, Odisha, Bihar, and probably to Varanasi as well. He also defeated Jayachandra of the Gahadavalas dynasty.
- Seven copper-plate inscriptions pertaining to his reign describe him *as a great military leader and a patron of learning. His victories over the kings of Gaur, Kamrupa, Kalinga and Kashi* have been mentioned in these inscriptions. He is also said to have erected pillars commemorating his military activities at Puri, Benares and Allahabad. He was the first Bengali ruler to extend his suzerainty beyond Benaras. Some inscriptions found in Gaya shortly after his reign attest to his rule in the Gaya region.
- On his accession, he assumed the title of *Ariraja-Madana-Sankara*. Along with the traditional title of *Gaureswara*, he also assumed the title *Paramvaishnava* in place of the earlier epithet of *Paramaeshwara* used by both Vijay Sena and Ballal Sena. This indicates that Lakshmana Sena was a devout Vaishnav, unlike his father and grandfather, who were proclaimed Shaivas. This is also supported by the fact that all the official proclamations from then on started with an invocation to Narayana.
- Lakshmana Sena's court was adorned by Jayadeva (the famous Vaishanava poet of Bengal and the author of *Geet Govinda*), Dhoyi and Umapati Dhar, among other distinguished poets. His prime minister, Halayudha, was himself a great poet. The king himself was a man of letters and according to tradition, completed the work *Adbhutsagara* begun by his father.
- During the later years of his reign, the disintegration of the Sena kingdom began. South Bengal, Orissa and Kamrupa threw away Sena suzerainty. There were also invasions by Central Asian invaders of Turkish origin and of Islamic faith.

Towards the beginning of the 13th century (around c. 1203–1204 CE), one of the generals of Muhammad Ghori, Muhammad Bin Baktiyar Khalji attacked Nabadwip and invaded Bengal and Bihar and annexed them to the Islmaic empire. He captured north-west Bengal, although eastern Bengal remained under Sena control. However, by the middle of 13th century, the Senas were overthrown by the Deva dynasty.

The Gangas/Chodagangas of Orissa

The Eastern Ganga dynasty, popularly known as the Chodagangas, were a Hindu dynasty. They reigned from the 11th century to the early 15th century at Kalinga, and their kingdom consisted of the whole of the modern-day state of Odisha as well as parts of West Bengal, Andhra Pradesh and Chhattisgarh. Their capital was known by the name Kalinganagara, which is the modern Srimukhalingam in Srikakulam district of Andhra Pradesh bordering Odisha. They are remembered as the builders of the Sun temple at Konark, which is an UNESCO World Heritage site. It is pertinent to note that the Kesaris, who used to rule Orissa before the Gangas, built the Lingaraja temple at Bhubaneshwar.

The dynasty was founded by King Anantavarman Chodaganga[1]. The Eastern Ganga rulers, naturally carried south Indian culture to Odisha, as they hailed from southern India and were matrimonially related to the Chola empire and Eastern Chalukyas. Interestingly, this influence is very well reflected in their currency too. This kingdom prospered through trade and commerce and the wealth was mostly used in the construction of temples.

Anantavarman Chodaganga (c. 1076–1150 CE)

- He assumed the title of *Trikalingadhipathi* in 1076 CE, that is, the ruler of the three Kalingas, which comprises of Kalinga proper (South), Utkal (North) and Kosal (West), and probably was the first king to rule all three divisions of Kalinga.
- He was a religious person as well as a great patron of art and literature. He was credited for having built the famous Jagannath temple of Puri in Odisha.

FIGURE 10.5 Sundial at Konark Sun temple, Puri

[1] He claimed lineage from the Western Ganga Dynasty (that ruled southern parts of modern Karnataka state from the 4th century to the end of the 10th century) and the Chola dynasty.

Narsimhadeva (c. 1238–1264 CE)

- Another important king of this dynasty who constructed the Sun temple of Konark which is an UNESCO World Heritage site.

FIGURE 10.6 Sun Temple at Konark

In the early 15th century, the rule of the dynasty came to end under the reign of King Bhanudeva IV (c. 1414–1434 CE). After the decline of the early Eastern Gangas reign, the Chalukyas of Vengi took control of the region.

Western Chalukyas of Kalyani / Later Western Chalukyas

The Chalukyas who ruled from Kalyani (modern Basavakalyan in Karnataka) between the 10th and the 12th centuries CE are referred to as the Later Western Chalukyas (*please refer to the earlier chapters for a discussion of the Chalukyas of Badami*). Their kingdom included most of western Deccan and southern India. As you may recall that prior to the rise of the Chalukyas of Kalyani, most of Deccan and central India was controlled by the Rashtrakuta empire of Manyakheta for over two centuries, but subsequently in 973 CE, following an invasion of Manyakheta by the Paramaras of Malwa and taking advantage of the confusion caused in the Rashtrakuta ranks by the same, a feudatory of the Rashtrakutas ruling from Bijapur region Taila or Tailapa II, defeated his overlords and made Manyakheta his capital. The dynasty expanded quickly and grew into an empire under Someshvara I, who moved the capital to Kalyani.

Tailapa-II (c. 957–997 CE)

- The founder of the later Western Chalukyas, who with the help of earlier Chalukya family and with the help of the Kadambas[2] not only recovered much of the lost territories of earlier Chalukyas but also consolidated his realm.

Satyasraya (c. 997–1008 CE)

- Taila was succeeded by his son Satyasraya, who defeated the Chola king, Rajaraja, who had invaded Satyasraya's region and thus conquered Rajaraja's territories.
- The successors of Satyasraya were respectively Dasavarman, Vikramaditya V and Jayasimha I (c. 1015–1042 CE). It is pertinent to note that Jayasimha repelled invasions from the north as well as southern invasions from the Chola king, Rajendra.

Someshvara-I (c. 1043–1068 CE)

- The son of Jayasimha, who expelled Rajadhiraja Chola. Some inscriptions state that '*he broke the line of succession of Rajendra Chola by killing him*'.
- According to tradition, it is believed that Someshvara I preferred his second and more able son Vikramaditya as his successor, but the latter declined the honour in favour of the elder son i.e., Somesvara II (c. 1068–1076 CE) and as a general of his brother's army Vikramaditya conquered the Cholas, Kerala and Ceylon. However, Somesvara II soon fell into bad ways and thus lost the loyalty of his brother, following which Vikramaditya started ruling the southern part of the kingdom independently.

Vikramaditya VI (c. 1076–1126 CE)

- The greatest ruler of this dynasty, who earned the title *Permadideva* and *Tribhuvanamalla* (meaning '*lord of three worlds*'.)
- Vikramaditya also received submission from the ruler of Konkan, and soon marched against Vira Rajendra Chola. The latter pled for peace by offering his daughter's hand to Vikramaditya. When Vira Rajendra died, Vikramaditya placed his brother-in-law, Adhi-Rajendra, on the throne of Cholas.
- After his brother-in-law was killed, Vikramaditya was defeated by the Eastern Chalukya king Jayasimha, and was given the governorship of Bellary. However, in c. 1076 CE, Vikramaditya reclaimed his power with the aid of the Hoysalas and ascended the throne as Vikramaditya VI. He introduced Chalukya–Vikrama era in c. 1076 CE.
- During the rule of Vikramaditya VI, the Western Chalukyas convincingly contended with the Cholas. They ruled over territories that spread over most of the Deccan, between the Narmada river in the north and the Kaveri river in the south. He had several queens who ably assisted him in administration.

---

[2] The Kadambas were rewarded with the control over Banavasi and Goa.

- The two great writers, named Bilhana and Vijnaneswara, flourished in the court of Vikramaditya VI. He was the hero of Bilhana's *Vikramankadeva Charitra*. Bilhana came to his court from Kashmir and compared his rule to Ramarajya.
- Vijnaneshwara, the noted jurist in his court, wrote *Mitakshara*, a commentary on *Yagnavalkya Smriti* (on Hindu family law). Of the king he wrote, '*A King like Vikramarka is neither to be seen nor heard of*'.
- Vikramaditya VI was a Shaiva by faith and his rule saw prolific temple-building activity. Notable constructions include the Mallikarjuna temple, the Mahadeva temple, the Kaitabheshvara temple and the Kalleshvara temple.

The next successor, Somesvara III, was more interested in literary matters and thus could not stop Vishnuvardhana Hoysala to grasp the opportunity to declare independence. The later rulers were not very capable either, and gradually the feudatories of the Chalukyas started declaring independence. However, for some brief time under the leadership of Somesvara IV, the son of Taila III, the Chalukyas were able to recover their territory. His suzerainty was acknowledged by many rulers such as the last Kalachuri ruler, Singhana and the Kadambas of both Goa and Banavasi, and the Pandyas of Uchchangi. But with the attack from the Hoysalas under Vira Ballala I and the Yadavas of Devagiri, the later Western Chalukya dynasty came to an end in about c. 1190 CE.

Developments in Art and Architecture, and Science and Technology

The growth in scientific pursuits unfortunately slowed down during this period. The growth of science and technology is linked with the growth of any society. However, as the society during this period became largely rigid and narrow in its outlook, scientific attitudes could not develop as well. As noted by the Central Asian scientist and scholar, Al Biruni, the *insular attitudes of the educated, in particular the Brahmanas, led a tremendous lack in inter-cultural scientific learning and collaboration*. Surgery declined, as the dissection of dead bodies was regarded as fit only for people of low castes such as barbers. Astronomy was now enveloped by astrology.

However, some advances were made in the field of mathematics as the 9th century *Ganitasarasangraha* of Mahaviracharya and the *Lilavati* of Bhaskar II were written during this period (c. 1150 CE), which remained standard text for a long time. Bhaskara II (c. 1114–1185 CE), the greatest mathematician of medieval India and astronomer, was born in Bijapur in modern Karnataka. His main work, the *Siddhanta Shiromani* (Sanskrit for '*Crown of Treatises*') is divided into four parts:

Parts of Siddhanta Shiromani	
(a) *Lilavati*	Deals with arithmetic and covers calculations, progressions, measurement, permutations and other topics.
(b) *Bijaganita*	Deals with algebra, and under this section, Bhaskara discusses concepts such as zero, infinity, positive and negative numbers and indeterminate equations including (the now called) Pell's equation.
(c) *Grahagaita*	Deals with the mathematics of the planets, and while treating the motion of planets, he considers their instantaneous speeds and also arrives at an approximation. Bhaskara accurately defined many astronomical quantities, including, for example, the length of the sidereal year, the time that is required for the Earth to orbit the Sun, as 365.2588 days.
(d) *Goladhyaya*	Deals with mathematics of the spheres.

He also wrote another treatise named the *Karana Kautuhala*. Bhaskara's work on calculus predates Newton and Leibniz by over half a millennium. He was perhaps the first to conceive the differential coefficient and differential calculus and its application to astronomical problems and computations.

In the field of medicine, certain minerals like mercury were discovered. Many books were written on plant sciences and for the treatment of animals, but not much research was done on the inter-breeding of horses and this further resulted in the perennial dependence of Indians on imports of horses from Central Asia.

The system of education, which had gradually developed in the earlier period continued without much change. The concept of mass education did not exist. Reading and writing was confined to a small section of the *Brahmanas* and the upper castes. The main subjects taught were the branches of Vedas and grammar. Education of a more formal kind with greater emphasis on secular subjects continued to be provided at some Buddhist viharas such as Nalanda, Vikramashila and Uddandapura monasteries of Bihar. Kashmir was another prominent centre of education and many Shaiva sects and centres of learning flourished during this period. A number of important *maths* (education centres) were set up at Madurai and Sringeri in south India. The various centres of education provided an impetus to discussions on religion and philosophy.

Religious Movements and Beliefs and Development in Philosophy

This period is marked by the revival and expansion of Hinduism and a continued decline of Buddhism and Jainism. Apart from the intellectual challenge posed to Buddhism and Jainism by the revived Hinduism, at certain occasions there were instances of violence and forcible occupations of their sacred places as well. Buddhism was merely confined to eastern India, specially patronised by the Palas. However, Buddhism during this era assumed forms which made it indistinguishable from Hinduism. Jainism continued to be popular, especially among the trading communities. The Chalukyan rulers of Gujarat patronised Jainism and it was during this time that the famous and magnificent Dilwara temples of Mount Abu were built.

The revival and expansion of Hinduism took many forms. Shiva and Vishnu became chief gods and magnificent temples were built to proclaim their supremacy. This also ushered an era of cultural synthesis. A typical and important characteristic of this period was the growth of the Bhakti movement in South India which was led by popular saints called *Nayannars* (worshippers of Shiva) and *Alvars* (worshippers of Vishnu). In Alvar Bhakti, the relationship between the devotee and Krishna was often expressed in terms of the lover-beloved or mother-child relationship, whereas in Nayannar Bhakti, the relationship between the god and the devotee was similar to that between master and slave. Thus, the Nayannars describe themselves as *atiyar* (servant). From the 7th century onwards, the cult of Bhakti began to dominate the religious life of the South Indians and these saints played a major role in propagating it. The word *Bhakti* comes from the root *bhaj*, which means to share or participate. Thus, the word *'bhakta'* implies one who shares or participates in the divine. These saints rejected austerities and spoke and wrote in local languages such as Tamil and Telugu, which not only made them popular but also allowed common people to join the Bhakti movement. They looked upon religion not as matter of cold, formal worship but based on a living bond between the god and the worshipper. These saints went from place to place carrying their message of love and devotion. They belonged to both upper castes and lower castes and also included women saints. Even though they disregarded the inequalities of caste, they did not oppose the caste system as such. The Bhakti movement, apart from bringing over many Buddhists and Jainas to the Hindu fold, won over many tribals as well.

Another popular movement which arose during the 12th century was the *Lingayat or Vir Shaiva* movement. Its founder was Basava and his nephew Channabasava, who lived at the court of the Kalachuri kings of Karnataka. The Lingayats were worshippers of Shiva and established their faith after bitter disputes with the Jainas. They strongly opposed the caste system and child marriage, and rejected feasts, fasts, pilgrimage and sacrifices. They supported widow remarriage.

It is also pertinent to mention the *Siddhas* (or *Sittars*) of Tamil Nadu, who held contrasting views with the Bhakti tradition, although some of their ideologies are considered to have originated during the first Sangam age. Their attitude against idol worship and their stress on yoga and right conduct distinguished them from the Bhakti cults. They believed in the oneness of the transcendental being (monotheism) in the world as well as in charity towards men. The Siddha saints were mostly Shaiva, who professed and practised an unorthodox type of *sadhana* (spiritual practices) to attain liberation. A *siddha* obtains yogic powers called *siddhi* by constant practice of certain yogic disciplines and *tapasya*. Along with that, they also used *rasayanas*, which were substances that were said to transform the body to make it potentially deathless, and a particular type of *pranayama* (breathing practice). The Siddhas are also believed to be the founders of *Varmam*, a kind of martial art for self-defence and medical treatment simultaneously. *Varmam* are specific points located in the human body, which, when pressed in different ways can give various results, such as disabling an attacker in self-defence, or balancing a physical condition as an easy first-aid medical treatment. The Tamil Siddhas were the first to develop *'naadi paarththal'* (pulse reading) to identify the origin of diseases. It is believed that this method was later adopted and used in Ayurveda.

In the period that the Bhakti movement was gaining popularity in south India, Tantra was gaining traction in northern India. They too denounced the caste system and the privileges claimed by the *Brahmanas*. Tantra, like Bhakti, was open to all. The most famous Hindu Yogi who adopted these practices was Goraknath and his followers came to be called *Nath Panthis*.

Many schools of philosophy came into existence in this period. *Moksha* (salvation) became the main subject of the *darshana* schools. Hindu philosophy is generally classified into six orthodox or classical schools (*astika*) and three heterodox (*nastika*) schools. The basic difference between these two branches of philosophy schools is based on the recognition of the Vedas: the orthodox[3] schools recognise the authority of the Vedas, while the heterodox schools do not believe in the authority of Vedas. Out of these nine systems, eight are atheistic as there is no place for God in them and only the Uttara Mimansa, which is also called Vedanta, has a place for God in it.

By the beginning of Christian era, six prominent schools of philosophy (*shatdarshan*) developed which are *Samkhya*, *Yoga*, *Nyaya*, *Vaisheshik*, *Purva Mimansa and Uttar Mimansa* (*Vedanta*):

Schools of Philosophy	
(a) *Samkhya*	Literally means 'count'. Oldest school of philosophy, founded by Kapila. • Samkhya is strongly dualist as its philosophy regards the universe as consisting of two realities, *Purusha* (consciousness) and *Prakriti* (matter), which is further composed of three basic gunas (elements), namely, *Tamas*, *Rajas and Sattva*. Purush cannot be modified or changed while prakriti brings change in all objects. • According to this school, a person can attain salvation through the acquisition of real knowledge and his participation in the life cycle can be ended forever. This knowledge can be acquired through *pratyaksha* (perception), *anumanya* (inference) and *shabda* (hearing). • Emphasises that it is self-knowledge that leads to liberation and not any exterior influence or agent. Self-knowledge can be attained by the means of concentration and meditation. • Samkhya forms the philosophical basis for Yoga. In Samkhya, the necessity of God is not felt for epistemological clarity about the interrelationship between higher self, individual self and the universe around us. According to this philosophy, the presence of divine agency is not essential for the creation of the world as the world owes its creation and evolution more to the nature or Prakriti than to God.

[3] Orthodox (Astika) schools, originally called Sanatana Dharma, are collectively referred to as Hinduism in modern times.

Schools of Philosophy	
(b) *Yoga*	The Yoga school founded by Patanjali, which presents a practical path for the realisation of the self-based on the method of physical and mental discipline by releasing *Purusha* from *Prakriti*. • Practice of control over pleasure, senses and bodily organs is central theme of this school. • In order to attain salvation, physical exercises in various *asanas* (postures) and *pranayama* (breathing exercises) are prescribed. It is believed that through these exercises, the mind gets diverted from worldly matters and achieves concentration. Yoga describes energy flowing through energy channels and concentrated in *chakras*. – *Hatha Yoga*: Hatha Yoga is about creating a body which is not a hurdle in one's life. The body becomes a stepping stone – not a hurdle, not a roadblock – in one's progress. – *Raja Yoga*: Classical yoga and *Astanga yoga* is a form of meditation which enriches the mind, wherein it is trained to stay focused at one point. It aims at the calming of the mind using a succession of steps, ultimately culminating in *samadhi*. • Yoga does not require belief in God, although such a belief is accepted as help in initial stage of mental concentration and control of mind. It thus admits the existence of God as a teacher and guide.
(c) *Nyaya*	Also known as School of Analysis, which developed as a system of logic by Gautama. Its principles are mentioned in *Nyaya Sutras*. • Nyaya philosophy believes in the supremacy of logic and adopts a scientific approach as it holds that nothing is acceptable unless it is in accordance with reason and experience. • Nyaya states that the world is real and the philosophy does not follow a monist view. • This school advocates the theory of *pramanas* (proofs), which are the means of obtaining true knowledge. According to it, the *pradhan pramana* or principal means of obtaining knowledge is *pratyaksha pramana* (knowledge obtained through the five senses). There are also other pramanas like *anumana* (inference, through which we can obtain true knowledge) and *shabda pramana* (a statement of an expert). • Many later philosophers claimed to belong to this school. For instance, Vatsyayan (who wrote *Nyaya Bhashya*), Udayan (who wrote *Kusumanjali*), and so on.
(d) *Vaisheshika*	This school propounded by Kannada gives importance to discussion of *dravya* or material elements. • This school propounded the atomic theory and can be marked as the beginning of the physics in ancient India. Earth, water, fire, air and ether (sky) are the aggregates, which combined give rise to new objects. • It signifies a realistic and objective way of looking at the universe.

Schools of Philosophy	
(e) *Mimamsa*	Also called *Purva Mimamsa* which literally signifies the art of reasoning and interpretation. • According to Mimamsa, the Vedas contain the eternal truth. In order to attain salvation, it strongly recommends the performance of *yagya* (Vedic sacrifices), which needed the services of the priests and legitimised the social distance between the different varnas. • This philosophy relies on the *Brahmanas* and the *Samhitas* of the Vedas. It is often argued that the *Brahmanas* wanted to maintain their ritual authority and preserve social hierarchy through the propagation of Mimamsa.
(f) *Vedanta*	Also known as *Uttara Mimamsa*. Vedanta signifies the end of the Veda. The *Brahmaputra* of Badarayana compiled in the 2nd century BCE formed its basic text. • According to Vedanta, the world is *Maya* (illusion) and there is only one reality, *Brahman*. Therefore, it lays emphasis on *brahmagyan*, and relies on the Upanishads. While Purva Mimamsa discusses the fire sacrifices of the Vedic rituals in the Samhitas and the Brahmanas, Vedanta throws light on the esoteric teachings of the Aranyakas (the forest scriptures) and the Upanishads. • Vedanta has its roots in Samkhya philosophy. The self or the *atman* (soul) is identical with *brahman*, and hence if a person acquires the knowledge of the self, he acquires the knowledge of brahman and thus attains salvation. • Both *brahman* and *atman* are eternal and indestructible. • The theory of *karma* is closely linked to Vedanta philosophy, which signifies that in his present birth a person has to bear the consequences of his actions performed in his previous birth. • The core message of Vedanta is that every action must be governed by the discriminating faculty that is the intellect. The mind can make mistakes, but the intellect lets us know if the action is in our interest or not. • The main traditions of Vedanta are: – Bhedabheda (difference and non-difference) by Nimbarka – Advaita (non-dualism) by Adi Shankaracharya. – Vishishtadvaita (qualified non-dualism) by Nathamuni, Yamuna and Ramanuja. – Tattvavada (Dvaita or dualism) by Madhvacharya. – Shuddhadvaita (pure non-dualism) by Vallabha. – Achintya-Bheda-Abheda (inconceivable difference and non-difference) by Chaitanya Mahaprabhu.

- Some of the prominent sub-branches for Vedanta are:
  - Absolute Monism or Advaita/non-dualist Vedanta of Shankara: Shankara was a major proponent of Vedanta in the 9th century. He considers *brahman* to be without any attributes and considers knowledge or *jnana* to be the chief means of salvation. Shankara argues that the *atman* is completely identical with *brahman*. He believed in only one reality. According to Shankara, *the atman experiences a false sense of*

plurality and individuality under the influence of the delusive power of maya. While maya has the ambiguous ontological status of being neither real nor unreal, the only true reality is *brahman* which is pure consciousness, eternal and unchanging. According to him, God and the created world are one and differences arise due to ignorance. He identifies two levels of reality – conventional reality and absolute reality. For instance, *he explains that a person looks at a coiled rope and thinks that it is a snake*. The rope seems like a real snake but it is not. Thus, ignorance is the reason for this mistake of taking conventional reality for absolute reality. The way for salvation is devotion to God and understanding the oneness of the atman with the brahman.

- *Visistadvaita Advaita* or qualified monism/non-dualism of Ramanuja: Ramanuja wrote a commentary on Vedanta in 12th century and combined Vaishnava *bhakti* with Upanishadic monism. He identifies the brahman with Vishnu, holding that *brahman* is *saguna* (possesses attributes), in contrast to Sankara's attributeless or *nirguna brahman*. The road to salvation lies in practising devotion or loving faith. Ramanuja asserts that the relationship between *brahman* and the *atman* is similar to relationship of a red rose and redness. *Just as the red rose cannot exist without redness, similarly brahman cannot exist without the atman*. Hence, according to Ramanuja, *atman* and *brahman* are distinct but inseparable.

- Dvaita of Madhva: The Dvaita or dualist school of Hindu Vedanta philosophy originated in 13th century South India with Sri Madhvacharya (Madhva). Madhva wrote commentaries on the Brahmasutra and Upanishads, and a work called the *Bharatatatparyanirnaya*, based on the *Puranas* and the epics. He considers God to be completely different from the individual soul and the world. He asserts that the individual soul has many defects, but it can attain near perfection by worshipping God. According to him, the relationship between God and the soul can best be described as a relationship between the master and servant. Madhva and his followers call their system *tattvavada* (the realist viewpoint). Madhva maintains that *even though living beings and inert matter are dependent upon brahman, such dependence differentiates them from Him and makes them discrete entities* (*tattvas*). Thus, reality in Madhva's system consists of three basic elements: God, the souls (*jivasi*) and insentient matter (*jada*). He views Vishnu as preeminent above all other deities on the basis of his unique characteristics.

It is interesting to note that the first four classical schools are not entirely based on Vedas but the last two, the Mimamsa and Vedanta, certainly rely on the Vedas.

Heterodox Schools of Indian Philosophy

Heterodox schools or unorthodox (*nastika*) schools of Indian philosophy do not accept the authority of the Vedas. Apart from the Buddhist and Jain philosophy, the following are the heterodox schools:

Charvaka School /Lokayata Philosophy

Its founder was Charvaka, the author of the *Barhaspatya Sutras* in the final centuries before the Common Era. It is characterised as a materialistic and atheistic school of thought. Lokayata refers to ideas derived from common people and it underlines the importance of intimate contact with the world (*loka*), while showing a lack of belief in the other world. It accepts direct perception as the surest method to prove the truth of anything. It thus recognises earth, water, fire and air, but not ether, as it cannot be known by perception. Charvaka insists on joyful living and is opposed to the quest for spiritual salvation. He denies the existence of any divine or supernatural agency and accepts the existence/reality of only those things which could be experienced by human senses organs. Thus, there was a clear lack of faith in the existence of *brahman* and God. According to Charvaka, the *Brahmanas* manufactured rituals for acquiring *dakshina* (gifts). Sanskrit poems and plays like the *Naisadha-carita, Prabodha-chandrodaya, Agama-dambara, Vidvanmoda-tarangini and Kadambari* contain representations of the Charvaka thought. The school is also mentioned in the works of Shatdarshan Samuchay and Sarvadarsanasangraha of Vidyaranya.

Ajivika School

It was founded by Gosala Maskariputra and is famous for its Niyati ("Fate") doctrine of absolute fatalism or determinism. According to this school, '*there is no reason or cause for the depravity of things; they deprave without reason or cause. There is also no cause for the purity of beings; they become pure without reason or cause.*' The Digha Nikaya, Anguttara Nikaya, Samyutta Nikaya, Sutrakritanga-sutra, Shilanka's commentary on the Sutrakritanga-sutra, Bhagavati-sutra, Nandi-sutra, and Abhayadeva's commentary on Samavayanga-sutra are considered to be its primary sources of knowledge. The oldest descriptions of the Ajivika fatalists and their founder, Gosala, can also be found in ancient Buddhist and Jaina scriptures.

Ajnana School

Founded by Sanjaya Belatthiputta, this school philosophy revolves around the notion that it is impossible to obtain knowledge of metaphysical nature or ascertain the truth value of philosophical propositions, and even if knowledge was possible, it was useless and disadvantageous for final salvation. The Ajanas viewpoints are recorded in Theravada Buddhism's Pali Canon in the Brahmajala Sutta, Samannaphala Sutta, and the Suyagadamga of Jainism.

The Islamic Conquest of North India and the Gangetic Plains

Rise and Spread of Islam

In the 7th century CE, a new religion called Islam was founded in Arabia by Muhammad (c. 570–632 CE), an Arab merchant from the city of Mecca who would later be known as the Prophet Muhammad. In a very short span of time, Islam carved out an empire extending from North Africa to the Iberian Peninsula, to Iran and India. This religion transformed the religious, political and social life, not only of the people of Arabia but also of many other parts of the world. Islam lays an emphasis upon the belief in one God (Allah) and its holy book, the Quran, which is considered as the supreme authority in Islam as, according to Muslims, it was revealed by Allah to the Prophet Muhammad. Every Muslim is asked *to pray five times a day, to fast during the month of Ramzan (or Ramadhan), to distribute alms and to make a pilgrimage to Mecca once in their lives*, if possible.

A Brief History of Islam

In c. 610 CE, Prophet Muhammad found himself receiving messages from Allah, and learned that he was a prophet in the same line as Moses and Jesus Christ. According to tradition, one morning Prophet Muhammad heard the voice of the angel Gabriel and, through him, Allah spoke words of wisdom. The words were first recited by Prophet Muhammad, later his disciples, and were later on recorded as text which came to be known as the Holy Quran. At first, the pagan Arabs were tolerant, but gradually, when the influence of Prophet Muhammad began to rise, they began to regard him and his followers with disdain and placed a trade embargo on them. Prophet was ridiculed in public. The slaves who followed him were beaten by their pagan masters who forced Prophet Muhammad and his followers to emigrate north to the oasis town of Medina in c. 622 CE, where they were welcomed by the local pagan and Jewish tribes. The year c. 622 CE is also known as the year of the *hijra*, or 'emigration', which also marks the beginning of the Muslim calendar. Just two year later, in c. 624 CE, a decisive battle known as the Battle of Badr was fought between Muslims led by Prophet Muhammad and the merchant caravans of the pagan Arabs. This was the first major battle in the Muslim conquest of Arabia and with gradual increasing influence of Prophet Muhammad, the Muslims expanded their territorial control over the area to the north of Medina till c. 628 CE. In c. 630 CE, Prophet Muhammad conquered his hometown of Mecca and over the next two years, sent his armies all over Western Arabia to conquer the remaining Pagan tribes.

After the death of the Prophet in c. 632 CE, the task of providing religious and political leadership to the Muslims passed on to the Caliphs (Islamic leaders) known as the Rashidun (rightly guided). The word Caliph is derived from the Arabic word 'Khalifa', which means 'deputy', and the title was given to the rulers who succeeded Prophet Muhammad. Between c. 632 and 661 CE, there were four pious Caliphs, all close companions of the Prophet. The first of these companions to be appointed

Caliph was Abu Bakr, who was one of Prophet Muhammad's father-in-law and had been the first man after Muhammad to convert to Islam. Abu Bakr's first task was to suppress a rebellion in Arabia (Wars of Apostasy) that had been started by various Arab tribes who had renounced their conversion to Islam after the death of the Prophet. Once these wars were completed, Abu-Bakr reunited the Arabian Peninsula and began the invasion of the two major superpowers of the region, the Byzantine Empire of the Mediterranean, and the Sassanid Empire of Persia. Both of these empires were in a weak state, having been in almost continuous war with each other for an entire century and were unable to mount much effective resistance. Abu Bakr died in c. 634 CE and the leadership passed to the next Caliph Umar, another early convert to Islam who had spent 17 years by Muhammad's side. During the Caliphate of Umar, Muslim armies conquered almost the entire Middle East, including the Levant, Egypt, and much of Persia. The rest of Persia was conquered under the reigns of the two subsequent Rashidun Caliphs, Uttman and Ali.

The Umayyad Caliphate (c. 661–750 CE) succeeded the pious Caliphs. The Umayyad dynasty gave stability and prosperity to the Caliphate and was followed by the Abbasid Caliphate (c. 750–1258 CE). During the time of later Abbasids, the Caliphs began to loose political control and independent Sultans (Muslim rulers) emerged in several regions.

The Age of Conflict (c. 1000–1200 CE)

The period from c. 1000 to 1200 CE witnessed many changes both in West and Central Asia, and in northern India as well. The continuous incursions of the Turkish tribesmen from central Asia, the mercenary character of the Turkish soldiers who switched loyalties often and the strife between the different Muslim sects and between the different regions made the period restless and gave it the tag of the 'age of conflict'. Towards the end of this period, there were a series of incursions of the Turks into northern India.

As a part of the expansion policy of the Umayyad Caliphate, the invasions started as early as the 8th century in India. Moreover, Arabs were also attracted by the wealth promised by India, since Arab merchants and sailors boasted of the great wealth of the Indian territories that they had witnessed in their journeys. In c. 712 CE, Arabs invaded India from the north-west region (Sindh) under Muhammad bin Qasim, who was a general of the Umayyad caliphate. However, the reason for the invasion of Sindh was to avenge the plunder of Arab ships by the pirates of Debal. When King Dahir refused to punish the pirates, Hajjaj (the governor of Iraq) dispatched an army under his nephew and son-in-law Muhammad bin Qasim. He arrived in Sind in c. 712 CE, and besieged Debal, which was situated on the sea coast. Then he annexed Nerun (Hyderabad) and Siwistan (Sehwan), followed by a decisive victory over King Daher at the fort of Raor near his capital Alor. Subsequently, Alor, Brahmanabad and Multan (near Indus river and parts of lower Punjab) were taken. The invading Arabs also killed a large number of fleeing soldiers. This military conquest is mentioned in the *Chachnama*, which is an early 13th century Persian translation of an old Arabic history of bin Qasim. Though his rule lasted only for two years, yet it greatly disturbed the economic life of Sindh and a large number of people and merchants fled from Sindh. However, many Arabs settled down in Sindh and the Arab influence continued for a long period.

The Ghaznavids and Mahmud of Ghazni

By the end of the 9th century CE, the Abbasid Caliphate was in decline and a large number of states under Islamised Turks were beginning to emerge. It is interesting to note that during the 9th century, the Turks had entered the Abbasid empire as palace guards and mercenary soldiers but they soon emerged as king-makers. These new rulers assumed title of *amir ul umra* (commander of commanders) at first, and later, Sultan. Towards the end of the 9th century, Trans Oxiana, Khorasan and parts of Iran were being ruled by the Samanids, who were Iranians by descent. The Samanids had frequent battles with Turkish tribesmen on their northern and eastern frontiers. It was during this struggle that a new type of soldiers known as the Ghazi emerged, who were fighters as well as missionaries. They acted as auxiliaries of the regular armies, and in lieu of regular salaries took recourse to plunder. The Ghazis took on the Turks in tough battles. In the course of time, many Turks became Muslims themselves, and these Islamised Turkish tribes emerged as the greatest defenders and crusaders of Islam.

In the 9th and 10th centuries, most of Afghanistan was under the control of the Samanids. Among the Samanid governors was a Turkish slave, Alptagin, who started as the governor of Balkh and in course of time established an independent Turkish dynasty with its capital at Ghazni, Afghanistan. He was succeeded by his slave and son-in-law, Subuktagin, who established his own rule in Ghazni in 977 CE. The Samanid kingdom soon ended, and the Ghaznavids took over the task of defending the Islamic lands from the central Asian tribesmen. In these circumstances, Subuktagin's son Mahmud ascended the throne (c. 998–1030 CE) at Ghazni (the present day South Kabul). He was 27 years old then, and the first ruler to get the title of 'Sultan'. Due to his stout defence against the central Asian Turkish tribal invaders, he was considered a hero of the Islamic people by medieval Muslim historians. He was also closely associated with the renaissance of the Persian (Iranian) spirit. In fact, Persian renaissance writer Firdausi was the poet laureate at the court of Mahmud, who glorified the ancient Iranian heroes. The Persian language and culture now became the language and culture of the Ghaznavid empire. Even Mahmud himself claimed descent from the legendary Iranian king, Afrasiyab. Thus, the Turks became not only Islamised but Persianised too. However, while Mahmud played an important role in the defence of the Islamic states against the Turkish tribes and in the Persian cultural renaissance, he plundered and destroyed Indian territory during his invasions.

Muhammad bin Qasim (c. 712 CE)

↓ – First Muslim invader who invaded Sindh.

The Ghaznavids Subuktagin (c. 977–998 CE)

- Hindu Shahi king, Jayapala, who held territories extending from Punjab and modern Afghanistan, was first to realise the danger posed by the Ghaznanids. He thus invaded Ghazni in alliance with the son of the former governor of Ghazni, but he had to suffer defeat and Subuktagin succeeded in forcing him into a humiliating treaty.

Mahmud of Ghazni (c. 998–1030 CE)

- During the period between c. 1000–1027 CE, he attacked India 17 times. He started his invasions in India during the period when the Rajput power had declined. The main reasons behind conquest of India by Mahmud Ghazni were:
  - Firstly, to accumulate the vast amount of wealth that existed in India. With the help of that wealth, he wanted to transform Ghazni, his capital city, into a region of formidable power in the entire central Asia. Also, with the help of his plundered wealth from India, he continued his struggle against his enemies in central Asia. As a matter of fact, his raids into India alternated with his battles in central Asia.
  - Secondly, to spread Islam and to destroy Hindu temples. In fact, he is also known as *shikan* or destroyer of images.
  - He also did not want to give time to the rulers in India to regroup and combine against him.
- It has been analysed that he always attacked India during the hot summer season. With the onset of monsoons, he would go back to Ghazni, probably to avoid the flooding rivers of Punjab so that his forces would not get trapped there.
- In c. 1000 CE, he first invaded modern Afghanistan and Pakistan and defeated the Hindu Shahi ruler Jayapala in the Battle of Waihind. It is believed that Jayapala burnt himself in the funeral pyre, unable to bear his disgrace.
- In the years c. 1004–1006 CE, Mahmud of Ghazni attacked the rulers of Multan.
- In c. 1008 CE, the Second Battle of Waihind between Mahmud of Ghazni and Anandapala (son of Jayapala) was fought near Peshawar. Even though Anandapala was supported by the Sultan of Multan and many princes of north-western India, like the rulers of Kannauj and Rajasthan and the *Khokhars* (a brave war tribe of Punjab), and despite his forces being numerically larger, he lost the war. One of the major reasons behind Mahmud's success was his fast moving cavalry, in comparison to the slow Indian troops, which were mainly driven by elephants. Strategically, he annexed Punjab to have easy access to India.
- In c. 1014 CE, Mahmud took Thaneshwar (near Delhi) and burnt the temple of Mathura.
- In c. 1018 CE, he sacked Kannauj by defeating its Chandella king, Vidhyadhara. In the same year he defeated and killed two more rulers, Hindu Shahi Trilochanapala and his son Bhimapala, thereby conquering Rahib and Lahore.

- In c. 1025 CE (his 16th expedition), he plundered the Somnath temple dedicated to Shiva in Kathiawar, Saurashtra. Mahmud captured the city after grim struggle, in which more than 50,000 defenders lost their lives. It is pertinent to note that Mahmud left Somnath after a fortnight when he came to know that the Chalukayan ruler of Gujarat, Bhima I, had completed preparations to confront him. It was Bhima I who repaired the Somnath temple.
- In c. 1026 CE, he returned and punished Jats for colluding against him.
- He patronised three important people:
  - Al Biruni – The scholar from central Asia, and the composer of the *Kitab-ul-Hind.*
  - Firdausi – The Persian poet called the *Homer of the East*, writer of the *Shahnama.*
- tbi – The court historian of Mahmud of Ghazni, writer of the *Kitab-ud-Yamni.*

In c. 1030 CE, Mahmud died, and following his death a powerful empire called the Seljuk empire came into being. This empire included Syria, Iran and Trans-Oxiaea, and contended with the Ghaznavids for the control of Khorasan. In a famous battle, Masud, the son of Mahmud, was completely defeated and he had to flee to Lahore for refuge. The Ghaznavid empire was now confined to Ghazni and the Punjab. Although the Ghaznavids continued to make plundering raids into the Gangetic valley and Rajputana, they were no longer in a position to pose a serious threat to India. In the field of culture, a process of interaction between Islam and Hindu religion and society started. Lahore emerged as a centre of Arabic and Persian languages. Muslim traders helped in augmenting the India's trade with the central and west Asian countries. Muslim religious preachers called the Sufis emerged during this era, who preached the message of love and humanity to all and were widely respected by both Hindus and Muslims.

Though the 17 invasions of India undertaken by Ghazni did not show any systematic effort to conquer the subcontinent, yet they proved very costly to Indian subcontinent. They not only exposed the inherent military weaknesses of Indian rulers but Ghazni's conquests, especially with the inclusion of Punjab and Afghanistan in his kingdom, made the Indian frontiers weak. His conquest opened the gates of India to be conquered from the north-west and this made it easier for other Afghan and Turkish rulers to enter India into the Gangetic valley at any time. One such ruler was Muhammad Ghori.

The Ghurid Dynasty and Muhammad Ghori

Many historians assert that the actual founder of the Islamic Empire in India was Shahabuddin Muhammad (also known as Mui'zz ud-din Muhammad bin Sam), popularly called Muhammad Ghori, who was the Sultan of the Ghurid empire along with his brother Ghiyath ud-din from c. 1173–1202 CE, and the supreme ruler of the Ghurid empire from c. 1202–1206 CE. He was one of the greatest rulers of the Ghurid dynasty, and is credited with laying the foundation of Muslim rule not only in India but also in South Asia, that lasted for several centuries. His kingdom included parts of modern-day Afghanistan, Bangladesh, Iran, India, Pakistan, Tajikistan and Turkmenistan.

Brief background of Ghurid Dynasty

We had just discussed about the establishment of the Seljuk empire which eclipsed the Ghaznavids. However, towards the middle of the 12th century, another group of Turkish tribesmen who were partly pagan and partly Buddhist, shattered the power of the Seljuk Turks. In this vacuum, two new powers rose to prominence, the Khwarizmi empire based in Iran and the Ghurid empire based in Ghur in north-west Afghanistan. It is pertinent to note that though the Ghurids had started as vassals of Ghazni, they soon overpowered them. The power of the Ghurids further increased under Sultan Alauddin who earned the title of *jahan-soz* (the world burner) since he ravaged Ghazni and burnt it to ground in revenge for the treatment that had been meted out to his brothers at Ghazni. Interestingly, the rising power of the Khwarizmi empire severely limited the central Asian ambition of the Ghurids as Khorasan (in western Asia), which was the bone of contention between the two, was soon conquered by Khwarizm Shah and thus the Ghurids were left with no option but to look for the expansion towards India.

In c. 1173 CE, Muhammad Ghori ascended the throne at Ghazni while his elder brother was ruling at Ghur. Ghori, being a very ambitious ruler, was thus naturally not satisfied with only Ghazni and wanted to expand his empire to get hold of more power and control. Being well aware of India's political, religious, social and military weaknesses, the desire to spread Islam in India and also the enormous wealth that India had, he thought of winning India. Thus, for all these reasons, he carried out a number of invasions to establish his rule over India. It is pertinent to note that unlike Mahmud of Ghazni, Muhammad Ghori was very much keen in establishing a permanent empire in India and not merely looting its wealth. His campaigns were well organised and whenever he conquered any territory, he left a general behind to govern it in his absence. His invasions resulted in the permanent establishment of the Turkish Sultanate in the region lying north of the Vindhya mountains. However, *as a warrior Mahmud of Ghazni was a more successful one, as he never suffered defeat in India or central Asia while Muhammad Ghori's political achievements in India were greater than that of Mahmud.* However, the political and military motives of the two were very different.

Mohd. Ghori (c. 1173–1206 CE)

- Real founder of the Islamic empire in India. There were as many as seven major invasions of Muhammad Ghori against India, and mostly he emerged as the winner.
- Conquest of Multan and Upper Sindh (c. 1175–1178 CE): In c. 1175 CE, he led his first expedition against Multan, which was largely successful. In the same campaign, he captured Uchch (in Upper Sindh) from the Bhatti Rajputs and established a fort there.

- Conquest of Gujarat (c. 1178 CE): Three years later, he again marched to conquer Gujarat but Solanki Bhima II, the Chalukya ruler of Gujarat defeated him at the battle of Kayadara (near to Mount Abu, about forty miles to the north-east of Anhilwara, the capital of Gujarat). However, undeterred at his defeats Muhammad Ghori did realise the necessity of creating a suitable base in Punjab before venturing on the further conquest of India.
- Conquest of Punjab and Lahore (c. 1179–1186 CE): He thus launched a campaign against the Ghaznavid possessions in Punjab. Consequently, he conquered Peshawar c. 1179 CE, Sindh in c. 1182 CE, Punjab and Lahore in c. 1186 CE. Thus by c. 1190 CE, Muhammad Ghori had secured Multan, Sindh and Punjab and was paving his way for a further thrust into the Gangetic Doab.
- First Battle of Tarain (c. 1191 CE): Ghori's possession of Punjab and his attempt to advance into the Gangetic Doab thus brought him into direct conflict with the iconic Rajput ruler, Prithivaraja Chauhan, who also wanted to extend his control over Punjab and Ganga valley after overrunning many small states in Rajputana, and capturing Delhi. The conflict started with claims of *Tabarhinda* (Bhatinda). In the first battle fought at Tarain (a place near Karnal in the present Haryana), Ghori's narrowly escaped death and his army was routed. Prithviraj conquered Bhatinda but did the mistake of not garrisoning it effectively which gave Ghori an opportunity to re-assemble his forces and make preparations for another advance into India.
- Second Battle of Tarain (c. 1192 CE): This battle is regarded as one of the turning points in Indian history, as Prithviraj Chauhan was defeated and Ghori emerged successful. Interestingly, the Indian forces were more in number but Turkish forces under Ghori were well organised with swift-moving cavalry. The bulky Indian forces were no match against the superior organisation, skill and speed of the Turkish cavalry. It is pertinent to note that the Turkish cavalry used two superior technologies, namely the use of horse shoes (which gave their horses a long life and protected their hooves) and the use of iron stirrups (which gave a good hold to the horse rider and a better striking power in the battle). A large number of Indian soldiers were killed. Prithviraj escaped, but was captured near Saraswati. He was allowed to rule over Ajmer for some time as the coins pertaining to this period bear legend *'Prithvirajadeva'* on one side and the words *'Sri Muhammad Sam'* on the other. However, soon after, Prithviraj was executed on the charges of conspiracy.
- Capture of Delhi and Ajmer: The Turkish army captured the fortresses of Hansi, Saraswati, Samana, Delhi and Ajmer.
- Battle of Chandwar (c. 1194 CE): Ghori defeated Jaichandra (the ruler of Kannauj) of the Gahadavalas dynasty. Thus, the battles of Tarain and Chandwar laid the foundations of Turkish rule in northern India. After this invasion, Qutab-ud-din Aibak was made the viceroy of Muhammad Ghori. After this, Ghori returned to Ghazni to carry out his

conquests in the western frontiers, leaving the affairs of India in the hands of his trusted slave general Qutab-ud-din Aibak, who continued his conquests in India.

- Conquests of Gujarat, Bundelkhand, Bengal and Bihar (c. 1195–1202 CE): In c. 1195 CE, Qutab-ud-din Aibak captured Aligarh and Ranthambore. He also attacked Bhima II, the Solanki king of Gujarat who defeated Aibak. Aibak, however, prevailed in his next battle with Bhima II and thus conquered Gujarat. He next conquered Bundelkhand, ruled by the Chandella Rajputs.
- Simultaneously, Muhammad Bakhtiyar Khalji (another general of Muhammad Ghori) conquered Bihar in 1197 CE and Bengal in 1202 CE and destroyed the universities of Nalanda and Vikramshila. Khalji thus became the *viceroy of Bengal* and *Bihar*.
- Revolt of Khokhars (c. 1205 CE): Ghori had to again come to India to crush the revolt of the Khokhars.
- However, in 1206 CE, Ghori was killed by someone near Dhamyak district of Jhelum (now in Pakistan) while going back to Ghazni. The reign of India passed on to *Aibak*, who laid the foundation of the Slave Dynasty.

QUESTIONS FROM LAST YEAR'S PRELIMS

1. Consider the following dynasties: **(2023)**

1. Hoysala
2. Gahadavala
3. Kakatiya
4. Yadava

How many of the above dynasties established their kingdoms in the early eighth century AD? **(2022)**

(a) Only one (b) Only two
(c) Only three (d) None

2. The world's second tallest statue in sitting pose of Ramanuja was inaugurated by the Prime Minister of India at Hyderabad recently. Which one of the following statements correctly represents the teachings of Ramanuja? **(2022)**

(a) The best means of salvation was devotion.
(b) Vedas are eternal, self-existent and wholly authoritative.
(c) Logical arguments were essential means for the highest bliss
(d) Salvation was to be obtained through meditation.

3. Consider the following pairs: **(2022)**

King	Dynasty
1. Nannuka	Chandela
2. Jayashakti	Paramara
3. Nagabhata II	Gurjara-Pratihara
4. Bhoja	Rashtrakuta

How many pairs given above are correctly matched:

(a) Only one pair
(b) Only two pairs
(c) Only three pairs
(d) All four pairs

4. With reference to the cultural history of medieval India, consider the following statements: **(2016)**

i. Siddhas (Sittars) of Tamil region were monotheistic and condemned idolatry.

ii. Lingayats of Kannada region questioned the theory of rebirth and rejected the caste hierarchy.

Which of the statement(s) given above is/are correct?

(a) i only (b) ii only
(c) Both i and ii (d) Neither i nor ii

5. Consider the following pairs: **(2016)**

Famous place	Region
(i) Bodhgaya	Baghelkhand
(ii) Khajuraho	Bundelkhand
(iii) Shirdi	Vidarbha
(iv) Nasik	Malwa
(v) Tirupati	Rayalaseema

Which of the pairs given above are correctly matched?

(a) i, ii and iv (b) ii, iii, iv and v
(c) ii and v only (d) i, iii, iv and v

6. Which one of the following pairs does not form part of the six systems of Indian Philosophy? **(2014)**

(a) Mimamsa and Vedanta
(b) Nyaya and Vaisheshika
(c) Lokayata and Kapalika
(d) Samkhya and Yoga

7. Consider the following statements: **(2014)**

(i) 'Bijak' is a composition of the teachings of Saint Dadu Dayal.

(ii) The Philosophy of Pushti Marg was propounded by Madhvacharya.

Which of the statement(s) given above is/are correct?

(a) i only (b) ii only
(c) Both i and ii (d) Neither i nor ii

8. With reference to the history of philosophical thought in India, consider the following statements regarding Samkhya school: **(2013)**

(i) Samkhya does not accept the theory of rebirth or transmigration of soul.

(ii) Samkhya holds that it is the self-knowledge that leads to liberation and not any exterior influence or agent.

Which of the statements given above is/are correct?

(a) i only (b) ii only
(c) Both i and ii (d) Neither i nor ii

9. Why did Buddhism start to decline in India in the early medieval times? **(2010)**

(i) Buddha was by that time considered as one of the incarnations of Vishnu and thus became a part of Vaishnavism.

(ii) The invading tribes from Central Asia till the time of the last Gupta king adopted Hinduism and persecuted Buddhists.

(iii) The kings of Gupta dynasty were strongly opposed to Buddhism.

Which of the statement(s) given above is/are correct?

(a) i only (b) i and iii only
(c) ii and iii only (d) i, ii and iii

10. Match List I with List II and select the correct answer using the code given below the lists: **(2009)**

List I (Famous Temple)	List II (State)
(a) Vidhyashankara temple	i. Andhra Pradesh
(b) Rajarani temple	ii. Karnataka
(c) Kendriya Mahadeo temple	iii. Madhya Pradesh
(d) Bhimesvara temple	iv. Orissa

Code:	A	B	C	D
(a)	ii	iv	iii	i
(b)	ii	iii	iv	i
(c)	i	iv	iii	ii
(d)	i	iii	iv	ii

11. Which one of the following sequences indicates the correct chronological order? **(2004)**

(a) Shankaracharya–Ramanuja–Chaitanya
(b) Ramanuja–Shankaracharya–Chaitanya
(c) Ramanuja–Chaitanya–Shankaracharya
(d) Shankaracharya–Chaitanya–Ramanuja

12. According to Mimamsa system of philosophy liberation is possible by means of **(1995)**

(a) Jnana (b) Bhakti
(c) Yoga (d) Karma

13. Who among the following were famous jurists of medieval India? **(1995)**

(i) Vijnanesvara
(ii) Hemadri
(iii) Rajasekhara
(iv) Jimutavahana

(a) i, ii and iii (b) ii, iii and iv
(c) i, ii and iv (d) i and iv

ANSWERS

1. (d)	2. (a)	3. (b)	4. (c)	5. (c)	6. (c)	7. (d)	8. (b)
9. (a)	10. (c)	11. (a)	12. (d)	13. (c)			

QUESTIONS FROM LAST YEAR'S MAINS

1. Give a brief account of the early medieval temple architecture of Kashmir. **(2015, History optional)**

2. Evaluate Rajtarangini as a source of history. **(2012, History optional)**

PRACTICE QUESTIONS – PRELIMS

1. Match the following:

(A) Mohammad bin Qasim (i) c. 712 CE
(B) Mahmud of Ghazni (ii) c. 1000 CE
(C) Mohd. Ghori (iii) c. 1175 CE
(D) Prithviraj Chauhan (iv) c. 1191 CE

(a) A–ii, B–i, C–iii, D–iv
(b) A–i, B–ii, C–iii, D–iv
(c) A–iv, B–iii, C–ii, D–i
(d) A–iii, B–i, C–ii, D–iv

2. Consider the following statements and mark the option which is correct.

(i) The First battle of Tarain was won by Prithviraj Chauhan.
(ii) The Battle of Waihind was won by Mahmud of Ghazni.
(iii) The Somnath temple was plundered by Mohd. Ghori.
(iv) Mohd. Ghori was defeated by the Gahadavalas ruler, Jaichandra.

(a) i and ii (b) All of the above
(c) ii, iii and iv (d) None of the above

3. Consider the following statements and mark the option which is correct.
(i) The Chalukya dynasty was founded by Taila II, with its capital at Kalyani.
(ii) The Second Battle of Tarain was won by Mahmud of Ghazni.
(iii) Vastupala, a minister of the Chauhans, built the famous Dilwara temple.

Which of the statement(s) given above is/are correct?
(a) i only (b) i and iii only
(c) ii and iii only (d) i, ii and iii

4. Which one of the following pairs form part of the heterodox school of Indian Philosophy?
(a) Mimamsa and Vaisheshika
(b) Yoga and Vedanta
(c) Lokayata and Ajivika
(d) Samkhya and Nyaya

5. Match List I with List II and select the correct answer using the code given below the lists:

List I (Famous Book)	List II (Author)
(a) Prithviraj Raso	i. Chand Bardai
(b) Rajataringini	ii. Bhaskara II
(c) Shahnama	iii. Kalhana
(d) Lilavati	iv. Firdausi

Code:	A	B	C	D
(a)	ii	iv	iii	i
(b)	ii	iii	iv	i
(c)	i	iv	iii	ii
(d)	i	iii	iv	ii

6. With reference to the history of philosophical thought in India, consider the following statements regarding Vedanta school:
(i) The theory of karma was closely linked to the Vedanta philosophy.
(ii) It lays emphasis on brahmagyan, hence relies on the Upanishad part of the Vedas.

Which of the statement(s) given above is/are correct?
(a) i only (b) ii only
(c) Both i and ii (d) Neither i nor ii

7. Consider the following statements and mark the option which is correct.
(i) The Lakshmana Temple was constructed during the reign of the Chandella ruler, Yashovarman.
(ii) The Vishvanatha Temple was constructed during the reign of the Chandella ruler, Dhanga.
(iii) The Kandariya Mahadeva temple was constructed during the reign of the Chandella ruler, Vidyadhara.

Which of the statement(s) given above is/are correct?
(a) i only (b) i and iii only
(c) ii and iii only (d) i, ii and iii

8. Consider the following statements and mark the option which is correct.
(i) Jayadeva, author of the Geet Govinda, was at the court of Lakshmana Sena.
(ii) Al Biruni wrote the Kitab-ud-Yamni.
(iii) Utbi wrote the Kitab-ul-Hind.

Which of the statement(s) given above is/are correct?
(a) i only (b) i and iii only
(c) ii and iii only (d) i, ii and iii

9. Consider the following statements and mark the correct option.
(i) Anangapala Tomara is widely believed as the ruler who established Delhi.
(ii) In the famous battle of Chandwar, Mohd. Ghori defeated the Gahadavalas ruler Jaichandra.

(iii) Vijay Sena was the founder of the Sena dynasty.

Which of the statement(s) given above is/are correct?

(a) i only (b) i and iii only
(c) ii and iii only (d) i, ii and iii

10. Consider the following statements and mark the option which is correct.

(i) The Vedanta of Shankara (Absolute Monism) considers brahman to be without any attributes and considers knowledge to be the chief means of salvation.

(ii) The Visistadvaita Advaita of Ramanuja considers brahman with attributes.

(iii) The Dvaita of Madhva considers God to be completely different from the individual soul and the world.

Which of the statement(s) given above is/are correct?

(a) i only (b) i and iii only
(c) ii and iii only (d) i, ii and iii

11. Consider the following statements and mark the option which is correct.

(i) Vikramaditya VI was the hero of Bilhana's Vikramankadeva Charitra.

(ii) The Siddhanta Shiromani was written by Lilavati.

Which of the statement(s) given above is/are correct?

(a) i only (b) Both i and ii
(c) Only ii (d) None

ANSWERS

1. (b) 2. (a) 3. (a) 4. (c) 5. (d) 6. (c) 7. (d) 8. (a)
9. (d) 10. (d) 11. (a)

PRACTICE QUESTIONS – MAINS

1. The battles of Tarain and Chandwar were turning points in the history of India. Do you agree? Explain with suitable reasoning.

2. Describe in detail the different schools of Indian philosophy, emphasising on the branches of the Vedanta school.

3. Science and education suffered after the Guptas, but there were considerable improvements in the field of mathematics. Elaborate.

CHAPTER 11

The Delhi Sultanate (c. 1206–1526 CE)

As we have discussed in the last chapter, invasions by Mahmud of Ghazni and Mohd. Ghori into India ultimately resulted in the establishment of the Delhi Sultanate. Five different dynasties – the Slave, the Khalji, the Tughlaq, the Sayyids and the Lodhi's are collectively referred to as the Delhi Sultanate. The rulers, termed as Sultans, were of Turkish and Afghan origin. Not only did they extend their rule over North India (i.e., Malwa and Gujarat), but they also penetrated into the Deccan and South India. The Sultanate's rule resulted in far-reaching changes in the Indian society, administration and cultural life.

Delhi Sultanate Period (c. 1206–1526 CE)

- Slave/Ilbari (c. 1206–1290 CE)
- Khalji (c. 1290–1320 CE)
- Tughlaq (c. 1320–1413 CE)
- Saiyyad (c. 1414–1451 CE)
- Lodhis (c. 1451–1526 CE)

Slave Dynasty/Ilbari/The Mameluk Sultans (c. 1206–1290 CE)

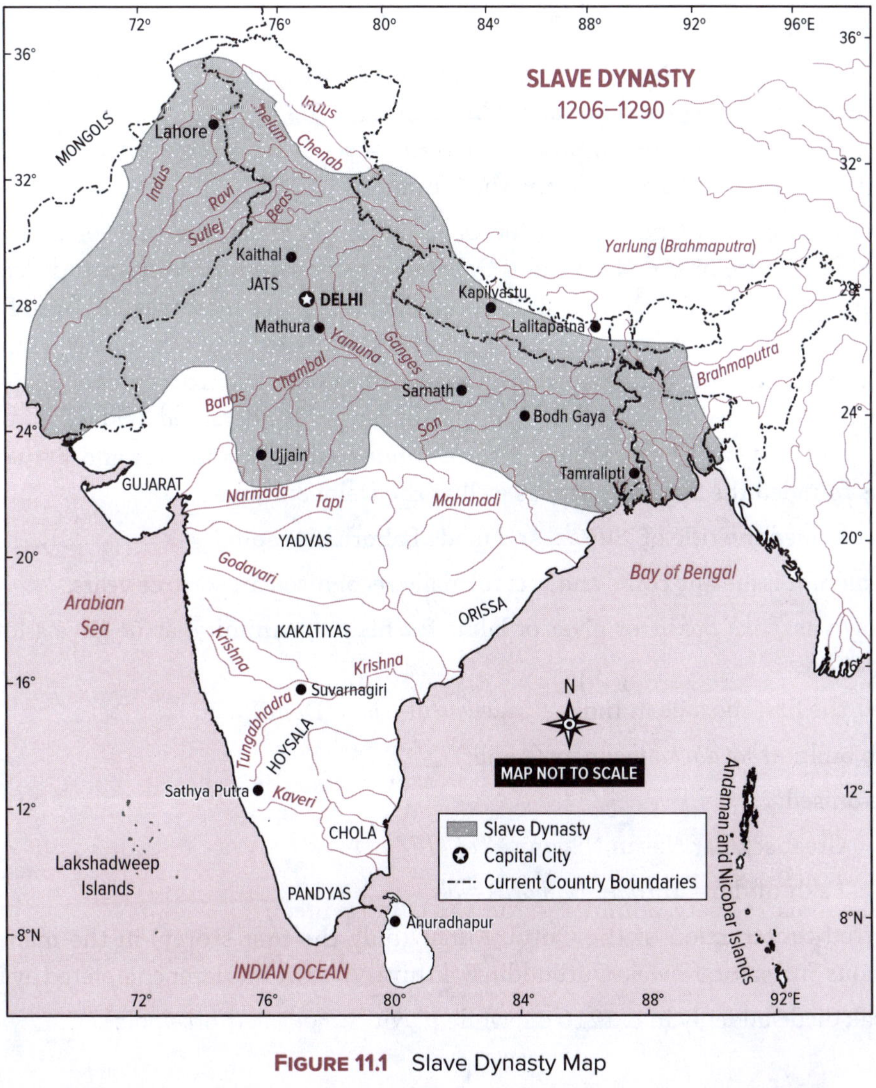

FIGURE 11.1 Slave Dynasty Map

The Slave dynasty was also called the Mameluk dynasty. *'Mameluk'* was the Arabic word meaning 'owned', used to distinguish the important Turkish slaves chiefly meant for military service from the lower slaves, who were used as domestic labour or artisans. In fact, three dynasties were established during this period. They were:

1. Qutbi dynasty (c. 1206–1211 CE) founded by Qutbuddin Aibak.
2. First Ilbari dynasty (c. 1211–1266 CE) founded by Iltutmish.
3. Second Ilbari dynasty (c. 1266–1290 CE) founded by Balban.

Qutub-ud-din Aibak (c. 1206–1210 CE)

- Founder of the Slave dynasty; considered by many scholars as the real founder of Muslim rule in India.
- He was a Turkish slave of Muhammad Ghori, who played an important role in the expansion of the Turkish Sultanate in India after the Battle of Tarain and was made the governor of Ghori's Indian possessions. He raised a standing army and established his hold over north India even during the lifetime of Ghori.
- After the death of Ghori in c. 1206 CE, Tajuddin Yaldauz, the ruler of Ghazni, claimed his rule over Delhi and Nasiruddin Qabacha, the governor of Multan and Uchch aspired for independence. Along with all this, he also had to face many revolts from Rajputs and other Indian chiefs. The successor of Jaichand, Harishchandra, had driven out the Turks from Badayun and Farukhabad. However, Aibak was able to win over his enemies by conciliatory measures as well as a display of power. He defeated Yaldauz and severed all connections with Ghazni. Aibak also re-conquered both Badayun and Farukhabad and thus founded the Slave dynasty as well as the Delhi Sultanate.
- He assumed the title of 'Sultan' and made Lahore his capital.
- He did not issue any coins and was formally recognised after three years.
- Known as *'Lakh Baksh'* or giver of lakhs for his magnanimity, as he gave a lot of liberal donations.
- Built the first mosque in India – *Quwwat-ul-Islam* (Delhi).
- Also built: *Arhai din ka jhonpara* (Ajmer).
- Patronised:
  - Great scholar Hasan Nizami – *Taj-ul-Massir*
  - Fakh-ul-din – *Tarikh-i-Mubarakshahi*
- Started construction of the Qutub Minar (only the first storey) in the memory of the famous Sufi saint, Khwaja Qutbuddin Bakthiyar Kaki (it was later completed by Iltutmish).
- Aibak died suddenly in c. 1210 CE, while playing *Chaugan* (horse polo).

Aram Shah (c. 1210 CE)

- Son of Qutbuddin Aibak, who succeeded his father but was an incapable ruler, and a weak and worthless young man. The Turkish amirs opposed him. He ruled for a mere eight months.
- The Turkish chiefs of Delhi invited the governor of Badayun, Iltutmish (son-in-law of Qutbuddin Aibak), to come to Delhi. Iltutmish disposed off Aram Shah and became the Sultan with the name of Shamsuddin. The credit of consolidating the Delhi Sultanate lies largely with him.

Iltutmish (c. 1210–1236 CE)

- The real consolidator of Turkish rule in India. He belonged to the Ilbari tribe and hence his dynasty also known as the Ilbari dynasty. Legends describe that his half-brothers sold him as a slave to Aibak, who made him his-son-in law by giving his daughter in marriage to him. Later, Aibak appointed him as the Iqtadar of Gwalior. After becoming Sultan, he shifted his capital from Lahore to Delhi.
- During the first 10 years of his reign, he concentrated on securing his throne from his rivals. The commanders of Muhammad Ghori like Yaldauz, Qabacha (of Multan) and Ali Mardan (of Bihar and Bengal) rose in defiance again. The chief of Jalore and Ranthambore joined Gwalior and Kalinjar in declaring their independence. Apart from this, the rising power of the Mongols under Chenghiz Khan threatened the North-West Frontier of the Sultanate.
- Iltutmish took up the task of consolidating his position. He defeated Yaldauz in c. 1215 CE in the Battle of Tarain. In c. 1217 CE, he drove away Qabacha from Punjab.
- In c. 1220 CE, Temujin, popularly known as Chengiz Khan, the leader of the Mongols, started invading Central Asia and destroyed the Khwarizm empire. Jalaluddin Mangbarani, the son of the Shah of Khwarizm, while escaping from the Mongols, sought shelter at Iltutmish's court, but Iltutmish refused to grant asylum to him. So, with his diplomatic skills, he prevented Mongol attack and saved India from the wrath of Chengiz Khan.
- From c. 1225 CE onwards, Iltutmish engaged his armies in suppressing the disturbances in the East. In c. 1226–1227 CE, Iltutmish sent a large army under his son Nasiruddin Mahmud, which defeated Iwaz Khan and brought Bengal and Bihar back into the Delhi Sultanate. Similarly, a campaign was also launched against the Rajput chiefs. Ranthambore was captured in c. 1226 CE and by c. 1231 CE, Iltutmish had established his authority over Mandor, Jalore, Bayana and Gwalior. He also attacked Nagda, the capital of Mewar, but had to retreat at the arrival of the Gujarat armies. As a revenge, he led an expedition against the Chalukyas of Gujarat but it was not successful.

- He divided his empire into *Iqtas* (assignment of land in lieu of salary). Every Iqtadars had to maintain law and order and collect revenue. After deducting own salary and expenses, they had to send the surplus to central government. As a matter of fact, the *Iqtadars* were transferable.
- Organised *Turkan-i-chahalgani*, a new class of ruling elite of forty powerful military leaders, the Forty. These were Turkish amirs (nobles) who advised and helped the Sultan in administering the Sultanate. After the death of Iltutmish, this group assumed great power in its hands. For a few years they decided on the selection of Sultans one after the other. The group was finally eliminated by Balban.
- His authority was recognised by the Abbasid Caliph of Baghdad in c. 1229 CE as he received the *mansur* (the letter of recognition/Investiture), by which he became the legal sovereign ruler of India.
- Issued purely Arabic coinage of silver *tanka* (first to do so) weighing 175 grams, which remains the basis of the modern rupee and copper *Jital*.
- Father of tomb building (Sultangarhi in Delhi); completed the construction of the Qutab Minar at Delhi, the tallest stone tower in India (238 ft.).
- Patronised Minhas-us-siraj (contemporary historian) who wrote *Tahaqqat-i-Nasuri*.
- Since he did not consider any of his sons worthy of the throne, he declared his daughter Razia as successor, deviating from normal practice. The nomination of a woman in preference to sons was a novel step.

Ruknuddin Firuz Shah (c. 1236 CE)

- Eldest son of Iltutmish who was put on the throne by nobles.
- Took rides on elephants in Delhi distributing gold and the government was handled by Shah Turkan (originally Turkish Maid).
- When the governor of Multan revolted, Ruknuddin marched to suppress that revolt. Using this opportunity, Raziya, with the support of amirs of Delhi, seized the throne of the Delhi Sultanate. Both Firuz Shah and Shah Turkan were put to death.

Razia Sultan (c. 1236–1239 CE)

- First and only female Muslim ruler of medieval India's Sultanate period.
- Discarded female apparel and *purdah*; she held court with her face unveiled. She began to adorn herself in male attire and rode out in public on an elephant, went for hunting, and led the army. This aroused resentment among the Turkish nobles.
- Her attempts to create a counter nobility of non-Turks invited the wrath of the Turkish *amirs*. They were particularly incensed over her decision to appoint an Abyssinian slave, Malik Jamaluddin Yaqut, to important office of the *Amir-i-akhur* (Superintendent of royal

horses). The recruitment of a few other non-Turks to important posts further inflamed matters. The nobility realised that, though a woman, Raziya was not willing to be a puppet in their hands, therefore the nobles started revolting against her in the provinces. The governor of Lahore was first to create trouble but was defeated.

- In c. 1240 CE, a serious rebellion broke out in Sirhind (Bhatinda) under Altuniya (governor). Raziya, alongside Yaqut, marched against Altuniya, but on the way Turkish followers of Altuniya murdered Yaqut and imprisoned Raziya. In the meantime, the Turkish nobles put Bahram, another son of Iltutmish, on the throne. However, Raziya won over her captor, Altuniya, and after marrying him proceeded to Delhi. But she was defeated and killed on the way by Bahram Shah.

Bahram Shah (c. 1240–1242 CE)

- The fall of Raziya paved the way for the ascendancy of 'the Forty'. In the next few years there ensued a struggle for supremacy between the Sultans and the nobles. Initially, the nobles helped Bahram to ascend the throne but gradually these nobles became disordered and constantly bickered among each other. It was during this period of unrest that he was murdered by his own army in c. 1242 CE.

Alauddin Masud Shah (c. 1242–1246 CE)

- Son of Ruknuddin Firuz Shah and nephew of Raziya Sultan. After his predecessor Bahram, was murdered by the army, the chiefs chose him to become the next ruler.
- However, he was more of a puppet for the chiefs, was considered incompetent and worthless and did not actually have much power or influence in the government. Instead, he became infamous for his fondness for entertainment and wine.
- By c. 1246 CE, the chiefs became upset with his increasing hunger for more power in the government, and replaced him with Nasiruddin Mahmud.

Nasiruddin Mahmud (c. 1246–1265 CE)

- Grandson of Iltutmish who was inexperienced and young and had ascended to the throne with the aid of Ulugh Khan/Balban (member of the *Chahalgani*), who himself assumed the position of Naib (deputy or regent). To further strengthen his position, he married his daughter to Nasiruddin. The real power during Mahmud reign lay in the hands of Balban.
- The growing authority of Balban alienated many of the Turkish chiefs and with a conspiracy in c. 1250 CE, they ousted Balban from his position and replaced him with Imaduddin Raihan, who was an Indian Muslim, as they could not agree among themselves which Turkish noble should succeed Balban's post. Balban agreed to step aside but carefully built his own group, and within a short span of one and a half years, won over some of his opponents. In due course of time, Balban was reinstated with even more powers and he even assumed the royal insignia, the chhatr.

- Mahmud died in c. 1265 CE and according to some historians such as Ibn Batuta and Isami, Balban poisoned his master Nasiruddin and ascended the throne.

Balban (c. 1266–1286 CE)

- Balban was undoubtedly one of the main architects of the Delhi Sultanate, particularly of its form of government and institutions. He asserted and enhanced the power of the monarchy. According to Balban, the Sultan was God's shadow on earth (*Zil-i-Ilahi*) and the recipient of divine grace (*Nibyabat-i-Khudai*). He ruled in an autocratic manner and worked hard to elevate the position of the Sultan.
- Balban's experience as the regent made him understand the problems of Delhi Sultanate. He knew that the real threat to the monarchy was from the nobles called the Forty. He was convinced that only by enhancing the power and authority of the monarchy he could solve this problem. He got every member of Iltutmish's family killed and gave a deadly blow to *Chahalgani*.
- Balban introduced rigorous court discipline and new customs such as *sijada* (prostration) and *paibos* (kissing the Sultan's feet) to prove his superiority over the nobles. In order to impress the people with the strength and awe of his government, Balban maintained a magnificent court and also introduced the Persian festival of *Nauroz*. He refused to laugh and joke in the court, and even gave up drinking wine so that no one may see him in a non-serious mood.
- He spared only the most obedient nobles and eliminated all others by fair or foul means. Haybat Khan, the governor of Oudh, was punished for killing a man who was drunk. Sher Khan, the governor of Bhatinda, was poisoned.
- He was deeply racist and excluded non-Turks from administration. He stood forth as the champion of Turkish nobility. Indian Muslims were not given important posts in the government. He appointed spies known as *Barids* to monitor the activities of the nobles.
- When Balban became the Sultan, his position was not secure. Many Turkish chiefs were hostile to him; the Mongols were looking forward for an opportunity to attack the Sultanate; the governors of the distant provinces were trying to become independent rulers while Indian rulers were also ready to revolt at the smallest opportunity. The law and order situation in the area around Delhi and in the Doab region had deteriorated. In the Ganga–Yamuna doab and Awadh, the roads were infested with the robbers and dacoits, because of which the communication with the eastern areas had become difficult. Some of the Rajput zamindars had set up forts in the area, and defied the government. The Mewatis had become so bold as to plunder people up to the outskirts of Delhi.
- To deal with these elements, Balban adopted a stern policy. He organised a strong centralised army, both to deal with internal disturbances, and to repel the Mongols who had entrenched themselves in the Punjab and posed a serious threat to the Delhi Sultanate.

- He separated the *Diwan-i-unzarat* (Finance Department) from the *Diwan-i-Arz* (Military Department). He reorganised the Diwan-i-arz and deployed the army in different parts of the country to put down rebellion. The disturbances in Mewat, Doab, Awadh and Katihar were ruthlessly suppressed. Balban also secured control over Ajmer and Nagaur in eastern Rajputana, but his attempts to capture Ranthambore and Gwalior failed. Instead of expanding his kingdom, Balban paid more attention to the restoration of law and order. Balban took severe action against the Mewatis and prevented such robberies. Robbers were mercilessly pursued and put to death. As a result, the roads became safe for travel.
- In c. 1279 CE, encouraged by the Mongol threats and the old age of the Sultan, the governor of Bengal, Tughril Beg, revolted, assumed the title of Sultan and had the khutba read in his name. Balban sent his forces to Bengal and had Tughril beheaded. Subsequently he appointed his own son Bughra Khan as the governor of Bengal. By all these harsh methods, Balban controlled the situation. He called himself *Nasir-amir-ul-momin* (Caliph's right hand man) and instructed the ulemas to confine themselves to religious affairs and not to interfere in political activities.
- He administered justice with extreme impartiality. For instance, Malik Baqbaq, the governor of Badaun, was publicly flogged for his cruelty towards his servants.
- Followed the policy of Blood and Iron. Developed an efficient spy system and kept himself well-informed by appointing spies in every department.
- Strengthened frontiers against the Mongols but even he could not fully defend northern India against the attacks of the Mongols. Moreover, by excluding the non-Turkish from positions of power and authority and by trusting only a very narrow racial group, he made many people dissatisfied.
- Patron of men of letters and showered special favours on Amir Khusrau.
- However, in the north-west, the Mongols reappeared and Balban sent his son, Prince Mahmud, against them. But the prince (Khan-i-Shahid) was killed in the battle and his death was a smashing blow to Balban. He died in c. 1287 CE.

Kaiqubad (c. 1287–1290 CE)

- Grandson of Balban, who was raised to the throne by nobles after Balban's death. However, he was soon replaced by his son, Kaimurs, who remained on the throne for a little over three months. In c. 1290 CE, Firoz, the *Ariz-i-Mumalik*, i.e., the Minister of War who later took the title of Jalaluddin Khalji, took a bold step by murdering Kaimurs and seized the throne. A group of Khalji nobles led by him established the Khalji dynasty. Some scholars call this event as the 'dynastic revolution' of c. 1290 CE, as it brought to an end the so-called slave dynasty and bought to the forefront the Khaljis.

Khalji Dynasty (c. 1290–1320 CE)

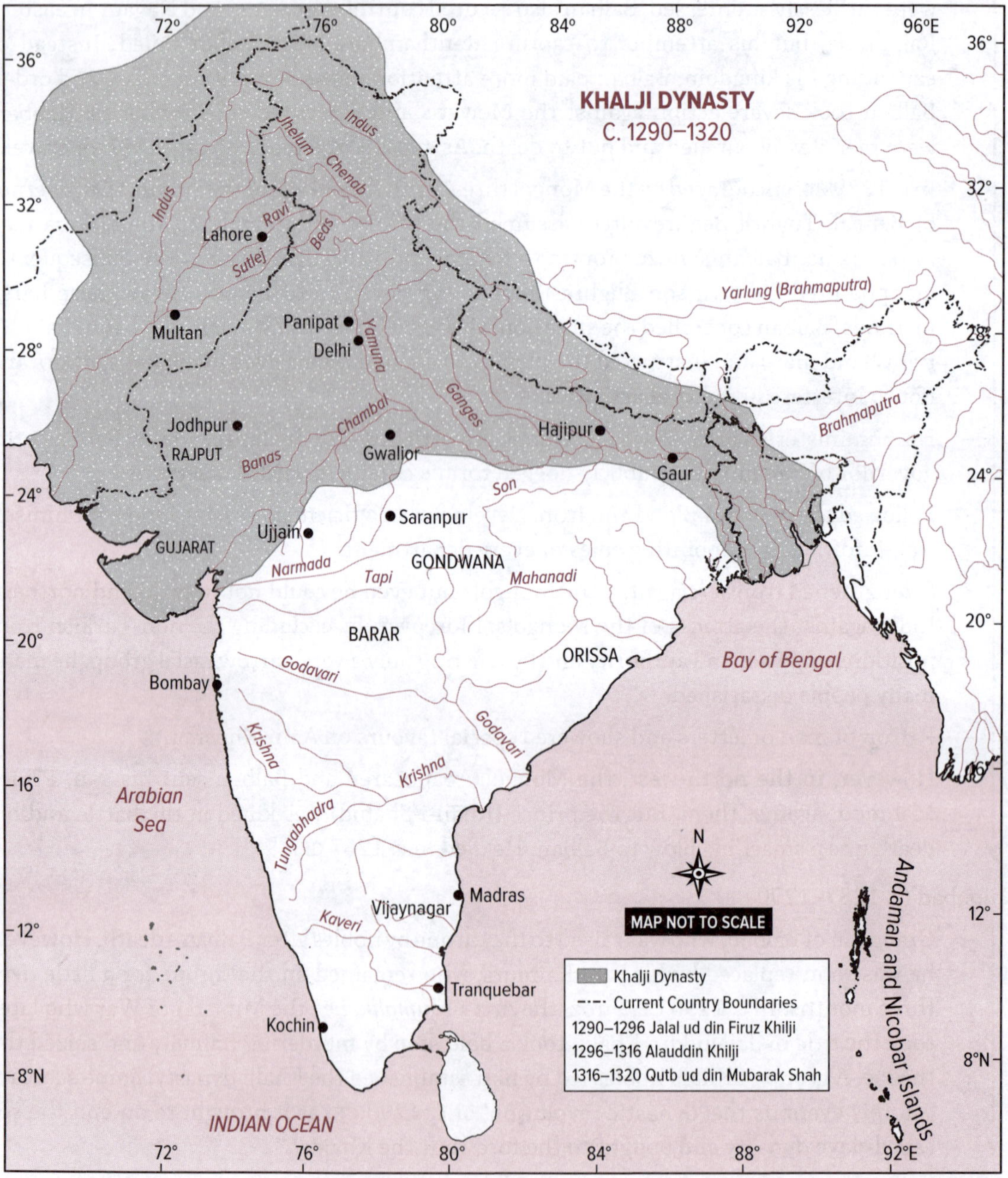

FIGURE 11.2 Khalji Dynasty

Jalauddin Khalji (c. 1290–1296 CE)

- Jalaluddin Khalji (Firoz) laid the foundation of the Khalji dynasty. He was seventy years old when he came to power and ruled only for a short span of six years. During Balban's reign, Jalaluddin had been the warden of the marches in north-west and had fought many successful battles against the Mongols.
- Repelled the attack of the Mongols under Abdullah and the Mongols who settled near Delhi were called the '*New Musalmans*'.
- He was generous and also the first sultan of the Delhi Sultanate to have a benevolent attitude towards Hindus. He clearly put forward the view that the state should be based on the willing support of the governed, and that since the large majority of the people in India were Hindus, the state in India could not be a truly Islamic state.
- He avoided harsh punishments, even to those who revolted against him. He not only forgave them but at times even rewarded them to win their support. However, his leniency was misunderstood as weakness by many people, including his supporters. When the *thugs* (robbers) looted the country, they were allowed to go after only a mere severe warning.
- Jalaluddin tried to win the goodwill of the nobility by adopting policy of tolerance. He retained the earlier nobility in his administration. For instance, Malik Chhajju, nephew of Balban, was allowed to remain the governor of Kara. When Chhajju revolted, it was suppressed, but he was pardoned. In c. 1292 CE, when Malik Chhajju revolted for the second time, he was replaced by his nephew and son-in-law, Alauddin Khalji.
- Married his daughter to Ulugh Khan, a descendant of Chengiz Khan (to win the Mongols' goodwill).
- During his reign in c. 1294 CE, Devagiri was invaded by Alauddin Khalji (Ali Gurshap) during the reception there in July c. 1296 CE, Alauddin Khalji treacherously murdered his father-in-law Jalaluddin Khalji near Kara and usurped the throne of Delhi. He proclaimed himself Sultan by winning over the nobles and soldiers to his side by lavish use of gold (accumulated from Devagiri).

Alauddin Khalji (c. 1296–1316 CE)

- Alauddin Khalji was Jalaluddin's ambitious nephew and son-in-law. He had helped his uncle in his struggle for power and was appointed as *Amir-i-Tuzuk* (Master of Ceremonies). He had two victorious expeditions during the reign of Jalaluddin. After the first expedition of Bhilsa (Vidisa) in c. 1292 CE, he was given the iqta of Awadh, in addition to that of Kara. He was also appointed *Arizi-i-Mumalik* (Minister of War). In c. 1294 CE, he led the first Turkish expedition to southern India and plundered Devagiri. The successful expedition proved that Alauddin was an able military commander and efficient organiser.

- Jalaluddin's policy of tolerance was reversed by Alauddin Khalji, who awarded drastic punishments to all those who dared to oppose him. He decided to revive Balban's policies of ruthless governance. He slaughtered the New Musalmans, and the old Balbani and Jalali nobles. He decided to curb the powers of the nobles and the interference of the *ulema* in the matters of the state. According to Barani, the author of *Tarikh-i-Firuz Shahi*, Alauddin was convinced that the general prosperity of the nobles, inter-marriages between noble families, inefficient spy-system and drinking liquor were the basic reasons for the rebellions. Therefore, he passed four ordinances.
  - He confiscated the properties of the nobles.
  - The intelligence system was reorganised and all the secret activities of the nobles were immediately reported to the Sultan.
  - The use of liquor and intoxicants was prohibited.
  - Social gatherings and festivities without the permission of Sultan were forbidden. By such harsh measures, his reign was free from rebellions.
- Alauddin established a huge permanent standing army to satisfy his ambition of conquest and to protect the country from Mongol invasion. Alauddin Khalji sent his army six times against the Mongols. The first two were successful. But the third Mongol invader, Khwaja, came up to Delhi and Alauddin had to return from Chittor in a haste in 1303 CE and had to seek refuge in a strongly guarded camp at the Siri Fort, which was still under construction. Meanwhile, the Mongols besieged Delhi and its environs, but were unable to breach Siri, forcing them to retreat. The next three Mongol invasions were also dealt with severely. Thousands of Mongols were killed. The north-western frontier was fortified and Ghazi Malik (Ghiyasuddin Tughlaq) was appointed as the Warden of Marches to protect the frontier.
- The military conquests of Alauddin Khalji include his expedition against Gujarat, Rajputana and the Deccan.
- Conquest of Gujarat: Alauddin first began his territorial conquest with a campaign against Gujarat in c. 1299 CE, which was ruled by the Vaghela king Rai Karan. The vast riches of Gujarat allured him first and foremost, and furthermore, it was also a strategic decision since the Gujarat wealth could pay for his future conquests while her seaports could ensure a regular supply of Arab horses for his army. An army under two of Alauddin's noted generals, Ulugh Khan and Nusarat Khan, marched against Gujarat. Rai Karan, the ruler of Gujarat fled, and the temple of Somnath was captured and destroyed. An enormous booty was collected. Even the wealthy Muslim merchants were not spared. Alauddin married the Raja's wife Kamla Bai and acquired Malik Kafur (a eunuch and great military general who later led the Khalji dynasty invasions to South India).

- Conquest of Rajputana: After the annexation of Gujarat, Alauddin turned his attention towards Rajputana.
    - Ranthambore: It was reputed to be the strongest fort of Rajasthan and had earlier defied Jalaluddin Khalji. The capture of Ranthambore was necessary to break the power and morale of the Rajputs. Hence, it was his first target. The immediate cause of attack was that the ruler of Ranthambore, Hamirdeva, gave shelter to two rebellious Mongol soldiers and refused to hand over them to the Khalji ruler. Hence an offensive was launched against Ranthambore. To begin with, the Khalji forces suffered losses. Nusrat Khan even lost his life. Finally, Alauddin himself had to come on the battlefield. However, in c. 1301 CE, the fort fell to Alauddin. Women committed jauhar or self- immolation (described by Amir Khusrau).
    - Chittor: In c. 1303 CE, Alauddin besieged Chittor, another powerful state of Rajputana. According to some scholars, Alauddin attacked Chittor because he coveted Padmini, the beautiful queen of Raja Ratan Singh. The Rajput women including Rani Padmini performed jauhar. This Padmini episode was graphically mentioned in the book *Padmavath,* written by Jayasi. According to Amir Khusrau, the Sultan ordered a general massacre of the civil population. Chittor was renamed Khizrabad after the name of Sultan's son Khizr Khan. Alauddin, however, had to return back quickly to Delhi as the Mongol army was advancing towards Delhi.
    - Malwa and others: In c. 1305 CE, the Khalji army under Ain-ul-Mulk captured Malwa. Other states such as Ujjain, Mandu, Dhar and Chanderi were also captured. After the conquest of Malwa, Alauddin sent Malik Kafur to the South and himself attacked Siwana. The ruler of Siwana, Raja Shital Deva, defended the fort bravely but was ultimately defeated. In c. 1311 CE, another Rajput kingdom, Jalore, was also captured. Thus by c. 1311 CE, Alauddin had completed the conquest of large parts of Rajputana and became the master of North India.
- Conquest of Deccan and South India: This region was ruled by four important dynasties
- *Yadavas of Devagiri*, *Kakatiyas of Warangal*, *Hoysalas of Dwarasamudra* and the *Pandyas of Madurai*. The expeditions to the south were sent under Malik Kafur, a trusted commander of Alauddin who held the office of the Naib.
    - His first target was Rai Karan (the earlier ruler of Gujarat), who had now occupied Baglana, and defeated him.
    - The second expedition was against Rai Ramachandra, the ruler of Devagiri in c. 1306– 1307 CE, who had earlier promised to pay tribute to Sultan but did not pay. Ramachandra surrendered after little resistance to Malik Kafur and was treated honourably. He was kept as a guest at Alauddin's court and was given a gift of one lakh tankas and the title of Rai Rayan. He was also given a district of Gujarat and

one of his daughters was married to Alauddin. Alauddin showed generosity towards Ramachandra because he wanted to have Ramachandra as an ally for campaigns in the South.

- In c. 1309 CE, Malik Kafur launched his campaign against Warangal in the Telengana area. Its ruler Pratab Rudradeva was defeated and enormous booty was collected from him while he agreed to pay regular tribute to the Sultan.
- Malik Kafur's next target was the Hoysala ruler Vira Ballala III in c. 1310 CE. He was defeated and a vast quantity of booty was seized and sent to Delhi.
- Kafur next marched against the Pandyas in c. 1311 CE. In the case of Pandyas, a direct decisive battle could not take place. Vira Pandya fled to the capital Madurai and Kafur plundered as much as he could, including a number of wealthy temples such as that of Chidambaram. According to Amir Khusrau, Malik Kafur reached as far as Rameshwaram and built a mosque there and returned to Delhi with 512 elephants, 7000 horses and 500 mans of precious stone. The Sultan honoured Malik Kafur by appointing him Naib Malik of the empire. Alauddin's forces under Malik Kafur continued to maintain a control over the Deccan kingdoms. Alauddin died in c. 1316 CE.

- Although the Sultan was illiterate, he patronised poets like Amir Khusrau and Mir Hasan Dehlvi. He also built a famous gateway known as Alai Darwaza, Hauz Khas, Mahal Hazaar Satoon, Jamait Khana Mosque, Alai Minar, and constructed a new capital at Siri.
- Alauddin adopted the title of *Sikander-i-Azam* and gave Amir Khusrau the title of *Tuti-i-Hind* (Parrot of India).
- Included non-Turks in his service.
- First ruler to fix land revenue in cash.
- His theory of kinship was secular and he proclaimed '*Kingship knows no Kinship*' and 'I do not know if this is lawful or unlawful, I do whatever I think to be good for the state'.
- Refuted the suzerainty of the Caliph and did not allow any power independence of the state to guide his policy. According to Barni, Alauddin wanted to join a new religion.

Qutbuddin Mubarak Shah (c. 1316–1320 CE)

- Following the death of Alauddin, the Delhi Sultanate was plunged into confusion. Malik Kafur sat on the throne for a few days, only to be deposed by Qutbuddin Mubarak Shah (one of the sons of Alauddin, who escaped the preying eyes of Malik Kafur).
- Declared himself Caliph and took title of *Al Wasiq Billah*.
- Cancelled all harsh regulations of his father.

- Although able to crush many revolts of his reign, he was not able to run the administration smoothly. For instance, during this period, rebellions broke out in Devagiri (Deogir) but were harshly suppressed.
- Qutbuddin Mubarak Shah was soon murdered and Khusrau ascended the throne.

Nasiruddin Khusrau Shah (c. 1320 CE)

- Killed Mubarak Shah; however, did not last long on the throne as some dissatisfied officers, led by Ghazi Malik, the governor of Dipalpur, killed Khusru Shah and ascended the throne of Delhi under the title of Ghiyasuddin Tughlaq in c. 1320 CE.
- Only Hindu convert to sit on the throne of Delhi.

Thus, only four years after the death of Alauddin, the Khalji dynasty came to end and power passed into the hands of the Tughlaqs.

Administration of Alauddin Khalji

a. Military Reforms: Alauddin was the first Sultan to have a large permanent standing army and paid them in cash from the royal treasury. He imported horses and according to historian Ferishta, he recruited 4,75,000 cavalrymen. An innovative *Chehra and Dagh System* was introduced by him wherein the *Chehra* (detailed description of each soldier) and *Dagh* (branding of horses) was maintained. In order to ensure maximum efficiency, a strict review of the army from time to time was carried out.

b. Market Reforms: Alauddin's measures to control the markets and price regulations were one of the most important policy initiatives of his reign and he is noted in history for the same. Since Alauddin wanted to maintain a large army, he therefore lowered and fixed the price of the commodities of daily use. Alauddin Khalji established four separate markets in Delhi,

   i. Grain market (*Mandi*) for grain.
   ii. Cloth and groceries market (*Sarai Adl*) for cloth, sugar, dried fruits, butter and oil.
   iii. Market for horses, slaves, cattle, etc.
   iv. Market for miscellaneous commodities.

   To ensure implementation, each market was under the control of a superintendent called *Shahna-i-Mandi* who was assisted by an intelligence officer. Apart from Shahna-i-Mandi, Alauddin received daily reports of the market from two other independent sources, *barids* (intelligence officer) and *munhiyans* (secret spies). The Sultan also sent slave boys to buy various commodities to check prices. Any violation of the Sultan's orders (such as if any shop keeper charged a higher price, or tried to cheat by using false weights and measures) resulted in harsh punishment, including expulsion from the capital, imposition of fine, imprisonment and mutilation. No hoarding was allowed and even during the famine the same price was maintained.

The supply of grain was ensured by holding stocks in government store houses. Regulations were issued to fix the price of all commodities. A separate department called *Diwani Riyasat* was created under an officer called *Naib-i-Riyasat*. Every merchant was registered under the Market Department. The sale of liquor and intoxicants was prohibited and gambling too was banned.

c. Land Revenue Administration: Alauddin Khalji was the first Sultan of Delhi who ordered for the measurement of land. Even the big landlords could not escape from paying land tax. Land revenue was collected in cash in order to enable the Sultan to pay the soldiers in cash. The state officials measured the cultivated land and fixed land revenue accordingly. *Biswa* was the standard unit of measurement. State demand was one fifth of the produce and along with it house tax (*Grahi*) and pasture tax (*Chari*) were imposed, but *Kismat-i-Khuti* (Headman's cess) was abolished. His land revenue reforms provided a basis for the future reforms of Sher Shah and Akbar. He centralised administration and even confiscated religious endowments and free lands (*Inam and Wakt*).

Tughlaq Dynasty (c. 1320–1414 CE)/Dynasty of Qaraunah Turks

The Tughlaqs were also known as the *Qaraunah Turks* as the father of Ghazi Malik was a Qaraunah Turk in origin.

Ghiyasuddin Tughlaq (c. 1320–1325 CE)

- Founder of the Tughlaq dynasty and the first Sultan to take the title of *Ghazi*/Slayer of Infidels.
- First Sultan to start irrigation works.
- Built a strong fort called Tughlaqabad near Delhi.
- Dispatched his son, Jauna Khan/Mohammad Bin Tughlaq, to re-establish authority in Warangal (Kakatiyas) and Madurai (Pandayas).
- Had a troublesome relationship with the Sufi saint, Sheikh Nizamuddin Aulia.
- Died due to the collapse of a wooden structure; some scholars like Ibn Batuta believe that his death was an act of sabotage orchestrated by his son Jauna Khan.

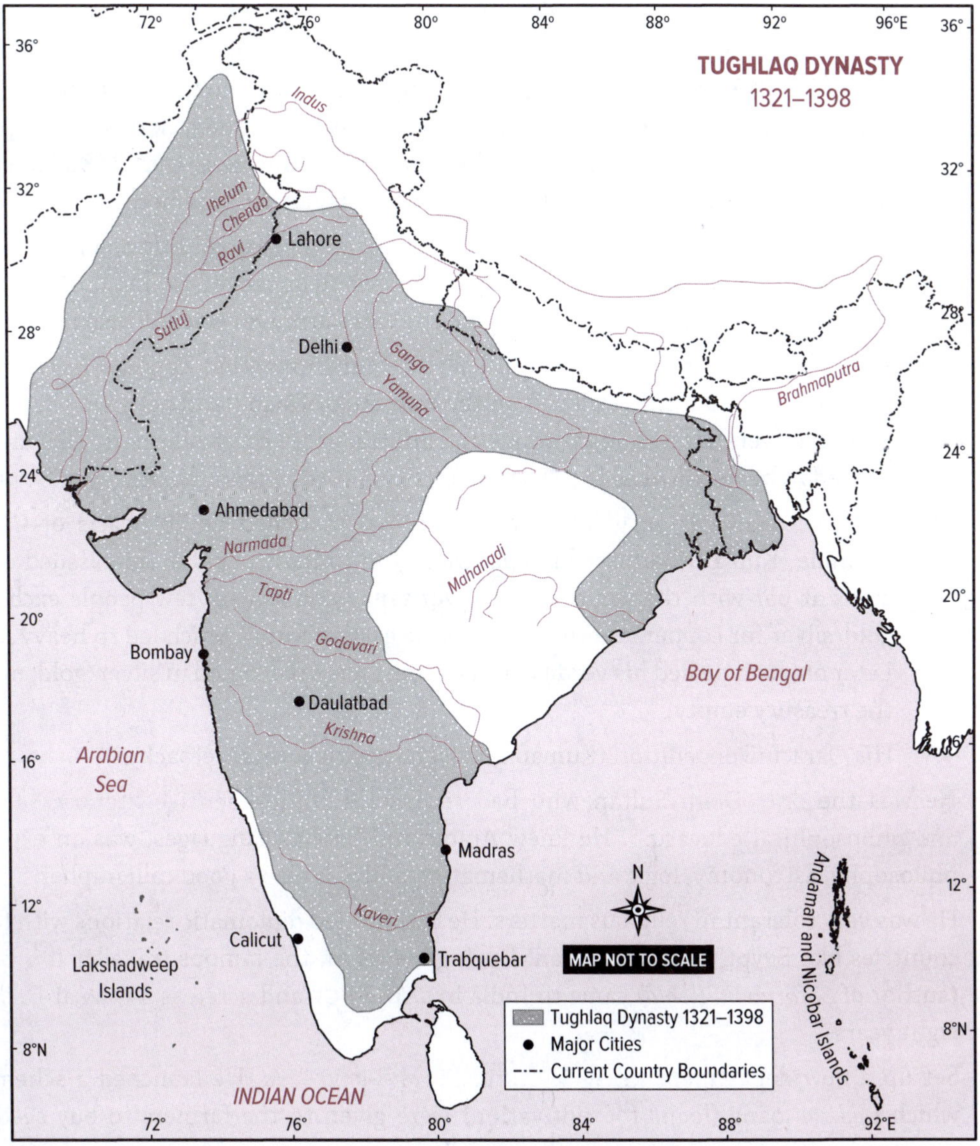

FIGURE 11.3 Tughlaq Dynasty Map

Mohammad Bin Tughlaq/Jauna Khan (c. 1325–1351 CE)

- He is considered an ill-fated idealist owing to his ambitious schemes and novel experiments, which ended in miserable failures because they were all far ahead of their time.

- Ziauddin Barni mentions his five experiments/campaigns:
    i. Transferred his capital from Delhi to Devagiri (Daulatabad) to have better administration, and forcibly moved the entire population to the new capital. But the capital shifted back to Delhi after two years because of the lack of water supply in Daulatabad. The distance between these two places was more than 1500 kilometres and many people died during the rigorous journey in the summer.
    ii. After repulsing an attack of Mongols, he planned to occupy Khurasan and Iraq. For this, he organised a huge army, but as conditions improved in Iraq, he abandoned the plan and disbanded the army (paid the extra army for one full year).
    iii. In order to overcome financial difficulties, Muhammad bin Tughlaq increased the land revenue (half the produce) on the farmers of Doab (land between Ganges and Yamuna rivers). It was an excessive and arbitrary step on the farmers. This measure proved to be ill-timed as the Doab was passing through famine, followed by plague.
    iv. Idea of token currency (using copper coins) modelled on the basis of Chinese example (Kublai Khan issued paper money in China). Tughlaq thus issued copper coins at par with the value of the silver tanka coins. Very few people exchanged gold/silver for copper and the tokens were easy to forge, which led to heavy losses. Later on, he repealed his verdict, and all coins were redeemed in silver/gold, making the treasury empty.
    v. His Qarachill expedition (Kumaon Hills) met with several setbacks.
- He was the only Delhi Sultan who had received a comprehensive literary, religious and philosophical education. He knew Arabic and Persian languages, was an expert in philosophy, astronomy, logic and mathematics, and was also a good calligrapher.
- He was very tolerant in religious matters. He maintained diplomatic relations with far off countries like Egypt, China and Iran. During his reign, the famous traveller Ibn Batuta (author of *Safarnama Rehla*) came to India in c. 1334 CE and acted as a *Qazi* at Delhi for eight years.
- Set up a new department of Agriculture, *Diwan-i-amir-kohi.* He launched a scheme by which *takkavi* loans (loans for cultivation) were given to the farmers to buy seed and to extend cultivation. A model farm under the state was created in an area of 64 square miles, for which the government spent seventy lakh tankas. This experiment was further continued by Firoz Tughlaq.
- Built the fort of Adilabad and the city of Jahanpanah.
- During his last days, the whole of South India became independent and three major states emerged:
    - Vijaynagar Kingdom – Harihara and Bukka (c. 1336 CE)

    - Bahmani Kingdom (Deccan) – Hasan Gangu (c. 1347 CE)
    - Sultanate of Madurai: The rebellion of Hasan Shah resulted in the establishment of the Madurai Sultanate.
- Along with Southern states, the governors of Oudh, Multan and Sindh revolted against the authority of Muhammad bin Tughlaq. In Gujarat, Taghi rose in revolt against the Sultan who spent nearly three years in chasing him.
- Muhammad bin Tughlaq's health became worse and he died in c. 1351 CE. According to Baduani, *the Sultan was freed from his people and the people from the Sultan*. According to Barani, Muhammad bin Tughlaq was a mixture of opposites. His reign marked the beginning of the process of its decline.

Firoz Shah Tughlaq (c. 1351–1388 CE)

- He had the *unique* distinction of being chosen as Sultan by the nobles. So, his policy aimed to appease the nobles, the army and theologicians.
- He appointed *Khan-i-Jahan* Maqbal, a Telugu Brahmin convert, as *Wazir* (prime minister). The Wazir helped the Sultan in his administration and maintained the prestige of the Sultanate during this period.
- After his accession, Firoz had to face the problem of preventing the disintegration of the Delhi Sultanate. Instead of reasserting his authority over the Deccan and south India, he tried to safeguard his authority over north India. He led two unsuccessful campaigns to Bengal, which, as a result, became free from the control of Delhi Sultanate.
- Firoz led a campaign against Jajnagar (modern Orissa). He returned with rich booty acquired from temples such as the Puri Jagannath temple. He marched against Nagarkot and made its ruler pay him tributes. During this campaign, the Sultan collected 1300 Sanskrit manuscripts from the Jawalamukhi temple library and got them translated into Persian by Arizuddin Khan 'Dalail-i-Firuz Shahi'. Firoz next marched against Thatta in the Sindh region and crushed a rebellion there.
- He strictly followed the advice of the *ulemas* in running the administration. As per the Islamic law, he levied the taxes. *Jaziya* was strictly imposed on non-Muslims. He treated Hindus as second grade citizens and adopted a very harsh attitude towards them (for instance a Brahmin was burnt publicly for questioning the Quran). In this respect, he was the precursor of Sikandar Lodhi and Aurangazeb. The special tax on 28 items was abolished by him since they were against Islamic law. He also prohibited Muslim women from going to worship at the grave of saints and also persecuted a number of heretical Muslim sects (Shia Muslims and Sufis).
- Had great regard for Caliph of Egypt and styled himself as his deputy and twice received robes of honour from him.

- He not only revived the *Iqtadari* system but also made it hereditary. Soldiers were given land assignments (jagir system), and even their recruitment was made hereditary.
- He was the first Sultan to impose *Sharb* (irrigation tax). But at the same time, he built number of canals and also set up a separate department of public works.
    - Sirsa to Hansi
    - Sutlej to Hansi: Longest canal (about 200 kilometres)
    - Yamuna to Hissar
- During his reign there were about 1200 fruit gardens in and around Delhi yielding good revenue:
    - *Kharaj* – 10% of produce
    - *Zakat* – Alms for Muslims
    - *Khams* – 20% spoils of war
- Introduced 2 new coins: *Adha* (50% Jital) and *Bitch* (23% Jital)
- He also developed royal factories called *karkhanas* in which thousands of slaves were employed, organised under the *Diwan-i-Bandagan* (department of slaves). The officer-in-charge was the *Wakil-i-dar*. He increased the number of slaves by capturing the defeated soldiers and young persons.
- About 300 new towns were built during his reign. The famous among them was Firozabad near Red Fort in Delhi, now called Firoz Shah Kotla, Hisar, Jaunpur (considered the Shiraz of the east).
- Old monuments like the Jama Masjid and the Qutab Minar (which was struck by lightning, and the fourth storey was subsequently replaced by two smaller ones) were repaired. Ashokan pillars from Topara and Meerut were brought to Delhi.
- A new department called *Diwan-i-Khairat* (Department of Charity) was created to take care of orphans and widows. Free hospitals like *Dar-ul-Shafa* and marriage bureaus for poor Muslims were also established.
- Firoz patronised scholars like Barani (famous historian who wrote *Tarikh-i-Firoz Shah* and *Futwa-i-Jahandari*) and Khwajja Abdul Malik Islami (who wrote *Futah-Us-Sulatin*). He himself wrote the *Futuhat-e-firozshahi*.
- When Firoz Shah Tughlaz died in c. 1388 CE, the struggle for power between the Sultan and the nobles started once again. His successors had to face the rebellion of the slaves created by Firoz.

Muhammad Khan

↓

Ghiyaddin Tughlaq Shah II

↓

Abu Bakr Shah

↓

Nasiruddin Muhammad (c. 1390–1398 CE)

- In the following years, the Delhi Sultanate had disintegrated further. Many provinces like Malwa and Gujarat declared their independence.
- Timur (Mongol leader of Central Asia, head of Chaghtai Turks, whose vast kingdom stretched from lower Volga to river Indus, incorporating modern Turkey, Iran, Transoxiana, Afghanistan, parts of Punjab, and who had already conquered Mesopotamia and Afghanistan) invaded India in c. 1398 CE, which further worsened the situation.
- When Timur entered Delhi, there was no opposition and he sacked Delhi for three days murdering thousands of people and looting enormous wealth. He withdrew from India in c. 1399 CE and his invasion delivered a death blow to the Tughlaq dynasty.

Daulat Khan

- Defeated by Khizr Khan who founded the Saiyyad Dynasty.

Sayyid Dynasty[1] (c. 1414–1451 CE)

Khizr Khan (c. 1414–1421 CE)

- Before his departure from India, Timur appointed Khizr Khan as the governor of Multan. He captured Delhi and founded the Sayyid dynasty in c. 1414 CE. However, he did not assume the title of Sultan but was comfortable with *Rayat-i-Ala*. Coins were struck and khutba was read in name of Timur, and after his death, in the name of his successor Shahrukh.
- Khizr Khan was the most competent Sayyid ruler. He tried to consolidate the Delhi Sultanate but could not do much and died in c. 1421 CE.

[1] The Sayyids derived their name from the Arabic title **"Sayyid,"** which means descendants of the Prophet and thus, they claimed lineage from the Prophet Muhammad, which lent them religious legitimacy and prestige. They commanded special respect in Muslim society and even Timur, who is known for brutal violence and slaughter, protected the life of Saiyyads during his invasion. The Sayyids used to put on a pointed cap (*kulah*) and were also thus known as '*Kulah Daran*' during the Delhi Sultanate.

Mubarak Shah (c. 1421–1433 CE)

- Khizr Khan was succeeded by his son, Mubarak Shah who discontinued his father's nominal allegiance to Timur.
- According to some historians, he was the 1st Sultan to appoint Hindu nobles to the court of Delhi.

Muhammad Shah (c. 1434–1443 CE)

- He was always busy acting against conspirators and gradually lost control over his nobles[2].
- Muhammad Shah died in 1445 and was succeeded by his son Alam Shah. He is remembered for his patronage of the arts and architecture. He commissioned several mosques and tombs, including his own tomb in the Lodi Gardens.

Alauddin Alam Shah (c. 1443–1451 CE)

- He proved to be an incompetent Sultan and the weakest of the Sayyid princes.
- Alam Shah's Wazir, Hamid Khan, invited Bahlol Lodhi to take charge of the army and after realising that it would be difficult to continue as Sultan, Alam Shah left for Badaun.

Lodhi Dynasty (c. 1451–1526 CE)

The Lodhis were the last ruling family of the Sultanate period and the first to be headed by the Afghans who were ruling over Sirhind when the Sayyids were in India.

Bahlol Lodhi (c. 1451–1489 CE)

- With the help of a few nobles, Bahlol Lodhi took charge of the army and became the Sultan. Thus, he laid the foundation of Lodhi dynasty.
- Sultan Bahlol Lodhi was a capable general and was well aware of the fact that to establish his control over Sultanate, he would require help and support of Afghan nobles. The Afghan nobles wanted Sultan to treat them as an equal partner rather than an absolute monarch. To placate them, Bahlol publicly declared that he considered himself one of the Afghan peers and not the king. He did not sit on the throne, nor did he insist on his nobles standing in his court. This policy worked well throughout his long reign and he did not face any trouble from his powerful Afghan nobles.
- He successfully suppressed the revolts in Mewat and Doab. In c. 1476 CE, he defeated the Sultan of Jaunpur and annexed it to Delhi Sultanate. He also brought the ruler of Kalpi and Dholpur under the suzerainty of Delhi. He annexed Sharqui dynasty and introduced Bahlol copper coins. However, he failed to re-occupy Bengal, Gujarat and the Deccan.

---

[2] Infact, all of the rulers of Sayyid dynasty tried to control rebellious regions like Katehar, Badaun, Etawah, Patiali, Gwalior, Kampil, Nagaur and Mewat, but they failed due to the conspiracy of the nobles.

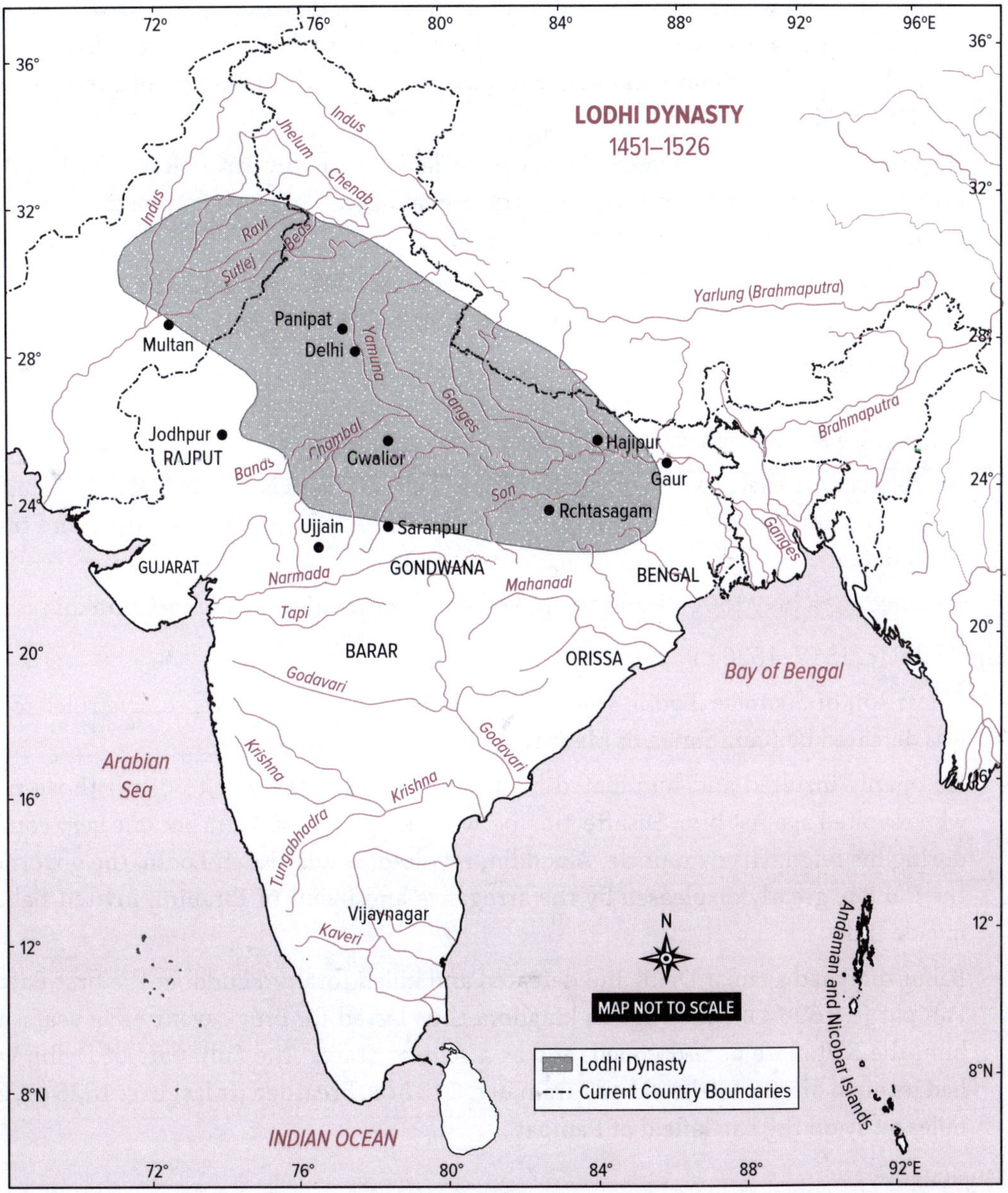

FIGURE 11.4 Lodhi Dynasty Map

Sikander Lodhi (c. 1489–1517 CE)

- He was the greatest and noblest of the three Lodhi rulers.
- His mother was a Hindu and his real name was Nizam Khan.

- He brought the whole of Bihar under his control, and defeated many Rajput chiefs. He attacked Bengal and forced its ruler to conclude a treaty with him, and extended his empire from the Punjab to Bihar including Dholpur, Narwar, and some parts of the kingdom of Gwalior and Nagor.
- He was a good administrator. Roads were laid and many irrigational facilities were provided for the benefit of the peasantry. He laid great emphasis on justice. During his reign, prices of commodities were very cheap.
- Introduced a new measurement yardstick, the *Gazz-i-Sikandari*, and a system of auditing of accounts.
- Despite certain laudable qualities, he was a bigot and showed little tolerance towards the non-Muslims. He destroyed many Hindu temples and imposed many restrictions on the Hindus. He re-imposed *jaziya* on non-Muslims.
- He believed in the superior position of the Sultan vis-a-vis the nobles. He compelled nobles and amirs to show formal respect to the Sultan in and outside darbar and treated them harshly.
- Founded Agra in c. 1504 CE and wrote Persian verses under the name 'Gulrakhi'.

Ibrahim Lodhi (c. 1517–1526 CE)

- Eldest son of Sikander Lodhi, who was not only arrogant but a repressive ruler too. He was defeated by Rana Sanga of Mewar.
- He openly insulted and humiliated his nobles in court and put to death those nobles who revolted against him. Disaffection between king and courtiers became very common during his reign. His own uncle, Alauddin, revolted. Daulat Khan Lodhi, the governor of the Punjab, greatly displeased by the arrogance and insult of Ibrahim, invited Babur to invade India.
- Babur marched against Delhi and defeated and killed Ibrahim Lodhi in the first Battle of Panipat (c. 1526 CE). The Afghan kingdom thus lasted for only seventy-five years. With him, the Sultanate period ended, and as a scholar states 'The Sultanate of Delhi, which had its birth on the battlefield of Tarain in c. 1192 CE, breathed its last in c. 1526 CE, a few miles away on the battlefield of Panipat'.

The Mughals

Administration Under Sultanate Period

The establishment and expansion of the Delhi Sultanate led to the evolution of a powerful and efficient administrative system. At its zenith, the Delhi Sultanate controlled almost the entire country as far south as Madurai. Even after its disintegration, the Delhi Sultanate and its administrative system made a powerful impact on the Indian provincial kingdoms, and later on the Mughal system of administration.

The Sultan

The title of 'Sultan' was started by Turkish rulers and Mahmud of Ghazni was the first to assume the title of Sultan. The Delhi Sultanate was an Islamic state with its religion as Islam. The Sultans considered themselves as representatives of the Caliph. They included the name of the Caliph in the *khutba* or prayer and inscribed it on their coins. This practice was even continued by Balban, who called himself the shadow of God. Iltutmish, Muhammad bin Tughlaq and Firoz Tughlaq obtained *mansur* (letter of investiture) from the Caliph. The office of the Sultan was the most important in the Sultanate and he was the ultimate authority for the military, legal and political matters. The dispensation of justice was another important function performed by the Sultan and he acted as a court of appeal. For instance, Balban dispensed justice with extreme impartiality, not sparing even the high officers of state. Muhammad bin Tughlaq even gave harsh punishments to *ulemas*, who were previously exempted.

There was no clear law of succession during this period. All the sons had equal claim to the throne. Interestingly, the idea of primogeniture was fully acceptable neither to the Muslims nor to the Hindus. Iltutmish even nominated his daughter in preference to his sons. But such nominations or successions were to be mostly accepted by the nobles. Sometimes, ulemas also played crucial role in getting a favourable public opinion. However, military superiority remained the main factor in matters of succession.

Central Administration

The Sultan was assisted by a number of ministers who headed different departments and aided in administration. These ministers were chosen by Sultan and they remained in office at his pleasure. The post of *Naib* was the most powerful one. The Naib practically enjoyed all the powers of the Sultan and exercised general control over all the departments. Next to him, was the *Wazir*, who headed the finance department called *Diwan-i-Wizarat*. A separate Auditor General for scrutinising expenditure and an accountant general for inspecting income worked under the Wazir. The period of Wazir-ship of Firuz Tughlaq Khan-i-Jahan is generally considered as the high watermark period of the Wazir's influence.

The military department was called *Diwan-i-Arz*. It was headed by the *Ariz-i-mumalik* who was responsible for recruiting the soldiers and administering the military department. It should be noted that the Ariz was not the commander-in-chief of the army, since the Sultan himself was the commander-in-chief of the armed forces. The military department was first set up by Balban and was further improved by Alauddin Khalji, who insisted on a regular muster of the armed forces. Alauddin introduced the Chehra and Dagh system, so that along with a descriptive roll of each soldier, a system of branding of the horses was also in place which would allow only good quality horses to be part of muster. He was also the first Sultan to pay his soldiers salary in cash. He also had the largest standing and efficient army of about three lakhs, which was definitely a main factor in containing the Mongol invasions along with his Deccan expansion. The Turks also maintained a large number of elephants properly trained for war purposes. However, there was predominance of the Cavalry which was considered more prestigious. At the time of Ghaznavids, Hindus were employed both in the infantry and cavalry but during the Sultanate period they were largely employed in the infantry.

Diwan-i-Rasalat was the department of religious affairs, which dealt with pious foundations and gave stipends to deserving scholars and men of piety. Grants were made by this department also for the construction and maintenance of mosques, tombs and madrasas. It was headed by chief *Sadr* who also functioned as Chief *Qazi,* as the head of the judicial department. Other judges or qazis were appointed in various parts of the Sultanate. Muslim personal law or *sharia* was followed in civil matters. The Hindus were governed by their own personal law and their cases were dispensed by the village panchayats. The criminal law was based on the rules and regulations made by the Sultans. The department of correspondence was called *Diwan-i-Insha.* All the correspondence between the ruler and the sovereigns of other states as well as with his subordinate officials was dealt with by this department.

Provincial Government

The provinces under the Delhi Sultanate were called *iqtas.* They were initially under the control of the nobles. But the governors of the provinces were called the *muqtis* or *walis.* They were to maintain law and order and collect the land revenue. The provinces were further divided into *shiqs,* which was under the control of the *shiqdar,* and the next division was *pargana,* comprising a number of villages and was headed by the *amil.* The villages were grouped into units of 100 or 84 (traditionally called *chaurasi*). The village remained the basic unit of the administration. The village headman was known as *muqaddam* or *chaudhri.* The village accountant was called *patwari.*

Iqtas (Province) ⟶ *muqtis or walis* (governor)

↓

shiqs (District) ⟶ *shiqdar*

↓

pargana (Sub-districts) ⟶ *amil*

↓

Village ⟶ *muqaddam or chaudhri*

Economy

After consolidating their position in India, the Delhi Sultans introduced reforms in the land revenue administration. The lands were classified into three categories:

1. *Iqta* land – Lands assigned to officials as iqtas instead of payment for their services.
2. *Khalisa* land – Land under the direct control of the Sultan and the revenues collected were spent for the maintenance of royal court and royal household.
3. *Inam* land – Land assigned or granted to religious leaders or religious institutions.

A class of *khuts* (smaller landlords) and Hindus *rais* (autonomous *rajas*) emerged, who not only enjoyed a higher standard of life but sometimes they misused their power and exploited the poor peasants. Stern actions were taken against them by Alauddin Khalji. However, the general peasantry paid one third of their produce as land revenue, and sometimes even one half of the produce. They also paid other taxes and always led a hand-to-mouth living. Frequent famines made their lives more miserable. However, Sultans like Muhammad bin Tughlaq and Firoz Tughlaq took efforts to enhance agricultural production by providing irrigational facilities and by providing *takkavi* loans. They also encouraged the farmers to cultivate superior crop like wheat instead of barley. Firoz encouraged the growth of horticulture. Muhammad bin Tughlaq created a separate agricultural department, *Diwan-i-Kohi.* The Sultan and his nobles took keen interest in improving the quality of fruits in India, especially melons and grapes. Ibn Batuta records in his texts that the soil was so fertile that it could produce two crops every year, rice being sown three times a year.

During the Sultanate period, the process of urbanisation gained momentum. A number of cities and towns had grown during this period. Lahore and Multan (in the north west), Broach, Cambay and Anhilwara (in the west), Kara and Lakhnauti in the east, Daulatabad, Delhi and Jaunpur were important among them. Delhi remained the largest city in the east. The growth of trade and commerce was described by contemporary writers. India exported a large number of commodities to the countries on the Persian Gulf and West Asia and also to South East Asian countries. Bengal (specially Sonargaon for muslin, i.e., fine cotton cloth) and the towns in Gujarat were famous for fine quality fabrics. Cambay in Gujarat was famous for textiles and for gold and silver work. India imported high grade textiles (satin, etc.), glassware and horses from West Asia. From China, it imported raw silk and porcelain. Overseas trade was under the control of Multanis (mostly Hindus) and Khurasanis (Afghan Muslims). Inland trade was dominated by Gujarati, Marwari and Muslim Bohra merchants. The merchants were extremely wealthy and lived a luxurious life. The Gujarati and Marwari merchants were mostly Jains and they spent large sums for the construction of temples.

Construction of roads and their maintenance facilitated for smooth transport and communication. Particularly, the royal roads were kept in good shape. In addition to royal road from Peshawar to Sonargaon, Muhammad bin Tughlaq built road to Daulatabad. *Sarais* or rest houses on the highways were maintained for the convenience of the travellers. There were also arrangements for posts to be carried very quickly from one part of the country to another with the help of relays of horses and runners who were posted every few kilometres.

Cotton textile and silk industry flourished in this period. Sericulture was introduced on a large scale, which made India less dependent on other countries for the import of raw silk. The paper industry had grown and there was an extensive use of paper from 14th and 15th centuries. Other crafts like leather-making, metal-crafts and carpet-weaving flourished due to the increasing demand. The royal *karkhanas* supplied the goods needed to the Sultan and his household. They manufactured costly articles made of gold, silver and gold ware. The nobles also aped the lifestyle of the Sultans and indulged in luxurious living. They were well paid and accumulated enormous wealth.

The system of coinage had also developed during the Delhi Sultanate. Iltutmish issued several types of silver *tankas*. One silver tanka was divided into 48 jitals during the Khalji rule and 50 jitals during the Tughlaq rule. Gold coins or *dinars* became popular during the reign of Alauddin Khalji after his South Indian conquests. Copper coins were less in number and dateless. Muhammad bin Tughlaq had not only experimented with token currency but also issued several types of gold and silver coins. They were minted at eight different places. At least twenty five varieties of gold coins were issued by him.

The Turks popularised a number of crafts and techniques such as:

a. Use of iron stirrup

b. Use of armour both for the horse and rider.

c. Improvement of *rahat* (Persian wheel through which water could be lifted from a deeper level for irrigation)

FIGURE 11.5 Persian Wheel

d. Paper-making, glass-making, the spinning wheel and an improved loom for weaving.

e. Use of superior mortar, which enabled the Turks to erect magnificent buildings based on the arch and dome.

Social System

There was little change in the structure of the Hindu society during this period. Traditional caste system with the Brahmins on the upper strata of the society was prevalent. The subservient position of women also continued and the practice of Sati was widely prevalent. Ibn Batuta had mentioned with horror the scene of a woman burning herself in the funeral pyre of her husband with great beating of drums. The Arabs and Turks brought the *purdah* system into India and the seclusion of women, and the wearing of purdah became widespread among the women in the upper Hindu classes of north India.

During the Sultanate period, the Muslim society remained divided into several ethnic and racial groups. The Turks, Iranians, Afghans, and Indian Muslims developed as exclusive groups and there were no intermarriages between them. Hindu converts from lower castes were also not given equal respect. The Muslim nobles occupied high offices and very rarely the Hindu nobles were given high position in the government. The Hindus were considered *zimmis* or protected people, for which they were forced to pay a tax called *jaziya.* In the beginning *jaziya* was collected as part of land tax. Firoz Tughlaq separated it from the land revenue and collected *jaziya* as a separate tax and levied it on Brahmans also.

Even though slavery had existed in India since ancient times, it flourished during the Sultanate period. There were slave markets for men and women and slaves were hired for varied jobs ranging from household chores to skilled professions. Firoz Shah Tughlaq had about 1,80,000 slaves.

Art and Architecture

The art and architecture of the Delhi Sultanate period was distinct from the Indian style. The Turks introduced arches, domes, lofty towers, or minarets and decorations using the Arabic script. They used the skill of the Indian stone-cutters. They also added colour to their buildings by using marbles, red and yellow sand stones.

In the beginning, they converted a number of Hindu temples into mosques. For instance, the Quwwat-ul-Islam mosque near Qutub Minar in Delhi was formerly a Vishnu temple. But later, they began to construct new structures. Their policy towards temples and places of Hindu worship forbade new places of worship but allowed the repair of old temples. The most magnificent building of the 13th century was the Qutub Minar, which was founded by Aibak and completed by Iltutmish. This 71 m tower was dedicated to the Sufi saint, Khwaja Qutbuddin Bakthiyar Kaki. The balconies of this tower were projected from the main building and it was the proof of the architectural skills of that period. Later, Alauddin Khalji added an entrance to the Qutub Minar called Alai Darwaza. The dome of this arch was built on scientific lines.

FIGURE 11.6 Qutub Minar

FIGURE 11.7 Alai Darwaza

The buildings of the Tughlaq period were constructed by combining arch and dome. They also used the cheaper and easily available grey colour stones. The palace complex called Tughlaqabad with its beautiful lake was built during the period of Ghiyasuddin Tughlaq. Muhammad bin Tughlaq built the tomb of Ghyasuddin on a high platform. The Kotla fort at Delhi was the creation of Firoz Tughlaq. The Lodhi garden in Delhi is an example of the architecture of the Lodhis.

Music

New musical instruments such as the *sarangi* and the *rabab* were introduced during this period. Amir Khusrau introduced many new *ragas* such as Ghora and Sanam. He evolved a new style of light music known as *qawwalis* by blending the Hindu and Iranian systems. The invention of sitar is also attributed to him. The Indian classical work, *Ragadarpan,* was translated into Persian during the reign of Firoz Tughlaq. Pir Bhodan, a Sufi saint, was one of the great musicians of this period. Raja Man Singh of Gwalior was a great lover of music. He encouraged the composition of a great musical work called *Man Kautuhal.*

Literature

The Delhi Sultans patronised learning and literature. Many of them had great love for Arabic and Persian literature. Learned men came from Persia and Persian language got encouragement from the rulers. Besides theology and poetry, the writing of history was also encouraged. Some of the Sultans had their own court historians. The most famous historians of this period were Hasan Nizami, Minhaj-us-Siraj, Ziauddin Barani and Shams Siraj Afif. Barani's *Tarikh-i-Firoz Shahi* contains the history of Tughlaq dynasty. Minhaj-us-Siraj wrote *Tabaqat-i-Nasari*, a general history of Muslim dynasties up to c. 1260 CE.

Amir Khusrau (c. 1252–1325 CE) was the most famous Persian writer of this period. He wrote a number of poems. He experimented with several poetical forms and created a new style of Persian poetry called *Sabaq-i-Hind* or the Indian style. He also wrote some Hindi verses. Amir Khusrau's *Khazain-ul-Futuh* speaks about Alauddin's conquests. His famous work, the *Tughlaq Nama,* deals with the rise of Ghyasuddin Tughlaq.

Sanskrit and Persian functioned as link languages in the Delhi Sultanate. Zia Nakshabi was the first to translate Sanskrit stories into Persian. The book *Tutu Nama* or the Book of the Parrot became popular and was translated into Turkish and later into many European languages. The famous *Rajatarangini* written by Kalhana belonged to the period of Zain-ul-Abidin, the ruler of Kashmir. Many Sanskrit works on medicine and music were translated into Persian. In Arabic, Alberuni's *Kitab-ul-Hind* is the most famous work. Regional languages also developed during this period. Chand Bardai was the famous Hindi poet of this period. Bengali literature had also developed and Nusrat Shah patronised the translation of Mahabaratha into Bengali.

Concept/Term	Meaning/Purpose
(a) *Majlis-i-Khalwat*	Council of friends and trusted officers who advised the Sultan, though their advice was not binding.
(b) Amirs/*Chahalgani*	Nobles/Group of Forty. Dominant during Iltutmish's reign; Balban crushed their power.
(c) *Diwan-i-Wizarat*	Finance department headed by *Wazir.* The Tughlaq period were the heydays of the *Wizarat.*

Concept/Term	Meaning/Purpose
(d) *Mustaufi-i- Mammalik*	Auditor general, responsible for state expenditure. In charge of accounts and receipts.
(e) *Khazin*	Treasurer
(f) *Bar-i-Khas*	The space where the Sultan received all his courtiers including *Khans, Maliks*.
(g) *Bar-i-Aam*	The place where the Sultan tried cases, received petitions and complaints from people.
(h) *Amir-i-Behr*	Controller of boats
(i) *Muhtasib*	Officer who kept strict watch over conduct of people
(j) *Diwan-i-Ishtihlqaq*	Department of charity and mint.
(k) *Amir-i-Haqib/Barbek*	Master of ceremonies.
(l) *Wakil-i-Dar*	Managed royal household.
(m) *Zawabit*	State laws
(n) *Jahandari*	Laws made by Sultans
(o) *Khet Batai*	Without separating anything, land revenue on basis of standing crop.
(p) *Lank Batai*	Without separating grain from chaff.
(q) *Ras Batai*	After separating grain from chaff.
(r) *Masahat*	On the basis of measurement of land
(s) *Umara*	Plural of *amirs*, *amir* means nobles or ruling groups in Delhi Sultanate.
(t) Ulema	Muslims of religious learning
(u) *Jaziya*	Personal and yearly tax on non-Muslims
(v) *Mameluks*	Slave officers
(w) Malik	One of the highest grades of the officers.
(x) *Fawazil*	Excess amount paid to the exchequer by the *iqtadars*.

QUESTIONS FROM LAST YEAR'S PRELIMS

1. With reference to Indian history, consider the following statements: **(2022)**

1. The first Mongol invasion of India happened during the reign of Jalal-ud-din Khalji.
2. During the reign of Ala-ud-din Khalji, one Mongol assault marched up to Delhi and besieged the city.
3. Muhammad-bin-Tughlaq temporarily lost portions of north-west of his kingdom to Mongols.

Which of the statements given above is/are correct?

(a) 1 and 2 (b) 2 only
(c) 1 and 3 (d) 3 only

2. With reference to Indian history, who of the following were known as "Kulah-Daran"? **(2022)**

(a) Arab merchants
(b) Qalandars
(c) Persian calligraphists
(d) Sayyids

3. Consider the following statements: **(2021)**

1. It was during the reign of Iltutmish that Chengiz Khan reached the Indus in pursuit of the fugitive Khwarezm prince.
2. It was during the reign of Muhammad bin Tughluq that Taimur occupied Multan and crossed the Indus.
3. It was during the reign of Deva Raya II of Vijayanagara Empire that Vasco da Gama reached the coast of Kerala.

Which of the statements given above is/are correct?

(a) 1 only (b) 1 and 2
(c) 3 only (d) 2 and 3

4. Consider the following statements: **(2019)**

1. In the revenue administration of Delhi Sultanate, the in-charge of revenue collection was known as 'Amil'.
2. The lqta system of Sultans of Delhi was an ancient indigenous institution.
3. The office of 'Mir Bakshi' came into existence during the reign of Khalji Sultans of Delhi.

Which of the statements given above is/are correct?

(a) 1 only (b) 1 and 2 only
(c) 3 only (d) 1, 2 and 3

5. Which one of the following is the correct chronological order of the Afghan rulers to the throne of Delhi? **(2006)**

(a) Sikander Shah-Ibrahim Lodhi-Bahlol Khan Lodhi
(b) Sikander Shah-Bahlol Khan Lodhi-Ibrahim Lodhi
(c) Bahlol Khan Lodhi-Sikander Shah-Ibrahim Lodhi
(d) Bahlol Khan Lodhi-Ibrahim Lodhi-Sikander Shah

6. Assertion (A): Muhammad bin Tughlaq issued a new gold coin which was called dinar by Ibn Batuta.

Reasoning (R): Muhammad bin Tughlaq wanted to issue token currency in gold coins to promote trade with West Asian and North African countries. **(2006)**

(a) Both A and R are true and R is the correct explanation of A
(b) Both A and R are true but R is not the correct explanation of A
(c) A is true but R is false
(d) A is false but R is true

7. Who was the last ruler of the Tughlaq dynasty of the Delhi Sultanate? **(2004)**

(a) Firoz Shah Tughlaq
(b) Ghiyasuddin Tughlaq
(c) Nasiruddin Mahmud
(d) Nasrat Shah

8. How did Sultan Qutbuddin Aibak die? **(2003)**

(a) He was treacherously stabbed to death by one of his ambitious nobles.
(b) He was killed in a battle with Tajuddin Yaldauz, the ruler of Ghazni, who entered into a contest with him over the capture of Punjab.
(c) He sustained injuries while besieging the fortress of Kalinjar in Bundelkhand and succumbed to them later.

(d) He died after a fall from his horse while playing Chaugan.

9. Alam Khan, one of those who invited Babur to invade India was **(2003)**

(a) An uncle of Ibrahim Lodhi and a pretender to the throne of Delhi.
(b) A cousin of Ibrahim Lodhi who was ill-treated and expelled from the country.
(c) The father of Dilawar Khan to whom cruel treatment was meted by Ibrahim Lodhi.
(d) A high official of Punjab province who was very discontented with Ibrahim Lodhi's treatment to his tribe.

10. The first writer to use Urdu as the medium of poetic expression was **(1999)**

(a) Amir Khusrau
(b) Mirza Ghalib
(c) Bahadur Shah Zafar
(d) Faiz

11. 'The king was freed from his people and they from their king' – On whose death did Badauni comment thus? **(1999)**

(a) Balban
(b) Aladdin Khalji
(c) Muhammad bin Tughlaq
(d) Firoz Shah Tughlaq

12. The Sultan of Delhi who is reputed to have built the biggest network of canals in India was **(1998)**

(a) Iltutmish
(b) Ghiyasuddin Tughlaq
(c) Firoz Shah Tughlaq
(d) Sikander Lodhi

13. Fawazil in the Sultanate period means **(1998)**

(a) Extra payment made to the nobles
(b) Revenue assigned in lieu of salary
(c) Excess amount paid to the exchequer by the iqtadars
(d) Illegal exactions extracted from the peasants

14. Consider the following: **(1998)**

1. Tughlaqabad Fort
2. Lodhi Garden
3. Qutub Minar
4. Fatehpur Sikri

The correct chronological order in which they were built is:

(a) 3, 1, 4, 2 (b) 3, 1, 2, 4
(c) 1, 3, 2, 4 (d) 1, 3, 4, 2

15. Assertion (A): At first the Turkish administration in India was essentially military.

Reasoning (R): The country was parcelled out as 'Iqtas' among leading military leaders. **(1998)**

(a) Both A and R are true and R is the correct explanation of A
(b) Both A and R are true but R is not the correct explanation of A
(c) A is true but R is false
(d) A is false but R is true

16. After consolidating his power, Balban assumed the grand title of **(1997)**

(a) Tute-i-Hind (b) Kaisar-i-Hind
(c) Zil-i-ilahi (d) Din-i-illahi

ANSWERS

1. (b)	2. (d)	3. (a)	4. (a)	5. (c)	6. (c)	7. (c)	8. (d)
9. (a)	10. (a)	11. (c)	12. (c)	13.(c)	14. (b)	15. (a)	16. (c)

QUESTIONS FROM LAST YEAR'S MAINS

1. Discuss in brief the land revenue system and judicial administration of the Delhi Sultanate. **(2015, History optional)**
2. Analyse the ordinances mentioned by Barani which Aladdin Khalji promulgated for market control. **(2014, History optional)**

PRACTICE QUESTIONS – PRELIMS

1. Match the following:

(A) Muhammad bin Tughlaq	(i) Market reforms
(B) Firoz Shah Tughlaq	(ii) Policy of Blood and Iron
(C) Balban	(iii) Department of Public works
(D) Alauddin Khalji	(iv) Shifted capital to Daulatabad

(a) (A)–ii, (B)–i, (C)–iii, (D)–iv
(b) (A)–i, (B)–ii, (C)–iii, (D)–iv
(c) (A)–iv, (B)–iii, (C)–ii, (D)–i
(d) (A)–iii, (B)–i, (C)–ii, (D)–iv

2. Consider the following statements and mark the option which is correct.
   (i) Iltumish introduced the Sajda and Paibos.
   (ii) Qutubuddin Aibak was the founder of the Slave Dynasty.
   (iii) Aibak died while playing Chaugan.
   (iv) Ilutmish constructed the Quwal-ul-Islam mosque at Delhi.

   (a) i and ii (b) All of the above
   (c) ii and iii (d) None of the above

3. Consider the following statements and mark the option which is correct.
   (i) Aibak was also known as Lakh Baksh.
   (ii) Ilutmish shifted his capital from Lahore to Delhi.
   (iii) Ilutmish introduced the Iqtadari system.

   Which of the statements given above is/are correct?
   (a) 1 only (b) 1 and 3 only
   (c) 2 and 3 only (d) 1, 2, and 3

4. Which one of the following is an incorrect statement?
   (a) Illutmish saved the Delhi Sultanate from the wrath of Chengiz Khan.
   (b) Illutmish completed the Qutub Minar started by Aibak.
   (c) Balban was a weak ruler who depended on nobles for everything.
   (d) Raziya Sultan was the first and the last Muslim female ruler of Sultanate period.

5. Match List I with List II and select the correct answer using the code given below the lists:

List I (Famous Book)	List II (Author)
(a) Tarikh-i-Firoz Shahi	1. Barani
(b) Khazain-ul-Futuh	2. Minhaj-us-Siraj
(c) Kitab-ul-Hind	3. Alberuni
(d) Tabaqat-i-Nasari	4. Amir Khusrau

Code:	A	B	C	D
(a)	2	4	3	1
(b)	2	3	4	1
(c)	1	4	3	2
(d)	1	3	4	2

6. Consider the following statements and identify the ruler.
(1) The Chehra and Dagh system was introduced by him.
(2) He broke the power of the Chahalgani/ the Group of Forty.
(3) He introduced market reforms.
(a) Balban
(b) Alauddin khalji
(c) Muhammad bin Tughlaq
(d) Jalauddin Khalji

7. Consider the following statements and identify the 'he'.
(i) He served before as regent to the earlier king.
(ii) He established the military department Diwan-i-arz.
(iii) He introduced the festival of Nauroz and Sajda and Paibos.
(a) Balban
(b) Alauddin Khalji
(c) Muhammad bin Tughlaq
(d) Jalauddin Khalji

8. What is the correct chronological order of annexation of the following states by Alauddin Khalji?
(i) Ranthambore
(ii) Gujarat
(iii) Chittor
(iv) Malwa
(v) Deccan
(a) i, ii, iii, iv, v (b) ii, i, iii, v, iv
(c) ii, i, iii, iv, v (d) i, ii, iv, iii, v

9. Consider the following statements and mark the option which is correct.
(i) Malik Kafur was a trusted aide of Alauddin Khalji who won for him Deccan and South India.
(ii) Ghiyasuddin Tughlaq had a troubled relationship with Saint Nizamuddin Aulia.
(iii) Khan-i-Jahan Maqbul was an able Wazir of Firoz Shah Tughlaq.

Which of the statements given above is/are correct?
(a) 1 only (b) 1 and 3 only
(c) 2 and 3 only (d) 1, 2, and 3

ANSWERS

1. (c) 2. (c) 3. (d) 4. (c) 5. (c) 6. (b) 7. (a) 8. (c)
9. (d)

PRACTICE QUESTIONS – MAINS

1. Why did the position of the nobles decline during the period of Alauddin Khalji and Balban? What measures did they take for curtailing the power of the Chahlgani?

2. Explain the various facets of administration during the Delhi Sultanate period.

3. Barani comments, 'The permanence of prices in the market was a wonder of the age'. Which ruler is her referring to? Elucidate the different measures taken by that ruler for such market reforms.

4. 'The king was freed from his people and they from their king', said Badauni on the death of Muhammad bin Tughlaq. Why did he say so? Explain, giving suitable examples.

CHAPTER

12

Provincial Kingdoms of Medieval India

As we have discussed earlier, the Delhi Sultanate expanded as a result of the annexation of the states like Bengal, Bihar, Gujarat, Malwa, various states of *Rajputana* (like Ranthambor, Jalore, Nagore, Ajmer), the Deccan states of Warangal, Telengana, the Yadavas of Devagiri, the southern states of the Hoysalas of Dwarsamudra and the Pandyas of Madurai. However, after the 13th century (around the reign of Firoz Shah Tughlaq), due to internal weaknesses, the process of disintegration of the Delhi Sultanate started. It was during this period that some of the provincial rulers declared their independence from the rule of the Sultanate and a large number of regional states arose. The establishment of Vijayanagar and the Bahmani kingdom were a result of the assertion of power by provincial officers, like Harihara and Bukka, and Alauddin Hasan Bahman Shah, respectively. Similarly, the Sultanates in Gujarat, Malwa, Bengal and Jaunpur near

FIGURE 12.1 Provincial Kingdoms

Varanasi, emerged as powerful provincial kingdoms. This constant evolution and development of provincial states can also be explained on the basis of growth of agriculture and agriculture-related activities as *wherever good agricultural activity took place, it not only fed the population but generated a large surplus that could be sold and wealth could be generated. This resulted in the rise of powerful sections in the society that controlled the agricultural surplus. Sometimes, some members of this powerful section asserted themselves and acquired political power and became kings and established ruling dynasties, whereas sometimes some groups came from outside who conquered the land, controlled the administration, and became powerful.*

An important point to note is that all these kingdoms had a regional history that pre-dated the Sultanate period. For instance, Bengal was an important regional kingdom in the 8th and the 9th centuries under the Palas and subsequently in the 12th century under the Senas. Similarly, four important kingdoms which arose after the decline of the Cholas and the Chalukyas were the Yadavas and Kakatiyas in the Deccan and the Pandyas and the Hoysalas in the region beyond Deccan. Even the regional state of Vijayanagar ruled over different cultural zones. Hence, it should be noted that these *provincial kingdoms never disappeared, though the regional dynasties gained and lost power, and the regions changed their geographical boundaries.* Even though these states did wage wars amongst themselves, they provided stability over their respective regions. These different regional dynasties had their own vibrant culture and exclusive art, literature and architecture forms, and they too influenced each other. Thus, these provincial kingdoms were not closed isolated areas, rather they were in continuous interaction – be it religious, cultural or economic – with another kingdoms. For instance, the early Vijayanagar rulers called themselves as Hindu Suratrana, meaning Hindu Sultan, where the term Sultan was borrowed from the Delhi Sultanate. Similarly, the Iqtadari system of the Delhi Sultanate influenced the administrative systems of the Vijayanagar and Bahmani kingdoms. There were well-established trade and commerce networks, and regular migration of artisans occurred from one region to another, as evident in the migration of the silk weavers – Pattanulkars – from the Gujarat region to the Vijayanagar state in the 15th century.

Deccan and Southern India

The Yadavas of Devagiri (c. 1187–1317 CE)

The Yadavas of Devagiri[1], also known as the **Sevuna/Seuna Dynasty**, ruled across the Deccan Plateau from the 12th to the 14th centuries and had their capital at **Devagiri** (present-day Daulatabad). They were the feudatories of Rashtrakutas and the Western Chalukyas, and with the decline of the latter, they emerged as independent rulers ruling over the parts of present-day Maharashtra, North Karnataka and Madhya Pradesh till their annexation by the **Khalji Sultanate** in 1317.

Bhillama (c. 1173–1191 CE)

- Was earlier the feudatory of the Chalukyan ruler Somesvara IV but later acquired independent status in CE 1187 and founded the Yadava or Seuna dynasty.
- Mutugi inscription mentions him as '***Chakravartin Yadava***'.
- He fought with the Hoysala king **Ballala II** to control the Chalukya capital Kalyani and defeated him **at Soratur**. In 1190, he took over the Chalukya capital of Kalyani and established **Devagiri** (now Daulatabad) as the Yadava dynasty's capital.

[1] The Yadavas of Devagiri claimed their descent from the epic hero Lord Krishna and were also known as Sevunas because they ruled over Sevuna, the region from Nasik to Devagiri. The Deolali inscription mentions the information about Yadava King Seunachandra II.

- He patronised the scholar **Bhaskara**, who was Nagarjuna's teacher.

Simhana II (c. 1200–1246 CE)

- The most powerful Yadava king who took the Yadava empire to pinnacle during his reign. He was an able general and led successful military campaigns against the Hoysalas, the Kakatiyas, the Paramaras and Chalukyas. During his reign, the Yadava boundaries extended to western Madhya Pradesh and Berar, southern Gujarat, parts of Maharashtra, Karnataka, the western half of Hyderabad State and the northern districts of Mysore.
- He patronised Sarangadeva (the author of *Sangita Ratnakar*), Cangadeva (famous astrologer) and Anantadeva (another famous astrologer who wrote commentaries on Brahmagupta's *Brahmasphutasiddhanta* and Varahamihira's *Brhajjataka*).

Ramchandra (c. 1291–1309 CE)

- Another prominent Yadava ruler who fought against the Vaghelas, Hoysalas, Kakatiyas and Paramaras. However, he was defeated by **Malik Kafur,** the general of Alauddin Khalji in 1308 and was imprisoned in Delhi.

Subsequently, the Yadava Kingdom was annexed by the Khalji Sultanate in 1317 and many years later, Muhammad Tughlaq of the Tughlaq dynasty renamed the city Daulatabad.

Contribution of the Yadavas

They were the patrons of the famous Gondeshwar Temple, the 12th century Hindu temple located in the Nashik district of Maharashtra which features **Panchayatana** plan, with a main shrine dedicated to Shiva. They were also the first major dynasty to use **Marathi** as an official language, as prior to them, the primary languages of the inscriptions were Kannada and Sanskrit.

Author	Literary Work
Mukundaraya	Vivekasindhu (in Marathi)
Hemadri (celebrated Sanskrit author who lived at the court of Ramchandra)	– Chaturanga Chintamani (encyclopaedic Sanskrit work) – Introduced Modi script for writing in Marathi from Ceylon and has left some valuable historical sketch of Yadava dynasty
Mahimabhatta	Lilacharita
Gnyaneshwar	Gnyaneshwari (a Marathi language commentary on Bhagwad Gita)
Chaundarasa	Dashakumara Charite
Achanna	Vardhamanapurana
Bhaskaracharya	Karnakutuhala and Siddhanta Shiromani
Sarangadeva	Sangeet Ratnakara (considered to be first book on music)
Kamalabhava	Santhishwarapurana

The Kakatiyas of Warangal (c. 1163–1323 CE)

The Kakatiyas were the feudatories of the Chalukyas of Kalyani and Kakati Rudradeva (Prataprudra I) is considered the founder of the Kakatiya Dynasty. They established their capital at Hanumakonda and Orugallu (Warangal) while their rule extended over the parts of present-day Telangana and Andhra Pradesh and parts of eastern Karnataka and southern Odisha. The famous **Kohinoor diamond** unearthed in Kollur on the banks of the Krishna River belonged to the Kakatiyas. They also patronised famous authors: **Jayapa Senani** who wrote *Geeta Ratnavali, Nritya Ratnavali and Vadya Ratnavali* and **Tikkana Somayaji** who wrote *Nirvachanottara Ramayanamu, Vijayasenamu, Kavivaagbandhamu* and *Krishnasatakamu.*

Prataprudra I (c. 1158–1195 CE)

- In c. 1162 CE, defeated the Chalukyan ruler Tailapa III and laid the foundation of the Kakatiyas and established Hanumakonda as its capital.
- The famous Palanadu war[2] took place during his period. Later, he also successfully captured Kurnool district from the Velananti chiefs around 1185 CE.
- **Anumakonda inscription** of Rudradeva (Prataparudra I) is considered the earliest known record that describes the Kakatiyas as a sovereign power. Along with this description, **Mangallu** and the **Bayyaram inscriptions** describe the Kakatiyas as a branch of the Rashtrakuta family.
- The famous Rudresvara temple dedicated to Lord **Shiva**, Vishnu and Surya was built in Anamakonda by him. He also authored the famous Sanskrit work ***'Nitisara'***.

Ganapati Deva (c. 1198–1262 CE)

- He was another important ruler of the dynasty who captured territories up to Kanchi from the Cholas and invaded Kalinga and Western Andhra.
- He shifted the capital from **Hanumakonda** to **Warangal**.
- Took the title of '*Rayagajekesari*'.
- He created the man-made **Pakhal Lake** in Warangal and issued ***'Abhya Sasanam'*** at Motupalli port. During his reign, one of his generals Recherla Rudra got built the '**Ramappa**' temple dedicated to Lord Shiva which, in 2021, was declared a UNESCO Heritage site. The temple is made up of granite and basalt and its foundation is built with the sandbox[3] technique.
- He also adorned the famous poet Tikkana Somayaji.

[2] In which a whole generation of Andhra warriors perished and Velananti chiefs were weakened and which later helped the Kakatiyas to take over their domain.

[3] It is a technique where the foundation pit is filled with a mixture of sand-lime, jaggery and black myrobalan fruit, which acts as a cushion in the event of earthquakes.

Rudrama Devi (c. 1262–1295 CE)

- She was the daughter of Ganapati and the **first woman** ruler of the Kakatiya Dynasty.
- Italian traveller **Marco Polo** visited during her reign and paid glorious tributes to her for excellent administration and rule, describing her as '*a lady of discretion, who always strove to achieve justice and equity*'.

Prataparudra II (c. 1295–1323 CE)

- His reign faced the Muslim invasions by **Allauddin Khilji** and **Gayasuddin Tughlaq**, which eventually led to the decline of the Kakatiyas.

The Hoysalas Dynasty (c. 1050–1355 CE)

The Hoysalas were originally the feudatories of **Western Chalukyas** who later established their independent kingdom with the capital at Halebidu and Belur and ruled over the parts of the present Karnataka and most of the Tamil region from the 10th to the 14th century. Their rule marked a golden age in the history of Karnataka as they were known for their significant contributions to art, architecture, and literature.

Vishnuvardhana (c. 1108–1152 CE)

- Was the first important ruler of this dynasty though was not its founder as the **Belur inscription** of his reign mentions Sala as the founder of the Hoysala Dynasty.
- He annexed the Gangavadi and parts of Nolambavadi from the Cholas in c. 1116 CE.
- He is also known as '*Bitti Deva*' and '*Talakadugond*'.
- Initially he was a Jain but later converted to Hinduism under the influence of **Ramanujacharya**.
- He patronised the famous mathematician Rajaditya and got built the Keerthi Narayana temple at Talakad, the Hoysaleswara Temple at Halebidu and the famous Vijayanarayana or the Chennakesava[4] Temple at Belur in 1117 CE.

Veera Ballala II (c. 1173–1220 CE)

- Another prominent ruler who retained the independence of the Hoysalas and fought wars with the Yadavas (defeated Billama V), Kalachuris, Pandyas of Madurai and the Western Chalukya Empire.
- He adorned the Jain poets Janna and Nemichandra and the Brahman poet Rudrabhatta.

[4] This was later repaired by the Vijayanagara Empire under the sponsorship of Harihara II. The temple, renowned for the 48 unique pillars inside the main hall, is a Hindu temple dedicated to Lord Vishnu on the banks of the Yagachi River in the Hassan district of Karnataka and includes themes from Shaivism, Shaktism, Jainism and Buddhism.

Narasimhan-II (c. 1220–1235 CE)

- He had to defend against the aggressive designs of the Yadava and the Pandya rulers. He lost the territory between Krishna and Tungabhadra to a Yadava ruler, Singhana. However, he defeated Maravarman Sundara Pandya and restored Rajaraja-III to the Chola throne.
- He erected the pillar of victory at Rameshwaram.

Narasimhan-III (c. 1263–1291 CE)

- In 1268 CE, he got built the famous Hindu temple Kesava Temple at Somanathapura on the banks of River **Kaveri** in Karnataka. The temple is built from soapstone and is known for its lathe-turned pillars, symmetrical architecture and intricate sculptures. It depicts the legends and spiritual stories from the Ramayana, the Puranas and the Mahabharata.

Ballala III (c. 1291–1342 CE)

- He was the last great ruler of the Hoysalas dynasty.
- However, in 1310 CE, he was defeated by Malik Kafur while in 1342 CE, he fell victim to the Sultans of Madurai and died at the battle of Madurai in 1343 CE.

Later, his son Ballala IV continued his struggles with his aggressive neighbours but could not achieve much and eventually with his death, the Hoysala rule came to an end.

Contribution of the Hoysalas

The Hoysalas paved the way for the rise of Mysore into a big Kingdom. The Hoysalas were great patrons of art, architecture and literature. They developed a distinct style of architecture known as the Hoysala School of Art.

Features of the Hoysala School of Art	
(a) Multiple shrines	They built multiple shrines around a central pillared hall and the shrines were made according to the stellate plan.
(b) Material	Soft soapstone (Chlorite schist) was the main building material.
(c) Decoration	Both the interior and exterior walls were intricately carved. Sculptures and jewellery were also decorated.
(d) Interconnectedness	All the chambers had Shikharas, which were interconnected by an arrangement of horizontal lines and mouldings.
(e) Jagati	The temples were built on an upraised platform known as Jagati, which was about 1 metre high.
(f) Zigzag pattern	The walls and stairs of the temple followed a zigzag pattern.

The Hoyasala period also saw the great enrichment of **Kannada** literature, the development of the **Champu style** and the **Saptapadi metre**.

Author	Literary Work
Janna	Yashodharacharite (It is the story of a king intending to perform a ritual sacrifice of two young boys to a local deity)
Rudrabhatta	Jagannatha Vijaya (It describes the fight of Krishna with the demon Banasura)
Harihara	Girijakalyana (It represents the marriage of Shiva and Parvati)
Madhvacharya	Rigbhshya
Vidyatirtha	Rudraprshnabhashya

The Later Pandyas (c. 1216–1345 CE)

Around the first quarter of the 13th century, taking advantage of the vacuum created by the decline of Cholas, the Pandya chieftains started ruling their regions independently. It is pertinent to note that during the reign of the Pandyas, the kingdom was co ruled among several royals, one of them enjoying primacy over the rest.

Maravarman Sundara Pandyan (c. 1216–1238 CE)

- The first independent significant Pandya ruler who laid the foundation for the Pandya revival. He celebrated his victory over Cholas by taking the title of *Sonadugondan* (Conqueror of Chola Country).
- He is the main protagonist of the Tamil historical novel *Kayalvizhi* by Akilan.

Sadaiyavarman Sundara Pandyan (c. 1251–1268 CE)

- Another illustrious ruler of the second Pandya kingdom who not only brought the entire Tamil Nadu under his rule but also exercised his authority up to Nellore in Andhra Pradesh.

Maravarman Kulasekhara Pandyan (c. 1268–1310 CE)

- After Sundarapandya, he ruled successfully for a period of 40 years, giving the country peace and prosperity. He was appointed the co-regent[5] by his father during the latter's reign and he actively supported his father in politics. According to his inscriptions, he defeated not only the Hoysalas and the Cholas but also Bhuvanaikabahu, the Sri Lankan ruler and conquered Simhala.
- He took the title of '*Kollamkondan*' meaning conqueror of Kollam and '*Konerinmaikondan*' meaning King without equal.
- The Venetian traveller Marco Polo visited the Pandyan territory during his reign and described Maravarman as Asiyar or Ashkar and also praised his administrative skills and the wealth of the Pandyan Empire. According to Marco Polo, the city of Kail or Kayal

[5] The practice of shared rule was common during the Pandyas and Maravarman Kulasekhara Pandyan shared his rule with Jatavarman Vira Pandyan, Maravarman Vikkiraman III and Jatavarman Sundara Pandyan II.

of the Pandyan Empire was very prosperous. The Persian historian Abdulla Wassaf also visited his kingdom and described the Tamil country as the most agreeable abode on Earth.

Jatavarman Veera Pandiyan (c. 1309–1345 CE)

- The last prominent Pandya ruler who was defeated by the Vijayanagara Empire in the 16th century, effectively ending the Pandya dynasty's rule in Madurai.
- He was also known for his battles against the Delhi Sultanate's forces, particularly the armies of Alauddin Khalji.

Contribution of the Later Pandyas

The later Pandyas were the pioneers in the field of cave temples in Tamil Nadu as they excavated a good number of cave temples in the southern region. Their one and only monolithic temple at Kalugumalai in Tirunelveli district is considered as one of the "jewels" of the south Indian architectural sculptures and considered to be the Ellora of the south as it is trenched out of the living rock as in the case of Ellora. Unfortunately, it was left unfinished and, if completed, it would have been the best among the monolithic structures of the south. Both cave temples and the structural temples are all made up of hard granite stones.

The Vijayanagar Kingdom (c. 1336–1672 CE)

The Vijayanagar kingdom constituted four dynasties – Sangama (c. 1336–1485 CE), Saluva (c. 1485–1503 CE), Tuluva (c. 1503–1570 CE) and Aravidu (till the end of the 17th century). There are varied sources for the study of the Vijayanagar kingdom, such as literary and archaeological sources, as well as numismatics. Krishnadevaraya's Amukthamalyada, Gangadevi's Maduravijayam and Allasani Peddanna's Manucharitam are some of the indigenous literature of this period. Many foreign travellers' valuable accounts on the socio-economic conditions of the Vijayanagar kingdom are also available, since they visited the Vijayanagar kingdom. This includes the Moroccan Ibn Batuta, Venetian Nicolo de Conti, Persian Abdur Razzak and the Portuguese Domingo Paes.

The copper plate inscriptions such as the Srirangam copper plates of Devaraya II provide the genealogy and achievements of Vijayanagar rulers. The Hampi ruins and other monuments of Vijayanagar provide information on the cultural contributions of the Vijayanagar rulers. The numerous coins issued by the Vijayanagar rulers contain figures and legends explaining their tittles and achievements. It is pertinent to note that the empire included people from different cultural regions – the Tamil, Telugu and Karnataka region – who all spoke different languages and belonged to different cultures.

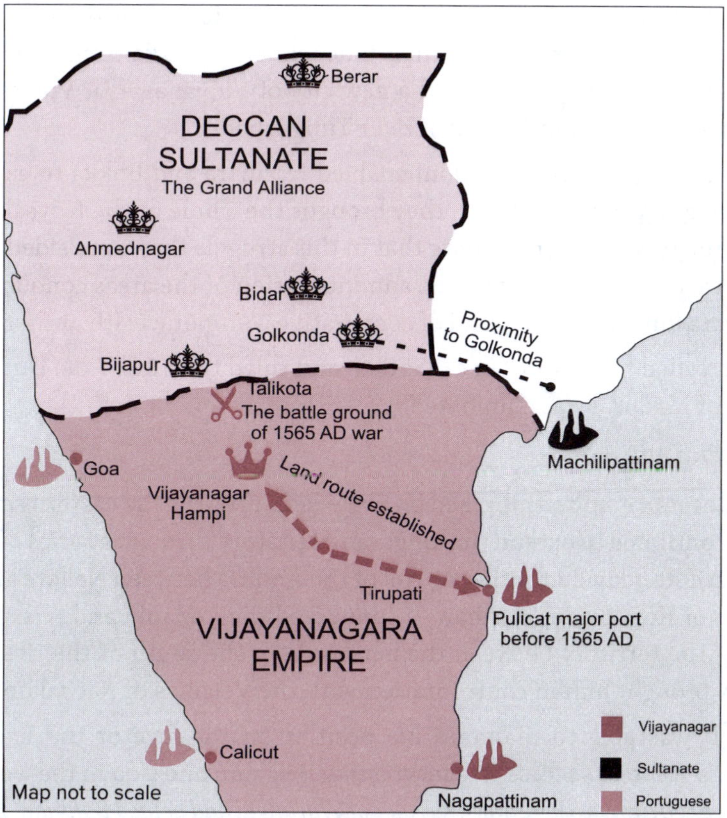

FIGURE 12.2 Map of Deccan Sultanate and Vijayanagar Empire

In the south, Vijayanagara's main rivals were the Sultans of Madurai and the struggle between them continued for almost four decades. By c. 1377 CE, the Sultanate of Madurai was wiped out and the Vijaynagara kingdom comprised the whole of south India up to Rameshwaram, including the Tamil country as well as that of the Cheras (Kerala). In the north, they had continuous hostility with the Bahmani Sultanate (this conflict will be dealt in detail later).

Sangama Dynasty

Harihara and Bukka (c. 1336–1377 CE)

- Founders of the Sangama dynasty of Vijayanagar kingdom.
- According to legends, they belonged to a family of five brothers and were originally feudatories of the Kakatiyas of Warangal and after their fall, they served as ministers in the Kampili state (modern Karnataka). When Kampili was overrun by Muhammad bin Tughlaq for giving refuge to a Muslim rebel, the two brothers were imprisoned and

converted to Islam. Later, they returned to the Hindu fold at the initiative of the saint Vidyaranya. They also proclaimed their independence and to commemorate the memory of their guru, the brothers founded a new city of Vidyanagar or Vijayanagara (meaning city of victory) on the south bank of river Tungabhadra.

- The decline of the Hoysala kingdom enabled Harihara and Bukka to expand their newly founded kingdom. By c. 1346 CE, they brought the whole of the Hoysala kingdom under their control. It is pertinent to note that in this struggle they were aided by their brothers who with their relations took up the administration of the areas conquered, and thus the Vijayanagara kingdom was a kind of cooperative commonwealth at first.
- Bukka succeeded his brother in c. 1356 CE and ruled till c. 1377 CE. During his reign, the Sultanate of Madurai was eliminated.

Harihara II (c. 1377–1406 CE)

- The Vijayanagara empire embarked on expansion towards the eastern sea coast under his reign. He continued to extend the kingdom's territory through a series of conflicts against the Reddis of Kondavidu for the control of the Andhra between Nellore and Kalinga. From the Reddis of Kondavidu, Harihara II conquered the Addanki and Srisailam areas as well as most of the territory between the peninsula to the south of the river Krishna, which eventually brought him in confrontation with the Velamas of Rachakonda (Telangana).
- Harihara II was able to maintain his position in the face of the Bahmani–Warangal alliance. His greatest success was in wresting Belgaum and Goa in the west from Bahmani Sultanate. According to legends, *the ruler of Warangal had helped Bahmani Sultanate founder, Hasan Gangu, in his struggle against Delhi, but his successor invaded Warangal and seized the stronghold of the Kaulas and the hill fort.* This alliance of Warangal and the Bahmani Sultanate lasted for over 50 years and was a major factor in the ability of Vijaynagara to overrun the Tungabhadra doab.

Deva Raya I (c. 1406–1422 CE)

- He was a very capable ruler noted for his military exploits and his support to irrigation works in his kingdom. He constructed a dam across river Tungabhadra to bring canals into the city to relieve the shortage of water. He also built a dam on the river Haridra for irrigation purposes.
- Throughout his reign, Deva Raya was continually at war with the Velamas of Telangana, the Bahmani Sultan of Gulbarga, the Reddis of Kondavidu and the traditional rivals of Vijayanagara, the Gajapatis of Kalinga.
- Early in his career, he was defeated by the Bahmani ruler Firoz Shah and had to not only pay a huge indemnity but also had to marry his daughter to the Sultan. But this marriage could buy peace only for a short time and later, with the ruler of Warangal on his side,

the balance of power in the Deccan tilted in favour of Deva Raya I. In c. 1420 CE, Firoz Shah invaded Pangal, which had been taken by Vijayanagar, but this time Deva Raya inflicted a shattering defeat on Firoz Shah. The two-year siege at Pangal ended in disaster for Firoz Shah's armies. The Sultan had to hand over the southern and eastern districts of his kingdom to Deva Raya I. Consequently, by c. 1422 CE, Deva Raya I came to control territory up to the Krishna–Tungabhadra doab including Pangal.

- He modernised the Vijayanagar army by improving the cavalry, employing Turkic archers and procuring horses from Arabia and Persia.
- He maintained a secular attitude in administrative matters. He had 10,000 Muslims in his army, being the first Vijaynagar king to do so. He had a mosque and a slaughterhouse constructed for the convenience of the Muslim soldiers in his army.
- Italian traveller, Nicolo Conti (in c. 1420 CE), and Russian merchant Nikitin (author of Voyage to India), visited during his reign. Nicolo Conti commented on Vijayanagara and Deva Raya I that '*In this city, there are 90,000 men fit to bear arms... their king is more powerful than all the kings of India*'.
- Deva Raya I was a patron of Kannada literature and architecture. There was a pearl hall where he honoured men of eminence. Madhura, a noted Jain poet, was in his court (and also in the court of his father King Harihara II). He wrote the Dharmanathapurana on the life of the 15th Jain Tirthankar in Kannada, as well as a poem in eulogy of Gommateshvara of Shravanabelagola.
- The noted Hazare Rama temple, an excellent example of Deccan architecture, was constructed during his rule. The credit for making the capital city of the Vijayanagar kingdom one of the biggest cities in the 15th century goes to him.

Deva Raya II (c. 1425–1446 CE)

- The greatest of the Sangama dynasty rulers who was an able administrator, an ambitious warrior and a man of letters. He authored well-known works in the Kannada language (Sobagina Sone and Amaruka) and in the Sanskrit language (Mahanataka Sudhanidhi). He also wrote a commentary on the Brahmasutra.
- Some of the most noted Kannada poets of the medieval period, such as Chamarasa and Kumara Vyasa gained his patronage. The Sanskrit poet Gunda Dimdima and gifted Telugu poet Kavisarvabhauma (Emperor among Poets) Srinatha, author of Haravilasam, were also present at his court.
- In case of secular literature, the noted South Indian mathematician, Parameshvara, from the Kerala school of astronomy and mathematics lived in his kingdom.
- He acquired the title of Gajabetegara, which literally means 'Hunter of Elephants', an honorific title that explained his addiction to hunting elephants or a metaphor referring

to his victories against enemies who were 'as strong as elephants'. Despite some reversals, Deva Raya II extended and held territories up to the Krishna river.

- According to an account of the visiting Persian chronicler Abdur Razzak, *Deva Raya II's empire extended from Ceylon to Gulbarga, and Orissa to the Malabar,* and according to Nicolo Conti, *the king levied tribute on Ceylon, Quilon, Pegu, Pulicat.*

The next dynasty, Saluva founded by Saluva Narasimha (the earlier king's minister) reigned only for a brief period (c. 1486–1509 CE).

Tuluvas Dynasty

Vira Narasimha Raya (c. 1505–1509 CE)

- He was the younger brother of Krishna Deva Raya who ascended the throne following the death of Tuluva Narasa Nayaka[6].

Krishna Deva Raya (c. 1509–1529 CE)

- The greatest of the Vijayanagar rulers, was also known as 'Abhinava Bhoja', 'Andhra Pitamah', 'Andhra Bhoja' (as he was great patron of literature and art). His imposing personality was accompanied by high intellectual quality.
- He was a great commander and an efficient administrator. He fought a series of wars with the independent kingdoms (Deccan Sultanates) that came up on the ruins of the Bahmani kingdom. The Muslim armies were decisively defeated in the battle of Diwani. Then he invaded the Raichur Doab and completely shattered the Adil Shahi forces of Bijapur first, attacked Gulbarga and captured the city of Raichur in c. 1520 CE, and set free the three Bahmani princess who were imprisoned there. He thus restored the Bahmani Sultanate to Muhammad Shah, and Krishna Deva himself took the title of Yavanarajya sthapanacharya. Krishna Deva Raya's Orissa campaign was also successful. He defeated the Gajapathi ruler Prataparudra and conquered the whole of Telangana. He compelled the ruler of Orissa to restore to Vijaynagar all the territories up to the river Krishna. He also maintained law and order and dealt with the Portuguese influence in the Deccan.
- He maintained friendly relations with the Portuguese. King Albuquerque sent his ambassadors to the court of Krishna Deva Raya. The Portuguese travellers Domingo Paes and Barbosa came to India during his reign.
- Though a Vaishnavite, he respected all religions. Eight eminent scholars of Telugu known as the 'Ashta diggajas' adorned his court:
    - Allasani Peddanna (the greatest, who was also called Andhrakavita Pitamaga); his important works include Manucharitam and Harikathasaram.

[6] Tuluva Narasa Nayaka was the commander of the Vijaynagar army under the rule of Saluva Narasimha Deva Raya from 1491-1503 CE.

- Tenali Ramakrishna, author of Panduranga Mahamatyam.
- Pingali Suranna, author of Garuda Puranam, Prabhavatee Pradyumnamu, Raghava Pandaveeyam *and* Kalapurnodayamu.

– He himself authored

- Amukthamalyadha (Telugu)
- Jambavati Kalyanam *and* Ushaparinayam (Sanskrit)

– He built some fine stone temples such as famous the Vittalaswamy and Hazara Ramaswamy temples at Vijayanagar. Apart from repairing many temples, he also added impressive gopurams or gateways to many important South Indian temples. The famous temple of Tirupati greatly developed during his period as the deity there was his titular deity.

– He also founded a suburban township near Vijayanagar called Nagalapuram after his mother. Some of the most detailed descriptions of Vijayanagar come from his period.

Achyuta Deva Raya (c. 1529–1542 CE)

– Was the younger brother of Krishna Deva Raya, who handpicked him to be his successor.

– A Portuguese traveller, Fernoa Nuniz, came to India during his reign.

– He patronised the Kannada poet Chatu Vittalanatha, the great singer and composer Purandaradasa (father of Carnatic music), and the Sanskrit scholar Rajanatha Dindima II.

– The Tiruvengalanatha temple, which is now popularly known by his name as the Achyutaraya temple, was built in Vijayanagar during his reign.

– Upon his death, the succession was disputed. His son, Venkata I (Venkata Raya or Venkatadri Raya), succeeded him, but he was a weak ruler and was killed six months later. Then Krishna Deva Raya's son Sada Siva Raya, finally became king while yet a child, under the regency of Aravidu Aliya Rama Raya, son-in-law of Krishna Deva Raya. The word 'Aliya' means 'son-in-law' in the Kannada language. Along with another brother, Venkatadri, the Aravidu brothers rose to prominence during the rule of Krishna Deva Raya. Rama Raya was a successful army general, able administrator and tactful diplomat who conducted many victorious campaigns during the rule of Krishna Deva Raya. Thus, after the demise of his illustrious father-in-law, as a member of the family, Rama Raya, began to wield great influence over the affairs of the state.

Sada Siva Raya (c. 1542–1570 CE)

– Last ruler of Tuluva dynasty.

– He was a puppet in the hands of his minister, Aliya Rama Raya, who was the de facto king. He removed the old nobility and replaced it with those loyal to him.

– Rama Raya tried to balance the Deccan powers by playing one against the other. For instance, *when the Nizam of Ahmadnagar and Qutabshahi of Golconda sought Rama Raya's help against Bijapur, Rama Raya secured the Raichur doab for his benefactors. Later in c. 1549 CE when the Adilshahi of Bijapur and Baridshahi of Bidar declared war on Nizamshahi of Ahmadnagar, Rama Raya fought on behalf of the Ahmadnagar ruler and secured the fort of Kalyana.* In c. 1557 CE, Rama Raya allied himself with Ali Adilshahi of Bijapur and Baridshahi of Bidar when the Sultan of Bijapur invaded Ahmadnagar.

- His constantly changing sides to improve his own position eventually prompted the Sultanates to form an alliance. The Deccan states (Bijapur, Ahmadnagar, Golkonda and Bidar, except Berar) thus formed a confederacy and inflicted a crushing blow on the Vijayanagar armies at Bannihatti in the battle of Talaikotta in c. 1565 CE. This battle is also known as Rakshasa Thangadi. Rama Raya was imprisoned and executed and the city of Vijayanagar was destroyed. The Battle of Bannihatti is generally considered to mark the end of the Vijayanagar Empire. It should be noted that Caesar Fredrick visited Vijaynagar after battle of Talaikotta.

However, the Vijayanagar kingdom continued to exist under the Aravidu dynasty, which ruled from Penukonda and later from Chandragiri (near Tirupati) for about another century. Thirumala, Sri Ranga and Venkata II were the important rulers of this dynasty. The last ruler of Vijayanagar kingdom was Sri Ranga III (c. 1642–1646 CE).

Administration of Vijaynagar Kingdom

There was a well-organised administration under the Vijayanagar kingdom. The Rayas (king) enjoyed absolute authority in executive, judicial and legislative matters. He was the highest court of appeal. In the matter of justice, harsh punishments such as mutilation and throwing to elephants were given. Succession to the throne was mostly on the principle of hereditary, but sometimes usurpation to the throne also occurred, such as when Saluva Narasimha came to power by ending the Sangama dynasty. The king was assisted by a council of ministers in his day-to-day administration.

The kingdom was divided into different administrative units called Mandalams, Nadus, sthalas, and finally into gramas. The governor of the Mandalam was called Mandaleswara or Nayak. Vijayanagar rulers gave full powers to the local authorities in the administration. It is pertinent to note that the Chola traditions of village self-government were considerably weakened under the Vijaynagar rulers. The growth of hereditary nayakships tended to curb their freedom and initiative.

The governors of the provinces were royal princes at first. Later, persons belonging to vassals of the ruling families and nobles were also appointed as governors. The provincial governors had a large measure of autonomy as they held their own courts, appointed their own officers, and maintained their own armies. At times, they even issued their own coins (though in small denominations).

The term for the provincial governor was not fixed and it depended on his ability and strength. Each governor paid a fixed contribution in men and money to the central government. Thus, it would not be totally wrong to assume that Vijaynagar was more a confederacy than a centralised empire.

Besides land revenue, tributes and gifts from vassals and feudal chiefs, customs collected at the ports, taxes on various professions, were other sources of income to the government. Land revenue was fixed at generally one sixth of the produce.

Army and Military Organisation

The conflict between Vijayanagar Empire and the Bahmani kingdom lasted for many years. The dispute over Raichur Doab, i.e., the region between the rivers Krishna and Tungabhadra and also over the fertile areas of Krishna–Godavari delta led to this long-drawn conflict. In order to wage continuous wars, there was a need to keep a large army. The Vijayanagar army was very well-organised and efficient. It consisted of the cavalry, infantry, artillery and elephants. High-breed horses were procured from foreign traders. The Vijayanagar rulers imported high quality horses from across the Arabian Sea from Arabia and other Gulf countries. The port of Malabar was the centre of this trade and trade in other luxury commodities. The Vijayanagar rulers always attempted to control the port of Malabar.

One of the important characteristics of the Vijayanagar administration was the amara-nayaka system. The top-grade officers of the army were known as Nayaks *or* Palaiyagars *or* Poligars. Interestingly, these officers were granted land (called amaram) in lieu of their services while soldiers were usually paid in cash. The nayaka was responsible for expanding agricultural activities in his amaram (area). He collected taxes in his area and with this income maintained his army, horses, elephants and weapons of warfare that he had to supply to the *raya* or the Vijayanagar ruler. The *nayaka* was also the commander of the forts. Some of the revenue was also used for the maintenance of temples and irrigation works. The *amara-nayakas* sent tribute to the king annually and personally appeared in the royal court with gifts to express their loyalty. It is noteworthy to add that in the 17th century, several of these nayakas such as those of Tanjore and Madurai became independent and established separate states and emerged as a powerful section that challenged the Vijayanagar authority, weakened its internal structures and contributed to the defeat of Vijayanagar in the battle of Talaikotta.

The Vijayanagar state also was familiar with the use of firearms and employed Turkish and Portuguese experts to train the soldiers in the latest weaponry of warfare. The walls of the forts were made thick to counter the firearms and special kinds of door with fortified wall fronts were constructed. On the walls of the forts, special kinds of big holes were made to rest the guns. Special kinds of *parapets* were constructed on the forts to put the canons on it. They had both small firearms such as rifles and pistols, and certain heavy arms such as cannons, which had to be put on a bullock cart or on an elephant and pushed into the battlefield.

Social Life

Allasani Peddanna in his Manucharitam refers to the existence of four castes – *Brahmins*, *Kshatriyas*, *Vaishyas*, and *Sudras* – in the Vijayanagar society. Foreign travellers left vivid accounts on the splendour of buildings and luxurious social life in the city of Vijayanagar. Paes mentions *the beautiful houses of the rich and the large number of their household servants*. Nicolo Conti refers *to the prevalence of slavery*. Silk and cotton clothes were mainly used for dress. Dancing, music, wrestling, gambling and cock-fighting were some of the common forms of amusement.

The Sangama rulers were chiefly Shaivites and Virupaksha was their family deity while other dynasties were Vaishnavites. Ramanuja's Srivaishnavism was very popular. It is pertinent to note that all kings were tolerant towards other religions. Barbosa referred to *the religious freedom enjoyed by everyone*. Regarding Krishna Deva Raya's tolerant attitude, Barbosa says, '*The king allows such freedom that every man may come and go and live according to his own creed, without suffering any annoyance, and without enquiry whether he is a Christian, Jew, Moor or heathen*'. Muslims were employed in the administration and they were freely allowed to build mosques and worship. As we have read earlier, Deva Raya II enrolled Muslims in his armed services, allotted them *jagirs*, and erected a mosque for their use in the city. A large number of temples were built during this period and numerous festivals were celebrated.

The position of women was not much improved. However, some of them were learned such as Gangadevi, wife of Kumarakampana, who authored the famous work Maduravijayam. Hannamma and Thirumalamma were two other famous poets. According to Portuguese traveller Nuniz, "*a large number of women were employed in the royal palaces as dancers, domestic servants and palanquin bearers. There were also wrestlers, astrologers and soothsayers among them. Some women were also appointed as accountants, judges, bailiffs, and watch women.*" Sahagaman, i.e., Sati was honoured. The practice of *devadasi* (attachment of dancing girls to temples) was in place. Even Paes refers to the *flourishing devadasi system* of this period. Polygamy was prevalent among the royal families. Interestingly, the temples were rich and also took active part in both internal and overseas trade.

Economy

According to the accounts of the foreign travelers, the Vijayanagar kingdom was one of the wealthiest kingdoms of the world at that time. Agriculture continued to be the chief occupation of the people. The Vijayanagar rulers provided a stimulus to its further growth by providing irrigation facilities. New tanks were built and dams were constructed across the rivers like Tungabhadra. Nuniz refers to *the excavation of canals*.

There were numerous industries and they were organised into guilds. Metal workers and other craftsmen flourished during this period. Diamond mines were located in Kurnool and Anantapur district. Vijayanagar was also a great centre of trade. According to Abdur Razzaq, the Ambassador from Iran, who visited the Indian subcontinent during the rule of Deva Raya II, "*in Vijayanagar, three kinds of coins were in use – Varaha, Dinara and Fanam. Of these, the Fanam*[7] *was most popular.*" The chief gold coin was the varaha but weights and measures varied from place to place. Inland, coastal and overseas trade led to the general prosperity. There were a number of seaports on the Malabar coast, the chief being Cannanore. Commercial contacts with Arabia, Persia, South Africa and Portugal on the west, and with Burma, the Malay peninsula and China on the east flourished. The chief items of exports were cotton and silk clothes, spices, rice, iron, saltpetre and sugar. The imports consisted of horses, pearls, copper, coral, mercury, China silk and velvet clothes. The art of shipbuilding had developed.

Cultural Contributions

The temple building activity further gained momentum during the Vijayanagar rule. The chief characteristics of the Vijayanagar architecture were the construction of tall Raya Gopurams or gateways and the Kalyanamandapam with carved pillars in the temple premises. The sculptures on the pillars were carved with distinctive features. The horse was the most common motif found on these pillars. Large *mandapams* contain one hundred pillars as well as one thousand pillars in some big temples. These *mandapams* were used for seating the deity on festival occasions. Also, many Amman shrines were added to the already existing temples during this period.

The most important temples of the Vijayanagar style were found in the Hampi ruins or the city of Vijayanagar. Vittalaswamy and Hazara Ramaswamy temples were the best examples of this style. The Varadharaja and Ekamparanatha temples at Kanchipuram stand as examples for the magnificence of the Vijayanagara style of temple architecture. The Raya Gopurams at Thiruvannamalai and Chidambaram speak of the glorious epoch of Vijayanagar. They were continued by the Nayak rulers in the later period. The metal images of Krishna Deva Raya and his queens at Tirupati are examples for casting of metal images. Music and dancing were also patronised by the rulers of Vijayanagar.

Different languages such as Sanskrit, Telugu, Kannada and Tamil flourished in the regions. There was a great development in Sanskrit and Telugu literature. The peak of literary achievement was reached during the reign of Krishna Deva Raya. He himself was a scholar in Sanskrit and Telugu. His famous court poet Allasani Peddanna was distinguished in Telugu literature. Thus, the cultural contributions of the Vijayanagar rulers were many-sided and remarkable.

---

[7] A small coin used in south India between the 9th and 19th centuries which weighed as little as 0.3 grams and had a diameter of less than a centimetre.

Key term/Concept	Meaning
(a) *Pradhani*	Prime minister
(b) *Raysani*	Recorded oral order of king
(c) *Karnikam*	Accountant
(d) *Kadamal, Irai, Vrai*	Kinds of taxes
(e) *Athavane*	Land revenue department
(f) *Mahanayakachara*	Acted as linkage between kings and villages
(g) *Padikaval*	Selling of policing rights
(h) *Talara*	Watchman

Bahmani Sultanate (c. 1347–1527 CE)

In the 14th century, along with Vijayanagar kingdom, another powerful kingdom arose in South India, which was the Bahmani Sultanate. As we can recall that, the Deccan region was a part of the provincial administration of the Delhi Sultanate. In order to establish a stable administration in the Deccan, Mohammad bin Tughlaq appointed amiran-i-sada also known as Sada Amir (administrative heads of hundred villages). From c. 1337 CE, the conflict between the officers in Deccan and Delhi Sultanate accelerated which ultimately resulted in the establishment of an independent state in the Deccan in c. 1347 CE with the capital at Gulbarga in Karnataka. Its founder, Hasan Gangu, assumed the title Alauddin Hasan Bahman Shah, as he traced his descent from the mythical hero of Iran, Bahman Shah, and the kingdom was named the Bahmani Sultanate after him. Since after Mohammad bin Tughlaq there were no attempts by the Delhi Sultanate to control the Deccan region, therefore, the Bahmani Sultans without any checks annexed the other parts of the kingdom too. One of the important acquisitions was the control over Dabhol, an important port on the west coast.

Alauddin Hasan Bahman Shah (c. 1347–1358 CE)

- Founder of the Bahmani Sultanate who was an Afghan adventurer, who began his career as a general serving under the Sultan Muhammad bin Tughlaq. Nazir Uddin Ismail Shah, who had revolted against the Delhi Sultanate, stepped down in favour of Bahman Shah. However, according to the historian Ferishta, his original name was Hasan Gangu, *as he had earlier served in the service of a brahmana named Gangu and he adopted the word 'Bahman Shah' as a tribute to his brahmana patron.*
- He had regular confrontations with the Vijaynagar kingdom and Warangal state. He led his first campaign against Warangal in c. 1350 CE and forced its ruler Kapaya Nayaka to cede to him the fortress of Kaulas.
- By the time of his death, the kingdom stretched from north to south from the Wenganga river to Krishna and east to west from Bhongir to Daulatabad.

Muhammad Shah I (c. 1358–1377 CE)

- Succeeded his father Bahman Shah.
- Was a great conqueror as well as a capable administrator. In fact, the administrative system established by him not only lasted for a long time under the Bahmani empire but it also impacted the administrative systems of neighbouring kingdoms too.
- Collaborated with a Persian architect named Rafi of Qazvin to construct the Grand Mosque of Gulbarga.

Taj-ud-din Firoz Shah (c. 1397–1422 CE)

- Considered as the most remarkable figure in the Bahmani Sultanate and greatest of them all.
- He started the Bahmani expansion towards Berar by defeating the Gond Raja Narsing Rai of Kherla. A huge amount of money, gold and silver was paid to Firuz and a daughter of Rai was married to him.
- Later, he invaded Vijaynagar with victories in c. 1398 CE and c. 1408 CE, but faced a defeat in c. 1420 CE at the hands of Deva Raya I.
- He was well acquainted with the religious sciences (commentaries on the Quran, jurisprudence) and natural sciences too (such as botany, geometry, logic, etc.).
- He was a good calligraphist and a poet and often composed extempore verses. According to Ferishta, he *was well versed not only in Telugu, Kannada and Marathi but also in Persian, Arabic and Turkish.*
- He encouraged the pursuit of astronomy and built an observatory near Daultabad.
- Inducted a large number of Hindus in his administration. It is said that it was from his time that the Deccan *brahmans* became dominant in administration.

Ahmah Shah Wali (c. 1422–1435 CE)

- After the defeat of Firuz Shah in c. 1420 CE, he was forced to abdicate in favour of his brother Ahmad Shah I who is called a saint (wali) on account of his association with the famous Sufi saint Gesu Daraz.
- He continued the struggle for the domination of the south eastern sea board and in order to punish the ruler of Warangal for siding with the Vijaynagar in the previous battle, he invaded Warangal (c. 1424–1425 CE), and defeated and killed its ruler and annexed most of its territories. After this, he turned his attention toward Malwa (c. 1425–1435 CE), Gondwana and the Konkan.
- He shifted the capital from Gulbarga to Bidar.

Humayun Shah (c. 1458–1461 CE)

- Greatly impressed with his military genius, Humayun appointed Mahmud Gawan (who later emerged as one of the most important personality of the Bahmani kingdom) as minister who initiated many reforms. After Humayun's death, Gawan became the guardian of his minor prince Nizam Shah (c. 1461–1463 CE) and had the reigns of the government in his hands. However, the young Sultan died in c. 1463 CE and his brother Muhammad Shah III who was aged only nine years (c. 1463–1482 CE) succeeded him, and Mahmud Gawan served as his prime minister. The power of the Bahmani kingdom reached its peak under the rule of Muhammad Shah III (all due to the advice and services of Mahmud Gawan). It extended from the Arabian sea to the Bay of Bengal. On the west, it extended from Goa to Bombay. On the east, it extended from Kakinada to the mouth of the river Krishna. The history of Bahmani kingdom after this period is actually the record of the achievements of Mahmud Gawan.

Mahmud Gawan (c. 1461–1481 CE)

- The Bahmani kingdom reached the height of its power and territorial limits under the able guidance of Mahmud Gawan. He was a Persian merchant who came to India (Deccan) at the age of 42 years and joined the services of Bahmani kingdom. He was granted the title of Malik-ul-Tujjar, i.e., 'Chief of the Merchants' by the Bahmani ruler, Humayun Shah. The sudden death of Humayun led to the coronation of his minor son Nizam Shah and a regency council was set for the administration of which Mahmud Gawan was an important member. Slowly, due to his personal qualities, he was made wazir (the prime minister) and was given the title of 'Khwaju-i-Jahan'.
- He was a learned person and possessed a great knowledge of mathematics. He not only controlled the kingdom in an efficient manner but also provided stability to it. Gawan carried out many internal administrative reforms and attempted to put an end to the strife in the nobility and to increase the control of Sultan over the nobles and provinces. He divided the kingdom into eight tarafs or provinces, each governed by a tarafdar. In order to curb the military power of the tarafdar, Gawan ordered that only one fort of each province was to be under the direct control of the provincial tarafdar. The remaining forts of the province were placed under a Qiladar or commander of the forts (who was appointed by the central Government). Allowances of the nobles were also reduced who shirked their responsibility.
- He was a military genius and waged successful wars against Vijayanagar, Orissa and the sea pirates on the Arabian sea. He conquered the Vijayanagar territories up to Kanchi. On the western coast, Goa and Dabhol were conquered. After gaining control over Goa and Dabhol, Bahmani strengthened its trading relations with Iran and Iraq.
- He introduced the use of gunpowder in the war against the Vijayanagar kings in Belgaum and invited Persian chemists to teach his soldiers the preparation and use of gunpowder.

- He also tried to settle the northern frontiers of the kingdom. With the help of the ruler of Gujarat, he defeated Mahmud Khalji of Malwa over the control of Berar. Thus, he expanded the Bahmani Empire through his conquests and diplomacy skills.
- He was a great patron of arts and made endowments to build a college at Bidar which was built in the Persian style of architecture. Some of the most famous scholars of the time belonging to Iran and Iraq came to this madarasa.
- One of the most difficult problems faced by the Bahmani kingdom was strife among nobles. The nobles were divided into Deccanis (oldtimers) and Afaqis (new-comers). Despite of being an Afaqi, Gawan was liberal and wanted a compromise between the *Afaqis* and the *Deccanis*. But unfortunately, the petty strife could not be stopped and the Deccani nobles plotted against Gawan and induced the young Sultan to punish him with a death sentence and had him executed in c. 1482 CE. Later, the Sultan regretted his hasty decision and buried his Prime Minister with honours.
- After Gawan's execution, the Bahmani kingdom began to disintegrate and the provincial governors declared their independence. During this period, the Vijayanagar king Krishna Deva Raya defeated the last remnant of the Bahmani Sultanate's power, after which the Bahmani Sultanate collapsed. After c. 1518 CE, the Sultanate broke up into five states: the Nizam Shahis of Ahmadnagar, the Adil Shahis of Bijapur, the Qutb Shahis of Golconda, and the Imad Shahis of Berar and the Barid Shahis of Bidar, which are collectively known as the 'Deccan Sultanates'.

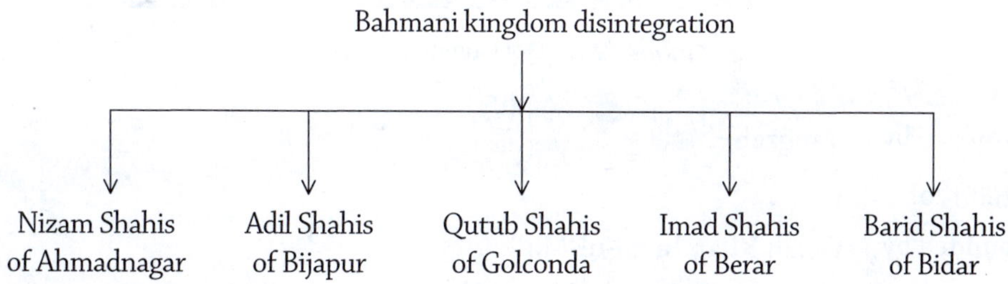

1. Nizam Shahis of Ahmadnagar
   - Founded by Ahmad Bahri.
   - Annexed by Shah Jahan.
2. Adil Shahis of Bijapur
   - Founded by Yusuf Adil Shah.
   - Mohd. Adil Shah built the world's second largest dome (Gol Gumbaz of Bijapur).
   - Another prominent ruler was Ibrahim Adil Shah II (c. 1580–1627 CE), the fifth king of the dynasty, known for religious tolerance and was given title of Jagadguru Budshah owing

to his belief in secularism. He tried to bring in cultural harmony between the Shias and the Sunnis and between Hindus and Muslims through music. He was a great lover of music, played musical instruments, sang and composed praises of Hindu deities *Saraswati* and *Ganapati*. He wrote the book Kitab-E-Navras (Book of Nine Rasas) in Dakhani. He maintained a large number of musicians (around 4000) at his court and the band of musicians was known as Lashkar-e-Nauras (Army of Nauras) as they were paid by the government regularly.

FIGURE 12.3 Gol Gumbaz, Bijapur

- Annexed by Aurangzeb.

3. Imad Shahis of Berar
   - Founded by Fatullah Khan Imad-ul-Mulk.
   - Later conquered by Nizam Shahi rulers of Ahmadnagar.
4. Qutb Shahis of Golconda
   - Founded by Quli Qtub Shah, who built the famous Golconda fort.
   - Mohd. Quli Qutb Shah.
     - Greatest of all Qutb Shahi who built the city of Hyderabad and 'Charminar'.
   - Kingdom annexed by Aurangzeb.
5. Barid Shahis of Bidar
   - Founded by Ali Barid.
   - Annexed by Adil Shahis of Bijapur.

Of these, the kingdoms of Ahmadnagar, Bijapur and Golconda played a leading role in the Deccan politics till their absorption in the Mughal Empire during the 17th century.

Conflict between the Vijaynagar Kingdom and Bahmani Sultanate

There were constant conflicts between the Vijayanagar kingdom and the Bahmani Sultanate as their interests clashed in three separate and distinct areas:

a. Over the control of the Raichur doab (between rivers Krishna and Tungabhadra): This area was fertile and rich in mineral resources. The famous diamond mines of Golconda were located in the eastern part of the doab region. The geography of both the kingdoms was such that expansion was possible only across Tungabhadra in the Deccan. It appears that the battles between the two were not conclusive and the status quo was mostly maintained. Sometimes, Bahmani had an advantage and sometimes, Vijayanagar had an advantage. For instance, in c. 1504 CE, the Bahmanis managed to reconquer the Raichur doab. However, with the ascent of Krishna Deva Raya, the Bahmanis lost Raichur, Mudkal, Nalgonda and other inland towns. As we have discussed earlier too, that the Raichur doab had been the bone of contention between the western Chalukyas and the Cholas in the earlier period and between the Yadavas and the Hoysalas in the later period.

b. The Krishna–Godavari basin: Apart from being very fertile, this region had the additional advantage of control of foreign trade (as this stretch of land contained numerous important ports that held the priced key of foreign trade).

c. Over the Marathwada region: In the Marathwada region, the main contention was for the control of the Konkan belt (a narrow strip of land between the Western Ghats and the sea) and the areas which gave access to it. The Konkan belt was extremely fertile and included with it the port of Goa which was an important outlet for export as well as import (especially of horses from Iraq and Iran).

Often, the battles between the Vijayanagar and the Bahamani states are perceived as Hindu–Muslim conflicts. However, the aforementioned reasons clearly point out that the struggle was not due to any religious differences but for territorial and economic motives. These military conflicts resulted in wide spread devastation of the contested areas and the neighbouring territories and a considerable loss of life and property. Continuous warfare exhausted the resources of both the states and weakened them. Another crucial cost of these wars was that both the powers were so involved amongst themselves that they never realised the increasing power of the Portuguese on the coast of south India.

It is also significant to mention that despite hostilities between the two states, there were times when they also co-operated with each other. For instance, Krishna Deva Raya supported some claimants to power in the Sultanates and took pride in the title '*establisher of the Yavana kingdom*'. Similarly, the Sultan of Bijapur intervened to resolve succession disputes in Vijayanagar following the death of Krishna Deva Raya. There was also sharing and exchange of ideas, especially in the field of art, literature and architecture.

Bahmani Administration

The Bahmani administrative system was well-organised. The Sultanate was divided into four (before Gawan; Gawan divided the Sultanate into eight units) administrative units called 'taraf' or provinces. These provinces were Daultabad, Bidar, Berar and Gulbarga. Muhammad I defeated the Vijayanagar kingdom and consequently Golconda was annexed to Bahmani Sultanate. Every province was under a tarafdar who was also called a subedar. In every province, a tract of land (Khalisa) was set apart from the jurisdiction of the tarafdar as it was used for meeting the expenses of the king and the royal household. Further, the salaries and obligations of every noble was fixed. Those nobles who kept 500 horses were given 1000,000 huns annually. If they were short of the stipulated troops, the tarafdar had to reimburse the amount to the central government. Nobles used to get their salary either in cash or in form of grant of land or 'jagir'. The Bahmanis were familiar with the use of firearms and they employed Turkish and Portuguese experts to train the soldiers in the latest weaponry of warfare.

Bahmani rulers depended for military support on his *amirs*. There were two groups in the ranks of *amirs*: one was the Deccanis who were immigrant Muslims and had been staying for a long time in the Deccan region, and the other was the Afaqis *or* Pardesis who had come from Central Asia, Iran and Iraq, and had settled in the Deccan region recently. There was always tension between these groups to appropriate better administrative positions. Because of their internal feuds, the stability of the Bahamani Sultanate was affected as we just discussed in the execution of Mahmud Gawan.

Key term	Meaning
(a) *Wazir-i-kul*	Prime Minister
(b) *Amir-i-kul*	Finance head
(c) *Wazir ashraf*	Foreign affairs and royal court
(d) *Sadar-i-jahan*	Head of judiciary and charities
(e) *Tarafdar*	Head of province

Western India – Gujarat, Malwa and Mewar

Gujarat

Gujarat was one of the richest provinces of the Delhi Sultanate on account of its handicrafts, fertile lands and flourishing seaports. Alauddin Khalji was the first Sultan to annex it to Delhi Sultanate (c. 1297 CE) and since then it remained under the Turkish governors of the Sultanate.

Under Firoz Tughlaq, Gujarat had a benign governor who, according to the historian Ferishta, *was highly liberal and encouraged the Hindu religion to a great extent*. He was succeeded by Zafar Khan, whose father Sadharan was a Rajput who converted to Islam, and had given his sister in marriage to Firoz Tughlaq. *After Timur's invasion*, in c. 1407 CE, Zafar Khan, who was then the governor, *proclaimed* himself an *independent* ruler. He assumed the title of Muzaffar Shah and founded the Muzaffarid dynasty.

Muzaffar Shah/Zafar Khan (c. 1407–1411 CE)

- Founder of Muzaffarid dynasty who declared independence from Delhi Sultanate when Delhi was in chaos after Timur's invasion.

Ahmed Shah (c. 1411–1441 CE)

- Grandson of Muzaffar Shah, who was the real founder of the kingdom of Gujarat as he not only controlled the nobility and settled the administration, but also expanded and consolidated the kingdom.
- He tried to extend his control over Rajput states in the Saurashtra region (Girnar), as well as those located on the Gujarat–Rajasthan border such as Jhalawar, Bundi and Dungarpur. He also attacked Sidhpur, the famous Hindu pilgrimage centre, and destroyed many beautiful temples. It is rather interesting to note that even though he pertained to be an orthodox Muslim who imposed jaziya on the Hindus in Gujarat and destroyed several temples, quite oppositely, he appointed Hindus to important administrative positions. For instance, his two ministers Manik Chand and Motichand both were Hindus.
- He fought equally fiercely against Hindu as well as Muslim rulers. His arch-enemies were the Muslim rulers of Malwa. The rivalry between Gujarat and Malwa was bitter and prevented both the regional states from concentrating on larger political gains in north Indian politics.
- Founded the city of Ahmedabad and made it his capital in c. 1413 CE (shifted earlier capital from Patan).
- Influenced by the Jaina architectural traditions of Gujarat (having exquisite features of slender turrets, exquisite stone-carving and highly ornate brackets), he built beautiful buildings, like the Jami Masjid (c. 1423 CE) and Teen Darwaza, and beautified the city with gardens, palaces and bazaars.
- He was also noted for imparting justice. For instance, he publicly executed his son-in-law who had murdered an innocent man.
- After the death of Ahmed Shah in c. 1441 CE, his eldest son Muhammad Shah ascended the throne, who was also known as Zar-Baksh. However, in c. 1451 CE, he was killed by conspirators. Muhammad Shah was followed by two weak rulers. Later, nobles raised Fateh Khan, a grandson of Ahmad Shah, to the throne. He took the title Mahmud Begarha and was the ablest ruler of his dynasty.

Mahmud Begarha (c. 1459–1511 CE)

- The most important ruler of Gujarat, under whom the Gujarat kingdom reached its maximum limit and emerged as one of the most powerful and well administered states in the country.
- He was called 'Begarha' as he had captured two powerful forts *or garhs*, Girnar (Junagarh) in Saurashtra and the fort of Champaner from the Rajputs in south Gujarat. However, according to another version, *he was called Begarha as his moustaches resembled the horns of a cow*.
- The strategic fort of Girnar was suitable not only for administering Saurashtra but also provided a base for operations against Sindh. Mahmud founded a new town called Mustafabad at the foot of the hill, which had many beautiful monuments and later became the second capital of Gujarat.
- Similarly, he besieged the fort of Champaner, which was crucial to control Malwa and Khandesh. Here too, Mahmud constructed a new town called Muhammadabad near Champaner and laid out many fine gardens.
- Mahmud sacked Dwarka primarily to check the menace of pirates who preyed on the pilgrims traveling to Mecca.
- In c. 1507 CE, Mahmud led an expedition against the Portuguese (who had settled on the western coast) to break their trade monopoly, which was causing immense harm to the Muslim traders. For this, he sought help of the ruler of Egypt but he was unsuccessful and finally he had to give the Portuguese a site for a factory in Diu.
- During his reign, trade and commerce prospered. He constructed many *caravan-sarais* and inns for the comfort of the travellers and tried to maintain roads safe for traffic.
- Though he himself had never received systematic education, yet he was a great patron of art and literature. Many works were translated from Arabic to Persian during his reign. His court poet was the Sanskrit scholar, Udayaraja, who wrote a book called the Raja-Vinoda on Mahmud Begarha.
- Interestingly, *Mahmud had a striking appearance as he had a flowing beard, which reached up to his waist, and his moustache was so long that he tied it over his head*. According to Barbosa, '*Mahmud was given some poison right from his childhood, so if a fly settled on his hand, it met instant death*'. He was also famous for his huge appetite.

Bahadur Shah (c. 1526 –1535 CE & 1536 –1537 CE)

- During his reign, Gujarat was under pressure from the expanding Mughal Empire under emperors Babur (died 1530) and Humayun (1530–1540), and from the Portuguese, who were establishing fortified settlements on the Gujarat coast to expand their power in India from their base in Goa.

- He sent an embassy to the Ottoman rule and sought his support against the Portuguese. The Turks reciprocated positively and in 1529, a strong fleet under Sulaiman Rais was dispatched to aid him. Two of the Turkish officials were given Indian names[8], and were appointed governors of Surat and Diu, respectively.
- In 1534, he signed the Treaty of Bassein with the Portuguese, through which he not only ceded Diu to the Portuguese, but also other territories of his empire such as Vasai and the islands that today form Mumbai. The Portuguese obtained Daman from the Shah in 1559.
- Another noteworthy incident during his reign was his seige of Chittor in 1534 in which Rani Karnavati sent *'Rakhi'*, the holy thread, to Humayun and requested for help. But, Humayun could not help in time and Karnavati performed Jauhar.
- In 1536, however, he was drowned during one of the scuffles which ensued with the Portuguese due to some misunderstanding.

Gujarat was annexed by Akbar in c. 1573 CE.

Malwa

Malwa was the south-western province of the Delhi Sultanate, which was conquered by Alauddin Khalji in c. 1310 CE and remained the part of the Delhi Sultanate till the death of Firoz Tughlaq.

It had a very strategic position as it was situated on the high plateau between the rivers Narmada and Tapti and hence commanded the trunk routes between Gujarat and northern India, as also between north and south India. So, if any of the powerful states of the region could extend its control over Malwa, it could dominate north India.

After the invasion of Timur, in c. 1401 CE, Dilawar Khan Ghori who belonged to the court of Firoz Shah Tughlaq, threw off his allegiance to Delhi, though he did not take the royal title of 'Sultan'. Dilawar shifted the capital from Dhar to Mandu, renaming it Shadiabad, the city of joy, which was highly defensible and which had a great deal of natural beauty. After the death of Dilawar Khan in c. 1405 CE, his son Alp Khan ascended the throne and acquired the title of Hoshang Shah.

Hoshang Shah (c. 1406–1435 CE)

- He was the first formally appointed Islamic king of Malwa who was a bold and ambitious ruler. An interesting account of his boldness could be ascertained by his rather unconventional way of obtaining the finest elephants from Odisha in c. 1421 CE, when the King of Odisha had refused to send him the best elephants. *He himself along with a thousand soldiers reached Jajpur in Odisha and disguised themselves as merchants of other things, including the king's favourite horses. When the king came to inspect the horses, Hoshang Shah's soldiers captured him and he let him free only after the king promised to gift 100 of the very best elephants and to let him out of Odisha safely.*

[8] Of these two, one of them was Rumi Khan who later earned a great name for himself as a master-gunner. He also repulsed the Portuguese attack on Diu in 1531.

- Despite being a warrior, he had a sympathetic heart and was dearly loved by his subjects. He adopted a broad policy of religious toleration as evident from the inscription of the Lalitpur temple which belonged to this period. It specifies that no restrictions were placed on the construction of temples. He also encouraged many Rajputs to settle in Malwa and extended his patronage to the Jains who were the principal commercial merchants and bankers of the area. For instance, two of the elder brothers of Rana Mokul of Mewar were granted jagirs in Malwa, and Nardeva Soni, a successful merchant, was his treasurer and adviser.
- He is also remembered for his wonderful taste in architecture. It was he who made Mandu one of the most impregnable forts of India. Hoshangabad in Madhya Pradesh (earlier called Narmadapur) was founded by Hoshang Shah.

Mahmud Khalji (c. 1436–1469 CE)

- Mahmud Khalji crowned himself Sultan after assassinating Mohammad, the son of the Hoshang Shah. It was under his reign that the Malwa Sultanate reached its greatest height.
- He was a restless and ambitious ruler who fought with almost all his neighbours – the ruler of Gujarat, the rajas of the Gondwana, and Orissa, the Bahmani Sultans, and even an unsuccessful campaign against the Delhi Sultanate. However, his prime targets were the south Rajputana states, specially Mewar. Mahmud Khalji fought with Rana Kumbha of Mewar, and both sides claimed victory. Rana Kumbha erected a tower of victory in Chittor, and the Sultan erected a seven-storied column at Mandu.

Ghiyas-ud-Din (c. 1469–1500 CE)

- Mahmud was succeeded by his eldest son Ghiyas-ud-Din, who was a pleasure seeker and devoted himself to women and music. He constructed the Jahaz Mahal for housing the women, numbering in thousands, of his harem.

FIGURE 12.4 Jahaz Mahal, Mandu

- Ghiyas-ud-Din was defeated by Rana Raimal of Chittor.

Mahmud Shah II (c. 1510–1531 CE)

- The last ruler of the Khalji dynasty of Malwa, who surrendered to Bahadur Shah, the sultan of Gujarat, after he lost the fort of Mandu in c. 1531 CE.
- During c. 1531–1537 CE, the kingdom was under the control of Bahadur Shah though the Mughal emperor Humayun captured it for a short period during c. 1535–1536 CE. In c. 1537 CE, Qadir Shah, an ex-officer of the previous Khalji dynasty, regained control over a part of the erstwhile kingdom. But in c. 1542 CE, Sher Shah Suri conquered the kingdom defeating him and appointed Shujaat Khan as the governor. His son, Baz Bahadur, declared himself independent in c. 1555 CE.

Baz Bahadur (c. 1555–1561 CE)

- He was the last sultan of Malwa, who was noted for his gift of music and poetry, and is known for his romantic liaison with queen Roopmati.
- In c. 1561 CE, Akbar's army led by Adham Khan and Pir Muhammad Khan attacked Malwa and defeated Baz Bahadur in the battle of Sarangpur. *One of the reasons for Adham Khan's attack seems to be his love for Rani Roopmati. Rani Roopmati poisoned herself upon hearing of the fall of Mandu and Baz Bahadur fled to Khandesh.*
- Akbar soon recalled Adham Khan and handed over command to Pir Muhammad, who attacked Khandesh and proceeded up to Burhanpur, but was soon defeated and killed by a coalition of three powers: Miran Mubarak Shah II of Khandesh, Tufal Khan of Berar and Baz Bahadur. The confederate army pursued the Mughals and drove them out of Malwa, and thus Baz Bahadur regained his kingdom for a brief period.
- However, in c. 1562 CE, Akbar sent another army led by Abdullah Khan which finally defeated Baz Bahadur, who fled to Chittor. He thus remained a fugitive at a number of courts until he surrendered in c. 1570 CE to Akbar at Nagaur and Malwa, thus became a subah of the Mughal empire.

Among the many buildings of splendid architectural beauty built in the fortified city of Mandu, the Jami Masjid, which was planned and begun by Hoshang Shah and completed by Mahmud Khalji, the Hindola Mahal, the Jahaz Mahal, Hoshang Shah's tomb, and Baz Bahadur's and Rani Rupamati's palaces are worth a visit. It is pertinent to note that unlike the Gujarat style of architecture, the Mandu architecture was massive due to use of lofty plinth for the buildings and there was a large-scale use of coloured and glazed tiles which provided variety to the buildings.

Mewar

Mewar or Udaipur Kingdom was originally called Medhpaat and over time, the name Medhpath became Mewar. Interestingly, the rulers of Mewar used the title 'Maharana' (Prime Minister or Custodian) instead of the typical title 'Maharaja' (King), as they believed themselves to be merely custodians of the Hindu civilisation epitomised in the temple of their lord Eklingaji (a manifestation of Lord Shiva), who was also called Medhpateshwar (Lord of Medhpath).

The rise of Mewar during the 15th century was an important factor in the political life of north India. The power of the Chauhans in Rajputana came to an end with the conquest of Ranthambhore by Alauddin Khalji. After being overrun by the armies of Alauddin Khalji, Mewar had become relatively insignificant. Later in c. 1335 CE, Rana Hammira (c. 1314–1378 CE) established the Second Guhila dynasty of Chittor and also became the progenitor of the Sisodia clan, a branch of the Guhilot clan, to which every succeeding Maharana of Mewar has belonged. He was the first ruler who started the use of title 'Rana' and also built the Annapoorna Mata temple, which is located in the Chittorgarh Fort in Rajasthan. After the assassination of Rana Hammira's grandson, Maharana Mokal, his son Rana Kumbha, ascended the throne of Mewar in c. 1433 CE.

Rana Kumbha (c. 1433–1468 CE)

- Rana Kumbha or Kumbhakarna Singh raised Mewar to the status of a power to be reckoned with and pulled it out of obscurity. He was a talented military commander and ruler who made his mark in the political as well as cultural field.
- After cautiously consolidating his position with great diplomacy and defeating his internal rivals, Rana Kumbha conquered states like Bundi, Kota, Chatsu, Malpura, Amber, Dungerpur, etc. Majority of these states accepted the suzerainty of Rana Kumbha and came under his political influence. He also annexed Sambhar, Didwana, Mandore, Nagaur, Ranthambore, Sirohi, Gagran, Ajmer, Mandalgarh, Abu, Toda, etc. to his kingdom.
- Rana Kumbha and Sultan Mahmud Khalji of Malwa had a history of tussle. Rana Kumbha had given shelter to a rival of Mahmud Khalji and even attempted to install him on the throne of Malwa. In retailation, Mahmud Khalji gave shelter and active encouragement to some of the rivals of the Rana, such as his brother Mokal. As we have discussed above, Rana Khumba and Mahmud Khalji fought against each other, and interestingly, both sides claimed victory. Kumbha erected a Victory Tower at Chittor a mark of victory of his conquests. He also consolidated the fortification of Chittor and constructed a road running through its seven doors.
- It is rather admirable of Rana Kumbha that although he was sorely pressed from all sides, he was largely able to maintain his position in Mewar. Though Kumbhalgarh was besieged a couple of times by Gujarat forces, and Mahmud Khalji was able to raid as far inland as Ajmer and install his own governor, Rana was able to repulse these attacks and retain possession of most of his conquests with the exception of some of the outlying areas such as Ranthambore.
- He was a great patron of art and literature and a great musician himself (he was a great veena player). He was acclaimed as 'Sangeet Shiromani' and wrote an outstanding treatise on Indian music titled *Sangeet-Raj* as well as other works like Sangeet Mimansa, Sangeet

Ratnakar *and* Sudprabandh. He also patronised great scholars such as Mahesh and Atri, the composers of the inscriptions of Victory Tower.

- He constructed the city of Basantpur. He built several inns, palaces, ponds, schools and temples. For the defence of the kingdom, he built five forts of Kumbhalgarh, Achalgarh, Maddan, Kolana and Vairat. He also gave patronage to many craftsmen and sculptors.
- Unfortunately, he was murdered by his own son Udai in order to gain the throne. Udai was however ousted by Maharana Raimal who was the younger son of Rana Kumbha. Later, after another unfortunate, long fratricidal conflict with his brothers, Rana Sanga (son of Raimal) became the ruler of Mewar.

Rana Sanga (c. 1508–1528 CE)

- Originally called Sangram Singh, the grandson of Rana Kumbha was a ferocious and brave Rajput ruler who fought several battles. He was a man of indomitable spirit and despite losing one arm, one eye and numerous other grave injuries, he carried on with great valour and established his supremacy over almost all Rajput states in Rajasthan.
- He was more of a visionary than a warrior. After the fall of the Gurjara–Pratihara kingdom, Rajputs all over northern India had broken up into various factions squabbling and quarrelling among themselves but he united the various factions under his able leadership.
- After first consolidating his power at Mewar, Rana Sanga moved his army against the internally troubled neighbouring kingdom of Malwa (as during this period Malwa was disintegrating).
- The ruler of Malwa, Mahmud II, was wary of his rival Rajput Wazir Medini Rai's power, so he sought assistance from both Sultan Ibrahim Lodhi of Delhi and Bahadur Shah of Gujarat. Rai, on his part, requested Sanga to come to his aid. Joined by Rajput rebels from within Malwa, Sanga's troops from Mewar not only defeated Malwa's army but also their supporting troops from Delhi. Thus, Malwa fell under Rana's military power. His chivalry was reflected when he treated Sultan Mahmud with generosity and restored his kingdom even when he was defeated and taken as a prisoner by Rana.
- He also defeated the Delhi Sultan Ibrahim Lodhi in c. 1518 CE at Ghatoli (near Gwalior). Lodhi, reportedly stunned by this Rajput aggression, moved again against Sanga's army in c. 1519 CE, but was humbled again at Dholpur. Lodi thus fought Sanga repeatedly, only to be defeated each time, losing much of his land in Rajputana, while the boundaries of Sanga's military influence came to extend within striking distance of Agra.
- According to some legends, it was on the invitation of Rana Sanga that Babur invaded India in c. 1526 CE. But just after a year, Rana Sanga fought against Babur in the famous battle of Khanwa near Fatehpur Sikri (c. 1527 CE). The Rajput forces of Rana Sanga,

supplemented by the contingents of Hasan Khan Mewati and the Afghan Mahmud Lodhi and Raja Medini Rai of Alwar, fought against Babur. The battle, which lasted for not more than 10 hours, was bitterly contested and became an exceedingly brutal affair. At a critical moment of battle, the defection of Silhadi and his contingent caused a split in the Rajput forces. Rana Sanga, while trying to rebuild his front, was wounded and fell unconscious from his horse. The Rajput army thought their leader was dead and fled in disorder, thus allowing the Mughals to win.

- Rana Sanga was whisked away to safety by the Rathore contingent from Marwar. Unwilling to admit defeat, he set out once more to rebuild his military and renew war with Babur. He vowed not to set foot in Chittor till Babur was defeated by him. In c. 1528 CE, he again fought Babur at Battle of Chanderi to help Medini Rai who was attacked by Babur. But he fell sick at Kalpi and died in his camp. It is speculated that he was poisoned by some of his nobles who thought that his renewal of war with Babur was suicidal.

It is pertinent to note that poet, saint and passionate devotee of Lord Krishna, the legendary Meera Bai, was the daughter-in-law of Maharana Sanga, and Maharana Pratap too belonged to his lineage.

North India: Kashmir

In Rajatarangini (a history of Kashmir written by Kalhana in the mid-12th century) it is stated that the valley of Kashmir was formerly a lake. According to Hindu mythology, *the lake was drained by the great rishi or sage, Kashyapa, son of Marichi (who in his turn was the son of Brahma), by cutting the gap in the hills at Baramulla (Varaha-mula). When Kashmir had been drained, Kashyapa asked Brahmans to settle there* and thus Kashmir valley was settled by Hindus in the initial phases. The beautiful kingdom of Kashmir was for long a forbidden land for all outsiders. Alberuni, the famous Arab traveller remarked in his work Al-Hind that *entry into Kashmir was not allowed even to the Hindus who were not known personally to the local nobles.*

In the 11th century, the rulers were followers of Shaivism, and Shaivism was the central religion in Kashmir. The oppressive taxation, corruption, internecine fights and rise of the Damaras (feudal lords) during the unpopular rule of the Lohara dynasty (c. 1003–1320 CE) paved way for foreign invasions of Kashmir. In c. 1320 CE, Suhadeva, the last king of the Lohara dynasty, fled Kashmir after Zulju (Dalucha), a Turkic–Mongol chief, led a savage raid on Kashmir. Zulju massacred the civilian population on a mass scale and did a lot of destruction. The hapless Kashmir government could offer no opposition and thus lost all credibility and public support. So, in c. 1339 CE, Shamsuddin Shah deposed the Shaiva ruler and became the ruler of Kashmir and from this period onwards, Islam started influencing the Kashmiri society. A group of Sufi saints known as the *Rishis* propagated a religion that combined features of Hinduism and Islam.

For instance, Islamic preacher Sheikh Nooruddin Noorani, who is traditionally revered by Hindus as *Nund Rishi*, combined elements of Kashmir Shaivism with Sufi mysticism in his discourses. Thus, in the 14th century under the influence of Sufi saints like Noorani, Islam gradually became the dominant religion in Kashmir.

Shamshuddin Shah Mir (c. 1339–1342 CE)

- He was the founder of the Shah Miri dynasty and was the first Muslim ruler of Kashmir.

Sikandar Shah (c. 1389–1413 CE)

- All other Sultans between c. 1354–1470 CE were tolerant of other religions, but Sultan Sikandar was an exception who was more of an iconoclast. He imposed taxes on non-Muslims, forced conversions to Islam, and earned the title But–Shikan for destroying idols.
- The state encouragement to Islam took an extreme turn during his reign as he issued an order that all Hindus, especially the Brahmanas living in his kingdom should embrace Islam or leave his kingdom. (It is perceived that *these orders were issued at the instance of his minister, Suha Bhatt, who was earlier a Hindu but had converted to Islam, and was bent on harassing his former co-religionists*).
- After the death of Sikander Shah, his son Ali Shah (c. 1413–1419 CE) ascended the throne, and after some years his brother Shah Khan ascended the throne under the title of Zain-ul-Abidin.

Zain-ul-Abidin (c. 1420–1470 CE)

- Known as Bud Shah (the Great Sultan) and as Akbar of Kashmir who was benevolent, liberal and an enlightened ruler.
- He reversed all the negative and bigoted policies of Sikandar Shah and brought back all the non-Muslims who had fled. He allowed the freedom to revert back to Hinduism to all those who were forcibly converted under any pressure. He even restored their liberties, abolished jaziya, and prohibited cow slaughter. As noted by Abul Fazal more than 100 years later, 'Kashmir had one hundred and fifty majestic temples', and it is most likely that they must have been restored under Zain-ul-Abidin.
- The Hindus occupied many high offices in his government. For instance, Sriya Bhatt was a minister of justice and court physician. Even Zainul's first two queens were Hindus, being the daughters of the Raja of Jammu.
- Though not a great warrior, he defeated the Mongol invasion of Ladakh, conquered the Baltistan area (called Tibbat-i-Khurd) and kept control over Jammu, Rajauri, etc. and thus unified the Kashmiri kingdom.
- He paid great attention towards the economic growth of Kashmir. The Sultan not only invited artists and craftsmen from Central Asia and Persia to train local artists in Kashmir

but also sent two persons to Samarkand to learn the arts of paper-making and book-binding. Under his rule, the arts of wood carving, stone-cutting and polishing, bottle-making, gold-beating, musket-making, art of manufacturing fireworks, shawl and carpet-weaving prospered.

- He contributed to the agricultural development of Kashmir by constructing dams and canals and initiated the maintenance of the agricultural records. During the period of famine and other natural calamities, relief in terms of loans and grains and fodder was provided to the peasants. He also introduced reforms in the currency, market control and fixed prices of the commodities. The Sultan also subsidised the import of the commodities that were scarce in the state. For instance, to make up for the shortage of salt, he imported salt from Ladakh and helped the traders in every possible way.
- He got built Zaina Lanka, the artificial island in the Wular Lake on which he built his palace and a mosque. He also founded the towns of Zaingir, Zainket and Zainpur. The striking feature of the Jama Masjid in Kashmir completed by Zain-ul-Abidin is similar to Buddhist pagodas with Persian style and also includes turrets in its architecture.

FIGURE 12.5 Jama Masjid, Srinagar

- He himself was a great scholar of Persian, Sanskrit, Tibetan and Kashmiri language and wrote poetry under the pen name 'Qutb'. He also gave patronage to Sanskrit and Persian scholars and under his patronage, the Mahabharat and Kalhana's Rajatarangini were translated into Persian and many Persian and Arabic works were translated into Hindi. He was also in touch with the leading rulers in other parts of not only India but Asia too.

After him, weak rulers ascended the throne of Kashmir and there was confusion. Taking advantage of this, Mirza Haider, a relative of Babur, occupied Kashmir. In c. 1586 CE, Akbar conquered Kashmir and made it a part of the Mughal Empire.

Eastern India: Jaunpur, Bengal, Assam and Orissa

Jaunpur

Jaunpur was a prosperous province in the eastern part of the Delhi Sultanate (near modern Varanasi on the banks of river Gomati). The governor of Jaunpur was Malik Sarwar, who was a prominent noble during Firoz Shah Tughlaq's period. In c. 1394 CE, Sultan Nasiruddin Mohammad Shah Tughlaq made him a minister and gave him the title of Sultanu-Sharq (the master of the east). Thereafter, he was known as *Malik Sarwar Sultanus Sharq*. After Timur's invasion and the weakening of the Delhi Sultanate, Malik Sarwar took advantage of a weak political situation and declared himself independent and extended his authority over Awadh and a large part of Ganga–Yamuna doab such as Kannauj, Kara, Sandeela, Dalmau, Bahraich, Bihar and Tirhut. Though Malik Sarwar did not assume the title of *Sultan*, he laid down the foundation of the Sharqi Dynasty.

FIGURE 12.6 Atala Masjid, Jaunpur

Jaunpur evolved a distinct architecture that is known as the Sharqi style of architecture. Jaunpur was known as the Shiraz of India. Most notable examples of Sharqi style of architecture in Jaunpur are the Atala Masjid, the Lal Darwaja Masjid and the Jama Masjid.

Malik Sarwar (c. 1394–1399 CE)

- Laid the foundation of the Sharqi dynasty.
- His authority was recognised by the Rai of Jajnagar and the ruler of Lakhnauti too.
- After his death, he was succeeded by his adopted son Malik Qaranfal, who took the title of Mubarak Shah.

Mubarak Shah (c. 1399–1402 CE)

- First ruler of Sharqi dynasty. During his reign, Mallu Iqbal (the powerful minister of the puppet Sultan of Delhi, Mahmud Tughlaq) tried to recover Jaunpur, but failed.

Ibrahim (c. 1402–1440 CE)

- He was the younger brother of Mubarak Shah, who ruled as Shams-ud-din Ibrahim Shah and proved to be the greatest ruler of the Sharqi dynasty, under whom Jaunpur became an important centre of learning.
- To the east, his kingdom extended to Bihar, and to the west, to Kannauj. During his reign, the relations between Delhi and Jaunpur became worse. He even led an expedition against Delhi but failed. He also threatened the Sultanate of Bengal under Raja Ganesha.
- He was a patron of Islamic learning and established a number of colleges for this purpose. A large number of scholarly works on Islamic theology and law was produced during his reign, which include the Hashiah-i-Hindi, the Bahar-ul-Mawwaj and the Fatwa-i-Ibrahim Shahi.
- During his reign, one of the most famous buildings, the Atala Masjid, was constructed at Jaunpur. Though the foundation of the Atala Masjid was laid by Firoz Shah Tughlaq in c. 1376 CE, it was completed only during the rule of Ibrahim Shah in c. 1408 CE. Another mosque, the Jhanjhiri Masjid, was also built by Ibrahim Shah in c. 1430 CE.

Mahmud Shah (c. 1440–1457 CE)

- Elder son of Ibrahim who conquered the fort of Chunar but could not conquer Kalpi.
- In c. 1452 CE, he invaded Delhi but was defeated by Bahlol Lodhi. Later, he made another attempt to conquer Delhi and marched into Etawah. Finally, he agreed to a treaty that accepted the right of Bahlol Lodhi over Shamsabad. But when Bahlol tried to take possession of Shamsabad, he was opposed by the forces of Jaunpur. Around this time, Mahmud Shah died. He was succeeded by his son Bhikhan, who assumed the title of Muhammad Shah.
- The Lal Darwaja Masjid (c. 1450 CE) was built during the reign of the Mahmud Shah.

Muhammad Shah (c. 1457–1458 CE)

- On assuming power in c. 1457 CE, he made peace with Bahlol Lodhi and recognised his right over Shamsabad.

- In c. 1458 CE, when he got his brother Hasan executed, his other brother Hussain revolted and proclaimed himself as the Sultan of Jaunpur under the title of Hussain Shah, and killed Muhammad Shah.

Hussain Shah Sharqi (c. 1458–1505 CE)

- The last ruler of the Sharqi dynasty, Hussain Shah, assumed the title of Gandharva and contributed significantly in the development of the khayal, a genre of Hindustani classical music. He also composed several new ragas (melodies). Most notable among these are *Malhar-syama, Gaur-syama, Bhopal-syama, Hussaini- or Jaunpuri-asavari* (presently known as Jaunpuri) and Jaunpuri-basant.
- It was during his reign that the Jama Masjid was built in c. 1470 CE and also a prolonged war with Bahlol Lodhi started.

Finally, Sikandar Lodhi who succeeded Bahlol Lodhi annexed Jaunpur. Hussain Shah died and the Sharqi dynasty came to an end.

Bengal

Bengal was an important regional kingdom under the Palas in the 8th century and the Senas in the 12th century. It was the easternmost province of the Delhi Sultanate. The long distance, uncomfortable climate and poor means of transport and communications (as much of its communication depended upon waterways) made it difficult for the Delhi Sultanate to control this province. Though Bengal was annexed to the Delhi Sultanate, a number of times it gained its independence. For instance, if we look through the pages of history, during the last decade of the 12th century CE, Muhammad Bin Bakhtiyar annexed Bengal to the conquered territories of Muhammad Ghori. But after his death, his successors declared their independence with the support of the local people. Later, Balban forced Bengal to accept the sovereignty of Delhi and appointed his son Bughra Khan as its governor. But after Balban's death, he declared his own independence. Ghiyasuddin Tughlaq tried to solve this problem by partitioning Bengal into three independent administrative divisions: Lakhnauti, Satgaon and Sonargaon. However, the problems remained as such. Muhammad bin Tughlaq tried to control Bengal, but in c. 1338 CE, when he was busy in suppressing rebellion in other parts of Sultanate, Bengal cut off its connection with Delhi. Finally, Bengal emerged as an independent regional state in the 14th century.

In c. 1342 CE, one of the nobles, Haji Ilyas Khan, united Bengal and became its ruler and laid the foundation of the Ilyas Shah dynasty. The Bengal Sultanate (which ruled for around 125 years though in phases) established by Ilyas Shah emerged as one of the leading diplomatic, economic and military powers in the subcontinent. Ilyas Shah and his successors embraced Indo-Aryanisation and adapted themselves to Bengali culture and society. Their kingdom was a melting pot for migrants from across the Muslim world and played a key role in the development of Bengali Muslim society. Pandua and Gaur, the capitals of Bengal were adorned with magnificent buildings. While Persian was the language of administration, Bengali developed as a regional language. The celebrated poet Maladhar Basu, compiler of Sri-Krishna-Vijaya, was patronised by the Sultans and was granted the title of Gunaraja Khan. His son was honoured with the title of Satyaraja Khan. Later, another prominent Hussain Shahi dynasty came to fore and after a brief period of 44 years, Bengal came under the authority of Sher Shah Suri, one of the most able Sur rulers who even ousted the Mughal ruler Humayun from Delhi.

Haji Shamsh-ud-din Ilyas Khan (c. 1342–1357 CE)

- Founder of Ilyas Shah dynasty. His most important legacy is that he unified the independent kingdom of Bengal. He extended the dominions in the west from Tirhut to Champaran and Gorakhpur, and finally up to Benaras. This brought him in conflict with Firoz Shah Tughlaq and to counter his increasing influence, Firoz Shah Tughlaq took Champaran and Gorakhpur and occupied the Bengali capital Pandua, and forced Ilyas to seek shelter in the strong fort of Ekdala. Ilyas Shah thus had to sign a treaty with Firoz Shah Tughlaq. According to this treaty, river Kosi was accepted as the boundary line between two kingdoms.
- With the establishment of friendly relations now with Delhi, Ilyas Shah was enabled to extend his control over the kingdom of Kamrupa (modern Assam). He tried to annex Bengal and raided Orissa and Tirhut and forced them to pay tribute. His campaigns were thus considered 'world-conquering' in the context of medieval Bengal and Ilyas Shah has been described as the Bengali equivalent of Alexander or Napoleon.
- He was a popular ruler and organised an inclusive and pluralistic administration. It is said that *when Firoz Shah Tughlaq was at Pandua, he tried to win over the inhabitants of the city to his side by giving liberal grants of land to the nobles, the clergy and other deserving people, but due to immense popularity of Ilyas Shah, Firoz Shah could not succeed.*
- Haji Iliyas died in c. 1357 CE and his son Sikandar succeeded the throne. During his reign too, Firoz Shah Tughlaq again tried to annex Bengal but Sikandar followed the tactics of his father and retreated to Ekdala. Firoz once again failed and had to retreat. After this, Bengal was left alone for about 200 years and was not invaded again till c. 1538 CE after the Mughals had established their power at Delhi.

Ghiyasuddin Azam (c. 1390–1411 CE)

- One of the important rulers of the Ilyas Shah dynasty who was known for his love for justice. It is said that *once he accidentally killed a son of a widow who filed a complaint with qazi. The Sultan when summoned to the court humbly appeared and paid fine imposed by the qazi. At the end of the trial, Azam told the qazi that had he not discharged his duties honestly, he would have had him beheaded.*
- Azam was a learned man and had close relations with the famous learned men of his times, including the famous Persian poet, Hafiz of Shiraz. He also maintained cordial

relations with China and a prosperous trading relationship existed between Bengal and China during his reign. The port of Chittagaong was an important trading centre. He also sent and received Chinese envoy and on request from the king of China, Azam also sent Buddhist monks to China.

- There was a brief spell of Hindu rule under Raja Ganesha (c. 1414–1435 CE), but later the rule of Ilyas Shahi dynasty was restored by Nasiruddin Mahmud Shah and his successors (c. 1435–1487 CE). However, for a short period of seven years, the Habshis came to rule over Bengal (c. 1487–1494 CE), who were then overthrown by Alauddin Hussain Shah. He later proved to be one of the most remarkable rulers of Bengal.

Alauddin Hussain Shah (c. 1494–1519 CE)

- Founder of the Hussain Shahi dynasty (c. 1494–1538 CE). He is considered as the greatest of all the sultans of Bengal as under him, not only did Bengal frontiers expand but he also brought a cultural renaissance in Bengal and the Bengali language enriched a lot.
- He conquered Kamarupa, Kamata, Jajnagar and Orissa, and extended the sultanate all the way to the port of Chittagong, which witnessed the arrival of the first Portuguese merchants.
- He was very efficient, liberal, and gave high administrative posts to Hindus. For instance, his wazir, chief physician, chief bodyguard, master of mint were all talented Hindus. He also paid great respect to the Vaishnavite saint Chaitanya. Even his private secretary Sanatan was a celebrated pious Vaishnava, as was his brother Rupa.
- He came into conflict with Sikandar Lodhi and had to make peace with him. On his death, in c. 1518 CE, his son Nasib Khan ascended the throne under the title of Nasir-ud-din Narrat Shah.

Nasiruddin Nasrat Shah (c. 1518–1533 CE)

- He married Ibrahim Lodi's daughter and gave refuge to the Afghan lords. During the invasion of Babur, however, he remained neutral. Later, Nasrat Shah made a treaty with Babur and saved Bengal from a Mughal invasion.
- He continued his father's expansionist policies, adding more territory to his sultanate early on in his reign, but after c. 1526 CE he had to contend with the Mughal ascendency, and also suffered a reversal at the hands of the Ahom kingdom. He was succeeded by his son Alauddin Firuz Shah, under whose reign the Bengal army entered Assam and reached Kaliabor, but he was assassinated by his uncle Ghiyasuddin Mahmud Shah.

Ghiyasuddin Mahmud Shah (c. 1533–1538 CE)

- The last Sultan of the Hussain Shahi dynasty, who ruled from Sonargaon and was a weak, pleasure-loving and easy-going ruler who according to many historians *neither had diplomatic foresight, nor any practical approach to the political problems which beset Bengal during his reign.*

- His reign was marked by rebellions, including those by Khuda Bakhsh Khan, his general and governor of the Chittagong area, and Makhdum Alam, the governor of Hajipur.
- During his reign in c. 1534 CE, the Portuguese who had earlier arrived in Chittagong, were captured and sent to Gaur as prisoners on charges of misbehaviour. But, even at the position of superiority, he reconciled with them and permitted them to establish factories at Chittagong and Hughli.
- Ghiyasuddin and his Portuguese allies were defeated by Sher Shah Suri and his Afghans in c. 1538 CE, as his appeals to Mughal Emperor Humayun went unanswered.

Bengal was thus annexed by Sher Shah Suri, who established the Sur empire. Later in c. 1586 CE, Akbar conquered Bengal, and made it into a suba (province). The establishment of Mughal control over Bengal coincided with the rise of agrarian settlements in the forested and marshy areas of south-eastern Bengal. Soon after, with the spread of rice cultivation, this area became heavily populated with the local communities of fisher folks and peasants. The Mughals established their capital in the heart of the eastern delta at Dhaka, where officials and functionaries were granted land grants and they settled there.

Assam

The history of Assam is the history of the confluence of the Tibeto-Burman (Sino-Tibetan), Indo-Aryan and Austroasiatic cultures, as well as the confluence of people from the east, west and the north. It is noteworthy that although invaded over the centuries, it was never a vassal or a colony to an external power until the Burmese in c. 1821 CE, and, subsequently, the British in c. 1826 CE after the famous Treaty of Yandaboo.

The Assamese history has been derived from multiple sources. For instance, proto-history has been reconstructed from folklore epics like Mahabharata, and two medieval texts compiled in the Assam region: *the* Kalika Purana *and the* Yogini Tantra, while the historical account of Ancient Assam begins with the establishment of Pushyavarman's Varman dynasty in the 4th century in the Kamarupa kingdom, which left behind a corpus of Kamarupa inscriptions on rock, copper plates, clay; royal grants, etc. There is also a mention of Kamarupa in Samudragupta's Allahabad pillar. During the medieval period, the Buranjis, chronicles written in the Ahom and the Assamese languages by the Ahom kings offer a lot of detail about the Assam of medieval India.

Since the time of Muhammad bin Bakhtiyar Khalji (c. 1207 CE as mentioned in the Kanai-boroxiboa rock inscription), the Muslim rulers of Bengal had tried to bring the Brahmaputra valley in modern Assam under their control, but had to suffer a series of disastrous defeats in this region which was little known to them. There were two warring kingdoms in north Bengal and Assam; Kamata, also known as Kamrupa in the west, and the Ahom kingdom in the east. The Ahoms were a Mongoloid tribe from north Burma who had succeeded in establishing a powerful kingdom in the 13th century, and had become Hinduised in course of time. In fact, the name Assam is derived from them.

Ilyas Shah invaded Kamata and he could penetrate up to Gauhati, but he could not hold the area, and the river Karatoya was accepted as the north-east boundary of Bengal. Later, the rulers of Kamata were gradually able to recover many areas on the eastern bank of the Karatoya. They also fought against the Ahoms. Having made both their neighbours into enemies, the Kamata rulers sealed their doom as Alauddin Hussain Shah, with the aid of Ahoms, attacked Kamata and destroyed the city of Kamatapur (near modern Cooch Bihar) and thus annexed the kingdom to Bengal, appointing one of his sons as governor of the area. However, an attack by Alauddin's son Nusrat Shah later was repulsed with considerable losses to him.

During this time, the eastern Brahmaputra valley was under Suhungmung (c. 1497–1539 CE), one of the greatest Ahom rulers. He was the first Ahom king to adopt a Hindu title, Svarga Narayana, indicating rapid Hinduisation of the Ahoms as well as a move towards an inclusive polity. The Ahom kings thus came to be known as the Svarga Dev (heaven-lord). He is also called the Dihingia Raja, as he made Bakata on the Dihing river his capital. He not only repulsed the Muslim attack, but also extended his kingdom in all directions. The Vaishnavite reformer, Shankardeva, belonged to his time and spread Vaishnavism in the area.

Orissa/Odisha

The Gangas of Orissa were succeeded by the Hindu Gajapati rulers (c. 1435–1541 CE) during medieval times who ruled over Kalinga (present Odisha), large parts of Andhra Pradesh, and West Bengal, and the eastern and central parts of Madhya Pradesh and Jharkhand. Gajapati etymologically means a king with an army of elephants. The *Gajapati* dynasty was established by Kapilendra Deva in c. 1435 CE, after the fall of the last eastern Ganga king, Bhanudeva IV. The dynasty is also known as a Suryavamsi dynasty. The Suryavamsi Gajapatis period in Odisha was marked by the popularity of the Bhakti movement under the influence of Sri Chaitanya, who arrived in the empire at the time of King Prataparudra and stayed for 18 long years at Puri, and by the construction of Jagannatha temples across the length and breadth of the empire. The *Gajapati* rulers were mainly instrumental in extending their rule in the south towards Karnataka, which brought them in conflict with Vijaynagar, the Reddis and the Bahmani Sultans. However, by the early 16th century, the *Gajapatis* lost great portions of their southern dominion to Vijayanagar and Golconda, and even the *Gajapatis* were dislodged by Bhoi dynasty.

Kapilendra Deva (c. 1435–1466 CE)

- First ruler of Gajapati dynasty. During his reign, his kingdom expanded from Ganga in the north to as far as Bidar in the south.
- In about c. 1450 CE, he installed his eldest son, Hamvira Deva, as the governor of Rajamundry and Kondavidu. He also ordered Hamvira to conquer Vijayanagar and the

Bahmani Sultanate. Hamvira successfully captured the Vijaynagar capital, Hampi, and forced the weak ruler Mallikarjuna Raya to pay yearly taxes. In c. 1460 CE Hamvira Deva's commander, Tamavupala, conquered the southern states of Udayagiri (Nellore district) and Chandragiri. The rock edicts of Srirangam temple near Trichinapalli indicate that *Hamvira Deva captured* as far as Trichinapalli, Tanjore and Arcot in south and in the c. 1464 CE assumed the title of Dakshina Kapileswara.

- Kapilendra Deva patronised Vaishnavism, expanded the Jagannath temple at Puri and constructed the Shaivite temple of Kapileswar in Bhubaneswar. He was a great patron of Vedic culture and himself wrote a Sanskrit play called Parshuram Bijaya. It was during his reign that Odia language was officially used as an administrative language and the famous Odia poet Sarala Das wrote the Odia Mahabharata.

Purushottama Deva (c. 1466–1497 CE)

- After the death of Kapilendra Deva, a succession war started among his sons and Purushottama Deva succeeded in securing the throne in c. 1484 CE by defeating Hamvira Deva. But, during this period, significant southern parts of the empire were lost to Saluva Narasimha, the ruler of Vijayanagar. However, by the time of his death, he managed to recover some of these territories.

Prataparudra Deva (c. 1497–1540 CE)

- Son of Purushottama Deva, during whose reign, Alauddin Husain Shah of Bengal attacked twice. In the latter campaign (c. 1508 CE), the Bengal army marched up to Puri.
- In c. 1512 CE, Krishna Deva Raya of the Vijayanagar empire invaded Kalinga and defeated the forces of the *Gajapati* Kingdom and in c. 1522 CE, Quli Qutb Shah of Golconda ousted the Odia army from the Krishna–Godavari tract.
- Prataparudra was highly influenced by the works of Chaitanya and he gave up the military tradition as he retired himself into the life of an ascetic leaving the future of the empire uncertain.

Later, in c. 1541 CE, Prataparudra Deva's minister Govinda Vidyadhara rebelled against his weak successors, and after murdering the two sons of Prataparudra Deva he established the Bhoi Dynasty. The Bhoi dynasty was short-lived and during this period the kingdom came into conflict with neighbouring kingdoms and reeled under civil wars. Later, history repeated itself as Mukunda Deva, a minister of the Bhoi dynasty came to throne in c. 1559 CE in a bloody coup, after assassinating the last two Bhoi kings and declaring himself the ruler of Odisha. Mukunda Deva is considered the last independent ruler of Odisha as the region saw a steady decline afterwards. In c. 1568 CE, Odisha came under the control of Sulaiman Khan Karrani of Karrani dynasty, who was the ruler of the Sultanate of Bengal. The year of c. 1568 CE is important in the history of Odisha, as Odisha never emerged as an independent kingdom again.

QUESTIONS FROM LAST YEAR'S PRELIMS

1. Who among the following rulers of the Vijayanagara Empire constructed a large dam across Tungabhadra River and a canal-cum-aqueduct several kilometers long from the river to the capital city? **(2023)**

(a) Devaraya I (b) Mallikarjuna
(c) Vira Vijaya (d) Virupaksha

2. Who among the following rulers of medieval Gujarat surrendered Diu to the Portuguese? **(2023)**

(a) Ahmad Shah
(b) Mahmud Begarha
(c) Bahadur Shah
(d) Muhammad Shah

3. Consider the following dynasties: **(2023)**

1. Hoysala
2. Gahadavala
3. Kakatiya
4. Yadava

How many of the above dynasties established their kingdoms in the early eighth century AD?

(a) Only one (b) Only two
(c) Only three (d) None

4. In medieval India, the term "Fanam" referred to: **(2022)**

(a) Clothing (b) Coins
(c) Ornaments (d) Weapons

5. According to the Portuguese writer Nuniz, the women in Vijayanagara Empire were expert in which of the following areas? **(2021)**

1. Wrestling
2. Astrology
3. Accounting
4. Soothsaying

Select the correct answer using the code given below:

(a) 1, 2 and 3 only
(b) 1, 3 and 4 only
(c) 2 and 4 only
(d) 1, 2, 3 and 4

6. Building 'Kalyaana Mandapas' was a notable feature in the temple construction in the kingdom of **(2019)**

(a) Chalukya
(b) Chandela
(c) Rashtrakuta
(d) Vijayanagara

7. Regarding the taxation system of Krishna Deva Raya, the ruler of Vijayanagar, consider the following statements: **(2016)**

1. The tax rate on land was fixed depending on the quality of the land.
2. Private owners of workshops paid an industries tax.

Which of the statement(s) given above is/are correct?

(a) 1 only (b) 2 only
(c) Both 1 and 2 (d) Neither 1 nor 2

8. Which one of the following was given classical language status recently? **(2015)**

(a) Odia (b) Konkani
(c) Bhojpuri (d) Assamese

9. Who of the following founded a new city on the south bank of a tributary to river Krishna and undertook to rule his new kingdom as the agent of a deity to whom all the land south of the river Krishna was supposed to belong? **(2015)**

(a) Amoghavarsha I
(b) Ballala II
(c) Harihara I

(d) Prataparudra II

10. In medieval India, the designations 'Mahattara' and 'Pattakila' were used for **(2014)**

(a) Military officers
(b) Village headmen
(c) Specialists in Vedic rituals
(d) Chiefs of craft guilds

11. With reference to the religious history of medieval India, the Sufi mystics were known to pursue which of following practices? **(2012)**

1. Meditation and control of breath.
2. Severe ascetic exercises in a lonely place.
3. Recitation of holy songs to arouse a state of ecstasy in their audience.

Select the correct answer using the codes given below:

(a) 1 and 2 only (b) 2 and 3 only
(c) 3 only (d) 1, 2 and 3

12. When Raja Wodeyar founded the kingdom of Mysore, who was the ruler of the Vijaynagar Empire? **(2006)**

(a) Sadashiva (b) Tirumala
(c) Ranga II (d) Venkata II

13. Consider the following statements: **(2004)**

1. Narasimha Saluva ended the Sangama dynasty and seized the throne for himself and started the Saluva dynasty.
2. Vira Narasimha deposed the last Saluva ruler and seized the throne for himself.
3. Vira Narasimha was succeeded by his younger brother, Krishna Deva Raya.
4. Krishana Deva Raya was succeeded by his half-brother, Achyuta Raya.

Which of the following statements given above are correct?

(a) 1, 2 and 3 only
(b) 2, 3 and 4 only
(c) 1 and 4
(d) 1, 2, 3 and 4

14. Assertion (A): Saluva Narasimha put an end to the old dynasty and assumed the royal title.

Reasoning (R): He wanted to save the kingdom from further degeneration and disintegration. **(2003)**

(a) Both A and R are true and R is the correct explanation of A.
(b) Both A and R are true but R is not the correct explanation of A.
(c) A is true but R is false.
(d) A is false but R is true.

15. Assertion (A): The Battle of Khanwa was certainly more decisive and significant than the First battle of Panipat.

Reasoning (R): Rana Sanga, the Rajput hero, was certainly a more formidable adversary than Ibrahim Lodhi. **(2001)**

(a) Both A and R are true and R is the correct explanation of A.
(b) Both A and R are true but R is not the correct explanation of A.
(c) A is true but R is false.
(d) A is false but R is true.

16. Which one of the following Muslim rulers was hailed as the 'Jagadguru' by his Muslim subjects because of his belief in secularism? **(2000)**

(a) Husain Shah
(b) Zain-ul-Abidin
(c) Ibrahim Adil Shah
(d) Mahmud II

17. Match the following: **(2000)**

(A)	Iqta	(i)	Marathas
(B)	Jagir	(i)	Delhi Sultans
(C)	Amaram	(iii)	Mughals

(D) Mokasa (iv) Vijayanagara
(a) (A)–iii, (B)–ii, (C)–i, (D)–iv
(b) (A)–ii, (B)–iii, (C)–iv, (D)–i
(c) (A)–ii, (B)–iii, (C)–i, (D)–iv
(d) (A)–iii, (B)–ii, (C)–iv, (D)–i

18. Consider the following statements:

The striking feature of the Jama Masjid in Kashmir completed by Zain-ul-Abidin include: **(1999)**

i. Turret
ii. Similarity with the Buddhist pagodas
iii. Persian style

(a) i alone (b) i, ii, and iii
(c) ii and iii (d) i and iii

19. One of the consistent features found in the history of southern India was the growth of small regional kingdoms rather than large empires because of **(1999)**

(a) The absence of minerals like iron.
(b) Too many divisions in the social structure.
(c) The absence of vast areas of fertile land.
(d) The scarcity of manpower.

20. Which one of the following monuments has a dome which is said to be one of the largest in the world? **(1995)**

(a) The Tomb of Sher Shah, Sasaram
(b) Jama Masjid
(c) Tomb of Ghiyasuddin Tughlaq
(d) Gol Gumbaz, Bijapur

ANSWERS

1. (a)	2. (c)	3. (d)	4. (b)	5. (d)	6. (d)	7. (c)	8. (a)
9. (c)	10. (b)	11. (d)	12. (c)	13. (d)	14. (c)	15. (a)	16. (c)
17. (b)	18. (b)	19. (c)	20. (d)				

QUESTIONS FROM LAST YEAR'S MAINS

1. Mention the salient features of the polity of Vijaynagar Empire under Krishna Deva Raya. **(2015, History optional)**

2. On the basis of contemporary sources evaluate the system of agriculture and irrigation of the Vijaynagar kingdom. **(2013, History optional)**

PRACTICE QUESTIONS – PRELIMS

1. Match the following:

(A) Harihara I and Bukka (i) Tuluva dynasty
(B) Krishan Deva Raya (ii) Founded Vijaynagar Empire

(C)	Rana Khumbha	(iii)	Sangeet Shiromani
(D)	Deva Raya II	(iv)	Famous poet Srinatha

(a) (A)–ii, (B)–i, (C)–iii, (D)–iv
(b) (A)–i, (B)–ii, (C)–iii, (D)–iv
(c) (A)–iv, (B)–iii, (C)–ii, (D)–i
(d) (A)–iii, (B)–i, (C)–ii, (D)–iv

2. Consider the following statements and mark the option which is correct.
(i) Alauddin Hasan was the founder of Bahmani Kingdom.
(ii) Krishna Deva Raya's court was adorned by the 'ashtadiggaja'.
(iii) During the reign of Immadi Narasimha, Vasco da Gama landed in Calicut.

(a) i and ii (b) All of the above
(c) ii and iii (d) None of the above

3. Consider the following statements and mark the option which is correct.
(i) Hamvira deva of Orissa was also known as Dakshina Kapileswara.
(ii) The Gajapati dynasty was established by Kapilendra Deva.
(iii) Suhungmung was one of the greatest Ahom rulers.

Which of the statement(s) given above is/are correct?
(a) 1 only (b) 1 and 3 only
(c) 2 and 3 only (d) 1, 2 and 3

4. Match List I with List II and select the correct answer using the code given below the lists:

List I	List II
(a) Nizamshahis	1. Ahmadnagar
(b) Adilshahis	2. Golconda
(c) Imadshahis	3. Berar
(d) Qutubshahis	4. Bijapur

Code:	A	B	C	D
(a)	2	4	3	1
(b)	2	3	4	1
(c)	1	4	3	2
(d)	1	3	4	2

5. Match List I with List II and select the correct answer using the code given below the lists:

List I (Famous Book)	List II (Author)
(a) Dharmanathapurana	1. Udayaraja
(b) Sri-Krishna-Vijaya	2. Madhura
(c) Haravilasam	3. Srinatha
(d) Raja-Vinoda	4. Maladhar Basu

Code:	A	B	C	D
(a)	2	4	3	1
(b)	2	3	4	1
(c)	1	4	3	2
(d)	1	3	4	2

6. Consider the following statements and identify the ruler:
(1) Was known as Bud Shah.
(2) He abolished jaziya and prohibited cow slaughter.
(3) He built Zaina Lanka, the artificial island in the Wular Lake.

(a) Mahmud Gawan
(b) Alauddin Khalji
(c) Zainul Abidin
(d) Ghiyasuddin Azam

ANSWERS

1. (a) 2. (b) 3. (d) 4. (c) 5. (a) 6. (c)

PRACTICE QUESTIONS – MAINS

1. Why was the control of Malwa important for establishing supremacy in north India? List the important rulers of Malwa and their key achievements in detail.
2. What were the main reasons of conflict between the Bahmanis and the Vijaynagar empire? Elaborate.
3. Mahmud Gawan was the chief architect of the Bahmani empire. Do you agree? Give suitable reasons.
4. Compare the Vijaynagar administration with Bahmani Sultanate's administration.

CHAPTER

13

The Mughals (c. 1526–1857 CE)

The Mughal Empire was founded by Babur, a Central Asian ruler who claimed lineage from Timur (the founder of the Timurid Empire) on his father's side and from Chagatai, the second son of the Mongol ruler Chengiz Khan, on his mother's side. It is noteworthy to add that due to the lineage of Timur, the Mughals are also referred as Timurids. In c. 1494 CE, Babur, at the meagre age of twelve ascended the throne at Farghana, a small principality in Transoxiana, after the death of his father. The situation in Central Asia was not stable and Babur lost both Farghana and Samarkand to the Uzbeks. Ousted from his ancestral domains in Central Asia, Babur was forced to move towards India. Like countless earlier invaders from Central Asia, Babur too was drawn towards India by the lure of its fabulous wealth.

Babur (c. 1526–1530 CE)

- Founder of Mughal Empire (descendants of Mongols).
- Worthy descendant of Timur, the Turk (father's side), and Chengiz Khan (mother's side).
- He became the Sultan of Farghana (Afghanistan) at an early age of 12, when his father Sultan Umar Shaikh Mirza died, but he was soon deprived of his kingdom by a distant relative with the aid of Uzbek chief Shibani Khan.
- He established himself first in Kabul (c. 1504 CE) and then pushed steadily southward into India from Afghanistan through the Khyber Pass. He was successful in capturing Bhira (c. 1519–1520 CE), Sialkot (c. 1520 CE) and Lahore (c. 1524 CE) in Punjab. Another reason for Babur coveting the Punjab *parganas* was the meagre income of Kabul, which was not sufficient to maintain an empire, and his apprehension of an Uzbek attack on Kabul. Thus, he considered India to be a good place to find refuge and develop a suitable base for operations against the Uzbeks. The unstable political situation in India after Sikandar Lodhi's death further aided in his entry.
- It is believed that he was invited to fight against Ibrahim Lodhi by Daulat Khan Lodhi (Governor of Punjab), Alam Khan (uncle of Ibrahim Lodhi) and Rana Sanga of Mewar.
- The First Battle of Panipat (c. 1526 CE): This was one of the decisive battles of Indian history, fought between Ibrahim Lodhi and Babur. Ibrahim Lodhi was defeated and Babur was not only able to take control of Delhi and Agra but also got the rich treasure of Lodhis. Some key aspects of this battle were:
    - Babur's soldiers were less in number (only 12,000 soldiers against Lodhi's troops of 100,000 soldiers) but the organisation of his army was far superior.
    - Great achievement of Babur's military tactics. He effectively applied the Rumi (Ottoman) method of warfare, also known as Tulguma system of warfare, wherein he encircled Ibrahim Lodhi's army from both flanks. From the centre, his cavalry mounted attack with arrows and gun-fires under expert Ottoman gunners Ustad Ali and Mustafa, whereas the trenches and barricades provided adequate defence against the march of the enemy.
    - Babur occupied Delhi and sent his son Humayun to seize Agra. Babur proclaimed himself as the '*Emperor of Hindustan*'.
- Victory at Panipat provided Babur a firm ground to consolidate his conquests but at the same time he was faced with new problems:
    - His nobles and commanders were eager to return to Central Asia because they did not like the climate of India. They also felt alienated culturally.
    - The Rajputs were rallying around under the leadership of Rana Sanga, the king of Mewar, and wanted to expel the Mughal forces.

- The Afghans, though defeated at Panipat, were still a formidable force in eastern parts of U.P., Bihar and Bengal. They were re-grouping to reclaim their lost powers.

Babur thus convinced his companions and nobles to stay back and help in consolidating the conquered territories. The nobles who were not inclined towards staying back were allowed to go back to Kabul. Even as he succeeded in this difficult task, he found himself inviting the hostilities of Rana Sanga. The Rana had expected Babur to return to Kabul, and his decision to remain in India was a big jolt to Rana Sanga's territorial ambitions. Thus, battle between the two became inevitable.

- Battle of Khanwa (c. 1527 CE, near Fatehpur Sikri): One of the most fiercely contested battles in Indian history, fought between Babur and Rana Sanga of Mewar and his allies. Rana Sanga was defeated and Babur's position in the Delhi–Agra region was secured. Some key aspects of this battle were:
  - Rana Sanga of Mewar enjoyed the support of a large number of Rajput chiefs, of which the prominent ones were of Jalore, Sirohi, Dungarpur and Amber, along with Raja Medini Rai of Chanderi in Malwa, Hasan Khan of Mewat and Mahmud Lodhi, the younger son of Sikander Lodhi.
  - Babur declared the war against Rana Sanga to be a *jihad* and adopted the tittle of Ghazi after the victory.
- Babur strengthened his position further by conquering the chain of forts in Gwalior, Dholpur, east of Agra and large parts of Alwar from Hasan Khan Mewati.
- Battle of Chanderi (c. 1528 CE): This battle was fought between Babur and Medini Rai, the Rajput ruler of Malwa. In spite of the great valour with which the Rajputs fought, Babur faced little difficulty in overcoming Medini Rai. With his defeat, resistance across Rajputana was completely shattered. Babur had to, however, cut short his plan of further campaigns in the area due to growing disturbances of the Afghans in eastern Uttar Pradesh.
- Battle of Ghagra (near Bihar, c. 1529 CE): This battle was fought between Babur and Mahmud Lodhi (brother of Ibrahim Lodhi, head of the Afghan chiefs, with the support of Nusrat Shah of Bengal). The Afghans had surrendered Delhi, but they were still powerful in the east (Bihar and parts of Jaunpur). Although Babur compelled the Bengal and the Afghan armies to retreat, he could not win a decisive victory. Shortly afterwards, Babur died in c. 1530 CE in Agra, while on his way to Kabul. He was buried in Arambagh in Agra, and later his body was taken to Kabul.
- Significance of Babur's advent into India:
  - Security from External Invasions from North-West Frontier: For the first time after the downfall of the Kushana Empire, Kabul and Gandhar became integral parts of

the Mughal Empire. This not only strengthened trans-Asian foreign trade (as these two cities were the starting points for caravans meant for China in the east and the Mediterranean seaports in the west) but also secured the North-West Frontier as they were the staging places for invasions.

- Established an all-India Empire by breaking the power of the Rajput confederacy.
- Introduced new mode of warfare and led to the popularisation of gun powder, cavalry and artillery in India. Although gunpowder was used earlier too in India, it is Babur who popularised its use.
- Re-established the authority of the king in Delhi, which had been eroded since the death of Firoz Shah Tughlaq.

– He led by example and was always prepared to share the hardships of his soldiers.

– Though an orthodox Sunni, he was neither bigoted nor led by religious divines. He was a devoted follower of Naqshbandiya Sufi Khwaja Ubaidullah Ahrar.

– He was deeply learned in Persian and Arabic, and is regarded as one of the two most famous writers of his mother tongue, Turkish. Indeed, he wrote his memoir in Turki called *Tuzuk-i-Babri*/*Babarnama* (translated into Persian by Abdur Rahim Khan-i-Khana) and also wrote *Masnavi*.

– He was a keen lover and observer of nature and has described the flora and fauna of India in considerable detail.

– Introduced Char-Baghs and symmetrically laid out gardens with running waters and fountains.

– Built two mosques, one at Panipat and another at Sambhat in Rohilkhand.

Humayun (c. 1530–1556 CE)

– Humayun was born to Mahim Begam and Babur and was the eldest son of Babur. 'Humayun' means 'fortune', but he remained the most unfortunate ruler of the Mughal Empire.

– He succeeded Babur at the young age of 23 and had to cope up with number of problems left behind by Babur. The main problems faced by Humayun were:

- The newly conquered territories and administration was not consolidated and the finances were precarious.
- Unlike Babur, Humayun did not command the respect and esteem of Mughal nobility. The Chaghatai nobles were not favourably inclined towards him and the Indian nobles, who had joined Babur's service, deserted the Mughals at Humayun's accession.
- He also had to confront the hostility of the Afghans and other prominent provincial rulers as they were not fully subdued. This included Sher Khan, a powerful Afghan of Bihar, and the provincial ruler of Gujarat, Bahadur Shah.

- As per the Timurid tradition, Humayun had to share power with his brothers which created multiple centres of power.
  - Kamran – Kabul, Qandahar and Punjab
  - Hindal – Alwar and Mewat
  - Mirza Aksari – Sambhal

- In c. 1532 CE at Daurah, he defeated the Afghan forces which had conquered Bihar and Jaunpur. Then, he besieged the powerful fort of Chunar from the Afghan *sardar* Sher Khan, which commanded the land and the river route between Agra and the east and was thus known as the gateway of eastern India. But in spite of the position of superiority, he made a treaty with rising Afghan leader Sher Khan, *leaving him in full control of area east of Banaras and also the possession of the fort in lieu of his loyalty, a mistake which cost him his empire later*. A probable reason for this hastiness was the advance of Bahadur Shah of Gujarat towards the Mughal frontiers, specially towards Malwa and Rajputana. In such a situation, Humayun was forced to rush back to Agra (c. 1532–1533 CE).
- Marching towards Malwa, Humanyun seized Mandu and then stormed Champaner and Ahmedabad. He appointed his younger brother Askari as viceroy of Gujarat and returned to Mandu. However, both Gujarat and Malwa were lost as quickly as they had been gained. Askari lacked experience and when Bahadur Shah moved towards Ahmedabad, he fled to Agra. The only advantage from the Gujarat campaign was that it destroyed forever the threat posed to the Mughals by Bahadur Shah and Humayun could concentrate all his resources against Sher Khan and the Afghans.
- Meanwhile, Sher Khan became the unquestioned master of Bihar. After equipping a new army, Humayun marched against Sher Khan and despite the best efforts by the master gunner, Rumi Khan, it took Humayun 6 months to besiege Chunar. Sher Khan captured the powerful fort of Rohtas by treachery, where he left his family safely and invaded Bengal and captured Gaur, its capital. He then made an offer to Humayun *that he would surrender Bihar and pay an annual tribute of 10 lakh dinars if he was allowed to retain Bengal.* But Humayun declined the offer as he did not want to lose Bengal, which was not only rich but was also a significant foreign trade centre.
- Battle of Chausa (near Buxar, c. 1539 CE): Humayun was defeated and Sher Khan adopted the title of Sher Shah. Humayun barely escaped with his life from the battle field, swimming across the river with the help of a water carrier.
- Battle of Bilgrama/Battle of Kannauj (c. 1540 CE): After the defeat at Chausa, only the fullest unity among the Timurid princes and the nobles could have saved the Mughals. Humayun reached Agra to negotiate with his brothers. But they were not cooperative, and Humayun could not get support of Kamran who moved out of Agra towards Lahore, leaving Humayun with small force. He thus was not able to prepare properly against Sher Khan.

The battle of Kannauj was bitterly contested. Both the younger brothers of Humayun, Askari and Hindal, fought valiantly, but Humayun was still thoroughly defeated by Sher Shah. This battle decided the issue between Sher Shah and the Mughals. Humayun now became a prince without a kingdom and he had to flee from Delhi, becoming an exile for the next fifteen years (c. 1540–1555 CE).

- He wandered about in Sindh (c. 1540 CE) and its neighbouring regions for next two and half years, trying different schemes to regain his kingdom. He married Hamida Banu Begum (daughter of Hindal's teacher) on his way to Sind. While they stayed at Amarkot, a Hindu kingdom ruled by Rana Prasad, Akbar was born in c. 1542 CE. Ultimately, Humayun sought shelter at the court of the Iranian king who forced him to convert to Shia faith (Mughals were otherwise Sunni), and recaptured Gandhar and Kabul with his help in c. 1545 CE.
- In c. 1555 CE, following the break-up of the Sur empire, Humayun defeated the Afghans and recovered the Mughal throne. But before he could consolidate his position, only after six months, he died from a fall from the staircase of his library at Sher Mandal at Delhi in c. 1556 CE. For him, it is said that '*he jumbled throughout life and was tumbled out of life*'.
- Bairam Khan, one of his faithful officers, helped him come back to India.
- His half-sister, Gulbadan Begum, wrote *Humayun-nama*.
- Humayun built a new city at Delhi which he named Dinapanah, and constructed the Jamali mosque and mosque of Isa Khan at Delhi.
- Humayun's tomb is called the prototype of the Taj Mahal, and was built by his widow Haji Begum.
- Humayun invited two Persian painters, Mir Sayyid Ali and Abdus Samad, and made them his court painters.

FIGURE 13.1 Humayun's Tomb, Delhi

The Afghan Interlude/Sur Interregnum (c. 1540–1555 CE)

Sher Shah Suri (c. 1486–1545 CE)

- Founder of the Sur dynasty and also the second Afghan Empire (after the Lodhis) whose original name was Farid. He was the son of Hasan Khan, a *jagirdar* of Sasaram in South Bihar (Jaunpur). Later, Farid served under the Afghan governor of Bihar, Bahar Khan Lohani, who gave him the title *Sher Khan* for his bravery (as he killed a tiger).
- He very effectively managed the *jagir* of his father and also acquired great military and administrative skills. He gradually increased his influence and defeated Sultan Mahmud Shah of Bengal (Battle of Surajgarh) and emerged as the most powerful Afghan military commander in the eastern provinces.
- As we have discussed earlier, this brought him in conflict with Mughal emperor Humayun and he adopted the title of Sher Shah after defeating Humayun in the Battle of Chausa, thus declaring himself as an independent king. He defeated Humayun again in the Battle of Kannauj and proclaimed himself as *Emperor of Hindustan* at the age of 54.
- Sher Shah followed Humayun on his flight till Sindh in the north-west. After expelling Humayun, he started consolidating his position in northern and eastern India. He defeated and conquered Malwa in c. 1542 CE, which was followed by Chanderi. In Rajasthan, he led campaigns against Marwar, Ranthambhore, Nagor, Ajmer, Jodhpur and Bikaner. He defeated Maldeo in the famous Battle of Samel around Ajmer (c. 1544 CE). He defeated rebellious Afghans in Bengal and by c. 1545 CE he had established himself as the supreme ruler from Sindh and Punjab to the whole of Rajputana in the west and Bengal in the east.
- His last campaign was against Kalinjar (Bundelkhand), in which he succeeded but died from an accidental explosion of gun powder in c. 1545 CE.
- Sher Shah, even though a pious Muslim, adopted a tolerant attitude towards other religions. He employed Hindus in important offices.
- He was also a patron of art and architecture and built a new city on the banks of the river Yamuna near Delhi. He built the Purana Qila (Old Fort), Sher Mandal, an octagonal building inside the Purana Qila complex, which later served as the library of Humayun, and his own mausoleum at Sasaram, which is considered as one of the master pieces of Indian architecture. He also built the Rohtas Fort (now a UNESCO World Heritage Site in Pakistan), many structures in the Rohtasgarh Fort in Bihar, and the Sher Shah Suri Masjid, in Patna. He built a new city, Bhera of modern day Pakistan, in c. 1545 CE and inside the city built the historical grand Sher Shah Suri Masjid.
- Sher Shah also patronised learned men. Malik Mohammad Jaysi completed his Padmavat during his reign. Famous historian, Abbas Khan Sarwani, wrote the Tarikh-i-Shershahi during his reign.

He was succeeded by his son Islam Shah (Jalal Khan), who had to face a number of conflicts with his brother Adil Khan, and many Afghan nobles. He died in c. 1553 CE and the Afghan empire was substantially weakened. The Sur domains were partitioned among relatives of Sher Shah (Punjab, Agra, Delhi, Bihar and eastern region). For instance, Punjab was taken by Sikander Sur who was later defeated by Humayun. Humayun thus gradually captured his lost kingdom.

Sher Shah's Administration (c. 1540–1545 CE)

Although his rule lasted for only five years, he organised a brilliant administrative system which served as inspiration to not only the Mughal administration but to the British too. The empire was divided into forty seven *sarkars*. Chief *Shiqdar* (law and order) and Chief *Munsif* (judge) were the two officers in charge of the administration in each *sarkar*. Each *sarkar* was divided into several *parganas*. *Shiqdar* (military officer), *Amil* (land revenue), *Fotedar* (treasurer) and *Karkuns* (accountants) were in charge of the administration of each *pargana*. *Mauza* (village) was the lowest level of administration.

There were also many administrative units called *iqtas*. The government was highly centralised and consisted of several departments. The king was assisted by four important ministers:

1. Diwan-i-Wizarat – Also called Wazir, in charge of Revenue and Finance.
2. Diwan-i-Ariz – In charge of the Army.
3. Diwan-i-Rasalat – Foreign Minister.
4. Diwan-i-Insha – Minister for Communications.

The land revenue administration was very well organised and revenue officers were called *Amils* while *Qanungo* were the officials in charge of maintaining revenue records. Sher Shah for the first time introduced a schedule of crop rates (*ray*). He improved land revenue system by adopting *Zabti-i-har-sal* (land assessment every year) and classified all cultivable lands into three heads (good, middle, bad). *Amils* used to oversee the measurement of land under cultivation for determining state share. The state's share was one third of the average produce and it was paid in cash or crop. Land was measured using Sikandari *gaz* (32 points). Sher Shah introduced two documents:

a. *Patta* (amount each peasant had to pay)
b. *Qabuliyat* (deed of agreement)

Sher Shah also introduced new copper coins called *Dam* and it is interesting to note that they were in circulation till c. 1835 CE. He was also the first ruler to introduce silver *Rupayia* (1 *Rupayia* = 64 *dams*) and gold coin (*Ashrafi/Mohur*). It is pertinent to note that while the term *Rupayia* had previously been used as a generic term for any silver coin, during his rule the term '*Rupayia*' came to be used as the name for a silver coin of a standard weight of 178 grains, which was the precursor of the modern rupee. Similarly, gold coins weighed 169 grains.

Sher Shah also improved the communications by building roads called arteries of the empire. He laid four important highways. They were:

1. Sonargaon to Sind: He restored the old imperial road (the Grant Trunk road by Ashoka) and also restored the *Uttarapatha* which connected Tamralipti (Bengal) to Purushpur (Peshawar).
2. Agra to Burhampur.
3. Jodhpur to Chittor.
4. Lahore to Multan.

He built *sarais* (rest houses) at the distance of every two *kos*, i.e., eight kms on the highways for the convenience of the travellers. These *sarais* were fortified lodging or inns where travellers could pass the night and also keep their goods in safe custody. Every *Sarai* had several watchmen under the control of a *shahna* (custodian). One of the foremost contributions of Sher Shah was his re-establishment of law and order across the empire. Police was efficiently reorganised and crime was less during his regime. He dealt sternly with robbers and *dacoits*, and with *zamindars* who refused to pay land revenue or disobeyed the orders of the government. Many of the *sarais* developed into market towns (*qasbas*) to which peasants flocked to sell their produce and these *sarais* were also used as stages for the news service or *dak-chowki*.

Sher Shah also introduced other reforms to promote growth of trade and commerce. For instance, in his entire empire, goods paid customs duty only at two places: goods produced in Bengal or imported from outside paid customs duty at the border of Bengal and Bihar at Sikrigali, and goods coming from West and Central Asia paid customs duty at the Indus. It is noteworthy to add that no one was allowed to levy customs at roads, ferries, or towns, or anywhere else. The duty was paid a second time at the time of sale. He directed his *amirs* to compel the people to treat merchants and travellers well in every way, and not to harm them at all. If a merchant died, they were not supposed to seize his goods as if they were unowned. In fact, he made the local village headmen (*muqaddams*) and *zamindars* responsible for any loss that the merchant suffered on the roads.

The military administration was also efficiently reorganised and Sher Shah revived Alauddin's *Chehra* and *Dagh* system. He personally supervised recruitment of soldiers and paid them directly. He divided the army into *sawars* (serving as linchpin of entire organisation), elephants and frontmen. He maintained his personal royal force called *Khasa Kail*.

He placed considerable emphasis on justice and considered *justice to be the most excellent of the religious rites*. He did not spare oppressors, whether they were high nobles, men of his own tribe or near relatives. *Qazis* were appointed at different places for justice and village *panchayats* and *zamindars* dealt with civil and criminal cases at the local level. In fact, his son Islam Shah took a big step towards dispensation of justice as he codified the laws.

Akbar (c. 1556–1605 CE)

- One of the greatest monarchs of the Mughal dynasty, who was the son of Humayun and Hamida Banu Begam, born at Amarkot in c. 1542 CE. When Humayun fled to Iran, young Akbar was captured by his uncle Kamran, but he treated him well. Akbar was re-united with his parents after the capture of Qandahar. When Humayun died, Akbar was at Kalanaur in the Punjab, commanding operations against the Afghan rebels there. He was thus crowned at Kalanaur (Punjab) in c. 1556 CE, at the age of 13 years by Bairam Khan.
- Regency period of Bairam Khan (c. 1556–1560 CE): Bairam Khan was Humayun's favourite officer and confidante, who served as Akbar's tutor as well as regent (*wazir*) of the kingdom with the title of *Khan-i-Khanan*, remaining at the helm of affairs of the Mughal Empire.
    - Bairam Khan represented Akbar in the Second Battle of Panipat (c. 1556 CE) with Hemu Vikramaditya (Wazir of Mohd. Shah Adil of Bengal) who led the Afghan forces who were posing a serious threat to the Mughal Empire.
    - Under guidance of Bairam Khan, the Mughals won a series of battles in quick succession and warded off other Afghan contenders like Sikander Sur. They captured Lahore, Multan, Ajmer, vanquished Ibrahim Sur and annexed Jaunpur, besides laying a successful siege to Gwalior fort, also under Afghan control.
    - During this phase, Bairam Khan emerged as the most powerful noble and started appointing his own supporters on important positions neglecting the old nobles. This caused resentment among other nobles who managed to influence Akbar as well. The problem was further aggravated by the growing arrogance of Bairam Khan. By now, weary of Bairam Khan's tutelage, Akbar also wanted to assume full control. He thus removed Bairam Khan, who revolted but was forced to submit. Akbar received him cordially, and gave him the option of serving at the court or anywhere outside it, or retiring to Mecca. He decided to go to Mecca but was assassinated at Patan near Ahmedabad by an Afghan who bore him a personal grudge. Bairam's wife and his son were brought to Agra. Akbar married his widow and took his infant son under his protection. His son later on became famous as the noted Hindi poet Abdur Rahim Khan-i-Khana, an influential noble under Akbar.
- Rebellion from Nobility: During Bairam Khan's rebellion, groups and individuals in the nobility had become politically active. They included Akbar's foster mother, Maham Anaga, and her relatives, especially her son, Adham Khan. In c. 1561 CE, Adham Khan was victorious at Malwa by defeating Baz Bahadur (an accomplished magician and poet). The Malwa queen Rupamati preferred to take her life than become a Mughal captive. Adham Khan followed his victory at Malwa with almost total massacre of the defending army, women and children, and sent only parts of the booty to Akbar. Removed from the command, he laid claim to the post of *wazir*, and when this was not conceded, he stabbed

the acting *wazir* in his office. Furious at his impropriety, Akbar had him thrown down from the Agra fort.

- Similarly, between c. 1561 and 1567 CE, Akbar was engulfed by serious challenge from his Uzbek (central Asian) nobles who broke out in rebellion several times. Many of them traced their descent from Uzbek chief who had driven Babur out of Samarkand and had come to India with Humayun. Uzbeks declared Mirza Hakim, governor of Kabul (his half-brother), as the emperor of Hindustan. A group of Timurid nobles, called *Mirzas*, also turned against the emperor. This was perhaps the most serious crisis Akbar had to face since Hemu's capture of Delhi. However, by sheer grit and determination along with a certain amount of luck, Akbar was able to overcome these multiple threats. Mirza Hakim was forced to withdraw to Kabul and the Mirzas were duly suppressed, while the Uzbeks were completely routed by c. 1567 CE.

– Early Expansion of Empire (c. 1560–1576 CE): He conquered northern India from Agra to Gujarat and then from Agra to Bengal. He strengthened the North-West Frontier. Later, he went to the Deccan.

– Conquest of Gwalior, Malwa and Gondwana: Akbar started his policy of expansion with central India. In c. 1559–1560 CE, the first expedition was sent to capture Gwalior before moving towards Malwa. As we have discussed above, in c. 1561 CE the Malwa ruler Baz Bahadur was defeated by Adham Khan, who fled towards Burhanpur. However, due to senseless cruelties of Adham Khan and his successor, there was a reaction against the Mughals which enabled Baz Bahadur to recover Malwa. After dealing with Bairam Khan's rebellion, Akbar sent another expedition to Malwa. Baz Bahadur had to flee, and for some time he took shelter with the Rana of Mewar. After wandering about from one area to another, he finally surrendered at Akbar's court and was enrolled as a Mughal mansabdar. Thus, Malwa came under Mughal authority.

- The kingdom of Gondwana (Garh-Katanga) included the Narmada valley and the northern portions of Madhya Pradesh and a number of Gond and Rajput principalities. It was an independent state in Central India ruled by Rani Durgavati, the Chandella princess from Mahoba, and the widow of Dalpat Shah, son of Sangram Shah. In c. 1564 CE, Asaf Khan, the Mughal governor of Allahabad, aroused by the stories of the fabulous wealth and beauty of the Rani attacked Gondwana. The Rani fought gallantly but lost the battle. She stabbed herself to death and Gondwana was annexed to the Mughal empire. Akbar later restored the kingdom to Chandra Shah, the younger son of Sangram Shah.

– Conquest of Rajasthan: It seems that Akbar was fully aware of the importance of Rajput kingdoms and wanted them as allies in his ambition of establishing a large empire. He tried to win over the Rajputs wherever possible and inducted them into Mughal service.

He also entered into matrimonial alliances with the Rajput rulers. For instance, *Raja Bharmal of Amber married his eldest daughter Jodha Bai to Akbar and Raja Bharmal himself, his son Bhagwan Das and grandson Man Singh joined the imperial Mughal service.* Akbar's military conquests were extensive.

- The Rajput kingdoms like Merta and Jodhpur were occupied without much resistance.
- Siege of Chittor (Mewar): A major step in his campaign against the Rajput states was the siege of Chittor, which held not only key to central Rajasthan but above all, it was a symbol of the Rajput spirit of resistance. In c. 1568 CE, Chittor fell after a gallant siege of six months. At the advice of his nobles, Rana Udai Singh retired to the hills, leaving the famous warriors, Jaimal and Patta, in charge of the fort. A large number of Rajput soldiers were killed in the war. However, it could not be fully subdued and some resistance from Mewar side continued for a long time. Later, Maharana Pratap, the ruler of Mewar, posed the most serious challenge to the Mughal emperor and did not submit before Akbar. In the famous Battle of Haldighati (c. 1576 CE), Rana Pratap was defeated by the Mughal army led by Man Singh.
- Following the defeat of Mewar, most of the leading Rajput rulers accepted Akbar's suzerainty. After the fall of Chittor, Ranthambhor (c. 1569 CE) and Kalinjar were captured. In c. 1570 CE, Marwar, Bikaner and Jaisalmer also submitted to Akbar. Thus by c. 1570 CE, Akbar had captured almost the whole of Rajasthan.
- One of most notable achievements of Akbar was that, in spite of the subjugation of the whole of Rajasthan, there was no hostility between the Rajputs and the Mughals. Akbar's Rajput policy was combined with a broad religious tolerance. He abolished the pilgrim tax (c. 1563 CE) and later the *jiziya* (c. 1564 CE). He also prohibited forcible conversion of prisoners of war. It is noteworthy to add that the Rajput policy of Akbar proved to be beneficial to the Mughal state as well as to the Rajputs. The alliance on one hand secured the services of the bravest warriors to the Mughals whereas on the other hand, it ensured peace in Rajasthan and many Rajput *mansabdars* were assigned their own territories as *Watan Jagir*, which was hereditary and non-transferable. They also rose to important positions in Mughal services.

– Conquest of Gujarat, Bihar and Bengal: Gujarat had been in a sorry state of affairs since the death of Bahadur Shah. Moreover, the Mirzas who had failed in their rebellion near Delhi had taken shelter in Gujarat. Akbar was not prepared for such a rich province to become a rival centre of power. In c. 1572 CE, Akbar advanced on Ahmedabad via Ajmer and defeated the Gujarat ruler Muzaffar Shah without any serious resistance. It was in order to commemorate the victory of Gujarat that Akbar built the Buland Darwaza at Fatehpur

Sikri. Surat, with a strong fortress, offered some resistance but was also captured. In a short time, most of the principalities of Gujarat were brought under his control. Akbar organised Gujarat into a province and placed it under Mirza Aziz Koka and returned to capital. However, just within six months various rebellious groups came together under Ikhitiyar ul Mulk and Mohammad Hussain Mirza and revolted against the Mughal rule. As a result, the Mughal governor had to cede a number of territories. Hearing the news, Akbar marched out of Agra at a rapid pace along with a few soldiers and managed to reach Ahmedabad in just 10 days. He quickly suppressed the rebellion in c. 1573 CE. After this, Akbar turned his attention to Bengal.

- Bihar and Bengal: The Afghans continued to dominate Bihar and Bengal. They had also overrun Orissa and killed its ruler. Internal fights among the Afghans, and the declaration of independence by the new ruler Daud Khan, gave Akbar the opportunity he was seeking. In c. 1574 CE, Akbar along with Khan-i-Khanan Munaim Khan, marched towards Bihar. In a short time, he captured Hajipur, Patna and Gaur (Bengal). Daud was forced to sue for peace but he soon rose in rebellion again. In a stiff battle in Bihar in c. 1576 CE, Daud Khan was defeated and executed on the spot. With this, the independent rule of Bengal was ended.

– Rebellions and Further Expansion of the Mughal Empire: Around c. 1580–1581 CE, a series of conflicts arose in some regions of the Mughal empire particularly in Bengal, Bihar, Gujarat and the north-west. The Afghans were at the root of these problems since they were overthrown everywhere by the Mughals. Apart from this, Akbar's policy of strict administration of *jagirs* including *strict enforcement of the dagh system or branding of horses and strict accounting of their income was also responsible for this*. This created dissatisfaction, and this discontentment was further fanned by some religious divines too who were unhappy at Akbar's liberal views, and at his policy of resuming the large revenue-free grants of lands which had been obtained by them, sometimes illegally.

- Due to the mishandling of the situation by local officers, Bengal and almost the whole of Bihar passed into the hands of the rebels. The rebels under leadership of Masum Khan Kabuli, Roshan Beg, Mirza Sharfuddin and Arab Bahadur declared Akbar's brother Mirza Hakim, who was in Kabul, as their king. Akbar immediately sent a large force under Raja Todar Mal and Shaikh Farid Bakshi and soon the Mughal forces were able to successfully crush the rebellion in Bihar, Bengal and adjoining regions. Raja Man Singh and Bhagwan Das offered stout defence to Mirza Hakim's attack on Lahore. Akbar crowned his success by marching to Kabul (c. 1581 CE), the first time an Indian ruler had entered this historic town. Akbar gave the charge of Kabul to his sister Bakhtunnisa Begum and later on, Raja Man Singh was appointed governor of Kabul and Kabul was handed over to him as *jagir*.

- Punjab and North West: In c. 1584 CE, the hereditary enemy of the Mughals, Abdullah Khan Uzbek overran Badakhshan which was being ruled by Timurid princes and it posed danger to Kabul too. Both Mirza Hakim and the Timurid princes ousted from Badakhshan now appealed to Akbar for help. Akbar immediately ordered Man Singh to march to Kabul, and he himself moved to Attok on the river Indus. In order to block all roads to the Uzbeks, he sent expeditions against Kashmir (c. 1586 CE) and against Baluchistan. The whole of Kashmir, including Ladakh and Baltistan (including Tibet Khurd and Buzurg), came under Mughal domination.
- Expeditions were also sent to clear the Khyber Pass, which had been blocked by rebellious tribesmen of *Roshanai*. *Roshanai* was a sect having a large following, which was established by a soldier called Pir Roshanai. His son Jalala was the head of the sect. Akbar gave the duty of suppressing the *Roshanais* to Zain Khan along with Sayid Khan Gakhar and Raja Birbal. In one of these expeditions, Akbar's favourite, Birbal, lost his life. Akbar deputed Raja Todar Mal and Raja Man Singh to suppress the rebellion and they forced the Roshanais to submit.
- In c. 1590 CE, Akbar appointed Khan-i-Khanan as the governor of Multan, giving him the responsibility of subduing Bilochis, a tribe in the Sindh region, and to conquer the whole territory. Finally, by c. 1595 CE, Mughal supremacy was established over the north-west region. In fact, Akbar stayed at Lahore till c. 1598 CE when the death of Abdullah Uzbek finally removed the threat of Uzbeks. The consolidation of the north-west and fixing a frontier of the empire were two of the major contributions of Akbar.
- Eastern, Western India and Deccan: After settling the affairs of the north-west, Akbar turned his attention towards the affairs of eastern and western India and the Deccan. In c. 1592 CE, the Mughal *mansabdar* Raja Man Singh brought the whole of Orissa, Cooch Bihar and parts of east Bengal, including Dacca, under the Mughal rule. Mirza Aziz Koka, the foster brother of Akbar, conquered Kathiawar in the west. In c. 1591 CE, Akbar adopted a policy of aggression towards Deccan and dispatched an expedition to Ahmednagar under the command of Prince Murad and Abdul Rahim Khan Khanan. In c. 1595 CE, the Mughal forces invaded Ahmednagar and Chand Bibi (the deceased Sultan's sister) was defeated. After heavy losses on both sides, a treaty was worked out and Chand Bibi ceded Berar to Mughals. After some time, Chand Bibi attacked Berar to take it back with support from Adilshahi and Qutabshahi. The Mughals suffered heavy losses but could retain their position. Meanwhile, serious differences between Murad and Abdul Rahim Khan Khanan weakened the Mughal position. Akbar, therefore, recalled Khan Khanan and deputed Abul Fazl to Deccan. After Prince Murad's death in c. 1598 CE, Prince Daniyal and Khan Khanan were sent to Deccan and Ahmednagar was again captured. Soon, Mughals also conquered Asirgarh and adjoining regions bringing them into direct conflict with the Marathas.

- In c. 1605 CE, Akbar died of dysentery and was buried at Sikandra.
- Akbar was not liked for his political ideology by Shaikh Ahmad Sirhindi (Sufi leader).
- Art and Architecture: During the reign of Akbar, many indigenous art styles were encouraged leading to the common use of sandstone, the use of arches (mainly in a decorative form) and the decoration that comprised mainly of boldly carved or inlaid patterns complemented by brightly coloured patterns on the interiors. He built the Agra fort in red sandstone. His other forts are at Lahore and Allahabad.
    - He built Fatehpur Sikri (city of victory) near Agra, and a palace-cum-fort complex in it. Many buildings in Gujarati and Bengali styles are found in this complex. The most magnificent building in it is the Jama Masjid and the gateway to it called Buland Darwaza (the Lofty Gate), made up of red sandstone, the height of which is 176 ft. It was built in c. 1572 CE to commemorate Akbar's victory over Gujarat. Other important buildings at Fatehpur Sikri are Jodha Bai's palace, the Panch Mahal with five storeys built in the plan of a Buddhist Vihara, the *Diwan-i-Khas*, the *Diwan-i-Aam* and Sheikh Salim Chisti's tomb.
    - Planned his own tomb at Sikandra (near Agra), which was completed by Jahangir.
    - Planned the temple of Govindadeva at Vrindavan.
    - Built the Jahangiri Mahal in Agra fort, according to Hindu design based on Man Mandir.

FIGURE 13.2 Buland Darwaza, Fatehpur Sikri

FIGURE 13.3 Panch Mahal, Fatehpur Sikri

FIGURE 13.4 Agra Fort

- Akbar commissioned the illustrations of several literary and religious texts. Illustrations of Persian versions of *Mahabharata* and *Ramayana* were produced in miniature form. At the behest of the crown prince Jahangir, Nizamuddin Panipati translated '*Yoga Vasistha*[1]' in 1597.
- Many other Indian fables became the miniature paintings in the art studio established by Akbar. Historical works such as the *Akbar Nama* also remained the main themes of Mughal paintings. One of the most important works, *Hamznama*, which consisted of 1200 paintings, belonged to his reign.
- He organised painting in imperial *karkhanas* and also introduced European style. Indian colours such as peacock blue, Indian red began to be used. He invited a large number of painters from different parts of the country to his court. Both Hindus and Muslims joined in this work. Mir Sayyid Ali, Abdal Samad, Farukh Beg, Bhusrau Kuli, Miskina, Jamshed Basawan and Daswant (painted *Razim Namah*, the Persian *Mahabharata*) were the prominent painters.
- Persian language became widespread in the Mughal Empire by the time of Akbar's reign. Apart from Abul Fazl and his brother Abul Faizi, Abdul Qadir Badauni (who wrote *Kitab-ul-Tawarikh*), Khwaja Nizamuddin Ahmad Harami (who wrote *Tabaquat-i-Akbari Tarikh Alfi*), Muntakhab ul-Akbari, Utbi and Naziri (leading Persian poets) were present at Akbar's court. From the time of Akbar, Hindi poets were attached to the Mughal court. The most influential Hindi poet was Tulsidas, who wrote the Hindi version of the Ramayana, the *Ramcharitmanas*.

Year	State Annexed/Important Event
c. 1556 CE	Second Battle of Panipat
c. 1560 CE	Expedition against Gwalior
c. 1561 CE	Expedition against Malwa
c. 1563 CE	Abolished the pilgrim tax
c. 1564 CE	Abolished the *jiziya* Expedition against Gondwana
c. 1568 CE	Expedition against Chittor
c. 1569 CE	Expedition against Ranthambhor
c. 1570 CE	Expedition against Marwar, Bikaner and Jaisalmer
c. 1571 CE	Shifted from Agra to Fatehpur Sikri

[1] *Yoga Vasistha*, originally written in Sanskrit by Valmiki recounts a discourse of the sage Vasistha to a young prince Rama, when the latter was in a dejected state. During the Mughal era, the book was translated into Persian several times under the reigns of Akbar, Jahangir and Darah Shikoh. The Persian translation is popularly known as the '*Jug Basisht*'.

Year	State Annexed/Important Event
c. 1572 CE	Expedition against Gujarat Construction of Buland Darwaza at Fatehpur Sikri to commensurate victory of Gujarat
c. 1574 CE	Expedition against Bihar and Bengal
c. 1576 CE	Battle of Haldighati
c. 1579 CE	Issued decree of infallibility (read the Khutba composed by Falzi in his own name)
c. 1581 CE	Expedition against Kabul
c. 1583 CE	Imposed ban on killing animals on certain days
c. 1585 CE	Ralph Fitch was the first Englishman to visit Akbar's court. Akbar transferred his capital to Lahore.
c. 1586 CE	Expedition against Kashmir and Baluchistan
c. 1591 CE	Expedition against Sindh
c. 1592 CE	Expedition against Orissa
c. 1595 CE	Expedition against Qandahara
c. 1593–1601 CE	Expedition against Deccan (Ahmednagar and Khandesh)
c. 1601 CE	Last campaign of Akbar was against Asirgarh Salim rebelled in Allahabad
c. 1605 CE	Death of Akbar

Interestingly, some of the contemporaries of Akbar (1556 to 1605) were Elizabeth of England, Shakespeare, Henry IV of France, first ruler of the Bourbon dynasty and Abbas the Great of Persia, the strongest ruler of the Safavid dynasty.

Administrative System Under the Akbar

Organisation of Government

The Mughals retained many features of the administrative system of the Sultanate and Sher Shah Suri's administration. The administration was highly centralised and the territories of the empire were divided into *Jagir*, *Khalisa* (income went directly to the royal exchequer) and *Inam* (lands allowed to learned and religious men).

Central Administration

Central Administration	
(i) The Emperor	The Emperor was the supreme head of the administration and controlled all military and judicial powers. All officers in Mughal administration owed their power and position to the Emperor. The Emperor had authority to appoint, promote and remove officials at his pleasure.
(ii) Wazir	(a) The position of the *wazir* was revived under the Mughals under whom various heads of departments functioned. He was the principal link between the ruler and the administration. (b) Babur's and Humayun's *wazir* enjoyed great powers. The period during which Bairam Khan (c. 1556–1560 CE) was regent of Akbar, saw the rise of the *wakil-wazir* with unlimited powers. (c) Akbar reorganised the central machinery of administration on the basis of the division of power between various departments, and of checks and balances. In his determination to curb the powers of the *wazir*, he took away the financial powers from him, which was a big jolt to the *wazir*'s power. While the post of *wakil* was not abolished, it was stripped of all power and became largely decorative. This post was given to important nobles from time to time, but they played little part in administration. Thus, the head of the revenue department continued to be *wazir*, but he was no longer the principal adviser to the ruler, but an expert in revenue affairs having title of *diwan* or *diwan-i-ala*. (d) The *diwan* used to inspect all transaction and payments in all departments and supervised the provincial *diwans*.
(iii) Mir Bakshi	(a) The head of the military administration was Mir Bakshi who was also considered as head of the nobility. (b) Recommendations for appointment to *mansabs* or for promotions were made to the emperor after duly endorsed by him only. Once the emperor accepted the recommendation, it was sent to the *diwan* for confirmation and for assigning a *jagir* to the appointee. (c) The Mir Bakshi was also the head of the intelligence and information agencies of the empire. *Barids* (intelligence officers) and *Waqia-navis* (news reporters) were posted to all the parts of the empire. Their reports were presented to the emperor at the court through Mir Bakshi. He kept a strict watch over proper maintenance of the sanctioned size of armed contingents and war equipage by the *mansabdars*.
(iv) Mir Saman	(a) The Mir Saman was the officer-in-charge of the royal household and royal *karkhanas*. He was responsible for all kinds of purchases, manufacturing of different articles for use, and their storage for the royal household. Only nobles who enjoyed the complete confidence of the emperor were appointed to this office. (b) The maintenance of etiquette at the court, the control of the royal body guard, etc., were all under his supervision.

Central Administration	
(v) Chief Qazi/ Sadrus Sudur	(a) The judicial department was headed by the chief *qazi*. This post was sometimes combined with that of the *Sadr-us Sudur* (Chief *Sadar*) was the head of the ecclesiastical department. (b) His chief duty was to protect the laws of the Shariat and he was also responsible for all charitable and religious endowments. (c) Interestingly, the chief *qazi* during Akbar's reign Abdun Nabi was accused of corruption. However, the promulgation of *Mahzar* in c. 1580 CE severely restricted his authority as according to *Mahzar*, *Akbar's view was to prevail in case of conflicting views among religious scholars*. Later, several restrictions were placed on the authority of the *Sadar* for award of revenue free grants also. Two striking features of *Inam* grants were: (i) Akbar granted *inam* lands to all persons, irrespective of their religious faith and beliefs. As a matter of fact, *Sanads* of grant to various Hindu *maths* made by Akbar are still preserved. (ii) Akbar made it a rule that half of the *inam* land should consist of cultivable wasteland. Thus, the *inam* holders were encouraged to extend cultivation.
(vi) *Muhtasibs*	They were the censors of public morals who were appointed to ensure the general observance of the rules of morality. They also used to examine weights and measures and enforce fair prices, etc.

It is pertinent to note that the doors of the nobility were open to everyone, whether Turks, Afghans, Persians, Hindustani, or Shaikhzadas (Indian Muslims), or Hindu Rajputs, and due to extremely high salaries of Mughal nobles, there was a brain drain in reverse as India attracted many talented persons from foreign lands to the Mughal court.

Provincial Administration

The Mughal empire was divided into twelve *subas* or provinces by Akbar. These were Allahabad, Agra, Awadh, Ajmer, Ahmedabad, Bihar, Bengal, Delhi, Kabul, Lahore, Malwa and Multan. Later on, Ahmednagar, Berar and Khandesh were added. With the expansion of Mughal empire, the number of provinces increased to twenty. The empire was divided into:

- *Suba* (province) ⟶ *Subedar* (Governor)

↓

- *Sarkar* (District) ⟶ *Faujdar* (Law and order) and *Amalguzar* (Assessment and collection of the land revenue)

↓

- *Parganas* (sub-districts) ⟶ *Shiqdar* (Executive officer)

↓

- Village ⟶ *Muqaddam* (village head man)

<table>
<tr><th colspan="2">Provincial Administration</th></tr>
<tr><td>(a) Suba</td><td>(a) Each suba was placed under a Subedar (provincial governor) who was directly appointed by the Emperor.
(b) The subedar was the head of the province and responsible for maintenance of general law and order. He was to encourage agriculture, trade and commerce, and take steps to enhance the revenue of the state. He was also to suppress rebellions and provide army for expeditions.
(c) The head of the revenue department in the suba was the Diwan. He was appointed by the Emperor and was an independent officer. He was to supervise the revenue collection in the suba and maintain accounts of all expenditures. He was also expected to increase the area under cultivation. In many cases, taccavi (advance loans) were given to peasants through his office.
(d) The Bakshi in the province performed the same functions as were performed by Mir Bakshi at the centre. He was appointed by the imperial court at the recommendation of the Mir Bakshi. He was responsible for checking and inspecting the horses and soldiers maintained by the mansabdars in the suba. He issued the pay bills of both the mansabdars and the soldiers. Often, his office was combined with Waqia-navis as his duty was also to inform the centre about the happenings in his province.
(e) The representative of the central Sadar at the provincial level was called Sadar. He was responsible for the welfare of those who were engaged in religious activities and learning. He also looked after the judicial department and in that capacity supervised the works of the Qazis.
(f) There were some other officers also who were appointed at the provincial level. Darogai-i-Dak was responsible for maintaining the communication channel. He used to pass on letters to the court through the Merwars (postal runners).</td></tr>
<tr><td>(b) Sarkar</td><td>(a) At the level of Sarkar, there were two important functionaries:
(i) the Faujdar: The primary duty of the Faujdar was to maintain law and order and safeguard the life and property of the residents of the areas under his jurisdiction. He also assisted in the timely collection of revenue whenever force was required
(ii) the Amalguzar: The Amalguzar or Amil was the revenue collector. His duty was to assess and supervise the revenue collection. He was expected to increase the land under cultivation and induce the peasants to pay revenue willingly. He used to maintain all accounts and send the daily receipt and expenditure report to the provincial Diwan.
(b) It should be noted that the Faujdari was an administrative division whereas Sarkar was a territorial and revenue division.</td></tr>
<tr><td>(c) Pargana</td><td>At the level of Pargana, the Shiqdar was the executive officer. He assisted the Amil in the task of revenue collection. The Quanungo kept all the records of land in the Pargana. The Kotwals were appointed mainly in towns by the imperial government and were in charge of law and order.</td></tr>
<tr><td>(d) Village</td><td>The Muqaddam was the village headman and the Patwari looked after the village revenue records. The services of the zamindars were utilised for the maintenance of law and order in their areas as well as in the collection of revenue.</td></tr>
</table>

The forts were placed under an officer called *Qiladar*. He was in charge of the general administration of the fort and the areas assigned in *jagir* to him.

The port administration was independent of the provincial authority. The governor of the port was called *Mutasaddi* who was directly appointed by the Emperor. The *Mutasaddi* collected taxes on merchandise and maintained a customs house. He also supervised the mint house at the port.

Land Revenue Administration

The land revenue system adopted by Akbar was largely based on Sher Shah's system but with slight modifications and was called *Zabti* or *Bandobast* system, which was further improved by Raja Todar Mal. Under this system, Todar Mal introduced a uniform system of land measurement, classification of land and fixation of rates. The revenue was one third of the average produce and was paid mostly in cash. In c. 1580 CE, Akbar introduced the *Dahsala System* under which revenue was fixed on the average yield of land assessed on the basis of past ten years (dah years). Later, a further improvement was made as not only local prices were taken into account, but *parganas* having the same type of productivity were grouped into separate assessment circles. A number of other assessment systems were also followed under Akbar. The most common, and perhaps, the oldest was called *batais or ghalla-bakhshi* wherein the produce was divided between the peasants and the state in fixed proportion. Another system was *nasaq or kankut* under which a rough appraisement on the basis of the inspection of the crops and past payments was made by the village as a whole.

The land was divided into four categories –

a. *Polaj* (cultivated every year).

b. *Parati* (fallow, once in two years): *Parati* land paid at the full *polaj* rate when it was cultivated.

c. *Chachar* (once in three or four years).

d. *Banjar* (once in five or more years).

Both *chachar* and *banjar* were assessed at concessional rates. Officials called *Karoris* were appointed all over India who were responsible for the collection of a crore of *dams* (Rs 2,50,000) and also audited the facts and figures supplied by the *Qanungos* (local hereditary officials of land record keeping). Akbar was deeply interested in the improvement and extension of cultivation. He asked the *Amil* (revenue officers) to act like a father to the peasants and to advance *taccavi* loans to the peasants for seeds, implements, animals, etc., in times of need and to recover them in easy instalments.

During the 17th century, two new crops, tobacco and maize were added. Potato and red chillies came later in the 18th century. But no new agricultural technique was introduced during this period. The peasants who owned the land they tilled were called *Khudkasht* who paid land revenue at customary rates.

Mansabdari System

Akbar introduced the *Mansabdari* system in his administration. Under this system, every officer (*Mansabdar*) was assigned a rank (*mansab*). The lowest rank was 10 and the highest was 5,000 for the nobles. Princes of royal blood received even higher ranks. For instance, Raja Man Singh and Mirza Aziz Koka were honoured with the rank of 7,000 each. The *mansab* rank was not hereditary. All appointments and promotions as well as dismissals were directly made by the emperor.

The ranks were further divided into two – *zat* and *sawar*. *Zat* means personal and apart from fixing the personal status of a person in the administration hierarchy, it also decided salary due to him. *Sawar* rank indicated the number of cavalrymen (*sawars*) a person was required to maintain. There were further three categories in every *mansab* (rank):

a. First category: A person who was required to maintain as many *sawars* as his *zat* rank. For example, in the first category, *zat* and *sawar* ranks were equal (7000/7000).

b. Second category: If the person maintained half or more *sawars* as his *zat* rank. For example, in the second category, *sawar* rank was lower than the *zat* but stopped at half, or fifty percent, of the *zat* rank (7000/4000).

c. Third category: If the person maintained less than half as his *zat* rank. For example, in the third category, *sawar* rank was lower than fifty percent of the *zat* rank (7000/3000).

Thus, the *sawar* rank was either equal or less than the *zat*. Even if the *sawar* rank was higher, the *mansabdar*'s position in the official hierarchy would not be affected. It would be decided by the *zat* rank. For example, a *mansabdar* with 4000 *zat* and 2000 *sawar* was higher in rank than a *mansabdar* of 3000 *zat* and 3000 *sawar*. Also, different terminologies were used for persons holding different ranks. For instance, persons holding 500 *zat* were called *mansabdars*, those from 500 to 2500 were called *amirs*, and those holding ranks of 2500 and above were called *amirl-i-umda* or *umda-i-azam*. Interestingly, an *amir* or an *amirl-i-umda* could have another *amir* or *mansabdar* serve under him but not so a *mansabdar*.

The *chehra* (descriptive roll of every soldier) and *dagh* system (branding of horses) was followed. Every noble had to bring his contingent for periodic inspection before persons appointed by the emperor for the purpose. Ideally, 10–20 rule was followed which meant that, for every 10 cavalrymen, the *Mansabdar* had to maintain 20 horses. Interestingly, a *sawar* with only one horse was considered to be only half a *sawar*.

In order to weaken the forces of tribalism and parochialism, adequate care was taken to draw mixed contingents of nobles from all the groups: Mughal, Pathan, Hindustani and Rajput. Apart from cavalrymen, bowmen, musketeers, sappers and miners were also recruited in the contingents.

Guns and siege guns for breaching forts were also maintained. The salary due to the soldiers was added to the personal salary of the *Mansabdar*, who was paid by assigning to him a *jagir* and sometimes in cash. The *Mansabdar* were paid handsomely. As a matter of fact, the Mughal *Mansabdars* formed the highest paid service in the world. In addition of meeting his personal expenses, the *Mansabdar* had to maintain a stipulated quota of horses, elephants, camels, mules and carts. However, later these were maintained centrally, but the *Mansabdar* had to pay for them out of his salary. The only drawback of Mughals was lack of a strong and effective navy.

The Jagirdari System

Iqta of the Sultanate period in a modified form became *Jagir* under the Mughals. The *Jagirdari* system, that is to say the system of assignment of revenue of a particular territory to the nobles for their services to the state was an integral part of the *Mansabdari* system. In case the payment was made through the assignment of a *jagir*, the office of the central *Diwan* would identify *parganas* the sum total of whose *Jama* was equal to the salary claim of the *Mansabdars*. *In case, the recorded Jama was in excess of salary claim the assignee was required to deposit the balance with the central treasury*. On the other hand, *if it was less than the salary claims the short fall was paid from the treasury*. There were various types of *jagirs:*

Different Types of *Jagirs*	
(a) *Tankha Jagirs*	Which were given in lieu of salaries and were transferable every three to four years.
(b) *Mashrut Jagirs*	Which were given on certain conditions.
(c) *Watan Jagirs*	Which were assigned to *zamindar* or *rajas* in their local dominions. *Watan Jagirs* were hereditary and non-transferable. When a *zamindar* was made a *Mansabdar*, he was given *Tankha Jagir* apart from his *Watan Jagir* at another place, if the salary of his rank was more than the income from his *Watan Jagir*.
(d) *Altamgha Jagirs*	Which were given to Muslim nobles in their family towns or place of birth.

Along with *Jagirdars*, there were *zamindars* who were the people who had hereditary rights over the produce of the land and claimed a direct share in the peasants produce which varied from 10% to 25% in different parts of the country. *Zamindars* also assisted the state and the *jagirdar* in the collection of land revenue. They had their own armed forces, and generally lived in forts or *grahis*, which was both a place of refuge and a status symbol. It should be noted that the *zamindar* was *not the 'owner' of all the lands comprising his zamindari*. The peasants who actually cultivated the land could not be dispossessed as long as they paid the land revenue. Thus, the *zamindars* and the peasants had their own hereditary rights in land. It is pertinent to note that apart from revenue collecting duties, Zamindars had to render military duties and perform *Khidmat* such as rendering soldiers to fill the ranks of royal army at times of need and offer gifts at the royal court.

Religious Policy

Akbar rose to fame in the pages of history due to his religious policy. Various factors were responsible for his religious ideas. The most important among them were his early contacts with the Sufi saints, the teachings of his tutor Abdul Latif, his marriage with Rajput women, his association with intellectual giants like Shaikh Mubarak and his two illustrious sons – Abul Faizi and Abul Fazl – and his ambition to establish an empire in Hindustan.

In the beginning of his life, Akbar was a pious Muslim. He regularly visited the shrine of Sheikh Muinuddin Chisti at Ajmer. Later, he became a sceptical Muslim. Soon after marrying Jodha Bai of Amber, he abolished the pilgrim tax and in c. 1562 CE, he abolished *jiziya*. He allowed his Hindu wives to worship their own gods. In c. 1575 CE, he constructed the *Ibadat Khana* (Hall of Prayers) at his new capital Fatehpur Sikri wherein Akbar invited learned scholars from all religions like Hinduism, Jainism, Christianity and Zoroastrianism and used to conduct religious discussions with them. Some of the scholars were:

- Pursottam Das – Hindu
- Dastur Maharji Rana – Parsi (of Navsari)
- Hira Vijaya Suri – Jain saint of Kathiawar
- Aquaviva and Monserrate – Christian (sent by the Portuguese on Akbar's request)

He disliked the interference of the Muslim *ulemas* in political matters. In c. 1579 CE, he issued the 'Infallibility Decree' by which he asserted his religious powers.

In c. 1582 CE, he promulgated a new religion called *Din-i-Ilahi*/*Tauhind-i-Ilahi* (Divine Monotheism), which believes in one God and in *Sul-i-Kul*/peace to all. It contained the good points of all religions and the basics were rational. However, his new faith proved to be a failure. It fizzled out after his death. Even during his lifetime, it had only followers including Birbal, Abul Fazl and Abul Faizi.

Akbar's Navratnas

Akbar, despite his illiteracy, was a great lover of the artists and intellectuals. His passion for knowledge and interest in learning from great minds attracted him to men of genius to his court. Nine of these courtiers were known as Akbar's *Navratnas* (or *nine jewels*):

Akbar's ***Navratnas***	
1. Abul Fazl	• Wrote *Ain-i-Akbari* and *Akbar Nama* • Led Mughal imperial army in its wars in Deccan. • Was murdered by Bir Singh Bundela, on the orders of Prince Salim.
2. Faizi	• Historian Abul Fazl's brother and Persian poet. • Translated *Lilavati* into Persian (a work on mathematics), and under his supervision, the Mahabharata was translated into the Persian language.

Akbar's *Navratnas*	
3. Fakir Aziao Din	He was a Sufi mystic and one of the chief advisors of Akbar.
4. Tansen	• Great musician, Hindu of Gwalior, served as a court musician to King Ramachandra who gave him the title of Tansen too. • Accepted Islam at the hand of great Sufi mystic saint Muhammad Ghaus of Gwalior. • It is believed that *he could bring rain and fire through singing the ragas Megh Malhar and Deepak,* respectively. • He composed *Dhrupada* on Hindu Gods and Goddesses along with inventing many ragas. • He also composed songs on his patrons. • Akbar gave him the honorific title *Mian.*
5. Raja Birbal/ Mahesh Das	• Courtier to whom Akbar gave the title of both Raja and Birbal. • Died fighting Yusuf Shahis on North West frontier.
6. Raja Todar Mal	• Finance minister, overlooked revenue system. • Introduced standard weights and measurements, revenue districts and officers. • Earlier worked under Sher Shah Suri. • In c. 1582 CE, Akbar bestowed on him the title of *Diwan-i-Ashraf.*
7. Raja Man Singh	Was a *Mansabdar*, grandson of Akbar's father-in-law and one of his trusted general.
8. Abdul Rahim Khan-i-Khanan	• Great poet • Son of Bairam Khan • Although a Muslim by birth, a devotee of Lord Krishna. • Translated *Babarnama* into Turki.
9. Mirza Aziz Koka	He was also known as Khan-i-Azam or Kotaltash and was one of the leading nobles, and also the foster brother of Akbar. He also served as the *Subedar* of Gujarat.

Mughal Dynasty after Akbar

Jahangir/Salim (c. 1605–1627 CE)

- Jodha Bai and Akbar's eldest son, was named Salim after blessings of Sheikh Salim Chisti.
- Revolted against Akbar in c. 1599 CE. After Akbar's death, he was crowned at Agra in c. 1605 CE, and assumed the title of Nur-ud-din Muhammad Jahangir (Conqueror of the World).
- In c. 1611 CE, he married Mehrunnisa (widow of Sher Afghani). He gave her title of Nur Jahan (Light of the World) and her father Gyas Beg was given title of *Itmaduddaulah*.

- Nur Jahan had great influence on Jahangir's life and dominated the royal household and set new fashions based on Persian traditions. She encouraged Persian art and culture in the court. She was given the status of *Padshah Begum* and was the only woman in Mughal Darbar. The coins were struck in her name and all royal *farmans* also had her name. She was a constant companion of Jahangir and even joined him in his hunting.
- A lot of members of her family benefited from this alliance. She got high positions for her father (chief *diwan*) and brother Asaf Khan (was appointed as *Khan-i-Saman*). In c. 1612 CE, Asaf Khan's daughter, Arjumand Banu Begum (later known as Mumtaz), married Jahangir's third son, prince Khurram (later Shah Jahan).
- Rebellions: Jahangir's rule witnessed a spate of rebellions. His eldest son Khusrau (son of Jahangir and Man Bai, daughter of Bhagwan Das) revolted but was defeated and imprisoned. The fifth Sikh *guru*, Arjun Dev, was beheaded for supporting the rebel prince Khusrau.
    - For the first 10 years, after Khurram's marriage to Mumtaz Mahal, there was practically a rule of alliance of Noor Jahan, her father, her brother Asaf Khan and Khurram. But problems arose when Noor Jahan married her daughter Ladli Begum (by Sher Afghani) to Jahangir's youngest son Shahryar, and now she supported him as the heir apparent. So, this drove Khurram (Shah Jahan) into rebellion against his father in c. 1622 CE, since he felt that Jahangir was completely under Nur Jahan's influence. However, some historians believe that Shah Jahan revolted against his father due to his personal ambitions. Jahangir had ordered Shah Jahan to go to Qandahar, which was besieged by the Persians but Shah Jahan was afraid that the campaign would be a long and difficult one and intrigues would be hatched against him during his absence from the court. Hence, he put forward a number of unreasonable demands such as full command of the army, which included the veterans of the Deccan, complete sway over the Punjab, and a number of other forts, etc. He was defeated by the forces led by Mahabat Khan. However, this rebellion kept the empire distracted for four years, i.e., till c. 1626 CE and resulted in the loss of Qandahar, and emboldened the Deccanis to recover all the territories surrendered to the Mughals.
- Mughal expansion under Jahangir: In c. 1615 CE, Amar Singh of Mewar (son of Maharana Pratap) submitted before him. Rana's son Karan Singh was made *Mansabdar* in the Mughal court.
    - In c. 1616 CE, with the help of Maratha *sardars* , Khan-i-Khanan inflicted a crushing defeat on the combined forces of Ahmednagar, Bijapur and Golconda.
    - In c. 1620 CE, Jahangir annexed Kangra. He was the first Muslim ruler to do so.
    - In c. 1622 CE, Qandahara was occupied by Shah Abbas of Persia.

- Conquest of Deccan: Jahangir decided to follow Akbar's expansionist policy in the Deccan. But Jahangir could achieve little success in it due to certain problems:
- He could not devote much attention in the crucial phase due to Khurram's revolt.
- The Mughal nobles were also involved in a number of intrigues and conflicts in Deccan.
- Due to the rise of Malik Ambar in Deccan: Malik Ambar, with the help of Marathas and the ruler of Bijapur Ibrahim Adil Shah, made it difficult for the Mughals to consolidate their position in Berar, Ahmednagar and Balaghat.

– After Jahangir's death in c. 1627 CE, Shah Jahan reached Agra and with the support of the nobles, chief *diwan* Asaf Khan and the army, Shah Jahan ascended the throne. Nur Jahan was given a pension and she lived a retired life till her death 18 years later.

– The British visited Machlipatnam during Jahangir's reign. Captain Hawkins (c. 1608–1611 CE) and Thomas Roe (c. 1615–1619 CE) visited his court. Thomas Roe got the *farman* for setting up an English factory at Surat.

– Jahangir had a chain of justice hung outside his palace.

– Jahangir mostly lived in Lahore and he forbade the killings of animals for food on Tuesday and Friday.

– Wrote the *Tuzuk-i-Jahangiri* (autobiography) in Persian, in which he described his drinking habit. He also patronised valuable dictionary *Farhang-i-Jahangiri*. During his reign, Abdul Hamid Lahori wrote *Padshah Namah* and Khafi Khan wrote *Muntakhab-i-Lubab*. He also patronised many scholars like Ghiyas Beg, Naqib Khan and Niamatullah.

– Art and Architecture during Jahangir's reign: The practice of putting up buildings in marble and decorating the walls with floral designs made of semi-precious stones (known as Pietra Durra) started during his reign.

FIGURE 13.5 Pietra Durra

FIGURE 13.6 Itmad-Ud Daulah Tomb, Agra

- Noor Jahan built the tomb of her father Itmad-ud-dulah at Agra.
- Jahangir built Moti Masjid at Lahore and his own mausoleum at Lahore. He laid a number of gardens such as the Shalimar and Nishant gardens in Kashmir.
- Mughal painting reached its zenith under Jahangir. He employed a number of painters like Abul Hasan, Bishan Das (regarded as master of portraits), Madhu, Anant, Manohar, Govardhan and Ustad Mansur (specialist in animal painting). The use of 'Halo' or 'Divine lights' behind king's head started under him. Apart from painting the scenes of hunting, battles and royal courts, progress was made in portrait painting and paintings of animals. It was under his rule that the emphasis shifted from illustrated manuscripts to album and individual portrait.

Shah Jahan (c. 1628–1658 CE)

- Also known as Khurram, whose mother was the Hindu Jagat Gosain, and was married to Arjumand Banu Begum (Mumtaz Mahal).
- He was crowned in Agra in c. 1628 CE; had to face instant revolt by Bundelas under Jujhar Singh and Khan Jahan Lodhi, the Mughal governor of the Deccan. Khan Jahan Lodhi, with the intention of securing help in times of necessity, gave away Balaghat to the Nizam Shah, to which Shah Jahan objected and ordered Khan Jahan Lodi to recover it. As the latter failed, Shah Jahan recalled him to court. Khan Jahan, however, turned hostile and

took shelter with Nizam Shah. This infuriated Shah Jahan and he decided to follow an aggressive policy to recover the lost territories of the Deccan.

- Shah Jahan's Deccan policy was more successful. Ascertaining the fact that there could be no peace for the Mughals in the Deccan as long as Ahmednagar continued as an independent state, he successfully isolated Ahmednagar by winning over Bijapur and the Marathas. Fath Khan, son of Malik Ambar, also made peace with the Mughals, and Mahabat Khan was appointed governor of Deccan. But the conflict with Deccan states continued. Finally, in c. 1636 CE, *ahdnama* (treaties) were signed with Bijapur and Golconda. The main points of agreement with Bijapur were:
  i. Adil Shah accepted the Mughal suzerainty
  ii. He was to pay 20 lakh rupees as indemnity
  iii. He was not to interfere in the affairs of Golconda
  iv. Mughal emperor was to arbitrate in case of any future dispute between Bijapur and Golconda
  v. Adil Shah was to help Mughals in conflict against Shahji Bhonsle (father of Shivaji)

In return for these, territory worth about 20 lakh *huns* annually belonging to Ahmednagar was ceded to Bijapur. Shah Jahan completed the settlement of the Deccan by entering into a treaty with Golconda as well. According to this treaty:

i. Golconda took oath of loyalty towards Mughal emperor. He agreed to include the name of the Mughal emperor in the *Khutba* and exclude the name of the Shah of Iran.
ii. Golconda agreed to pay two lakh *huns* per year to the Mughals.

These treaties ended the conflicts in the Deccan. The Mughals could have large parts of Southern India under their domination, and peace with the Mughals enabled the Deccani states to expand their territories towards the south. However, rapid expansion weakened the internal cohesion of the Deccan states and ambitious nobles like Shahji and his son Shivaji in Bijapur, Mir Jumla in Golconda, started carving out spheres of influence for themselves and this again created a conflicting atmosphere in Deccan. In c. 1656 CE, following the death of Muhammad Adil Shah, a distinct change came in Mughal policy and the treaties were ignored. The justification provided by Mughals was that both these states had made extensive conquests in Karnataka and that 'compensation' was due to the Mughals on the ground that the two states were Mughal vassals, and their conquests had been made possible due to the benevolent neutrality on the part of the Mughals. Now, Shah Jahan asked his son Aurangzeb to conquer and annex the territories of Deccan kingdoms. However, this change did not benefit the Mughal empire in any substantial way, in fact it created more problems for future.

- In c. 1632 CE, Shah Jahan defeated the Portuguese near Hughli due to the regular abuse of trading privilege by them.

- In c. 1639 CE, Shah Jahan secured Qandahara and immediately fortified it, but Persia wrested Qandahara from Mughals. In c. 1649 CE. Shah Jahan launched a prolonged campaign in the North-West Frontier to recover Qandahara and other ancestral lands, but all the campaigns failed. Gradually Shah Jahan realised the futility of his ambition and stopped fighting. Thus, there was the permanent loss of Qandahara.
- Shah Jahan's reign is considered the 'The Golden age' of the Mughal Empire. He built:
  - Taj Mahal: Counted among seven wonders of the world and considered a jewel of the builder's art. The construction was commissioned in c. 1631 CE and was constructed in 22 years. The architectural design was prepared by Ustad Isa and Isa Muhammad Effendi, while the main dome was designed by Ismail Khan.
  - Mosque-building reached its peak during Shah Jahan's reign. He built the Moti Masjid at Agra (built entirely in white marble), the Sheesh Mahal and Mussaman Burj at Agra (where he spent his last years in captivity), while the Jama Masjid at Delhi was built in red stone.

FIGURE 13.7 Taj Mahal, Agra

  - The climax of fort-building reached during the reign of Shah Jahan. The famous Red Fort at Delhi with its Rang Mahal, Diwan-i-Am and Diwan-i-Khas was his creation. He also built the Jama Masjid in Delhi, Shalimar Bagh in Lahore and the city of Shahjahanabad. He also got Bebadal Khan to build the Peacock Throne, on which is inscribed the Amir Khusrao couplet: *'If there is a paradise on earth, it is here'*.

FIGURE 13.8 Red Fort, Delhi

- Shah Jahan also patronised many writers and historians like Inayat Khan, who wrote *Shah Jahan Nama*. His son Dara Shikoh translated the Bhagavat Gita and Upanishads into the Persian language.

– His reign is described by:
  - French travellers – Bernier and Tavernier
  - Italian traveller – Manucci
  - Peter Mundy described famine during Shah Jahan's time.

– Shah Jahan's sudden illness in c. 1657 CE plunged the empire into a civil war (c. 1657–1659 CE) among his four sons, who were located in the following places:
  - Dara Shikoh (eldest and crown prince), based in Delhi, supported by Jahanara, the daughter of Jahangir.
  - Shuja, the governor of Bengal.
  - Aurangzeb, the governor of Deccan, supported by Roshanara.
  - Murad Baksh, the governor of Malwa and Gujarat

– At first, Shuja declared himself the emperor, but he was defeated by Sulaiman Sheikh, son of Dara Shikoh with the aid of Mirza Raja Jai Singh. Aurangzeb and Murad agreed to partition the empire and both defeated Raja Jaswant Singh (ruler of Jodhpur) and Qasim Khan at the Battle of Dharmat (in c. 1658 CE).

- Later, just after a month, the Battle of Samugarh (c. 1658 CE) was fought between Aurangzeb and Dara in which, due to divided counsel and underestimation of Aurangzeb by Dara, Dara Shikoh lost the battle. This practically decided the issue of succession. Aurangzeb also treacherously imprisoned Murad and sent him to Gwalior jail, where he was killed two years later. Aurangzeb soon crowned himself with the title of 'Alamgir' (conqueror of the world), but the civil war continued for more than two years.
- In c. 1658 CE the Battle of Khajwah (near Allahabad) was fought between Aurangzeb and Shuja in which again Aurangzeb emerged victorious.
- The Battle of Deorai (c. 1659 CE) was the last major battle Dara fought against Aurangzeb, in which he was again defeated and he had to flee to Afghanistan. On his way in the Bolan Pass, a treacherous chief imprisoned him and handed him over to Aurangzeb who had him executed, and later, his son Sulaiman Sheikh too. Interestingly, after the Battle of Deorai, the second coronation of Aurangzeb happened.
- Aurangzeb made Shah Jahan prisoner in Agra Fort, where he was looked after by his daughter Jahanara till his death in c. 1666 CE.
- Aurangazeb emerged victorious in this struggle. He entered the Agra Fort after defeating Dara and forced Shah Jahan to surrender. Shah Jahan was confined to the Agra fort and put under vigil. But he was not ill-treated. Shah Jahan lived for eight long years lovingly nursed by his daughter Jahanara. He died in c. 1666 CE and was buried beside his wife's grave in the Taj Mahal.
- The financial *bickering between father and son* form a large part of Aurangzeb's correspondence, known as *Adab-i-Alamgiri*.

Aurangzeb (c. 1658–1707 CE)

- Was one of the ablest of the Mughal emperors under whom the Mughal empire reached its greatest territorial limits and emerged as the largest single state ever known in India from the dawn of history to the rise of British power.
- Reign:
  - First 25 years in north India, when Maratha power under Shivaji emerged.
  - Last 25 years in Deccan.
- Northern Conquest: Aurangzeb could expand Mughal power in Assam in the north-east region. In c. 1662 CE, Mir Jumla, Aurangzeb's ablest general and the governor of Bengal, led the expedition against the Ahoms. Despite concluding a favourable treaty, Mughals suffered heavy losses and Jumla died in c. 1663 CE on his way back to Dacca. Another notable achievement in north-east was capture of island of Sondip and Chittagong in c. 1664 CE under Shaista Khan, the new governor of Bengal, who also chastised the Arakanese pirates. However, the Ahom kingdom could not be controlled for long and

the Mughal *faujdars* had to face resistance and regular conflicts. Thus, by c. 1680 CE, the Ahoms succeeded in capturing Kamrupa and Mughal control over the territory ended.

– Conquest of Deccan: Prof. Satish Chandra identifies four distinct phases in Aurangzeb's policy towards the Deccan states:

A. Phase I (c. 1658–1668 CE)

- The main attempt was to recover from Bijapur the territories belonging to the Ahmednagar state, surrendered to it by the treaty of c. 1636 CE.
- Led by Jai Singh, the governor of Deccan. The focus was to get hold of the territories of Kalyani, Bidar and Parenda from Bijapur.
- The Mughals failed to lay siege on Bijapur in c. 1665 CE and Jai Singh died in c. 1667 CE.
- However, Sholapur was secured by bribery in c. 1668 CE.

B. Phase II (c. 1668–1684 CE)

- The Marathas were considered as the major danger in the Deccan and efforts were made to pressurise Bijapur and Golconda into joining hands with the Mughals against Shivaji and then against his son Sambhaji. Thus, during this phase, attempts were made to secure the help of the Deccan states against Marathas.
- This shift in Mughal policy was due to the death of Adil Shah of Bijapur, the growing power of Shivaji, and the increasing influence of the brothers Akhanna and Madanna in Golconda administration, but Aurangzeb's efforts to contain the Marathas were not very successful as the tripartite alliance between Golcanda, Shivaji and Bijapur did not allow Aurangzeb to have his way.
- In c. 1679–1680 CE, desperate effort by Mughal viceroy Diler Khan to capture Bijapur failed due to this tripartite alliance.

C. Phase III (c. 1686–1687 CE)

- Aurangzeb followed the policy of outright annexation of the Deccan states. He personally supervised the siege of Bijapur (c. 1686 CE) and Golconda (c. 1687 CE), along with the territory of Karnataka. Aurangzeb made Khirki, founded by Malik Ambar, the capital of Mughal Deccan and named it Aurangabad.

D. Phase IV (c.1687–1707 CE)

- Aurangzeb spent most of his time in Deccan and despite of the conflict with Marathas, he managed to keep the region under Mughal control. It was during this period that Sambhaji (Shivaji's son) was captured and executed at Sangameshwar. But after his death in c. 1707 CE (at Aurangabad in Deccan), the Marathas reasserted their independence and succeeded within a short span of time.

- In fact, the destruction of the Deccan kingdoms was a political blunder on the part of Aurangzeb as with the fall of the Deccan Sultanate, the barrier between the Mughals and the Marathas was removed and there ensued a direct confrontation between them. Also, his Deccan campaigns exhausted the Mughal treasury. According to J.N. Sarkar, *the Deccan ulcer ruined Aurangzeb*.

– Religious policy and rebelions: Various rebellions took place during his reign due to his harsh religious policy. This included the rebellions of the Jat peasantry at Mathura (under their leader Gokla in c. 1669 CE, under Rajaram in c. 1685 CE, and under Churaman in c. 1691 CE), the Satnami peasantry in Punjab, and the Bundelas in Bundelkhand (under king Chatrasaal) in c. 1672 CE.

- Aurangzeb was a staunch and orthodox Muslim in his personal life and his ideal was to transform India into an Islamic state. Initially, Aurangzeb banned the construction of new Hindu temples and the repair of old temples, but later he gradually started destroying Hindu temples. The celebrated temples of Keshava Rai at Mathura (built by Bir Singh Deo Bundela in the reign of Jahangir) and the Vishwanath temple at Banaras were reduced to ruins and mosques erected in their place. In c. 1679 CE, he reimposed *jiziya* and pilgrim tax.
- He was also not tolerant of other Muslim sects. The celebration of Muharram was stopped. In fact, his invasions against the Deccan sultanates were partly due to his hatred of the Shia faith. In c. 1675 CE, he executed the ninth Sikh Guru, Tegh Bahadur, which resulted in the rebellion of the Sikh community against him.
- He gave excessive powers to the office of *Muhtasib*, the officer entrusted to enforce moral codes and *shara*. Throughout his kingdom, drinking was prohibited and cultivation and the use of *bhang* and other drugs were banned. He also forbade music in the Mughal court and discontinued the practice of *Jharokha darshan* (as he considered it a superstitious practice and against Islam) and the system of weighing the emperor in gold, the celebration of *Dasarah*, forbade astrologers from preparing *almanacs*, forbade the use of Kalma inscribed on his coins, abolished Nauroz (as it was a Zoroastrian practice favoured by the Safavid rulers of Iran) and also forbade Sati.
- However, it is also believed that he also issued secular decrees, called *zawabit* which sometimes along with supplementing the *shara*, often modified it in view of the conditions prevalent in India. Another interesting and notable point is that the largest number of Persian works on classical Indian music were written in Aurangzeb's reign and that Aurangzeb himself was proficient in playing the *veena*.

– Aurangzeb's Rajput policy also alienated the Rajputs and they gradually lost their position in the administrative set up. Aurangzeb's policy towards Marwar and Mewar was clumsy and blundering and brought no advantage of any kind to the Mughals. He wanted to divide the Marwar state between the two principal claimants, and in the process alienated both, as also the ruler of Mewar who considered Mughal interference in such matters to be a dangerous precedent. The breach with Mewar and the long drawn-out war which followed damaged the moral standing of the Mughal state.

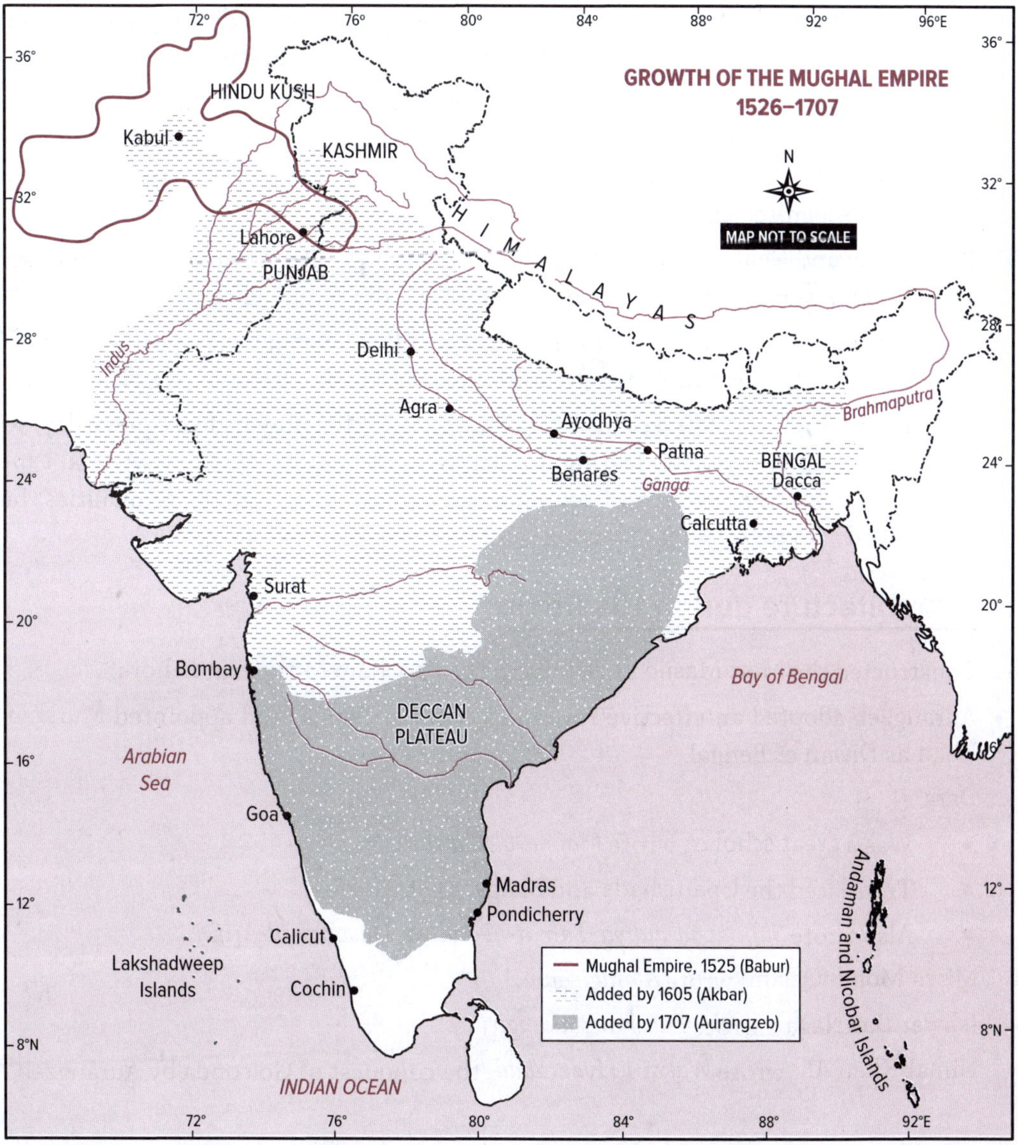

FIGURE 13.9 Growth of Mughal Empire

- On the death of Raja Jaswant Singh of Marwar in c. 1678 CE, Aurangzeb gave the *tika* of Jodhpur to his nephew, Inder Singh, instead of his son Ajit Singh. The dispute escalated when Ajit Singh's younger brother died. Aurangzeb sent a force to capture the two queens and Ajit from the Rathor mansion in Shahjahanabad, but his attempt was rebuffed by Durgadas Rathor, a senior officer of the former ruler who initially used gunfire in retaliation and eventually escaped from the city to Jodhpur along with Ajit and the two queens, who were disguised as men. A loyal nanny of Ajit Singh left behind her own son at the mansion as Ajit Singh.
- Rana Raj Singh of Mewar sided with Rani Hadi and the young prince Ajit Singh. In c. 1679 CE, Aurangzeb attacked Mewar and the Rajputs had to retire to the hills, from where they engaged in sporadic guerrilla warfare. Finally, in c. 1698 CE, Ajit Singh was recognised as the ruler of Marwar.

– Personality and Character of Aurangzeb: In his private life, Aurangzeb was industrious, disciplined, was very simple in food, dressing, and did not at all consume wine.

- He was learned and proficient in Arabic and Persian languages and was a great lover of books. He patronised the greatest digest of Muslim law in India, *Fatwa-i-Alamgiri*.
- He was highly devoted to his religion and conducted prayers five times a day, strictly observing the Ramzan fasting. In fact, he earned money for his personal expenses by copying the *Quran* and selling those copies. Due to all these qualities, he was called *Darvesh*/*Zindapir* (a living saint).

Art and Architecture during His Reign

– Constructed the Moti Masjid at Delhi and the Badshahi Mosque at Lahore.

– Aurangzeb adopted an effective revenue system at Bengal and appointed Murshid Quli Khan as Diwan of Bengal.

– Dara

- Was a great scholar, wrote *Majma-ul-Bahrain*
- Translated the Upanishads and Bhagvat Gita
- Also wrote *Safinat-ul-auliya*, *Sainat-ul-Auliya*, *Hasanat-ul-Arifin*

– Mirza Mohd. Qasim: wrote *Alamgirnama*

– Ishwar Das Nagar: wrote *Fatuhat-i-alamgiri*

– Nimat Khan Ali: wrote *Wakai-i-Hyderabad*, the conquest of Golconda by Aurangzeb

Economic and Social Life Under the Mughals

The Mughal period saw important social and economic developments. During this period, many European travellers and traders came to India and their accounts contain a lot of information about the socio-economic conditions of India. In general, they described the wealth and prosperity of India and also the luxurious life of the aristocratic classes. On the other side, they also mentioned the poverty and sufferings of the ordinary people such as peasants and artisans. Nikitin observed *that the people of Deccan were bare-footed and it might be due to high cost of leather*.

Growth of Trade

The Indian trading classes were large in numbers, well-spread throughout the country and were well organised and highly professional. *Seth*, *bohra* traders specialised in long distance trade while local traders were called *banik*. Another class of traders known as *banjaras* were specialised in carrying bulk goods and used to move to long distances with their goods on the back of oxen. Interestingly, the trading community did not belong to one caste or religion. For instance, the Gujarati merchants included Hindus, Jains and Muslims, in Rajasthan Oswals, Maheshwaris and Agarwals came to be called the Marwaris, while in south India, the Chettis on the Coramandal coast and the Muslim merchants of Malabar formed important trading communities.

Just like communities, different regions emerged as prominent trading stations. For instance:

- Bengal exported sugar, rice, as well as delicate muslin and silk.
- The Coromandal coast became a centre of textile production.
- Gujarat was an entry point of foreign goods. From there, fine textiles and silk were taken to north India. Indigo and food grains were exported from north India through Gujarat. It was also the distribution centre for the luxury products of Kashmir such as shawls and carpets.

India, during the Mughal period, witnessed further intensification of her foreign trade owing to the advent of the European trading companies and their direct participation in the Euro-Asian and Intra-Asian trade. India had trade relations with central Asia, Persia and Europe. Her major export included textiles, saltpetre, sugar, opium and spices. In comparison to her export, her imports were limited to select commodities like war horses, luxury items such as ivory, silver, silk, porcelain, good quality wine, carpets, perfume, glass, watches, silver utensils, tin and copper, etc. The movement of goods occurred through a complex network, linking wholesalers with merchants down to the regional and local levels through agents (*gumashtas*) and commission agents (*dalals*). The movement of goods was also facilitated by the growth of a financial system which permitted easy transmission of money from one part of the country to another. This was done through the use of *hundis*, a paper document promising payment of money after a fixed period of time at a discount and certain place. The *hundis* often included insurance which was charged at different rates on the basis of value of the goods, destination, means of transport (land, river, or sea), etc. The *sarrafs* (*shroffs*) who specialised in changing money, also specialised in dealing with *hundis*. In the process, they also acted as private banks as they lent money to nobles and kept their money too. By means of *hundis*, they created credit which supplemented the money in circulation.

The trading community in India, especially in the port towns, included some of the richest merchants who were comparable to merchant princes of Europe such as Virji Vohra, Abdul Ghafur Bohra, Malay Chetti of the Coromandel coast, Kashi Viranna and Sunca Rama Chetti. Each community of merchants had its leader known as *nagarseth*, who could intercede with the local officials on their behalf. In fact, there were instances of strikes by merchants in Ahmedabad to stress their points of view.

Growth of Administration: *Mansabdari* System and the Mughal Army

The *mansab* and *jagir* systems under the Mughals evolved through the time. As we have discussed earlier, the mansabdari system, evolved by Akbar, was the basis of civil and military administrations under the Mughals. Jahangir introduced a new provision in the *sawar* rank. According to it, a part of *sawar* rank was termed *du-aspa sih-aspa* in case of select *mansabdars*. He probably introduced this provision to promote nobles of his confidence and strengthen them militarily. By this provision, he could increase the military strength of his nobles without effecting any change in their *zat* rank and for this part, additional payment at the same rate of 8,000 *dams* per *sawar* was sanctioned. Thus, if the *sawar* rank was 4000 out of which 1000 was *du-aspa sihaspa*, the salary for this *sawar* was calculated as 3,000 × 8,000 + (1,000 × 8,000 × 2) = 40,000,000 *dams*. Without *du-aspa sih-aspa*, salary for the 4,000 *sawar* would have stood at (4,000 × 8,000) = 32,000,000 *dams*. Thus, the *mansabdar* was to maintain double the number of *sawars* for the *duaspa sih-aspa* category and was paid for it.

Shah Jahan introduced the month-scale in the *mansabdari* system to compensate the gap between *Jama* (estimated income) and *hasil* (actual realisation). As we know, the *mansabdars* were generally paid through revenue assignments, i.e., *jagirs*. The biggest problem was that calculation was made on the basis of the expected income (*Jama*) from the *jagir* during one year. It was noticed that the actual revenue collection (*hasil*) always fell short of the estimated income. In such a situation, the *mansabdar*'s salary was fixed by a method called month-scale. Thus, if a *jagir* yielded only half of the *Jama*, it was called *Shashmaha* (six monthly), and if it yielded only one fourth, it was called *Sihmaha* (three monthly). The month scale was applied to cash salaries also. There were deductions from the sanctioned pay also. During the reign of Shah Jahan, the *mansabdars* were allowed to maintain 1/5 to 1/3 of the sanctioned strength of the *sawar* rank without any accompanying reduction in their claim on the maintenance amount for the *sawar* rank.

Later, Aurangzeb continued with all these changes and created an additional rank called *Mashrut* (conditional). This was an attempt to increase the *sawar* rank of the *mansabdar* temporarily. Aurangzeb added one another deduction called *Khurak-i-dawwab*, towards meeting the cost for feed of animals in the imperial stables.

European Factories during Mughal Rule	
Portuguese	(a) Goa (captured from the ruler of Bijapur by Albuquerque in 1510 and became the capital of the Portuguese Empire in the East). (b) Subsequently on the west coast, Daman, Salsette and Bombay and on the east coast Santhome near Madras and Hugli in Bengal had become Portuguese settlements.
Dutch	(a) Masulipatam (1605) (b) Pulicat (1610) (c) Surat (1616) (d) Bimilipatam (1641) (e) Karaikal (1645) (f) Chinsura (1653) (g) Kasimbazar, Baranagore, Patna, Balasore, Nagapattinam (all in 1658) (h) Cochin (1663)
Danes	(a) Tranquebar in Tamilnadu (1620) (b) Serampore in Bengal (Danes HQ).
French	(a) Surat (1668) (b) Masulipatnam (1669) (c) Pondicherry, a small village then (1673) (d) Chandernagore in Bengal (1690) (e) Mahe in the Malabar, Yanam in Coromandal (both in 1725) (f) Karaikal (1739).
English	(a) Surat (1612) (b) Madras (1639) also known as Fort St George (c) Bombay (1668) (d) Calcutta (1690) also known as Fort William in Bengal.

Prominent European Travellers

European Traveller	Time Period	Visited during the reign of (Dynasty/Ruler)	Literature/Remarks
Nicolo De Conti (Venetian)	1420–1421	Vijayanagara (Deva Raya I)	'*De varietate fortunae*' ('On the Vicissitudes of Fortune')
Athanasius Nikitin (Russian)	1470–1474	Bahmani (Muhammad III)	'*The Journey Beyond Three Seas*'
Domingo Paes (Portuguese)	1520–1522	Vijayanagara (Krishna Deva Raya)	'Chronica dos reis de Bisnaga' ('Chronicle of the Vijayanagar Kings')
Duarte Barbosa (Portuguese)	1500–1516	Vijayanagara (Krishna Deva Raya)	'The Book of Duarte Barbosa, An Account of the Countries bordering on the Indian Ocean and their Inhabitants'
Fernao Nuniz (Portuguese)	1535–1537	Tuluva dynasty (Achyutdeva Raya)	Mentions cultural aspects of the empire, admires the jewels worn of women and how women were appointed in the King's service.
William Hawkins (British)	1608–1611	Mughal Emperor (Jahangir)	Acquired formal approval for the establishment of an English factory at Surat.
Sir Thomas Roe (British)	1615–1619	Mughal Emperor (Jahangir)	'*Journal of the Mission to the Mogul Empire*'.
Peter Mundy (Italian)	1630–1634	Mughal Emperor (Shah Jahan)	'*The Levelling Sea*' (a concise biography of Peter Mundy).
Jean Baptiste Tavernier (French)	1638–1643	Mughal Emperor (Shah Jahan)	'*Travels in India*' (elaborately discussed diamonds and diamond mines of India).
Nicolao Manucci (Italian)	1653–1708	Mughal Emperor (Aurangzeb)	'*History of the Mogul Dynasty in India, 1399–1657*'
Francois Bernier (French)	1656–1717	Mughal Emperor (Aurangzeb)	• '*Travels in the Mogul Empire, A.D. 1656–1668*' • '*The History of the Late Revolution of the Empire of the Great Mogol*'

QUESTIONS FROM LAST YEAR'S PRELIMS

1. "Yogavasistha" was translated into Persian by Nizamuddin Panipati during the reign of: **(2022)**

(a) Akbar (b) Humayun
(c) Shahjahan (d) Aurangzeb

2. With reference to medieval India, which one of the following is the correct sequence in ascending order in terms of size? **(2021)**

(a) Paragana-Sarkar-Suba
(b) Sarkar-Paragana-Suba
(c) Suba-Sarkar-Paragana
(d) Paragana-Suba-Sarkar

3. With reference to Mughal India, what is/are the difference/differences between Jagirdar and Zamindar? **(2019)**

(1) Jagirdars were holders of land assignments in lieu of judicial and police duties, whereas Zamindars were holders of revenue rights without obligation to perform any duty other than revenue collection.
(2) Land assignments to Jagirdars were hereditary and revenue rights of Zamindars were not hereditary.

Select the correct answer using the code given below.

(a) 1 only (b) 2 only
(c) Both 1 and 2 (d) Neither 1 nor 2

4. With reference to Mian Tansen, which one of the following statements is not correct? **(2019)**

(a) Tansen was the title given to him by Emperor Akbar.
(b) Tansen composed Dhrupads on Hindu gods and goddesses.
(c) Tansen composed songs on his patrons.
(d) Tansen invented many Ragas.

5. Who among the following Mughal Emperors shifted emphasis from illustrated manuscripts to album and individual portrait? **(2019)**

(a) Humayun
(b) Akbar
(c) Jahangir
(d) Shah Jahan

6. With reference to the cultural history of India, consider the following statements: **(2018)**

1. White marble was used in making Buland Darwaza and Khankah at Fatehpur Sikri.
2. Red sandstone and marble were used in making Bara Imamabara and Rumi Darwaza at Lucknow.

Which of the statements given above is/are correct?

(a) 1 only
(b) 2 only
(c) Both 1 and 2
(d) Neither 1 nor 2

7. Which one of the following foreign travellers elaborately discussed diamonds and diamond mines of India? **(2018)**

(a) Francois Bernier
(b) Jean-Baptiste Tavernier
(c) Jean de Thevenot
(d) Abbe Barthelemy Carre

8. *Banjaras* during the medieval period of Indian history were generally: **(2016)**

(a) Agriculturists
(b) Warriors
(c) Weavers
(d) Traders

9. Consider the following:

The arrival of Babur into India led to the **(2015)**

i. Introduction of gunpowder in the subcontinent.

ii. Introduction of arch and dome architecture in the region's architecture.

iii. Establishment of the Timurid dynasty in the region.

Select the correct answer using the codes given below:

(a) i and ii only (b) iii only

(c) i and iii only (d) i, ii, and iiii

10. Ibadat Khana at Fatehpur Sikri was **(2014)**

(a) The mosque for the use of royal family.

(b) Akbar's private chamber prayer.

(c) The hall in which Akbar held discussions with scholars of various religions.

(d) The room in which the nobles belonging to different religions gathered to discuss religious affairs.

11. Consider the following: **(2012)**

i. Assessment of the land revenue on the basis of nature of the soil and the quality of crops.

ii. Use of mobile cannons in warfare.

iii. Cultivation of tobacco and red chillies.

Which of the above was/were introduced into India by the English?

(a) i only (b) i and ii

(c) ii and iii (d) None

12. During the time of which Mughal Emperor did the English East India Company establish its first factory in India? **(2008)**

(a) Akbar (b) Humayun

(c) Jahangir (d) Aurangzeb

13. Which one of the following was the first fort constructed by the British in India? **(2007)**

(a) Fort William (b) Fort St. George

(c) Fort St. David (d) Fort St. Angelo

14. In Indian history, who was Abdul Hamid Lahori? **(2006)**

(a) An important military commander during Akbar's reign.

(b) An official historian of the reign of Shah Jahan.

(c) An important noble and confidant of Aurangzeb.

(d) A chronicler and poet during the reign of Muhammad Shah.

15. Bhakta Tukaram was a contemporary of which Mugal Emperor? **(2006)**

(a) Babar (b) Akbar

(c) Jahangir (d) Aurangzeb

16. How did the dynasty of Nizam Shahis of Ahmad Nagar come to an end? **(2004)**

(a) Ahmad Nagar was annexed to Mughal Empire and Husain Shah was consigned to life imprisonment.

(b) Mughal troops destroyed Daulatabad fort and killed Nizam-ul-Mulk of Ahmednagar.

(c) Fateh Khan usurped the throne from Nizam-ul-Mulk.

(d) Malik Amber was defeated in a battle with Mughals in 1631 and the entire royal family was killed by the Mughal troops.

17. Assertion (A): Emperor Akbar marched towards Afghanistan in 1581 with a huge Army.

Reason (R): He was on his way to reclaim his ancestral country of Farghana in Central Asia. **(2003)**

(a) Both A and R are true and R is the correct explanation of A
(b) Both A and R are true but R is not the correct explanation of A
(c) A is true but R is false
(d) A is false but R is true

18. The motive behind Shah Jahan's Balkh campaign was to **(2002)**
(a) Secure a friendly ruler in Balkh and Badakshan which bordered Kabul.
(b) Conquer Samarkand and Farghana, the Mughal homelands.
(c) Fix the Mughal frontier on scientific lines, the Amu Daria.
(d) Expand the Mughal Empire beyond the sub-continent.

19. Assertion (A): The Battle of Khanwa was certainly more decisive and significant than the first Battle of Panipat.

Reason (R): Rana Sanga, the Rajput hero, was certainly a more formidable adversary than Ibrahim Lodhi. **(2001)**
(a) Both A and R are true and R is the correct explanation of A
(b) Both A and R are true but R is not the correct explanation of A
(c) A is true but R is false
(d) A is false but R is true

20. Assertion (A): During the time of Akbar, for every ten cavalrymen, the *mansabdars* had to maintain twenty horses.

Reason (R): Horses had to be rested while on march and replacements were necessary in times of war. **(1999)**
(a) Both A and R are true and R is the correct explanation of A
(b) Both A and R are true but R is not the correct explanation of A
(c) A is true but R is false
(d) A is false but R is true

21. Which one of the following pairs is not correctly matched? **(1999)**
(a) Jahangir: William Hawkins.
(b) Akbar: Sir Thomas Roe.
(c) Shah Jahan: Tavernier.
(d) Aurangzeb: Manucci.

22. Consider the following statements:

Ahadis were those troopers who **(1998)**
(i) offered their services singly.
(ii) did not attach themselves to any chief.
(iii) had the emperor as their immediate colonel.
(iv) attached themselves to Mirzas.

Of these statements
(a) i, iii, and iv are correct
(b) i, ii and iii are correct
(c) ii and iii are correct
(d) i and iv are correct

23. The loss of Qandahar was a big blow to the Mughal empire from the view point of **(1998)**
(a) Natural resources
(b) Buffer territory
(c) Communication
(d) Strategic stronghold

24. The head of the military department under the recognised central machinery of administration during Akbar's reign was **(1997)**
(a) Diwan
(b) Mir Bakshi
(c) Mir Saman
(d) Bakshi

25. In medieval India, the *Mansabdari* system was introduced mainly for **(1996)**
(a) Making recruitments to the army
(b) Facilitating revenue collection
(c) Ensuring religious harmony
(d) Effecting clean administration

26. Nastaliq was, **(1996)**
(a) A Persian script used in medieval India
(b) A raga composed by Tansen
(c) A cess levied by the Mughal rulers
(d) A manual of code of conduct for the Ulemmas

ANSWERS

1. (a)	2. (a)	3. (c)	4. (d)	5. (b)	6. (d)	7. (b)	8. (d)
9. (a)	10. (c)	11. (d)	12. (c)	13. (b)	14. (b)	15. (c)	16. (a)
17. (c)	18. (a)	19. (a)	20. (d)	21. (b)	22. (b)	23. (d)	24. (b)
25. (d)	26. (a)						

QUESTIONS FROM LAST YEAR'S MAINS

1. Persian literary sources of medieval India reflect the spirit of the age. Comment. **(2020 GS1)**

2. Why should the 16th century be regarded as the period of Indian Renaissance? **(2015, History optional)**

3. How was the *Iqta* system of the Sultans different from the *Jagir* system under the Mughals? **(2014, History optional)**

PRACTICE QUESTIONS – PRELIMS

1. Match List I with List II and select the correct answer using the code given below the lists:

List I	List II
(a) Akbar	i. Moti Masjid at Agra
(b) Humayun	ii. Buland darwaza
(c) Jahangir	iii. Jamali Mosque
(d) Shah Jahan	iv. Climax of painting

Code:	A	B	C	D
(a)	ii	iv	iii	i
(b)	ii	iii	iv	i
(c)	i	iv	iii	ii
(d)	i	iii	iv	ii

2. Match List I with List II and select the correct answer using the code given below the lists:

List I (Famous Book)	List II (Author)
(a) *Shah Jahan Nama*	i. Inayat Khan
(b) *Ain-i-Akbari*	ii. Jahangir
(c) *Humayun-nama*	iii. Gulbadan Begam
(d) *Tuzuk-i-Jahangiri*	iv. Abul Fazl

Code:	A	B	C	D
(a)	ii	iv	iii	i
(b)	ii	iii	iv	i
(c)	i	iv	iii	ii
(d)	i	iii	iv	ii

ANSWERS

1. (b) 2. (c)

PRACTICE QUESTIONS – MAINS

1. Explain the innovative practices of Mughals in case of military organisation focusing on the *Mansabdari* system.
2. What were the main contributions of the Mughals in the field of art and architecture? Elaborate.
3. It is said of Humayun that 'he jumbled throughout his life and finally tumbled out of his life'. Do you agree? Give suitable reasons.
4. Sher Shah's administration was the foundation for both Mughal as well as British administration. Elucidate.

CHAPTER

14

The Later Mughals, the Marathas and Other Provincial Kingdoms

As we have discussed earlier, even during the long and strong reign of Emperor Aurangzeb, the unity and stability of the Mughal Empire was shaken. However, in spite of these setbacks, the Mughal army and administration was still quite efficient at the time of his death in c. 1707 CE. This year is generally referred as the differentiating year to separate the era of the great Mughals from that of the lesser Mughals, also known as the Later Mughals. The Mughal Empire declined rapidly after the death of Aurangzeb and it was in no position to militarily enforce its regulations on the other parts of the empire. As a result, many provincial governors started to assert their authority. Many kingdoms that were earlier subjugated by the Mughals also started proclaiming independence. In due course of time, they gained independent status. The period between c. 1707 CE and c. 1761 CE (*the time of Aurangzeb's death to the period when the Third Battle of Panipat took place, wherein Ahmad Shah Abdali defeated the Maratha chiefs*) witnessed the resurgence of regional identities and highlighted a sorry state of affairs for the once mighty Mughals. The Mughal court became the scene of factions among the nobles.

In c. 1707 CE, when Aurangzeb died, a war of succession broke out among his three surviving sons, Muazzam (the governor of Kabul), Muhammad Kam Bakhsh (the governor of Deccan) and Muhammad Azam Shah (the governor of Gujarat). Finally, Muazzam emerged victorious after defeating Muhammad Azam Shah in the Battle of Jajau, and ascended the throne with the title of Bahadur Shah I.

The Later Mughals

Bahadur Shah I/Muazzam/Shah Alam I (c. 1707–1712 CE)

- Ascended the throne with the title of 'Bahadur Shah', at the age of 63 years.
- He followed a policy of compromise towards the nobles, granting them appropriate territories and postings, pardoning even those nobles who had supported his rivals. However, due to his reckless grants of *jagirs* and promotions, the position of the state finances worsened. Historians often believe that the real power was in the hands of his *Wazir*, Zulfiqar Khan.
- He adopted a more tolerant attitude towards Hindus. He never abolished the *jizya,* but the efforts to collect the tax were not that steadfast.
- During his reign, the independence of Mewar and Marwar was acknowledged. However, the settlement could not restore these states to become fully-committed warriors for the Mughal cause.
- The Emperor's policy towards the Marathas was also that of half-hearted conciliation as he released Shahu, but did not recognise him as the rightful Maratha king. Similarly, he granted Marathas *sardeshmukhi* of Deccan, but failed to grant them *chauth* and thus could not satisfy them fully. The Marathas, thus continued to fight among themselves as well as against the Mughals in the Deccan.
- He was however, successful in conciliating the Bundela chief, Chattrasal and the Jat chief, Churaman who also joined him in the campaign against the Sikhs. He gave a high *mansab* to Guru Govind Singh, but there was rebellion of Banda Bahadur and it was during the course of his campaign against Banda Bahadur, he died in c. 1712 CE.
- Mughal historians like Khafi Khan gave him the title of '*Shah-i-Bekhabar*'.

Jahandar Shah (c. 1712–1713 CE)

- With the death of Bahadur Shah, a new style of politics emerged in Mughals' political sphere. Now, the nobles became direct aspirants to the throne and they utilised the princes as mere pawns to capture authoritarian positions. Thus, the nobles became 'king makers' and the kings mere 'puppets' in their hands.

- Jahandar Shah was the first puppet ruler in Mughal India. He ascended the throne because of the support of the most powerful Iranian noble and his *Wazir*, Zulfiqar Khan, who had the reins of the executive in his hands.
- Zulfiqar Khan reversed many policies of Aurangzeb and also tried to establish friendly relations with the Rajputs, the Marathas and different Hindu chieftains. He abolished the *jizya* and accorded title of '*Mirza Raj Sawai*' on Jai Singh of Ambar and gave the *title* of '*Maharaja*' to Ajit Singh. He also granted the *chauth* and *sardeshmukhi* of Deccan to Shahu, along with reconciling with Churaman Jat and Chhatrasal Bundela. However, the old policy of suppression was continued against Banda Bahadur and the Sikhs.
- Zulfiqar Khan also made earnest attempts to improve the finances of the empire by checking the reckless grants of *jagirs* and offices while also compelling the *Mansabdars* to maintain the official quota of troops. But he is infamous in history for introducing the evil practice of *Ijarah (revenue farming)*.
- Lal Kanwar (a dancing girl), Jahandar Shah's favourite lady, dominated the court.

Farrukh Siyar (c. 1713–1719 CE)

- Brother of Jahandar Shah, who defeated Jahandar Shah at Agra in c. 1713 CE.
- He came to the throne with the help of Saiyyad brothers (the king makers), who promoted the policies initiated earlier by Zulfiqar Khan, but had him murdered and appointed themselves to key positions:
    - Saiyyad Abdullah Khan – *Wazir*
    - Hussain Ali Khan – *Mir Bakshi*
- The Saiyyad brothers tried to reconcile with the Rajputs, the Marathas and the Jats, and were also able to suppress the Sikh revolt. It was during Farrukh Siyar's reign that Banda Bahadur, the Sikh leader, was executed.
- In c. 1717 CE, the Emperor heedlessly granted to East India Company many trading privileges, including the exemption from custom duties for its trade through Bengal.
- Saiyyad brothers completely abolished *jaziya* and also abolished pilgrimage tax at a number of places.
- However, due to the overwhelming powers of Saiyyad brothers, friction arose between Farrukh Siyar and the Saiyyad brothers. The emperor thrice plotted against Saiyyad brothers, but failed to overpower them.
- In the meantime, in c. 1719 CE, the Saiyyad brothers forged an alliance with Balaji Vishwanath, by which they succeeded in receiving Marathas active armed assistance in the struggle for supremacy going on in Delhi while in lieu of this favour Marathas gained

many concessions. Eventually, with the help of the Maratha troops, the Saiyyad brothers killed Farrukh Siyar.

- The murder of Farrukh Siyar created a wave of revulsion against the Saiyyads among the various factions of nobility, who were also jealous of their growing power.

Rafi-us-Darajat (c. 1719 CE)

- Placed by Saiyyad brothers in place of Farrukh Siyar. In fact, the Saiyyad brothers raised to the throne three young princes in quick succession within a short span of eight months in c. 1719 CE.
- Died of consumption (tuberculosis) within four months.
- During his reign, Nikusiyar (grandson of Aurangzeb) revolted and set up himself as Emperor at Agra with the help of Mitrasen (a Nagar Brahmin).

Rafi-us-Daula (c. 1719 CE)

- Hussain Ali Khan marched upon Agra and took Nikusiyar as prisoner.
- Given the title of Shah Jahan II.
- Shortest reign; died very quickly as he too suffered from consumption (tuberculosis).

Mohd. Shah Rangeela/Roshan Akhtar (c. 1719–1748 CE)

- Son of Jahan Shah (brother of Jahandar Shah), who loved dancing and was himself an expert Kathak dancer.
- Under the leadership of the Nizam-ul-Mulk, Chin Qilich Khan and his father's cousin Muhammad Amin Khan, he was successful in dislodging the Saiyyad brothers in c. 1720 CE. Hussain Ali was murdered and Abdullah Khan was made a prisoner. He appointed Mohd. Amin Khan (who had killed Hussain Ali) as *wazir* under title of *Itmad-ud-Daula*.
- However, autonomous states emerged under his reign:
- Nizam-ul-Mulk – Deccan
- Saadat Khan – Awadh
- Murshid Quli Khan – Bengal, Bihar and Orissa
- The weakness of the empire was exposed when Nadir Shah not only invaded India but also imprisoned the Mughal Emperor and looted Delhi in c. 1739 CE.
  - Nadir Shah Invasion (c. 1739 CE): Nadir Shah was the Emperor of Iran who rose from being the son of poor shepherd to a national hero by driving the Afghans out of Iran.
- Reasons for invasion:
  - Mohd. Shah Rangeela suddenly withdrew his ambassador from the Persian court and snapped all diplomatic ties with that country after Nadir Shah came to power

in c. 1736 CE. He sent three envoys to the Mughal court and his third envoy was detained by Rangeela, which probably infuriated him.
    - Also, **Rangeela gave shelter** to some Afghan nobles who had escaped from Nadir Shah when he had invaded Afghanistan.
    - Nizam-ul-Mulk and Saadat Khan sent special messages to Nadir Shah **inviting him** to invade India.
- Course of Nadir Shah's Invasion:
    - He captured Jallalabad, Peshawar and proceeded towards Lahore.
    - Zakariya Khan, the governor of Lahore, surrendered without much fight.
    - Nadir struck a gold coin and read *khutba* in his name.
    - Nadir and Mohd. Shah met at **Karnal** on c. 1739 CE, but Mohd. Shah was defeated and he agreed to pay an indemnity of Rs. 25 crore, and trans-Indus provinces including Sindh, western Punjab, and Kabul were ceded to him. Nadir Shah's troops remained in the capital until the money was paid and indulged in a **gruesome massacre** of the general population, including women and children at Delhi.
    - He also **took away** the famous **Kohinoor Diamond.**
    - He was an able general and administrator, but an inhumane butcher in the course of war.
- **Ahmad Shah Abdali raided** the kingdom for the **first time** during his reign as well.

Ahmad Shah (c. 1748–1757 CE)

- Born to Mohd. Shah Rangeela (only son) through a dancing girl named Kudsiya Begam.
- **Ahmad Shah Abdali invaded Delhi** many times, and Punjab along with Multan was ceded to him.
- The **Marathas** snatched **Malwa** and Bundelkhand.
- It is believed that his *Wazir*, Imad-ul-Mulk, had him blinded and imprisoned him at Salimgarh.

Alamgir II (c. 1754–1759 CE)

- Son of Jahandar Singh.
- **Repeated invasions** of Ahmad Shah Abdali.
- The famous **Battle of Plassey** (c. 1757 CE) was fought during his tenure.
- He was also murdered by his *Wazir* Imad-ul-Mulk.

FIGURE 14.1 Battle of Plassey inscribed at the base row of temple of the Malla dynasty at Bishnupur in India

Aligauhar/Shah Alam II (c. 1759–1806 CE)

- During his reign, his power was so depleted that it led to a saying in Persian, *'Sultanat-e-Shah Alam, Az Dilli ta Palam'*, meaning, *'The kingdom of Shah Alam is from Delhi to Palam'*, Palam being a suburb of Delhi.
- Due to the fear of his *Wazir*, he remained a refugee with Shuja-ud-Daula of Awadh from c. 1761 CE until c. 1764 CE. He did not return to Delhi till c. 1771 CE, when the Marathas re-established their hold and invited him to the capital.
- The Third Battle of Panipat (c. 1761 CE) was fought during his reign (between the Marathas and Ahmad Shah Abdali).
- He also participated in the Battle of Buxar (c. 1764 CE) along with the combined armies of Mir Qasim, the Nawab of Bengal and Shuja-ud-Daula, the Nawab of Awadh, against the British East India Company. But he was defeated and was forced to sign the Treaty of Allahabad (c. 1765 CE), under which the diwani[1] of Bengal (which included Bihar and Odisha) was granted to the British East India Company.

Akbar II (c. 1806–1837 CE)

- Remained only under British protection as in c. 1803 CE, the British had captured Delhi.
- He conferred the title of 'Raja' on Ram Mohan Roy.

---

[1] Revenue collection rights.

- He was a great poet and is credited with the introduction of the Hindu-Muslim unity festival *Phool Walon Ki Sair*.

Bahadur Shah II/Zafar (c. 1837–1857 CE)

- The last Mughal Emperor who was more a nominal head than anything else, as the Mughal Empire existed in name only and his authority was limited only to the city of Delhi (Shahjahanbad).

FIGURE 14.2 Bahadur Shah Zafar

- He was an accomplished Urdu poet using 'Zafar' (meaning victory) as his pen name, and wrote many Urdu ghazals.
- Participated in the revolt of c. 1857 CE; after the revolt, he was deported to Rangoon, where he died in c. 1862 CE.

Decline of the Mughals

The causes for the decline and the downfall of the Mughal Empire was the combination of varied political, social and economic factors:

Factors Responsible for the Decline of the Mughals	
(a) Weak successors	• None of Aurangzeb's successors could give any stability to the empire. • They were absolutely inefficient and most of them were mere puppets in the hands of powerful nobles who often ran the administration on their behalf. • None of them had the ability to overcome the centrifugal forces to unite the empire. • The wars of succession that plagued Delhi from c. 1707 to 1719 CE gradually weakened the empire.
(b) Role of nobility	• Another crucial factor for the disintegration of the Mughal Empire was the constant infighting between the nobles. They had assumed a lot of powers and the course of politics and state activities were guided by their individual interests. • The Mughal court consisted of four groups of nobles: - the *Turanis*, - the *Iranis*, - the *Afghans*, and - the *Indian born Muslims*. With the accession of weak rulers at the centre, these four groups fought amongst themselves for more power, *jagirs* and high offices. They, thus eventually weakened the Empire.
(c) Ineffective Mughal army, neglect of naval power and foreign invasions	• The Mughal army gradually became inefficient and demotivated after losing many important battles. • The neglect of naval power by the Mughals also cost them dearly. • Further, the external invasions of Nadir Shah and Ahmad Shah Abdali not only took a heavy toll of the imperial treasury but also exposed the inefficiencies of the Mughal military and political administration.
(d) Lack of strong finances	Due to the emergence of many autonomous states, the revenue sources depleted, and due to continuous wars, the treasury was further emptied.
(e) Orthodox rule of Aurangzeb	To some extent, the religious and Deccan policies of Aurangzeb contributed to the empire's decline. He was ambitious and wanted to increase the geographical limits of his empire without taking into consideration the practicability of such moves. His hard-headed attitude towards the Marathas, Rajputs and the Jats turned away the loyal warriors, and he went on making more enemies without having strong alliances. His religious policy too alienated the Hindus, which certainly had an adverse effect on the stability of the empire.

Mughal Administration

Key term/Concept	Meaning
(a) Mir Bakshi	Head of military, pay and accounts office
(b) Khan-i-Saman	Head of imperial household
(c) Chief Qazi	Head of judiciary department
(d) Mir Maal	Lord privy seal
(e) Mustaufi	Auditor general
(f) Mushriff	Revenue secretary
(g) Waqa-i-Navis	News reporter
(h) Mir Arz	In-charge of petitions
(i) Mir Tozak	Master of ceremonies
(j) Amul Guzar	Head of revenue administration in *parganas*
(k) Bitakchi	Writer/record keeper
(l) Shiqdar/Shikdar	In-charge of law and order
(m) Nasq/Kankut	Wherein estimate was made of the produce by government officials
(n) Muqtai	Fixed revenue demand leased in cash
(o) Dahsala/Zabti system	Average produce per *bigha* of each category of land was ascertained based on past 10 years' produce. – One third of the average produce per *bigha* of land in respect to various crops in various categories of land, fixed as state demand. – Adopted by East India company in the Ryotwari system.

Rise of Regional Polities and States

The gradual weakening of the central Mughal authority further resulted in the creation of different provincial kingdoms. Interestingly, the Mughal court also did not oppose the formation of these states as its chief concerns at that point of time was two-fold: firstly, assurance of the flow of the necessary revenue from the provinces and secondly, the maintenance of at least the semblance of imperial unity and both of these concerns were being met by these new states.

The states that arose in India during the phase of Mughal decline and the following century (between c. 1700 and 1850 CE) varied greatly in terms of their state resources, essential character and their life span. For instance, a state such as Hyderabad had been in a region where there had been an older regional tradition of provincial states in the immediate pre-Mughal period too, whereas many of the other post-Mughal states were based on either ethnic or sectarian groupings such as the Jats, the Marathas and the Sikhs. However, each of the contenders in the regions, in proportion to their strength, looked for and seized opportunities to establish their dominance over the others in the neighbourhood. Thus, the regional states of this period can be divided into three categories:

Categories of Regional States	
(a) States formed by former Mughal nobles	• There were some states whose founders were important high *mansab* Mughal nobles, who, on the basis of their growing strength and administrative ability, established some of the formidable provincial kingdoms. • Though, they had declared independence from Mughal rule, yet they never broke formal ties from the Mughal state. • Some of the prominent states in this category were Bengal whose founder was Murshid Quli Khan, Awadh whose founder was Saadat Khan and Hyderabad whose founder was Nizam-ul-Mulk Asaf Jah. All three of these founder members were either former governors of these provinces or powerful members of the Mughal nobility. • An interesting aspect pertaining to administration of these states was that in these states, many reforms were undertaken in the field of revenue assessment and even the *zamindari* system. For instance in these states, revenue was collected with great strictness in cash from all *zamindars* and as a result of this, many *zamindars* had to eventually borrow money and thus, there was rise of the moneylenders or *mahajans* and bankers in these states since both the state and the landed class depended on them for loans. Gradually, there was a rise in the status of these bankers who not only became powerful but also started to influence the administration which further led to development of a new system known as *Ijaradari system* wherein the state auctioned its right to collect taxes to the highest bidders known as *Ijaredars*, who were usually bankers and *mahajans* while in turn, the state was assured of a fixed income. • It is however pertinent to note that this system was not promoted during Mughal rule as there were chances that those who collected the tax would collect much more than fixed settled amount, exploiting the peasants, while giving less to the state, thereby causing losses to the state revenue.
(b) *Watan jagirs*	The second category of regional states in the 18th century was those states who had previously served extremely well under the Mughals and as a result were allowed to enjoy considerable autonomy in their watan jagirs such as the Rajput states.
(c) Rebellious states	The third category of regional states was those that had emerged after rebelling against the Mughal authority. The Sikhs, the Jats and the Marathas belonged to this group, and out of them, the Marathas over the course of time emerged as a formidable power.

The Marathas

The single most important power that emerged in the fading shadow of the Mughal dynasty was the Marathas. Various factors contributed to the rise of the Marathas in the 16th and

17th centuries. The physical environment of the Maratha country, such as mountainous regions and dense forests, probably resulted in shaping certain peculiar qualities among the Marathas. For instance, this difficult terrain made the Maratha soldiers expert in guerilla tactics. The Marathas held important positions in the administrative and military systems of Deccan Sultanates of Bijapur and Ahmadnagar, which offered them a first-hand experience of administration, further facilitating in the emergence and organisation of the Maratha state. Also, the spread of the Bhakti movement in Maharashtra under the influence of spiritual leaders like Tukaram, Ramdas, Vaman Pandit and Eknath fostered social unity among them and the much-required political unity was conferred by Shahji Bhonsle and his son Shivaji. Seizing upon the opportunity of disintegration of the Mughal empire, the Marathas began their northward expansion and overran Malwa, Gujarat and Bundelkhand, and in due course of time posed a formidable challenge to the authority of the Mughals.

Shivaji and Rise of Marathas

Shivaji Raje Bhonsle (c. 1674–1680 CE)

- Born in the hill fortress of Shivmer in Poona on February 19, 1630 CE.

FIGURE 14.3 Statue of Shivaji Bhonsle, also known as Chhatrapati Shivaji Maharaj

- Belonged to the Bhonsle clan of Marathas.
- Father – Shahji Bhonsle (was a military commander under the Nizam Shahi ruler of Ahmednagar, but after the fall of Ahmednagar, he had transferred his services to Bijapur).

- Mother – Jijabai.
- Named 'Shiva' after the local goddess 'Shivai'.
- Shivaji was greatly influenced by Jijabai (his mother), Dadaji Kondev (his teacher), Sufi saint Pir Shaikh Yacub, Guru Ramdas, Tukaram (Bhakti Saint) and the Hazrat Baba of Ratnagiri. The *Ramayana* and the *Mahabharata also had a great influence* on the development of his personality.
- He started his career as an independent young prince at Poona after inheriting the *jagir* of Poona from his father in c. 1637 CE. After the death of his guardian, Dadaji Kondadev in c. 1647 CE, Shivaji assumed full charge of his *jagir*.
- In c. 1646 CE, he captured Torna *from* the ruler of Bijapur and with the booty he built the fort of Raigarh. He also captured Javli from a Maratha chief named Chanda Rao More. This made him the master of the Mavala region.
- By c. 1654 CE, Shivaji had captured forts in the Western Ghats and along the Konkan coast. Shivaji and his elder brother defeated invading armies of Adil Shah and secured the release of their father.
- He also raided Portuguese settlement at Daman and received tribute from them.
- Battle of Pratapgarh (c. 1659 CE): Fought between Afzal Khan (represented Adil Shah of Bijapur) and Shivaji, in which Shivaji killed Afzal Khan with his tiger claws and became a local hero. The military conquests of Shivaji made him a legendary figure in the Maratha region and as a result many locals came forward to join his army.
- Battle of Kolhapur: Fought between General Rustemjaman (represented Adil Shah of Bijapur) and Shivaji. The victory of Shivaji alarmed Aurangzeb, but he still considered Shivaji nothing more than a mountain rat.
- Battle of Pavankhind (c. 1660 CE): Fought between Siddi Johar (represented Adil Shah of Bijapur) and Shivaji. A truce was made between Shivaji and Adil Shah through Shahji, thus acknowledging and formally recognising the independence of Shivaji's kingdom.
- In c. 1660 CE, Aurangzeb sent the Mughal governor of the Deccan, Shaista Khan, against Shivaji. Shivaji suffered a defeat at the hands of the Mughal forces and lost Poona, but war continued till c. 1663 CE. In c. 1663 CE, Shivaji carried out a daring night attack on the camp of Shaista Khan, injuring Khan and killing his son. This daring attack affected the prestige of Khan and he was recalled by Aurangzeb and sent to Bengal as punishment.
- In c. 1664 CE, Shivaji sacked the rich port of Surat. This plundering of Surat, an important Mughal trading city, enraged Aurangzeb and he sent Raja Jai Singh of Amber and Diler Khan to destroy the Maratha power. Due to their elaborate preparations they succeeded in sieging the Purander fort[2]. Shivaji then opened negotiations with Jai Singh and the

[2] Where Shivaji had lodged his family and treasure.

Treaty of Purander was signed in c. 1665 CE. According to this treaty, *Shivaji was asked to surrender 23 forts to the Mughals out of the 35 forts he held, and the remaining 12 forts were to remain with Shivaji on the condition of service and loyalty to the Mughal empire*. On the other hand, the Mughals recognised the right of Shivaji to hold certain parts of the Bijapur kingdom. Once Shivaji declined from personal service of the Mughals, his minor son Sambhaji was granted a *mansab* of 5000.

- According to some legends, in c. 1665 CE, Shivaji visited Agra with his son but were humiliated by Aurangzeb who put them under house arrest. It is believed that his plan was to send Shivaji to Qandahara, but Shivaji escaped along with his son while disguised as a palanquin bearer.
- Aurangzeb was exasperated and he gave him the title of Raja and Jagir of Berar.
- Between c. 1667 and 1669 CE, Shivaji adopted a low profile and built his army. In c. 1670 CE, he recovered most of his lost forts and sacked Surat for the second time.
- He defeated Mughals in the Battle of Salher (c. 1672 CE) and crowned himself at Raigarh and assumed the title Maharaja Chattrapati.
- Towards end of c. 1676 CE, Shivaji launched a wave of conquests in southern India's Carnatic region and captured the forts of Vellore and Ginjee, which served as the Maratha's capital for nine years.
- He died due to fever in c. 1680 CE, at the age of 53, after ruling for only six years. In this short time, he founded the Maratha kingdom, which dominated western India for a century and a half.
- Shivaji promoted Sanskrit, but respected all religions and opposed forced conversion.

Sambhaji (c. 1681–1689 CE)

- Many Maratha chiefs did not support Sambhaji and instead lent support to Rajaram, the other son of Shivaji. This internal conflict weakened Maratha power.
- Was nicknamed as *'Kalusha'*, meaning Instigator of strife.
- Prince Akbar, the rebellious son of Aurangzeb, took shelter with him and in a pursuing battle at Sangmeshwar in c. 1689 CE, he was defeated by the Mughal commander Muqqarrab Khan and was killed along with his personal counselor, Kavi Kalash.
- Widow of Sambhaji, Yesubai could not protect the fort of Raigarh, and she along with her son, Shahu were made prisoners.

Rajaram (c. 1689–1707 CE)

- Younger brother of Sambhaji, who never sat on the throne as he claimed that he was ruling on behalf of Shahu.

- Shifted his headquarters to Ginjee. After the Mughals conquered Ginjee, he fled to Vishalgarh and then to Satara, giving *Hukumat Panha* (King status) to Peshwa Ramchandra Pant.
- During his reign, devoted Maratha leaders like Ramchandra Pant, Prahlad Niraji and Dhanaji Jadhav created havoc among Mughals.
- Died in c. 1700 CE; his widow Tarabai assumed control in the name of her infant son Shivaji II.
- Around same time, Shahu was released by Zulfiqar Khan hoping for a civil war among Marathas. As expected, the Mughals succeeded in dividing the Marathas into two rival camps – one under Tara Bai and the other under Sambhaji's son, Shahu. Tarabai sent Dhanaji Jhadav to oust Shahu from Maharashtra, but Dhanaji was won over by Shahu. In c. 1707 CE, with the help of a Chitpavan Brahman named Balaji Vishwanath, Shahu was successful in defeating Tarabai at the Battle of Khed and she went away to Kolhapur, establishing the Royal House of Kolhapur.

Shahu (c. 1707–1749 CE)

- During his reign, the states of Satara and Kolhapur came into being. By c. 1710 CE, two separate principalities had become an established fact, eventually confirmed by the Treaty of Warna in c. 1731 CE.
- The period was also marked by the ascendancy of a lineage of Chitpavan Brahmin ministers, who held the title of *Peshwa* (chief minister) and virtually came to control central authority in the Maratha state, reducing the Bhonsles to mere figureheads. In fact, the first truly prominent figure of this line was Balaji Vishwanath, who had helped Shahu in his rise to power.
- In c. 1719 CE, Shahu, under the advice of Peshwa Balaji Vishwanath, assisted the Saiyyad brothers in the execution of Farukkh Siyar and got his mother released. Soon after, he declared *Swaraja*/the Independence of Maratha land.

Rajaram II/Ramraja (c. 1749–1777 CE)

- Adopted son of Shahu, who was presented by Tarabai as the grandson of Rajaram and herself to grab power after Shahu's death. After being sidelined, she stated that he was only an imposter. However, Peshwa Baji Rao retained him as the titular Chattrapati.

The power of the Chhatrapati was almost totally overshadowed by that of the Peshwa.

Royal House of Kolhapur

Shivaji II (c. 1710–1714 CE)

- Son of Queen Tarabai and Rajaram, and was under the regency of Queen Tarabai.

Sambhaji II (c. 1714–1760 CE)

- Son of Rajaram from his second wife Rajabai, who deposed Shivaji II and Tarabai.
- He signed the Treaty of Warna in c. 1731 CE with his cousin Shahu to formalise the two separate seats of the Bhonsle family.

The British sent expeditions against Kolhapur in c. 1765 CE and c. 1792 CE. However, after the collapse of the Maratha confederacy in c. 1812 CE, the state eventually entered into treaty with the British.

The Office of the Peshwa (c. 1640–1818 CE)

The word *'Peshwa'* probably originated in Persian, meaning 'foremost', and was introduced in Deccan by the Muslim rulers. The duties of a Peshwa were equal to that of a Prime Minister.

Sonopant Dabir (c. 1640–1652 CE)

- First unofficial Peshwa

Shyampant Kulkarni Ranzekar (c. 1652–1657 CE)

- Was Peshwa under Shahji Bhonsle

Moropant Trimbak Pingle (c. 1657–1683 CE)

- Was appointed Peshwa by Chhatrapati Shivaji

Moreshwar Pingale (c. 1683–1689 CE)

- Was Peshwa under Sambhaji

Ramchandra Pant Amatya (c. 1689–1708 CE)

- Peshwa under Rajaram, and when Rajaram had to escape to Ginjee in c. 1689 CE, he gave *Hukumat Panha* (King status) to Pant before leaving.
- Was an able administrator as he managed the state under many challenges like the influx of Mughals, betrayal from *Vatandars* (local *satraps* under Marathas), and socio-economic challenges like the scarcity of food.
- Acted as 'shadow/proxy king', and got military help from great Maratha warriors Santaji Ghorpade and Dhanaji Jadhav.
- In c. 1698 CE, Rajaram offered the post of Peshwa to his wife Tarabai, and he happily stepped down. Meanwhile, Tarabai gave him an important position in the senior administration of the Maratha state.
- Wrote *Adnyapatra*, in which he explained different techniques of war, maintenance of forts and administration.
- Since he owed loyalty to Tarabai against Shahuji, he was sidelined after arrival of Shahuji in c. 1707 CE.

Balaji Vishwanath Bhatt (c. 1713–1719 CE)

- He belonged to the Bhatt family of Shri Vardhan in the Konkan region. He is known in history for making the post of the Peshwa hereditary, and for making the position as one of the most important and powerful ones in the Maratha administration.
- He played a crucial role in the civil war as he sought the support of all Maratha leaders for appointment of Shahu and thus helped Shahu become the Maratha ruler.
- In c. 1719 CE, Balaji Vishwanath was also successful in obtaining certain crucial Maratha rights from the then Mughal Emperor, Farrukh Siyar, such as the recognition of Shahu as the Maratha king and the permission to collect *chauth* and *sardeshmukhi* from the six Mughal provinces of the Deccan, including the Carnatic and Mysore.
- The Chapekar brothers and Nana Sahib belonged to this family.
- Negotiated with Kanhoji Angre (admiral of the navy and an ally of Tarabai) and gradually succeeded in winning over Kanhoji to become the admiral (*Sarkhel*) of Shahu's navy.
- Assisted Saiyyad brothers in dethroning Farrukh Siyar from Delhi.

Baji Rao I (c. 1720–1740 CE)

- Eldest son of Balaji Vishwanath who succeeded him as Peshwa at the young age of twenty. He was the most famous of all nine Peshwas and also known as '*Thorale*', meaning 'Elder' Baji Rao. He was one of the greatest exponents of guerrilla tactics after Shivaji.
- During his lifetime, he never lost a battle and the Maratha power reached its zenith under him. He formulated the policy of Northward expansion so that the Maratha flag would fly from Krishna to Attock.

FIGURE 14.4 Equestrian statue of Peshwa Bajirao I outside the Shaniwar Wada fort at Pune, Maharashtra

- He preached and popularised the idea of *Hindu-pad-padshahi* (Hindu Empire) to secure the support of the Hindu chiefs against the common enemy, the Mughals.
- His arch rival in Deccan was Nizam-ul-Mulk, who continuously plotted intrigues with the Raja of Kolhapur against Baji Rao and Shahu. Baji Rao, however, defeated the Nizam on both occasions when they fought at Palkhed and Bhopal, and compelled him to grant *chauth* and *sardeshmukhi* of the six provinces of Deccan.
- In c. 1722 CE, he captured Salsette and Bassein from the Portuguese.
- He shifted the administrative capital from Satara to Pune in c. 1728 CE.
- Two famous lines pertaining to him are:
  - Shahu (to Bajirao): '*You are a worthy son of worthy father*'.
  - Bajirao (to Shahu): '*Let us strike at the root and the branches will fall apart themselves*'.
- He initiated the system of confederacy among the Maratha chiefs. Under this system, each Maratha chief could administer his assigned territory autonomously. Consequently, many Maratha families became prominent and established their authority in different parts of India. They were the Gaekwads at Baroda, the Bhonsles at Nagpur, the Holkars at Indore, the Scindias at Gwalior and the Peshwas at Poona.

Balaji Baji Rao I/Nana Sahib I (c. 1740–1761 CE)

- Balaji Baji Rao succeeded his father as Peshwa at the young age of nineteen and was appointed as Peshwa by Shahuji.
- It was during his reign that the Maratha king Shahu died in c. 1749 CE without an issue. His nominated successor, Ramaraja, was even though accepted by Balaji Baji Rao but gradually the supreme power of Maratha confederacy passed into the hands of Peshwa (by the Sangola Agreement of c. 1750 CE).
- He defeated Bengal Nawab Alivardi Khan and about one third of the Indian sub-continent came under the rule of Marathas.
- In c. 1752 CE, the Peshwa entered into an agreement with the Mughal Emperor. According to this agreement, '*the Peshwa gave assurance to the Mughal Emperor that he would protect the Mughal Empire from internal and external enemies for which the chauth of the north-west provinces and the total revenue of the Agra and Ajmer provinces would be collected by the Marathas*'.
- Honouring this agreement only, Marathas fought the Third Battle of Panipat (c. 1761 CE) when Ahmad Shah Abdali invaded India. However, in this battle, the Marathas were defeated and many Maratha leaders and soldiers died. Unable to cope with the defeat and the loss of his son, Vishwasrao, and his brother, Sadashivrao Bhau, Balaji Baji Rao soon after died.

- The defeat of Panipat not only checked the expansion of Marathas but also fragmented the empire since after the battle, the Marathas never fought again as one unit. Meanwhile, the branches of the Bhonsle family relocated to Kolhapur and Nagpur, while the main line remained in the Deccan heartland, at Satara.

Madhav Rao (c. 1761–1772 CE)

- Was a remarkable Peshwa who within a short period of 11 years restored the lost fortunes of the Maratha Empire.
- He not only defeated the Nizam but also compelled the Haidar Ali of Mysore to pay tribute, while reasserting control over northern India by defeating the Rohillas and subjugating the Rajput state and Jat chiefs.
- In c. 1772 CE, he brought back Emperor Shah Alam to Delhi.
- Saw the division of Maratha kingdom into semi independent states. Of these, the most important were the Gaikwads (Gaekwars), the Holkars and the Scindias.

Raghunath Rao (c. 1772–1773 CE)

- After Madhav Rao's death (c. 1772 CE), struggle for power ensued between Raghunath Rao, the younger brother of Nana Sahib and Narayan Rao, the younger brother of Madhav Rao.

Narayan Rao (c. 1772–1773 CE)

- He was killed on Raghunath Rao's orders in c. 1773 CE.

Raghunath Rao (c. 1773–1774 CE)

- Seized the throne but was not recognised by the Emperor and overthrown.

Sawai Madhav Rao (c. 1774–1795 CE)

- Son of Narayan Rao, who was merely 40 days old when crowned as Peshwa. The empire was managed by Nana Phadnavis, an able administrator and warrior par excellence with the help of a twelve member regency council called the *Barbhai Council*.
- Out of frustration, Raghunath Rao went to British for help which resulted in the First Anglo-Maratha war (c. 1775–1782 CE). At the famous battle of Talegaon (c. 1776 CE), Nana Phadnavis defeated the British and the famous treaty of Purandhar (c. 1776 CE) and the treaty of Salbai (c. 1782 CE) were signed. The treaty virtually restored the status quo except the fact that the English retained Salsette and dropped the cause of Raghunath Rao.
- It was after death of Nana Phadnavis in c. 1800 CE that the Marathas could not sustain against the British and could never regain their past glory.

Baji Rao II (c. 1796–1818 CE)

- Son of Raghunath Rao and the last Peshwa.
- Weakest and most incompetent Peshwa who signed the humiliating Treaty of Bassein with the British (c. 1802 CE), which gave the British effective control of not only the Maratha region but also of Deccan and western India.
- He was defeated by the East India Company in the Third Anglo-Maratha War in c. 1818 CE after which he was pensioned off and the Peshwa's territory in central Maharashtra was annexed to the British East India Company's Bombay province.
- Later, his adopted son Nana Sahib (alias Dhondu Pant) participated in the famous Revolt of 1857 against the British.

However, even the Marathas could not succeed in preventing the establishment of British power in India. One of the important reasons behind this was that there was lack of unity among the Maratha chiefs. Also, in comparison with British, their army was ill-equipped and still relied on old fighting methods.

Maratha Confederacy

Maratha Confederacy	
(a) Peshwas of Poona	Already discussed above.
(b) The Gaikwads of Baroda	• The Gaikwads had gathered prominence in c. 1720 CE. Initially, they were subordinate not only to the Bhonsles but also to the powerful Dabhade family. But, after the death of Shahu, the power of the Peshwas was further enhanced, thereby improving the position of the Gaikwads and by the early 1750s, Peshwa recognised their rights on the large portion of the revenues of Gujarat. • The Gaikwads, thus established their capital at Baroda. Gradually, in c. 1752 CE, they expelled the Mughal governor of the Gujarat province from the capital, Ahmedabad, which eventually resulted in realignment in the network of trade and consumption in the area. • One of the most prominent rulers was Damaji (c. 1768 CE), who was later succeeded by Fateh Singh (c. 1771–1789 CE). Fateh Singh broke out of the hold of the Peshwa in the late 1770s and early 1780s, and negotiated a settlement with the English East India Company, which eventually led to increased British interference in his affairs. Thus, by c. 1800 CE, instead of the Peshwa, the British were the final arbiters in determining succession among the Gaikwads who eventually became their subordinate rulers in the 19th century. • It is pertinent to mention that Sayaji Rao belonging to this dynasty gave scholarship to Dr. Ambedkar.

Maratha Confederacy	
(c) The Holkars of Indore	• The Holkars achieved marked and rapid rise in their status and wealth in short span of time. Though starting initially with very little political power, the Holkars consolidated their position at Indore by the c. 1730s under the able guidance of their prominent ruler, Malhar Rao Holkar who secured a large share of the *chauth* collection in Malwa, eastern Gujarat and Khandesh. • Later, his successors too consolidated and spread the hold of Holkars along with controlling the important trade routes as well as the crucial trading centre of Burhanpur. One of such prominent successors was iconic Ahalya Bai, his son's widow who ruled Indore from c. 1765 to 1794 CE and brought great glory to the Holkars.
(d) The Bhonsles of Nagpur	The Bhonsles of Nagpur were clearly subordinate to the Satara rulers. An important ruler from this line was Raghuji Bhonsle (c. 1727–1755 CE), who was responsible for the Maratha incursions on Bengal and Bihar in the 1740s and early 1750s. He occupied Orissa from Nawab Alivardi Khan.
(e) The Scindias of Gwalior	• In the decades following the Third Battle of Panipat (c. 1761 CE), the Scindias carved a prominent place for themselves in north India. Like the Holkars, the Scindias were also based largely in central India, first at Ujjain, and later (from the last quarter of the 18th century) in Gwalior. • The family's fortunes were consolidated during the long reign of Mahadaji Scindia (c. 1761–1794 CE), who was an effective and innovative military commander. He organised a powerful European style army employing a large number of European officers, soldiers, and gunners and consisting equally of Hindu and Muslim soldiers. He also established his own ordinance factories near Agra. • In the mid-1780s, the Mughal Emperor Shah Alam II made him the *Naib-i Munaib*, meaning deputy regent of his affairs and thus his influence was noticed not only across the provinces of Delhi and Agra but also on Rajasthan and Gujarat, making him the most formidable Maratha leader of that era. It is believed that even the officials of the East India Company were very cautious in dealing with him however, his relations with the acting Peshwa, Nana Phadnavis of Pune and Holkar of Indore, were fraught with tensions. • The momentum generated by Mahadaji could not be unfortunately maintained by his successor Daulat Rao Scindia (c. 1794–1827 CE), who was defeated by the British and forced to surrender his territories.

An interesting point to note here is that the Mughal system of honours and titles, as well as Mughal derived administrative terminology and fiscal practices, continued despite the decline of imperial power. Even in the phase of Mughal decline, the Mughal symbols held a special significance. For instance, after recapturing Gwalior from the British, Mahadaji Scindia took special care to have his control of the town sanctioned by the Mughal Emperor. Equally, he zealously guarded the privileges and titles granted to him by Shah Alam, such as *amir al-umara* (head of the amirs) and *na'ib wakii-i mutlaq* (deputy regent). In this case, he was not alone, as instances of states that wholly threw off all pretences of allegiance to the Mughals are found rarely in the 18th century.

Shivaji's Administration

Administration

Shivaji was a great administrator who laid the foundations of a sound system of administration. The administrative system of the Marathas was very much influenced by the administrative system of the Mughals and the Deccani states (adopted by Malik Amber of Ahmednagar and Mahmud Gawan of Bahmani Kingdom). The Maratha Kingdom was known as *Swarajya* or *Mulk-e-Kadim*.

(i) Central Administration

The king was the pivot of the government, who was assisted by a council of ministers called the *Ashtapradhan*. Each one headed a department and was directly responsible to Shivaji. It is also pertinent to note that under Shivaji, these offices were neither hereditary nor permanent and were also frequently transferred.

Ashthapradhan	
(a) *Peshwa*	• *Pant Pradhan*, who looked after finance and general administration. • Later, the office of Peshwa became more powerful and functioned more as the prime minister. • There was also great focus on intelligence and a centralised intelligence department was created.
(b) *Sar-i-Naubat or Senapati*	Military commander, an honorary post.
(c) *Amatya/Majumdar*	Accountant General.
(d) *Waqenavis*	Intelligence and police, posts, historical archives and household affairs.
(e) *Surnavis or Chitnis or Sachiv*	General Secretary who also overlooked official correspondence.
(f) *Sumant/Dabir*	Master of ceremonies and Foreign Affairs.
(g) *Nyayadish*	Justice.
(h) *Pandit Rao*	Charities and ecclesiastical affairs.

Hierarchy of officers from top to bottom was:

Peshwa ⟶ Majumdar ⟶ Sachiv ⟶ Mantri

It is pertinent to note that all the ministers except *Pandita Rao* and *Nyayadhish* participated in war. The *Ashtapradhan* was not a creation of Shivaji and many of these officers such as *Peshwa, Majumdar, Waqai navis, Dabir* and *Surnavis* had existed earlier under the Deccani rulers too. Each of the *Ashtapradhan* was assisted by eight assistants namely *Diwan, Majumdar, Fadnis* (used to respond to the letters of commanders of the forts), *Sabnis, Karkhanis, Chitnis* (dealt with all diplomatic correspondences and wrote all royal letters), *Jamadar* and *Potnis* (looked after the income and expenditure of the royal treasury).

Prants (Province) ⟶ *Subedar* (Governor) supervised by *Sarsubedar*

↓

Tarfs (District) ⟶ *Havaldar* (Law and order)

↓

Parganas (Sub-districts) ⟶ *Deshpande* (Account and record keeper) and *Deshmukh* (Law and order)

↓

Mauzas (Village) ⟶ *Kulkarni* (Account and record keeper) and *Patil* (Law and order)

(ii) Provincial and Local Administration

The provincial administration was also patterned largely on the Deccani and Mughal system. Shivaji reorganised and renamed certain provinces. The provinces were known as *Prants*, which were under the charge of the *Subedar*. The *Sarsubedar* used to control and supervise the work of the *subedar*. After *Prants* came the *Tarfs*, which were headed by a *havaldar*. *Mauzas* or villages were the lowest unit of administration. The police officer in rural area was called *Faujdar* and in urban area was called *Kotwal*. Under the Marathas, performance-based Brahmin elites called *Kamvishdar* manned the central bureaucracy and the local administration and used to enjoy wide powers of tax assessment and collection. They kept records, adjudicated cases, and provided information about local conditions to the superior officials. Interestingly, the office of British District Collector was modelled on the *Kamvishdar*.

Army

Shivaji was a military genius and his army was very well organised. The Marathas were pioneers of commando actions. The regular standing army known as *Paga* consisted of about 30,000 to 40,000 cavalry supervised by the *havaldar*, who were given fixed salaries. The lowest head of the cavalry was called *Naik*. In fact, all the war horses belonged to the state. There were two divisions in the Maratha cavalry:

1. *Bargirs*: Equipped and paid by the state.
2. *Silahdars*: Maintained by the nobles.

The Marathas were famous for guerrilla warfare, along with the use of an innovative weapon, the *Bagh naka*, meaning tiger claw. The infantry was highly mobile and light, and the Mavli foot soldiers played an important role in the infantry. Interestingly, at the time of exigencies, peasants also functioned as part time soldiers as they used to work for eight months in the field and performed war duty in four months. Shivaji also built a powerful navy[3] for the purpose of guarding the Maratha ports, thereby checking piracy, and collecting customs duties from the incoming and outgoing ships. In the military operations of the Marathas, the forts also played an important role. Each fort was put under the charge of three officers of equal rank (*Sabnis, Kardadar, Sar-i-naubat*) for mutual check and as a precaution against treachery.

Revenue

The revenue system of Shivaji was also largely based on that of the Mughals and Deccani states such as that of Malik Amber of Ahmednagar. Land was measured by using the measuring rod called *lathi* and were classified into three categories – paddy fields, garden lands and hilly tracts. Shivaji drastically reduced the powers of the existing *Deshmukhs* and *Kulkarnis* and appointed his own revenue officials called *karkuns*. Shivaji strongly discouraged revenue farming. The Marathas employed a special script known as the 'Modi script' in the documents of the revenue and administrative records.

Chauth and *sardeshmukhi* were two major sources of revenue and it is interesting to note that these taxes were collected not in the Maratha kingdom but in the neighbouring territories of the Mughal empire or Deccan sultanates.

1. *Chauth:* One fourth (1/4th of the land revenue) paid to the Marathas in order to avoid the Maratha raids.
2. *Sardeshmukhi* was an additional levy of ten percent, that is, 1/10 of standard land revenue on those lands on which the Marathas claimed hereditary rights.

Bengal

In 1705, Aurangzeb appointed Murshid Quli Khan as Governor of Bengal and later placed Orissa, too, under his authority. Murshid Quli Khan shifted capital from Dacca to Murshidabad and, after the death of Aurangzeb, founded an independent state and became virtually independent

[3] Later, Balaji Vishwanath built naval bases at Konkan, Khanderi and Vijayadurg.

but kept on sending tribute to the Mughal emperor. After his death in 1727, his son-in-law Shuja-ud-din started ruling Bengal. However, in 1739, Ali Vardi Khan deposed the family of Shuja-ud-din and became the Nawab himself.

These Nawabs brought stability and peace to Bengal and, at the same time, promoted agriculture, trade and industry. During their reign, equal opportunities were given to both Hindus and Muslims in the administration. But, the Nawabs could not foresee the long-term implications of the presence of the European trading companies. Their ignorance of contemporary world affairs cost them a lot as they were totally ignorant about the devastation caused by the western trading companies in Africa and Latin America. Also, they neglected to build a strong army and failed to check the growing corruption among their officials. The foreign trading companies, especially English East India Company, took full advantage of their weakness and thus started interfering in their affairs. The successor of Ali Vardi Khan, Siraj-ud-daulah had to fight the English East India Company over the trading rights and his defeat at the Battle of Plassey in 1757 paved the way for subjugation of Bengal as well as India, the details of which will be subsequently discussed in the last chapter.

Awadh

The weakened control of the Mughals also resulted in the emergence of the provincial kingdom of Awadh (1722) under governor Saadat Khan, popularly known as Burhan ul Mulk, who was an energetic, bold and intelligent ruler. He not only disciplined the rebellious zamindars but also improved the lot of the peasants by levying equitable land revenue. His administration was efficient and troops were well paid, well armed and well trained. Before his death in 1739, Saadat Khan made his position hereditary. His successors Safdar Jung and Asaf ud Daulah not only played a very decisive role in the politics of northern India but also gave a long-term administrative stability to the Awadh province. Under the Nawabs, firstly Faizabad and then Lucknow emerged as the centres of cultural excellence comparable to Delhi in the spheres of arts, literature and crafts. Regional architecture also reflected itself in the form of *Imambarah's* and certain other buildings. In fact, the evolution of dance form Kathak was the outcome of this cultural synthesis.

Punjab

Even though the Mughal forces suppressed the Sikhs under Banda Bahadur and later executed him, yet the Sikh resistance against the Mughal authority continued. After the invasions of Nadir Shah and Ahmad Shah Abdali, the Sikhs once again asserted their authority and organised themselves into 12 *misls* or confederacies ruled by chiefs who exercised control over different

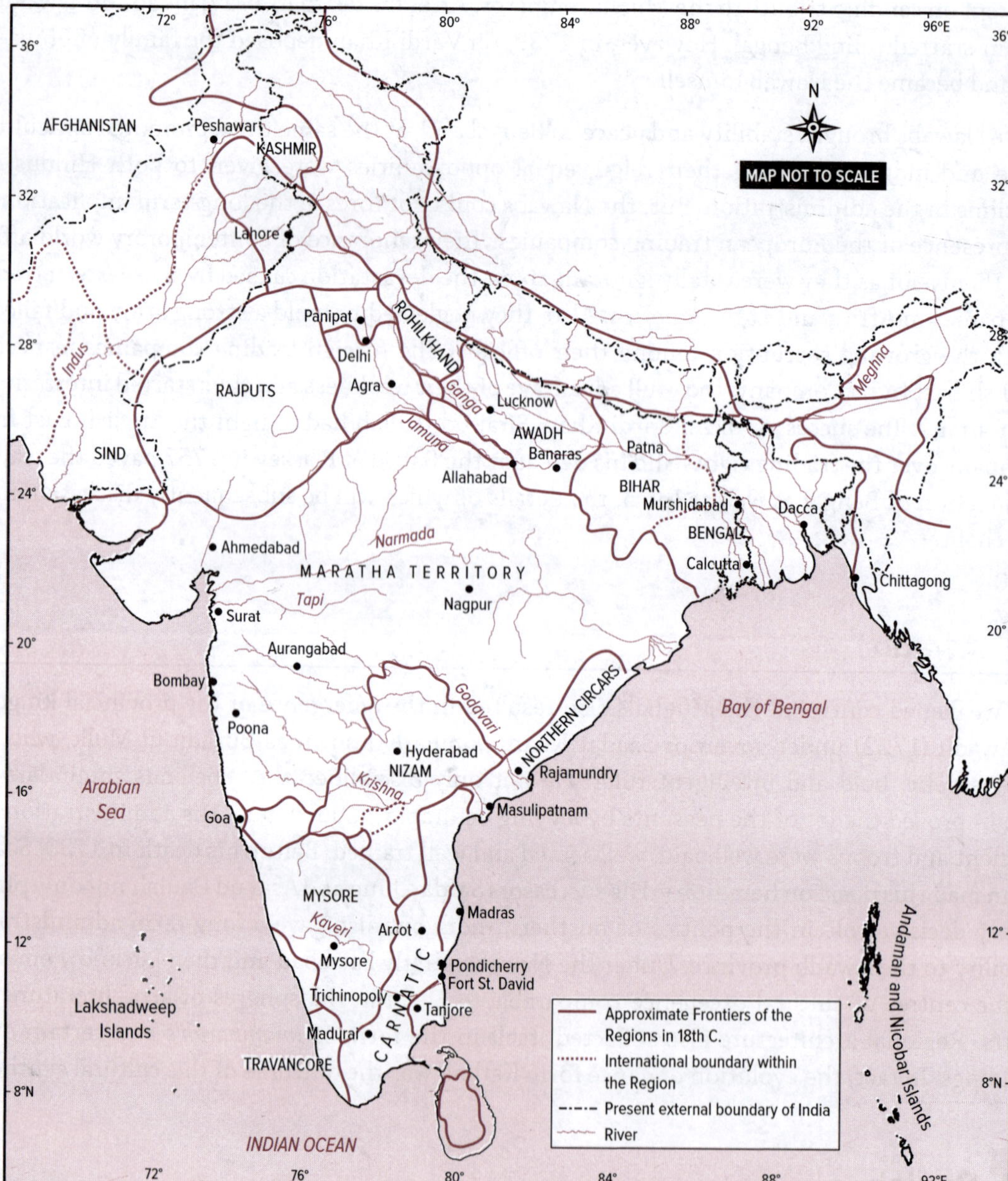

FIGURE 14.5 Regional Powers of the 18th Century

parts of the kingdom. It was one such chief, Ranjit Singh, of the Sukerchakia *misl*, who eventually welded these principalities into a larger entity, lasting though for a brief time. He captured Lahore in 1799 and Amritsar in 1802. Later, he conquered Kashmir, Peshawar and Multan. His rise to power was based on superior military force, partly serviced by European mercenaries, intelligent application of the principles of statecraft and by the strategic location of his territories. It is said that he possessed the second best army in Asia, next only to English East India company army. By 1809, he was the undisputed master of the most of Punjab. His effective rule lasted four decades, from 1799 to 1839. However, within 10 years of his death, the British annexed Punjab, the details of which, along with the annexation of Sindh, will be further discussed later in the last chapter.

Rajputs

Rajputs had proved to be a great support to the Mughals, specially in control of the peripheral areas. However, during the reign of Aurangzeb, the Mughal relations with Rajputs suffered, particularly over the issue of Aurangzeb's interference in the succession dispute of Marwar. His support to the rival candidate antagonised the Rajputs and his occupation of Jodhpur further put a dent on the Mughal-Rajput relation, alienating the Rajputs totally from the Mughal rule. However, most of the larger Rajput states, like other regional states, were constantly involved in petty quarrels and civil wars. In fact, Ajit Singh of Marwar was killed by his own son.

One of the principalities that came into prominence in the early 18th century was of Jaipur (earlier Amber) located in eastern Rajasthan. Its remarkable ruler Sawai Jai Singh (1699–1743, after whom Jaipur came to be named) was a distinguished statesman and reformer. He tried to enforce a law to reduce lavish expenditure which a Rajput had to incur on a daughter's marriage, which often indirectly resulted in female infanticide. Interestingly, he was a great astronomer and a man of science in an age when Indians were oblivious to scientific progress. He erected observatories with accurate and advanced instruments, some of them of his own invention at Jaipur, Delhi, Mathura, Ujjain and Varanasi. He drew up a set of tables, titled *Zij Muhammadshahi*, to enable people to make astronomical observations and, as a matter of fact, his own astronomical observations were remarkably accurate. He got translated Euclid's 'Elements of Geometry' into Sanskrit along with Napier's work on construction and use of logarithms and other various works on trigonometry. But after his death, the second half of the 18th century was marked by an economic depression on account of a series of crop failures in the 1750s and 60s, which further led to the decline of political power of Jaipur and it became a vulnerable target for the ambitions of the Marathas, and of Mahadaji Sindhia in particular.

Jats

The Jats were an agriculturist and pastoral caste who inhabited the region around Delhi, Agra and Mathura. Caste affinity with their zamindars brought solidarity within the community and they began to revolt against the Mughal state from the times of Jahangir. In fact, the first revolt of the Jat peasants took place in 1669 and the Emperor himself had to proceed to suppress the rebellion.

Later, using the discontent of their peasants against Mughal state, local zamindar, first Gokala and then Rajaram and Churaman Jat founded the Jat kingdom at Bharatpur. However, the Jat power reached its highest glory under king Suraj Mal (1756–63) who consolidated the Jat power during his reign and compelled the Mughal authorities to recognise him. He was not only an extremely able administrator, wise statesman but a great warrior too. He successfully withstood Ahmad Shah Abdali's army siege and supported the Marathas in the Third Battle of Panipat. He tried to centralise his powers and bring key reforms in the administration by reducing the state's dependence on the over mighty kinsmen, by raising an army with foreigners and introducing the Mughal system of revenue collection. But, with his untimely death, there was a virtual collapse of Jat state.

Rohilkhand and Farrukhabad

A couple of small Afghan kingdoms were also established in north India following the weakening of the Mughal empire. The Afghans were bands of roving warlords who had initially started migrating to India from the 15th century. In the 18th century, due to political instability and economic dislocations in Afghanistan, Afghani's migration to India increased. Also, the breakdown of authority in north India that followed Nadir Shah's invasion gave opportunity to another Afghan leader, Ali Muhammad Khan, to establish a small kingdom of Rohilkhand at the foothills of the Himalayas between the Ganga in the south and the Kumaon hills in the north, with its capital at first at Aolan in Bareilly and later at Rampur. But, the new kingdom had hardly any influence, as it suffered heavily at the hands of stronger neighbouring powers like Awadh, the Jats and later the English.

Another independent Afghan kingdom to the east of Delhi in the area around Farrukhabad (between Aligarh and Kanpur) was established by Ahmad Khan Bangash, during the reigns of Farrukhsiyar and Muhammad Shah. Both the Rohillas and Bangash helped Ahmad Shah Abdali during the Third Battle of Panipat, but their power declined quickly as Abdali retired from the Indian stage, leaving Najib-ud-daula in charge of affairs at Delhi.

South India

In the south, several states did make a determined effort during this period to consolidate their power by the use of access to sea and ports. Principal among these were Travancore in Kerala under Martanda Varma and Rama Varma, and Mysore under Haidar Ali and Tipu Sultan. However, these states rose to prominence only in the latter half of the 18th century, or at least after c. 1740 CE. Before them, there were three formidable powers[4] in the south:

[4] It is pertinent to note that neither of these rulers, while establishing dynastic succession, claimed full sovereignty and continued to present themselves as representatives of Mughal authority.

(a) The Marathas who were present both at Thanjavur and elsewhere,

(b) Sadullah Khan of Arcot (or Carnatic) who had ruled the Arcot principality around the 1700s, and

(c) The Nizam-ul-Mulk of Hyderabad who had consolidated his position at Hyderabad by the 1740s.

However, in the second half of the 18th century, the power of all three of these declined. The succession struggle at Arcot in the 1740s and early 1750s emptied the state coffers and its rulers succumbed to financial manipulation by private British merchants, to whom they were increasingly in debt for war expenses. Similarly, in the c. 1750s after the death of its founder, Nizam-ul-Mulk, the power of Hyderabad also declined. Regarding the fate of Marathas, we have already discussed.

Hyderabad

The state of Hyderabad was founded by *wazir* Chin Qilich Khan himself, who was one of the leading nobles of the post-Aurangzeb era and had earlier played a key role in the overthrow of the Saiyyad brothers. However, frustrated by his failure to reform the administration under Emperor Muhammad Shah, he relinquished his office of *waziriyat* and, in 1724, marched south to establish the state of Hyderabad in the Deccan and took the title of *Nizam-ul-Mulk Asaf Jah*. Similar on the lines of Murshid Quli Khan of Bengal, he never openly declared his independence from Mughals but acted more like a sovereign ruler who waged wars, concluded peace, conferred titles, and gave *jagirs* and offices without any reference to Delhi. He established an orderly administration in the Deccan and successfully not only kept the defaulting zamindars in line but also kept the powerful Marathas out of his dominions. However, after his death in 1748, the power of Hyderabad also declined and the state was not able to maintain its affairs independently. The control of the coastal districts was quickly lost, leaving the kingdom in economic loss.

Mysore

Originally, a vice royalty under the Vijaynagara empire in the 16th century, Mysore emerged as an important state under the rulers of the Wodeyar dynasty, such as Kanthirava Narasaraja and Chikka Devaraja. However, it reached its real period of glory under Haidar Ali, a cavalry commander of migrant origin, who assumed effective power in the kingdom in 1761 when he took over the political power in Mysore by ousting the corrupt *dalwai*, i.e. the prime minister Nanjraj (who had, in the meanwhile, usurped real power in the state by reducing the Wodeyar's to mere figureheads).

Haidar modernised his army with French experts and infused European discipline into the Mysore army which was organised on a European model through the system of *risalas*, with a clear chain of command going up to the top commander, i.e. the Sultan himself. He, and later his son Tipu

Sultan (around 1782), made attempts to consolidate Mysore and make it a kingdom with access to not one but both coasts of peninsular India. In fact, they were relatively successful against the Kodavas (the inhabitants of the upland kingdom of Kodagu, i.e. Coorg), Coastal Karnataka and northern Kerala, enabling Tipu to open diplomatic and commercial relations on his own with the Middle East. However, both Haidar and Tipu were always resisted by Poligars, the local chiefs, the Marathas and top of that, they had to also face formidable military adversary in the form of the English East India Company. Their detailed rivalry culminating in Anglo-Mysore wars will will be discussed in the last chapter.

Travancore

Martanda Varma, who ruled Travancore (southern Kerala state of Venad) from 1729 to 1758, initiated many measures to strengthen his authority so as to build a substantial standing army, reducing the power of the Nayar aristocracy on which the rulers of the area had earlier depended militarily, and fortifying the northern limits of his kingdom at the so-called "Travancore line." In order to limit European involvement in trade, he extended patronage to the Syrian Christians, a large trading community within his domains and also organised a strong army on the western model with the help of European officers. He defeated the Dutch and ended their political power in Kerala.In order to further keep the trade under his watch, he declared many goods as royal monopoly items, requiring a license for trade, such as pepper. He also built roads, canals and undertook many irrigation works. These policies were also continued by Martanda's successor, Rama Varma (1758–98), who was himself a poet, scholar, and a man of great knowledge. He conversed fluently in English, took keen interest in European affairs and regularly read newspapers and journals published in London. The 18th century saw a remarkable revival in Malayalam literature and Trivandrum, the capital of Travancore, became a famous centre of Sanskrit scholarship. However, around 1766, the kingdom of Travancore had to face invasions from Mysore which affected the state as Haidar Ali was able to annex northern Kerala upto Cochin.

QUESTIONS FROM LAST YEAR'S PRELIMS

1. With reference to Indian history, which of the following statements is/are correct? **(2021)**

1. The Nizamat of Arcot emerged out of Hyderabad State.
2. The Mysore Kingdom emerged out of Vijayanagara Empire.
3. Rohilkhand Kingdom was formed out of the territories occupied by Ahmad Shah Durrani.

Select the correct answer using the code given below:

(a) 1 and 2 (b) 2 only
(c) 2 and 3 (d) 3 only

2. What was the immediate reason for Ahmad Shah Abdali to invade India and fight the Third Battle of Panipat? **(2010)**

(a) He wanted to avenge the expulsion by Marathas of his viceroy Timur Shah from Lahore.

(b) The frustrated governor of Jullundhar, Adina Beg Khan, invited him to invade Punjab.
(c) He wanted to punish Mughal administration for non-payment of the revenues of the Chahar Mahal (Gujarat, Aurangabad, Sialkot and Pasrur).
(d) He wanted to annex all the fertile plains of Punjab, up to the borders of Delhi to his kingdom.

3. With reference to Sree Shakti Puraskar, for which one of the following is 'Devi Ahalya Bai Holkar Award' given? **(2009)**
(a) Administrative skills
(b) Achievements in Scientific Research
(c) Achievements in Sports and Games
(d) Courage and Valour

4. The Battle of Dharmat was fought between **(2003)**
(a) Mohammed Ghori and Jai Chand
(b) Babur and the Afghans
(c) Aurangzeb and Dara Shikoh
(d) Ahmed Shah Durrani and the Marathas

5. How did Mughal Emperor Jahandar Shah's reign come to an early end? **(2003)**
(a) He was deposed by his *wazir*.
(b) He died due to a slip while climbing down steps.
(c) He was defeated by his nephew in a battle.
(d) He died of sickness due to too much consumption of wine.

6. Assertion (A): Shah Alam II spent the initial years as an Emperor far away from his capital.

Reason (R): There was always a burning danger of foreign invasion from the North-West Frontier. **(2003)**
(a) Both A and R is true and R is the correct explanation of A
(b) Both A and R is true but R is not the correct explanation of A
(c) A is true but R is false
(d) A is false but R is true

7. Assertion (A): The Marathas emerged as the strongest native power in India after the decline of the Mughal empire.

Reason (R): The Marathas were the first to have a clear concept of a united Indian nation. **(2003)**
(a) Both A and R is true and R is the correct explanation of A
(b) Both A and R is true but R is not the correct explanation of A
(c) A is true but R is false
(d) A is false but R is true

8. Who among the following streamlined the Maratha administration after Sambhaji? **(2000)**
(a) Rajaram
(b) Balaji Vishwanath
(c) Ganga Bai
(d) Nanaji Deshmukh

9. The member of Shivaji's *Ashtapradhan* who looked after foreign affairs was: **(1998)**
(a) Peshwa (b) Sachiv
(c) Pandit Rao (d) Sumant

10. Match List I with List II and select the correct answer using the code given below the lists: **(1998)**

List I	List II
A. 1556	i. Battle of Haldi Ghati
B. 1600	ii. Nadir Shah's capture of Delhi
C. 1686	iii. Death of Shivaji
D. 1739	iv. Grant of Charter to East India Company
	v. Accession of Akbar

Code:	A	B	C	D
(a)	iii	iv	ii	i
(b)	v	iv	iii	ii
(c)	v	ii	i	iv
(d)	i	v	iii	ii

11. The 'Modi script' was employed in the documents of the: **(1995)**
(a) Wodeyars
(b) Zamorins
(c) Hoysalas
(d) Marathas

12. *Ashtapradhan* was a council of ministers: **(1995)**
(a) in the Gupta administration
(b) in the Chola administration
(c) in the Vijaynagar administration
(d) in the Maratha administration

ANSWERS

1. (b)	2. (d)	3. (d)	4. (c)	5. (c)	6. (c)	7. (c)	8. (b)
9. (d)	10. (b)	11. (d)	12. (d)				

QUESTIONS FROM LAST YEAR'S MAINS

1. Clarify how mid-eighteenth century India was beset with the spectre of a fragmented polity. **(2017 GS1)**

2. Krishnadeva Raya, the King of Vijayanagar, was not only an accomplished scholar himself but was also a great patron of learning and literature. Discuss. **(2016 GS1)**

3. Compare the Peshwa's bureaucratic management with that of the Imperial Mughal administration. **(2015, History optional)**

4. Give the social background to the rise of the Maratha movement during the seventeenth century. **(2012, History optional)**

PRACTICE QUESTIONS – PRELIMS

1. Match List I with List II and select the correct answer using the code given below the lists:

List I	List II
(a) Peshwa	i. Prime Minister
(b) Nyayadish	ii. Finance Minister
(c) Pandit Rao	iii. Religion Minister
(d) Sachiv	iv. Chief Judge

Code:	A	B	C	D
(a)	ii	iv	iii	i
(b)	ii	iii	iv	i
(c)	i	iv	iii	ii
(d)	i	iii	iv	ii

2. Match List I with List II and select the correct answer using the code given below the lists:

List I	List II
(a) *Shah-e-Bekhabar*	1. Saiyyad Brothers
(b) *Kalusha*	2. Bahadur Shah
(c) *Thorale*	3. Sambhaji
(d) *King Makers*	4. Baji Rao I

Code:	A	B	C	D
(a)	ii	iv	iii	i
(b)	ii	iii	iv	i
(c)	i	iv	iii	ii
(d)	i	iii	iv	ii

3. Consider the following:

i. The Third battle of Panipat was fought in c. 1761 CE was fought between the Marathas and Ahmad Shah Abdali.
ii. Shah Alam participated in the Battle of Buxar in c. 1764 CE.
iii. Jahandar Shah participated in the Battle of Plassey in c. 1757 CE.

Select the incorrect answer using the codes given below:

(a) i and ii only (b) iii only
(c) i and iii only (d) i, ii and iii

4. Consider the following:

1. Jahandar Shah introduced the evil practice of *Ijarah*, i.e., Revenue farming.
2. Farrukh Siyar came to the throne with the help of Zulfikar Khan.

Select the correct answer using the codes given below:

(a) 1 and 2 only (b) 1 only
(c) 2 only (d) None

5. Match List I with List II and select the correct answer using the code given below the lists:

List I	List II
(a) *Mir Bakshi*	i. Head of Military
(b) *Mushriff*	ii. Master of Ceremonies
(c) *Shiqdar*	iii. In-charge of law and order
(d) *Mir Tozak*	iv. Revenue Secretary

Code:	A	B	C	D
(a)	ii	iv	iii	i
(b)	ii	iii	iv	i
(c)	i	iv	iii	ii
(d)	i	iii	iv	ii

6. Match List I with List II and select the correct answer using the code given below the lists:

List I	List II
(a) The Gaikwads of Baroda	i. Mahadaji
(b) The Holkars of Indore	ii. Damaji
(c) The Bhonsles of Nagpur	iii. Raghuji
(d) The Scindias of Gwalior	iv. Malhar Rao

Code:	A	B	C	D
(a)	ii	iv	iii	i
(b)	ii	iii	iv	i
(c)	i	iv	iii	ii
(d)	i	iii	iv	ii

7. Consider the following:

i. The Battle of Pratapgarh was fought between Afzal Khan and Shivaji.
ii. The Battle of Plassey was fought during the reign of Alamgir II.
iii. Nana Phadnavis defeated the British and signed the Treaty of Purandhar of c. 1776 CE.

Select the correct answer using the codes given below:

(a) i and ii only (b) iii only
(c) i and iii only (d) i, ii and iii

8. Consider the following:

i. Murshid Quli Khan was the ruler of Awadh.
ii. Safdar Jung was the ruler of Bengal.

Select the correct answer using the codes given below:
(a) i and ii only
(b) i only
(c) ii only
(d) None

9. Match List I with List II and select the correct answer using the code given below the lists:

List I	List II
(a) Hindu Padshahi	i. Baji Rao I
(b) Hereditaryship of Peshwa	ii. Rama Chandra Pant
(c) Third Anglo–Maratha War	iii. Baji Rao II
(d) Wrote *Adnyapatra*	iv. Balaji Vishwanath

Code:	A	B	C	D
(a)	ii	iv	iii	i
(b)	ii	iii	iv	i
(c)	i	iv	iii	ii
(d)	i	iii	iv	ii

ANSWERS

1. (c) 2. (b) 3. (b) 4. (b) 5. (d) 6. (a) 7. (d) 8. (d)
9. (c)

PRACTICE QUESTIONS – MAINS

1. Explain the reasons for the decline of Mughals.

2. The Maratha system of administration was quite effective. Explain the major tenets of administration of the Marathas.

3. The office of the Peshwa overshadowed the office of the Chattrapati in the later times. Do you agree? Give reasons for your answer.

CHAPTER 15

Bhakti and Other Important Religious Movements

An important landmark in the cultural history of medieval India was the silent revolution in the society known as the Bhakti Movement. The term '*Bhakti*' symbolises 'devotion or passionate love for the Divine'. Its meaning has, however, evolved with time, along with the concept of Bhakti itself. Since the times of the Indo-Aryans and the sacred texts, i.e., the Vedas, the meaning of Bhakti as a tradition has varied. The Vedic period, with its focused image of the rishi or the seer (a visionary figure who was able to communicate with and about the various gods of the Vedic pantheon through a complex system of rituals; Moksha could be attained through the precise performance of these rituals), did contain the seeds of the Bhakti movement, but it was clearly not the true depiction. This process of 'adoration of a personal god' started during the course of the 6th century BCE, with the rise of the heterodox movements of Buddhism and Jainism. For instance, under *Mahayana Buddhism*, the worship of the Buddha started in his *avalokita* (gracious) *form*. The worship of Vishnu too started around the same time, which was popularised to a great extent by the Gupta kings, who supported the pantheon of gods (*Vishnu*, the cosmic king; *Shiva*, the great yogi and ascetic; and his feminine counterpart, *Shakti*, or divine energy) through the worship of divine images (puja), the *Puranas* (mythological compositions about the gods). The Gupta kings also built temples dedicated to these gods and patronised the various devotional groups.

The Bhakti Movement in South India

However, what is known today as the Bhakti Movement had its genesis in southern India in the 7th and 12th century CE. It was in south India that Bhakti grew from a religious tradition to a popular movement, based on notions of religious equality and broad-based social participation. It is characterised by the writings of its poet-saints, the *Shaivaite Nayannars*[1] and the *Vaishnavaite Alvars*[2], who preached the Bhakti cult under the Pallavas, Pandyas and the Cholas. They disregarded[3] the austerities preached by the Jains and the Buddhists along with rejecting their fatalistic and atheistic traditions and preached that personal devotion to god was the only means of salvation. They extolled passionate devotional love for the Divine and stressed on the fact that Moksha (liberation from the cycle of rebirth) could be attained not by following rules, regulations, or social order, but through simple devotion to the divine. It is pertinent to note that the compositions of Alvars and Nayannars at times commanded equal significance as the Vedas. For instance, one of the major anthologies of compositions by the Alvars, '*the Nalayira Divyaprabandham*', was frequently described as the Tamil Veda. The Bhakti saints usually emerged from lower castes, preached a religion which was non–ritualistic and open to all without any distinction of caste or creed, taught in the local vernacular languages, and encouraged women to join in the gatherings. For instance, the compositions of Andal, a woman Alvar were quite popular while another woman Karaikal Ammaiyar was a devoted Nayannar who adopted the path of extreme asceticism. These ideas of Bhakti were carried to the north by saints as well as by scholars.

[1] Those who are immersed in the devotion to Shiva. There were 63 Nayannar, who belonged to different caste backgrounds such as Brahmanas, potters, hunters, peasants, soldiers, untouchable workers. The best known among them were Appar, Sambhandar, Sundarar and Malvikkasagar. There are two sets of compilations of their songs – Tenvaram and Tiruvacakam.

[2] Ardent devotees of Vishnu. There were 12 Alvars, who came from divergent backgrounds, the best known being Periyalvar, his daughter Andal, Tondaradippodi Alvar and Nammalvar. By the 10th century, the compositions of 12 Alvars were compiled in an anthology known as 'Nalayira Divya Pradandham', the 'Four Thousand Sacred Compositions'.

[3] The hostility against the Buddhist and Jain traditions was primarily on account of the competition between members of different religious traditions for royal patronage.

The Devotee and the Lord

This is a composition of Manikkavasagar:

Into my vile body of flesh
You came, as though it were a temple of gold,
And soothed me wholly and saved me,
O Lord of Grace, O Gem most Pure,
Sorrow and birth and death and illusion
You took from me, and set me free.
O Bliss! O Light! I have taken refuge in You,
And never can I be parted from You.

However, the South India bhakti movement had its limitations as it never consciously opposed Brahmanism or the Varna and caste systems at the social level. It only emphasised on the idea that Bhakti as a mode of worship should be accessible to all or it provided an alternate avenue of worship to the Shudras while it continued to function within the social structure of caste system and the lower castes continued to suffer from various social disabilities. Inspite of the emphasis on Bhakti as the superior mode of worship, there was no elimination of Brahmanical rituals such as worship of idols, recitation of the Vedic mantras and pilgrimages to the sacred places. In fact, their main targets were the Buddhists and Jains and not the Brahmanas and this perhaps was the reason why the Brahman-dominated temples played an important role in the growth of the South Indian Bhakti Movement.

The Bhakti Movement in North India

The evolution of Bhakti Movement in medieval India gained momentum in the northern parts of the country during the 12th–17th century CE. But, interestingly, it differed greatly from the southern Bhakti Movement. The Bhakti Movement in the north included socio-religious movements linked to one of the acharyas from the south. Hence the Bhakti Movement in north India is sometimes seen as a continuation of the movement that originated in the south. For instance, like the South Indian bhakti movement, the Vaishnava bhakti movements of North India, though egalitarian in the religious sphere, never denounced the caste system, the authority of Brahmanical scriptures and the Brahmanical privileges as such. Despite similarities in the traditions of the two regions, the idea of bhakti varied in terms of the teachings of each of the saints. The northern medieval Bhakti Movement was influenced by the spread of Islam in India. The significant characteristics of Islam such as Monotheism or belief in one God, equality and brotherhood of man, and rejection of rituals and class divisions greatly influenced the Bhakti Movement of this era. Further, the preaching of Sufi teachers shaped the thinking of Bhakti reformers like Ramananda, Kabir and Nanak, as the Bhakti Movement also led to certain reforms in the society.

There are varied reasons behind the origins of the Bhakti Movement. Some scholars consider the rise of the Bhakti Movement as a reaction against feudal oppression and against conformist Rajput–Brahman domination as was evident in the anti-feudal tone in the poetry of some Bhakti saints like Kabir, Nanak, Chaitanya and Tulsidas. Another group of scholars thought that the socio-economic changes in the early medieval period led to the emergence of this movement.

According to them, '*during the 13th and 14th centuries, the demand for manufactured goods, luxuries and other artisanal goods increased, leading to a movement of artisans into the cities. The movement gained support from these classes of the society as these groups were dissatisfied with the low status accorded to them by the Brahmanical system, and hence they turned towards Bhakti since it focused on equality*'. Though there is no single opinion about the origins of the Bhakti Movement, there is unanimity of thought over the fact that the Bhakti Movement focused on the message of equality and devotional surrender to a personally conceived supreme God.

The Bhakti movement is also divided into two different ideological streams of *'Saguna' and 'Nirguna'*.

Saguna	Nirguna
Saguna represented those poet-saints who composed verses extolling a god with attributes or form.	*Nirguna* represented those poet-saints who extolled god without and beyond all attributes or form. They are also known as Monotheistic Bhakti saints.
Major proponents: Tulsidas, Surdas, Chaitanya and Meera.	Major proponents: Kabir and Nanak.
• The Saguna poet-saints upheld the caste system and supported the supremacy of the Brahmans. • They preached a religion of surrender and simple faith in a personal god while also supporting idol worship.	• On the other hand, the Nirguna poet-saints rejected the varnashrama and the authority of the Brahmans and all conventions based on caste distinctions along with the practice of idolatry. • They gave more importance to the personal experience with god and even though they called their god using different names and titles, yet their god was non-incarnate, formless, eternal and ineffable. • It seemed that their ideas were a synthesis of the three traditions; the Vaishnava concept of Bhakti, the *Nathpanthi* movement and Sufism. Thus, though they had adopted the notion of *bhakti* from Vaishnavism, they gave it a *nirguna* orientation.

It is also interesting to note that there was an ideological affinity between both *Saguna* and *Nirguna* poet-saints as evident in their verses wherein they frequently mentioned each other's teachings and influence. Also, while the differences between these two branches are indeed important, their overarching similarities cannot be minimised:

a. Both focused on a personal relationship with the Divine and believed in singular devotion and love for God.

b. Both were highly critical of ritual observances as were fostered by the Brahman priests and as a matter of fact, many poet-saints, specially in northern areas, were themselves of lower caste lineages.

c. Another commonality between the two was their usage of the vernacular or regional languages of the masses, as opposed to the sacred language 'Sanskrit' of the elite priests. They composed their poems in popular languages and dialects spoken across India which further enabled them to transmit their ideas among the various lower classes and masses.

Salient Features of Bhakti Movement

(a) The Bhakti reformers preached the principles of monotheism (oneness of God) and criticized idol worship.

(b) They believed in freedom from the cycle of life and death and advocated that the salvation could be attained only by deep devotion and faith in God.

(c) They emphasized that for obtaining the bliss and grace of God, one should self-surrender while they also believed in the importance of 'Gurus' who acted as guides and preceptors.

(d) They advocated the principle of universal brotherhood.

(e) They condemned ritualism, pilgrimages and fasts. Arguing that all living beings, including humans, were god's children, they also strongly denounced caste system which divided people according to their birth.

(f) They stressed the singing of hymns with deep devotion and without considering any language as sacred, they composed poems in the language of the common people.

Prominent Leaders of the Bhakti Movement

1. Sankaracharya (c. 788–820 CE)

- Distinguished philosopher, great thinker and one of the mystic Bhakti poet-saint leader of the 8th century, who gave a new orientation to Hinduism.
- He was born in Kaladi (Kerala) and propounded the *Advaita* (Monism) philosophy and *Nirgunabrahman* (god without attributes).

FIGURE 15.1 Sankaracharya

- In Advaita, the reality of the world is denied and *Brahman* is considered as the only reality. It is only *Brahman* at its base that gives it its reality.
- His famous quotes include, '*Brahma Satyam Jagat Mithya Jivo Brahmatra Naparaha*', meaning, 'The Absolute Spirit is the reality, the world of appearance is *Maya*' and '*Ekameva Adviteeyam* Brahma' meaning 'The absolute is one alone, not two[4]'.

*'The **analogy** given for Advaita is the famous **analogy of** the **snake** and the **rope**. In the dark, we may mistake a rope for a snake and for a time take it to be a real snake. But soon we realise that it is in fact only a rope. Once we know it to be a rope, we do not see the snake anymore. The rope had never existed, it was purely in our minds. Similarly, if knowledge of Brahman is attained, the illusion of the body and the world will vanish'.*

[4] He further explained it with the example that 'as there may be many stalks of sugarcane, but the juice from all of them has the same sweetness. Similarly, beings are many, but their breath is the same; nations are many, but the Earth is one'. In this manner, Sankara proclaimed to the world that it is unity that underlines the apparent diversity.

- He stressed that *gyaan* (knowledge) alone can lead to salvation.
- Wrote commentary on the *Bhagvat Gita*, on the *Brahmasutra* and the *Upanishads*, and wrote books like:
  (a) Upadesh Shastri
  (b) Vivek Chudamani
  (c) Bhaja Govindum Stotra
- Established *mathas* at Sringiri, Dwarka, Puri and Badrinath.

2. Ramanuja (c. 1017–1137 CE)
   - 12th century Bhakti saint poet who was born at Sriperumbudur near modern Chennai. He was deeply influenced by the Alvars and inspired the new strand of bhakti which developed in north India subsequently.
   - He opposed the *mayavada* of Shankara and advocated the philosophy of *Vishista Advaitavada* (qualified monism), and founded the Shrivaishnava sect. According to him, God is *Saguna Brahman* and the creative process including all the objects in creation are real and not illusory as was held by Sankaracharya. Therefore, According to Ramanuja God, soul, matter are real. However, God is inner substance and the rest are his attributes.
   - In Vishista Advaita, the universe and *Brahman* are also considered two equally real entities, as in dualism, but here the universe is not separate from *Brahman* but is formed out of *Brahman*. The *Brahman* is considered as a personal god with omniscient qualities who has created the world out of his own self. Thus, the world bears to *Brahman* the relation of the part to the whole, or the relation of a 'qualified effect' to the base (hence qualified monism).

FIGURE 15.2 Ramanuja

*'The famous **analogy given** for this is the **sea and wave** – Brahman is the sea and the objects of the world, both non-living and the living souls, are like waves upon this sea. All waves are ultimately the sea only, but as long as we see the wave, we think it to be different from the sea. The wave is of name and form only. Other analogies given for this are **gold** and **gold jewellery**, **clay** and **clay pots**, the **spider** and his **web**, etc'.*

- Ramanuja defined *Brahman* as an entirely personal God and considered it to be Vishnu or one of his avatars. He believed that Vishnu has all the qualities of a personal God like omniscience, omnipotence, etc. and he has created the world out of his love for humans, and he also controls the world at every step. Thus, the duty of humans is to love and worship Lord Vishnu so that he will grant deliverance when their worship has ripened.
- Even though the practice of religion in Vishista Advaita is similar to Dualism yet they have a major difference that 'mankind enjoys a higher status than in pure dualistic worship and is nearer to God'. Thus, in *Vishista Advaita*, although both the world and *Brahman* are considered equally real, they are not considered two separate entities as in Dualism.
- He was also firm supporter of *prabattimarga* or the path of self-surrender to God and invited the downtrodden to *Vaishnavism* and advocated salvation by bhakti. However, it is pertinent to note here that though he advocated bhakti as a mode of worship accessible to all including the Shudras and even the outcastes, and he himself did not observe caste distinctions and tried to eradicate untouchability yet he did not support the idea of lower castes having access to Vedas.
- He wrote:
  (a) Sribhashya
  (b) Vedanta Dipa
  (c) Gita Bhasya
  (d) Vedantasara

3. Madhavacharya (c. 1238–1317 CE)

- In the 13th century, Madhava from Kannada region propagated *Dvaita* or the dualism of the *Jivatma* and *Paramatma*. His philosophical system was based on the Bhagvata Purana. According to tenets of this philosophy, the world is not an illusion but a reality and full of real distinction.

FIGURE 15.3 Madhavacharya

*'According to Madhava, **Brahman** and the **universe** are considered to be two equally real entities who are not **related in any way**. The God of dualism is the Hindu God, Vishnu who has created the universe, and the universe stands separate from God and in an inferior position to God with no link between the two. Vishnu controls the universe and all world events, and the duty of all persons is to worship and pray to god'.*

- God, soul and matter are all unique in nature, and hence they are irreducible to each other.
- He also founded the *Brahma Sampradya*.
- Like Ramanuja, he also supported the belief that bhakti provided alternative avenue of worship to the Shudras but he too did not disputed the orthodox Brahmanical restriction on the Vedic study by the Shudras.

4. Nimbraka

- Younger contemporary of Ramanuja who propounded the *Dvaita advaita* philosophy and the philosophy of *Bheda Abheda* (difference/non-difference). According to him, *Brahman* or the supreme soul transforms itself into the souls of the world, which are therefore real, distinct and different from *Brahman*. Like Vishista Advaita, the *Bheda Abheda* school also believes that the world and *Brahman* are both equally real, and that the world is a part of *Brahman*. The difference is on emphasis only. The same analogy of sea and wave, clay and pot, etc. is used here.

*'A particular **analogy of Bhed Abheda** is the sun and the **sun beam**. The sun beam cannot be called separate from the sun, it arises from the sun, and is attached to it. Yet it is not the sun either, it is only a part of the sun, a reflection of the sun, and it gives only a part view of the sun. Hence the world also is but a manifestation of Brahman, but it is a very small manifestation, and the difference with Brahman is very large'.*

- Preacher of Vaishnavite Bhakti in the Telangana region who believed that people were trapped in physical bodies constricted by *prakrti* (matter) and that only by surrender to Radha-Krishna and not through their own efforts could they attain the necessary grace for liberation from rebirth.
- He also founded the *Sanak Sampradaya*.

5. Vallabhacharya (c. 1479–1531 CE)

- Born in Benaras to a Telugu Brahman family in the 15th century who propagated his doctrine of *bhakti* (devotion) through god Krishna whom he fondly addressed as Shrinath ji. He lived at the court of Krishnadeva Raya and Chaitanya Mahaprabhu was one of his worthy contemporaries.
- He founded *Pushtimarga i.e.* ('the Path of Grace'), a path that teaches a devotee how to offer selfless love and devotion to Shrinath ji without seeking anything in return except love.
- He propounded the philosophy of *Shudhadvaita* (pure monism) which forms the basis of Pushtimarg devotional practice. As in *Vishista Advaita*, *Shudh Advaita* too indicates that the entire universe is the manifestation of *Brahman*. The universe exists as it were as an aspect of *Brahman* without undergoing any change. We can consider it like the two sides of a coin, with *Brahman* as one side and the universe another side. There is no change – the universe is a part of the coin that is *Brahman*. Hence, this is called '*Shudh Advaita*' because it is said that *there is only one and there is no change*.

FIGURE 15.4 Vallabhacharya

- However, it is pertinent to note that though Shudh Advaita calls itself monism, it does recognise the presence of both the universe and Brahman, being equally real. Hence, there exist two realities. Even if we say that the universe is a part of Brahman, it exists as a different reality from *Brahman*. A branch of Vishista Advaita recognises both the universe and Brahman as being two equally real existences, though it emphasises the non-difference more by saying that the universe is an inseparable, unchanged aspect of Brahman. Hence, it tends more towards pure Advaita than the Vishista Advaita of Ramanuja.
- He also founded the *Rudra Sampradya*.
- He along with his disciple Surdas[5] was largely instrumental in popularising the Krishna cult in north India.

6. Basavana (c. 1106 – 1167/1168 CE)
   - A 12th century saint-poet, social reformer, and philosopher who laid the foundation of the Virashava tradition in Karnataka. His followers were known as Virashaivas (heroes of Shiva) or Lingayats[6] (wearer of the linga).
   - A Brahman by birth, he was a minister in the court of the Kalachuri ruler King Bijjala (1157–1167) who used his poetry, known as **Vachanaas**, an innovative literary form

[5] Surdas (1483–1563) was Krishna bhakti saint who even though was blind popularised Krishna cult.

[6] Lingayats continue to be an important community in Karnataka and they are strict monotheists as they worship Shiva in his manifestation as a linga and men usually wear a small linga in a silver case on a loop strung over the left shoulder. They believe that on death the devotees will be united with the Shiva and will not return to this world. Therefore, they do not practise funerary rites such as cremation, prescribed in the Dharmashastras, instead they ceremonially bury their dead.

composed in simple Kannada language, to **raise societal consciousness**. In fact, he rejected all sorts of social or gender discrimination, superstitions, and rituals and subsequently his followers, the Lingayats, challenged the idea of caste, theory of rebirth and pollution attributed to certain groups. They were also firm supporters of post-puberty marriage and the remarriage of widows.

- He is credited with several major Lingayat works such as the *Shat-Sthala-Vachana, Kala-jnana-Vachana, Mantra-Gopya, Ghatna Chakra-Vachana, and Raja-yoga-Vachana.*
- His spiritual discipline was based on the principles of Arivu (true knowledge), Achara (right conduct), and Anubhava (divine experience).
- He established the **Anubhava Mantapa,** a common forum for all to discuss the prevailing problems of **social, economic and political strata** including religious and spiritual principles along with personal problems. Thus, it was the first and foremost **Parliament of India,** where **Sharana**s (citizens of welfare society) sat together and discussed the socialistic principles of a democratic society 'Kalyana Rajya'. As a matter of fact, all the discussions of Sharanas were written in the form of **Vachanas.**

Rituals and the Real World

Here is a vachana composed by Basavanna:

When they see a serpent carved in stone they pour milk on it.
If a real serpent comes they say: "Kill. Kill."
To the servant of the god who could eat if served they say: "Go away! Go away!"
But to the image of the god which cannot eat they offer dishes of food.

7. Vidyapati (c. 1352–1448 CE)

- Vidyapati was a 14th century Maithili poet known for his poetry dedicated to Shiva, whom he addressed as Ugna.

8. Sankaradeva (c. 1449-1568 CE)

- Introduced bhakti both in the Brahmaputra valley as well as in Cooch-Behar. Preached absolute devotion to Vishnu and his incarnation, Krishna. He composed poems and plays in Assamese and founded the institution of '*Satra*[7]' or '*namghars*', houses of recitation and

[7] The Satra, literally meaning 'holy areas', is a network of decentralised monasteries each headed by a Guru (teacher) designated as the *Satradhikar*. The Namghars are an 'extended wing' or a 'miniature replica' of the Satra institution.

prayer where people of all classes assembled for religious as well as social purposes. Later, the *Satras* grew into full fledged monasteries. The sect formed by him was later known as *Mahapurashiya Dharma*.

The Bhakti Movement in Maharashtra

The Bhakti movement in Maharashtra centred around the shrine of *Vithoba* or *Vitthal*, the residing deity of Pandharpur, who was regarded as a manifestation of Krishna. That is why it is also known as the Pandharpur movement, which led to great cultural and social development in Maharashtra such as the development of Marathi literature, elevation in the status of women, breaking of caste barriers, etc. In Maharashtra, the Bhakti Movement drew its inspiration from the *Bhagavata Purana* and the Shiva Nathpanthis. The Bhakti Movement is broadly divided into two sects:

a. *Varakaris*: The mild devotees of God Vitthala of Pandharpur, who are more emotional, theoretical and abstract in their view-point and who insisted on annual pilgrimage to Pandharpur.

b. *Dharakaris*: The heroic followers of the cult of Ramadasa, the devotee of God Rama, who are more rational, practical and concrete in their thoughts.

The difference between the two schools, however, is only apparent, and the realisation of God as the highest end of human life is common aim of both. The great saints belonging to the Vithoba cult were Jnaneswar/Jnanadeva, Namdeva and Tukaram.

9. Jnaneswara or Jnanadeva (c. 1275–1296 CE)

- A 13th century mystical poet-saint of Maharashtra, whose commentary on the Bhagvat Gita called *Jnanesvari* served as a foundation of the bhakti ideology in Maharashtra. He was also the author of many hymns called *abhangs*.
- He had also composed '*Amritanubhava*' ('Immortal Experience'), based on the philosophy of the Upanishads and '*Haripatha*', a song praising the Hari i.e., Vishnu.
- He was staunch critic of caste distinctions and believed that the only way to attain God was through Bhakti.

10. Namdeva (c. 1270–1350 CE)

- He was a poet-saint from Maharashtra belonging to the 14th century, who according to tradition was a tailor who had taken to banditry before he became a saint. It is interesting to note that while he is remembered in the north Indian monotheistic tradition as a *nirguna* saint, in Maharashtra he is considered to be part of the Varkari tradition meaning 'the *Pilgrims Path*', one of the Vaishnava devotional tradition.
- He is considered one of the five revered *gurus* in the *Dadupanth* tradition within Hinduism, the other four being Dadu, Kabir, Ravidas and Hardas. It is believed that his *Abhangas* were included in the *Guru Granth Sahib*.

FIGURE 15.5 Commemorative postal stamp of India depicting Bhagat Namdev, also known as Sant Namdeo

- His Marathi poetry and community-driven bhajan singing sessions attracted individuals from diverse classes and castes and breathes a spirit of intense love and dedication to god.
- His companions during worship sessions included:
  - (i) Kanhopatra (a dancing girl),
  - (ii) Sena (a barber),
  - (iii) Savata (a gardener),
  - (iv) Chokhamela (an untouchable),
  - (v) Janabai (a maid),
  - (vi) Gora (a potter),
  - (vii) Narahari (a goldsmith), and
  - (viii) Jnanesvar (also known as Dnyandev, a Brahmin).

11. Sant Eknath (c. 1533–1599 CE)

- He was a Marathi poet-saint and scholar of the Varkari sampradaya and Vaishnavism, the branch of Hinduism that reveres the deity Vishnu and his different incarnations or avatars.
- He developed enriched Marathi literature and is often seen as a bridge between his predecessors – Dnyaneshwar and Namdeva – and the later Tukaram and Ramdas. He is best known for his translations of various Sanskrit texts into Marathi, a vernacular version of the *Ramayana*, and his restored edition of the then-corrupted Marathi literature classic, the *Jnaneshvari* written by eminent poet-saint Jnaneshvar.

FIGURE 15.6 Shrine of Sant Eknath on the banks of river Godavri, Aurangabad

- He also tried to shift the emphasis of Marathi literature from spiritual to narrative compositions and introduced a new form of Marathi religious song called *Bharood*.
- He is believed to be a family man and was renowned for resolving the conflicts between householder duties and the demands of religious devotion. He emphasised that stay in monasteries or resignation from the world are not necessary for leading a religious life.
- He tirelessly worked towards bringing *bhakti* within the reach and understanding of ordinary people, including outcastes and women. He was also firmly against any sort of distinctions and through his own life and writings, he rejected such differences and spread the message that there was no distinction in God's eyes between Brahman and outcaste or between Hindu and Muslim.

12. Tukaram (c. 1608–1650 CE)
    - Tukaram was a poet-saint of the Bhakti movement in Maharashtra in 17th century who is believed to be a contemporary of Maratha Shivaji and saints like Eknath and Ramdas. He devoted his poetry to Vitthala or Vithoba, an avatar of the Hindu God Vishnu. According to tradition, he belonged to Kunbi, a lower caste and was part of the egalitarian Varkari devotionalism tradition.
    - He is best known for his *Abangas* (*dohas*) in Marathi, which are rich heritage of the gatha-devotional poetry and was also responsible for creating a background for Maratha nationalism, '*Parmaratha*'.
    - Stressing on community-oriented worship with spiritual songs known as kirtans, he preached the virtue of piety, forgiveness and peace of mind.

FIGURE 15.7 Tukaram

Questioning the Social Order

This is an *abhang* (Marathi devotional hymn) of Sant Tukaram:

He who identifies with the battered and the beaten
Mark him as a saint
For God is with him

He holds
Every forsaken man
Close to his heart
He treats
A slave
As his own son

Says Tuka
I won't be tired to repeat again
Such a man
Is God
In person.

Here is an *abhang* composed by Chokhamela's son:

You made us low caste,
Why don't you face that fact, Great Lord?
Our whole life – left-over food to eat.
You should be ashamed of this.

You have eaten in our home.
How can you deny it?
Chokha's (son) Karmamela asks
Why did you give me life?

Ramdasa (c. 1608–1681 CE)

- He was the famed spiritual Guru and guide of Shivaji and is believed to have contributed in the building of the Maratha empire under Shivaji.
- He wrote *Dasabodha* (a treatise on the Advaita Vedanta in the Marathi language and deals with a wide range of subjects on the spiritual life: true and false knowledge, necessity of a Guru, characteristics of a Guru, the qualifications of a true disciple, Maya, necessity of spiritual disciplines, bhakti and liberation). His other notable works are *Karunashtaken*, *Manache Sloka* and *Janasvabhavagosanvi*.
- He was against all distinctions based on caste and creed and greatly encouraged the participation of women in religious work.

Non Sectarian Bhakti Movement

In the 14th and 15th centuries, Ramananda, Kabir and Nanak emerged as the great apostles of the Bhakti cult who carved a complete new path and perspective towards Bhakti. Unlike the early reformers, they were not linked with any particular religion and were totally against rituals and ceremonies. They believed in one God and condemned polytheism along with denouncing all forms of idolatry. They emphasised greatly on the fundamental unity of all religions and urged the common people to shed age-old superstitions and attain salvation through bhakti or pure devotion. They were all also monotheists as they uncompromisingly believed in one God which, as rightly described by Guru Nanak, was non-incarnate and formless (*nirankar*), eternal (*akal*) and ineffable (*alakh*). Interestingly, quite often Kabir called God as Ram, but he himself made it clear that the Ram he was devoted to was not the son of King Dashratha but a formless, non-incarnate

God. In addition to the oneness of god and nirguna bhakti, the monotheists also emphasised on the importance of repetition of divine name, spiritual guru, community singing of devotional songs (*kirtan*) and companionship of saints (*satsang*). They composed their teachings in popular languages and a mixture of different dialects spoken for the propagation of their non conformist ideas among the masses in various regions. Also most of these saints were not ascetics and led worldly life and were married. The Non Sectarian movement was very popular among masses and it broke territorial barriers. For instance a mid 17th century Maharashtrian saint Tukaram looked upon himself as an admirer and follower of Kabir, even almost two hundred years after Kabir. It is also interesting to note that ironically, later the followers of each of the major figures in the monotheistic movement like Kabir, Raidas and nanak gradually organised themselves into exclusive sectarian orders called panths like Kabir panth, Raidasi panth, Nanak panth.

14. Ramananda (c. 1400–1476 CE)

- Considered to be the link between the Bhakti movement of south India and north India, Ramananda was a 15th century poet-saint who was born in Allahabad and later, founded his own sect and preached his principles in Hindi at Benaras and Agra. He is considered as the link between the south Indian bhakti tradition and North Indian Vaishnava bhakti. His followers are called *Ramanandis*. A hymn attributed to him was incorporated in the *Adi Granth*.
- He was originally a follower of Ramanuja except that he opposed the interdiction on inter caste dining and rejected the monopoly of Sanskrit language over the teaching of religious texts. Thus, he, like the other monotheist *bhakti* saints, rejected caste hierarchies and preached in the local languages to popularise his teachings.
- He preached against the formalism of the orthodox cult and founded a new school of Vaishnavism based on the gospel of love and devotion. One of his most outstanding contribution was the abolition of distinctions of caste among his followers.
- He put emphasis on *bhakti* and avoided both *gyana marg* and *karma marg*. He is identified as the founder of the Ram cult in north India as his object of *bhakti* was Ram since he worshiped Ram and Sita.

'Let no one ask a man's caste or with whom he eats.
If a man is devoted to Hari, he becomes Hari's own'.

-- ***Ramananda***

- Gave rise to two schools of thought:
  - (a) Orthodox school – Represented by Nabhadas, Tulsidas
  - (b) Liberal – Represented by Kabir, Nanak and others
- Other followers included:
  - (c) Raidasa – A cobbler whose songs are included in the Guru Granth Sahib.
  - (d) Kabir – A weaver who preached that Ram, Rahim and Allah are all the same.
  - (e) Sena – A barber
  - (f) Sadhana – A butcher
  - (e) Dhanna – A 15th century Jat peasant from Rajasthan
  - (f) Naraharai – A goldsmith
  - (g) Pipa A Rajput prince

15. Kabir (c. 1440–1518 CE)

- One of the most famous disciples of Ramananda who belonged to 15th century and whose iconic verses are found in the Sikh holy scripture, *Adi Granth*.

FIGURE 15.8 Kabir

- According to tradition, it is believed that he was born near Varanasi to a Brahman widow, but was brought up by a Muslim weavers[8] couple. He had an innate religious passion and possessed an inquiring mind, and while in Benares, learnt both about Hinduism and Islamic teachings too.
- He laid great emphasis on the equality of man before God and was a great critic of idolatry, rituals, the caste system especially the practice of untouchability. He utilised ridicule as a powerful method for denouncing orthodox Brahmanism.
- He was quite familiar with yogic practices and regarded devotion to god as an effective means of salvation and urged his disciples that to achieve this one must have a pure heart, free from dishonesty, cruelty, hypocrisy and insincerity. He considered neither asceticism nor book knowledge important for true knowledge.
- One of the main objectives of Kabir was to reconcile Hindus and Muslims and establish harmony between the two sects. He emphasised on the essential oneness of all religions by describing Hindus and Muslims '*as pots of the same clay*'. To him '*Rama and Allah, temple and mosque*' were the same.
- Kabir is still regarded as the greatest of the mystic saints and his followers are called *Kabirpanthis*. Among those who were influenced by Kabir were
  - (i) Raidas[9], who was a tanner by caste from Benares,
  - (ii) Guru Nanak, who was a Khatri merchant from Punjab, and
  - (iii) Dhanna, who was a Jat peasant from Rajasthan.
- Most of the compositions of Kabir are compiled in *Bijak*. He also utilised a specific style known as '*ulatbansi*' (upside down sayings containing paradoxes and enigmas) which are written in a form in which everyday meanings are inverted.

16. Guru Nanak (c. 1469–1539 CE)

- The first Sikh Guru and founder of the Sikhism, who was also a *Nirguna* Bhakti saint and social reformer. According to him, the Absolute or '*rab*' had no gender or form. He proposed a simple way of connecting with the Divine by remembering and repeating the Divine Name, expressing ideas through hymns called '*shabad*[10]'.
- He was born in a Khatri household in the village of Talwandi (now called Nankana), on the banks of the river Ravi in c. 1469 CE. His father was an accountant, and even Nanak was trained in Persian to follow his father's footsteps, but he was inclined towards mysticism.

---

[8] Julaha – indigenous converts to Islam

[9] According to some traditions, he was the preceptor of Mirabai.

[10] Guru Nanak would sing these compositions in various ragas while his attendant Mardana played the rabab.

FIGURE 15.9 Guru Nanak

- He preached about the unity of god and opposed all sort of distinctions be it religious rivalries or caste distinctions and condemned the formalism and ritualism of both Islam and Hinduism. The sacred space created by Guru Nanak was known as dharmsala which is now known as Gurudwara.
- He laid great emphasis on the purity of character and conduct and considered both of them to be the first essential condition of approaching God. He also stressed on the need of a guru for guidance. Like Kabir, he advocated a middle path in which spiritual life could be combined with the duties of the householder. He used the terms '*nam, dan* and *insan*' meaning right worship, welfare of others and purity of conduct. His teachings are now remembered as '*nam-japna, kirt-karna* and *vand-chhakna*' signifying the importance of right belief and worship, honest living and helping others.

17. Dadu Dayal (c. 1544–1603 CE)

- '*Dadu*' means 'brother', and '*Dayal*' means 'the compassionate one'. Dadu Dayal is one of the major representatives of the *Nirguna Sant* traditions in Northern India. He believed that '*devotion to God should transcend religious or sectarian affiliation, and that devotees should become non-sectarian or nipakh*'.
- According to tradition, he was a saint from Gujarat, who spent the best part of his spiritual life in Rajasthan. His followers came to be known as the *Dadupanthis* who set up ashrams known as *Thambas* around the region.
- It is believed that Emperor Akbar and Kabir were two of his prominent followers.

Vaishnavite Movement

Apart from the non-sectarian movement, the Bhakti Movement in north India developed around the worship of Ram and Krishna, two of the incarnations of the God Vishnu. Saint-poet Tulsidas was the leading light of the Ram cult. His great poem, the *Ramacharitamanasa*, popularly called *Tulsi-krita Ramayana*, is very popular among Hindu devotees till date, in which he portrays Sri Ram as all virtuous and all powerful and the very embodiment of the Supreme Reality (*Parambrahma*).

On the other hand, the followers of the Krishna cult founded the Radha Ballabhi sect under Hari Vamsa in c. 1585 CE. In the early 16th century, Vallabacharya, a popular bhakti saint popularised the Krishna bhakti cult. He was followed by Surdas[11] (c. 1483–1563 CE) and Mirabai (c. 1503–1573 CE). Sur Das wrote *Sursagar, Surasaravali and Sahitya Lahiri* in *Brajbhasha*, which is full of verses on the charm of Lord Krishna and his beloved Radha. Mirabai, the daughter-in-law of Rana Sanga, was a great devotee of Krishna, and she became popular in Rajasthan for her bhajans. Later, the exponents of the Ram cult and the Krishna cult among the Vaishnavas branched off into a number of sects and creeds.

The Vaishnava Bhakti Movement in Bengal was very different from that in north and south India. The Vaishnava Bhakti tradition of the *Bhagavata Purana*, and the *Sahajiya Buddhist* and *Nathpanthi traditions* influenced this Bhakti movement. These traditions focused on the esoteric and emotional aspects of devotion. In the 12th century, Jayadeva, an important bhakti saint in this tradition highlighted the mystical dimension of love with reference to Krishna and Radha. Another popular bhakti saint from the region was Chaitanya who was even considered as an incarnation of Krishna.

18. Chaitanya Mahaprabhu (c. 1486–1533 CE)

- 16th century saint and social reformer of Bengal, who popularised the Krishna cult in Bengal. He was even looked upon as an *avatar* (incarnation) of Krishna. Under his able guidance, the Bhakti Movement in Bengal developed into a reform movement as it questioned social division on the basis of caste. It is believed that he was greatly influenced by the philosophical school of Madhava.
- Popularised the *Sankirtan/Kirtan system* (group devotional songs accompanied with ecstatic dancing). He believed that through song and dance, love and devotion, a devotee can feel the presence of God.
- He proclaimed universal brotherhood of man and emphasised on love and peace condemning all sorts of distinctions based on religion and caste in the sphere of devotional singing thereby accepting disciples from all classes and castes. In fact, one of his favourite

[11] Unlike Kabir and Guru Nanak who rejected all orthodox religions, both Surdas and Tulsidas accepted beliefs and practices but wanted to make these accessible to all. Tulsidas conceived God in form of Rama and his composition Ramcharitmanas written in Awadhi is a fine expression of his devotion.

disciple was Haridas, who was a Muslim. He was also highly empathetic towards the suffering of other people, especially that of the poor and the weak.

- However, he did not give up traditional Brahmanical values altogether as he upheld the caste prejudices of his Brahman disciples against the lower caste disciples. He sent six of his Sanskrit knowing Brahmin *Goswamin* disciples to Vrindavan who later established a religious order which recognised caste restrictions in its devotional practices and rituals.
- The biography of Chaitanya was written by Krishnadas Kaviraj.

FIGURE 15.10 Sri Chaitanya's Statue at Gupta Vrindavan in Puri, Odisha

19. Narsingh Mehta (c. 1414–1481 CE)
    - Saint from Gujarat who wrote songs in Gujarati depicting the love of Radha–Krishna.
    - Author of Mahatma Gandhi's favorite *bhajan* – '*Vaishanava jan ko*' and gave the famous statement '*They are Vaishnavas who understand the pain of others*'.
20. Saint Tyagaraja (c. 1767–1847 CE)
    - One of the most precious jewel of Carnatic trinity[12] who was highly instrumental in the development of the classical devotional music tradition and considered as one of the greatest composers of Carnatic music, who had composed thousands of devotional compositions, mostly in Telugu in praise of Lord Ram.
    - He did not consider music as a fine art but as the easiest path to attain salvation.
    - He was a musical genius and composed the famous *Pancharatna Kritis* (meaning five gems) in the traditional Ghana ragas namely Natta, Gaula, Arabhi, Varali and Sriraga.

[12] The three jewels of Carnatic trinity are Tyagaraja, Muthuswami Dikshitar and Syama Sastri.

19. Tallapaka Annamacharya (c. 1408–1503 CE)
   - Was a 15th-century Telugu poet-saint and musician who was an ardent devotee of the Hindu god Lord Venkateshwara.
   - He was a pioneer in both devotional music *sankirtans* and also in field of opposition to social evils such as the practice of untouchability.

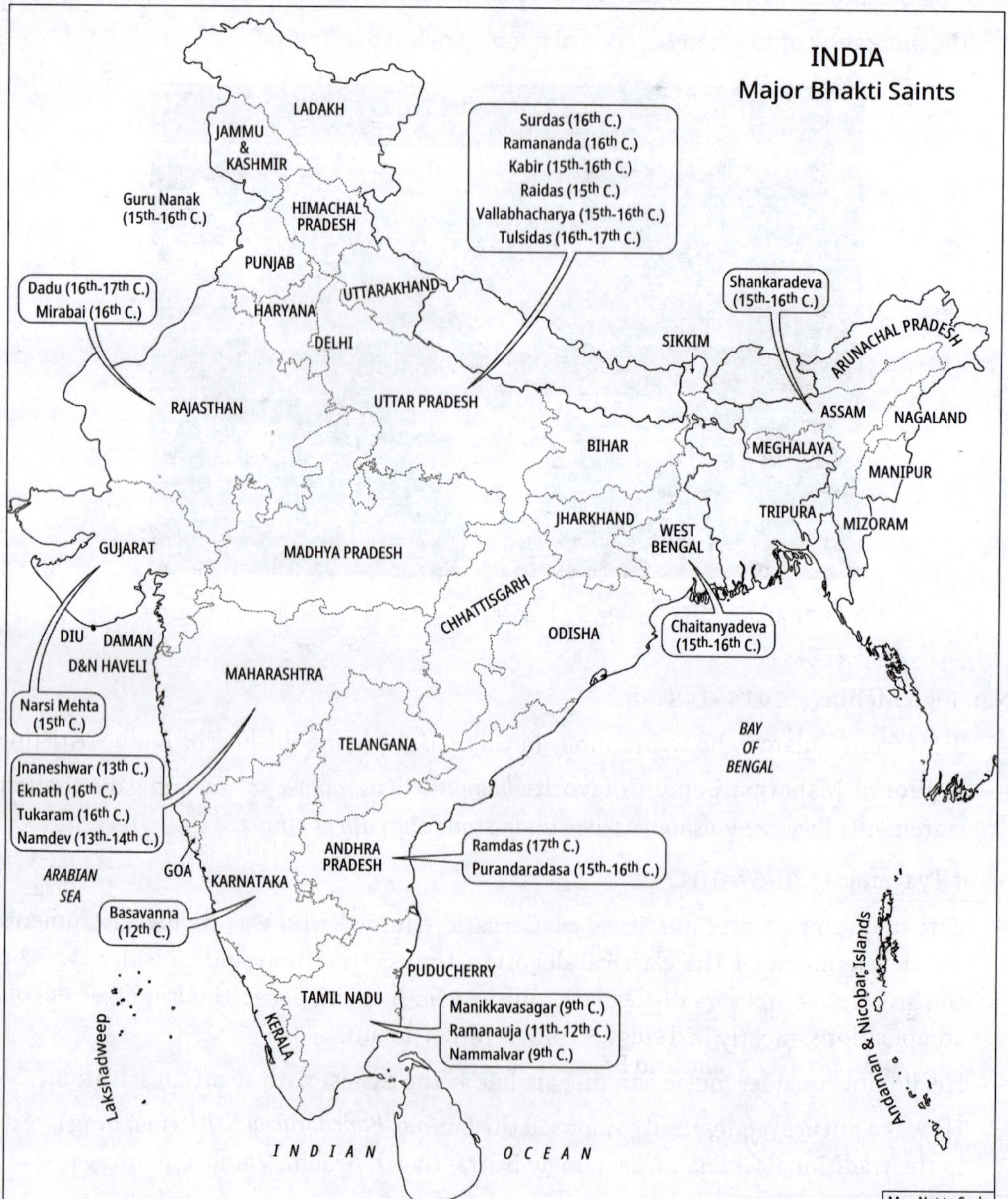

Sufism

The word 'sufi' is derived from '*suf*', which means wool in Arabic, referring to the simple cloaks worn by the early Muslim ascetics. It also means 'purity', and thus the Sufis can be understood as the people who kept their heart pure and through their ascetic practices could communicate with God. It is pertinent to note that the terms *Sufi*, *Darvesh*, *Wali* and *Faqir* are often used interchangeably for representing Muslim saints who could develop their intuitive faculties through contemplation, ascetic exercises, renunciation and self-denial.

Salient Features of Sufism

(a) God, man and the relation of love between God and man is fundamental to Sufism. They sought union with the God as a lover seeks his beloved.

(b) The ideas of *ruh* (soul), *qurbat* (divine proximity) and *hulul* (infusion of the divine spirit), *Ishq* (divine love) and *Fana* (self-annihilation) are central to the theory of Sufism.

(c) According to Sufism, love of God meant the love of humanity and thus, they stressed on the fact that service to God is nothing but service to humanity. The Sufi saints, transcending all religious and communal distinctions, have often worked for promoting the interest of humanity at large.

(d) The Sufis also regard God as the supreme beauty, and draw an analogy between the God and themselves as that of *Mashuq* and the *Ashiqs*. They not only admire God, but also take delight in his thought and concentrate their attention on him only.

(e) Sufism also lays stress on self-discipline and considers sense of perception as an essential condition to gain the knowledge of God.

(f) Other key ideas emphasised by Sufism are good actions, prayers, pilgrimages, meditation, repentance for sins, charity, fasting and suppression of passions by ascetic practices.

(g) Unlike orthodox Muslims who lay emphasis on external conduct, the Sufis on the other hand lay stress on inner purity. They, thus represent the inward or esoteric, mystical side of Islam.

Background History

It is believed that Sufism or mysticism emerged in the 8th century, and the early known Sufis were Rabia al-Adawiya, Al-Junaid and Bayazid Bastami. However, it evolved into a well-developed movement by the end of the 11th century. One of the oldest Sufis in the sub-continent was Al Hujwiri, *author of Kashf-ul Mahjub*[13], who had established himself in north India and was buried in

[13] A famous Persian treatise on Sufism.

Lahore. By the 12th century, the Sufis were organised in *Silsilahs*[14] (i.e. , sufi orders, which basically represented an unbreakable chain between the *Pir*, the teacher and the *murids*, the disciples) who passes through *maqamat* (various stages) in this process of experiencing communion with the divine. The activities of the various Sufi orders were centred around *khanqah*[15] (the hospice) which was led by the *shaikh*, *pir*, or *murshid* (teacher), who lived with his murids (disciples) and laid down rules for spiritual conduct and interaction between inmates as well as between lay persons and the teacher. Gradually, the *khanqahs* emerged as important centres of learning and preaching. Many Sufis enjoyed the *sama* or musical congregation in their khanqahs. In fact, *qawwali* developed during this period only. On the death of the pir, his *dargah*, i.e. , the tomb or shrine, became a centre for his disciples and followers and the *ziyarat* or pilgrimage to the tombs of the Sufi saints soon emerged as an important form of ritual pilgrimage. The four most popular *Silsilahs* among these were the *Chistis*, *Suhrawardis*, *Qadiriyahs* and *Naqshbandis*.

Four Most Popular Silsilahs	
The Chisti Silsilah	• The Chisti order was established in India by Khwaja Muinuddin Chishti also known as *Gharib Nawaz (comforter of the poor)*, who probably moved to India during the time of invasion of Muhammad Ghori and settled in Ajmer around c. 1206 CE. Since, his attitude towards non-Muslims was one of tolerance and he was not actively involved in conversion, he won the respect of both Muslims and non-Muslims. • His fame grew more after his death in c. 1235 CE, when his grave was visited by the then Sultan Muhammad Tughlaq, after which the mosque and the dome were erected by Mahmud Khalji of Malwa in the 15th century. Later, after the support of Mughal Emperor Akbar, the patronage to the *dargah* reached unprecedented heights. The Chisti presence in Delhi was established by Qutbuddin Bakhtiyar Kaki under the patronage of Sultanate ruler Illtutmish. • The Chistis believed in: a. Simplicity of life, humility and selfless devotion to God. They believe that renunciation of worldly possessions is crucial for both the control of the senses as well as for leading a spiritual life. b. Love as the bond between god and the individual soul, and adopting an attitude of benevolence towards all. c. The tolerance between people of different faiths, and acceptance of disciples irrespective of their religious beliefs.

[14] The word *Silsilah* literally means a chain, signifying a continuous link between master and discipline, stretching as an unbroken spiritual genealogy to the Prophet Mohammad. It was through this channel that spiritual power and blessings were transmitted to devotees. Each *Silsilah* prescribed a different method (*tariqa*) of instruction and ritual practice.

[15] The centre of the activities of a Sufi order, a place where pir imparted spiritual training to his disciples and held their assemblies. At times these places also served as the house of rest for travellers.

Four Most Popular Silsilahs	
	d. Use of simple language and the refusal to accept any grant for their maintenance from the Sultans. e. The highest form of devotion to God was to redress the misery of those in distress, fulfilling the need of the helpless and to feed the hungry. • Apart from Muinuddin Chisti, the other important Chistis were: (a) Khalifa Khwaja Fariduddin Masud (c. 1175–1265 CE): Also known as Ganj-i-Shakar, and more popularly as Baba Farid. He was strongly against association with the rich and ruling class and his verses were later incorporated in the Guru Granth Sahib. (b) Nizamuddin Auliya (c. 1238–1325 CE): He brought humanism at the forefront of Sufism and laid down six principles for a seeker of God: (i) Solitary life (ii) Physical purity and cleanliness (iii) Fasting (iv) Priority of the beloved over anything else (v) Following the '*Shaikh*' or spiritual master (vi) To regard God above the two worlds. Interestingly, even though he was widely respected by the masses yet he had a conflicting relationship with different Sultans such as Mubarak Khalji and Ghiyasauddin Tughlaq. He saw the reigns of seven successive Sultans of Delhi, but he is known for avoiding the company of kings and nobles and never visiting courts. Prominent poets Amir Khusrau, Amir Hasan Sijzi and court historian Ziyauddin Barani were all disciples of Nizamuddin Auliya. Amir Khusrau gave a unique form to the Chisti '*sama*' by introducing the '*qual*', a hymn sung at the opening or closing of qawwali. (c) Nasiruddin Chiragh-i-Dehlavi: A disciple of Nizamuddin Auliya. (d) Shaikh Burhanuddin Gharib: He established the Chisti order in the 13th century in the Deccan. (e) Muhammad Banda Nawaz: One of the famous pirs of the Deccan city of Bijapur region.
The Suhrawardi Silsilah	• The order which is noted for the severity of its spiritual discipline was founded by Shihabuddin Suhrawardi in Baghdad and was established in India by Bahauddin Zakariya (1182–1262). He openly supported the-then Sultan Ilutmish who in turn accorded the title of Shaikh-ul Islam. • Unlike the Chistis, the Suhrawardis accepted maintenance grants from the Sultans and took active part in politics too. They were active in Punjab and Sindh as compared to the Chistis, who were active in Delhi, Rajasthan and parts of the western Gangetic plains, and in the later years in the eastern regions of the Gangetic plain (Bihar and Bengal) and into the Deccan.

<table>
<tr><th colspan="2">Four Most Popular Silsilahs</th></tr>
<tr><td></td><td>• Suhrawardis believed that
(a) A Sufi should possess the three attributes of property, knowledge and hal (mystical enlightenment). They however, did not support excessive austerities or self–mortification.
(b) They stressed on the observance or external forms of religious belief and advocated a combination of ilm (scholarship) with mysticism.</td></tr>
<tr><td>The Naqshbandi Silsilah</td><td>• This Silsilah was established in India by Khwaja Bahauddin Naqshbandi, and later on, propagated by his successors, Sheikh Baqi Billah and Shaikh Ahmad Sirhindi (1563–1624).
• They were also known as the 'silent sufis' due to their practice of silent meditation of the heart.
• The mystics of this Silsilah stressed on:
(a) The observance of the shariat law in its purest form and denounced all innovations or biddat. They attempted to purge Islam from all liberal, and according to them, 'un-Islamic' practices.
(b) Contrary to the Chistis, they maintained that the relationship between man and God was that of the slave and the master and not of a lover and beloved.
(c) They criticised the liberal policies of Akbar such as the high status accorded by Akbar to many non-Muslims, the withdrawal of the jizya and the ban on cow slaughter.
(d) They opposed the listening of sama (religious music) and the practice of pilgrimage to the tombs of saints, and strongly opposed interaction with Hindus and Shias.
• However, after the death of Sirhindi, the order was represented by two important mystics each having a different approach:
(e) Conservative approach under the leadership of Shaj Waliullah
(f) Liberal approach under the leadership of Mirza Mazhar Jan-i-Jahan.</td></tr>
<tr><td>The Qadri Silsilah</td><td>• The Quadiriyya Silsilah, which was popular in Punjab, was initiated during the Mughal rule under the teachings of Sheikh Abdul Qadir and his sons, Shaikh Niamtullah, Mukhdum Muhammad Jilani and Miyan Mir. Another important pir of this order was Shah Badakhshani. They had enrolled the Mughal princess Jahanara and her brother Dara as disciples.
• The pirs of this Silsilah believed in:
(a) The concept of Wahdat al Wajud meaning 'Unity of Existence' or 'Unity of Being', that is to say, God and his creation are one and similar.
(b) The pirs of this order dismissed Orthodox elements.</td></tr>
</table>

It is pertinent to note that during the medieval period, while there was a constant tension between the liberal and orthodox views in Islam, the Sufis featured on both sides. For instance, there were the *Chistis* who held a liberal view and argued in favour of assimilation of local traditions, while there were *Naqshbandi* Silsilah proponents who held the orthodox view of *shariat* and argued that through the other Silsilahs, the purity of Islam was being diluted. But the majority of the Sufis found resonance with the liberal opinion that argued against the narrow definition of Islamic laws by the ulema. It is also important to mention another group of radical Sufis, who were mystics who initiated movements based on a radical interpretation of Sufi ideals and observed extreme forms of asceticism, often known by the names of *Qalandars*, *Madaris*, *Malangs*, *Haidaris*. Since they deliberately defied Sharia, they were often referred to as *be-Sharia* in contrast to the *ba-Sharia* Sufis who complied with it.

Impact of Sufism

a. The liberal and unorthodox features of Sufism had a profound influence on medieval Bhakti saints. In the later period, the Sufi doctrines influenced the religious perspective of the rulers along with reminding them of their moral obligations. For instance, the Mughal emperor, Akbar's religious outlook and religious policies were shaped a lot under Sufism.

b. Sufism took roots in both rural and urban areas and exercised a deep social, political and cultural influence on the masses. It helped create a new world order in which spiritual bliss was the ultimate goal and the masses could raise their voice against all forms of orthodoxy, religious formalism, falsehood and hypocrisy. In a world torn by strife and conflict, the Sufis tried to bring peace and harmony.

c. The most important contribution of Sufism is that it helped to bridge the gap between the Hindu–Muslim prejudices and could bring both these communities closer to each other. Through Sufism and the Bhakti cult, a bond of solidarity and brotherhood was forged between these two religious communities. It is pertinent to note that the Sufi saints are revered even today by not only Muslims but by a large number of Hindus also, and their tombs have become popular places of pilgrimage for both communities.

Key Term/Concept	Meaning
(a) Kanqah	Pir or the preceptor who lived in a hospice and followed certain practices of Sufism
(b) Sama	Religious music, which led to ecstasy
(c) Tauba	Repentance over bad deeds
(d) Vara	Non-acceptance of what was not given freely
(e) Julad	Kindness
(f) Fakr	Poverty
(g) Suhr	To observe tolerance
(h) Sukar	Acceptance of obligation

(i) Khauf	Symbolises fear
(j) Tawakkhul	To observe contentment
(k) Riza	Surrender to achieve salvation
(l) Ziyarat	Practice of visiting tombs
(m) Ba-shara	Who followed Islamic law
(n) Beshara	Who are not bound by the Sharait law

Sikh Movement

The Sikh Movement had origins in the medieval period when saint-preacher Guru Nanak, founded the Sikh religion, which started as a minor religion, but developed into a prominent religion over the centuries. There were ten recognised living Gurus in the Nanak line:

1. Guru Nanak (c. 1469–1539 CE):
   - Founder of Sikhism, who was born in Talwandi near Lahore in a respectable family of accountants.
   - Rejected the authority of the Vedas and preached the new idea of God as the supreme, universal, all-powerful, truthful, formless, fearless, without hate, self-existent, ever-lasting creator of all things, the eternal and absolute truth.
   - He denounced caste distinctions and rituals like bathing in holy rivers, and promoted equality of all human beings, including women. He argued that the caste and honour should be judged by the acts or the deeds of individuals. He lay emphasis on concepts of justice, righteousness and liberty.
   - His conception of religion was very practical and sternly ethical. He encouraged people to give up selfishness, falsehood and hypocrisy and advised them to lead a life of truth, honesty and kindness. He guided people to follow the principles of conduct and worship: *sach* (truth), *halal* (lawful earning), *khair* (wishing well of others), *niyat* (right intention) and service to the lord. '*Abide pure amidst the impurities of the world*' was one of his famous sayings.
   - His philosophy consists of three basic elements: a leading charismatic personality (*the Guru*), ideology (*Shabad*) and organisation (*Sangat*).
   - He repudiated idol worship and did not favour pilgrimage, nor did he accept the theory of incarnation. He condemned formalism and ritualism.
   - He introduced the concept of *Langar* (a community kitchen).
   - His main teachings can be summarised as:
     - Faith in one true lord

- Worship of the name
- Necessity of the guru in worship of the name

– God conceptualised as *Nirguna* (attribute less) and *Nirankar* (formless)

2. Guru Angad (c. 1539–1552 CE)
   - His real name was Bhai Lehna.
   - He standardised and popularised the Gurumukhi script of the Punjabi language.
   - He established new religious institutions to strengthen the base of Sikhism and opened many new schools.
   - He popularised and expanded the institution of Guru ka Langar.
   - He started the tradition of *Mall Akhara* for physical as well as spiritual development.
3. Guru Amardas (c. 1552–1574 CE)
   - He reformed the Langar and gave more importance to it.
   - Divided his spiritual empire into 22 parts called *Manjis*, each under a Sikh and also *Piri* system.
   - Strengthened the Langar community kitchen system.
   - Preached against the Hindu society's *sati* system (the act of burning alive of a wife at the pyre of her deceased husband), advocated widow-remarriage and asked the women to discard the *purdah* (veil worn by women).
   - Asked Akbar to remove the toll-tax (pilgrim's tax) for non-Muslims while crossing Yamuna and Ganges rivers.
4. Guru Ramdas (c. 1574–1581 CE)
   - Composed the four *Lawans* (stanzas) of the *Anand Karaj*, a distinct marriage code for Sikhs separate from the orthodox and traditional Hindu Vedic system.
   - Had very cordial relations with Akbar. Akbar granted him a plot of land where the Harmandir Sahib was later constructed. Interestingly, the first brick of Harmandir Sahib was laid down by Hazi Mian Mir (a Muslim).
   - Guru Ramdas also laid the foundation stone of Chak Ramdas or Ramdas Pur, now called Amritsar.
   - Strongly decried superstitions, caste system and pilgrimages.
5. Guru Arjun Dev (c. 1581–1606 CE)
   - Compiled the *Adi Granth*, i.e., *Guru Granth Sahib*, and installed it at Sri Harmandir Sahib.
   - Completed construction of Amritsar, Taran and Kartarpur.
   - Executed by Jahangir for helping his rebellious son Khusrau, and was thus hailed as the first martyr of the Sikh religion, and as *Shaheedan-de-Sartaj* (The crown of martyrs).

6. Guru Har Govind (c. 1606–1644 CE)
   - Longest tenure as Guru. He transformed Sikhs into a militant community, established the *Akal Takht*, and fortified Amritsar.
   - Waged wars against rulers Jahangir and Shah Jahan, and defeated a Mughal army at Sangrama.
   - Took the title of *Sachcha Padshah*.
   - Shifted his headquarters to Kartarpur.
   - Was the proprietor of the concept of *miri* and *piri* (keeping two knives).
7. Guru Har Rai (c. 1644–1661 CE)
   - Gave shelter to Dara Shikoh (brother of Aurangzeb, and his rival to the throne), and thus was persecuted by Aurangzeb, who framed charges of anti-Islamic blasphemy against the Guru and the Guru Granth Sahib.
8. Guru Har Kishan (c. 1661–1664 CE)
   - Was forcibly summoned to Delhi, the imperial capital of Aurangzeb, under framed charges.
   - According to tradition, he died at a young age of 8 years due to smallpox, which he contracted while healing the sick people during an epidemic.
9. Guru Tegh Bahadur (c. 1665–1675 CE)
   - Revolted against Aurangzeb, but was executed by him and was beheaded before the public in Delhi's Chandni Chowk in 1675 CE. The Sis Ganj Sahib Gurudwara stands at the site of his martyrdom today.
   - He appointed Banda Bahadur as the military leader of the Sikhs.
   - Credited with spread Sikhism to Bihar and Assam.
10. Guru Gobind Singh (c. 1675–1708 CE)
    - Last Sikh Guru in human form, who passed the Guruship of the Sikhs to the *Guru Granth Sahib*. He died of complications from stab wounds inflicted by an Afghan, believed to have been sent by the Mughal governor, Wazir Khan.
    - Was born in Patna and organised the Sikhs as community at warriors and called them Khalsa in c. 1699 CE.
    - To create a sense of unity among the Sikhs, the Guru started some practices which were to be followed by Sikhs. These were: initiation through baptism by the double-edged sword, wearing uncut hair, carrying arms and adopting the epithet Singh as part of the name.
    - He selected five persons known as the *Panj piyare* (the five beloved), and requested them to administer the *pahul* (*amrit chakhha*) to him.
    - Compiled the supplementary granth of *Deswan Padshan Ka Granth*.

Importance of the Bhakti Movement

Impact of the Bhakti Movement

(a) Bhakti movement could uplift the position of women and members of the lower strata of the society. It could also provide them an inclusive path to spiritual salvation, which was otherwise considered attainable only by people of the first three orders in the social hierarchy.

(b) Since various preachers of Bhakti Movement spoke and wrote in the regional languages, it provided an impetus for the development of regional languages such as Hindi, Marathi, Bengali, Kannada, etc.

(c) The Bhakti movement provided a simple religion to the people, which was without complicated rituals or dogmas. It helped in the development of a new philosophy of a life of charity and service to fellow human beings.

(d) The synthesis of Bhakti tradition and Sufism also helped in fostering of unity among the two communities, Hindu and Muslims. Also, with the mutual influence and interaction of Sufism and Bhakti traditions even the masses got an opportunity to understand each other's religious traditions and practices, which not only resulted in appreciation for each other traditions but also developed a feeling of mutual respect among each other. In fact, a best example of this interaction and synthesis was the emergence of Urdu as a new language.

Women in the Bhakti Movement

In the Bhakti Movement, a significant role was also played by female poet-saints. However, it is pertinent to note that many of these women saints had to struggle for acceptance within the otherwise largely male-dominated movement and it was only through demonstration of their utter devotion to the Divine, their outstanding poetry and stubborn insistence of their spiritual equality with their contemporaries, they were able to garner acceptance and more egalitarian access to the Divine.

It is also interesting to note that since most of the bhakti poetry was grounded in the everyday familiar language of the ordinary people, the women bhaktas wrote more around the same issues such as the obstacles faced by them at home, family tensions, the absent husband, meaningless household chores, and restrictions of married life, including their status as married women. In many cases, the women saints rejected traditional women's roles and societal norms and left their husbands and homes altogether to become wandering bhaktas, while in some other instances, they tried to engage in Bhakti without discarding their household roles. Interestingly, conforming still largely to the patriarchal ideology that upheld the chaste and dutiful wife as ideal, these women transferred the object of their devotion and their duties as the 'lovers' or 'wives' to their Divine Lover or Husband. In fact, from 6th to 13th centuries far greater number of women took part in the movement's earlier development, while during the later centuries, male bhaktas and saints dominated the Bhakti scene.

Some of the prominent female Bhaktas are:

a. Akkamahadevi: A 12th century bhakti saint who belonged to the southern region of Karnataka and earned the honorific title *'Akka' meaning 'elder sister'* from prominent philosophers of her time Basavanna, Chenna Basavanna, Prabhudeva and Madivalayya. She was as an ardent devotee of Shiva whom she addressed as *Chennamallikarjuna*.

b. Janabai: Was born around 13th century in Maharashtra in a low caste Sudra family. Coincidentally, she worked in the household of one of the most revered bhakti poets, saint Namdeva, and though she never had any formal schooling, she composed over 300 poems focusing on varied aspects pertaining to her life be it domestic chores or about the restrictions she faced as a low caste woman.

c. Mirabai or Mira: She is known for her devotional songs pertaining to Lord Krishna and interestingly her poetry portrays a unique relationship with Krishna as she is not only

FIGURE 15.11 Mirabai

being portrayed as the devoted bride of Krishna, but Krishna is also portrayed as in pursuit of Mira. Mira belonged to a high class ruling Rajput family and was married to the son of Rana Sanga of Mewar at an early age but she was not interested in household life and eventually, she left her husband and family and went on a pilgrimage to various places associated with her divine husband, Krishna. Though she was rejected initially being a woman, yet Mirabai's reputation of devotion, piety and intellectual astuteness eventually led to her inclusion within the community of the saints of Brindavan.

d. Bahinabai or Bahina: She was a poet-saint from 17th century Maharashtra, who wrote different *abangas*, women's folk songs, that portray the working life of woman, especially in the fields.

QUESTIONS FROM LAST YEAR'S PRELIMS

1. The world's second tallest statue in sitting pose of Ramanuja was inaugurated by the Prime Minister of India at Hyderabad recently. Which one of the following statements correctly represents the teachings of Ramanuja? **(2022)**

(a) The best means of salvation was devotion.

(b) Vedas are eternal, self-existent and wholly authoritative.

(c) Logical arguments were essential means for the highest bliss

(d) Salvation was to be obtained through meditation.

2. Consider the following statements: **(2019)**

1. Saint Nimbarka was a contemporary of Akbar.
2. Saint Kabir was greatly influenced by Shaikh Ahmad Sirhindi. Which of the statements given above is/are correct?

(a) 1 only (b) 2 only

(c) Both 1 and 2 (d) Neither 1 nor 2

3. With reference to cultural history of India, consider the following statements: **(2018)**

1. Most of the Tyagaraja Kritis are devotional songs in praise of Lord Krishna.
2. Tyagaraja created several new ragas.
3. Annamacharya and Tyagaraja are contemporaries.
4. Annamacharya kirtanas are devotional songs in praise of Lord Venkateshwara.

Which of the statements given above are correct?

(a) 1 and 3 only (b) 2 and 4 only

(c) 1, 2 and 3 (d) 2, 3 and 4

4. Consider the following statements: **(2014)**

i. 'Bijak' is a composition of the teachings of Saint Dadu Dayal.

ii. The philosophy of Pushti Marg was propounded by Madhvacharya.

Which of the statements given above is/are correct?

(a) i only (b) ii only

(c) Both i and ii (d) Neither i nor ii

5. Consider the following Bhakti Saints: **(2013)**

i. Dadu Dayal

ii. Guru Nanak

iii. Tyagaraja

Who among the above was/were preaching when the Lodhi dynasty fell and Babur took over?

(a) i and iii (b) ii only
(c) ii and iii (d) i and ii

6. Among the following, who was not a proponent of Bhakti cult? **(2010)**
(a) Nagarjuna (b) Tukaram
(c) Tyagaraja (d) Vallabhacharya

7. Anekantavada is a core theory and philosophy of which one of the following? **(2009)**
(a) Buddhism (b) Jainism
(c) Sikhism (d) Vaishnavism

8. Bhakta Tukaram was a contemporary of which Mughal Emperor? **(2006)**
(a) Babur (b) Akbar
(c) Jahangir (d) Aurangzeb

9. Which one of the following sequences indicates the correct chronological order? **(2004)**
(a) Shankaracharya – Ramanuja – Chaitanya
(b) Ramanuja – Shankaracharya – Chaitanya
(c) Ramanuja – Chaitanya – Shankaracharya
(d) Shankaracharya – Chaitanya – Ramanuja

10. Consider the following statements about the Sikh Gurus: **(2004)**
i. Banda Bahadur was appointed as the military leader of the Sikhs by Guru Tegh Bahadur.
ii. Guru Arjun Dev became the Sikh Guru after Guru Ram Das.
iii. Guru Arjun Dev gave to Sikhs their own script, Guru Mukhi.

Which of the statements given above is/are correct?
(a) i only (b) ii and iii
(c) i and iii (d) i and ii

11. Who among the following was the first Bhakti saint to use Hindi for the propagation of his message? **(2002)**
(a) Dadu (b) Kabir
(c) Ramananda (d) Tulsidas

12. With reference to Sufism in Indian history, consider the following statements: **(2002)**
i. Shaikh Ahmad Sarhandi was a contemporary of Ibrahim Lodhi.
ii. Shaikh Nasruddin Chirag-i-Dehlavi was a disciple of Shaikh Nizamuddin Auliya.
iii. Aurangzeb was a contemporary of Shaikh Salim Chisti.
iv. The Qadiri order of Sufis was first introduced in India by Shaikh Niamtullah and Makhdum Muhammad Jilani.

Which of these statements are correct?
(a) i and ii (b) i and iii
(c) ii and iii (d) ii and iv

13. Match List I with List II and select the correct answer using the code given below the lists: **(2001)**

List I (Bhakti Saint)	List II (Profession)
(a) Namdeva	i. Barber
(b) Kabir	ii. Weaver
(c) Ravidas	iii. Tailor
(d) Sena	iv. Cobbler

Code:	A	B	C	D
(a)	ii	iii	i	iv
(b)	iii	ii	iv	i
(c)	iii	ii	i	iv
(d)	ii	iii	iv	i

14. Assertion (A): The sponsor and the most prominent figure of the Chisti order of Sufis in India is Khwaja Moinuddin Chisti.

Reason (R): The Chisti order takes its name from a village Chisti in Ajmer. **(1997)**

(a) Both A and R are true and R is the correct explanation of A
(b) Both A and R are true but R is not the correct explanation of A
(c) A is true but R is false
(d) A is false but R is true

15. Prem Vatika, the poems on the life of Krishna, was composed by: **(1996)**
(a) Bihari (b) Surdas
(c) Raskhan (d) Kabir

16. The Sufi Saint who maintained that devotional music was one way of coming close to God was **(1996)**
(a) Muin-ud-din Chisti
(b) Baba Farid
(c) Saiyyad Muhammad Gesudaraz
(d) Shah Alam Bukhari

ANSWERS

1. (a)	2. (d)	3. (b)	4. (d)	5.(b)	6. (a)	7. (b)	8. (c)
9. (a)	10. (d)	11. (c)	12. (d)	13. (b)	14. (c)	15. (c)	16. (b)

QUESTIONS FROM LAST YEAR'S MAINS

1. Evaluate the nature of the Bhakti Literature and its contribution to Indian culture. **(2021 GS1)**

2. The Bhakti movement received a remarkable re-orientation with the advent of Sri Chaitanya Mahaprabhu. Discuss. **(2018 GS1)**

3. Sufis and medieval saints failed to modify either religious ideas and practices or the outward structure of Hindu/Muslim societies to any appreciable extent. Comment. **(2014 GS1)**

4. Evaluate the contribution of Vaishnava saints to the growth of medieval Bhakti literature. **(2014, History optional)**

5. Discuss and evaluate critically various trends in the historiography of Bhakti. **(2013, History optional)**

PRACTICE QUESTIONS – PRELIMS

1. Match List I with List II and select the correct answer using the code given below the lists:

List I	List II
(a) Bengal	i. Chaitanya
(b) Sri Perumbudur	ii. Ramananda
(c) Amritsar	iii. Ramanuja
(d) Benaras	iv. Ramdas

Code:	A	B	C	D
(a)	ii	iv	iii	i
(b)	ii	iii	iv	i
(c)	i	iv	iii	ii
(d)	i	iii	iv	ii

2. Who among the following was not an exponent of the Bhakti Movement in northern India?

(a) Nanak (b) Shankaracharya
(c) Ramananda (d) Kabir

3. Consider the following:
i. The pioneer in preaching Nirguna Bhakti in medieval India was Ramananda.
ii. Surdas was the blind poet who worshipped Krishna.
iii. Shankaracharya established four mathas in the four corners of India.

Select the correct answer using the codes given below:
(a) i and ii only (b) iii only
(c) i and iii only (d) i, ii and iii

4. Match List I with List II and select the correct answer using the code given below the lists:

List I	List II
(a) Tawakkhul	i. Teacher
(b) Beshara	ii. To observe contentment
(c) Bashara	iii. Bound by Shariat Law
(d) Wali	iv. Not bound by Shariat Law

Code:	A	B	C	D
(a)	ii	iv	iii	i
(b)	ii	iii	iv	i
(c)	i	iv	iii	ii
(d)	i	iii	iv	ii

5. Match List I with List II and select the correct answer using the code given below the lists:

List I	List II
(a) Guru Nanak	i. Introduced the concept of Langar
(b) Guru Arjun Dev	ii. Khalsa
(c) Guru Ram Das	iii. Anand Karaj
(d) Guru Gobind Singh	iv. Compiled Guru Granth Sahib

Code:	A	B	C	D
(a)	ii	iv	iii	i
(b)	ii	iii	iv	i
(c)	i	iv	iii	ii
(d)	i	iii	iv	ii

6. Consider the following:
i. Aurangzeb executed Guru Angad.
ii. Guru Arjun Dev was executed by Jahangir.

Select the incorrect answer using the codes given below:
(a) i and ii only (b) i only
(c) ii only (d) None

ANSWERS

1. (d) 2. (b) 3. (d) 4.(a) 5. (c) 6. (b)

PRACTICE QUESTIONS – MAINS

1. Delineate the role of Sikh Gurus in the development of Sikhism.

2. Bhakti Movement and Sufism were both categorical in promoting Hindu–Muslim unity. Do you agree? Substantiate your answer with examples.

3. Maharashtra has a rich tradition of Bhakti saints, and the Maratha rulers have also promoted Bhakti cults. Elaborate with examples.

CHAPTER

16

The Advent of Europeans

With the discovery of a new sea route via Cape of Good Hope by Vasco da Gama[1] in 1498, many trading companies came to India and established their trading centres. At the outset, they entered India as traders but with the passage of time, in order to safeguard their commercial interests, they tried to dominate the politics of India. Thus, the commercial rivalry among the European powers led to political rivalry and this not only brought them in conflict with each other but with Indian rulers too.

---

[1] Vasco da Gama landed in Calicut in 1498 during the reign of Tuluva Narsa Nayaka, who was the father of Vira Narasimha, the founder of the Tuluva dynasty.

The Portuguese

The Portuguese hold the distinction of being the first Europeans to reach India and ironically, were also the last to leave in 1961, when Indian Government took the reigns of Goa, Daman and Diu from them. **Prince Henry** of Portugal encouraged voyages for discovery of a sea route to India. The first Portuguese who succeeded in reaching the Cape of Good Hope was **Bartholomew Diaz** in 1487. Later, following his footsteps, **Vasco da Gama** reached the port of **Calicut** on 21 May 1498, making it a landmark day in the history of India's maritime trade. He was warmly received by **Zamorin**, the Hindu ruler of Calicut, and he returned to Portugal the next year making huge profits. The Portuguese established trading stations at **Calicut, Cannanore** and **Cochin** (first Portuguese fort) with the dream of monopolising eastern trade and excluding their competitors, especially the Arabs.

The first governor of the Portuguese in India was **Francisco de Almeida** who pursued the famous '**Blue Water Policy**' through which he advocated 'making Portuguese the master of the Indian Ocean by being powerful at sea instead of building fortresses on Indian land'. Later in 1510, the second governor, **Alfonso de Albuquerque**, the real founder of the Portuguese power, captured Goa from the ruler of Bijapur (during reign of Sikander Lodhi), and thereafter Goa became the capital of the Portuguese settlements in India and, interestingly, also the first territory to be under Europeans since the times of Alexander. Albuquerque not only captured Malacca and Ceylon but also gained strategic control of the Indian Ocean by establishing Portuguese bases overlooking all the entrances to the sea such as Malabar, Ormuz, East Africa and the Red Sea. He also encouraged his countrymen to marry Indian women probably to secure permanent Portuguese population in India. At the time of his death in 1515, he left the Portuguese as the strongest naval power in India.

In 1530, **Nino da Cunha** acquired Diu and Bassein from Bahadur Shah of Gujarat. Later, Portuguese settlements were also established in Daman, Salsette and Bombay on the west coast and at San Thome near Chennai and Hooghli in Bengal on the east coast. However, the Portuguese power declined in India by the end of the 16th century and they lost all their possessions in India **except** Goa, Diu and Daman. The Portuguese acts of piracy and prosecution of Muslims brought them in conflict with the Mughals. In 1631, the Portuguese lost Hooghly during the reign of **Shah Jahan**. In 1661, the Portuguese king gave **Bombay** as a gift to **Charles II** of **England** for marrying his sister. In 1663, the Dutch ousted the Portuguese from the Malabar Coast. The Marathas captured Salsette and Bassein in 1739 and Portuguese power declined substantially, never coming back to its glory days.

Reasons for Decline of the Portuguese

- **Emergence of More Powerful Trading Competitors such as the English and the Dutch**: Gradually, other European traders like the Dutch and the English emerged on the scene, and due to fierce struggle for control of trade among them, the less resourceful and comparatively weak Portuguese had to give up its territories to its opponents. Also, the emergence of powerful dynasties circumventing the Indian Ocean, like Persia and Egypt, caused a setback to the monopoly of the Portuguese over the Indo-European trade. The rise of conflicts with strong local powers such as the Marathas further endangered their position.

- **Religious Intolerance**: The religious policies of the Portuguese further weakened their position in the Indian subcontinent, because with their proselytising activities and antagonistic attitude towards Muslims, they alienated both Hindus and Muslims. The Jesuit activities gave rise to political fears, and some instances of forceful conversion to Christianity added fuel to the fire.
- **Clandestine Practices in Trade and Piracy**: Due to their dishonest trade practices and sea piracy, the Portuguese were resented by all, ranging from the mighty Mughals to rulers of small states along with the other European competitors too. The regular naval assaults by the Portuguese brought them in conflict with all these powers and, thus, further weakened Portuguese territorial occupation.
- **Discovery of Brazil**: It diverted the focus of Portugal to the West as it was easy for them to colonise Brazil, devoid of any other troubling competition. Brazil soon emerged as an economic centre of the overseas empire of Portugal, gradually superseding Goa.

Portuguese Gifts to India

- Cultivation of tobacco and potato
- First printing press in India (1556)
- First scientific work on Indian medicinal plants
- Introduced various military innovation techniques like body armour, matchlock men and drilling groups of infantry

The Dutch

The first Dutch expedition which reached the East Indies was led by **Cornelis de Houtman** in 1596. In March 1602, the Dutch East India Company amalgamating many other trading companies was formed. Interestingly, it is often considered to be not only the first multinational corporation in the world but also the first company to issue stock. In 1605, the Dutch set up their first factory at **Masulipatnam** (Andhra Pradesh). Other Dutch factories were at Pulicat, Chinsurah (Gustavus fort), Kasim Bazar, Patna, Balasore, Surat, Karaikal, Nagapattinam and Cochin. In fact, **Pulicat** emerged as the headquarters of Dutch operations in India and from 1617, the Chief of Pulicat also functioned as the Dutch Governor in India, and the factory at Pulicat was known as **Fort Geldria**. However, Pulicat was later replaced by **Nagapattinam**, which they had captured from the Portuguese.

The credit of dislodging the Portuguese from India's maritime trade and establishing Indian textiles as the premier export of India goes to the Dutch. In 1619, the Dutch company conquered Java, and by 1623 effectively controlled the **English** competition in the Malaya Archipelago (though by the infamous massacre of Englishmen at Amboyna). Soon, the Dutch monopolised the trade in black pepper and spices though they also traded in cotton, indigo, rice, silk and opium. The Anglo–Dutch rivalry lasted for about 7 decades during which period the **Dutch** lost their settlements to the **British** one by one and the final collapse of the Dutch came with their defeat by English in the **Battle of Biderra** in 1759.

The English

The **English East India Company** was established on 31 December 1600 as 'The Company of Merchants of London Trading into the East Indies' by a royal Charter issued by Queen **Elizabeth I**. Initially, the company had rights of exclusive trading for fifteen years, but in 1609 CE, through a fresh charter, the monopoly of the company was extended indefinitely. In 1609 itself, Captain **William Hawkins** arrived at the court of Mughal Emperor **Jahangir** to seek permission to establish a *factory* (store house of goods) in Surat. But, it was refused by the Mughal Emperor due to **Portuguese** opposition. The English, thus, started trading at Masulipatnam (located on the southeastern coast) in 1611, which was developed into a factory in 1616. However, in 1612, impressed by the defeat of the Portuguese at the hands of Captain **Thomas Best** in the sea off Surat, Jahangir issued a *farman* (permission letter) to the English and they established a trading factory in Surat in 1613. Later in 1615, Sir **Thomas Roe** came to the Mughal court as the ambassador of James I, the King of England, and obtained permission from Jahangir to establish English trading factories at Agra, Ahmedabad and Broach.

- The company's position was further improved in 1632 when they earned the privilege of trading freely in the ports of Golconda through the ***golden farman*** issued to them by the Sultan of Golconda. The Company established its first factory in East India at **Balasore** (Orissa) in **1633**.
- In 1639, **Francis Day** obtained the site of Madras from Raja of Chandragiri[2] (which was later renamed as **Fort St. George**). Madras soon replaced Masulipatnam as the headquarters of English in the Coromandel Coast.
- The English East India Company acquired Bombay from Charles II, the then King of England on lease at an annual rent of £10 in 1668 and Bombay became the headquarters of the company in the west coast.
- In 1690, **Job Charnock**, an agent of the East India Company, purchased three villages, namely Sutanuti, Gobindapur and Kalikata, which, in course of time, grew into the city of Calcutta (**Fort William**, renamed after the English King, William III) and which later became the capital of British India.

[2] On a plot of land leased from a representative of the Vijayanagara empire.

- The factories and trading centres that the English established all along the sea coast of India were, thus, grouped under three presidencies, namely Bombay, Madras (**Fort St. George**) and Calcutta (**Fort William**).
- In 1701, Emperor **Aurangzeb** ordered the general arrest of all the Europeans in India due to their aggressiveness on mughal ships and territory but the English could be controlled only for a short time. In 1715, an English surgeon, **William Hamilton**, cured Mughal Emperor **Farukhsiyar** of a disease and as result of this, in 1717, the English mission led by the Governor of Calcutta, **John Surman** secured three valuable *farmans*, which were also regarded as **Magna Carta** of the company (since they provided a large number of trade concessions to Company at Bengal, Gujarat and Hyderabad).

Important highlights of 1717 Magna Carta of the Company

- The Company's imports and exports were exempted from additional customs duties excepting the earlier settled annual payment of ₹3,000.
- The Company was permitted to issue dastaks (passes) for the movement of their goods.
- The Company was permitted to rent more lands around Calcutta.
- The Company was permitted to mint its own coins and it was decreed that the coins minted by the company at Bombay were a legal currency throughout the Mughal empire.
- In Hyderabad, the Company retained its existing privilege of no duties and had to pay only for the prevailing rent for Madras.
- In Surat, for an annual payment of ₹10,000 the Company could secure exemption from levy of all duties.

The Danes (from Denmark)

The Danes formed an East India Company in 1616. They established a settlement at Tranquebar (Tamil Nadu) in 1620 and at Serampore (Bengal) in 1676. Serampore was their headquarters in India. However, they failed to strengthen themselves and were forced to sell all their settlements of India to the British in 1845. They are known more for their **missionary activities** than commerce.

The French

The French were the **last** Europeans to arrive in India for sharing the fruits of Indo-European trade. The French East India Company *La compagnie des Indes Orientales* was formed in 1664 by **Colbert**, a minister under Louis XIV. In 1668, **François Caron** established the first French factory in India at Surat and then, in 1669, **Marcara**, a Persian who accompanied Caron, succeeded in establishing another factory at Masulipatinam. Later, in 1673 **François Martin** founded **Pondicherry** (Fort

Louis), the headquarters of the French possessions in India and became its first governor too. He gradually transformed Pondicherry from a small fishing village to a flourishing and important port town. In 1690, Chandernagore (in Bengal) was acquired from Shaista Khan, the Mughal governor. Other French factories in India were Mahe, Balasore, Qasim Bazar and Karaikal. The French had to face perpetual conflict from both the Dutch and the English. The arrival of **Dupleix** as the French Governor in India in 1742 saw the beginning of **Anglo–French** conflict that resulted in the famous ***Carnatic* Wars**.

Anglo–French Rivalry

In the beginning of the 18th century, the English and the French were competing with each other to establish their supremacy in India. The Anglo–French rivalry, taking the form of three ***Carnatic* Wars**, were decisive in terms of the British conquest in south India. *Carnatic* was the name given by the Europeans to the Coromandel Coast and its nearby hinterland. A part of the fallout of the events of the Carnatic Wars was that the weaknesses of the Indian regional powers, in particular their inability to make naval interventions and the ineffectiveness of their large unorganised, indisciplined armies against smaller European forces became manifest and this had grave implications in the political history of the rest of the 18th century.

First Carnatic War (1746–1748)

English under **Commodore Barnett** captured French ships

Dupleix (French Governor of Pondicherry)

(a) Appealed for help to French Governor of Mauritius La Bourdonnais

(b) Madras was captured by French

Cause of the First *Carnatic* War

The First Carnatic War was the Indian theatre of war for the **Austrian succession**. In 1742, war broke out between **France** and **Britain** in Europe over the **Austrian** War of Succession and in 1746 the English Navy under **Commodore Barnett** started the war in India by seizing some French ships. France retaliated by seizing **Madras** (St. George) with the help of the fleet from Mauritius, under French Governor Admiral La Bourbonnais while the English sought help from the Nawab of *Carnatic* **Anwar-ud-din**.

The English under Commodore Barnett captured the French ships.

Important Battles and Treaty Pertaining to the First Carnatic War

1.a **Battle of Adyar** (1746, also known as Battle of St. Thome which exposed the indiscipline of Indian Army): It was fought between the **French** and **Mehfuz Khan** (representative of Nawab **Anwar-ud-din**) to capture/restore Madras in which a small disciplined French army defeated a much larger unorganised Indian army.

Later, in 1748, the Austrian war of succession ended in Europe, so battle also stopped in India, resulting in the Treaty of Aix-la-Chapelle.

1.b **Treaty of Aix-la-Chapelle** (1748) →
- Madras was restored to English.
- Louis-burg in North America was given to France.

Second Carnatic War (1749–1754)
- **English** supported **Nasir Jung** for Hyderabad and Nawab **Anwar-ud-din** for Carnatic
- **Dupleix** supported **Muzzaffar Jung** for Hyderabad and **Chanda Sahib** for Carnatic

Cause of the Second *Carnatic* War

Both the French and English wanted to increase their political influence in southern India so they frequently indulged in interfering in local dynastic disputes. When the Nizam of Hyderabad died in 1748, it resulted in a war of succession among different contenders to the throne, similarly in the *Carnatic*, the appointment of Anwar-ud-din as the Nawab was resented by Chanda Sahib. This all culminated in the Second *Carnatic* War as both the English and French supported opposite camps.

Important Battles and Treaty Pertaining to the Second Carnatic War

2.a Battle of Ambur (1749)

The **French** side defeated Nawab Anwar-ud-din at Ambur and his son Mohammed Ali escaped to Tiruchirappalli for safety and surrendered to the English. Meanwhile, Chanda Sahib, the Nawab of *Carnatic*, rewarded Dupleix by giving Valudanoor, Villianoor and Bahur, near Pondicherry and marched towards Tiruchirappalli to capture Muhammed Ali. Since Nasir Jung (British ally) lost his life in an encounter in 1750, Muzaffar Jung became Nizam and he amply rewarded the French.

2.b Battle of Arcot (1751)

Robert Clive (an English officer) suggested a plan to attack **Arcot** (capital of *Carnatic*), which was approved by Governor Saunders, and he sent a small army with Robert Clive and Major Lawrence. Clive captured Arcot and earned the tag of Hero of Arcot. Meanwhile, French forces and Chanda Sahib were defeated at Arni and Kaveripakkam and Chanda Sahib was beheaded in 1752. Since, Dupleix failed to capture Tiruchirappalli, and also due to heavy financial losses, he was recalled to France in 1754. Godeheu succeeded Dupleix as the French Governor and he adopted a policy of negotiations with the English.

2.c Treaty of Pondicherry

- The English and the French agreed not to interfere in the quarrels of the native states.
- The English emerged as the real winner in *Carnatic*, but still French possessions were given back to France, and each party was left in possession of the territories actually occupied by them at the time of the treaty.

A key change in Indian authority during the course of the Second *Carnatic* War was that it became dependent on European support, and regional rulers like Muhammad Ali (*Carnatic*) and Salabat Jung (Hyderabad) functioned more as clients rather than patrons to these European powers.

Third Carnatic War (1756–1763)

French **Count de Lally** captured English Fort St. David and recalled Bussy (French General in Hyderabad) to assist him at Madras. Due to this mistake, French lost political influence in Hyderabad. Later, Lally lost Madras too.

English attacked Northern Circars when Bussy left and forced **Salabat Jung** (Nizam of Hyderabad) to change sides.

The Third *Carnatic* War decisively put an end to the French ambitions in India, and its political influence completely disappeared after the war. Henceforth, the French, like the Portuguese, the Dutch and the Danes, were confined to only commercial pursuits and that too in a small periphery. Hereafter, the **English** emerged as supreme power across the Indian subcontinent. It is pertinent to note that unlike the earlier two *Carnatic* wars, which were limited to Deccan only, the Third *Carnatic* War spread to Bengal too.

Cause of the Third *Carnatic* War

- As a result of the Seven Year's War (1756–63) in Europe, the French and English settlements in India also became involved in open hostilities.

Important Battles and Treaty Pertaining to the Third Carnatic War

3.a. **Battle of Wandiwash** (1760): The French under Counte de Lally were defeated by Sir Eyre Coote at Wandiwash (in Tamil Nadu) and this battle gave the British trading company a far superior position in India compared to the other Europeans. Later, in 1761, the French had to eventually surrender Pondicherry too. The Battle of Wandiwash is regarded as an equally decisive battle as the Battle of Plassey (1757) in terms of the British conquest of India because with their victory at Wandiwash, the British could eliminate their last, most important and strong European rival, that is, the French, from the Indian subcontinent (since they had already defeated the Dutch at the Battle of Biderra in 1759). With this win, they clearly emerged as a supreme European power across the Indian subcontinent.

3.b. **Treaty of Paris**

- Pondicherry, Karaikal and other French possessions were returned to the French on condition that they should not fortify them.

Causes for the English Success and French Failure in Anglo–French Rivalry

- Commercial and naval superiority of the English, combined with good leadership skills of able commanders such as Robert Clive, Sir Eyre Coote and Major Lawrence as compared to only a few such as Dupleix on the French side. Difference of opinion between the French generals at times also hampered their military strategies.
- Private nature of the English Company with less governmental control aided in quick decision-making as opposed to the French Company, which being state concern, had to face more controls and regulations which at times, resulted in delayed decision-making. Also, at certain instances, the French could not muster adequate support at the right time from the French government.
- The French had support only in the Deccan but the English had a strong base and larger resources at its command in Bengal.
- The English had three important ports – Calcutta, Bombay and Madras – but the French had only Pondicherry.
- England's victory in the European wars decided the destiny of the French in India.

The Conquest of Bengal

The **struggle with the French** for supremacy in south India marked the first phase of the British conquest of India and proceeding further in the sequence of events, the **conquest of Bengal** proved to be the second and the most decisive step. Bengal was one of the most fertile and richest of India's provinces, and the English East India Company had highly profitable trading interests in the province as Bengal goods came to comprise nearly 60 per cent of English imports from Asia. As we have earlier discussed that, through the royal *farman* of **1717**, the Company secured valuable trading privileges but this *farman*, however, became a **perpetual source of conflict** between the Company and the Nawabs of Bengal.

The *farman* granted the Company the freedom to export and import their goods in Bengal without paying taxes and also the right to issue passes or *dastaks* for the movement of such goods. It is pertinent to note that, though the Company's servants were also permitted to trade but they were not covered by this *farman* and were required to pay taxes as Indian merchants. Since, the Nawabs on multiple occasions had refused to extend the duty-free provision to private trade of the Company officials, the latter, therefore took to rampant misuse of *dastaks*, which led to development of hostilities towards each other. Matters came to a head in **1756**, when young **Siraj-ud-Daulah** succeeded his grandfather, **Alivardi Khan**, and threatened the lucrative English private trade by stopping all misuse of *dastaks*. The breaking point came with the grant of asylum to Krishna Ballabh, who was charged with fraud by the Nawab and the new fortifications at Calcutta by the Company without taking Nawab's permission.

Background of Battle of Plassey (1757)

Paved the way for foundation of British Rule in India.

In Bengal, as we have already discussed:

Murshid Quli Khan

↓

Shuja-ud-din Khan (son-in-law of Murshid Quli Khan)

↓

Sarfaraz Khan (son)

↓

Alivardi Khan

↓

Death of Alivardi Khan

↓

Siraj-ud-Daulah (Alivardi's Grandson)

- As compared to Alivardi Khan, Siraj-ud-Daulah was a young, inexperienced and quick-tempered ruler, who had to face continuous opposition from **Ghasiti Begum** (widow of Alivardi Khan), **Shaukat Jung** (his rival cousin, who was also Nawab of Purnea) and **Mir Jafar** (rebellious commander of the army whom Siraj-ud-Daulah dismissed and replaced with Mir Madan).

↓

- Came in conflict with British as he was against misuse of **dastaks** (that is, seals of trading).
- Prevented British from fortifying **Fort William** (Calcutta).
- Attacked English factory at Kasimbazar on British refusal of fortifying and occupied the Fort William on 20 June 1756. Some references of Black Hole tragedy (wherein, many English prisoners were holed up in one room and as a consequence they died of suffocation).
- He then retired from Calcutta to celebrate his easy victory, letting the English escape with their ships to Fulta near the sea protected by their naval superiority, a mistake for which he paid dearly later.

This precipitated in a crisis, and in the meantime, the English organised a web of intrigue and treachery with the leading men of the Nawab's court such as **Mir Jafar** (Commander in chief of Siraj), **Khadim Khan** (commanded large number of the Nawab's troops), **Manik Chand** (Officer in charge of Calcutta), **Amichand** (Rich merchant), **Jagat Seth** (Biggest banker of Bengal) and **Robert Clive** along with **Admiral Watson** now arrived with a strong force from Madras. Clive reconquered Calcutta in the beginning of 1757 and apprehensive of an Afghan attack under Abdali, Siraj now preferred a negotiated settlement, but a confident Clive decided on a *coup d'etat* and conspired to replace Siraj with Mir Jafar resulting in the fateful **Battle of Plassey** which marked the beginning of political rule of the Company and laid the foundation of the British empire in India.

Battle of Plassey (23 June 1757)

↓

Siraj-ud-Daulah (was captured and executed by Miran, Mir Jafar's son).	Robert Clive and Mir Jafar (Commander-in-chief of Siraj).

- Was a battle only in name as the English victory in the battle was predecided, much before the first shot was fired since a major part of the Nawab's army remained inactive and took no part in the fighting. It was not a great battle but was rather a great betrayal.
- Only a small group of Nawab soldiers led by Mir Madan and Mohan Lal fought bravely but could hardly bring a difference to the outcome of the battle, that is, victory of English and Mir Jafar.
- The Nawab was forced to flee and was captured and put to death by Miran, Mir Jafar's son.

Outcomes of Battle of Plassey

- The English proclaimed **Mir Jafar** as Nawab of Bengal and indulged in plunder of vast resources of Bengal, often referred to as the '**Plassey Plunder**'.

- The Company was granted undisputed monopoly over the right to free trade in **Bengal, Bihar** and **Orissa**. It also received the *zamindari* of the 24 *Parganas* near Calcutta and a whopping sum of ₹17,700,000 as compensation for the attack on Calcutta.
- In addition, Mir Jafar also paid large sums of bribes disguised as 'gifts' to the high officials of the Company. Clive himself got a personal jagir and over ₹2 million.
- Moreover, it led to the tacit understanding that British officials and merchants would no longer be asked to pay any taxes on their private trade.
- Robert Clive was appointed Governor of Bengal (1758–60) and he consolidated the British power both in Bengal and in the Deccan.

Significance of Battle of Plassey

- Immense **historical importance** as it paved the way for the British mastery of Bengal and eventually whole of India. Boosted British prestige and at a single stroke raised them to the status of a major contender for the Indian Empire.
- The **economic significance** of Battle of Plassey was far greater than the immediate political one. The rich revenues of Bengal enabled them to organise a strong army, and thus also, played a decisive role in Anglo-French struggle.
- Brought major change in the nature and structure of British trade as prior to 1757, the English trade in Bengal was largely financed through import of bullion from England, but after 1757, interestingly not only bullion import stopped but reversely bullion was exported from Bengal to China and other parts of India, which gave a competitive advantage to the English Company over its European rivals.

"Night of Eternal gloom for India"

-- ***Poet Nabin Chandra Sen***

"Bengal in particular was not to know peace again until it had been bleed white"

-- ***British historians Edward Thompson and G. T. Garrett***

> *"The single aim of the Company officials was to grasp all they could; to use Mir Jafar as a golden sack into which they could dip their hands at pleasure"*
> -- ***Colonel Malleson***

Mir Jafar

- Mir Jafar soon discovered that his treasury was getting emptied by not only the unnecessary regular presents and bribes to the Company officials but also due to the unreasonable demands of the Company officials as they wanted Bengal to pay for the expenses of the Bombay and Madras Presidencies and purchase out of Bengal's revenue all the Company's exports from India, which were almost impossible for him to meet.
- The Company officials too started criticizing Nawab for his incapacity in fulfilling their expectations and thus, in 1760, he was forced to resign in favour of his son-in-law Mir Qasim.

Mir Qasim

- Mir Qasim on securing the throne, rewarded Company by granting the **zamindari** of the districts of Burdwan, Midnapore, and Chittagong, and also gave handsome presents totalling around ₹29 lakhs to higher officials. But, he was not as docile as British had hoped.
- He was an able, efficient and a strong ruler who soon emerged as a threat to English position in Bengal. He tried to maintain public order, increase revenues by removing corruption from the administration, raise a modern and disciplined army on European lines and also tried to free himself from English control.
- In order to ward off company's influence, he shifted his capital from Murshidabad to Munger and also established a gun factory at Munger.
- He tried to check the misuse of the *farman* of 1717 by the Company officials through which they not only used to evade customs duty but also compelled the Indian artisans, peasants and merchants to sell their goods cheap but forced them to buy dear from them. This used to hurt the Indian merchants as they had to pay taxes from which the foreigners got complete exemption from. Thus, in order to address the recurrent problem of misuse of *dastaks* by the Company officials while giving his own subjects a concession that the English had seized by force, he took the drastic step of **abolishing all duties** on internal trade, thus, providing a equal level playing field to Indian merchants too. The English, however, did not like this display of independence and as a retaliatory measure, again replaced him with Mir Jafar.

Mir Jafar

- In 1763, Mir Jafar was again placed on the throne and again huge sums were extorted from him by Company Officials.
- After Mir Jafar's death, British placed his second son **Nizam-ud-Daulah** on the throne.

Nizam-ud-Daulah

- He was made to sign a new treaty with British through which, most of the army of Nawab was disbanded and he was required to administer Bengal through a Deputy *Subahdar* (nominated by the Company and who could not be dismissed without its approval). The Company, thus gained supreme control over the *nizamat* that is, administration of Bengal specially over the law and order and criminal justice.
- In December 1763, **Mir Qasim** fled from Bengal and tried to form a grand alliance with the fugitive Mughal Emperor **Shah Alam II** and Nawab of Awadh **Shuja-ud-Daulah** against the British. The three allies clashed with the Company's army at Battle of Buxar but were thoroughly defeated.

Battle of Buxar (1764): made the English virtually the masters of Bengal, Bihar and Orissa

Battle of Buxar (22 October 1764)

- Mir Qasim, Mughal Emperor Shah Alam II and Shuja-ud-Daulah (Nawab of Awadh)
- English led by Major Hector Munro

Outcome and Significance of the Battle of Buxar

- One of the most **decisive battles** of Indian history as it demonstrated the superiority of English arms over the combined army of two of the major Indian powers and firmly established the British as masters of Bengal, Bihar and Orissa and placed Awadh at their mercy.
- The victory of British in Battle of Buxar not only **confirmed** the verdict of Plassey, that is, establishing the British as one of the prominent political powers in India but also somehow sealed the fate of India by demonstrating superiority of Company over the other Indian contenders.
- **Treaty of Allahabad** (1765): Victory of British made it *defacto* power in Bengal; however, the Treaty of Allahabad converted the company into *dejure* power too as through this treaty, Mughal Emperor Shah Alam II legitimised the company's control over Bengal.

- Shah Alam II was forced to grant the **diwani rights** (that is, revenue collecting rights) of **Bengal, Bihar** and **Orissa** to the English. The districts of Kara and Allahabad were given to Shah Alam II and English accorded pension of ₹26 lakhs per year to him.
- Province of Awadh was returned to Nawab Shuja-ud-Daulah but he had to pay war indemnity of ₹50 lakhs to English. A British resident was posted at his court and he was forced to maintain English troops for the defence of his state. The Company also secured free trading rights in Awadh (a clause which in later years created tensions and prepared the grounds for annexation of Awadh itself).
- The **British resident** posted at the court of Murshidabad, thereafter became the locus of real administrative power in the province, and thus from Bengal started the system of indirect rule or **Dual Government**.

Dual Government (1765–72)

- Robert Clive introduced a new administrative system in Bengal called the **Dual Government** or the rule of two in which:
  - Nominal Head – **Nawab of Bengal**
  - Real **Power – EIC (East India Company)**

This dual government was ended later by **Warren Hastings** in 1772.

- Dual Government can also be understood as dual system of administration, wherein the East India Company was enjoying all the politico-military-economic authority in Bengal while the Nawab of Bengal was only a nominal/titular head.
- The East India Company became real masters of Bengal at least from 1765 as they controlled the finances and army of the province directly and its administration indirectly. The Nawab and his officials had the responsibility of administration but not the power to discharge it. On the other hand, the British had all the power without any responsibility.
- In this kind of arrangement[3]:
  - British army was in sole control of Bengal defence.
  - Supreme political power was in British hands.
  - As the *Diwan*, Company directly collected revenues.
  - Through right to nominate the Deputy *Subahdar*, it controlled the *nizamat*, that is, judicial and police functions.

---

[3] Interestingly, under this system, the same person acted in Bengal as the deputy *Diwan* on behalf of the Company and as deputy *Subahdar* on behalf of the Nawab.

Impact of Dual Government

- It resulted in great exploitation of the people of Bengal as neither the Company nor the Nawab cared for their welfare. The Company officials used its politico-military-economic authority to exploit the peasants, craftsman and traders which further resulted in ruining of Indian agriculture and handicrafts industry.
- The Company starting draining Bengal of its wealth as the Company officials used Bengal wealth to not only finance Indian trade but also wars fought on Indian soil. They stopped sending money from England to purchase Indian goods, rather they started purchasing the Indian goods from the revenues of Bengal and sold them abroad. In three years (1766 to 1768) alone, nearly 5.7 million pounds were drained from Bengal.
- The abuses of Dual Government and drain of wealth further led to the impoverishment of the people of Bengal and when in 1770 Bengal suffered from famine, then its effects on the already exhausted population were a lot gruesome and it proved to be one of the most terrible famines known in Indian history resulting in annihilation of about one-third of Bengal's population.

The Conquest of Mysore

In the 16th century, after the famous **Battle of Talikota** (1565), the great kingdom of **Vijayanagara** disintegrated and many small kingdoms emerged from its remnants. Mysore was one such independent kingdom ruled by Hindu Wodeyar dynasty. We have already discussed how during the second half of the 18th century, under the able leadership of **Hyder Ali**, and later his son **Tipu Sultan**, Mysore emerged as a formidable power in south India, much to the annoyance of the British who considered it as a major threat to their expansion plans. Hyder Ali was an **able general** who strengthened his army by including French soldiers and also set up an arms factory at **Dindigul**. He also maintained tight control over the rich trade of the Malabar coast, which was another cause of concern for the British.

First Anglo–Mysore War (1767–69)

After the conquest of Bengal, the British were looking for ways to further their conquests and expand their influence. Hyder Ali was already having disputes with his neighbouring states such as the Nizam of Hyderabad, Nawab of Arcot and Marathas due to clash of territorial interests. Taking advantage of their hostilities, the British in 1766 entered into a treaty with the **Nizam of Hyderabad** to help him in attacking Hyder Ali in lieu of cession of the region of *Northern Circars*. The Nizam, the English and the Marathas allied together against Hyder Ali resulting in the First Anglo–Mysore War.

First Anglo-Mysore War (1767–1769)

Rapid rise of Haider Ali naturally excited the jealousy of the **Marathas**, **Nizam of Hyderabad** and the **English**. They joined together and formed a triple alliance and declared a war on Haider Ali.

Haider Ali

However, by considerable tact and diplomacy, Hyder Ali won over the Marathas and Nizam and the First Mysore War ended with the **defeat of the British** and they were forced to sign the Treaty of Madras.

1.a Treaty of Madras

Both sides restored each other's conquest and promised mutual help[4] in case of an attack by a third party.

Second Anglo–Mysore War (1780–84): During the Time of Lord Warren Hastings

Mysore was attacked by the Marathas in 1771 and as per the terms of the Treaty of Madras, the English were supposed to help Hyder Ali. However, the British under Verelst did not come to his help. So, this added to the already created rift between the two. Hyder Ali, thus, wanted an opportunity to strike at the English. During the course of the American War of Independence, there was an outbreak of hostilities in India too between the English and the French (who were allies of Hyder).

Immediate Cause of the Second Anglo–Mysore War

When **Mahe**, a French possession in the dominion of Hyder Ali was attacked by the **English**, Hyder Ali considered it as a direct challenge to his authority. He formed a grand alliance with the **Nizam of Hyderabad** and the **Marathas** against the British in 1779 and declared war on the English in 1780, when without Hyder's permission, the British led their forces through his territory to capture Guntur in the northern *Circars*. Hyder Ali defeated English force in *Carnatic* under **Colonel Baillie** and captured **Arcot** in 1780. However, by a clever stroke of diplomacy in 1781, **Warren Hastings** divided the confederacy, consequently isolating Hyder without any alliance. He was, thus, defeated by Sir Eyre Coote at **Porto Novo** in 1781.

---

[4] However, after only eleven years, the Second Anglo–Mysore War broke out.

Second Anglo-Mysore War (1780–1784)

English
English under **Sir Eyre Coote** defeated Haider Ali at Porto Novo in 1781.

Haider Ali
Haider Ali defeated English force in Carnatic and made them surrender but was defeated at Porto Novo. Also in the meantime, Haider Ali died of cancer in 1782. His son, **Tipu Sultan** continued the war with English for more than 2 years.

2.a Treaty of Mangalore (1784)

Fed up with inconclusive war, both sides opted for peace under the Treaty of Mangalore wherein both sides agreed to exchange the captured territories and war prisoners.

Third Anglo–Mysore War (1790–92): During the Time of Lord Cornwallis

The peace of 1784 was not able to permanently end the traditional hostility between Tipu Sultan and the East India Company. After the Second Anglo–Mysore War, Tipu Sultan undertook several internal reforms to strengthen the state of Mysore. He also made attempts to seek external assistance against the British by sending envoys to **Turkey** (1784–85) and **France** (1787). All of these acts alarmed the British and especially worried its Governor General Cornwallis, who after his debacle in the American War of Independence, did not want to take any risk in India. Cornwallis was, thus, waiting for an opportunity to wipe out the challenge of Tipu forever. In 1789, the British also secured the necessary support[5] of the Nizam of Hyderabad and the Marathas since they were also anxious about Mysore's rise.

Immediate Cause of the Third Anglo–Mysore War

In April 1790, Tipu attacked his neighbouring state **Travancore**, which was an ally of the British. The British used this act as a pretext for declaring war on Mysore in May 1790. The Third Anglo–Mysore War was fought in three phases:

- The first phase commenced when the Governor of Madras, **Medows**, initially directed the campaign to invade Mysore but Tipu's rapid movements halted the progress of the English troops and inflicted heavy losses on them.

[5] However, interestingly after the conclusion of war the British gave only a small territory on the banks of river Krishna to the Nizam of Hyderabad and on similar lines offered a negligible area of land to Marathas on the banks of Tungabhadra which the Marathas refused to accept. That is why even Cornwallis commented on the Third Anglo–Mysore War that *"we have crippled our enemy effectively without making our friends too formidable"*.

- The second phase of the war started when in the meantime, **Cornwallis** himself assumed command in December 1790 and Marching from Vellore, he captured Bangalore in March 1791, but Tipu's brilliant strategies prolonged the war and Cornwallis was forced to retreat to Mangalore due to lack of provisions.
- The third phase of the war began when timely aid from the **Marathas** with plenty of provisions helped Cornwallis to resume his campaign and he marched against Seringapatnam again. Unfortunately, now Tipu was at a disadvantage and the English forces quickly occupied the hill forts near Seringapatnam and seized it in February 1792.

Third Anglo-Mysore War (1790–1792)

↓

English along with **Nizam of Hyderabad** and **Marathas**
English under Cornwallis defeated Tipu Sultan and captured Bangalore.

Tipu Sultan

3.a Treaty of Seringapatnam (1792)

- Tipu Sultan lost almost ½ of his territory, that is, Malabar, Coorg, Dindigul, Baramahal (now Salem and Erode).
- He was compelled to pay huge war indemnity of ₹3 crore and had to surrender two of his sons as hostages to the English until he paid the indemnity.
- Both the sides agreed to release the prisoners of war.

Fourth Anglo–Mysore War (1799): During the Time of Lord Wellesley

The Third Anglo–Mysore War had dealt a severe blow to Mysore's dominant position in the south and Tipu Sultan too was never able to reconcile with the loss of half of his territory. He, therefore, worked incessantly to make Mysore a strong state. He also wanted to avenge his humiliating defeat and the harsh terms imposed on him by the British. He, thus, not only entered into negotiations for an alliance with revolutionary **France** (1798) but also sent missions to **Afghanistan, Arabia** and **Turkey** to forge an anti-British alliance. In fact, he started a **Jacobian Club** at Seringapatnam where even the flag of the French Republic was hoisted and the tree of Liberty was planted. Later, Tipu also received a friendly letter from **Napoleon** (who was in Egypt at that time). This increased the suspicions of Lord **Wellesley** who wanted to prevent any possibility of the French re-entering India and he was now more than determined to annihilate Tipu Sultan completely.

Immediate Cause of the Fourth Anglo–Mysore War

Tipu refused to accept the Subsidiary Alliance of Lord Wellesley. As a part of his strategy, Wellesley tried to revive the **Triple Alliance** of 1790 with the Marathas. Though his proposal was not accepted by the **Marathas**, they, however, promised to remain neutral. Meanwhile, a subsidiary alliance with the **Nizam of Hyderabad** was concluded by the British and consequently French force at Hyderabad was disbanded. Knowing fully well that proud Tipu Sultan would never agree to a subsidiary alliance, Wellesley asked him to dismiss the French, to receive an English envoy, and to make terms with the Company and its allies. As expected, Tipu refused to accept the humiliating terms and proudly declared that it was *better to die like a soldier, than to live a miserable dependent on the infidels, in the list of their pensioned rajas and nawabs*, and thus the Fourth Anglo–Mysore War started. The war was brief but fierce and decisive. As planned, the Bombay army under **General Stuart** invaded Mysore from the west while the Madras army, which was led by the Governor-General's brother, **Arthur Wellesley**, forced Tipu to retreat to his capital Seringapatnam. Unable to receive French help on time, on 4 May 1799, Tipu met a hero's end while defending his capital.

Fourth Anglo-Mysore War (1799)

English
English under Wellesley, General Stuart and General Harris defeated Tipu Sultan and besieged Seringapatnam.

Tipu Sultan

Results of the War[6]

- **Tipu Sultan** fought bravely but died in the battle and English annexed large portions of **Mysore**. Central part of Mysore was given to **Krishna Raja** of **Wodeyar's dynasty**, a five-year-old boy who was descendant of the dethroned Hindu Raja and Purnaiya, the previous minister was made *diwan*. Tipu's family was removed from Seringapatnam and sent to Vellore prison.
- The remaining parts of the kingdom, nearly half of Tipu Sultan's dominions, were divided between the British and their ally, the Nizam. The whole of Canara, Wynad, Coimbatore, Dharmapuri and Seringapatnam were retained by the British, whereas the Nizam was given the areas around Gooty and a part of Chittoor and Chitaldurg districts.

[6] An important result of the Fourth Anglo–Mysore War was the complete elimination of the **French threat** to British supremacy in India.

- A **British resident** was stationed at Mysore and a special treaty of **Subsidiary Alliance** was imposed on the new Raja. Under the system, Mysore would not henceforth enter into any relationship with any other European powers, a contingent of Company army would be stationed in Mysore and the provision for its maintenance would come from its treasury. Also, the Governor General was authorised to take over the administration of the state in case of necessity, using which **William Bentinck** in 1831 took control of Mysore on grounds of misgovernance. Later, however, in 1881, Lord **Ripon** restored the kingdom to its ruler.

British Struggle with Marathas

After the conquest of Bengal and Mysore, the **Marathas** were the only major Indian power left outside the sphere of British control. Meanwhile, with the growth of the Company's cotton trade with China through Bombay, control of Deccan (which was under the control of the Marathas) was a crucial requirement for the Company. A succession dispute among Marathas provided the first opportunity to the British for intervention which resulted in the First Anglo–Maratha War, a series of battles between 1775 and 1782 in which the British were ultimately defeated.

First Anglo–Maratha War (1775–82): During the Reign of Warren Hastings

In 1772, **Madhava Rao** (Maratha Peshwa) died who had no issue. **Narayan Rao**, the younger brother of Madhava Rao, succeeded him to the throne but his uncle Raghunath Rao alias Raghoba murdered him and announced himself the next Peshwa, but Maratha leaders disregarded the authority of Raghoba and under able leadership of **Nana Phadnavis** appointed **Madhava Rao Narayana**, the infant son of Narayan Rao.

- Infuriated by this harsh treatment, Raghoba went to the British to seek their help for obtaining Peshwaship. To fructify their agreement, the **Treaty of Surat** (1775) was signed between Raghoba and the Bombay Governor, without the knowledge of Warren Hastings under which Raghoba agreed to hand over islands of Salsette and Bassein to the British along with parts of revenues from the districts of Surat and Bharuch. In return, the British promised him a support of 2,500 soldiers.
- When the news of this treaty reached Calcutta, Governor General Warren Hastings strongly condemned the decision of Bombay Governor to indulge in the fight against the Marathas (as by the *Regulating Act of 1773*, it was imperative for the Bombay and Madras Councils to get their actions ratified by the Calcutta Council which was headed by Governor General Warren Hastings). Since, Hastings wanted to consolidate the control over the newly acquired province of Bengal first, he sent his representative **Colonel Upton** to settle the issue in 1776. Colonel Upton cancelled the Treaty of Surat and

concluded the **Treaty of Purandhar** (1776) with **Nana Phadnavis**, which was much to the advantage of the Marathas and eventually raised the position of Nana Phadnavis among the Marathas. According to this treaty:

- Madhava Rao Narayana was accepted as the new Peshwa and the English withdrew their support from Raghunath Rao.
- The British, however, retained Salsette along with Broach.

– However, the **Bombay Council** authorities rejected the **Treaty of Purandhar** and kept giving refuge to Raghunath Rao. They even appealed against the Treaty of Purandhar to the Court of Directors in London. The Court of Directors, thus, did not recognise the Treaty of Purandhar and nullified it. Subsequently, Warren Hastings too discarded the Treaty of Purandar as a *scrap of paper* and sanctioned operations against the Marathas.

– In the meantime, the British forces sent by the Bombay Government were defeated by the Marathas under the able leadership of Mahadji Scindia at the **Battle at Talegaon** (1776). Mahadji Scindia lured the British army into the ghats (valleys) near Talegaon and after trapping them from all sides, attacked their base camp. He also made use of *scorched earth policy* technique wherein all the farmlands were burned and wells were poisoned cutting their necessary food and water supplies.

– Subsequently, by January 1779, the English **retreated** and surrendered near the village of *Wadgaon* and the Company had to sign the humiliating **Treaty of Wadgaon** (1779) that forced the Bombay government to relinquish all territories acquired by the East India Company since 1775.

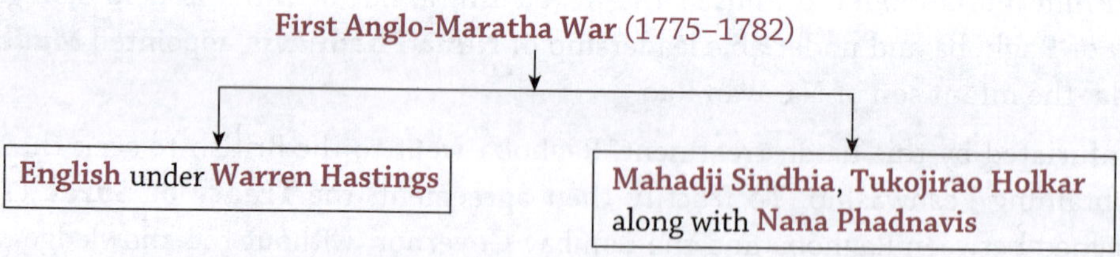

– However, Warren Hastings again refused to accept the Treaty of Wadgaon by taking the plea that Bombay Council had no legal powers to sign such treaty and acting swiftly in February 1779, he dispatched British troops under the command of **Colonel Goddard** who captured Ahmedabad, and Bassein in 1780 and **Captain Popham** who defeated the Maratha chief, Mahadji Scindia, in a number of small battles and captured Gwalior in 1781. But the English could not stage a final victory, and war with different ups and downs on both sides continued till 1782.

– By this time, the hostile camp against Warren Hastings in the Calcutta Council became active and lodged a complaint against him at the Court of Directors. The English Company was also involved in the **Second Anglo-Mysore War** against Hyder Ali (1780–84) at the same time and, thus, realised that it was almost impossible to continue wars in two different fronts against two formidable enemies. Realising the complexities of the situation, the British proposed for peace with Mahadji Scindia. Scindia accepted the proposal and, thus, in May 1782, the **Treaty of Salbai** was signed between **Warren Hastings** and Mahadji Scindia. According to provisions of this treaty:

- English returned all the Maratha territories except Salsette.
- Raghunath Rao was pensioned off and Madhav Rao Narayana was accepted as the Peshwa.

Critical Examination of Treaty of Salbai (1782)

In immediate terms, it may appear that the **Treaty of Salbai** (1782) was not advantageous to the East India Company as its provisions were quite similar to **Treaty of Purandar** (1776) which was discarded by the Company six years ago. On the face of it, it may appear that accepting a similar treaty after suffering huge financial and military loss was no way a good deal for the British but in terms of the long run, the Treaty of Salbai proved to be much more beneficial to the British than the Marathas as it provided the British **20 years of peace** with the Marathas which also enabled them to concentrate all its energies against **Mysore**. The Treaty of Salbai guaranteed the Company crucial support of the Marathas, without which it was impossible for the British to defeat Tipu Sultan in the **Third** and **Fourth Anglo-Mysore Wars**. Thus, the British were not only able to save themselves from the combined opposition of Indian powers but also succeeded in dividing the Indian powers that eventually led to the consolidation and establishment of the British Empire in India.

Second Anglo–Maratha War (1803–05): During the Reign of Lord Wellesley

The Marathas remained largely disunited since the Third Battle of Panipat (1761). The great Maratha statesman **Nana Phadnavis** kept the internal differences of Marathas in check, but with his death in 1800 it appears even wisdom and moderation too departed from Maratha land. In April 1801, **Peshwa Baji Rao II** who lacked political wisdom got **Vithoji**, the brother of **Jaswant Rao Holkar**, murdered. This triggered a war between the Holkar and the Peshwa, who was also supported by Daulat Rao Sindhia. **Holkar** defeated the combined forces of Scindia and the Peshwa and seized the city of Poona. With rich booty, Holkar returned to his capital but the scared and weak ruler **Peshwa Baji Rao II** fled to Bassein and approached the English for protection where he signed with them the **Treaty of Bassein** (1802) which was a **subsidiary alliance** treaty according to which:

- The Peshwa agreed to keep a permanent subsidiary force in his capital at Poona and for the upkeep of this force agreed to surrender to East India Company, the city of Surat and neighbouring territory yielding revenue of ₹26 lakh.

- A English resident was stationed at Poona.
- Peshwa surrendered his foreign policy to British control and agreed to not to enter in any offensive or defensive alliances without the permission of the Company.
- He also agreed not to keep in employment any other Europeans.

As an immediate response to the Treaty of Bassein, the British troops marched under the command of **Arthur Wellesley** towards Poona and restored the **Peshwa** to his position.

But the proud Maratha chiefs **Daulat Rao Sindhia** and **Raghoji Bhonsle** took the Treaty of Bassein as an insult to the national honour of the Marathas. Soon the forces of both the chieftains were united and they crossed the River Narmada. Lord **Wellesley** seized this opportunity and declared war in August 1803 and this way the Second Anglo–Maratha War was started.

Second Anglo-Maratha War (1803–1805)

English under **Wellesley** defeated	**Daulat Rao Sindhia**, **Raghoji Bhonsle** and later **Yashwant Rao Holkar**

- **Arthur Wellesley** captured Ahmednagar in August 1803 and defeated the combined forces of **Sindhia** and **Bhonsle** at Assaye near Aurangabad. Subsequently, Arthur Wellesley carried the war into Bhonsle's territory and completely defeated the Maratha forces on the plains of Argaon. As a result, the **Treaty of Deogaon** was signed between Bhonsle and Wellesley according to which Bhonsle signed the subsidiary treaty, which forced him to give up the province of Cuttack in Orissa.
- In the north, **Lord Lake** routed **Scindia's** army at Laswari in November 1803 and occupied Aligarh, Delhi and Agra. He took the Mughal Emperor **Shah Alam II** under British protection. **Scindia** too had to sign a type of subsidiary treaty known as the **Treaty of Surji–Arjungaon** with the British.
- Wellesley now turned his attention towards **Yashwant Rao Holkar**, but Holkar proved more than a match for the British. Using traditional Maratha tactics of guerrilla warfare and in alliance with the **Jats**, he remained unsubdued. His ally, the **Raja of Bharatpur**, inflicted heavy losses on Lake who unsuccessfully attempted to storm his fort. The **British**, thus, **failed** to comprehensively defeat **Holkar**, and since all these wars meant huge expenses for the Company and also the Court of Directors were dissatisfied with the forward policy of Lord Wellesley, he was recalled from India. The Company then made peace with Holkar by the **Treaty of Rajpurghat** (Dec. 1805) giving back to him most of his territories.

Significance of the Treaty of Bassein for the British (1802)

Even though the treaty was signed by a Peshwa who lacked political authority, but the direct and indirect implications of the Treaty of Bassein were of immense benefit to the **East India Company**. The provision of keeping British troops permanently in Poona proved to be a decision of great strategical benefit to the English as now the Company's troops were more evenly spread across the Deccan and with this newly added advantage of swift movement of English troops in times of need to any place, the Company was in a better position to expand its sphere of influence in the neighbouring areas. Also, the provisions of Treaty of Bassein subjugated the entire **Maratha** kingdom as even though titular but still theoretically Peshwa was the head of the entire Maratha Empire. So, the Treaty of Bassein paved the way for making the East India Company into strongest political power in not only western India but also the whole of India as well since Marathas were the only major Indian power left outside the sphere of British control and now with their subjugation too, there was hardly any other native power left in India who could stand up against British.

Third Anglo–Maratha War (1817–18): During the Reign of Lord Hastings

Even though the Second Anglo–Maratha War had shattered the power of the Maratha chiefs somehow their spirit of fight was still alive within them. The **Maratha chiefs** did not want to surrender their great tradition of independence without a struggle, and hence they made a desperate last attempt to regain their independence and lost prestige in 1817. But before that an important event had a prominent role to play in the **Third Anglo–Maratha War**, and that was the **Pindari War** (1816–18).

Pindari War (1816–18)

The Maratha army used to have two components, regular forces and irregular forces. The regular forces were maintained by the state and were given arms, horses and salary, whereas the **Pindaris** formed part of irregular forces who used to bring their own horses and weapons, did not receive any salary from the state but in lieu of that used to get the opportunity to plunder the conquered territory after the war. After the Second Anglo–Maratha War, when the Marathas accepted the Subsidiary Alliance system, they had to **disband** these irregular forces. Having lost their traditional profession, Pindaris took to **highway robberies**. They were mostly active in the areas of Rajputana and the Central Provinces and subsisted on plunder. It is worth mentioning that even though being mercenaries, the Pindaris never helped the British and also noteworthy is the fact that they did not belong to any particular caste or creed and their leaders belonged to both the Hindu as well as the Muslim communities, who had thousands of followers. Chief leaders amongst the Pindaris were **Wasil Muhammad**, **Chitu** and **Karim Khan**. In 1812, the Pindaris plundered the districts of Mirzapur and Shahabad, and in 1815 they raided the Nizam's dominions.

In 1816, they plundered the Northern Circars. All these plundering activities of seemingly lawless Pindaris caught the attention of Governor General **Lord Hastings** who viewed these activities of Pindaris as a direct challenge to British Paramountcy. Thus, in 1816, he determined to suppress the Pindaris and assembled a large force to round up and exterminate their chiefs.

Pindari War (1816–18)

English under lord **Hastings** defeated Pindaris	**Pindaris** Major leaders were **Karim Khan** (submitted but was offered estate) **Wasil Muhammad** (forced to lay down arms and died in captivity) **Chitu** (defeated but was probably killed by a tiger in a forest)

- By 1818, the **Pindaris** were mostly suppressed and all their bands disintegrated. **Karim Khan** was given a small estate in the Gorakhpur district of the United Provinces. **Wasil Muhammad** took refuge in the Scindia camp, but the latter handed him over to the British and Wasil committed suicide in captivity while **Chitu** escaped to the forest, where probably a tiger killed him.
- Even though the Pindari War was won by British, yet it created a rift between the Company and the Marathas. When the military campaign was organised against the Pindaris, the Company had expected full Maratha support for the same but since the Pindaris were former Maratha soldiers only, the Maratha commanders were somewhere emotionally attached to them.
- Subsequently, Lord Hastings accused the Marathas of not supporting the Anti-Pindari Campaign whole-heartedly. He, thus, asked them to sign a new treaty providing greater control and when the Maratha chiefs hesitated, it became one of the reasons for Hastings to declare a war on them. Thus, the Anti-Pindari War merged into the Third Anglo–Maratha War.

Immediate Cause of the Third Anglo–Maratha War (1817–18)

Peshwa **Baji Rao II**, fed up with the rigid control of the British Resident, made a last attempt to regain his independence and took the lead in organising a united front of the Maratha chiefs against the British resulting in the Third Anglo–Maratha War.

Third Anglo-Maratha War (1817–1818)

↓

English under Hastings defeated the Marathas	Baji Rao II, Appa Sahib, Malhar Rao Holkar and Daulat Rao Sindia

- The **Peshwa**, thus, attacked the **British Residency** at Poona in November 1817, but was defeated at a place called Kirkee. His territories were annexed and the Presidency of Bombay was enlarged subsequently.
- Similarly, the Bhonsle chief, **Appa Sahib** of Nagpur, refused to abide by the **Treaty of Nagpur** (1816) signed by him with the British and hereafter, attacked the **Residency** at Nagpur. The **Battle of Sitabuldi** was fought between him and the British in November 1817, but he too was defeated.
- **Malhar Rao Holkar** too was defeated by the British on 21 December 1817 at Baroda.
- **Lord Hastings** also compelled the **Scindia** to accept British suzerainty and he surrendered Ajmer to the British who gave it further to the Nawab of Bhopal, who had also accepted the British suzerainty.
- The **Gaekwar** of **Baroda** too accepted the Subsidiary Alliance and handed over certain areas of Ahmedabad to the British.

Therefore, by December 1817, the dream of a mighty Maratha Confederacy was finally shattered and British emerged as the paramount power[7] in India.

Results of the War

- To satisfy Maratha pride, a small state of Satara was created under **Pratap Singh**, a descendent of Shivaji, but he ruled it as a complete dependent of the British.
- The **Peshwa** was dethroned and pensioned off at Bithur near Kanpur. Peshwaship itself was abolished.
- An indirect result of the war was that with the downfall of the Marathas, the Rajputana states who had been dominated for several decades by the Scindia and Holkar, too readily accepted British supremacy.

---

[7] The year **1818**, thus, proved to be a significant year for both India and the British as the entire Indian subcontinent excepting the Punjab and Sindh had been brought under British control, making them the **paramount power** in India.

Causes of the Defeat of the Marathas

- **Lack of Capable Leadership**: Towards the end of the 18th century, the Marathas unfortunately lost nearly all of their wise and experienced leaders such as **Peshwa Madhav Rao II**, **Nana Phadnavis**, **Mahadji Scindia**, **Tukoji Holkar** and **Ahilyabai Holkar**. These leaders had earlier kept the Maratha confederacy together and had provided efficient leadership. But, with their demise, the later Maratha leaders were not able to fill in their worthy shoes and, thus, it proved to be a huge cost for the Maratha state.
- **Lack of Unity and Coordination amongst Maratha Chiefs**: The Maratha Confederacy consisted of five major chiefs, being the Peshwa at Poona, the Gaekwad at Baroda, the Scindia at Gwalior, the Holkar at Indore and the Bhonsle at Nagpur, the Peshwa being the nominal head of the confederacy. But, more often the chiefs were engaged in bitter fratricidal strife, totally ignoring the real danger from the rapidly advancing British. For instance, when the Scindia and Bhonsle fought the British, the Holkar stood on the sidelines while the Gaekwad gave help to the British. Consequently, when the Holkar fought against the British, the Bhonsle and Scindia refused to help the Holkar. Had they fought as a united front against their common enemy the British in the early stages, the outcome of the wars would have been definitely different.
- **Military weakness of the Marathas**: Though Marathas were great warriors full of personal prowess and valour, they were still inferior to the English in terms of artillery, organisation of the forces and in disciplined action. The Maratha use of age-old warfare techniques was no match against British sophisticated modern warfare methodology. Along with it, the well-knit spy system and better diplomatic skills of the British to win over allies helped them to isolate their adversary.
- **Failure to estimate correctly the political and diplomatic strategy of the British**: Maratha chiefs somehow lived in the false belief that the Company being primarily a trading body was a transitory power, while Mysore, Nizam of Hyderabad and other native powers were their real enemies. This proved to be a costly mistake for both Marathas and the rest of the rulers too.

The Conquest of Sindh

Since the 18th century, Sindh was ruled by some Baluchi chiefs collectively known as '**Amirs of Sindh**'. The East India Company had tried as early as 1758 to open a factory at the strategic port of Tatta, situated in the Indus Delta in Sindh. Trade relations thus established continued till 1775, when, owing to the discouraging attitude of the new ruler, **Sarfaraz Khan**, the factory was abandoned. However, owing to political turmoil in Sindh, all relations of the British with

Sindh thus came to an end and were revived only after two decades owing to European political developments.

- In June 1807, **Napolean** concluded the alliance of Tilsit with **Alexander I** of Russia, one of the details of which was a combined invasion of India by the land route. To provide against this fresh danger, it was thought necessary to have a barrier between British India and Russia. Accordingly, **Lord Minto I** dispatched missions, namely that of Metcalfe to Lahore, Elphinstone to Kabul and Malcolm to Tehran and Mr Hankey Smith to Sindh. Consequently, in 1809 a '**Treaty of Eternal Friendship**' was concluded with Amirs of Sindh. By this treaty, both sides agreed to maintain territorial integrity and unity of each other and also to exclude **French** from Sindh.
- This treaty was renewed in 1820 with the addition of some new articles which excluded the **Americans** also and purported to resolve some border disputes on the side of Kutch.
- Again to counteract and check the influence of Russia through Persia, the British decided to collect political and geographical information of the region for possibilities of future military movements. Thus, in 1831, the British sent Lieutenant **Alexander Burnes** out to India to explore the possibilities of navigation of the river Indus for the purposes of commercial intercourse between Northern India and Britain.
- Further in 1832, Lord **William Bentinck** sent Henry Pottinger to Sindh, who negotiated a **treaty with Amirs** through which the Company gained a number of commercial privileges as the lower part of the Indus and the whole of the Sutlej were thrown open to English trade.
- In order to further consolidate their position in Sindh, the English were looking for an opportunity which they got, when Maharaja Ranjit Singh of Punjab captured a frontier town of Sindh. Lord **Auckland** offered protection to the Amirs but forced them to sign a new treaty in 1838 under which the Company troops were kept in Sindh at the Amir's expense. The treaty also permitted the English to intervene in the disputes between the Amirs and the Sikhs, along with stationing of a British resident. Thus, very cleverly Sindh was turned into a British protectorate.
- Gradually in 1839, Sindh was made to accept Subsidiary Alliance and later acting quite cheap British even forced the Amirs to pay for their Afghan adventure too.
- However, to counter-balance their defeat in the **First Anglo-Afghan War** (1839–42), and to uplift his already precarious position due to the Afghan reverses, **Lord Ellenborough** chanced upon the easy target of Sindh since it was going through a period of internal turmoil and chaos due to certain succession dispute after the death of an Amir. Ellenborough imposed a totally outrageous treaty on Sindh and made the Amirs to cede more provinces.

- In 1842, Sir **Charles Napier** was appointed as British resident in place of Major James Outram. Napier, thereafter, unnecessarily provoked the Amirs, and in 1843 destructed their famous desert fortress Imamgarh. In retaliation to this, the **Baluchis** attacked the British resident and declared war on the British. The **Battle of Miani** ensued in which the Baluchi army was defeated by Napier and some Amirs had to surrender. Later, the **Battle of Dubbo** happened in which Napier defeated the Amir of Mirpur Sher Muhammad resulting in the formal **annexation of Sindh** (1843).
- Napier was appointed as the first Governor of Sindh and interestingly he sent a telegram to the British headquarters exclaiming, "I have Sin(ne)d". Thus, in spite of previous assurances that territorial integrity would be always respected, Sindh was annexed. Napier had himself written in his diary, *"We have no right to seize Sindh, yet we shall do so, and a very advantageous, useful humane piece of rascality it will be."*

Critical Examination of Annexation of Sindh (1843)

Most historians believe that the pretexts and causes for the annexation of Sindh were deliberately manufactured by the British. They thus univocally condemned the Annexation of Sindh and considered it as a political sequential to the First Anglo–Afghan War, which if we analyse closely seems to be a quite justified theory. In 1838, to counter the Russian influence, Shah Shuja was placed on the Afghan throne, but since he was a mere puppet of the East India Company, a popular uprising against him broke out and the First Anglo–Afghan War (1839–42) started in which the Company was badly defeated. This notably broke the myth of English invincibility and also emboldened many rebellions in India as witnessed in the ranks of Madras army and in the Scindia territory. The British thought that these dissensions could only be countered by restoring the myth of English invincibility. Thus, they chanced upon the easy target of Sindh. Even the British official Elphinstone statement read, *"Coming from Afghanistan, when a bully was knocked in the street, he went home to beat his wife in revenge,"* confirms this inference.

Causes for Annexation of Sindh (1843)

- Commercial possibilities of the River Indus.
- British fear of expansion of Russian Empire towards the east.
- British desire to increase influence in Persia and Afghanistan through control over Sindh.

The Conquest of Punjab

In the late 18th century, the consolidation of Sikh power had taken place under Maharaja **Ranjit Singh**, who was a capable ruler and administrator. During his lifetime, there was no major tension between Punjab and the British. In fact, in order to counter the Russian threat and to maintain Sikh state as a buffer between Company's north Indian possessions on the one end and the Muslim powers in Persia and Afghanistan on the other, **Lord William Bentinck** negotiated friendly relations with both Ranjit Singh and also with the Amirs of Sind and as an initial measure, an exchange of gifts took place between Lahore, the capital of Punjab, and Calcutta, the seat of the Governor-General. It was then followed by the meeting of **Bentinck** and **Ranjit Singh** (1831) at Ropar on the banks of the River Sutlej amidst great show and splendour. Both sides mutually promised perpetual friendship and respect for each other's territorial integrity and unity. They also concluded a commercial treaty known as **Indus Navigation Treaty** through which River Sutlej was also opened for navigation. We have already discussed above that a similar kind of treaty was also concluded with the Amirs of Sind. In 1838, a **Tripartite treaty** was signed by East India Company, Ranjit Singh and Shah Shuja of Afghanistan, and all parties professed friendship and agreed to respect each other's territorial integrity and unity.

Background of Anglo-Sikh Wars

Things took a sudden turn in 1839 when **Ranjit Singh** died. His death was followed by **political instability**. A number of people ascended the throne in quick succession and the whole region was plunged into prolonged and bloody succession battles resulting in the breakdown of the delicate balance of power that Ranjit Singh had carefully maintained between the hereditary Sikh chieftains and the Punjabi and Dogra faction of nobles. After the death of Ranjit Singh, the next three rulers Kharak Singh, Nau Nihal Singh and Sher Singh were **murdered** within next 6 years (1839–45).

- In such an unstable environment, without much effective control over the army, **Dalip Singh**, the 5-year-old son of Ranjit Singh, ascended the throne in 1843, under the regency of **Rani Jindan** and guardianship of wazir **Hira Singh Dogra**. But, by now the Khalsa Army became a power onto itself and began to control Punjabi politics. Hira Singh soon fell a victim to this power struggle and was assassinated in 1844. He was succeeded by new wazir **Jawahar Singh**, the brother of **Rani Jindan**, but he remained for all practical purposes, a puppet in the hands of the army.
- The British were now concerned about these new developments of continuous political instability in Punjab and increasing political influence of the Khalsa Army since all these issues were threatening their scheme of a strong buffer state. Meanwhile, British encirclement of Punjab had started from 1833, when they had appointed British residents at Ludhiana and Sindh.
- Hereafter, when the situation in Punjab did not stabilise and even **Jawahar Singh** was executed by the army in 1845, the English started preparations for war. Barracks for additional troops were built in a forward area and additional regiments began to be despatched to the Punjab frontier. The Punjab army, now convinced that the British were

determined to occupy Punjab, took counter-measures and when they learnt that British Commander in chief, Lord **Hugh Gough** and Governor General Lord **Harding** were marching towards Ferozepur, they decided to strike and war between the two was thus declared on 13 December, 1845.

First Anglo Sikh War (1845–1846)

English under Hardinge defeated Sikhs

Sikh Chiefs fought under the name of Dalip Singh and Rani Jindan.

A series of battles that happened during the course between the British and Sikhs form part of the First **Anglo-Sikh War** (1845–46):

- **Battle of Mudki** (1845): It was fought between **Lal Singh** (Prime Minister of Sikhs) and Lord **Hugh Gough** in which the Sikh Army was defeated.
- **Battle of Ferozeshah** (1845): It was fought between the Sikh Army under **Tej Singh** (got defeated) and the **British**
- **Battle of Baddowal** (1846): It was fought between **Ranjodh Singh Majithia** (got defeated) and **Harry Smith**.
- **Battle of Guns/Battle of Sobraon** (1846): One of the decisive battles fought between the British (**Harry Smith**) and **Sikhs**. The British emerged victorious and they not only crossed Sutlej but occupied Lahore too.

This resulted in signing of **Treaty of Lahore** (1846) according to which:

- **Jalandhar Daob** was given to the British along with a demand for payment of ₹1.5 crores to the British. Sikhs paid only half of this amount and for settling the rest they sold **Kashmir** to the **British** who sold it further to the Raja of Jammu, Gulab Singh Dogra, for a cash payment of ₹5 million.
- Appointment of British Resident at Lahore (**Sir Henry Lawrence**), with a strong British force stationed there.
- Punjab army was reduced to 20,000 infantry and 12,000 cavalry.
- Dalip Singh was allowed to retain his throne, but was to be advised and guided by an English resident.

Rani Jindan, who was acting as regent of her son, Dalip Singh, had believed that, as stipulated in the treaty of Lahore, the British force would eventually leave Lahore. But the British, instead of quitting, started strengthening their authority over Lahore administration. This led to the signing of the **Treaty of Bhairowal** (1846) also known as the Second Treaty of Lahore through which **Rani Jindan** was removed and a regency council for Punjab was set up (consisting of eight

Sikh Sardars and presided over by Sir Henry Lawrence) and moreover, the British were permitted to station their troops in any part of the state and the Sikh authorities had to even pay for their maintenance. Thus, the Treaty of Bhairowal transformed the Sikh kingdom into a virtual British protectorate and hence the grounds for another confrontation were set.

Second Anglo–Sikh War (1848–49)

In order to avenge humiliation of the first war and also bad treatment accorded to Rani Jindan, Punjabis rose up in numerous local revolts. Two of the prominent revolts were led by Sikh governors **Mul Raj** of Multan and **Chattar Singh** Attariwala of Haripur near Lahore. Lord **Dalhousie** seized this opportunity to annex Punjab and thus, this way the **Second Anglo–Sikh War** started.

Second Anglo-Sikh War (1848–1849)

- **English** under **Dalhousie** defeated Sikhs
- Two Prominent Sikh governors:
  a) **Mul raj** of Multan
  b) **Chattar Singh Attariwala** of Haripur, near Lahore

In the first two rounds of the battle at Ramnagar in November 1848 and at Chillianwala in January 1849, the British suffered heavy losses but this was soon reversed in February-March, when the rebel Sardars had to surrender one after another.

The Second Anglo–Punjab War thus resulted in **annexation of Punjab** by Lord Dalhousie in 1849 and Dalip Singh and Rani Jindan were transported to England. A board of **three Commissioners** was established consisting of:

- Henry Lawrence
- John Lawrence
- Charles G Mansel

In 1853, this board was abolished and Sir **John Lawrence** was appointed as Chief Commissioner for Punjab who was subsequently made Lieutenant Governor of Punjab in 1859.

The conquest of Punjab was followed by the annexation of several other princely states such as Satara (1848), Jaitpur, Sambalpur (Orissa), Jhansi (1853), Nagpur (1854) and Awadh (1856) on the basis of Lord **Dalhousie's** infamous **Doctrine of Lapse**. Thus by 1857, the British had annexed 63 per cent of the territories of the Indian subcontinent and brought under its authority 78 per cent of the population while the rest remained under the Indian princes who were autonomous only in name.

Ideology of Expansion: Annexation Through Diplomatic Alliances and Administrative Policies

The Conquest of India by the British was carried out using a two-pronged approach. The first approach being annexation by means of defeating Indian states in different **wars and battles** to emerge as paramount power in the Indian subcontinent, while the second approach focused on making effective use of **diplomatic alliances and administrative policies** to fulfil its dream of imperial expansion and consolidation of British paramountcy. Some of the effective diplomatic and administrative policies utilised by British were as follows:

- **The policy of Ring Fence**: This policy was initiated by **Lord Warren Hastings** (1772–85) and was aimed at creating buffer zones to defend the Company's frontiers. The friendly native states were used as a buffer to keep the unfriendly states away. It can also be understood as a policy of defence of British's neighbours' frontiers for safeguarding their own territories. The policy is clearly evident in Warren Hastings' action of creating Awadh as a buffer and securing Awadh frontiers in order to ward off the influence of Marathas and Mysore. Interestingly, though the buffer states were promised military assistance against external aggression, yet they were required to pay for the maintenance and expenses of the defending army.
- **Subsidiary Alliance**: The Subsidiary Alliance system was introduced by **Lord Wellesley** (1798–1805) and was in fact an extension of the policy of ring fence. It is rather interesting to note that the basic principles of Subsidiary Alliance were first formulated by French Governor **Dupleix** in southern India when he initiated the practice of lending European troops to his native allies in return for fixed amount of money. The **English** thereafter adopted and expanded the system. The system was initially based on the idea of supporting a friendly native ruler in his wars and battles which over the course of time gradually modified in reducing the subsidiary states to a position of dependence on the Company's support. Under this system, **subsidiary agreements** (*sanads*) were entered between the British and the local Indian rulers according to which the British agreed to protect the Indian rulers against **external threats** and **internal disorders** but, in return:
    - The Indian rulers who accepted the Subsidiary Alliance system were to agree to the stationing of **permanent subsidiary British force** in his capital for whose maintenance they would pay a subsidy to the British. The Indian state was called '**the protected state**' and the British hereinafter were referred to as '**the paramount power**'.
    - The protected state should give money or was asked to surrender a part of its territory yielding revenue equal to the cost of maintaining subsidiary force to the British.
    - The ruler under the system of alliance had to completely **surrender his foreign relations** to the East India Company. He could neither enter into offensive or

defensive alliance with any other power nor can fight a war or sign peace without **prior permission** from the British Company.

- The Indian ruler could **not employ** any European in his service without the prior approval of the British.
- A **British resident** was stationed at these subsidiary states. While the British promised to adopt a policy of non-interference in the internal matters of the protected state, in reality they seldom followed it.

The **Nizam of Hyderabad** (1798) was first to enter into a subsidiary alliance with the English (1798), followed by Tanjore (1799), Awadh (1801), the Scindhias (1804), the Rajput states of Jodhpur, Jaipur, Bundi, the ruler of Bharatpur (1818) and the Holkars (1818). It is noteworthy to add that **Tipu Sultan** rejected it summarily but eventually with his defeat in the Fourth Anglo–Mysore War, Mysore was brought under the Subsidiary Alliance system (1799), while **Baji Rao II**, the Maratha leader, entered into it (Treaty of Bassein, 1802) in a futile attempt to regain control over his warring chiefs.

Wellesley's Subsidiary system is regarded as one of the master strokes of British imperialism. This system was suited best to the advantage of the British as:

- It gradually and discreetly disarmed the Native states resulting in considerable loss of their autonomy, which further aided in enhancing the clout of British paramountcy.
- It increased the military strength of the Company in India at the expense of the protected states. The system enabled the Company to maintain large force without incurring any additional cost. Moreover, this force could be used at shortest possible notice against its Indian and non-Indian enemies.
- This system enabled the Company to weed out the foreign influence from the Indian courts.

It thus helped in the expansion of the British Empire in India by bringing new territories under its influence without even fighting any battle or spending any penny enabling the British to become the paramount power in India.

- The **Doctrine of Lapse**: It was an annexation policy devised by Lord **Dalhousie** (1848–56). There was a widespread custom of adoption to secure an heir in the absence of a natural successor, that is, son among the Indian rulers. However, with his principle of Doctrine of Lapse, Dalhousie refused to recognise the authority of succession of an adopted heir. He cunningly maintained that there was a difference in principle between the right to inherit private property and the right to govern. As per his policy of Doctrine of Lapse:
    - Any Indian state under the direct influence of the British East India Company, or as a vassal state under the British Subsidiary System, would be **automatically annexed** if the ruler died without a natural male heir or was either incompetent and did not have natural heirs to the throne.

- In other words, the sovereignty of a native state lapsed to the paramount power in absence of natural heirs in a ruling family.
- Thus, by the Doctrine of Lapse not only the long-established right of the Indian sovereigns without an heir to choose a successor was taken over, but the British also took over the authority of deciding the competence of the Indian rulers.

With the help of the policy of Doctrine of Lapse, the Company annexed the states of Satara (1848), Jaitpur, Sambalpur (Orissa), Jhansi, Nagpur (1854) and Awadh (1856).

Reasons for the Success of the British

In less than a century, the British not only established but also consolidated their power over India. For this, they made use of each possible tactic available at their disposal ranging from diplomatic alliances, to exertion of military power to utilisation of administrative policies to at times also, using unjustified reasons to finally emerge as supreme rulers of India. However, there were certain factors responsible for the success of the British in the conquest of India:

- **Lack of political unity and statesmanship among Indian states**: After the political power vacuum created by the Mughal decline, no single regional Indian state could rise up to the occasion. Some regional Indian states like Mysore, Marathas and Punjab possessed the capability to counter British influence but they were so busy fighting with each other that they failed to foresee the dangers arising from the growing political clout of the British. At the critical time, they could **not unite** against the common foreign enemy and, thus, eventually had to surrender before the British one after another. Also, in the 18th century, they **lacked** the **statesmanship** of having a vision and consciousness of one nation, which eventually hurt them all.
- **Use of superior warfare techniques, modernised arms and ammunition along with brilliant leadership**: Having witnessed the Industrial Revolution in 16th century, the British had the advantage of the latest and most sophisticated weapons. As a matter of fact, their firearms were much better in terms of firing and in range as compared to Indian firearms. The English also had the advantage of brilliant leaders both in the political and military field. **Robert Clive**, **Warren Hastings**, **Cornwallis**, **Dalhousie**, **Wellesley**, Sir **Eyre Coote**, Lord **Lake** all had the foresight and sharpness of mind to lead from the front. Even though the Indian side too had some gems of leaders like Hyder Ali, Tipu Sultan, Nana Phadnavis, Mahadji Scindia and Yashwant Rao Holkar but they often had to face the crunch of talented second line commanders. The Company's military power that held the key to its political dominance was predicated not only on the superior fighting skills but also on effective recruitment strategies. Also, their civil administration was integrated with the military administration and this generated important fiscal and logistical benefits.

- **Better military discipline, training and regular salary to the troops**: It is indeed interesting to note that the British troops consisted of many Indian natives only. The high quality of military training imparted by British officers transformed these natives into well-disciplined troops who won for British so many wars and battles. A regular system of payment of salaries ensured their loyalty towards the English. The Indian armies, on the other hand, were inadequately trained and poorly paid, who often were no match for the disciplined and well-trained British troops.
- **Effective use of diplomatic policies like subsidiary alliance and doctrine of lapse**: These policies proved to be more effective instruments than bloody battles and wars for expanding the colonial footprint of the British. These diplomatic treaties not only allowed the British to establish their **spheres of influence** but also at the same time saved them precious millions required for maintaining their troops. Later, the British used one or the other excuse to insubordinate that state completely. The insubordination of states of Hyderabad, Awadh and Mysore is a clear testimony to this fact.
- **Benefit from Britain's global profile**: The British East India Company could always rely on huge assets that Britain possessed and could be used to bail the Company out if the occasion so demanded.

Chronological Order of Major Events

First Carnatic War (1746–48)

- Dupleix and Barnett
- Battle of Adyar
- Treaty of Aix-La-Chapelle (1748)

Second Carnatic War (1748–54)

- Dupleix + Chanda Sahib + Muzzafar Jang vs English + Nasir Jung + Nawab Anwar-ud-din
- Battle of Ambur (1749)
- Battle of Arcot (1751)
- Treaty of Pondicherry

Third Carnatic War (1756–63)

- Count de Lally (French) vs General Eyre Coote (English)
- Battle of Wandiwash (1760)
- Treaty of Paris

Battle of Plassey (1757)

↓ – Siraj-ud-Daulah vs Robert Clive + Mir Jafar

Battle of Buxar (1764)

- Mir Qasim + Shuja-ud-Daulah + Shah-Alam II vs English + Mir Jafar
- Treaty of Allahabad (1765)

First Anglo–Mysore War (1767–69)

- Hyder Ali vs English
- Treaty of Madras (1769)

First Anglo–Maratha War (1775–82)

- Maratha Nana Padhnavis vs English + Raghoba (Under Lord Warren Hastings).
- Treaty of Surat (1775)
- Battle of Talegaon (1776)
- Treaty of Purandhar (1776)
- Treaty of Salbai (1782)

Second Anglo–Mysore War (1780–84)

- Hyder Ali vs English
- Treaty of Mangalore (1784)

Third Anglo–Mysore War (1790–92)

- Tipu Sultan vs English + Nizam + Marathas (under Cornwallis)
- Treaty of Seringapatnam (1792)

Fourth Anglo–Mysore War (1799)

↓ – Tipu Sultan + French vs English (under Lord Wellesley)

Second Maratha War (1803–05)

- Baji Rao II + British vs Holkar + Sindhia (under Lord Wellesley).
- Treaty of Bassein (1802)
- Treaty of Rajpuraghat (1806)

Pindari War (1816–18)

↓ – British vs Pindari

Third Maratha War (1817–18)

↓ – Baji Rao II + Daulat Rao + Appa Sahib + Malhar Rao vs British (under Lord Hastings)

Annexation of Sindh (1843)

↓

First Anglo–Sikh War (1845–46)

↓

Second Anglo–Sikh War (1848–49)

QUESTIONS FROM LAST YEAR'S PRELIMS

1. With reference to Indian history, consider the following statements: **(2022)**

1. The Dutch established their factories/warehouses on the east coast on lands granted to them by Gajapati rulers.
2. Alfonso de Albuquerque captured Goa from the Bijapur Sultanate.
3. The English East India Company established a factory at Madras on a plot of land leased from a representative of the Vijayanagara empire.

Which of the statements given above are correct?

(a) 1 and 2 only (b) 2 and 3 only
(c) 1 and 3 only (d) 1, 2 and 3

2. In the first quarter of seventeenth century, in which of the following was/were the factory/factories of the English East India Company located? **(2021)**

1. Broach
2. Chicacole
3. Trichinopoly

Select the correct answer using the code given below:

(a) 1 only (b) 1 and 2
(c) 3 only (d) 2 and 3

3. Consider the following statements: **(2021)**

1. It was during the reign of Iltutmish that Chengiz Khan reached the Indus in pursuit of the fugitive Khwarezm prince.
2. It was during the reign of Muhammad bin Tughluq that Taimur occupied Multan and crossed the Indus.
3. It was during the reign of Deva Raya II of Vijayanagara Empire that Vasco da Gama reached the coast of Kerala.

Which of the statements given above is/are correct?

(a) 1 only (b) 1 and 2
(c) 3 only (d) 2 and 3

4. The staple commodities of export by the English East India Company from Bengal in the middle of the 18th century were: **(2018)**

(a) Raw cotton, oil-seeds and opium
(b) Sugar, salt, zinc and lead
(c) Copper, silver, gold, spices and tea
(d) Cotton, silk, saltpetre and opium

5. With reference to Pondicherry (now Puducherry), consider the following statements: **(2010)**

1. The first European power to occupy Pondicherry were the Portuguese.
2. The second European power to occupy Pondicherry were the French.
3. The English never occupied Pondicherry.

Which of the statements given above is/are correct?

(a) 1 only
(b) 2 and 3 only
(c) 3 only
(d) 1, 2 and 3

6. The ruler of which one of the following states was removed from power by the British on the pretext of misgovernance? **(2008)**

(a) Awadh (b) Jhansi
(c) French (d) Satara

7. Who among the following Europeans were the last to come to pre-Independence of India as traders? **(2008)**

(a) Dutch (b) English
(c) French (d) Portuguese

8. Consider the following statements: **(2008)**

1. Robert Clive was the first Governor-General of Bengal.
2. William Bentinck was the first Governor-General of India.

Which of the statements given above is/are correct?

(a) 1 only
(b) 2 only
(c) Both 1 and 2
(d) Neither 1 nor 2

9. Which of the following was the first fort constructed by the British in India? **(2008)**

(a) Fort William
(b) Fort St. George
(c) Fort St. David
(d) Fort St. Angelo

10. Consider the following statements: **(2004)**

1. In the Third Battle of Panipat, Ahmad Shah Abdali defeated Ibrahim Lodi.
2. Tipu Sultan was killed in the Third Anglo–Mysore War.
3. Mir Jafar entered in a conspiracy with the English for the defeat of Nawab Siraj ud-Daulah in the Battle of Plassey.

Which of the statements given above is/are correct?

(a) 1, 2 and 3 (b) 3 only
(c) 2 and 3 (d) None

11. Which of the following pairs are correctly matched? **(2004)**

List I	List II
1. AD 1767–69	First Anglo–Maratha War
2. AD 1790–92	Third Mysore War
3. AD 1824–26	First Anglo–Burmese War
4. AD 1845–46	Second Sikh War

Select the correct answer using the codes given below:

Codes:

(a) 2 and 4 (b) 3 and 4
(c) 1 and 2 (d) 2 and 3

12. With reference to the entry of European powers into India which of the following is not correct? **(2003)**

(a) The Portuguese captured Goa in 1499.
(b) The English opened their first factory in south Indian at Masulipatnam.
(c) In Eastern India, the English company opened its first factory in Orissa in 1633.
(d) Under the leadership of Dupleix, the French occupied Madras in 1746.

13. In India, among the following locations, the Dutch established their earliest factory at **(2003)**

(a) Surat (b) Pulicat
(c) Cochin (d) Cossimbazar

ANSWERS

1. (b)	2. (a)	3. (a)	4. (d)	5. (a)	6. (a)	7. (c)	8. (b)
9. (b)	10. (b)	11. (d)	12. (a)	13. (b)			

QUESTIONS FROM LAST YEAR'S MAINS

1. Critically examine the following statements in about 150 words each:

(a) "Annexation of Punjab was part of a broad north-west frontier policy set in motion after the exit of Maharaja Ranjit Singh." **(2015, History optional).**

2. Critically examine the following statements in about 150 words each:

(a) "Plassey did not complete the British conquest of India. Had the English been convincingly defeated in any subsequent battle in India, then (the battle of) Plassey would have remained as a minor episode in the history of India." **(2014, History optional)**

PRACTICE QUESTIONS – PRELIMS

1. Match List I with List II and select the correct answer using the code given below the lists:

List I	List II
A. Ist Mysore War	1. Treaty of Salbai
B. IInd Mysore War	2. Treaty of Madras
C. IIIrd Mysore War	3. Treaty of Mangalore
D. Ist Maratha War	4. Treaty of Seringapatnam

Code:	A	B	C	D
(a)	2	4	3	1
(b)	2	3	4	1
(c)	1	4	3	2
(d)	1	3	4	2

2. Who among the following was appointed as Chief Commissioner of board in Punjab in c.1853 CE?

(a) John Lawrence
(b) Henry Lawrence
(c) Charles G Mansel
(d) Charles Napier

3. Consider the following:

1. The Treaty of Aix la Chapelle was signed after Ist Carnatic War.
2. The Treaty of Pondicherry was signed after IInd Carnatic War.
3. The Treaty of Paris was signed after IIIrd Carnatic War.

Select the correct answer using the codes given below:

(a) 1 and 2 only (b) 3 only
(c) 1 and 3 only (d) 1, 2 and 3

4. Match List I with List II and select the correct answer using the code given below the lists:

List I	List II
A. Battle of Plassey	1. Ranjeet Singh Maihithia vs Harry Smith
B. Battle of Buxar	2. Siraj ud-daulah vs Robert Clive + Mir Jafar
C. Battle of Talegaon	3. Shuja-ud-daulah +Shah-Alam II vs English + Mir Jafar
D. Battle of Buddewal	4. Marathas vs English

Code:	A	B	C	D
(a)	2	4	3	1
(b)	2	3	4	1
(c)	1	4	3	2
(d)	1	3	4	2

5. Match List I with List II and select the correct answer using the code given below the lists:

List I	List II
A. Dual Government	1. Robert Clive
B. Ist Maratha War	2. Lord Hastings
C. IInd Maratha War	3. Lord Wellesley
D. IIIrd Maratha War	4. Lord Warren Hastings

Code:	A	B	C	D
(a)	2	4	3	1
(b)	2	3	4	1
(c)	1	4	3	2
(d)	1	3	4	2

6. Arrange the following chronologically:

a. Battle of Plassey
b. Carnatic Wars
c. Ist Mysore War
d. Ist Maratha War

(a) a, b, c, d (b) b, a, c, d
(c) a, b, d, c (d) b, a, d, c

ANSWERS

1. (b) 2. (a) 3. (d) 4.(a) 5. (c) 6. (b)

PRACTICE QUESTIONS – MAINS

1. Both Haider Ali and Nana Phadnavis could not reap much dividends from their early victory over the British. Do you agree? Substantiate your answer.

2. Explain the conquest of India by British citing important wars and treaties.